Kalman Filter: Recent Advances and Applications

Edited by
Victor M. Moreno
and
Alberto Pigazo

Kalman Filter: Recent Advances and Applications
Victor M. Moreno and Alberto Pigazo

Republished by InTech
Janeza Trdine 9, 51000 Rijeka, Croatia

Additional hard copies can be obtained from orders@intechopen.com

p. cm.
ISBN 978-953-307-000-1
1. Kalman Filter: Recent Advances and Applications, Victor M. Moreno and Alberto Pigazo

For EU product safety concerns:
IN TECH d.o.o., Prolaz Marije Krucifikse Kozulić 3, 51000 Rijeka, Croatia,
info@intechopen.com or visit our website at intechopen.com.

Meet the editors

Víctor M. Moreno (A'01–M'01) received the M.Sc. and Ph.D. degrees in physics (electronics) from the University of Cantabria, Santander, Spain, in 1980 and 1994, respectively.He is currently an Associate Professor in the Department of Electronics and Computers, University of Cantabria, and teaches electronics, power electronics, and signal processing techniques at the School of Nautical Studies. His main research interests include electrical power quality, electromagnetic compatibility (EMC), digital signal processing, and digital control of power converters.Dr. Moreno has been a member of the IEEE Power Electronics Society (PELS) since 2001, and contributes as an author and reviewer for IEEE journals and conferences. His Ph.D. thesis, entitled "Distributed Measurement and Analysis System for Power Quality in Electrical Grids Applying Kalman Filtering" received the Viesgo Award in 1994.

Alberto Pigazo received the M.Sc. and Ph.D. degrees in physics (electronics) from the University of Cantabria, Santander, Spain, in 1997 and 2004 respectively, where he is currently an Associate Professor teaching courses in electronics and power electronics. He was a guest researcher at the Power Electronics Laboratory (Politechnic of Bari, Italy) and a guest professor at the Dept. of Energy Technology (Aalborg University, Denmark) and the Chair of Power Electronics (Christian-Albrecht University of Kiel, Germany). His main research interests include electrical power quality and digital signal processing techniques applied to the control of power converters, having an h-index equal to 12. Dr. Pigazo is member of the IEEE Industrial Electronics Society (IES), the Editorial Board of the IEEE Industrial Electronics Magazine, and the IEEE IES Technical Committee on Renewable Energy Systems.

Preface

The discussion about the manned spacecraft program was initiated at NASA in 1959. Only one year later, Dr. Kalman and Dr. Schmidt linked the linear Kalman filter and the perturbation theory in order to obtain the Kalman-Schmidt filter, currently known as the extended Kalman filter. This approach would be implemented in 1961 using an IBM 704 computer (running at approximately 4000 operations per second) for simulation purposes, and subsequently, in July 1969, for making the descent of the Apollo 11 lunar module to the Moon possible.

The seminal Kalman filter paper, entitled *A new approach to linear filtering and prediction problems,* and published in 1960, reformulated the Wiener problem and proposed a new solution based on state transition, avoiding the stationary limitations of the Wiener filter and giving a more suitable algorithm to be implemented in computers. This paper concludes with a prophetic sentence: "... The Wiener problem is shown to be closely connected to other problems in the theory of control. Much remains to be done to exploit these connections."

The aim of this book is to provide an overview of recent developments in Kalman filter theory and their applications in engineering and scientific fields. The book is divided into 24 chapters and organized in five blocks corresponding to recent advances in Kalman filtering theory, applications in medical and biological sciences, tracking and positioning systems, electrical engineering and, finally, industrial processes and communication networks.

Various Kalman filtering techniques applied to non-linear and/or non-gaussian systems are discussed in chapters 1-5 of this book. Unscented and robust Kalman filters are introduced and their adaptive versions proposed. Fuzzy sets are also employed in order to improve the filtering performance. Kalman filters, as described in chapters 6-9, can also be employed in medical and biological sciences allowing medical diagnosis and monitoring techniques, such as Electroencephalograms (EEGs), to be improved. Classical applications of Kalman filters, those relating to tracking and positioning systems, are also included in this book (chapters 10-15). New applications in cellular and wireless networks and personal navigation systems are shown. Kalman filters have also been applied to evaluation of the power quality in electrical grids and estimation of variables in electrical motors. These applications are shown in chapters 16-19 of this book. Chapters 20-24 propose Kalman Filtering applications in industrial processes, such as fault detection diagnosis and measurements during manufacturing processes. Communication systems are also treated, such as the case of video coding and channel tracking.

The Kalman filter has been successfully employed in diverse knowledge areas over the last 50 years and these chapters review its recent applications. We hope the selected works will be useful for readers, contributing to future developments and improvements of this filtering technique.

Editors

Víctor M. Moreno
Dept. of Electronics and Computers
University of Cantabria
Spain

Alberto Pigazo
Dept. of Electronics and Computers
University of Cantabria
Spain

Contents

Recent Advances

1

Adaptive Unscented Kalman Filter and Its Applications in Nonlinear Control

Jianda Han, Qi Song and Yuqing He
State Key Laboratory of Robotics
Shenyang Institute of Automation
Chinese Academy of Sciences
P.R.China

1. Introduction

Active estimation is becoming a more important issue in control theory and its application, especially in the nonlinear control of uncertain systems, such as robots and unmanned vehicles where time-varying parameters and uncertainties exist extensively in the dynamics and working environment.

Among the available techniques for active modeling, Neural Networks (NN) and NN-based self learning have been proposed as one of the most effective approaches in 1990s (Pesonen et al., 2004). However the problems involved in NN, such as training data selection, online guaranteed convergence, robustness, reliability and real-time implementation, still remain open and limit its application in real systems, especially those requiring high reliable control.

Most recently, the encouraging achievements in sequential estimation makes it becoming an important direction for online modeling and model-reference control (Napolitano, et al., 2000). Among stochastic estimations, the most popular one for nonlinear system is the Extended Kalman Filter (EKF). Although widely used, EKF suffers from the deficiencies including the requirement of sufficient differentiability of the state dynamics, the susceptibility to bias and divergence during the estimation. Unscented Kalman Filter (UKF) (Julier et al., 1995; Wan & Van der Merwe, 2000) provides a derivative-free way to the state parameter estimation of nonlinear systems by introducing the so called 'unscented transformation', while achieving the second-order accuracy (the accuracy of EKF is first order) with the same computational complexity as that of EKF.

Although the nonlinear state dynamics are used without linearization and the calculations on Jacobians or Hessians are not involved, UKF still falls into the framework of Kalman-type filters, which can only achieve good performance under *a priori* assumptions (Jazwinski, 1970), which includes: 1) accurate reference models, 2) complete information of the noise distribution, and 3) proper initial conditions. However, such *a priori* knowledge is often not accurate, or even not available in practice. The normal UKF will suffer from performance degradation or even instability due to the mismatch between the *a priori* assumptions and the real ones within the system to be controlled.

One of the approaches solving this problem is to introduce adaptive mechanism into a normal filter, i.e., the adaptive law automatically tunes the filter parameters to match the real statistics that are insufficiently known as *a priori*. During the past decade, there have been some investigations in the area of adaptive filter, and most of them are constructed with respect to the KF or EKF. Mohamed et al. (Mohamed et al., 1999) studied the performance of multiple-model-based adaptive Kalman Filter for vehicle navigation using GPS. Loebis et al. (Loebis et al., 2004) proposed an adaptive EKF algorithm, which adjusted the measurement noise covariance matrix by fuzzy logic. Other works can also be seen in references (Noriega & Pasupathy, 1997; Mehra, 1970; Hu et al., 2003; Chaer et al., 1997; Garcia-Velo, 1997). As far as the adaptive UKF (AUKF) is concerned, the most-often-mentioned scheme was proposed by Lee and Alfriend (Lee & Alfriend, 2004), where the Maybeck's method (Maybeck, 1979) was modified by maximum-likelihood principle to estimate the error covariance matrix, and this estimator was further integrated into the normal UKF as the adaptive mechanism.

In this Chapter, we first introduce the normal UKF algorithm. Then, two adaptive UKFs, which are the MIT-rule-based AUKF (MIT-AUKF) and master-slave AUKF (MS-AUKF), are proposed and analyzed in detail. In the MIT-AUKF: a cost function is first constructed from the error between the covariance matrix of innovation and their corresponding estimations; then, an MIT-like adaptive law is designed to online update the covariance of the process noise with the purpose of minimizing the cost function; and finally, the updated covariance is fed back into the normal UKF to realize the adaptive performance. The MS-AUKF, on the other hand, is composed of two parallel UKFs, where the master UKF is used to estimate the states or parameters as a normal UKF, and the slave one is dedicated to estimating the noise covariance matrix for the master UKF.

In order to demonstrate their applications, the proposed AUKFs are tested with respect to the dynamics of an omni-directional mobile robot and a model unmanned helicopter. The improvements achieved from the adaptive mechanisms are demonstrated by the comparisons between the simulation results of the AUKFs and those of the normal UKF. Moreover, the integration of AUKF into robust control scheme is also introduced in the end.

The Chapter is organized as follows: the unscented transformation (UT) and normal UKF are introduced in Section II. The MIT-AUKF and MS-AUKF are described in Section III and IV respectively. Simulations on both UKF and AUKF with respect to the joint estimation of states and parameters, as well as the integration of AUKF into robust control, are provided in Section V, followed by the conclusions.

2. UT and normal UKF

Instead of propagating the Gaussian variables through the first-order linearization model as EKF does, UKF uses the Unscented Transformation (UT) to handle the nonlinear plant directly. UT provides an approach to approximate the statistics of a nonlinear transformation like Eq. (1) by a finite set of 'sigma points'.

$$\kappa = g(\delta) \tag{1}$$

where $g(\cdot)$ is a nonlinear function, and δ denotes an $n\times 1$ stochastic variable with the mean of $\bar{\delta}$ and the covariance of P_δ.

In order to calculate the propagation statistics of δ through $g(\cdot)$, i.e., the mean ($\bar{\kappa}$) and covariance (P_κ) of the output κ, the UT uses the following steps (see Fig. 1 also).

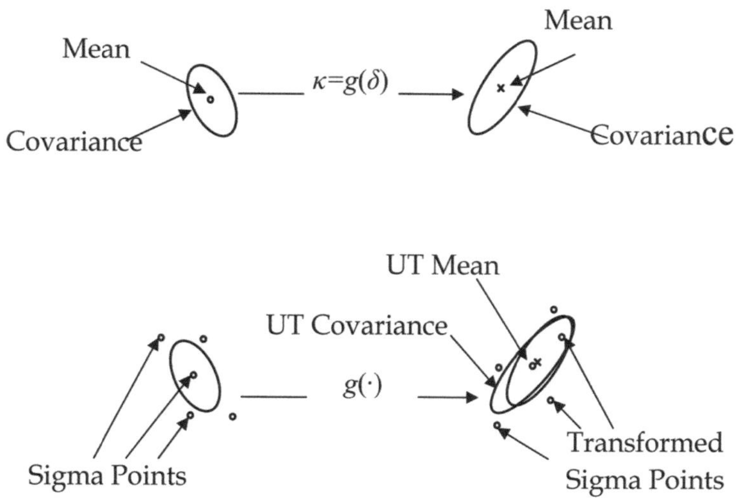

Fig. 1. Unscented Transformation

***UT-I:* Definition of Sigma Points**

The distribution of κ can be approximated by a finite set of sigma points. These sigma points are calculated from the *a priori* mean and covariance of δ by the following equations,

$$\begin{cases} \chi_0 = \bar{\delta} \\ \chi_i = \bar{\delta} + (\sqrt{(L+\lambda)P_\delta})_{i,:} & i = 1,\cdots,L \\ \chi_i = \bar{\delta} - (\sqrt{(L+\lambda)P_\delta})_{i-l,:} & i = L+1,\cdots,2L \end{cases} \tag{2}$$

$$\lambda = L(\alpha^2 - 1) \tag{3}$$

where $(\cdot)_i$ denotes the ith row of matrix $(\cdot)$, L is the number of sigma point, α and λ are both constants, and α determines the spread of the sigma points.

***UT-II:* Propagating of Sigma Points**

Computing the transformation from the input δ-space to the output κ-space of each sigma point by Eq. (1), i.e.,

$$\gamma_i = g(\chi_i) \qquad i = 1,\cdots,2L \tag{4}$$

***UT-III:* Calculating the Mean and Covariance of output κ**

$$\begin{cases} \bar{\kappa} = \sum_{i=0}^{2L} w_i^m \gamma_i \\ P_\kappa = \sum_{i=0}^{2L} w_i^c (\gamma_i - \bar{\kappa})(\gamma_i - \bar{\kappa})^T \end{cases} \tag{5}$$

where the weights of w_i^m and w_i^c are calculated by

$$\begin{cases} w_0^m = \dfrac{\lambda}{L+\lambda} \\ w_0^c = \dfrac{\lambda}{L+\lambda} + (1-\alpha^2+\beta) \\ w_i^m = w_i^c = \dfrac{1}{2(L+\lambda)} \qquad i = 1,\cdots,2L \end{cases} \tag{6}$$

and β is a constant with the purpose of incorporating part of the prior knowledge of the distribution of δ. It has been proved that, for Gaussian distributions, $\beta = 2$ is optimal (Van der Merwe & Wan, 2001).

With respect to the control application of a nonlinear system of Eq. (7),

$$\begin{cases} x_{k+1} = f(x_k) + w_k \\ y_k = h(x_k) + v_k \end{cases} \tag{7}$$

where $x_k \in R^n$, and $y_k \in R^m$ are respectively, the state and output vector at time k; w_k and v_k are the process and measurement noise vector, which are both assumed to be Gaussian white noise with zero mean and covariance R_w and R_v; the normal UKF can be deduced as followings.

***UKF-I:* Initialization**

$$\begin{cases} x_0 = E[x_0] \\ P_0 = E[(x_0 - \bar{x}_0)(x_0 - \bar{x}_0)^T] \end{cases} \tag{8}$$

where $E[\cdot]$ denotes the mean of $[\cdot]$

***UKF-II:* Sigma Points Calculation in the *k*-th time instant**

$$\chi_{k-1} = \left[\bar{x}_{k-1}, \bar{x}_{k-1} + \sqrt{(L+\lambda)P_{k-1}}, \bar{x}_{k-1} - \sqrt{(L+\lambda)P_{k-1}} \right] \tag{9}$$

***UKF-III:* Time Update**

$$\begin{cases} \chi^*_{k|k-1} = f(\chi_{k-1}) \\ \bar{x}_{k|k-1} = \sum_{i=0}^{2L} w_i^m \chi^*_{i,k|k-1} \\ P_{k|k-1} = \sum_{i=0}^{2L} w_i^c (\chi^*_{i,k|k-1} - \bar{x}_{k|k-1})(\chi^*_{i,k|k-1} - \bar{x}_{k|k-1})^T + Q^w \\ \chi_{k|k-1} = \left[\bar{x}_{k|k-1}, \bar{x}_{k|k-1} + \sqrt{(L+\lambda)P_{k|k-1}}, \bar{x}_{k|k-1} - \sqrt{(L+\lambda)P_{k|k-1}} \right] \\ \gamma_{k|k-1} = h(\chi_{k|k-1}) \\ \bar{y}_{k|k-1} = \sum_{i=0}^{2L} w_i^m \gamma_{i,k|k-1} \end{cases} \tag{10}$$

UKF-IV: **Measurement Update**

$$\begin{cases} P_{\bar{y}_k \bar{y}_k} = \sum_{i=0}^{2L} w_i^c (\gamma_{i,k|k-1} - \bar{y}_{k|k-1})(\gamma_{i,k|k-1} - \bar{y}_{k|k-1})^T + Q^v \\ P_{\bar{x}_k \bar{y}_k} = \sum_{i=0}^{2L} w_i^c (\chi_{i,k|k-1} - \bar{x}_{k|k-1})(\gamma_{i,k|k-1} - \bar{y}_{k|k-1})^T \\ K_k = P_{\bar{x}_k \bar{y}_k} P_{\bar{y}_k \bar{y}_k}^{-1} \\ P_k = P_{k|k-1} - K_k P_{\bar{y}_k \bar{y}_k} K_k^T \\ \bar{x}_k = \bar{x}_{k|k-1} + K_k (y_k - \bar{y}_{k|k-1}) \end{cases} \tag{11}$$

where Q^w and Q^v are the process and measurement noise covariance respectively, both of which are assumed to be known as *a priori*. The parameter a is usually set within [0.0001, 1].

3. MIT-AUKF

It is the same as KF to a linear system, UKF suffers performance degradation or even losing stability if the *a priori* knowledge of Q^w and Q^v in Eq.(10) and Eq.(11) mismatches the relative ones in real system denoted as R_w and R_v in the following sections. To avoid this problem, a MIT-rule-based approach is introduced in this section.

3.1 Parameters to be turned adaptively

From the previous introduction, there are six parameters need to be selected in UKF, including the initial state x_0, initial covariance P_0, process noise covariance Q^w, measurement noise covariance Q^v, and UT parameters a and β. The x_0 and P_0, however, usually have asymptotically negligible influence on the estimation results as more data are handled with time proceeding. And the values of a and β only affect the higher order terms of the nonlinear estimation but have little relation with the estimation accuracy or stability of UKF. Thus, the covariance matrices Q^w and Q^v are the only possible parameters which the adaptive law could update for improving the performance of UKF. Indeed, the selection of Q^w and Q^v does have significant influence on UKF. If Q^w and/or Q^v are too small at the beginning of the estimation process, the uncertainty tube around the estimated value will probably tighten and a biased solution might appear. On the other hand, too large Q^w and/or Q^v will probably result in filter divergence.

In this section, the adaptive UKF adjusting the process noise covariance Q^w will be introduced. And without losing the generality, the case of adjusting Q^v can be conducted in a similar way.

3.2 Cost function

In order to update the Q^w in time, most adaptive filters tried to minimize the time-averaged innovations, i.e., the measured outputs and their estimated values. However, the computation of minimum innovations is time consuming and the results may be different from the 'true' values. Here, we propose a recursive algorithm to minimize the difference between the filter-computed and the actual innovation covariance.

The time-averaged approximation of innovation covariance is defined as

$$S_k = \frac{1}{N}\sum_{i=k-N}^{k-1} v_i v_i^T \tag{12}$$

where N is the size of the estimation window, v_i is the innovation and can be written as,

$$v_i = y_i - \overline{y}_{i|i-1} \tag{13}$$

where y_i and $\overline{y}_{i|i-1}$ are respectively, the real measurement and its estimated value. From Eq.(11) of the standard UKF, the computed innovation covariance can be obtained as,

$$\hat{S}_k = P_{\overline{y}_k \overline{y}_k} = \sum_{i=0}^{2L} w_i^c (\gamma_{i,k|k-1} - \overline{y}_{k|k-1})(\gamma_{i,k|k-1} - \overline{y}_{k|k-1})^T + Q^v \tag{14}$$

Then, the criterion for adaptive UKF is to minimize the following cost function,

$$V_k = tr(\Delta S_k^2) = tr\left[(S_k - \hat{S}_k)^2\right] \tag{15}$$

3.3 MIT-AUKF algorithm

The MIT rule is used in this section to derive the adaptive law. With the MIT rule, the parameters are adjusted in the negative gradient direction of the criterion function, i.e.,

$$\dot{q}_k^m = -\eta_k \frac{\partial V_k}{\partial q_k^m} \tag{16}$$

where q_k^m is the m-th diagonal element of the process-noise covariance matrix at time k, i.e.,

$$Q_k^w = \begin{bmatrix} q_k^1 & \cdots & 0 \\ \vdots & \ddots & \vdots \\ 0 & \cdots & q_k^n \end{bmatrix}$$

and η is the tuning rate that determines the convergence speed, and it is assumed to satisfy the following conditions,

$$q_k^m = q_{k-1}^m - \eta_k \frac{\partial J_k}{\partial q_k^m} \cdot T \tag{17}$$

Eq.(16) leads to the following recursive scheme with respect to discrete time application,

$$q_k^m = q_{k-1}^m - \eta \frac{\partial V_k}{\partial q_{k-1}^m} \cdot T \tag{18}$$

where T is the sampling time. In order to calculate Eq. (18), the partial derivative of V_k with respect to q_k^m needs to be calculated. From Eq. (15), we have

$$\frac{\partial V_k}{\partial q_{k-1}^m} = \frac{\partial}{\partial q_{k-1}^m}\left(\sum_{i=1}^{m}(\Delta S_k)_{i,:}(\Delta S_k)_{:,i}\right) = \sum_{i=1}^{m}\left[\left(\frac{\partial(\Delta S_k)_{i,:}^T}{\partial q_{k-1}^m}\right)^T (\Delta S_k)_{:,i} + (\Delta S_k)_{i,:}\frac{\partial(\Delta S_k)_{:,i}}{\partial q_{k-1}^m}\right] \tag{19}$$

$$\frac{\partial(\Delta S_k)_{i,:}^T}{\partial q_{k-1}^m} = \frac{\partial(\Delta S_k)_{:,i}}{\partial q_{k-1}^m} = \frac{\partial}{\partial q_{k-1}^m}\left[(S_k)_{:,i} - (\hat{S}_k)_{:,i}\right] = \frac{\partial(S_k)_{:,i}}{\partial q_{k-1}^m} - \frac{\partial(\hat{S}_k)_{:,i}}{\partial q_{k-1}^m} \tag{20}$$

where $(\Delta S_k)_{i,:}$ and $(\Delta S_k)_{:,j}$ denote the ith row and jth column of matrix ΔS_k respectively. From Eq.(12) and (13), the first term of Eq.(20) is obtained as follows,

$$\frac{\partial(S_k)_{:,i}}{\partial q_{k-1}^m} = \frac{1}{N}\sum_{j=k-N+1}^{k}\left[-\frac{\partial(\bar{y}_{j|j-1,i})}{\partial q_{k-1}^m}(y_j - \bar{y}_{j|j-1})^T - (y_{j,i} - \bar{y}_{j|j-1,i})\frac{\partial(\bar{y}_{j|j-1}^T)}{\partial q_{k-1}^m}\right] \tag{21}$$

And the second term of Eq.(20) can be obtained from Eq.(14),

$$\frac{\partial(\hat{S}_k)_{:,i}}{\partial q_k^m} = \sum_{j=0}^{2n} w_i^c\left[-\frac{\partial \bar{y}_{k|k-1}}{\partial q_k^m}(\gamma_{j,k|k-1} - \bar{y}_{k|k-1})_{:,i}^T - (\gamma_{j,k|k-1} - \bar{y}_{k|k-1})\frac{\partial \bar{y}_{k|k-1,i}^T}{\partial q_k^m}\right] \tag{22}$$

Thus, the recursive algorithm for the gradient of innovation vector (InV) can be formulated as follows,

***InV-I:* Initialization**

$$\begin{cases} \dfrac{\partial \bar{x}_0}{\partial q_k^m} = 0 \\ \dfrac{\partial P_0}{\partial q_k^m} = 0 \end{cases} \tag{23}$$

InV-II: **Derivative of Sigma Points**

$$\begin{cases} \dfrac{\partial \chi_{0,k-1}}{\partial q_{k-1}^{m}} = \dfrac{\partial \overline{x}_{k-1}}{\partial q_{k-1}^{m}} \\ \dfrac{\partial \chi_{i,k-1}}{\partial q_{k-1}^{m}} = \dfrac{\partial \overline{x}_{k-1}}{\partial q_{k-1}^{m}} + \sqrt{L+\lambda}\cdot(\dfrac{\partial \sqrt{P_{k-1}}}{\partial q_{k-1}^{m}})_i, \quad i=1,\ldots,L \\ \dfrac{\partial \chi_{i,k-1}}{\partial q_{k-1}^{m}} = \dfrac{\partial \overline{x}_{k-1}}{\partial q_{k-1}^{m}} - \sqrt{L+\lambda}\cdot(\dfrac{\partial \sqrt{P_{k-1}}}{\partial q_{k-1}^{m}})_{i-n}, i=L+1,\ldots,2L \end{cases} \tag{24}$$

InV-III: **Derivative Propagation**

$$\begin{cases} \dfrac{\partial \chi_{i,k|k-1}^{*}}{\partial q_{k-1}^{m}} = \left.\dfrac{\partial f}{\partial x}\right|_{x=\chi_{i,k-1}} \cdot \dfrac{\partial \chi_{i,k-1}}{\partial q_{k-1}^{m}} \\ \dfrac{\partial \overline{x}_{k|k-1}}{\partial q_{k-1}^{m}} = \sum_{i=0}^{2L} w_i^m \dfrac{\partial \chi_{i,k|k-1}^{*}}{\partial q_{k-1}^{m}} \\ \dfrac{\partial P_{k|k-1}}{\partial q_{k-1}^{m}} = \sum_{i=0}^{2L} w_i^c \left\{ \left(\dfrac{\partial \chi_{i,k|k-1}^{*}}{\partial q_{k-1}^{m}} - \dfrac{\partial \overline{x}_{k|k-1}}{\partial q_{k-1}^{m}} \right) (\chi_{i,k|k-1}^{*} - \overline{x}_{k|k-1})^T + \right. \\ \qquad \left. (\chi_{i,k|k-1}^{*} - \overline{x}_{k|k-1}) \left(\dfrac{\partial \chi_{i,k|k-1}^{*}}{\partial q_{k-1}^{m}} - \dfrac{\partial \overline{x}_{k|k-1}}{\partial q_{k-1}^{m}} \right)^T \right\} \end{cases} \tag{25a}$$

$$\begin{cases} \dfrac{\partial \chi_{0,k|k-1}}{\partial q_{k-1}^{m}} = \dfrac{\partial \overline{x}_{k|k-1}}{\partial q_{k-1}^{m}} \\ \dfrac{\partial \chi_{i,k|k-1}}{\partial q_{k-1}^{m}} = \dfrac{\partial \overline{x}_{k|k-1}}{\partial q_{k-1}^{m}} + \sqrt{L+\lambda}(\dfrac{\partial \sqrt{P_{k|k-1}}}{\partial q_{k-1}^{m}})_i, \quad i=1,\ldots,L \\ \dfrac{\partial \chi_{i,k|k-1}}{\partial q_{k-1}^{m}} = \dfrac{\partial \overline{x}_{k|k-1}}{\partial q_{k-1}^{m}} - \sqrt{L+\lambda}(\dfrac{\partial \sqrt{P_{k|k-1}}}{\partial q_{k-1}^{m}})_{i-n}, i=L+1,\ldots,2L \end{cases} \tag{25b}$$

InV-IV: **Interested Derivative**

$$\begin{cases} \dfrac{\partial \gamma_{i,k|k-1}}{\partial q_{k-1}^{m}} = \left.\dfrac{\partial h}{\partial x}\right|_{x=\chi_{i,k|k-1}} \cdot \dfrac{\partial \chi_{i,k|k-1}}{\partial q_{k-1}^{m}} \\ \dfrac{\partial \overline{y}_{k|k-1}}{\partial q_{k-1}^{m}} = \sum_{i=0}^{2L} w_i^m \dfrac{\partial \gamma_{i,k|k-1}}{\partial q_{k-1}^{m}} \end{cases} \tag{26}$$

***InV-V:* Derivative Update**

$$\begin{cases} \dfrac{\partial P_{k|k-1}}{\partial q_k^m} = I \\ \dfrac{\partial \chi_{i,k|k-1}}{\partial q_k^m} = \sqrt{L+\lambda}(\dfrac{\partial \sqrt{P_{k|k-1}}}{\partial q_k^m})_i, \quad i = 1,\ldots,L \\ \dfrac{\partial \chi_{i,k|k-1}}{\partial q_k^m} = -\sqrt{L+\lambda}(\dfrac{\partial \sqrt{P_{k|k-1}}}{\partial q_k^m})_{i-n}, i = L+1,\ldots,2L \\ \dfrac{\partial \gamma_{i,k|k-1}}{\partial q_k^m} = \dfrac{\partial h}{\partial x}\bigg|_{x=\chi_{i,k|k-1}} \cdot \dfrac{\partial \chi_{i,k|k-1}}{\partial q_k^m} \\ \dfrac{\partial \overline{y}_{k|k-1}}{\partial q_k^m} = \sum_{i=0}^{2L} w_i^m \dfrac{\partial \gamma_{i,k|k-1}}{\partial q_k^m} \\ \dfrac{\partial P_{\overline{y}_k\overline{y}_k}}{\partial q_k^m} = \sum_{i=0}^{2L} w_i^c \left\{ \left(\dfrac{\partial \gamma_{i,k|k-1}}{\partial q_k^m} - \dfrac{\partial \overline{y}_{k|k-1}}{\partial q_k^m} \right) (\gamma_{i,k|k-1} - \overline{y}_{k|k-1})^T \right. \\ \qquad \left. + (\gamma_{i,k|k-1} - \overline{y}_{k|k-1}) \left(\dfrac{\partial \gamma_{i,k|k-1}}{\partial q_k^m} - \dfrac{\partial \overline{y}_{k|k-1}}{\partial q_k^m} \right)^T \right\} + \dfrac{\partial Q^w}{\partial q_k^m} \\ \dfrac{\partial P_{\overline{x}_k\overline{y}_k}}{\partial q_k^m} = \sum_{i=0}^{2L} w_i^c \left\{ \left(\dfrac{\partial \chi_{i,k|k-1}}{\partial q_k^m} - \dfrac{\partial \overline{x}_{k|k-1}}{\partial q_k^m} \right) (\gamma_{i,k|k-1} - \overline{y}_{k|k-1})^T \right. \\ \qquad \left. + (\chi_{i,k|k-1} - \overline{x}_{k|k-1}) \cdot \left(\dfrac{\partial \gamma_{i,k|k-1}}{\partial q_k^m} - \dfrac{\partial \overline{y}_{k|k-1}}{\partial q_k^m} \right)^T \right\} \end{cases} \tag{27a}$$

$$\begin{cases} \dfrac{\partial K_k}{\partial q_k^m} = \dfrac{\partial P_{\overline{x}_k\overline{y}_k}}{\partial q_k^m} P_{\overline{y}_k\overline{y}_k}^{-1} - P_{\overline{x}_k\overline{y}_k} P_{\overline{y}_k\overline{y}_k}^{-1} \dfrac{\partial P_{\overline{y}_k\overline{y}_k}}{\partial q_k^m} P_{\overline{y}_k\overline{y}_k}^{-1} \\ \dfrac{\partial P_k}{\partial q_k^m} = \dfrac{\partial P_{k|k-1}}{\partial q_k^m} - \dfrac{\partial K_k}{\partial q_k^m} P_{\overline{x}_k\overline{y}_k}^T - K_k \left(\dfrac{\partial P_{\overline{x}_k\overline{y}_k}}{\partial q_k^m} \right)^T \\ \dfrac{\partial \overline{x}_k}{\partial q_k^m} = \dfrac{\partial \overline{x}_{k|k-1}}{\partial q_k^m} + \dfrac{\partial K_k}{\partial q_k^m}(y_k - \overline{y}_{k|k-1}) - K_k \dfrac{\partial \overline{y}_{k|k-1}}{\partial q_k^m} \end{cases} \tag{27b}$$

where

$$P_{k|k-1} = \sum_{i=0}^{2L} w_i^c (\chi_{i,k|k-1}^* - \overline{x}_{k|k-1})(\chi_{i,k|k-1}^* - \overline{x}_{k|k-1})^T + Q_k^w$$

Finally, the procedure of MIT-AUKF can be concluded as:

***MIT-AUKF-I:* Initialization**

Initialize the UKF algorithm from Eq.(8) and the gradient of Eq.(23), and let

$$\begin{cases} Q_0^w = \bar{Q}^w \\ Q^v = \bar{Q}^v \end{cases}$$

***MIT-AUKF-II:* Sigma Points Calculation at the *k*-th time instant**

Compute the sigma points as Eq.(9) and the derivative update of Eq.(24).

***MIT-AUKF-III:* Time Update**

Obtain the time update of UKF as Eq. (10) and compute the derivative update of Eq. (25).

***MIT-AUKF-IV:* Update Process Noise Covariance Matrix**

Compute the interested derivative with Eq.(26) and obtain new process noise covariance matrix by Eq.(18-22).

***UKF-IV:* Measurement Update**

Complete the measurement update as Eq.(11) and the last update of Eq.(27).

4. MS-AUKF

In the MIT-AUKF, the partial derivative of $\hat{S}_k$ with respect to q_k^m has to be calculated as Eq. (22), which will introduce a relative large computational burden. In this section, another AUKF scheme with master-slave structure is proposed with the purpose of avoiding the complicated calculation.

Shown in Fig.2, the proposed MS-AUKF is composed of two parallel UKFs. At every timestep, the master UKF estimates the states/parameters using the noise covariance obtained by the slave UKF, while the slave UKF estimates the noise covariance using the innovations generated by the master UKF. It should be noted that the two UKFs are independent in the MS-AUKF structure. Thus, the slave UKF can be replaced by another simple filter such as KF to save the computational burden in time-critical application.

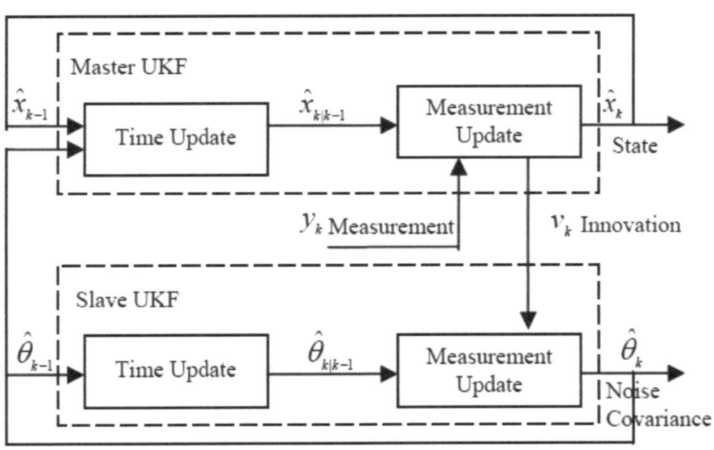

Fig. 2. The Structure of MS-AUKF

In the proposed scheme, the calculation of the master UKF is the same as that of a normal UKF. The slave UKF, on the other hand, needs to estimate the noise covariance. In this section, without losing the generality, the slave UKF is described to estimate the measurement covariance matrix, here, we use the θ_k^i to denote the ith diagonal element of matrix Q_k^v, i.e.,

$$Q_k^v = \begin{bmatrix} \theta_k^1 & \cdots & 0 \\ \vdots & \ddots & \vdots \\ 0 & \cdots & \theta_k^m \end{bmatrix} \tag{28}$$

In the case that the dynamics of θ are clearly known, i.e.,

$$\theta_k = f(\theta_{k-1}) + w_{\theta k} \tag{29}$$

then Eq.(29) can be directly used as the reference model of the slave UKF. While the dynamics of θ are unknown, we can use a noise-actuated model like Eq.(30) instead.

$$\theta_k = \theta_{k-1} + w_{\theta k} \tag{30}$$

where $w_{\theta k}$ is supposed to be Gaussian white noise with zero mean.
The innovation covariance generated by the master UKF is taken as the observation signal for the slave UKF, and then according to Eq.(11), the observation model can be described as,

$$\bar{S}_k = g(\theta_k) = diag\left[\sum_{i=0}^{2n} w_i^c (\gamma_{i,k|k-1} - \bar{y}_{k|k-1})(\gamma_{i,k|k-1} - \bar{y}_{k|k-1})^T + Q_{k-1}^v\right] \tag{31}$$

The measurement of $\hat{S}_k$ received by the slave UKF is,

$$S_k = diag\left[v_k v_k^T\right] \tag{32}$$

$$v_k = y_k - \bar{y}_{k|k-1} \tag{33}$$

where v_k is innovation, and y_k is the real measurements in Eq.(11).
Therefore, the recursive algorithm of the slave UKF can be formulated as,

***Slave-I:* Initialization**

$$\begin{cases} \hat{\theta}_0 = E[\theta_0] \\ P_{\theta_0} = E\left[(\theta_0 - \hat{\theta}_0)(\theta_0 - \hat{\theta}_0)^T\right] \end{cases} \tag{34}$$

***Slave-II:* Sigma Points Calculation**

$$\vartheta_{k-1} = [\hat{\theta}_{k-1}, \hat{\theta}_{k-1} + \sqrt{(1+\lambda)P_{\theta_{k-1}}}, \hat{\theta}_{k-1} - \sqrt{(1+\lambda)P_{\theta_{k-1}}}] \tag{35}$$

Slave-III: **Time Update**

$$\begin{cases} \vartheta_{k|k-1} = f_\theta(\vartheta_{k-1}) \\ \hat{\theta}_{k|k-1} = \sum_{i=0}^{2n} w_{\theta_i}^m \vartheta_{i,k|k-1}^* \\ P_{\theta_{k|k-1}} = \sum_{i=0}^{2n} w_{\theta_i}^m (\vartheta_{i,k|k-1}^* - \hat{\theta}_{k|k-1})(\vartheta_{i,k|k-1}^* - \hat{\theta}_{k|k-1})^T + Q^\theta \\ \vartheta_{k|k-1} = [\hat{\theta}_{k|k-1}, \hat{\theta}_{k|k-1} + \sqrt{(1+\lambda)P_{\theta_{k|k-1}}}, \hat{\theta}_{k|k-1} - \sqrt{(1+\lambda)P_{\theta_{k|k-1}}}] \\ \varsigma_{k|k-1} = g(\vartheta_{k|k-1}) \\ \hat{S}_{k|k-1} = \sum_{i=0}^{2n} w_{\theta_i}^m \varsigma_{i,k|k-1} \end{cases} \tag{36}$$

Slave-IV: **Measurement Update**

$$\begin{cases} P_{S_k S_k} = \sum_{i=0}^{2n} w_{\theta_i}^c (\varsigma_{i,k|k-1} - \hat{S}_{k|k-1})(\varsigma_{i,k|k-1} - \hat{S}_{k|k-1})^T + R^\theta \\ P_{\theta_k S_k} = \sum_{i=0}^{2n} w_{\theta_i}^c (\vartheta_{i,k|k-1} - \hat{\theta}_{k|k-1})(\vartheta_{i,k|k-1} - \hat{\theta}_{k|k-1})^T + R^\theta \\ K_{\theta_k} = P_{\theta_k S_k} P_{S_k S_k}^{-1} \\ \hat{\theta}_k = \hat{\theta}_{k|k-1} + K_{\theta_k}(S_k - \hat{S}_{k|k-1}), \quad P_{\theta_k} = P_{\theta_{k|k-1}} - K_{\theta_k} P_{S_k S_k} K_{\theta_k}^T \end{cases} \tag{37}$$

where Q^θ and $R^\theta$are respectively the process and measurement noise covariance matrix, and the weights can be calculated by Eq.(6).
Finally, the procedure of the MS-AUKF can be easily obtained by directly combining the four steps of UKF as Eq.(8) - (11) and the slave UKF as Eq.(34) - (37).

5. Application of AUKF

In this section, we introduce the applications of the proposed AUKFs on the dynamics of both a ground mobile robot and a model helicopter, to demonstrate the performance of the AUKFs in state/parameter estimation and control.

5.1 State estimation

First, the simulations of applying the two AUKFs to state estimation are conducted with respect to the dynamics of the omni-directional ground mobile robot developed in Shenyang Institute of Automation, CAS (See Fig. 3) (Song, 2002),

$$\begin{cases} (2Mr^2 + 3i_n I_w)\ddot{x}_w + 3i_n^2 I_w \dot{y}_w \dot{\varphi}_w + 3i_n^2 c\dot{x}_w = nr(\beta_1 u_1 + 2u_2 \cos\varphi_w + \beta_2 u_3) \\ (2Mr^2 + 3i_n I_w)\ddot{y}_w - 3i_n^2 I_w \dot{x}_w \dot{\varphi}_w + 3i_n^2 c\dot{y}_w = nr(\beta_3 u_1 + 2u_2 \sin\varphi_w + \beta_4 u_3) \\ (3i_n I_w L^2 + I_v r^2)\ddot{\varphi}_w + 3i_n^2 cL^2 \dot{\varphi}_w = nrL(-u_1 - u_2 - u_3) \end{cases} \tag{38}$$

$$\begin{cases} \beta_1 = -\sqrt{3}\sin\varphi_w - \cos\varphi_w \\ \beta_2 = \sqrt{3}\sin\varphi_w - \cos\varphi_w \\ \beta_4 = -\sqrt{3}\cos\varphi_w - \sin\varphi_w \\ \beta_3 = \sqrt{3}\cos\varphi_w - \sin\varphi_w \end{cases} \tag{39}$$

where x_w, y_w, and φ_w respectively represent the displacements in the *x*-, *y*-direction and the rotation; u_1, u_2, and u_3 are the actuated torques on each joint. Other parameters in Eq. (38) and Eq. (39) are listed in Table 1.

Fig. 3. 3-DOF Omni-Directional Mobile Robot

Symbols	Physical Meanings	Values in Simulations
c	Friction Coefficient	0.0009kgm2/s
Iw	Inertia on motor axis	0.0036 kgm2
M	Mass	120kg
Iv	Inertia	45 kgm2
r	Wheel Radius	0.06m
L	Centroid-wheel distance	0.273m
in	Motor gear radio	15

Table 1. Mobile Robot Parameters

The state and measurement vectors are selected as follows,

$$\begin{cases} \vec{x} = [x_w, y_w, \phi_w, \dot{x}_w, \dot{y}_w, \dot{\phi}_w]^T \\ y = [\dot{x}_w, \dot{y}_w, \dot{\phi}_w]^T \end{cases} \tag{40}$$

The sampling interval is set as T=0.01s. During the simulation, measurements are corrupted by an zero mean white noise with covariance $R_v = \text{diag}\{10^{-8}; 10^{-8}; 10^{-8}\}$. The UKF parameters are designed as,

$$\begin{cases} \hat{x}_0 = x_{T_0} \\ \hat{P}_0 = diag\{10^{-8},10^{-8},10^{-8},10^{-8},10^{-8},10^{-8}\} \\ Q^v = R_v \\ \alpha = 1 \\ \beta = 2 \end{cases} \tag{41}$$

In order to demonstrate the performance of the AUKFs, we assume an abrupt change occurring with the process noise at the time of t=10s, i.e., the *a priori* knowledge is no longer match the real one after t=10s,

$$R_w = \begin{cases} diag\{10^{-12},10^{-12},10^{-12},10^{-8},10^{-8},10^{-8}\} & t < 10s \\ diag\{10^{-10},10^{-10},10^{-10},10^{-6},10^{-6},10^{-6}\} & t \geq 10s \end{cases} \tag{42}$$

In all of the three UKFs, i.e., the normal UKF, MIT-AUKF and MS-AUKF, the *a priori* process noise covariance is set as $Q = diag\{10^{-12}, 10^{-12}, 10^{-12}, 10^{-8}, 10^{-8}, 10^{-8}\}$.
The velocity estimation errors of the three UKFs, under the same noise change of Eq.(42) at t =10s, are illustrated in Fig. 4, where the parameters required by the MIT-AUKF and MSAUKF are respectively selected as Eq.(43) and (44),

$$\eta = 10^{-12} \tag{43}$$

$$\begin{cases} \theta_0 = \left[10^{-12},10^{-12},10^{-12},10^{-8},10^{-8},10^{-8}\right]^T \\ P_{\theta_0} = diag\left\{10^{-16},10^{-16},10^{-16},10^{-16},10^{-16},10^{-16}\right\} \\ Q_\theta^w = diag\left\{10^{-24},10^{-24},10^{-24},10^{-21},10^{-21},10^{-21}\right\} \\ Q_\theta^n = diag\left\{2\times10^{-16},2\times10^{-16},2\times10^{-16}\right\} \end{cases} \tag{44}$$

From Fig. 4, we can see that, with incorrect *a priori* noise statistic information, the normal UKF can not produce satisfying estimations due to the violation of the optimality conditions. On the contrary, the estimation errors of the two proposed AUKF are quickly convergent due to the performance of the adaptive laws.

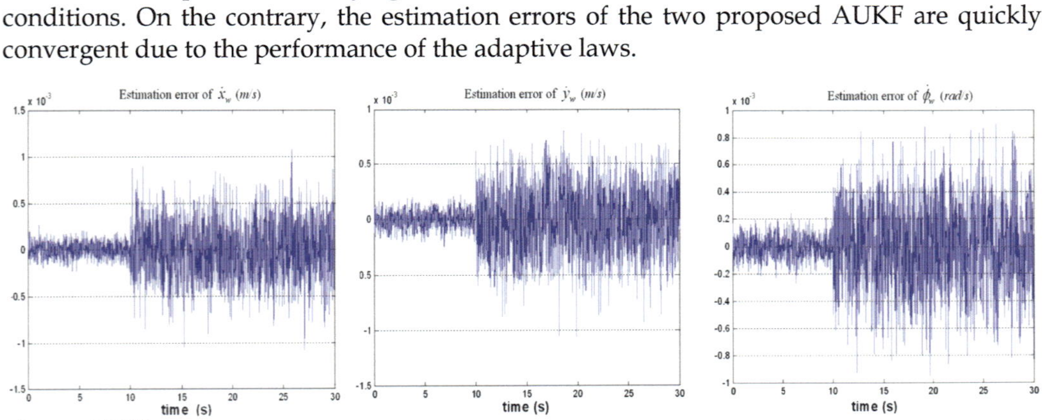

a) normal UKF

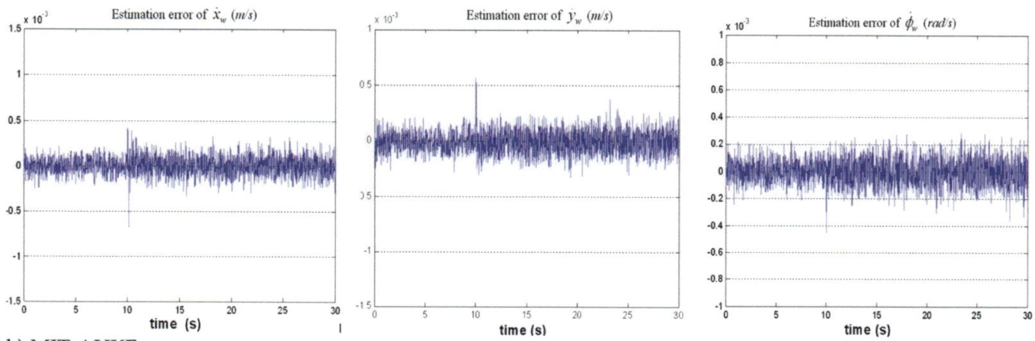

b) MIT-AUKF

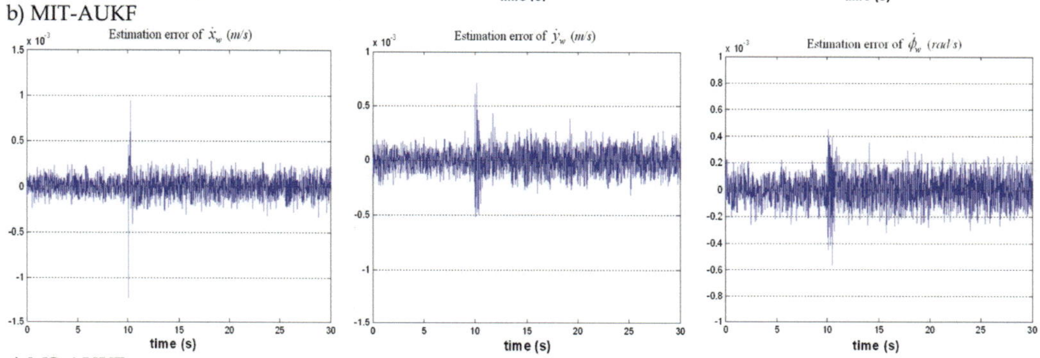

c) MS-AUKF

Fig. 4. Velocity Estimation Errors With Respect To Changing Process Noise Covariance

5.2 Performance comparison

In this section, we compare the performance of the three UKFs in two aspects: 1) estimation precision, and 2) computational time. In order to quantify the estimation precision, the following criterion is defined,

$$J_{ac} = \sqrt{\frac{1}{N_k}\sum_{k=1}^{N_k}(x_k - \overline{x}_k)^2} \tag{45}$$

where N_k is the number of sample points, x_k is the real state or parameter, $\overline{x}_k$ is the estimated state or parameter.

		Normal UKF	MIT-AUKF	MS-AUKF
Computational Time		8.83	45.52	14.94
After the changing of the process noise covariance	ER of $\dot{x}_w$	0.00020	0.000070	0.000079
	ER of $\dot{y}_w$	0.00021	0.000071	0.000076
	ER $\dot{\varphi}_w$	0.00020	0.000071	0.000076

*ER means Estimation error

Table 2. Performance comparison of the two AUKFs

Table-2 shows the performance comparison of the three AUKFs, where the unit of the computational time has been ignored since the simulations are conducted by MATLAB, but the ratio among the three can indicate the complexity of AUKF with respect to that of the normal UKF. From Table-2, we can conclude that: 1) the computational time of the MSAUKF is almost one-third of that of MIT-AUKF, but one times longer than that of normal UKF because two UKFs have to be calculated in the MS-UKF. The accuracy of the MS-AUKF is about 2.5 times higher than that of normal UKF. The MIT-AUKF, although suffering from the most complicated computation, achieves the best accuracy among the three UKFs, and about 7% more accuracy than that of MS-AUKF.

5.3 Disturbance estimation

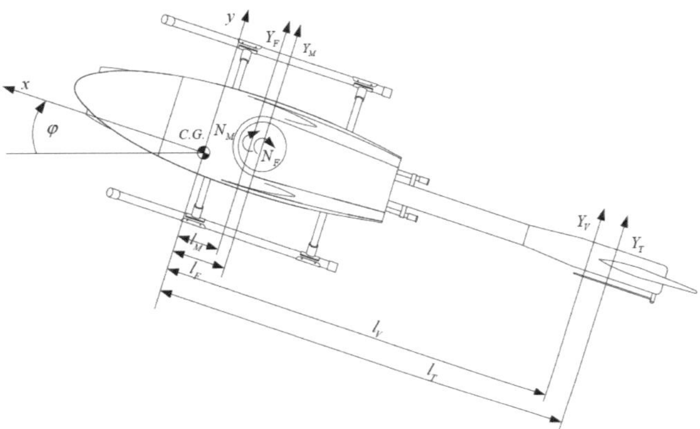

(a)Planform

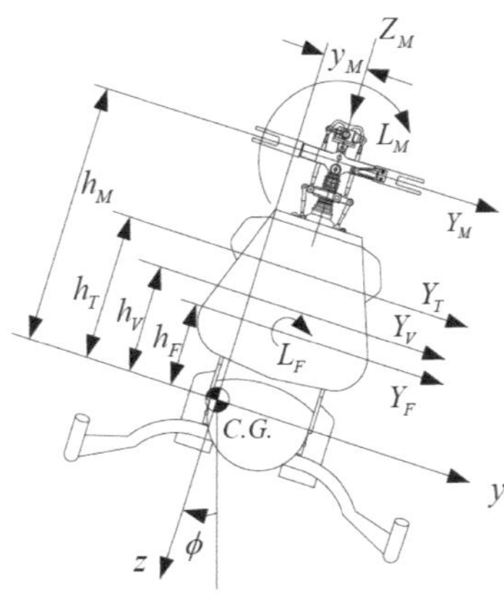

(b) Back view

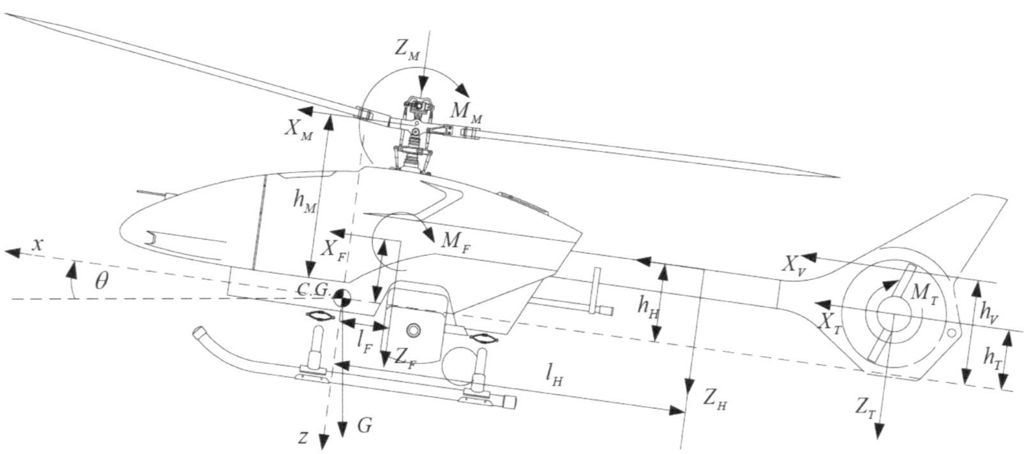

(c) Side view

Fig. 5. Model Helicopter

In this section, we investigate the disturbance and state estimation of an unmanned helicopter. The dynamics of a model helicopter can be described as (see Fig.5, and Koo & Sastry, 1998; He & Han, 2007),

$$\begin{bmatrix} \dot{p} \\ \dot{v}^p \\ \dot{\Theta} \\ \dot{\omega}^b \end{bmatrix} = \begin{bmatrix} v^p \\ \frac{1}{m} W f^b \\ \Psi \omega^b \\ J^{-1}(\tau^b - \omega^b \times J\omega^b) \end{bmatrix} \tag{46}$$

$$f^b = \begin{bmatrix} -T_M \sin a_{1s} \\ T_M \sin b_{1s} + T_T \\ -T_M \cos a_{1s} \cos b_{1s} \end{bmatrix} + W^T \begin{bmatrix} 0 \\ 0 \\ mg \end{bmatrix} + \Delta_1$$
$$\tau^b = \begin{bmatrix} S_{L_1} b_{1s} + S_{L_2} Q_M \\ S_{M_1} a_{1s} + S_{M_2} T_M + S_{M_3} Q_T \\ S_{N_1} Q_M + S_{N_2} T_T \end{bmatrix} + \begin{bmatrix} T_M \sin b_{1s} h_M - T_M \cos a_{1s} \cos b_{1s} y_M + T_T h_T \\ T_M \sin a_{1s} h_M - T_M \cos a_{1s} \cos b_{1s} l_M \\ -T_M \sin b_{1s} l_M - T_T l_T \end{bmatrix} + \Delta_2 \tag{47}$$

where $p \in R^3$ and $v_p \in R^3$ are the position and velocity vector of the center of mass in inertia frame; $W \in SO(3)$ is the rotation matrix of the body frame relative to the inertia frame; ω_b is angular velocity vector; $\Theta = [\varphi\ \theta\ \psi]^T$ is Euler angle vector; m and J are respectively, the mass and inertia of the helicopter; Ψ is the transformation matrix from angular velocity to angular position; f^b and τ^b are force and moment acted on the helicopter in body frame including disturbances; the subscript M and T denote the main and tail rotor respectively; T and Q are respectively, the force and torque generated by main or tail rotor; a_{1s} and b_{1s}, are respectively, the longitudinal and lateral tilt of the tip path plane of the main rotor with respect to shaft; h_M, y_M, h_T, l_M, l_T are constants indicating the distances as Fig.5; Δ_1 and Δ_2 denote the unmodeled dynamics.

The forces T and the moments Q in Eq. (47) can be further calculated by

$$T_i = \frac{R_{1i}^3 - R_{0i}^3}{3} m_3 \theta_{ci} + \frac{m_3 m_6}{2}\left(R_{1i}^2 - R_{0i}^2\right) - \frac{m_3}{8\pi\Omega_i^2}\{\frac{2}{15 m_2^2 \theta_{ci}^2} \times$$
$$\left(\left(3m_2 R_{1i}\theta_{ci} - 2m_5\right)\left(m_2 R_{1i}\theta_{ci} + m_5\right)^{3/2} - \left(3m_2 R_{0i}\theta_{ci} - 2m_5\right)\left(m_2 R_{0i}\theta_{ci} + m_5\right)^{3/2}\right)\}$$

$$Q_i = n_1 n_7 \frac{R_{1i}^3 - R_{0i}^3}{3} - \frac{n_1 n_9}{2}\left(R_{1i}^3 - R_{0i}^3\right) + \frac{c_d n_1}{4}\left(R_{1i}^4 - R_{0i}^4\right) +$$
$$\frac{2 n_1 n_8}{105 m_4^3}\left\{\left(15 m_4^2 R_{1i}^2 - 12 m_4 m_5 R_{1i} + 8 m_5^2\right)\left(m_4 R_{1i} + m_5\right)^{3/2} - \right. \tag{48}$$
$$\left. \left(15 m_4^2 R_{0i}^2 - 12 m_4 m_5 R_{0i} + 8 m_5^2\right)\left(m_4 R_{0i} + m_5\right)^{3/2}\right\} +$$
$$\frac{2 n_1 n_{10}}{15 m_4^3}\left\{\left(\left(3 m_2 R_{1i} - 2m_5\right)\left(m_2 R_{1i} + m_5\right)^{3/2} - \right.\right.$$
$$\left.\left.\left(3 m_2 R_{0i} - 2m_5\right)\left(m_2 R_{0i} + m_5\right)^{3/2}\right)\right\}$$

where $m_1 \sim m_6$, $n_1 \sim n_{10}$ are aerodynamics-related coefficients and the detailed description can be found in reference (Shim, 2000). These coefficients are time-varying and can not be accurately determined.
It can be seen that the complete dynamics of Eq.(48) is too complicated to be used for controller design. Hence, it has to be simplified before using as a reference model of control. But the simplification will definitely introduce extra uncertainties besides the aerodynamics related disturbances, both of which need the controller to handle and overcome. One of the simplified models of aerodynamics-generated force/torque is like,

$$f^b = \begin{bmatrix} -T_M a_{1s} \\ T_M b_{1s} + T_T \\ -T_M \end{bmatrix} + R^T \begin{bmatrix} 0 \\ 0 \\ mg \end{bmatrix} + \Delta_1$$

$$\tau^b = \begin{bmatrix} S_{L1} b_{1s} + S_{L2} Q_M + T_M b_{1s} h_M - T_M y_M + T_T h_T \\ S_{M1} a_{1s} + S_{M2} T_M + S_{M3} Q_T + T_M a_{1s} h_M - T_M l_M \\ S_{N1} Q_M + S_{N2} T_T + -T_M b_{1s} l_M - T_T l_T \end{bmatrix} + \Delta_2 \tag{49}$$

$$T_M = S_{T_M 1}\theta_M + S_{T_M 2},\ T_T = S_{T_T}\theta_T + S_{T_T 2},\ Q_M = S_{Q_M 1}\theta_M + S_{Q_M 2},\ Q_T = S_{Q_T}\theta_T + S_{Q_T 2}$$

And in the following simulation, we use the proposed MIT-AUKF algorithm to estimate the system states and the modeling error, and the estimated results are further used in an adaptive controller to attenuate the influence of uncertainties and disturbances in section 5.4. The simulation is conducted on the yaw dynamics of Eq.(50), which can be obtained by Eq.(46)-(49) (Song & Han, 2007),

$$\ddot{\psi} = a_1\dot{\psi} + a_2\dot{\psi}^2 + b_1(S_{M_1}a_{1s} + S_{M_2}T_M + S_{M_3}Q_T) + b_2(S_{N_1}Q_M + S_{N_2}T_T) + b_3 \tag{50}$$

where

$$\ddot{\psi} = a_1\psi + a_2\dot{\psi} + b_1(S_{M_1}a_{1s} + S_{M_2}T_M + S_{M_3}Q_T) + b_2(S_{N_1}Q_M + S_{N_2}T_T) + b_3$$

$$a_1 = (\dot{\phi}\sin\phi\cos\phi - \dot{\theta}\sin^2\phi\cos\phi)(I_x - I_y)/I_z + \dot{\theta}\tan\theta -$$
$$(\dot{\theta}\cos^2\phi\tan\phi + \dot{\phi}\sin\phi\cos\phi)(I_y - I_x)/I_z$$

$$a_2 = \sin\theta\sin\phi\cos\phi(I_y - I_x)/I_z - \sin\theta\sin\phi\cos\phi(I_x - I_z)/I_y$$

$$b_1 = \sin\phi\sec\theta/I_y$$

$$b_2 = \cos\phi\sec\theta/I_z$$

$$b_3 = \dot{\theta}\dot{\phi}(\sin^2\phi\sec\theta(I_x - I_z)/I_y + \cos^2\phi\sec\theta(I_y - I_x)/I_z + \sec\theta)$$

The state and the measurement vector of AUKF are selected as,

$$\begin{cases} x = [\psi \quad \dot{\psi}] \\ y = [\psi \quad \dot{\psi}] \end{cases} \tag{51}$$

The sampling interval is T=0.02s. The measurements are corrupted by a zero mean additive white noise with covariance,

$$R_v = diag\{10^{-10}, 10^{-10}\} \tag{52}$$

The AUKF parameters are selected as,

$$\begin{cases} x_0 = x_{T_0} \\ \hat{P}_0 = diag\{10^{-14}, 10^{-10}\} \\ Q^v = R_v \\ a = 1, \beta = 1 \end{cases} \tag{53}$$

$$\eta = \begin{bmatrix} 10^{-25} & 0 & 0 \\ 0 & 10^{-25} & 0 \\ 0 & 0 & 10^{-20} \end{bmatrix}$$

Assume an abrupt change occuring with respect to the process noise covariance at t=10s, i.e.,

$$Q_t = \begin{cases} diag\{10^{-14}, 10^{-10}\} & t < 10s \\ diag\{10^{-12}, 10^{-8}\} & t \geq 10s \end{cases} \tag{54}$$

while the prior knowledge remain unchanged during the estimation. The estimation results obtained by both the MIT-AUKF and normal UKF are presented in Fig. 6, where we can see that the state estimated by AUKF is not influenced by the noise covariance changed at t=10s. But for the state estimated by normal UKF, it starts to bias from its true value at t=10s.

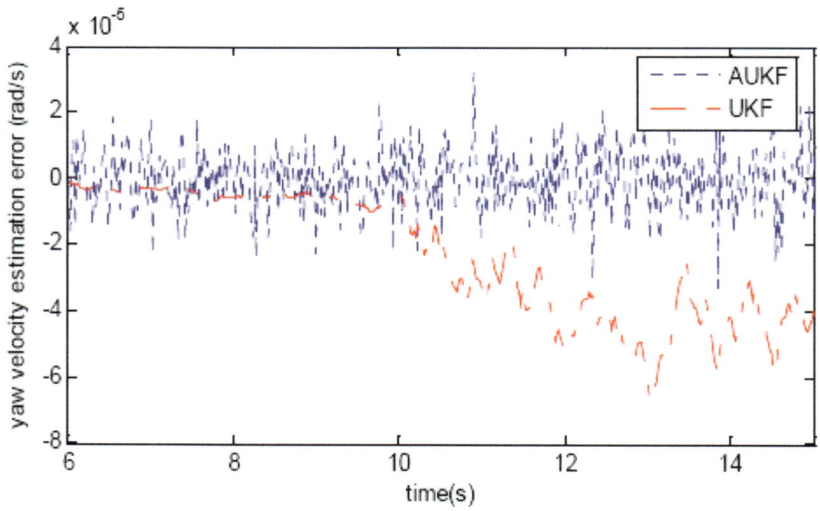

Fig. 6. State Estimation with Respect to Changing Process Noise Covariance

Besides the state estimation, parameter estimation is also tested and compared between the MIT-AUKF and normal UKF. In order to estimate the model error, an extended reference model is proposed as Eq.(55), where the model error is treated as an extra parameter driven by noise.

$$\begin{cases} \dot{\psi} = \dot{\psi} + w_1 \\ \ddot{\psi} = f(p_2, \dot{p}_2, \psi, \dot{\psi}, u) + \zeta + w_2 \\ \dot{\zeta} = w_3 \end{cases} \tag{55}$$

where $[\psi, \dot{\psi}, \zeta]^T$ is the vector to be estimated, and ζ presents model error plus disturbance, w_1, w_2 and w_3 are the process noises, $f(.)$ can be found in the following Eq. (59). By assuming that the model error changes at t = 10s, i.e.,

$$\begin{cases} \zeta = 0 & t < 6s \\ \zeta = 15.6 & t \geq 6s \end{cases} \tag{56}$$

and the state vector is subject to zero mean additive white noises with covariance,

$$Q_T^a = diag\{10^{-14}, 10^{-10}, 10^{-20}\} \tag{57}$$

Fig. 7 presents the results of disturbance estimation, from which we can see that the standard UKF cannot track the abrupt change due to the lower pseudonoise intensity. As for the adaptive UKF, the intensity of the pseudonoise increases during the parameter updates by the proposed adaptive mechanism. This accelerates the convergence of the model error estimation and makes the AUKF successfully track the abrupt change after a short period (about 1 second) of adaptation.

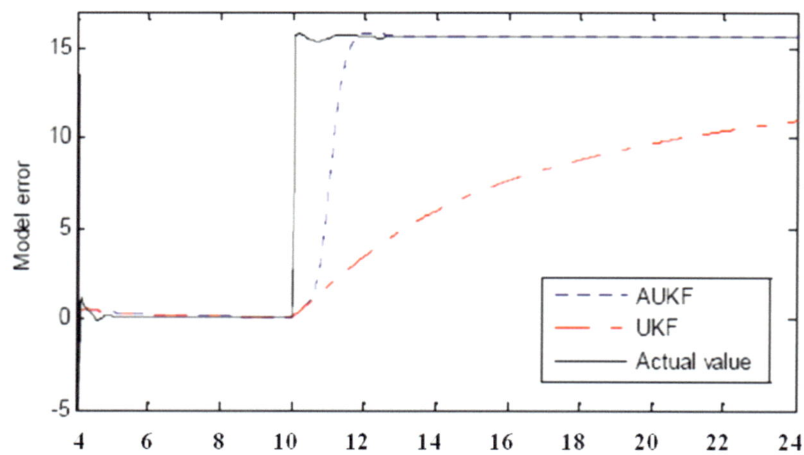

Fig. 7. Comparison of Disturbance Estimation When Noise Covariance Changing

5.4 Active estimation enhanced control

In order to design a tracking controller involving active estimation for robustness enhancement, we use the feedback linearization method to divide the helicopter dynamics into two parts: position dynamics and yaw dynamics. It can be proved that Eq.(46), (47) and (49) can be transformed into the following form (He & Han, 2007),

$$\begin{aligned} \ddot{p}_1 &= p_2 + \Delta_1 \\ \ddot{p}_2 &= f_2(p_1, \dot{p}_1, p_2, \dot{p}_2) + g_2(p_1, \dot{p}_1, p_2, \dot{p}_2)u + h_2(p_1, \dot{p}_1, p_2, \dot{p}_2)\Delta_2 \end{aligned} \tag{58}$$

$$\ddot{\psi} = f_3(p_2, \dot{p}_2, \psi, \dot{\psi}) + g_3(p_2, \dot{p}_2, \psi, \dot{\psi})u + \zeta \tag{59}$$

where Eq.(59) is the same as that in Eq. (55), and

$$f_2 = \frac{2\dot{T}_M}{M} R(\omega^b \times [0\,0\,1]^T) + \frac{T_M}{M} R[\omega^b \times (\omega^b \times [0\,0\,1]^T)] - \frac{T_M}{M} R\{[J^{-1}(\omega^b \times J\omega^b)] \times [0\,0\,1]^T\}$$

$$g_2 = \frac{1}{M}[T_M R\bar{J} \quad R[0\,0\,1]^T]; h_2 = \frac{T_M}{M} R\bar{J}, \bar{J} = J\begin{bmatrix} 0 & 1 & 0 \\ -1 & 0 & 0 \\ 0 & 0 & 0 \end{bmatrix}$$

$$\begin{aligned} f_3 = & -[0 \quad \sin\phi/\cos\theta \quad \cos\phi/\cos\theta] J^{-1}(\omega^b \times J\omega^b) + \\ & q\dot{\phi}\cos\phi/\cos\theta + q\dot{\theta}\sin\theta\sin\phi/\cos^2\theta - \\ & r\dot{\phi}\sin\phi/\cos\theta + r\dot{\theta}\sin\theta\cos\phi/\cos^2\theta \\ g_3 = & [0 \quad \sin\phi/\cos\theta \quad \cos\phi/\cos\theta] J^{-1}, \\ u = & [(\tau^b)^T \quad \ddot{Z}]^T \end{aligned}$$

The disturbances of Δ_1 and $h_2\Delta_1$ can be measured by linear accelerometers, but we can not obtain the disturbance ζ since the angular acceleration is difficult to measure (He & Han, 2007). In this section, we use the estimated disturbances ζ in section 5.3 into the acceleration feedback control (AFC) scheme, proposed in He and Han's paper (He & Han, 2007) and shown as Fig. 8, to attenuate its influence on the closed loop performance. And the detailed designing processes are as follows,

Step I:

Design a nonlinear H∞ controller with measurable disturbances of (58) based on He's AFC based controller design method by taking $u_1 = g_2(p_1, \dot{p}_1, p_2, \dot{p}_2)u$ as independent inputs.

Step II:

With respect Eq. (59), design the following feedback linearization controller with estimated disturbances of (59) by taking $u_2 = g_3(p_2, \dot{p}_2, \psi, \dot{\psi})u$ as independent inputs.

$$u_2 = -f_3(p_2, \dot{p}_2, \psi, \dot{\psi}) - \hat{\zeta} \tag{60}$$

where k_1 and k_2 are positive constant; $\hat{\zeta}$ is the estimated disturbance and can be obtained by construct a dynamic model as Eq. (55).

Step III:

Obtain the control input u,

$$u = \begin{bmatrix} g_2(p_1, \dot{p}_1, p_2, \dot{p}_2) \\ g_3(p_2, \dot{p}_2, \psi, \dot{\psi}) \end{bmatrix}^{-1} \begin{bmatrix} u_1 \\ u_2 \end{bmatrix} \tag{61}$$

Step IV:

Compute the real inputs as Eq. (49) and Eq. (61). ■

The estimator parameters are the same as Eq. (57). And the following parameters are selected to construct the preceding controller,

$$k_1 = k_2 = 4$$

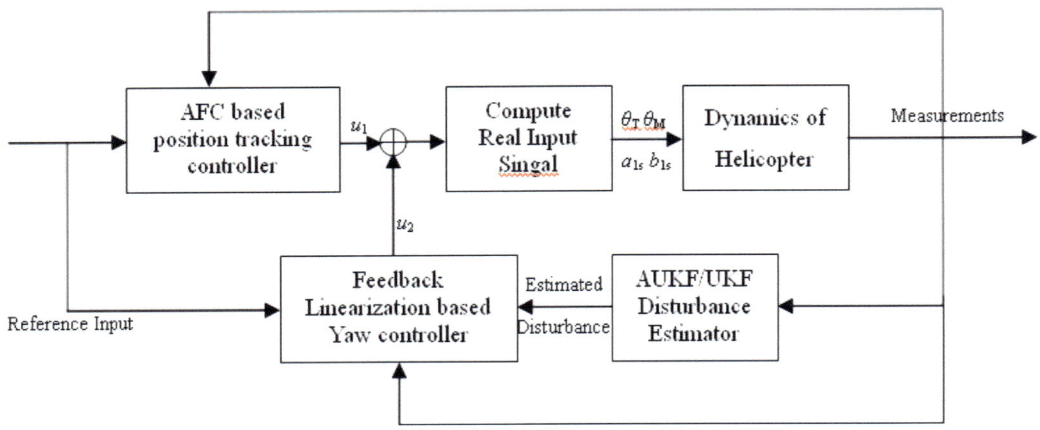

Fig. 8. Tracking Controller Structure of Model Helicopter

Fig. 9 shows the time response of the closed loop. From which, with the AUKF estimator, the yaw angle can go back to the desired value more quickly that that of UKF, and thus, it is clear that the controller with the AUKF has better attenuation disturbance performance.

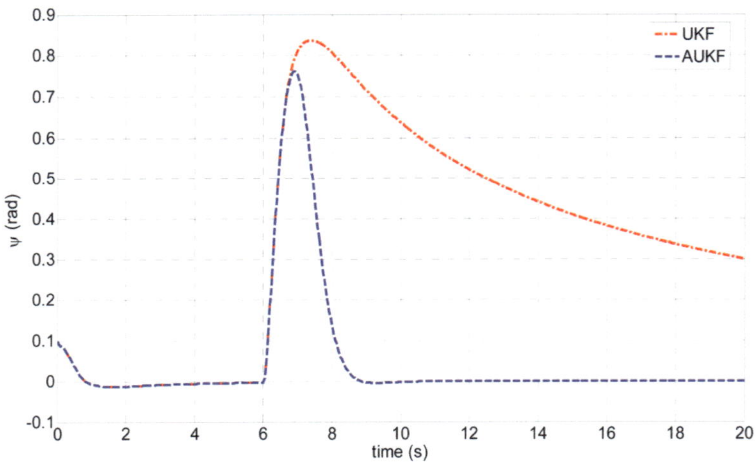

Fig. 9. Time Response of Yaw Angle With Tracking Controller

6. Conclusions

In this Chapter, two adaptive Unscented Kalman Filters (AUKFs), named MIT rule based AUKF and master-slave AUKF, are introduced respectively with the purpose of handling time-varying or uncertain noise distribution. According to the simulation results conducted on omni-directional mobile robot and model helicopter, we can conclude the followings:

1. With incorrect *a priori* statistic information, the AUKFs perform much better than the normal UKF does.
2. Although achieving a little higher estimation precision than the MS-AUKF does, the MITAUK suffers more complicated calculations. That means, the MS-AUKF is appropriate for the application where computation resources are critical. The MS-AUKF, on the other hand, would meet the requirement of high precision estimation.

3. The proposed AUKF is feasible to be integrated into robust control scheme, to effectively reject the uncertainty/disturbance that are difficult for actually measured or off-line modelled.

7. References

Chaer, W. S.; Bishop, R. H. & Ghosh, J. (1997). A mixture-of-experts framework for adaptive Kalman filtering. *IEEE Transactions on Systems, Man and Cybemetics, Part B: Cybemetics*, Vol. 27, No. 3, pp. 452-464

El-Fattah, Y. M. (1983). Recursive self-tuning algorithm for adaptive Kalman filtering. *IEE Proceedings*, Vol. 130, No. 6, pp. 341-344

Garcia-Velo, J. (1997). Determination of noise covariances for extended Kalman filter parameter estimators to account for modeling errors, Ph.D. thesis, University of Cincinnati

He, Y. Q. & Han. J. D. (2007). Acceleration Feedback Enhanced H∞ Disturbance Attenuation Control, *The 33rd Annual Conference of the IEEE Industrial Electronics Society (IECON)*, pp. 839-844, Taipei

Hu, C.; Chen, W.; Chen,Y. & Liu., D. (2003). Adaptive Kalman filtering for vehicle navigation. *Journal of Global Positioning Systems*, Vol. 2, No. 1, pp. 42-47

Jazwinski, A. H. (1970). "Stochastic processes and filtering theory," Academic Press, New York, 1970.

Julier, S. J.; Uhlmann, J. K. & Durrant-Whyte, H. F. (1995). A new approach for filtering nonlinear systems. *Proceedings of the American Control Conference*, pp. 1628-1632, Seattle

Koo, T. & Sastry, S. (1998). Output tracking control design of a helicopter model based on approximated linearization, *Proceedings of the 37th IEEE conference on Decision & Control*, pp. 3625-3640, Tampa

Lee, D. J. & Alfriend, K. T. (2004). Adaptive sigma point filtering for state and parameter estimation. *AIAA/AAS Astrodynamics Specialist Conference and Exhibit*, pp. 1-20, Rhode Island

Ljung, L. (1977). Analysis of recursive stochastic algorithms. *IEEE Transactions on Automatic Control*, Vol. 22, No. 4, pp. 551-575

Loebis, D.; Sutton, R.; Chudley, J.; & Naeem, W. (2004). Adaptive tuning of a Kalman filter via fuzzy logic for an intelligent AUV navigation system, *Control Engineering Practice*, Vol. 12, No. 12, pp. 1531-1539

Maybeck, P. S. (1979). *Stochastic Models, Estimation and Control.* New York: Academic Press

Mehra, R. K. (1970). On the identification of variances and adaptive Kalman filtering. *IEEE Transactions on Automatic Control*, Vol. 15, No. 2, pp. 175-184

Mohamed, A. H. & Schwarz, K. P. (1999). Adaptive Kalman filtering for INS/GPS. *Journal of Geodesy*, Vol. 73, No. 4, pp. 193-203

Napolitano, M.; An, Y. & Seanor, B. (2000). A Fault Tolerance Flight Control System for Sensor and Actuator Failures Using Neural Networks. *Aircraft Design*, 2000, 3(2): 103-128.

Noriega,G. & Pasupathy, S. (1997). Adaptive Estimation of Noise Covariance Matrices in Real-Time Preprocessing of Geophysical Data. *IEEE Transactions on Geoscience and Remote Sensing*, Vol. 35, No. 5, pp. 1146-1159

Pesonen, U.; Steck, J & Rokhsaz K. (2004). Adaptive neural network inverse controller for general aviation safety. *Journal of Guidance, Control, and Dynamics*, 2004, 27(3): 434-443

Shim, D. H. (2000). Hierarchical flight control system synthesis for rotorcraft-based unmanned aerial vehicles. Ph.D. thesis, University of California

Song, Q. & Han, J. D. (2007). A novel adaptive unscented Kalman filter for nonlinear estimation. Proceedings of the 46th IEEE Conference on Decision and Control, pp. 4293-4298. New Orleans

Song, Y. X. (2002). *Study on trajectory tracking control of mobile robot with orthogonal wheeled assemblies.* Ph.D. thesis, Shenyang Institute of Automation, Chinese Academy of Sciences

Van der Merwe, R. &Wan, E. A. (2001). The squre-root unscented Kalman filter for state and paramter estimation, *Proceedings of the IEEE International Conference on Acoustics, Speech, and Signal Processing*, pp. 3461-3464. Soat Late City

Wan, E. A. & Van der Merwe, R. (2000). The unscented Kalman filter for nonlinear estimation. *Proceeding of the Symposium 2000 on Adaptive System for Signal Processing, Communication and Control (AS-SPCC)*, pp. 153-158. Lake Louise

2

MMSE-Based Filtering for Linear and Nonlinear Systems in the Presence of Non-Gaussian System and Measurement Noise

I. Bilik[1] and J. Tabrikian[2]
[1]Dept. of Electrical and Computer Engineering, University of Massachusetts, Dartmouth, MA,
[2]Dept. of Electrical and Computer Engineering, Ben-Gurion University of the Negev,
[1]USA
[2]Israel

1. Introduction

This chapter addresses the problems of minimum mean square error (MMSE) estimation in non-Gaussian linear and nonlinear systems. In many scientific and practical problems (such as control, astronomy, economic data analysis, communication and radar surveillance), estimation of time-varying system state using a sequence of noisy measurements is performed using the dynamic state-space (DSS) modeling approach. In the DSS approach, the time-varying dynamics of an unobserved state are characterized by the state vector. In most problems, the Bayesian approach can be efficiently used for system state estimation. The posterior probability density function (PDF), which contains the complete statistical information for the system state estimation, can be used for optimal (in any sense) state estimation [1]. Unfortunately, many practical applications, such as target tracking in radar systems are nonlinear and non-Gaussian. Thus, in maneuvering target tracking applications, a heavy-tailed distribution is usually used to model the abrupt changes of the system state due to target maneuver [2]. In addition, changes in the target aspect toward the radar may cause irregular electromagnetic wave reections, resulting significant variations of radar reections [3]. This phenomenon gives rise to outliers in angle tracking, and it is referred to as target glint [4]. It was found that glint has a long-tailed PDF [3], [5], and its distribution can be modeled by mixture of a zero-mean, small-variance Gaussian and a heavy-tailed Laplacian [6]. The Gaussian mixture model (GMM) with two mixture components is widely used in the literature for abrupt changes of the system state and glint noise modeling [3], [7]. This model consists of one small variance Gaussian with high probability and one large variance Gaussian with low probability of occurrence. The nonlinearity behavior in target tracking systems is due to the fact that the target dynamics are usually modeled in Cartesian

---

Reprinted, with permission, from IEEE Trans. Aerospace and Electronic Systems, references [39] and [45]

coordinates, while the observation model is in polar coordinates. There is no general analytic expression for the posterior PDF in nonlinear problems and only suboptimal estimation algorithms have been studied [1]. The extended Kalman filter (EKF) is the most popular approach for recursive nonlinear estimation [8], [9]. The main idea of the EKF is based on a first-order linearization of the model where the posterior PDF and the system and measurement noises are assumed to be Gaussian. The nonlinearity of the measurement model leads to non-Gaussian, multi-modal PDF of the system state, even when the system and the measurement noises are Gaussian. The Gaussian approximation of this multi-modal distribution leads to poor tracking performance. The unscented Kalman filter (UKF) approximates the PDF at the output of the nonlinear transformation using deterministic sampling [10]-[11]. The advantage of the UKF over the EKF stems from the fact that it does not involve approximation of the nonlinear model per se [12], [13]. The UKF provides an unbiased estimate, however its convergence is slow [13]. Many researchers addressed the problem of filtering in non-Gaussian models. One of the effective algorithms in the non-Gaussian problems is the Masreliez filter [14], [15] that employs a nonlinear "score-function", calculated from known *a-priori* noise statistics. The score-function is customized for the noise statistics and has to be redesigned for each application. The main disadvantage of this approach is that it involves a computationally expensive score function calculation [6]. In [16], the Masreliez filter was used in the target tracking problem with glint noise. Recently, a few new filtering approaches have been proposed for the problem of target tracking. One of them is the multiple modeling (MM) approach, in which the time-varying motion of the maneuvering target is described by multiple models [17]. In this approach, the non-Gaussian system is represented by a mixture of parallel Gaussian-distributed modes [8]. Using the Bayesian framework, the posterior PDF of the system state is obtained as a mixture of conditional estimates with *a-priori* probabilities of each mode [18]. Various filters are used for mode-conditioned state estimation. For example, the Gaussian sum filter (GSF), was implemented in [8], [19] using a bank of KFs. The EKF and Masreliez filters were used as mode-conditioned filters for the nonlinear problems of target tracking in [6], [16], [20]. The main drawback of the MM approach is the exponential growth of the number of the modes, and exponentially increasing number of mode-conditioned filters [18], [21]. Therefore, optimal algorithms, such as the GSF, are impractical. The direct approximation methods for target tracking in the presence of clutter with GMM distribution approximation were proposed in [22]-[28]. The joint probabilistic data association (JPDA) [18] and global nearest neighbor (GNN) [25] approximate the entire GMM by a single Gaussian, loosing important information contained in other mixture components. The multiple hypothesis tracking (MHT) [26] and mixture reduction (MR) methods [22], employ *ad-hoc* joining and clustering preserving mean and covariance of the original distribution. The direct approximation algorithms are generally computationally efficient, however, they are suboptimal due to the *ad-hoc* mixture approximation methods and lead to degraded target tracking performance. A suboptimal, computationally-efficient interacting MM (IMM) algorithm was successfully applied to the maneuvering target tracking problem [18], [29], [30]. In [7], [16], [20] the IMM algorithm with EKFs and Masreliez filters were implemented for maneuvering target tracking in the presence of glint noise. The IMM algorithm with greater number of modes was proposed in [31] for non-Gaussian system and measurement noise. In the recent decade, a new class of filtering methods has been proposed based on the sequential Monte Carlo (MC) approach. The sequential importance sampling technique forms the basis for most MC techniques [32]. In these techniques, the filtering is performed recursively generating MC samples of the state variables. These methods are often very exible in non-Gaussian problems due to the nature of the MC simulations [33]. One of the popular techniques of this approach is the PF, which is a suboptimal estimator that approximates the posterior distribution by a set of random samples with associated weights. The PF models the posterior distribution using discrete random samples rather than using an analytic model [34]. The Gaussian sum particle filter (GSPF) [35] implements the PF assuming Gaussian mixture distributions for the system and measurement noises. The GSPF generalizes the GSF introducing a new model order reduction method. Thus, the model order of the system state PDF remains constant over iterations, discarding mixands with small weights. The PF has been extensively used for maneuvering target tracking (e.g. [2]). In [36], the PF was applied to the problem of tracking in glint noise environment. As it was shown in [37] and [38], the PF outperforms the IMM algorithm when the likelihood function is multi-modal. Different application-driven PFs are presented in the literature, but there is no precise rule, which type of PF should be used in each application. This implies that no rigorous PF exists, which is one of the disadvantages of the PF approach. In this chapter, two recursive methods, based on the MMSE estimator of the GMM distributed state vector, are presented. The first is Gaussian mixture Kalman filter (GMKF), derived in [39], [40], for a linear model with non-Gaussian system and measurement noise. This algorithm relies on the fact that any PDF can be closely approximated by a mixture of finite number of Gaussians [41]. A greedy EM-based model order reduction method for the problem of exponential model order growth, discussed in [18], [21] and [19], is derived. The greedy learning algorithm controls the GMM order of the system state PDF, which might vary over the iterations, but remains finite. The EM-based model order reduction method is optimal with respect to the Kullback-Leibler divergence (KLD), that is, it minimizes the KLD of the reduced-order estimated PDF from the "true" PDF of the system state. The GMKF addresses a general estimation problem with non-Gaussian system and measurement noise, modeled by the GMM. This problem is of a great practical interest, for example, in maneuvering target tracking in the presence of glint noise [31]. The second recursive algorithm, named as nonlinear GMKF (NL-GMKF), extends the GMKF to nonlinear models [44]-[46]. The NL-GMKF considers the case of non-Gaussian system and measurement noises as well as non-Gaussian posterior PDF of the state vector. The expected significance of the NL-GMKF is in practical applications of low to moderate maneuvering target tracking, when maneuver detection is difficult. The advantage of the NL-GMKF over other tracking algorithms is significant especially in the presence of glint measurement noise with small probability of detection and high significance. The correlation between the statistics of glint noise and maneuver (that characterizes a maneuvering target consisting of multiple scattering centers) makes the problem of maneuvering target tracking in the presence of glint noise extremely challenging, due to the difficulty of maneuver and glint detection and filtering simultaneously. The NL-GMKF does not require prior knowledge of the target dynamics such as coordinated turn model, therefore, it might be useful when tracking targets with a complicated maneuvering profile that cannot be modeled by a finite set of simple dynamic models.

2. DSS model

A. Linear model

Consider a state sequence $\{\mathbf{s}[n], n = 0, 1, 2, ...\}$ and observations $\{\mathbf{x}[n], n = 0, 1, 2, ...\}$ whose time evolution and observation equations are described by the following linear non-Gaussian model

$$\mathbf{s}[n] = \mathbf{A}[n]\mathbf{s}[n-1] + \mathbf{u}[n] \ , \tag{1}$$

$$\mathbf{x}[n] = \mathbf{H}[n]\mathbf{s}[n] + \mathbf{w}[n] \ , \tag{2}$$

where the state transition matrices, $\mathbf{A}[n]$, and the observation matrices, $\mathbf{H}[n]$, are known. The initial state $\mathbf{s}[-1]$, the zero-mean driving noise $\mathbf{u}[n]$, and the zero-mean measurement noise $\mathbf{w}[n]$ are independent with the following distributions

$$\mathbf{s}[-1] \sim GMM(\alpha_{\mathbf{s}l}[-1], \boldsymbol{\mu}_{\mathbf{s}l}[-1], \boldsymbol{\Gamma}_{\mathbf{s}l}[-1]; l = 1, \ldots, L) \ , \tag{3}$$

$$\mathbf{u}[n] \sim GMM(\alpha_{\mathbf{u}k}[n], \boldsymbol{\mu}_{\mathbf{u}k}[n], \boldsymbol{\Gamma}_{\mathbf{u}k}[n]; k = 1, \ldots, K) \ , \tag{4}$$

$$\mathbf{w}[n] \sim GMM(\alpha_{\mathbf{w}m}[n], \boldsymbol{\mu}_{\mathbf{w}m}[n], \boldsymbol{\Gamma}_{\mathbf{w}m}[n]; m = 1, \ldots, M) \ , \tag{5}$$

where $GMM(\alpha_j, \boldsymbol{\mu}_j, \boldsymbol{\Gamma}_j, j = 1,..., J)$ denotes a Jth-order proper complex Gaussian mixture distribution with weights, $\{\alpha_j\}_{j=1}^J$, mean vectors, $\{\boldsymbol{\mu}_j\}_{j=1}^J$, and covariance matrices, $\{\boldsymbol{\Gamma}_j\}_{j=1}^J$. The driving noise $\mathbf{u}[n]$ and the measurement noise $\mathbf{w}[n]$ are temporally independent, i.e. $\mathbf{u}[n]$ and $\mathbf{u}[n']$, and $\mathbf{w}[n]$ and $\mathbf{w}[n']$ are mutually independent for any time instances $n = 0, 1, 2,..., n' = 0, 1, 2, ...; n \neq n'$. The PDF of a GMM-distributed random vector $\mathbf{y} \sim GMM(\alpha_{\mathbf{y}j}, \boldsymbol{\mu}_{\mathbf{y}j}, \boldsymbol{\Gamma}_{\mathbf{y}j}; j = 1,..., J)$ is given by

$$f_{\mathbf{y}}(\mathbf{y}) = \sum_{j=1}^{J} \alpha_{\mathbf{y}j} \Phi(\mathbf{y}; \boldsymbol{\theta}_j) \ , \tag{6}$$

where $\Phi(\mathbf{y}; \boldsymbol{\theta}_j)$ is a Gaussian PDF and $\boldsymbol{\theta}_j$ contains the mean vector, $\boldsymbol{\mu}_{\mathbf{y}j}$ and the covariance matrix, $\boldsymbol{\Gamma}_{\mathbf{y}j}$. In the following, we will use the term Gaussian for proper Gaussian distributions.

B. Non-linear model

The nonlinear and non-Gaussian DSS model is:

$$\mathbf{s}[n] = \mathbf{a}(\mathbf{s}[n-1], \mathbf{u}[n]) \ , \tag{7}$$

$$\mathbf{x}[n] = \mathbf{h}(\mathbf{s}[n], \mathbf{w}[n]) \ , \tag{8}$$

where the nonlinear transition function, $\mathbf{a}(\cdot,\cdot)$, and the observation function, $\mathbf{h}(\cdot,\cdot)$, are assumed to be known. The system and measurement noise are non-Gaussian with known PDFs. The driving noise, $\mathbf{u}[n]$, and the measurement noise, $\mathbf{w}[n]$, are temporally independent, i.e. $\mathbf{u}[n]$ and $\mathbf{u}[n']$, and $\mathbf{w}[n]$ and $\mathbf{w}[n']$ are mutually independent for any time instances $n = 0, 1, 2,...; n' = 0, 1, 2,... ; n \neq n'$. The initial state, $\mathbf{s}[-1]$, the driving noise, $\mathbf{u}[n]$, and the measurement noise, $\mathbf{w}[n]$, are independent. The initial state distribution is modeled in (3).

3. MMSE-based filters

Let $\hat{\mathbf{s}}[n|p]$ denote the MMSE estimator of $\mathbf{s}[n]$ from $\mathcal{X}[p]$ where $\mathcal{X}[p] \triangleq (\mathbf{x}^T[0], \mathbf{x}^T[1], \ldots, \mathbf{x}^T[p])^T$. The notation $\hat{\mathbf{s}}[n|n-1]$ stands for one-step prediction of the state vector $\mathbf{s}[n]$ from data $\mathcal{X}[n-1]$. The objective of this section is to derive recursive methods for estimation of $\mathbf{s}[n]$ from the observed data $\mathcal{X}[n]$ for the linear and nonlinear non-Gaussian models. To this end, the MMSE criterion resulting in the conditional mean estimator

$$\hat{\mathbf{s}}[n|n] \triangleq E[\mathbf{s}[n]|\mathcal{X}[n]] , \tag{9}$$

is employed.

A. GMKF

For the linear DSS model, stated in Section IIA, the MMSE estimator of the state vector $\mathbf{s}[n]$ from the measurements $\mathcal{X}[n]$ can be implemented by the following recursive algorithm, named as GSF.

GSF Theorem

1. Initialization:

Initialize the GMM parameters of the state vector at time instance $n = -1$ for $l = 1,\ldots, L$.

$$\alpha_{\mathbf{s}}[-1|-1, \eta_l[-1]] = \alpha_{\mathbf{s}l}[-1] , \tag{10}$$

$$\boldsymbol{\mu}_{\mathbf{s}}[-1|-1, \eta_l[-1]] = \boldsymbol{\mu}_{\mathbf{s}l}[-1] , \tag{11}$$

$$\boldsymbol{\Gamma}_{\mathbf{s}}[-1|-1, \eta_l[-1]] = \boldsymbol{\Gamma}_{\mathbf{s}l}[-1] , \tag{12}$$

where $\eta_{sl}[n]$, $l = 1,\ldots, L$ is the random mixture indicator [47]-[48].

Set $n = 0$.

2. Prediction

2a. Predicted state PDF parameters:

$$\boldsymbol{\theta}[n|n-1] = \{\boldsymbol{\alpha}_{\mathbf{s}}[n|n-1, \tilde{\eta}_{lk}[n]], \boldsymbol{\mu}_{\mathbf{s}}[n|n-1, \tilde{\eta}_{lk}[n]], \boldsymbol{\Gamma}_{\mathbf{s}}[n|n-1, \tilde{\eta}_{lk}[n]]\}_{(l,k)=(1,1)}^{(L,K)}$$

in which

$$\alpha_{\mathbf{s}}[n|n-1, \tilde{\eta}_{lk}[n]] = \alpha_{\mathbf{s}}[n-1|n-1, \eta_l[n-1]]\alpha_{\mathbf{u}k}[n] , \tag{13}$$

$$\boldsymbol{\mu}_{\mathbf{s}}[n|n-1, \tilde{\eta}_{lk}[n]] = \mathbf{A}[n]\boldsymbol{\mu}_{\mathbf{s}}[n-1|n-1, \eta_l[n-1]] + \boldsymbol{\mu}_{\mathbf{u}k}[n] , \tag{14}$$

$$\boldsymbol{\Gamma}_{\mathbf{s}}[n|n-1, \tilde{\eta}_{lk}[n]] = \mathbf{A}[n]\boldsymbol{\Gamma}_{\mathbf{s}}[n-1|n-1, \eta_l[n-1]]\mathbf{A}^H[n] + \boldsymbol{\Gamma}_{\mathbf{u}k}[n] . \tag{15}$$

The PDFs of the state and system noise are modeled by GMM of order L and K, respectively, and therefore in the prediction stage, the number of mixture components grows to LK. The random indicator for this mixture is denoted as $\tilde{\eta}_{lk}[n]$, $l = 1,\ldots, L$; $k = 1,\ldots,K$.

2b. Prediction of the state vector:

$$\hat{\mathbf{s}}[n|n-1] = \sum_{l=1}^{L}\sum_{k=1}^{K} \alpha_{\mathbf{s}}[n|n-1, \tilde{\eta}_{lk}[n]]\boldsymbol{\mu}_{\mathbf{s}}[n|n-1, \tilde{\eta}_{lk}[n]] . \tag{16}$$

2c. Prediction of the measurements vector and innovation calculation:
The MMSE prediction of $\mathbf{x}[n]$ from $\mathcal{X}[n-1]$ is

$$\hat{\mathbf{x}}[n|n-1] \triangleq E(\mathbf{x}[n]|\mathcal{X}[n-1]) = \mathbf{A}[n]\hat{\mathbf{s}}[n|n-1] \; . \tag{17}$$

Define the innovation process $\tilde{\mathbf{x}}[n]$ as

$$\tilde{\mathbf{x}}[n] \triangleq \mathbf{x}[n] - \hat{\mathbf{x}}[n|n-1] \; .$$

The mixture parameters of the conditional PDF $\tilde{\mathbf{x}}[n] \,|\, \mathcal{X}[n-1]$ are defined as follows: $\boldsymbol{\theta}_{lkm}[n] = \{\boldsymbol{\mu}_{\tilde{\mathbf{x}}}[n \,|\, n-1, \bar{\eta}_{lkm}[n]], \boldsymbol{\Gamma}_{\tilde{\mathbf{x}}}[n \,|\, n-1, \bar{\eta}_{lkm}[n]]\}$ and

$$\alpha_{\tilde{\mathbf{x}}}[n|n-1, \bar{\eta}_{lkm}[n]] = \alpha_{\mathbf{s}}[n|n-1, \bar{\eta}_{lk}[n]] \cdot \alpha_{\mathbf{w}m}[n] \; , \tag{18}$$

$$\boldsymbol{\mu}_{\tilde{\mathbf{x}}}[n|n-1, \bar{\eta}_{lkm}[n]] = \mathbf{H}[n]\left(\boldsymbol{\mu}_{\mathbf{s}}[n|n-1, \bar{\eta}_{lk}[n]] - \hat{\mathbf{s}}[n|n-1]\right) + \boldsymbol{\mu}_{\mathbf{w}m}[n] \; , \tag{19}$$

$$\boldsymbol{\Gamma}_{\tilde{\mathbf{x}}}[n|n-1, \bar{\eta}_{lkm}[n]] = \mathbf{H}[n]\boldsymbol{\Gamma}_{\mathbf{s}}[n|n-1, \bar{\eta}_{lk}[n]]\mathbf{H}^H[n] + \boldsymbol{\Gamma}_{\mathbf{w}m}[n] \; , \tag{20}$$

3. Kalman gain:

$$\begin{aligned}\mathbf{K}_{lkm}[n] = &\left(\boldsymbol{\Gamma}_{\mathbf{s}}[n|n-1, \bar{\eta}_{lkm}[n]]\mathbf{H}^H[n] + \left(\boldsymbol{\mu}_{\mathbf{s}}[n|n-1, \bar{\eta}_{lkm}[n]] - \hat{\mathbf{s}}[n|n-1]\right)\boldsymbol{\mu}_{\mathbf{w}m}[n]\right) \\ &\cdot \left(\mathbf{H}[n]\boldsymbol{\Gamma}_{\mathbf{s}}[n|n-1, \bar{\eta}_{lkm}[n]]\mathbf{H}^H[n] + \boldsymbol{\Gamma}_{\mathbf{w}m}[n]\right)^{-1} \; .\end{aligned} \tag{21}$$

The measurement noise PDF is modeled by GMM of order M, and therefore at the estimation stage the number of mixture components grows to LKM. The random indicator for this mixture is denoted as $\bar{\eta}_{lkm}[n]$, $l = 1,\dots, L$; $k = 1,\dots, K$; $m = 1,\dots, M$.

4. Estimation
4a. Estimated state mixture parameters:

$$\bar{\boldsymbol{\theta}}[n|n] \triangleq \{\alpha_{\mathbf{s}}[n|n, \bar{\eta}_{lkm}[n]], \boldsymbol{\mu}_{\mathbf{s}}[n|n, \bar{\eta}_{lkm}[n]], \boldsymbol{\Gamma}_{\mathbf{s}}[n|n, \bar{\eta}_{lkm}[n]]\}_{(l,k,m)=(1,1,1)}^{(L,K,M)} \tag{22}$$

where

$$\alpha_{\mathbf{s}}[n|n, \bar{\eta}_{lkm}[n]] = \frac{\alpha_{\tilde{\mathbf{x}}}[n|n-1, \bar{\eta}_{lkm}[n]]\Phi(\tilde{\mathbf{x}}[n]; \boldsymbol{\theta}_{lkm}[n])}{\sum_{l'=1}^{L}\sum_{k'=1}^{K}\sum_{m'=1}^{M} \alpha_{\tilde{\mathbf{x}}}[n|n-1, \bar{\eta}_{l'k'm'}[n]]\Phi(\tilde{\mathbf{x}}[n]; \boldsymbol{\theta}_{l'k'm'}[n])} \; , \tag{23}$$

$$\boldsymbol{\mu}_{\mathbf{s}}[n|n, \bar{\eta}_{lkm}[n]] = \boldsymbol{\mu}_{\mathbf{s}}[n|n-1, \bar{\eta}_{lkm}[n]] + \mathbf{K}_{lkm}[n]\left(\tilde{\mathbf{x}}[n] - \boldsymbol{\mu}_{\tilde{\mathbf{x}}}[n|n-1, \bar{\eta}_{lkm}[n]]\right) \; , \tag{24}$$

$$\begin{aligned}\boldsymbol{\Gamma}_{\mathbf{s}}[n|n, \bar{\eta}_{lkm}[n]] = &\left(\mathbf{I} - \mathbf{K}_{lkm}[n]\mathbf{H}[n]\right)\boldsymbol{\Gamma}_{\mathbf{s}}[n|n-1, \bar{\eta}_{lk}[n]] + \mathbf{K}_{lkm}[n]\left(\boldsymbol{\mu}_{\mathbf{s}}[n|n-1, \bar{\eta}_{lk}[n]] - \hat{\mathbf{s}}[n|n-1]\right)\boldsymbol{\mu}_{\mathbf{w}m}[n] \; , \\ &\forall l = 1,\dots,L; \; k = 1,\dots,K; \; m = 1,\dots,M \; ,\end{aligned} \tag{25}$$

4b. Estimation of the state vector:

$$\hat{\mathbf{s}}[n|n] = \sum_{l=1}^{L}\sum_{k=1}^{K}\sum_{m=1}^{M} \alpha_{\mathbf{s}}[n|n, \bar{\eta}_{lkm}[n]]\boldsymbol{\mu}_{\mathbf{s}}[n|n, \bar{\eta}_{lkm}[n]] \; , \tag{26}$$

5. Set $n \to n+1$, go to step 2.
Note that according to this theorem, the model order grows during the prediction (stage 2) due to the non-Gaussian system noise, and during the estimation (stage 4) due to the non-Gaussian measurement noise. The GMKF algorithm consists of the GSF followed by a model order reduction algorithm implemented after the estimation stage:

$$\begin{aligned}\boldsymbol{\theta}[n|n] &\triangleq \{\alpha_{\mathbf{s}}[n|n,\eta_l[n]], \boldsymbol{\mu}_{\mathbf{s}}[n|n,\eta_l[n]], \boldsymbol{\Gamma}_{\mathbf{s}}[n|n,\eta_l[n]]\}_{l=1}^{L} \\ &= EM_{LKM\to L}\left(\{\alpha_{\mathbf{s}}[n|n,\bar{\eta}_{lkm}[n]], \boldsymbol{\mu}_{\mathbf{s}}[n|n,\bar{\eta}_{lkm}[n]], \boldsymbol{\Gamma}_{\mathbf{s}}[n|n,\bar{\eta}_{lkm}[n]]\}_{(l,k,m)=(1,1,1)}^{(L,K,M)}\right) .\end{aligned} \tag{27}$$

The operator $EM_{LKM\to L}$ means that the parameters of an L-order GMM are estimated via synthetic data generation according to the GMM PDF with LKM components. Note that in general, the GMM order of the posterior state PDF can vary from iteration to iteration. The GMKF stages that are similar to the KF (see e.g. [49]) are schematically presented in Fig. 1.
Proof: In the following, an algorithm for obtaining $\hat{\mathbf{s}}[n|n]$ is developed from $\hat{\mathbf{s}}[n-1|n-1]$. Let the MMSE prediction of $\mathbf{x}[n]$ from $\mathcal{X}[n-1]$ be defined as

$$\hat{\mathbf{x}}[n|n-1] \triangleq E(\mathbf{x}[n]|\mathcal{X}[n-1]) , \tag{28}$$

and the innovation process be

$$\tilde{\mathbf{x}}[n] \triangleq \mathbf{x}[n] - \hat{\mathbf{x}}[n|n-1] . \tag{29}$$

If the transformation $\mathcal{X}[n] \leftrightarrow [\mathcal{X}^T[n-1], \tilde{\mathbf{x}}^T[n]]^T$ is one-to-one, then the conditional distribution of $\mathbf{s}[n]|\mathcal{X}[n]$ is identical to the conditional distribution of $\mathbf{s}[n]|\mathcal{X}[n-1], \tilde{\mathbf{x}}[n]$. The vector $\hat{\mathbf{x}}[n|n-1]$ is calculated using (2) and the statistical independence between $\mathcal{X}[n-1]$ and the zero-mean measurement noise $\mathbf{w}[n]$, as follows:

$$\hat{\mathbf{x}}[n|n-1] = E(\mathbf{x}[n]|\mathcal{X}[n-1]) = E(\mathbf{H}[n]\mathbf{s}[n] + \mathbf{w}[n]|\mathcal{X}[n-1]) = \mathbf{H}[n]\hat{\mathbf{s}}[n|n-1] ,$$

where $\hat{\mathbf{s}}[n|n-1]$ is the prediction of the state vector at time instance n, from data $\mathcal{X}[n-1]$, obtained by using (1):

$$\hat{\mathbf{s}}[n|n-1] = E(\mathbf{s}[n]|\mathcal{X}[n-1]) = \mathbf{A}[n]\hat{\mathbf{s}}[n-1|n-1] , \tag{30}$$

where $\hat{\mathbf{s}}[n-1|n-1]$ is the conditional mean estimator of the state vector $\mathbf{s}[n-1]$ from data $\mathcal{X}[n-1]$. The innovation process in (29) can be expressed using (1), (2) and (30), as

$$\begin{aligned}\tilde{\mathbf{x}}[n] &= \mathbf{H}[n](\mathbf{s}[n] - \hat{\mathbf{s}}[n|n-1]) + \mathbf{w}[n] \\ &= \mathbf{H}[n]\left(\mathbf{A}[n]\left(\mathbf{s}[n-1] - \hat{\mathbf{s}}[n-1|n-1]\right) + \mathbf{u}[n]\right) + \mathbf{w}[n] .\end{aligned} \tag{31}$$

Using (1), (30) and (31) it can be obtained that

$$\mathbf{y}[n] \triangleq \begin{bmatrix} \mathbf{s}[n] \\ \tilde{\mathbf{x}}[n] \end{bmatrix} = \begin{bmatrix} \mathbf{A}[n] & \mathbf{I} & \mathbf{0} \\ \mathbf{H}[n]\mathbf{A}[n] & \mathbf{H}[n] & \mathbf{I} \end{bmatrix} \begin{bmatrix} \mathbf{s}[n-1] \\ \mathbf{u}[n] \\ \mathbf{w}[n] \end{bmatrix} - \begin{bmatrix} \mathbf{0} \\ \mathbf{H}[n]\hat{\mathbf{s}}[n|n-1] \end{bmatrix} . \tag{32}$$

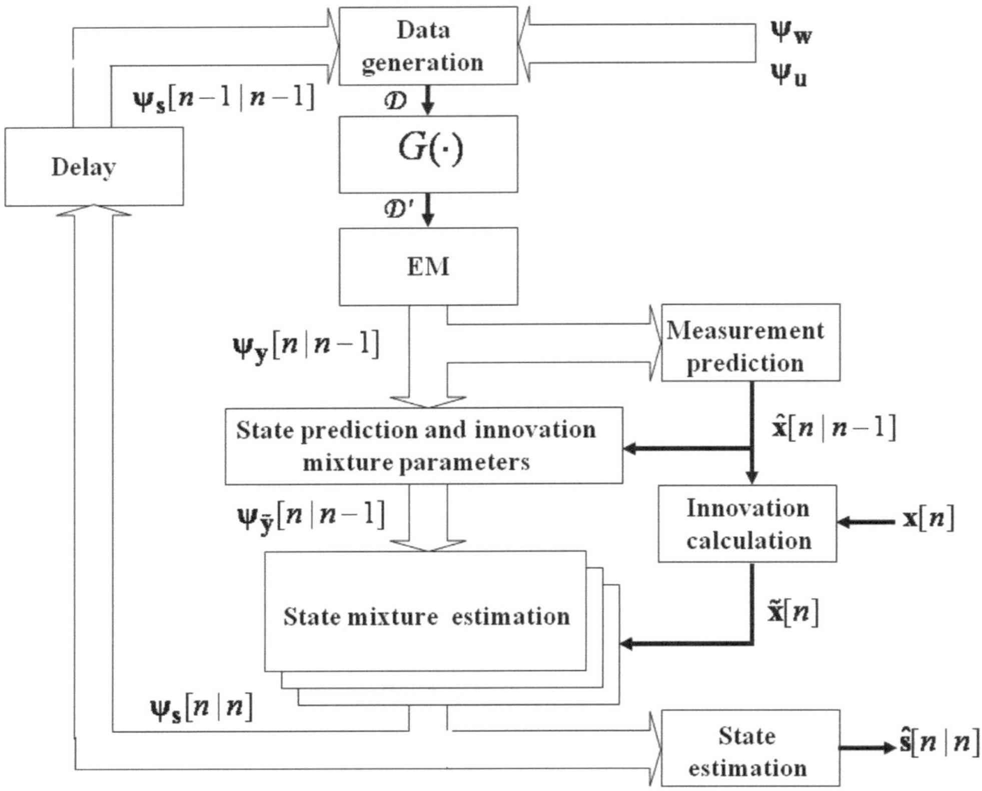

Fig. 1. GMKF schematic diagram.

The conditional distribution of $\begin{bmatrix} \mathbf{s}[n-1] \\ \mathbf{u}[n] \\ \mathbf{w}[n] \end{bmatrix}$ given $\mathcal{X}[n-1]$ is GMM of order *LKM*, because $\mathbf{s}[n-1]$, $\mathbf{u}[n]$ and $\mathbf{w}[n]$ are independent, $\mathbf{s}[n-1] \mid \mathcal{X}[n-1]$ is GMM distributed of order *L*, $\mathbf{u}[n]$ is GMM distributed of order *K*, and $\mathbf{w}[n]$ is GMM distributed of order *M*. According to (32), $\mathbf{y}[n]$ is a linear transformation of $\begin{bmatrix} \mathbf{s}[n-1] \\ \mathbf{u}[n] \\ \mathbf{w}[n] \end{bmatrix}$ and therefore, using Proposition 2 in the appendix, the conditional distribution of $\mathbf{y}[n]$ given $\mathcal{X}[n-1]$ is also GMM of order *LKM*:

$$\mathbf{y}[n]|\mathcal{X}[n-1] \sim GMM\left(\alpha_{\mathbf{y}}[n|n-1,\bar{\eta}_{lkm}[n]], \boldsymbol{\mu}_{\mathbf{y}}[n|n-1,\bar{\eta}_{lkm}[n]], \boldsymbol{\Gamma}_{\mathbf{y}}[n|n-1,\bar{\eta}_{lkm}[n]], \right. \\ \left. l=1,\ldots,L;\ k=1,\ldots,K;\ m=1,\ldots,M\right), \quad (33)$$

where

$$\boldsymbol{\mu}_{\mathbf{y}}[n|n-1,\bar{\eta}_{lkm}[n]] \triangleq \begin{bmatrix} \boldsymbol{\mu}_{\mathbf{s}}[n|n-1,\bar{\eta}_{lkm}[n]] \\ \boldsymbol{\mu}_{\tilde{\mathbf{x}}}[n|n-1,\bar{\eta}_{lkm}[n]] \end{bmatrix}, \quad (34)$$

$$\boldsymbol{\Gamma}_{\mathbf{y}}[n|n-1,\bar{\eta}_{lkm}[n]] \triangleq \begin{bmatrix} \boldsymbol{\Gamma}_{\mathbf{s}}[n|n-1,\bar{\eta}_{lkm}[n]] & \boldsymbol{\Gamma}_{\mathbf{s}\tilde{\mathbf{x}}}[n|n-1,\bar{\eta}_{lkm}[n]] \\ \boldsymbol{\Gamma}_{\tilde{\mathbf{x}}\mathbf{s}}[n|n-1,\bar{\eta}_{lkm}[n]] & \boldsymbol{\Gamma}_{\tilde{\mathbf{x}}}[n|n-1,\bar{\eta}_{lkm}[n]] \end{bmatrix}, \quad (35)$$

and $\boldsymbol{\mu}_{\mathbf{s}}[n|n-1, \bar{\eta}_{lkm}[n]]$ is the MMSE estimator of $\mathbf{s}[n]$ from $\mathcal{X}[n-1]$ given the *lkm*th mixture indicator $\bar{\eta}_{lkm}[n]$, defined as

$$\boldsymbol{\mu}_{\mathbf{s}}[n|n-1, \bar{\eta}_{lkm}[n]] = E[\mathbf{s}[n]|\mathcal{X}[n-1], \bar{\eta}_{lkm}[n]] \; . \tag{36}$$

As mentioned above, the distribution of $\mathbf{s}[n]|\mathcal{X}[n]$ is identical to the distribution of $\mathbf{s}[n]|\mathcal{X}[n-1], \tilde{\mathbf{x}}[n]$. Since $\mathbf{s}[n]$ and $\tilde{\mathbf{x}}[n]$ given $\mathcal{X}[n-1]$ are jointly GMM of order *LKM*, then the conditional distribution of $\mathbf{s}[n]|\mathcal{X}[n]$ is GMM:

$$\begin{aligned}\mathbf{s}[n]|\mathcal{X}[n] \sim GMM\,(&\alpha_{\mathbf{s}}[n|n, \bar{\eta}_{lkm}[n]], \boldsymbol{\mu}_{\mathbf{s}}[n|n, \bar{\eta}_{lkm}[n]], \mathbf{M}[n|n, \bar{\eta}_{lkm}[n]],\\ &l = 1, \ldots, L; k = 1, \ldots, K; m = 1, \ldots, M) \;,\end{aligned} \tag{37}$$

where the parameters of this conditional distribution are given by

$$\tilde{\boldsymbol{\theta}}[n|n] \triangleq \{\alpha_{\mathbf{s}}[n|n, \bar{\eta}_{lkm}[n]], \boldsymbol{\mu}_{\mathbf{s}}[n|n, \bar{\eta}_{lkm}[n]], \boldsymbol{\Gamma}_{\mathbf{s}}[n|n, \bar{\eta}_{lkm}[n]]\}_{(l,k,m)=(1,1,1)}^{(L,K,M)} \; . \tag{38}$$

In the following, expressions for the parameters in $\tilde{\boldsymbol{\theta}}[n|n]$ are derived. Using the Bayesian rule, the estimated mixture weights are given by

$$\alpha_{\mathbf{s}}[n|n, \bar{\eta}_{lkm}[n]] = \frac{\alpha_{\tilde{\mathbf{x}}}[n|n-1, \bar{\eta}_{lkm}[n]]\Phi(\tilde{\mathbf{x}}[n]; \boldsymbol{\theta}_{lkm}[n])}{\sum_{l'=1}^{L}\sum_{k'=1}^{K}\sum_{m'=1}^{M} \alpha_{\tilde{\mathbf{x}}}[n|n-1, \bar{\eta}_{l'k'm'}[n]]\Phi(\tilde{\mathbf{x}}[n]; \boldsymbol{\theta}_{l'k'm'}[n])} \; . \tag{39}$$

The relation between the parameters of the *lkm*th mixture component in the conditional distribution of $\mathbf{s}[n], \tilde{\mathbf{x}}[n]|\mathcal{X}[n-1]$ and in the conditional distribution of $\mathbf{s}[n]|\mathcal{X}[n-1], \tilde{\mathbf{x}}[n]$ is obtained below. For any random mixture indicator $\bar{\eta}_{lkm}[n]$, the vectors $\mathbf{s}[n]$ and $\tilde{\mathbf{x}}[n]$ given $\mathcal{X}[n-1]$, are jointly Gaussian. Therefore, the MMSE estimator of $\mathbf{s}[n]$ from $\mathcal{X}[n]$, given the *lkm*th mixture indicator $\eta_{lkm}[n]$ is obtained using (36) as:

$$\begin{aligned}\boldsymbol{\mu}_{\mathbf{s}}[n|n, \bar{\eta}_{lkm}[n]] = E\;&[\mathbf{s}[n]|\mathcal{X}[n-1], \tilde{\mathbf{x}}[n], \bar{\eta}_{lkm}[n]] = E[\mathbf{s}[n]|\mathcal{X}[n-1], \bar{\eta}_{lk}[n]]\\ &+ \boldsymbol{\Gamma}_{\mathbf{s}\tilde{\mathbf{x}}}[n|n-1, \bar{\eta}_{lkm}[n]]\boldsymbol{\Gamma}_{\tilde{\mathbf{x}}}^{-1}[n|n-1, \bar{\eta}_{lkm}[n]]\,(\tilde{\mathbf{x}}[n] - \boldsymbol{\mu}_{\tilde{\mathbf{x}}}[n|n-1, \bar{\eta}_{lkm}[n]]) \;,\end{aligned} \tag{40}$$

where $\boldsymbol{\Gamma}_{\tilde{\mathbf{x}}}[n|n-1, \bar{\eta}_{lkm}[n]]$ and $\boldsymbol{\Gamma}_{\mathbf{s}\tilde{\mathbf{x}}}[n|n-1, \bar{\eta}_{lkm}[n]]$ are the *lkm*th covariance and cross-covariance matrices of the conditional distribution of $\tilde{\mathbf{x}}[n]|\mathcal{X}[n-1]$, respectively. The covariance matrix $\boldsymbol{\Gamma}_{\mathbf{s}}[n|n, \bar{\eta}_{lkm}[n]]$ can be obtained as

$$\begin{aligned}\boldsymbol{\Gamma}_{\mathbf{s}}[n|n, \bar{\eta}_{lkm}[n]] &= \operatorname{cov}(\mathbf{s}[n]|\tilde{\mathbf{x}}[n], \mathcal{X}[n-1], \bar{\eta}_{lkm}[n]) = \operatorname{cov}(\mathbf{s}[n]|\mathcal{X}[n-1], \bar{\eta}_{lk}[n])\\ &\quad -\boldsymbol{\Gamma}_{\tilde{\mathbf{x}}\mathbf{s}}^{H}[n|n-1, \bar{\eta}_{lkm}[n]]\boldsymbol{\Gamma}_{\tilde{\mathbf{x}}}^{-1}[n|n-1, \bar{\eta}_{lkm}[n]]\boldsymbol{\Gamma}_{\tilde{\mathbf{x}}\mathbf{s}}[n|n-1, \bar{\eta}_{lkm}[n]] \; .\end{aligned} \tag{41}$$

Following the conventions of the KF, the *lkm*th Kalman gain notation corresponding to the *lkm*th mixture component, is defined as

$$\mathbf{K}_{lkm}[n] \triangleq \boldsymbol{\Gamma}_{\tilde{\mathbf{x}}\mathbf{s}}^{H}[n|n-1, \bar{\eta}_{lkm}[n]]\boldsymbol{\Gamma}_{\tilde{\mathbf{x}}}^{-1}[n|n-1, \bar{\eta}_{lkm}[n]] \; . \tag{42}$$

Using (42), expressions (40) and (41) can be rewritten as

$$\boldsymbol{\mu}_{\mathbf{s}}[n|n,\bar{\eta}_{lkm}[n]] = \boldsymbol{\mu}_{\mathbf{s}}[n|n-1,\tilde{\eta}_{lk}[n]] + \mathbf{K}_{lkm}[n]\left(\tilde{\mathbf{x}}[n] - \boldsymbol{\mu}_{\tilde{\mathbf{x}}}[n|n-1,\bar{\eta}_{lkm}[n]]\right), \quad (43)$$

$$\boldsymbol{\Gamma}_{\mathbf{s}}[n|n,\bar{\eta}_{lkm}[n]] = \boldsymbol{\Gamma}_{\mathbf{s}}[n|n-1,\tilde{\eta}_{lk}[n]] - \mathbf{K}_{lkm}[n]\boldsymbol{\Gamma}_{\tilde{\mathbf{x}}\mathbf{s}}[n|n-1,\bar{\eta}_{lkm}[n]]\,. \quad (44)$$

The first terms in the RHS of (43) and (44) are the statistics of the predicted state vector. These terms are calculated using Lemma 1.

Lemma 1: The conditional distribution of the state vector $\mathbf{s}[n]$ given $\mathcal{X}[n-1]$ is

$$\mathbf{s}[n]|\mathcal{X}[n-1] \sim GMM\left(\alpha_{\mathbf{s}}[n|n-1,\tilde{\eta}_{lk}[n]], \boldsymbol{\mu}_{\mathbf{s}}[n|n-1,\tilde{\eta}_{lk}[n]], \boldsymbol{\Gamma}_{\mathbf{s}}[n|n-1,\tilde{\eta}_{lk}[n]], \; l=1,\ldots,L\right),$$

where the predicted state mixture weights, mean vector and covariance matrix of the *lk*th mixture component are

$$\alpha_{\mathbf{s}}[n|n-1,\tilde{\eta}_{lk}[n]] = \alpha_{\mathbf{s}}[n-1|n-1,\eta_l[n-1]]\alpha_{\mathbf{u}k}[n]\,, \quad (45)$$

$$\boldsymbol{\mu}_{\mathbf{s}}[n|n-1,\tilde{\eta}_{lk}[n]] = E(\mathbf{s}[n]|\mathcal{X}[n-1],\tilde{\eta}_{lk}[n]) = \mathbf{A}[n]\boldsymbol{\mu}_{\mathbf{s}}[n-1|n-1,\eta_l[n-1]] + \boldsymbol{\mu}_{\mathbf{u}k}[n]\,, \quad (46)$$

$$\boldsymbol{\Gamma}_{\mathbf{s}}[n|n-1,\tilde{\eta}_{lk}[n]] = \mathrm{cov}(\mathbf{s}[n]|\mathcal{X}[n-1],\tilde{\eta}_{lk}[n]) = \mathbf{A}[n]\boldsymbol{\Gamma}_{\mathbf{s}}[n-1|n-1,\eta_l[n-1]]\mathbf{A}^H[n] + \boldsymbol{\Gamma}_{\mathbf{u}k}[n]\,. \quad (47)$$

Proof: According to (1), $\mathbf{s}[n]$ is the sum of two statistically independent GMM-distributed random variables $\mathbf{A}[n]\mathbf{s}[n-1]$ and $\mathbf{u}[n]$. The system noise, $\mathbf{u}[n]$ is independent of $\mathcal{X}[n-1]$, because it is an i.i.d. sequence independent of the state vector at the previous time instance. Therefore, (45)-(47) can be directly obtained from (1) and Proposition 2 in the appendix. □

Lemma 1 proves the state mixture prediction in (13)-(15). Using Proposition 1 in the appendix and the parameters of the conditional state distribution of $\mathbf{s}[n]$ given $\mathcal{X}[n-1]$ obtained in Lemma 1, the state prediction is

$$\hat{\mathbf{s}}[n|n-1] = \sum_{l=1}^{L}\sum_{k=1}^{K} \alpha_{\mathbf{s}}[n|n-1,\tilde{\eta}_{lk}[n]]\boldsymbol{\mu}_{\mathbf{s}}[n|n-1,\tilde{\eta}_{lk}[n]]\,,$$

which proves the state vector prediction in (16). In order to calculate the second terms in the RHS of (43) and (44), the conditional statistics of the innovation process $\tilde{\mathbf{x}}[n]\,|\,\mathcal{X}[n-1]$ are required.

Lemma 2: The conditional distribution of the innovation process $\tilde{\mathbf{x}}[n]$, defined in (29), given $\mathcal{X}[n-1]$, is GMM of order *LKM*:

$$\tilde{\mathbf{x}}[n]|\mathcal{X}[n-1] \sim GMM\left(\alpha_{\tilde{\mathbf{x}}}[n|n-1,\bar{\eta}_{lkm}[n]], \boldsymbol{\mu}_{\tilde{\mathbf{x}}}[n|n-1,\bar{\eta}_{lkm}[n]], \boldsymbol{\Gamma}_{\tilde{\mathbf{x}}}[n|n-1,\bar{\eta}_{lkm}[n]]; \; l=1,\ldots,L; k=1,\ldots,K; m=1,\ldots,M\right), \quad (48)$$

where the mixture parameters are

$$\begin{aligned} \alpha_{\tilde{\mathbf{x}}}[n|n-1,\bar{\eta}_{lkm}[n]] &= \alpha_{\mathbf{s}}[n|n-1,\tilde{\eta}_{lk}[n]]\cdot\alpha_{\mathbf{w}m}[n]\,, \\ \boldsymbol{\mu}_{\tilde{\mathbf{x}}}[n|n-1,\bar{\eta}_{lkm}[n]] &= \mathbf{H}[n]\left(\boldsymbol{\mu}_{\mathbf{s}}[n|n-1,\tilde{\eta}_{lk}[n]] - \hat{\mathbf{s}}[n|n-1]\right) + \boldsymbol{\mu}_{\mathbf{w}m}[n]\,, \\ \boldsymbol{\Gamma}_{\tilde{\mathbf{x}}}[n|n-1,\bar{\eta}_{lkm}[n]] &= \mathbf{H}[n]\mathbf{M}[n|n-1,\tilde{\eta}_{lk}[n]]\mathbf{H}^H[n] + \boldsymbol{\Gamma}_{\mathbf{w}m}[n]\,. \end{aligned}$$

Proof: According to (31), the innovation process is a linear transformation of $\mathbf{s}[n-1]$, $\mathbf{u}[n]$ and $\mathbf{w}[n]$. Using the statistical properties of the system state, and system and measurement noises, the conditional distribution of the innovation process $\tilde{\mathbf{x}}[n]$ given $\mathcal{X}[n-1]$ is GMM of order *LKM*. The mixture weights, mean vectors and covariance matrices of the *lkm*th mixture component in the conditional PDF of the innovation process are calculated using (31) and Proposition 2 in the appendix, as follows:

$$\alpha_{\tilde{\mathbf{x}}}[n|n-1,\bar{\eta}_{lkm}[n]] = \alpha_{\mathbf{s}}[n|n-1,\tilde{\eta}_{lk}[n]]\cdot\alpha_{\mathbf{w}m}[n]\ , \tag{49}$$

$$\begin{aligned}\boldsymbol{\mu}_{\tilde{\mathbf{x}}}[n|n-1,\bar{\eta}_{lkm}[n]] &= E(\tilde{\mathbf{x}}[n]|\mathcal{X}[n-1],\bar{\eta}_{lkm}[n]) \qquad (50)\\ &= \mathbf{H}[n]\left(E[\mathbf{s}[n]|\mathcal{X}[n-1],\tilde{\eta}_{lk}[n]]-\hat{\mathbf{s}}[n|n-1]\right)+E[\mathbf{w}[n]|\mathcal{X}[n-1],\bar{\eta}_{lkm}[n]]\\ &= \mathbf{H}[n](\boldsymbol{\mu}_{\mathbf{s}}[n|n-1,\tilde{\eta}_{lk}[n]]-\hat{\mathbf{s}}[n|n-1])+\boldsymbol{\mu}_{\mathbf{w}m}[n], \qquad (51)\end{aligned}$$

$$\begin{aligned}\boldsymbol{\Gamma}_{\tilde{\mathbf{x}}}[n|n-1,\bar{\eta}_{lkm}[n]] &= \mathrm{cov}(\tilde{\mathbf{x}}[n]|\mathcal{X}[n-1],\bar{\eta}_{lkm}[n])\\ &= \mathbf{H}[n]\mathrm{cov}\left(\mathbf{s}[n]|\mathcal{X}[n-1],\bar{\eta}_{lkm}[n]\right)\mathbf{H}^H[n]+\mathrm{cov}\left(\mathbf{w}[n]|\mathcal{X}[n-1],\bar{\eta}_{lk}[n]\right) \qquad (52)\\ &= \mathbf{H}[n]\mathbf{M}[n|n-1,\tilde{\eta}_{lk}[n]]\mathbf{H}^H[n]+\boldsymbol{\Gamma}_{\mathbf{w}m}[n]\ ,\end{aligned}$$

where $\alpha_{\mathbf{s}}[n|n-1, \tilde{\eta}_{lk}[n]]$, $\boldsymbol{\mu}_{\mathbf{s}}[n|n-1, \tilde{\eta}_{lk}[n]]$ and $\mathbf{M}[n|n-1, \tilde{\eta}_{lk}[n]]$ are obtained using Lemma 1. □

In the definition of the Kalman gain in (42), the cross-covariance matrix $\boldsymbol{\Gamma}_{\mathbf{s}\tilde{\mathbf{x}}}[n|n-1, \bar{\eta}_{lkm}[n]]$ is required. According to (32) and Proposition 2 in the appendix, the joint distribution of $\mathbf{s}[n]$ and $\tilde{\mathbf{x}}[n]$ given $\mathcal{X}[n-1]$ is GMM of order *LKM* whose *lkm*th cross-covariance matrix $\boldsymbol{\Gamma}_{\mathbf{s}\tilde{\mathbf{x}}}[n|n-1, \bar{\eta}_{lkm}[n]]$, defined in (35), is

$$\boldsymbol{\Gamma}_{\mathbf{s}\tilde{\mathbf{x}}}[n|n-1,\bar{\eta}_{lkm}[n]] = \mathrm{cov}\left(\mathbf{s}[n],\tilde{\mathbf{x}}[n]|\mathcal{X}[n-1],\bar{\eta}_{lkm}[n]\right)\ . \tag{53}$$

By substitution of (31) into (53) we obtain

$$\begin{aligned}\boldsymbol{\Gamma}_{\mathbf{s}\tilde{\mathbf{x}}}[n|n-1,\bar{\eta}_{lkm}[n]] &= \mathrm{cov}\left(\mathbf{s}[n],(\mathbf{H}[n](\mathbf{s}[n]-\hat{\mathbf{s}}[n|n-1])+\mathbf{w}[n])\,|\mathcal{X}[n-1],\bar{\eta}_{lkm}[n]\right)\\ &= \mathrm{cov}\left(\mathbf{s}[n]|\mathcal{X}[n-1],\tilde{\eta}_{lk}[n]\right)\mathbf{H}^H[n]+E\left[(\mathbf{s}[n]-\hat{\mathbf{s}}[n|n-1])\mathbf{w}^H[n]|\mathcal{X}[n-1],\bar{\eta}_{lkm}[n]\right] \qquad (54)\end{aligned}$$

$$=\boldsymbol{\Gamma}_{\mathbf{s}}[n|n-1,\tilde{\eta}_{lk}[n]]\mathbf{H}^H[n]+\left(\boldsymbol{\mu}_{\mathbf{s}}[n|n-1,\tilde{\eta}_{lk}[n]]-\hat{\mathbf{s}}[n|n-1]\right)\boldsymbol{\mu}^H_{\mathbf{w}m}[n]\ . \tag{55}$$

where (54) is obtained under the assumption that $\mathbf{w}[n]$ is independent of $\mathbf{s}[n]$, and since $\hat{\mathbf{s}}[n|n-1]$ given $\mathcal{X}[n-1]$ is deterministic. Using (52) and (55), the Kalman gain defined in (42), can be rewritten as

$$\begin{aligned}\mathbf{K}_{lkm}[n] &= \left(\boldsymbol{\Gamma}_{\mathbf{s}}[n|n-1,\tilde{\eta}_{lk}[n]]\mathbf{H}^H[n]+(\boldsymbol{\mu}_{\mathbf{s}}[n|n-1,\tilde{\eta}_{lk}[n]]-\hat{\mathbf{s}}[n|n-1])\,\boldsymbol{\mu}^H_{\mathbf{w}m}[n]\right)\\ &\quad\cdot\left(\mathbf{H}[n]\boldsymbol{\Gamma}_{\mathbf{s}}[n|n-1,\tilde{\eta}_{lk}[n]]\mathbf{H}^H[n]+\boldsymbol{\Gamma}_{\mathbf{w}m}[n]\right)^{-1}\ .\end{aligned} \tag{56}$$

Equation (56) proves the Kalman gain equation in (21). Finally, using (44) and (55), $\boldsymbol{\Gamma}_{\mathbf{s}}[n|n, \bar{\eta}_{lkm}[n]]$ can be expressed as

$$\boldsymbol{\Gamma}_{\mathbf{s}}[n|n,\bar{\eta}_{lkm}[n]] = (\mathbf{I}-\mathbf{K}_{lkm}[n]\mathbf{H}[n])\,\boldsymbol{\Gamma}_{\mathbf{s}}[n|n-1,\tilde{\eta}_{lk}[n]]\ . \tag{57}$$

Equations (39), (43), and (44) prove the estimated mixture statistics in (23), (24) and (25). Using the estimated parameters of the distribution in (37), the MMSE state estimation is

$$\hat{\mathbf{s}}[n|n] = \sum_{l=1}^{L}\sum_{k=1}^{K}\sum_{m=1}^{M} \alpha_{\mathbf{s}}[n|n,\bar{\eta}_{lkm}]\boldsymbol{\mu}_{\mathbf{s}}[n|n,\bar{\eta}_{lkm}[n]] ,$$

which proves the state vector estimate in (26). This result is identical to the GSF presented in [19]. The GSF derived here suffers from exponential model order growth over the iterations. The system state PDF order grows twice: during prediction stage, derived in Lemma 1, and during the innovation process in Lemma 2. Section C.A presents a new model order reduction algorithm, which is optimal in the KLD sense. □

The proof for this theorem appears also in [42]-[43], for the case of non-stationary Gaussian noise processes with Markov noise statistics and Gaussian initial conditions. The assumption of mutually-independent i.i.d. noises enables to provide a simpler closed-form solution.

Model order reduction

In [19] it was shown that the use of GMM distributions for the system state, measurement and system noises results in exponential growth of the number of the mixture components over iterations, and therefore, the GSF is impractical [18],[21]. Several suboptimal techniques for model order reduction have been presented in [21]. In this section, an optimal model order reduction algorithm based on the minimization of the KLD is proposed. The model order reduction stage is implemented once at the end of each iteration. The main idea of the proposed model order reduction scheme is to approximate the posterior *LKM* order system state distribution $\bar{f}_{\mathbf{s}[n]|\mathcal{X}[n]}(\cdot)$ by a reduced order GMM $f_{\mathbf{s}[n]|\mathcal{X}[n]}(\cdot)$. Estimation of the reduced order distribution involves minimization of the distance between the estimated and the "true" PDFs. The KLD is widely used to measure the distance between distributions:

$$KLD\left(\bar{f}_{\mathbf{s}[n]|\mathcal{X}[n]}(\mathbf{s}[n],\bar{\boldsymbol{\theta}}[n|n])||f_{\mathbf{s}[n]|\mathcal{X}[n]}(\mathbf{s}[n],\boldsymbol{\theta}[n|n])\right) = \int_{\boldsymbol{\xi}} \bar{f}_{\mathbf{s}[n]|\mathcal{X}[n]}(\boldsymbol{\xi},\bar{\boldsymbol{\theta}}[n|n]) \log \frac{\bar{f}_{\mathbf{s}[n]|\mathcal{X}[n]}(\boldsymbol{\xi},\bar{\boldsymbol{\theta}}[n|n])}{f_{\mathbf{s}[n]|\mathcal{X}[n]}(\boldsymbol{\xi},\boldsymbol{\theta}[n|n])} d\boldsymbol{\xi} .$$

This induces that our main goal is to obtain:

$$\boldsymbol{\theta}[n|n] = \arg\min_{\boldsymbol{\theta}} KLD\left(\bar{f}_{\mathbf{s}[n]|\mathcal{X}[n]}(\mathbf{s}[n],\bar{\boldsymbol{\theta}})||f_{\mathbf{s}[n]|\mathcal{X}[n]}(\mathbf{s}[n],\boldsymbol{\theta}[n|n])\right) . \quad (58)$$

In [50], [51], it is shown that this minimization problem can equivalently be solved using Monte-Carlo realizations by the maximization of the likelihood function:

$$\boldsymbol{\theta}[n|n] = \arg\max_{\boldsymbol{\theta}} \lim_{J\to\infty} \prod_{j=1}^{J} f_{\mathbf{s}[n]|\mathcal{X}[n]}(\mathbf{s}_j,\boldsymbol{\theta}) , \quad (59)$$

where $\mathbf{s}_j$, j = 1,..., J are artificial samples generated from the distribution $\bar{f}_{\mathbf{s}[n]|\mathcal{X}[n]}(\mathbf{s}[n], \bar{\boldsymbol{\theta}}[n|n])$. Note that the size of the artificial data is theoretically unlimited and it is practically set according to the processor computational resources. There is no closed form solution for this maximization problem and the maximization can be carried out by the EM algorithm [50], using the following iterative expressions for mixture parameters estimation:

$$\begin{aligned} P(l|\mathbf{s}_j) &= \frac{\alpha_{\mathbf{s}}[n-1|n-1,\eta_l[n-1]]}{\Phi(\mathbf{s}_j;\boldsymbol{\theta}_l)} , \ \forall l=1,\ldots,L , j=1,\ldots,J \\ \alpha_{\mathbf{s}}[n|n,\eta_l[n]] &= \frac{1}{J}\sum_{j=1}^{J} P(l|\mathbf{s}_j) , \end{aligned}$$

$$\boldsymbol{\mu}_{\mathbf{s}}[n|n,\eta_l[n]] = \frac{\sum_{j=1}^{J} P(l|\mathbf{s}_j)\mathbf{s}_j}{\sum_{j=1}^{J} P(l|\mathbf{s}_j)},$$

$$\boldsymbol{\Gamma}_{\mathbf{s}}[n|n,\eta_l[n]] = \frac{\sum_{j=1}^{J} P(l|\mathbf{s}_j)(\mathbf{s}_j - \boldsymbol{\mu}_{\mathbf{s}}[n|n,\eta_l[n]])(\mathbf{s}_j - \boldsymbol{\mu}_{\mathbf{s}}[n|n,\eta_l[n]])^H}{\sum_{j=1}^{J} P(l|\mathbf{s}_j)},$$

where $\boldsymbol{\theta}_l = \{\boldsymbol{\mu}_{\mathbf{s}}[n|n, \eta_l[n]], \boldsymbol{\Gamma}_{\mathbf{s}}[n|n, \eta_l[n]]\}$ and $\Phi(\mathbf{s}_j; \boldsymbol{\theta}_l)$ was defined in (6). One of the computationally efficient variations of the EM algorithm is the greedy EM algorithm, which iteratively minimizes the KLD of the estimated from the "true" distributions. The resulting reduced order mixture estimated using the greedy EM algorithm [51] is:

$$\mathbf{s}[n]|\mathcal{X}[n] \sim GMM\left(\alpha_{\mathbf{s}}[n|n,\eta_l[n]], \boldsymbol{\mu}_{\mathbf{s}}[n|n,\eta_l[n]], \boldsymbol{\Gamma}_{\mathbf{s}}[n|n,\eta_l[n]]\ ;\ l = 1,\ldots,L\right).$$

Note that in general, the number of the mixture components may vary with n. Thus, the GMM order might be obtained using model order selection algorithms, such as the minimum description length (MDL) [52]. Alternatively, L can be set as an upper bound on the number of mixture components in the conditional PDF of $\mathbf{s}[n] \mid \mathcal{X}[n]$. Note that the EM role in the proposed order reduction scheme differs from the off-line EM algorithm presented in [21]. The proposed KLD-based model order reduction stage can be summarized as follows:

1. Generate J samples $\{\mathbf{s}_j\}_{j=1}^{J}$ from the distribution of $\mathbf{s}[n] \mid \mathcal{X}[n]$, obtained by the GSF at the end of the estimated stage:

$$\mathbf{s}[n]|\mathcal{X}[n] \sim GMM\left(\alpha_{\mathbf{s}}[n|n,\bar{\eta}_{lkm}[n]], \boldsymbol{\mu}_{\mathbf{s}}[n|n,\bar{\eta}_{lkm}[n]], \boldsymbol{\Gamma}_{\mathbf{s}}[n|n,\bar{\eta}_{lkm}[n]],\ l = 1,\ldots,L; k = 1,\ldots,K; m = 1,\ldots,M\right)$$

2. Estimate a reduced order GMM with L mixture components using the greedy EM algorithm as follows [50], [51]:
   a. Initialization: calculate the ML estimation of the first Gaussian parameters, $\hat{\boldsymbol{\theta}}_0$, using the training data set, $\{\mathbf{s}_j\}_{j=1}^{J}$ in order to obtain $f_{\mathbf{s}}^{(\tilde{K}=0)}(\mathbf{s})$. Set $\tilde{K} = 1$.
   b. Generate a new mixture by

$$f_{\mathbf{s}}^{(\tilde{K})}(\mathbf{s}) = (1 - \hat{\alpha}_{\mathbf{s}}^{(\tilde{K})}) f_{\mathbf{s}}^{(\tilde{K}-1)}(\mathbf{s}) + \hat{\alpha}_{\mathbf{s}}^{(\tilde{K})} \Phi(\mathbf{s}, \hat{\boldsymbol{\theta}}_{\tilde{K}}), \tag{60}$$

   where $\hat{\boldsymbol{\theta}}_{\tilde{K}}$ and $\hat{\alpha}_{\mathbf{s}}^{(\tilde{K})}$ are numerically obtained by:

$$\{\hat{\boldsymbol{\theta}}_{\tilde{K}}, \hat{\alpha}_{\mathbf{s}}^{(\tilde{K})}\} = \arg\max_{\boldsymbol{\theta},\alpha} \sum_{j=1}^{J} \log\left[(1-\alpha) f_{\mathbf{s}}^{(\tilde{K}-1)}(\mathbf{s}_j) + \alpha\Phi(\mathbf{s}_j, \boldsymbol{\theta})\right]. \tag{61}$$

   See [51] for further details.
   c. Apply the EM algorithm on the mixture $f_{\mathbf{s}}^{(\tilde{K})}(\mathbf{s})$, initialized by the mixture parameters, obtained in the previous step.

d. If the log-likelihood function in (60) does not significantly increase, set $f_{\mathbf{s}[n]\,|\,\mathcal{X}[n]}(\cdot\,|\,\mathcal{X}[n]) = f_{\mathbf{s}}^{(\tilde{K})}(\cdot)$; otherwise, set $\tilde{K} = \tilde{K} + 1$ and return to step (b).

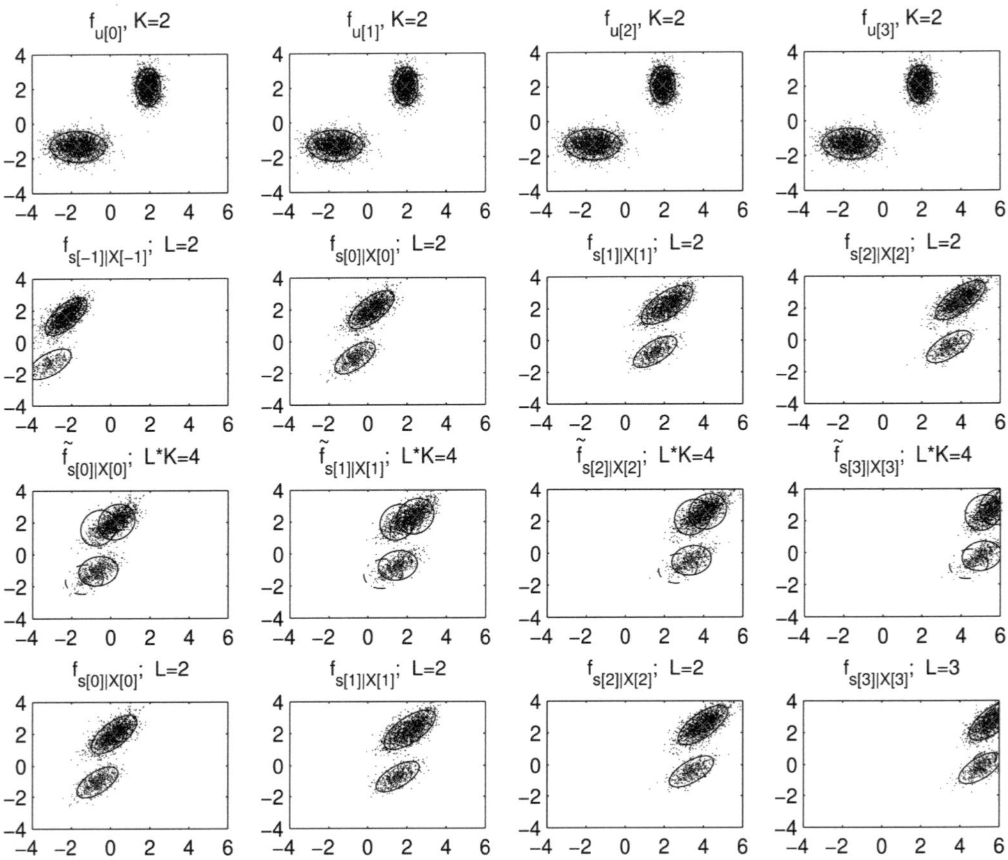

Fig. 2. The model order reduction procedure over 4 time instances.

The KLD-based model order reduction stage is illustrated via a two-dimensional example in Fig. 2. The figure shows the mixture order evaluation over iterations. The measurement noise was assumed to be zero-mean Gaussian. Fig. 2 shows a sequence of four time instances from $n = 0$ to $n = 3$. The corresponding two-dimensional data is represented by dots. The distribution of the system noise $\mathbf{u}[n]$ with two mixture components is shown in the first row of Fig. 2. The estimated distribution of the system state $\mathbf{s}[n-1]\,|\,\mathcal{X}[n-1]$ at the previous time instance is shown in the second row. The distribution of the estimated system state with increased model order $\mathbf{s}[n]\,|\,\mathcal{X}[n]$ is shown in the third row. The mixture components of this distribution are obtained from the convolution of the mixture components in the first two rows. The figure shows that the mixture order grows at this convolution stage. The data are generated from the distributions of the system state prediction on the third row, and new distributions with reduced order are estimated from the generated data. The reduced-order conditional distributions of the system state given the data at time instance n, $\mathbf{s}[n]\,|\,\mathcal{X}[n]$, are shown in the last row. The figure shows that no significant information was lost during the model order reduction process, and the reduced order distribution adequately represents the data distribution. Next, the KLD was used to evaluate the distortion caused by the mixture order reduction procedure. A Gaussian measurement noise was assumed also in this example, i.e. $M = 1$. The system noise was modeled as GMM of order two. The proposed KLD-based model order reduction method was compared to the MR clustering method proposed in [22]. The first row in Fig. 3 shows the PDF of the system state in sequential steps. The uncertainty ellipses represent Gaussians with means marked by 'x' and their widths correspond to 2σ (2 standard deviations). Ellipses with solid, and dashed-dot lines correspond to mixture component weights satisfying: $\alpha_s[n \mid n, \eta_l[n]] > 0.01$, and $\alpha_s[n \mid n, \eta_l[n]] \leq 0.01$, respectively. Thus, the system state order grows from 4 to 32 over four iterations. The second line in Fig. 3 shows the reduced order GMM at the output of the KLD based model order reduction stage. The third line on Fig. 3 shows the reduced order GMM at the output of the MR algorithm. The figure shows significant difference between the mixtures obtained by the two methods. The KLD of the reduced-order GMM from the exponentially growing order GMM was calculated according to the following procedure:

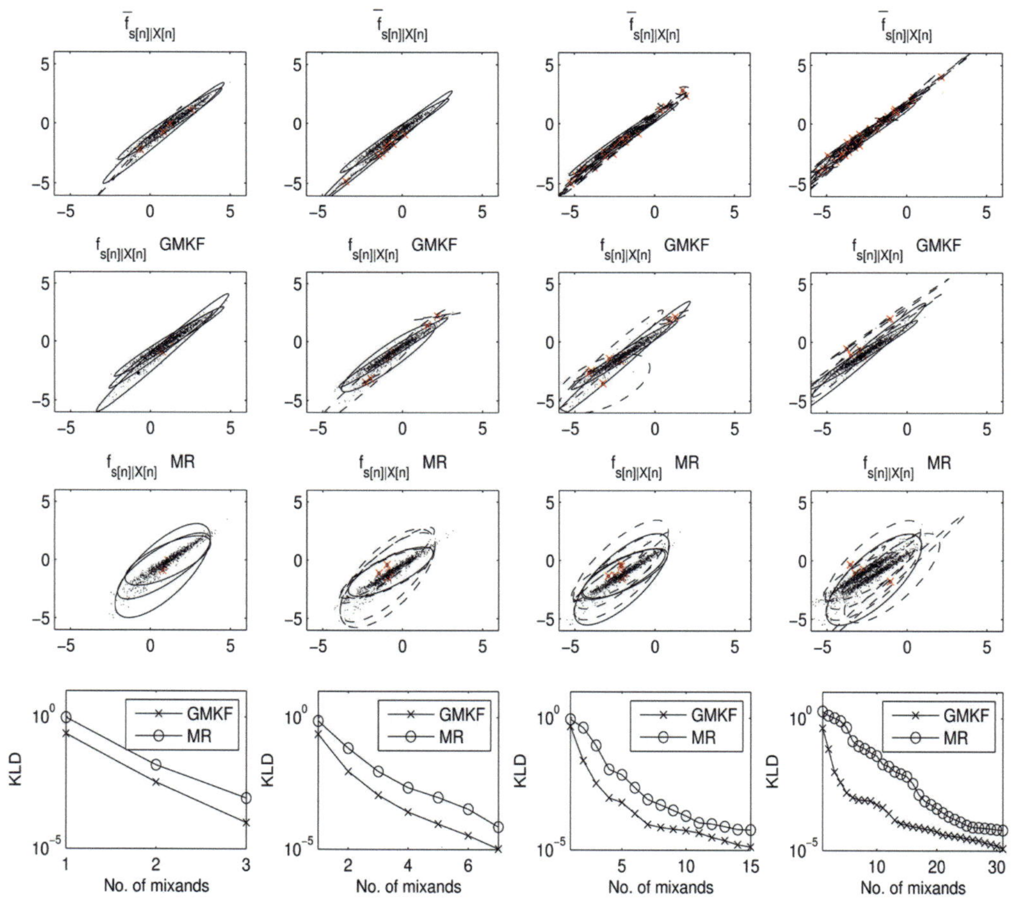

Fig. 3. KLD between system state distributions, obtained with and without model order reduction stage over 4 time instances.

- Sample artificial data vectors $\mathbf{s}_j$, $\forall j = 1,\dots, J$ from the increased order GMM, representing the posterior state PDF.
- Evaluate the KLD using Monte-Carlo simulations:

$$KLD(\bar{f}_{\mathbf{s}[n]|\mathcal{X}[n]}|f_{\mathbf{s}[n]|\mathcal{X}[n]}) \simeq \frac{1}{J}\sum_{j=1}^{J}\log\frac{\bar{f}_{\mathbf{s}[n]|\mathcal{X}[n]}(\mathbf{s}_j)}{f_{\mathbf{s}[n]|\mathcal{X}[n]}(\mathbf{s}_j)}\ .$$

In this example, the artificial data size was chosen to be $J = 5000$. The KLD between these distributions is shown at the last row as a function of the mixture order of $f_{\mathbf{s}[n]|\mathcal{X}[n]}$ for the two tested model order reduction methods. It is shown that for the proposed model order reduction method (a) the KLD decreases when the mixture order grows, (b) the proposed model order reduction method outperforms the *ad-hoc* MR method in the KLD sense. Fig. 3 shows that the distribution obtained by the proposed model order reduction method, represents the data fairly good.

B. NL-GMKF

In this section, the recursive NL-GMKF for the nonlinear and non-Gaussian model described in Section IIB, is derived based on the MMSE criterion.

Summary

The following summarizes the NL-GMKF for recursive estimation of $\mathbf{s}[n]$ from $\mathcal{X}[n]$.

1. Initialization:

Initialize the L-order GMM parameters of the state vector at time instance $n = -1$.

$$\begin{aligned}\alpha_{\mathbf{s}}[-1|-1,\eta_{\mathbf{s}l}[-1]] &= \alpha_{\mathbf{s}l}[-1]\ ,\\ \boldsymbol{\mu}_{\mathbf{s}}[-1|-1,\eta_{\mathbf{s}l}[-1]] &= \boldsymbol{\mu}_{\mathbf{s}l}[-1]\ ,\\ \boldsymbol{\Gamma}_{\mathbf{s}}[-1|-1,\eta_{\mathbf{s}l}[-1]] &= \boldsymbol{\Gamma}_{\mathbf{s}l}[-1]\ .\end{aligned}$$

Set $n = 0$.

2. Mixture parameters of the state and measurement prediction:

- Generate an artificial data set $\mathcal{D}$ from the conditional distribution of $\begin{bmatrix}\mathbf{s}[n-1]\\ \mathbf{u}[n]\\ \mathbf{w}[n]\end{bmatrix}$ given $\mathcal{X}[n-1]$, according to the PDF of $\mathbf{s}[n-1]|\mathcal{X}[n-1]$ from the previous step and PDFs of $\mathbf{u}[n]$ and $\mathbf{w}[n]$.
- Apply the nonlinear function $\mathbf{G}(\cdot) = \begin{bmatrix}\mathbf{a}(\cdot,\cdot)\\ \mathbf{h}(\mathbf{a}(\cdot,\cdot),\cdot)\end{bmatrix}$ on $\mathcal{D}$ and obtain a new artificial data set $\mathcal{D}'$.
- Model the conditional distribution of $\mathbf{y}[n]$ given $\mathcal{X}[n-1]$ using the new artificial data $\mathcal{D}'$ by GMM of order L to obtain the parameters of $\psi_{\mathbf{y}}[n|n-1]$:

$$\psi_{\mathbf{y}}[n|n-1] \triangleq \left\{\alpha_{\mathbf{y}}[n|n-1,\eta_l[n]], \boldsymbol{\mu}_{\mathbf{y}}[n|n-1,\eta_l[n]], \boldsymbol{\Gamma}_{\mathbf{y}}[n|n-1,\eta_l[n]]\right\}_{l=1}^{L}\ , \tag{62}$$

where

$$\boldsymbol{\mu}_{\mathbf{y}}[n|n-1,\eta_l[n]] \triangleq \begin{bmatrix}\boldsymbol{\mu}_{\mathbf{s}}[n|n-1,\eta_l[n]]\\ \boldsymbol{\mu}_{\mathbf{x}}[n|n-1,\eta_l[n]]\end{bmatrix}\ , \tag{63}$$

and

$$\boldsymbol{\Gamma}_{\mathbf{y}}[n|n-1,\eta_l[n]] = \begin{bmatrix} \boldsymbol{\Gamma}_{\mathbf{s}}[n|n-1,\eta_l[n]] & \boldsymbol{\Gamma}_{\mathbf{sx}}[n|n-1,\eta_l[n]] \\ \boldsymbol{\Gamma}_{\mathbf{sx}}^H[n|n-1,\eta_l[n]] & \boldsymbol{\Gamma}_{\mathbf{x}}[n|n-1,\eta_l[n]] \end{bmatrix} . \tag{64}$$

3. Innovation:
Calculate the innovation vector:

$$\tilde{\mathbf{x}}[n] = \mathbf{x}[n] - \hat{\mathbf{x}}[n|n-1] , \tag{65}$$

where

$$\hat{\mathbf{x}}[n|n-1] = \sum_{l=1}^{L} \alpha_{\mathbf{y}}[n|n-1,\eta_l[n]]\boldsymbol{\mu}_{\mathbf{x}}[n|n-1,\eta_l[n]] . \tag{66}$$

4. PDF parameters of the state prediction and the innovation:
Obtain the parameters

$$\boldsymbol{\psi}_{\tilde{\mathbf{y}}}[n|n-1] = \left\{\alpha_{\tilde{\mathbf{y}}}[n|n-1,\eta_l[n]], \boldsymbol{\mu}_{\tilde{\mathbf{y}}}[n|n-1,\eta_l[n]], \boldsymbol{\Gamma}_{\tilde{\mathbf{y}}}[n|n-1,\eta_l[n]]\right\}_{l=1}^{L} , \tag{67}$$

where

$$\boldsymbol{\mu}_{\tilde{\mathbf{y}}}[n|n-1,\eta_l[n]] = \begin{bmatrix} \boldsymbol{\mu}_{\mathbf{s}}[n|n-1,\eta_l[n]] \\ \boldsymbol{\mu}_{\tilde{\mathbf{x}}}[n|n-1,\eta_l[n]] \end{bmatrix} = \boldsymbol{\mu}_{\mathbf{y}}[n|n-1,\eta_l[n]] - \begin{bmatrix} \mathbf{0} \\ \hat{\mathbf{x}}[n|n-1] \end{bmatrix} , \tag{68}$$

$$\boldsymbol{\Gamma}_{\tilde{\mathbf{y}}}[n|n-1,\eta_l[n]] = \begin{bmatrix} \boldsymbol{\Gamma}_{\mathbf{s}}[n|n-1,\eta_l[n]] & \boldsymbol{\Gamma}_{\mathbf{s}\tilde{\mathbf{x}}}[n|n-1,\eta_l[n]] \\ \boldsymbol{\Gamma}_{\mathbf{s}\tilde{\mathbf{x}}}^H[n|n-1,\eta_l[n]] & \boldsymbol{\Gamma}_{\tilde{\mathbf{x}}}[n|n-1,\eta_l[n]] \end{bmatrix} = \boldsymbol{\Gamma}_{\mathbf{y}}[n|n-1,\eta_l[n]] , \tag{69}$$

$$\alpha_{\tilde{\mathbf{y}}}[n|n-1,\eta_l[n]] = \alpha_{\mathbf{y}}[n|n-1,\eta_l[n]] , \tag{70}$$

5. Kalman gains:
Calculate the Kalman gains

$$\mathbf{K}_l[n] \triangleq \boldsymbol{\Gamma}_{\mathbf{s}\tilde{\mathbf{x}}}[n|n-1,\eta_l[n]]\boldsymbol{\Gamma}_{\tilde{\mathbf{x}}}^{-1}[n|n-1,\eta_l[n]] . \tag{71}$$

6. Estimation
6a. Estimated state mixture parameters:
Obtain the estimated state mixture parameters:

$$\boldsymbol{\psi}_{\mathbf{s}}[n|n] \triangleq \{\alpha_{\mathbf{s}}[n|n,\eta_l[n]], \boldsymbol{\mu}_{\mathbf{s}}[n|n,\eta_l[n]], \boldsymbol{\Gamma}_{\mathbf{s}}[n|n,\eta_l[n]]\}_{l=1}^{L} , \tag{72}$$

where

$$\boldsymbol{\mu}_{\mathbf{s}}[n|n,\eta_l[n]] = \boldsymbol{\mu}_{\mathbf{s}}[n|n-1,\eta_l[n]] + \mathbf{K}_l[n]\left(\tilde{\mathbf{x}}[n] - \boldsymbol{\mu}_{\tilde{\mathbf{x}}}[n|n-1,\eta_l[n]]\right) , \tag{73}$$

$$\boldsymbol{\Gamma}_{\mathbf{s}}[n|n,\eta_l[n]] = \boldsymbol{\Gamma}_{\mathbf{s}}[n|n-1,\eta_l[n]] - \mathbf{K}_l[n]\boldsymbol{\Gamma}_{\tilde{\mathbf{x}}\mathbf{s}}[n|n-1,\eta_l[n]] , \tag{74}$$

$$\alpha_{\mathbf{s}}[n|n,\eta_l[n]] = \frac{\alpha_{\tilde{\mathbf{y}}}[n|n-1,\eta_l[n]]\Phi(\tilde{\mathbf{x}}[n];\boldsymbol{\theta}_{\tilde{\mathbf{x}}l}[n|n-1])}{\sum_{l'=1}^{L}\alpha_{\tilde{\mathbf{y}}}[n|n-1,\eta_{l'}[n]]\Phi(\tilde{\mathbf{x}}[n];\boldsymbol{\theta}_{\tilde{\mathbf{x}}l'}[n|n-1])}, \tag{75}$$

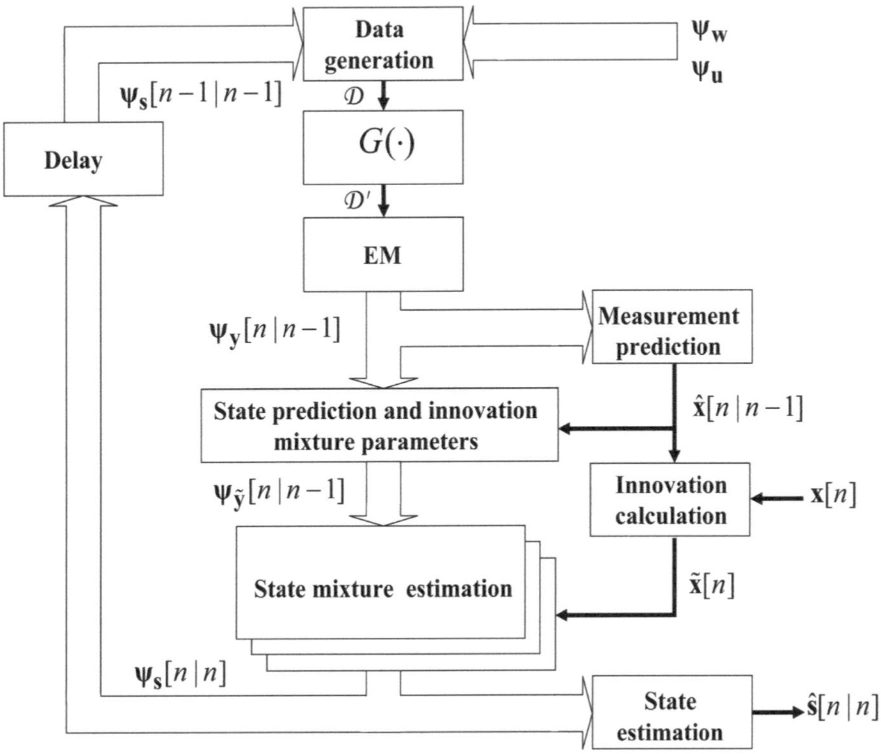

Fig. 4. NL-GMKF schematic diagram.

6b. Estimation of the state vector:
Obtain the system state estimation:

$$\hat{\mathbf{s}}[n|n]=\sum_{l=1}^{L}\alpha_{\mathbf{s}}[n|n,\eta_l[n]]\boldsymbol{\mu}_{\mathbf{s}}[n|n,\eta_l[n]]\ . \tag{76}$$

7. Set $n \rightarrow n+1$, go to step 2.
The NL-GMKF algorithm is schematically presented in Fig. 4.

Derivation

Let $\hat{\mathbf{x}}[n|n-1]$ denote the MMSE estimator of $\mathbf{x}[n]$ from $\mathcal{X}[n-1]$ using (8), $\hat{\mathbf{x}}[n|n-1]$ is given by

$$\hat{\mathbf{x}}[n|n-1] = E(\mathbf{x}[n]|\mathcal{X}[n-1]) = E(\mathbf{h}(\mathbf{s}[n],\mathbf{w}[n])|\mathcal{X}[n-1])\ , \tag{77}$$

and the innovation process defined as $\tilde{\mathbf{x}}[n]$, is given by

$$\tilde{\mathbf{x}}[n] = \mathbf{x}[n] - \hat{\mathbf{x}}[n|n-1] = \mathbf{h}(\mathbf{s}[n],\mathbf{w}[n]) - \hat{\mathbf{x}}[n|n-1]\ . \tag{78}$$

If the transformation $\mathcal{X}[n] \leftrightarrow [\mathcal{X}^T[n-1], \tilde{\mathbf{x}}^T[n]]^T$ is one-to-one, then the conditional distribution of $\mathbf{s}[n] | \mathcal{X}[n]$ is identical to the conditional distribution of $\mathbf{s}[n] | X[n-1], \tilde{\mathbf{x}}[n]$. Since $\mathbf{s}[n]$ and $\tilde{\mathbf{x}}[n]$ given $\mathcal{X}[n-1]$ are assumed to be jointly GMM of order L, the conditional distribution of $\mathbf{s}[n] | \tilde{\mathbf{x}}[n], \mathcal{X}[n-1]$ given the random mixture indicator $\eta_l[n]$ [47], is Gaussian. Therefore, the conditional distribution of $\mathbf{s}[n] | \mathcal{X}[n]$ is GMM of order L:

$$\mathbf{s}[n]|\mathcal{X}[n] \sim GMM\left(\alpha_{\mathbf{s}}[n|n, \eta_l[n]], \boldsymbol{\mu}_{\mathbf{s}}[n|n, \eta_l[n]], \boldsymbol{\Gamma}_{\mathbf{s}}[n|n, \eta_l[n]]; l = 1, \ldots, L\right) . \tag{79}$$

In the following, the parameters of this conditional distribution, $\psi_{\mathbf{s}}[n|n]$, where

$$\psi_{\mathbf{s}}[n|n] \triangleq \{\alpha_{\mathbf{s}}[n|n, \eta_l[n]], \boldsymbol{\mu}_{\mathbf{s}}[n|n, \eta_l[n]], \boldsymbol{\Gamma}_{\mathbf{s}}[n|n, \eta_l[n]]\}_{l=1}^{L} , \tag{80}$$

are derived. Since the conditional distribution of $(\mathbf{s}[n], \tilde{\mathbf{x}}[n])$ given the random mixture indicator $\eta_l[n]$, is jointly Gaussian, then the mean vector $\boldsymbol{\mu}_{\mathbf{s}}[n | n, \eta_l[n]]$ and covariance matrix $\boldsymbol{\Gamma}_{\mathbf{s}}[n | n, \eta_l[n]]$ can be obtained as

$$\begin{aligned}\boldsymbol{\mu}_{\mathbf{s}}[n|n, \eta_l[n]] &= E[\mathbf{s}[n]|\tilde{\mathbf{x}}[n], \mathcal{X}[n-1], \eta_l[n]] \\ &= E[\mathbf{s}[n]|\mathcal{X}[n-1], \eta_l[n]] + \boldsymbol{\Gamma}_{\mathbf{s}\tilde{\mathbf{x}}}[n|n-1, \eta_l[n]]\boldsymbol{\Gamma}_{\tilde{\mathbf{x}}}^{-1}[n|n-1, \eta_l[n]]\left(\tilde{\mathbf{x}}[n] - \boldsymbol{\mu}_{\tilde{\mathbf{x}}}[n|n-1, \eta_l[n]]\right) .\end{aligned} \tag{81}$$

$$\begin{aligned}\boldsymbol{\Gamma}_{\mathbf{s}}[n|n, \eta_l[n]] &= \mathrm{cov}(\mathbf{s}[n]|\tilde{\mathbf{x}}[n], \mathcal{X}[n-1], \eta_l[n]) \\ &= \mathrm{cov}(\mathbf{s}[n]|\mathcal{X}[n-1], \eta_l[n]) - \boldsymbol{\Gamma}_{\mathbf{s}\tilde{\mathbf{x}}}[n|n-1, \eta_l[n]]\boldsymbol{\Gamma}_{\tilde{\mathbf{x}}}^{-1}[n|n-1, \eta_l[n]]\boldsymbol{\Gamma}_{\mathbf{s}\tilde{\mathbf{x}}}^{H}[n|n-1, \eta_l[n]] ,\end{aligned} \tag{82}$$

where

$$\begin{aligned}\boldsymbol{\mu}_{\tilde{\mathbf{x}}}[n|n-1, \eta_l[n]] &= E[\tilde{\mathbf{x}}[n]|\mathcal{X}[n-1], \eta_l[n]] \\ \boldsymbol{\Gamma}_{\tilde{\mathbf{x}}}[n|n-1, \eta_l[n]] &= \mathrm{cov}(\tilde{\mathbf{x}}[n]|\mathcal{X}[n-1], \eta_l[n]) \\ \boldsymbol{\Gamma}_{\mathbf{s}\tilde{\mathbf{x}}}[n|n-1, \eta_l[n]] &= \mathrm{cov}(\mathbf{s}[n], \tilde{\mathbf{x}}[n]|\mathcal{X}[n-1], \eta_l[n]) .\end{aligned} \tag{83}$$

Following the conventions of the KF, the lth Kalman gain corresponding to the lth mixture component, is defined as

$$\boldsymbol{\mu}_{\mathbf{s}}[n|n, \eta_l[n]] = \boldsymbol{\mu}_{\mathbf{s}}[n|n-1, \eta_l[n]] + \mathbf{K}_l[n]\left(\tilde{\mathbf{x}}[n] - \boldsymbol{\mu}_{\tilde{\mathbf{x}}}[n|n-1, \eta_l[n]]\right) , \tag{84}$$

Using (84), Eqs. (81) and (82) can be rewritten as

$$\boldsymbol{\mu}_{\mathbf{s}}[n|n, \eta_l[n]] = \boldsymbol{\mu}_{\mathbf{s}}[n|n-1, \eta_l[n]] + \mathbf{K}_l[n]\left(\tilde{\mathbf{x}}[n] - \boldsymbol{\mu}_{\tilde{\mathbf{x}}}[n|n-1, \eta_l[n]]\right) , \tag{85}$$

$$\boldsymbol{\Gamma}_{\mathbf{s}}[n|n, \eta_l[n]] = \boldsymbol{\Gamma}_{\mathbf{s}}[n|n-1, \eta_l[n]] - \mathbf{K}_l[n]\boldsymbol{\Gamma}_{\tilde{\mathbf{x}}\mathbf{s}}[n|n-1, \eta_l[n]] . \tag{86}$$

In the following, the parameters required in (85) and (86), are obtained. Let $\mathbf{y}[n] \triangleq \begin{bmatrix} \mathbf{s}[n] \\ \mathbf{x}[n] \end{bmatrix}$ and $\tilde{\mathbf{y}}[n] \triangleq \begin{bmatrix} \mathbf{s}[n] \\ \tilde{\mathbf{x}}[n] \end{bmatrix}$. Then, by using (7), (8) and (78) one obtains

$$\mathbf{y}[n] = \begin{bmatrix} \mathbf{a}(\mathbf{s}[n-1], \mathbf{u}[n]) \\ \mathbf{h}(\mathbf{a}(\mathbf{s}[n-1], \mathbf{u}[n]), \mathbf{w}[n]) \end{bmatrix} = \mathbf{G}\left(\begin{bmatrix} \mathbf{s}[n-1] \\ \mathbf{u}[n] \\ \mathbf{w}[n] \end{bmatrix}\right) . \tag{87}$$

and

$$\tilde{\mathbf{y}}[n] = \mathbf{y}[n] - \begin{bmatrix} \mathbf{0} \\ \hat{\mathbf{x}}[n|n-1] \end{bmatrix} = \mathbf{G}\left(\begin{bmatrix} \mathbf{s}[n-1] \\ \mathbf{u}[n] \\ \mathbf{w}[n] \end{bmatrix}\right) - \begin{bmatrix} \mathbf{0} \\ \hat{\mathbf{x}}[n|n-1] \end{bmatrix}. \quad (88)$$

Since $\tilde{\mathbf{y}}[n]$, is a linear transformation of $\mathbf{y}[n]$, then the vectors $\mathbf{s}[n]$ and $\tilde{\mathbf{x}}[n]$ given $\mathcal{X}[n-1]$ are jointly GMM of order L, that is, the conditional distribution of $\tilde{\mathbf{y}}[n]$ given $\mathcal{X}[n-1]$ can be modeled by an L-order GMM with parameters:

$$\boldsymbol{\psi}_{\tilde{\mathbf{y}}}[n|n-1] = \left\{\alpha_{\tilde{\mathbf{y}}}[n|n-1,\eta_l[n]], \boldsymbol{\mu}_{\tilde{\mathbf{y}}}[n|n-1,\eta_l[n]], \boldsymbol{\Gamma}_{\tilde{\mathbf{y}}}[n|n-1,\eta_l[n]]\right\}_{l=1}^{L}, \quad (89)$$

where

$$\boldsymbol{\mu}_{\tilde{\mathbf{y}}}[n|n-1,\eta_l[n]] \triangleq \begin{bmatrix} \boldsymbol{\mu}_{\mathbf{s}}[n|n-1,\eta_l[n]] \\ \boldsymbol{\mu}_{\tilde{\mathbf{x}}}[n|n-1,\eta_l[n]] \end{bmatrix}, \quad (90)$$

$$\boldsymbol{\Gamma}_{\tilde{\mathbf{y}}}[n|n-1,\eta_l[n]] \triangleq \begin{bmatrix} \boldsymbol{\Gamma}_{\mathbf{s}}[n|n-1,\eta_l[n]] & \boldsymbol{\Gamma}_{\mathbf{s}\tilde{\mathbf{x}}}[n|n-1,\eta_l[n]] \\ \boldsymbol{\Gamma}_{\mathbf{s}\tilde{\mathbf{x}}}^H[n|n-1,\eta_l[n]] & \boldsymbol{\Gamma}_{\tilde{\mathbf{x}}}[n|n-1,\eta_l[n]] \end{bmatrix}. \quad (91)$$

Using the properties of the jointly GMM-distributed random processes, $\mathbf{s}[n]\,|\,\mathcal{X}[n-1]$ and $\tilde{\mathbf{x}}[n]\,|\,\mathcal{X}[n-1]$, the mixture weights can be obtained as:

$$\alpha_{\mathbf{s}}[n|n,\eta_l[n]] = \frac{\alpha_{\tilde{\mathbf{y}}}[n|n-1,\eta_l[n]]\Phi(\tilde{\mathbf{x}}[n];\boldsymbol{\theta}_{\tilde{\mathbf{x}}l}[n|n-1])}{\sum_{l'=1}^{L}\alpha_{\tilde{\mathbf{y}}}[n|n-1,\eta_{l'}[n]]\Phi(\tilde{\mathbf{x}}[n];\boldsymbol{\theta}_{\tilde{\mathbf{x}}l'}[n|n-1])}, \quad (92)$$

where

$$\boldsymbol{\theta}_{\tilde{\mathbf{x}}l}[n|n-1] = \{\boldsymbol{\mu}_{\tilde{\mathbf{x}}}[n|n-1,\eta_l[n]], \boldsymbol{\Gamma}_{\tilde{\mathbf{x}}}[n|n-1,\eta_l[n]]\}. \quad (93)$$

Therefore, one can calculate the PDF parameters of $\mathbf{s}[n]\,|\,\mathcal{X}[n]$, given in (85), (86) and (92), using the parameters of the distribution $\tilde{\mathbf{y}}[n]\,|\,\mathcal{X}[n-1]$ obtained in the following. The conditional PDF of $\mathbf{y}[n]\,|\,\mathcal{X}[n-1]$ is modeled by GMM of order L with parameters:

$$\boldsymbol{\psi}_{\mathbf{y}}[n|n-1] \triangleq \left\{\alpha_{\mathbf{y}}[n|n-1,\eta_l[n]], \boldsymbol{\mu}_{\mathbf{y}}[n|n-1,\eta_l[n]], \boldsymbol{\Gamma}_{\mathbf{y}}[n|n-1,\eta_l[n]]\right\}_{l=1}^{L}, \quad (94)$$

where

$$\boldsymbol{\mu}_{\mathbf{y}}[n|n-1,\eta_l[n]] \triangleq \begin{bmatrix} \boldsymbol{\mu}_{\mathbf{s}}[n|n-1,\eta_l[n]] \\ \boldsymbol{\mu}_{\mathbf{x}}[n|n-1,\eta_l[n]] \end{bmatrix}, \quad (95)$$

and

$$\boldsymbol{\Gamma}_{\mathbf{y}}[n|n-1,\eta_l[n]] = \begin{bmatrix} \boldsymbol{\Gamma}_{\mathbf{s}}[n|n-1,\eta_l[n]] & \boldsymbol{\Gamma}_{\mathbf{s}\mathbf{x}}[n|n-1,\eta_l[n]] \\ \boldsymbol{\Gamma}_{\mathbf{s}\mathbf{x}}^H[n|n-1,\eta_l[n]] & \boldsymbol{\Gamma}_{\mathbf{x}}[n|n-1,\eta_l[n]] \end{bmatrix}. \quad (96)$$

Eqs. (94), (95), and (96) provides (62), (63), and (64). Since $\hat{\mathbf{x}}[n\,|\,n-1]$ depends on $\mathcal{X}[n-1]$ only, then from (88) we conclude that the conditional PDF of $\tilde{\mathbf{y}}[n]\,|\,\mathcal{X}[n-1]$ is shifted by $\begin{bmatrix} \mathbf{0} \\ \hat{\mathbf{x}}[n|n-1] \end{bmatrix}$ compared to the conditional PDF of $\mathbf{y}[n]\,|\,\mathcal{X}[n-1]$:

$$\boldsymbol{\mu}_{\tilde{\mathbf{y}}}[n|n-1,\eta_l[n]] = \boldsymbol{\mu}_{\mathbf{y}}[n|n-1,\eta_l[n]] - \begin{bmatrix} \mathbf{0} \\ \hat{\mathbf{x}}[n|n-1] \end{bmatrix}, \tag{97}$$

$$\boldsymbol{\Gamma}_{\tilde{\mathbf{y}}}[n|n-1,\eta_l[n]] = \boldsymbol{\Gamma}_{\mathbf{y}}[n|n-1,\eta_l[n]], \tag{98}$$

$$\alpha_{\tilde{\mathbf{y}}}[n|n-1,\eta_l[n]] = \alpha_{\mathbf{y}}[n|n-1,\eta_l[n]], \tag{99}$$

and

$$\boldsymbol{\mu}_{\tilde{\mathbf{x}}}[n|n-1,\eta_l[n]] = \boldsymbol{\mu}_{\mathbf{x}}[n|n-1,\eta_l[n]] - \hat{\mathbf{x}}[n|n-1]. \tag{100}$$

Hence the mixture weights and covariance matrices in $\psi_{\mathbf{y}}[n|n-1]$ and $\psi_{\tilde{\mathbf{y}}}[n|n-1]$ are identical except the means as described in (100). Since the function $\mathbf{G}(\cdot)$ is nonlinear, the parameters of the conditional distribution of $\tilde{\mathbf{y}}[n]|\mathcal{X}[n-1]$ cannot be obtained analytically. Alternatively, the MC approach can be implemented. Thus, an artificial data set $\mathcal{D}$ is obtained from the conditional distribution of $\begin{bmatrix} \mathbf{s}[n-1] \\ \mathbf{u}[n] \\ \mathbf{w}[n] \end{bmatrix}$, given $\mathcal{X}[n-1]$. Next, the nonlinear function $\mathbf{G}(\cdot)$ is applied on the data set $\mathcal{D}$ to obtain a new artificial data set $\mathcal{D}'$, which is used to obtain the PDF parameters of $\tilde{\mathbf{y}}[n]|\mathcal{X}[n-1]$, i.e. $\psi_{\tilde{\mathbf{y}}}[n|n-1]$. The statistical parameters required for calculation of (84), (85) and (86) can be obtained from the parameters of $\psi_{\tilde{\mathbf{y}}}[n|n-1]$ in (89). The measurement prediction is calculated as a conditional mean estimator of $\mathbf{x}[n]$ given $\mathcal{X}[n-1]$, using parameters obtained in (95) and (96) as follows

$$\hat{\mathbf{x}}[n|n-1] = \sum_{l=1}^{L} \alpha_{\mathbf{y}}[n|n-1,\eta_l[n]]\boldsymbol{\mu}_{\mathbf{x}}[n|n-1,\eta_l[n]]. \tag{101}$$

The MMSE estimator in (9) is obtained using (85) and (92) as follows:

$$\hat{\mathbf{s}}[n|n] = \sum_{l=1}^{L} \alpha_{\mathbf{s}}[n|n,\eta_l[n]]\boldsymbol{\mu}_{\mathbf{s}}[n|n,\eta_l[n]]. \tag{102}$$

This completes the derivation of the NL-GMKF. Note that the GMM order of the conditional distribution $\mathbf{y}[n]|\mathcal{X}[n-1]$ might be obtained using model order selection algorithms, such as the minimum description length (MDL) [52]. Alternatively, L can be set as an upper bound on the number of mixture components in the conditional PDF. In this work, the vector parameter $\psi_{\tilde{\mathbf{y}}}[n|n-1]$ is obtained from the data $\mathcal{D}'$using the greedy EM algorithm [50]. The greedy learning algorithm controls the GMM order of the estimated PDF, which varies over the iterations. In [51] it was shown that the greedy EM algorithm is insensitive to the initialization. The PDF estimation using the greedy EM algorithm appears in [51], [50] and is summarized in the appendix.

4. Simulation results

A. GMKF

In the following scenarios, the estimation performance of the GMKF is evaluated for different linear DSS models, and compared to the IMM, PF and GSPF in terms of root-mean-square error (RMSE) of the estimate of the first element in the state vector. Additionally, the performance of the GMKF is compared to the GSF with clustering MR algorithm [22]. In these scenarios, the standard sampling importance resampling (SIR) PF was used [1] with 10000 particles. In the scenarios with real-valued Gaussian measurement noise, a common IMM algorithm was used [18]. The number of models corresponds to the number of mixture components in the PDF of the system noise. The GMKF performance is evaluated for various system noise PDFs and it is tested for N = 100 time instances. For estimation performance evaluation, each test was performed over 100 trials. In the first three scenarios, a practical application of maneuvering radar target tracking is addressed. In these scenarios, the state vector is composed of the target range and radial velocity, where the target range is observed by the radar. The DSS and measurement models are given by:

$$\begin{aligned} \begin{bmatrix} r[n] \\ \dot{r}[n] \end{bmatrix} &= \begin{bmatrix} 1 & T \\ 0 & 1 \end{bmatrix} \cdot \begin{bmatrix} r[n-1] \\ \dot{r}[n-1] \end{bmatrix} + \mathbf{u}[n] \\ x[n] &= \begin{bmatrix} 1 & 0 \end{bmatrix} \cdot \begin{bmatrix} r[n] \\ \dot{r}[n] \end{bmatrix} + w[n] , \end{aligned} \tag{103}$$

where T = 0.1 *sec* is the sampling interval. Thus, the state transition matrix and the measurement matrix are given by $\mathbf{A}[n] = \begin{bmatrix} 1 & 0.1 \\ 0 & 1 \end{bmatrix}$ and $\mathbf{H}[n] = [\ 1\ 0\ ]$, respectively. The conditional distribution of $\mathbf{s}[n] \,|\, \mathcal{X}[n]$ was assumed to be real-valued GMM of order L = 16. The GMKF is initialized at time instance n = -1 with $\alpha_{\mathbf{s}}[-1 \,|\, -1, \eta_l[-1]] = \frac{1}{L}$, $\boldsymbol{\mu}_{\mathbf{s}}[-1 \,|\, -1, \eta_l[-1]] = \mathbf{0}$, $\boldsymbol{\Gamma}_{\mathbf{s}}[-1 \,|\, -1, \eta_l[-1]] = \rho\mathbf{I}$ for $l = 1,\ldots, L$, where ρ is a large number. For the GSPF, the conditional distribution of the state vector $\mathbf{s}[n]$, given $\mathcal{X}[n]$ was assumed to be GMM of order L = 16, and the number of particles for each Gaussian in the mixture was chosen to be 2000. For the GSF with MR algorithm, the number of mixture components at the output of the MR was selected to be the same as in the GMKF.

A.1 Maneuvering target tracking

The measurement noise, $w[n]$, was assumed to be zero-mean Gaussian $\boldsymbol{\theta}_w = \{\mu_w = 0,\ \sigma_w^2 = 0.1\}$. The target maneuvers (timevarying acceleration) are simulated by white-noise acceleration [61]. This model is commonly used for small, random maneuvers which are usually modeled by zero-mean Gaussian system noise with time-varying variance: $\mathbf{u}[n] \sim \mathcal{N}(\mathbf{0}, \beta[n]\mathbf{I})$, $\forall n = 0, 1, 2,\ldots$, where $\beta[n]$ controls the target maneuvering. In the first part of the simulation ($n = 0,\ldots, 21$) this parameter was $\beta[n] = 0.01$ to represent approximately constant-acceleration. In the second part of the simulation $n = 22,\ldots, 82$, the target's time-varying acceleration was simulated by a random vector with "wider" Gaussian, defined by $\beta[n] = 1$. For the GMKF, the GSPF and the GSF with MR, the system noise was modeled by GMM with two mixture components:

$$f_{\mathbf{u}}(\mathbf{u}) = (1-\alpha_{\mathbf{u}})\Phi(\mathbf{u}, \boldsymbol{\theta}_{\mathbf{u}1}) + \alpha_{\mathbf{u}}\Phi(\mathbf{u}, \boldsymbol{\theta}_{\mathbf{u}2}) \ , \quad \forall n = 0, 1, 2, \ldots$$

where $\alpha_{\mathbf{u}}$ = 0.2. For the PF, the system noise is modeled by a single Gaussian with the following first and second order statistics:

$$\begin{aligned} \bar{\boldsymbol{\mu}}_{\mathbf{u}} &= (1-\alpha_{\mathbf{u}})\boldsymbol{\mu}_{\mathbf{u}1} + \alpha_{\mathbf{u}}\boldsymbol{\mu}_{\mathbf{u}2} \ , \\ \bar{\boldsymbol{\Gamma}}_{\mathbf{u}} &= (1-\alpha_{\mathbf{u}})\boldsymbol{\Gamma}_{\mathbf{u}1} + \alpha_{\mathbf{u}}\boldsymbol{\Gamma}_{\mathbf{u}2} + (1-\alpha_{\mathbf{u}})\boldsymbol{\mu}_{\mathbf{u}1}\boldsymbol{\mu}_{\mathbf{u}1}^T + \alpha_{\mathbf{u}}\boldsymbol{\mu}_{\mathbf{u}2}\boldsymbol{\mu}_{\mathbf{u}2}^T - \bar{\boldsymbol{\mu}}_{\mathbf{u}}\bar{\boldsymbol{\mu}}_{\mathbf{u}}^T \ . \end{aligned} \tag{104}$$

The IMM consisted of two KFs, which correspond to the two modes characterized by the following system and measurement noise parameters:

- Mode 1: non-maneuvering - $\boldsymbol{\theta}_{\mathbf{u}1}$, $\boldsymbol{\theta}_w = \{0, 0.1\}$,
- Mode 2: maneuvering - $\boldsymbol{\theta}_{\mathbf{u}2}$, $\boldsymbol{\theta}_w = \{0, 0.1\}$.

The transition probability matrix between the two models was selected to match the transition probabilities to the mean sojourn time in each mode [18]:

$$\pi_1 = \begin{bmatrix} 0.95 & 0.05 \\ 0.02 & 0.98 \end{bmatrix}, \tag{105}$$

which corresponds to 20 samples in first and 60 in a second mode. Note that the estimation performances of the IMM were weakly sensitive to small changes of the transition probabilities. The range and velocity estimate RMSE of GMKF, IMM, PF, GSPF, and MR are presented in Fig. 5. This figure shows that in the first part of the simulation (non-maneuvering target), the estimation RMSEs of all the tested methods are close. However, beyond the switching point (maneuvering target), the GMKF outperforms the other tested algorithms.

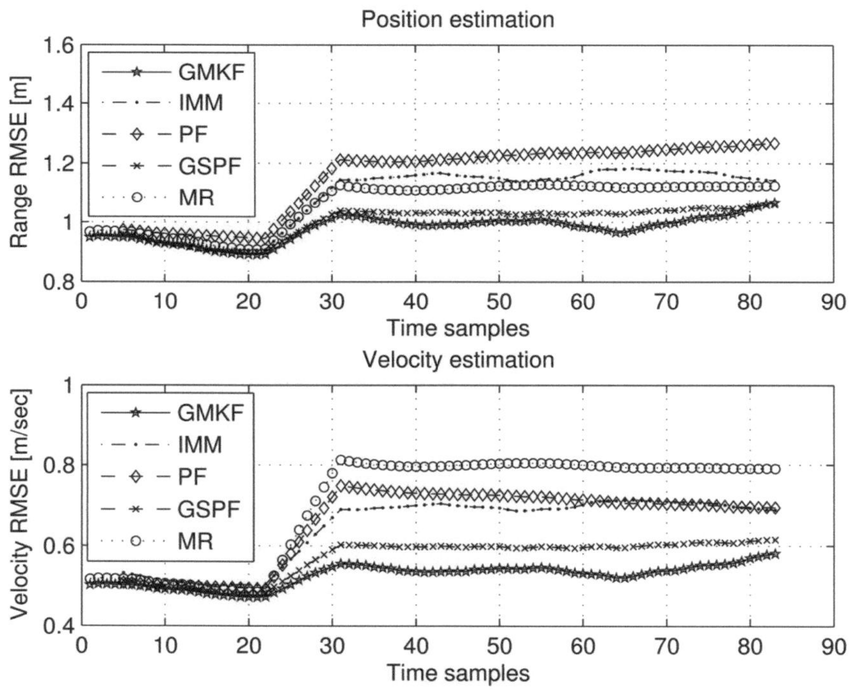

Fig. 5. GMKF vs. IMM, PF, GSPF, and MR for maneuvering target tracking.

A.2 Comparison with the GSF

The estimation performance of the GMKF is compared to the GSF (GMKF without the order reduction stage), which is optimal (but computationally impractical) in the MMSE sense. The measurement noise, $w[n]$, was assumed to be real-valued zero-mean Gaussian with variance σ_w^2 = 0.1. The target maneuvers are modeled by GMM with two mixture components:

$$f_{\mathbf{u}}(\mathbf{u}) = (1-\alpha_{\mathbf{u}})\Phi(\mathbf{u},\boldsymbol{\theta}_{\mathbf{u}1}) + \alpha_{\mathbf{u}}\Phi(\mathbf{u},\boldsymbol{\theta}_{\mathbf{u}2})\ ,\ \ \forall n = 0,1,2,\ldots$$

where

$$\boldsymbol{\theta}_{\mathbf{u}1} = \{\boldsymbol{\mu}_{\mathbf{u}1} = \mathbf{0}, \boldsymbol{\Gamma}_{\mathbf{u}1} = diag\left([0\ \ 0.01]\right)\}\ ,\ \boldsymbol{\theta}_{\mathbf{u}2} = \{\boldsymbol{\mu}_{\mathbf{u}2} = \mathbf{0}, \boldsymbol{\Gamma}_{\mathbf{u}2} = diag\left([0\ \ 1]\right)\}\ .$$

and $\alpha_{\mathbf{u}} = 0.2$. As it was shown in Section III-A, the GSF is optimal with respect to the MMSE, but it is impractical due to the model order growth. Therefore, the estimation RMSE of the GSF can be interpreted as a lower bound for the RMSE of GMKF. The range estimation performance of the GMKF and the GSF are shown in Fig. 6 for maneuvering target tracking. The GMKF performance is evaluated for $N = 13$ only, because longer runs are computationally impractical due to exponential model order growth. This figure shows that the GMKF performance is close to the lower bound provided by the GSF which is the exact MMSE.

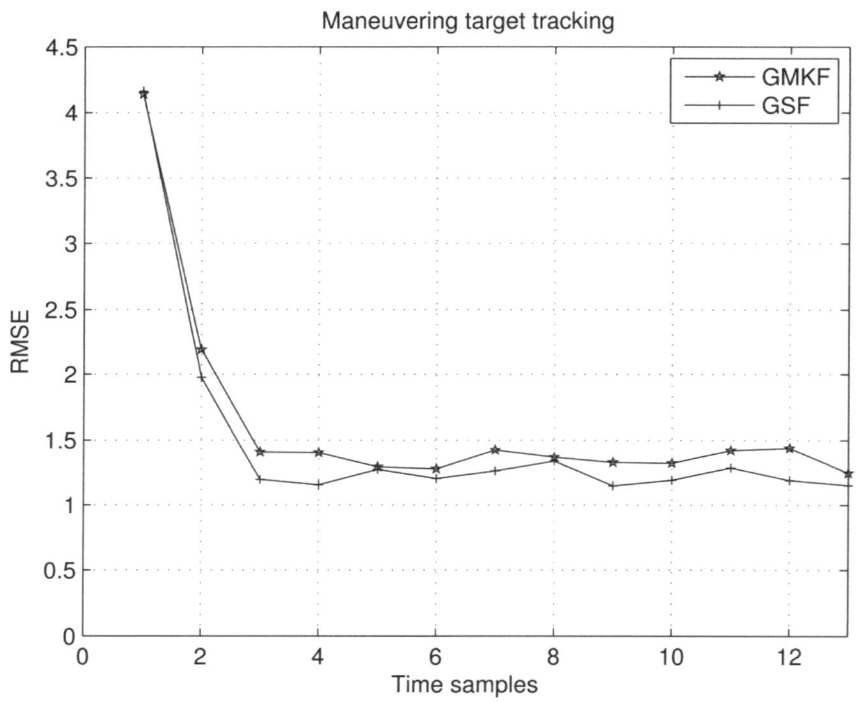

Fig. 6. GMKF vs. GSF for maneuvering target tracking.

A.3 Non-Gaussian glint measurement noise

The Middleton class-A model is widely used for glint measurement noise [3], [62]. This model consists of one Gaussian with high probability of occurrence and small variance and another with small probability of occurrence and very high variance:

$$f_{w[n]}(w) = \alpha_w \Phi(w,\boldsymbol{\theta}_{w_1}) + (1-\alpha_w)\Phi(w,\boldsymbol{\theta}_{w_2})\ ,\ n = 0,\ldots,N-1\ ,$$

where $\alpha_w = 0.9$, $\boldsymbol{\theta}_{w1} = \{\mu_{w1} = 0,\ \sigma_{w1}^2 = 0.01\}$, $\boldsymbol{\theta}_{w2} = \{\mu_{w2} = 0,\ \sigma_{w2}^2 = 1\}$. For the PF, the measurement noise is modeled by a single Gaussian with the following first and second order statistics:

$$\begin{aligned}\bar{\mu}_w &= (1-\alpha_w)\mu_{w1} + \alpha_w \mu_{w2} \, , \\ \bar{\sigma}_w^2 &= (1-\alpha_w)\sigma_{w1}^2 + \alpha_w \sigma_{w2}^2 + (1-\alpha_w)\mu_{w1}\mu_{w1}^T + \alpha_w \mu_{w2}\mu_{w2}^T - \bar{\mu}_w \bar{\mu}_w^T \, ,\end{aligned} \tag{106}$$

The IMM [20] with 2 modes was used in this scenario. These modes are characterized by the following measurement and system noises parameters:

- Mode 1: no glint: $\boldsymbol{\theta}_\mathbf{u} = \{\mathbf{0}, diag([1\ 1])\}, \boldsymbol{\theta}_{w_1} = \{\mu_{w1} = 0, \sigma_{w1}^2 = 0.01\}$,
- Mode 2: glint : $\boldsymbol{\theta}_\mathbf{u} = \{\mathbf{0}, diag([1\ 1])\}, \boldsymbol{\theta}_{w_2} = \{\mu_{w2} = 0\ , \sigma_{w2}^2 = 1\}$.

In this scenario, it was assumed that the glint is time-independent. Therefore, the transition probability matrix between the two models is [20]:

$$\pi_2 = \begin{bmatrix} (1-\alpha_w) & \alpha_w \\ (1-\alpha_w) & \alpha_w \end{bmatrix} . \tag{107}$$

The estimation performances of GMKF, IMM, PF, GSPF, and MR are presented in Fig. 7. This figure shows that the GMKF outperforms the other tested algorithms.

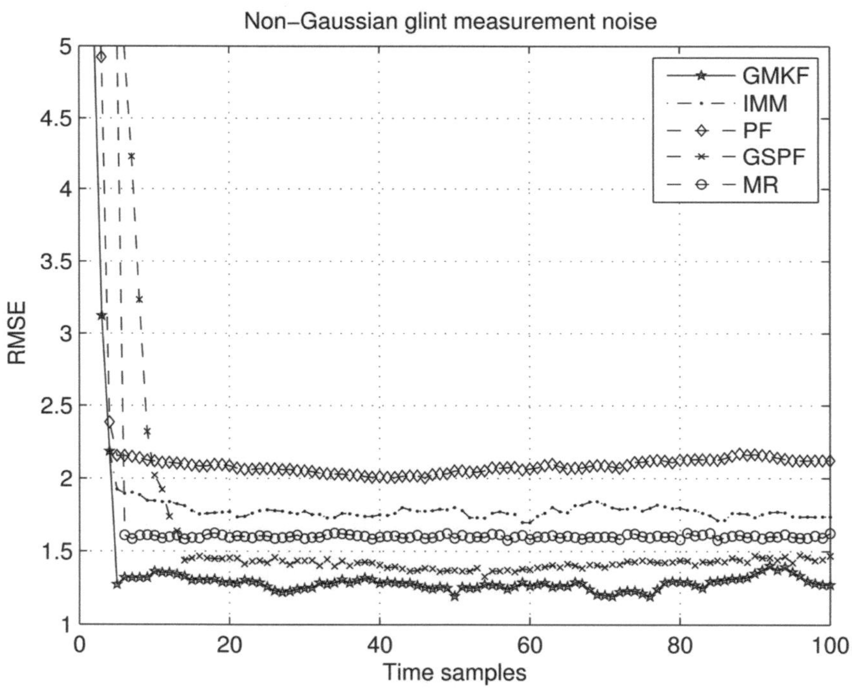

Fig. 7. GMKF vs. IMM, PF, GSPF, and MR for non-Gaussian glint measurement noise.

A.4 GMKF sensitivity

The main motivation of this test is to show that the estimation performance of the GMKF is weakly sensitive to the assumed GMM order of the posterior distribution. In addition, the sensitivity of the GMKF performance to the size of the artificial data used in the model order reduction algorithm, is tested. The DSS model, used in the previous scenario was adopted here. It was assumed that the elements of the system noise $\mathbf{u}[n] = [u_1[n]\ u_2[n]]^T$ are independent where $u_1[n]$ and $u_2[n]$ are Laplacian-distributed with marginal PDFs

$f_{u_i[n]}(u) = \frac{1}{2b_i}e^{-b_i|u|}$, $n = 0,...,N-1$, $i = 1, 2$, where $b_1 = 0.3$ and $b_2 = 0.4$. The measurement noise, $w[n]$, was assumed to be zero-mean Gaussian with variance $\sigma_w^2 = 0.1$. The Laplacian PDF of the system noise vector is approximated by a GMM of order $K = 16$. Fig. 8 shows that for any number of Gaussians in the mixture, the GMKF estimation performance improves as the size of the artificial data in the EM stage increases. It can be observed that the estimation performance improves to a turning point, from which the estimation performance degrades. The reason for the estimation performance degradation is the overfitting problem [63]. The threshold for the number of the components in the mixture increases with the size of the artificial data used in the EM stage. This figure shows that only a minor improvement in the estimation performance is achieved with increase of the GMM order.

B. NL-GMKF

In this section, the NL-GMKF performance is evaluated using the following nonlinear DSS model with non-Gaussian driving and measurement noise distributions.

Maneuvering target tracking model

Maneuvering target tracking involves modeling of a maneuver control signal, which is unknown to the tracker. Typically, the control signal is modeled as a random process [18], [64]. Most maneuver models assume that target maneuvering is uncoupled in Cartesian coordinates. The well-known Singer model [65] assumes that the target acceleration is a zero-mean first-order Markov process. In this example, a two-dimensional target tracking problem is addressed. The two-dimensional time-varying target dynamics can be described by the system state vector, which consists of the target position $[r_x\, r_y]^T$, velocity $[\dot{r}_x\, \dot{r}_y]^T$, and acceleration $[\ddot{r}_x\, \ddot{r}_y]^T$:

$$\mathbf{s}[n] = \left[r_x[n],\ r_y[n],\ \dot{r}_x[n],\ \dot{r}_y[n],\ \ddot{r}_x[n],\ \ddot{r}_y[n]\right]^T .$$

The discrete-time Singer model is described by the linear transition function:

$$\mathbf{a}(\mathbf{s}[n-1], \mathbf{u}[n]) = \begin{bmatrix} 1 & 0 & T & 0 & c_1 & 0 \\ 0 & 1 & 0 & T & 0 & c_1 \\ 0 & 0 & 1 & 0 & c_2 & 0 \\ 0 & 0 & 0 & 1 & 0 & c_2 \\ 0 & 0 & 0 & 0 & e^{-\delta T} & 0 \\ 0 & 0 & 0 & 0 & 0 & e^{-\delta T} \end{bmatrix} \mathbf{s}[n-1] + \begin{bmatrix} 0 & 0 \\ 0 & 0 \\ 0 & 0 \\ 0 & 0 \\ 1 & 0 \\ 0 & 1 \end{bmatrix} \mathbf{u}[n] ,$$

where

$$\begin{aligned} c_1 &= \frac{T}{\delta} - \frac{1 - e^{-\delta T}}{\delta^2} \\ c_2 &= \frac{1 - e^{-\delta T}}{\delta} , \end{aligned}$$

T is the sampling interval, and $\delta = \frac{1}{\tau}$ is reciprocal of the maneuver time constant τ, that describes the maneuver duration. Note that this model can describe both maneuvering and nonmaneuvering motions. Thus, as maneuver time decreases, the Singer model reduces to the constant velocity (CV) model, and as the maneuver time increases, the Singer model reduces to the constant acceleration (CA) model. According to the Singer model, the target position change is determined by its velocity, the target velocity change is determined by its

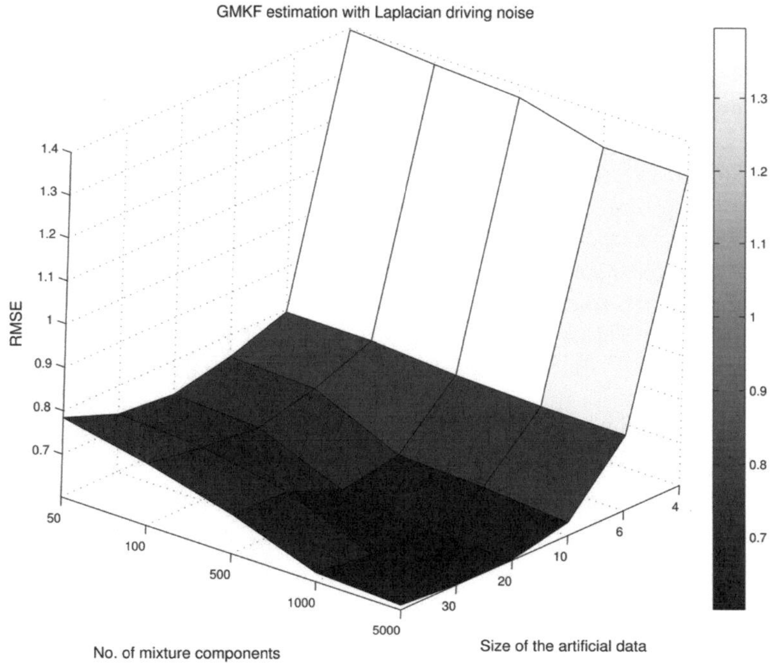

Fig. 8. GMKF sensitivity testing.

acceleration, and the acceleration change is driven by the system noise. Therefore, an alternative way to model target maneuver is to model abrupt changes of target acceleration that corresponds to increased variance of the system noise.

Observation model

The measurements from a typical two-dimensional radar consist of the target range and bearing. Therefore, the measurement equation is nonlinear. Assuming that the radar is placed at the origin $(x, y) = (0, 0)$, the radar measurements: range, $r[n]$, and bearing, $\beta[n]$, of the target are described by the measurement function

$$\mathbf{h}\left(\mathbf{s}[n],\ \mathbf{w}[n]\right) = \begin{bmatrix} \left(r_x^2[n] + r_y^2[n]\right)^{\frac{1}{2}} \\ \arctan\left(\frac{r_y[n]}{r_x[n]}\right) \end{bmatrix} + \mathbf{w}[n]\ ,$$

where $\mathbf{w}[n]$ is a zero-mean additive noise.

Glint noise model

The mixture approach is widely used in modeling the non-Gaussian glint noise. The glint is Gaussian-like around the mean and has a non-Gaussian, long-tailed nature in the tail region [3]. The data at the tail region represent outliers caused by the glint spikes. The outliers with low occurrence probability have a significant inuence on the conventional target tracking algorithms, such as the KF. In [3], [16] and [36], the glint noise was modeled as a mixture of two zero-mean Gaussians, where the outliers were represented by a zero-mean Gaussian with large (comparing to the thermal noise) covariance matrix. In [6] and [20], it was proposed to model the heavy-tailed distribution of the glint noise for each measurement component as a mixture of a zero-mean Gaussian noise with high occurrence probability and a Laplacian noise with low probability of occurrence:

$$f_w(w) = (1-\alpha_w)\Phi(w, \boldsymbol{\theta}_{w1}) + \alpha_w \mathcal{L}(w, \boldsymbol{\theta}_{w2}) \;, \tag{108}$$

where α_w is the glint probability, and $\mathcal{L}(w, \boldsymbol{\theta}_{w2})$ is the Laplacian PDF in which $\boldsymbol{\theta}_{w2}$ contains the mean and the variance. The estimation performance of the NL-GMKF was compared to PF, IMM-EKF, UKF, and GSPF. The performances were tested for N = 150 time instances with sampling interval T = 1 sec. The following target tracking cases were tested:

1. Nonmaneuvering target tracking in the presence of glint measurement noise
2. Maneuvering target tracking with Gaussian measurement noise
3. Maneuvering target tracking in the presence of glint measurement noise
4. Maneuvering target tracking in the presence of glint measurement noise, whose statistics depend on the target maneuver
5. Coordinated turn (CT) maneuvering target tracking in the presence of Gaussian or glint measurement noise.

Table 1 shows time-varying statistical parameters of the system and measurement noises for the first four scenarios. In these scenarios, the target maneuver was modeled by Gaussian-distributed system noise with time-varying variance and the following parameters:

- Stages 1 and 3: $\boldsymbol{\theta}_{\mathbf{u}1} = \{\boldsymbol{\mu}_{\mathbf{u}1}, \Gamma_{\mathbf{u}1}\}$, where $\boldsymbol{\mu}_{\mathbf{u}1} = \mathbf{0}$, $\Gamma_{\mathbf{u}1}^{1/2} = diag\left([1m/sec^2, 1m/sec^2]\right)$.
- Stage 2: $\boldsymbol{\theta}_{\mathbf{u}2} = \{\boldsymbol{\mu}_{\mathbf{u}2}, \Gamma_{\mathbf{u}2}\}$, where $\boldsymbol{\mu}_{\mathbf{u}2} = \mathbf{0}$, $\Gamma_{\mathbf{u}2} = \xi^2\Gamma_{\mathbf{u}1}$.

Scenario	Noises	Stage 1 $1 \le n \le 50$	Stage 2 $51 \le n \le 100$	Stage 3 $101 \le n \le 150$
1	System Measurement	$\boldsymbol{\theta}_{\mathbf{u}1}$ $\boldsymbol{\theta}_{\mathbf{w}1}, \boldsymbol{\theta}_{\mathbf{w}2}$ $\psi = 5,\ \alpha_{\mathbf{w}} = 0.3$	$\boldsymbol{\theta}_{\mathbf{u}1}$, $\boldsymbol{\theta}_{\mathbf{w}1}, \boldsymbol{\theta}_{\mathbf{w}2}$, $\psi = 5,\ \alpha_{\mathbf{w}} = 0.3$	$\boldsymbol{\theta}_{\mathbf{u}1}$ $\boldsymbol{\theta}_{\mathbf{w}1}, \boldsymbol{\theta}_{\mathbf{w}2}$ $\psi = 5,\ \alpha_{\mathbf{w}} = 0.3$
2	System Measurement	$\boldsymbol{\theta}_{\mathbf{u}1}$ $\boldsymbol{\theta}_{\mathbf{w}1},\ \alpha_{\mathbf{w}} = 0$	$\boldsymbol{\theta}_{\mathbf{u}2},\ \xi = 10$ $\boldsymbol{\theta}_{\mathbf{w}1},\ \alpha_{\mathbf{w}} = 0$	$\boldsymbol{\theta}_{\mathbf{u}1}$ $\boldsymbol{\theta}_{\mathbf{w}1},\ \alpha_{\mathbf{w}} = 0$
3	System Measurement	$\boldsymbol{\theta}_{\mathbf{u}1}$ $\boldsymbol{\theta}_{\mathbf{w}1}, \boldsymbol{\theta}_{\mathbf{w}2}$ $\psi = 5,\ \alpha_{\mathbf{w}} = 0.3$	$\boldsymbol{\theta}_{\mathbf{u}2},\ \xi = 10$ $\boldsymbol{\theta}_{\mathbf{w}1}, \boldsymbol{\theta}_{\mathbf{w}2}$ $\psi = 5,\ \alpha_{\mathbf{w}} = 0.3$	$\boldsymbol{\theta}_{\mathbf{u}1}$ $\boldsymbol{\theta}_{\mathbf{w}1}, \boldsymbol{\theta}_{\mathbf{w}2}$ $\psi = 5,\ \alpha_{\mathbf{w}} = 0.3$
4	System Measurement	$\boldsymbol{\theta}_{\mathbf{u}1}$ $\boldsymbol{\theta}_{\mathbf{w}1},\ \alpha_{\mathbf{w}} = 0$	$\boldsymbol{\theta}_{\mathbf{u}2},\ \xi = 10$ $\boldsymbol{\theta}_{\mathbf{w}1}, \boldsymbol{\theta}_{\mathbf{w}2}$, $\psi = 5,\ \alpha_{\mathbf{w}} = 0.3$	$\boldsymbol{\theta}_{\mathbf{u}1}$ $\boldsymbol{\theta}_{\mathbf{w}1},\ \alpha_{\mathbf{w}} = 0$

Table 1.Parameters of the system and measurement noise for scenarios 1-4

The following parameters for the measurement noise in (108) were selected in all the scenarios: $\boldsymbol{\theta}_{\mathbf{w}i} = \{\boldsymbol{\mu}_{\mathbf{w}i}, \boldsymbol{\Gamma}_{\mathbf{w}i}\}$, i = 1, 2, where $\boldsymbol{\mu}_{\mathbf{w}1} = \boldsymbol{\mu}_{\mathbf{w}2} = 0$, $\Gamma_{\mathbf{w}1}^{1/2} = diag\,([10m, 0.5mrad])$, and $\boldsymbol{\Gamma}_{\mathbf{w}2} = \psi^2\boldsymbol{\Gamma}_{\mathbf{w}1}$. In the first two scenarios, target tracking performances were evaluated for a variety of glint noise statistics and maneuvering levels, respectively. In the first scenario, tracking performances of the different methods are evaluated for different probabilities of glint, $\alpha_{\mathbf{w}}$, and different glint noise levels, ψ in the range of [1, 10]. In the second scenario, maneuver cases [18], [31], starting from low maneuvering target (commercial aircraft) to extremely highly maneuvering target, modeled by different values of ξ in the range [1, 100], were tested. Thus, ξ = 1 models extremely low acceleration standard deviation (STD) of about 0.1g, and ξ = 100 models extremely high acceleration STD of about 10g. In all the scenarios, the initial target position, velocity and acceleration were as follows:

$$\mathbf{s}[-1] \quad = \quad \left[5km,\ 5km,\ -100m/sec,\ 0m/sec,\ 0m/sec^2,\ 0m/sec^2\right]^T \;.$$

For performance evaluation, the RMSE of the two-dimensional target position $\mathbf{r}[n] = [r_x[n]\ r_y[n]]^T$ and velocity $\dot{\mathbf{r}}[n] = [\dot{r}_x[n]\ \dot{\mathbf{r}}_y[n]]^T$ estimates were evaluated. The mean RMSE of the range and velocity estimation, defined as

$$||\hat{\mathbf{r}}[n] - \mathbf{r}[n]|| = \left((\hat{r}_x[n] - r_x[n])^2 + (\hat{r}_y[n] - r_y[n])^2\right)^{\frac{1}{2}} ,$$
$$||\hat{\dot{\mathbf{r}}}[n] - \dot{\mathbf{r}}[n]|| = \left((\hat{\dot{r}}_x[n] - \dot{r}_x[n])^2 + (\hat{\dot{r}}_y[n] - \dot{r}_y[n])^2\right)^{\frac{1}{2}} ,$$

are evaluated in the following scenarios using 100 trials. In all the tests, the NL-GMKF was initialized at time instance n = -1 with

$$\begin{aligned} \alpha_{\mathbf{s}l}[-1] &= \frac{1}{L} , \\ \boldsymbol{\mu}_{\mathbf{s}l}[-1] &= \mathbf{0} , \\ \boldsymbol{\Gamma}_{\mathbf{s}l}[-1] &= \rho\mathbf{I} , \forall l = 1, \ldots, L \end{aligned}$$

where ρ is a large number, and $\mathbf{I}$ is an identity matrix. For the NL-GMKF and the GSPF, the conditional distribution of the state vector $\mathbf{s}[n]$, given $\mathcal{X}[n]$ was assumed to be GMM of order L = 16. For the GSPF, the number of particles for each Gaussian in the mixture was chosen to be 400 (totally 6400 particles). Addressing the nonlinear problem, the GSPF was implemented using first-order linearization in the time-update stage [35]. In the following tests, the standard sampling importance resampling (SIR) PF with 10000 particles was implemented [1]. For the PF, UKF and the GSPF, the first and second order statistics of the state vector $\mathbf{s}[n]$, given $\mathcal{X}[n]$ were initialized with

$$\boldsymbol{\mu}_{\mathbf{s}}[-1|-1] = \mathbf{0} ,$$
$$\boldsymbol{\Gamma}_{\mathbf{s}}[-1|-1] = \rho\mathbf{I} .$$

In the UKF [55], the parameter that determines the spread of the sigma points was set to α = 0.95. The scaling parameter, k, was set to 0, and the parameter β, used to incorporate prior knowledge of the distribution [55], was set to 2.

B.1 Nonmaneuvering target tracking in the presence of glint measurement noise

The tracking performance of the NL-GMKF in the presence of non-Gaussian glint noise is tested in this scenario. A nonmaneuvering target was considered in order to evaluate the inuence of the non-Gaussian measurement noise on the tracking performance. In practice, this situation might occur when glint noise arises due to environmental factors such as turbulence and vibration and not due to target maneuver [53], [54]. Tracking performances of the tested algorithms are evaluated for various levels of glint noise covariance and its probabilities. In the NL-GMKF, the system noise was assumed to be Gaussian with parameters $\boldsymbol{\theta}_{\mathbf{u}1}$. The measurement noise was modeled by the mixture in (108), with parameters defined in Table 1. The IMM consisted of two EKFs, which correspond to the two modes characterized by the following system and measurement noise parameters:

- Mode 1: no glint: $\boldsymbol{\theta}_{\mathbf{u}1}$, $\boldsymbol{\theta}_{\mathbf{w}1}$,
- Mode 2: glint: $\boldsymbol{\theta}_{\mathbf{u}1}$, $\boldsymbol{\theta}_{\mathbf{w}2}$.

In this scenario, it assumed that the glint is time-independent. Therefore, the transition probability matrix between the two models is [20]

$$\pi_2 = \begin{bmatrix} (1-\alpha_{\mathbf{w}}) & \alpha_{\mathbf{w}} \\ (1-\alpha_{\mathbf{w}}) & \alpha_{\mathbf{w}} \end{bmatrix}. \quad (109)$$

The tracking performances of the NL-GMKF, PF, IMM-EKF, UKF and GSPF in terms of mean RMSE, are shown in Fig. 9 for the two-dimensional position and velocity. It can be observed that the NL-GMKF outperforms the other tested algorithms. The tracking performances as a function of the glint probability, α_{w}, and glint level, ψ, at time instance n = 75 are shown in Figs. 10 and 11, respectively. It can be observed that the NL-GMKF outperforms the other tested algorithms for the tested probabilities of glint and the tested glint levels. Note that the estimation performance of the NL-GMKF remains almost constant across the entire range of the tested probability of glint and glint level.

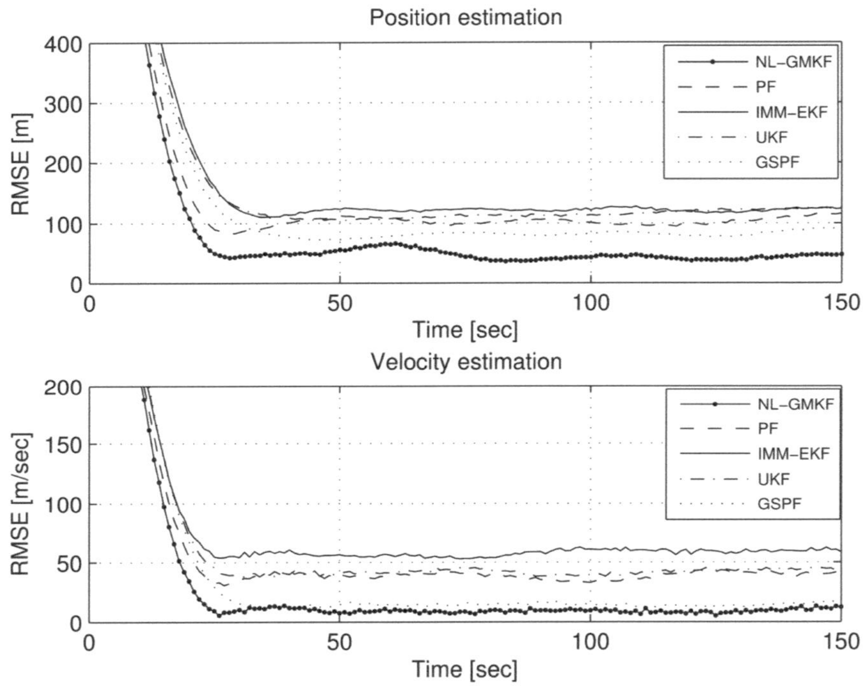

Fig. 9. Tracking performance of NL-GMKF, PF, IMM-EKF, UKF and GSPF in the presence of glint noise with probability of $\alpha_{\mathrm{w}} = 0.3$, and glint noise level of $\psi = 5$.

B.2 Maneuvering target tracking

In this scenario, target tracking performances of the NL-GMKF without glint noise are evaluated for a wide range of maneuvers, from low, hardly detectable, to very high. The glint produced by small targets at long distances may be negligible and target tracking errors arises solely due to target maneuver. The tracking performance of the NL-GMKF is tested in a wide range of maneuvers in order to test its ability to track highly maneuverable targets as well as slow maneuverable targets with low probability of maneuver detection. In this example, the maneuvering target was simulated during the second interval of the simulation. In the NL-GMKF, the system noise statistics were modeled by the mixture of two components:

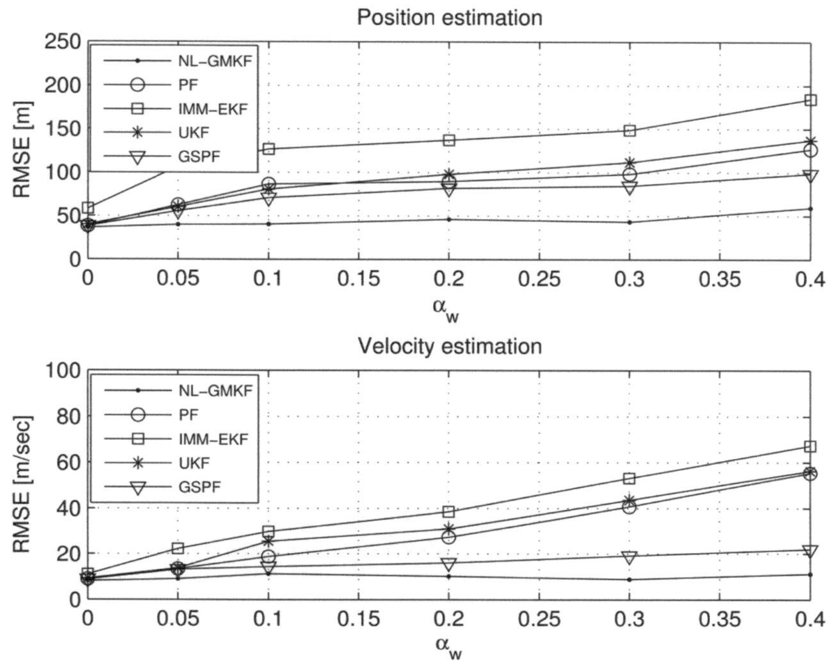

Fig. 10. Tracking performance of NL-GMKF, PF, IMM-EKF, UKF and GSPF vs. glint noise probability with glint noise level $\psi = 5$ at time instance $n = 75$.

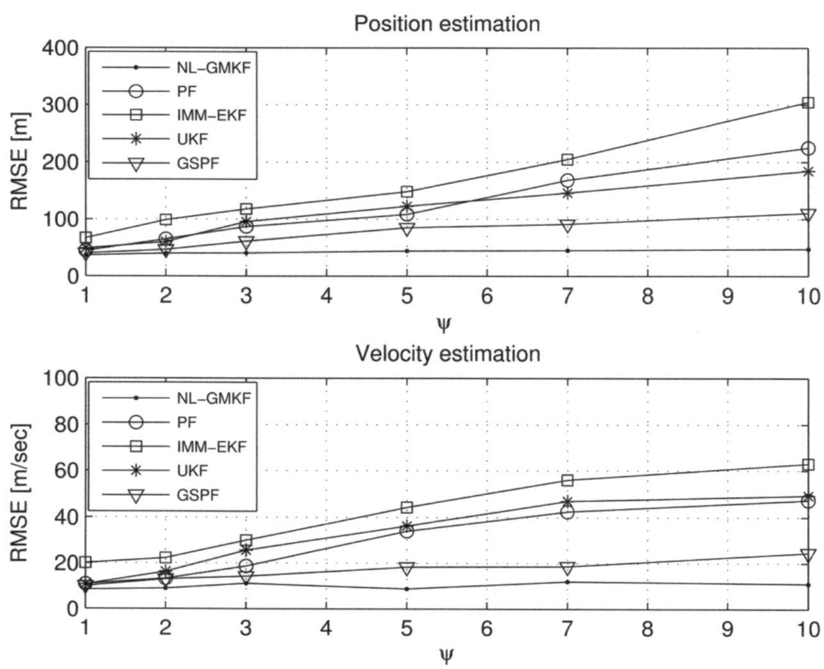

Fig. 11. Tracking performance of NL-GMKF, PF, IMM-EKF, UKF and GSPF as a function of glint noise level with probability of glint $\alpha_w = 0.3$ at time instance $n = 75$.

$$f_{\mathbf{u}}(\mathbf{u}) = (1-\alpha_{\mathbf{u}})\Phi(\mathbf{u},\boldsymbol{\theta}_{\mathbf{u}1}) + \alpha_{\mathbf{u}}\Phi(\mathbf{u},\boldsymbol{\theta}_{\mathbf{u}2}) \ , \ \ \forall n = 0,1,2,\dots \ , \tag{110}$$

and the probability of target maneuver was selected to be $\alpha_{\mathbf{u}} = 0.2$. The measurement noise model was assumed to be Gaussian with parameters $\boldsymbol{\theta}_{\mathbf{w}1}$. The IMM consisted of two EKFs, which correspond to the two modes characterized by the following system and measurement noise parameters:

- Mode 1: nonmaneuvering - $\boldsymbol{\theta}_{\mathbf{u}1}$, $\boldsymbol{\theta}_{\mathbf{w}1}$,
- Mode 2: maneuvering - $\boldsymbol{\theta}_{\mathbf{u}2}$, $\boldsymbol{\theta}_{\mathbf{w}1}$.

The first model represents the target motion in the first and third parts of the simulation, and the second represents the target motion in the second part. The transition probability matrix between the two models was selected to match the transition probabilities to the mean sojourn time in each mode [18]:

$$\pi_1 = \begin{bmatrix} 0.98 & 0.02 \\ 0.02 & 0.98 \end{bmatrix} , \tag{111}$$

which corresponds to 50 samples at each mode. The estimation performance of the IMM was found to be weakly sensitive to small changes of the transition probabilities. The tracking performances of the NL-GMKF, PF, IMM-EKF, UKF, and GSPF in terms of mean RMSE are presented in Fig. 12. This figure shows the mean RMSE of the target position and velocity estimation. It can be observed that at the first and the third parts of the simulation (nonmaneuvering target), the estimation performances of the tested algorithms are close. However, at the second part of the simulation (maneuvering target), the NL-GMKF outperforms the other tested algorithms. It is expected that the estimation errors in tracking highly maneuvering targets would be larger. However, high maneuvers can be easily detected and the estimation errors can be significantly reduced using a proper model. A more challenging scenario arises when tracking slow-maneuvering targets with low probability of maneuver detection. In this case, large errors may be due to mismatch in the model. These situations can be modeled by small covariance matrices of the system noise representing the maneuver, $\boldsymbol{\Gamma}_{\mathbf{u}2}$, which is determined by ξ. The tracking performance of the proposed NL-GMKF at time instance n = 75 as a function of the maneuvering level, ξ, is tested and presented in Fig. 13 for accelerations in the range $0.1g$ – $10g$, which covers the entire range of maneuvering aircrafts [7]. This figure shows that the NL-GMKF outperforms the other tested algorithms for all tested maneuvering levels. This figure also shows that the performance of the NL-GMKF is almost constant for all tested maneuvering levels while the tracking performances of other tested algorithms degrade for higher maneuvering levels.

B.3 Maneuvering target tracking in the presence of glint measurement noise

In this example, maneuvering target tracking in the presence of glint noise was tested. It is assumed that the glint noise arises due to environmental factors such as turbulence and vibration and not due to target maneuver per se, and thus it is present during the entire simulation and its statistics are independent of the target maneuver. This scenario occurs in tracking close targets (such as a group of aircrafts) [20], [53], [54] and tests the effect of the glint noise on tracking the maneuvering target with various levels of maneuverability. The target maneuvering during the second interval, modeled by zero-mean Gaussian system noise with time-varying statistics described in scenario 2 with $\xi = 10$, was considered in this example. In the NL-GMKF, the statistics of the system noise used in scenario 2 was adopted.

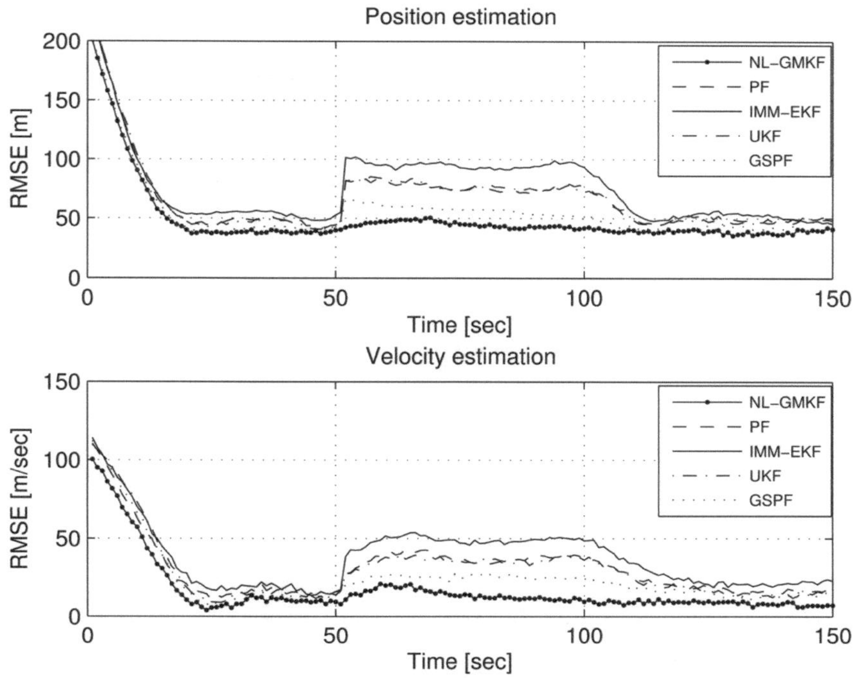

Fig. 12. Tracking performance of NL-GMKF, PF, IMM-EKF, UKF and GSPF in the presence of maneuvering during $n \in [50, 100]$ with $\xi = 10$.

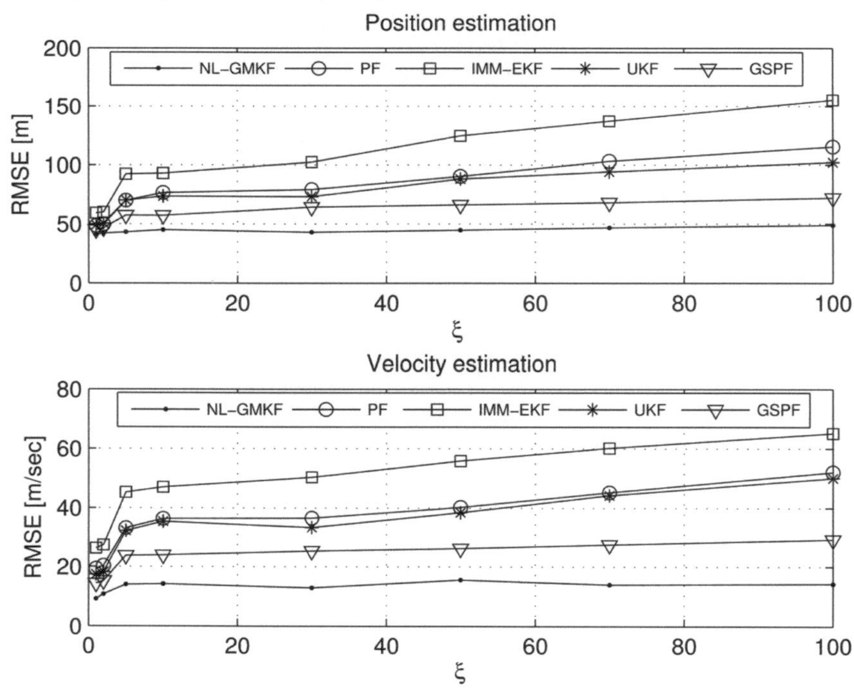

Fig. 13. Tracking performance of NL-GMKF, PF, IMM-EKF, UKF, and GSPF in the presence of maneuvering target for various levels of maneuver at time instance $n = 75$.

The measurement noise was modeled by the mixture in (108), with parameters defined in Table 1. The IMM-EKF algorithm for maneuvering target in the presence of glint noise was implemented using an efficient layered implementation [31]. According to this scheme, two sets of modes are used. One corresponds to the presence or absence of target maneuvering and the other to the presence or absence of glint. Therefore, the IMM is implemented with four modes with transition matrices, defined in (107), (111) according to [31]. The parameters of the measurement and system noise were identical to those defined in scenarios 1 and 2, respectively. The IMM consisted of four EKFs, which correspond to the four modes characterized by the following system and measurement noise parameters:

- Mode 1: nonmaneuvering and no glint - $\boldsymbol{\theta}_{\mathbf{u}1}$, $\boldsymbol{\theta}_{\mathbf{w}1}$,
- Mode 2: maneuvering and no glint - $\boldsymbol{\theta}_{\mathbf{u}2}$, $\boldsymbol{\theta}_{\mathbf{w}1}$,
- Mode 3: nonmaneuvering and glint - $\boldsymbol{\theta}_{\mathbf{u}1}$, $\boldsymbol{\theta}_{\mathbf{w}2}$,
- Mode 4: maneuvering and glint - $\boldsymbol{\theta}_{\mathbf{u}2}$, $\boldsymbol{\theta}_{\mathbf{w}2}$.

The tracking performances of the NL-GMKF, PF, IMM-EKF, UKF and GSPF in terms of mean RMSE for a maneuvering target with glint are shown in Fig. 14. It can be observed that the NL-GMKF outperforms the other tested algorithms during the entire simulation interval.

B.4 Maneuvering target tracking in the presence of correlated statistics of glint noise

In this example, a scenario of great practical interest in which the statistics of the glint noise and the target maneuver are correlated, was tested. In target tracking, changes in the target aspect with respect to the radar due to maneuver dramatically increases the radar cross section uctuations resulting in significant glint noise [20], [53]-[57]. Therefore, glint noise increases dramatically during the maneuver. This scenario is modeled by correlated time-variations of the statistics of the measurement noise and the system noise. In this example, it was assumed that there is no glint noise during nonmaneuvering parts of the simulation (first and third parts), while it is present during the maneuvering part of the simulation (second part). The models for the tested tracking algorithms presented in the previous scenario, are adopted here too. The tracking performances of NLGMKF, PF, IMM-EKF, UKF, and GSPF of the maneuvering target with glint, are shown in Fig. 15 in terms of mean RMSE of the two-dimensional position and velocity. It can be observed that the NL-GMKF outperforms the other tested algorithms during the entire simulation interval. Note that in contrast to other tested scenarios, the performance of the NL-GMKF degrades at the switching point (comparing to almost constant performance obtained in the previous examples in Figs. 9, 12, and 14). This behavior occurs due to simultaneous changes in the system and measurement noise statistics and the difficulty to associate those changes, expressed by the innovation vector statistics, with glint noise or target maneuver. Fig. 16 shows the tracking performances for various combinations of maneuvers and glint noise levels. One can notice that the tracking performance of the NL-GMKF does not monotonically decrease as a function of ξ or ψ. This phenomenon can be explained by the difficulties of the NL-GMKF to associate the increase in the innovation process variance to glint or to target maneuver. Note that Fig. 16 is in conformance with results in scenarios 1 and 2. The first column in Fig. 16 (ξ = 1) corresponds to the NL-GMKF performance in the non-maneuvering scenario shown in Fig. 11, and the first row in Fig. 16 (ψ= 1) corresponds to the NLGMKF performance in the scenario without glint noise shown in Fig. 13. The NL-GMKF provides higher performance than the other tested algorithms, since it employs prior knowledge on the non-Gaussian PDF of system and measurement noise by approximating

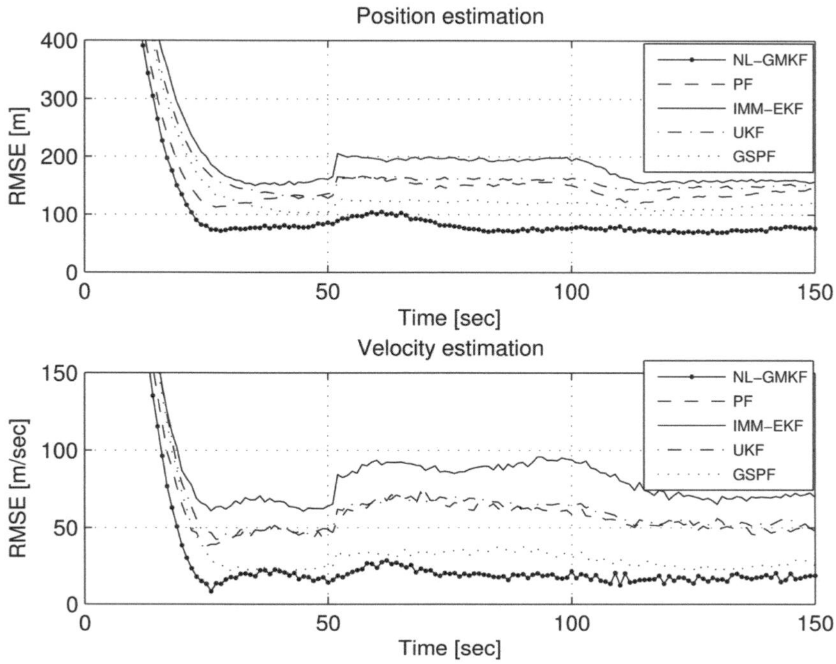

Fig. 14. Tracking performance of NL-GMKF, PF, IMM-EKF, UKF and GSPF in the presence of maneuvering target during $n \in [50, 100]$ with $\xi = 10$, and glint noise probability $\alpha_w = 0.3$ with glint noise level $\psi = 5$.

the non-Gaussian system state PDF by GMM and it does not attempt to estimate their parameters from the data. Therefore, performance degradation of the NL-GMKF in maneuvering or glint noise scenarios is due to reduction of information carried by the system model or measurements during maneuvering or glint samples, while in the other tested algorithms, it is due to modeling mismatch.

B.5 Coordinated turn

In this example, we consider a scenario in which the target maneuver is modeled by motion dynamics and not by increased system noise level. In air traffic control applications, the motion of the civil aircraft can be modeled by combination of intervals of constant velocity (CV) motion and intervals of CT with constant turning speed and a constant angular rate [18], [58]-[60]. In the considered scenario, the radar is positioned at [0*m*, 0*m*], and the target initial position at time $t = 0$ is [5*km*, 5*km*]. During the first 10 seconds, the target approaches the radar along the y-axis with constant speed of 100*m/sec*. Next, the target executes a coordinated turn during 10 seconds with angular velocity of $\frac{3\pi}{20}$ *rad/sec*, which corresponds to acceleration of about 4.5g. Finally, the target continues at constant speed of 100*m/sec* motion along x-axis for the next 10 seconds. The target trajectory is shown in Fig. 17. Two scenarios with Gaussian and glint measurement noise correlated to the maneuver statistics, were considered. In the first scenario, a zero-mean Gaussian measurement noise, defined in scenario 1, was considered during the entire simulation. In the second scenario, it was assumed that there is no glint noise during the CV intervals of the target motion and the glint noise increases during the CT interval. The measurement noise PDF in the 3 stages of

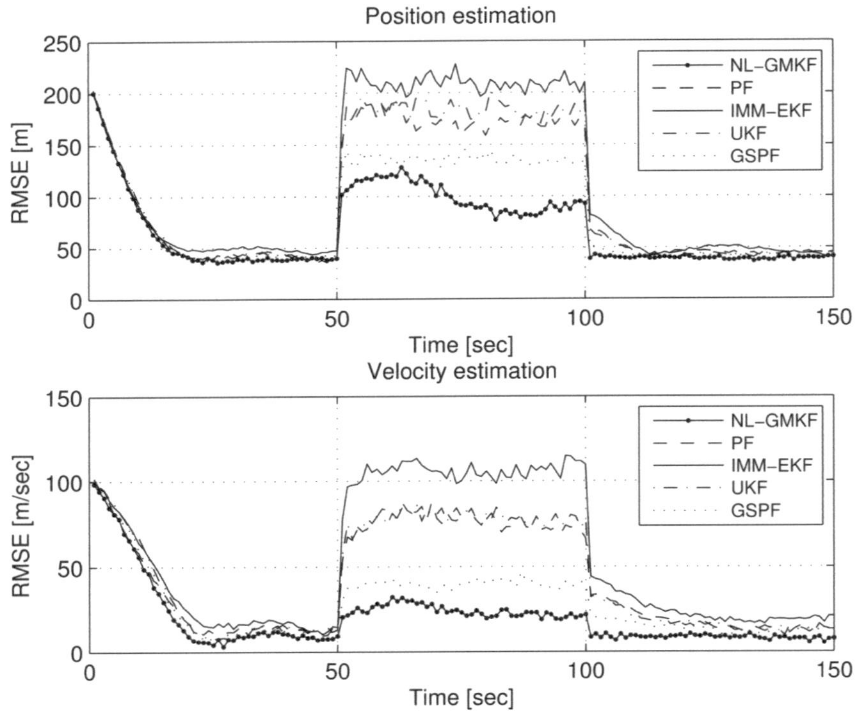

Fig. 15. Tracking performance of NL-GMKF, PF, IMM-EKF, UKF and GSPF in the presence of maneuvering target during $n \in [50, 100]$ with $\xi = 10$, and glint noise with probability $\alpha_w = 0.3$ with glint noise level $\psi = 5$ during $n \in [50, 100]$ with correlated statistics.

target maneuver was taken according to the 3 stages of scenario 4. In the NL-GMKF, the statistics of the measurement noise, considered in scenario 3, was adopted here. The statistics of the system noise were modeled by a mixture of two components, as modeled in scenario 2. The covariance matrix of the second mixture component was selected to be $\mathbf{\Gamma}_{\mathbf{u}2}^{\frac{1}{2}} = diag\ ([50m/sec^2, 50m/sec^2])$. Two types of IMM-EKF algorithms were tested in this scenario: IMM-EKF$^{(1)}$ consists of two CV kinematics models with different system noise levels (similar to the IMM-EKF that was used in scenario 4), and IMM-EKF$^{(2)}$ consists of the CV and the CT models [18]. The IMM-EKF$^{(1)}$ parameters were set to be similar to the IMM-EKF in scenarios 2 and 4, respectively. The covariance matrix of the system noise in the second mode of the IMM-EKF$^{(1)}$ was set to: $\mathbf{\Gamma}_{\mathbf{u}2}^{\frac{1}{2}} = diag\ ([50m/sec^2, 50m/sec^2])$. The first mode of the IMM-EKF$^{(2)}$ is similar to mode 1 of the IMM-EKF in scenario 4. In the second mode of the IMM-EKF$^{(2)}$, the CT model [18] was incorporated by including the turn rate as part of the state vector. The system noise standard deviations of the CT model were $0.5m/sec^2$ and $0.03rad/sec$. The transition probability matrix, defined in (111) was used for the IMM-EKF$^{(2)}$. The tracking performance of the NL-GMKF and IMM-EKFs algorithms for non-glint and glint scenarios are shown in the first and the second columns of Fig. 17, respectively. The two-dimensional CV-CT-CV trajectories estimated by the NL-GMKF and the IMM-EKFs, are shown in the first to third rows. The estimation performances of the tested algorithms as a function of time are shown in Fig. 18. This figure shows that performances of the NL-GMKF and the IMM-EKF$^{(2)}$ are similar and that both outperform the IMM-EKF$^{(1)}$ in the first scenario.

However, the NL-GMKF outperforms both IMM-EKF algorithms in the second scenario, in the presence of glint noise during the CT interval. It should be noted that the model of IMM-EKF$^{(2)}$ is tailored to specific scenarios of CV and CT, while the NL-GMKF does not use such prior information. The use of CV and CT models can enable using smaller system noise variance and could be simply incorporated within the NL-GMKF. However, such a prior information increases the algorithm sensitivity to other types of target maneuvering. The target position and velocity estimation RMSEs in this scenario are slightly higher than the corresponding RMSEs presented in Fig. 16 due to modeling mismatch. Finally, the tracking performance of the NL-GMKF was evaluated for a scenario with longer maneuvering duration with the same high acceleration. This scenario models higher maneuvering intensity. In this scenario, the target executes a coordinated turn during 50 seconds with acceleration magnitude of about 4.5g. As in the previous case, the acceleration vector varies, and this variation is not modeled in the NL-GMKF. The estimation performances of the tested algorithms as a function of time are shown in Fig. 19. This figure shows that performances of the NL-GMKF and the IMM-EKF$^{(2)}$ are similar and both of them outperform the IMM-EKF$^{(1)}$ in the first scenario, while the NL-GMKF outperforms both IMM-EKF algorithms in the second scenario, in the presence of glint noise during the CT interval.

B.6 NL-GMKF sensitivity

The main motivation of this test is to show that the performance of the NL-GMKF is weakly sensitive to the assumed GMM order of the posterior distribution. In addition, the sensitivity of the NL-GMKF performance to the size of the artificial data used in greedy EM learning, is tested. Note that the size of the artificial data is theoretically unlimited and it is practically set according to the processor computational resources [40]. The scenario 4 is considered here and the position estimation performance at time instance n = 75 is used for sensitivity testing. Fig. 20 shows that for the tested number of Gaussians in the mixture, the NL-GMKF estimation performance improves as the size of the artificial data in the EM stage increases. It can be observed that the estimation performance improves to a turning point, from which the estimation performance degrades. The reason for the estimation performance degradation is the overfitting problem [63]. The threshold for the number of the components in the mixture increases with the size of the artificial data used in the EM stage. This figure shows that only a minor improvement in the estimation performance is achieved with increase of the GMM order.

5. Conclusions

Two new recursive filters, named as GMKF and NL-GMKF, for linear and nonlinear, non-Gaussian problems were presented in this chapter. The GMKF algorithm consists of the GSF followed by an efficient model order reduction method. The GSF provides a rigorous solution for state vector estimation in a linear DSS model with GMM-distributed system and measurement noises and it generalizes the original KF to GMMs. Practical implementation of the optimal GSF is limited due to the exponential model order growth. The GMKF solves this problem via an efficient model order reduction method. The problem of exponential growth of the model order was solved via the mixture PDF estimation at each step using the greedy EM algorithm. It was shown that greedy EM-based order reduction scheme does not signi_cantly reduce the GMKF estimation performance. The estimation performance of the GMKF was tested for non-Gaussian cases using simulations, and it was shown that the GMKF outperforms the PF, IMM and the KF. However this superiority comes at the cost of the extra computational complexity caused by the use of EM for model order reduction procedure. The NL-GMKF was also derived based on the MMSE criterion. It assumes a nonlinear DSS model with general non-Gaussian distributions for the system and measurement noise. The posterior distribution of the state vector is modeled by GMM whose parameters are determined to minimize its estimated KLD from the true distribution. The NL-GMKF was applied to a nonlinear problem of maneuvering radar target tracking in the presence of glint noise. The performance of the derived NL-GMKF was evaluated via simulations and compared to the PF, the IMM-EKF and the EKF. The simulations showed that the NL-GMKF outperforms the PF, the IMM-EKF and the EKF in the considered cases.

APPENDIX

Proposition 1: Consider two M-order jointly GMM-distributed random variables $\mathbf{x}$ and $\mathbf{y}$ whose joint distribution can be written as

$$\begin{bmatrix} \mathbf{x} \\ \mathbf{y} \end{bmatrix} \sim GMM\left(\alpha_m, \begin{bmatrix} \boldsymbol{\mu}_{\mathbf{x}m} \\ \boldsymbol{\mu}_{\mathbf{y}m} \end{bmatrix}, \begin{bmatrix} \boldsymbol{\Gamma}_{\mathbf{x}m} & \boldsymbol{\Gamma}_{\mathbf{xy}m} \\ \boldsymbol{\Gamma}_{\mathbf{yx}m} & \boldsymbol{\Gamma}_{\mathbf{y}m} \end{bmatrix}; m = 1, \ldots, M\right) . \tag{112}$$

The MMSE estimator of $\mathbf{y}$ from $\mathbf{x}$ is

$$E(\mathbf{y}|\mathbf{x}) = \frac{1}{\sum\limits_{m'=1}^{M} \alpha_{m'} \Phi(\mathbf{x}; \boldsymbol{\theta}_{m'})} \sum_{m=1}^{M} \alpha_m \Phi(\mathbf{x}; \boldsymbol{\theta}_m) \left[\boldsymbol{\mu}_{\mathbf{y}m} + \boldsymbol{\Gamma}_{\mathbf{yx}m} \boldsymbol{\Gamma}_{\mathbf{x}m}^{-1} (\mathbf{x} - \boldsymbol{\mu}_{\mathbf{x}m})\right] , \tag{113}$$

where $\boldsymbol{\theta}_m$ consists of the mean and covariance matrix of the mth mixture component of the PDF of $\mathbf{x}$.

The proof of this proposition can be obtained by noting that $E(\mathbf{y} \mid \mathbf{x}) = E_{\eta_m} E_{\mathbf{y} \mid \mathbf{x}, \eta_m}(\mathbf{y} \mid \mathbf{x}, \eta_m)$ where η_m is the random mixture indicator of the mth Gaussian [47]. Therefore, the conditional distribution of $\mathbf{y} \mid \mathbf{x}, \eta_m$ is Gaussian, and this implies that the MMSE estimator of a GMM-distributed random vector is a weighted sum of linear MMSE (LMMSE) estimators. Note that the MMSE in (113) is nonlinear for $M > 1$, as expected in non-Gaussian problems.

Proposition 2: Consider two statistically independent GMM-distributed random vectors $\mathbf{x} \sim GMM(\alpha_{\mathbf{x}k}, \boldsymbol{\mu}_{\mathbf{x}k}, \boldsymbol{\Gamma}_{\mathbf{x}k}; k = 1,\ldots, K)$ and $\mathbf{y} \sim GMM(\alpha_{\mathbf{y}l}, \boldsymbol{\mu}_{\mathbf{y}l}, \boldsymbol{\Gamma}_{\mathbf{y}l}; l = 1,\ldots, L)$. The random vector $\mathbf{z}$, defined as:

$$\mathbf{z} = \mathbf{A}_\mathbf{x}\mathbf{x} + \mathbf{A}_\mathbf{y}\mathbf{y} + \mathbf{b} , \tag{114}$$

is GMM-distributed of order $J = KL$: $\mathbf{z} \sim GMM(\alpha_{\mathbf{z}j}, \boldsymbol{\mu}_{\mathbf{z}j}, \boldsymbol{\Gamma}_{\mathbf{z}j}; j = 1,\ldots, J)$, with

$$\alpha_{\mathbf{z}j} = \alpha_{\mathbf{x}k}\alpha_{\mathbf{y}l} , \tag{115}$$

$$\boldsymbol{\mu}_{\mathbf{z}j} = \mathbf{A}_\mathbf{x}\boldsymbol{\mu}_{\mathbf{x}k} + \mathbf{A}_\mathbf{y}\boldsymbol{\mu}_{\mathbf{y}l} + \mathbf{b} , \tag{116}$$

$$\boldsymbol{\Gamma}_{\mathbf{z}j} = \mathbf{A}_\mathbf{x}\boldsymbol{\Gamma}_{\mathbf{x}k}\mathbf{A}_\mathbf{x}^H + \mathbf{A}_\mathbf{y}\boldsymbol{\Gamma}_{\mathbf{y}l}\mathbf{A}_\mathbf{y}^H , \tag{117}$$

where the matrices $\mathbf{A_x}$, $\mathbf{A_y}$ and the vector $\mathbf{b}$ are deterministic. The index j represents the combination of (k, l), through the relation: $j = (k - 1)L + l$.

Proof of Proposition 2

Equation (114) can be rewritten as

$$\mathbf{z} = \begin{bmatrix} \mathbf{A_x} & \mathbf{A_y} \end{bmatrix} \begin{bmatrix} \mathbf{x} \\ \mathbf{y} \end{bmatrix} + \mathbf{b} \ . \tag{118}$$

The vectors $\mathbf{x}$ and $\mathbf{y}$ are GMM-distributed of order K and L, respectively, and thus $\mathbf{v} = \begin{bmatrix} \mathbf{x} \\ \mathbf{y} \end{bmatrix}$ is GMM-distributed of order LK. Using GMM definition in (6), the PDF of $\mathbf{v}$ can be rewritten as

$$f_{\mathbf{v}}(\mathbf{v}) = \sum_{l=1}^{L} \sum_{k=1}^{K} \alpha_{\mathbf{x}k} \alpha_{\mathbf{y}l} \Phi(\mathbf{x}, \boldsymbol{\theta}_{\mathbf{x}k}) \Phi(\mathbf{y}, \boldsymbol{\theta}_{\mathbf{y}l}) \ . \tag{119}$$

From (119) it can be easily obtained that the weight of the lkth mixture component is $\alpha_{\mathbf{v}lk} = \alpha_{\mathbf{x}k}\alpha_{\mathbf{y}l}$. Since $\mathbf{z}$ is a linear transformation of the GMM-distributed random vector $\mathbf{v}$, therefore $\mathbf{z}$ is GMM-distributed of order LK. Hence, the lkth mixture weight in the distribution of $\mathbf{z}$ is

$$\alpha_{\mathbf{z}lk} = \alpha_{\mathbf{v}lk} = \alpha_{\mathbf{x}k}\alpha_{\mathbf{y}l} \ . \tag{120}$$

Let $\tilde{\eta}_{lk}$ denote the random mixture indicator in the PDF of $\mathbf{z}$. Using (118) and (119), the mean vector of the lkth mixture component is

$$\begin{aligned} \boldsymbol{\mu}_{\mathbf{z}lk} &= E\left[\left(\begin{bmatrix} \mathbf{A_x} & \mathbf{A_y} \end{bmatrix} \begin{bmatrix} \mathbf{x} \\ \mathbf{y} \end{bmatrix} + \mathbf{b}\right) \middle| \tilde{\eta}_{lk}\right] = \begin{bmatrix} \mathbf{A_x} & \mathbf{A_y} \end{bmatrix} \begin{bmatrix} E[\mathbf{x}|\tilde{\eta}_{lk}] \\ E[\mathbf{y}|\tilde{\eta}_{lk}] \end{bmatrix} + \mathbf{b} \\ &= \mathbf{A_x}\boldsymbol{\mu}_{\mathbf{x}k} + \mathbf{A_y}\boldsymbol{\mu}_{\mathbf{y}l} + \mathbf{b} \ . \end{aligned} \tag{121}$$

Similarly, the covariance matrix of the lkth mixture component is

$$\begin{aligned} \boldsymbol{\Gamma}_{\mathbf{z}lk} &= \mathrm{cov}\left(\left(\begin{bmatrix} \mathbf{A_x} & \mathbf{A_y} \end{bmatrix} \begin{bmatrix} \mathbf{x} \\ \mathbf{y} \end{bmatrix} + \mathbf{b}\right) |\tilde{\eta}_{lk}\right) = \mathrm{cov}\left(\mathbf{A_x}\mathbf{x} + \mathbf{A_y}\mathbf{y}|\tilde{\eta}_{lk}\right) \\ &= \mathbf{A_x}\boldsymbol{\Gamma}_{\mathbf{x}k}\mathbf{A_x}^H + \mathbf{A_y}\boldsymbol{\Gamma}_{\mathbf{y}k}\mathbf{A_y}^H \ , \end{aligned} \tag{122}$$

where the cross-covariance of $\mathbf{x}$ and $\mathbf{y}$ vanishes, because $\mathbf{x}$ and $\mathbf{y}$, conditioned on the Gaussian indicator, $\tilde{\eta}_{lk}$, are statistically independent.

6. References

[1] S. Arulampalam, S. Maskell, N. Gordon, and T. Clapp, "A tutorial on particle filters for on-line nonlinear/non-Gaussian Bayesian tracking," *IEEE Trans. Signal Processing*, vol. 50, pp. 174-188, 2002.

[2] N. Ikoma, N. Ichimura, T. Higuchi, and H. Maeda, "Particle filter based method for maneuvering target tracking," *IEEE International Workshop on Intelligent Signal Processing,* Hungary, pp. 3-8, 2001.
[3] G. Hewer, R. Martin, and J. Zeh, "Robust preprocessing for Kalman filtering of glint noise," *IEEE Trans. AES,* vol. 23, pp. 120-128, 1987.
[4] D. Howard, "Radar target glint in tracking and guidance system based on echo signal phase distortion," *Proc. on National Electronics Conference,* pp. 840-849, 1959.
[5] B. Borden and M. Mumford, "A statistical glint/radar cross section target model," *IEEE Trans. AES,* vol. 19, no. 1, pp. 781-785, 1983.
[6] W. Wu and P. Cheng, "Nonlinear IMM algorithm for maneuvering target tracking," *IEEE Trans. AES,* vol. 30, pp. 875-884, 1994.
[7] X. Li and V. Jilkov, "Survey of maneuvering target tracking. Part V: Multiple-model methods," *IEEE Trans. AES,* vol. 41, no. 4, pp. 1255-1320, 2005.
[8] B. Anderson and J. Moore, *Optimal filtering.* Prentice-Hall 1979.
[9] A. Jazwinski, "Stochastic processes and filtering theory," *Academic Press,* NY, 1970.
[10] S. Julier and J. Uhlmann, "A new extension of the Kalman filter to nonlinear systems," *Proc. The 11th Int. Symp. on Aerospace/Defence Sensing, Simulation and Controls.,* 1997.
[11] S. Haykin, *Kalman Filtering and Neural Networks.* pp. 221-280, Wiley Publishing, 2001.
[12] M. Vemula, M. Bugallo, and P. Djuric, "Performance comparison of Gaussian-based filters using information measures," *IEEE Signal Processing Letters,* vol. 14, no. 12, pp. 1-4, 2007.
[13] A. Farina, B. Ristic, and D. Benvenuti, "Tracking a ballistic target: comparison of several nonlinear filters," *IEEE Trans. AES,* vol. 38, no. 3, pp. 854-867, 2002.
[14] C. Masreliez, "Approximate non-Gaussian filtering with linear state and observation relations," *IEEE Trans. Automatic Control,* AC-20, pp. 107-110, 1975.
[15] C. Masreliez and R. Martin, "Robust Bayesian estimation for the linear model and robustifying the Kalman filter," *IEEE Trans. Automatic Control,* AC-22, pp. 361-371, 1975.
[16] W. Wu, "Target tracking with glint noise," *IEEE Trans. AES,* vol. 29, pp. 174-185, 1993.
[17] D. Magill, "Optimal adaptive estimation of sampled stochastic processes," *IEEE Trans. Automat. Control,* vol. 10, no. 1, pp. 434-439, 1965.
[18] Y. Bar-Shalom and X. Li, Estimation with Applications to Tracking and Navigation. Artech House, NY, 2001.
[19] D. Alspach and H. Sorenson, "nonlinear Bayesian estimation using Gaussian sum approximation," *IEEE Trans. Automat. Control,* vol. AC-17, pp. 439-448, 1972.
[20] E. Daeipour and Y. Bar-Shalom, "An interacting multiple model approach for target tracking with glint noise," *IEEE Trans. AES,* vol. 31, no. 2, pp. 706-715, 1995.
[21] F. Gustafsson, *Adaptive filtering and change detection.* John Wiley & Sons, NY, 2000.
[22] D. Salmond, "Mixture reduction algorithms for target tracking in clutter," *SPIE Signal and Data Processing of Small Targets, 1305,* pp. 434-445, 1990.
[23] L. Pao, "Multisensor multitarget mixture reduction algorithms for tracking," *Jour. Guidamce, Control, and Dynamics,* vol. 17, no. 6, pp. 1205-1211, 1994.
[24] Y. Bar-Shalom and L. Xiao-Rong, *Multitarget Multisensor Tracking: Principles and Techniques.* Storrs. CT: YBS Publishing, 1995.
[25] S. Blackman and R. Popoli, *Design and Analysis of Modern tracking Systems.* Norwood. MA: Artech House, 1999.

[26] S. Blackman, *Multiple-Target Tracking with Radar Applications.* Norwood, MA: Artech House, 1986.

[27] J. Williams and P. Maybeck, "Cost-function-based hypothesis control techniques for multiple hypothesis tracking," *Mathematical and Computer Modelling,* vol. 43, Iss. 9-10, pp. 976-989, 2006.

[28] P. Maybeck and B. Smith, "Multiple model tracker based on Gaussian mixture reduction for maneuvering targets in clutter," *Proc. 7th Int. Conference on Information Fusion,* pp. 40-47, 2005.

[29] H. Blom and Y. Bar-Shalom, "The interacting multiple model algorithm with markovian switching coefficients," *IEEE Trans. Automat. Control,* vol. 33, no. 8, pp. 780-783, 1988.

[30] E. Mazor, A. Averbuch, Y. Bar-Shalom, and J. Dayan, "Interacting multiple model methods in target tracking: a survey," *IEEE Trans. AES,* vol. 34, no. 1, pp. 103-123, 1998.

[31] E. Daeipour and Y. Bar-Shalom, "IMM tracking of maneuvering targets in the presence of glint," *IEEE Trans. AES,* vol. 34, no. 3, pp. 996-1002, 1998.

[32] A. Doucet, N. de Freitas, and N. Gordon, *An introduction to sequential Monte Carlo methods.* New York: Springer-Verlag 2001.

[33] R. Chen and N. Liu, "Mixture Kalman filter," *Journal of Royal Statistical Society,* vol. 62, part 3, pp. 493-508, 2000.

[34] P. Djurić, N. Kotecha, N. Zhang, Y. Huang, T. Chirmai, M. Bugallo, and N. Miguez, "Particle filtering," *IEEE Signal Processing Magazine,* pp. 19-38, 2003.

[35] N. Kotecha and P. Djurić, "Gaussian sum particle filtering,"*IEEE Trans. Signal Processing,* vol. 51, no. 10, pp. 2602-2612, 2003.

[36] H. Hu, Z. Jing, A. Li, S. Hu, and H. Tian, "An MCMC-based particle filter for tracking target in glint noise environment," *Journal of Systems Engineering and Electronics,* vol. 16, no. 2, pp. 305-309, 2005.

[37] T. Ho and B. Chen, "Novel extended Viterbi-based multiple model algorithms for state estimation of discrete-time systems with Markov jump parameters," *IEEE Trans. Signal Proc.,* vol. 54, no. 2, pp. 393-404, 2006.

[38] N. Bergman, A. Doucet and N. Gordon, "Optimal estimation and Cram_er-Rao bounds for partial non-Gaussian state space models," *Ann. Inst. Statist. Math.,* vol. 53, no. 1, pp. 97-112, 2001.

[39] I.Bilik and J. Tabrikian, "MMSE-based tracking filter with non-Gaussian process and measurement noises," *IEEE Trans. on Aerospace and Electronic Systems, in press.*

[40] I. Bilik and J. Tabrikian, "Optimal recursive filtering using Gaussian mixture model," *Proc. IEEE Workshop on Statistical Signal Processing,* pp. 399-403, 2005.

[41] N. Li and A. Barron, "Mixture density estimation," In Advances in Neural Information Processing Systems 12. The MIT Press, 2002.

[42] G. Ackerson and K. Fu, "On State Estimation in Switching Environments," *IEEE Trans. AC,* vol.15, no. 1, pp. 10-17, 1970.

[43] J. Tugnait and A. Haddad, "Adaptive estimation in linear systems with unknown markovian noise statistics," *IEEE Trans. on Information Theory,* vol. 26, no. 1, pp. 66-78, 1980.

[44] I. Bilik and J. Tabrikian, "Maneuvering target tracking using the nonlinear non-Gaussian Kalman filter," *Proc. of ICASSP,* vol. III, pp. 724 - 727 May 2006.

[45] I. Bilik and J. Tabrikian, "Target tracking with nonlinear Gaussian mixture Kalman filter," *Trans. on Aerospace and Electronic Systems, in press.*

[46] I. Bilik and J. Tabrikian, "Target tracking in glint noise environment using nonlinear non-Gaussian Kalman filter," *Proc. IEEE International Radar Conference,* pp 24-27, April 2006.

[47] K. Todros and J. Tabrikian, "Application of Gaussian mixture model for blind separation of mixture models," *Proc. of ICA 2004, Granada,* pp. 392-395, 2004.

[48] K. Todros and J. Tabrikian, "Blind Separation of Independent Sources Using Gaussian Mixture Model," *IEEE Trans. Sig. Proc.,* vol. 55, no. 7, pp. 3645-3658, 2007.

[49] S. Kay, *Fundamentals of Statistical Signal Processing.* vol. I, Prentice Hall, Upper Saddle River, NJ, 1998.

[50] D. A. Reynolds, *A Gaussian mixture modeling approach to text-independent speaker identification,* Ph.D. Dissertation, Georgia Institute of Technology, 1992.

[51] J. Verbeek, N. Vlassis, and B. Kröse, "Efficient greedy learning of Gaussian mixture models," *Neural Computations,* MIT Press, 2002.

[52] P. Stoica and Y. Selen, "Model-order selection: a review of information criterion rules," *IEEE Signal Processing Mag.,* 36-47, 2004.

[53] F. Xiaobin, H. Peikang, and F. Zhengfang, "Analysis spectral-power-density of glint of radar-extended target," *Proc. on CIE Radar Conf.,* pp. 1128-1331, 2001.

[54] S. Xiaoli, L. Yongcai, W. Xinmin, and W. Changqing, "Angular glint of aircraft formation and its applications," *Proc. ICMA 2007,* pp. 1334-1339, 2007.

[55] E. Wan and R. van der Merwe, "The unscented Kalman filter for nonlinear estimation," *Proc. Adaptive Systems for Signal Processing, Communications, and Control Symposium,* pp. 153-158, 2000.

[56] J. Lindsay, "Angular glint and the moving, rotating, complex radar target," *IEEE Trans. AES,* vol. 4, no. 2, pp. 164-173, 1968.

[57] G. Sandhu and A. Sauylor, "A real-time statistical radar target model," *IEEE Trans. AES,* vol. 21, no. 4, pp. 490-507, 1985.

[58] X. Yuan, C. Han, Z. Duan, and M. Lei, "Comparison and choice of models in tracking target with coordinated turn," *Proc. FUSION07,* pp. 1497-1502, 2005.

[59] X. Li and Y. Bar-Shalom, "Design of interacting multiple model algorithm for tracking in air traffic control systems," *Proc. 32 Conf. on Design and Control,* pp. 906-911, 1993.

[60] M. Morelande and N. Gordon, "Target tracking through a coordinated turn," *Proc. ICASSP 2005,* vol. IV, pp. 21-24, 2005.

[61] X. Rong and V. Jilkov, "Survey of maneuvering target tracking-Part I: Dynamic models," *IEEE Trans. Aerospace and Electronic Systems,* vol. 39, no. 4, 2003.

[62] D. Middleton, "Statistical-physical model of electromagnetic interference," *IEEE Trans. Eletromagn. Compat.* vol. EMC-19, no. 3, pp. 106-126, 1977.

[63] R. Duda, P. Hart, and D. Stork, *Pattern Classification.* A Wiley-Intersience Publication, 2001.

[64] X. Li and V. Jilkov, "Survey of maneuvering target tracking. Part I: Dynamic models," *IEEE Trans. AES,* vol. 39, no. 4, 2003.

[65] R. Singer, "Estimating optimal tracking filter performance for manned maneuvering target," *IEEE Trans. AES,* vol. 6, pp. 473-483, 1970.

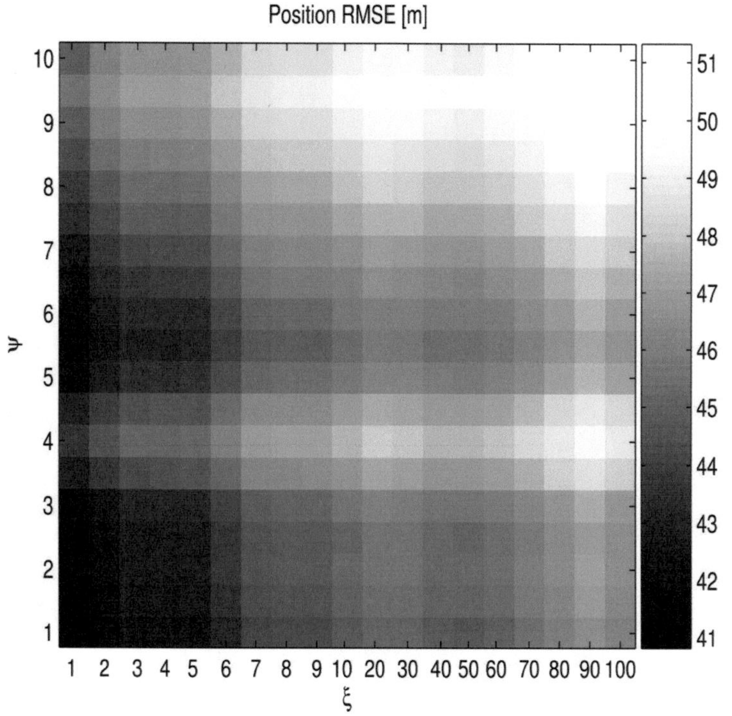

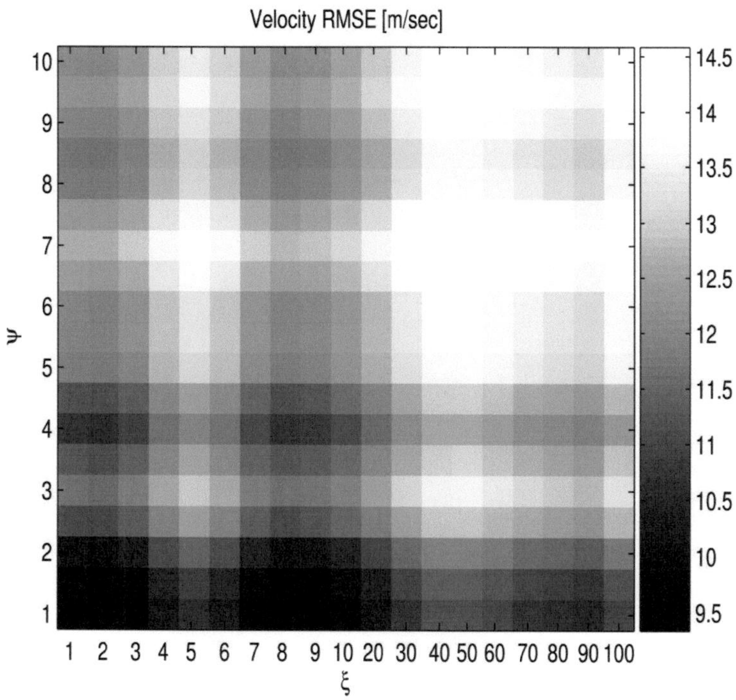

Fig. 16. Tracking performance of NL-GMKF in the presence of maneuvering target with glint noise during the second interval at time instance $n = 75$ and $\alpha_w = 0.3$.

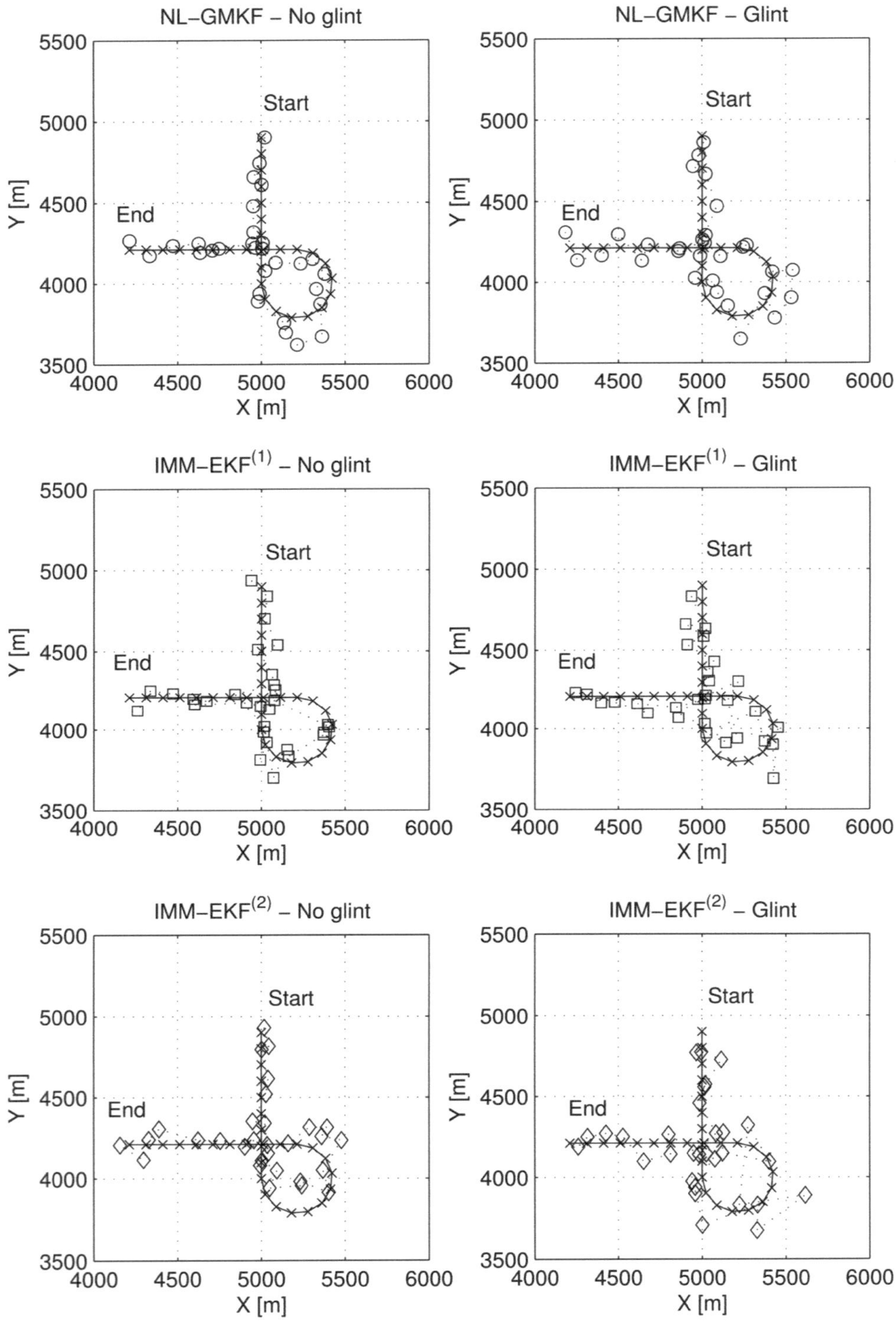

Fig. 17. Tracking performance of NL-GMKF compared to IMM-EKF(1) and IMM-EKF(2) in a CV-CT-CV scenario, with and without glint during the CT period.

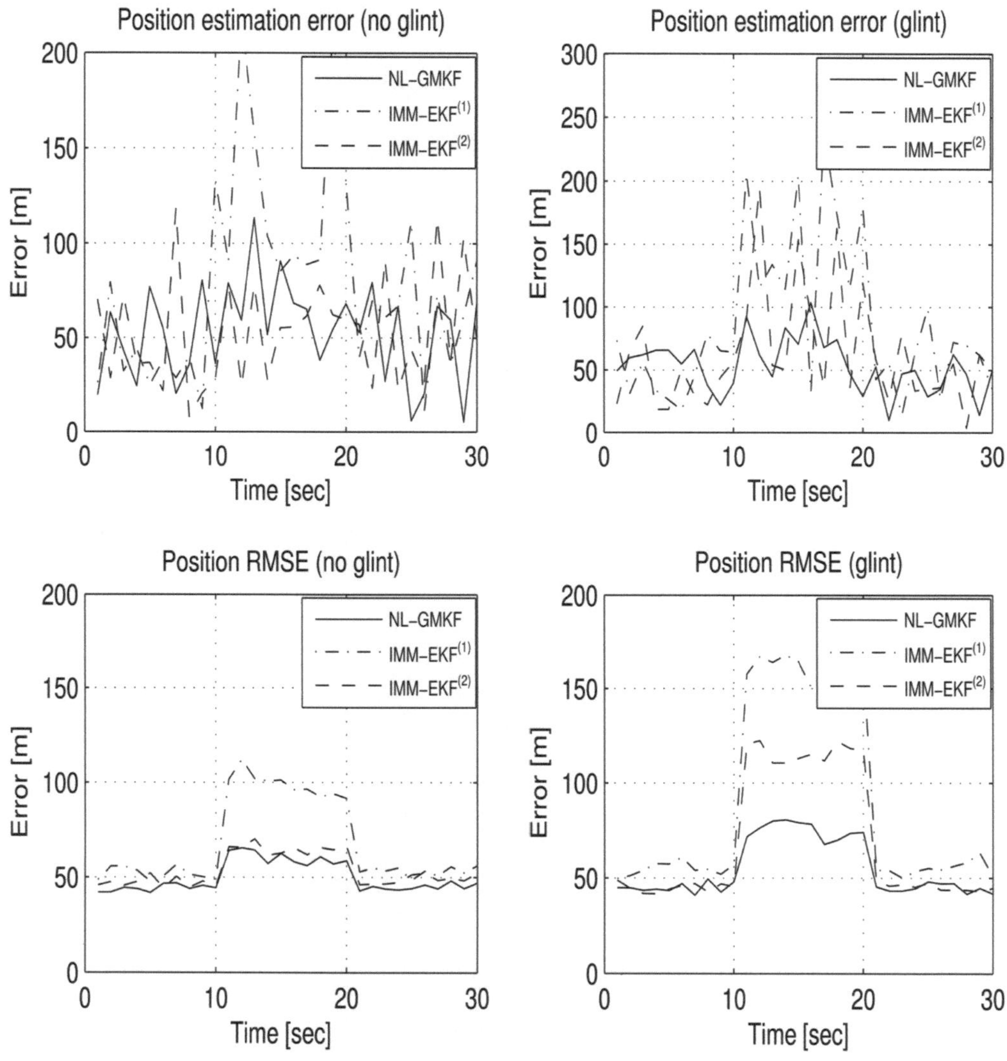

Fig. 18. Tracking performance of NL-GMKF, IMM-EKF(1) and IMM-EKF(2) in a CV-CT-CV scenario, without and with glint noise with probability $\alpha_w = 0.3$ and glint noise level $\psi = 5$ during the CT period.

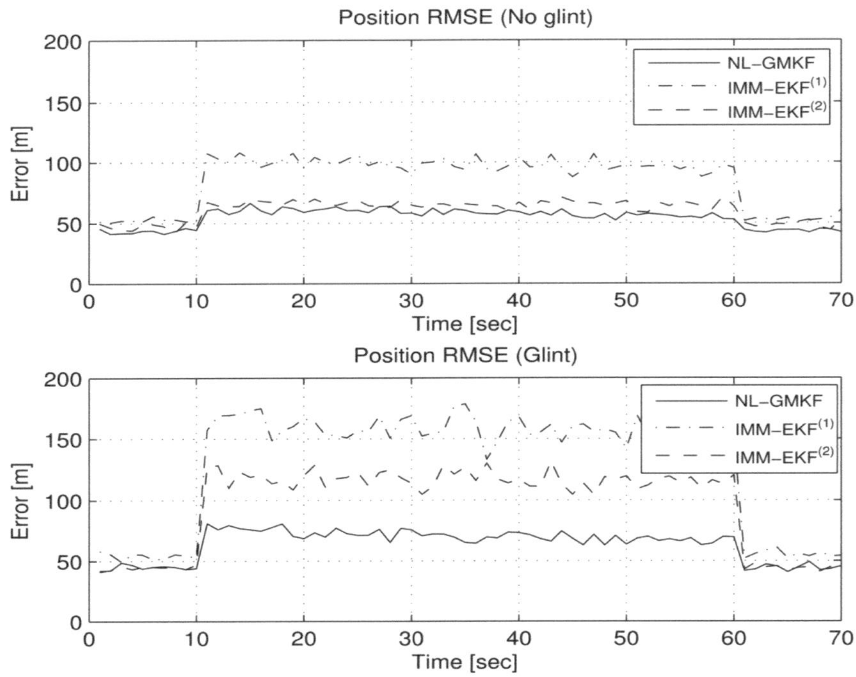

Fig. 19. Tracking performance of NL-GMKF, IMM-EKF(1) and IMM-EKF(2) in a CV-CT-CV high maneuver intensity scenario, without and with glint noise with probability $\alpha_w = 0.3$ and glint noise level $\psi = 5$ during the CT period.

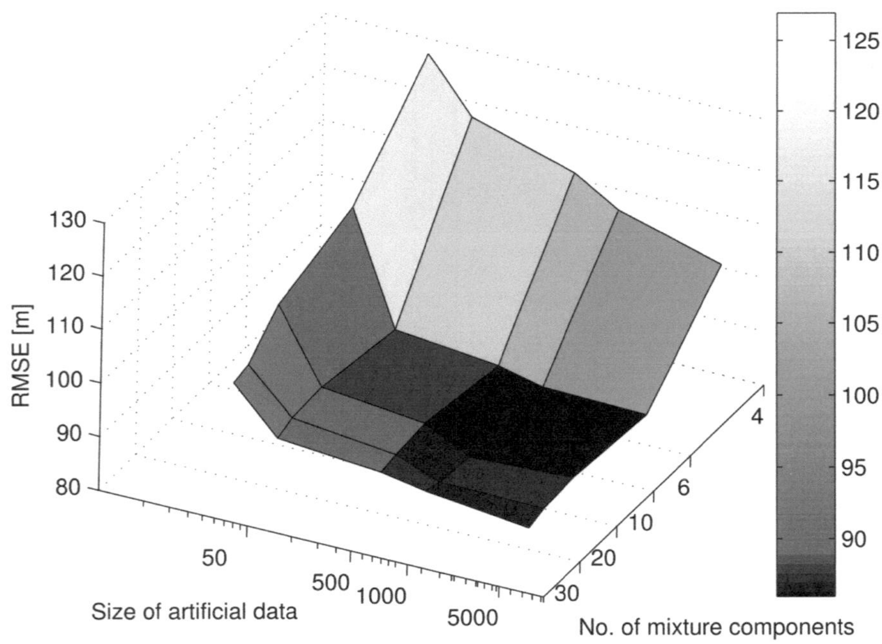

Fig. 20. NL-GMKF sensitivity testing.

3

Kalman Filter in Control and Modeling

Mouna Ghanai[1] and Kheireddine Chafaa[2]
[1]*University of Batna, Electronics Department, 05000, Batna*
[2]*University of M'sila, Electronics Department, 28000, M'sila, Algeria*

1. Introduction

Originaly, a filter is a physical device for removing unwanted components of mixtures (gas, liquid, solid). In the area of telecommunications, signals are mixtures of different frequencies, and the term of filter is used to describe the attenuation of the unwanted frequencies. Since 1940, the concept of a filter was extended to the separation of signals from noise. With Kalman filter, the meaning of filter is well beyond the notion of separation. It also includes the solution of an inversion problem, in which one knows how to represent the measurable variables as functions of variables of principle interest.
Least squares method proposed by Carl Friedrich Gauss in 1795 was the first method for forming an optimal estimate from noisy data, and it provides an important connection between the experimental and theoretical sciences.
Before Kalman, Norbert Wiener proposed his famous filter called Wiener filter which was restricted only to stationary scalar signals and noises, the solution obtained by this filter is not recursive and needs the storing of the entire pas observed data.
Kalman filter is a generalization of Wiener filter. The significance of this filter is in its ability to accommodate vector signals and noises which may be non stationary. The solution is recursive in that each update estimate of the state is computed from the previous estimate and the new input data, so, contrary to Wiener filter, only the previous estimate requires storage, so Kalman filter eliminate the need for storing the entire pas observed data.
In this chapter, we present two important applications of Kalman filter. In the first one we show how this filter can be used as an adaptive controller system (Chafaa et al., 2006). Studies proposed in this part illustrate a structure for the control of a positional system towards a mobile target in a three dimensional space (see Fig.1). In the presence of a random disturbances (white noise) or when few system parameters change, the use of an adaptive and optimal controller turns out necessary (Mudi & Nikhil, 1999; Zdzislaw, 2005). In this case we are choosing to use Kalman filter as a controller. This technique is based on the theory of Kalman's filtering (Kalman, 1960; Eubank, 2006), it transforms Kalman's filter into a Kalman controller.
In the second application we give the use of such filter in estimating the membership functions of fuzzy sets in order to obtain a fuzzy model (Chafaa et al., 2007). Fuzzy modelling is an effective tool for the approximation of nonlinear systems. Takagi-Sugeno (TS) model is widely used fuzzy modeling technique (Takagi & Sugeno, 1986; Angelov & Filev, 2004). The TS model utilizes the idea of linearization in a fuzzily defined region of the state space. Due to the fuzzy regions, the nonlinear system is decomposed into a multi-

model structure consisting of linear models that are not necessarily independent (Johansen & Babuska, 2003). A TS fuzzy model is usually constructed in two steps: Step 1: Determine the membership functions of the antecedents; Step 2: Estimate the parameters of the consequent functions.
One of the most techniques used to release the first step is the fuzzy clustering in the Cartesian product-space of the inputs and outputs (Babuska & Verbruggen, 1995; Babuska & Verbruggen, 1997; Bezdek & Dunn, 1975). As the consequent functions are usually chosen to be linear in their parameters, the second step is done by standard linear least-squares methods (Babuska & Verbruggen, 1997; Babuska et al., 1998).
Many clustering algorithms can be found in the literature, they are based on the optimization of fuzzy C-means functional (Nascimento et al., 2003). Some of them utilize an Euclidian distance norm (Bezdek et al., 1987; Hathaway & Bezdek, 1991) in which the detected clusters have an hyperspherical shapes, i.e., clusters whose surfaces of constant membership are hyperspheres. Others extend the Euclidian distance norm to an adaptive distance norm (Bezdek & Dunn, 1975; Gustafson & Kessel, 1997; Gath & Geva, 1998) in order to detect clusters of different geometrical shapes in one data set.

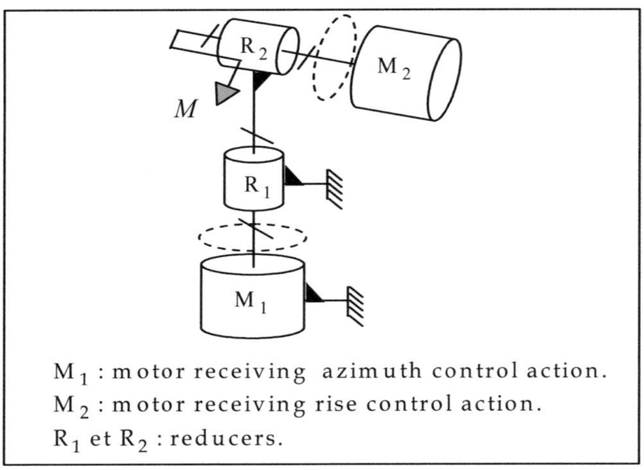

Fig. 1. Positioning system

Fuzzy clustering in the Cartesian product-space of the inputs and the outputs has been extensively used to obtain the antecedent membership functions (Babuska & Verbruggen, 1997; Babuska, 1998; Sugeno & Yasukawa, 1993). Attractive features of this approach are the simultaneous identification of the antecedent membership functions along with the consequent local linear models and the implicit regularization (Johansen& Babuska, 2003).
By clustering in the product-space, multidimensional fuzzy sets are initially obtained, which are either used in the model directly or after projection onto the individual antecedent variables (regressors). As it is generally difficult to interpret multidimensional fuzzy sets, projected one-dimensional fuzzy sets are usually preferred.
Babuska and Verbruggen (Babuska & Verbruggen, 1997) proposed a fuzzy modeling scheme based on Gustafson-Kessel clustering algorithm (GKCA) to estimate the premise membership functions and on least-squares method to estimate the parameters of the consequence functions. Abony et al (Abonyi et al., 2002) proposed to use the Gath-Geva

(GG) clustering algorithm instead of GKCA method, because with GG method, the parameters of the univariate membership functions can directly be derived from the parameters of the clusters.
In this part, a fuzzy modeling algorithm combining GKCA and Kalman filter (KF) is proposed (Chafaa et al., 2007). We use GKCA in order to detect clusters of different geometrical shapes in the data set and to obtain the point-wise membership functions of the premise. After that a Kalman filter is introduced to estimate the parameters of the premise membership functions and those of the consequence functions. In the premise part, the membership functions are triangular functions, then Kalman filter will estimate the parameters of a straight line functions by using the data corresponding to the premise membership functions defined point-wise, but in the consequence part, Kalman filter will be used as a linear regression to estimate the parameters of the TS fuzzy model using the input-output data set.

2. Kalman controller for target tracking system

2.1 Target tracking system

A target tracking system is a system for which inputs are the azimuth and rise, and outputs are the control actions for locating the motors. The target moves through azimuth-rise space. Two dc-motors adjust the platform position constantly towards the target (Chafaa et al., 2006; Brookner, 1998). The platform can be any directional system which can turn up exactly towards the target; such system can be a Laser, a video camera or an antenna. We suppose that we have a potentiometric system which can discover the direction of the platform towards the target (Ogata, 1970). The Radar sends azimuth and rise coordinates to the target tracking system in the end of every time interval, we calculate the current error and its variation in the platform position. Then, a Kalman controller determines the control actions for dc-motors, one action for azimuth motor and the other one for rise motor. These actions are going to reposition the platform as shown in Fig. 2. We can control independently the azimuth and rise positions by applying the same algorithm twice, it facilitates us calculations.

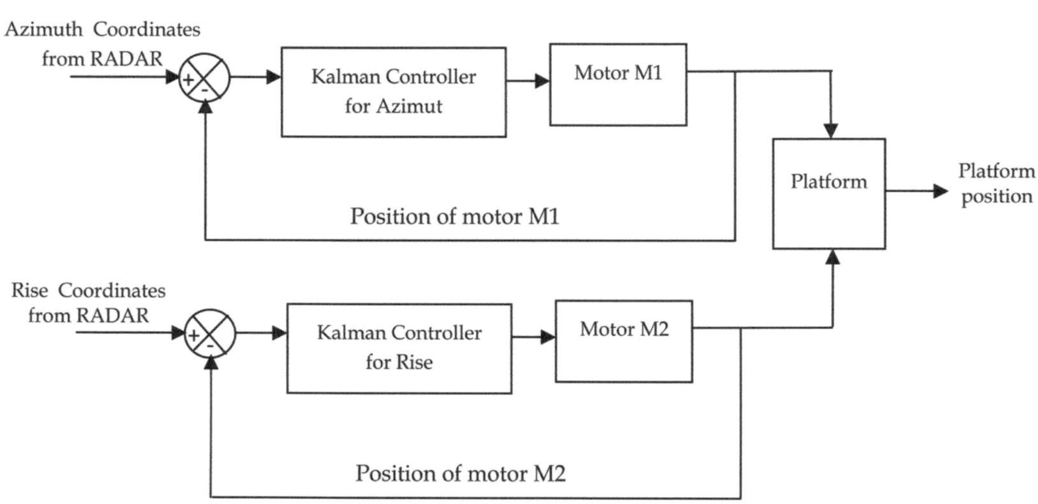

Fig. 2. Control system

2.2 Kalman controller

The Kalman filter is used for estimating or predicting the next stage of a system based on a moving average of measurements driven by white noise, which is completely unpredictable. It needs a model of the relationship between inputs and outputs to provide feedback signals but it can follow changes in noise statistics quite well. The Kalman filter is an optimum estimator that estimates the state of a linear system developing dynamically through time. An optimum estimator can be defined as an algorithm that processes all the available data to yield an estimate of the "state" of a system whilst at the same time estimating some predefined optimality criterion.

In this section we will conceive another type of controllers called "Kalman Controller" or "Kalman Filter controller". This technique consists to achieve a one-dimensional Kalman Filter acting as an alternative controller, i.e., it can provides the control actions to the dc-motor in addition to its filtering function (Kosko, 1992).

In the discrete state space formulation, the state and measurement equations for the controllers are given by:

$$\begin{aligned} x_{k+1} &= Gx_k + Hc_k + w_k \\ z_k &= Cx_k + v_k \end{aligned} \tag{1}$$

Our proposed control structure contains two Kalman controllers, one for azimuth (Azimuth controller) and another for rise (rise controller). Since the two controllers act independently, so we can assume them to have one-dimensional models such that :

$$G = H = C = 1 \tag{2}$$

Since the state is a control action, so we can take the input c_k to be :

$$c_k = e_k + \dot{e}_k \tag{3}$$

Let x_{k+1} denotes the control action necessary at the moment k to exactly lock onto the target at the moment k+1. Then, the controller output at the moment k will be considered equal the prediction $u_k = \hat{x}_{k+1/k}$

Let us note that:

$$\begin{aligned} e_k &= x_k - \hat{x}_{k/k-1} \\ \dot{e}_k &= e_k - e_{k-1} \end{aligned} \tag{4}$$

By substitution of 2 and 3 in 1 we obtain the new state equation:

$$x_{k+1} = x_k + e_k + \dot{e}_k + w_k \tag{5}$$

where w_k represents a white noise that models target acceleration or other unmodeled effects. The new equation of measurements is

$$\begin{aligned} z_k &= x_k + v_k \\ &= \hat{x}_{k/k-1} + e_k + v_k \\ &= \hat{x}_{k/k-1} + v'_k \end{aligned} \tag{6}$$

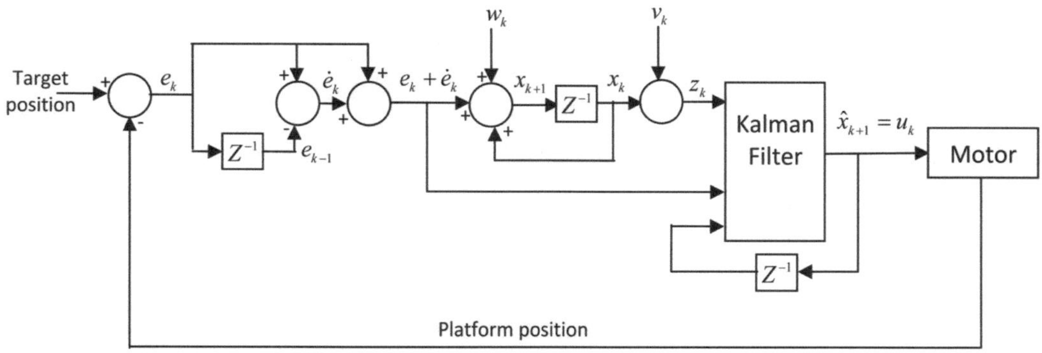

Fig. 3. Control system

Since we assume that e_k and v_k are uncorrelated, the variance of v'_k is:

$$\begin{aligned} R'_k &= E\left[v_k'^2\right] \\ &= E\left[\left(e_k + v_k\right)^2\right] \\ &= E\left[e_k^2\right] + E\left[v_k^2\right] \\ &= P_{k/k-1} + R_k \end{aligned} \tag{7}$$

The recursive equations of Kalman Filter take the following general form:

$$\begin{aligned} \hat{x}_{k+1/k} &= G\hat{x}_{k/k} + HU_k \\ P_{k/k-1} &= GP_{k-1/k-1}G^T + Q_{k-1} \\ K_k &= P_{k/k-1}C^T\left[CP_{k/k-1}C^T + R_k\right]^{-1} \\ \hat{x}_{k/k} &= \hat{x}_{k/k-1} + K_k\left[z_k - C\hat{x}_{k/k-1}\right] \\ P_{k/k} &= P_{k/k-1} - K_kCP_{k/k-1} \end{aligned} \tag{8}$$

To obtain the one-dimensional Kalman controller, we substitute 2, 3, 6 and 7 in 8, and then we obtain it under the following form:

$$\begin{aligned} u_k &= \hat{x}_{k/k} + e_k + \dot{e}_k \\ P_{k/k-1} &= P_{k-1/k-1} + Q_{k-1} \\ K_k &= \frac{P_{k/k-1}}{R'_k} \\ \hat{x}_{k/k} &= u_{k-1} + K_k v'_k \\ P_{k/k} &= \left[1 - K_k\right]P_{k/k-1} \end{aligned} \tag{9}$$

Figure 3 illustrates the detailed structure of Kalman controller. The simulation results of this controller are presented in figures 4 and 5, where we see in figure 4 that the load disturbance is rejected and in figure 5 the tracking is carried out.

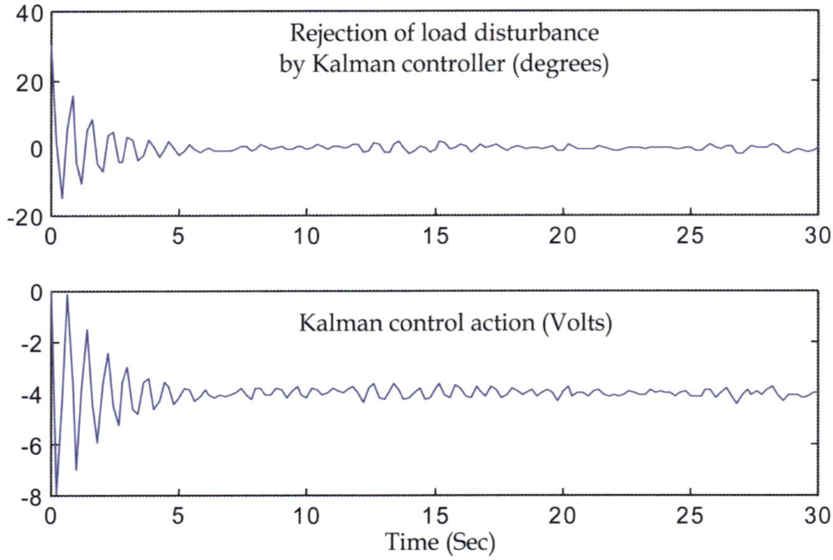

Fig. 4. System response and Kalman control action to a strong load disturbance

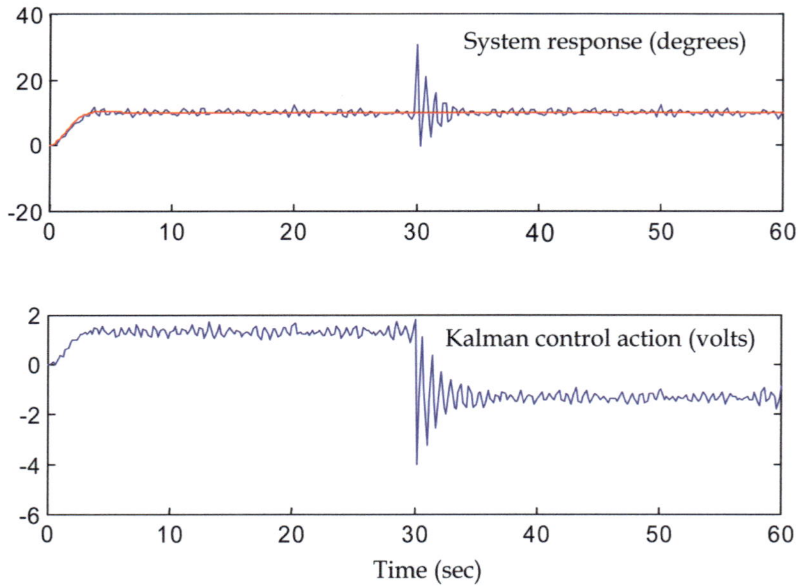

Fig. 5. System response and Kalman control action to a step input and a strong load disturbance

3. Fuzzy modeling and identification

3.1 Takagi-Sugeno fuzzy models

The TS fuzzy model can represent or model any unknown nonlinear system $y = f(\boldsymbol{x})$, based on some available input-output data $\boldsymbol{x}_k = \left[x_{1k}, x_{2k}, \ldots, x_{nk}\right]^T$ and y_k. The index k denotes the individual data samples and n the number of regressors.

In the TS fuzzy model, the rule consequents are crisp functions of the model inputs:

$$R_i : IF\ \boldsymbol{x}\ is\ \boldsymbol{A}_i(\boldsymbol{x})\ THEN\ y_i = \boldsymbol{a}_i^T \boldsymbol{x} + b_i \qquad i = 1,2,...c \tag{10}$$

Where x is $n \times 1$ input variable, $y_i \in R$ is the output variable. $n \times 1$ vector $\boldsymbol{a}_i$ and $b_i \in R$ are the TS parameters. R_i denotes the ith rule and c is the number of rules in the rule base. $\boldsymbol{A}_i$ is the premise multivariable membership function of the ith rule. $\boldsymbol{\theta}_i = \left[\boldsymbol{a}_i \ \ b_i\right]^T$ is the parameter vector of the ith rule.
The premise proposition " $\boldsymbol{x}\ is\ \boldsymbol{A}_i(\boldsymbol{x})$ " can be expressed as a logical combination of propositions with univariate fuzzy sets defined for the individual components of $\boldsymbol{x}$, usually in the following conjunctive form (Kukolj & Levi, 2004) :

$$R_i : IF\ x_1\ is\ A_{i1}(x_1)\ AND......AND\ x_n\ is\ A_{in}(x_n)\ THEN\ y_i = \boldsymbol{a}_i^T \boldsymbol{x} + b_i \qquad i = 1,2,...c \tag{11}$$

the degree of fulfilment of the rule is calculated as the product of the individual membership degrees :

$$\beta_i(\boldsymbol{x}) = \prod_{j=1}^{n} \mu_{A_{ij}}(\boldsymbol{x}) \tag{12}$$

where $\mu_{A_{ij}}(\boldsymbol{x})$ is the membership function of the fuzzy set A_{ij} .
The inference is reduced to the fuzzy-mean defuzzification formula (Takagi & Sugeno, 1986 ; Kukolj & Levi, 2004) :

$$y = \frac{\sum_{i=1}^{c} \beta_i(\boldsymbol{x})\left(\boldsymbol{a}_i^T \boldsymbol{x} + b_i\right)}{\sum_{i=1}^{c} \beta_i(\boldsymbol{x})} \tag{13}$$

From (11) and (13), it is noted that TS fuzzy model approximates a nonlinear system with a combination of several linear systems by decomposing fuzzily the whole input space into several partial spaces and representing each input-output space with each linear equation.

3.2 New fuzzy modeling algorithm

The structure of the proposed algorithm is presented in Fig. 6. The identification algorithm proceeds in three steps:

1. from the input-output sequences $\left\{(x_k, y_k\right\}_{k=1}^{N}$, partition the data into a set of local linear submodels by using GKCA in the product space $\boldsymbol{X} \times \boldsymbol{Y}$
2. Obtain the membership functions for the premise variables by using cluster projections and Kalman filtering.
3. Estimate the consequent parameters by Kalman filter algorithm.

The three procedures are repeated to find the appropriate number of clusters c as shown in Fig. 6 in which the performance index used is the mean squared error (MSE), so when $\text{MSE} \le \varepsilon$ the loop is stopped and the optimal c is obtained.

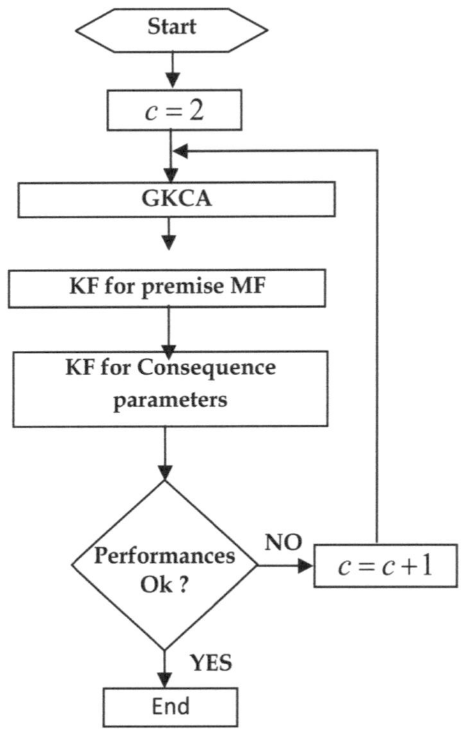

Fig. 6. Structure of the proposed fuzzy modeling

A. Fuzzy clustering

Clustering of numerical data forms the basis of many classification and system modeling algorithms (Bezdek & Dunn, 1975; Babuska et al., 1998). The purpose of clustering is to distil natural grouping of data from a large data set, producing a concise representation of a system's behavior. In particular, The GKCA has been widely studied and applied by many researchers (Bezdek et al., 1987; Hathaway & Bezdek, 1991). The GKCA is an iterative optimization algorithm that minimizes the cost function:

$$J = \sum_{i=1}^{c}\sum_{k=1}^{N} \mu_{ik}^{m} (\boldsymbol{z}_k - \boldsymbol{v}_i)^T \boldsymbol{M}_i (\boldsymbol{z}_k - \boldsymbol{v}_i) \tag{14}$$

where N is the number of data points, c is the number of clusters, $\boldsymbol{z}_k$ is the k 'th data point, $\boldsymbol{v}_i$ is the i 'th cluster center, μ_{ik} is the degree of membership of the k 'th data in the i 'th cluster, M_i is the norm-inducing matrix of the i 'th cluster and m is a weighting exponent which determines the fuzziness of the resulting clusters (typically $m = 2$).

In this work, the GKCA is applied in order to obtain the fuzzy partition matrix $\boldsymbol{U} = \left[\mu_{ik}\right]_{c\times N}$, with $\mu_{ik} \in \left[0 \quad 1\right]$ is a membership degree.

B. Premise membership functions

The premise membership functions can be obtained from the results of fuzzy clustering by projecting the fuzzy sets defined point-wise in the partition matrix onto the premise variables x_j, $1 \le j \le n$. The TS rules are then expressed in the conjunctive form as in (11).

In order to obtain membership functions for the premise fuzzy sets $A_{ij}, 1 \le i \le c, 1 \le j \le n$, the multidimensional fuzzy set defined point-wise in the ith row of the partition matrix is projected onto the regressors x_j. Note that the resulting membership functions are defined point-wise, for the identification data only and may be nonconvex, which is caused by the probabilistic constraint in most fuzzy clustering algorithms and by the noise in the data (Babuska et al., 1998).

In order to obtain a prediction model or a model suitable for control purposes, the premise membership functions must be expressed in a form that allows computation of the membership degrees, also for input data not contained in the data set. To achieve this step, we propose to use Kalman filter to approximate the point-wise defined membership functions by some suitable straight line functions (triangular functions) as depicted in Fig. 7.

The Kalman filtering process is a recursive minimum mean square estimation procedure (Kalman, 1960; Mohinder & Angus, 2001). Each update estimate of the parameter vector corresponding to a straight line equation is computed from the previous estimate and the new input data (here the input data are the point-wise values of the membership functions). In this sense we propose to use Kalman filter as a linear regression as follows : Consider $2cn$ sets, each set represent the linear part of the point-wise set of a certain premise membership function. The linear part is obtained by taking the α -cut of the considered membership function. So we obtain $2cn$ parameter vectors (one for each set). In each set we will have N_j data (samples), where j denotes the jth set.

Then each set can be modeled by the following measurement equation:

$$\begin{aligned} y_{k_j}^j &= a^j x_{k_j} + b^j + v_{k_j} & j = 1,2,\dots,2cn \\ &= \begin{bmatrix} x_{k_j} & 1 \end{bmatrix} \begin{bmatrix} a^j \\ b^j \end{bmatrix} + v_{k_j} & k_j = 1,2,\dots,N_j \\ &= \boldsymbol{C}_{k_j}^j \boldsymbol{\theta}_{k_j}^j + v_{k_j} \end{aligned} \tag{15}$$

where $\boldsymbol{C}_{k_j}^j$ is the observation vector at the moment k_j, $\boldsymbol{\theta}_{k_j}^j = \begin{bmatrix} a^j & b^j \end{bmatrix}^T$ is the parameter vector, v_{k_j} is the measurement noise, N_j is the number of data (samples) in the jth set and the superscript j denotes the jth straight line regression. For simplicity, we will denote k_j by k. From equation (15), $\boldsymbol{\theta}_k^j$ will be considered as a state variable, so the state equation will be

$$\boldsymbol{\theta}_k^j = \boldsymbol{A}^j \boldsymbol{\theta}_{k-1}^j + \boldsymbol{w}_{k-1}^j \qquad j = 1,2,\dots,2cn \tag{16}$$

where $\boldsymbol{A}^j$ is an 2×2 state transition matrix, and $\boldsymbol{w}_k^j$ is the state noise and $\boldsymbol{\theta}_k^j$ is the value of the state variable at the moment k.

The state noise and the measurement noise are assumed to be statistically independent (Haykin, 2001) and can be modeled as zero mean, white noise processes whose covariances are given as

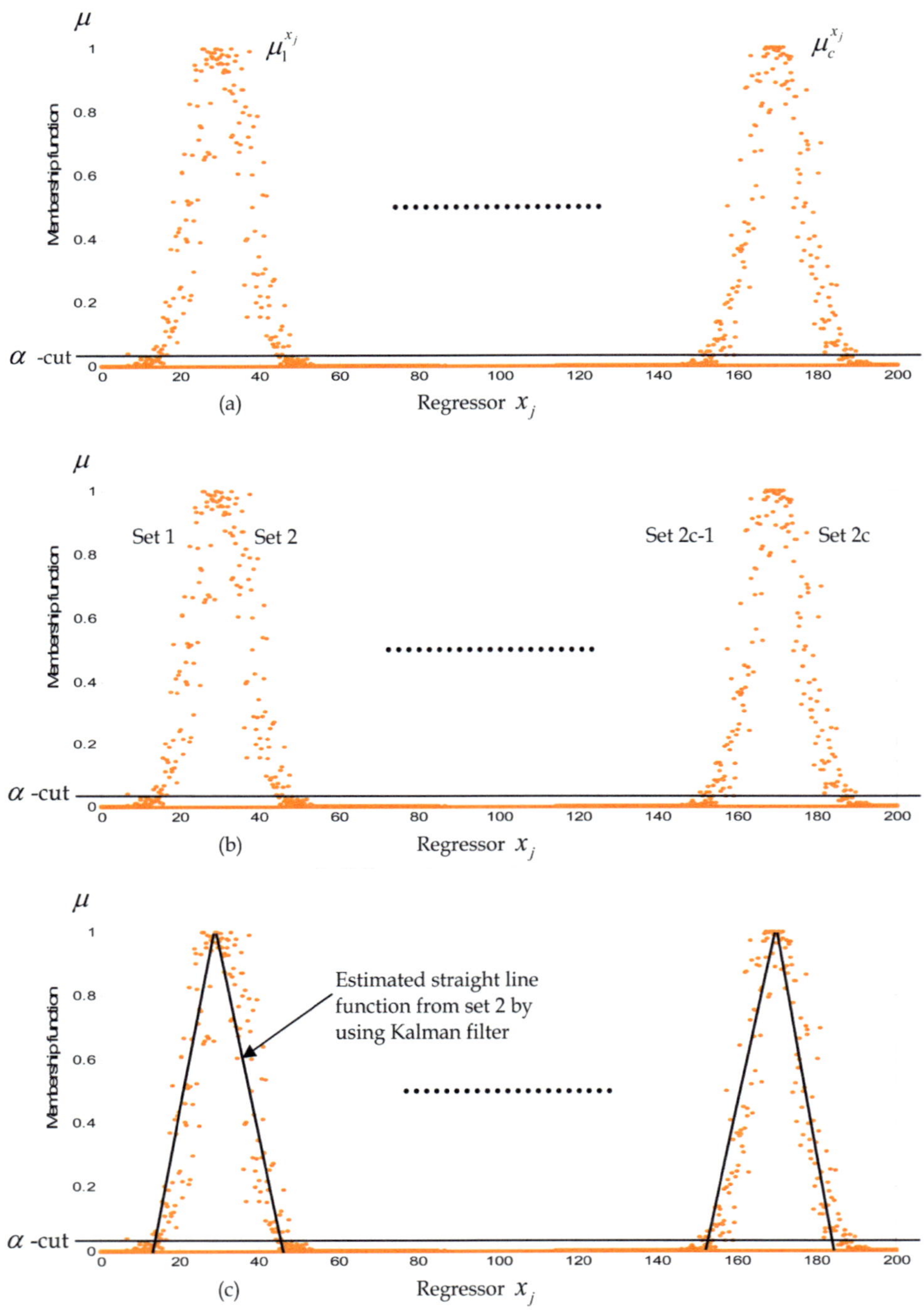

Fig. 7. Determination of premise membership functions :
(a) Premiss MF defined point-wise for the regressors x_j, j=1,2,...n
(b) Division of each membership function into 2 sets (2c sets are obtained for each x_j and 2cnsets are obtained for all regressors)
(c) Approximation of each set by a straight line function by using Kalman filter

$$E\left[\boldsymbol{w}_i^T \boldsymbol{w}_j\right] = \begin{cases} \boldsymbol{Q} & i = j \\ 0 & i \neq j \end{cases}$$
$$E\left[v_i v_j\right] = \begin{cases} r & i = j \\ 0 & i \neq j \end{cases} \quad (17)$$
$$E\left[\boldsymbol{w}_i v_j\right] = 0 \quad \forall i, j$$

By recurrence proceeding, the update state equation and the predicted measure will be given by the following equations:

$$\hat{\boldsymbol{\theta}}_{k/k-1}^j = \boldsymbol{A}\hat{\boldsymbol{\theta}}_{k-1/k-1}^j \quad (18)$$

$$\hat{y}_k^j = \boldsymbol{C}_k^j \hat{\boldsymbol{\theta}}_{k/k-1}^j \quad (19)$$

Now that the model representation of the parameter vectors is complete, the training of the parameters via Kalman filter technique is in order. The update of the parameters is according to the following recursion:

$$\hat{\boldsymbol{\theta}}_{k/k}^j = \hat{\boldsymbol{\theta}}_{k/k-1}^j + \boldsymbol{K}_k^j \left(y_k^j - \boldsymbol{C}_k^j \hat{\boldsymbol{\theta}}_{k/k-1}^j\right) \quad (20)$$

where $\boldsymbol{K}_k$ is the computed Kalman gain. The computed Kalman gain can be viewed as an adaptive learning rate (Tzeng et al., 1994) ant its computation is according to the following steps :

$$\boldsymbol{K}_k^j = \boldsymbol{P}_{k/k-1}^j \boldsymbol{C}_k^{jT} \left(\boldsymbol{C}_k^j \boldsymbol{P}_{k/k-1}^j \boldsymbol{C}_k^{jT} + r\right)^{-1} \quad (21)$$

$$\boldsymbol{P}_{k/k-1}^j = \boldsymbol{A}^j \boldsymbol{P}_{k-1/k-1}^j \boldsymbol{A}^{jT} + \boldsymbol{Q} \quad (22)$$

$$\boldsymbol{P}_{k/k}^j = \boldsymbol{P}_{k/k-1}^j - \boldsymbol{K}_k^j \boldsymbol{C}_k^j \boldsymbol{P}_{k/k-1}^j \quad (23)$$

where $\boldsymbol{P}_{k/k-1}^j = E\left[\left(\boldsymbol{\theta}_k^j - \hat{\boldsymbol{\theta}}_{k/k-1}^j\right)\left(\boldsymbol{\theta}_k^j - \hat{\boldsymbol{\theta}}_{k/k-1}^j\right)^T\right]$ and $\boldsymbol{P}_{k/k}^j = E\left[\left(\boldsymbol{\theta}_k^j - \hat{\boldsymbol{\theta}}_{k/k}^j\right)\left(\boldsymbol{\theta}_k^j - \hat{\boldsymbol{\theta}}_{k/k}^j\right)^T\right]$ are the one step predicted and filter estimate error covariance matrices, respectively.
To simplify the implementation of the Kalman filtering technique, we assume that $\boldsymbol{A}^j = \boldsymbol{I}$ where $\boldsymbol{I}$ is a unit matrix ; $\boldsymbol{Q}$ and r are an assigned variances of the process noise and measurement noise, respectively. The initial parameters values are set to be random numbers.

C. Estimating consequent parameters

There are several methods to obtain the consequent parameters (Angelov & Filev, 2004; Babuska & Verbruggen, 1997; Abonyi et al., 2002). In part we propose an algorithm based also on KF that can compute directly the consequent parameters from the data set and the estimated premise membership functions.

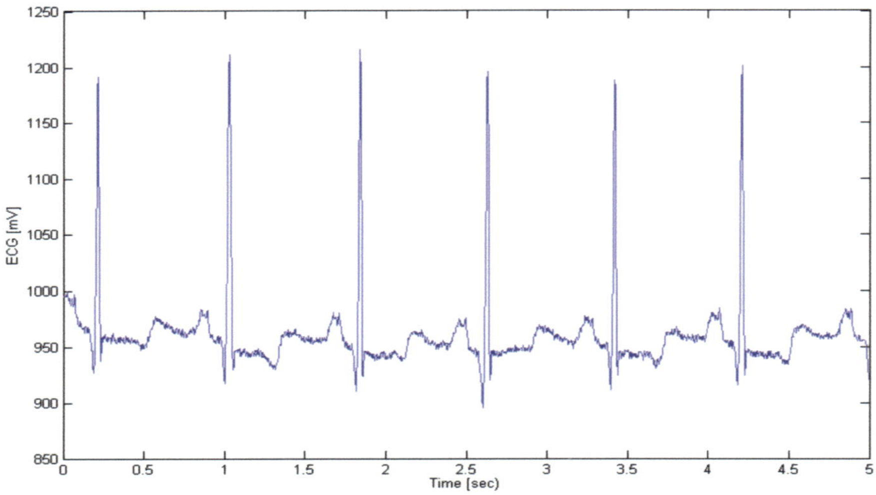

Fig. 8. ECG signal

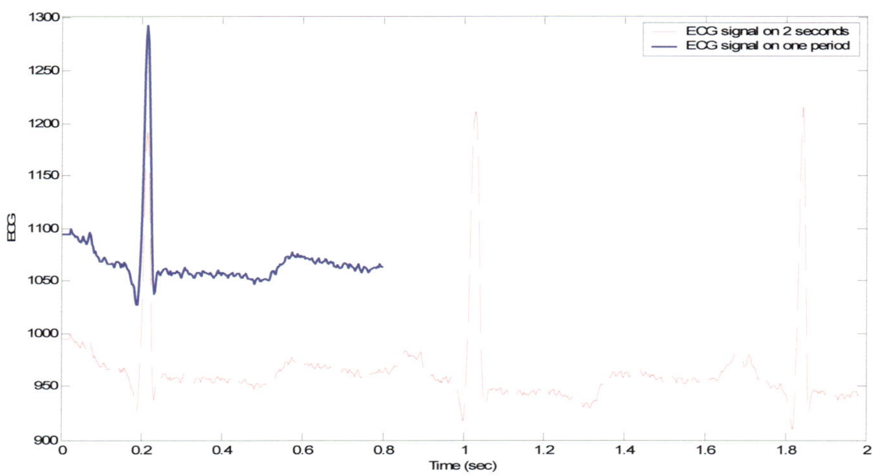

Fig. 9. Extraction of one period ECG signal

From equation (13) we have

$$y = \sum_{i=1}^{c} \varphi_i(\boldsymbol{x})\left(\boldsymbol{a}_i^T \boldsymbol{x} + b_i\right) \tag{24}$$

where $\varphi_i(\boldsymbol{x}) = \dfrac{\beta_i(\boldsymbol{x})}{\sum_{i=1}^{c} \beta_i(\boldsymbol{x})}$ is the normalized activation value of the ith rule. The development of (24) gives

$$y = \left[\varphi_1(\boldsymbol{x})[\boldsymbol{x} \quad 1] \quad \varphi_2(\boldsymbol{x})[\boldsymbol{x} \quad 1] \quad .... \quad \varphi_c(\boldsymbol{x})[\boldsymbol{x} \quad 1]\right] \begin{bmatrix} a_1 \\ b_1 \\ \vdots \\ a_c \\ b_c \end{bmatrix} \tag{25}$$

Let $\boldsymbol{\Theta} = \left[a_1 \quad b_1 \quad ... \quad a_c \quad b_c\right]^T$ the $c(n+1)\times 1$ TS parameters vector and let the extended vector $\boldsymbol{x}_e = [\boldsymbol{x} \quad 1]$ with dimension $1\times(n+1)$, also if we put $\boldsymbol{C} = [\varphi_1 \boldsymbol{x}_e \quad \varphi_2 \boldsymbol{x}_e \quad .... \quad \varphi_c \boldsymbol{x}_e]$, then equation (25) can be rewritten as follows :

$$y = \boldsymbol{C\Theta} \tag{26}$$

with $\boldsymbol{C}$ is an $1\times(n+1)c$ vector.

To apply Kalman filter, we must introduce the measurement noise v_k, so the measurement equation corresponding to (27) at the moment k will take the following form :

$$y_k = \boldsymbol{C}_k \boldsymbol{\Theta}_k + v_k \tag{27}$$

then, we can consider that the state variable is $\boldsymbol{\Theta}_k$, so the state equation will take the following expression :

$$\boldsymbol{\Theta}_k = \boldsymbol{A\Theta}_{k-1} + \boldsymbol{w}_{k-1} \tag{28}$$

where $\boldsymbol{A}$ is an $c(n+1)\times c(n+1)$ transition matrix and $\boldsymbol{w}_k$ is a state noise. v_k and $\boldsymbol{w}_k$ must satisfy some conditions as cited in the previous subsection.

Now we can apply Kalman filter to estimate the TS parameter vector $\boldsymbol{\Theta}_k$ as follows:

$$\hat{\boldsymbol{\Theta}}_{k/k-1} = \boldsymbol{A}\hat{\boldsymbol{\Theta}}_{k-1/k-1} \tag{29}$$

$$\boldsymbol{P}_{k/k-1} = \boldsymbol{A} \ \boldsymbol{P}_{k-1/k-1}\boldsymbol{A}^T + \boldsymbol{Q} \tag{30}$$

$$\boldsymbol{K}_k = \boldsymbol{P}_{k/k-1}\boldsymbol{C}_k^T \left(\boldsymbol{C}_k \boldsymbol{P}_{k/k-1}\boldsymbol{C}_k^T + r\right)^{-1} \tag{31}$$

$$\hat{\boldsymbol{\Theta}}_{k/k} = \hat{\boldsymbol{\theta}}_{k/k-1} + \boldsymbol{K}_k \left(y_k - \boldsymbol{C}_k \hat{\boldsymbol{\Theta}}_{k/k-1}\right) \tag{32}$$

$$\boldsymbol{P}_{k/k} = \boldsymbol{P}_{k/k-1} - \boldsymbol{K}_k \boldsymbol{C}_k \boldsymbol{P}_{k/k-1} \tag{33}$$

where $\hat{\boldsymbol{\Theta}}_k$ is the estimated value of $\hat{\boldsymbol{\Theta}}_k$ and $\boldsymbol{K}_k$ is the computed Kalman gain, $\boldsymbol{P}_{k/k-1}$ and $\boldsymbol{P}_{k/k}$ are the one step predicted and filter estimate error covariance matrices, respectively. Also, for simplicity we will take $\boldsymbol{A} = \boldsymbol{I}$.

3.3 Application

In order to illustrate the effectiveness of the proposed method, we consider the problem of approximating the electrocardiogram (ECG) signal. The ECG is the graphical representation

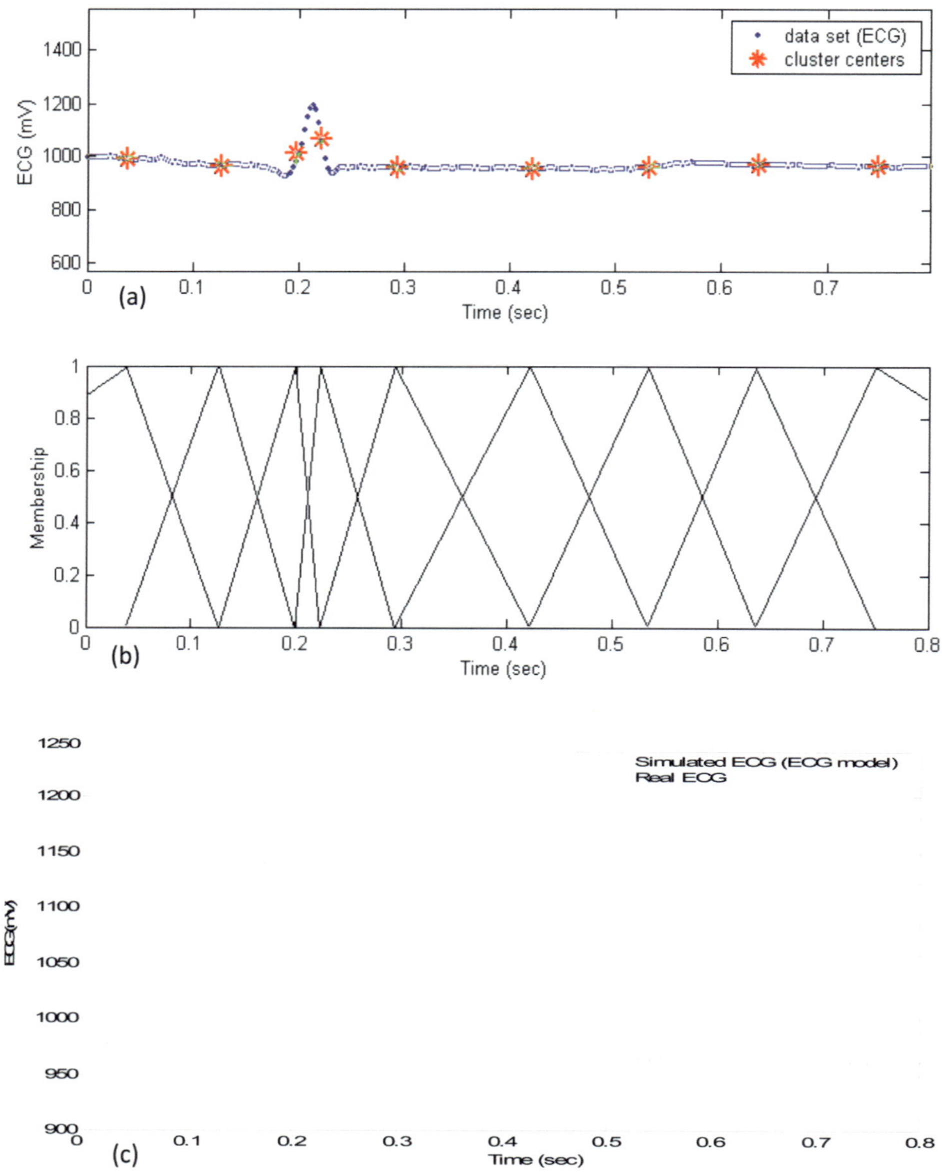

Fig. 10. (a) Clustering result for the ECG signal
(b) Obtained membership function
(c) Performance of our model for the ECG signal.

of the electrical activity generated by the heart. This activity shows dynamical behavior which is neither periodic nor deterministically chaotic.
To avoid the confusion between the two proposed Kalman filters, we will denote KF1 the filter used for premise membership functions and KF2 the filter used for the consequence parameters.
The considered ECG signal is taken from a publically available database of MIT (see figure 8). Before structure identification, extraction of one period ECG is done (see figure 9). In the

structure identification of the proposed method, 9 clusters are detected as shown in Fig. 10(a). By taking the projection of U on x, taking an $\alpha - cut = 0.1$ and by applying Kalman filter KF1, the premise membership functions are obtained (see figure 10(b)). The resulting model using our strategy is as follows:

$$R_i : If \ x \ is \ A_i, \ Then \ y = a_i x + b_i \qquad i = 1, 2, ..., 9 \tag{34}$$

where A_i are the obtained premise membership functions, and a_i, b_i are the TS parameters to be estimated. After applying Kalman filter KF2, the TS parameters of the fuzzy model are obtained and presented in the antecedent membership function. The ECG signal and the simulated ECG signal (ECG model) are shown in Figure 10(c).

4. Conclusion

Investigations presented in this chapter were divided into two parts. In the first part, Kalman filter was used as an alternative controller. The main idea of this technique is to transform the Kalman filter from a state estimator to a control action estimator. We developed a Kalman controller system for real-time target tracking. According to our simulation results, we can say that this type of controller is very robust to load and stochastic disturbances.

In the second part, a fuzzy modelling algorithm is proposed and its validity is verified through computer simulations. This new algorithm has an excellent capacity to describe a given system. We have showed that Kalman filter can be used with fuzzy clustering to obtain a useful method to fuzzy modeling. The proposed algorithm is composed of three steps: 1) fuzzy clustering; 2) determination of premise membership functions; 3) estimation of the TS parameters. In the first step, the GKCA algorithm was used in order to detect clusters of different shapes. In the second step, a Kalman filter has been used in order to estimate the parameter values of the premise membership functions by considering the point-wise defined membership functions as a training sets. In the third step, Kalman filter is also used as a linear regression to efficiently choose the parameter values of the consequent part (TS parameters) of the fuzzy model from the input output data of the identified system. Consequently, the hybrid clustering and Kalman filter method can be efficiently constructed. The performances of the proposed modeling technique was demonstrated on modeling of ECG signal.

5. References

Abonyi, J., Babuska, R. & Szeifert, F. (2002). Modified Gath-Geva Fuzzy Clustering for Identification of Takagi-Sugeno Fuzzy Models. *IEEE Transactions on Systems, Man and Cybernetics. Part B*, Vol. 32, No. 5, (October 2002) 612-621

Angelov, P. P. & Filev, D. P. (2004). An approach to online identification of Takagi-Sugeno fuzzy models. *IEEE Transactions on Systems, Man and Cybernetics*. Part B: Vol. 34, No. 1, (February 2004) 484-498

Babuska, R. (1998). *Fuzzy modeling for control*. Nowell, MA: Kluwer

Babuska, R.; Roubos, J. A. & Verbruggen, H. B. (1998). Identification of MIMO Systems by Input-Output TS Fuzzy Models, *IEEE International Conference on Fuzzy Fystems*, Vol. 1, pp. 657-662, Anchorage, 1998

Babuska, R. & Verbruggen, H. B. (1995). Identification of composite linear models via fuzzy clustering, *Proceedings of European Control Conference*, pp. 1207-1212, Rome, Italy, 1995

Babuska, R. & Verbruggen, H. B. (1997). Constructing fuzzy models by product space clustering, *In Fuzzy Model Identification, Selected Approaches,* Hellendoorn, H.& Driankov, D., (Ed.Berlin, Germany : Springer-Verlag) 53-90

Bezdek, J. C. & Dunn, J. C. (1975). Optimal Fuzzy Partitions : A Heuristic for Estimating the Parameters in a Mixture of Normal Distribution. *IEEE Transactions on Computers C-24,* (1975) 835-838

Bezdek, J. C.; Hathaway, R. J.; Howard, R. E.; Wilson, C. A. & Windham, M. P. (1987). Local convergence analysis of a grouped version of coordinate descent. *Journal of Optimization Theory and Application,* Vol. 3, No. 54, (1987) 471-477

Brookner, E. (1998). *Tracking and kalman filtering made easy,* john wiley & sons

Chafaa, K.; Ghanai, M. & Benmahammed, K. (2005). Control structures of target tracking system. *Association for the advancement of modelling and simulation techniques in entreprises' A.M.S.E, Advances in Modelling and Analysis C,* Vol. 60, No. 4, (2005) 59-73, ISSN 1240-4535.

Chafaa, K.; Ghanai, M. & Benmahammed, K. (2007). Fuzzy modeling using Kalman filter. *IET Control theory and applications,* Vol. 1, No. 1, (January 2007) 58-64

Eubank, R. L. (2006). *A Kalman filter primer,* Taylor & Francis Group

Gath, I. & Geva, A. B. (1998). Unsupervised optimal fuzzy clustering. *IEEE Transactions on Pattern Anal. Machine Intell.,* Vol. 7, (1998) 773-781

Gustafson, D. E. & Kessel, W. C. (1997). Fuzzy clustering with a fuzzy covariance matrix, *Proceedings IEEE CDC,* pp. 761-766, 1979.

Hathaway, R. J. & Bezdek, J. C. (1991). Grouped coordinate minimization using newton's method for Inexact minimization in one vector coordinate. *Journal of Optimization Theory and Applications,* Vol. 3, No. 71, (1991) 503-516

Haykin, S. (2001). *Kalman Filtering and Neural Networks,* John wiley & Sons

Johansen, T. A. & Babuska, R. (2003). Multiobjective identification of Takagi-Sugeno fuzzy models. *IEEE Transactions on Fuzzy Systems,* Vol. 11, No. 6, (December 2003) 847-860

Kalman, R. E. (1960). A new approach to linear filtering and prediction problems. *Transactions of the ASME, journal of the basic engineering,* (1960)

Kosko, B. (1992). Neural networks and Fuzzy systems, Prentice Hall

Kukolj, D.& Levi, E. (2004). Identification of complex systems based on neural and Takagi-Sugeno fuzzy model. *IEEE Transactions on Systems, Man and Cybernetics. Part B,* Vol. 34, No 1, (February 2004) 272-282

Mohinder, S. G. & Angus, A. P. (2001). Kalman Filtering: Theory and Practice Using Matlab, *John Wiley & Sons*

Mudi Rajani, K. & Nikhil Pal, R. (1999). A robust self-tuning scheme for PI and PD type fuzzy controllers. *IEEE transactions on fuzzy systems,* Vol. 7, No. 1, (February 1999) 2-16

Nascimento, S.; Mirkin, B. & Pives, F. M. (2003). Modeling proportional membership in fuzzy clustering. *IEEE Transactions on Fuzzy Systems.* Vol. 11, No. 2, (April 2003) 173-186

Ogata, K. (1970). *Modern control engineering,* Prentice Hall

Sugeno, M. & Yasukawa, T. (1993). A Fuzzy-logic based approach to qualitative modelling. *IEEE Transactions on Fuzzy Systems,* Vol. 1, (January 1993) 7-31

Takagi, T. & Sugeno, M. (1986). Fuzzy Identification of Systems and its Applications to Modeling and Control. *IEEE Transactions on. Systems Man and Cybernetics.* Vol. SMC-15, (Jan./Feb, 1986) 116-132

Tzeng, Y. C.; Chen, K. S.; Kao, W. L. & Fung, A. K. (1994). A dynamical learning neural network for remote sensing applicationsn. *IEEE Transactions on Geoscience, Remote Sensing,* Vol. 32, No. 5, (September 1994) 1096-1102

Zdzislaw, B. (2005). *Modern control theory,* Springer-Verlag Berlin Heidelberg

4

Extended Kalman Filter Based Fuzzy Adaptive Filter

Wai Kit Wong and Heng Siong Lim
Faculty of Engineering and Technology, Multimedia University, Jln Ayer Keroh Lama, 75450 Melaka, Malaysia

1. Introduction

In classical logic, every statement is either true or false, i.e., it has a truth value of 1 or 0. Classical sets impose rigid membership requirements. Fuzzy logic, which is the principle of imprecise knowledge, was introduced by Lofti A. Zadeh in 1965 (Zadeh, L. A., 1965). It is an extension of classical logic dealing with the partial truth concept. Every statement in fuzzy logic is a matter of degree and exact reasoning is viewed as a limiting case of approximate reasoning. In fuzzy logic, classical/Boolean truth value is replaced with degree of truth. Degree of truth denotes the extent to which a proposition is true. In fuzzy logic, the degree of truth of a proposition may be any real number between 0 and 1, inclusive. This fuzzy truth represents membership in vaguely defined sets, not likelihood of some event or condition.

Fuzzy logic allows for set membership values between and including 0 and 1, shades of grey as well as black and white, and in its linguistic form, imprecise concepts like "slightly", "quite" and "very". Specifically it allows partial membership in a set. It is related to fuzzy sets and possibility theory. Fuzzy sets are an extension of classical set theory and are used in fuzzy logic (Zadeh, L. A., 1975). In classical set theory, the membership of elements in relation to a set is assessed in a crisp condition: either belongs to or not. In contrast, fuzzy set theory allows the gradual assessment of the membership of elements in relation to a set, with the aid of a membership function μ. A membership function may act as an indicator function, mapping all elements of fuzzy sets to real numbered value in the interval 0 and 1: $\mu \rightarrow [0,1]$. In general, there are 6 types of membership functions as depicted in Fig. 1.

2. Fuzzy logic system

A fuzzy logic system is composed of four principal components: a fuzzifier, a fuzzy rule base, a fuzzy inference engine and a defuzzifier (Mendel, J. M., 1995). It is an information processing system. Fig. 2 depicts a fuzzy logic system that is widely used in fuzzy logic controllers and signal processing applications.

The crisp inputs s, are first converted into fuzzy quantities u. This process is known as fuzzification, where a fuzzifier transforms crisp input values into linguistic values. Input values are translated into linguistic concepts, which are represented by fuzzy sets. Rules may be provided by experts or can be extracted from numerical data. In either case, engineering rules are expressed as a collection of IF-THEN statements. The inference engine

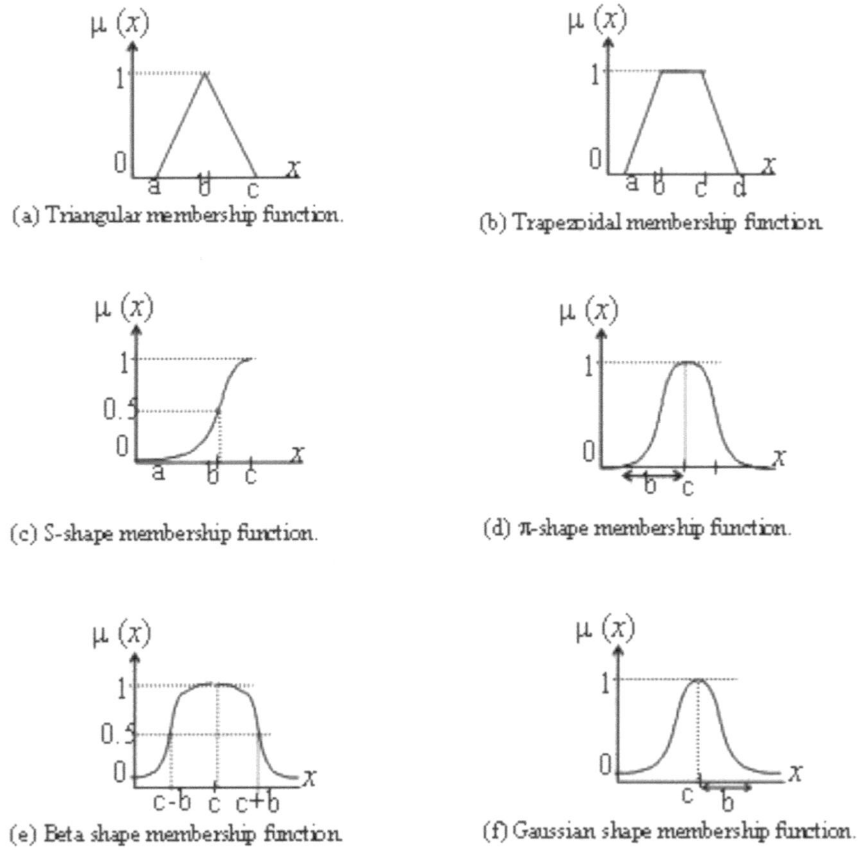

Fig. 1. Types of membership functions

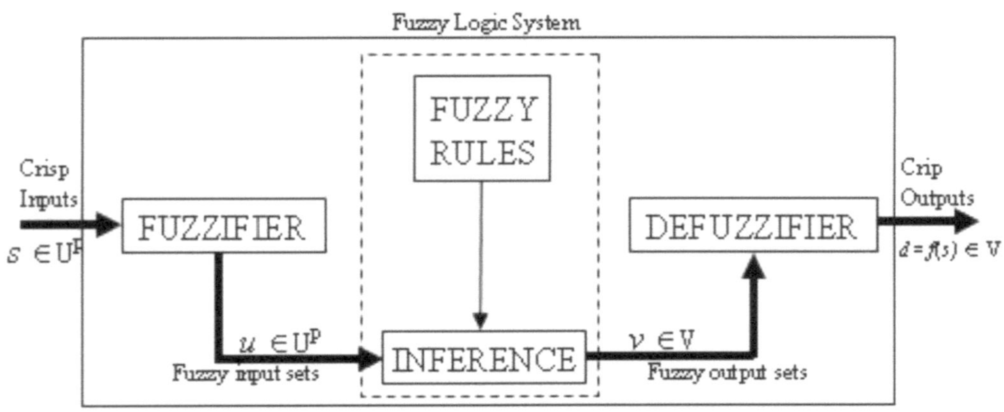

Fig. 2. Fuzzy logic system (Mendel, J.M., 1995)

of the fuzzy logic system maps fuzzy sets *u* into fuzzy sets *v*. It handles the way in which rules are combined. The defuzzifier maps output sets into crisp numbers. This mapping can be expressed quantitatively as $d = f(s)$. We shall consider an example of a simple temperature regulator that uses a fan. Fig. 3 shows the fuzzy sets and the membership functions for the input temperature.

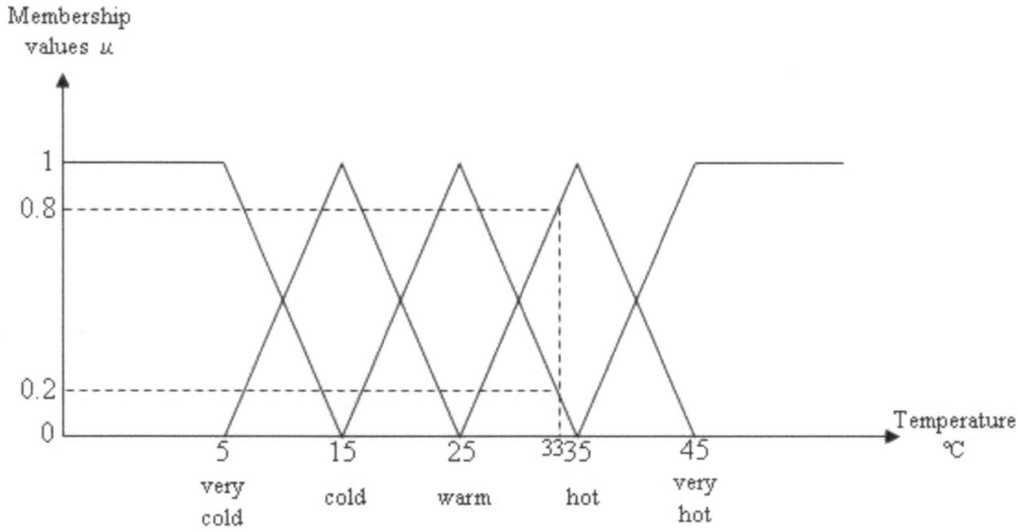

Fig. 3. Fuzzy sets of a simple temperature regulator that use a fan

A membership function μ_x, for $x \in X$, quantifies the grade of membership of the elements x to the fundamental set X. An element mapping to the value 0 means that the member is not included in the given set, 1 describes a fully included member. Values strictly between 0 and 1 characterize the fuzzy members. Membership functions are applied to the measurement and the degree of truth in each determined premise. According to Fig.3, if the input temperature s is 33°C, after fuzzification, the membership value that s belongs to warm and hot temperature are $\mu_{warm} = 0.2$ and $\mu_{hot} = 0.8$ respectively.

The fuzzy rules may be provided by a human expert, or can be extracted from numerical input-output data pairs. In either case, engineering rules are expressed as a collection of IF-THEN statements, i.e.,

"IF temperature is very hot THEN speed maximum fan."
"IF temperature is hot THEN speed medium high fan."
"IF temperature is warm THEN maintain medium fan."
"IF temperature is cold THEN turn down medium low fan."
"IF temperature is very cold THEN stop fan."

These rules reveal that we will need an understanding of (Mendel, J.M., 1995):

1. Linguistic variables versus numerical values of the variable, e.g., very hot versus 45°C.
2. Quantifying linguistic variables. E.g., u may have a finite number of linguistic terms associated with it, ranging from very hot to very cold, which is fuzzifying using fuzzy membership functions. There is no unique membership function in a situation and it is primarily subjective in nature. But this does not mean that membership function can be assigned arbitrarily, it is rather on the basis of application-specific criteria. Some of the commonly used membership functions are shown in Fig. 1 (Chen, S., 1990).
3. Implications, which is the relationship between two statements where the truth of one suggests the truth of the other, e.g., "IF temperature is warm THEN maintain medium

fan." Here, the truth of temperature is warm suggests the fan to maintain in medium speed.

4. Logical connections for linguistic variables, e.g., "and", "or", etc. "IF temperature is very hot and humidity is high, THEN speed medium high fan." Humidity is another fuzzy set. The fan speeds to medium high only when the two conditions are fulfilled.

Inference is the act or process of drawing a conclusion based solely on the fuzzy rules, e.g., u has $\mu_{warm} = 0.2$ and $\mu_{hot} = 0.8$, inference machine will draw a conclusion that the temperature is hot since $\mu_{hot} > \mu_{warm}$. Defuzzifier converts the fuzzy value into a "crisp" value. The defuzzifier maps output sets v into crisp numbers d. In the example mentioned above, v is speed medium high fan, when map into crisp number, d is the supply voltage value to the fan (e.g., 80 volts).

In summary, once the fuzzy rules have been established, the fuzzy logic system could map crisp inputs s into crisp outputs d. The mapping can be expressed quantitatively as $d = f(s)$. The fuzzifier maps crisp numbers s into fuzzy sets u in order to activate fuzzy rules that are in terms of linguistic variables, which have fuzzy sets associated with them. The inference machine maps fuzzy sets u into fuzzy sets v. It deals with the process in which rules are combined. The defuzzifier maps output sets v into crisp numbers d. In the sub-section below, we will discuss a well-known fuzzy logic system, which is the Takagi-Sugeno Kang (TSK) fuzzy logic system.

2.1 Takagi Sugeno Kang (TSK) fuzzy logic system

The Takagi-Sugeno Kang (TSK) fuzzy model is a universal approximator of the continuous real functions that are defined in a closed and bounded subset of n-dimensional real number $\Re^n$. This strong property of the TSK model finds several applications in modeling dynamical systems (Mastorakis, N.E., 2004). A TSK fuzzy logic system is described by fuzzy IF-THEN rules which represent input/output relations of a system. The most widely used TSK fuzzy logic system is the first-order TSK fuzzy logic system. It has a rule base of M rules, each having p antecedents, where the l-th rule is expressed as:

R^l: IF x_1 is F_1^l and x_2 is F_2^l and ...and x_p is F_p^l

THEN $y^l = c_0^l + c_1^l x_1 + c_2^l x_2 + \ldots + c_p^l x_p$

in which l=1, 2,..., M; c_j^l is the consequent parameter, for j=0,1,...,p; x_j is the input to the fuzzy logic system; y^l is the output of the l-th IF-THEN rule; and F_j^l is the fuzzy sets, for j=0,1,...,p. The final output of the unnormalized first order TSK model is inferred as (Tanaka, K., 1998):

$$r = \sum_{l=1}^{M} f^l y^l \tag{1.1}$$

where f^l are rule firing strengths defined as:

$$f^l = \mathcal{T}_{j=1}^{p} \mu_{F_j^l}(x_j) \tag{1.2}$$

and $\mathcal{T}$ denotes a t-norm. t-norm is the short form of triangular norm. It is a kind of function used in multi-valued logic, especially in fuzzy logic. t-norm generalizes intersection in a lattice and AND in logic. The most often used t-norms are:

minimum t-norm : $\mathcal{T}_{min}(a,b) = \min\{a,b\}$

product t-norm : $\mathcal{T}_{prod}(a,b) = a.b$

drastic t-norm : $\mathcal{T}_{-1}(a,b) = \begin{cases} a \;, & \text{if } b = 1 \\ b \;, & \text{if } a = 1 \\ 0 & else \end{cases}$

When Gaussian membership functions

$$\mu_{F_j^l}(x_j) = \exp\left[-\frac{1}{2}\left(\frac{x_j - m_j^l}{\sigma_j^l} \right)^2 \right] \tag{1.3}$$

and product t-norm are used, (1.1) can be expressed as:

$$r = \sum_{l=1}^{M} y^l \prod_{j=1}^{p} \exp\left[-\frac{1}{2}\left(\frac{x_j - m_j^l}{\sigma_j^l} \right)^2 \right] \tag{1.4}$$

where m_j^l and σ_j^l are the centre and width of the l-th fuzzy set F_j^l, respectively.

2.2 Application of fuzzy logic system

Fuzzy logic systems deal with reasoning with fuzzy sets, fuzzy rules, and estimated sampled functions from linguistic input to linguistic output. Fuzzy logic systems are successful in the field of control especially the feed back control of some physical and chemical processes like electric current, temperature, motion of machines and flow of liquids or gas. Fuzzy logic principles are also be applied in fuzzy software engineering that incorporate fuzziness in data and programs and fuzzy database systems in the field of economics, management and medicines (Gupta, M.M., 1994[a], Gupta, M.M., 1994[b], Jang, J.S.R., 1993, Kaufmann, A., 1988). Recently, some automotive industry products and consumer electronics in the market have moved into fuzzy logic technology, and the outcome of the products has significant performance improvement (Al-Holou, N., 2002, Eichfeld, H., 1996).

Fuzzy logic systems are nonlinear systems and they are capable of inferring complex nonlinear relationships between input and output variables (Mendel, J.M., 1997). The non-linearity property is particularly important when the underlying physical mechanism to be modeled is inherently nonlinear. The system can 'learn' the non-linear mapping by being presented with a sequence of input signals and desired response pairs, which are used in conjunction with an optimization algorithm to determine the values of the system parameters. This is one of the most commonly used learning paradigms, called *supervised learning*. Even if the process to be modeled is non-stationary, the system can be updated to reflect the changing statistics of the process. Unlike conventional stochastic models used to model such processes, fuzzy logic systems do not make any assumptions regarding the structure of the process, nor do they invoke any kind of probabilistic distribution model, i.e., they belong to the general family of model free, data driven, non-parametric methods.

However, conventional fuzzy systems have limitation of low capabilities for learning and adaptation. An improvement done in (Gupta, M.M.,1991) combines conventional fuzzy technology with neural network technology to form an innovative technological field, so called fuzzy neural networks (FNNs). Fuzzy mathematics gives an inference mechanism for approximate reasoning under cognitive uncertainty, while neural networks have the abilities of pattern recognition, optimization and decision making (Bhatti, S.S., 2002). A combination of these two technological innovations give birth to a new technology in which the explicit knowledge representation of fuzzy logic is improved by the learning power of simulated neural networks (Bhatti, S.S., 2002). Fuzzy basis function network (FBFN) is one of the FNNs that are used for information processing. It rediscovers some interesting advantages of a fuzzy system. One is the universal approximation capability, and the other is learning and adaptation, which have not been dealt with in fuzzy systems. Fuzzy adaptive equalizers are based on such technology. This technology is also capable of dealing with nonlinearity and uncertainty.

3. Equalizer

Consider, for example, a communication system which consists of a transmitter, communication channel, receiver, and equalizer connected together as shown in Fig. 4. The term equalizer in communication system is commonly refer to a device that place after the receiver designed to equalize the channel characteristics and extract out information send by transmitter side from noise and distortion.

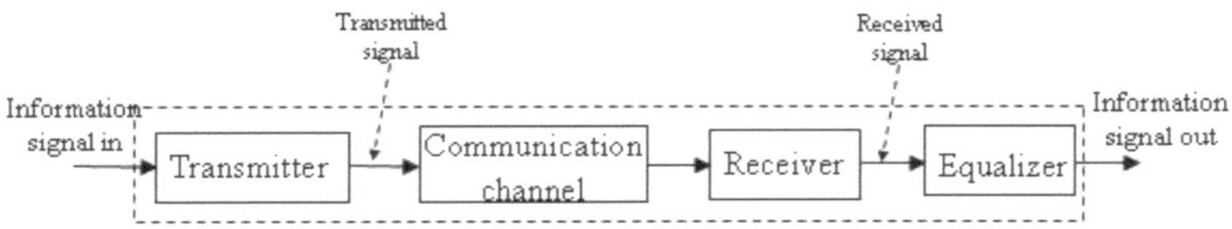

Fig. 4. Block diagram of a communication system

The main problem that has to be considered in communication system involves the fading and intersymbol interference (ISI), which is generated by multipath propagation effects and its resulting delay spread. Sometimes, there are obstacles and reflectors in the communication channel. The transmitted signal arrives at the receiver from various directions over a multiplicity of paths. Such a phenomenon is called multipath. It is an unpredictable set of reflections from direct waves and each with its own degree of attenuation and delay.

In communication channel, multiple reflections of the transmitted signal may arrive at the receiver at different times, this can result in intersymbol interference (or bits "crashing" into one another) which the receiver cannot sort out. This time dispersion of the channel is called multipath delay spread which is an important parameter to degrade the performance of communication systems.Besides signal distortion due to multipath propagation, noise is the most crucial factor that degrades the performance of communication systems. Since communication systems have such a lot of undesired distortions, equalizers are designed to compensate these distortions.

3.1 Optimal equalizer (MAP equalizer)

Maximum a-posteriori (MAP) equalizer is the optimal equalizer based on maximum a posteriori probability estimation. MAP equalization requires the knowledge of the conditional probability density function (PDF) of the received signal given the transmitted signal pattern. Assume that we want to estimate an unobservable population θ on the basis of observations y. Let f be the sampling distribution of y, so that $f(y \mid \theta)$ is a conditional PDF, summarizing our knowledge provided by the data y conditioned on knowing θ. Then the function:

$$\theta \mapsto f(y \mid \theta) \tag{1.5}$$

is known as the likelihood function and the estimate (Kay, S.M., 1993):

$$\hat{\theta}_{ML}(y) = \arg \max_{\theta} f(y \mid \theta) \tag{1.6}$$

as the maximum likelihood estimate of θ. Now, assume that a prior distribution g over θ exists. Applying Bayesian statistics, we may treat θ as a random variable with posterior distribution as:

$$\theta \mapsto \frac{f(y \mid \theta)g(\theta)}{\int_{\theta} f(y \mid \theta)g(\theta)d\theta} \tag{1.7}$$

This is an application of Bayes' theorem. The method of maximum a-posteriori estimation is then estimates θ as the mode of the posterior distribution with:

$$\hat{\theta}_{MAP}(y) = \arg \max_{\theta} \frac{f(y \mid \theta)g(\theta)}{\int_{\theta} f(y \mid \theta)g(\theta)d\theta} = \arg \max_{\theta} f(y \mid \theta)g(\theta) \tag{1.8}$$

MAP estimate of θ coincides with maximum likelihood estimate when the prior distribution function g is uniform. The geometric formulation of MAP equalizer is given below.

3.2 Geometric formulation for MAP equalizer

The geometric formulation of the MAP equalizer is shown in (Chen, S., 1990) and (Chen, S., 1991). We are using the same notation as in those studies and we define:

$$P_{\eta,\tau}(1) = \{\hat{\mathrm{x}}(k) \in \Re^{\eta} \mid s(k-\tau) = 1\} \tag{1.9}$$

and

$$P_{\eta,\tau}(-1) = \{\hat{\mathrm{x}}(k) \in \Re^{\eta} \mid s(k-\tau) = -1\} \tag{1.10}$$

where η is the order, τ is the lag of the equalizer, $\Re$ is any real number,

$$\hat{\mathrm{x}}(k) = [\hat{x}(k) \quad \hat{x}(k-1) \quad \ldots \quad \hat{x}(k-\eta+1)]^T \tag{1.11}$$

$\hat{x}(k)$ is the noise-free output of the rake receiver, and $P_{\eta,\tau}(1)$ and $P_{\eta,\tau}(-1)$ are two sets of possible noise free output vectors $\hat{\mathrm{x}}(k)$ that can be produced from input sequences containing $s(k-\tau) = 1$ and $s(k-\tau) = -1$, respectively. Let:

$$\mathrm{x}(k) = [x(k) \quad x(k-1) \quad \ldots \quad x(k-\eta+1)]^T \tag{1.12}$$

be the observed output vector with noise, $p_1[\mathrm{x}(k) \mid \hat{\mathrm{x}}(k) \in P_{\eta,\tau}(1)]$ and $p_{-1}[\mathrm{x}(k) \mid \hat{\mathrm{x}}(k) \in P_{\eta,\tau}(-1)]$ be the conditional probability density functions of $x(k)$ given $\hat{\mathrm{x}}(k) \in P_{\eta,\tau}(1)$ and $\hat{\mathrm{x}}(k) \in P_{\eta,\tau}(-1)$ respectively. It was shown in (Chen, S., 1990) and (Chen, S., 1991), which the MAP equalizer is defined by:

$$f_{opt}(\mathrm{x}(k)) = \mathrm{sgn}[p_1(\mathrm{x}(k) \mid \hat{\mathrm{x}}(k) \in P_{\eta,\tau}(1)) - p_{-1}(\mathrm{x}(k) \mid \hat{\mathrm{x}}(k) \in P_{\eta,\tau}(-1))] \tag{1.13}$$

This optimal equalizer achieves the minimum bit error rate for the given order η and τ, where sgn(q) = 1 (-1), if $q \geq 0$ ($q<0$). If the noise is Gaussian and with covariance matrix:

$$Q = E\{[(n(k) \quad \ldots \quad n(k-\eta+1)][n(k) \quad \ldots \quad n(k-\eta+1)]^T\} \tag{1.14}$$

Then from $x(k) = \hat{x}(k) + n(k)$, we have:

$$p_1(\mathrm{x}(k) \mid \hat{\mathrm{x}}(k) \in P_{\eta,\tau}(1)) - p_{-1}(\mathrm{x}(k) \mid \hat{\mathrm{x}}(k) \in P_{\eta,\tau}(-1))$$

$$= \sum \exp\left[-\frac{1}{2}(\mathrm{x}(k) - \hat{\mathrm{x}}_+)^T Q^{-1}(\mathrm{x}(k) - \hat{\mathrm{x}}_+)\right] - \sum \exp\left[-\frac{1}{2}(\mathrm{x}(k) - \hat{\mathrm{x}}_-)^T Q^{-1}(\mathrm{x}(k) - \hat{\mathrm{x}}_-)\right] \tag{1.15}$$

where the first summation is over all the positive noise free points $\hat{\mathrm{x}}_+ \in P_{\eta,\tau}(1)$ whereas the second summation is over all the negative noise free points $\hat{\mathrm{x}}_- \in P_{\eta,\tau}(-1)$.

In practice, it is difficult to know or predict the PDF of the transmitted or received signals, and MAP equalizer is too complex for practical use. Therefore, attention has been given to the design of sub-optimum equalizers such as adaptive equalizers that are practical and have near optimal performance.

4. Adaptive equalizer

Adaptive equalizers are sub-optimum equalizers that rely on a recursive algorithm to perform satisfactory information extraction in a communication system in which the statistical characteristics about the input-output signal are not known. The algorithm will start from some predetermined set of initial conditions, representing whatever the system knows about the communication channel. In a stationary communication channel, after successive iterations of the algorithm, the equalizer will converges to the optimum solution in some statistical sense. In a non-stationary communication channel, the algorithm will also have the ability to track time variations in the statistic of the input data (Haykin, S. 2002). Some adaptive equalizers examples are shown below:

4.1 Transversal equalizer

Digital equalizer is well known and was already described in 1940 by H. J. Kallman in (Kallman, H.J., 1940). The invention relates to a simple and linear transversal equalizer for processing an analog signal with a number of stages to which level control devices are connected by uniformly spaced taps in a non-dispersive delay line. The transversal equalizer is typically implemented using digital circuitry, charged-coupled devices, or surface-acoustic wave devices. Due to its versatility and ease of implementation, the transversal equalizer has emerged as an essential signal processing structure in a wide variety of applications.

In signal processing, transversal equalizer is also known as tapped-delay line equalizer or finite-duration impulse response (FIR) equalizer (Proakis, J.G.,1995). The structure of an adaptive transversal equalizer is depicted in Fig. 5:

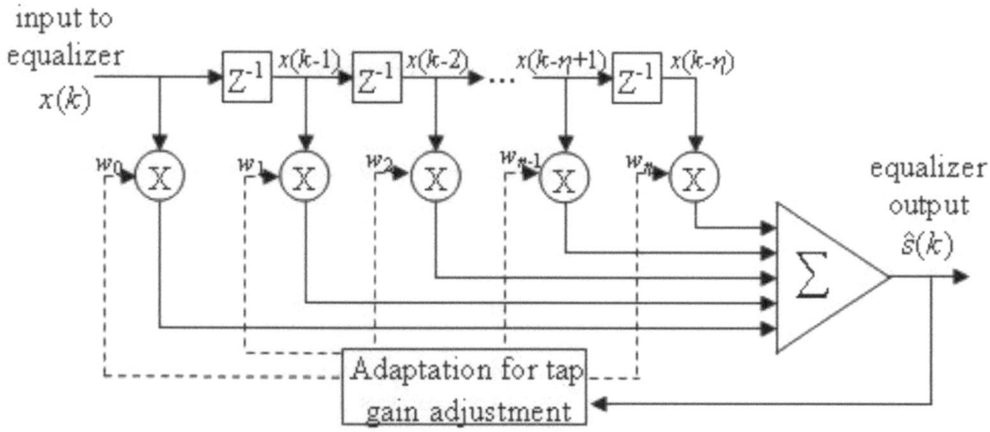

Fig. 5. Structure of transversal equalizer

The output of the transversal equalizer is given by:

$$\hat{s}(k) = \sum_{l=0}^{\eta} w_l x(k-l) . \tag{1.16}$$

where w_l is the l-th tap weight and η is the order of the equalizer. The weights of the equalizer can be optimized by minimizing some criterion functions. Two popular choices for the adaptation algorithm are the RLS and LMS algorithm.

4.2 Decision feedback equalizer

Another sub-optimum adaptive equalizer is the decision feedback equalizer (DFE). DFE utilizes two transversal equalizers: a feedforward transversal equalizer and a feedback transversal equalizer (Sailer, T.M., 2001). The DFE uses previous symbol estimates for interference cancellation of ISI corrupted data transmission. When the symbol estimates are correct, they have the advantage of not being corrupted by additive channel noise, giving the DFE a performance advantage over other linear structures. However, if the symbol estimates are incorrect, there is the danger of error propagation leading to catastrophic performance. The structure of DFE is shown in Fig. 6:

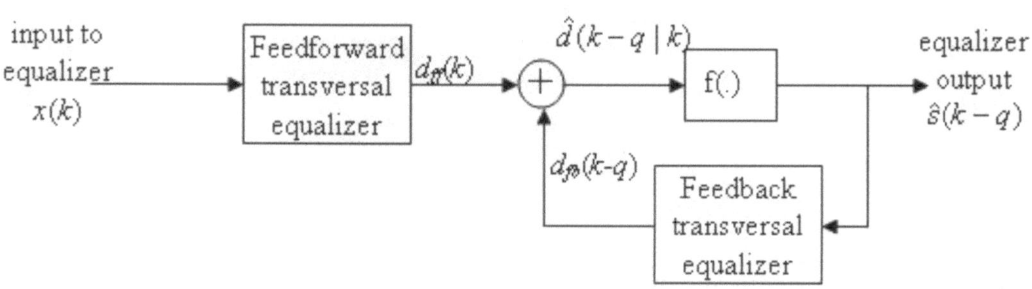

Fig. 6. Structure of decision feedback equalizer

where f(.) is a decision device and $x(k)$ is the input to the feedforward transversal equalizer. From the output of the feedforward transversal equalizer, $d_{ff}(k)$, the interference from previously detected symbols are removed via the output of the feedback transversal equalizer, $d_{fb}(k-q)$. The difference between these two transversal equalizer outputs constitutes an estimate of the transmitted symbol, $\hat{d}(k-q\,|\,k)$. This estimate is sometimes called *soft estimate*, since it is not yet quantized. The decision device quantizes the soft estimate and the resulting *hard estimate*, $\hat{s}(k-q)$ becomes the input of the feedback transversal equalizer. The constant q is known as the decision delay or the smoothing lag. It specifies how many future measurements are being processed before a decision is made on the present symbol.

4.3 Volterra series expansion equalizer

Since the optimal decision boundary is normally nonlinear for communication channel equalization problem, linear equalization methods are no longer adequate for the task. In this case, nonlinear equalizers that have the ability to perform nonlinear input-output mapping can be applied to minimize the error probability. In this and the following two subsections, we discuss three nonlinear channel equalization methods, namely the Volterra series expansion, the radial basis function and the multilayer perceptrons. The Volterra series expansion equalizer is a nonlinear equalizer based on the Volterra series functional representation from mathematics (Kong, X., 2004).

Let $x[n]$ and $y[n]$ represent the input and output signals, respectively, of a discrete time and causal nonlinear system. The Volterra series expansion for $y[n]$ using $x[n]$ is given by (Mathews, V.J., 1991):

$$y[n] = h_0 + \sum_{m_1=0}^{\infty} h_1[m_1]x[n-m_1] + \sum_{m_1=0}^{\infty}\sum_{m_2=0}^{\infty} h_2[m_1,m_2]x[n-m_1]x[n-m_2] + \ldots$$

$$+ \sum_{m_1=0}^{\infty}\sum_{m_2=0}^{\infty}\ldots\sum_{m_p=0}^{\infty} h_p[m_1,m_2,\ldots,m_p]x[n-m_1]x[n-m_2]\ldots x[n-m_p] + \ldots \qquad (1.17)$$

where $h_p[m_1,m_2,\ldots,m_p]$ is known as the p-th order Volterra kernel of the system. $h_p[m_1,m_2,\ldots,m_p]$ can be optimized by minimizing some criterion functions. Among the most commonly used algorithm are the recursive least squares (RLS) and least mean squares (LMS) algorithms. Without any loss of generality, it is assumed that the Volterra kernels are symmetric, in which $h_p[m_1,m_2,\ldots,m_p]$ is left unchanged for any of the possible p! permutations of the indices $m_1,m_2,\ldots,m_p$ (Mathews, V.J., 1991).

Since an infinite series expansion like (1.17) is not useful in channel equalization, we may work with truncated Volterra series expansion (Mathews, V.J., 1991):

$$y[n] = \sum_{m_1=0}^{N-1} h_1[m_1]x[n-m_1] + \sum_{m_1=0}^{N-1}\sum_{m_2=0}^{N-1} h_2[m_1,m_2]x[n-m_1]x[n-m_2] + \ldots$$

$$+ \sum_{m_1=0}^{N-1}\sum_{m_2=0}^{N-1}\ldots\sum_{m_p=0}^{N-1} h_p[m_1,m_2,\ldots,m_p]x[n-m_1]x[n-m_2]\ldots x[n-m_p] \qquad (1.18)$$

where $h_0 = 0$ (without loss of generality (Mathews, V.J., 1991)). Note that there are $O(N^P)$ coefficients in this polynomial expansion. One big disadvantage for the model as in (1.18) is that the complexity of implementing equalizers using this model can be very large even for moderately large values of N and P. Consequently, most Volterra series expansions system involve low order model.

4.4 Radial basis function equalizer

A radial basis function (RBF) equalizer is a neural network equalizer whose outputs are a linear combination of the hidden layer functions (Mulgrew, B., 1996). It is trained to perform a mapping from an m-dimensional input space to an n-dimensional output space. The structure of RBF equalizer is shown in Fig. 7 below.

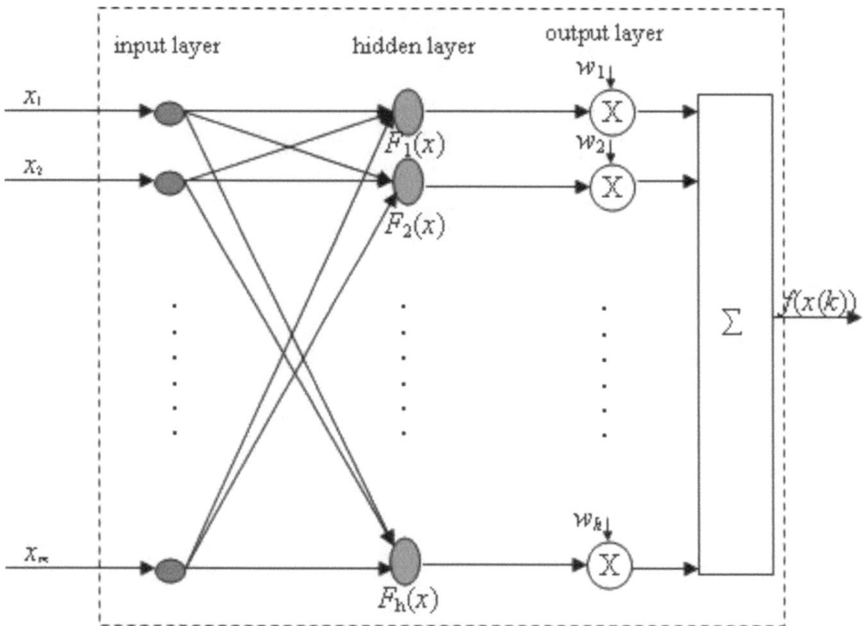

Fig. 7. Structure of radial basis function equalizer

Mathematically, the output of a RBF equalizer is,

$$f(x(k)) = \sum_{l=1}^{h} w_l F_l(\boldsymbol{x}) \tag{1.19}$$

where the basis function F is a sigmoidal function

$$F(\boldsymbol{x}) = \exp\left(-\frac{1}{\sigma_l^2} \left\| \boldsymbol{x} - \mu_l \right\|^2 \right) \tag{1.20}$$

$\boldsymbol{x}$ is the input vector of the equalizer $[x_1 \ x_2 \ \ldots \ x_m]$, h indicates the total number of hidden neurons, μ_l and σ_l refer to the center and width of the l-th hidden neuron. $\| . \|$ is the Euclidean norm. The coefficient w_l is the weight of the l-th hidden neuron to the output neuron.

4.5 Multilayer perceptrons equalizer

Another approach for nonlinear channel equalization using neural network is the multilayer perceptrons (MLP) equalizer. A typical MLP equalizer consists of a set of source nodes forming the input layer, one or more hidden layers of computation nodes, and an output layer of nodes. The input signal propagates through the MLP equalizer layer-by-layer. The signal-flow of such an equalizer is shown in Fig. 9. In between the input layer and the output layer are the hidden layers of the MLP equalizer. The MLP equalizer has L layers of synaptic connections and L+1 layers of neurons.

In (Seung, S., 2002), back propagation algorithm is used in multilayer perceptrons network. Assume there are no biases, the network is diagrammed as:

$$x^0 \xrightarrow{W^1} x^1 \xrightarrow{W^2} \cdots \xrightarrow{W^L} x^L \tag{1.21}$$

where $x^l \in \Re^{n_l}$ for all l = 0,1, …, L; $x^l = [x_1^l \; x_2^l \ldots x_h^l]$ and W^l is an $n_l \times n_{l-1}$ matrix for all l = 0,1, …, L. n_l is the number of hidden neurons in l-th layer. There are L + 1 layers of neurons. The input vector x^0 is transformed into the output vector x^L by evaluating the equation:

$$x_i^l = \sum_{j=1}^{n_l - 1} W_{ij}^l x_j^{l-1} \quad \text{for } l = 1 \text{ to } L. \tag{1.22}$$

The actual output of the equalizer is

$$f(x(k)) = \sum_{i=1}^{h} x_i^L \tag{1.23}$$

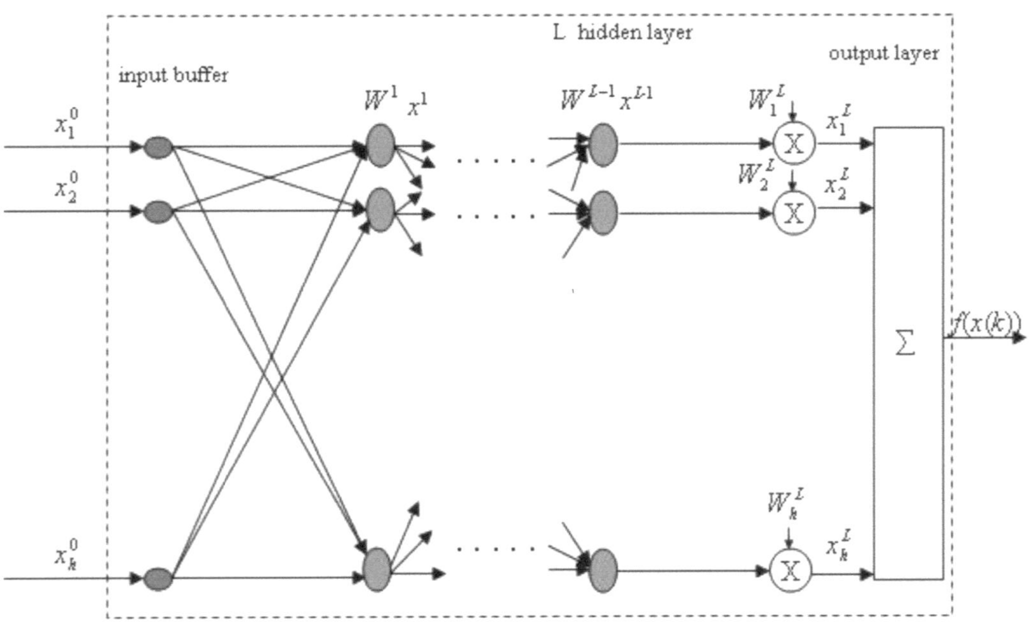

Fig. 9. Structure of multilayer perceptron equalizer

Two types of linear adaptive equalizer had been discussed, namely transversal equalizer and decision feedback equalizer; at the meantime, three types of nonlinear channel are also discussed, namely Volterra series expansion equalizer, radial basis function equalizer and multilayer perceptron equalizer. Normally, complex communication channels are nonlinear channel. Therefore most of the adaptive equalizers used today are nonlinear adaptive equalizer, because they not only dealing well with linear channel characteristic, but nonlinear channel as well. Since nonlinear channels include a very broad spectrum of nonlinear distortion, it is difficult to comment on which nonlinear adaptive equalizer is dominantly better than the others. So, it is good to try out new nonlinear adaptive equalizer for communication channel equalization. Fuzzy adaptive equalizer is such a new nonlinear equalizer.

5. Fuzzy adaptive equalizer

Fuzzy adaptive equalizers are adaptive equalizers that apply the concepts of fuzzy logic. Fuzzy adaptive equalizers are information processors that make use of both linguistic (in the form of fuzzy IF-THEN rules) and numerical information (in the form of input-output pairs). The main merits of using fuzzy adaptive equalizers are nonlinear and simple in design, which linguistic information from human experts can be directly incorporated into the equalizer. If no linguistic information is available, the fuzzy adaptive equalizers become well-defined nonlinear adaptive equalizers (similar to the polynomial, neural nets, or radial basis function adaptive equalizers). The adaptive algorithms adjust the parameters of the membership functions which characterize the fuzzy concepts in the IF-THEN rules, by minimizing some criterion function.

Fuzzy adaptive equalizer, as a fuzzy basis function expansions system, can be represented as two-layered feedforward network structure (Wang, L.X., 1992[b]). On the basis of this idea, the fuzzy adaptive equalizer can be trained to realize the desired input-output relationship using various learning algorithms such as least mean squares (LMS), recursive least squares (RLS) and extended Kalman filter (EKF) adaptation algorithms. Fig. 10 shows the schematic diagram of fuzzy adaptive equalizer. The inputs to the fuzzy adaptive equalizer [$x(k)$, $x(k-1)$,..., $x(k-n+1)$] are the receiver's outputs. The task of the fuzzy adaptive equalizer at the sampling instant k is to produce an estimate of the transmitted symbol $\hat{s}(k-d)$, using the information contained in [$x(k)$, $x(k-1)$,..., $x(k-n+1)$] where the integer n and d are the order and lag of the equalizer respectively.

A fuzzy adaptive equalizer is functionally equivalent to a fuzzy basis function network (FBFN) with the form given in (1.24) to (1.27). It can be shown that the input-output equations of a fuzzy adaptive equalizer with singleton fuzzifier, product inference and centroid defuzzifier can be expressed as:

$$f(x(k)) = \frac{\sum_{l=1}^{M} \theta^l \left(\prod_{i=1}^{n} \mu_{F_i^l}(x_i) \right)}{\sum_{l=1}^{M} \left(\prod_{i=1}^{n} \mu_{F_i^l}(x_i) \right)} = \sum_{l=1}^{M} \theta^l \phi^l(\mathrm{x}) \tag{1.24}$$

$$\text{where} \quad \phi^l(\mathrm{x}) = \frac{\prod_{i=1}^{n} \mu_{F_i^l}(x_i)}{\sum_{l=1}^{M}\left(\prod_{i=1}^{n} \mu_{F_i^l}(x_i)\right)} \tag{1.25}$$

$\phi^l(\mathrm{x})$ are called the fuzzy basis functions. Equation (1.24) gives an expression for fuzzy adaptive equalizer as shown in Fig.10. $\boldsymbol{x} = [x_1\ x_2\ \ldots x_{n-1}] = [x(k)\ x(k\text{-}1)\ \ldots\ x(k\text{-}n\text{+}1)]$ is the vector of inputs to the fuzzy adaptive equalizer. In particular, if a Gaussian radial basis function is chosen as the membership function, then

$$\phi^l(\mathrm{x}) = \frac{u_l(\mathrm{x})}{\sum_{l=1}^{M} u_l(\mathrm{x})} \tag{1.26}$$

$$\text{where} \quad u_l(x) = \left(\prod_{i=1}^{n} \mu_{F_i^l}(x_i)\right) = \prod_{i=1}^{n} \exp\left(-\frac{1}{2}\left(\frac{x_i - \tilde{x}_i^l}{\sigma_i^l}\right)\right) \tag{1.27}$$

$u_l(x)$ is the membership function after product inference, $\tilde{x}_i^l$ is the center of the i-th membership function and σ_i^l represents the width of the i-th membership function. In the next two sections, we will discuss two examples of fuzzy adaptive equalizers that were proposed in (Wang, L.X., 1993) for nonlinear channel equalization.

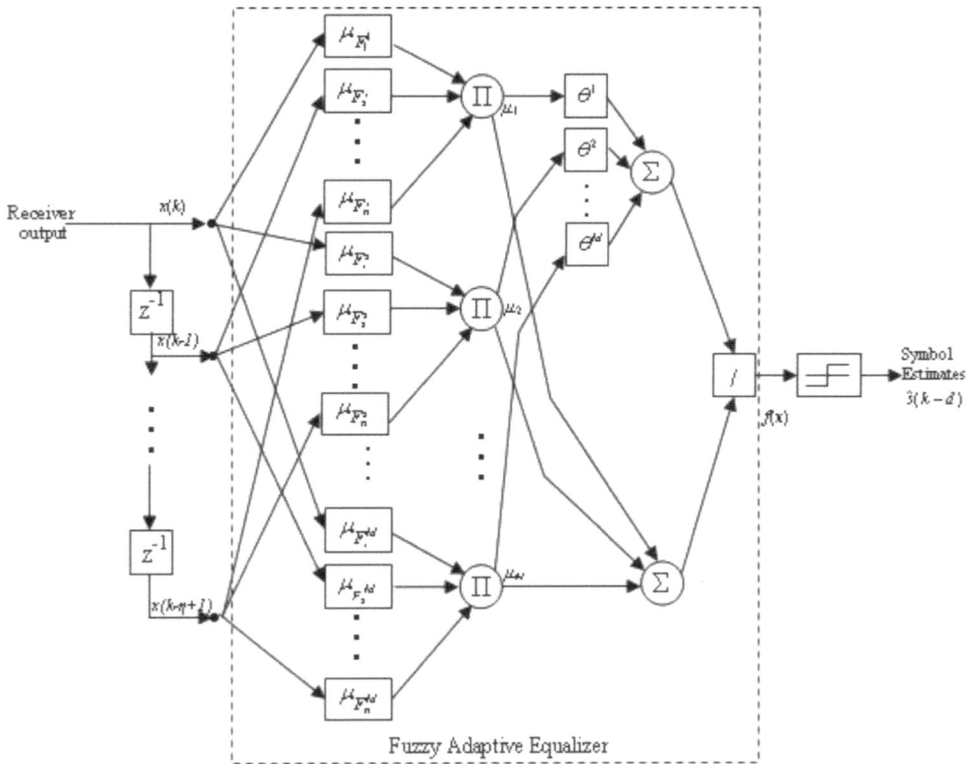

Fig. 10. Schematic diagram of fuzzy adaptive equalizer.

6. RLS based fuzzy adaptive equalizer

In (Wang, L.X., 1993), the RLS based fuzzy adaptive equalizer is used to solve the following problem. Consider a real-valued vector input sequence $[x(k)]$ and a real-valued scalar sequence $[d(k)]$, where $k=0,1,2,\dots$ is the time index, and $x(k) \in U \equiv [C_1^-, C_1^+] \times [C_2^-, C_2^+] \times \dots \times [C_n^-, C_n^+] \subset \Re^n$. U and $\Re$ are the input and output spaces of the equalizer respectively. At each time point k, the values of $x(k)$ and $d(k)$ are given. The problem to be solved is to determine a fuzzy adaptive equalizer $f_k : U \subset \Re^n \to \Re$ such that:

$$J(k) = \sum_{i=0}^{k} \lambda^{k-i} [d(i) - f_k(x(i))]^2 \tag{1.28}$$

is minimized, where $\lambda \in (0,1]$ is a forgetting factor.

6.1 Design procedure of the RLS based fuzzy adaptive equalizer

Step 1: m_i fuzzy sets are defined in each interval $\left[C_i^-, C_i^+\right]$ of the input space U, which are labeled as F_i^{ji} ($i = 1, 2, \dots, n$; $ji = 1, 2, \dots, m_i$; ji is a single index, i.e., $j1$ is an index which takes values from 1 to m_1 for $i=1$), in the following way: the m_i membership functions $\mu_{F_i^{ji}}$ cover the interval $\left[C_i^-, C_i^+\right]$ in the sense that for each $x_i \in \left[C_i^-, C_i^+\right]$ there exist at least one $\mu_{F_i^{ji}}(x_i) \neq 0$. These membership functions are fixed and will not change during the adaptation procedure.

Step 2: A set of $\prod_{i=1}^{n} m_i$ fuzzy IF-THEN rules is constructed in the following form:

$$R^{(j1,\dots,jn)} : \text{IF } x_1 \text{ is } F_1^{j1} \text{ and } \dots \text{ and } x_n \text{ is } F_n^{jn}, \text{ THEN } d \text{ is } G^{(j1,\dots,jn)}. \tag{1.29}$$

where $\mathrm{x} = \left[x_1, \dots, x_n\right]^T = \left[x(k), \dots, x(k-n+1)\right]^T \in U$ is the equalizer input, $d \in \Re$ is the equalizer output, $ji = 1, 2, \dots, m_i$ with $i = 1, 2, \dots, n$, F_i^{ji}'s are the same labels of the fuzzy sets defined in Step 1, and the $G^{(j1,\dots,jn)}$'s are labels of fuzzy sets defined in the output space which are determined in the following way: if there are linguistic rules from human experts in the form of (1.29), $G^{(j1,\dots,jn)}$ is set to the corresponding linguistic terms of these rules; otherwise, $\mu_{G^{(j1,\dots,jn)}}$ is set to an arbitrary membership function over the output space $\Re$. It is in this way that linguistic rules are incorporated into the fuzzy adaptive equalizer.

Step 3: The filter output f_k is calculated based on the $\prod_{i=1}^{n} m_i$ rules in step 2 as follows:

$$f_k(\mathrm{x}) = \frac{\sum_{j1=1}^{m_1} \dots \sum_{jn=1}^{m_n} \theta^{(j1,\dots,jn)} \left(\mu_{F_1^{j1}}(x_1) \dots \mu_{F_n^{jn}}(x_n)\right)}{\sum_{j1=1}^{m_1} \dots \sum_{jn=1}^{m_n} \left(\mu_{F_1^{j1}}(x_1) \dots \mu_{F_n^{jn}}(x_n)\right)} \tag{1.30}$$

where $\mathrm{x} = [x_1,...,x_n]^T = [x(k),...,x(k-n+1)]^T \in U$, $\mu_{F_i^{ji}}$'s are membership functions defined in Step 1, and $\theta^{(j1,...,jn)} \in \Re$ is the point at which $\mu_{G^{(j1,...,jn)}}$ achieves its maximum value. Due to the way in which the $\mu_{F_i^{ji}}$'s are defined in Step 1, the denominator of (1.30) is nonzero for all the points of *U*; therefore the filter f_k of (1.30) is well defined. For a given input $\mathrm{x} \in U$, the equalizer output is determined as a weighted average of the $\prod_{i=1}^{n} m_i$ points $\theta^{(j1,...,jn)}$ in the output space at which the fuzzy sets $G^{(j1,...,jn)}$ of the THEN parts of the $\prod_{i=1}^{n} m_i$ rules have maximum membership values; and, the weight $\mu_{F_1^{j1}}(x_1)...\mu_{F_n^{jn}}(x_n)$ for $\theta^{(j1,...,jn)}$ is proportional to the membership values of which $\boldsymbol{x}$ satisfies the IF part of $R^{(j1,...,jn)}$.

6.2 Parameter adaptation of the RLS based fuzzy adaptive equalizer

In (1.30), the weights $\mu_{F_1^{j1}}(x_1)...\mu_{F_n^{jn}}(x_n)$ are fixed functions of $\boldsymbol{x}$; therefore the free design parameters of the fuzzy adaptive equalizer are the $\theta^{(j1,...,jn)}$'s which are collected as a $\prod_{i=1}^{n} m_i$ - dimensional vector (Wang, L.X., 1993):

$$\theta = [\theta^{(1,1,...,1)},...,\theta^{(m_1,1,...,1)},\theta^{(1,2,...,1)},...,\theta^{(m_1,2,1,...,1)},...,\theta^{(1,m_2,1,...,1)},...,\theta^{(m_1,m_2,1,...,1)},..., \theta^{(1,m_2,...,m_n)},...,\theta^{(m_1,m_2,...,m_n)}]^T \quad (1.31)$$

The fuzzy basis function is defined by

$$p^{(j1,...,jn)}(\mathrm{x}) = \frac{\mu_{F_1^{j1}}(x_1)...\mu_{F_n^{jn}}(x_n)}{\sum_{j1=1}^{m_1}...\sum_{jn=1}^{m_n}\left(\mu_{F_1^{j1}}(x_1)...\mu_{F_n^{jn}}(x_n)\right)} \quad (1.32)$$

and they are collected as a $\prod_{i=1}^{n} m_i$ -dimensional vector $\boldsymbol{p}(\boldsymbol{x})$ in the same ordering as the $\boldsymbol{\theta}$ of (1.31), i.e.,

$$\mathrm{p}(\mathrm{x}) = (p^{(1,1,...,1)}(\mathrm{x}),..., p^{(m_1,1,...,1)}(\mathrm{x}), p^{(1,2,1,...,1)}(\mathrm{x}),..., p^{(m_1,2,1,...,1)}(\mathrm{x}),..., p^{(1,m_1,1,...,1)}(\mathrm{x})$$

$$,..., p^{(m_1,m_2,1,...,1)}(\mathrm{x}),..., p^{(1,m_2,...,m_n)}(\mathrm{x}),..., p^{(m_1,m_2,...,m_n)}(\mathrm{x}))^T \quad (1.33)$$

Based on (1.31) and (1.33), (1.30) can be rewritten as:

$$f_k(\boldsymbol{x}) = \mathrm{p}^T(\mathrm{x})\theta \quad (1.34)$$

The following RLS algorithm is used to update θ. The initial estimate of $\boldsymbol{\theta}$, $\boldsymbol{\theta}(0)$, is determined as in Step 2, and $P(0)=\sigma I$, where σ is a small positive constant, and I is the $\prod_{i=1}^{n} m_i$ -by- $\prod_{i=1}^{n} m_i$ identity matrix. At each time point k=1,2, ..., the following equation are computed:

$$\phi(k) = \mathrm{p}(\mathrm{x}(k)) \tag{1.35}$$

$$P(k) = \frac{1}{\lambda}\left[P(k-1) - P(k-1)\phi(k)[\lambda + \phi^T(k)P(k-1)\phi(k)]^{-1}\phi^T(k)P(k-1)\right] \tag{1.36}$$

$$K(k) = P(k-1)\phi(k)[\lambda + \phi^T(k)P(k-1)\phi(k)]^{-1} \tag{1.37}$$

$$\theta(k) = \theta(k-1) + K(k)(d(k) - \phi^T(k)\theta(k-1)) \tag{1.38}$$

where $\boldsymbol{x}(k)$ is the real-valued input vector and $d(k)$ is the real-valued desired output scalar sequence. $\mathrm{p}(\mathrm{x}(k))$ is defined in (1.33), and λ is the forgetting factor. Some comments on the RLS based fuzzy adaptive equalizer are given in the next sub-section.

6.3 Comments on RLS based fuzzy adaptive equalizer

The RLS algorithm, (1.36) - (1.38) are obtained by minimizing the recursive least squares criterion, $J(k) = \sum_{i=0}^{k} \lambda^{k-i}[d(i) - f_k(\mathrm{x}(i))]^2$, with f_k constrained to be the form of (1.34). Because f_k is linear in the parameter, the derivation of (1.36) - (1.38) is the same as that for the FIR linear adaptive filter (Cowan, C.F.N., 1985).

Equations (1.36) - (1.38) can be viewed as updating the $\prod_{i=1}^{n} m_i$ rules in the form of (1.29) by changing the centers $\theta^{(j1,\dots,jn)}$ of the THEN parts of these rules in the direction that minimizing the criterion function $J(k)$ as in (1.28). Only these centers are allowed to change. The membership functions $\mu_{F_i^{ji}}$ of the IF parts of the rules are fixed at the very beginning and are not allowed to change. Hence, a good choice of the membership functions is very important to the success of the entire equalizer. However, in the next section, LMS based fuzzy adaptive equalizer will lighten this constraint by allowing $\mu_{F_i^{ji}}$'s also to change during the adaptation process.

It was proven in (Wang, L.X., 1992[a]) and (Wang, L.X., 1992[b]) that the equalizers (1.30) are universal approximators; i.e. for any real continuous function g on the compact set U, there exists a function in the form of (1.30) such that it can uniformly approximate g over U to an arbitrary accuracy. Therefore, this fuzzy adaptive equalizer is a powerful nonlinear adaptive equalizer in the sense that it has the capability of performing very difficult nonlinear equalization operation. This type of fuzzy adaptive equalizer performs two operations on the input vector $\boldsymbol{x}$: first, it performs a nonlinear transformation $\boldsymbol{p}(.)$ on $\boldsymbol{x}$; then the equalizer output is obtained as a linear combination of these transformed signals. The fuzzy adaptive equalizer is similar to the radial basis function (Chen, S., 1991), (Powell, M.J.D., 1987) and potential function (Meisel, W.S., 1969) approaches.

Linguistic information (in the form of fuzzy IF-THEN rules of (1.30)) and numerical information (in the form of desired input-output pairs $\boldsymbol{x}(k)$, $d(k)$) are combined into the equalizer in the following way: In Step 2-3, linguistic IF-THEN rules are directly incorporated into the equalizer (1.30) by constructing the initial equalizer based on the linguistic rules. During the parameter adaptation, numerical pairs ($\boldsymbol{x}(k)$, $d(k)$) are

incorporated into the equalizer by updating the equalizer parameters such that the equalizer output "matches" the input-output pairs in the sense of minimizing (1.28).
A nonlinear equalizer which is linear in the parameter is obtained by fixing the fuzzy membership functions on the input space U at the very beginning. So, the fast-convergent RLS algorithm could be used in the adaptation process, but has to include all the $\prod_{i=1}^{n} m_i$ possible rules in the equalizer because if a region of U is not covered by any rules and an input x to the equalizer happens to be in that region, then the equalizer response will be very poor. So, for problems of high dimension η and large m_i, the computations involved in this type of fuzzy adaptive equalizer are with higher complexity, because at each time point k, we need to perform the $\prod_{i=1}^{n} m_i$ -dimensional matrix-to vector multiplications of (1.36)-(1.38), and to evaluate the values of the $\prod_{i=1}^{n} m_i$ fuzzy basis functions of (1.35). Although these computations are highly parallelizable, we may not be able to use the equalizer in some practical situations where computing power is limited. Therefore, a LMS based fuzzy adaptive equalizer is developed in (Wang, L.X., 1993), which involves much less computation.

7. LMS based fuzzy adaptive equalizer

In (Wang, L.X., 1993), the LMS fuzzy adaptive equalizer solves the following problem. Consider the same input and output sequence, $x(k)$ and $d(k)$ as in RLS based fuzzy adaptive equalizer. At each time point k=1,2,..., a fuzzy adaptive equalizer is required to determine $f_k : U \rightarrow R$ such that

$$L = E[(d(k) - f_k(\mathrm{x}(k)))^2] \tag{1.39}$$

is minimized.

7.1 Design procedure of the LMS based fuzzy adaptive equalizer

Step 1: M fuzzy sets F_i^l in each interval $\left[C_i^-, C_i^+\right]$ of U are defined with the following Gaussian membership functions:

$$\mu_{F_i^l} = \exp\left[-\frac{1}{2}\left(\frac{x_i - \tilde{x}_i^l}{\sigma_i^l}\right)^2\right] \tag{1.40}$$

where l = 1, 2, ..., M, i = 1, 2, ..., n, $x_i \in \left[C_i^-, C_i^+\right]$, and $\tilde{x}_i^l$ and σ_i^l are free parameters which will be updated in the LMS adaptation process.
Step 2: A set of M fuzzy IF-THEN rules is constructed in the following form:

$$R^l : \text{IF } x_1 \text{ is } F_1^l \text{ and } \ldots \text{ and } x_n \text{ is } F_n^l, \text{THEN } d \text{ is } G^l. \tag{1.41}$$

where $\mathrm{x} = [x_1, \ldots, x_n]^T = [x(k), \ldots, x(k-n+1)]^T \in U$, $d \in \Re$, F_i^l are defined in Step 1, $M \leq \prod_{i=1}^{n} m_i$ and G^l's are fuzzy sets defined in $\Re$ which are determined as follows: if there are linguistic rules in the form of (1.41), set F_i^l and G^l to be the labels of these linguistic rules; otherwise, choose μ_{G^l} and the parameters $\tilde{x}_i^l$ and σ_i^l arbitrarily. The parameters of membership functions $\mu_{F_i^l}$ and μ_{G^l} in these rules will change during the LMS adaptation process. Hence, the rules constructed in this step are initial rules of the fuzzy adaptive equalizer. Similar to RLS based fuzzy adaptive equalizer, linguistic rules are incorporated into the LMS based fuzzy adaptive equalizer by constructing the initial equalizer based on these rules.

Step 3: The filter $f_k:U\rightarrow R$ is constructed based on the M rules of Step 2 as follows:

$$f_k(\mathrm{x}) = \frac{\sum_{l=1}^{M} \theta^l \left(\prod_{i=1}^{n} \mu_{F_i^l}(x_i) \right)}{\sum_{l=1}^{M} \left(\prod_{i=1}^{n} \mu_{F_i^l}(x_i) \right)} \tag{1.42}$$

where $\mathrm{x} = [x_1,\dots,x_n]^T = [x(k),\dots,x(k-n+1)]^T \in U$, $\mu_{F_i^l}$'s are the Gaussian membership functions of (1.40), and $\theta^l \in \Re$ is any point at which μ_{G^l} achieves its maximum value. The equalizer in (1.42) is constructed in the same way as (1.30), and shares the same interpretation. Because the membership functions $\mu_{F_i^l}(x_i)$ is chosen to be Gaussian functions, which are nonzero for any $x_i \in [C_i^-, C_i^+]$, the denominator of (1.42) is nonzero for any $\mathrm{x} \in U$; therefore the equalizer in (1.42) is well defined. Because the θ^l as well as $\tilde{x}_i^l$ and σ_i^l are free parameters, the equalizer is nonlinear in the parameters.

7.2 Parameter adaptation of the LMS based fuzzy adaptive

The following LMS algorithm (Wang, L.X., 1993) is used to update the LMS based fuzzy adaptive equalizer parameters: θ^l, $\tilde{x}_i^l$ and σ_i^l. The initial $\theta^l(0)$, $\tilde{x}_i^l(0)$ and $\sigma_i^l(0)$ are determined in Step 2. At each time point $k = 1, 2, \dots$, do the following:

$$\theta^l(k) = \theta^l(k-1) + \alpha[d(k) - f_k] \frac{a^l(k-1)}{b(k-1)} \tag{1.43}$$

$$\tilde{x}_i^l(k) = \tilde{x}_i^l(k-1) + \alpha[d(k) - f_k] \frac{\theta^l(k-1) - f_k}{b(k-1)} a^l(k-1) \frac{x_i(k) - \tilde{x}_i^l(k-1)}{\left(\sigma_i^l(k-1)\right)^2} \tag{1.44}$$

$$\sigma_i^l(k) = \sigma_i^l(k-1) + \alpha[d(k) - f_k] \frac{\theta^l(k-1) - f_k}{b(k-1)} a^l(k-1) \frac{\left(x_i(k) - \tilde{x}_i^l(k-1)\right)^2}{\left(\sigma_i^l(k-1)\right)^3} \tag{1.45}$$

where $a^l(k-1) = \prod_{i=1}^{n} \exp\left[-\frac{1}{2} \left(\frac{x_i(k) - \tilde{x}_i^l(k-1)}{\sigma_i^l(k-1)} \right)^2 \right]$, $b(k-1) = \sum_{l=1}^{M} a^l(k-1)$, and

$f_k = \frac{\sum_{l=1}^{M} \theta^l a^l(k-1)}{b(k-1)}$. a is a small positive step size, l = 1, 2, …, M, and i =1, 2, …,n. Equations (1.43) - (1.45) are obtained by taking the gradient of L(ignore the expectation E) as in (1.39) with respect to the parameters and using the specific formula of (1.42) and (1.40). Some comments on the LMS based fuzzy adaptive equalizer are given in the next sub-section.

7.3 Comments on LMS based fuzzy adaptive equalizer

From Steps 2 and 3, the initial LMS based fuzzy adaptive equalizer is constructed based on linguistic rules from human experts and some arbitrary rules (in the sense that the parameters of membership functions $\mu_{F_i^l}$ and μ_{G^l} which characterize these rules are chosen arbitrarily). Both sets of rules are updated during the LMS adaptation process, changing the parameters in the direction of minimizing (1.39). Since minimizing (1.39) can be viewed as matching the input-output pairs $\{x(k),d(k)\}$, the LMS based fuzzy adaptive equalizer can be said to combine both linguistic and numerical information in its design.

LMS algorithm is a gradient algorithm. Therefore, a good choice of initial parameters is very important for its convergence. Since linguistic information is used to choose the initial parameters, the adaptation process will converge faster if the linguistic rules give good instructions for how the equalizer should perform, i.e., good description of the input-output pairs $\{x(k),d(k)\}$. Although LMS algorithm in general is slow to converge, LMS algorithm in fuzzy adaptive equalizer may converge fast, provided that there are sufficient linguistic rules.

A novel fuzzy adaptive equalizer that uses the extended Kalman filter (EKF) adaptation algorithm will be discussed in the next section. As compared to RLS and LMS based fuzzy adaptive equalizer, EKF based fuzzy adaptive equalizer has the merits of faster convergent speed and lower steady state bit error rate.

8. Extended Kalman Filter based Fuzzy Adaptive Equalizer (EKFAE)

Kalman filter is an efficient recursive filter which estimates the state of a dynamic system from a series of incomplete and noisy measurements (Kalman, R.E., 1960). Kalman filter is widely used in engineering applications from radar to computer vision and it is an important topic in control theory and control system engineering. For example, in a radar application, to track a target, information about the location, speed, and acceleration of the target is measured with a great deal of corruption by noise at any time instant. The Kalman filter exploits the dynamics of the target, which govern its time evolution, to remove the effects of the noise and obtain a good estimate of the location of the target at the past time (interpolation or smoothing process), present time (filtering process) or at future time (prediction process).

The Kalman filter is a recursive estimator. Only the estimated state from the previous time step and the current measurement are required to compute the estimate of the current state. In contrast to batch estimation techniques, no history of observation and/or estimates is required. Kalman filter has two distinct phases, which is the *predict phase* and the *update phase* (Kay, S.M., 1993). The predict phase uses the estimate from the previous time step to produce an estimate of the current state. For update phase, measurement information from

the current time step is used to refine this prediction to arrive at a new and more accurate estimate (Kay, S.M., 1993).
Kalman filter may be thought of as a sequential minimum mean square error (MMSE) estimator of a signal embedded in noise, where the signal is characterized by a dynamical or state model. If the signal and noise are jointly Gaussian, then the Kalman filter is an optimal MMSE estimator, if not, it is the optimal linear minimum mean square error (LMMSE) estimator (Kay, S.M., 1993).
The basic Kalman filter is limited to a linear assumption. However most of the real world systems are nonlinear. The nonlinearity can be associated either with the process model or with the observation model or with both. In the extended Kalman filter (EKF), the state transition and observation models need not be a linear function of the state but may instead be the differentiable functions. The functions used to compute the predicted filter state and predicted measurement cannot be applied to the covariance directly. Instead a matrix of partial derivatives, so called the Jacobian is computed. At each time step, the Jacobian is evaluated with current predicted states. This process essentially linearizes the nonlinear function around the current estimate. This result in the following extended Kalman filter equations:

Kalman Gain Matrix

$$\mathbf{G}_{\alpha}(k) = \mathbf{E}_{\alpha}(k-1)\mathbf{\Omega}_{\alpha}^{T}(k)[\mathbf{\Omega}_{\alpha}(k)\mathbf{E}_{\alpha}(k-1)\mathbf{\Omega}_{\alpha}^{T}(k) + N]^{-1} \tag{1.46}$$

(Posterior) error covariance matrix

$$\mathbf{E}_{\alpha}(k) = \mathbf{E}_{\alpha}(k-1) - \mathbf{G}_{\alpha}(k)\mathbf{\Omega}_{\alpha}(k)\mathbf{E}_{\alpha}(k-1) \tag{1.47}$$

Correction

$$\boldsymbol{\alpha}(k) = \boldsymbol{\alpha}(k-1) + \mathbf{G}_{\alpha}(k)\left[d(k) - f(\boldsymbol{x}(k))\right] \tag{1.48}$$

where k is the discrete time index;
$\boldsymbol{\alpha}(k)$ is the equalizer parameter;
$\mathbf{\Omega}_{\alpha}(k)$ is the Jacobian of the equalizer parameter;
$\boldsymbol{x}(k)$ is the equalizer input vector at time k;
$d(k)$ is the desired output at time k;
$f(\boldsymbol{x}(k))$ is the equalizer output at time k;
N is the measurement noise covariance.
Our extended Kalman filter based fuzzy adaptive equalizer (EKFAE) solves the following problem. Consider a real-valued scalar sequence $[d(k)]$, where k =0,1,2,... is the time index, and $\boldsymbol{x}(k) \in U \equiv [C_1^-, C_1^+] \times [C_2^-, C_2^+] \times ... \times [C_n^-, C_n^+] \subset \Re^n$. U and $\Re^n$ are the input and output spaces of the equalizer respectively. At each time point k=0,1,2,..., we are using EKF algorithm to determine an adaptive equalizer $f_k : U \subset \Re^n \to \Re$ such that the mean square error:

$$\text{MSE} = E\{[d(k) - f_k(\boldsymbol{x}(k))]^2\} \tag{1.49}$$

is minimized.

8.1 Design procedure of the EKFAE

The EKFAE is constructed with three steps:

1. Define M fuzzy sets F_i^l for each interval $[C_i^-, C_i^+]$ of the input space, U, with Gaussian membership functions (Gupta, M.M., 2003):

$$\mu_{F_i^l} = \exp\left[-\frac{1}{2}\left(\frac{x_i - \tilde{x}_i^l}{\sigma_i^l}\right)^2\right] \tag{1.50}$$

where $l = 1,2,\ldots,M$, $i = 1,2,\ldots,n$, $x_i = x(k - I + 1)$ is the input to the equalizer, $\tilde{x}_i^l$ is the center of the i-th membership function in the l-th rule and σ_i^l represents the width of the i-th membership function in the l-th rule. $\tilde{x}_i^l$ and σ_i^l are free parameters which will be optimized using the EKF adaptation algorithm. The reason we choose Gaussian membership functions rather than triangular, trapezoidal, etc. is because, it can be shown by using Stone Weierstrass theorem, the Gaussian network is a universal approximator that can be used to uniformly approximate continuous functions on a compact set (Wang, L.X., 1992a, Gupta, M.M., 2003). However, if other types of membership functions are employed in such a network, the universal approximation capability may not be easily verified, and in the meantime, large number of rules may be needed to carry out a function approximation.

2. Construct a set of changeable fuzzy IF-THEN rules either by linguistic information or numerical information from the matching input-output data pairs:

$$R^l : \text{IF } x_1 \text{ is } F_1^l \text{ and } \ldots \text{ and } x_n \text{ is } F_n^l, \text{ THEN } d \text{ is } G^l. \tag{1.51}$$

where $d \in \Re$ is the desired output, F_i^l s' are defined in Step 1, G^l's are fuzzy sets defined in R^l which are determined as follows : if there are linguistic rules in the form of (1.51), set F_i^ls and G^l to be the labels of these linguistic rules, otherwise, choose μ_{G^l} and the parameters $\tilde{x}_i^l$ and σ_i^l arbitrarily. These parameters will change during the adaptation process. The rules constructed in this step are initial rules of the fuzzy adaptive equalizer. We may incorporate the linguistic rules into the EKFAE by constructing the initial equalizer base on these rules.

3. Construct the equalizer $f(x)$ base on the set of M rules by using product inference and centroid defuzzification (Gupta, M.M., 2003):

$$f(x) = \frac{\sum_{l=1}^{M} \theta^l \left(\prod_{i=1}^{n} \mu_{F_i^l}(x_i)\right)}{\sum_{l=1}^{M} \left(\prod_{i=1}^{n} \mu_{F_i^l}(x_i)\right)} \tag{1.52}$$

where $\boldsymbol{x} = [x_1, \ldots, x_n]^T$, $\mu_{F_i^l}$s are the Gaussian membership functions defined in (1.50), and $\theta^l \in \Re$ is the value which μ_{G^l} achieves its maximum. Since we pick our membership function, $\mu_{F_i^l}(x_i)$ to be Gaussian function which is nonzero for any $x_i \in [C_i^-, C_i^+]$, the denominator of (1.52) is nonzero for any $x \in U$. Therefore (1.52) is well defined. Since θ^l as well as $\tilde{x}_i^l$ and σ_i^l are free parameters, the equalizer (1.52) is nonlinear in the parameters.

4. The EKF algorithm as stated in (1.46), (1.47) and (1.48) is used to update the equalizer parameters $\theta^l, \tilde{x}_i^l$ and σ_i^l iteratively. This involves the computation of the Jacobian $\Omega(k)$, which is obtained as the linearization about the current value of the nonlinear parameters (θ^l, $\tilde{x}_i^l$ and σ_i^l). The Jacobians $\Omega_\theta, \Omega_{\sigma_i}$ and $\Omega_{\tilde{x}_i}$ are calculated in Appendix 1.

Let $$a^l(k-1) = \prod_{i=1}^{n} \exp\left[-\frac{1}{2}\left(\frac{x_i(k) - \tilde{x}_i^l(k-1)}{\sigma_i^l(k-1)} \right)^2 \right] \quad (1.53)$$

$$b(k-1) = \sum_{l=1}^{M} a^l(k-1) \quad (1.54)$$

$$c^l(k-1) = \frac{\left(x_i - \tilde{x}_i^l\right)^2}{\left(\sigma_i^l\right)^3} \quad (1.55)$$

$$e^l(k-1) = \frac{\left(x_i - \tilde{x}_i^l\right)}{\left(\sigma_i^l\right)^2} \quad (1.56)$$

To update parameter θ^l, we use the following EKF procedure,

$$\Omega_{\theta^l} = \frac{a^l(k-1)}{b(k-1)}, \quad \text{for } l = 1,\ldots, M \quad (1.57)$$

$$\mathbf{\Omega}_\theta = [\Omega_{\theta^1}\ \Omega_{\theta^2}\ \ldots\ \Omega_{\theta^M}]$$

$$\mathbf{G}_\theta(k) = \mathbf{E}_\theta(k-1)\mathbf{\Omega}_\theta^T(k)\left[\mathbf{\Omega}_\theta(k)\mathbf{E}_\theta(k-1)\mathbf{\Omega}_\theta^T(k) + N \right]^{-1} \quad (1.58)$$

$$\mathbf{E}_\theta(k) = \mathbf{E}_\theta(k-1) - \mathbf{G}_\theta(k)\mathbf{\Omega}_\theta(k)\mathbf{E}_\theta(k-1) \quad (1.59)$$

$$\boldsymbol{\theta}(k) = \boldsymbol{\theta}(k-1) + \mathbf{G}_\theta(k)\left[d(k) - f(\boldsymbol{x}(k))\right], \text{ where } \boldsymbol{\theta} = [\theta^1\ \theta^2\ \ldots\ \theta^M] \quad (1.60)$$

To update parameter σ_i^l, we use the following EKF procedure,

$$\Omega_{\sigma_i^l} = \frac{\left[\theta^l - f_k(x(k))\right]a^l(k-1)c^l(k-1)}{b(k-1)}, \quad \text{for } l = 1,\ldots, M \quad (1.61)$$

$$\mathbf{\Omega}_{\sigma_i} = [\Omega_{\sigma_i^1} \ \Omega_{\sigma_i^2} \ \ldots \ \Omega_{\sigma_i^M}]$$

$$\mathbf{G}_{\sigma_i}(k) = \mathbf{E}_{\sigma_i}(k-1)\mathbf{\Omega}_{\sigma_i}{}^T(k)\left[\mathbf{\Omega}_{\sigma_i}(k)\mathbf{E}_{\sigma_i}(k-1)\mathbf{\Omega}_{\sigma_i}{}^T(k) + N\right]^{-1} \quad (1.62)$$

$$\mathbf{E}_{\sigma_i}(k) = \mathbf{E}_{\sigma_i}(k-1) - \mathbf{G}_{\sigma_i}(k)\mathbf{\Omega}_{\sigma_i}(k)\mathbf{E}_{\sigma_i}(k-1) \quad (1.63)$$

$$\boldsymbol{\sigma}_i(k) = \boldsymbol{\sigma}_i(k-1) + \mathbf{G}_{\sigma_i}(k)\left[d(k) - f(\boldsymbol{x}(k))\right], \text{ where } \boldsymbol{\sigma}_i = [\sigma_i^1 \ \sigma_i^2 \ \ldots \ \sigma_i^M] \quad (1.64)$$

To update parameter $\tilde{x}_i^l$, we use the following EKF procedure,

$$\Omega_{\tilde{x}_i^l} = \frac{\left[\theta^l - f_k(x(k))\right]a^l(k-1)e^l(k-1)}{b(k-1)}, \text{ for } l = 1,\ldots, M \quad (1.65)$$

$$\mathbf{\Omega}_{\tilde{x}_i} = [\Omega_{\tilde{x}_i^1} \ \Omega_{\tilde{x}_i^2} \ \ldots \ \Omega_{\tilde{x}_i^M}]$$

$$\mathbf{G}_{\tilde{x}_i}(k) = \mathbf{E}_{\tilde{x}_i}(k-1)\mathbf{\Omega}_{\tilde{x}_i}{}^T(k)\left[\mathbf{\Omega}_{\tilde{x}_i}(k)\mathbf{E}_{\tilde{x}_i}(k-1)\mathbf{\Omega}_{\tilde{x}_i}{}^T(k) + N\right]^{-1} \quad (1.66)$$

$$\mathbf{E}_{\tilde{x}_i}(k) = \mathbf{E}_{\tilde{x}_i}(k-1) - \mathbf{G}_{\tilde{x}_i}(k)\mathbf{\Omega}_{\tilde{x}_i}(k)\mathbf{E}_{\tilde{x}_i}(k-1) \quad (1.67)$$

$$\tilde{\boldsymbol{x}}_i(k) = \tilde{\boldsymbol{x}}_i(k-1) + \mathbf{G}_{\tilde{x}_i}(k)\left[d(k) - f(\boldsymbol{x}(k))\right], \text{ where } \tilde{\boldsymbol{x}}_i = [\tilde{x}_i^1 \ \tilde{x}_i^2 \ \ldots \ \tilde{x}_i^M] \quad (1.68)$$

The EKFAE algorithm is summarized in Table 1.

<u>Initialize</u> The number of iteration, n. $\boldsymbol{\theta} = [\theta^1 \theta^2 \ldots \theta^M]$ in the range of [-0.5,0.5], $\boldsymbol{\sigma}_i = [\sigma_i^1 \ \sigma_i^2 \ \ldots \ \sigma_i^M]$ in the range of [0.1,0.3], $\tilde{\boldsymbol{x}}_i = [\tilde{x}_i^1 \ \tilde{x}_i^2 \ \ldots \ \tilde{x}_i^M]$ in the range of [-2.0,2.0], and $\mathbf{E}_\theta(0)$, $\mathbf{E}_{\sigma_i}(0)$ and $\mathbf{E}_{\tilde{x}_i}(0)$ each equals to an identity matrix of $M \times M$ elements.
<u>For k=1,2,...,n, do</u> 1. Calculate $\mu_{F_i^l}$ using (1.50), and $a^l(k-1)$, $b^l(k-1)$, $c^l(k-1)$ and $e^l(k-1)$ using (1.53)-(1.56). 2. Calculate the Jacobians $\Omega_\theta(k)$, $\Omega_{\sigma_i}(k)$ and $\Omega_{x_i}(k)$ using (1.57), (1.61) and (1.65) respectively. 3. Calculate the Kalman gain matrices $\mathbf{G}_\theta(k)$, $\mathbf{G}_{\sigma_i}(k)$ and $\mathbf{G}_{\tilde{x}_i}(k)$ using (1.58), (1.62) and (1.66) respectively. 4. Update the error covariance matrices $\mathbf{E}_\theta(k)$, $\mathbf{E}_{\sigma_i}(k)$ and $\mathbf{E}_{\tilde{x}_i}(k)$ using (1.59), (1.63) and (1.67) respectively. 5. Update the parameters, $\boldsymbol{\theta}(k)$, $\boldsymbol{\sigma}_i(k)$ and $\tilde{\boldsymbol{x}}_i(k)$, using (1.60), (1.64) and (1.68) respectively.

Table 1. The EKFAE algorithm

9. Performance evaluation

In this section, we investigate the performance EKFAE and three other types of short listed adaptive equalizers, namely: decision feedback recursive least-squares adaptive equalizer, recursive least squares (RLS) based FAE and least mean squares (LMS) based FAE in terms of convergence speed and steady-state bit error rate (BER). We consider an arbitrary communication channel with transfer function $h(z) = 1 + 0.5z^{-1} + 0.3z^{-2} - 0.1z^{-3}$. Spread spectrum modulation/demodulation technique is use with spreading sequence [1 1 -1 1]. The DF-RLS adaptive equalizer has a number of forward taps $N_f = 2$ and number of feedback taps $N_b = 2$, while the order and lag of the FAEs are n=2 and d=0 respectively. The background noise is modeled as zero mean Gaussian with variance σ^2. As shown in Section 1.11, a smaller number of rules can be used to reduce the computational complexity of the FAEs. To ensure a fair comparison of the different FAEs, we have considered M = 25 rules for the EKFAE, the RLS-based FAE ($m_1 = m_2 = 5$) and the LMS-based FAE. We have also compared the performance of those equalizers with the optimum MAP equalizer that achieves the minimum probability of error.

Example 1. We first consider the situation where there is no linguistic information for the FAEs. We randomly set $\theta^l(0)$ in [-0.5 0.5], $\tilde{x}_i^l(0)$ in [-2.0 2.0] and $\sigma_i^l(0)$ in [0.1 0.3]. For the EKFAE, we set N = 0.999 and $E(0) = I$, where I is an identity matrix of $M \times M$. For the LMS-based FAE, we set the step size for adaptation, $\alpha = 0.05$. For DF-RLS equalizer and the RLS-based FAE, we set the forgetting factor, $\lambda = 0.999$ and $\sigma = 0.01$. When signal to noise ratio equals to 10dB, we plot the convergence curves for these equalizers in Fig. 12. Around 30 times of experiments were simulated in order to obtain the convergence curves. The simulation results show that without using any linguistic information, the EKFAE is a well performing nonlinear adaptive equalizer. The EKFAE achieves the fastest convergent speed. The EKFAE also outperforms the DF-RLS adaptive equalizer, RLS-based FAE and LMS-based FAE in term of steady-state BER.

Example 2. Next, we incorporate some linguistic information about the decision region into the fuzzy adaptive equalizers. For EKFAE and LMS-based FAE, the first M = 25 training data pairs are used to construct the initial fuzzy rules. In particular, the centers of the fuzzy antecedents $\tilde{x}^l = [\tilde{x}_1^l \; \tilde{x}_2^l]$ are set to the received signals $\left[x(l) \;\; x(l-1)\right]$ where $l = 1,2,\ldots,M$. Similarly, the centers of the fuzzy consequences θ^l are set to the corresponding scaled desired data, $\beta d(l)$, where $l = 1,2,\ldots,M$. In the simulation, we use $\beta = 0.5$. For RLS-based FAE, we use the same 25 training data pairs to construct the initial fuzzy rules. The centers for the fuzzy antecedents, $\tilde{x}_i^{ji}$ =-1.6, -0.8, 0, 0.8, 1.6 are fixed and will not change during the adaptation, where ji=1,2,...,5 and i=1,2. The decision region of the RLS-based FAE can be partitioned as shown in Fig. 11. Every section corresponds to a certain fuzzy rule. The initial fuzzy rules can be constructed as follows: if the equalizer inputs $\left[x(l) \;\; x(l-1)\right]$ fall in the region that corresponds to the rule $R^{(j1,j2)}$, then set the center of the fuzzy consequence $\theta^{(j1,j2)}$ to the corresponding scaled desired data, $\beta d(l)$. For the region that the 25 received signal does not fall in, we choose $\theta^{(j1,j2)}$ arbitrarily in [-0.3 0.3]. Other parameters remain the same as in *Example 1.* When signal to noise ratio equals to 10 dB, we plot the convergence curves for the three equalizers in Fig. 13. Around 30 times of experiments were simulated in order to obtain the convergence curves. The simulation results show that by incorporating some noisy linguistic information about the decision region into the equalizers, the convergence rates of the three fuzzy adaptive equalizers are greatly improved. We observed that EKFAE achieves the fastest convergence and lowest steady-state BER compared with the LMS-based FAE and RLS-based FAE.

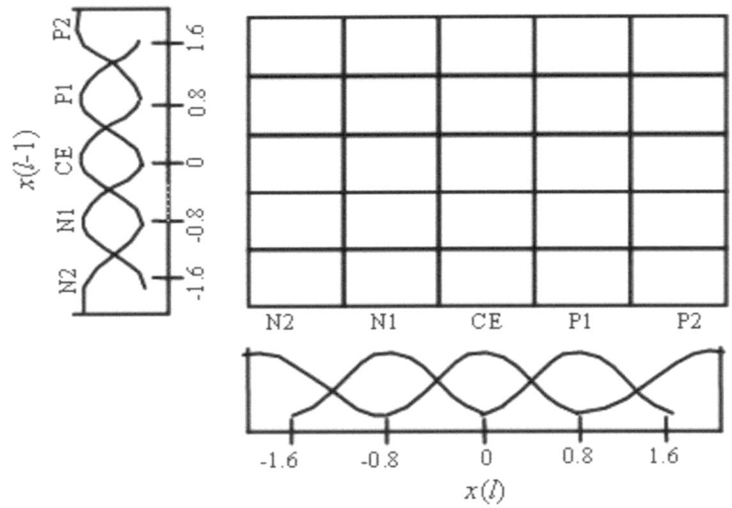

Fig. 11. Construction of fuzzy rules for the fuzzy RLS-based FAE.

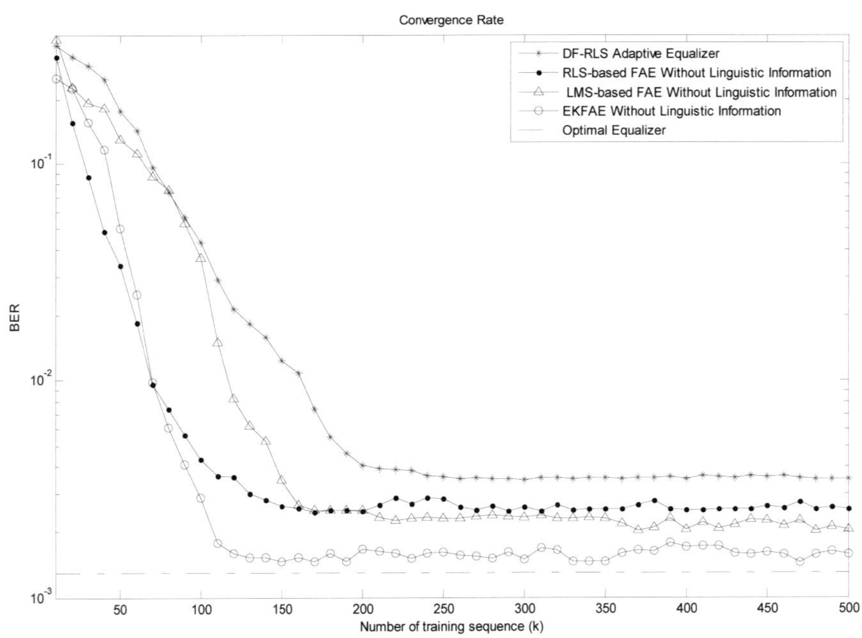

Fig. 12. Convergence rate for DF-RLS adaptive equalizers and 3 types of fuzzy adaptive equalizers without linguistic information.

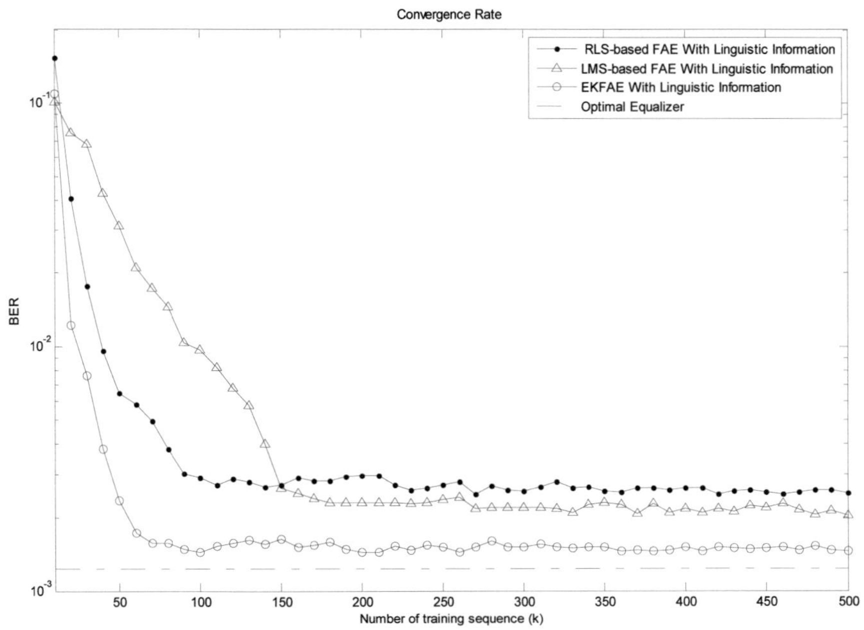

Fig. 13. Convergence rate for 3 types of fuzzy adaptive equalizers with linguistic information.

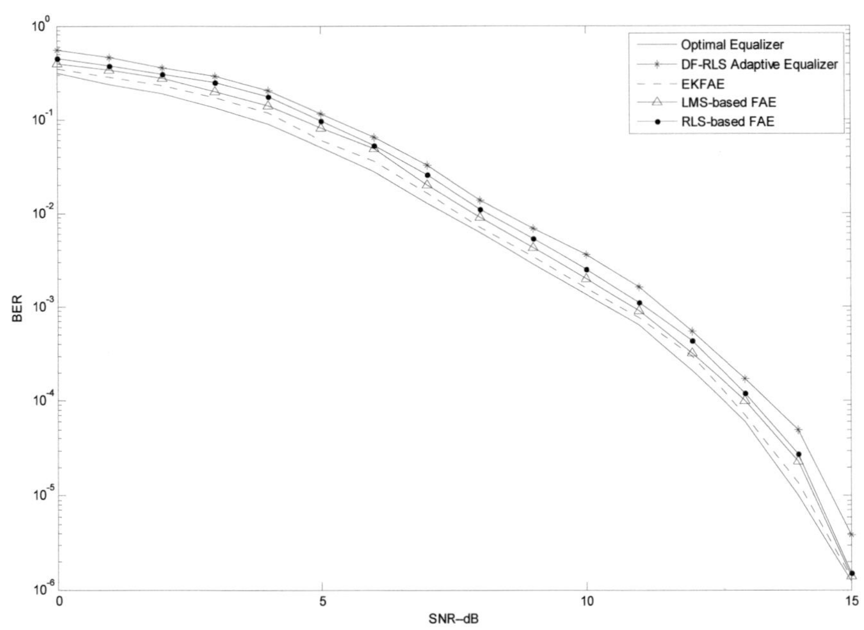

Fig. 14. The bit error rate vs. signal to noise ratio plots of DF-RLS equalizer, EKFAE, RLS-based FAE, LMS-based FAE, and the optimal MAP equalizer

Example 3. Finally, the bit error rates of DF-RLS adaptive equalizer, EKFAE, LMS-based FAE and RLS-based FAE are compared with the maximum-a-posteriori probability (MAP) equalizer that has the minimum probability of error. Fig. 14 shows the bit error rates of the optimum MAP equalizer and the EKFAE for different signal to noise ratios. We see that the bit error rate of the EKFAE is the closest to the optimal one.

10. Computational complexity

In this section, we study the computational complexity of the DF-RLS adaptive equalizer and the three FAEs (i.e., RLS, LMS and EKF based FAEs). During the training process of DF-RLS adaptive equalizer, LMS-based FAE, RLS-based FAE and EKFAE, the computational requirement for one training iteration is summarized and listed in Table 2..

The computational requirements for the adaptive equalizers are dependent on the order of the equalizers (N_f and N_b for DF-RLS adaptive equalizer and n for FAEs) and the number of rules ($m^n = m_1.m_2.....m_n$ for RLS-based FAE and M for LMS-based FAE and EKFAE). If we set the adaptive equalizer with the same order (N_f+N_b = n), then N_f+N_b << m^n and M. Hence from Table 2, we can see that DF-RLS adaptive equalizer has the least time complexity among the adaptive equalizers. The computational complexity of the LMS based FAE is on the order of O(nM) while EKFAE is on the order of O(nM^2) during training. EKFAE has higher time complexity compared to LMS based FAE. RLS based FAE is on the order of O(m^{2n}). If we set m^n = M, then RLS based FAE is on the order of (O(M^2)). Among the three FAEs, EKFAE has the high computational requirement for training process (O(nM^2)), followed by RLS based FAE (O(M^2)),whereas LMS-based FAE has the lowest computational requirement for training process (O(nM)) .

After DF-RLS adaptive equalizer, LMS-based FAE, RLS-based FAE and EKFAE complete their training, their parameters are fixed and the actual estimation for desired symbol goes on. The computational complexity per estimated symbol for the above equalizers is listed in Table 3. From Table 3, DF-RLS adaptive equalizer has the least time complexity if N_f+ N_b = n. We can observe that both LMS based FAE and EKFAE are in the same time complexity category (O(nM)) in symbol estimation after the training process stopped. Since m^n = M, RLS based FAE with O(nm^n) is in the same time complexity category with EKFAE (O(nM)) for symbol estimation. We can conclude that the DF-RLS adaptive has the least time complexity, whereas the three FAEs are in the same time complexity category involved for estimation of one desired symbol if we set N_f+ N_b = n, m=m_1=m_2=…=m_n >1 and m^n = M.

Equalizer Type	Addition/Subtraction	Multiplication	Division	e^{-x}
DF-RLS adaptive equalizer	$4(N_f+N_b)^2+(N_f+N_b)$	$5(N_f+N_b)^2+6(N_f+N_b)-1$	2	0
RLS-based FAE	$4m^{2n}+(1+n)m^n-1$	$5m^{2n}+(6+3n)m^n$	$(1+n)m^n+2$	nm^n
LMS-based FAE	$(9n+4)M-2$	$(16n+2)M$	$(5n+1)M+1$	nM
EKFAE	$(8n+4)M^2+(3n+2)M-2$	$(8n+4)M^2+(21n+3)M$	$(5n+1)M+2n+2$	nM

Table 2. Computational requirements for DF-RLS adaptive equalizer, RLS-based FAE and EKFAE for 1 training iteration.

Equalizer Type	Addition/Subtraction	Multiplication	Division	e^{-x}
DF-RLS adaptive equalizer	N_f+N_b-1	N_f+N_b	0	0
RLS based FAE	$(n+2)m^n-2$	$(3n+3)m^n$	$(n+1)m^n$	nm^n
LMS-based FAE	$(n+2)M-2$	$4nM$	$nM+1$	nM
EKFAE	$(n+2)M-2$	$4nM$	$nM+1$	nM

Table 3. Computational requirements for DF-RLS adaptive equalizer, RLS-based FAE and EKFAE per desired symbol estimation

11. Number of rules

In this section, we investigate the number of rules required for the FAEs. The design parameters of the proposed equalizer are the number of fuzzy IF-THEN rules, M, and the initial values of the parameters $\tilde{\mathbf{X}}$, $\boldsymbol{\sigma}$ and $\boldsymbol{\theta}$. If the channel impulse response is known at the receiver, the exact number of rules, M can be calculated as:

$$M = 2^{L+n} \tag{1.69}$$

where L is the ISI span (in bits) and n denotes the order of the equalizer. The ISI span, L, depends on the length of the channel impulse response, N, and the length of the spreading sequence, N_s. For $N = 1$, $L = 1$; for $1 < N \leq N_s + 1$, $L = 2$; for $N_s + 1 < N \leq 2N_s + 1$, $L = 3$; and so on. We shall look at one example.

Consider a channel with impulse response $h(z) = 1 + 0.5z^{-1} + 0.3z^{-2} - 0.1z^{-3}$. The spreading sequence is [1 1 -1 1]. The order and lag of the EKFAE are $n = 2$ and $d = 0$, respectively. In this case, the number of noiseless equalizer input signal states is $M = 2^{2+2} = 16$. Fig. 15a shows the noiseless signal states. When noise is added, the equalizer inputs form 16 clusters with centers equal to the noiseless states. The noisy signal states are illustrated in Fig. 15b. Since there are 16 clusters and one fuzzy rule is required to cater for one cluster, a total of 16 fuzzy rules are needed. It is shown in (Patra, S.K., 1998) that the FAE is optimal when the number of rules is equal to the number of noiseless states, and the parameters, $\tilde{\mathbf{x}}$, $\boldsymbol{\sigma}$ and $\boldsymbol{\theta}$, are set to the locations of the noiseless states, the standard deviation of the noise, and the corresponding desired data symbols of the noiseless states, respectively.

However, in practice, the channel impulse response is unknown at the receiver. To determine a suitable number of rules for the EKFAE, the channel impulse response has to be estimated first. Next, by using the same channel as above, we study the effects of the channel estimation on the performance of the EKFAE. The BER performances of the EKFAE in different channel conditions are plotted against the estimated initial rules in Fig. 16. When the number of rules is 16 the equalizer achieves the optimum performance. Also, when the number of rules is more than 10, the BER performance is very near to optimum. The general conclusion is, the number of rules need not be equal to the optimum number of rules exactly. Consequently, the EKFAE is robust against the channel estimation error. From our experience, using 70% of the optimum number of rules is often sufficient to give good results.

When the channel is unknown, the initial values of the parameters $\tilde{\mathbf{X}}$, $\boldsymbol{\sigma}$ and $\boldsymbol{\theta}$, are set randomly in their valid range. Then, these parameters are optimized by the EKF adaptation algorithm in the MMSE sense. From extensive experiments, the EKFAE never failed to converge with random initial values. However, faster convergence can be achieved if some knowledge about the channel is incorporated into the setting of the initial parameter values.

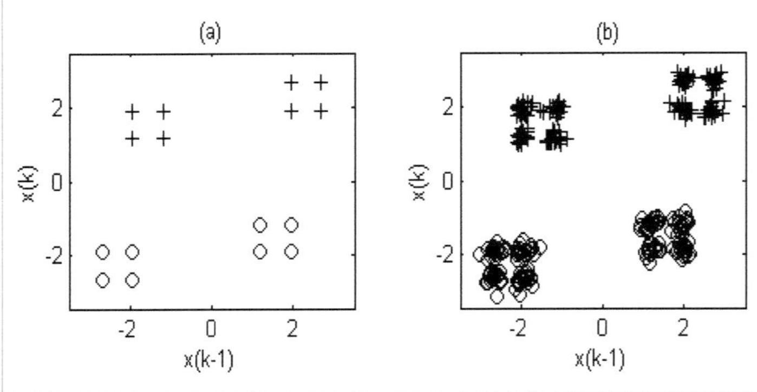

Fig. 15. Equalizer input signal states. The "+" and "o" denote the signals corresponding to "+1" and "-1" desired data bits, respectively. (a) Noiseless states. (b) Noisy states.

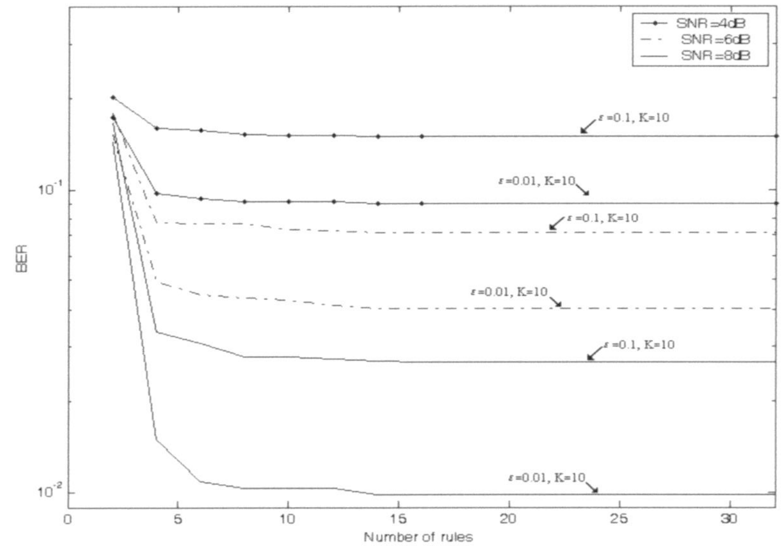

Fig. 16. The BER performances of the EKFAE in different SNRs versus number of initial rules

12. Summary

Fundamentals of fuzzy logic, fuzzy logic system, equalizer, adaptive equalizer and fuzzy adaptive equalizer are described in this chapter. A new fuzzy adaptive equalizer with extended Kalman filter adaptation (EKFAE) had been derived in this chapter for communication channel equalization. The merits of EKFAE as compared with three other types of short listed adaptive equalizers, namely: decision feedback recursive least-squares adaptive equalizer, recursive least squares (RLS) based FAE and least mean squares (LMS) based FAE are faster convergent speed and lower steady state BER. Simulation results in

Section 1.9 show that EKFAE converges fastest without using any linguistic information. By incorporating some linguistic rules about the equalizer inputs into EKFAE, the adaptation speed is greatly improved. The steady state BER of EKFAE is very close to that of the optimal equalizer. The computational requirements for those adaptive equalizers in consideration (DF-RLS adaptive equalizer, RLS, LMS and EKF based FAEs) are calculated out. The number of rules required for the FAEs are also investigated.

13. References

Al-Holou, N. T., Lahdhiri, Joo, D., Weaver, J., Al-Abbas, F. (2002). Sliding mode neural network inference fuzzy logic control for active suspension systems. *IEEE Trans. on Fuzzy Syst.*.p.p.234-247.

Bhatti, S. S. (2002). What is neuro fuzzy-logic? *The Tribune (Chandigarh, India).*

Chen, S., Gibson, G.J., Cowan, C.F.N., Grant, P.M. (1990). Adaptive Equalization of Finite Nonlinear Channels Using Multilayer Perceptrons. *Signal Processing, Vol. 20,* p.p.107-119.

Chen, S., Gibson, G. J., Cowan, C. F. N., Grant, P. M. (1991). Reconstruction of binary signals using an adaptive radial-basis-function equalizer. *Signal Processing, Vol. 22.* p.p.77-93.

Cowan, C. F. N., Grant, P. M. (1985). Adaptive Filters. *Englewood Cliffs, NJ: Prentice Hall.*

Eichfeld, H., Kunermund, T., Menke, M. (1996). A 12b general-purpose fuzzy logic controller chip. *IEEE Trans. on Fuzzy Syst., Vol. 4.* p.p.460-475.

Gupta, M. M., Qi, J. (1991). Theory of T-norms and fuzzy inference methods. *Fuzzy sets and systems, Vol. 40.* p.p.431-450.

Gupta, M. M., Rao, D. H. (1994a). Neuro-Control Systems: Theory and Applications. *IEEE Press, NJ.*

Gupta, M. M., Rao, D. H. (1994b). On the principles of fuzzy neural networks. *Fuzzy sets and systems, Vol. 61.* p.p.1-18.

Gupta, M. M., Jin, L., Homma, N. (2003). Static And Dynamic Neural Networks, From Fundamentals to Advanced Theory. *IEEE Press, John Wiley & Sons Inc.*

Haykin, S. (2002). Adaptive Filter Theory. *4th Ed. Prentice Hall.*

Jang, J. S. R., Sun, C. T. (1993). Functional equivalence between radial basis-function networks and fuzzy inference systems. *IEEE Trans. on Neural Networks 4(1).* p.p.156-159.

Kallman, H. J. (1940). Transversal filters. *Proc. IRE, Vol. 28.* p.p.302-310.

Kalman, R. E. (1960). A new Approach to Linear Filtering and Prediction Problems. *Trans. of the ASME, Journal of Basic Engineering, Vol. 82.* p.p.35-45.

Kaufmann, A., Gupta, M. M. (1988). Fuzzy Mathematical Models in Engineering and Management Science. *Elsevier, Amsterdan.*

Kay, S. M. (1993). Fundamentals Of Statistical Signal Processing: Estimation Theory. *Prentice Hall Signal Processing Series, Vol. 1.* p.p.419-477.

Kong, X., Han, C., Wei, R. (2004). A Stable Total Least Square Adaptive Algorithm for the Nonlinear Volterra Filter. *The 7th International Conference on Information Fusion, Stockholm, Sweden, Jun 28- July 1,2004.* p.p.518-522.

Mastorakis, N. E. (2004). Modeling Dynamical Systems via the Takagi-Sugeno Fuzzy Model. *Procs. of the 4th WSEAS Int. Conf. on Fuzzy sets and Fuzzy Systems, Udine, Italy.*

Mathews, V. J. (1991). Adaptive polynomial filters. *IEEE Signal Processing Magazine, Vol.8, No.3,* p.p.10-26.

Meisel, W. S. (1969). Potential functions in mathematical pattern recognition. *IEEE Trans. Comput., Vol. 18, No. 10.* p.p.911-918.

Mendel, J. M. (1995). Fuzzy Logic Systems for Engineering: A Tutorial. *Proceedings of the IEEE, Vol. 83, No. 3.* p.p.345-377.

Mendel , J. M., Mouzouris, G. C. (1997). Designing Fuzzy Logic Systems. *IEEE Trans. on Circuits and Systems II : Analog and Digital Signal Processing, Vol.44, No.11.*

Patra, S. K., Mulgrew B. (1998). Efficient architecture for Bayesian Equalization Using Fuzzy Filters. *IEEE Trans. Circuits and Systems-II: Analog and Digital Signal Processing, Vol. 45.* p.p.812-820.

Powell, M. J. D. (1987). Radial basis functions for multivariable interpolation: A review. *Algorithms for Approximation, J. C. Mason and M. G. Cox, Eds. Oxford: Oxford University Press.* p.p.143-167.

Proakis, J. G. (1995). Digital Communications. *3rd ed. New York: McGraw-Hill.*

Sailer, T.M. (2001). Decision Feedback Equalization for Powerline and HIPERLAN. *PhD thesis, Swiss Federal Institute of Technology Zurich. Diss. ETH No. 13970.*

Seung, S. (2002). Multilayer perceptrons and backpropagation learning. *9.641 Lecture4.* 1-6. Source from: http://hebb.mit.edu/courses/9.641/2002/lectures/lecture04.pdf

Tanaka, K., Sugeno, M. (1998). Introduction to fuzzy modeling. *Fuzzy Syst. Modeling and Control, H. T. Nguyen and M. Sugeno, Eds. Boston, MA: Kluwer.* p.p.63-89.

Wang, L. X. (1992a). Fuzzy systems are universal approximators. *Proc. IEEE Conf. Fuzzy Systems (San Diego).* p.p.1163-1170.

Wang, L. X., Mendel, J. M. (1992b). Fuzzy Basis Function, Universal Approximation, and Orthogonal Least Squares Learning. *IEEE Trans. on Neural Networks, Vol. 3, No. 5.* p.p.807-814.

Wang, L. X., Mendel, J. M. (1993). Fuzzy Adaptive Filters, with Application to Nonlinear Channel Equalization. *IEEE Trans. On Fuzzy Systems, Vol. 1, No. 3.* p.p.161-170.

Zadeh, L. A. (1965). Fuzzy sets. *Information and Control 8.* p.p.338-353.

Zadeh, L. A. (1975). The concept of a linguistic variable and its application to approximate reasoning. *Information Sciences, Vol. 8.* p.p.199-249.

Appendix 1:

Derivation of Extended Kalman Filter based adaptation algorithm for fuzzy adaptive equalizer.

$$\text{Let} \quad a^l(k-1) = \prod_{i=1}^{\eta} \exp\left[-\frac{1}{2}\left(\frac{x_i(k)-\tilde{x}_i^l(k-1)}{\sigma_i^l(k-1)}\right)^2\right] \tag{A1.1}$$

$$b(k-1) = \sum_{l=1}^{M} a^l(k-1) \tag{A1.2}$$

$$c^l(k-1) = \frac{\left(x_i - \tilde{x}_i^l\right)^2}{\left(\sigma_i^l\right)^3} \tag{A1.3}$$

$$e^l(k-1) = \frac{\left(x_i - \tilde{x}_i^l\right)}{\left(\sigma_i^l\right)^2} \tag{A1.4}$$

Therefore, the equalizer output as from equation (1.52) becomes:

$$f_k(x(k)) = \frac{\sum_{l=1}^{M} \theta^l \left(\prod_{i=1}^{\eta} \mu_{F_i^l}(x_i)\right)}{\sum_{l=1}^{M}\left(\prod_{i=1}^{\eta} \mu_{F_i^l}(x_i)\right)} = \frac{\sum_{l=1}^{M} \theta^l \left(\prod_{i=1}^{\eta} \exp\left[-\frac{1}{2}\left(\frac{x_i - \tilde{x}_i^l}{\sigma_i^l}\right)^2\right]\right)}{\sum_{l=1}^{M}\left(\prod_{i=1}^{\eta} \exp\left[-\frac{1}{2}\left(\frac{x_i - \tilde{x}_i^l}{\sigma_i^l}\right)^2\right]\right)} = \frac{\sum_{l=1}^{M} \theta^l a^l(k-1)}{b(k-1)} \tag{A1.5}$$

The computation of the Jacobian $\Omega(k)$ requires the evolution of the partial derivatives of $f_k(x(k))$ vs. the parameters of the fuzzy network:

$$\Omega_{\theta^l} = \frac{\partial f_k(x(k))}{\partial \theta^l} = \frac{\partial}{\partial \theta^l}\left(\frac{\sum_{l=1}^{M}\theta^l a^l(k-1)}{b(k-1)}\right) = \frac{a^l(k-1)}{b(k-1)} \tag{A1.6}$$

$$\Omega_{\sigma_i^l} = \frac{\partial f_k(x(k))}{\partial \sigma_i^l} = \frac{\partial f_k(x(k))}{\partial \mu_{F_i^l}} \times \frac{\partial \mu_{F_i^l}}{\partial \sigma_i^l}$$

since
$$\frac{\partial f_k(x(k))}{\partial \mu_{F_i^l}} = \frac{\partial}{\partial \mu_{F_i^l}}\left(\frac{\sum_{l=1}^{M}\theta^l \prod_{j=1}^{\eta}\mu_{F_j^l}}{\sum_{l=1}^{M}\prod_{j=1}^{\eta}\mu_{F_j^l}}\right) = \frac{\sum_{l=1}^{M}\prod_{j=1}^{\eta}\mu_{F_j^l}\,\theta^l \prod_{\substack{j\neq i\\ j=1}}^{\eta}\mu_{F_j^l} - \sum_{l=1}^{M}\theta^l \prod_{j=1}^{\eta}\mu_{F_j^l}\prod_{\substack{j\neq i\\ j=1}}^{\eta}\mu_{F_j^l}}{\left(\sum_{l=1}^{M}\prod_{j=1}^{\eta}\mu_{F_j^l}\right)^2}$$

$$= \frac{\prod_{\substack{j\neq i\\ j=1}}^{\eta}\mu_{F_j^l}\left[\theta^l\left(\sum_{l=1}^{M}\prod_{j=1}^{\eta}\mu_{F_j^l}\right) - \sum_{l=1}^{M}\theta^l\prod_{j=1}^{\eta}\mu_{F_j^l}\right]}{\left(\sum_{l=1}^{M}\prod_{j=1}^{\eta}\mu_{F_j^l}\right)^2} = \frac{\prod_{\substack{j\neq i\\ j=1}}^{\eta}\mu_{F_j^l}}{\sum_{l=1}^{M}\prod_{j=1}^{\eta}\mu_{F_j^l}}\left[\theta^l - f_k(x(k))\right]$$

and
$$\frac{\partial \mu_{F_i^l}}{\partial \sigma_i^l} = \frac{\partial}{\partial \sigma_i^l}\left(\exp\left[-\frac{1}{2}\left(\frac{x_i-\tilde{x}_i^l}{\sigma_i^l}\right)^2\right]\right)$$

$$\frac{\partial \mu_{F_i^l}}{\partial \sigma_i^l} = \exp\left[-\frac{1}{2}\left(\frac{x_i-\tilde{x}_i^l}{\sigma_i^l}\right)^2\right] \times \frac{\partial}{\partial \sigma_i^l}\left(-\frac{1}{2}\left(\frac{x_i-\tilde{x}_i^l}{\sigma_i^l}\right)^2\right)$$

$$= \exp\left[-\frac{1}{2}\left(\frac{x_i-\tilde{x}_i^l}{\sigma_i^l}\right)^2\right] \times \left(-\frac{1}{2}\right) \times \left(x_i-\tilde{x}_i^l\right)^2 \times \frac{\partial}{\partial \sigma_i^l}\left(\frac{1}{\left(\sigma_i^l\right)^2}\right)$$

$$= \frac{\left(x_i-\tilde{x}_i^l\right)^2}{\left(\sigma_i^l\right)^3}\exp\left[-\frac{1}{2}\left(\frac{x_i-\tilde{x}_i^l}{\sigma_i^l}\right)^2\right] = \mu_{F_i^l}\frac{\left(x_i-\tilde{x}_i^l\right)^2}{\left(\sigma_i^l\right)^3}$$

Therefore,

$$\Omega_{\sigma_i^l} = \frac{\prod_{\substack{j\neq i\\ j=1}}^{\eta}\mu_{F_j^l}}{\sum_{l=1}^{M}\prod_{j=1}^{\eta}\mu_{F_j^l}} \times \left[\theta^l - f_k(x(k))\right] \times \mu_{F_i^l} \times \frac{\left(x_i-\tilde{x}_i^l\right)^2}{\left(\sigma_i^l\right)^3} = \frac{\left[\theta^l - f_k(x(k))\right]\prod_{j=1}^{\eta}\mu_{F_j^l}\,\frac{\left(x_i-\tilde{x}_i^l\right)^2}{\left(\sigma_i^l\right)^3}}{\sum_{l=1}^{M}\prod_{j=1}^{\eta}\mu_{F_j^l}}$$

$$=\frac{\left[\theta^l - f_k(x(k))\right]a^l(k-1)c^l(k-1)}{b(k-1)} \tag{A1.7}$$

$$\Omega_{\tilde{x}_i^l} = \frac{\partial f_k(x(k))}{\partial \tilde{x}_i^l} = \frac{\partial f_k(x(k))}{\partial \mu_{F_i^l}} \times \frac{\partial \mu_{F_i^l}}{\partial \tilde{x}_i^l}$$

since $\dfrac{\partial f_k(x(k))}{\partial \mu_{F_i^l}} = \dfrac{\prod_{\substack{j\neq i \\ j=1}}^{\eta} \mu_{F_j^l}}{\sum_{l=1}^{M} \mu_{F_j^l}} \left[\theta^l - f_k(x(k))\right]$

and
$$\frac{\partial}{\partial \tilde{x}_i^l}\left(\exp\left[-\frac{1}{2}\left(\frac{x_i-\tilde{x}_i^l}{\sigma_i^l}\right)^2\right]\right) = \exp\left[-\frac{1}{2}\left(\frac{x_i-\tilde{x}_i^l}{\sigma_i^l}\right)^2\right] \times \frac{\partial}{\partial \tilde{x}_i^l}\left(-\frac{1}{2}\left(\frac{x_i-\tilde{x}_i^l}{\sigma_i^l}\right)^2\right)$$

$$= \exp\left[-\frac{1}{2}\left(\frac{x_i-\tilde{x}_i^l}{\sigma_i^l}\right)^2\right] \times \left(-\frac{1}{2\left(\sigma_i^l\right)^2}\right) \times \frac{\partial}{\partial \tilde{x}_i^l}\left(x_i-\tilde{x}_i^l\right)^2$$

$$= \exp\left[-\frac{1}{2}\left(\frac{x_i-\tilde{x}_i^l}{\sigma_i^l}\right)^2\right] \frac{\left(x_i-\tilde{x}_i^l\right)}{\left(\sigma_i^l\right)^2}$$

$$= \mu_{F_i^l} \frac{\left(x_i - x_i^l\right)}{\left(\sigma_i^l\right)^2}$$

Therefore,

$$\Omega_{\tilde{x}_i^l} = \frac{\prod_{\substack{j\neq i \\ j=1}}^{\eta} \mu_{F_j^l}}{\sum_{l=1}^{M}\prod_{j=1}^{\eta} \mu_{F_j^l}} \times \left[\theta^l - f_k(x(k))\right] \times \mu_{F_j^l} \times \frac{\left(x_i-\tilde{x}_i^l\right)}{\left(\sigma_i^l\right)^2}$$

$$= \frac{\left[\theta^l - f_k(x(k))\right]\prod_{j=1}^{\eta} \mu_{F_j^l} \dfrac{\left(x_i-\tilde{x}_i^l\right)}{\left(\sigma_i^l\right)^2}}{\sum_{l=1}^{M}\prod_{j=1}^{\eta} \mu_{F_j^l}}$$

$$= \frac{\left[\theta^l - f_k(x(k))\right]a^l(k-1)e^l(k-1)}{b(k-1)} \tag{A1.8}$$

5

Adaptive Robust Extended Kalman Filter

Kai Xiong[1], Hongyue Zhang[2] and Liangdong Liu[1]
[1]*National Laboratory of Space Intelligent Control, Beijing Institute of Control Engineering,*
[2]*School of Automation Science and Electrical Engineering, Beihang University, China*

1. Introduction

The extended Kalman filter (EKF) is one of the most widely used methods for state estimation with communication and aerospace applications based on its apparent simplicity and tractability (Shi et al., 2002; Bolognani et al., 2003; Wu et al., 2004). However, for an EKF to guarantee satisfactory performance, the system model should be known exactly. Unknown external disturbances may result in the inaccuracy of the state estimate, even cause divergence.

This difficulty has been recognized in the literature (Reif & Unbehauen, 1999; Reif et al., 2000), and several schemes have been developed to overcome it. A traditional approach to improve the performance of the filter is the 'covariance setting' technique, where a positive definite estimation error covariance matrix is chosen by the filter designer (Einicke et al., 2003; Bolognani et al., 2003). As it is difficult to manually tune the covariance matrix for dynamic system, adaptive extended Kalman filter (AEKF) approaches for online estimation of the covariance matrix have been adopted (Kim & ILTIS, 2004; Yu et al., 2005; Ahn & Won, 2006). However, only in some special cases, the optimal estimation of the covariance matrix can be obtained. And inaccurate approximation of the covariance matrix may blur the state estimate.

Recently, the robust H_∞ filter has received considerable attention (Theodor et al., 1994; Shen & Deng, 1999; Zhang et al., 2005; Tseng & Chen, 2001). The robust filters take different forms depending on what kind of disturbances are accounted for, while the general performance criterion of the filters is to guarantee a bounded energy gain from the worst possible disturbance to the estimation error. Although the robust extended Kalman filter (REKF) has been deeply investigated (Einicke & White, 1999; Reif et al., 1999; Seo et al., 2006), how to prescribe the level of disturbances attenuation is still an open problem. In general, the selection of the attenuation level can be seen as a tradeoff between the optimality and the robustness. In other words, the robustness of the REKF is obtained at the expense of optimality.

This chapter reviews the adaptive robust extended Kalman filter (AREKF), an effective algorithm which will remain stable in the presence of unknown disturbances, and yield accurate estimates in the absence of disturbances (Xiong et al., 2008). The key idea of the AREKF is to design the estimator based on the stability analysis, and determine whether the error covariance matrix should be reset according to the magnitude of the innovation.

Further analysis shows that the filter can guarantee boundedness of the estimation error despite the unknown disturbances as well as the linearization error. Unlike the AEKF, the calculated innovation is not adopted directly to tune the error covariance matrix, but used as an indicator of the necessity of resetting the covariance matrix, so that the covariance matrix will be reset only when large disturbance occurs. The AREKF can be seen as a REKF with time-varying attenuation level. In comparison with the REKF, the advantage of the AREKF is that the robust behavior is achieved without decreasing accuracy. In addition, no complicated computation procedures are required to implement the AREKF.

The AREKF particularly suits for state estimation in nonlinear stochastic system with large external disturbance. This chapter describes the application of the algorithm to autonomous astronomical navigation for orbit maneuvering spacecraft. The problem is to determine the position vector of the spacecraft according to the spacecraft dynamic model and the measurements from the earth sensor and the star sensor. We consider the case in which the spacecraft performs thrust maneuvers but the unknown acceleration produced by the thruster firings is not known. The unknown acceleration, which may seriously impact the positioning accuracy, is treated as disturbances in the design of the AREKF. Numerical example shows that the AREKF outperforms the usual EKF, the REKF and the AEKF.

The structure of this chapter is as follows. In Section 2, the stability of the REKF is analyzed based on some standard results about the boundedness of stochastic processes. It is specified that the stability of the REKF is not guaranteed. In Section 3, the AREKF is derived to ensure the stability of the filter. The autonomous navigation system that consists of the earth sensor and the star sensor is described in Section 4. In Section 5, the high performance of the AREKF is illustrated through simulations in comparison with the usual EKF, the REKF and the AEKF. Some conclusions are drawn in Section 6.

2. Problem statement

2.1 REKF algorithm

The considered nonlinear discrete-time system is represented by

$$\boldsymbol{x}_t = f(\boldsymbol{x}_{t-1}) + \boldsymbol{w}_t \tag{1}$$

$$\boldsymbol{y}_t = h(\boldsymbol{x}_t) + \boldsymbol{v}_t \tag{2}$$

where $\boldsymbol{x}_t \in \boldsymbol{R}^l$ and $\boldsymbol{y}_t \in \boldsymbol{R}^m$ denote the state and measurement vectors at time instant t. $f(.)$ is a function that describes the dynamics of the state vector. $h(.)$ is a function that describes the relation between the state vector and the measurement vector. The function $f(.)$ and $h(.)$ are assumed to be continuously differentiable. w_t and v_t are uncorrelated zero mean white noise processes with covariance matrices $\boldsymbol{Q}_t$ and $\boldsymbol{R}_t$ respectively.

The structure of the standard REKF algorithm is presented as follows (Einicke & White, 1999):

Prediction: The one-step prediction of $\hat{\boldsymbol{x}}_{t|t-1}$ and its corresponding error covariance matrix $\boldsymbol{\Sigma}_{t|t-1}$ are

$$\hat{\boldsymbol{x}}_{t|t-1} = f(\hat{\boldsymbol{x}}_{t-1}) \tag{3}$$

$$P_{t|t-1} = F_t P_{t-1} F_t^T + Q_t \tag{4}$$

$$\Sigma_{t|t-1} = (P_{t|t-1}^{-1} - \gamma^{-2} L_t^T L_t)^{-1} \tag{5}$$

where $F_t = \left.\frac{\partial f(x)}{\partial x}\right|_{x=\hat{x}_{t-1}}$ is the Jacobian matrix of $f(x_{t-1})$, $L_t \in R^{l \times l}$ is designed as identity matrix I, and the tuning parameter γ is found by searching over $\gamma \neq 0$ such that $\Sigma_{t|t-1} > 0$.

Update: The estimate of state $\hat{x}_t$ and the estimation error covariance matrix P_t are

$$\hat{x}_t = \hat{x}_{t|t-1} + K_t[y_t - h(\hat{x}_{t|t-1})] \tag{6}$$

$$K_t = \Sigma_{t|t-1} H_t^T P_{y,t}^{-1} \tag{7}$$

$$P_{y,t} = H_t \Sigma_{t|t-1} H_t^T + R_t \tag{8}$$

$$P_t = (\Sigma_{t|t-1}^{-1} + H_t^T R_t^{-1} H_t)^{-1} \tag{9}$$

where $H_t = \left.\frac{\partial h(x)}{\partial x}\right|_{x=\hat{x}_{t|t-1}}$ is the Jacobian matrix of $h(x_t)$.

Apparently, the structure of the REKF is similar to that of the EKF, and if $\gamma \to \infty$, the REKF reverts to the EKF. The design objective of the REKF is to guarantee the norm of the transfer function between the estimation error and the external disturbances (modeling errors and system noises) to be less than a prescribed attenuation level γ

$$\frac{\|L_t \tilde{x}_t\|^2}{\|w_t\|^2 + \|\Delta_t\|^2 + \|v_t\|^2} \leq \gamma^2 \tag{10}$$

where $\|x\|$ is 2-norm of vector x, $\tilde{x}_t = x_t - \hat{x}_t$ is the estimation error, and Δ_t represents the model error caused by the linearization error or unknown exogenous inputs.

It can be seen from (10) that the tuning parameter γ in (5) describes the ability of the filter to minimize the effects of the disturbances on the estimation errors. Decreasing γ will enhance robustness of the filter. However, as is pointed out in (Einicke & White, 1999), when a minimum possible γ is adopted, the accuracy of the filter will be decreased. Another limitation of the REKF will be specified in the next sub-section.

2.2 Stability analysis

The stability analysis of the REKF is based on the following lemma. The inequalities with random variables in this paper hold with probability one.

Lemma 1: Assume that ξ_t is the stochastic process and there is a stochastic process $V(\xi_t)$ as well as the real numbers $v_{\min} > 0$, $v_{\max} > 0$, $\mu > 0$ and $0 < \lambda \leq 1$ such that $\forall t$

$$v_{\min}\left\|\xi_t\right\|^2 \le V(\xi_t) \le v_{\max}\left\|\xi_t\right\|^2 \tag{10}$$

and

$$E[V(\xi_t) \mid \xi_{t-1}] - V(\xi_{t-1}) \le \mu - \lambda V(\xi_{t-1}) \tag{11}$$

are fulfilled. Then the stochastic process ξ_t is bounded in mean square, i.e.

$$E\{\left\|\xi_t\right\|^2\} \le \frac{v_{\max}}{v_{\min}} E\{\left\|\xi_0\right\|^2\}(1-\lambda)^t + \frac{\mu}{v_{\min}} \sum_{i=1}^{t-1}(1-\lambda)^i \tag{12}$$

The proof of Lemma 1 is given in (Reif & Unbehauen, 1999; Tarn & Rasis, 1976).
During the stability analysis, the Lyapunov function $V(\xi_t)$ that represents the energy of ξ_t should be chosen by the user. Certainly, a properly chosen $V(\xi_t)$ may facilitate the analysis. The numbers v_{min} and v_{max} define the low bound and the upper bound of $V(\xi_t)$ respectively. The lemma specified that if the difference between the conditional expectations of $V(\xi_t)$ and $V(\xi_{t-1})$ is not larger than a positive constant μ minus the product of $V(\xi_{t-1})$ and another constant λ, then ξ_t will be bounded. Intuitively, if the condition (11) is fulfilled, the energy of ξ_t will not increase arbitrarily.
The prediction error of the REKF is defined as

$$\tilde{\boldsymbol{x}}_{t|t-1} = \boldsymbol{x}_t - \hat{\boldsymbol{x}}_{t|t-1} \tag{13}$$

Substitute (1) and (3) into (13), the prediction error can be written as

$$\tilde{\boldsymbol{x}}_{t|t-1} = f(\boldsymbol{x}_{t-1}) + \boldsymbol{w}_t - f(\hat{\boldsymbol{x}}_{t-1}) \tag{14}$$

Then the predication error of the REKF is transformed to an equivalent formulation that is easy to handle

$$\tilde{\boldsymbol{x}}_{t|t-1} = \boldsymbol{\beta}_t \boldsymbol{F}_t \tilde{\boldsymbol{x}}_{t-1} + \boldsymbol{w}_t \tag{15}$$

where $\boldsymbol{\beta}_t = diag(\beta_{1,t},\cdots,\beta_{l,t})$ is unknown time-varying matrix used to scale the prediction error caused by the linearization error and the unknown exogenous inputs. Similar formulation has been used in (Boutayeb & Aubry, 1999) and (Xiong et al., 2006) to analyze the stability of the EKF and the UKF respectively. Using (17), the real error covariance matrix of the prediction error can be approximated by

$$\begin{aligned}\overline{\boldsymbol{\Sigma}}_{t|t-1} &= E(\tilde{\boldsymbol{x}}_{t|t-1}\tilde{\boldsymbol{x}}_{t|t-1}^T \mid \tilde{\boldsymbol{x}}_{t-1}) = E[(\boldsymbol{\beta}_t \boldsymbol{F}_t \tilde{\boldsymbol{x}}_{t-1} + \boldsymbol{w}_t)(\boldsymbol{\beta}_t \boldsymbol{F}_t \tilde{\boldsymbol{x}}_{t-1} + \boldsymbol{w}_t)^T \mid \tilde{\boldsymbol{x}}_{t-1}] \\ &= \boldsymbol{\beta}_t \boldsymbol{F}_t \boldsymbol{P}_{t-1} \boldsymbol{F}_t^T \boldsymbol{\beta}_t + \boldsymbol{Q}_t \end{aligned} \tag{16}$$

With these prerequisites, the sufficient conditions to ensure stability of the REKF are demonstrated in the following theorem.
Theorem 1. Consider the nonlinear stochastic system given by (1)-(2) with linear measurement $h(\boldsymbol{x}_t) = \boldsymbol{H}_t \boldsymbol{x}_t$, and the REKF as stated by (3)-(9). Let the following assumptions hold for every $t \ge 0$

1. There are real numbers $f_{\min}$, $f_{\max}$, $\beta_{\min}$, $\beta_{\max}$, $h_{\min}$, $h_{\max}$, such that:

$$f_{\min}^2 I \le \boldsymbol{F}_t \boldsymbol{F}_t^T \le f_{\max}^2 I,\ \beta_{\min}^2 I \le \boldsymbol{\beta}_t \boldsymbol{\beta}_t^T \le \beta_{\max}^2 I,\ h_{\min}^2 I \le \boldsymbol{H}_t \boldsymbol{H}_t^T \le h_{\max}^2 I \tag{17}$$

2. There are real numbers $p_{\min}$, $p_{\max}$, $r_{\min}$, $r_{\max}$, $q_{\max}$, such that:

$$p_{\min} I \le \boldsymbol{P}_t \le p_{\max} I,\ r_{\min} I \le \boldsymbol{R}_t \le r_{\max} I,\ \boldsymbol{Q}_t \le q_{\max} I \tag{18}$$

3. The following matrix in-equation is fulfilled

$$\boldsymbol{\Sigma}_{t|t-1} > \overline{\boldsymbol{\Sigma}}_{t|t-1} \tag{19}$$

Then there are real numbers $\mu_{\max} > 0$, $0 < \lambda_{\min} \le 1$, such that

$$E\{\|\widetilde{\boldsymbol{x}}_t\|^2\} \le \frac{p_{\max}}{p_{\min}} E\{\|\widetilde{\boldsymbol{x}}_0\|^2\}(1-\lambda_{\min})^t + \frac{\mu_{\max}}{p_{\min}} \sum_{i=1}^{t-1} (1-\lambda_{\min})^i \tag{20}$$

The proof of Theorem 1 can be found in Appendix. The measurement equation is assumed to be linear to simplify the deduction. Nevertheless, the following analysis is expected to remain valid for the system with nonlinear measurement equation if the linearization error of the measurement equation is negligible.

It is clarified in Theorem 1 that under sufficient condition (17)-(19), estimation error of the REKF will remain bounded, and the effect of the initial error $\widetilde{\boldsymbol{x}}_0$ on the super-bound of $\widetilde{\boldsymbol{x}}_t$ will diminish as time goes on. In (17), the matrices $\boldsymbol{F}_t$, $\boldsymbol{\beta}_t$ and $\boldsymbol{H}_t$ are assumed to be bounded. Nevertheless, there are no limitations about the magnitude of the bounds. In general, when the REKF is used in physical processes with finite energy, it is reasonable to assume that $\boldsymbol{\beta}_t$ is bounded, and the assumption can be verified in practice. In (18), the condition $p_{\min}\boldsymbol{I} \le \boldsymbol{P}_t \le p_{\max}\boldsymbol{I}$ is related to the observability property of the linearized system and related discussion can be seen in (Reif & Unbehauen, 1999; Boutayeb & Aubry, 1999). The inequalities $r_{\min}\boldsymbol{I} \le \boldsymbol{R}_t \le r_{\max}\boldsymbol{I}$ and $\boldsymbol{Q}_t \le q_{\max}\boldsymbol{I}$ are trivially true.

Equation (19) is the key condition of Theorem 1. It can be interpreted as follows: to ensure the stability of the filter, the calculated covariance matrix $\boldsymbol{\Sigma}_{t|t-1}$ should be larger than the real one. This conclusion is similar with the traditional perspective that enlarging the covariance matrices may enhance the filter stability (Einicke et al, 2003; Bolognani et al, 2003; Boutayeb & Aubry, 1999). As unknown matrix $\boldsymbol{\beta}_t$ may be rather large in the presence of large unknown inputs, from (16), the condition (19) may be violated and stability of the filter can not be guaranteed. A remedy to this potential problem is to tune the parameter γ. From (5), with $\boldsymbol{L}_t = I$, in order for $\boldsymbol{\Sigma}_{t|t-1} - \overline{\boldsymbol{\Sigma}}_{t|t-1}$ to be positive definite, it requires

$$(\boldsymbol{P}_{t|t-1}^{-1} - \gamma^{-2}\boldsymbol{I})^{-1} - \overline{\boldsymbol{\Sigma}}_{t|t-1} > 0 \Rightarrow \boldsymbol{P}_{t|t-1}^{-1} - \overline{\boldsymbol{\Sigma}}_{t|t-1}^{-1} < \gamma^{-2}\boldsymbol{I}$$

$$\Rightarrow \gamma^{-2} > \max[\mathrm{eig}(\boldsymbol{P}_{t|t-1}^{-1} - \overline{\boldsymbol{\Sigma}}_{t|t-1}^{-1})] \tag{21}$$

where $\max[\mathrm{eig}(\boldsymbol{A})]$ denotes the minimum eigenvalue of the matrix $\boldsymbol{A}$. If $\max[\mathrm{eig}(\boldsymbol{P}_{t|t-1}^{-1} - \overline{\boldsymbol{\Sigma}}_{t|t-1}^{-1})] \le 0$, (21) is bound to be fulfilled. Otherwise, the chosen γ should satisfy

$$\gamma < \{\max[\mathrm{eig}(\boldsymbol{P}_{t|t-1}^{-1} - \overline{\boldsymbol{\Sigma}}_{t|t-1}^{-1})]\}^{-0.5} \tag{22}$$

Hence, γ should be small enough to improve the stability of the REKF. This requirement is consistent with the design criterion of the robust H_∞ filter that the prescribed attenuation level γ should be as small as possible (Tseng & Chen, 2001). However, in order for the error covariance matrix $\boldsymbol{\Sigma}_{t|t-1}$ to be positive definite, it requires

$$\boldsymbol{P}_{t|t-1}^{-1} - \gamma^{-2}\boldsymbol{I} > 0 \Rightarrow \gamma > \{\max[\mathrm{eig}(\boldsymbol{P}_{t|t-1})]\}^{0.5} \tag{23}$$

Obviously, if $\{\max[\mathrm{eig}(\boldsymbol{P}_{t|t-1})]\}^{0.5} > \{\max[\mathrm{eig}(\boldsymbol{P}_{t|t-1}^{-1} - \overline{\boldsymbol{\Sigma}}_{t|t-1}^{-1})]\}^{-0.5}$, it will be difficult to find an appropriate γ to stabilize the filter, i.e., stability of the REKF is not guaranteed.

According to (10), for a fixed γ which is chosen to ensure $\boldsymbol{\Sigma}_{t|t-1} > 0$, the bound of the estimation error $\|\boldsymbol{L}_t\tilde{\boldsymbol{x}}_t\|^2$ will be enlarged in the presence of large linearization error or unknown exogenous inputs. And large deviation of the estimated state from the real one will further augment the linearization error. If this trend is not terminated, the filter will fail to converge. Hence, as can be seen from (23), ability of the REKF to minimize the energy of the estimation error is limited by the maximum eigenvalue of $\boldsymbol{P}_{t|t-1}$.

3. The AREKF algorithm

In order to guarantee the stability of the filter, a novel method is proposed to design the REKF. From Theorem 1, the bound of $\tilde{\boldsymbol{x}}_t$ can be controlled by enlarging the calculated covariance matrix $\boldsymbol{\Sigma}_{t|t-1}$. For the REKF, $\boldsymbol{\Sigma}_{t|t-1}$ will be enlarged by decreasing γ. However, it may be impossible to choose a suitable γ such that $\boldsymbol{\Sigma}_{t|t-1}$ is sufficiently large when $\boldsymbol{L}_t = I$. In fact, this problem can be solved if the matrix $\boldsymbol{L}_t$ in (5) is designed as

$$\boldsymbol{L}_t = \gamma(\boldsymbol{P}_{t|t-1}^{-1} - \lambda_t^{-1}\boldsymbol{P}_{t|t-1}^{-1})^{1/2} \tag{24}$$

where $(\cdot)^{1/2}$ denotes the matrix square root, and λ_t is a tuning parameter which should be large enough such that the following inequation is fulfilled

$$\overline{\boldsymbol{\Sigma}}_{t||t-1} < \lambda_t \boldsymbol{P}_{t|t-1} \tag{25}$$

With this design, the difficulty of tuning the prescribed level γ is avoid, and λ_t should be tuned instead of γ to obtain better robust behaviour. A practice way to tune the parameter λ_t is given in the next sub-section. Substitute (24) into (5), it is easy to verify that the sufficient condition (19) in Theorem 1 is fulfilled.

Nevertheless, the use of the upper bound $\lambda_t\boldsymbol{P}_{t|t-1}$ may be too conservative. Too much emphasis is placed in accommodating the worst case (the largest linearization error) at the expense of optimality. In order to improve stability of the filter without decreasing accuracy, an adaptive scheme to adjust $\boldsymbol{\Sigma}_{t|t-1}$ in response to the changing environment is given as follows

$$\boldsymbol{\Sigma}_{t|t-1} = \begin{cases} \boldsymbol{P}_{t|t-1}, & \boldsymbol{P}_{y,t} > \alpha \overline{\boldsymbol{P}}_{y,t} \\ (\boldsymbol{P}_{t|t-1}^{-1} - \gamma^{-2} \boldsymbol{L}_t^T \boldsymbol{L}_t)^{-1}, & otherwise \end{cases} \tag{26}$$

where $\overline{\boldsymbol{P}}_{y,t} = E(\widetilde{\boldsymbol{y}}_t \widetilde{\boldsymbol{y}}_t^T \mid \widetilde{\boldsymbol{x}}_{t-1})$ is the real covariance matrix of the innovation $\widetilde{\boldsymbol{y}}_t = \boldsymbol{y}_t - \boldsymbol{H}_t \hat{\boldsymbol{x}}_{t|t-1}$. The parameter $\alpha > 0$ is introduced to provide an extra degree of freedom to tune the threshold during the implementation process. Although $\overline{\boldsymbol{P}}_{y,t}$ is unknown in practice, it can be estimated by

$$\overline{\boldsymbol{P}}_{y,t} \approx \begin{cases} \widetilde{\boldsymbol{y}}_t \widetilde{\boldsymbol{y}}_t^T, & t = 0 \\ \dfrac{\rho \overline{\boldsymbol{P}}_{y,t-1} + \widetilde{\boldsymbol{y}}_t \widetilde{\boldsymbol{y}}_t^T}{\rho + 1}, & t > 0 \end{cases} \tag{27}$$

where $\rho = 0.98$ is a forgetting factor (Bai, 1999).

The adaptive robust extended Kalman filter (AREKF) has the structure of the REKF, except that the prediction error covariance is calculated by (26) instead of (5). With this particular design, when there is large innovation, $\boldsymbol{\Sigma}_{t|t-1}$ will be set to $(\boldsymbol{P}_{t|t-1}^{-1} - \gamma^{-2} \boldsymbol{L}_t^T \boldsymbol{L}_t)^{-1}$ to prevent filter divergence. On the other hand, when the innovation is rather small, $\boldsymbol{\Sigma}_{t|t-1}$ will be set to $\boldsymbol{P}_{t|t-1}$ so that it will not distort the estimation. The stability of the proposed algorithm is analyzed as follows.

Theorem 2. Consider the nonlinear stochastic system given by (1)-(2) with linear measurement $h(\boldsymbol{x}_t) = \boldsymbol{H}_t \boldsymbol{x}_t$. Assume that rank($\boldsymbol{H}_t$) = l and $\alpha = 1$, and the real error covariance matrix $E(\widetilde{\boldsymbol{x}}_{t|t-1} \widetilde{\boldsymbol{x}}_{t|t-1}^T \mid \widetilde{\boldsymbol{x}}_{t-1})$ is approximated by $\overline{\boldsymbol{\Sigma}}_{t|t-1}$. The AREKF is stated by (3), (4), (6)-(9), (24) and (26). Let the following assumptions hold for every $t \ge 0$

1. There are real numbers f_{min}, f_{max}, β_{min}, β_{max}, h_{min}, h_{max}, such that:

$$f_{\min}^2 \boldsymbol{I} \le \boldsymbol{F}_t \boldsymbol{F}_t^T \le f_{\max}^2 \boldsymbol{I}, \ \beta_{\min}^2 \boldsymbol{I} \le \boldsymbol{\beta}_t \boldsymbol{\beta}_t^T \le \beta_{\max}^2 \boldsymbol{I}, \ h_{\min}^2 \boldsymbol{I} \le \boldsymbol{H}_t \boldsymbol{H}_t^T \le h_{\max}^2 \boldsymbol{I} \tag{28}$$

2. There are real numbers p_{min}, p_{max}, r_{min}, r_{max}, q_{max}, such that:

$$p_{\min} \boldsymbol{I} \le \boldsymbol{P}_t \le p_{\max} \boldsymbol{I}, \ r_{\min} \boldsymbol{I} \le \boldsymbol{R}_t \le r_{\max} \boldsymbol{I}, \ \boldsymbol{Q}_t \le q_{\max} \boldsymbol{I} \tag{29}$$

Then there are real numbers $\mu_{\max} > 0$, $0 < \lambda_{\min} \le 1$, such that

$$E\{\|\widetilde{\boldsymbol{x}}_t\|^2\} \le \frac{p_{\max}}{p_{\min}} E\{\|\widetilde{\boldsymbol{x}}_0\|^2\}(1 - \lambda_{\min})^t + \frac{\mu_{\max}}{p_{\min}} \sum_{i=1}^{t-1} (1 - \lambda_{\min})^i \tag{30}$$

Proof: The proof of Theorem 2 is similar to that of Theorem 1, except that the sufficient condition shown in (19) is verified according to (24) and (26).

From (2) and (16), the real covariance matrix of the innovation is expressed as

$$\overline{\boldsymbol{P}}_{y,t} = \mathrm{E}[(\boldsymbol{y}_t - \boldsymbol{H}_t \hat{\boldsymbol{x}}_{t|t-1})(\boldsymbol{y}_t - \boldsymbol{H}_t \hat{\boldsymbol{x}}_{t|t-1})^T \mid \widetilde{\boldsymbol{x}}_{t-1}]$$

$$= \mathrm{E}[(\boldsymbol{H}_t\tilde{\boldsymbol{x}}_{t|t-1} + \boldsymbol{v}_t)(\boldsymbol{H}_t\tilde{\boldsymbol{x}}_{t|t-1} + \boldsymbol{v}_t)^T \mid \tilde{\boldsymbol{x}}_{t-1}]$$

$$= \boldsymbol{H}_t\overline{\boldsymbol{\Sigma}}_{t|t-1}\boldsymbol{H}_t^T + \boldsymbol{R}_t \tag{31}$$

From (8) and (31), we have

$$\boldsymbol{P}_{y,t} - \overline{\boldsymbol{P}}_{y,t} = \boldsymbol{H}_t(\boldsymbol{\Sigma}_{t|t-1} - \overline{\boldsymbol{\Sigma}}_{t|t-1})\boldsymbol{H}_t^T \tag{32}$$

As the rank of the measurement matrix $\boldsymbol{H}_t$ is assumed to be l and α is assumed to be 1, if $\boldsymbol{P}_{y,t} > \overline{\boldsymbol{P}}_{y,t}$, the condition $\boldsymbol{\Sigma}_{t|t-1} > \overline{\boldsymbol{\Sigma}}_{t|t-1}$ is fulfilled. Otherwise, if the inequation $\boldsymbol{P}_{y,t} > \overline{\boldsymbol{P}}_{y,t}$ is not fulfilled, inserting (24) into (26), we have

$$\boldsymbol{\Sigma}_{t|t-1} - \overline{\boldsymbol{\Sigma}}_{t|t-1} = \lambda_t\boldsymbol{P}_{t|t-1} - \overline{\boldsymbol{\Sigma}}_{t|t-1} > 0 \tag{33}$$

Therefore, the condition (19) can always be satisfied. Then the theorem can be proved following the proof process of Theorem 1.

Remarks:

1) This theorem shows that the stability of the proposed algorithm can be ensured with the assumption rank($\boldsymbol{H}_t$) = l. Nevertheless, the AREKF can be used even if rank($\boldsymbol{H}_t$) < l. According to (28), if the hypothesis $\boldsymbol{P}_{y,t} > \overline{\boldsymbol{P}}_{y,t}$ is not satisfied, then the condition $\boldsymbol{\Sigma}_{t|t-1} > \overline{\boldsymbol{\Sigma}}_{t|t-1}$ is bound to be violated. In other words, it indicates that the stability of the filter is not guaranteed. Thus it is proper to adopt the robust filtering technique to adjust the covariance matrix $\boldsymbol{\Sigma}_{t|t-1}$ when $\boldsymbol{P}_{y,t} > \overline{\boldsymbol{P}}_{y,t}$ is not satisfied.

2) The small positive number α in (26) is introduced to avoid resetting the covariance matrix $\boldsymbol{\Sigma}_{t|t-1}$ frequently. Note that the condition $\boldsymbol{\Sigma}_{t|t-1} > \overline{\boldsymbol{\Sigma}}_{t|t-1}$ is sufficient but not necessary to ensure stability of the filter. Numerical simulations have shown that even if the condition is not globally satisfied as $\alpha < 1$, the AREKF can tolerate much higher prediction error than the REKF and the traditional EKF.

3) The key idea of the AREKF is to design the estimator based on the stability analysis, and determine whether the error covariance matrix $\boldsymbol{\Sigma}_{t|t-1}$ should be reset according to the hypothesis test. Unlike the REKF, the proposed algorithm is designed based on the tuning parameter λ_t instead of the prescribed attenuation level γ. Sufficient large λ_t can generally be found for practical systems with finite energy. In contrast, as discussed earlier, it may be impossible to obtain appropriate γ for the REKF. Thus, the proposed technique is more efficient to prevent instability in the case of large predication error. In addition, as the AREKF switches between the REKF and the traditional EKF under the control of the innovation covariance $\overline{\boldsymbol{P}}_{y,t}$, and it will not work in the REKF mode unless the estimated covariance $\overline{\boldsymbol{P}}_{y,t}$ exceeds the threshold $\alpha\boldsymbol{P}_{y,t}$, it is expected to be more accurate than the traditional REKF in the case of negligible predication error.

4) Note that the estimate of $\overline{\boldsymbol{P}}_{y,t}$ is not adopted directly in the algorithm, but used as an indicator of the filter instability. Even if the covariance matrix $\boldsymbol{\Sigma}_{t|t-1}$ is reset inappropriately

due to the inaccurate approximation in (27), as $(\boldsymbol{P}_{t|t-1}^{-1} - \gamma^{-2}\boldsymbol{L}_t^T \boldsymbol{L}_t)^{-1} > \boldsymbol{P}_{t|t-1}$, from (19) in Theorem 1, it will not affect the stability of the filter. Certainly, in order to avoid decreasing accuracy of the filter, the parameter α should be fine tuned so that $\boldsymbol{\Sigma}_{t|t-1}$ will not be reset frequently.

5) In fact, the estimation errors of the EKF and the UKF can be written as a uniform formulation which is similar to (A.3) (See (Xiong, 2006) for more explanations about the reformulation). Hence, conclusions as shown in Theorem 1 and Theorem 2 can also be drawn for the UKF, and the proof goes roughly the same as those shown in this paper.

6) A robust adaptive Kalman filter for linear systems with stochastic uncertainties has been proposed in (Wang & Balakrishnan, 1999). The key idea of the algorithm is to minimize the mean square estimation error, and a convex optimization problem should be solved according to the time-varying model and the measurements at each step of the algorithm. In contrast, the purpose of this paper is to provide a technique to stabilize the filter for nonlinear systems with external disturbances, and the hypothesis test is adopted to control the error covariance matrix of the estimator.

7) This section provides a technique to enhance the ability of the EKF to handle large external disturbances. In the presence of both model-plant mismatch and disturbances, other methods should be used together with the proposed technique to design the estimator. The most popular method to account for the model mismatch is to estimate the error terms adaptively and compensate the mismatch effect according to the estimates (Kwon, 2006). Another effective method is the extended robust H_∞ filter technique developed in (Seo et al., 2006). When this technique is adopted, several terms that scale the magnitude of the model error should be added in the error covariance matrix of the filter.

8) Although the paper focus on the external disturbance in state equation, the result in this paper can be extended to the systems with disturbance in measurement equations, and the innovation covariance matrix $\boldsymbol{P}_{y,t}$ may play a similar role to the error covariance matrix $\boldsymbol{\Sigma}_{t|t-1}$ in ensuring the filter stability. In other words, enlarging the covariance matrix of the innovation could enhance ability of the filter to handle large prediction errors in the innovation. However, if both the state equation and the measurement equation are nonlinear, the stability analysis will be more complicated. Further works are required to give some principles for the design of $\boldsymbol{P}_{y,t}$.

4. The autonomous navigation system

Currently, the orbit of a spacecraft is determined by earth stations, which require expensive equipments and extensive ground operations. As the number of the satellites increases, the number of the earth stations and system maintenance cost may increase significantly. This problem can be partly solved by using the autonomous navigation technique (Wiegand, 1996; Ma & Zhai, 2004; Huang et al., 2004).

The usefulness of autonomy has been recognized in the literature and several studies have been done to realize the autonomous navigation. The EKF forms the basis of many spacecraft navigation algorithm today (Vasile et al., 2002; Psiaki & Hinks, 2007; Nolet, 2007). Here we study the astronomical navigation technique method that employs the earth sensor and the star sensor. The basic measurement of the navigation system is illustrated in Fig.1.

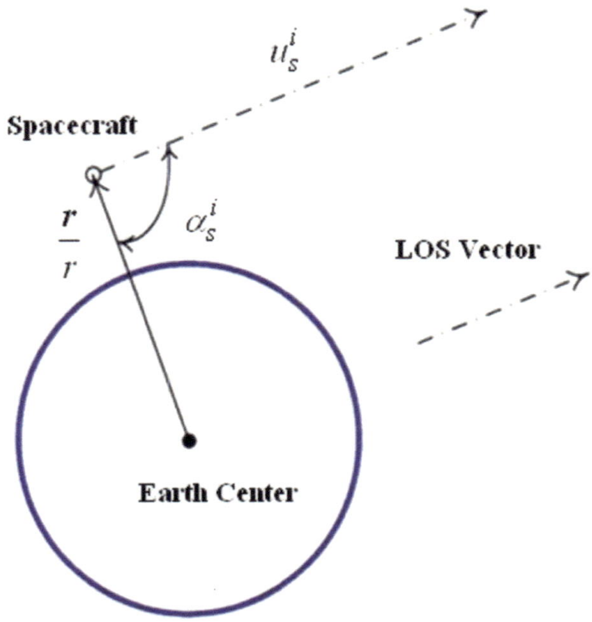

Fig. 1. The angle between the satellite position vector and the LOS vector

In Fig.1, $\boldsymbol{r}/r$ is the unit position vector that points from the center of Earth to the spacecraft. It can be obtained from the earth sensor. $\boldsymbol{u}_s^i$ is the line of sight (LOS) vector that points from the spacecraft to the star. It can be obtained from the star sensor. α_s is the angle between the unit position vector $\boldsymbol{r}/r$ and the LOS vector $\boldsymbol{u}_s^i$. The measurement α_s does not depend on the estimate of the spacecraft attitude.

Then we define the state vector, the dynamic model and the measurement model that are used in the spacecraft navigation filter. The spacecraft navigation filter uses the following 6-dimensional state vector

$$\boldsymbol{x}_t = [\boldsymbol{r} \quad \dot{\boldsymbol{r}}]^T \tag{34}$$

where $\boldsymbol{r} = [r_x \quad r_y \quad r_z]^T$ is the position vector of the spacecraft in Earth-centered inertial (ECI) coordinates, $\dot{\boldsymbol{r}} = [v_x \quad v_y \quad v_z]^T$ is the velocity vectors of the spacecraft in ECI coordinates.

The orbital dynamic model is written in the form of (1) with the function $f(\boldsymbol{x}_{t-1})$ as follows (Zhang & Fang, 2003)

$$f(\boldsymbol{x}_{t-1}) = \boldsymbol{x}_{t-1} + \varphi(\boldsymbol{x}_{t-1})\Delta t \tag{35}$$

where the propagation period Δt is defined as the time between two predictions, and

$$\varphi(\boldsymbol{x}_{t-1}) = \begin{bmatrix} v_x \\ v_y \\ v_z \\ -\frac{\mu r_x}{r^3}[1+\frac{3}{2}J_2(\frac{R_e}{r})^2(1-5\frac{r_z^2}{r^2})] \\ -\frac{\mu r_y}{r^3}[1+\frac{3}{2}J_2(\frac{R_e}{r})^2(1-5\frac{r_z^2}{r^2})] \\ -\frac{\mu r_z}{r^3}[1+\frac{3}{2}J_2(\frac{R_e}{r})^2(3-5\frac{r_{z,i}^2}{r^2})] \end{bmatrix} \tag{36}$$

μ is the Earth's gravitational constant, R_e is the radius of Earth, $r_i = (r_x^2 + r_y^2 + r_z^2)^{0.5}$ is the distance of the satellite from the center of Earth. Although the motion of the spacecraft is affected by the Earth's non-spherical mass distribution, atmospheric dray, solar radiation pressure and the forces caused by the thruster firings, the dynamic model in the algorithm is limit to the two-body equations of motion augmented by J2 perturbations. For most Earth-orbiting satellites that are placed in a set orbit with no mission operations deviating from that orbit, the unmodeled terms are relative small and their effects are represented as the process noise w_t.

The measurement equation is written in the form of (2) with the function $h(\boldsymbol{x}_t)$ as follows (Wei, 2004)

$$h(\boldsymbol{x}_t) = \begin{bmatrix} \alpha_s^1 \\ \alpha_s^2 \end{bmatrix} \tag{37}$$

where

$$\alpha_s^i = \arccos(-\frac{\boldsymbol{u}_s^i \cdot \boldsymbol{r}}{|\boldsymbol{r}|}), i = 1,2 \tag{38}$$

The superscript i is used to distinguish the measurements obtained from different star sensors.

Based on the previous state equation and measurement equation, the standard EKF can be used to estimate the position and velocity vector of the spacecraft. Note that the unknown acceleration produced by the thruster firings is not taken into consideration in the orbital dynamic model. Hence, the standard algorithm is only valid for one specific orbit. If a spacecraft's mission requires it to maneuver at some point, such as merely changing its location along the orbit track or possibly altering its entire orbit shape, the unknown acceleration, which can be seen as the external disturbances of the navigation system, will degrades the performance of the EKF.

In order to achieve better accuracy, the AREKF is adopted in this Section. For a maneuvering spacecraft, the filter innovation $\tilde{\boldsymbol{y}}_t$ will be enlarged due to the unknown acceleration. From (26), if the covariance matrix $\overline{\boldsymbol{P}}_{y,t}$ calculated according to $\tilde{\boldsymbol{y}}_t$ exceed the specified threshold $\frac{1}{\alpha}\overline{\boldsymbol{P}}_{y,t}$, the matrix $\boldsymbol{\Sigma}_{t|t-1}$ will be reset as $(\boldsymbol{P}_{t|t-1}^{-1}-\gamma^{-2}\boldsymbol{L}_t^T\boldsymbol{L}_t)^{-1}$ such that the effect of the measurements to correct the state estimate will be reinforce. On the other hand, when the spacecraft stop maneuvering, the innovation will decrease as the filter goes on, and from (26), the original $\boldsymbol{P}_{t|t-1}$ will be used to calculate the gain $\boldsymbol{K}_t$, such that the information contained in the orbital dynamic model will be fully used to handle the unfavorable effect of the measurement noise.

5. Simulation

The autonomous navigation system described in Section 4 is considered in this sub-section to demonstrate the improvement of the AREKF over the EKF, the REKF and the AEKF. The simulated truth orbital states are obtained by using a high accurate numerical orbit propagator, and the simulated measurements are obtained according to the simulated states and the measurement model. The simulated measurements are processed by different filters to obtain the state estimates. The estimates are compared with the simulated states to evaluate the performance of the filter.

The numerical simulation is implemented under the following assumptions. An Earth-orbiting satellite performs maneuver from 7293s to 8373s and from 11279s to 12068s. The height of the perigee of the orbit is raised from 500km to 2000km. The measurement precisions are 0.02° for earth sensor and 5" for star sensor. The measurements are used to correct the predicted state $\hat{\boldsymbol{x}}_{t|t-1}$ with a sampling interval of 100s. The initial position error and the corresponding error covariance matrix of the filters are list below

$$\tilde{\boldsymbol{x}}_0=[p_r \quad p_r \quad p_r \quad p_v \quad p_v \quad p_v]^{\mathrm{T}} \tag{39}$$

$$\boldsymbol{P}_0=diag([p_r^2 \quad p_r^2 \quad p_r^2 \quad p_v^2 \quad p_v^2 \quad p_v^2]) \tag{40}$$

where p_r = 5000m, p_v = 10m/s. The process noise covariance matrix is set to

$$\boldsymbol{Q}_k=diag([q_r^2 \quad q_r^2 \quad q_r^2 \quad q_v^2 \quad q_v^2 \quad q_v^2]) \tag{41}$$

where $q_r = 2\times10^{-5}$m, $q_v = 2\times10^{-4}$m/s.

The proposed AREKF can cope with the large linearization error caused by the initial error or the external disturbances. As the effect of the initial estimation error on the performance of the nonlinear filter has been analyze in (Xiong et al., 2006), here emphasis is on the impact of the disturbances, i.e., the unknown acceleration produced by the thruster firings.

First, the usual EKF is performed to estimate the position and the velocity of the maneuvering spacecraft according to (3), (4), (6)-(9) with the covariance matrix $\boldsymbol{\Sigma}_{t|t-1}=\boldsymbol{P}_{t|t-1}$. The result obtained from the EKF serves as a baseline reference for the comparison. The estimation errors are plotted versus time in Fig.2. Obviously, the performance of the EKF is seriously degraded due to the unknown acceleration in dynamic model. It indicates that this algorithm is sensitive to the disturbances. In addition, the root mean square (RMS) error of the EKF is computed from the data collected in the last 2000s of the simulation. The equation to compute RMS error can be expressed as

$$\sigma_i = \sqrt{\frac{1}{n-1}\sum_{t=T-n}^{T}(r_{i,t} - \hat{r}_{i,t})^2} \text{ , } i = x, y, z, n = 2000 \tag{42}$$

where T is the time of the simulation. In order to facilitate the comparison, the square root of σ_x, σ_y and σ_z are computed by using the following equation

$$\sigma_p = \sqrt{\sigma_x^2 + \sigma_y^2 + \sigma_z^2} \tag{43}$$

The RMS errors of the filters are summarized in Table 1.

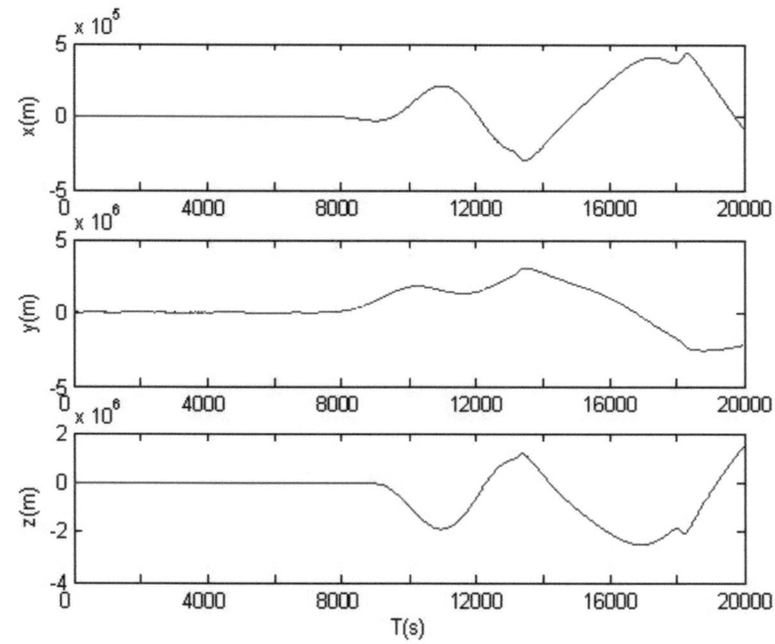

Fig. 2. Estimation error of the EKF

Second, the REKF is implemented according to (3)-(9). It was found that $\gamma = 8000$ is sufficient to satisfy the condition $\gamma > \{\max[\text{eig}(\boldsymbol{P}_{t|t-1})]\}^{0.5}$ for the entire run. Fig.3 shows the graph of the position error of the REKF, and the RMS error of the REKF is listed in Table1 1. Although the RMS error is slightly reduced by using the REKF instead of the EKF, performance of the REKF is also severely degraded by the disturbance. As the ability of the REKF to tolerant large disturbances is limited by the scaling parameter γ, which is chosen to ensure $\boldsymbol{\Sigma}_{t|t-1} > 0$, there is a potential problem of instability in the method. From (22) and (23), it is difficult to choose an appropriate γ such that $\boldsymbol{\Sigma}_{t|t-1} > \overline{\boldsymbol{\Sigma}}_{t|t-1}$ is fulfilled when the magnitude of the disturbances is rather large. Surely, the problem can be partly solved be choosing time-vary scaling parameter γ (Fu et al, 2001). However, additional computation is required to implement this technique. In addition, the performance of the REKF may be improved by tuning the noise covariance matrices $\boldsymbol{Q}_t$ and $\boldsymbol{R}_t$. However, in general, it is difficult to obtain appropriate $\boldsymbol{Q}_t$ and $\boldsymbol{R}_t$.

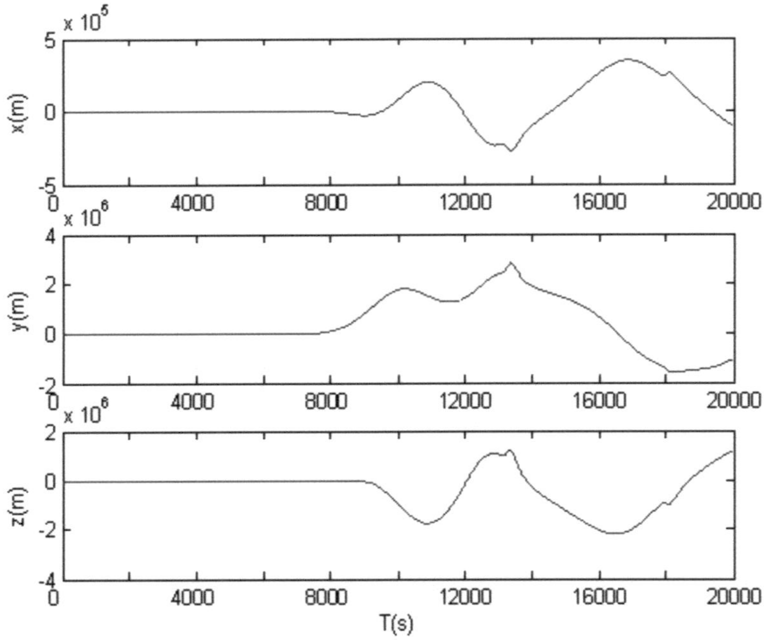

Fig. 3. Estimation error of the REKF

In order to clarify the superiority of the proposed algorithm, the AREKF is also compared with the AEKF proposed in (Moghaddamjoo & Kirlin, 1989) and developed in (Ashokaraj et al, 2002). A brief description of the AEKF is collected in the Appendix. It is shown in (Ashokaraj et al, 2002) that the performance of the AEKF is superior to that of the EKF. The AEKF algorithm can be implemented by using (3), (A.16), (A.17) and (6)-(9). For estimation of $\hat{\boldsymbol{Q}}_t$, the matrix $\boldsymbol{A}$ and $\boldsymbol{B}$ in (A17) are set to be

$$\boldsymbol{A} = a \times \begin{bmatrix} 0 & 0 & 0 & 1/\sqrt{2} & 0 & 1/\sqrt{2} \\ 0 & 0 & 0 & 0 & 1 & 0 \end{bmatrix}^T, \ \boldsymbol{B} = \boldsymbol{A}^T \tag{44}$$

where $a = 1.5$. The parameter k in (A.16) is set to be 2, i.e., $\hat{\boldsymbol{Q}}_t$ is determined by

$$\hat{\boldsymbol{Q}}_t = \hat{\boldsymbol{Q}}_{t-1} \exp[\boldsymbol{H}_t (\boldsymbol{C}_{y,1} + \boldsymbol{C}_{y,2}) \boldsymbol{C}_{y,0}^{-1} \boldsymbol{H}_t^T] \tag{45}$$

$\boldsymbol{C}_{y,i}$ (i = 1,2) is estimated by

$$\boldsymbol{C}_{y,i} = \frac{1}{N-1} \sum_{j=t-N+1}^{t} \tilde{\boldsymbol{y}}_j \tilde{\boldsymbol{y}}_{j-i}^T \tag{46}$$

The window size N is set to be 15 for this simulation. The performance of the AEKF is shown in Fig.4 and Table 1. The estimation result of the AEKF is better than those of the EKF and the REKF. It shows that the AEKF is more effective to eliminate the unfavorable effect of the considered disturbances in comparison with the EKF and the REKF. However, the error curves also fluctuate widely during the maneuver. On the other hand, it is specified in (Xiong et al., 2008) the AEKF is somewhat less accurate than the standard EKF when there are no disturbances in dynamic model, for the noise covariance matrix is reset to the estimated value $\hat{\boldsymbol{Q}}_t$ in every step of the filter, and $\hat{\boldsymbol{Q}}_t$ which may deviate from its true value due to the inaccuracy of the state estimate. In addition, to implement the adaptive EKF, many tuning parameters (such k, N and the elements in matrices $\boldsymbol{A}$ and $\boldsymbol{B}$) have to be designed. In contrast, for the AREKF, only parameters λ_t and α should be tuned. And from (26), the covariance matrix $\boldsymbol{\Sigma}_{t|t-1}$ will not be reset unless $\overline{\boldsymbol{P}}_{y,t}$ is enlarged sufficiently due to the disturbances.

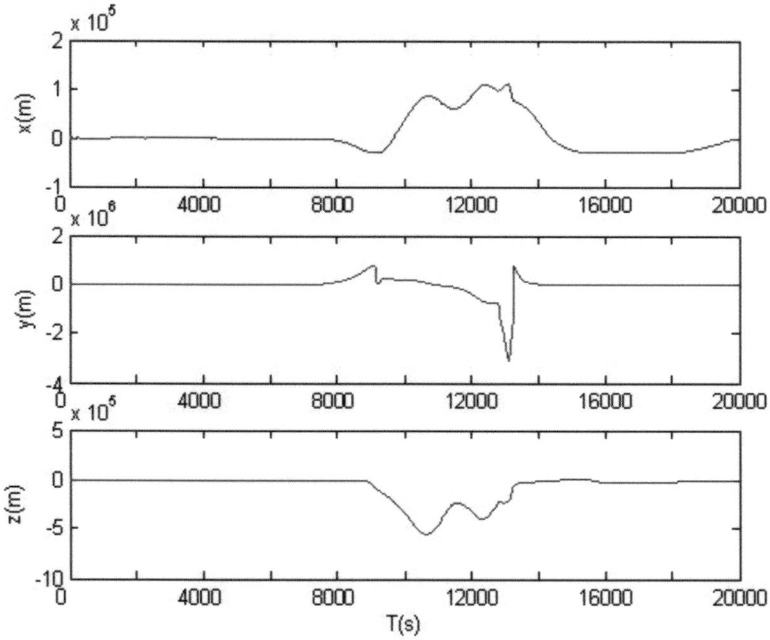

Fig. 4. Estimation error of the AEKF

Finally, we illustrate the application of the AREKF. The only difference from the REKF is that the prediction error covariance matrix is calculated by (26) instead of (5). As explained in Section 3, the design of the parameter λ_t is crucial to control the accuracy and stability of the filter. In order to obtain appropriate λ_t, λ_t is tuned according to trace of the covariance matrix $\overline{\boldsymbol{P}}_{y,t}$ calculated from the innovation $\tilde{\boldsymbol{y}}_t$. In this scenario, λ_t is set to be

$$\lambda_t = \frac{\mathrm{trace}(\overline{\boldsymbol{P}}_{y,t})}{\mathrm{trace}(\boldsymbol{P}_{y,t})} \tag{47}$$

and α is set to be 0.2 to avoid resetting $\Sigma_{t|t-1}$ frequently when the disturbances are rather small. The estimation errors of the AREKF are plotted in Fig.5.

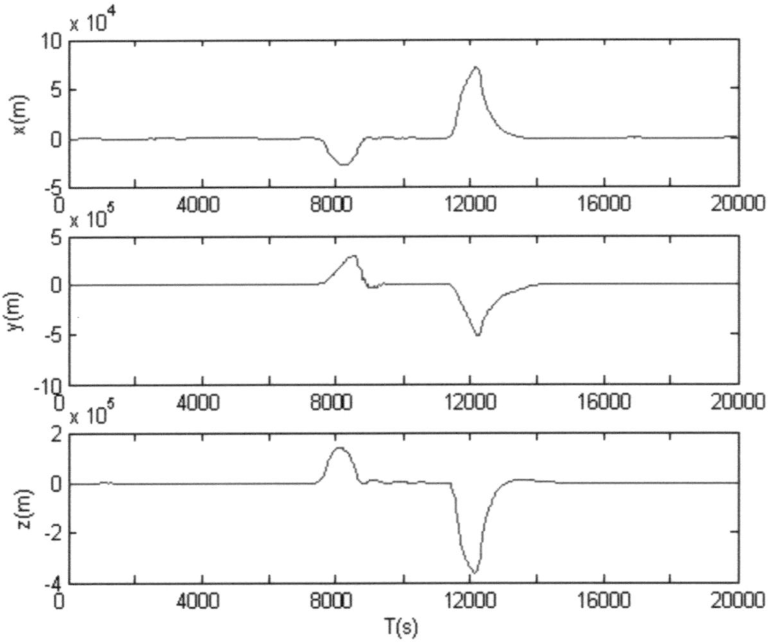

Fig. 5. Estimation error of the AREKF

As we expected, the proposed algorithm is robust enough to cope with the disturbances. Unlike the AEKF, the covariance matrix of the AREKF is reset only when the disturbances are large enough. Since the impact of the disturbances is partly eliminated, it is not surprising that the accuracy of the autonomous navigation system is further improved by using the AREKF instead of the AEKF. From Fig. 2-5 and Table 1, it is evident that the proposed method outperforms the usual EKF, the REKF and the AEKF in the presence of large external disturbances. The RMS error of the AREKF for the considered navigation system is on the order of 200m.

Filtering Algorithm	RMS error (18000s < t < 20000s)			
	σ_x (m)	σ_y (m)	σ_z (m)	σ_p (m)
EKF	0.2771×10^6	2.4096×10^6	1.2367×10^6	2.7175×10^6
REKF	0.1382×10^6	1.4027×10^6	0.7055×10^6	1.5762×10^6
AEKF	1.9091×10^4	1.2786×10^4	0.6441×10^4	2.3863×10^4
AREKF	126.1731	143.1503	69.5699	203.1050

Table 1. Performance Comparison of the Filtering Algorithms

6. Conclusion

The AREKF is proposed here as a modification of the REKF, that switches between the REKF mode and the normal EKF mode under the control of the innovation. In the presence of large external disturbances, the proposed algorithm is more effective than the REKF to ensure boundedness of the estimation error. On the other hand, in the absence of disturbances, it can yield more accurate estimates. In comparison with the adaptive EKF, the main advantage of the AREKF is its ease of application, as few parameters need to be tuned for the design of the estimator. The proposed method is successfully applied to determine the position and velocity of the orbit maneuvering spacecraft based on the information obtain from the earth sensor and the star sensor. Numerical simulation shows that the AREKF is more effective than the EKF, the REKF and the AEKF to eliminate the unfavorable effect of the unknown acceleration produced by the thruster firings.

In addition, the adaptive robust filtering technique is expected to be effective to improve the stability of other nonlinear filters, such as the unscented Kalman filter (UKF) and the particle filter.

7. Appendix

7.1 Proof of Theorem 1

Proof: First, choose the Lyapunov function

$$V_t(\tilde{\boldsymbol{x}}_t) = \tilde{\boldsymbol{x}}_t^T \boldsymbol{P}_t^{-1} \tilde{\boldsymbol{x}}_t \tag{A.1}$$

Because of (16), we have the bounds for the function $V_t(\tilde{\boldsymbol{x}}_t)$

$$\frac{1}{p_{\max}} \|\tilde{\boldsymbol{x}}_t\|^2 \le V_t(\tilde{\boldsymbol{x}}_t) \le \frac{1}{p_{\min}} \|\tilde{\boldsymbol{x}}_t\|^2 \tag{A.2}$$

i.e., (10) hold with $v_{\min} = \frac{1}{p_{\max}}$ and $v_{\max} = \frac{1}{p_{\min}}$. To satisfy the requirement (11) for the application of Lemma 1, it needs an upper bound on $\mathrm{E}[V_t(\tilde{\boldsymbol{x}}_t) \mid \tilde{\boldsymbol{x}}_{t-1}] - V_{t-1}(\tilde{\boldsymbol{x}}_{t-1})$.

From (5), (13) and (2), estimation error of the REKF can be written as

$$\tilde{\boldsymbol{x}}_t = \boldsymbol{\beta}_t \boldsymbol{F}_t \tilde{\boldsymbol{x}}_{t-1} - \boldsymbol{K}_t \boldsymbol{H}_t \boldsymbol{\beta}_t \boldsymbol{F}_t \tilde{\boldsymbol{x}}_{t-1} + (\boldsymbol{I} - \boldsymbol{K}_t \boldsymbol{H}_t) \boldsymbol{w}_t - \boldsymbol{K}_t \boldsymbol{v}_t \tag{A.3}$$

Substitute (A.3) into (A.1), and taking the conditional expectation yields:

$$\begin{aligned}\mathrm{E}[V_t(\tilde{\boldsymbol{x}}_t) \mid \tilde{\boldsymbol{x}}_{t-1}] = \mathrm{E}[&(\boldsymbol{\beta}_t \boldsymbol{F}_t \tilde{\boldsymbol{x}}_{t-1})^T \boldsymbol{P}_t^{-1} (\boldsymbol{\beta}_t \boldsymbol{F}_t \tilde{\boldsymbol{x}}_{t-1}) - (\boldsymbol{K}_t \boldsymbol{H}_t \boldsymbol{\beta}_t \boldsymbol{F}_t \tilde{\boldsymbol{x}}_{t-1})^T \boldsymbol{P}_t^{-1} (\boldsymbol{\beta}_t \boldsymbol{F}_t \tilde{\boldsymbol{x}}_{t-1}) - \\ &(\boldsymbol{\beta}_t \boldsymbol{F}_t \tilde{\boldsymbol{x}}_{t-1})^T \boldsymbol{P}_t^{-1} (\boldsymbol{K}_t \boldsymbol{H}_t \boldsymbol{\beta}_t \boldsymbol{F}_t \tilde{\boldsymbol{x}}_{t-1}) + (\boldsymbol{K}_t \boldsymbol{H}_t \boldsymbol{\beta}_t \boldsymbol{F}_t \tilde{\boldsymbol{x}}_{t-1})^T \boldsymbol{P}_t^{-1} (\boldsymbol{K}_t \boldsymbol{H}_t \boldsymbol{\beta}_t \boldsymbol{F}_t \tilde{\boldsymbol{x}}_{t-1}) + \\ &\boldsymbol{w}_t^T (\boldsymbol{I} - \boldsymbol{K}_t \boldsymbol{H}_t)^T \boldsymbol{P}_t^{-1} (\boldsymbol{I} - \boldsymbol{K}_t \boldsymbol{H}_t) \boldsymbol{w}_t + \boldsymbol{v}_t^T \boldsymbol{K}_t^T \boldsymbol{P}_t^{-1} \boldsymbol{K}_t \boldsymbol{v}_t \mid \tilde{\boldsymbol{x}}_{t-1}]\end{aligned} \tag{A.4}$$

Using (6) and (7), it can be verified that

$$\boldsymbol{K}_t = \boldsymbol{P}_t \boldsymbol{H}_t^T \boldsymbol{R}_t^{-1}$$

And then (A.4) becomes

$$\mathrm{E}[V_t(\tilde{\boldsymbol{x}}_t) \mid \tilde{\boldsymbol{x}}_{t-1}] = \tilde{\boldsymbol{x}}_{t-1}^T \boldsymbol{F}_t^T \boldsymbol{\beta}_t [\boldsymbol{\Sigma}_{t|t-1}^{-1} - \boldsymbol{H}_t^T (\boldsymbol{R}_t^{-1} - \boldsymbol{R}_t^{-1} \boldsymbol{H}_t \boldsymbol{P}_t \boldsymbol{H}_t^T \boldsymbol{R}_t^{-1}) \boldsymbol{H}_t] \boldsymbol{\beta}_t \boldsymbol{F}_t \tilde{\boldsymbol{x}}_{t-1} + \boldsymbol{\mu}_t \tag{A.5}$$

where

$$\boldsymbol{\mu}_t = \mathrm{E}[\boldsymbol{w}_t^T (\boldsymbol{I} - \boldsymbol{K}_t \boldsymbol{H}_t)^T \boldsymbol{P}_t^{-1} (\boldsymbol{I} - \boldsymbol{K}_t \boldsymbol{H}_t) \boldsymbol{w}_t + \boldsymbol{v}_t^T \boldsymbol{K}_t^T \boldsymbol{P}_t^{-1} \boldsymbol{K}_t \boldsymbol{v}_t] \tag{A.6}$$

It can be seen from (14) and condition (17) that

$$\boldsymbol{\Sigma}_{t|t-1} \geq \boldsymbol{\beta}_t \boldsymbol{F}_t \boldsymbol{P}_{t-1} \boldsymbol{F}_t^T \boldsymbol{\beta}_t + \boldsymbol{Q}_t \geq \boldsymbol{\beta}_t \boldsymbol{F}_t \boldsymbol{P}_{t-1} \boldsymbol{F}_t^T \boldsymbol{\beta}_t \tag{A.7}$$

In addition, it is easy to verified that

$$\boldsymbol{R}_t^{-1} - \boldsymbol{R}_t^{-1} \boldsymbol{H}_t \boldsymbol{P}_t \boldsymbol{H}_t^T \boldsymbol{R}_t^{-1} = (\boldsymbol{H}_t \boldsymbol{\Sigma}_{t|t-1} \boldsymbol{H}_t^T + \boldsymbol{R}_t)^{-1} \tag{A.8}$$

Using (A.7) and (A.8), we have

$$\mathrm{E}[V_t(\tilde{\boldsymbol{x}}_t) \mid \tilde{\boldsymbol{x}}_{t-1}] \leq \tilde{\boldsymbol{x}}_{t-1}^T \boldsymbol{P}_{t-1}^{-1} \tilde{\boldsymbol{x}}_{t-1} - \tilde{\boldsymbol{x}}_{t-1}^T \boldsymbol{F}_t^T \boldsymbol{\beta}_t \boldsymbol{H}_t^T (\boldsymbol{H}_t \boldsymbol{\Sigma}_{t|t-1} \boldsymbol{H}_t^T + \boldsymbol{R}_t)^{-1} \boldsymbol{H}_t \boldsymbol{\beta}_t \boldsymbol{F}_t \tilde{\boldsymbol{x}}_{t-1} + \boldsymbol{\mu}_t \tag{A.9}$$

Subtracting $V_{t-1}(\tilde{\boldsymbol{x}}_{t-1})$ from both sides of (A.9), we establish that

$$\mathrm{E}[V_t(\tilde{\boldsymbol{x}}_t) \mid \tilde{\boldsymbol{x}}_{t-1}] - V_{t-1}(\tilde{\boldsymbol{x}}_{t-1}) \leq \mu_t - \lambda_t V_{t-1}(\tilde{\boldsymbol{x}}_{t-1}) \tag{A.10}$$

where

$$\lambda_t = [\tilde{\boldsymbol{x}}_{t-1}^T \boldsymbol{F}_t^T \boldsymbol{\beta}_t \boldsymbol{H}_t^T (\boldsymbol{H}_t \boldsymbol{\Sigma}_{t|t-1} \boldsymbol{H}_t^T + \boldsymbol{R}_t)^{-1} \boldsymbol{H}_t \boldsymbol{\beta}_t \boldsymbol{F}_t \tilde{\boldsymbol{x}}_{t-1}] / V_{t-1}(\tilde{\boldsymbol{x}}_{t-1}) \tag{A.11}$$

The aim of the following deduction is to determine domains of μ_t and λ_t. Because both sides of (A.6) are scalars, taking the trace of the equation will not change its value. Under assumption (15) and (16), we obtain

$$\begin{aligned}
\mu_t &\leq tr[(\boldsymbol{P}_t^{-1} + \boldsymbol{H}_t^T \boldsymbol{K}_t^T \boldsymbol{P}_t^{-1} \boldsymbol{K}_t \boldsymbol{H}_t) \boldsymbol{Q}_t] + tr(\boldsymbol{K}_t^T \boldsymbol{P}_t^{-1} \boldsymbol{K}_t \boldsymbol{R}_t) \\
&= tr[(\boldsymbol{P}_t^{-1} + \boldsymbol{H}_t^T \boldsymbol{R}_t^{-1} \boldsymbol{H}_t \boldsymbol{P}_t \boldsymbol{H}_t^T \boldsymbol{R}_t^{-1} \boldsymbol{H}_t) \boldsymbol{Q}_t] + tr(\boldsymbol{R}_t^{-1} \boldsymbol{H}_t \boldsymbol{P}_t \boldsymbol{H}_t^T) \\
&\leq (p_{\min}^{-1} + h_{\max}^4 r_{\min}^{-2} p_{\max}) q_{\max} l + h_{\max}^2 p_{\max} r_{\min}^{-1} m \\
&\overset{\Delta}{=} \mu_{\max}
\end{aligned} \tag{A.12}$$

Obviously, $\mu_{\max} > 0$. Applying the matrix inversion lemma (see, e.g., (Lewis, 1986), Appendix A2, p.347) yields:

$$\begin{aligned}
& V_{t-1}(\tilde{\boldsymbol{x}}_{t-1}) - \lambda_t V_{t-1}(\tilde{\boldsymbol{x}}_{t-1}) \\
&= \tilde{\boldsymbol{x}}_{t-1}^T [\boldsymbol{P}_{t-1}^{-1} - \boldsymbol{F}_t^T \boldsymbol{\beta}_t \boldsymbol{H}_t^T (\boldsymbol{H}_t \boldsymbol{\Sigma}_{t|t-1} \boldsymbol{H}_t^T + \boldsymbol{R}_t)^{-1} \boldsymbol{H}_t \boldsymbol{\beta}_t \boldsymbol{F}_t] \tilde{\boldsymbol{x}}_{t-1} \\
&> \tilde{\boldsymbol{x}}_{t-1}^T [\boldsymbol{P}_{t-1}^{-1} - \boldsymbol{F}_t^T \boldsymbol{\beta}_t \boldsymbol{H}_t^T (\boldsymbol{H}_t \boldsymbol{P}_{t|t-1} \boldsymbol{H}_t^T + \boldsymbol{R}_t)^{-1} \boldsymbol{H}_t \boldsymbol{\beta}_t \boldsymbol{F}_t] \tilde{\boldsymbol{x}}_{t-1} \\
&= \tilde{\boldsymbol{x}}_{t-1}^T [\boldsymbol{P}_{t-1} + \boldsymbol{P}_{t-1} \boldsymbol{F}_t^T \boldsymbol{\beta}_t \boldsymbol{H}_t^T (\boldsymbol{H}_t \boldsymbol{Q}_t \boldsymbol{H}_t^T + \boldsymbol{R}_t)^{-1} \boldsymbol{H}_t \boldsymbol{\beta}_t \boldsymbol{F}_t \boldsymbol{P}_{t-1}]^{-1} \tilde{\boldsymbol{x}}_{t-1} > 0
\end{aligned} \tag{A.13}$$

Hence, $\lambda_t < 1$. Under assumption (15) and (16),

$$\lambda_t \geq p_{\min}(h_{\min}\beta_{\min}f_{\min})^2[p_{\max}(h_{\max}\beta_{\max}f_{\max})^2 + q_{\max}h_{\max}^2 + r_{\max}]^{-1}$$

$$\overset{\Delta}{=}\lambda_{\min} > 0 \tag{A.14}$$

Then we obtain the following inequality

$$\mathrm{E}[V_t(\tilde{\boldsymbol{x}}_t) \mid \tilde{\boldsymbol{x}}_{t-1}] - V_{t-1}(\tilde{\boldsymbol{x}}_{t-1}) \leq \mu_{\max} - \lambda_{\min}V_{t-1}(\tilde{\boldsymbol{x}}_{t-1}) \tag{A.15}$$

Where $\mu_{\max} > 0$, $0 < \lambda_{\min} < 1$. Finally, applying Lemma 1, we can draw a conclusion that the estimation error $\tilde{\boldsymbol{x}}_t$ is bounded in mean square.

7.2 The AEKF algorithm

The key idea of the AEKF is to stabilize the filter under any unknown external disturbances by adjusting the noise covariance matrix $\boldsymbol{Q}_t$. In other words, $\boldsymbol{Q}_t$ is modified to insert a negative feedback in the estimation process such that the property of the filter will be optimized.

The difference between the AEKF and the traditional EKF is that the prediction error covariance matrix of the AEKF is calculated as

$$\boldsymbol{\Sigma}_{t|t-1} = \boldsymbol{F}_t\boldsymbol{P}_{t-1}\boldsymbol{F}_t^T + \hat{\boldsymbol{Q}}_t \tag{A.16}$$

And $\hat{\boldsymbol{Q}}_t$ is adjusted according to the innovation of the filter

$$\hat{\boldsymbol{Q}}_t = \hat{\boldsymbol{Q}}_{t-1}\exp[\boldsymbol{A}(\sum_{i=1}^{k}\boldsymbol{C}_{y,i})\boldsymbol{C}_{y,0}^{-1}\boldsymbol{B}^T] \tag{A.17}$$

where $\boldsymbol{C}_{y,i} = \mathrm{E}(\tilde{\boldsymbol{y}}_t\tilde{\boldsymbol{y}}_{t-i}^T)$ is the autocorrelation of the innovation $\tilde{\boldsymbol{y}}_t$, $\boldsymbol{A}$ and $\boldsymbol{B}$ are coefficient matrices which should be found experimentally, and their dimensions are $(l \times m)$. It is suggested in (Psiaki & Hinks, 2007) to choose a small number of autocorrelation k.

In this method, $\hat{\boldsymbol{Q}}_t$ is used to control the Kalman gain $\boldsymbol{K}_t$ adaptively. From (A.16), when the estimate of $\boldsymbol{C}_{y,i}$ increases, $\hat{\boldsymbol{Q}}_t$ will be increased. On the other hand, when $\boldsymbol{C}_{y,i}$ decreases, $\hat{\boldsymbol{Q}}_t$ will be decreased. This behaviour can be seen as a negative feedback which has a stabilizing role in the performance of the algorithm (See (Psiaki & Hinks, 2007) for more explanations).

8. Acknowledgment

This work was supported in part by China Natural Science Foundation (No. 60702019).

9. References

Ahn, H.S. & Won, C. H. (2006). Fast alignment using rotation vector and adaptive Kalman Filter, *IEEE Transactions on Aerospace and Electronic Systems*, Vol. 42, pp. 70-83

Ashokaraj, I. A. R.; Silson, P. M. G.; Tsourdos, A. & White, B. A. (2002). Implementation of an adaptive EKF to multiple low cost navigation sensors in wheeled mobile robots, Seventh International Conference on Control, Automation, Robotics and Vision, Singapore, pp. 608-612

Bai, M.; Zhou, D. H. & Schwarz, H. (1999). Identification of generalized friction for an experimental planar two-link flexible manipulator using strong tracking filter, *IEEE Transactions on Robotics and Automation*, Vol. 15, pp. 362-369

Bolognani, S.; Tubiana, L. & Zigliotto, M. (2003). EKF-based sensorless IPM synchronous motor drive for flux-weakening applications, *IEEE Transactions on Industry Applications*, Vol. 39, pp. 768-775

Bolognani, S.; Tubiana, L. & Zigliotto, M. (2003). Extended Kalman filter tuning in sensorless PMSM drives, *IEEE Transactions on Industry Applications*, Vol. 39, pp. 1741-1747

Boutayeb, M. & Aubry, D. (1999). A strong tracking extended Kalman observer for nonlinear discrete-time systems, *IEEE Transactions on Automatic Control*, Vol. 44, pp. 1550-1556

Einicke, G. A. & White, L. B. (1999). Robust extended Kalman filtering, *IEEE Transactions on Signal Processing*, Vol. 47, pp. 2596-2599

Einicke, G. A.; White, L. B. & Bitmead, R. R. (2003). The use of fake algebraic Riccati equations for co-channel demodulation, *IEEE Transactions on Signal Processing*, Vol. 51, pp. 2288-2293

Fu, M.; Souza, C. E. & Luo, Z. (2001). Finite-Horizon Robust Kalman Filter Design, *IEEE Transactions on Signal Processing*, Vol. 49, pp. 2103-2112

Huang, X.; Cui, H. & Cui, P. (2004). An autonomous optical navigation and guidance for soft landing on asteroids, *Acta Astronautica*, Vol. 54, pp. 763-771

Kim, S. J. & Iltis, R. A. (2004). STAP for GPS receiver synchronization, *IEEE Transactions on Aerospace and Electronic System*, Vol. 40, pp. 132-144

Kwon, S. J. (2006). Robust Kalman filtering with perturbation estimation process for uncertain systems, *IEE Proc.-Control Theory Appl.*, Vol. 153, pp. 600-606

Lewis, F. L. (1986). *Optimal Estimation*, New York, Wiley

Ma, D. M. & Zhai, S. Y. (2004). Sun-synchronous satellite orbit determination, *Acta Astronautica*, Vol. 54, pp. 245-251

Moghaddamjoo, A. & Kirlin, R. L. (1989). Robust adaptive Kalman filtering with unknown inputs, *IEEE Transactions on Acoustics, Speech and Signal Processing*, Vol. 37, pp. 1166-1175

Nolet, S. (2007). The SPHERES navigation system: from early development to on-orbit testing, *AIAA Guidance, Navigation and Control Conference and Exhibit*, Hilton Head, South Carolina

Psiaki, M. L. & Hinks, J. C. (2007). Autonomous lunar orbit determination using star occultation measurements, *AIAA Guidance, Navigation and Control Conference and Exhhibit*, Hilton Head, South Carolina

Reif, K.; Sonnemann, F. & Unbehauen, R. (1999). Nonlinear state observation using H_∞ -filtering Riccati design, *IEEE Transactions on Automatic Control*, Vol. 44, pp.203-208

Reif, K. & Unbehauen, R. (1999). Stochastic stability of the discrete-time extended Kalman filter, *IEEE Transactions on Automatic Control*, Vol. 44, pp. 714-728

Reif, K.; Gunther, S. & Unbehauen, R. (2000). Stochastic stability of the continuous-time extended Kalman filter, *IEE Proc.-Control Theory Appl.*, Vol. 147, pp. 45-52

Seo, J.; Yu, M. J.; Park, C. G. & Lee, G. L. (2006). An extended robust H_∞ filter for nonlinear constrained uncertain systems, *IEEE Transactions on Signal Processing*, Vol. 54, pp. 4471-4475

Shen, X. & Deng, L. (1999). A dynamic system approach to speech enhancement using the H_∞ filtering algorithm, *IEEE Transactions on Speech and Audio Processing*, Vol. 7, pp. 391-399

Shi, K. L.; Chan, T. F.; Wong, Y. K. & Ho, S. L. (2002). Speed estimation of an induction motor drive using an optimized extended Kalman filter, *IEEE Transactions on Industrial Electronics*, Vol. 49, pp. 124-133

Tarn, T. J. & Rasis, Y. (1976). Observers for nonlinear stochastic systems, *IEEE Transactions on Automatic Control*, Vol. 21, pp. 441-448

Theodor, Y.; Shaked, U. & Souza, C. E. (1994). A game theory approach to robust discrete-time H_∞-estimation, *IEEE Transactions on Signal Processing*, Vol. 42, pp. 1486-1495

Tseng, C. S. & Chen, B. S. (2001). H_∞ fuzzy estimation for a class of nonlinear discrete-time dynamic systems, *IEEE Transactions on Signal Processing*, Vol. 49, pp. 2605-2619

Vasile, M.; Sironi, F. & Bernelli-Zazzera, F. (2002). Deep space autonomous orbit determination using CCD, *AIAA/AAS Astrodynamics Specialist Conference and Exhibit*, California

Wang, F. & Balakrishnan, V. (1999). Robust adaptive Kalman filters for linear time-varying systems with stochastic parametric uncertainties, *Proceedings of the American Control Conference*, California, pp.440-444

Wei, C. L.; Li, Y. & Chen, Y. Q. (2004). Spacecraft autonomous navigation based on ultraviolet sensors, *Aerospace Control*, Vol. 22, pp. 35-39

Wiegand, M. (1996). Autonomous satellite navigation via Kalman filtering of magnetometer data, *Acta Astronautica*, Vol. 38, pp. 395-403

Wu, S.; Hong, L. & Layne, J. R. (2004). 2D rigid-body target modeling for tracking and identification with GMTI/HRR measurements, *IEE Proc.-Control Theory Appl.*, Vol. 151, pp. 429-438

Xiong, K.; Zhang, H. Y. & Chan, C. W. (2006). Performance evaluation of UKF-based nonlinear filtering, *Automatica*, Vol. 42, pp. 261-270

Xiong, K.; Zhang, H. Y. & Liu, L. D. (2008). Adaptive robust extended Kalman filter for nonlinear stochastic systems, *IET Control Theory & Applications*, Vol. 2, pp. 239-250

Yu, K. K. C.; Watson, N. R. & Arrillaga, J. (2005). A adaptive Kalman filter for dynamic harmonic state estimation and harmonic injection tracking, *IEEE Transactions on Power Delivery*, Vol. 20, pp. 1577-1584

Zhang, W.; Chen, B. S. & Tseng, C. S. (2005). Robust H_∞ filtering for nonlinear stochastic systems, *IEEE Transactions on Signal Processing*, Vol. 53, pp. 589-598

Zhang, Y. & Fang, J. (2003). Simulation and research on the satellite autonomous celestial navigation based on the perturbative orbit, *Chinese Space Science and Technology*, pp. 57-63

Medical and Biological Sciences

6

Use of Constrained Nonlinear Kalman Filtering to Detect Pathological Constriction of Cerebral Arterial Blood Vessels

Federico S. Cattivelli[2], Shadnaz Asgari[1], Paul Vespa[3], Ali H. Sayed[2], Marvin Bergsneider[1] and Xiao Hu[1],
[1]*Neural Systems and Dynamics Lab, Department of Neurosurgery, University of California,*
[2]*Adaptive Systems Lab, Department of Electrical Engineering, University of California,*
[3]*Neurocritical Care Program, Department of Neurosurgery, University of California, Los Angeles, USA*

1. Introduction

Aneurysmal subarachnoid hemorrhage (aSAH) is a significant health care problem because of its high morbidity and mortality rates. Survivors of initial hemorrhage are susceptible to many forms of delayed but treatable secondary injuries, among which delayed ischemic neurological deficit (DIND) caused by vasospasm is the leading cause of morbidity and mortality. It is known that between 5 and 10% of hospitalized SAH patients die from vasospasm. What makes vasospasm interesting is that to some extent it is predictable, preventable and treatable [1].

Cerebral vasospasm is defined as the narrowing of the contrast medium column in the major cerebral arteries as evidenced in angiograms. It usually starts 3 to 5 days following bleeding showing a maximal reduction of the affected vessel lumen during Days 5 to 14 and can slowly resolve after weeks in some cases [2]. Prediction of cerebral vasospasm after aSAH is still challenging although there exist several ways of approaching it. Some patient-related factors, such as initial clinical grade of aSAH [3], size and location of aneurysm [4], age [5], and sex [6] were found predictive of cerebral vasospasm from epidemiological studies. However, these measures can be too general to be useful for individuals.

A. Detecting vasospasm

Various diagnostic neurological imaging modalities can potentially be used as indicators of vasospasm. Conventional angiography is the gold standard of confirming the narrowing of large arteries. However, it is an invasive technique, since it requires the insertion of a catheter into a peripheral artery and the addition of a dye for correct visualization. Angiography is not suitable for continuous monitoring, and can also miss small vasospastic vessels. Clinical scales, such as Fisher score [4] that quantifies total amount of subarachnoid blood on the initial CT scan, are predictive of vasospasm to some extent. However, they do not take into consideration the amount of blood removed by surgery, which has been shown to reduce the incidence of vasospasm. CT perfusion, single-photon emission computed

tomography (SPECT) and MRI perfusion/diffusion imaging methods have the advantage of being noninvasive. However, their limitations include possible irradiation of head, cost, inconvenience of transporting ICU patients, general availability and possible delay of prediction after significant tissue ischemia is already present. More regional methods such as bedside intracerebral microdialysis have also been proposed [7], which seem appropriate for detecting focal vasospasm. However, microdialysis needs insertion of a probe to observe metabolic parameters changes in the tissue that may become ischemic [7]. In addition, an appropriate selection of which region to probe is needed. Finally, a delay of prediction may be present because of its reliance on the changed tissue metabolic patterns.
The only noninvasive and easy-to-access clinical way of predicting vasospasm, at present, is to use Transcranial Doppler (TCD) measurement of blood flow velocities in conductive cerebral arteries including middle cerebral artery (MCA), anterior cerebral artery (ACA) and intracranial carotid artery (ICA) [8], [9], [10]. Prediction of vasospasm using this conventional TCD assessment is based on absolute values of velocity (> 120 cm/s indicating medium vasospasm, > 200 cm/s indicative of severe vasospasm). These criteria are based on a very simplified view of the complex cerebral hemodynamics that cerebral flow velocity (CBFV) is inversely related to square of the vessel radius. It has been demonstrated that this relationship only partially holds when vasospasm is not severe [11]. The actual relation between CBFV and arterial radius r is as follows

$$CBFV = \frac{CBF}{\pi r^2}$$

where CBF is the Cerebral Blood Flow. In severe cases, a diminishing CBF is concomitant with a decreasing CBFV, which would have been taken as a recovery sign from vasospasm without knowledge of CBF. Additionally, systemic vascular effect has also been shown to affect the absolute blood flow velocity where hypertensive patients have a lower CBFV such that assessment of these patients are more prone to false negative results [12]. Another limitation of relying on the inverse relationship between vessel radii and flow velocity is that vasospasm can be detected only after certain degree of vessel radii change hence compromising its predictive power.
An alternative method that is used often in practice is the evaluation of the Lindegaard ratio [13] which is an empirical approach and does not give exact information about the actual radii of the vessels as Angiography does, and also the thresholds defined for predicting the outcome are rather ad-hoc and may change for different patients.
In this work we resort to a different approach to estimate the radii of the arteries without directly measuring them. It constitutes a model-based approach where state-estimation is applied to estimate physiological variables of interest such as arterial radii. The objective is to obtain a better estimation than that offered by the Lindegaard ratio, avoid the invasiveness of Angiography, and at the same time allow for continuous monitoring and possibly prediction of future spastic states.

2. Methodology

It is apparent from the above discussion that in order to increase the predictive power of TCD based vasospasm assessment, additional measurements including arterial blood pressure (ABP) and intracranial pressure (ICP) are needed. ICP is informative for two reasons: 1) ICP directly affects cerebral perfusion pressure, whose fluctuation is one of CBF autoregulation stimuli, and autoregulation will modulate the relationship between CBFV and cerebral vasculature radii; 2) CBF changes lead to cerebral blood volume changes and thus ICP changes. Hence, ICP carries information about both CBF and cerebrospinal fluid (CSF) circulatory systems. In addition to more measurements, the dynamic changes in signals instead of absolute CBFV values shall be explored. However, what is less apparent is how to integrate all these added measurements such that dynamics can be properly characterized to provide predictive information.

Mathematical modeling of a complex system is useful in elucidating the internal factors that are causative of observed behaviors of the system. In a pure deterministic situation, such internal factors alone can determine the current state of system. The system in this study is the coupled CBF and CSF circulatory system, which is complex and distributed in nature. A mathematical model of such a system is inevitably imperfect and hence has uncertainties. Thus, when trying to assess internal states of a system from external observations, it is imperative to address the imperfectness of the model in statistical sense. This treatment then results in a model-based data fusion approach, or equivalently in an engineering term, a stochastic state estimation approach. Cerebral vasculature radii dynamics provide internal information that can potentially lead to a more straightforward and efficient way of predicting vasospasm offering considerable advantage than predicting vasospasm based on any single measurement of the system.

Three components are needed to construct such a state estimator for vasospasm prediction as described in our previous work [14]:

- A mathematical model of cerebral hemodynamics (Sec. III)
- A model-training (or parameter estimation) approach (Sec. IV)
- A nonlinear state-estimation approach (Sec. V)

The first component is a mathematical model of the integrated cerebral blood and CSF circulatory systems. Among many published models, those proposed in a series work of Ursino [15], [16], [17], [18], [19], [20], [21], [22] are appropriate ones because all the key known physiological factors are included in these models that regulate CBF and their interactions with the CSF circulation. However, one issue still remains regarding the complexity of the model if one chooses to model the vasospasm directly. Trade-off is usually justified between the complexity and the accuracy of the model because a state estimator is easier to be built on a simpler model as there would be fewer parameters to be estimated and the numerical stability of the estimator would be better. We approached this problem by a simulation study where signals simulated using a complete model including a direct modeling of vasospasm are used to test a state estimator based on a simplified model without components of vasospasm. This will be illustrated in Section VI.

The second component is the parametrization of the model using individual patient's measurement. This is essentially a nonlinear optimization problem. We will briefly describe in Section IV our solution that utilizes a combined global random search of parameter space and a local gradient based search to fine tune the parameters found by the global search. Particularly, we chose the differential evolution (DE) algorithm in the present work [23]. This algorithm has been used successfully as a global search technique for parameterizing mathematical models encountered in various fields [24], [25], [26].

Once an individualized model is obtained, the third step is to simulate the model and adjust its estimated state variables based on the error between the simulated and the measured output of the model. The adjustment of state variable is necessary because any inaccuracy of the model, any physiological changes of parameters with time, or the accumulated error of numerical integrator can drive the simulated results erroneous. The celebrated Kalman filter (KF) [27] is a better solution because errors sensed in the simulated output are then used to correct the state estimation at every measurement moment. The KF is an optimal state estimator for linear Gaussian systems. Even though it is well known that such optimality is lost for a nonlinear dynamic system, almost all of the recently proposed nonlinear state estimators still follow [28], [29], [30], [31] the KF's general schema to achieve a suboptimal solution for such systems although they differ in the particular form of propagating the statistics of state variables. In essence, one could chose any of the above nonlinear estimators for the vasospasm detection problem. However, all these filters have usually derived the Kalman gain in an unconstrained fashion, meaning that no domain knowledge has been used to define a feasible range of solutions for states and model parameters. In an intracranial pressure dynamic model, such physiological constraints usually exist for state variables as well as for model parameters. Therefore, a regularization of the state estimation process can be achieved by incorporating constraints in the derivation of the Kalman gain. A quadratic programming technique can be used to solve the resultant constraint optimization problem, which is applicable to any nonlinear state estimators.

In summary, we propose a model-based approach to integrate ABP, ICP, and CBFV signals so that a hidden variable useful for characterizing the narrowing process of cerebral arteries can be obtained for detecting this process before any clinical symptoms appear. This approach is comprised of a physiology-driven mathematical model of CBF and CSF circulatory systems, a parameter estimation module that provides appropriate values for unknown model parameters, and a state updating algorithm based on KF-like nonlinear estimators (see Fig. 1). In the following, brief technical descriptions of modeling, parametrization, and state estimation are provided. A simulation study will be introduced to illustrate the feasibility of using a simplified model to drive the state estimation process. The effectiveness of the whole system will be illustrated using data from patients who developed vasospasm.

All the variables mentioned in this work correspond to time domain signals, sampled at 1Hz. The mathematical models used in this work have inputs, outputs, state variables and parameters. The input in this case is Arterial Blood Pressure (ABP), and the outputs are Intracranial Pressure (ICP) and Cerebral Blood Flow Velocity (CBFV). We assume measurements of all inputs and outputs are available. The models have several parameters which are in general unknown. An example of a parameter is the nominal value of a vessel resistance. The states typically represent some physiological variables which may not be measured directly, such as arterial radii of the vessels, compartment compliances, etc, and therefore need to be estimated.

Note that the parameter estimation and state estimation could be combined into one step, by posing the problem as a joint parameter-state estimation. Note however that this requires knowing the dynamics of the model parameters a-priori. Another technique that makes the same assumption is dual estimation. None of these topics are discussed in this work, and the reader is referred to [32] for more information.

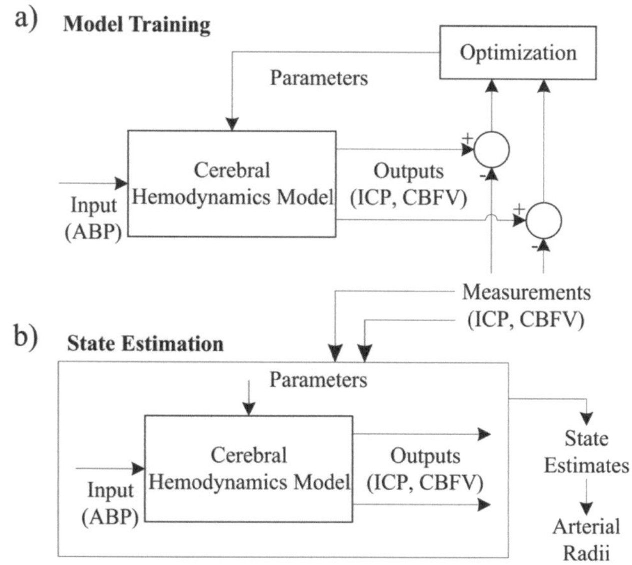

Fig. 1. Methodology involving a mathematical model, model training (or parameter estimation) and nonlinear state estimation.

3. Mathematical models of cerebral hemodynamics

We will introduce a complete dynamic model of CSF circulation, CBF circulation, and cerebral vasospasm. This model will be simulated with realistic parameters to provide ground truth data for validating the proposed state estimation approach. We will then present a systematic way of simplifying this model at different levels of complexity.

The proposed methodology for the estimation of arterial radii is based on continuous time measurements of CBFV, ABP and ICP. This methodology relies heavily on mathematical models that relate these quantities, together with the desired arterial radii. For our purpose, a good mathematical model should provide good correlation with observed quantities, and at the same time have low complexity to allow fast training and state estimation, and avoid possible instability. In general, these two characteristics will contradict each other, i.e., a less complex model will be less able to capture the interrelations between all the variables.

Another limitation of the approach is that even if we have a good model that closely matches the observed variables, it is virtually impossible to obtain continuous measurements of the actual arterial radii to compare them with the estimates. Hence, in this work we propose a simulationbased approach as follows: we develop a mathematical model of cerebral hemodynamics that is more general than previous models, and takes into account mechanisms such as Autoregulation and vasospasm. We will denote this model as Model 1. Then, we will use Model 1 to generate artificial data for different values of spasm severity. Next, we will develop a second model, denoted as Model 2, to estimate the arterial radii from Model 1 based on its outputs. As mentioned before, we want Model 2 to be simple, in order to reduce the complexity of the parameter and state estimation. This simulation-based approach will give us good insight into how capable simple models are of predicting states from more complex ones, and is the first step towards the application of the state estimation on actual patient data.

The mathematical models derived in this work are based on the models proposed by Ursino *et al.* These models were first introduced in [16], [17], [18]. Our work is based on the model of [16]. One inconvenience of the model in [16] is that it does not model vasospasm, which makes it inappropriate for the generation of data at different levels of spasm. Vasospasm was modeled in the work by Lodi and Ursino [19], but unfortunately several simplifications were introduced to the original Ursino model, such as a much simpler Autoregulation mechanism, and collapsing of the small and large arterial sections into one single section. Hence, we combined the two aforementioned models into one more general model that takes into account vasospasm, has a detailed Autoregulation mechanism, and has four sections: namely those corresponding to the large arteries (MCA, ACA, PCA), followed by the large pial arteries, small pial arteries and capillaries, and finally the venous compartment. We refer to this model as Model 1, and present it in the form of an electrical circuit in Fig. 2.

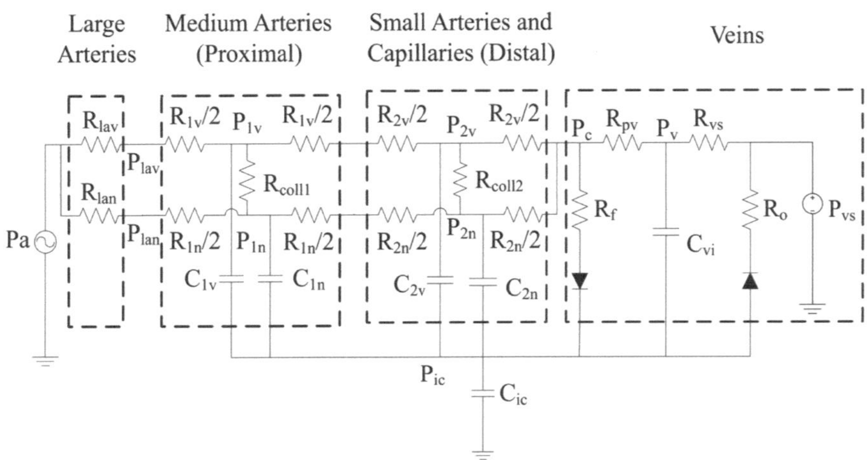

Fig. 2. Model 1, which is a combination of models published in [16] and [19].

Next we introduced several simplifications to Model 1, namely collapsing small and large pial arterial sections into one, a simpler Autoregulation mechanism, and assuming Pv=Pic. We also added one capacitance at the large arteries to obtain a state variable that allowed us to obtain the desired MCA radius. We refer to this model as Model 2, and present it in the form of an electrical circuit in Fig. 3.

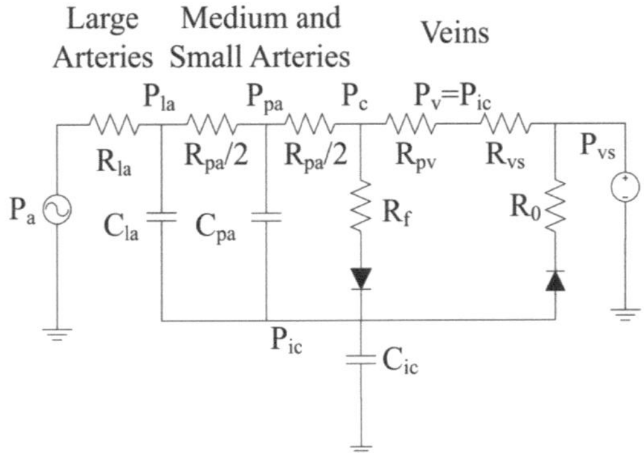

Fig. 3. Model 2, which is a simplified version of Model 1.

The details of models 1 and 2 can be found in [33] and are omitted from this work due to space considerations. Slight modifications were introduced to the models in [33] and will appear in future publications.

4. Parameter estimation

Fig. 1a shows the Model Training scenario. A model such as the ones described in Section III is used to generate artificial outputs (ICP and CBFV), and the measurements of these outputs are subtracted to generate an error signal. An optimization block is used to select the set of parameters that minimizes some cost function that depends on the error. For instance, in our case we use the cost function

$$J(\theta) = \sum_{l=1}^{L} \sum_{n=1}^{N} w_l(n) \left[y_l(n) - \hat{y}_l(n, \theta) \right]^2 \tag{1}$$

where N is the total number of measurements, L is the total number of outputs, θ is the unknown parameter vector, $y_l(n)$ is the nth measurement of output l, $\hat{y}_l(n, \theta)$ is the nth output l generated by the model using parameter θ, and $w_l(n)$ is some weighting function. In our case, we use the weighting function that weights every variable inversely proportional to the square of signal sample $y_l(n)$.

The models considered in this work are nonlinear, and hence (1) will in general be a nonconvex function of θ. As such, algorithms based on gradient descent are not guaranteed to converge to a global optimum. Hence, the optimization is done in two steps as proposed in [14]. First, a global search is performed using a genetic algorithm known as Differential Evolution (DE) [23], which has low complexity and good convergence. After the global search, a local search is performed using a standard gradient descent algorithm through the MATLAB Optimization Toolbox. Further details of this approach can be found in [14].

5. Non-linear state estimation

A. Kalman Filter-like state estimation for nonlinear models

Extensive treatments of the Kalman filter can be found in many standard text books [34], [35], [36], [37]. The extension of the Kalman Filter to nonlinear systems is required for detecting cerebrovascular radii changes. Consider a mathematical model of the system as follows

$$\mathbf{x}_{n+1} = F(\mathbf{x}_n, \mathbf{u}_n, \mathbf{w}_n) \tag{2}$$

and its measurement function as

$$\mathbf{y}_n = H(\mathbf{x}_n, \mathbf{u}_n, v_n) \tag{3}$$

where x_n, u_n, and w_n are the state variables, input, and state noise, respectively at time instant n. y_n and v_n are the model output and observation noise, respectively. For the continuous-time systems studied here (see Section 3), x_{n+1} is obtained by the numerical integration procedure with x_n, u_n and w_n as inputs.

The optimal estimate of the state variables $\mathbf{x}_n$ in the least mean squares sense, given the observation of $\mathbf{y}_i$, $i = 1, ..., n$, is the conditional expectation $E(\mathbf{x}_n \mid \mathbf{y}_i, i = 1, ..., n)$. The most significant contribution of the KF is that it realizes a recursive procedure to obtain this conditional expectation exactly for a linear system with jointly Gaussian initial states and noise variables. However, this optimality is not retained in general for nonlinear systems. Instead, several extensions of the linear Kalman Filter can be used to obtain a suboptimal solution for nonlinear systems. A typical approach to solve the problem is to use the Extended Kalman Filter (EKF), which has the disadvantage of requiring the Jacobian matrix of the system, its calculation being error prone. Derivative-free state estimation approaches in non-linear systems have also been proposed, for example, the Unscented Kalman Filter [38] and the DD1 and DD2 filters [31], which have been shown to provide better performance than the EKF. We give a brief introduction of the general paradigm of the Kalman filter in this section so that the links between the nonlinear and linear Kalman filters can be clearly observed.

In the subsequent mathematical developments, the notation $\hat{x}_{i|j}$ is used to denote an estimate of $\mathbf{x}_i$ based on the measurements up to discrete time j, and the operator * denotes conjugate transposition.

Let $\hat{x}_{n|n-1}$ denote the prior estimation of $\mathbf{x}_n$, namely

$$\hat{\mathbf{x}}_{n|n-1} \quad = \quad E[\mathbf{x}_n|\mathbf{y}_0, \ldots, \mathbf{y}_{n-1}]$$

where $E[\cdot]$ is the expectation operator, and define the error quantity $\tilde{\mathbf{x}}_{n|n-1} = \mathbf{x}_n - \hat{\mathbf{x}}_{n|n-1}$ with its associated covariance matrix as

$$P_{\tilde{\mathbf{x}}_{n|n-1}} = E(x_n - \hat{\mathbf{x}}_{n|n-1})(x_n - \hat{\mathbf{x}}_{n|n-1})^*$$

Similarly, let $\hat{y}_{n|n-1}$ denote the prior estimation of $\mathbf{y}_n$ and define the innovation sequence

$$\mathbf{e}_n = \mathbf{y}_n - \hat{\mathbf{y}}_{n|n-1}$$

with covariance

$$R_{\mathbf{e},n} = E\mathbf{e}_n\mathbf{e}_n^*$$

At time n, a new measurement $\mathbf{y}_n$ is collected to derive a better estimation of $\mathbf{x}_n$. For nonlinear filters, the assumption is that the random variables $\mathbf{x}_n$ and $\mathbf{y}_n$ are jointly Gaussian. When two random variables x and y are jointly Gaussian, it is well known that the optimal estimator of x given y is affine [36], [39]. Thus, in the case of a Gaussian system, it can be shown that the estimate of $\hat{x}_{n|n}$ can be obtained from $\hat{x}_{n|n-1}$ and the difference between the measured $\mathbf{y}_n$ and $\hat{y}_{n|n-1}$ such that

$$\hat{\mathbf{x}}_{n|n} = \hat{\mathbf{x}}_{n|n-1} + K_n \left(\mathbf{y}_n - \hat{\mathbf{y}}_{n|n-1}\right) , \tag{4}$$

where K_n is termed Kalman gain, which, for both linear and nonlinear systems, can be optimally calculated as

$$K_n = E[\tilde{\mathbf{x}}_{n|n-1}\mathbf{e}_n]R_{\mathbf{e},n}^{-1} \tag{5}$$

where $E[\tilde{\mathbf{x}}_{n|n-1}\mathbf{e}_n]$ is the cross covariance between $\tilde{x}_{n|n-1}$ and $\mathbf{e}_n$. Moreover, the state error covariance can be updated from

$$P_{\tilde{\mathbf{x}}_{n|n}} = P_{\tilde{\mathbf{x}}_{n|n-1}} - K_n R_{\mathbf{e},n} K_n^*$$

Equation (4), used to obtain $\hat{x}_{n|n}$ from $\hat{x}_{n|n-1}$, is usually called measurement update since the upgrade of the prior estimate to a better posterior estimate is achieved with the arrival of a new measurement. The optimal choices for the remaining quantities are:

$$\hat{\mathbf{x}}_{n+1|n} \quad = \quad E[F(\mathbf{x}_n, u_n, \mathbf{w}_n)|\mathbf{y}_0, \ldots, \mathbf{y}_n] \tag{6}$$

which requires the calculation of the conditional probability of $\mathbf{x}_n$ given the measurements up to time n. This step is usually called time-update. The prediction of the measurement can be calculated in a similar fashion as

$$\hat{\mathbf{y}}_{n|n-1} \quad = \quad E[H(\mathbf{x}_n, u_n, v_n)|\mathbf{y}_0, \ldots, \mathbf{y}_{n-1}] \tag{7}$$

Having obtained $\hat{x}_{n+1|n}$, $\hat{y}_{n+1|n}$ and their covariances, the next run of measurement-updates can be carried out. The whole iteration procedure then continues. The above equations allow us to recursively compute the state estimates $\hat{x}_{n|n}$. Note that we have not assumed linearity of the model, and our only assumption was that the states and measurements are jointly Gaussian.

The time update step in the general Kalman filter paradigm is essentially the propagation of the expectation and the covariances of random variables through functions. A difficulty arises in general when calculating (6) and (7) since the value of $\mathbf{x}_n$ is unknown. Different nonlinear Kalman filters address this propagation problem in different ways while the measurement update is conducted in the same fashion. Nonlinear Kalman-like estimators such as the Extended Kalman Filter (EKF) use the following approximations

$$\hat{\mathbf{x}}_{n+1|n} \approx F(\hat{\mathbf{x}}_{n|n}, u_n, \bar{\mathbf{v}}) \qquad \hat{\mathbf{y}}_{n|n-1} \approx H(\hat{\mathbf{x}}_{n|n-1}, u_n, \bar{\mathbf{w}})$$

The Unscented Kalman filter [38], [32] uses the so-called sigma points, $\chi_{0,i|i} = \hat{x}_{i|i}$, $\chi_{n,i|i} = \hat{x}_{i|i} + \left[\sqrt{(L+\lambda)P_{i|i}}\right]_n$, $n = 1, \ldots, L$ and $\chi_{n,i|i} = \hat{x}_{i|i} - \left[\sqrt{(L+\lambda)P_{i|i}}\right]_n$, $n = L+1, \ldots, 2L$, where $\lambda = \alpha^2(L+\kappa) - L$, α and κ are two constant parameters. Then the sigma points are propagated through the nonlinear function f, and the resulting points are aggregated to obtain an approximation for the mean of the output of the function, as follows:

$$\chi_{n,i+1|i} = f(\chi_{n,i|i}, u_i)$$

$$\hat{x}_{i+1|i} \approx \sum_{n=0}^{2L} W_n \chi_{n,i+1|i}$$

In the next two sections, we will briefly describe a different approach based on the DD1 filter [31].

B. DD1 filter

DD1 and DD2 filters were introduced by Norgaard [31], and approximate the nonlinear transformations using a multidimensional extension of Stirling's interpolation formula. As in Unscented filters, the DD1 and DD2 filters do not require calculation or evaluation of the derivatives of the nonlinear functions. Also, they have been shown to outperform the EKF in several situations.

The basic principle behind DD1 and DD2 filters is that a nonlinear function $f(x)$ can be approximated as

$$f(x) \approx f(\bar{x}) + f'_{DD}(\bar{x})(x-\bar{x}) + \frac{1}{2} f''_{DD}(\bar{x})(x-\bar{x})^2 \ldots$$

where

$$f'_{DD}(x) = \frac{f(x+h) - f(x-h)}{2h} \quad \text{and} \quad f''_{DD}(x) = \frac{f(x+h) + f(x-h) - 2f(x)}{h^2} \tag{8}$$

Given a random variable $\mathbf{x}$, with mean $E(\mathbf{x}) = \bar{x}$ and covariance $Cov(\mathbf{x}) = E(\mathbf{x}-\bar{x})(\mathbf{x}-\bar{x})^* = P_x$, and an arbitrary function $f(.)$, we would like to determine $E(\mathbf{y}) = \bar{y}$ and $Cov(\mathbf{y}) = P_y$, where $\mathbf{y} = f(\mathbf{x})$. In other words, we are interested in propagating the mean and covariance of a random variable through a possibly nonlinear function f. When f is linear, the answer is given by the Kalman filter.

Define a random variable $\mathbf{z} = S_x^{-1}\mathbf{x}$,, where S_x is a Cholesky factor of P_x, i.e., $P_x = S_x S_x^*$. Then we have that $P_z = I$. Moreover, define a function $\tilde{f}(\mathbf{z}) = f(S_x^{-1}\mathbf{x}) = f(\mathbf{x})$. To first order, we can approximate:

$$\mathbf{y} = \tilde{f}(\mathbf{z}) = \tilde{f}(\bar{z} + \Delta\mathbf{z}) \approx \tilde{f}(\bar{z}) + \tilde{f}'_{DD}(\bar{z})\Delta\mathbf{z} \tag{9}$$

where $\Delta\mathbf{z} \triangleq \mathbf{z} - E\mathbf{z}$ is a zero-mean random variable. Thus, taking expectation of (9), to first order we obtain:

$$\bar{y} \approx f(\bar{x}) \tag{10}$$

In order to propagate the covariance matrix, the same first order approximation leads us to

$$P_y = E[(\mathbf{y}-\bar{y})(\mathbf{y}-\bar{y})^*] \approx E[\tilde{f}'_{DD}(\bar{z})\Delta\mathbf{z}(\tilde{f}'_{DD}(\bar{z})\Delta\mathbf{z})^*]$$

Noting that $E\Delta\mathbf{z} = I$, and using (8) we obtain

$$P_y \approx \frac{1}{4h^2}[f(\bar{x}+hS_x) - f(\bar{x}-hS_x)][f(\bar{x}+hS_x) - f(\bar{x}-hS_x)]^*$$

In the general case where $\mathbf{x}$ has size n, [31] shows that P_y and the cross covariance P_{xy} can be obtained from

$$P_y \approx \frac{1}{4h^2}\sum_{p=1}^{n}[f(\bar{x}+hs_{x,p}) - f(\bar{x}-hs_{x,p})][f(\bar{x}+hs_{x,p}) - f(\bar{x}-hs_{x,p})]^* \tag{11}$$

$$P_{xy} \approx \frac{1}{2h}\sum_{p=1}^{n} s_{x,p}[f(\bar{x}+hs_{x,p}) - f(\bar{x}-hs_{x,p})]^* \tag{12}$$

where $s_{x,p}$ is the pth column of S_x.

The DD1 filter uses the same approximation as the EKF for the a-priori update, namely

$$\hat{\mathbf{x}}_{n+1|n} = F(\hat{\mathbf{x}}_{n|n}, u_n, \bar{w}_n)$$

and the output estimate is given by

$$\hat{\mathbf{y}}_{n|n-1} = H(\hat{\mathbf{x}}_{n|n-1}, u_n, \bar{v}_n)$$

The Kalman gain is computed from

$$K_n = P_{\mathbf{xe},n} R_{\mathbf{e},n}^{-1}$$

where $R_{\mathbf{e},n}$ and the cross covariance $P_{\mathbf{xe},n}$ are obtained from (11) and (12), respectively, by propagating $(\hat{x}_{n|n-1}, u_n, \mathbf{v}_n)$ through the function H. For these calculations, an estimate of $P_{\tilde{\mathbf{x}}_{n|n-1}}$ is required, which is obtained from (11) by propagating $(\hat{x}_{n-1|n-1}, u_{n-1}, \mathbf{w}_{n-1})$ through the function F. The measurement update is the same as in the linear case, namely,

$$\begin{aligned} \hat{\mathbf{x}}_{n|n} &= \hat{\mathbf{x}}_{n|n-1} + K_n(y_n - \hat{\mathbf{y}}_{n|n-1}) \\ P_{\hat{\mathbf{x}}_{n|n}} &= P_{\hat{\mathbf{x}}_{n|n-1}} - K_n R_{\mathbf{e},n} K_n^* \end{aligned} \tag{13}$$

C. Constrained Kalman Filter

Physical and physiological boundaries on some state variables and model parameters exist in the present model. However, it can be noted that the equation to update state variables can result in posterior estimates well beyond those boundaries. Hence, adding constraints to the original problem of optimizing K_n is necessary. It is shown that this can be formulated as a quadratic programming problem for which efficient algorithms exist. Quadratic programming solves the following problem

$$\min_{\theta \in R^n} J(\theta) = \frac{1}{2}\theta^T H \theta + w^T \theta \tag{14}$$

$$A_i \theta = b_i, \quad i = 1, \cdots, n_e \tag{15}$$

$$A_i \theta \leq b_i, \quad i = n_e + 1, \cdots, n_p \tag{16}$$

where H, w, A, and b are known quantities. A_i is the ith row of constraint matrix A and b_i is the ith element of b. In the above formulation, there are n_e equality and $n_p - n_e$ inequality constraints. To formulate the calculation of K_n as a QP problem, it should be realized that K_n is an optimal solution of linear least mean square problem, i.e.,

$$\min_{K_n} TrE[\mathbf{x}_n - \hat{\mathbf{x}}_{n|n-1} - K_n(\mathbf{y}_n - \hat{\mathbf{y}}_{n|n-1})][\mathbf{x}_n - \hat{\mathbf{x}}_{n|n-1} - K_n(\mathbf{y}_n - \hat{\mathbf{y}}_{n|n-1})]^T \tag{17}$$

where $Tr[\cdot]$ is the trace of a matrix. The above equation can be further simplified since all the variables involved are real. With definitions of $\tilde{x} = \mathbf{x}_n - \hat{x}_{n|n-1}$ and $\tilde{y} = \mathbf{y}_n - \hat{y}_{n|n-1}$, it follows

$$\min_{K_n} Tr\left[E\tilde{\mathbf{x}}\tilde{\mathbf{x}}^T + K_n E\tilde{\mathbf{y}}\tilde{\mathbf{y}}^T K_n^T - 2K_n E\tilde{\mathbf{y}}\tilde{\mathbf{x}}^T\right]. \tag{18}$$

Denoting the ith row of K_n as $K_{n,i}$ and the dimension of state variable as d, the above problem can be decomposed into d independent subproblems as

$$\min_{K_{n,i}} E\tilde{\mathbf{x}}_{\mathbf{i}}^2 + K_{n,i}E\tilde{\mathbf{y}}\tilde{\mathbf{y}}^T K_{n,i}^T - 2K_{n,i}E\tilde{\mathbf{y}}\tilde{\mathbf{x}}_{\mathbf{i}}^T \tag{19}$$

which is equivalently

$$\min_{K_{n,i}} \frac{1}{2}K_{n,i}E\tilde{\mathbf{y}}\tilde{\mathbf{y}}^T K_{n,i}^T + (-K_{n,i})E\tilde{\mathbf{y}}\tilde{\mathbf{x}}_{\mathbf{i}}^T \tag{20}$$

hence θ in Eq 14 is $-K_{n,i}^T$. Now suppose that the $\mathbf{x}_n$ is constrained by $[l^{(i)}, u^{(i)}]$, which leads to

$$l^{(i)} \leq \hat{\mathbf{x}}_{n|n-1,i} + K_{n,i}(\mathbf{y}_n - \hat{\mathbf{y}}_{n|n-1}) \leq u^{(i)} \ , \tag{21}$$

simple manipulations lead to the standard form of inequity constraints as

$$K_{n,i}(\mathbf{y}_n - \hat{\mathbf{y}}_{n|n-1}) \leq u^{(i)} - \hat{\mathbf{x}}_{n|n-1,i} \tag{22}$$

$$K_{n,i}(\hat{\mathbf{y}}_{n|n-1} - \mathbf{y}_n) \leq \hat{\mathbf{x}}_{n|n-1,i} - l^{(i)} \ . \tag{23}$$

This clearly indicates that $K_{n,i}$ can be calculated by solving a QP problem instead of the original unconstrained least mean square solution.

6. Numerical simulation

Our goal is to use a mathematical model of cerebral hemodynamics, combined with a stateestimation approach which, using signals produced by a human patient, will allow us to estimate the hidden states of the patient.

In Section 3 we discussed two models of cerebral hemodynamics. Model 1 is a more general version of the model presented in [16], where it was shown that the results obtained through this model are in accordance with expected human responses. This model has ten state variables and several unknown parameters. Thus, if we were to use Model 1 for our state-estimation approach, the technique would become computationally complex and error prone, making Model 1 a poor candidate for our state estimation approach.

Model 2 is a simpler model, with only four state variables, namely P_{la}, P_{pa}, P_{ic} and C_{pa}. Thus this model is more amenable to our estimation approach and will be more robust to model mismatch.

It is, however, interesting to analyze how accurate is Model 2 in modeling the human cerebral hemodynamics. In other words, will Model 2 be able to detect changes in arterial radius as well as Model 1 would? To answer this question, we propose the following approach. We assume that Model 1 is the "true" model, and use it to generate artificial ICP and CBFV signals at different spastic levels. Subsequently, we apply our state-estimation approach using Model 2, on the signals generated by Model 1, and use the resulting state estimates to obtain estimates of arterial radius.

Figure 4 shows the estimation results (from [33]). The solid blue curve shows the actual value of the radius introduced artificially in Model 1, and the red dashed curve shows the radius estimated by Model 2 through measurement of the ICP and CBFV signals produced by Model 1. We observe that Model 2 is able to accurately track the changes in radius. Thus Model 2 is a good candidate for our state estimation approach.

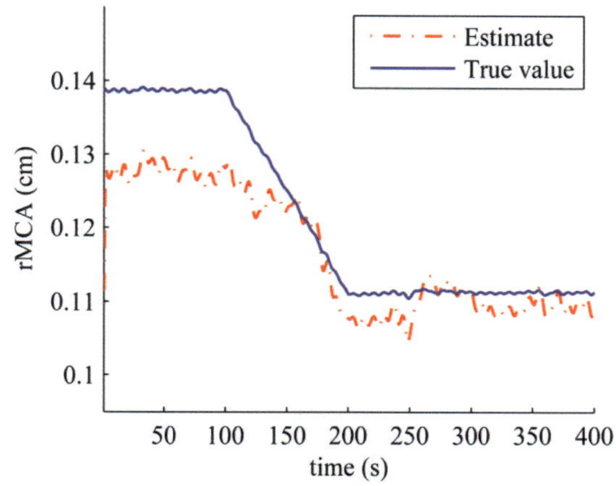

Fig. 4. Arterial radii artificially introduced in Model 1 ("true" model) and estimated through Model 2.

In the following section we will show the estimation results obtained using real patient data instead of artificial data generated by a model. We will use Model 2 as our state-estimation model.

7. Results with real patient data

We now present our state estimation results using real patient data. We show results on two patients who suffered Subarachnoid Hemorrhage (SAH), and were admitted to the Neurocritical care unit at the UCLA Medical Center in 2007. Both patients have continuous recordings of ICP, ABP and CBFV measured at the right MCA, on different days after the initial SAH. Typically, two recording sessions were obtained each day, one in the morning and one in the afternoon. The TCD monitoring and data collection were approved by the UCLA IRB with signed consent form from patients' next-of-kin.

The length of each recording varies, but typically includes between 10 minutes to 1 hour of usable data. The first patient, which we will refer to as "Patient A", had recordings on days 1, 3, 4, 5, 7, and 8 after the initial SAH. Days 1, 3, 4 and 8 have two sessions each. We will denote each recording session by the letter of the patient followed by the day after SAH, and then the session number on that day. Thus, the recordings of Patient A are labelled as A1-1, A1-2, A3-1, A3-2, A4-1, A4-2, A5-1, A7-1, A8-1 and A8-2. We will refer to the second patient as "Patient B", which has recordings B4-2, B5-1, B5-2, B6-1, B8-1, B10-1. This patient had an additional recording on day 4 after SAH, which was excluded since it did not include enough clean data for processing, due to either movement artifacts or noisy use of the TCD probe.

For each recording, we processed the data as follows. For each session, we extracted 300 seconds of clean data, including continuous ICP, CBFV at the right MCA and ABP. The 300 seconds were extracted by observing that the signals were clean enough, that there were no transient artifacts due to placement of the TCD probe, and that no significant movement artifacts were present. After we extracted the signals, we downsampled the signals to 1Hz sampling rate, previously using a lowpass filter to avoid aliasing. Note that this downsampling process keeps only average information of the signals, and the pulsatility information is destroyed.

After we obtained the downsampled signals, we applied our parameter estimation approach on the 300 seconds obtained from the first session available for that patient. That is, we used session A1-1 to estimate the parameters for patient A, and session B4-2 to estimate the parameters of patient B. Then we kept those same initial parameters constant for all the remaining sessions. The rationale behind this choice is that in the earliest recording, the patient is more likely not to have developed vasospasm. Typically vasospasm takes 3 to 4 days to develop. Thus, for patient A, it is very likely that the recording on day 1 will not include the effects of vasospasm. Then we will obtain a set of parameters that is representative of the "normal" state, without spasm. Then, a subsequent recording with a spastic state should be detected since it would deviate from the "normal" conditions. Unfortunately, for patient B, the earliest recording available is on day 4, indicating that the spasm may be present already (though we will argue later that this is not the case). Thus, if we train in a state that already includes the spasm, we may not be able to detect the subsequent changes. In summary, it is important to train the model as soon as possible after the initial SAH, to allow the system to learn the model parameters in normal conditions.

After learning the model parameters on the first available recording, we proceeded to estimate the states of the model using two different approaches: a DD1 filter, and a DD1 filter with constraints on the states, denoted by QCKF. The details of the constraints will be presented in future publications.

Figure 5 shows the estimated radius for every session of patient A, both for the DD1 and QCKF filters. We can observe that according to our predictions, this patient had an evolving vasospasm starting on day 1, session 2, after the initial SAH. This spasm get accentuated on day 4, where it reaches less than half of its initial value. Then there is a slight recovery up to day 7, though the spasm is still considered severe. On day 8, session 2, the radius of the artery recovers to normal values, indicating the possibility of an angioplasty (surgery used to return arterial radius to normal).

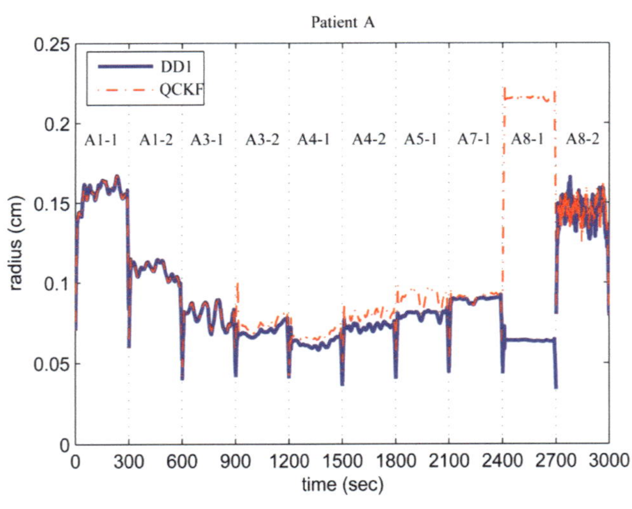

Fig. 5. Estimated radii for all sessions of patient A, for DD1 and QCKF filters.

Figure 6 shows the measured ICP and CBFV against the signals estimated through our state estimation approach, both for DD1 and QCKF. We can observe that for both methods, the observed and estimated ICP have good agreement. This is not the case for CBFV, where some discrepancies are observed. For instance, for session A7-1, DD1 has a significant disagreement with the actual signals. Note, however, how the QCKF approach is able to reduce this difference, by constraining the states to be within allowed values. On session A8-2, both filters have a significant difference with the true values, which is due to the fact that the CBFV is significantly increased from the normal values, thus questioning whether the estimates obtained in Fig. 5 for session A8-2 are accurate or not. Note that the two filters also disagree on the radius estimates of session A8-1. The output estimates provided by the QCKF are closer to the actual measurements on this session, thus we could conclude that the QCKF is providing better estimates of the radius, and that the angioplasty was performed before session A8-1.

Note also that the changes in ICP and CBFV do not seem to follow the trend of the vasospasm, which shows how powerful the proposed technique is. The mathematical models employed capture several complex inter-relationships between ICP, ABP and CBFV that are not evident at simple sight.

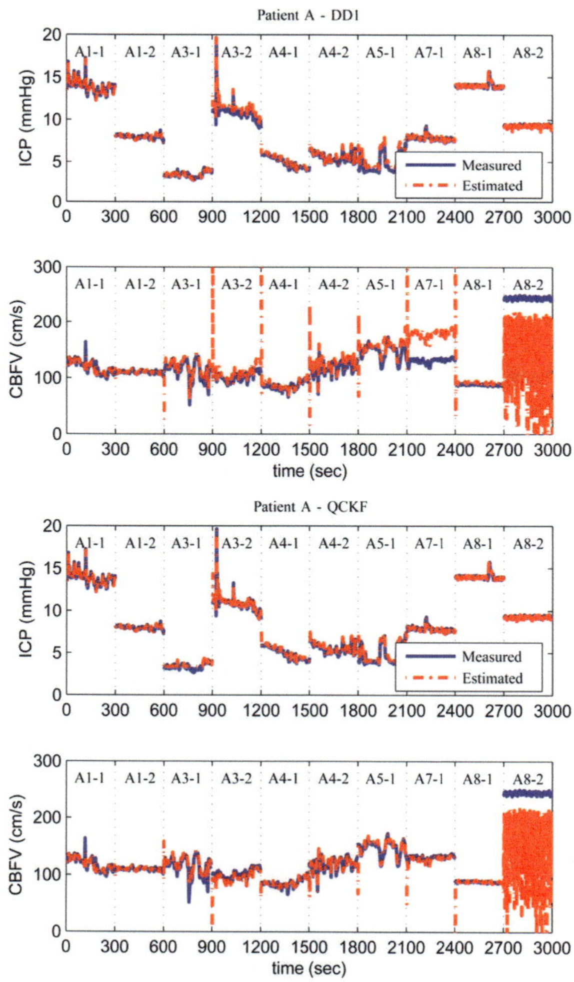

Fig. 6. Actual and estimated outputs (ICP, CBFV) for patient A, using DD1 filter (top two plots) and QCKF filter (bottom two plots).

The estimation results obtained for patient B are shown in Fig. 7, for the QCKF filter. The results obtained through DD1 filtering are similar. It can be observed that the patient did not suffer from significant changes in arterial radius. This indicates that either the patient did not suffer from vasospasm after SAH, or that the patient already had vasospasm on day 4 where the training was made, and the spasm did not improve in subsequent days. Angiographic evidence shows that the patient did have a mild vasospasm, supporting the second hypothesis.

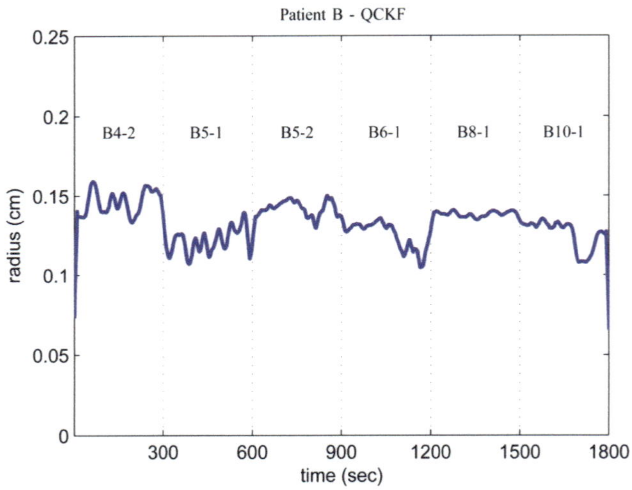

Fig. 7. Estimated radius for patient B, using QCKF filters.

Fig. 8 shows the measured and estimated outputs for Patient B, where a good match is observed for all recordings. Note again how big changes in CBFV and ICP do not influence the arterial radius estimates considerably, as is expected from this patient.

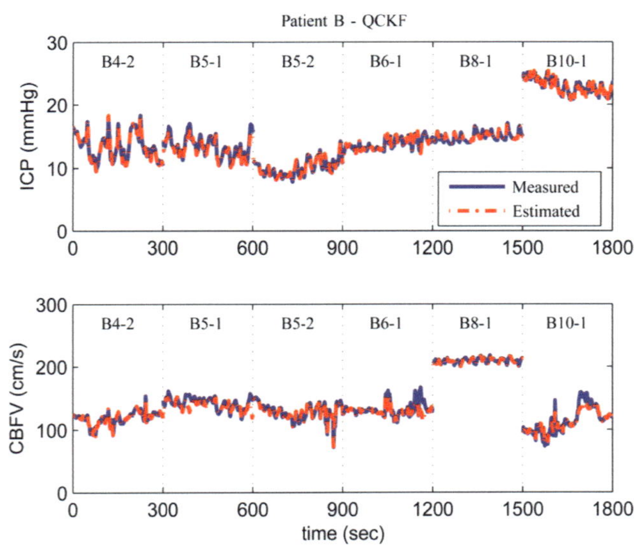

Fig. 8. Actual and estimated outputs (ICP, CBFV) for patient B, using the QCKF filter.

8. Discussion and conclusions

Estimation of lumped cerebral arterial radius is important for healthcare monitoring in ICU patients, specially for detecting the presence of vasospasm following Subarachnoid Hemorrhage. A technique for continuous monitoring based on available measurements without introducing any additional invasive technique is very attractive, and would allow detection of vasospasm earlier and more accurately than other methods such as angiography.

Our proposed estimation approach uses a combination of parameter estimation and state estimation techniques, and relies heavily on mathematical models of cerebral hemodynamics.We presented two models based on previous work by Ursino et. al, and showed through simulation how a simpler Model 2, with only four state-variables could predict changes in arterial radius from the signals generated through Model 1. We showed how to estimate the parameters of Model 1 through a non-linear least-squares technique, and how we trained the model on the first available recording of every patient. Then we applied our state-estimation approach using DD1 filtering, and a DD1 filter with constraints (QCKF). We showed that our approach detected the presence of vasospasm for Patient A, and observed a radius evolution that matches the expected results. The QCKF produced smaller errors in the output estimation, indicating that constraining the states to be within reasonable limits may improve the accuracy of the estimation. We also estimated the arterial radius for Patient B, which had a constant mild vasospasm throughout the recordings.

In essence, we have shown the potential of Kalman-like state-estimators for nonlinear models. This application could potentially save lives by predicting post-SAH vasospasm before other techniques would.

9. References

[1] R. L. Macdonald and B. Weir, *Cerebral Vasospasm*. San Diego, CA: Academic Press, 2001.

[2] M. R. Mayberg, H. H. Batjer, R. Dacey, M. Diringer, E. C. Haley, R. C. Heros, L. L. Sternau, J. Torner, J. Adams, H. P., W. Feinberg, and et al., "Guidelines for the management of aneurysmal subarachnoid hemorrhage. a statement for healthcare professionals from a special writing group of the stroke council, american heart association," *Circulation*, vol. 90, no. 5, pp. 2592–605, 1994.

[3] D. Chyatte and J. Sundt, T. M., "Cerebral vasospasm after subarachnoid hemorrhage," *Mayo Clin Proc*, vol. 59, no. 7, pp. 498–505, 1984.

[4] C. M. Fisher, J. P. Kistler, and J. M. Davis, "Relation of cerebral vasospasm to subarachnoid hemorrhage visualized by computerized tomographic scanning," *Neurosurgery*, vol. 6, no. 1, pp. 1–9, 1980.

[5] M. T. Torbey, T. K. Hauser, A. Bhardwaj, M. A.Williams, J. A. Ulatowski, M. A. Mirski, and A. Y. Razumovsky, "Effect of age on cerebral blood flow velocity and incidence of vasospasm after aneurysmal subarachnoid hemorrhage," *Stroke*, vol. 32, no. 9, pp. 2005–11, 2001.

[6] J. R. Ostergaard, "Risk factors in intracranial saccular aneurysms. aspects on the formation and rupture of aneurysms, and development of cerebral vasospasm," *Acta Neurol Scand*, vol. 80, no. 2, pp. 81–98, 1989.

[7] L. Persson, J. Valtysson, P. Enblad, P. E. Warme, K. Cesarini, A. Lewen, and L. Hillered, "Neurochemical monitoring using intracerebral microdialysis in patients with subarachnoid hemorrhage," *J Neurosurg*, vol. 84, no. 4, pp. 606–16, 1996.

[8] R. Aaslid, "Transcranial doppler assessment of cerebral vasospasm," *Eur J Ultrasound*, vol. 16, no. 1-2, pp. 3–10, 2002.

[9] R. W. Seiler, P. Grolimund, R. Aaslid, P. Huber, and H. Nornes, "Cerebral vasospasm evaluated by transcranial ultrasound correlated with clinical grade and ct-visualized subarachnoid hemorrhage," *J Neurosurg*, vol. 64, no. 4, pp. 594–600, 1986.

[10] L. N. Sekhar, L. R. Wechsler, H. Yonas, K. Luyckx, and W. Obrist, "Value of transcranial doppler examination in the diagnosis of cerebral vasospasm after subarachnoid hemorrhage," *Neurosurgery*, vol. 22, no. 5, pp. 813–21, 1988.

[11] C. A. Lodi and M. Ursino, "Hemodynamic effect of cerebral vasospasm in humans: a modeling study," *Ann Biomed Eng*, vol. 27, no. 2, pp. 257–73, 1999.

[12] A. Ekelund, H. Saveland, B. Romner, and L. Brandt, "Transcranial doppler ultrasound in hypertensive versus normotensive patients after aneurysmal subarachnoid hemorrhage," *Stroke*, vol. 26, no. 11, pp. 2071–4, 1995.

[13] K. Lindegaard, H. Nornes, S. Bakke, W. Sorteberg, and P. Nakstad, "Cerebral vasospasm after subarachnoid haemorrhage investigated by means of transcranial doppler ultrasound," *Acta Neurchir Suppl (Wien)*, vol. 42, pp. 81–84, 1988.

[14] X. Hu, V. Nenov, M. Bergsneider, T. Glenn, P. Vespa, and N. Martin, "Estimation of hidden state variables of the intracranial system using constrained nonlinear kalman filters," *IEEE Trans. Biomedical Engineering*, vol. 54, no. 4, pp. 597–610, April 2007.

[15] M. Ursino, "A mathematical study of human intracranial hydrodynamics part i - the cerebrospinal fluid pulse pressure," *Annals of Biomedical Engineering*, vol. 16, pp. 379–401, 1988.

[16] M. Ursino and P. D. Giammarco, "A mathematical model of the relationship between cerebral blood volume and intracranial pressure changes: The generation of plateau waves," *Annals of Biomedical Engineering*, vol. 19, pp. 15–42, 1991.

[17] M. Ursino and C. A. Lodi, "A simple mathematical model of the interaction between intracranial pressure and cerebral hemodynamics," *J. Applied Physiology*, vol. 82, pp. 1256–1269, 1997.

[18] ——, "Interaction among autoregulation, co2 reactivity, and intracranial pressure: A mathematical model," *Am. J. Physiol. Heart Circ. Physiol.*, vol. 274, pp. H1715–H1728, 1998.

[19] C. A. Lodi and M. Ursino, "Hemodynamic effect of cerebral vasospasm in humans: A modeling study," *Annals of Biomedical Engineering*, vol. 27, pp. 257–273, 1999.

[20] C. A. Lodi, A. Ter Minassian, L. Beydon, and M. Ursino, "Modeling cerebral autoregulation and co2 reactivity in patients with severe head injury," *Am J Physiol*, vol. 274, no. 5 Pt 2, pp. H1729-41, 1998.

[21] M. Ursino, M. Iezzi, and N. Stocchetti, "Intracranial pressure dynamics in patients with acute brain damage: a critical analysis with the aid of a mathematical model," *IEEE Transactions on Biomedical Engineering*, vol. 42, no. 6, pp. 529-40, 1995.

[22] M. Ursino, C. A. Lodi, S. Rossi, and N. Stocchetti, "Estimation of the main factors affecting icp dynamics by mathematical analysis of pvi tests," *Acta Neurochir Suppl (Wien)*, vol. 71, pp. 306-9, 1998.

[23] R. Storn and K. Price, "Differential evolution: A simple and efficient adaptive scheme for global optimization over continuous spaces," *J. Global Optimization*, vol. 11, pp. 341-359, 1997.

[24] P. Charusanti, X. Hu, L. Chen, D. Neuhauser, and r. DiStefano, J. J., "A mathematical model of bcr-abl autophosphorylation, signaling through the crkl pathway, and gleevec dynamics in chronic myeloid leukemia," *Discrete and Continuous Dynamical Systems Series B*, vol. 4, no. 1, pp. 99-114, 2004.

[25] S. L. Cheng and C. Hwang, "Optimal approximation of linear systems by a differential evolution algorithm," *IEEE Transactions on Systems Man and Cybernetics Part a-Systems and Humans*, vol. 31, no. 6, pp. 698-707, 2001.

[26] J. P. Chiou and F. S.Wang, "Estimation of monod model parameters by hybrid differential evolution," *Bioprocess and Biosystems Engineering*, vol. 24, no. 2, pp. 109-113, 2001.

[27] R. Kalman, "A new approach to linear filtering and prediction problems," *Transactions of the ASME. Series D, Journal of Basical Engineering*, vol. 82, pp. 34-45, 1960.

[28] N. J. Gordon, D. J. Salmond, and A. F. M. Smith, "Novel approach to nonlinear/non-gaussian bayesian state estimation," *IEE Proceedings-F Radar & Signal Processing*, vol. 140, no. 2, pp. 107-13, 1993.

[29] S. Julier, J. Uhlmann, and H. F. Durrant-Whyte, "A new method for the nonlinear transformation of means and covariances in filters and estimators," *IEEE Transactions on Automatic Control*, vol. 45, no. 3, pp. 477-482, 2000.

[30] S. J. Julier and J. K. Uhlmann, "Unscented filtering and nonlinear estimation," *Proceedings of the IEEE*, vol. 92, no. 3, pp. 401-422, 2004.

[31] M. Norgaard, N. Poulsen, and O. Ravn, "New developments in state estimation for nonlinear systems," *Automatica*, vol. 36, no. 11, pp. 1627-1638, 2000.

[32] S. H. ed., Kalman Filtering and Neural Networks. NY: Wiley, 2001.

[33] F. S. Cattivelli, A. H. Sayed, X. Hu, D. Lee, and P. Vespa, "Mathematical models of cerebral hemodynamics for detection of vasospasm in major cerebral arteries," *to appear, Acta Neurochirurgica (Wien)*, 2009.

[34] P. Zarchan and H. Musoff, *Fundamentals of Kalman filtering : a practical approach*, ser. Progress in astronautics and aeronautics ; v. 190. Reston, Va.: American Institute of Aeronautics and Astronautics, 2000.

[35] T. Kailath, A. H. Sayed, and B. Hassibi, *Linear Estimation*. NJ: Prentice Hall, 2000.

[36] A. H. Sayed, *Fundamentals of Adaptive Filtering*. NJ: Wiley, 2003.
[37] C. K. Chui and G. Chen, *Kalman filtering : with real-time applications*, 3rd ed., ser. Springer series in information sciences ; 17. Berlin ; New York: Springer, 1999.
[38] E. A. Wan and R. van der Merwe, "The unscented kalman filter for nonlinear estimation," in *Proc. IEEE Adaptive Systems for Signal Proc., Comm., and Control Symposium*, 2000, pp. 153–158.
[39] A. H. Sayed, *Adaptive Filters*. NJ: Wiley, 2008.

7

The Use of Kalman Filter in Biomedical Signal Processing

Vangelis P. Oikonomou, Alexandros T. Tzallas, Spiros Konitsiotis, Dimitrios G. Tsalikakis and Dimitrios I. Fotiadis
Department of Computer Science, University of Ioannina
GR 45110 Ioannina, Greece

1.Introduction

The Kalman Filter (KF) is a powerful tool in the analysis of the evolution of a dynamical model in time. The filter provides with a flexible manner to obtain recursive estimation of the parameters, which are optimal in the mean square error sense. The properties of KF along with the simplicity of the derived equations make it valuable in the analysis of signals. In this chapter an overview of the Kalman Filter, its properties and its applications is presented. More specifically, we focus on the application of Kalman Filter in the Electroencephalogram (EEG) processing, addressing extensions of Kalman Filter such as the Kalman Smoother (KS) in the time varying autoregressive (TVAR) model. The model can be written in a state - space form and the employment of KF provides with an estimation of the AR parameters which can be used for the estimation of the non - stationary signal. It is also demonstrated how these parameters can be used as input features of the signal in a clustering approach.

The Kalman Filter is an estimator with interesting properties like optimality in the Minimum Mean Square Error (MMSE). After its discovery in 1960 (Kalman, 1960), this estimator has been used in many fields of engineering such as control theory, communication systems, speech processing, biomedical signal processing, etc. An analogous estimator has been proposed for the smoothing problem (Rauch et al., 1963), which includes three different types of smoothers, namely fixed-lag, fixed-point and fixed interval (Anderson & Moore, 1979; Brown, 1983). In this chapter we address the fixed interval smoother. The difference between the two estimators, the Kalman Filter and the Kalman Smoother, it is related on how they use the observations to perform estimation. The Kalman Filter uses only the past and the present observations to perform estimation, while the Kalman Smoother uses also the future observations for the estimation. This means that the Kalman Filter is used for on - line processing while the Kalman Smoother for batch processing. The derivations of these two estimators is presented in (Kay, 1993; Grewal & Andrews, 2001; Haykin, 2001). Both estimators are recursive in nature. This means that the estimate of the present state is updated using the previous state only and not the entire past states. The Kalman Filter is not only an estimator but also a learning method (Grewal & Andrews, 2001; Bishop, 2006). The observations are used to learn the states of the model. The Kalman Filter is also a computational tool and some problems may exist due to the finite precision arithmetic of the computers.

The Kalman Filter and the Kalman Smoother have been extensively used in biomedical signal processing. The general idea is to propose a model for the observations, in most cases linear, where some parameters must be estimated. To be able to apply the Kalman Filter or the Kalman Smoother the model for the observations must be written in a state - space form. A state - space model is represented by two equations. One equation, which describes the evolution of the parameters, and a second equation, which describes the relation of the parameters with the observations:

$$\mathbf{x}_t = A\mathbf{x}_{t-1} + \mathbf{w}_t, \tag{1}$$

$$\mathbf{y}_t = C\mathbf{x}_t + \mathbf{v}_t. \tag{2}$$

These two equations represent a state - space model. In the above model $\mathbf{x}_t$ are the parameters in time t, $\mathbf{y}_t$ are the observations, $\mathbf{w}_t$ is the state noise with zero mean and covariance matrix C_w, $\mathbf{v}_t$ is the observation noise with zero mean and covariance matrix C_v, A is the state transition matrix and C is the observation matrix. In the above model the matrices A and C are assumed to be known, as well as the covariance matrices C_v and C_w. However, in reality we are not able to know exactly the above matrices. In that case some assumptions are considered for the model. For example we can assume that the evolution of the parameters is a random walk procedure (Tarvainen et al., 2004), i.e. $A=I$, where I is the identity matrix, or we restrict the matrix A to be a diagonal one (Oikonomou et al., 2007). Also, these matrices can be estimated through an estimation procedure like the EM algorithm (Shumway & Stoffer, 1982; Khan & Dutt, 2007).

In (Sayadi & Shamsollahi, 2008) the authors proposed a non linear model for the electrocardiogram (ECG) signal. They use the model for ECG denoising and compression. To estimate the model parameters they use a modified version of the Kalman Filter, the Extended Kalman Filter (EKF) (Haykin, 2001). In (Kazemi et al., 2008) the authors use the Kalman Filter to detect and extract periodic noise from the ECG. In (Georgiadis et al., 2005; Georgiadis et al., 2007) they assumed that the Evoked Potentials in the Electroencephalogram can be represented as a linear combination of basis functions. The coefficients of the basis functions are assumed to change with time. This assumption lead to the use of the Kalman Filter to estimate the coefficients of the basis functions. In (Oikonomou & Fotiadis, 2005) the authors use the Kalman Smoother to estimate the sources of a dynamic version of a Bayesian PCA. They applied the method to the extraction of fetal EEG.

Besides these applications of the Kalman Filter and the Kalman Smoother for Biomedical Signal Processing, there is a particular application which has been attracted special interest, especially because at the end a time varying spectrum is obtained. This application concerns the use of parametric models such as the AR and ARMA models. In this chapter we will focus on the time varying AR model. The time varying autoregressive (TVAR) model is an AR model where the AR coefficients evolve in time. The parametric spectrum analysis is used to overcome the limited frequency resolution of FFT based methods. The spectral density can be calculated at each frequency point using the model parameters. The TVAR model has been used for EEG spike detection (Oikonomou et al., 2007), for time varying - spectrum estimation of Event Related Synchronization (ERS) and Desynchronization (ERD) (Khan & Dutt, 2007), for the calculation of coherence in the analysis of biomedical signals such EEG and ECG (Arnold et al., 1998) and for time varying spectrum estimation of intracranial pressure signals from patients with traumatic brain injury (Aboy et al., 2005). In the above studies the TVAR coefficients have been estimated using the Kalman Filter or the Kalman Smoother, while in (Khan & Dutt, 2007) the EM algorithm is used to estimate the parameters of the model.

2. The time varying AR model and Kalman filter

We assume that our signal can be described by an AR model given by:

$$y(t) = \sum_{i=1}^{p} a(i)y(t-i) + e(t), \tag{3}$$

where p is the order of the AR model, $y(t)$ is the observation in time t, $a(i)$ are the AR coefficients and $e(t)$ is the driving noise, which is Gaussian with zero mean and variance σ_e^2. If we let the AR coefficients to vary in time then we have the following equation for the AR model:

$$y(t) = \sum_{i=1}^{p} a_t(i)y(t-i) + e(t), \tag{4}$$

which can be written in vector notation as:

$$y(t) = \mathbf{h}_t\mathbf{a}_t + e(t), \tag{5}$$

where the vector $\mathbf{h}_t$ contains the past observations [$y(t$-1),... , $y(t$-$p)$] and the vector $\mathbf{a}_t$ the AR coefficients in time t. This model is called the time-varying AR model (TVAR). If we restrict the time evolution of TVAR coefficients to be linear, then we have:

$$\mathbf{a}_t = A\mathbf{a}_{t-1} + \mathbf{w}_t, \tag{6}$$

where A is the state transition matrix and $\mathbf{w}_t$ is the state noise which follows the Gaussian distribution with zero mean and covariance matrix Q. The equations (5) and (6) correspond to a state - space model. Now, given the observations $\mathbf{Y}_{1:k} = [y(1),...,y(k)]$ we want to obtain estimates of the TVAR coefficients. This can be done using the Kalman Filter. The Kalman Filter gives the optimal estimates in the mean square error sense. In the estimation procedure we are interested in two quantities, the expectation of conditional states $\mathbf{a}_{t|k} = E\{\mathbf{a}_t \mid \mathbf{Y}_{1:k}\}$ and the error covariance of them $P_{t|k} = E\{(\mathbf{a}_t - \mathbf{a}_{t|k})(\mathbf{a}_t - \mathbf{a}_{t|k})^T \mid \mathbf{Y}_{1:k}\}$. These quantities are obtained using the following equations:

$$\mathbf{a}_{t|t-1} = A\mathbf{a}_{t-1|t-1}, \tag{7}$$

$$P_{t|t-1} = AP_{t-1|t-1}A^T + Q, \tag{8}$$

$$K_t = P_{t|t-1}\mathbf{h}_t^T(\sigma_e^2 + \mathbf{h}_t P_{t|t-1}\mathbf{h}_t')^{-1}, \tag{9}$$

$$\mathbf{a}_{t|t} = \mathbf{a}_{t-1|t-1} + K_t(y(t) - \mathbf{h}_t\mathbf{a}_{t|t-1}), \tag{10}$$

$$P_{t|t} = (I - K_t\mathbf{h}_t^T)P_{t|t-1}, \tag{11}$$

with initial condition $\mathbf{a}_{1|0} = \boldsymbol{\mu}$ and $P_{t|t-1} = \Sigma$, where $\boldsymbol{\mu}$ and Σ are the initial conditions for the states. For more information on how these equations have been derived the interested reader can look in (Kay, 1993; Haykin, 2001). From these equations we can observe how the Kalman Filter is working. To estimate the current state $\mathbf{a}_{t|t}$ a prediction step to obtain the predictive state $\mathbf{a}_{t|t-1}$ based only on the previous state $\mathbf{a}_{t-1|t-1}$ is performed. After that a correction step takes place using the present observation $y(t)$ and the predictive state. Also, we can observe that the update equation for the covariance matrix is $P_{t|t}$ calculated as the difference of two matrices (see Eq. (11)). This can lead to numerical problems and destroy the symmetry of the matrix. To avoid these problems the update equation of covariance $P_{t|t}$ is replaced with the so called Joseph form (Brown, 1983):

$$P_{t|t} = (I - K_t \mathbf{h}_t^T) P_{t|t-1} (I - K_t \mathbf{h}_t^T)^T + \sigma_e^2 K_t K_t^T . \tag{12}$$

Now, the covariance matrix is calculated by adding two matrices. The state at time t using only the observations until time t, $\mathbf{Y}_{1:t}$, is estimated. When all the observations are available, $\mathbf{Y}_{1:N}$, to estimate the state at time t the Kalman Smoother is used. The update smoothing equations are:

$$J_{t-1} = P_{t-1|t-1} A^T P_{t|t-1}^{-1}, \tag{13}$$

$$\mathbf{a}_{t-1|N} = \mathbf{a}_{t-1|t-1} + J_{t-1}(\mathbf{a}_{t|N} - A\mathbf{a}_{t-1|t-1}), \tag{14}$$

$$P_{t-1|N} = P_{t-1|t-1} + + J_{t-1}(P_{t|T} - P_{t|t-1}) J_{t-1}^T . \tag{15}$$

The derivation of those equations is explained in (Haykin, 2001). The equations of Kalman Filter, together with the above smoothing equations, consist the Kalman Smoother. In general to apply the Kalman Filter or the Kalman Smoother to a model, we must write the model in a state - space form. After that the above equations can be applied easily. However, there are several parameters which are assumed known before the application of the update equations. These parameters are the state transition matrix A, the covariance of the state noise Q, the variance of the driving noise σ_e^2, and the initial conditions, $\theta = \{A, Q, \sigma_e^2, \boldsymbol{\mu}, \Sigma\}$. The parameters θ can be tuned based on some empirical knowledge (Oikonomou et al., 2007) or define a function of parameters and perform optimization to obtain the optimal values of the parameters like the EM algorithm (Khan & Dutt, 2007). In the next section the EM algorithm is described to tune the parameters θ. The EM algorithm was introduced in (Dempster et al., 1977) and has been used for the optimization of linear state - space model for the first time in (Shumway & Stoffer, 1982).

3. The EM algorithm and the Kalman smoother

The EM algorithm is a procedure to perform maximum likelihood estimation. The objective of the algorithm is to maximize the likelihood of the observations, $\mathbf{Y}_{1:N}$, in the presence of hidden variables, $\mathbf{a}_{t|N}$, t = 1, ..., N. The maximization is performed with respect to the parameters θ, θ_{ML}=max$_\theta$ log $p(\mathbf{Y}_{1:N} | \theta)$, where $p(\mathbf{Y}_{1:N} | \theta)$ is the probability density function of the observations, which is called likelihood, when it is seen as a function of the parameters θ. Direct maximization cannot be performed because the hidden variables are not available.

The maximization must be done with respect to the hidden variables, in our case the time varying AR coefficients, and the model parameters. The EM algorithm is an iterative scheme consisting of two steps, the E-step and the M-step. In the E-step the expected values of the hidden variables are evaluated and in the M-step the maximization is performed with respect to the model parameters. To perform the E-step the expected complete log-likelihood must be calculated as follows:

$$F = E\left\{\log p(\mathbf{Y}_{1:N}, \mathbf{a}_{1:N|N}) \middle| \mathbf{Y}_{1:N}\right\}. \tag{16}$$

The expected likelihood depends on three quantities:

$$\mathbf{a}_{t|N} = E\left\{\mathbf{a}_t \middle| \mathbf{Y}_{1:N}\right\}, \tag{17}$$

$$S_{t|N} = E\left\{\mathbf{a}_t \mathbf{a}_t^T \middle| \mathbf{Y}_{1:N}\right\} = P_{t|N} + \mathbf{a}_{t|N}\mathbf{a}_{t|N}^T, \tag{18}$$

$$S_{t,t-1|N} = E\left\{\mathbf{a}_t \mathbf{a}_{t-1}^T \middle| \mathbf{Y}_{1:N}\right\} = P_{t,t-1|N} + \mathbf{a}_{t|N}\mathbf{a}_{t-1|N}^T \tag{19}$$

The first two quantities can be calculated using the Kalman Smoother equations, while for the calculation of the last quantity we use the following equation (Bishop, 2006):

$$P_{t,t-1|N} = J_{t-1}P_{t|N}. \tag{20}$$

The M - step involves direct differentiation of F with respect to the parameters θ. The estimates for the model parameters θ are given as:

$$A_{new} = [\sum_{t=2}^{N} S_{t,t-1|N}][\sum_{t=2}^{N} S_{t-1|N}]^{-1}, \tag{21}$$

$$Q_{new} = [1/(N-1)][\sum_{t=2}^{N} S_{t|N} - A_{new}\sum_{t=2}^{N} S_{t-1,t|N}], \tag{22}$$

$$\sigma_e^2 = (1/N)\sum_{t=1}^{N}(y_t^2 - 2\mathbf{h}_t^T\mathbf{a}_{t|N}y_t + \mathbf{a}_{t|N}^T S_{t|N}\mathbf{a}_{t|N}), \tag{23}$$

$$\mu_{new} = \mathbf{a}_{1|N}, \tag{24}$$

$$\Sigma_{new} = P_{1|N}. \tag{25}$$

In the presented model the EM algorithm consists of two iterative steps. First, the application of the Kalman Smoother, using the parameters from the previous step, to obtain the expected statistics, and second maximization of the expected log - likelihood with respect to the parameters. These two steps are applied iteratively until convergence of the likelihood. As we can see the use of EM algorithm needs statistics which can be obtained only with the Kalman Smoother, and not using the Kalman Filter. The use of the Kalman Filter for the calculations of these statistics leads to suboptimal procedures. At the end of the EM algorithm we obtain the TVAR coefficients, which can be used to obtain a time varying spectrum, given by:

$$P(t,f)=\frac{\sigma_e^2}{\left|1-\sum_{j=1}^{p}a_{t|N}(j)e^{-i2\pi j\frac{f}{f_s}}\right|^2}, \tag{26}$$

where f_s is the sampling frequency.

4. Biomedical signal processing: an application to EEG

4.1 The EEG signal

The electroencephalogram can be roughly defined as the signal which corresponds to the mean electrical activity of the brain in different locations of the head. More specifically, it is the sum of the extracellular current flows in a large group of neurons. It can be acquired using either intracranial electrodes inside the brain or scalp electrodes on the surface of the head (Niedermeyer & Lopes da Silva, 1993). The EEG has been found to be a valuable tool in the diagnosis of numerous brain disorders. Nowadays, the EEG recording is a routine clinical procedure and is widely regarded as the physiological "gold standard" to monitor and quantify levels of drowsiness and wakefulness but also for detection of epileptic spikes and seizures and generally for the diagnosis of epilepsy (Tzallas et al., 2006). The electric activity of the brain is usually divided into three categories: 1) bioelectric events produced by single neurons, 2) spontaneous activity, and 3) evoked potentials. EEG spontaneous activity is measured on the scalp or on the brain. Clinically meaningfull frequencies lie between 0.1 Hz and 100 Hz. In more restricted sense, the frequency range is classified into several frequency components, or delta rhythm (δ: 0.5-4 Hz), theta rhythm (θ: 4-8 Hz), alpha rhythm (α: 8-13 Hz), beta rhythm (β: 13-30 Hz), and gamma rhythm (γ: 30-60 Hz) (Niedermeyer & Lopes da Silva, 1993).

The properties of the EEG signal can be described as complex (Niedermeyer & Lopes da Silva, 1993; Thakor & Tong, 2004). The EEG complexity originates from the intricate neural system. Traditionally, the spontaneous EEG is characterized as a linear stochastic process with similarities to noise. From the signal processing view, EEG has the following properties (Thakor & Tong, 2004): (a) Noisy and pseudo-stochastic: The EEG is often between 10-300μV, which is easily affected by various physiological and electrical noises. Meanwhile, artefacts from electrocardiogram (ECG), electrooculogram (EOG), electromyogram (EMG), and recording systems can also contaminate the signals. Even the EEG shows a high degree of randomness and nonstationarity. (b) Time-varying and nonstationary: EEG is not a stationary process; it varies with the physiological states. The waveforms may include a complex of regular sinusoidal waves, irregular spikes/polyspikes, or spindles/polyspindles. In most pathological conditions, such as epileptic seizures, the EEG may show evident singularity or nonstationarity. In practice, EEG is considered as a stationary process over a relatively short period (approximately 3.5sec for routine spontaneous EEG) (Goel et al., 1996). (c) High nonlinearity: Although the traditional linear models of EEG still play significant roles in EEG analysis and diagnosis, EEG is a nonlinear process (Palu, 1996). This kind of nonlinearity is also time-, state-, and site-dependent (Pijn et al., 1991).

One of the most important challenges of EEG analysis is the quantification of the manifestations of epilepsy (Niedermeyer & Lopes da Silva, 1993; Thakor & Tong, 2004). The main goal is to establish a correlation between the EEG and clinical or pharmacological conditions. One of the possible approaches is based on the properties of the inter-ictal EEG (electrical activity measured between seizures), which typically consists of linear stochastic background fluctuations interspersed with transient nonlinear spikes, sharp waves or spikes-and-wave complexes (Tzallas et al., 2006). These transient potentials originate as a result of a simultaneous pathological discharge of neurons within a volume of at least several mm^3. The traditional definition of a spike is based on its amplitude, duration, sharpness, and emergence from its background (Wilson & Emerson, 2002). However, automatic epileptic spike detection systems based on this direct approach suffer from false detections in the presence of numerous types of artefacts and non-epileptic transients (Wilson & Emerson, 2002; Tzallas et al., 2006). This shortcoming is particularly acute for long-term EEG monitoring of epileptic patients, which became common in 1980s (Waterhouse, 2003; Mormann et al., 2007).

There has also been a challenge to find functional cerebral activation indices for cognitive processes involved in a given task. The EEG is a continuous measure over time and can be used to study ongoing activity in the brain while subjects perform long-lasting and/or variable tasks. The alpha rhythm of the EEG is predominantly observed over the posterior cortex (Lähteenmäki et al., 1999). This rhythm correlates with relaxation, and for this reason it has been interpreted as a sign of inhibition of activity in the areas over which it has been recorded. Activation of the cortex causes a desynchronization of the alpha band, i.e. its amplitude decreases, while alpha synchronization denotes the increase of alpha activity (Pfurtscheller & Aranibar, 1977; Pfurtscheller, 1989). When alpha desynchronization or synchronization is related to an internally or externally paced event, it is called as event-related desynchronization (ERD) (Pfurtscheller, 1977) or event-related synchronization (ERS), respectively. The quantification of ERD/ERS requires the comparison of two different experimental conditions. ERD and ERS are defined as the relative difference in the EEG alpha power between the reference recorded before each event and the actual event.

ERD/ERS is, thus, a 'within-subject' measure of cortical activation and is expressed as a percentage. ERD and ERS can be either externally (by stimuli) or internally (by voluntary behavior) paced and they have a specific topographical distribution depending upon the state of the brain, stimulus paradigm and modality (Pfurtscheller, 1989). ERD has been observed e.g. during complex auditory stimulation (Krause et al., 1994), during cognitive and attentional tasks, and during voluntary movement tasks (Pfurtscheller, 1977). The ERD/ERS of the lower alpha frequencies (8–10 Hz) has been claimed to reflect non-specific cognitive functions, such as sustained attention, while that of the upper alpha frequencies (10–12 Hz) appears to reflect stimulus-related, i.e. task-specific cognitive processes.

We apply the TVAR model for EEG spike identification and ERS/ERD frequency tracking. For both problems the algorithms have been initialized as follows. First when using the Kalman Smoother alone the state transition matrix has been set to be the identity matrix. The covariance of the state noise was assumed diagonal with the same element in the diagonal, σ_w^2. This parameter has been adjusted based on visual analysis of the data. When using the Kalman Smoother with the EM, the algorithm has been initialized as follows: To obtain an initial estimate of the covariance of state noise, the signal has been divided into overlapped segments. In each segment we find the AR coefficients using the Matlab's `aryule` function. We set the matrix $A=I$ and from the local estimates of AR coefficients we find an initial estimate for the covariance of state noise. For EEG spike identification experiments the model order was set to 2, while in the ERD/ERS experiments the model order was set to 5.

These values have been found to work well, based on visual analysis of the available datasets.

4.2 Application of the TVAR model to EEG spike identification

The EEG data used is part of the dataset described in (Oikonomou et al., 2007). The EM algorithm for the state - space model in the problem of EEG spike identification is applied. After the calculation of TVAR coefficients the time varying spectrum is calculated. The time varying spectrum is used to identify the EEG spike. In Fig. (1) an EEG segment with four spikes is depicted. Three of them can be identified easily, while one of them is not so easily to be identified. In Fig (1) we show the EEG segment, the time varying spectrum and a zoom of time varying spectrum in the region of interest. In this case the region of interest is the frequency range where a spike can be observed. According to (Pinault et al., 2001) this range is from 5-20 Hz. We can observe that the time varying spectrum give us an indication for the spike position. We observe that the first three spikes are identified in the frequency around 10 Hz, while the last spike is observed around 6-7 Hz. This difference between the spikes can be justified by taking into account the waveform morphology of the spikes. The first three spikes have similar morphology and they differ from the last spike.

In Fig. (2) we show the EEG segment, the time varying spectrum and a zoom of time varying spectrum using the Kalman Smoother. In that case we assume that the TVAR coefficients evolve in time according to a random walk. The covariance of the state noise in that case is tuned based on visual analysis and is set equal to $10^{-3}I$, where I is the identity matrix. We can observe that using only the Kalman Smoother we place some restrictions on the model. The state transition matrix was set equal to the identity matrix and we assume that the covariance of the state noise is diagonal with the same element in the diagonal (isotropic model). These restrictions are not based on some optimization procedure but on assumptions that we make for the model to make it simpler, i.e. it is more easily to find, through visual analysis, the isotropic covariance to have a meaningful solution of the Kalman Smoother than the full covariance. In Fig. (3) the Instantaneous Frequency (IF) using the Kalman Smoother (Fig. 3a) and the EM with Kalman Smoother (Fig. 3b) are shown. In the results we define the IF as the frequency where the maximum value of a time varying spectrum is located. It is clear that the use of EM gives better estimation of IF. It is interesting here to note how the IF is changing during the spike. The slow rise of IF few msec before the appearance of a spike could represent the accumulation of excitatory postsynaptic potentials from dendritic spines of pyramidal neurons from the epileptic brain. In the case of isolated spikes the activity is self-restricted and does not spread to involve adjacent brain areas. It is interesting, in the case of a series of spikes, that the rise in the frequency persists for the duration of the event. This finding might have important implications in the prediction of epileptic crisis or "epileptic events".

The TVAR coefficients, besides the estimation of the time varying spectrum, can be used as features of the signal and can be used for classification or clustering purposes. In the case of EEG signal clustering, the number of clusters is assumed to be two, one cluster for the spike and one cluster for the background activity. For the clustering the `netlab` toolbox is used (Nabney & Bishop, 2004) and the clustering method was based on the gaussian mixture models. In Fig. (4) we see the results of clustering in an EEG signal. We can see that the clustering have correctly identified the EEG samples which belong to the spikes.

4.3 Application to event related synchronization / desynchronization

The event related phenomena represent frequency changes of the ongoing EEG activity. A decrease of power in a given frequency band is called event related desynchronization (ERD) and an increase event related synchronization (ERS). ERS/ERD phenomena are generated by changes in one or more parameters which control oscillations in neuronal networks (Pfurtscheller & Lopes da Silva, 1999). When we refer to ERS/ERD is necessary to specify the frequency band. In our experiments this frequency band is 10 Hz, which corresponds to the alpha rhythm band. The ERS/ERD phenomena are related to frequency changes, which can be detected by frequency analysis. The TVAR model is used here to produce the time varying spectrum, which is helpful in the analysis of the ERS/ERD.

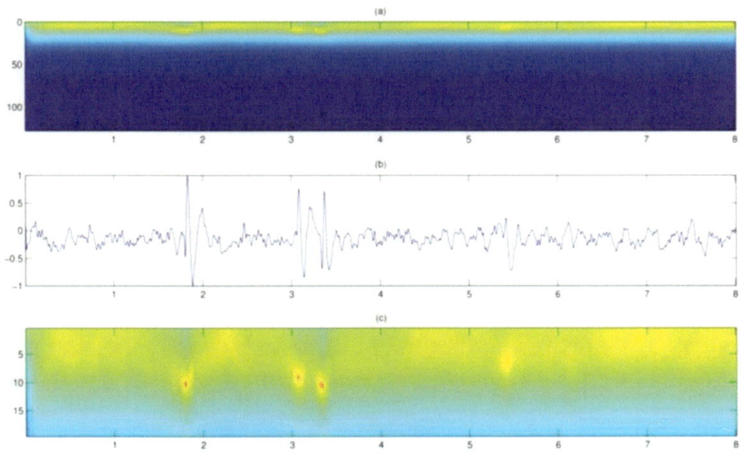

Fig. 1. Example of spike identification using the EM and Kalman Smoother, x - axis corresponds to time and y- axis corresponds to frequency. (a) The time varying spectrum. (b) The EEG signal. (c) Zoom in the frequency range 5-20 Hz.

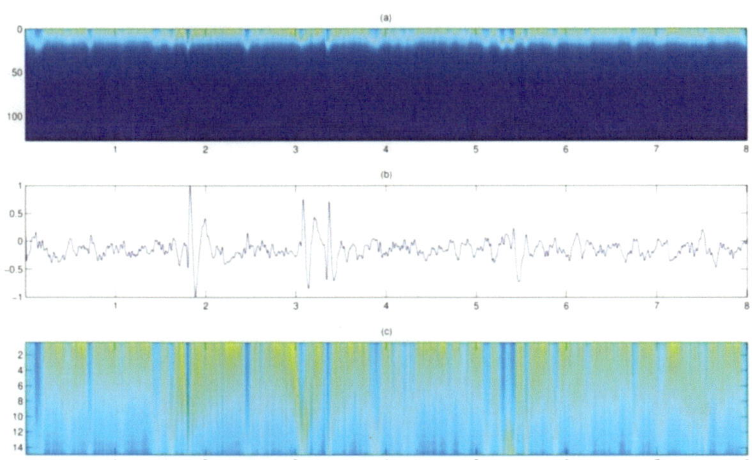

Fig. 2. Example of spike identification using the Kalman Smoother. (a) The time varying spectrum, x - axis corresponds to time and y- axis corresponds to frequency. (b) The EEG signal. (c) Zoom in the frequency range 5-20 Hz.

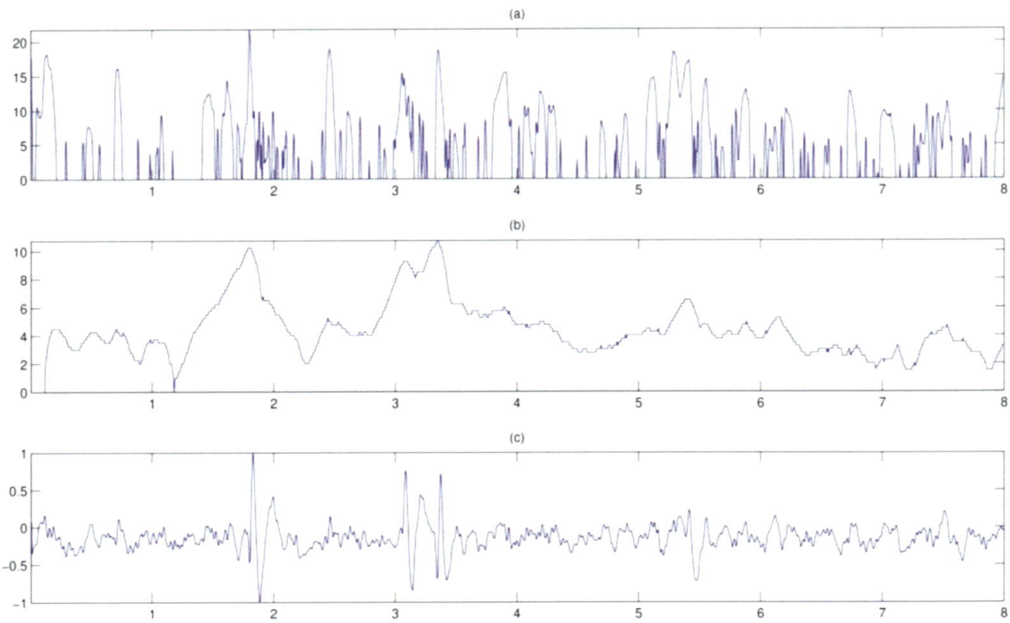

Fig. 3. Instantaneous Frequency. (a) Kalman Smoother, x - axis corresponds to time and y - axis to the IF value, (b) Kalman Smoother with EM, x - axis corresponds to time and y - axis to the IF value, (c) EEG signal, x - axis corresponds to time and y - axis to the signal amplitude.

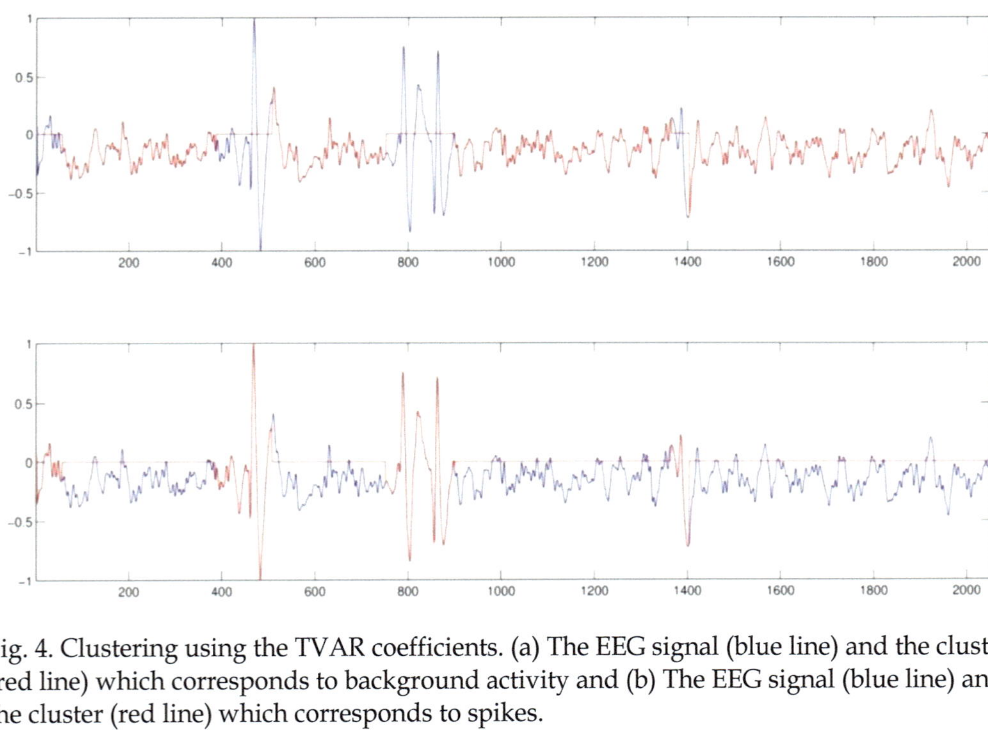

Fig. 4. Clustering using the TVAR coefficients. (a) The EEG signal (blue line) and the cluster (red line) which corresponds to background activity and (b) The EEG signal (blue line) and the cluster (red line) which corresponds to spikes.

The dataset used in this section is the motor imagery dataset provided by the Gratz University of Technology (Blankertz et al., 2004). In this experiment the subject was asked to control a feedback bar by means of imagery left or right hand movements. Two bipolar EEG channels, C3 and C4, have been used to obtain the EEG signals. The dataset consists of 280 trials of 9sec. The first 2sec was quite, at t=2sec an acoustic stimulus indicates the beginning of the trial, and at t=3sec an arrow was displayed as cue. At the same time the subject was asked to move the bar on the direction of the cue. The EEG signal was sampled at 128 Hz and it was filtered between 0.5 and 30 Hz.

The TVAR model has been applied to these trials using the Kalman Smoother only and the Kalman Smoother together with the EM algorithm. In the case of using only the Kalman Smoother some simplifications of the model are introduced. This restricts the number of parameters that must be known before the Kalman Smoother. The state noise is assumed to have diagonal covariance and the same element in the diagonal, i.e. $Q = \sigma_w^2 I$. Based on visual analysis of the data $\sigma_w^2 = 0.001$. Also the state transition matrix has been set to the identity matrix, i.e $A=I$. The model order for both methods has been set equal to 5. The initial state and covariance was set to zero and identity matrix, respectively.

A trial from the dataset with the extracted IF using the Kalman Smoother and Kalman Smoother with EM is shown in Fig. (5). It is clear that both methods track well the frequency evolution. However, the Kalman Smoother with EM produces smoother estimates than using the Kalman Smoother alone. Also, at Fig. (6) the time varying spectrums of both methods are presented. It is clear that the Kalman Smoother alone produces a noisy spectrum. All these observations can be justified by the fact that the Kalman Smoother alone imposes constraints on the state evolution model, in contrast to the Kalman Smoother with EM where such constraints do not exist.

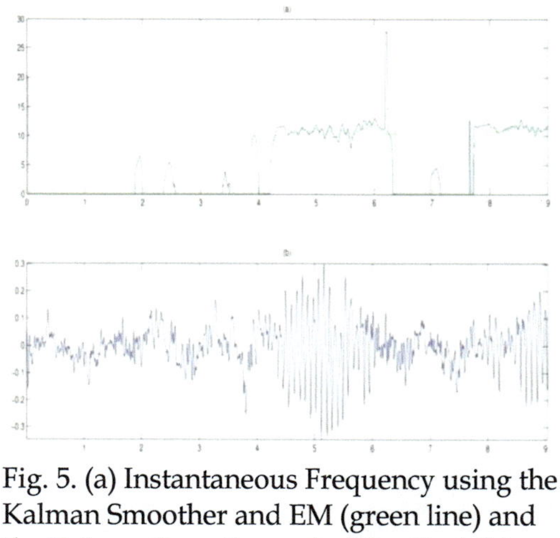

Fig. 5. (a) Instantaneous Frequency using the Kalman Smoother and EM (green line) and the Kalman Smoother only (blue line) (b) Trial data.

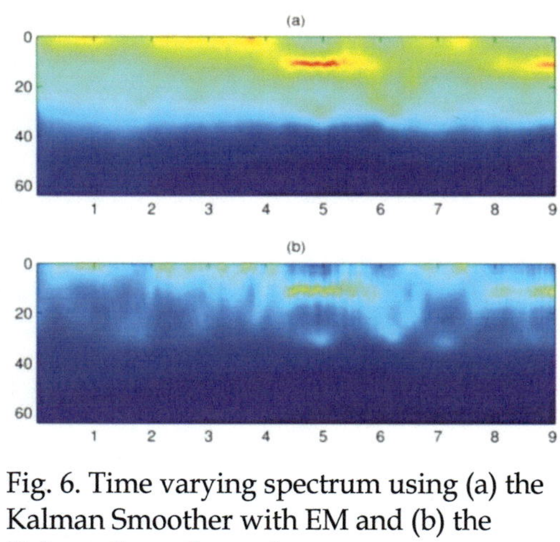

Fig. 6. Time varying spectrum using (a) the Kalman Smoother with EM and (b) the Kalman Smoother only

For each trial the time varying spectrum has been calculated using the TVAR coefficients. Also, for each trial the Instantaneous Frequency (IF) has been extracted from the time varying spectrum. The mean spectrum of trials is presented in Figs. (8,9) for the left hand movement. In Fig. (7) the mean Instantaneous Frequency is presented. We can observe that at channel C3 there is a decrease in IF from 8 Hz to 6 Hz at the beginning of the trial, t=2sec. Some milliseconds after that the IF increases to 8 Hz (t=3sec), where it stays for the rest of the trial. For the C4 channel we can observe that the IF decreases at the presentation of the acoustic stimulus, which indicates the beginning of the trial. Then from t=2sec to t=3sec the IF increases, to start to decrease from t=3sec to t=4sec. At t=4sec, the IF increases up to 6 Hz. Comparing the Kalman Smoother and the Kalman Smoother with EM we can observe that the Kalman Smoother gives noisy estimates of the time varying spectrum and IF. This change in frequency can be justified as reorganization of the brain neurons activity due to

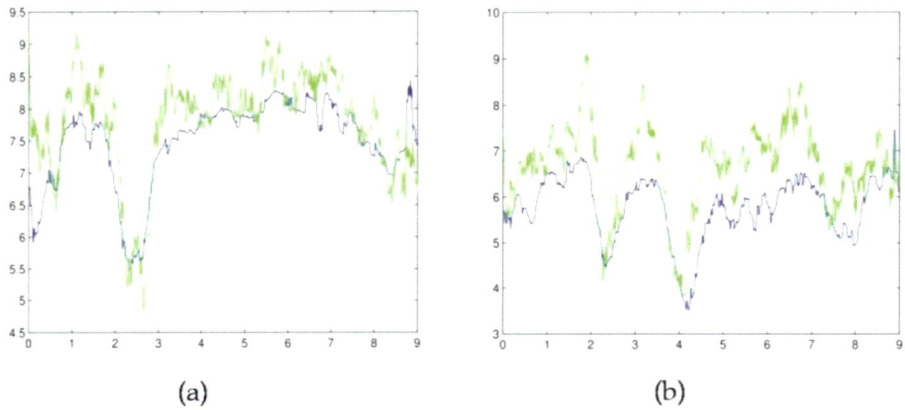

Fig. 7. Mean Instantaneous Frequency for left hand movement. (a) Channel C3. (b) Channel C4. In both figures the blue line corresponds to the Kalman Smoother with EM and green line to the Kalman Smoother only.

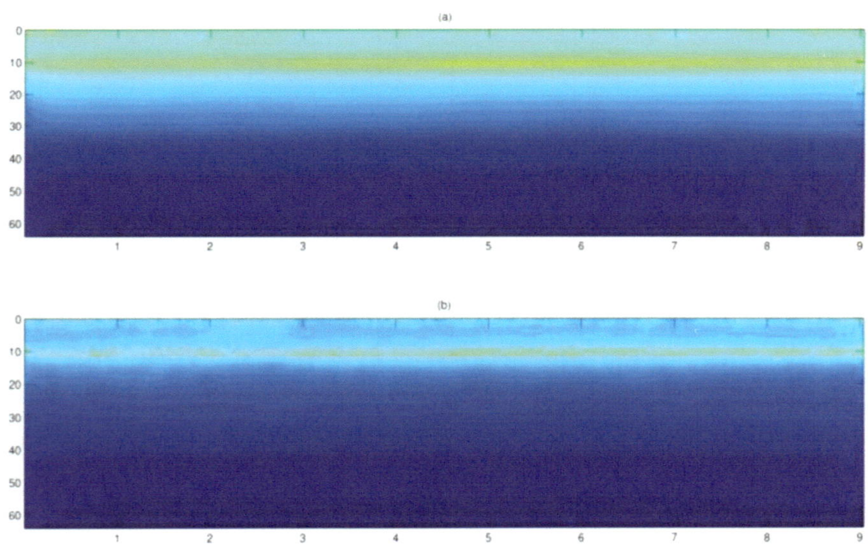

Fig. 8. Mean time varying PSD (Power Spectrum Density) for channel C3 in left hand movement. (a) Kalman Smoother with EM, (b) Kalman Smoother only.

the stimulus. It is clear that a change in IF is observed at t=2sec for both channels C3 and C4. However, at t=3sec there is a difference, a change in IF is observed only for channel C4. At the presentation of cue both brain positions are activated. However, after the cue is presented activation is observed only at C4 (t=3sec). The term activation is used here to describe a change in IF. In Figs. (10,11 and 12) the IF and the mean time varying spectrums for the right hand movements are shown. Similar conclusions can be extracted if we take into the account the hemispherical asymmetry of the brain due to the motor imagery experiment, i.e. we can see similarities in Fig. (7b) and in Fig. (10a). In both cases there is an increase in IF from t=2sec to t=3sec, and after that there is a decrease from t=3sec to t=4sec.

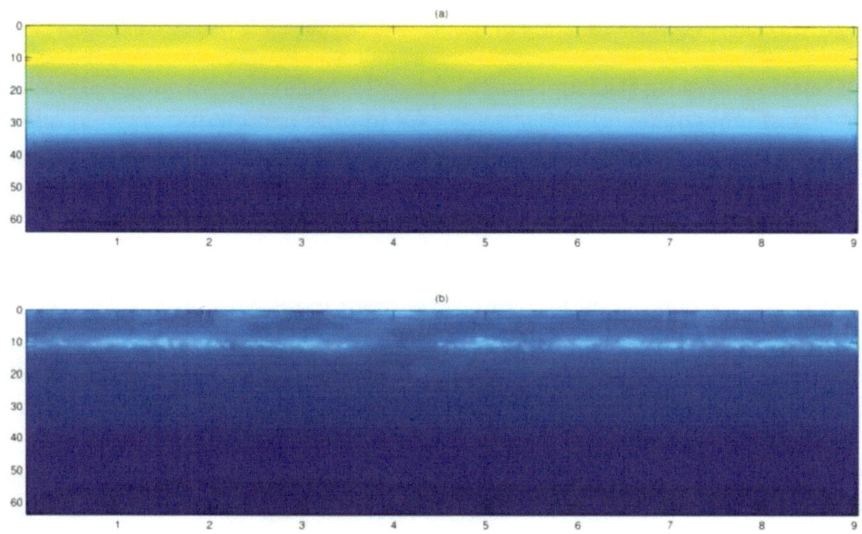

Fig. 9. Mean PSD (Power Spectrum Density) for channel C4 in left hand movement. (a) Kalman Smoother with EM, (b) Kalman Smoother only.

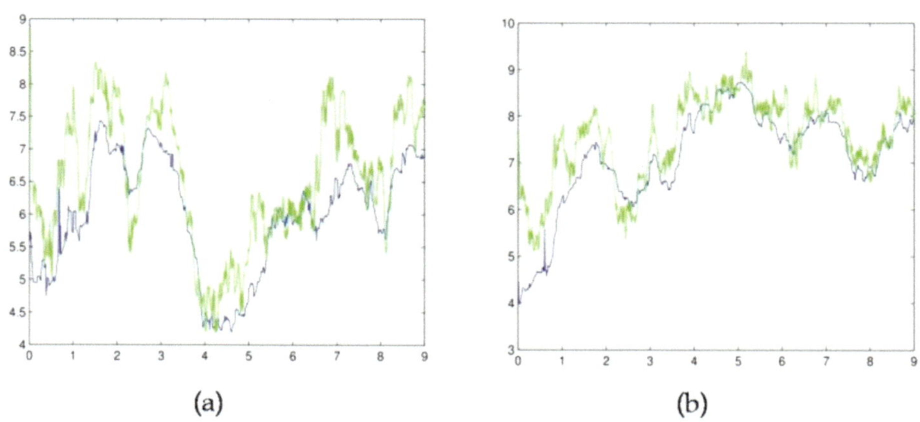

Fig. 10. Mean Instantaneous Frequency for right hand movement. (a) Channel C3. (b) Channel C4. In both figures the blue line corresponds to the Kalman Smoother with EM and green line to the Kalman Smoother only.

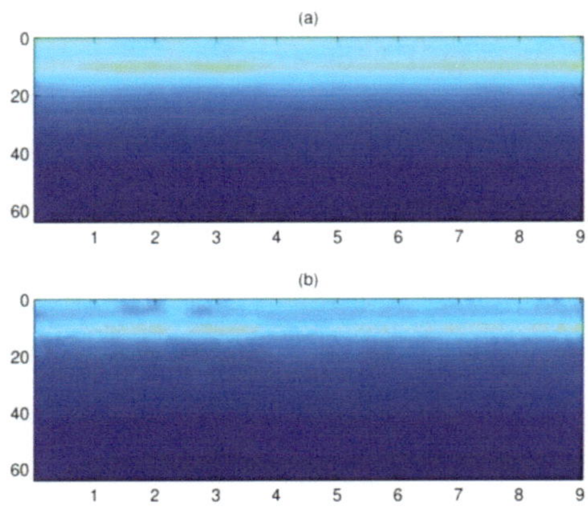

Fig. 11. Mean time varying PSD for channel C3 in right hand movement. (a) Kalman Smoother with EM, (b) Kalman Smoother only.

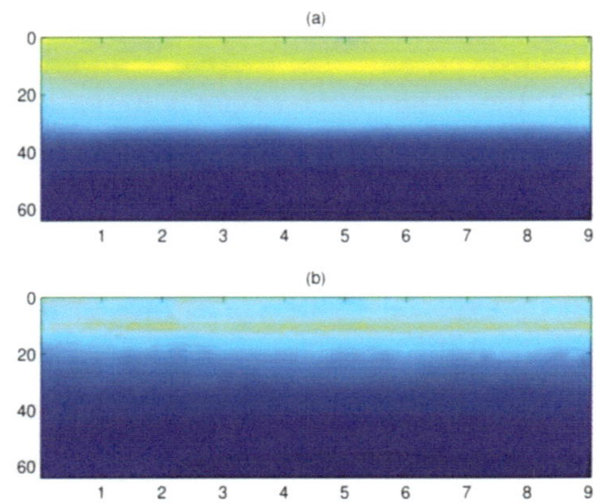

Fig. 12. Mean time varying PSD for channel C4 in right hand movement. (a) Kalman Smoother with EM, (b) Kalman Smoother only.

5. Discussion

In this chapter the Kalman Smoother, with or without the EM algorithm, has been used for the processing of the EEG signal in two cases, epileptic form spike identification and ERD/ERD analysis. Use of the Kalman Smoother forces to some simplifications of the model. This is performed in order to decrease the number of parameters which must be tuned. Based on the assumptions that the state transition matrix is the identity and the covariance is diagonal with the same element on the diagonal, there is one parameter to be tuned, the variance of the state noise. The value of this parameter defines how smooth or rough will be the evolution of states, in our case the TVAR coefficients. Large values of variance indicate rough estimates for the TVAR coefficients. This has as a result a noisy time varying spectrum. Small values indicated smooth estimates for the TVAR coefficients and hence a smooth time varying spectrum. The value of this parameter depends on the problem. In the case where we expect that the time varying spectrum is smooth, a small value for the variance of the state noise is preferable.

However, the parameters can be estimated based on some optimization procedure like the EM algorithm. The EM algorithm provides with estimates of the parameters. So the tuning of the parameters is done automatically based on the dataset, without manual settings. This fact permits the use of full covariance for the state noise and a general transition state matrix. As a consequence the model is more flexible because of the different types of state noise.

We observe that the Kalman Smoother with EM provides with smoother estimates than using the Kalman Smoother alone. This happens because the first approach can capture the patterns of the signal more accurately. In the estimation of the IF in the spike problem it is observed that the IF starts to increase before the appearance of the spike. Also, in the ERD/ERS analysis we observe that the IF is modulated when some events take place on the experiment, like the sound at t=2sec which denotes the beginning of the trial. In both problems we observe that the IF is a good measure to track changes in EEG activity.

The Kalman Smoother or the Kalman Filter can be used for the estimation of time varying AR coefficients. The use of TVAR model is twofold. First, the TVAR coefficients can be used for the estimation of the time varying spectrum. Usually, the Power Spectrum Density (PSD) estimation of biomedical signals is performed using classical techniques based on Fourier Transform which presents two problems: the frequency resolution and the assumption of stationarity. To overcome the problem of frequency resolution a parametric approach based on AR model can be used. However, the assumption of stationarity restricts the use of a parametric model to stationary signals. A solution to these problems is provided by the TVAR model. Second, the TVAR coefficients can be used as input for classification or clustering purposes. The use of AR model is not restrictive and other parametric models such as ARMA can be used for time varying spectrum estimation (Tarvainen et al., 2004).
Besides the particular application of the Kalman Filter or the Kalman Smoother for time varying spectrum estimation there is another application. In this a parameterization of the model is assumed, i.e. the signal is assumed to be a linear combination of basis functions. This signal is observed in additive noise. Assuming that the parameters are evolving in time the Kalman Filter or Smoother can be used to produce the evolution of the parameters in time. At the end an estimate of the signal can produced. This approach have been applied for the estimation of evoked potentials (Georgiadis et al., 2005; Georgiadis et al., 2007).

6. Conclusions

In this chapter we presented how the Kalman Filter and the Kalman Smoother is used for time varying spectrum estimation. The estimation of spectrum is based on a parametric model, a TVAR model. Given the evolution between the states, the Kalman Filter can be used to estimate the AR coefficients which evolve in time. At the end of this procedure a time varying spectrum is calculated. In the case where all the observations are available before the application of the estimation procedure, the Kalman Smoother can be used instead of the Kalman Filter. However, in that case, on line processing of the data cannot be done. When we are interested for batch processing the Kalman Smoother with the EM algorithm is a valuable tool. The use of EM algorithm leads to a process which does not depend on manual settings, which usually are not optimal. The main idea behind the use of Kalman Filter is to propose a model for the problem under consideration, which depends on some parameters. If we let the parameters of the model to change in time then the estimation of the parameters can be performed using the Kalman Filter. If the linearity assumption does not hold then some modifications of the Kalman Filter can be used such as the Extended Kalman Filter.

7. References

Aboy, M., Marquez, O.W., McNames, J., Hornero, R., Trong, T. & Goldstein, B. (2005). Adaptive modeling and spectral estimation of nonstationary biomedical signals based on Kalman filtering. *IEEE Trans Biomed Eng* 52(8): 1485-9.

Anderson, B.D.O. & Moore, J.B. (1979). Optimal Filtering, Englewood Cliffs, NJ: Prentice-Hall.

Arnold, M., Miltner, W.H., Witte, H., Bauer, R. & Braun, C. (1998). Adaptive AR modeling of nonstationary time series by means of Kalman filtering. *IEEE Trans Biomed Eng* 45(5): 553-62.

Bishop, C.M. (2006). Pattern recognition and machine learning, Springer.

Blankertz, B., Muller, K.R., Curio, G., Vaughan, T.M., Schalk, G., Wolpaw, J.R., Schlogl, A., Neuper, C., Pfurtscheller, G., Hinterberger, T., Schroder, M. & Birbaumer, N. (2004). The BCI Competition 2003: progress and perspectives in detection and discrimination of EEG single trials. *IEEE Trans Biomed Eng* 51(6): 1044-51.

Brown, R.G. (1983). Introduction to random signal analysis and Kalman filtering, Wiley New York.

Dempster, A.P., Laird, N.M. & Rubin, D.B. (1977). Maximum Likelihood from Incomplete Data Via Em Algorithm. *Journal of the Royal Statistical Society Series B-Methodological* 39(1): 1-38.

Georgiadis, S.D., Ranta-Aho, P.O., Tarvainen, M.P. & Karjalainen, P.A. (2007). A subspace method for dynamical estimation of evoked potentials. *Comput Intell Neurosci*: 61916.

Georgiadis, S.D., Ranta-aho, P.O., Tarvainen, M.R. & Karjalainen, P.A. (2005). Single-trial dynamical estimation of event-related potentials: A Kalman filter-based approach. *IEEE Trans Biomed Eng* 52(8): 1397-1406.

Goel, V., Brambrink, A.M., Baykal, A., Koehler, R.C., Hanley, D.F. & Thakor, N.V. (1996). Dominant frequency analysis of EEG reveals brain's response during injury and recovery. *IEEE Trans Biomed Eng* 43(11): 1083-92.

Grewal, M.S. & Andrews, A.P. (2001). Kalman Filtering: Theory and Practice Using MATLAB, Wiley.

Haykin, S.S. (2001). Kalman Filtering and Neural Networks, Wiley Chichester.

Kalman, R.E. (1960). A New Approach to Linear Filtering and Prediction Problems. *Transaction of the ASME* 82: 35-45.

Kay, S.M. (1993). Fundamentals of statistical signal processing. Englewood Cliffs, N.J., PTR Prentice-Hall.

Kazemi, R., Farsi, A., Ghaed, M.H. & Karimi-Ghartemani, M. (2008). Detection and extraction of periodic noises in audio and biomedical signals using Kalman filter. *Signal Processing* 88(8): 2114-2121.

Khan, M.E. & Dutt, D.N. (2007). An expectation-maximization algorithm based Kalman smoother approach for event-related desynchronization (ERD) estimation from EEG. *IEEE Trans Biomed Eng* 54(7): 1191-1198.

Krause, C.M., Lang, H.A., Laine, M., Helle, S.I., Kuusisto, M.J. & Pörn, B. (1994). Event-related desynchronization evoked by auditory stimuli. *Brain Topography* 7(2): 107-112.

Lähteenmäki, P.M., Krause, C.M., Sillanmäki, L., Salmi, T.T. & Lang, A.H. (1999). Event-related alpha synchronization/desynchronization in a memory-search task in adolescent survivors of childhood cancer. *Clinical Neurophysiology* 110(12): 2064-2073.

Mormann, F., Andrzejak, R.G., Elger, C.E. & Lehnertz, K. (2007). Seizure prediction: the long and winding road. *Brain* 130: 314-333.

Nabney, I. & Bishop, C. (2004). "Netlab toolbox." from http://www.ncrg.aston.ac.uk/netlab/.

Niedermeyer, E. & Lopes da Silva, F.H. (1993). Electroencephalography: basic principles, clinical applications, and related fields. Baltimore, William &Wikins

Oikonomou, V.P. & Fotiadis, D.I. (2005). A Bayesian PCA Approach for Fetal ECG extraction for Biomedical Signal Denoising *Conf Proc Eur Med Biol Eng (EMBEC'05)*, Prague, Czech Republic.

Oikonomou, V.P., Tzallas, A.T. & Fotiadis, D.I. (2007). A Kalman filter based methodology for EEG spike enhancement. *Computer Methods and Programs in Biomedicine* 85(2): 101-108.

Palu, M. (1996). Nonlinearity in normal human EEG: cycles, temporal asymmetry, nonstationarity and randomness, not chaos, Springer. 75: 389-396.

Pfurtscheller, G. (1977). Graphical display and statistical evaluation of event-related desynchronization (ERD). *Electroencephalogr Clin Neurophysiol* 43(5): 757-60.

Pfurtscheller, G. (1989). Spatiotemporal analysis of alpha frequency components with the ERD technique. *Brain Topogr* 2(1-2): 3-8.

Pfurtscheller, G. & Aranibar, A. (1977). Event-related cortical desynchronization detected by power measurements of scalp EEG. *Electroencephalogr Clin Neurophysiol* 42(6): 817-26.

Pfurtscheller, G. & Lopes da Silva, F.H. (1999). Event-related EEG/MEG synchronization and desynchronization: basic principles. *Clin Neurophysiol* 110(11): 1842-57.

Pijn, J.P., Van Neerven, J., Noest, A. & Lopes da Silva, F.H. (1991). Chaos or noise in EEG signals; dependence on state and brain site. *Electroencephalogr Clin Neurophysiol* 79(5): 371-81.

Pinault, D., Vergnes, M. & Marescaux, C. (2001). Medium-voltage 5-9-Hz oscillations give rise to spike-and-wave discharges in a genetic model of absence epilepsy: in vivo dual extracellular recording of thalamic relay and reticular neurons. *Neuroscience* 105(1): 181-201.

Rauch, H., Missiles, L., Co, S. & Alto, P. (1963). Solutions to the linear smoothing problem. *IEEE Trans Automatic Control* 8(4): 371-372.

Sayadi, O. & Shamsollahi, M.B. (2008). ECG denoising and compression using a modified extended Kalman filter structure. *IEEE Trans Biomed Eng* 55(9): 2240-8.

Shumway, R.H. & Stoffer, D.S. (1982). An approach to time series smoothing and forecasting using the EM algorithm. *Journal of the Times Series Analysis* 3(4): 253-264.

Tarvainen, M.P., Hiltunen, J.K., Ranta-aho, P.O. & Karjalainen, P.A. (2004). Estimation of nonstationary EEG with Kalman smoother approach: an application to event-related synchronization (ERS). *IEEE Trans Biomed Eng* 51(3): 516-24.

Thakor, N.V. & Tong, S. (2004). Advances in quantitative electroencephalogram analysis methods. *Annu Rev Biomed Eng* 6: 453-95.

Tzallas, A.T., Karvelis, P.S., Katsis, C.D., Fotiadis, D.I., Giannopoulos, S. & Konitsiotis, S. (2006). A method for classification of transient events in EEG recordings: application to epilepsy diagnosis. *Methods Inf Med* 45(6): 610-21.

Waterhouse, E. (2003). New horizons in ambulatory electroencephalography. *IEEE Eng Med Biol Mag* 22(3): 74-80.

Wilson, S.B. & Emerson, R. (2002). Spike detection: a review and comparison of algorithms. *Clin Neurophysiol* 113(12): 1873-81.

8

Extended Kalman Filtering for the Modeling and Estimation of ICG Pharmacokinetics in Cancerous Tumors using NIR Measurements

Burak Alacam and Birsen Yazıcı
Rensselaer Polytechnic Institute
NY, USA

1. Introduction

Near infrared (NIR) diffuse optical imaging and spectroscopy methods provide quantitative functional information that cannot be obtained by the conventional radiological methods (Yodh & Chance, 1995; Intes & Chance, 2005; Boas et al., 2001a). NIR techniques can provide *in vivo* measurements of the oxygenation and vascularization states, uptake and release of optical contrast agents, and chromophore concentrations with high sensitivity. In particular, NIR diffuse optical techniques in conjunction with optical contrast agents have the potential to characterize angiogenesis, and to differentiate between malignant and benign tumors (Hawrys & Sevick-Muraca, 2000; Furukawa et al., 1995; Chen et al., 2003; Becker et al., 1997). Among many commercially available optical contrast agents, only indocyanine green (ICG) is approved for human use by the Food and Drug Administration (El Deosky et al., 1999; Hansen et al, 1993; Shinohara et al., 1996). ICG is a blood pooling agent that has different delivery behaviour between normal and cancer vasculature. In normal tissue, ICG acts as a blood flow indicator in tight capillaries of normal vessel. However in tumor, ICG may act as a diffusible (extravascular) flow in leaky capillary of vessels (Alacam et al., 2006; Cuccia et al., 2003; Ntziachristos et al., 2000; Vaupel et al., 1991). Therefore, pharmacokinetics of ICG has the potential to provide new tools for tumor detection, diagnosis, and staging.

A number of research groups reported compartmental modeling of ICG time-kinetic measurements using NIR methods for tumor diagnosis in animal and human subjects (Gurfinkel et al., 2000; Cuccia et al., 2003; Intes et al., 2003; Milstein et al., 2005). A compartmental model is a mathematical description of the concentrations of contrast agents in which each compartment represents a kinetically distinct tissue type (Tornoe, 2002; Anderson, 1983; Cobelli et al., 2000). It consists of a set of coupled ordinary differential equations (ODE) and a measurement model. Coefficients of the ODE's are the physiological parameters of interest that represent rates of exchange between different compartments. These parameters are non-linearly related to the total concentration of ICG measured by NIR methods. Furthermore, concentration of ICG in each compartment cannot be directly measured non-invasively by NIR techniques, making the pharmacokinetic parameter estimation a highly non-linear problem.

Current methods of ICG compartmental modeling involve curve fitting methods and various techniques for solving differential equations. Gurfinkel et al. presented a two-compartment model for ICG kinetics, and estimated model parameters (Gurfinkel et al., 2000). The measurements were obtained using a frequency domain photon migration system coupled with a charge-coupled device. The pharmacokinetic parameters were estimated for each pixel based on a curve fitting method. This study indicated that model parameters show no difference in the ICG uptake rates between normal and diseased tissue. Cuccia et al. presented a study of the dynamics of ICG in an adenocarcinoma rat tumor model (Cuccia et al., 2003). A two-compartment model describing the ICG dynamics was used to quantify physiologic parameters related to capillary permeability. The ICG concentration curves were fitted to the compartmental model using a non-linear least squares Levenberg-Marquart algorithm. It was shown that different tumor types have different capillary permeability rates. Intes et al. presented the uptake of ICG by breast tumors using a continuous wave diffuse optical tomography apparatus (Intes et al., 2003). A two-compartment model was used to analyze the pharmacokinetics of ICG. A curve fitting algorithm, namely the non-linear Nelder-Mead simplex search, was used to estimate the pharmacokinetic parameters. This study showed that the malignant cases exhibit slower rate constants (uptake and outflow) as compared to healthy tissue. Milstein et al. presented a Bayesian tomographic image reconstruction method to form pharmacokinetic-rate images of optical fluorophores based on fluorescence diffuse optical tomography (Milstein et al., 2005). Numerical simulations show that the method provides good contrast. However, no real data experiments were presented to study the diagnostic value of spatially resolved pharmacokinetic-rates.

While the studies described above demonstrate the feasibility of the ICG pharmacokinetics in tumor characterization; due to the highly non-linear nature of the pharmacokinetic parameter estimation, variation in parameter values from one subject to another, and sparse data available in clinical and laboratory settings, a systematic and robust approach is needed to model, estimate and analyze ICG pharmacokinetics.

In this chapter, we first present a two-compartmental model for the ICG pharmacokinetics in cancerous tumors. The model captures the transportation of ICG between the vascular and extravascular compartments. We next introduce an extended Kalman filtering (EKF) framework for the estimation of pharmacokinetic-rate parameters and the ICG concentrations in different compartments. The EKF offers a recursive estimation framework with numerous advantages for ICG pharmacokinetic modeling. These include: i) effective modeling of multiple compartments, and multiple measurement systems governed by coupled ordinary differential equations, in the presence of measurement noise and uncertainties in the compartmental model dynamics; ii) simultaneous estimation of pharmacokinetic model parameters and ICG concentrations in each compartment, which are not accessible *in vivo* by means of NIR techniques; iii) recursive estimation of time-varying pharmacokinetic model parameters; iv) statistical validation of estimated concentrations and error bounds on the pharmacokinetic parameter estimates; v) incorporation of available a priori information about the initial conditions of the permeability rates into the estimation procedure; vi) potential real-time monitoring of ICG pharmacokinetic parameters and ICG concentrations in different compartments due to the recursive nature of the EKF estimation method.

We tested our approach using the ICG concentration data acquired from four Fisher rats carrying adenocarcinoma tumor cells. The two-compartment model, composed of plasma and extracellular-extravascular space (EES), was fitted to the data, and pharmacokinetic model parameters and concentrations in different compartments were estimated using the EKF framework. We then used the model parameters to differentiate between two types of cancerous tumors. Our study suggests that the permeability rates out of the vasculature are higher in edematous tumors as compared to necrotic tumors. Additionally, we observe that in the two-compartment model, the ICG concentration curve is higher in the EES compartment in edematous tumors.

Next, we describe a method of forming pharmacokinetic-rate images, and present spatially resolved pharmacokinetic-rates of ICG using *in vivo* NIR data acquired from three patients with breast tumors. We first reconstructed a set of spatio-temporally resolved ICG concentration images based on differential diffuse optical tomography (Ntziachristos et al., 1999). We modeled the ICG pharmacokinetics by the two-compartment model. Next, we estimated the ICG pharmacokinetic-rates and the concentrations in different compartments based on the EKF framework. The pharmacokinetic-rate images show that the rates from the tumor region and outside the tumor region are statistically different.

The chapter is organized as follows: In Section 2, we present the two-compartment model for the ICG pharmacokinetics in tissue, and the state-space representation of the compartmental model. In Section 3, we introduce the EKF framework for the estimation of ICG pharmacokinetics. In Section 4, we present the estimation of ICG pharmacokinetics in Fischer rat data. In Section 5, we present the reconstruction of ICG pharmacokinetic-rate images using the EKF framework; and the spatially resolved ICG pharmacokinetic-rate images from *in vivo* breast data. Finally, we summarize the Chapter in Section 6.

2. Pharmacokinetic modeling of ICG

2.1 Indocyanine green

ICG is an optical dye commonly used in retinopathy and hepatic diagnostics. Given its low toxicity and FDA approval, it has recently been utilized as a blood pooling agent for the detection and diagnosis of cancerous tumors by means of NIR optical methods. The absorption peak of ICG is 805 nm and the fluorescence peak is at 830 nm. ICG has strong affinity for blood proteins. In plasma, ICG is near-completely bound, primarily to albumin. As a result, its *in vivo* kinetics is similar to those of a 70 kD molecule, although it has a molecular weight of about 700 D (Hansen et al., 1993; Shinohara et al,. 1996; ElDeosky et al., 1999; Li et al., 1995, Yates et al., 1983).

ICG is eliminated from the body primarily through the bile. Outside of the circulatory system, it is not available for removal until it returns to the system. The kinetics of this transition offers a potential means of non-invasively assessing the leakiness of large molecules from the microvasculature; this permeability is a characteristic of the poorly developed vasculature observed in angiogenesis. The increase in local microvasculature density is also expected to induce increased perturbation in the optical signal from intercapillary ICG.

There are some differences in the delivery of ICG between normal and cancerous vasculature. In normal tissue, ICG acts as a blood flow indicator in tight capillaries of normal vessels. However in tumors, ICG may act as a diffusible (extravascular) flow in the leaky capillary of cancer vessels. To investigate the validity of this hypothesis, one has to employ at least a two-compartment model composed of plasma and EES. Additionally, the permeability rate is expected to increase as the malignancy advances (Alacam et al., 2006;

Cuccia et al., 2003; Intes et al., 2003). Fig. 1 (a) and (b) illustrates the ICG flow for healthy and malignant tissue, respectively.

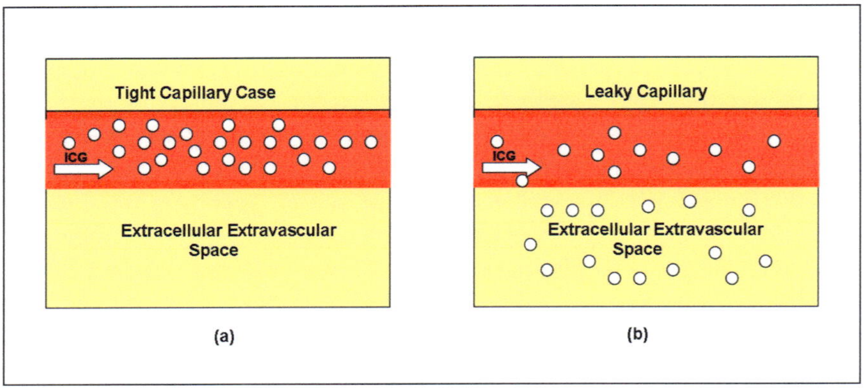

Fig. 1. An illustration of the ICG flow (a) in tight capillary of normal vessel, (b) in permeable capillary of tumor tissue.

2.2 Two-compartment model for the ICG pharmacokinetics

Compartmental modeling allows relatively simple and effective mathematical representation of complex biological responses due to contrast agents and drugs. A region of interest is assumed to consist of a number of compartments, generally representing a volume or a group of similar tissues into which the contrast agent is distributed. The concentration change in a specific compartment is modeled as a result of the exchange of contrast agent between connected compartments. These changes are modeled by a collection of coupled ODEs; each equation describing the time change dictated by the biological laws that govern the concentration exchanges between the interacting compartments (Tornoe, 2002; Anderson, 1983; Jacquez, 1972; Cobelli et al., 2000).

In Alacam et al 2006, we presented 3 different compartment models for the ICG pharmacokinetics and determined that the optimal model is the two-compartment model using the Bayesian information criteria (BIC) (Schwarz, 1978; Box et al., 1994; Akaike, 1980). In order to calculate the BIC for different compartmental models, we first derived a likelihood function for the EKF. The derivation is based on maximum likelihood estimation of the parameters in the Kalman filtering framework given as in (Harvey, 1993; Sallas & Harville, 1988). In the two-compartment model, the tumor region is assumed to be composed of plasma and the EES compartments (Alacam et al., 2006; Tofts et al., 1999; Tofts, 1997; Cuccia et al., 2003). The EES is defined as the region that lies outside of both the vascular region and the tumor cells. We consider transcapillary leakage to occur only at the tumor site. We also assume that a small perturbation of the global plasma concentration does not affect the bulk removal. Fig. 2 shows the block diagram of the two-compartment model for the ICG pharmacokinetics.

Let C_p and C_e denote the ICG concentrations in plasma and the EES, respectively. Then the two-compartment ICG chemical transport equations are given as follows:

The leakage into and the drainage out of plasma:

$$\frac{dC_p(t)}{dt} = k_b C_e(t) - k_a C_p(t) - k_{out} C_p(t) \tag{1}$$

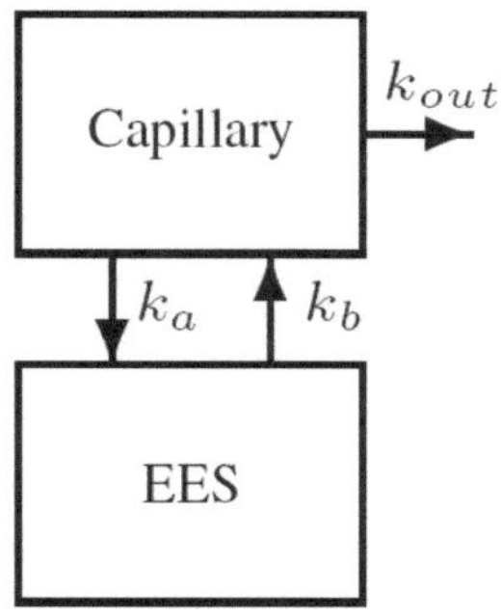

Fig. 2. Block diagram of the two-compartment model for ICG pharmacokinetics.

The leakage into and the drainage out of the EES:

$$\frac{dC_e(t)}{dt} = k_a C_p(t) - k_b C_e(t) \tag{2}$$

The parameters k_a and k_b govern the leakage into and the drainage out of the EES, respectively. The parameter k_{out} describes the ICG elimination from the body through kidneys and liver.

Actual bulk ICG concentration in the tissue measured by NIR is a linear combination of plasma and EES ICG concentrations given by:

$$m(t) = v_p C_p(t) + v_e C_e(t) \tag{3}$$

where the parameters v_p and v_e denote plasma and the EES volume fractions, respectively.

3. Extended Kalman filtering for the ICG pharmacokinetics

For the rest of the chapter, all matrices and vectors are denoted in boldface and scalar quantities are denoted in non-boldface notation.

3.1 State-space representation of the ICG pharmacokinetics

Coupled differential equations resulting from the two-compartment modeling of the ICG pharmacokinetics can be expressed in state-space representation as follows:

$$\begin{gathered}\begin{bmatrix} dC_e(t) \\ dC_p(t) \end{bmatrix} = \begin{bmatrix} -k_b & k_a \\ k_b & -(k_a + k_{out}) \end{bmatrix} \begin{bmatrix} C_e(t) \\ C_p(t) \end{bmatrix} + d\mathbf{B}(t) \\ m(t) = \begin{bmatrix} v_e & v_p \end{bmatrix} \begin{bmatrix} C_e(t) \\ C_p(t) \end{bmatrix} + \eta(t) \end{gathered} \tag{4}$$

where $dB(t)$ is the Weiner process increment, $d\mathbf{B}(t) = \omega(t)dt$. Here, $\omega(t)$ and $\eta(t)$ can be thought of as uncorrelated zero mean Gaussian process with covariance matrix Q, and variance σ^2, respectively.

In vector-matrix notation, the continuous time state-space representation for the n-compartment model is given by:

$$\begin{aligned} d\mathbf{C}(t) &= \boldsymbol{\kappa}(\boldsymbol{\alpha})\mathbf{C}(t)dt + d\mathbf{B}(t) \\ m(t) &= \mathbf{V}(\boldsymbol{\alpha})\mathbf{C}(t) + \eta(t) \end{aligned} \tag{5}$$

In Equation (5), *C(t)* denotes the concentration vector; $\boldsymbol{\alpha}$ is the parameter vector whose elements are the pharmacokinetic rates and the volume fractions; $\boldsymbol{\kappa}(\boldsymbol{\alpha})$ is the system matrix; and $\mathbf{V}(\boldsymbol{\alpha})$ is the measurement matrix. For example the parameter vector $\boldsymbol{\alpha}$ for the two-compartment model is given by

$$\boldsymbol{\alpha} = \begin{bmatrix} k_a & k_b & k_{out} & v_e & v_p \end{bmatrix} \tag{6}$$

The ICG measurements in Equation (5) are collected at discrete time instances, $t=kT$, k=0,1, ..., where T is the sampling period. Therefore, the continuous model described in Equation (14) has to be discretized. To simplify our notation, we shall use $\mathbf{C}(k) = \mathbf{C}(kT)$ and $m(k) = m(kT)$. The discrete state space system and the measurement models are given as follows:

$$\begin{aligned} \mathbf{C}(k+1) &= \boldsymbol{\kappa}_d(\boldsymbol{\alpha})\mathbf{C}(k) + \boldsymbol{\omega}(k) \\ m(k) &= \mathbf{V}_d(\boldsymbol{\alpha})\mathbf{C}(k) + \eta(k) \end{aligned} \tag{7}$$

where $\boldsymbol{\kappa}_d(\boldsymbol{\alpha}) = e^{\boldsymbol{\kappa}(\boldsymbol{\alpha})T}$ is the discrete-time system matrix and $\mathbf{V}_d(\boldsymbol{\alpha}) = \mathbf{V}(\boldsymbol{\alpha})$ is the discrete-time measurement matrix. $\omega(k)$ and $\eta(k)$ are zero mean Gaussian white noise processes with covariance matrix $\mathbf{Q}_d$ and variance σ_d^2, respectively. Discretization of state-space models can be found in various system theory books, see for example (Chen, 1999)

An explicit form of the discrete state space model for the two-compartment case is given as follows:

$$\begin{aligned} \begin{bmatrix} C_e(k+1) \\ C_p(k+1) \end{bmatrix} &= \begin{bmatrix} \tau_{11} & \tau_{12} \\ \tau_{21} & \tau_{22} \end{bmatrix} \begin{bmatrix} C_e(k) \\ C_p(k) \end{bmatrix} + \boldsymbol{\omega}(k) \\ m(k) &= \begin{bmatrix} v_e & v_p \end{bmatrix} \begin{bmatrix} C_e(k) \\ C_p(k) \end{bmatrix} + \eta(k) \end{aligned} \tag{8}$$

where τ_{ij} is the ith row and j^{th} column entry of the system matrix $\boldsymbol{\kappa}_d(\boldsymbol{\alpha})$. Note that the matrix entry is an exponential function of the parameters k_a and k_b and k_{out}.. To simplify the estimation process, we shall first estimate the matrix entries, τ_{ij}, and then compute the pharmacokinetic rates for each compartmental model.

3.2 Modeling of ICG pharmacokinetic rates and concentrations as unknown states

The Kalman filter provides a recursive method to estimate the states in state-space models, in which the states are driven by noise, and the measurements are collected in the presence of measurement noise (Zarchan, 2000; Chui & Chen, 1999; Catlin, 1989). In the case of non-linear state-space models, the EKF linearizes the model around the current state estimate, and then applies the KF to the resulting linear model. The EKF framework is also utilized for the joint estimation of the unknown system and/or measurement parameters and states. In a linear state-space model when both states and system parameters are unknown, the linear state-space model can be regarded as a non-linear model in which the linear system parameters and states are combined to form the new states of the non-linear model. This system is then linearized and solved for the unknown states using the KF estimator. We consider a linear Taylor approximation of the non-linear model. The details of the linearization procedure and a general discussion on EKF can be found in (Chui & Chen, 1999; Lyung, 1979; Togneri & Deng, 2003; Nelson & Stear, 1976).

In our problem, the objective is to simultaneously estimate the states, i.e., the ICG concentrations in each compartment, and the system and measurement parameters, i.e., the pharmacokinetic parameters and the volume fractions. Let $\boldsymbol{\theta}$ denote the discrete-time parameter vector of the pharmacokinetic rates and volume fractions. For example, in the two-compartment model, $\boldsymbol{\theta}$ is given by

$$\boldsymbol{\theta} = \begin{bmatrix} \tau_{11} & \tau_{12} & \tau_{21} & \tau_{22} & v_e & v_p \end{bmatrix} \tag{9}$$

In order to estimate $\boldsymbol{\theta}$ within the EKF framework, the following dynamic model is introduced:

$$\boldsymbol{\theta}(k+1) = \boldsymbol{\theta}(k) + \boldsymbol{\zeta}(k) \tag{10}$$

where $\boldsymbol{\zeta}(k)$ is a zero mean white noise process with covariance matrix S_d (Chui and Chen, 1999). Here, $\boldsymbol{\theta}(k)$ can be thought of as the kth update of the parameter rather than its value at time k.

We append the parameter vector $\boldsymbol{\theta}(k+1)$ to the ICG concentration vector $\mathbf{C}(k+1)$ to form the new non-linear state-space model given by

$$\begin{aligned} \begin{bmatrix} \mathbf{C}(k+1) \\ \boldsymbol{\theta}(k+1) \end{bmatrix} &= \begin{bmatrix} \mathbf{K}(\boldsymbol{\theta})\mathbf{C}(k) \\ \boldsymbol{\theta}(k) \end{bmatrix} + \begin{bmatrix} \boldsymbol{\omega}(k) \\ \boldsymbol{\zeta}(k) \end{bmatrix} \\ m(k) &= \begin{bmatrix} V_d(\boldsymbol{\theta}) & 0 \end{bmatrix} \begin{bmatrix} \mathbf{C}(k) \\ \boldsymbol{\theta}(k) \end{bmatrix} + \eta(k) \end{aligned} \tag{11}$$

where $\mathbf{K}(\boldsymbol{\theta}) = \boldsymbol{\kappa}_d(\boldsymbol{\alpha})$.

3.3 Joint estimation of ICG concentrations, pharmacokinetic parameters, and volume fractions within EKF framework

In this section we will summarize the major steps of the EKF estimator for the joint estimation of ICG concentrations and compartmental model parameters. Let the subscript $k\,|\,t$ denote the estimate at time k given all the measurements up to time t. Then the 1-step ahead prediction of the ICG concentrations and the compartmental model parameters are given as follows:

$$\begin{bmatrix} \hat{\mathbf{C}} \\ \hat{\boldsymbol{\theta}} \end{bmatrix}_{k|k-1} = \begin{bmatrix} \mathbf{K}(\hat{\boldsymbol{\theta}})\hat{\mathbf{C}} \\ \hat{\boldsymbol{\theta}} \end{bmatrix}_{k-1|k-1} \tag{12}$$

For the two-compartment model, Equation (12) becomes

$$\begin{bmatrix} \hat{C}_e \\ \hat{C}_p \\ \hat{\boldsymbol{\theta}} \end{bmatrix} = \begin{bmatrix} \hat{\tau}_{11}\hat{C}_e + \hat{\tau}_{12}\hat{C}_p \\ \hat{\tau}_{21}\hat{C}_e + \hat{\tau}_{22}\hat{C}_p \end{bmatrix}_{k-1|k-1} \tag{13}$$

The error covariance matrix, $\mathbf{P}_{k|k-1}$, of the 1-step ahead predictions is given as follows:

$$\mathbf{P}_{k|k-1}=\mathbf{J}_{k-1}\mathbf{P}_{k-1|k-1}\mathbf{J}_{k-1}^{T}+\begin{bmatrix}\mathbf{Q}_d & 0\\ 0 & \mathbf{S}_d\end{bmatrix} \tag{14}$$

where $\mathbf{J}_k$ is the Jacobian of the non-linear EKF system function at time k. Explicitly, it is given by:

$$\mathbf{J}_k=\begin{bmatrix}\mathbf{K}(\hat{\boldsymbol{\theta}}) & \frac{\partial}{\partial\boldsymbol{\theta}}\left[\mathbf{K}(\hat{\boldsymbol{\theta}}_n)\hat{\mathbf{C}}\right]\\ \mathbf{0} & \mathbf{I}\end{bmatrix}_{k|k} \tag{15}$$

where $\mathbf{0}$ and $\mathbf{I}$ denote zero and identity matrices, respectively. The Jacobian matrix for the two-compartment model becomes

$$\mathbf{J}_k=\begin{bmatrix}\begin{pmatrix}\hat{\tau}_{11} & \hat{\tau}_{12}\\ \hat{\tau}_{21} & \hat{\tau}_{22}\end{pmatrix} & \begin{pmatrix}\hat{C}_e & \hat{C}_p & 0 & 0 & 0 & 0\\ 0 & 0 & \hat{C}_e & \hat{C}_p & 0 & 0\end{pmatrix}\\ \mathbf{0}_{6\times2} & \mathbf{I}_{6\times6}\end{bmatrix}_{k|k} \tag{16}$$

The 1-step ahead predictions are updated to the kth-step estimates by means of the Kalman gain matrix which are given by

$$\mathbf{G}_k=\mathbf{P}_{k|k-1}\boldsymbol{\Lambda}^T[\boldsymbol{\Lambda}\mathbf{P}_{k|k-1}\boldsymbol{\Lambda}^T+\sigma_k^2]^{-1} \tag{17}$$

where $\boldsymbol{\Lambda}$ is the following vector:

$$\boldsymbol{\Lambda}=\begin{bmatrix}\mathbf{V}_d(\hat{\boldsymbol{\theta}}) & \frac{\partial}{\partial\boldsymbol{\theta}_n}\left[\mathbf{V}_d(\hat{\boldsymbol{\theta}})\hat{\mathbf{C}}\right]\end{bmatrix}_{k|k-1} \tag{18}$$

For the two-compartment model the $\boldsymbol{\Lambda}$ vector becomes

$$\boldsymbol{\Lambda}=\begin{bmatrix}\hat{v}_e & \hat{v}_p & 0 & 0 & 0 & 0 & \hat{C}_e & \hat{C}_p\end{bmatrix} \tag{19}$$

The kth-step estimate of the concentrations and the parameters are obtained using

$$\begin{bmatrix}\hat{\mathbf{C}}\\ \hat{\boldsymbol{\theta}}\end{bmatrix}_{k|k}=\begin{bmatrix}\hat{\mathbf{C}}\\ \hat{\boldsymbol{\theta}}\end{bmatrix}_{k|k-1}+G_k\left(m(k)-\left[\mathbf{V}_d(\hat{\boldsymbol{\theta}})\hat{\mathbf{C}}\right]_{k|k-1}\right) \tag{20}$$

The initialization and the convergence properties of the EKF can be found in (Alacam et al., 2006; Chui and Chen, 1999; Ljung, 1979; La Scala et al., 1996; Boutayeb et al., 1997).

4. Estimation of ICG pharmacokinetics in Fischer rat data

We applied the proposed EKF framework to the pharmacokinetic analysis of ICG data obtained from four Fischer rats with adenocarcinoma. R3230ac adenocarcinoma cells were injected below the skin into four Fischer rats 3 weeks prior to measurements. The tumor size for the rats varies in diameter from 5 to 30 mm. Measurements were conducted with a combined frequency-domain and steady-state optical technique that facilitates rapid measurement of tissue absorption. Frequency domain measurements were obtained at 674, 800, 849, 898, and 915 nm, modulated at frequencies from 50 to 601 MHz, sweeping a total of 233 frequencies. Tumors were also imaged by use of contrast-enhanced magnetic resonance imaging and coregistered with the location of the optical probe. In addition, a broadband continuous wave reflectance measurement spanning the range 650-1000 nm was performed with a spectrometer. With the reduced-scattering coefficient spectrum and diffusion theory, the broadband reflectance spectra were converted to absorption coefficient spectra. The absolute concentration of ICG, together with oxy-hemoglobin, deoxy-hemoglobin, and water were calculated by using multiple linear regressions of ICG extinction coefficient spectra to the calculated absorption spectrum at approximately every second for ten minutes. A detailed discussion of the measurement process and apparatus can be found in (Bevilacqua et al., 1988; Jacubowski, 2002).

Fig. 3 presents the ICG concentrations from four different rats. Tumors in Rat 1 and 2 are classified as necrotic because of their low tissue oxy-hemoglobin, low total hemoglobin, and low gadolinium-diethylene-triamine penta-acetic acid (Gd-DTPA) enhancement levels. Tumors in Rat 3 and 4 are classified as edematous due to their high water content (Merritt et al., 2003). It can be observed from Fig. 3 that the necrotic cases display low peak ICG concentration values and slowly rising slopes unlike the edematous cases with high peak values and sharp rising slopes.

We estimated the pharmacokinetic rates for the two-compartment model (Alacam et al., 2006).

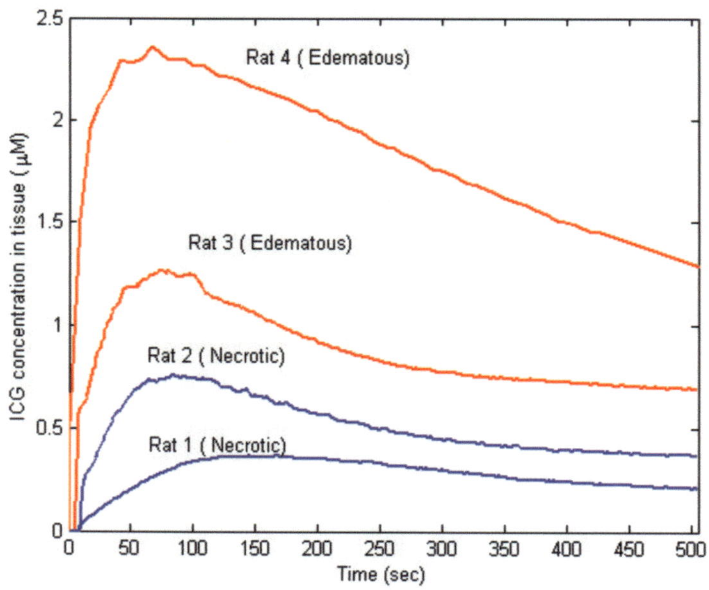

Fig. 3. ICG concentrations measured in tissue for four different rat tumors.

	k_a $(sec^{-1}10^{-2})$	k_b $(sec^{-1}10^{-2})$	k_{out} $(sec^{-1}10^{-3})$	v_e (10^{-2})	v_p (10^{-2})
Rat 1 (Necrotic)	2.47±0.043	1.06±0.052	4.61±0.073	21.8±1.92	1.41±0.053
Rat 2 (Necrotic)	3.54±0.082	2.98±0.086	4.83±0.092	25.4±3.49	2.42±0.088
Rat 3 (Edematous)	6.90±0.101	4.93±0.072	3.95±0.048	30.4±2.81	4.84±0.120
Rat 4 (Edematous)	8.40±0.114	7.77±0.091	4.02±0.068	53.0±4.73	7.03±0.321

Table 1. Estimated pharmacokinetic rates and volume fractions for the two-compartment model.

Table 1 presents the estimated pharmacokinetic rates and volume fractions using the EKF algorithm. The rate of leakage into the EES from the capillary, k_a, range from 0.0247 to 0.0840 1/sec and the rate of drainage out of the EES and into the capillary, k_b, range from 0.0106 to 0.0777 1/sec. Note that the permeability rates for the necrotic cases are lower than the ones observed for the edematous cases. Additionally, the estimated values for the pharmacokinetic rates are much higher than the normal tissue values due to the increased leakiness of the blood vessels around the tumor region (Alacam et al., 2006; Cuccia et al., 2003; Su et al., 1998). The estimated plasma volume fractions agrees with the values reported earlier (Cuccia et al., 2003), and the values presented in the literature (Fishkin et al., 1997; Buckley, 2002). These results confirm that v_p can be large in tumors and that its magnitude varies with respect to the stage of the tumor (Tofts, 1997). The estimated values of the EES volume fraction, v_e, range from 0.218 to 0.53, in agreement with the 0.2 to 0.5 range reported earlier (Tofts et al., 1999). Note that these results are valid only for the ICG pharmacokinetics in tumor cells R3230ac, adenocarcinoma and may not be generalized for other types of contrast agents or tumor types.

Figure 4 shows the estimated ICG concentrations in plasma and the EES compartments for the two-compartment model for Rats 1 to 4. Note that initial estimates of concentrations are noisy due to the limited data used in the recursive EKF estimation. This can be improved by Kalman backward smoothing (Gelb, 1989). The peak values of the plasma concentration, C_p, range from 2.72 μM to 4.28 μM. The absolute value of the concentrations may not be very useful. However, concentration of ICG in a compartment relative to the one in another compartment may provide useful information. We consider the ratio of the peak concentrations in plasma and the EES as a potential parameter to discriminate different tumors. The peak C_p/C_e ratio for Rats 1 to 4 is 0.551, 0.593, 0.787, and 1.151, respectively. This ratio is higher in edematous cases consistent with the fact that ICG-albumin leaks more into the EES in edematous tumors. Additionally, the ICG concentration in plasma decays faster than the ICG concentration in the EES due to its elimination through the liver and kidneys.

5. Pharmacokinetic-rate images of indocyanine green from *in vivo* breast data

In this section, we present a method of forming pharmacokinetic-rate images, and spatially resolved pharmacokinetic-rates of ICG using *in vivo* NIR data acquired from three patients with breast tumors.

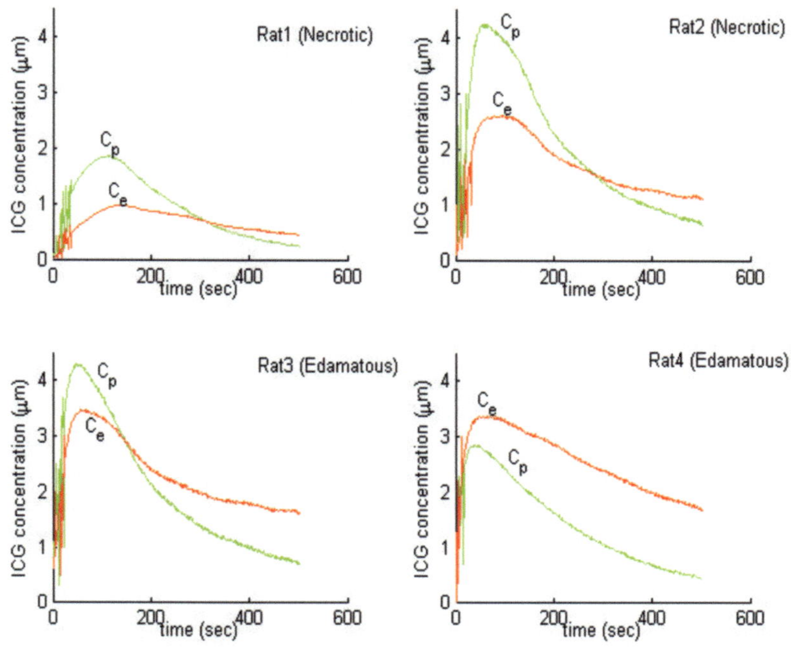

Fig. 4. ICG concentrations in plasma, $C_p(t)$ and EES, $C_e(t)$, for four different rats. (a) Rat1, (b) Rat2, (c) Rat3, and (d) Rat4.

5.1 NIR apparatus and patient information

We used the data collected with a continuous wave (CW) NIR imaging apparatus. The apparatus had 16 light sources, which are tungsten bulbs with less than 1 watt of output power. They were located on a circular holder at an equal distance from each other with 22.5 degrees apart. Sixteen detectors, namely, silicon photodiodes, are situated in the same plane. The breast was arranged in a pendular geometry with the source-detector probes gently touching its surface. The detectors used the same positions as the sources to collect the light originating from one source at a time. Only the signals from the farthest 11 detectors were used in the analysis. A band pass filter at 805 nm, the absorption peak of ICG, was placed in front of the sources to select the desired wavelength. A set of data for one source was collected every 500 ms. Total time for a whole scan of the breast including 16 sources and 16 detectors was about 8.8 seconds. A more detailed explanation of the apparatus and the data collection procedure can be found in (Nioka et al., 1997).

Three different patients with different tumor types were included in the study. Measurements were made before the biopsy to avoid modification of the blood volume and flow in the tumor region. First case, (Case 1), was fibroadenoma, which corresponds to a mass estimated to be 1-2 cm in diameter within a breast of 9 cm diameter located at 6-7 o'clock. Second case, (Case 2), was adenocarcinoma corresponding to a tumor estimated to be 2-3 cm in diameter within a breast of 7.7 cm diameter located at 4-5 o'clock. The third case, (Case 3), was invasive ductal carcinoma, which corresponds to a mass estimated to be 4 by 3 cm located at 6 o'clock. Table 2 describes the tumor information for each patient. *A priori* information on the location and size of the tumor was obtained by palpation and the diagnostic information was derived *a posteriori* from biopsy and surgery. ICG was injected intravenously by bolus with a concentration of 0.25 mg per 1/kg of body weight. Data acquisition started before the injection of ICG and continued for 10 minutes.

	Tumor Type	Tumor Size	Tumor Location
Case 1	Fibroadenoma	1-2 cm	6-7 o'clock
Case 2	Adenocarcinoma	2-3 cm	4-5 o'clock
Case 3	Invasive Ductal Carcinoma	4 by 3 cm	6 o'clock

Table 2. Tumor Information for each patient.

5.2 Reconstruction of bulk ICG concentration images

In our data collection process, a sequence of boundary measurements was collected over a period of time. Each set of measurements was used to form a frame of the ICG concentration images. The resulting sequence of ICG concentration images were then used to form pharmacokinetic-rate images. To reconstruct each frame of the ICG concentration images, we used the differential diffuse optical tomography (DDOT) technique (Alacam et al., 2008, Intes et al., 2003; Ntziachristos et al., 1999).

In DDOT, two sets of excitation measurements are collected corresponding to before and after the ICG injection, and the ICG concentration is determined by the perturbation method (Intes et al., 2003; Ntziachristos et al., 1999). The photon propagation before and after the injection is modeled by the following diffusion equations:

$$\nabla . D_x(r)\nabla\Phi_x^{\pm}(r,\omega) - (\mu_{ax}^{\pm}(r) + j\omega / c)\Phi_x^{\pm}(r,\omega) = 0 \qquad r \in \Omega \subset R^3 \tag{21}$$

with Robin-type boundary conditions (Arridge, 1999).

Here x stands for the excitation, c is the speed of light inside the medium Ω ; Ω denotes the modulation frequency of the source, $\mu_{ax}^{-}(r)$ and $\mu_{ax}^{+}(r)$ are the absorption coefficients before and after the ICG injection, $D_x(r)$ is the diffusion coefficient which is assumed independent of $\mu_{ax}^{\pm}(r)$, known but not necessarily constant, $\Phi_x^{\pm}(r,\omega)$ denotes optical field at location r before and after the ICG injection.

The absorption coefficient after the injection $\mu_{ax}^{+}(r)$ is modeled as a sum of the absorption coefficient of the medium before the ICG injection $\mu_{ax}^{-}(r)$ and the perturbation caused by the ICG $\Delta\mu_{ax}(r)$:

$$\Delta\mu_{ax}(r) = \mu_{ax}^{+}(r) - \mu_{ax}^{-}(r) \qquad r \in \Omega \subset R^3 \tag{22}$$

The forward model, given in Equation (21) is based on the first order Rytov approximation (Intes et al., 2003). We discretize the forward model and relate the relative absorption coefficients of voxels in the imaging volume to Rytov-type measurements by a system of linear equations. Let $\Psi_x(\omega, r_d, r_s)$ denote the Rytov-type measurements at location r_d due to source at r_s. The linearized relationship between the differential absorption coefficient and measurements is given by (O'Leary, 1996)

$$\Psi_x(\omega, r_d, r_s) = -\frac{1}{\Phi_x^{-}(\omega, r_d, r_s)} \int_{\Omega} G_x^{-}(r, \omega; r_d) \Phi_x^{-}(r, \omega; r_s) \frac{c\Delta\mu_{ax}(r)}{D_x} d^3 r \tag{23}$$

where $\Phi_x^-(r,\omega;r_s)$ is the photon density obtained at the excitation wavelength before ICG injection.

$\int_\Omega G_x^-(r,\omega;r_d)$ is the Green's function of Equation (21) for a source at r_s before the injection describing the propagation of light from the heterogeneity r to the detector at r_d.

We approximated the shape of the breast as a cylinder and used the Kirchhoff approximation (Ripoll et al., 2001a; Ripoll et al., 2001b) for diffuse waves to model the interaction of light with boundaries. In order to account for the biological noise, we implemented the forward model with coupling coefficient technique (Boas et al., 2001b).

We addressed the inverse problem of recovering $\Delta\mu_{ax}(r)$ from Rytov-measurements using the singular value decomposition of the Moore-Penrose generalized system. We used a zeroth-order Tikhonov regularization to stabilize the inversion procedure. We applied the L-curve method to an experimental model reconstruction and determined the best regularization parameter using a curvature function as described in (Hansen & O'Leary, 1993). A detailed discussion of the forward and inverse models used for the reconstruction of differential absorption coefficients $\Delta\mu_{ax}(r)$ can be found in (Intes et al., 2003).

To construct a set of ICG concentration images, we used the linear relationship between the differential absorption coefficients and ICG concentrations (Landsman et al., 1976):

$$\Delta\mu_a(r) = \ln 10 \varepsilon_\lambda m(r) \tag{24}$$

where ε_λ is the extinction coefficient of ICG at the wavelength 805nm, *m(r)* is the bulk ICG concentration in the tissue.

Using the method outlined above, we reconstructed a sequence of ICG concentration images. Fig., 5-7 show a set of images reconstructed from *in vivo* breast data for Case 1, 2,

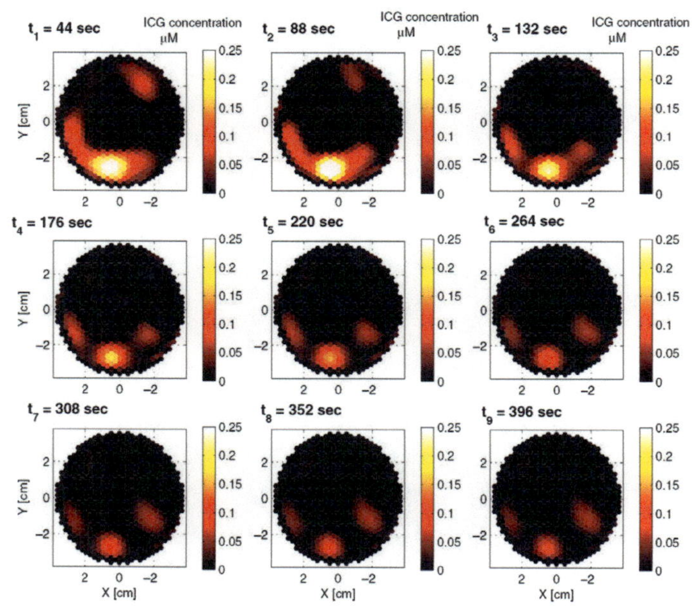

Fig. 5. ICG concentration images for a set of time instants for Case 1.

and 3, respectively. Although only 9 images are displayed, there are approximately 50 images for each case, each corresponding to a different time instant. Each image is composed of 649 voxels. Note that the ICG concentration images in Fig.5-7 represent the bulk ICG concentrations in the tissue, not the ICG concentrations in plasma or the EES compartments.

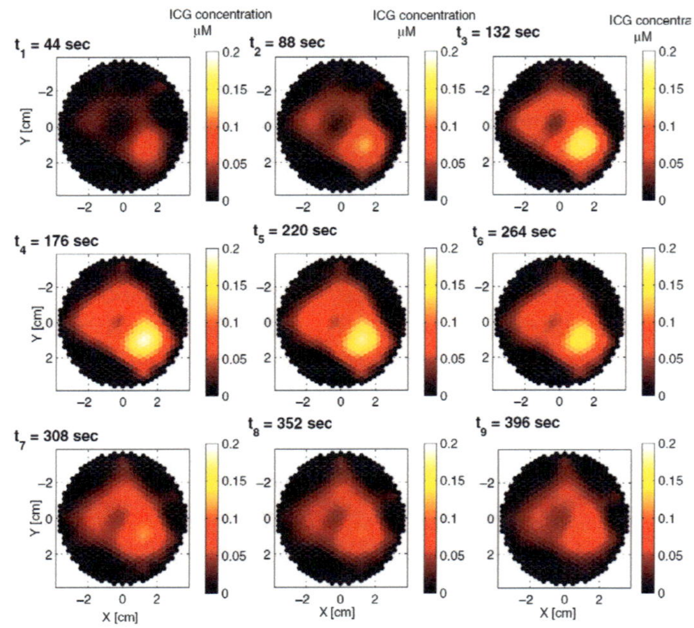

Fig. 6. ICG concentration images for a set of time instants for Case 2.

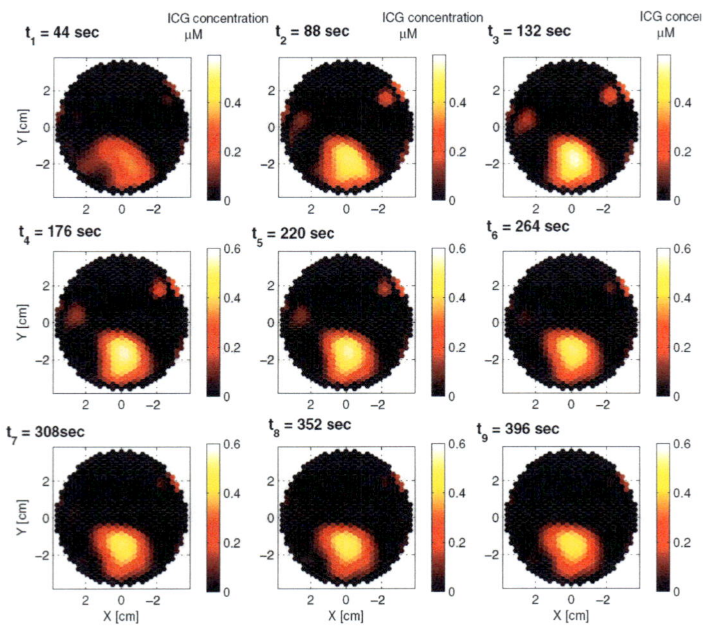

Fig. 7. ICG concentration images for a set of time instants for Case 3.

5.3 Reconstruction of ICG pharmacokinetics from *in vivo* breast data

Our objective is to model the pharmacokinetics of ICG at each voxel of ICG concentration images using the two-compartment model described in Section 2. To do so, we first extracted the time varying ICG concentration curves for each voxel from the sequence of ICG concentration images.

We then fit the two-compartment model to each time course data using the EKF framework; and estimated k_a, k_b, k_{out}, and the ICG concentrations in plasma and the EES. We chose the initial values within the biological limits that lead to minimum norm error covariance matrix for the EKF estimation. The images of k_a, and k_b for each case are shown in Fig. 8(a)-(b), 9(a)-(b), and 10(a)-(b), respectively.

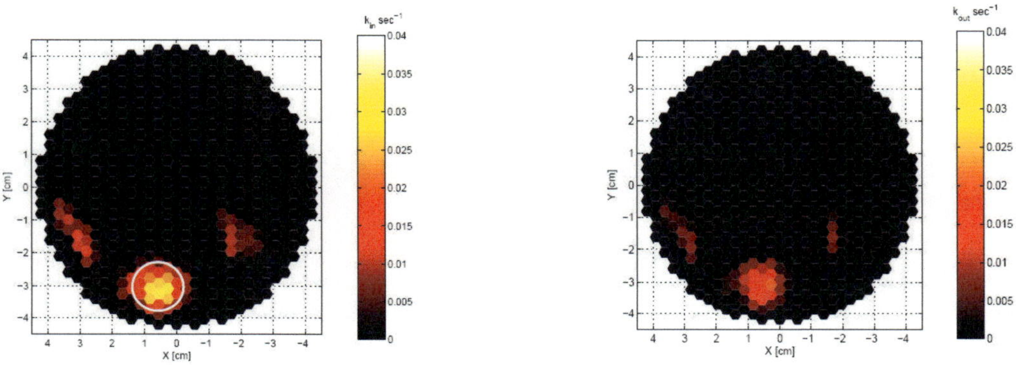

Fig. 8. Pharmacokinetic-rate images, (a) k_a, and (b) k_b for Case 1. The k_a images are shown with approximate tumor location and size.

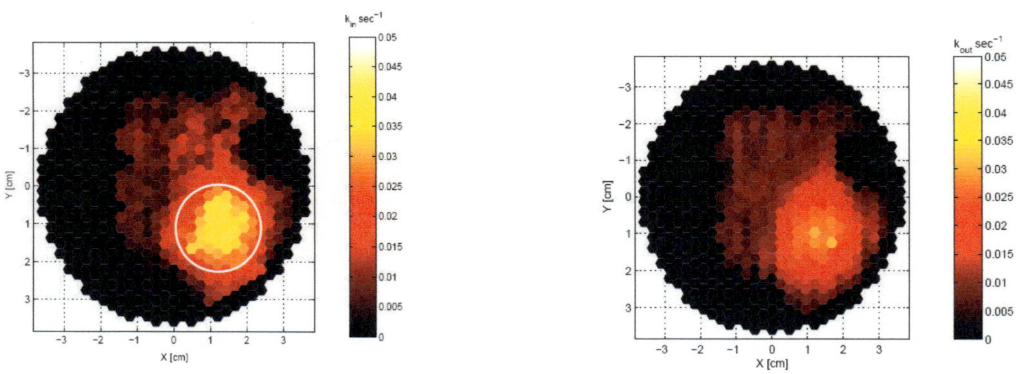

(a) (b)

Fig. 9. Pharmacokinetic-rate images, (a) k_a, and (b) k_b for Case 2. The k_a images are shown with approximate tumor location and size.

Using the *a priori* and *a posteriori* information on the location, and the size of the tumors, we plotted an ellipse (or a circle) to identify the approximate location and size of the tumor in the pharmacokinetic-rate images. We note that the radii of the ellipses were chosen large enough to include the tumor boundaries. Fig. 8(a), 9(a), and 10(a) present the k_a images with approximate tumor location and size for Case 1, 2, and 3, respectively. The consistency of

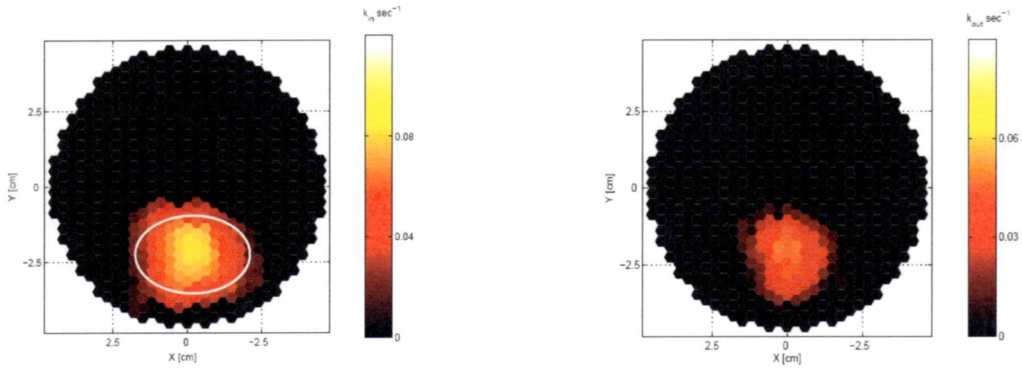

(a) (b)

Fig. 10. Pharmacokinetic-rate images, (a) k_a, and (b) k_b for Case 2. The k_a images are shown with approximate tumor location and size.

the bright regions in the k_a images, and circular/elliptical regions drawn based on the *a priori* and *a posteriori* information shows that the pharmacokinetic-rate images may provide good localization of tumors. Table 3 shows the mean values (± spatial standard deviation) of the pharmacokinetic-rates for the tumor region and outside the tumor region for all three cases. The pharmacokinetic rates are higher for Case 3 (invasive ductal carcinoma), for both the tumor region and outside the tumor region as compared to Case 2 (adenocarcinoma). Similarly, the kinetic rates are higher for Case 2 (adenocarcinoma), as compared to Case 1 (fibroadenoma) for both the tumor region and outside the tumor region. This observation shows that high mean values of k_a and k_b may be indicative of tumor aggressiveness. Additionally, we constructed the ICG concentration images for plasma and the EES compartments. Figures 11-16 show the ICG concentration in plasma and the EES for 3 different time instants for Case 1, 2, and 3, respectively.

	k_a $(sec^{-1}10^{-2})$		k_b $(sec^{-1}10^{-2})$		k_{out} $(sec^{-1}10^{-3})$	
	Inside	Outside	Inside	Outside	Inside	Outside
Case 1	2.14±0.018	0.73±0.011	1.24±0.069	0.43±0.013	4.11±0.057	3.87±0.012
Case 2	2.92±0.076	1.14±0.052	1.58±0.051	0.65±0.036	3.94±0.081	4.12±0.047
Case 3	6.87±0.093	3.06±0.015	4.96±0.048	1.66±0.072	4.49±0.056	4.46±0.081

Table 3. Mean and standard deviation of pharmacokinetic-rates for the tumor region and outside the tumor region

Our results show that the pharmacokinetic-rates are higher around the tumor region agreeing with the fact that permeability increases around the tumor region due to compromised capillaries of tumor vessels. We also observed that ICG concentrations in plasma and the EES compartments are higher around the tumors agreeing with the hypothesis that around the tumor region ICG may act as a diffusible extravascular flow in leaky capillary of tumor vessels.

6. Conclusion

We presented a two- compartmental model, and an EKF framework for (i) the estimation of bulk ICG pharmacokinetics and (ii) the reconstruction of ICG pharmacokinetic-rate images and concentration images in different compartments. We tested our approach in data obtained from Fischer rats with adenocarcinoma cells and estimated pharmacokinetic rates and volume fractions. The estimated parameters indicate that the permeability rates are higher for edematous cases as compared to the necrotic tumors.

We also presented pharmacokinetic-rate images of ICG using the *in vivo* data acquired from three patients with breast tumors. To form pharmacokinetic-rate images, we used the differential diffuse optical tomography technique. Along with the pharmacokinetic-rates, we also reconstructed the ICG concentration images in plasma and EES compartments. The ICG concentration images in plasma and the EES compartments show that the concentration of ICG is higher in the tumor region agreeing with the hypothesis that around the tumor region ICG may act as a diffusible extravascular flow in leaky capillary of tumor vessels.

While the two-compartment model is sufficient to model the ICG pharmacokinetics, higher-order compartmental models may be advantageous for modeling the pharmacokinetics of functionalized optical contrast agents that actively accumulate or activate in diseased tissue. In the future, we plan to apply higher order compartmental models and the EFK framework to estimate the pharmacokinetics of newly developed optical fluorophores approved for human and/or animal use.

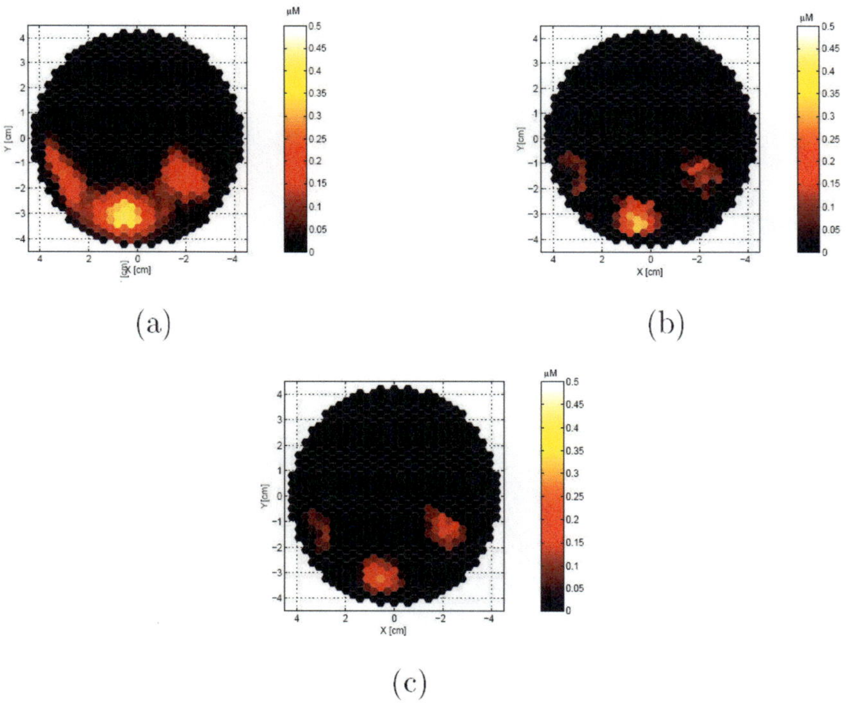

Fig. 11. ICG concentration images in plasma for Case 1 for (a) 246.4th, (b) 334.4th, and (c) 422.4th seconds.

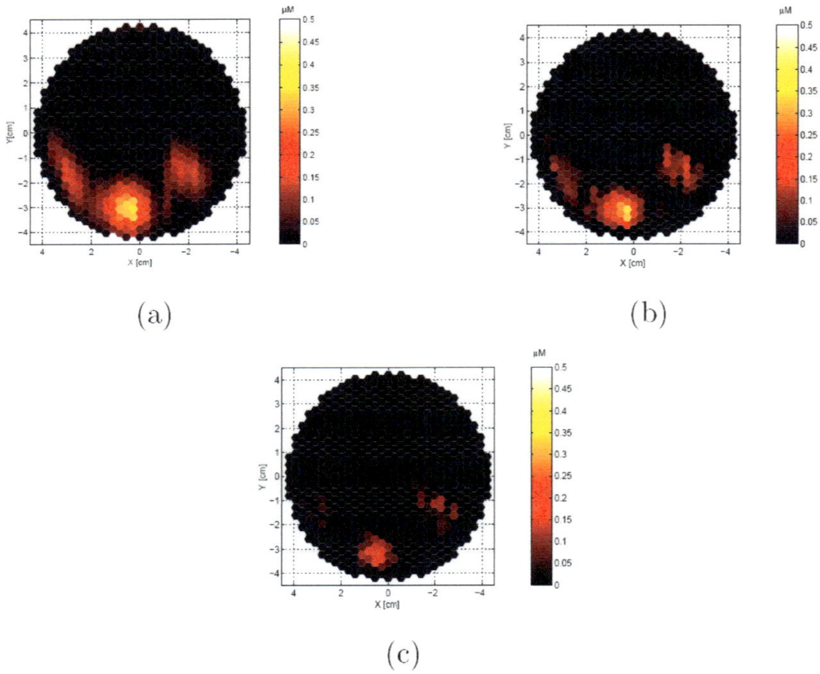

Fig. 12. ICG concentration images in the EES for Case 1 for (a) 246.4th, (b) 334.4th, and (c) 422.4th seconds.

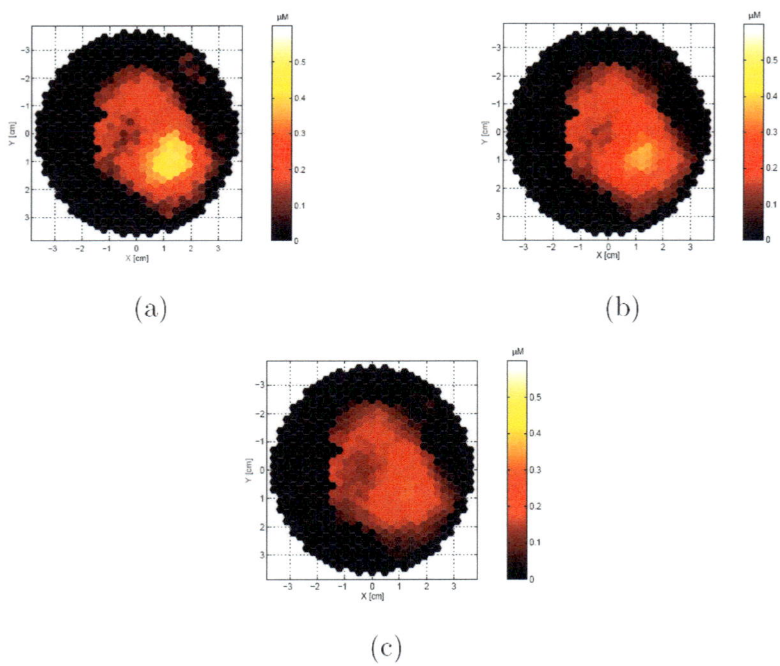

Fig. 13. ICG concentration images in plasma for Case 2 for (a) 228.8th, (b) 316.8th, and (c) 404.8th seconds.

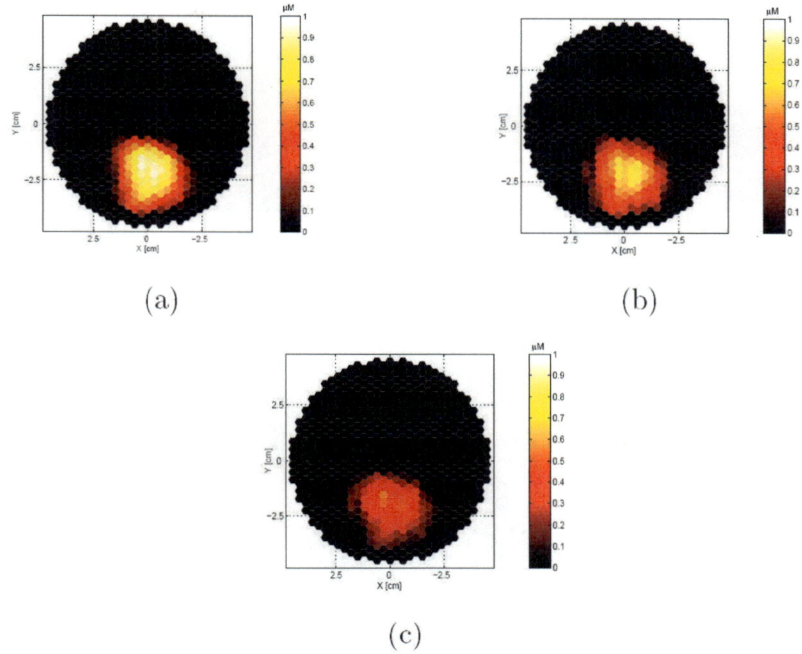

Fig. 14. ICG concentration images in the EES for Case 2 for (a) 228.8th, (b) 316.8th, and (c) 404.8th seconds.

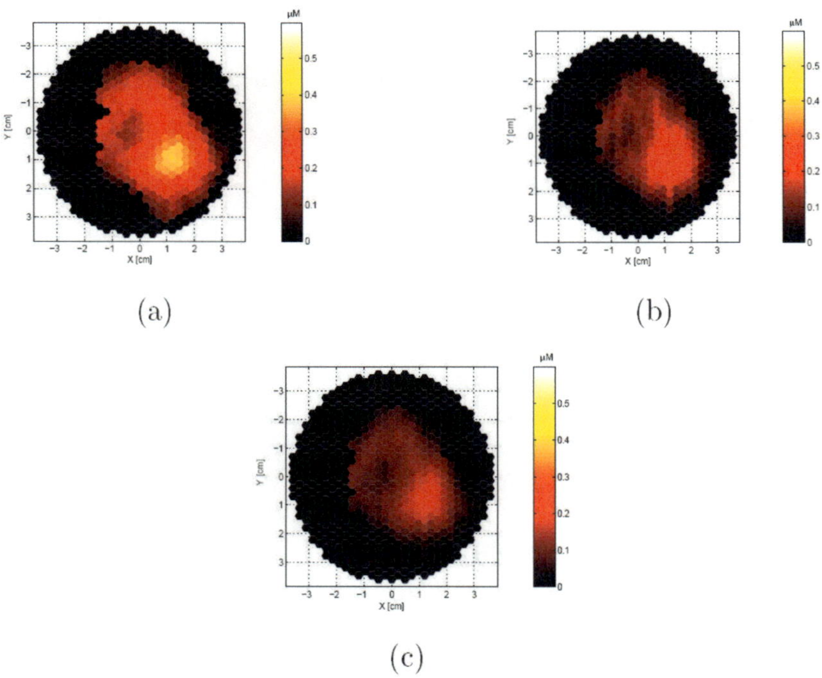

Fig. 15. ICG concentration images in plasma for Case 3 for (a) 246.4th, (b) 378.4th, and (c) 510.4th seconds.

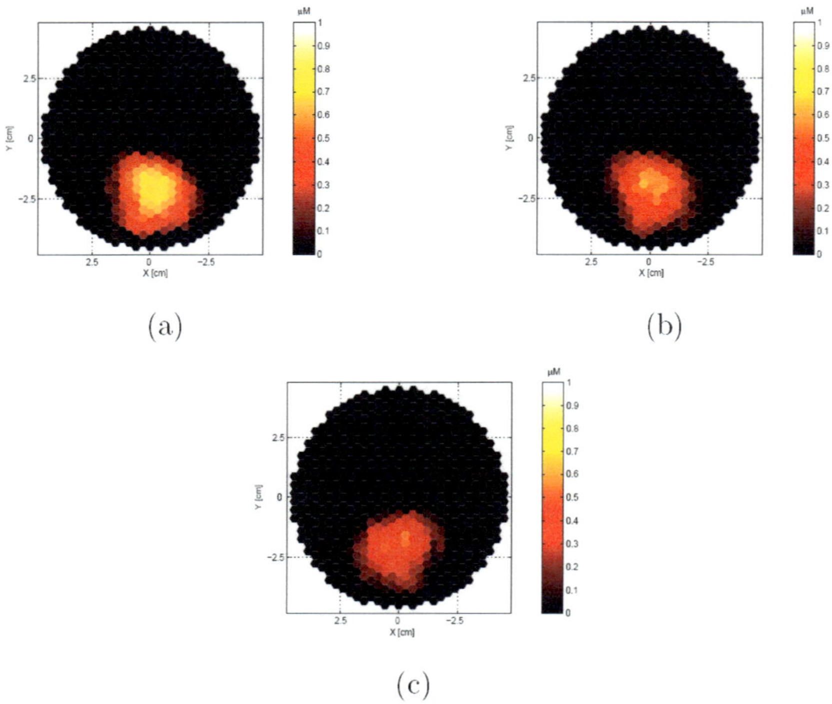

Fig. 16. ICG concentration images in plasma for Case 3 for (a) 246.4th, (b) 378.4th, and (c) 510.4th seconds.

7. References

Akaike, H. (1980). *Likelihood and the Bayes Procedure,* Bayesian Statistics, Univ. Press, Valencia, Spain

Alacam, B.; Yazici B.; Intes, X. & Chance, B. (2006). Extended Kalman filtering for the modeling and analysis of ICG pharmacokinetics in cancerous tumors using NIR optical methods. *Trans. IEEE Biomed. Eng.,* Vol. 53, pp. 1861–1871

Alacam, B.; Yazici, B.; Intes, X.; Chance, B.; & Nokia S. (2008). Pharmacokinetic-rate Images of Indocyanine Green for Breast Tumors using Near Infrared Optical Methods. *Physics in Medicine and Biology,* Vol. 53, No: 4, pp. 837-859

Anderson, D. H. (1983). *Lecture Notes in Biomathematics: Compartmental Modeling and Tracer Kinetics,* Springer-Verlag, Berlin

Arridge, S. R. (1999). Optical tomography in medical imaging. *Inverse Prob.,* Vol. 15, pp. 41–93

Becker, A.; Schneider, G.; Riefke, B.; Licha, K. & Semmler W. (1999). Localization of near-infrared contrast agents in tumors by intravital microscopy, *Proc. SPIE,* Vol. 3568, pp. 112-118

Bevilacqua, F.; Berger, A. J.; Cerussi, A. E.; Jakubowski, D. & Tromberg B. J. (2000). Broadband absorption spectroscopy in turbid media by combined frequency-domain and steady-state methods. *Appl. Opt.*, Vol. 39, pp. 6498-6507

Boas, D.; Gaudette, T. & Arridge, S. (2001a). Simultaneous imaging and optode calibration with diffuse optical tomography. *Opt. Exp.* Vol. 8 pp. 263–270

Boas, D.; Brooks, D.; Miller, E.; DiMarzio, C.; Kilmer, M. & Gaudette, R. (2001b). Imaging the body with diffuse optical tomography. *IEEE Signal Proc Magazine*, Vol. 18, pp. 57-74

Boutayeb, M.; Rafaralahy, H. & Darouach M. (1997). Convergence analysis of the Extended Kalman Filter used as an observer for nonlinear deterministic discrete-time systems. *IEEE Transactions on Automatic Control*, Vol. 42 No. 4, pp. 581-586

Box, G. E. P.; Jenkins, G. M. & Reinsel G.C. (1994). *Time Series Analysis: Forecasting and Control*, Third edition, Prentice Hall, New York

Buckley, D. L. (2002). Uncertainty in the analysis of tracer kinetics using dynamic contrast-enhanced T1-weighted MRI. *Magn. Reson. Med.*, Vol. 47, pp. 601-606

Catlin, C. E. (1989). *Estimation, Control, and the Discrete Kalman Filter*, Springer, New York

Chen, C. (1999). *Linear System Theory and Design*, Oxford University Press, New York

Chen, Y.; Liu, Q.; Huang, P.; Hyman, S.; Intes, X.; Lee, W. & Chance, B. (2003). Assessment of tumor angiogenesis using fluorescence contrast agents, *Proc. of the SPIE*, Vol. 5254 No. 1, pp. 296-301

Chui, C.K. & Chen, G. (1999). *Kalman Filtering with real time applications*, Springer, Berlin, 1999

Cobelli, C.; Foster, D. & Toffolo G. (2000). *Tracer Kinetics in Biomedical Research: from Data to Model*, Kluwer Academic/Plenum, New York

Cuccia, D.J.; Bevilacqua, F.; Durkin, A. J.; Merritt, S.; Tromberg, B. J.; Gulsen, G.; Yu, H.; Wang, J. & Nalcioglu O. (2003). In vivo quantification of optical contrast agent dynamics in rat tumors by use of diffuse optical spectroscopy with magnetic resonance imaging coregistration. *Applied Optics*, Vol. 42, No. 1, pp. 2940-2950

El Deosky, A.; Seifalian, A.; Cope, M.; Delpy, D. & Davidson B. (1999). Experimental study of liver dysfunction evaluated by direct Indocyanine green clearance using near infrared spectroscopy. *Br. J. Surg.*, Vol. 86, pp. 1005-1011

Fishkin, J. B.; Coquoz, O.; Anderson, E.; Brenner, M. & Tromberg B. J. (1997). Frequency-domain photon migration measurements of normal and malignant tissue optical properties in a human subject. *Appl. Opt.*, Vol. 36, pp. 10-20

Furukawa, K.; Crean, D. H.; Mang, T. S.; Kato, H. & Dougherty T. J. (1995). Fluorescence detection of premalignant, malignant, and micrometastatic disease using hexylpyropheophorbide, *Proc. SPIE*, Vol. 2371, pp. 510-514.

Gelb, A. (1989). *Applied Optimal Estimation*, M.I.T. Press, Cambridge

Gurfinkel, M.; Thompson, A. B.; Ralston, W.; Troy, T. L.; Moore, A. L.; Moore, T. A.; Gust, J. D.; Tatman, D.; Reynolds, J. S.; Muggenburg Nikula, B.K.; Pandey, R.; Mayer, R. H.;

Hawrysz, D. J. & Sevick-Muraca E. M. (2000). Pharmacokinetics of ICG and HPPH-car for the detection of normal and tumor tissue using fluorescence, near-infrared reflectance imaging: a case study. *Photochem Photobiol.*, Vol. 72, pp. 94-102

Hansen, D.; Spence, A.; Carski, T. & Berger M. (1993). ICG staining and demarcation of tumor margins in a rat glioma model. *Surg. Neurol*, Vol. 40, pp. 451-456.

Hansen, P. & O'Leary, D. (1993). The use of the *L*-curve in the regularization of discrete ill-posed problems. *SIAM J. Sci. Comput.* Vol. 14, pp. 1487–1503

Harvey, A. (1993). *Time Series Models*, MIT Press

Hawrys, D. & Sevick-Muraca, E. (2000). Developments toward diagnostic breast cancer imaging using Near-Infrared optical measurements and fluorescent contrast agents. *Neoplasia*, Vol. 2, pp. 388-417

Intes, X..; Ripoll, J.; Chen, Y.; Nioka, S.; Yodh, A. G. & Chance, B. (2003). Continuous-wave optical breast imaging enhanced with Indocyanine Green. *Med. Phys*, Vol. 30-6, pp.1039-1047

Intes, X. & Chance, B. (2005). Non-PET functional imaging techniques: optical.. *Radio. Clin. North Am.* Vol.43., pp.221-234

Jacquez, J. A. (1972). *Compartmental Analysis in Biology and Medicine: Kinetics of Distribution of Tracer-labeled Materials*, Elsevier Pub. Co., New York

Jakubowski, D. J. (2002). *Development of broadband quantitative tissue optical spectroscopy for the non-invasive characterization of breast disease*, Beckman Laser Institute, University of California, Irvine

La Scala, B. F. & Bitmead, R. R. (March 1996). Design of an extended Kalman filter frequency tracer. *IEEE Tran. On Sig. Proc.*, Vol. 44, No. 3, pp. 739-742

Landsman, M. L. J.; Kwant, G.; Mook, G. A. & Zijlstra, W. G. (1976). Light-absorbing properties, stability, and spectral stabilization of indocyanine green. *J. Appl. Physiol.*, Vol. 40, pp. 575–583

Li, X.; Beauvoit, B.; White, R.; Nioka, S.; Chance, B. & Yodh, A. (1995). Tumor localization using fluorescence of ICG in rat models, *Proc. SPIE*, Vol. 2389, pp. 789-797

Ljung, L. (1979). Asymptotic Behavior of the Extended Kalman Filter as a Parameter Estimator for Linear Systems. *IEEE Tran. Automa. Cont.*, Vol. AC-24-1, pp. 36-50

Merritt, S.; Bevilacqua, F.; Durkin, A. J.; Cuccia, D. J.; Lanning, R.; Tromberg, B. J.; Gulsen, G.; Yu, H.; Wang, J. & Nalcioglu O. (2003). Monitoring tumor physiology using near-infrared spectroscopy and MRI coregistration. *Appl. Opt.*, Vol. 42, pp. 2951-2959

Milstein, A. B.; Webb, K. J. & Bouman, C. A., (2005). Estimation of kinetic model parameters in fluorescence optical diffusion tomography *J. Opt. Soc. Am,.* Vol. 22, pp. 1357-1368

Nelson, L. & Stear, E. (1976). The Simultaneous On-Line Estimation of Parameters and States in Linear Systems. *IEEE Tran. on Auto. Control*, Vol.21, pp. 94-98.

Nioka, S.; Yung, Y.; Schnall, M.; Zhao, S.; Orel, S.; Xie, C.; Chance, B. & Solin, S. (1997) .Optical imaging of breast tumor by means of continuous waves. *Adv. Exp. Med. Biol.* Vol. 411, pp. 227–232

Ntziachristos, V.; Chance, B. & Yodh, A. (1999). Differential diffuse optical tomography, *Opt. Exp.* Vol. pp. 5230–5242

Ntziachristos, V.; Yodh, A. G.; Schnall, M. & Chance, B., (2000). Concurrent MRI and diffuse optical tomography of breast after indocyanine green enhancement. *Med. Sci.*, Vol. 97, pp. 2767–2772

O'Leary, M. (1996). Imaging with diffuse photon density waves, *PhD Thesis,* Department of Physics & Astronomy, University of Pennsylvania

Ripoll, J.; Ntziachristos, V.; Carminati, R. & Nieto-Vesperinas, M. (2001a). Kirchhoff approximation for diffusive waves. *Phys. Rev.*, Vol. 64, pp. 051917

Ripoll, J.; Ntziachristos, V.; Culver, J. P.; Pattanayak, D. N.; Yodh, A. G. & Nieto-Vesperinas, M. (2001b). Recovery of optical parameters in multiplelayered diffusive media: theory and experiments. *J. Opt. Soc. Am.*, Vol. 18, pp. 821–830

Sallas, W.M. & Harville, D.A. (1998). *Noninformative Priors and Restricted Maximum Likelihood Estimation in the Kalman Filter.* in J.C. Spall (Ed.), *Bayesian Analysis of Time Series and Dynamic Models*, New York: Marcel-Dekker, Inc.

Schwarz, G. (1978). Estimating the dimensions of a model. *Annals. of Stat.*, Vol. 6, pp. 461-464

Shinohara, H.; Tanaka, A.; Kitai, T.; Yanabu, N.; Inomoto, T.; Satoh, S.; Hatano, E.; Yamaoka, Y. & Hirao, K. (1996). Direct measurement of hepatic indocyanine green clearance with near-infrared spectroscopy: separate evaluation of uptake and removal. *Hepatology*, Vol. 23, pp. 137-144

Su, M. Y.; Muhler, A.; Lao, X. & Nalcioglu, O. (1998). Tumor characterization with dynamic contrast-enhanced MRI using MR contrast agents of various molecular weights. *Magn. Reson. Med.*, Vol. 39, pp. 259-269

Tofts, P. S. (1997). Modeling tracer kinetics in dynamic Gd-DTPA MR imaging. *J. Magn Reson. Imag.*, Vol. 7, pp. 91-101

Tofts. P. S.; Phil, D.; Brix, G.; Buckley, D. L.; Evelhoch, J. L.; Henderson, E.; Knopp, M. V.; Larsson, H. B. W.; Lee, T.; Mayr, N. A.; Parker, G. J. M.; Port, R. E.; Taylor, J. & Weisskoff, R. M. (1999). Estimating Kinetic Parameters From Dynamic Contrast-Enhanced T1-Weighted MRI of a Diffusable Tracer: Standardized Quantities and Symbols. *Jour. Mag. Res. Ima*, Vol. 10, pp. 223-232

Togneri, R. & Deng, L. (2003). Joint State and Parameter Estimation for a Target-Directed Nonlinear Dynamic System Model. *IEEE Tran. on Sig. Proc.,* Vol. 51, No. 12, pp. 3061-3070

Tornoe C. W. (2002). *Grey-Box PK/PD Modeling of Insulin*, M.S. Thesis

Vaupel, P.; Schlenger, K.; Knoop, C. & Hockel, M. (1991). Oxygenation of human tumors: evaluation of tissue oxygen distribution in breast cancers by computerized O2 tension measurements. *Cancer Res.*, Vol. 51, pp. 3316–3322

Yates, M. S.; Bowmer, C. J. & Emmerson, J. (1983). The plasma clearance of indocyanine green in rats with acute renal failure: effect of dose and route of administration. *Biochem. Pharmacol*, Vol. 32, pp. 3109-3114

Yodh, A. & Chance, B. (1995). Spectroscopy and imaging with diffusing light. *Phys. Today*,Vol. 48. No. 3, pp. 34-40

Zarchan, P. (2000). *Fundamentals of Kalman Filtering: a Practical Approach*, American Institute of Aeronautics and Astronautics, Reston

9

Dual Unscented Kalman Filter and Its Applications to Respiratory System Modelling

Esra Saatci[1] and Aydin Akan[2]
[1]*Istanbul Kultur University*
[2]*Istanbul University*
Turkey

1. Introduction

Unscented Kalman Filter (UKF) (Julier & Uhlmann, 1997) was developed as an improvement of Extended Kalman Filter (EKF) (Grewal & Andrews, 2001) for discrete-time filtering of the nonlinear dynamic systems. Comparison between different statistical approaches on the state and parameter estimation of the dynamic systems revealed that the performance of UKF is superior to EKF in many Kalman Filter (KF) applications (Chow et al., 2007); (Xiong et al., 2006); (Wan & Merwe, 2001); (Kandepu et al., 2008). Nonlinear dynamic systems with uncertain observations were often appeared in, for instance, communication systems (Wan & Merwe, 2001), medical systems (Polak & Mroczka, 2006) and machine learning (Chen, 2003). Medical systems, described by stochastic difference equations with measurement models including nonlinear and non-Gaussian components, are good candidates for the UKF analysis. Although there are many medical signal applications of Kalman Filters (KF); (Vauhkonen et al., 1998) and EKF (Avendano et al., 2006), some medical diagnostic and therapeutic measures are processed by UKF from indirect sensor measurements including statistical brain signal analysis to study cognitive brain functions by Electroencephalography (EEG) and functional Magnetic Resonance Imaging (fMRI) (Brochwell et al., 2007), ECG model-based denoising (Sameni et al., 2007), medical image processing (Ijaz et al., 2008), and evoke potential analysis in the neuroscience. These works demonstrated that UKF can be considered as an effective framework for medical signal analysing, modelling and filtering. Also, it was shown that UKF is a promising alternative in a variety of applications' domains including state and parameter estimation simultaneously which is dual estimation.

Respiratory mechanics is the dynamic relationship between appropriate pressures and flows in the respiratory system and assessment of it is an important problem in the diagnosis and monitoring of respiratory disorders, especially of Chronic Obstructive Pulmonary Disease (COPD). The primarily goal on the determination of the respiratory mechanics is the computation, or estimation, of the respiratory parameters non-invasively, continuously, effectively and without any patient cooperation. Direct approach to this problem is the measurement of the mechanics by the lung catheter or the alveolar capsule (Bates & Lutchen, 2005). However, these direct measurement methods are invasive and not suitable for continuous monitoring. On the other hand, the studies revealed that analysis of pressure and flow signals measured at the airway opening represent the respiratory parameters in question while isolation of the peripheral information on the mechanics remains challenging (Bates & Lutchen, 2005). To achieve the goal of extracting the mechanical information from the measured pressure and flow signals at the mouth, investigators are now using advanced system identification techniques in frequency-domain, time-domain or time-frequency domain (Yuan et al., 1998); (Lutchen & Costa, 1990).

In the literature, common approach to respiratory mechanics determination is the inverse modelling of the respiratory system in the frequency-domain by measured overall impedance over the range of frequencies (Hellinckx et al., 2001). Although, the parameters of the inverse model is assumed to correspond to the physiologically important quantities, due to the simplifications on the model, interpretation of the parameters are not straightforward. Thus, determining the physiologically relevant information requires realistic multi-parameter models incorporating dynamic and nonlinear nature of the respiratory system. Measured data fitting to such a nonlinear model is very difficult in frequency-domain (Nucci et al., 2002). Moreover, most patients with COPD require artificial ventilatory supports that apply a positive pressure to the airway opening of the patient to assist ventilatory muscles and patient-ventilator interaction is a time-varying system (Nucci et al., 2002).

These shortcomings of frequency-domain analysis of the respiratory system led us to implement time-domain methods for the determination of the respiratory mechanics. Recently presented nonlinear dynamic RC model of the respiratory system (Saatci & Akan, 2007) and multi-parameter well-known Mead model (Diong et al., 2007) were selected for the inverse modelling of the respiratory system in the time-domain. Dual UKF method was applied to the respiratory models to estimate the states as well as the parameters. Time series were measured from both the COPD patients and healthy subjects and artificially produced by the model equations. The reason to use dual estimation was the complications of the model's state and measurement equations and nonlinear relationship between the parameters and the states of the respiratory models. In this respect, first, in the Section 3 EKF, UKF principles will be given briefly, and dual UKF algorithm will be discussed in details. Used respiratory models will be presented in the Section 4 and Section 5 is devoted to the estimation of the states and parameters of the models. Finally, results are given in Section 6 and in Section 7 conclusions are drawn.

2. Kalman filtering

EKF and UKF are the Bayesian data analysis based practical methods for the nonlinear system modelling from the observed data using probability models for both the unobserved states and the unknown system parameters. Many of the practical systems can be represented by the following state-space model:

$$\mathbf{x}_k = f_k\left(\mathbf{x}_{k-1}, \boldsymbol{\theta}, \mathbf{u}_k\right) + \mathbf{q}_k \tag{1}$$

$$\mathbf{z}_k = h_k\left(\mathbf{x}_k, \boldsymbol{\theta}, \mathbf{u}_k\right) + \mathbf{r}_k \tag{2}$$

where $f(\bullet)$ and $h(\bullet)$ are the generally nonlinear functions. $\mathbf{q}_k$ and $\mathbf{r}_k$ the are additive state and observation noises respectively. $\mathbf{u}_k$ is devoted to the known inputs and $\boldsymbol{\theta}$ is the unknown parameter vector of interest.

In the statistical analysis terms above equations are called state-observation models of the practical system and represented as the distributions $\mathbf{Pr}(\mathbf{x}_k/\mathbf{x}_{k-1},\boldsymbol{\theta})$ for the state vector $\mathbf{x}_k$ and $\mathbf{Pr}(\mathbf{z}_k/\mathbf{x}_k,\boldsymbol{\theta})$ for the observation equation. From the Bayesian perspective, the solution of (1) and (2) is to recursively estimate the state vector $\mathbf{x}_k$ and/or parameter vector $\boldsymbol{\theta}$ given the observations $\mathbf{Z}_k = \{\mathbf{z}_i\}_{i=1}^{k}$. Once the initial distributions $\mathbf{Pr}(\mathbf{x}_0,\boldsymbol{\theta})$ and $\mathbf{Pr}(\mathbf{x}_0/\mathbf{z}_0)$ are given, filtering posterior distribution $\mathbf{Pr}(\mathbf{x}_k/\mathbf{Z}_k,\boldsymbol{\theta})$ can be obtained recursively by two steps: prediction and filtering. In the prediction step with the help of Markov property of the state vector $\mathbf{x}_k$ predictive distribution $\mathbf{Pr}(\mathbf{x}_k/\mathbf{Z}_{k-1})$ is compute by:

$$\mathbf{Pr}(\mathbf{x}_k/\mathbf{Z}_{k-1},\boldsymbol{\theta}) = \int \mathbf{Pr}(\mathbf{x}_k/\mathbf{x}_{k-1},\boldsymbol{\theta})\mathbf{Pr}(\mathbf{x}_{k-1}/\mathbf{Z}_{k-1},\boldsymbol{\theta})d\mathbf{x}_{k-1} \quad (3)$$

In the filtering step posterior distribution is obtained based on the predictive distribution via Bayes' rule:

$$\begin{aligned}\mathbf{Pr}(\mathbf{x}_k/\mathbf{Z}_k,\boldsymbol{\theta}) &= \mathbf{Pr}(\mathbf{z}_k/\mathbf{x}_k,\boldsymbol{\theta})\mathbf{Pr}(\mathbf{x}_k/\mathbf{Z}_{k-1},\boldsymbol{\theta})/\mathbf{Pr}(z_k/Z_{k-1}) \\ &\propto \mathbf{Pr}(\mathbf{z}_k/\mathbf{x}_k,\boldsymbol{\theta})\mathbf{Pr}(\mathbf{x}_k/\mathbf{Z}_{k-1},\boldsymbol{\theta})\end{aligned} \quad (4)$$

Equations (3) and (4) constitute the recursive Bayesian estimation and are optimum in the sense that it seeks the posterior distribution which integrated and uses all of available information expressed by probabilities. However, direct computation of these disributions is not easy due to large state-observation space and multidimensional integrals. Thus above expression is considered as the theoretic foundation for the estimation problem and computations of the predictive and posterior distributions require certain limitations to the model.

2.1 Extended Kalman filter

If the model equations (1) and (2) were to be in the linear form and the process and observation noises were assumed to be zero-mean white Gaussian noises, $\mathbf{q}_k \sim N[0,Q]$ and $\mathbf{r}_k \sim N[0,R]$, celebrated Kalman Filter would be the Minimum Variance Unbiased Estimation (MVUE) providing an exact solution for the linear system with relatively easy matrix calculations. However, if the linearity and Gaussian distribution assumptions were violated, different approaches would be required to overcome the filtering problem (Arulampalam et al., 2002).

One of the methods developed for the solution of the nonlinear but Gaussian distributed systems is the EKF. In the EKF, nonlinearity is overcome by locally linearization of the model equations. Due to the Gaussian assumption of the posterior distribution, EKF works well for some types of nonlinear problems, but it may provide a poor performance in some cases when the true posterior is non-Gaussian. Thus, with the linearization and Gaussian assumption of the distributions, the EKF equations derived from the Kalman Filter theory are:

Prediction step:

$$\begin{aligned}\mathbf{x}_{k/k-1} &= f_k\left(\mathbf{x}_{k-1/k-1},\boldsymbol{\theta},\mathbf{u}_{k-1}\right) \\ \mathbf{P}_{k/k-1} &= \mathbf{F}_k\mathbf{P}_{k-1/k-1}\mathbf{F}_k^T + \mathbf{Q}\end{aligned} \quad (5)$$

Filtering step:

$$K_k = \mathbf{P}_{k/k-1}\mathbf{H}_k^T\left(\mathbf{H}_k\mathbf{P}_{k/k-1}\mathbf{H}_k^T + \mathbf{R}\right)^{-1}$$
$$\mathbf{x}_{k/k} = \mathbf{x}_{k/k-1} + K_k\left(\mathbf{z}_k - h_k\left(\mathbf{x}_{k/k-1}, \boldsymbol{\theta}, \mathbf{u}_k\right)\right) \tag{6}$$
$$\mathbf{P}_{k/k} = \left(I - K_k\mathbf{H}_k\right)\mathbf{P}_{k/k-1}$$

where $\mathbf{F}_k$ and $\mathbf{H}_k$ matrices are defined as:

$$\mathbf{F}_k = \frac{df_k\left(\mathbf{x}, \boldsymbol{\theta}, \mathbf{u}_{k-1}\right)}{d\mathbf{x}}\bigg|_{\mathbf{x}=\mathbf{x}_{k-1/k-1}} \tag{7}$$

$$\mathbf{H}_k = \frac{dh_k\left(\mathbf{x}, \boldsymbol{\theta}, \mathbf{u}_k\right)}{d\mathbf{x}}\bigg|_{\mathbf{x}=\mathbf{x}_{k/k-1}} \tag{8}$$

2.2 Unscented Kalman filter

Different from EKF, UKF is global method which attempts to solve whole posterior distribution by deterministic sampling approximation. Unscented Transformation (UT) where so-called sigma points are the deterministic samples from posterior distribution and propagate the information of the data through nonlinear transformation is the theory behind UKF. Thus, based on Kalman Theory, implementation of UKF can be summarized as follows:

Step 1: Initialization and weights calculations:

Draw N_x - dimensional particles $\mathbf{x}_0 = \left\{x_0^{(i)}\right\}_{i=1}^{N_x}$ from the prior distribution $\mathbf{Pr}(\mathbf{x}_0, \boldsymbol{\theta}) = \mathrm{N}(\mathbf{x}_0, \mathbf{P}_0)$.

$$w_m^{(i)} = \lambda/(N_x + \lambda) \qquad i = 0$$
$$w_c^{(i)} = \lambda/(N_x + \lambda) + \left(1 - \alpha^2 + \beta\right) \qquad i = 0$$
$$w_m^{(i)} = w_c^{(i)} = 1/2(N_x + \lambda) \qquad i = 1, \ldots 2N_x$$

where $\lambda = \alpha^2(N_x + \kappa) - N_x$ is the composite scaling parameter and determines the spread of the sigma points around $\mathbf{x}_k$. α, β and κ are the parameters for scaling and prior distribution of $\mathbf{x}_0$.

For $k = 1, \ldots \infty$

Step 2: Sigma points calculations 1:

$$\aleph_{k-1}^{(i)} = \mathbf{x}_{k-1} \qquad i = 0$$
$$\aleph_{k-1}^{(i)} = \mathbf{x}_{k-1} + \left(\sqrt{(N_x + \lambda)\mathbf{P}_{k-1}}\right)_{(i)} \qquad i = 1, \ldots N_x$$
$$\aleph_{k-1}^{(i)} = \mathbf{x}_{k-1} - \left(\sqrt{(N_x + \lambda)\mathbf{P}_{k-1}}\right)_{(i)} \qquad i = N_x + 1, \ldots 2N_x$$

where $\left(\sqrt{(N_x + \lambda)\mathbf{P}_{k-1}}\right)_{(i)}$ is the i th column of the matrix.

Step 3: Prediction:

$$\aleph_{k/k-1}^{(i)} = f_k\left(\aleph_{k-1}^{(i)}, \boldsymbol{\theta}, \mathbf{u}_{k-1}\right) \quad i = 0, \ldots 2N_x$$

$$\mathbf{x}_{k/k-1} = \sum_{i=0}^{2N_x} w_m^{(i)} \aleph_{k/k-1}^{(i)}$$

$$\mathbf{P}_{k/k-1} = \sum_{i=0}^{2N_x} w_c^{(i)} \left(\aleph_{k/k-1}^{(i)} - \mathbf{x}_{k/k-1}\right)\left(\aleph_{k/k-1}^{(i)} - \mathbf{x}_{k/k-1}\right)^T + \mathbf{Q}$$

Step 4: Sigma points calculations 2:

$$\aleph_{k/k-1}^{(i)*} = \mathbf{x}_{k/k-1} \qquad i = 0$$

$$\aleph_{k/k-1}^{(i)*} = \mathbf{x}_{k/k-1} + \left(\sqrt{(N_x + \lambda)\mathbf{P}_{k/k-1}}\right)_{(i)} \qquad i = 1, \dots N_x$$

$$\aleph_{k/k-1}^{(i)*} = \mathbf{x}_{k/k-1} - \left(\sqrt{(N_x + \lambda)\mathbf{P}_{k/k-1}}\right)_{(i)} \qquad i = N_x + 1, \dots 2N_x$$

Step 5: Filtering:

$$Z_{k/k-1}^{(i)} = h_k\left(\aleph_{k/k-1}^{(i)*}, \boldsymbol{\theta}, \mathbf{u}_{k-1}\right)$$

$$\mathbf{z}_{k/k-1} = \sum_{i=0}^{2N_x} w_m^{(i)} Z_{k/k-1}^{(i)}$$

$$\mathbf{P}_{zz} = \sum_{i=0}^{2N_x} w_c^{(i)} \left(Z_{k/k-1}^{(i)} - \mathbf{z}_{k/k-1}\right)\left(Z_{k/k-1}^{(i)} - \mathbf{z}_{k/k-1}\right)^T + \mathbf{R}$$

$$\mathbf{P}_{xz} = \sum_{i=0}^{2N_x} w_c^{(i)} \left(\aleph_{k/k-1}^{(i)*} - \mathbf{x}_{k/k-1}\right)\left(Z_{k/k-1}^{(i)} - \mathbf{z}_{k/k-1}\right)^T$$

$$K_k = \mathbf{P}_{xz}\mathbf{P}_{zz}^{-1}$$

$$\mathbf{x}_k = \mathbf{x}_{k/k-1} + K_k\left(\mathbf{z}_k - \mathbf{z}_{k/k-1}\right)$$

$$\mathbf{P}_k = \mathbf{P}_{k/k-1} - K_k \mathbf{P}_{zz} K_k^T$$

Above algorithm is based on the conventional UKF, however there are variant UKF algorithms proposed in the literature. For instance, Unscented Particle Filter (UPF) is the most important one among them. In UPF, UKF is used to optimize the sampling stage of the Particle Filter (PF) by generating the required samples from $\mathbf{Pr}(\mathbf{x}_k/\mathbf{Z}_k, \boldsymbol{\theta})$ rather than $\mathbf{Pr}(\mathbf{x}_k/\mathbf{x}_{k-1}, \boldsymbol{\theta})$. As PF makes no assumption on the form of the probability densities in question, UPF is most suited to non-Gaussian systems. Another variant of UKF is the square-root implementation of the UKF algorithm where *Cholesky factor* is used for the matrix square-root of the state/parameter covariance matrix. Then the *Cholesky factor* is propagated via *QR decomposition* in subsequent iterations. This form of the UKF algorithm is mostly required where the convergence speed or execution duration is important.

2.3 Dual unscented Kalman filter

System identification often requires simultaneous state and parameter estimation from observed noisy data. If the parameters are assumed to have a prior distribution, $\mathbf{Pr}(\boldsymbol{\theta})$ Bayesian approach can be also applied to the parameter estimation. Therefore UKF equations above are modified for the dual estimation problem in order to extend the advantages of UKF method to the parameter estimation. There are two common

approaches for the simultaneous estimation: estimation with two different state-observation models or estimation by augmented state model with common observation model. First called dual UKF incorporates two distinct sequential filters, one estimating the true states and the other estimating the parameters. Later is called joint UKF and implementation not much differs from the UKF algorithm.
If the parameters of the dynamic system are considered as time-invariant random variables that need to be estimated, time-update should allow no changes beyond the effects of state noise. That is modelled as a first-order Markov process:

$$\boldsymbol{\theta}_{k+1} = \boldsymbol{\theta}_k + \mathbf{q}_p^k \tag{9}$$

where $\mathbf{q}_p^k \sim N\left[0, Q_p\right]$ is the parameter process noise and assumed to be zero-mean white Gaussian noise.
However, expression in (9) may not suitable for the systems where the parameters are actually constant unknowns. Thus, for those systems the parameter state noise is not existed at all and should not be added to the model. The parameter time-update becomes:

$$\boldsymbol{\theta}_{k+1} = \boldsymbol{\theta}_k \tag{10}$$

This form of the state equation of the parameters considerably simplifies the UKF algorithm. Thus, in the dual UKF algorithm, at the parameter estimation stage step 2 and step 3 are replaced by the equation (5) where $f(\bullet)$ and $\mathbf{F}_k$ are the identity matrices.
Constraints due to the physical limitations on the parameters are also applied to the dual estimation problem. Parameter constraints are usually represented by the box constraints ($\boldsymbol{\theta}_\mathbf{L} \le \boldsymbol{\theta} \le \boldsymbol{\theta}_\mathbf{H}$). In the respiratory models, parameters are assumed to be positive real numbers, thus the constraints are defined as $0 \le \boldsymbol{\theta} \le \infty$. Modifications to the dual algorithm should be made due to the constraints in the models. In the algorithm, after the sigma pints were calculated (Step 2) and the Prediction step (Step 3), constrained sigma points were obtained with the projection method explained in (Moradkhani et al., 2005). The new constrained sigma points are defined as $\aleph_{k-1}^{(i),C} = P\left(\aleph_{k-1}^{(i)}\right)$ and $\aleph_{k/k-1}^{(i),C} = P\left(\aleph_{k/k-1}^{(i)}\right)$.

3. Respiratory models

Respiratory models express the viscoelastic and mechanic properties of the airways, lung and chestwall and these properties are usually represented by the electrical elements. Elemental equations define the relationship between appropriate pressures and volumetric flow at the specific regions of respiratory system whereas the system state and measurement equations are the mathematical descriptions of the whole system behaviour. Theoretical and experimental studies reveal that respiratory system models may be linear and nonlinear in both state and parameters depending on the system identification technique, considered disease conditions and experimental methodology (Polak & Mroczka, 2006); (Bates & Lutchen, 2005); (Avanzolini et al., 1995). For the interested reader, discussion and comparisons on the linear and nonlinear models can be found in the literature (Diong et al., 2007); (Yuan et al., 1998). In this work well-known multi-parameter linear Mead model and recently presented nonlinear RC model were used to model the respiratory system. The presented nonlinear model is the simplified model by (Athanasiades et al., 2000). The motivation behind to use this nonlinear model was that, first it includes nonlinearities as well as time-varying nature of the respiratory system, second model states and measurements mimic the COPD patients data under non-invasive ventilatory support.

3.1 Mead respiratory model

Mead respiratory model with non-invasive ventilatory pressure effect, $P_{ven}(t)$ and muscular pressure effect, $P_{mus}(t)$ is shown in Fig. 1a. In the model, R_c and R_p are the resistances of the central and peripheral airways respectively. Airway flow inertance is represented as L and compliances include bronchial tube compliance C_b, lung compliance C_l, and chestwall compliance C_w.

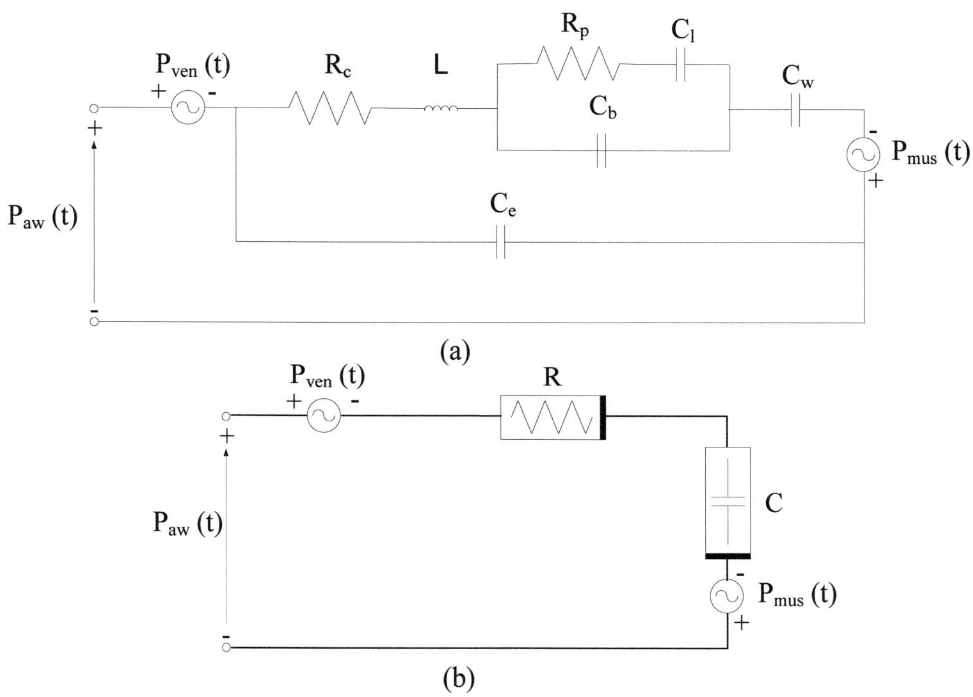

Fig. 1. (a) Mead respiratory model and (b) Nonlinear RC model of the respiratory system. Non-invasive ventilatory pressure effect, $P_{ven}(t)$ and muscular pressure effect, $P_{mus}(t)$ is added to the models.

Since the pressure measured at the airway opening is composed of relatively small part of the patient's effort and big part of the non-invasive ventilatory support, a series of the independent pressure sources are added to the model to mimic the muscular pressure effect and ventilatory effects. $P_{mus}(t)$ is direct effects of the patients inspiratory muscles and can be approximated by the second-order polynominal function (Yamada & Du, 2000):

$$P_{mus}(t) = \begin{cases} -P_{mus\,\mathbf{max}}(1-t/T_I)^2 + P_{mus\,\mathbf{max}} & 0 \le t \le T_I \\ P_{mus\,\mathbf{max}} e^{-t/\tau_m} & T_I \le t \le T \end{cases} \tag{11}$$

where $P_{mus\,\mathbf{max}}$ represents the effect of maximal patient's effort and added to the unknown parameter vector. T_I and T are the inspiration duration time and total duration of one cycle respiration respectively. They are set to constant values in the algorithm. τ_m is the inspiratory muscles relaxation time constant and determines the patient-ventilator asynchrony. τ_m is also set to $60\ ms$ constant value in the simulations.
Non-invasive ventilator pressure is simulated as an exponential function (Yamada & Du, 2000):

$$P_{ven}(t)=\begin{cases} PEEP & 0\le t\le t_{trig} \\ P_{ps}\left(1-e^{-t/\tau_{vi}}\right) & t_{trig}\le t\le T_I \\ P_{ps}e^{-t/\tau_{ve}} & T_I\le t\le T \end{cases} \tag{12}$$

where P_{ps} represents the maximum inspiration pressure set on the non-invasive ventilator. Depended upon the patient's established values, P_{ps} is taken between $8\,cmH_20$ - $15\,cmH_20$ and Positive End Expiration Pressure (PEEP) is set to $0\,cmH_20$ - $4\,cmH_20$. Ventilator inspiration time constant τ_{vi} corresponds the flow acceleration speed of the ventilator, whereas ventilator expiration time constant τ_{ve} is the ventilator deceleration speed and contributes to the small pressure rise at the termination of the inspiration. Both τ_{vi} and τ_{ve} were set to $0.006\,s$. The inspiration trigger delay of the ventilator t_{trig} was set to $20\,ms$ corresponding to the real world scenario.
Above set values for $P_{mus}(t)$ and $P_{ven}(t)$ were applied to simulations where artificially produced data and COPD patient's data were used. For the healthy subject's data $P_{ven}(t)$ was not included to the respiration model.
In the Mead model, parameter vector and state vector can be defined respectively as: $\boldsymbol{\theta}_k=\begin{bmatrix}R_c & L & C_l & C_b & R_p & C_w & C_e & P_{mus\,\mathbf{max}}\end{bmatrix}^T$, $\mathbf{x}_s^k=\begin{bmatrix}\dot{V}_L^k & P_{C_l}^k & P_{C_b}^k & P_{C_w}^k & P_{C_e}^k\end{bmatrix}^T$. Then, with the help of basic electrical circuits rules and first-order Taylor series expansion the state-observation equations of the state vector in the discrete-time become:

$$\mathbf{x}_s^{k+1}=\begin{bmatrix}1-R_c/L & 0 & -1/L & -1/L & 1/L \\ 0 & 1-1/R_pC_l & 1/R_pC_l & 0 & 0 \\ 1/C_b & 1/R_pC_b & 1-1/R_pC_b & 0 & 0 \\ 1/C_w & 0 & 0 & 1 & 0 \\ -1/C_e & 0 & 0 & 0 & 1\end{bmatrix}\mathbf{x}_s^k+\begin{bmatrix}0\\0\\0\\0\\1/C_e\end{bmatrix}\dot{V}_k+\begin{bmatrix}1\\0\\0\\0\\0\end{bmatrix}P_{mus}^k+\mathbf{q}_{ms}^k \tag{13}$$

$$\mathbf{z}_s^k=\begin{bmatrix}0 & 0 & 0 & 0 & 1\end{bmatrix}\mathbf{x}_s^k+P_{ven}^k+\mathbf{r}_{ms}^k \tag{14}$$

where k is the discrete-time index and we assumed that initial state vector $\mathbf{x}_s^0$ is 5-dimentional random vector with mean $E\left[\mathbf{x}_s^0\right]=\bar{\mathbf{x}}_s$ and covariance $E\left[\left(\mathbf{x}_s^0-\bar{\mathbf{x}}_s\right)\left(\mathbf{x}_s^0-\bar{\mathbf{x}}_s\right)^T\right]=P_s^0$, measurement noise and state noise are zero-mean white Gaussian noises, $\mathbf{q}_{ms}^k\sim N[0,Q_{ms}]$ and $\mathbf{r}_{ms}^k\sim N[0,R_{ms}]$. $\dot{V}_k$ is the measured airway flow sequence.

In order to define state-observation equations of the parameter vector, we assume that the parameters are first-order Markov process, but there is no uncertainty in the state $\mathbf{q}_{vp}^{k} \cong 0$. This means parameters are actually time-invariant. Thus the state-observation equations of the parameters are in the form as:

$$\boldsymbol{\theta}_{k+1} = \boldsymbol{\theta}_k \tag{15}$$

$$\mathbf{x}_s^{k+1} = h_k\left(\mathbf{x}_s^k, \boldsymbol{\theta}_k, \dot{V}_k, P_{mus}^k\right) + \mathbf{r}_{mp}^k \tag{16}$$

where we assumed that initial state vector $\boldsymbol{\theta}_0$ is 8-dimentional random vector with mean $E[\boldsymbol{\theta}_0] = \overline{\boldsymbol{\theta}}_0$ and covariance $E\left[\left(\boldsymbol{\theta}_0 - \overline{\boldsymbol{\theta}}_0\right)\left(\boldsymbol{\theta}_0 - \overline{\boldsymbol{\theta}}_0\right)^T\right] = P_p^0$, measurement noise is zero-mean white Gaussion noises, $\mathbf{r}_{mp}^k \sim N\left[0, R_{mp}\right]$.

3.2 Nonlinear RC respiratory model

Fig. 1b shows the nonlinear RC respiratory model with non-invasive ventilatory pressure effect, $P_{ven}(t)$ and muscular pressure effect, $P_{mus}(t)$. In the model R represents the upper airway resistance as the biggest contribution to the resistive pressure lost comes from the upper airways. Rohrer's equation is used to compose the relation between airway flow $\dot{V}(t)$ and mouth pressure $P_{aw}(t)$. Thus resistive pressure lost and dynamic pressure across the nonlinear compliance C in the model can be given respectively as:

$$P_r(t) = \left(A_u + K_u\left|\dot{V}(t)\right|\right)\dot{V}(t) \tag{17}$$

$$P_c(t) = A_l e^{K_l V(t)} + B_l \tag{18}$$

where $V(t)$ represents the gas volume changes above Residual Volume in the lungs. In (7) and (8) A_u, K_u, A_l, K_l, B_l together with $P_{mus\,\mathbf{max}}$ constitute the unknown parameter vector to be estimated.

In the nonlinear RC model, parameter vector and state vector can be defined respectively as: $\boldsymbol{\theta}_k = \begin{bmatrix} A_u & K_u & A_l & K_l & B_l & P_{mus\,\mathbf{max}} \end{bmatrix}^T$, $\mathbf{x}_s^k = \left[V^k\right]^T$. If the circuit theory rules are applied to the nonlinear RC circuits and elemental equations are written for nonlinear R and C elements below state-observation equations in discrete-time are given for the states of the circuits:

$$\mathbf{x}_s^{k+1} = V^k + \dot{V}^k + \mathbf{q}_{ns}^k \tag{19}$$

$$\mathbf{z}^k = \left(A_u + K_u\left|\dot{V}^k\right|\right)\dot{V}^k + A_l e^{K_l V^k} + B_l + P_{ven}^k - P_{mus}^k + \mathbf{r}_{ns}^k \tag{20}$$

where same assumptions on the state are applied to (19) and (20). Measurement noise and state noise are zero-mean white Gaussion noises, $\mathbf{q}_{ns}^k \sim N\left[0, Q_{ns}\right]$ and $\mathbf{r}_{ns}^k \sim N\left[0, R_{ns}\right]$. $\mathbf{z}^k$ is the measured mouth pressure sequence (discrete form of $P_{aw}(t)$).

Parameter model state equation of the nonlinear RC model is the same as the linear Mead model parameter equation (15) due to the same assumptions whereas (20) is used for the parameter model observation equation.

4. Dual UKF based respiratory model parameter estimation

Respiratory models, illustrated in Fig. 1 are composed of the electrical elements that have the unknown parameters. Discrete-time equations (13) - (16) were driven from Mead respiratory model and equations (15), (19) and (20) constitute non-linear RC respiratory model state-observation equations. The common way to model the respiratory system is to estimate the model parameters. The states are also required in order to implement Bayesian data analysis. Then, the respiratory model parameter estimation problem becomes dual recursive nonlinear inference problem from the noisy observed time series.

4.1 Data acquisition and pre-processing

In Mead model two state-observation equations for the states and parameters required to use dual UKF evaluation whereas joint UKF method was used for the nonlinear RC model. Both model parameters and states were estimated by *i)* artificially produced data that mimic the respiratory diseased patients, *ii)* data acquired from COPD patients and *iii)* data recorded from healthy subjects. Artificial airway flow was simulated as a sinusoidal signal with maximum flow of $0.6\,l/s$ and sampling rate was $100\,Hz$. Inspiration time T_I was taken as $1\,s$ while total breath cycle was $3\,s$. The states and observations were computed by (13), (14), (19), (20) and the parameters shown in the Table 1. After the observation sequence was obtained the zero-mean white Gaussian observation noises with $R_{ms} = 0.02\,I_{5\times5}$ and $R_{ns} = 0.02$ were added to the Mead model and nonlinear RC model respectively.

Simulation	Parameter	Value	Model	Parameter	Value
Non-invasive Ventilator Pressure Simulation	$PEEP$	$4\,cmH_2O$	Mead Model Parameters $\boldsymbol{\theta}$	R_c	$1.9601\,cmH_2O\cdot s\cdot l^{-1}$
	P_{ps}	$6\,cmH_2O$		L	$20.772\,cmH_2O\cdot s^2\cdot l^{-1}$
	τ_{vi}	$0.006\,s$		C_l	$4.5182\,l\cdot cmH_2O^{-1}$
	τ_{ve}	$0.006\,s$		C_b	$6.6670\,l\cdot cmH_2O^{-1}$
	t_{trig}	$N/10$		R_p	$4.7039\,cmH_2O\cdot s\cdot l^{-1}$
	N_I	$N/3$		C_w	$7.56\,l\cdot cmH_2O^{-1}$
	N	300 points		C_e	$40.589\,l\cdot cmH_2O^{-1}$
Muscular Pressure Simulation	$P_{mus\,\mathbf{max}}$	$1.2\,cmH_2O$	Nonlinear RC Model Parameters $\boldsymbol{\theta}$	A_u	$3.1\,cmH_2O\cdot s\cdot l^{-1}$
	τ_m	$60\,ms$		K_u	$0.32\,cmH_2O\cdot s^2\cdot l^{-2}$
Common Parameters	f_s	100 Hz		A_l	$0.5\,cmH_2O$
	$\mathbf{R}_s$	$0.02\,I$		K_l	0.2
	$\mathbf{Q}_s$	$0.01\,I$		B_l	$0\,cmH_2O$

Table 1. Parameters of the artificial respiratory signal.

Seven male and one female patients with COPD and four male and two female healthy non-smoking subjects (without any respiratory disease) were recruited. Patients were on non-invasive ventilator (Respironics Inc. BIPAP S/T IPAP - $8-15\,cmH_20$, PEEP - $0-4\,cmH_20$)

via facemask (Respironics Inc. Spectrum size medium and small). Mask pressure and airway flow were measured by pneumotachograph and pressure transducer system (Hans Rudolph Inc. Research pneumotachograph system). Sampling rate was 100 *Hz*. During acquisition, subjects were awake and in supine position breathing though the facemask. At least 10 breathing cycle of airway flow mask pressure and lung volume (integration of airflow) signals were recorded by data acquisition system (National Instrument DAQCard-6036E ADC-16bit) to the computer for the offline signal processing.
The airflow signal was first software filtered to remove high frequency noise with 8th order Butterworth low-pass filter with cut-off frequency of 50 *Hz* and then processed to detect the breathing cycle onset and end. Recorded signals were divided by breathing cycles with the consideration of ventilator trigger time, inspiration time and expiration time. Five clear breathing cycles were chosen for the offline signal processing step.
Dual UKF and joint UKF algorithm are applied to the pre-processed respiratory signals as explained in the section (3.2) and (3.3). Parameter constraints information was also incorporated in the dual UKF and EKF algorithm.

4.2 UKF and EKF parameter selection

Although there is no defined criteria for the estimator parameter selection, incorporating the model knowledge with the observation method some information can be drawn. In the both model the state transitions were obtained from the discretization of the continuous-time model equations by first-order Taylor series. The truncation error ($O(\Delta t^2)$) is the most contribution error in the process equation. Thus based on $\Delta t = 1/100\,s$, process noise covariance matrices for the states were $\mathbf{Q}_{ms} = 10^{-4} I_{5\times 5}$ and $\mathbf{Q}_{ns} = \begin{bmatrix} \mathbf{10^{-4}} & 0 \\ 0 & \mathbf{0} \end{bmatrix}$. In the UKF algorithm initial error covariance matrices for both models were $\mathbf{P}_0^{ms} = \mathbf{Q}_{ms}$ and $\mathbf{P}_0^{ns} = \mathbf{Q}_{ns}$ whereas in EKF in order to have some convergences in the parameters, initial error covariance were set to higher values such as $\mathbf{P}_0^{ms} = 10^6 \mathbf{Q}_{ms}$, and $\mathbf{P}_0^{ns} = 10^2 \mathbf{Q}_{ns}$. Observation noise covariance matrices were set with the convergence considerations to $\mathbf{R}_{ms} = \mathbf{R}_{ns} = 0.9$ for both models and for both estimators. Since the errors driven from the measurement equipment treats relatively low variances (accuracy of the equipments are in the range of %3), such a high choice of observation noise demonstrated the bigger uncertainty in the model fit to the measured noisy time-series. On the other hand in Mead model, the parameter observation error covariance matrix was set to the state process error covariance matrix due to the same equations.
Parameter and state initial values were found to be the most important settings. Especially the success of EKF was very much depended on the initial values. For the Mead model the initials were selected with regard to the convergences. Thus the set of initials for the Mead model were drawn from $\mathbf{x}_0^s = \mathbf{0}$, $\mathbf{x}_0^p \sim N[1,1]$ for UKF algorithm and $\mathbf{x}_0^s = \mathbf{0}$, $\mathbf{x}_0^p \sim N[1,2]$ for EKF algorithm. For the nonlinear RC model initials were the same for the states, but for the parameters, the $\mathbf{x}_0^p \sim N[0,1]$ was set in the both estimator algorithms.
Furthermore, UKF algorithm parameters were set according to the minimum Mean Squared Error (MSE) computed in the artificial data run. Monte Carlo simulations were performed with 100 run by artificial data series. $\alpha = 0.1$ for the parameters whereas $\alpha = 0.9$ for the states. κ, the secondary adjustment parameter was set to 1.1 for the minimum MSE. Finally, $\beta = 2$ indicating that the actual acquired signals were Gaussian distributed.

5. Results

5.1 MSE for the Mead and nonlinear RC models

MSE is the important showing for the performance comparison of both estimators. It was calculated with the Monte Carlo simulations and plotted against the data points. Figs. 2 and 3 show the MSE curves for the Mead and nonlinear RC models respectively. Both UKF and EKF estimates converge to single points through time-steps. Compared to Figs 2 and 3, although Mead model convergences are faster than nonlinear RC model convergences, approximations are better in the nonlinear RC model meaning that corresponding MSEs are lower. However, parameters K_u , K_l in the nonlinear RC model and $P_{mus\,\mathbf{max}}$ in the Mead model show very irregular results that demonstrate very slow or no convergence at all. This can be explained by the parameters interaction in the model structure. Parameter K_u is effected by the uncertainty of the airway flow, $\dot{V}^k$ by nonlinear fashion and K_l is in the direct relation with the estimated state V^k. On the other hand, parameter L is found to be the less identifiable parameter, apart from C_e. Since the state transition model of $P_{mus\,\mathbf{max}}$ includes L in the Mead model, $P_{mus\,\mathbf{max}}$ uncertainty is mostly effected by this parameter, therefore, degeneracy of the convergence happened.

It is apparent from the Figures that UKF converge faster than EKF for the Mead model. However, for the nonlinear model, EKF showed surprisingly no convergence at all for the nonlinear parameters A_l, K_l and B_l. This could be the consequence of the changes in the expiration. As it is noted convergences are distorted when the expiration begins and at the

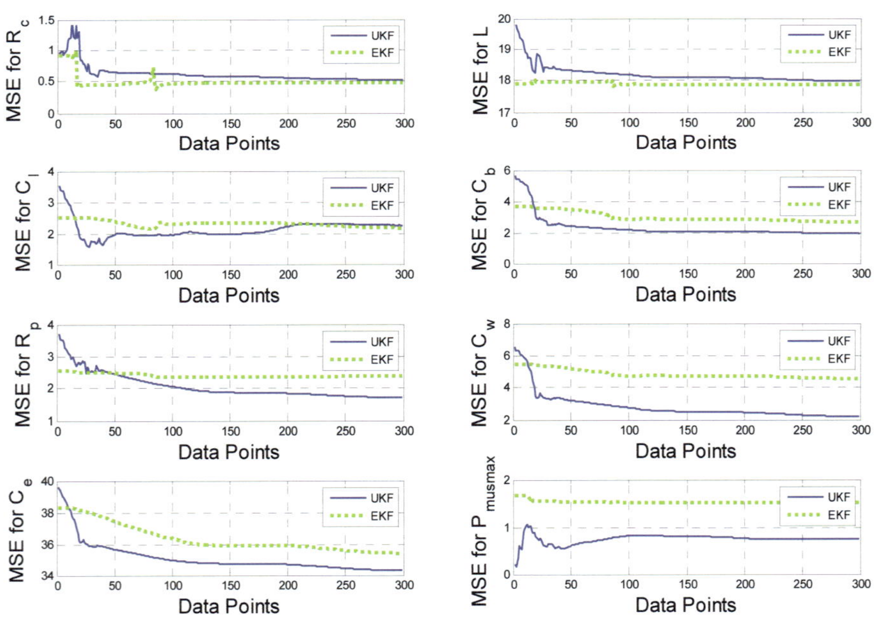

Fig. 2. MSE curves belongs to Mead model parameters (produced by artificial data). Curves were calculated by 100 run Monte Carlo simulations. Continuous and dashed lines represent the UKF and EKF estimates respectively.

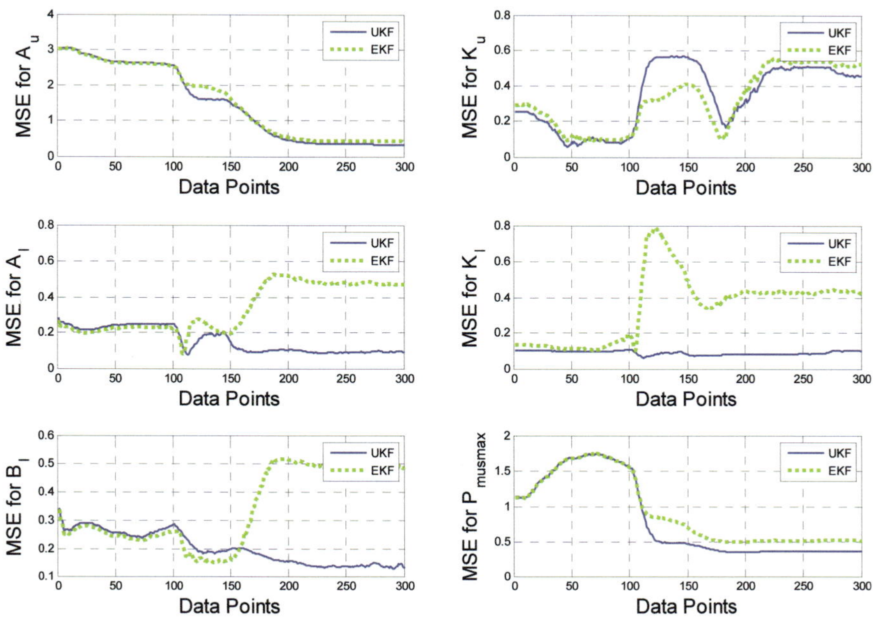

Fig. 3. MSE curves belongs to nonlinear RC model parameters (produced by artificial data). Curves were calculated by 100 run Monte Carlo simulations. Continuous and dashed lines represent the UKF and EKF estimates respectively.

expiration side only the nonlinear parameters govern the equations leaving muscular and ventilatory effects without contribution. Also, in line with our previous study (Saatci & Akan, 2007) in the nonlinear RC model, the most robust parameter is the parameter $P_{mus\,\mathbf{max}}$ for the artificial data sequence.

5.2 Convergence of the parameters for the measured respiratory signals

To illustrate the performance of the UKF and EKF estimators for the case of measured signals, parameters were estimated from acquired respiratory signals. Both UKF and EKF were evaluated with both model and for COPD patients' data and for healthy subjects' data. Figs 4 and 5 show Mead model UKF and EKF parameter convergence curves produced by the representative COPD patient's data respectively. Estimations from five different breath cycles were plotted on the same figure to illustrate the similarities and differences between breath cycles. Figs 6 and 7 show the plots of the same patients' parameters for the nonlinear RC model. Parameters' convergence curves produced by the healthy subject's data were plotted in the Figs 8 and 9 corresponding to the Mead model and in the Figs 10 and 11 for the nonlinear RC model.

First, it should be noted that since the Figs 4, 5, 6, 7 belong to the same COPD patient's data and it is expected to see compatible parameter values that at least indicate the patient's actual respiratory condition. First, if we compare Fig. 4 and Fig. 5 for some parameters EKF doesn't seem to converge at all in the Mead model. Since the initial value is very important for the EKF to converge, initial error covariance matrix was set to high values ($\mathbf{P}_0^{mp} = 10^1$ and $\mathbf{P}_0^{np} = 10^1$) in order to compensate the initial uncertainty. Thus, although consistency between breath cycles is accomplished in the EKF, the actual convergences don't go very far from the initial values. However for the nonlinear RC model case (Figs. 6 and 7), the parameter estimates of EKF and UKF is not only consistent but also very selective. Breath-to-breath variations existed for $P_{mus\,\mathbf{max}}$ could be the consequence of the variations in the patient's breath cycle.

If healthy subject's data is examined, it could be seen that convergence problems of the EKF resulted in again unexpected values in the Mead model (Figs 8 and 9). However, subject's data sequence fit to nonlinear RC model successfully. From the estimated values of the parameters it is apparent that UKF and EKF perform identical for the nonlinear RC model in both COPD patient's data and healthy subject's data.

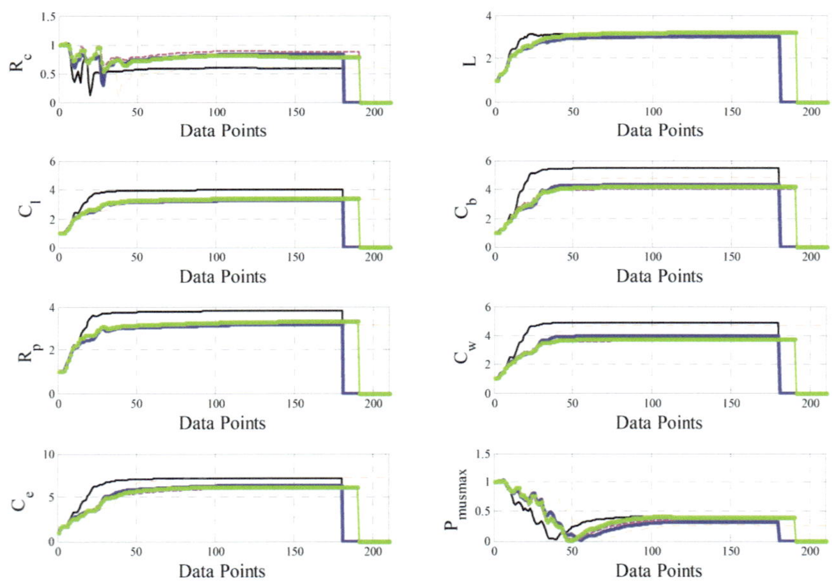

Fig. 4. Mead model UKF parameter convergence curves (produced by the representative COPD patient's data). Estimations from five different breath cycles were plotted on the same figure to illustrate the similarities and differences between breath cycles

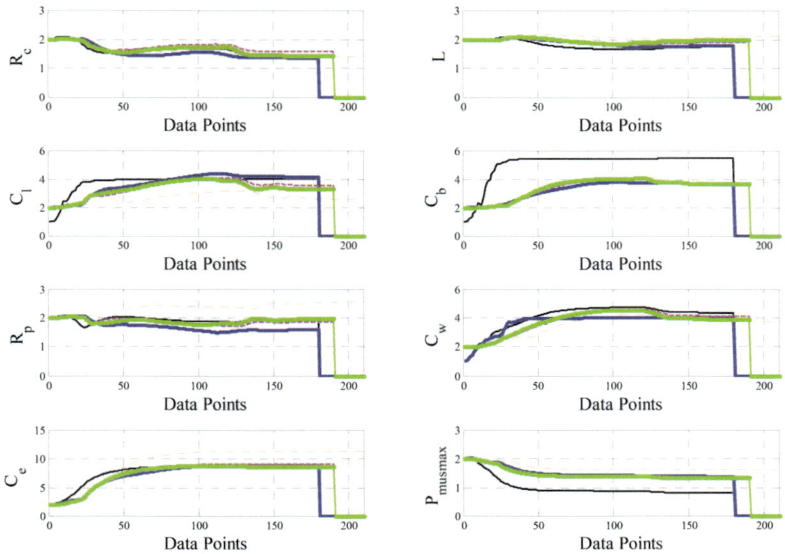

Fig. 5. Mead model EKF parameter convergence curves (produced by the representative COPD patient's data). Estimations from five different breath cycles were plotted on the same figure to illustrate the similarities and differences between breath cycles

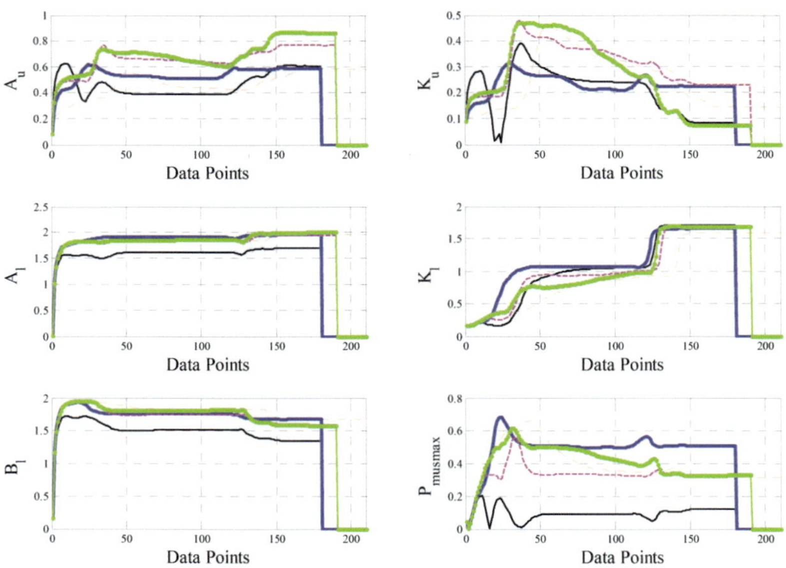

Fig. 6. Nonlinear RC model UKF parameter convergence curves (produced by the representative COPD patient's data). Estimations from five different breath cycles were plotted on the same figure to illustrate the similarities and differences between breath cycles

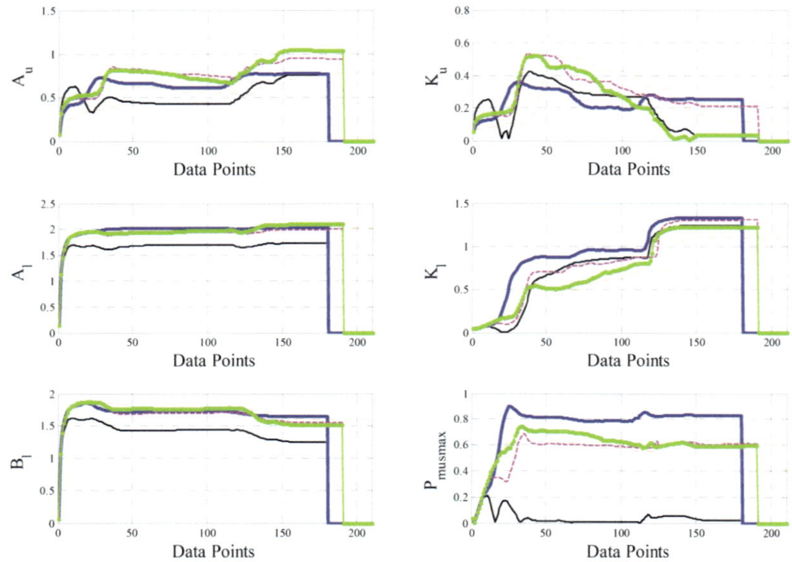

Fig. 7. Nonlinear RC model EKF parameter convergence curves (produced by the representative COPD patient's data). Estimations from five different breath cycles were plotted on the same figure to illustrate the similarities and differences between breath cycles

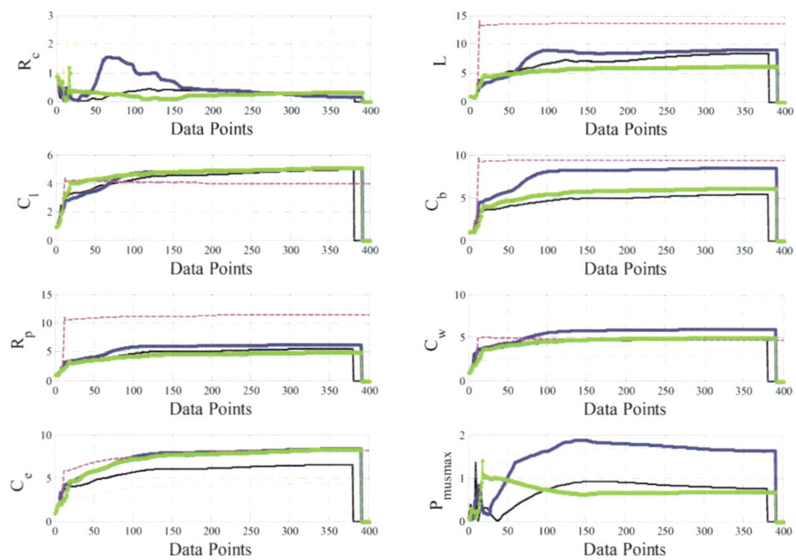

Fig. 8. Mead model UKF parameter convergence curves (produced by the representative healthy subject's data). Estimations from five different breath cycles were plotted on the same figure to illustrate the similarities and differences between breath cycles

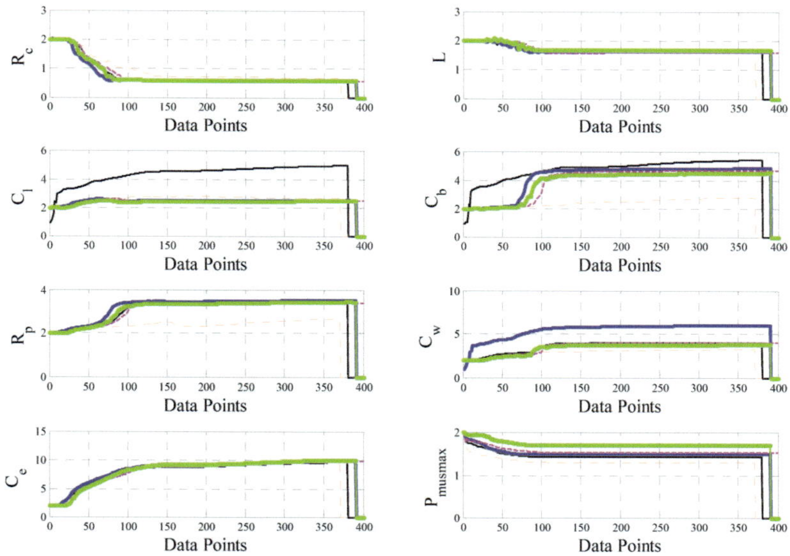

Fig. 9. Mead model EKF parameter convergence curves (produced by the representative healthy subject's data). Estimations from five different breath cycles were plotted on the same figure to illustrate the similarities and differences between breath cycles

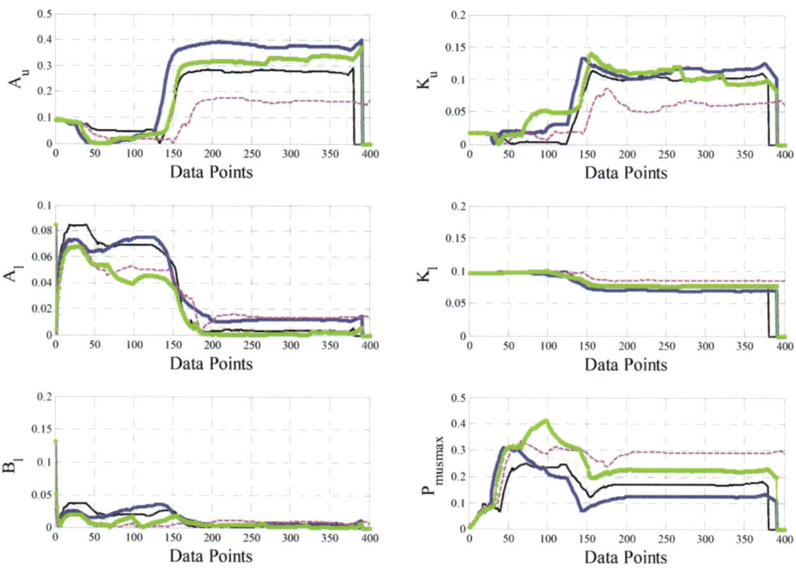

Fig. 10. Nonlinear RC model UKF parameter convergence curves (produced by the representative healthy subject's data). Estimations from five different breath cycles were plotted on the same figure to illustrate the similarities and differences between breath cycles

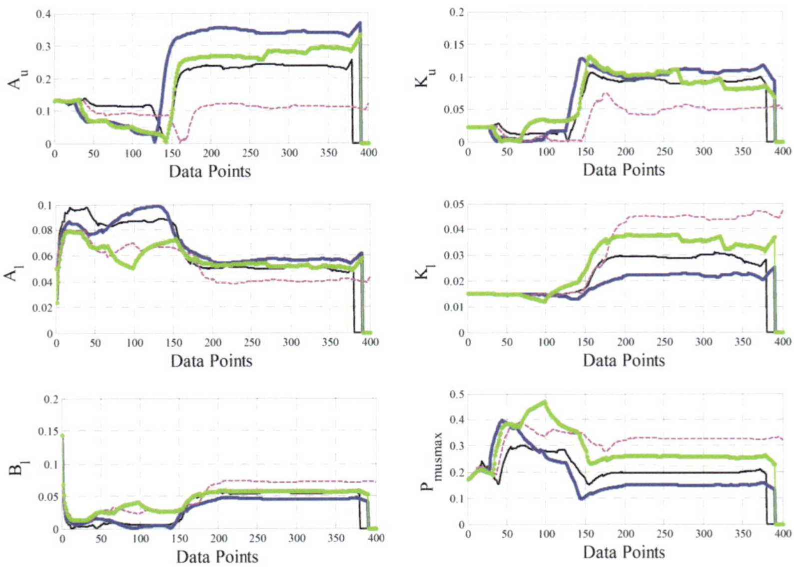

Fig. 11. Nonlinear RC model EKF parameter convergence curves (produced by the representative healthy subject's data). Estimations from five different breath cycles were plotted on the same figure to illustrate the similarities and differences between breath cycles

5.3 Convergence of the states for the measured respiratory signals

Reproducibility of the defined states of the respiratory models was also verified by comparing the state estimates produced for five breath cycles. Figures 12 and 13 show the Mead model states of the COPD patient corresponding to UKF and EKF estimates respectively. Healthy subject's figures are given in the Figs 14 and 15. Comparing to both figures, contrary to parameter estimates EKF seems to be more successful than UKF in the time-varying state estimation. For instance, state $\dot{V}_L^k$ could be estimated nothing but noise by UKF in the Mead model. Moreover, tracking of the states $P_{C_l}^k$, $P_{C_b}^k$ and $P_{C_w}^k$ converged to unexpectively more negative pressure values by UKF. However, incorporating the model equations together with the lung tissue, small airways and chest wall pressure effects it is expected to see pressure rise at the inspiration and pressure decrease at the expiration. Thus, especially EKF tracks produced from healthy subject's data (Fig. 15) report the expected state pressure waveforms in the Mead model.

In the nonlinear RC model case, both estimation methods again demonstrate the same sate tracks. Figs 16 and 17 are the evident of the UKF and EKF success on the state estimation. Tracks show expected lung volume, above Residual Volume, V_L^k as it increases through inspiration and decreases to zero at the end of expiration.

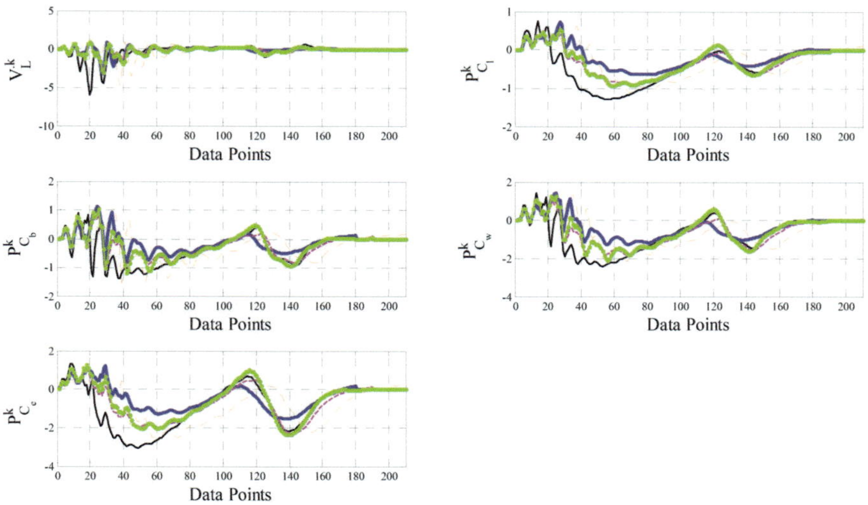

Fig. 12. Mead model UKF state convergence curves (produced by the representative COPD patient's data). Estimations from five different breath cycles were plotted on the same figure to illustrate the similarities and differences between breath cycles

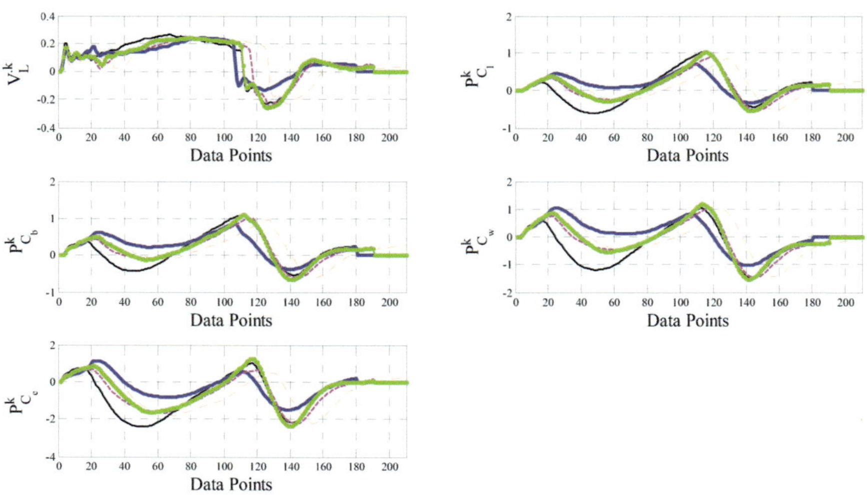

Fig. 13. Mead model EKF state convergence curves (produced by the representative COPD patient's data). Estimations from five different breath cycles were plotted on the same figure to illustrate the similarities and differences between breath cycles

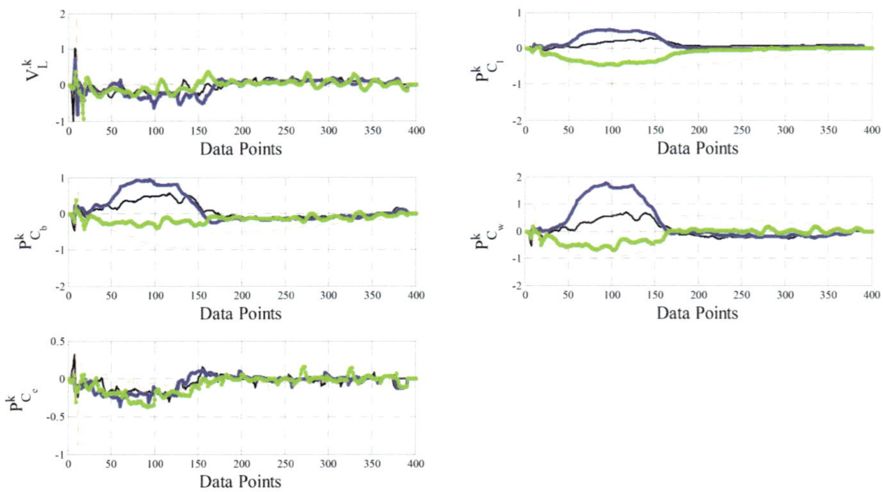

Fig. 14. Mead model UKF state convergence curves (produced by the representative healthy subject's data). Estimations from five different breath cycles were plotted on the same figure to illustrate the similarities and differences between breath cycles

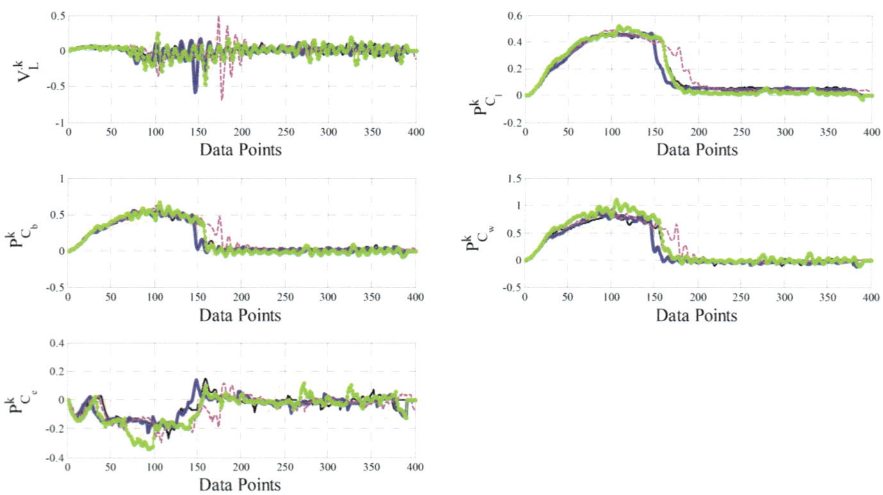

Fig. 15. Mead model EKF state convergence curves (produced by the representative healthy subject's data). Estimations from five different breath cycles were plotted on the same figure to illustrate the similarities and differences between breath cycles

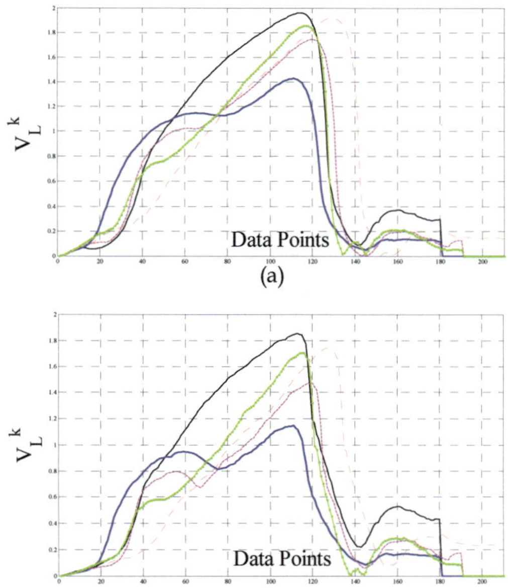

(b)

Fig. 16. Nonlinear RC model (a) UKF and (b) EKF parameter convergence curves (produced by the representative COPD patient's data). Estimations from five different breath cycles were plotted on the same figure.

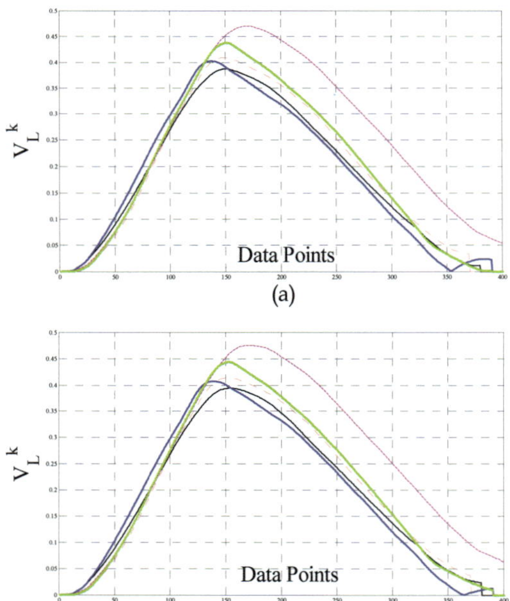

(b)

Fig. 17. Nonlinear RC model (a) UKF and (b) EKF parameter convergence curves (produced by the representative healthy subject's data). Estimations from five different breath cycles were plotted on the same figure.

6. Conclusion

Common problem in the respiratory model parameter estimates is the lack of information on the uncertainty (or residuals) between measured airway pressure and used model. As the model has more degree of freedom (incorporates more parameter (Avanzolini et al., 1995) or incorporates the nonlinearity (Athanasiades et al., 2000)) the uncertainties approaches to the statistical noise that is usually Gaussian distributed. Here, we started with the assumption that the residuals are the white Gaussian noises and estimation and measured noisy time series can be fit to the respiratory models by the estimation methods. Thus, unscented Kalman filter (UKF) was employed as an inverse solver to estimate the time-invariant parameters and time-varying states in the linear Mead model and the nonlinear RC model. Illustrative comparison between UKF and conventional EKF was also performed with the respiratory model applications. The convergence results of the parameters demonstrated the performance gains over EKF only in the Mead model. UKF is known to make more accurate results only if the kurtosis and higher order moments of the parameters' errors are significant. This fact is one indication of why the UKF doesn't perform better than EKF in the nonlinear RC model parameter and state estimation.

It is also experienced that the tuning of EKF is more difficult than UKF even though UKF has more tuning parameter. For the real respiratory signals, initial parameter and state vectors may require small adjustments for the proper convergences of the parameters.

7. References

Athanasiades, A.; Ghorbel, F. & Clark, J.W. (2000). Energy analysis of a nonlinear model of the normal human lung. *Journal of Biological Systems*, Vol.8, 115-139, ISSN 02183390

Arulampalam, M.S.; Maskell, S.; Gordon, N. & Clapp, T. (2002). A tutorial on particle filters for online nonlinear/non-Gaussian Bayesian tracking. *IEEE Transactions on Signal Processing*, Vol.50, No.2, February 174-188, ISSN 10535888

Avanzolini, G.; Barbini, P.; Cappello, A. & Cevenini, G. (1995). Influence of flow pattern on the parameter estimates of a simple breathing mechanics model. *IEEE Transactions on Biomedical Engineering*, Vol.42, No.4, April 394-402, ISSN 00189284

Avendano, L.E.; Castellanos, C.G. & Ferrero, J.M. (2006). Spectrum estimation and adaptive denoising of electrocardiographic signals using Kalman filters. *Computers in Cardiology*, Vol.33, 925-928, ISSN 02766547

Bates, J.H.Y. & Lutchen K.R. (2005). The interface between measurement and modelling of peripheral lung mechanics. *Respiratory Physiology & Neurobiology*, Vol.148, 153-164,

Brochwell, A.E., Kass, R.E. & Schwartz, A.B. (2007). Statistical signal processing and the motor cortex. *Proceedings of the IEEE*, Vol.95, No.5, May 881-898, ISSN 00189219

Chen, Z. (2003). Bayesian filtering: from Kalman filters to particle filters, and beyond. tech. rep. Adaptive Syst. Lab., McMaster University, Hamilton, ON, Canada

Chow, S.; Ferrer, E. & Nesselroade, J.R. (2007). An unscented Kalman filter approach to the estimation of nonlinear dynamical systems models. *Multivariate Behavioral Research*, Vol.42, Issue.2, June 283-321, ISSN 15327906

Diong, B., Nazeran, H., Nava, P. & Goldman M. (2007). Modeling human respiratory impedance. *IEEE Engineering in Medicine and Biology Magazine*, Vol.26, January 48-55, ISSN 07395175

Grewal, M.S. & Andrews, A.P. (2001). *Kalman Filtering: Theory and Practice*, Wiley, ISBN 0471392545, USA

Hellinckx, J.; Cauberghs, M. & De Boeck, K. (2001). Evaluation of impulse oscillation system: comparison with forced oscillation technique and body plethysmography. *European Respiratory Journal*, Vol.18, 564-570

Ijaz, U.Z.; Khambampati, A.K.; Lee, J.S.; Kim, S. & Kim, K.Y. (2008). Nonstationary phase boundary estimation in electrical impedance tomography using unscented Kalman filter. *Journal of Computational Physics*, Vol.227, 7089-7112, ISSN 00219991

Julier, S.J. & Uhlmann, J.K. (1997). A new extension of the Kalman filter to nonlinear systems. *Proceedings of Int. Symp. Aerospace/Defence Sensing, Simul. and Controls*, Orlando, FL

Kandepu, R.; Foss, B. & Imsland, L. (2008). Applying the unscented Kalman filter for nonlinear state estimation. *Journal of Process Control*, Vol.18, 753-768, ISSN 09591524

Lutchen, K.R. & Costa, K.D. (1990). Physiological interpretations based on lumped element models fit to respiratory impedance data: use of forward-inverse modelling. *IEEE Transactions on Biomedical Engineering*, Vol.37, No.11, November 1076-1086, ISSN 00189294

Moradkhani, H.; Sorooshian, S.; Gupta, H.V. & Houser, P.R. (2005). Dual state-parameter estimation of hydrological models using ensemble Kalman filter. *Advances in Water Resources*, Vol.28, 135-147, ISSN 03091708

Nucci, G.; Tessarin, S. & Cobelli, C. (2002). A morphometric model of lung mechanics for time-domain analysis of alveolar pressures during mechanical ventilation. *Annals of Biomedical Engineering*, Vol.30, 537-545, ISSN 00906964

Polak, A.G. & Mroczka J. (2006). Nonlinear model for mechanical ventilation of human lungs. *Computers in Biology and Medicine*, Vol.36, 41-58, ISSN 00104825

Saatci, E. & Akan, A. (2007). Lung model parameter estimation by unscented Kalman filter. *Proceedings of the 29th Annual International Conference of the IEEE EMBS*, Lyon, France, August 2556-2559

Sameni, R.; Shamsollahi, M.B.; Jutten, C. & Clifford G.D. (2007). A nonlinear Bayesian filtering framework for ECG denoising. *IEEE Transactions on Biomedical Engineering*, Vol.54, No.12, December 2172-1285, ISSN 00189294

Vauhkonen, M.; Karjalainen, P.A. & Kaipio, J.P. (1998). A Kalman filter approach to track fast impedance changes in electrical impedance tomography. *IEEE Transactions on Biomedical Engineering*, Vol.45, No.4, April 486-493, ISSN 00189294

Wan, E.A. & Merwe, van der R. (2001). The unscented Kalman filter, In: *Kalman Filtering and Neural Networks*, Simon Haykin, (Ed.), 221-283, Wiley, ISBN 0471369981, NewYork

Xiong, K.; Zhang, H.Y. & Chan, C.W. (2006). Performance evaluation of UKF- based nonlinear filtering. *Automatica*, Vol.42, 261-270, ISSN 00051098

Yamada, Y. & Du, H.L. (2000). Analysis of the mechanisms of expiratory asynchrony in pressure support ventilation: a mathematical approach. *Journal of Applied Physiology*, Vol.88, 2143-2150, ISSN 87507587

Yuan, H.; Suki, B. & Lutchen, K.R. (1998). Sensitivity analysis for evaluating nonlinear models of lung mechanics. *Annals of Biomedical Engineering*, Vol.26, 230-241, ISSN 00906964

Tracking and Positioning

10

Position and Velocity Tracking in Cellular Networks Using the Kalman Filter

Mohammed Olama[1], Seddik Djouadi[2], Charalambos Charalambous[3], Ioannis Papageorgiou[3] and Teja Kuruganti[1]
[1]Oak Ridge National Laboratory
[2]University of Tennessee
[3]University of Cyprus
[1,2]USA,
[3]Cyprus

1. Introduction

"Access to the right information anytime, anywhere" is becoming the new driving force for the information technology revolution. The "right" information's relevance is based on the user's profile and his/her current geographical position and/or time. Location Based Service (LBS) is an innovative technology that provides information or makes information available based on the geographical location of the mobile user. Analysts predict that LBSs will lead to new applications, generating billions of US dollars worldwide (Leite, 2001; Searle, 2001).

The need for an efficient and accurate mobile station (MS) positioning system is growing day by day. The ability to pinpoint the location of an individual has an obvious and vital value in the context of emergency services (Chan, 2003; Olama et al., 2008). Pinpointing the location of people and other valuable assets also opens the door to a new world of previously unimagined information services and m-commerce probabilities. For example, availability of services like "Where is the nearest ATM?", "Check traffic conditions on the highway on my route", "Find a parking lot nearby", as well as answers to "Where is my advisor?", and "Where is my car?" will be an everyday rule in our lives (Charalambous & Panayiotou, 2004).

A technology independent LBS architecture can be considered as comprised by three main parts (Girodon, 2002): A user requesting information, a mobile network operator and its partners, and several content providers (e.g. data, maps). The subscriber requests a personalized service dependant on his geographic location. The system will ask the Location Services Manager (which is in charge of handling requests, i.e., send/receive to the Location Calculator and the Content Providers) to pinpoint the location of the mobile. The Location Services Manager (LSM), using the Location Calculator, will ask the Content Provider (CP) to supply qualified information according to the mobile's geographical position. The LSM will eventually receive the answer from the CP and send it to the mobile, performing the essential data translations. Fig. 1 outlines the precedent concept.

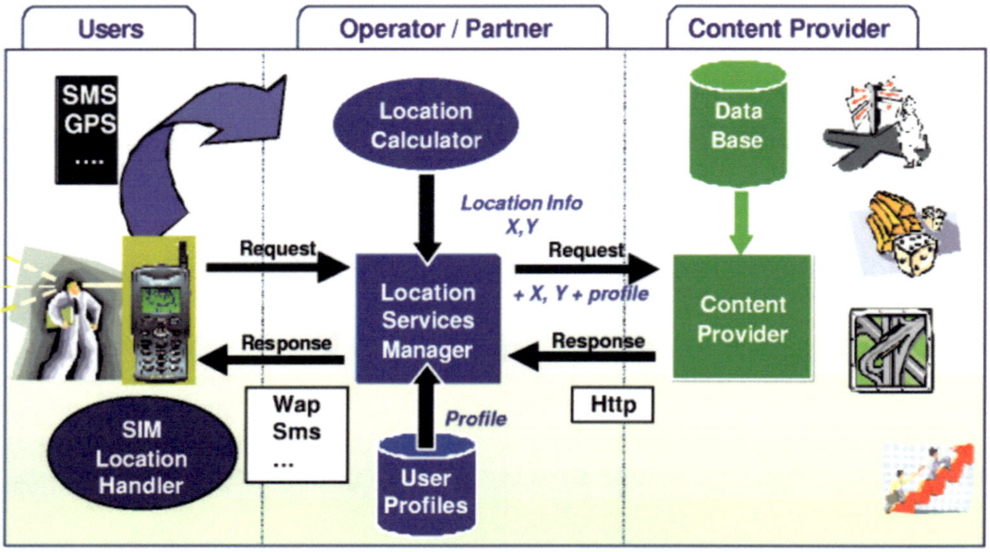

Fig. 1. Technology independent LBS architecture (Charalambous & Panayiotou, 2004)

For effective provision of LBS, one has to provide an accurate location, as well as suitable information for users required by the corresponding service, with minimal expenditure. Thus, there are three main technology issues that have to be resolved for LBS: positioning technology, application technology, and location services (Dru & Saada, 2001).
A very important technology is of course the positioning technology, the way to find out the location of a mobile device accurately. Due to the unique characteristics of the cellular environment, it is a great challenge to locate the user precisely. However, in many cases, application technology and location services are important consideration of LBS. Application technology manages the geographic information and delivers the customer requests to the appropriate service provider, thus it constitutes the communication system involved. LBS uses the geographic information to provide geographically sensitive information and services. Location-based applications and services are not sensitive to the type of location technology that is used - they merely rely on reasonably accurate geographic coordinates (Chan, 2003).
This chapter is structured as follows: In Section 2, we describe the use and applications of LBSs. The current location determination technologies and standards are presented in Section 3. In Section 4 we describe the mathematical models used for the location and velocity estimation algorithms. An initial attempt for MS location estimation via received signal level using the maximum likelihood estimation (MLE) approach and triangulation is presented in Sections 5. Since the former approach lacks acceptable accuracy for demanding services as numerical results reveal, the extended Kalman filter (EKF) approach, which is the main topic in this chapter, is introduced in Sections 6. In Section 7 we present numerical results. Section 8 provides concluding remarks.

2. Location based services and applications

Several market studies predicted that mobile location services will grow highly in the next few years (Leite, 2001; Searle, 2001). There are three major market drivers for LBS. These can

be identified as commercial, technological, and regulatory drivers. Regulatory is primarily the driver for the US, whereas in Europe and elsewhere LBS is mainly commercially and technologically driven.
In the US, regulatory requirements for emergency calls in cellular systems were first established in 1996 with the Federal Communications Commission (FCC) mandating all wireless service providers to provide public safety answering points with information to locate an emergency 911 (E-911) caller with an accuracy of 100 meters for 67% of the cases (FCC Docket No.96-264, Revision of the Commission Rule to ensure compatibility with Enhanced 911 emergency calling system, FCC Reports and Orders, 1996.). It is also expected that the FCC will tighten its requirements in the near future (Reed et al., 1998). The E-911 mandate distinguishes between wireline and wireless calls and the wireless E-911 mandate is separated into two Phases. Phase I requires that the call taker automatically receives the wireless call-back number and delivers the location of the cell tower handling the call, and Phase II allows call takers to receive both the caller's wireless phone number and their location information with prescribed accuracy.
In Europe, LBS is mainly driven by location-based value-added services, with the E112 emergency service only appearing recently on the political agenda. In contrast to the US, there is neither a distinction between mobile and fixed operator obligations nor a mention of any prescribed accuracy levels. In 2000, the European Commission launched a Coordination Group on Access to Location Information by Emergency Services (CGALIES: http://www.telematica.de/cgalies/) and project Location of Cellular Users for Emergency Services (LOCUS: http://www.telematica.de/locus/) to advise the European Union on implementing 112 emergency calling services, to actively involve the relevant players, and to develop a consensus on relevant implementation issues. In 2002, the Council and the European Parliament adopted the new regulatory package to enter into force by 24 July 2003. Even though, a recent Recommendation (Commission Recommendation of 25 July 2003 (2003/558/EC) Official Journal of the European Union, Erkki Liikanen) recommended a review of the situation in 2005.
LBSs can be categorized in different ways depending on the classification condition. We propose four main categories of LBS: Information, Safety, Monitoring and Operator Services (Dru & Saada, 2001). Information services include, among many others, finding the nearest service, accessing traffic news, getting navigation help, advertising and locating individuals. They are considered to be one of the most promising services in terms of global revenue (i.e. operators, developers, providers). Information services can penetrate in three kinds of relationships. First, the "Business to Consumer" relationship is targeted in means of local product promotion or advertising promotions, perhaps in exchange with lower monthly subscriptions, as long as privacy is not violated. In "Consumer to Business" relationship, users might require information about local services (restaurants, gas stations, pharmacies, etc.) or local traffic information. Last, in "Consumer to Consumer" relationship the subscriber can locate friends, family members, or more generally members of a desirable community.
Safety services include public and private emergency services for both pedestrians and drivers. As previously mentioned, public emergency services have already been regulated in the US and in Europe. These services do not require a subscription, can be accessed by any mobile subscriber, and do not generate a profit for the operators. Emergency roadside assistance for drivers appears to be one of the most promising of the safety services in terms of operator revenue.

Monitoring mainly covers "Business to Business" services, e.g. operating fleet management applications, and tracking the location of external resources to optimize their use and control or ensure their safety. External resources include individuals (truck drivers, delivery personnel, maintenance technicians, etc) and objects (cars, trucks, trailers, containers).
Moreover, user location information can be used to improve the way that services are implemented in areas such as quality of service, optimization of radio resources (handover and channel allocation) and pricing. Location-based pricing has been identified as one of the most promising applications in Operator Services in Europe.
Many other applications, such as vehicle fleet management, location sensitive billing, intelligent transport systems, fraud protection, and mobile yellow pages have driven the cellular industry to research new and promising technologies for MS positioning (Olama et al., 2008).

3. Location determination technologies and standards

Location Determination Technologies (LDTs) are the heart of LBSs. They are methods that use the signals of the cellular system to find the location of a mobile station, thus they are used to solve the so-called Automatic Location Identification (ALI) problem. Since cellular systems were not originally designed for positioning, the implementation of different location techniques may require various hardware and/or software modifications to the handset, network or both.
Based on the functions of the MS and the network, implementation of a location method belongs to one of the following categories (Cellular Location Technology, IST-2000-25382-CELLO Project, 2001): Network-based, Mobile-based, Mobile-assisted, and Network-assisted. In network-based implementation one or several base stations (BSs) make the necessary measurements and send the measurement results to a location centre where the position is calculated. Network-based implementation does not require any changes to existing handsets, which is a significant advantage compared to mobile-based or most mobile-assisted solutions.
In mobile-based implementation the MS makes measurements and position determination. This allows positioning in idle mode by measuring control channels which are continuously transmitted. Some assisting information, e.g. BS coordinates, might be needed from the network to enable location determination in the MS. Mobile-based implementation does not support legacy handsets. Mobile-assisted implementation includes solutions where the MS makes measurements and sends the results to a location centre in the network for further processing. Thus, the computational burden is transferred to a location centre where powerful processors are available. However, signaling delay and signaling load increase compared to a mobile-based solution, especially if the location result is needed at MS. Although mobile-assisted solutions typically do not support legacy handsets, it is possible to use the measurement reports that are continuously sent by handsets to the network in active mode. Last, network-assisted methods include those where the main functions take place at the MS but there is also some assistance from the network.
LDTs are mainly separated into two categories: Satellite and Cellular LDTs (Cellular Location Technology, IST-2000-25382-CELLO Project, 2001). Satellite LDTs (see Fig. 2) are based on the principle of measuring the interval of time a set of signals spend travelling from a set of orbiting satellites to a receiver on or near the surface of earth. The main satellite LDTs are GPS, AGPS, DGPS, GLONASS and Galileo.

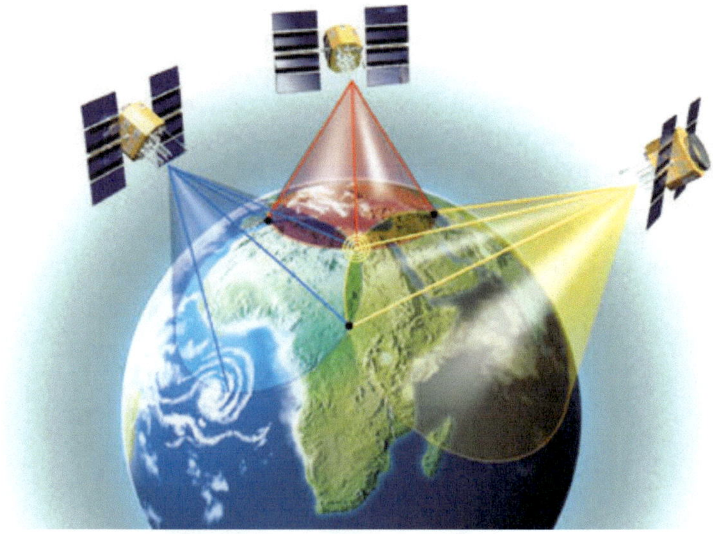

Fig. 2. Satellite LDTs based on triangulation

On the other hand, Cellular LDTs, which are addressed in this chapter, refer to the set of location techniques used by cellular networks, i.e. these methods use the signals of the cellular system to find the location of a MS. The main Cellular LDTs are Cell-ID (or Cell Of Origin (COO)), Received Signal Level (RSL), Angle Of Arrival (AOA), Uplink Time Difference of Arrival (TDOA), and Downlink Observed Time Differences (Cellular Location Technology, IST-2000-25382-CELLO Project, 2001). Additionally, there have been reported many hybrid solutions of the preceding methods, as well as a Database Correlation Method and a Signal Pattern Recognition method. Most of these LDTs make use of the triangulation concept, that is, they calculate the most possible MS location based on existing signal information for known locations (such as BSs). Such signal information might be the signal level from/to a BS or the propagation time from/to a BS (so-called Time of Arrival (TOA)). It is not the purpose of this chapter to separately address each one of these methods. On the contrary, we will focus on the general characteristics of the main methods and point out advantages and disadvantages of each method.

The simplest method for locating a MS is Cell-ID. If someone knows the cell area in which the MS is being used, then the position of the BS antenna can be used as an estimate of the MS location as described in Fig. 3. An advantage of this method is that no calculations are needed to obtain location information. Thus, Cell-ID based location is fast and suitable for applications requiring high capacity. The drawback is that accuracy is directly dependent on cell radius, which can be very large especially in rural areas. Accuracy can be improved using information of cell coverage area (e.g. sector cells), timing advance (TA) in GSM or round trip time (RTT) in UMTS and Network Measurement Reports (NMRs).

Angle of Arrival (AOA) technique is based on angle-calculation of the signal as it arrives at a base station. This angle defines a line out of each BS. A minimum of two BSs is required to determine the position of the mobile phone, which is located at the intersection of these lines as shown in Fig. 4. The technique relies on the technology of antenna arrays. In an array, the antennas are separated by a small distance and a measurable difference in arrival times and electrical phase received at each antenna are used to estimate the direction at which the transmission is originating. Achieved accuracy depends on the number of available measurements, geometry of BSs around the MS and multipath propagation. Since AOA method needs line-of-sight propagation conditions to obtain correct location estimates, it is clearly not the method of choice in dense urban areas where line of sight to two BSs is seldom present. A major barrier to implement AOA method in existing 2G networks is the need for an antenna array at each BS. It would be very expensive to build an overlay of AOA sensors to existing cellular network. In addition to financial issues, AOA method may have a capacity problem as it requires the co-ordination of almost simultaneous measurements at several BS sites. However, AOA surpasses in supporting legacy handsets.

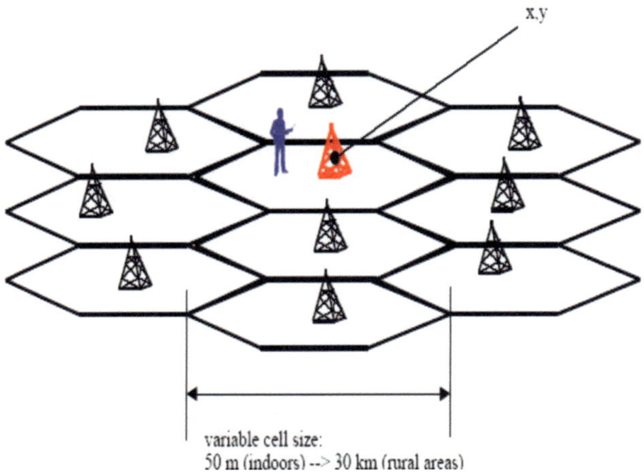

Fig. 3. Cell-ID LDT

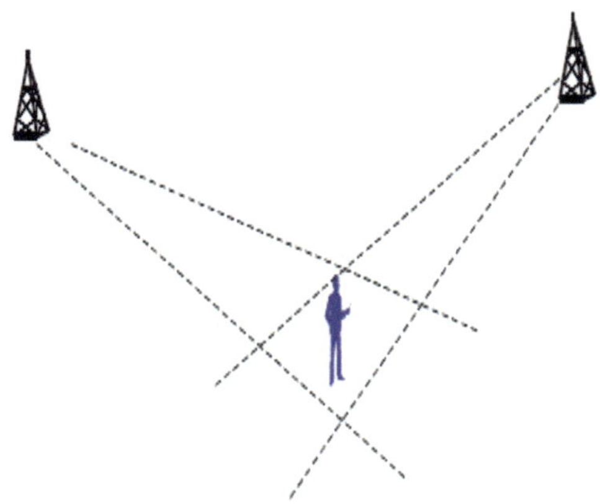

Fig. 4. AOA LDT

Signal time of arrival (TOA) measurements, performed either at the BSs or at the MS, can be used for positioning. Absolute TOA measurements are directly related to the BS-MS distances and three measurements are needed for unique 2-dimensional (2-D) location. However, if the BSs and the MS are not synchronized (do not have a common time reference, such as GSM and UMTS FDD networks), absolute TOA is difficult to measure, thus TOA measurements can only be used in differential manner .Two such measurements then define a hyperbola, and four measurements are needed for unambiguous 2-D location.

But, in any case (uplink or downlink), a common time reference (e.g. a GPS receiver) is needed at all BSs for accurate measurements. Consider that 1 microsecond error equals 300 meters measurement error. Additionally, in any case, location measurement units (LMUs) are required in the network (Symmetricom, 2002), which accurately measure TOA in Uplink measurements or exact OTD in Downlink measurements, process the measurements, receive measurement requests and provide measurement data. Even the inherent synchronization of a network (e.g. existing CDMA systems) is not adequate for location purposes, and this additional timing equipment is required. The required infrastructure has an important cost effect.

In uplink Time Difference of Arrival (TDOA), measurements are performed at the BSs, thus it's a network-based technique. This technique has two drawbacks compared to downlink method: It is only possible to perform the measurements in dedicated mode and there may be capacity problems. The advantage is that due to the network-based implementation, uplink TOA supports legacy phones. The location of a MS is accomplished by forcing the MS to request a handover to several neighbouring BSs. The MS then sends access bursts and TOA measurements are made from these bursts. As mentioned above, LMUs accurately measure the arrival time of the bursts. In the downlink time difference techniques, the MS observes time differences of signals from several BSs. These signals are typically control channel signals and therefore the MS can perform the measurements in idle mode as well as in dedicated mode. The clock differences of the BSs can be solved by LMUs of known location which continuously measure the observed time differences.

The accuracy of all time difference based techniques depends on several factors. The accuracy of an individual time difference measurement depends on signal bandwidth and multipath propagation. When the signal bandwidth is not large enough the time resolution in timing measurements is not adequate for the needed accuracy. On the other hand, multipath propagation imposes a significant difficulty on finding the earliest arriving signal component. In GSM and UMTS standardization, the downlink techniques are called Enhanced Observed Time Differences (E-OTD) and Observed Time Difference of Arrival (OTDOA), respectively.

The LDT we chose to present in this chapter is the Received Signal Level (RSL) method which makes use of power signal information. Using signal strength from the control channels of several BSs, the distances between the MS and the BSs can be estimated using a suitable propagation model. Assuming 2-D geometry, an omni-directional BS antenna, and free-space propagation conditions, signal level contours around BSs are circles. If signal levels from three different BSs are known, the location of the MS can be determined as the unique intersection point of the three circles. However, practical propagation conditions especially in urban areas are far from free-space propagation. Therefore, an environment-dependent propagation models should be used. In urban areas the received signal level decreases more rapidly with distance than in open areas.

Multipath fading and shadowing poses a problem for distance estimation based on signal level. The instantaneous, narrowband signal level may vary by as much as 30-40 dB over a distance of only a fraction of the wavelength. Random variations of this order of magnitude cause very large errors in distance estimates. However, fast fading can be smoothed out by averaging the signal strength over time and frequency band. Time-averaging only has a minor effect, due to the motion in the surrounding environment, if the MS is stationary. Contrary to fast fading, the random variations caused by shadowing can not be compensated. Thus, the variations in antenna orientation and local shadowing conditions around the MS (indoors, inside a vehicle etc.) are seen as random errors in distance estimates and consequently in position estimate. Location accuracy also depends on the accuracy of the propagation model and the number of available measurements.

Signal strength method is easy to implement in GSM, based on measurement reports that are continuously transmitted from the MS back to the network in active mode. Therefore, it does not require any changes to existing phones, and is often called a network-based method although it is the MS that performs the measurements. An alternative implementation is to modify the MSs to enable sending measurement reports in idle mode also. GSM phones with this capability are already available. An advantage of this technique is that in the GSM network, every MS measures the signal levels from up to seven BSs at 0.48-second intervals to facilitate handover. Signal strength is an easy and low-cost method to enhance the accuracy of pure cell-ID based location. Table 1 serves as a comparison of the above mentioned techniques.

Method	Accuracy		Response	Costs (Operator)	Modifications	
	Urban	Rural			Handset	Network
Cell-ID	Moderate	Poor	Fast	Low	-	SW
RSL	Good	Poor	Fast	Low	-	SW
TDOA	Good	Poor	Moderate	Moderate	-	SW/HW1
E-OTD	Good	Poor	Moderate	Moderate/High	SW	SW/HW2
AOA	Good	Poor	Moderate	High	-	SW/HW3
GPS	Moderate	Good	Slow	Low	SW/HW4	-

Table 1. LDTs comparison (Charalambous & Panayiotou, 2004).

In conclusion, no single technique is superior in terms of accuracy, response delay, coverage, capacity, and implementation costs. The choice of a LDT will depend on the importance of each parameter to the decision maker. There are considerable obstacles to location estimation (Romdhani & Trad, 2002). Achieving accurate location of a mobile system remains a challenge considering the sources of error in location estimation. The main obstacles are multipath propagation, non-line-of-sight (NLOS) conditions, geometric dilution of precision (GDOP), and lack of bandwidth. In the next section, we describe the mathematical models used for the location and velocity estimation algorithms which are based on RSL method.

4. System mathematical models

4.1 The lognormal propagation channel model

Here we consider a 2-D geometry with the MS located at (x_0, y_0) and the BSs located at $\left((x_{BS_1}, y_{BS_1}), (x_{BS_2}, y_{BS_2}), \ldots, (x_{BS_B}, y_{BS_B})\right)$. The general lognormal propagation channel model is described by (Rappaport, 2002)

$$PL_b^s(d_b) = PL(d_{0_b}) + 10\varepsilon_b \log\left(\frac{d_b}{d_{0_b}}\right) + X_b^s \tag{1}$$

where $d_b \geq d_{0_b}$, $s \in \{1,2,..,S\}$, $b \in \{1,2,..,B\}$, $PL_b^s(d_b)$ is the path loss (PL) from the bth BS at distance d_b for the sth sample, d_{0_b} is the reference distance, ε_b is the path loss exponent and

$X_b^s \sim \mathcal{N}(0;\sigma_b^2)$ is a Gaussian random variable (RV) represents the shadowing variance due to gross variations in the terrain profile and changes in the local topography. The reference distance d_{0_b} is necessary since the equation of PL is not valid for zero distance. It depends on the cell size and can be calculated through the free-space PL or through measurements. Thus, the reference distance must be in the far field of the transmitting antenna, for the free-space propagation to be valid. The path loss exponent ε_b indicates the rate at which the PL increases with distance and it depends on the specific propagation environment. For example, in free space ε_b = 2, and when obstructions are present ε_b has a larger value as described in Table 2.

ENVIRONMENT	PATH LOSS EXPONENT
Free- space	2
Urban area cellular radio	2.7 to 3.5
Shadowed urban cellular radio	3 to 5
In-Building Line-of-Sight	1.6 to 1.8
Obstructed in building	4 to 6
Obstructed in factory	2 to 3

Table 2. Path loss exponents for different propagation environments (Rappaport, 2002)

In cellular networks, the MS preserves and frequently updates, in idle and active mode, the received power of the strongest non-serving BSs (e.g., in GSM the 6 strongest (3GPP TS 05.08 V8.19.0, 2004)) in addition to the one of the serving cell. Exploiting these measurements from surrounding BSs lead to estimate the location of the MS. The MLE approach described in Section 5 that employs this channel model is used to estimate the MS location.

Note that this channel model assumes there is always a line-of-sight (LOS) between the transmitting and receiving antennas, which are not the case in common wireless systems such as urban environments. In the next section, we consider a more realistic channel model (Aulin's scattering model), which takes into account the multipath properties and NLOS condition usually encountered in wireless networks.

4.2 Aulin's scattering model

The basic 3-dimentional (3-D) wireless scattering channel model described by (Aulin, 1979), which assumes that the electric field, denoted by $E(t)$, at any receiving point (x_0, y_0, z_0) is the resultant of P plane waves (see Fig. 5), in which the receiver moves in the X-Y plane having velocity υ in a direction making an angle γ with the X-axis, is given by

$$E(t) = \sum_{n=1}^{P} E_n(t) = \sum_{n=1}^{P} r_n \cos(\omega_c t + \omega_n t + \theta_n) + e(t) \tag{2}$$

where

$$\omega_n = \frac{2\pi\upsilon}{\lambda}(\cos(\gamma - \alpha_n)\cos\beta_n),$$
$$\theta_n = -\frac{2\pi}{\lambda}(x_0 \cos\alpha_n \cos\beta_n + y_0 \sin\alpha_n \cos\beta_n + z_0 \sin\beta_n) + \phi_n \tag{3}$$

and α_n, β_n are spatial angles of arrival, ω_n is the Doppler shift, θ_n is the phase shift, r_n is the amplitude, ϕ_n is the phase of the nth component, λ is the wavelength, $e(t)$ is a white Gaussian noise, and P is the total number of paths. It can be seen from (3) that the Doppler and phase shifts depend on the velocity and location of the receiver, respectively. Aulin's model postulates knowledge of the instantaneous received field at the MS, which is obtained through the circuitry of the mobile unit. It takes into account NLOS condition as well as multipath propagation environments.

Clearly, (2) assumes transmission of a narrowband signal. This assumption is valid only when the signal bandwidth is smaller than the coherence bandwidth of the channel. Nevertheless, the above model is not restrictive since it can be modified to represent a wideband transmission by including multiple time-delayed echoes. In this case, the delay spread has to be estimated. A sounding device is usually dedicated to estimating the time delay of each discrete path such as the Rake receiver (Sklar, 2001).

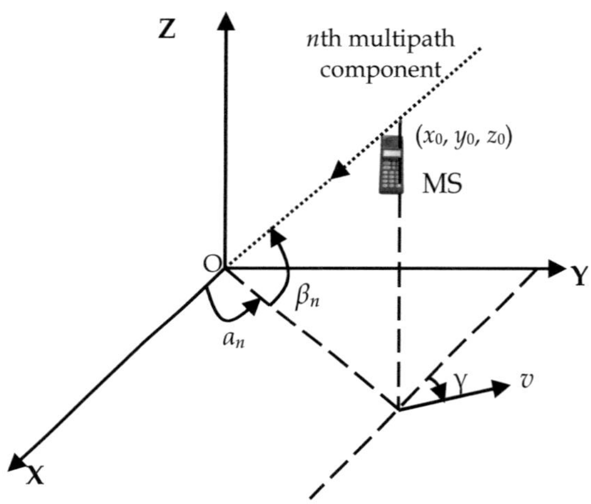

Fig. 5. Aulin's 3-D multipath channel model (Aulin, 1979)

It can be seen that the noisy instantaneous received field in (2) depends parametrically on the location and velocity of the receiver. Consequently, this expression is used to estimate the MS location and velocity by using the EKF. Next, we formulate the location estimation as a filtering problem in state-space form (Kailath, 1976). The general form, once discretized, is given by

$$\begin{aligned} \mathbf{x}_k &= \mathbf{f}(\mathbf{x}_{k-1}, \mathbf{w}_{k-1}) \\ \mathbf{z}_k &= \mathbf{h}(\mathbf{x}_k, \mathbf{v}_k) \end{aligned} \tag{4}$$

where $\mathbf{f}(.,.)$ and $\mathbf{h}(.,.)$ are known vector functions, k is the estimation step, $\mathbf{z}_k$ are the output measurements at time step k, and $\mathbf{x}_k$ is the system state at time step k and must not be confused with location coordinates. Further, $\mathbf{w}_k$ and $\mathbf{v}_k$ are the discrete zero-mean, independent state and measurement noise processes, with covariance matrices $\mathbf{Q}$ and $\mathbf{R}$, respectively.

Now let $\mathbf{x}_k = \left[x_k, \dot{x}_k, y_k, \dot{y}_k\right]^T$ denote the state of the MS at time k, where x_k and y_k are the Cartesian coordinates of the MS, $\dot{x}_k$ and $\dot{y}_k$ are the velocities of the MS in the X and Y directions, respectively. If we choose the case where the velocity of the MS is not known and is subject to unknown accelerations, then the dynamics of the MS can be written as (Gustafsson et al., 2002)

$$\mathbf{x}_k = \begin{bmatrix} x_k \\ \dot{x}_k \\ y_k \\ \dot{y}_k \end{bmatrix} = \begin{bmatrix} 1 & \Delta_k & 0 & 0 \\ 0 & 1 & 0 & 0 \\ 0 & 0 & 1 & \Delta_k \\ 0 & 0 & 0 & 1 \end{bmatrix} \begin{bmatrix} x_{k-1} \\ \dot{x}_{k-1} \\ y_{k-1} \\ \dot{y}_{k-1} \end{bmatrix} + \begin{bmatrix} \Delta_k^2/2 & 0 \\ \Delta_k & 0 \\ 0 & \Delta_k^2/2 \\ 0 & \Delta_k \end{bmatrix} \begin{bmatrix} w_{k-1,1} \\ w_{k-1,2} \end{bmatrix} \tag{5}$$

where Δ_k is a (possibly non-uniform) measurement interval between time k -1 and k. The measurement equation can be found from Aulin's scattering model (2) and (3), which can be written in discrete form as

$$z_k = h(\mathbf{x}_k, v_k) = \sum_{n=1}^{P} r_{n_k} \cos\left(\omega_c t_k + \omega_{n_k} t_k + \theta_{n_k}\right) + v(t_k) \tag{6}$$

where

$$\begin{aligned} \omega_{n_k} &= \frac{2\pi\sqrt{\dot{x}_k^2 + \dot{y}_k^2}}{\lambda}\left(\cos(\gamma_k - \alpha_{n_k})\cos\beta_{n_k}\right), \\ \theta_{n_k} &= \frac{-2\pi}{\lambda}\left(x_k \cos\alpha_{n_k} \cos\beta_{n_k} + y_k \sin\alpha_{n_k} \cos\beta_{n_k} + z_0 \sin\beta_{n_k}\right) + \phi_{n_k} \end{aligned} \tag{7}$$

Clearly, the measurement equation $h(.,.)$ is a nonlinear function of the state-space vector, as observed in (6) and (7). If we assume perfect knowledge of the channel, which is attainable either through channel estimation at the receiver (e.g., GSM receiver), or through various estimation techniques (e.g., least-squares, ML), then this problem falls under the broad area of nonlinear parameter estimation from noisy data which can be solved using the EKF as described in Section 6. The MLE algorithm that employs the lognormal propagation channel model is discussed in the next section.

5. RSL location estimation via MLE

The main idea of the algorithm described in this section is to use MLE with the distances of the MS from the BSs as parameters. That is, based on the power measurements, which constitute the experiment sample, we will calculate the distances that maximize the likelihood function. As the size of the sample increases, the accuracy of the estimation increases. Further, triangulation is performed for the most possible MS location.

5.1 MLE Theory

Consider a random sample of the measured quantity $X = X_1, X_2, \ldots, X_N$ and let θ be the parameter to be estimated. The likelihood function

$$L(X;\theta) = f(X_1, X_2, \ldots, X_N, \theta) \tag{8}$$

is another way of writing the probability density function (PDF), but the observations are fixed and the parameter is freely varying. Thus, the likelihood function reflects the likelihood of a given X arising for different values of θ. Given the sample, we are looking for that parameter value $\hat{\theta}$ that maximizes the likelihood of the sample occurrence as (Eliason, 1993)

$$\hat{\theta} = \arg\max_{\theta} L(X;\theta) \tag{9}$$

For convenience, we can maximize the so-called log-likelihood function log $L(X;\theta)$. The derivative of the log-likelihood function

$$\frac{\partial}{\partial\theta}(\log L(X;\theta)) \tag{10}$$

is called score function. The score function must satisfy the sufficient first and second order conditions for a maximum.

5.2 Location estimation via MLE

In this section, the MLE method that employs the lognormal propagation channel model described in section 4.1 is considered for the MS location estimation (Olama et al., 2008). This method exploits the received power measurements at the MS which are available from network measurement reports (NMRs). Thus, we write the likelihood function and then maximize it with respect to the distances $\boldsymbol{\theta} = \mathbf{d} = (d_1, d_2, .. d_B)$ from each BS, where $\boldsymbol{\theta}$ is the parameter to be estimated. The ML estimator, denoted by $\hat{\boldsymbol{\theta}} = \hat{\mathbf{d}} = (\hat{d}_1, \hat{d}_2, .., \hat{d}_B)$, represents the most possible MS/BS distances based on the measurements available at the MS.

Consider the measurement vector for the sth sample from all BSs, denoted by $\mathbf{PL}^s(\mathbf{d}) = (PL_1^s(d_1), PL_2^s(d_2), .., PL_B^s(d_B))$. The distribution function for this vector is the B-variate normal distribution given by

$$p(\mathbf{PL}^s(\mathbf{d}) \mid \boldsymbol{\theta}) = (2\pi)^{-B/2} (\det(\Sigma_s))^{-1/2} \exp\left(-\frac{1}{2}\left(\left(\mathbf{PL}^s(\mathbf{d}) - \overline{\mathbf{PL}}^s(\mathbf{d})\right)^T \boldsymbol{\Sigma}_s^{-1} \left(\mathbf{PL}^s(\mathbf{d}) - \overline{\mathbf{PL}}^s(\mathbf{d})\right)\right)\right) \tag{11}$$

where $\mathbf{PL}^s(\mathbf{d}) \sim \mathcal{N}_B\left(\overline{\mathbf{PL}}^s(\mathbf{d}); \boldsymbol{\Sigma}_s\right)$, $\overline{\mathbf{PL}}^s(\mathbf{d}) = \left(\overline{PL}_1^s(d_1), \overline{PL}_2^s(d_2), .., \overline{PL}_B^s(d_B)\right)$ is the mean path loss from each BS, and $\boldsymbol{\Sigma}_s$ is the covariance matrix. Assuming the noise is independent identically distributed (iid), then the logarithm likelihood function is the log product of the sample likelihood functions given by

$$L(\boldsymbol{\theta} \mid \mathbf{PL}^s(\mathbf{d})) = \log\left(\frac{1}{(2\pi)^{SB/2} (\det(\boldsymbol{\Sigma}_s))^{S/2}} \right) - \sum_{s=1}^{S} \left(\left(\mathbf{PL}^s(\mathbf{d}) - \overline{\mathbf{PL}}^s(\mathbf{d})\right)^T \frac{\boldsymbol{\Sigma}_s^{-1}}{2} \left(\mathbf{PL}^s(\mathbf{d}) - \overline{\mathbf{PL}}^s(\mathbf{d})\right)\right) \tag{12}$$

where S is the total number of samples. Maximizing (12) first with respect to $\overline{\mathbf{PL}}^s(\mathbf{d})$, the score function yields

$$\hat{\overline{PL}}_b(d_b) = \frac{1}{S}\sum_{s=1}^{S} PL_b^s(d_b), \quad \forall b \in \{1,2,..,B\} \tag{13}$$

Solving for $\hat{\mathbf{d}}$ using the invariance property of the MLE (Zehna, 1966), it can be shown that

$$\hat{d}_b = 10\exp\left\{\frac{1}{10\varepsilon_b}\left[\frac{1}{S}\sum_{s=1}^{S} PL_b^s(d_b) - PL(d_{0_b})\right]\right\} \tag{14}$$

is the MLE for the distance of the bth BS from the MS. Next, we perform triangulation using the least squares error method (Wong et al., 2000) to estimate the MS location (x_0, y_0), by solving

$$\arg\min_{x_0, y_0}\left\{\sum_{b=1}^{B}\left(d_b - \hat{d}_b\right)^2\right\} \tag{15}$$

5.3 Numerical results

In this example we employ a typical, yet realistic, simulation setup. The service area consists of a 19 cell cluster as configured in Fig. 6. The BSs are placed over a uniform hexagonal pattern of cells which are centrally equipped with omni-directional antennas. MSs are placed randomly in the central cell and the number of arranged users is 1000. The type of used environments is designated by the values of d_{0_b}, σ_b, ε_b (all previously defined in section 4.1) and cell radii R_b.
Path-loss exponent ε_b and path-loss variance values σ_b^2 were taken the same (σ_b = 8 dB, ε_b = 3.5, for all b (ETSI TR 101 115 V8.2.0 (2000-04), Annex V.A)), though cell radii R_b and reference distance d_{0_b} values are different for urban and suburban environments having values R_b =500, 2500m, d_{0_b} =50, 100m, respectively (ETSI TR 101 115 V8.2.0 (2000-04), Annex V.A)). The number of samples S is 20, the number of BSs for triangulation is 3 to 7 and the radio-frequency is 900MHz. We illustrate the 67% and 95% cumulative distribution function (CDF) values for urban and suburban environments and different number of BSs. E.g., a 67% CDF value X (meters) is equal to the probability $\Pr(\text{Error} < X(\text{meters})) = 0.67$.

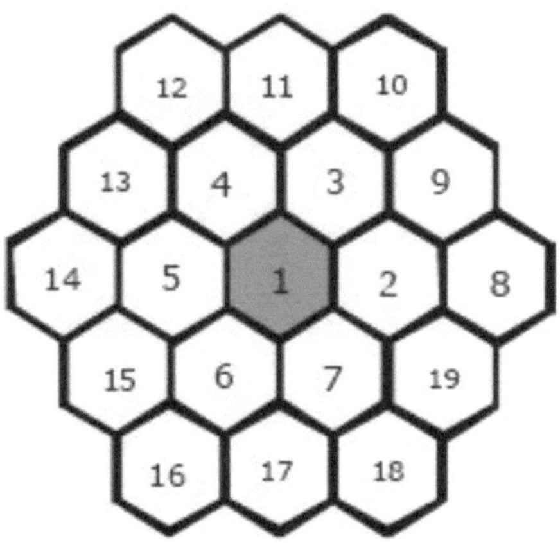

Fig. 6. Configuration of the cell arrangement

Fig. 7 shows numerical results in urban and suburban environments, respectively. It is observed that in urban environments the method's accuracy is below the FCC mandate for network-based solutions, and accuracy is improved as more BSs are incorporated. Results in suburban environments are also satisfactory; however accuracy degrades as the cell radii increases. This is due to the increasing error imposed by triangulation. It has been also observed that the accuracy increases as the number of samples, S, increases and as σ_b and ε_b decrease, as expected.

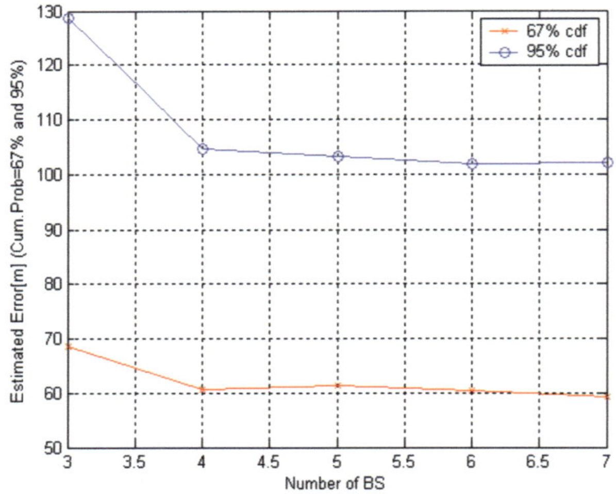

(a)

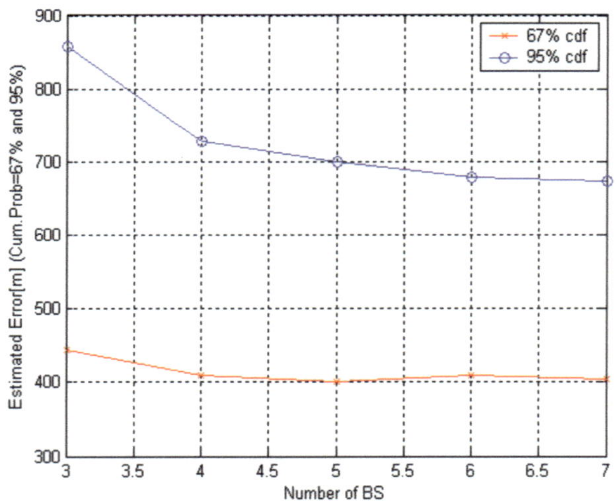

(b)

Fig. 7. 67% and 95% CDF of the ML estimate and 3 to 7 BSs for (a) Urban and (b) Suburban environments (Papageorgiou et al., 2005)

The maximum likelihood function concept is illustrated in Fig. 8. Instead of the separate likelihood functions, the overall likelihood function is considered. We show graphs of the likelihood function for one, two and three BSs. For one BS, the likelihood function is a 3-D Gaussian PDF which is maximized for distance $\hat{d}_1$ as shown in Fig. 8(a). For two BSs, the

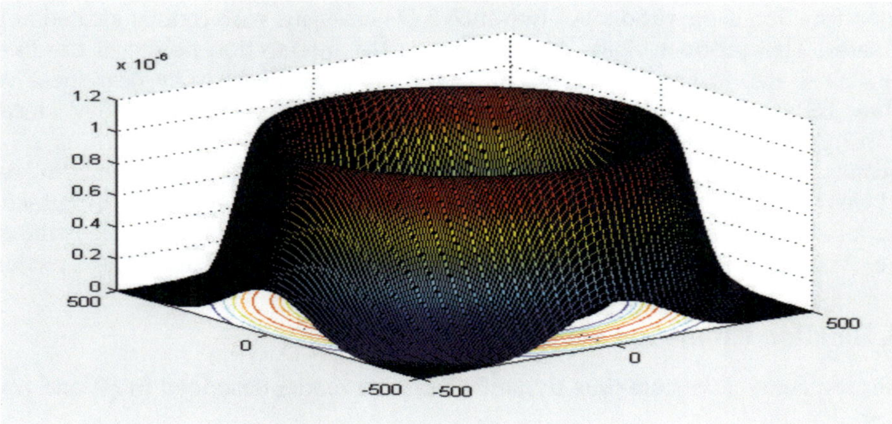

(a)

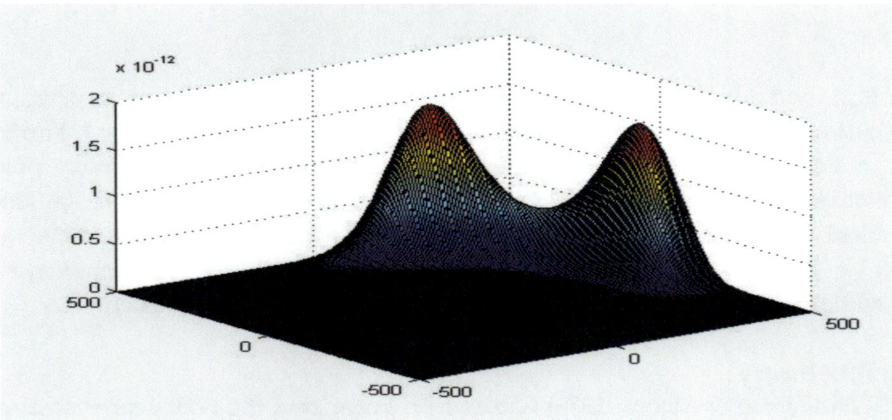

(b)

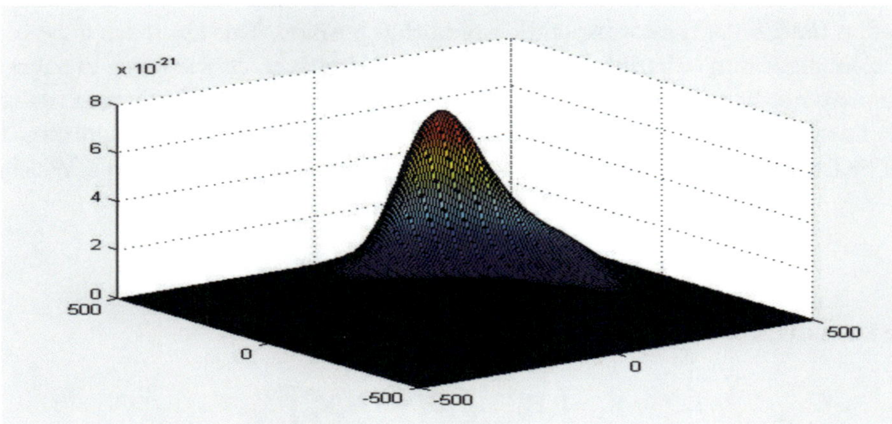

(c)

Fig. 8. The overall likelihood function for (a) 1 BS, (b) 2 BSs, and (c) 3 BSs (Charalambous & Panayiotou, 2004) likelihood function is the product of two such 3-D Gaussians with centres located at the BSs co-ordinates. This product yields two vertices at the intersection points of the likelihood functions as shown in Fig. 8(b). The true location is more likely to be near these vertices. With three BSs, there is only one vertex which represents the most probable MS location as shown in Fig. 8(c).

In realistic NLOS and multipath conditions the method will not perform so well. Nevertheless, it can be used as the initial estimator for the EKF approach, discussed in the next section, to find a more accurate estimator. The EKF approach that employs the channel model of Aulin to estimate the MS location and velocity is discussed in the next section.

6. RSL location estimation via the EKF

Consider the general discrete-time dynamical system model described in (4) and rewritten herein as

$$\begin{aligned} \mathbf{x}_k &= \mathbf{f}(\mathbf{x}_{k-1}, \mathbf{w}_{k-1}) \\ \mathbf{z}_k &= \mathbf{h}(\mathbf{x}_k, \mathbf{v}_k) \end{aligned} \tag{16}$$

where $\mathbf{f}(.,.)$ and $\mathbf{h}(.,.)$ are known vector functions, k is the estimation step, $\mathbf{z}_k$ are the output measurements at time step k, and $\mathbf{x}_k$ is the system state at time step k. Further, $\mathbf{w}_k$ and $\mathbf{v}_k$ are the discrete zero-mean, independent state and measurement noise processes, with covariance matrices $\mathbf{Q}$ and $\mathbf{R}$, respectively, and are assumed to be mutually independent. The set of entire measurements from the initial time step to time step k is denoted by $\mathbf{Z}_k = \{\mathbf{z}_i\}_{i=1}^{k}$. The initial state of the system $\mathbf{x}_0$ is given as a Gaussian random vector, with mean m_0 and covariance V_0, with V_0 symmetric and positive definite.

6.1 The EKF theory

The EKF (Anderson & Moore, 1979) is based on linearizing the nonlinear system models around the previous estimate. In other words, we only consider a linear Taylor approximation of the system function at the previous state estimate and that of the observation function at the corresponding predicted position. This approach gives a simple and efficient algorithm to handle a nonlinear model. However, convergence to a reasonable estimate may not be obtained if the initial guess is poor or if the disturbances are so large that the linearization is inadequate to describe the system. The general algorithm for the discrete EKF can be described by the time-update equations given as (Bishop & Welch, 2003)

$$\begin{aligned} \tilde{\mathbf{x}}_k &= \mathbf{f}(\hat{\mathbf{x}}_{k-1}, 0) \\ \tilde{\mathbf{P}}_k &= \mathbf{A}_k \hat{\mathbf{P}}_{k-1} \mathbf{A}_k^T + \mathbf{W}_k \mathbf{Q}_{k-1} \mathbf{W}_k^T \end{aligned} \tag{17}$$

and the measurement-update equations given as

$$\begin{aligned} \mathbf{K}_k &= \tilde{\mathbf{P}}_k \mathbf{H}_k^T \left[\mathbf{H}_k \tilde{\mathbf{P}}_k \mathbf{H}_k^T + \mathbf{V}_k \mathbf{R}_k \mathbf{V}_k^T \right]^{-1} \\ \hat{\mathbf{x}}_k &= \tilde{\mathbf{x}}_k + \mathbf{K}_k (\mathbf{z}_k - \mathbf{h}(\tilde{\mathbf{x}}_k, 0)) \\ \hat{\mathbf{P}}_k &= (\mathbf{I} - \mathbf{K}_k \mathbf{H}_k) \tilde{\mathbf{P}}_k \end{aligned} \tag{18}$$

where

$$\mathbf{A}_k = \frac{\partial \mathbf{f}}{\partial \mathbf{x}}(\hat{\mathbf{x}}_{k-1},0), \qquad \mathbf{W}_k = \frac{\partial \mathbf{f}}{\partial \mathbf{w}}(\hat{\mathbf{x}}_{k-1},0),$$
$$\mathbf{V}_k = \frac{\partial \mathbf{h}}{\partial v}(\hat{\mathbf{x}}_k,0), \qquad \mathbf{H}_k = \frac{\partial \mathbf{h}}{\partial \mathbf{x}}(\hat{\mathbf{x}}_k,0) \tag{19}$$

$\mathbf{K}$ is the gain matrix and $\mathbf{P}$ the estimation error covariance. The notation $\tilde{\mathbf{x}}_k$ denotes the a priori state estimate at step k and $\hat{\mathbf{x}}_k$ the a posteriori state estimate given measurement $\mathbf{z}_k$. $\tilde{\mathbf{P}}_k$ and $\hat{\mathbf{P}}_k$ are defined similarly.

6.2 Location estimation via the EKF

In this section, we employ the wave scattering model of Aulin (described in Section 4.2) in the EKF framework. We apply the general algorithm for the discrete EKF in (17)-(19) to our system model in (5)-(7) in which the state equation, $\mathbf{x}_k = \mathbf{f}(\mathbf{x}_{k-1}, \mathbf{w}_{k-1})$, is represented by the dynamics of the MS described in (5) and the measurement equation, $\mathbf{z}_k = \mathbf{h}(\mathbf{x}_k, \mathbf{v}_k)$, is represented by the discrete-time Aulin's scattering model described in (6) and (7). The result is given as (Olama et al., 2008)

$$\begin{aligned}
\tilde{\mathbf{x}}_k &= \mathbf{A}_k \hat{\mathbf{x}}_{k-1} \\
\tilde{\mathbf{P}}_k &= \mathbf{A}_k \hat{\mathbf{P}}_{k-1} \mathbf{A}_k^T + \mathbf{W}_k \mathbf{Q}_{k-1} \mathbf{W}_k^T \\
\mathbf{K}_k &= \tilde{\mathbf{P}}_k \mathbf{H}_k^T \left[\mathbf{H}_k \tilde{\mathbf{P}}_k \mathbf{H}_k^T + \mathbf{V}_k \mathbf{R}_k \mathbf{V}_k^T \right]^{-1} \\
\hat{\mathbf{x}}_k &= \tilde{\mathbf{x}}_k + \mathbf{K}_k (z_k - h(\tilde{\mathbf{x}}_k, 0)) \\
\hat{\mathbf{P}}_k &= (\mathbf{I} - \mathbf{K}_k \mathbf{H}_k) \tilde{\mathbf{P}}_k
\end{aligned} \tag{20}$$

where

$$\mathbf{A}_k = \frac{\partial \mathbf{f}}{\partial \mathbf{x}}(\hat{\mathbf{x}}_{k-1},0) = \begin{bmatrix} 1 & \Delta_k & 0 & 0 \\ 0 & 1 & 0 & 0 \\ 0 & 0 & 1 & \Delta_k \\ 0 & 0 & 0 & 1 \end{bmatrix}, \quad \mathbf{W}_k = \frac{\partial \mathbf{f}}{\partial \mathbf{w}}(\hat{\mathbf{x}}_{k-1},0) = \begin{bmatrix} \Delta_k^2/2 & 0 \\ \Delta_k & 0 \\ 0 & \Delta_k^2/2 \\ 0 & \Delta_k \end{bmatrix}, \quad \mathbf{V}_k = \frac{\partial h}{\partial v}(\hat{\mathbf{x}}_k,0) = 1,$$

$$\begin{aligned}
\mathbf{H}_k &= \frac{\partial h}{\partial \mathbf{x}}(\hat{\mathbf{x}}_k,0) = \left[H1_k \quad H2_k \quad H3_k \quad H4_k \right], \\
H1_k &= \sum_{n=1}^{P} \left[r_{n_k} \sin\left(\omega_c t_k + \omega_{n_k} t_k + \theta_{n_k}\right) \left(\frac{2\pi}{\lambda} \cos\left(\alpha_{n_k}\right) \cos\left(\beta_{n_k}\right) \right) \right] \\
H2_k &= \sum_{n=1}^{P} \left[\begin{array}{l} -r_{n_k} \sin\left(\omega_c t_k + \omega_{n_k} t_k + \theta_{n_k}\right) \left(\dfrac{2\pi t}{\lambda \sqrt{\dot{x}_k^2 + \dot{y}_k^2}} \cos\left(\beta_{n_k}\right) \right) \\ \left(\dot{x}_k \cos\left(\gamma_k - \alpha_{n_k}\right) + \dot{y}_k \sin\left(\gamma_k - \alpha_{n_k}\right) \right) \end{array} \right] \\
H3_k &= \sum_{n=1}^{P} \left[r_{n_k} \sin\left(\omega_c t_k + \omega_{n_k} t_k + \theta_{n_k}\right) \left(\frac{2\pi}{\lambda} \sin\left(\alpha_{n_k}\right) \cos\left(\beta_{n_k}\right) \right) \right] \\
H4_k &= \sum_{n=1}^{P} \left[\begin{array}{l} -r_{n_k} \sin\left(\omega_c t_k + \omega_{n_k} t_k + \theta_{n_k}\right) \left(\dfrac{2\pi t}{\lambda \sqrt{\dot{x}_k^2 + \dot{y}_k^2}} \cos\left(\beta_{n_k}\right) \right) \\ \left(\dot{y}_k \cos\left(\gamma_k - \alpha_{n_k}\right) - \dot{x}_k \sin\left(\gamma_k - \alpha_{n_k}\right) \right) \end{array} \right]
\end{aligned} \tag{21}$$

and $\gamma_k = \arctan(\dot{y}_k / \dot{x}_k)$. As in any nonlinear estimation problem, the convergence of the EKF to the true value of the location depends on the initial parameter value; therefore we first develop the MLE approach to obtain an initial estimator of adequate accuracy for the EKF. This hybrid algorithm, as numerical results indicate in the next section, has improved accuracy for the final MS location estimate.

The EKF approach takes into account NLOS condition as well as multipath propagation environments. It requires only one BS to estimate the MS location instead of at least three BSs as found in the MLE approach and in the literature (Hellebrandt & Scheibenbogen, 1999). However, an initial MS location estimate that requires at least three BSs, such as the MLE and triangulation method, will improve the convergence of the EKF.

7. Numerical results

In this numerical example, the EKF is employed utilizing the initial estimate as the first location estimate. Specifically, the first MLE algorithm passes its estimate to the EKF algorithm for final estimation and more precise location estimates. It will be shown that this approach corrects the initial estimate of the ML at a high level of accuracy.

The simulation setup for the initial estimate (MLE approach) remains the same; only now the number of BSs for triangulation is typically 5, and we are trying to locate a single MS. However, the simulated environment is determined by the environment-dependent parameters. All urban, suburban and rural (R_b =15000m, d_{0_b} =500m (ETSI TR 101 115 V8.2.0 (2000-04), Annex V.A.) environments have been considered, though only results for the rural case are illustrated due to space limitations. We choose the case when the velocity is not known to estimate the final location and velocity of the moving MS, and for simplicity, we assume zero acceleration.

As previously stated, we assume adequate channel knowledge, i.e., $\alpha_n, \beta_n, \phi_n, r_n$ are known. The number of paths P and the distributions of the envelopes r_n in (2) depend on the considered environment (Parsons, 1992). For urban areas $P \geq 6$ and the envelopes are Rayleigh distributed due to NLOS conditions. In urban and suburban areas typical values of P are 2-6 and the envelopes are taken from the Nakagami distribution with appropriate parameter value (ETSI TR 101 115 V8.2.0 (2000-04), Annex V.A.). Lastly, f_c = 2000Hz for simulation reasons.

Considering the rural environment, Fig. 9 illustrates the convergence of EKF to the real position and velocity of a moving MS. The relevant values are marked on the figure; these are the real position, estimated position, initial and final estimate errors. We observe that the final estimator is of high accuracy, if the initial estimate is used as the initial state of the algorithm. Specifically, the accuracy is below 10m most of the time; here it is 1.4m in comparison to the initial estimate accuracy of 1151m. This is due to the appropriateness of Aulin's channel model and the efficiency of Kalman Filtering in this particular application. In suburban and rural environments the results are even better, as expected. Moreover, it has been observed that the consistency and performance of the method are very high.

Fig. 10 illustrates the 67% and 95% CDF values of the final estimate in rural environment (the worst case of all), for different number of BSs used in triangulation. It is clear that the EKF approach achieves the FCC mandates for network-based solutions. The high accuracy, consistency and performance of the method, makes it suitable to be used in any LBSs, and particularly those which require high accuracy, such as emergency services.

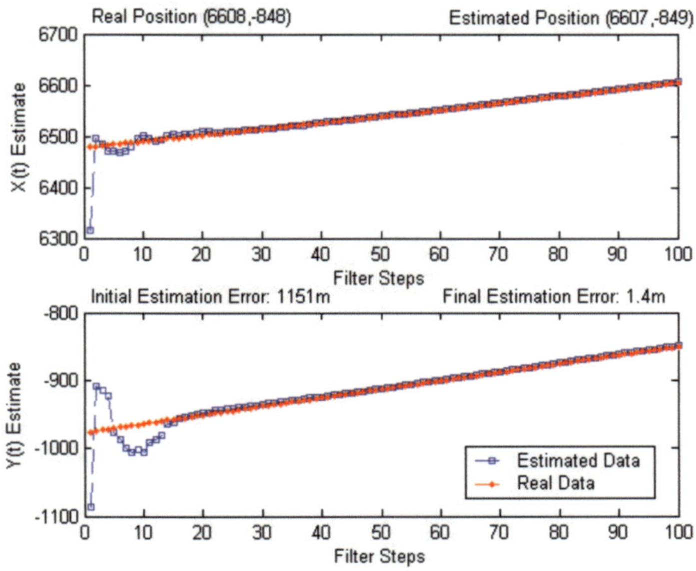

(a)

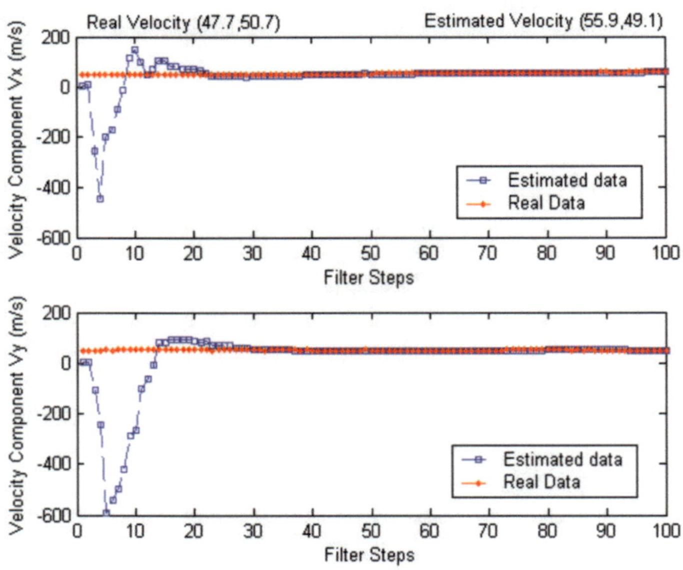

(b)

Fig. 9. Mobile (a) location and (b) velocity estimation in rural environment (Papageorgiou et al., 2005)

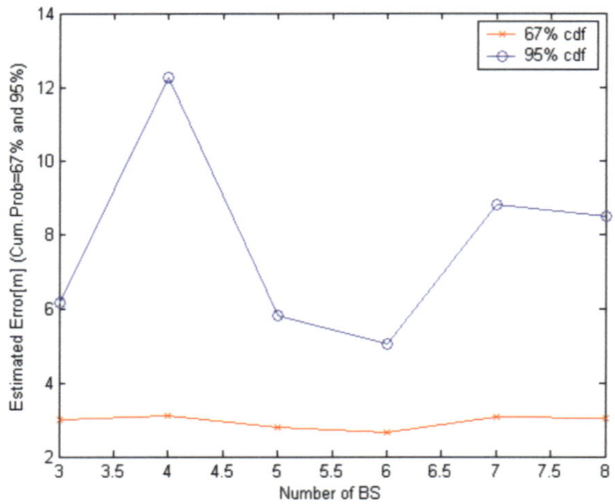

Fig. 10. 67% and 95% CDF of the final estimate using 3 to 8 BSs: Rural environment (Papageorgiou et al., 2005)

8. Conclusion

In this chapter, two estimation approaches are introduced to track the position and velocity of a MS in a cellular network. They are based on lognormal shadowing and Aulin's scattering models combined with the MLE and the EKF estimation algorithms, respectively. According to Aulin's channel model, the instantaneous electric field is a nonlinear function of the MS location and velocity. Consequently, the EKF is employed for the estimation process. Since the EKF approach is sensitive to the initial condition, we propose to use the ML estimate that employs the lognormal channel model, as the initial EKF state. Numerical results for typical simulations show that they are highly accurate and consistent.
These methods also excel in using inherent features of the cellular system, i.e., they support existing network infrastructure and channel signalling. The assumptions are knowledge of the channel and access to the instantaneous received field, which are obtained through channel sounding samples from the receiver circuitry. Future work will focus on generating efficient channel estimation algorithms, to remove the assumption on partial knowledge of the channel. Work on building a pilot application to test the performance of the EKF in realistic conditions is on-going together with the incorporation of channel model parameters estimation algorithms. Another direction in future work is to use more advanced filtering techniques such as the unscented Kalman filter (Julier & Uhlmann, 1997) and the particle filter (Arulampalam et al., 2002), which are not based upon the principal of linearising the nonlinear state and measurement models using Taylor series expansions as the EKF. Some preliminary results for MS location and velocity estimation algorithm based on particle filtering are presented in (Olama et al., 2007; Olama et al., 2008).

9. Acknowledgments

This chapter has been co-authored by employees of UT-Battelle, LLC, under contract DE-AC05-00OR22725 with the U.S. Department of Energy. Accordingly, the United States

10. References

Anderson, B.D. & Moore, J.B. (1979). *Optimal Filtering*, Prentice-Hall, Englewood Cliffs, New Jersey

Arulampalam, M.; Maskell, S.; Gordon, N. & Clapp, T. (2002). A tutorial on particle filters for online nonlinear/non-Gassian Bayesian tracking, *IEEE Transactions on Signal Processing*, Vol. 50, No. 2, Feb. 2002, pp. 174-188

Aulin, T. (1979), A modified model for fading signal at a mobile radio channel, *IEEE Transactions on Vehicle Technology*, Vol. 28, No. 3, Aug. 1979, pp. 182-203

Bishop, G. & Welch, G. (2003). *An Introduction to the Kalman Filter*, Department of Computer Science, University of North Carolina at Chapel Hill

Chan, N. (2003). *Introduction to Location-Based Service*, Department of Electronic Engineering, The Chinese University of Hong Kong

Charalambous C. D. & Panayiotou C. (2004). Development and Deployment of Location Based Services in Wireless Networks, Technical Report, Department of Electrical and Computer Engineering, University of Cyprus

Dru, M.A. & Saada, S. (2001). *Location-Based Mobile Services: The Essentials*, Alcatel Telecommunications Review, (first quarter, 2001), pp. 71-76

Eliason, S.R. (1993). *Maximum Likelihood Estimation: Logic and Practice*, SAGE, ISBN 0803941072, 9780803941076

Girodon, S. (2002). *Location based Services*, High Technologies Report, IAE Aix en Provence

Gustafsson, F.; Gunnarsson F.; Bergman N.; Forssell U.; Jansson J.; Karlsson R. & Nordlund P. (2002). Particle filters for positioning, navigation, and tracking, *IEEE Transactions on Signal Processing*, Vol. 50, No. 2, pp. 425-437

Hellebrandt, M. & Scheibenbogen, M. (1999). Location tracking of mobiles in cellular radio networks, *IEEE Transactions on Vehicle Technology*, Vol. 48, No. 5, pp. 1558-1562

Julier, S.J. & Uhlmann, J.K. (1997). A new extension of the Kalman filter to nonlinear systems, *Proceedings of the 11th International Symposium on Aerospace/Defence Sensing, Simulation and Controls*, Vol. Multi Sensor Fusion, Tracking and Resource Management II, Orlando, Florida

Kailath, T. (1976). *Lectures on Linear Least-Squares Estimation*, Springer, New York

Leite, F.S. (2001). *Mobility - The Shape of Things to Come*, IMT 200 Project Manager, ITU

Olama, M.M.; Djouadi, S.M.; Charalambous, C.D. & Papageorgiou, I.G. (2008), Position and velocity tracking in mobile networks using particle and Kalman filtering with comparison, *IEEE Transactions on Vehicle Technology*, Vol. 57, No. 2, pp. 1001 - 1010

Olama, M.M.; Djouadi, S.M.; Charalambous, C.D. & Papageorgiou, I.G. (2007), Estimation of position and velocity in multipath wireless networks from received signal measurements, *Proceedings of the 46th IEEE Conference on Decision and Control*, pp. 4590-4595

Papageorgiou, I.; Charalambous, C. & Panayiotou, C. (2005). An enhanced received signal level cellular location determination method via maximum likelihood and Kalman filtering, *Proceeding of the Wireless Communications and Networking Conference (WCNC)*, Vol. 4, pp. 2524-2529

Parsons, J.D. (1992). *The Mobile Radio Propagation Channel*, 2nd Edition, Wiley, ISBN: 978-0-471-98857-1

Rappaport, T.S. (2002). *Wireless Communications: Principles and Practice.* 2nd Edition, Prentice Hall

Reed, J.; Krizman, K.; Woerner, B. & Rappaport, T. (1998). An overview of the challenges and progress in meeting the E-911 requirement for location service, *IEEE Communication Magazine*, vol. 36, pp. 30-37

Romdhani, L. & Trad, A. (2002). *Mobile Location Estimation Approaches*, University of Nice Sophia-Antipolis, Technical Report for the Mobile Networks Module

Searle, M. (2001). *Location Based Services*, InSig Presentation

Sklar, B. (2001). *Digital Communications: Fundamentals and Applications*, 2nd Edition, Prentice Hall

Symmetricom (2002). *Location of Mobile Handsets-The Role of Synchronization and Location Monitoring Units*, White Paper

Wong, C.; Lee, M. & Chan, R. (2000). GSM-Based Mobile Positioning Using WAP, *Proceedings of the Wireless Communications and Networking Conference (WCNC)*, Vol. 2, pp. 874-878

Zehna, P. (1966). Invariance of Maximum Likelihood Estimators, *Annals of Mathematical Statistics*, Vol. 37, No. 3, pp. 744

11

Dead-Reckoning Method for Personal Navigation Systems Using Kalman Filtering Techniques to Augment Inertial/Magnetic Sensing

Angelo Maria Sabatini
ARTS Lab, Scuola Superiore Sant'Anna, Pisa, Italy

1. Introduction

Sensing techniques and computer algorithms help relieve demands in answering three questions that are crucial to navigation problem solving: "where am I?", "where am I going?", and "how should I get there?". The question "where am I?", namely localization, is addressed in this paper, in regard to the development of personal navigation systems (PNS) for determining a human walker's position and orientation. Biomedical applications of PNS technology, the ones we are mainly interested in, may include ambulatory monitoring systems for assessing the physical activity behavior of persons with disabilities and chronic health conditions, orientation & mobility aids for the blind or visually impaired, assistance services for frail seniors with compound problems of memory loss and disorientation.

In principle, PNS would provide the localization data in any environment, and at any time. Design criteria, in terms of, e.g., portability, accuracy, availability, cost, hindrance to the natural walking pattern, and the idiosyncrasies of the environment where the user walks greatly concur in practice to restrict the choice of sensing techniques and computational methods suited to implement PNS. Localization in outdoor environments is easy to solve using Global Positioning System (GPS) technology, despite that a number of serious shortcomings exist: loss of satellite track, when direct line of sight with the GPS constellation is precluded by obstructions, inability to provide static heading information, significant power consumption. When localization in indoor environments is pursued and GPS is therefore useless, other externally-referenced sensing techniques are available (video movement-sensing, infrared, ultrasound); however, their operation is typically based on complex and costly measuring hardware, dense environment infrastructure, not to mention the severely limited properties of the external sources themselves, in terms of, e.g., range, field-of-view and so forth.

Internally-referenced sensing techniques, namely inertial sensing, used in association with a relative-measurement approach, namely dead-reckoning (DR), can be a useful navigation alternative for implementing self-contained PNS (Fang et al., 2005). Being internally referenced and immune to interference and shadowing, inertial sensors (accelerometers and gyros) sense movement, in principle, without restrictions in the spatial domain (Welch &

Foxlin, 2002). The main problem of a dead-reckoning approach to localization based on inertial sensing is represented by the need to time-integrate the inertial measurements, which include any superimposed sensor drift and noise. Hence, the localization errors tend to grow unbounded over time, with the position errors growing at a faster rate than the orientation errors (Foxlin, 2002). Another drawback is that the integration has to be started from initial conditions, which inertial sensors cannot help establishing, or disambiguating completely. Earth's magnetic field sensing - an externally-referenced sensing technique whose source is virtually available anywhere on the Earth's surface - can help mitigate the integration errors and specify the absolute orientation. Inertial and magnetic sensors are thus an interesting sensor suite for PNS; recent technological advances have enabled fully integrated inertial/magnetic measurement units (IMMU) with form factors, cost and metrological specifications suited to studies in the field of human movement (Yun & Bachmann, 2006).

In this chapter we present a shoe-mounted inertial/magnetic sensor system to estimate the three-dimensional (3D) path traveled by the foot instep of an ambulating person. Central to our approach are the computer algorithms which estimate the IMMU orientation in the 3D space via a quaternion-based adaptive Extended Kalman Filtering (EKF), and determine the traveled path by stride-wise strap-down double integration of foot accelerations resolved in the navigation frame. In order to make the filtering process robust against the disturbances which may affect the IMMU sensors , several tricks are incorporated in the developed EKF:

- adaptation of the measurement noise covariance matrix during EKF runs;
- adaptive alternation between initialization and run of the EKF, so as to refine the estimation of either the rotation quaternion or the magnetic sensor bias vector - this is based on stance/swing phase gait detection driven by gyroscopic data, and accelerometric/magnetic measurement validation;
- bias-correction of the magnetic sensor measurements before using them for initializing each EKF run;
- stride-wise integration of gravity-compensated acceleration components with zero velocity updates performed once every movement epoch is detected.

2. Related work

Most PNS pursue the following approach to locate the position of the user: the displacement from the previous known position is computed from the step length of the user and his heading. Suppose a sensor, e.g., an accelerometer, is used to detect a step (many PNS are waist-mounted, in the belief that the dynamics of human movements is less challenging in those body parts where amplitude range and frequency content of sensed accelerations are limited). The vertical acceleration measured by a waist-mounted accelerometer takes its maximal absolute value when each foot hits the ground. The step time can thus be estimated by peak detection algorithms. The step length is usually either predetermined and entered by the user as a calibration factor (electronic pedometer), or estimated on the basis of simple biomechanical models. Provided that the step length is multiplied by the number of detected steps, the traveled distance is then computed.

In (Ladetto & Merminod, 2002), a walking model is used to predict the relationship between step time and step length in normal walking patterns. Similarly, the existence of simple relationships between step time, RMS value of the norm of the waist acceleration, and step length during normal walking is exploited in (Perrin et al., 2000). The main difficulties with the model-based approach to step length estimation are: the need for individual adaptations to, e.g., the walked surface (uphill/level/downhill walking) and its nature; the difficulty to encompass the large variety of motor patterns that, especially in crowded environments, a human walker produces to functionally move his body. As for the former point, additional sensor systems have to be deployed for in-line parametric model calibration, e.g., GPS and altimeters; as for the latter point, pattern recognition algorithms have to be implemented to discriminate walking from non-walking activities, e.g., side-stepping. Most PNS use a magnetic compass as a heading sensor (Ladetto & Merminod, 2002; Lee & Maze, 2002; Jirawimut et al., 2003). The accelerometers are used in these systems to perform the important task of tilt compensation, so as to project the measured Earth's magnetic field vector in the horizontal plane. However, since the Earth's magnetic field is weak and it can be easily masked and unpredictably distorted by any sort of natural or man-made magnetic disturbance, computational intelligence is mandatory in the design of complementary filtering algorithms which help improve the accuracy of compass heading determination using additional sensors, e.g., gyros, GPS or both.

An alternative approach to locate the position of the user is by strap-down integration (Elwell, 1999). The problems with this approach are due to the tendency of DR errors to grow over time - either errors incurred in estimating the absolute orientation of the navigation sensor, or errors incurred in performing the double-integration of gravity-compensated linear accelerations. In spite that the human body dynamics is more challenging at the foot level than it is at the waist level, the foot is a convenient location for PNS mounting when the goal is to measure directly the traveled distance (Sabatini et al., 2005). In particular, we may take advantage of the fact that the foot is stationary during the stance phase of gait. When the PNS is stationary, zero velocity updates (velocity errors can be reset with each stride), and zero attitude updates (gyro bias drift can be estimated and subtracted from gyro sensor output) can be performed. The benefits of these procedures are examined in (Sabatini, 2005), which highlights the importance that strap-down integration of inertial measurements is performed in a stride-wise fashion. When the foot is stationary, gravimetric tilt sensing, alone or combined with compass heading determination, helps establish the initial conditions needed to carry out another round of strap-down integration during the next gait cycle.

In (Sabatini et al., 2005), a sensor unit, which is composed of one uni-axis gyro, oriented in the medio-lateral direction, and one bi-axis accelerometer, with sensitive axes embedded in the vertical plane, is fastened to the foot instep in order to estimate a number of spatio-temporal features of gait, including walked distance, average walking speed, incline of the walked surface, stride length, stride time, and relative stance. The angular velocity measured by the gyro is used to perform gait segmentation in different phases, including the phase when the sensor unit alignment is performed by gravimetric tilt sensing. Treadmill walking trials attest the good accuracy of the proposed approach. The main limitation is that the system is blind to changes in the direction of displacement. These limitations can be overcome, in principle, when a fully integrated IMMU is considered, as it is in (Veltink et al., 2003) where, although experimental waveforms of the foot Euler angles are reported, no experimental results are offered in terms of user localization. Another interesting solution is described in (Stirling et., 2005), where the sensing hardware includes a pair of dual-axis accelerometers, with sensitive axes that are either collinear (X-axis) or parallel (Y-axis), and a dual-axis magnetic sensor. The accelerometers are offset to allow angular acceleration measurement. Since the sensor orientation is computed from a stride-wise double-integration of acceleration data, however, the overall accuracy of the system may be less than the accuracy achievable with a more expensive gyro-based IMMU.

3. Method

3.1 The strap-down approach to inertial navigation

Suppose a coordinate system attached to a rigid body in space - the body frame *B*, and an Earth's reference frame *E* are introduced. For the orientation and position of the rigid body to be determined, the orientation of the axes of *B* with respect to the *E*, and the origin of *B* relative to *E* need to be specified. Be $\vec{\mathbf{x}}$ a 3×1 column-vector, which is resolved along the axes of *B* and *E*, to yield $\vec{\mathbf{x}}^B$ and $\vec{\mathbf{x}}^E$, respectively:

$$\vec{\mathbf{x}}^B = \overset{E\to B}{C}\,\vec{\mathbf{x}}^E \tag{1}$$

where $\overset{E\to B}{C}$ is the direction cosine matrix (DCM) for the transformation from *E* to *B*.

Directly or through using attitude parameterizations based on, e.g., the orientation vector or the rotation quaternion, the DCM can be numerically determined by integrating a system of first-order differential equations that involve the components of the instantaneous angular velocity vector $\vec{\boldsymbol{\omega}}^B = [p, q, r]^T$, which can be measured by a tri-axis gyro strapped to the rigid body (Sabatini, 2006); the initial conditions needed to integrate these equations are assumed to be known or measurable during the alignment process. Alternately, the DCM can be determined by vector matching in *E* and *B* (Shuster and Oh, 1981). Vector matching, also known as Wahba's problem, matches two non-collinear vectors that are known in *E* and are measured in *B* - the Earth's gravity field $\vec{\mathbf{g}}^E = [0,0,g]^T$ (g = 9.81 m/s^2 is the gravity acceleration) and the Earth's magnetic field $\vec{\mathbf{h}}^E = [h_x, 0, h_z]^T$, both normalized to have unit norm, are two these *reference* vectors; aiding sensors, such as a tri-axis accelerometer and a tri-axis magnetic sensor, can thus be strapped to the rigid body, in order to resolve, respectively, the Earth's gravity and magnetic fields as unit-norm *observation* vectors in *B*. Vector matching may help solve the alignment process and is, in principle, an alternative to using gyros for DCM determination when the body accelerations, due to its own movement, are negligible in comparison with gravity (Gebre-Egziabher et al., 2000).

The estimated DCM is used to perform the process of gravity-compensation in the accelerometer output signals:

$$\vec{\mathbf{a}}_o^E(t) = \overset{B\to E}{C}(t)\,\vec{\mathbf{a}}^B(t) - \vec{\mathbf{g}}^E \tag{2}$$

Finally, the velocity $\vec{\mathbf{v}}_o{}^E(t)$ and position of the rigid body $\vec{\mathbf{p}}_o{}^E(t)$ are determined by single and double integration of (2), respectively.

The strap-down approach to inertial navigation as summarized above is deceptively simple. The computations of the integrals that are involved in determining the orientation from measured angular velocities, and determining the linear velocity/displacement from gravity-compensated accelerations are susceptible to several error sources, including the sensors' bias offset, drift, calibration errors, and the random-walk errors associated with

wideband noise integration. Also, the influence of body movements and external magnetic disturbances on the accuracy of accelerometers and magnetic sensors to sense the reference Earth's gravity and magnetic fields greatly contribute to the overall error budget.
It is then difficult that high performance in orientation/position determination are achieved by relying on IMMU sensors, the stand-alone accuracy and run-to-run stability of which are poor. In literature, the commonest approaches to enhance the achievable navigation performance consist of integrating additional sensorial resources, e.g., GPS into the navigation system hardware, managing the sensor fusion via sophisticated Kalman filters running in the navigation system software, or both (Foxlin, 2002; Ladetto & Merminod, 2002). Our approach is to use unaided inertial/magnetic sensing, in combination with an EKF for orientation determination. The structure of the developed EKF and the tricks introduced to enhance the filter performance are described in the next Section.

3.2 Implementation

The flow of information underlying the strap-down approach to inertial navigation we propose for the shoe-mounted IMMU described in this paper is sketched in Fig. 1.

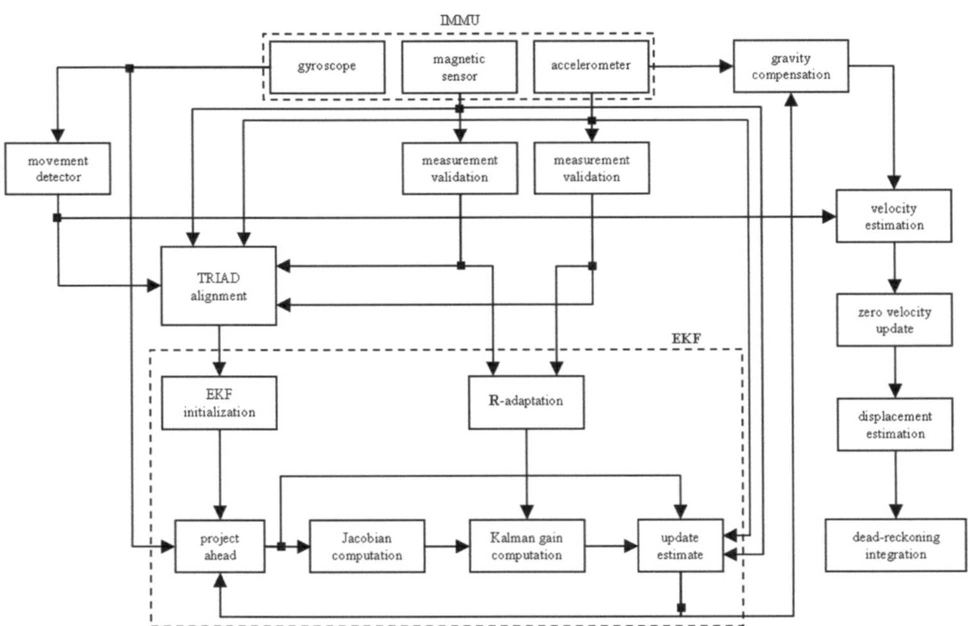

Fig. 1. Information flow for the proposed dead-reckoning algorithm of personal navigation.

The attitude parameterization we choose is the quaternion $\mathbf{q} = [\vec{\mathbf{e}}^T, q_4]^T$ associated to the rotation from B to E ($\vec{\mathbf{e}} = [q_1, q_2, q_3]^T$ is the vector part and q_4 is the scalar part of the quaternion). The rigid body angular movement obeys the vector differential equation

$$\frac{d}{dt}\mathbf{q} = \mathbf{\Omega}\left[\vec{\boldsymbol{\omega}}^B\right]\mathbf{q} = \begin{bmatrix} 0 & -r & q & p \\ r & 0 & -p & q \\ -q & p & 0 & r \\ p & q & r & 0 \end{bmatrix}\mathbf{q} \tag{3}$$

whose discrete-time model is

$$\begin{cases} \mathbf{q}_{k+1} = \exp(\boldsymbol{\Omega}_k T_s)\, \mathbf{q}_k, \quad k = 0,1,... \\ \mathbf{q}_0 = \mathbf{q}(0), \end{cases} \tag{4}$$

where T_s is the system's sampling interval. The quaternion is determined at time instants kT_s, starting from initial conditions $\mathbf{q}_0$ obtained in the alignment process. For (4) to be valid, the angular velocity $\vec{\boldsymbol{\omega}}_k$ is to be approximately constant in the interval $[kT_s, (k+1)T_s]$. The DCM is a homogeneous quadratic function of the components of $\mathbf{q}$:

$$\overset{E\to B}{C}(\mathbf{q}) = \left(q_0^2 - \|\vec{\mathbf{e}}\|^2\right)\mathbf{I}_{3\times 3} - 2q_4 \begin{bmatrix} 0 & -q_3 & q_2 \\ q_3 & 0 & -q_1 \\ -q_2 & q_1 & 0 \end{bmatrix} + 2\vec{\mathbf{e}}\vec{\mathbf{e}}^T \tag{5}$$

which is used for updating the DCM, once that the solution of (4) has progressed in time.
In this paper the alignment process is performed using the TRIAD algorithm (Shuster & Oh, 1981). Given two *reference* unit vectors, namely $\vec{\mathbf{v}}_1$ and $\vec{\mathbf{v}}_2$, and two *observation* unit vectors, namely $\vec{\mathbf{w}}_1$ and $\vec{\mathbf{w}}_2$, the DCM is estimated by the TRIAD algorithm as follows:

$$\overset{E\to B}{C}_{est} = [\vec{\mathbf{s}}_1 \;\; \vec{\mathbf{s}}_2 \;\; \vec{\mathbf{s}}_3][\vec{\mathbf{r}}_1 \;\; \vec{\mathbf{r}}_2 \;\; \vec{\mathbf{r}}_3]^T \tag{6}$$

where:

$$\begin{aligned} \vec{\mathbf{r}}_1 &= \vec{\mathbf{v}}_1 \\ \vec{\mathbf{r}}_2 &= \vec{\mathbf{v}}_1 \times \vec{\mathbf{v}}_2 \\ \vec{\mathbf{r}}_3 &= \vec{\mathbf{r}}_1 \times \vec{\mathbf{r}}_2 \end{aligned} \tag{7}$$

and:

$$\begin{aligned} \vec{\mathbf{s}}_1 &= \vec{\mathbf{w}}_1 \\ \vec{\mathbf{s}}_2 &= \vec{\mathbf{w}}_1 \times \vec{\mathbf{w}}_2 \\ \vec{\mathbf{s}}_3 &= \vec{\mathbf{s}}_1 \times \vec{\mathbf{s}}_2 \end{aligned} \tag{8}$$

where × denotes the cross vector product. Suppose that the accelerometer and magnetic sensor measurement noises are modeled as Gaussian white noises, with null mean and covariance matrices $\Sigma_a = \sigma_a^2 \mathbf{I}$ and $\Sigma_h = \sigma_h^2 \mathbf{I}$, respectively (**I** is the 3×3 identity matrix). The covariance matrix of the TRIAD-related quaternion is known to be a function of the observation vectors and sensor noise variances (Shuster & Oh, 1981):

$$P^{TRIAD} = f\left(\vec{\mathbf{w}}_1, \vec{\mathbf{w}}_2, \sigma_1^2, \sigma_2^2\right) \tag{9}$$

where $\sigma_1^2 = \sigma_a^2, \sigma_2^2 = \sigma_h^2$ or $\sigma_1^2 = \sigma_h^2, \sigma_2^2 = \sigma_a^2$; it can be used for EKF initialization at first contact.
The minute body movements at the time of alignment acts to increase σ_a over the noise floor that is measured when the tri-axis accelerometer stands motionless on the calibration bench. More importantly, the accuracy of the TRIAD-quaternion is actually dependent on

whether systematic errors affect the observation vectors, which invalidates the assumption that the sensor measurements are unbiased. Suppose, indeed, that the tri-axis magnetic sensor output is expressed by

$$\vec{\mathbf{m}}={}^{m}\mathbf{K}\overset{E\to B}{C}(\mathbf{q})\vec{\mathbf{h}}^{E}+{}^{h}\vec{\mathbf{b}}+{}^{h}\vec{\mathbf{v}} \tag{10}$$

where ${}^{m}\mathbf{K}$ is the scale factor matrix (ideally, ${}^{m}\mathbf{K}=\mathbf{I}$); ${}^{h}\vec{\mathbf{b}}$ is the bias vector (ideally, it is null); ${}^{h}\vec{\mathbf{v}}$ is the zero-mean magnetic sensor measurement noise. Even though it is carefully calibrated against the effects of sensor electronic offset and scale factor drifts, and the effects of so-called hard and soft irons due to sensor placement on the human body, the tri-axis magnetic sensor is vulnerable to either static or time-varying external magnetic disturbances near or within the measurement space (Sabatini, 2006). The following discrete-time random-walk model is used to describe the dynamics of the (time-varying) bias vector:

$${}^{h}\vec{\mathbf{b}}_{k+1}={}^{h}\vec{\mathbf{b}}_{k}+{}^{h}\vec{\mathbf{w}}_{k} \tag{11}$$

where ${}^{h}\vec{\mathbf{w}}_{k}$ is a zero-mean white noise process with covariance matrix ${}^{m}\mathbf{\Sigma}=\sigma_{w}^{2}\mathbf{I}$.
The state vector of the developed EKF includes the rotation quaternion and the magnetic bias vector. The state transition vector equation is

$$\vec{\mathbf{x}}_{k+1}=\begin{bmatrix}\mathbf{q}_{k+1}\\ {}^{h}\vec{\mathbf{b}}_{k+1}\end{bmatrix}=\Phi(T_s,\vec{\boldsymbol{\omega}}_k)\vec{\mathbf{x}}_k+\vec{\mathbf{w}}_k=\begin{bmatrix}\exp(\Omega_k T_s) & \mathbf{0}\\ \mathbf{0} & \mathbf{I}\end{bmatrix}\begin{bmatrix}\mathbf{q}_k\\ {}^{h}\vec{\mathbf{b}}_k\end{bmatrix}+\begin{bmatrix}{}^{q}\vec{\mathbf{w}}_k\\ {}^{h}\vec{\mathbf{w}}_k\end{bmatrix} \tag{12}$$

where $\mathbf{0}$ is the 3×3 null matrix and

$${}^{q}\vec{\mathbf{w}}_k=-\frac{T_s}{2}\Xi_k{}^{g}\vec{\mathbf{v}}_k=-\frac{T_s}{2}\begin{bmatrix}[\vec{\mathbf{e}}_k\times]+q_{0k}\mathbf{I}\\ -\vec{\mathbf{e}}_k^{T}\end{bmatrix}{}^{g}\vec{\mathbf{v}}_k \tag{13}$$

where the operator

$$[\vec{\mathbf{e}}_k\times]=\begin{bmatrix}0 & -e_z & e_y\\ e_z & 0 & -e_x\\ -e_y & e_x & 0\end{bmatrix} \tag{14}$$

represents the cross vector product.
${}^{g}\vec{\mathbf{v}}_k$ is the gyro measurement noise, assumed to be a zero-mean white Gaussian process, with covariance matrix ${}^{g}\mathbf{\Sigma}_k=\sigma_g^2\mathbf{I}$. The process noise covariance matrix $\mathbf{Q}_k$ has the following expression:

$$\mathbf{Q}_k=\begin{bmatrix}(T_s/2)^2\Xi_k\mathbf{\Sigma}_g\Xi_k^T & \mathbf{0}\\ \mathbf{0} & {}^{m}\mathbf{\Sigma}_k\end{bmatrix} \tag{15}$$

The measurement model is given by

$$\vec{\mathbf{z}}_{k+1}=\begin{bmatrix}{}^{h}\vec{\mathbf{m}}_{k+1}\\ {}^{a}\vec{\mathbf{m}}_{k+1}\end{bmatrix}=\mathbf{f}\left[\vec{\mathbf{x}}_{k+1}\right]+\vec{\mathbf{v}}_{k+1}=\begin{bmatrix}\overset{E\to B}{C}(\mathbf{q}_{k+1})\vec{\mathbf{h}}^{E}\\ \overset{E\to B}{C}(\mathbf{q}_{k+1})\vec{\mathbf{g}}^{E}\end{bmatrix}+\begin{bmatrix}{}^{h}\vec{\mathbf{b}}_{k+1}\\ \mathbf{0}\end{bmatrix}+\begin{bmatrix}{}^{h}\vec{\mathbf{v}}_{k+1}\\ {}^{a}\vec{\mathbf{v}}_{k+1}\end{bmatrix} \tag{16}$$

The covariance matrix of the measurement model $\mathbf{R}_{k+1}$ is

$$\mathbf{R}_{k+1} = \begin{bmatrix} {}^{h}\mathbf{R}_{k+1} & \mathbf{0} \\ \mathbf{0} & {}^{a}\mathbf{R}_{k+1} \end{bmatrix} \tag{17}$$

Underlying (17) is the assumption that the magnetic sensor and accelerometer measurement noise ${}^{h}\vec{\mathbf{v}}_{k+1}$ and ${}^{a}\vec{\mathbf{v}}_{k+1}$ are uncorrelated zero-mean white noise processes, the covariance matrices of which are ${}^{h}\mathbf{R}_{k+1} = {}^{R}\sigma_h^2\mathbf{I}$ and ${}^{a}\mathbf{R}_{k+1} = {}^{R}\sigma_a^2\mathbf{I}$, respectively.

Before the current measurement $\vec{\mathbf{z}}_{k+1}$ is incorporated in the filtering process to drive the state vector update, a mechanism of adaptation of the measurement noise covariance matrix is implemented. In our approach, the deviation of the sensed magnetic field magnitude from the local earth's magnetic field magnitude is tested and the following adaptation mechanism is then implemented:

$${}^{R}\sigma_h^2 = \begin{cases} \sigma_{ho}^2 \left| \dfrac{\left\| \vec{\mathbf{m}}_{k+1} \right\|}{\left\| \vec{\mathbf{h}} \right\|} - 1 \right|, & \left| \left\| \vec{\mathbf{m}}_{k+1} \right\| - \left\| \vec{\mathbf{h}} \right\| \right| < \varepsilon_m \\ \infty \text{ (measurement rejected)}, & \text{otherwise} \end{cases} \tag{18}$$

Moreover, the measured acceleration magnitude is tested in advance for the absence of significant deviations from gravity; if persistent for some specified time interval, this absence is considered the sign that the body is at rest. If not so, the observation variance ${}^{R}\sigma_a^2$ is set to extremely high values:

$${}^{R}\sigma_a^2 = \begin{cases} \sigma_a^2, & \left| \left\| \vec{\mathbf{a}}_{j+1} \right\| - \left\| \vec{\mathbf{g}} \right\| \right| < \varepsilon_a \quad \forall j \in [k - k_a, k] \\ \infty \text{ (measurement rejected)}, & \text{otherwise} \end{cases} \tag{19}$$

Because of the non-linear nature of the measurement model (16), the EKF approach requires that a first-order Taylor-Mac Laurin expansion is carried out around the current state estimate by computing the Jacobian matrix:

$$\mathbf{F}_{k+1} = \frac{\partial}{\partial \vec{\mathbf{x}}_{k+1}} \vec{\mathbf{z}}_{k+1} \bigg|_{\vec{\mathbf{x}}_{k+1} = \vec{\mathbf{x}}_{k+1}^{-}} \tag{20}$$

For the sake of reader's convenience, the EKF equations are summarized below. We remind that the superscript – in the following equations stands for *a priori* estimate at time t_{k+1}, before the current measurement $\vec{\mathbf{z}}_{k+1}$ is used in the computation of the *a posteriori* estimate.

- Compute the *a priori* state estimate:

$$\vec{\mathbf{x}}_{k+1}^{-} = \Phi(T_s, \vec{\boldsymbol{\omega}}_k)\vec{\mathbf{x}}_k$$

- Compute the *a priori* error covariance matrix

$$\mathbf{P}_{k+1}^{-} = \Phi(T_s, \vec{\boldsymbol{\omega}}_k)\mathbf{P}_k\Phi(T_s, \vec{\boldsymbol{\omega}}_k)^T + \mathbf{Q}_k$$

- Compute the Kalman gain

$$\mathbf{K}_{k+1} = \mathbf{P}_{k+1}^{-}\mathbf{F}_{k+1}^{T}\left(\mathbf{F}_{k+1}\mathbf{P}_{k+1}^{-}\mathbf{F}_{k+1}^{T} + \mathbf{R}_{k+1}\right)^{-1}$$

- Compute the *a posteriori* state estimate

$$\vec{\mathbf{x}}_{k+1} = \vec{\mathbf{x}}_{k+1}^{-} + \mathbf{K}_{k+1}\left[\vec{\mathbf{z}}_{k+1} - \mathbf{f}\left(\vec{\mathbf{x}}_{k+1}^{-}\right)\right]$$

- Compute the *a posteriori* error covariance matrix

$$\mathbf{P}_{k+1} = \mathbf{P}_{k+1}^{-} - \mathbf{K}_{k+1}\mathbf{F}_{k+1}\mathbf{P}_{k+1}^{-}$$

Although similar in principle, the developed EKF is different in several regards from the EKF described in (Sabatini, 2006). First, the accelerometer bias vector is not part of the state vector; second, the test (18) does not include the condition on the dip angle, namely the angle between the sensed gravity and magnetic fields; third, the magnetic sensor variance in (18) is made to increase over σ_{ho}^2 based on the magnitude of sub-threshold magnetic disturbances.

More importantly, a central role in the EKF operation is now played by the action of the movement detector, Fig. 1. The gyro output signal feeds the movement detector, the function of which is to discriminate conditions of presence and absence of movement by submitting the norm of the measured angular velocity vector to a threshold-based detector. The movement detector helps identify, in each gait cycle, the time interval between heel-off and foot-flat, when the foot instep swings and gyro data can be exploited by the EKF to update the estimate of the state vector. Conversely, when the foot instep is detected to be steady at 0 °/s, the EKF does not run and its initialization at first contact is performed by applying the TRIAD algorithm to the aiding sensors' information available before the heel-off transition, in preparation for the next gait cycle.

It is the outcome of the measurement validation tests (18)-(19) which drives the alternation between EKF initializations during stance and EKF runs during swings. If the test (19) fails at the time when the movement detector signals the transition from absence to presence of movement, the EKF initialization is not actually carried out, and the EKF processing is extended to the following gait cycle. Conversely, upon successful termination of the test (19), it is the outcome of the test (18) to prescribe whether body-fixed magnetic sensor measurements are subject to bias compensation before applying the TRIAD algorithm. Whilst no bias compensation takes place when the test (18) is successfully terminated, the estimate of the bias vector delivered by the EKF at the time when the test (18) fails is used for compensation purposes in what we call the iterated-TRIAD algorithm. The movement detector may be unable to cope with small changes of orientation when non-walking activities, e.g., foot shuffling during rest periods, are chained with epochs of normal walking; hence, the EKF-estimated bias vector has to be resolved in B without knowing the rotation quaternion, which is, indeed, the quantity that the TRIAD algorithm would determine using quasi-static acceleration and bias-corrected magnetic field measurements. The estimate of the state vector delivered by the EKF at the time when the test (18) fails helps correct body-fixed magnetic sensor measurements before applying the TRIAD algorithm. The quaternion determined by the TRIAD algorithm is then used to refine the estimate of the bias vector in B, before applying the TRIAD algorithm again. The interplay between applications of the TRIAD algorithm and refinements of the bias vector estimate resolved in *B* proceeds iteratively, until convergence is reached – this occurs either when the difference between rotation quaternions determined in successive iterations is smaller than a given threshold, or when a maximum number of iterations is elapsed.

The gravity compensation of acceleration components is performed using the rotation quaternion estimated from the EKF. In order to maximally benefit from the zero velocity update, the velocity estimate is reset with each time interval between heel-off and foot flat (determined by the movement detector), before embarking in the second integration which helps update the position of the foot instep relative to *E* from its most recent position fix.

3.3 Experimental validation

The dead-reckoning navigation algorithm was tested in a series of walking trials with data acquired from a shoe-mounted IMMU, Fig. 2.

A MicroStrain 3DM-GX1 sensor device embedded with a tri-axis gyro, accelerometer, and magnetic sensor (MicroStrain Inc., Williston, VT, U.S.A.) was placed on the instep of the (left) foot and attached snugly to the shoe under the shoe-laces. The device was interfaced to a PC via a serial communication interface (RS232 communication protocol, baud rate: 115.200 bps). The raw sensory data were delivered at a sampling rate of about 77 Hz, and submitted to off-line processing using Matlab v. 6.0. After the raw data were filtered with a second-order forward-backward low-pass Butterworth filter (cut-off frequency: 10 Hz), the rotation quaternion was determined by directly time-propagating (4) over the whole data-set. Zero velocity updates applied to gravity-compensated acceleration components and successive integration of detrended velocity components enabled to produce the displacements of the foot instep from the start position.

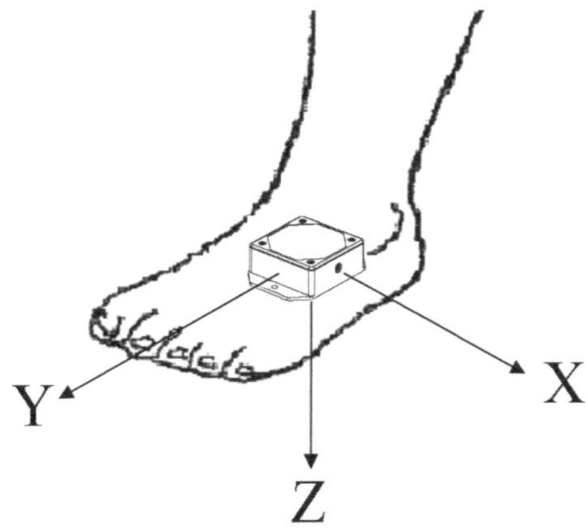

Fig. 2. Shoe-mounted IMMU, with the body-fixed reference frame superimposed.

Two EKF implementations were considered, henceforth called Method A and Method B. The difference between them was that the alternation between EKF initializations during stance and EKF runs during swings was adaptive, since it was based on the outcome of the measurement validation tests (18)-(19), and required to perform bias compensation of body-fixed magnetic sensor measurements, as prescribed by the TRIAD algorithm (Method A); conversely, the alternation was not adaptive and the TRIAD algorithm was applied without bias compensation in Method B.

The experimental validation consisted of walking along an outdoor path whose length was about 680 m, with overall changes in altitude of about 40 m. The path was walked in about 13 min. The instructions to the user were to walk in a stop-and-go fashion: walk ten consecutive strides before taking a brief rest, then walk ten consecutive strides, and so forth. The walker was also asked to turn around on himself at some point along the path, and the path traveled so far was then traced back. The truth-reference trajectory was constructed using a handheld GPS receiver (eMap, Garmin International Inc., Olathe, Kansas, U.S.A.), which was manually commanded by the user to store a way-point any time he rested between successive blocks of ten strides. In the open environment where the experiment was performed, the number of satellites in view was always between 5 and 7, hence the GPS receiver worked in nearly optimal conditions.

The EKF parameters were hand-crafted carefully by standard trial-and-error procedures. In our testing environment, a good parameter setting was the following: $\sigma_g = 0.6\ °/\text{s}$, $\sigma_w = 1$ mGauss, $\sigma_{ho} = 1$ mGauss, $\sigma_a = 10$ mg. Additionally, as for the measurement validation tests (18)-(19), we choose $\varepsilon_m = 10$ mGauss, $\varepsilon_a = 0.1$ m/s^2, and $k_a T_s = 0.1$ s.

The filtering performance metrics was based on the root mean square (RMS) of the horizontal and vertical positioning error Δp_h and Δp_v, respectively, which were computed, together with the three-dimensional positioning error Δp.

4. Results

The time functions of the angular velocity (vector norm and X-axis component) sensed by the tri-axis gyro in two movement epochs occurring during the outdoor walking trial are reported in Fig. 3. The two movement epochs correspond to a representative downhill gait cycle, and to the user's turn-around maneuver.

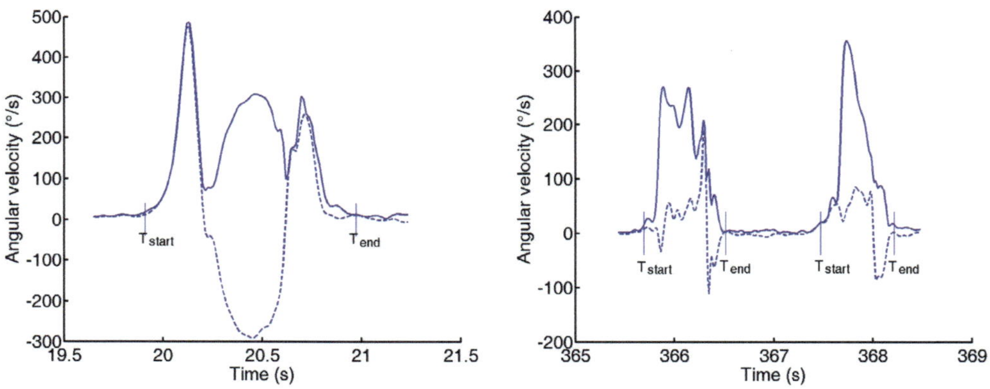

Fig. 3. Time function of the angular velocity sensed by the tri-axis gyro.
Solid line: vector norm; dashed line: X-axis component.
(a): representative gait cycle;
(b): movement patterns acquired during the turning around maneuver, see text.

The vector norms of the acceleration and magnetic field sensed by the aiding sensors are plotted against the times of alignment at which they are measured in Figs. 4-5.

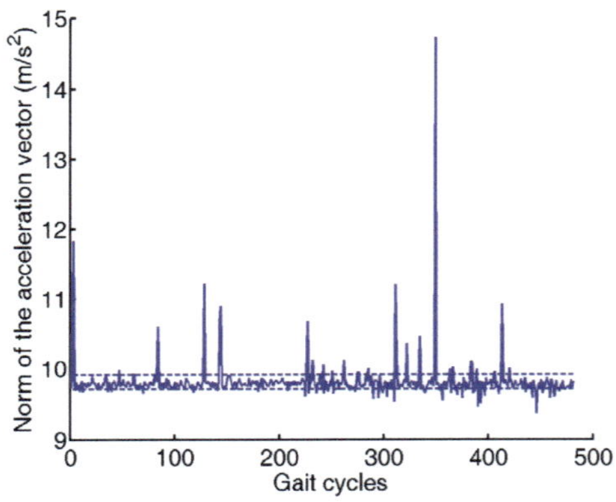

Fig. 4. Vector norm of the acceleration sensed by the tri-axis accelerometer at the time of alignment, as a function of the number of gait cycles.

The number of rejections issued by the measurement validation tests, normalized to the 481 movement epochs detected by the movement detector, are 7%, 21% and 1.25% (h-rejections, g-rejections and h/g-rejections). The EKF runs may thus have different durations: in particular, for Method A, the duration of each run depends whether (19) accepts the gravity read-out from the accelerometer at start and end times, which leads to the time function plotted in Fig. 6.

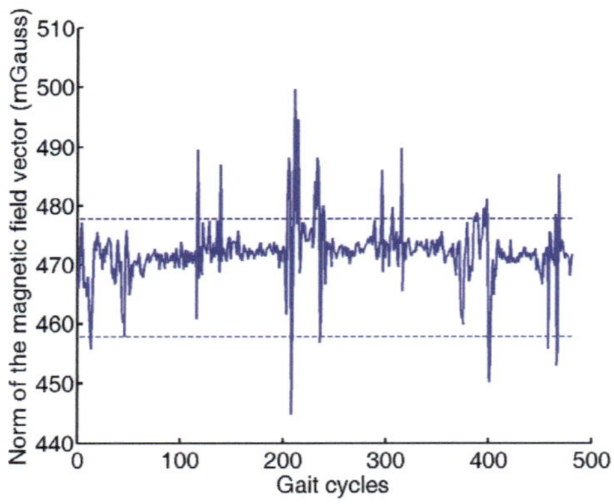

Fig. 5. Vector norm of the magnetic field sensed by the tri-axis magnetic sensor at the time of alignment, as a function of the number of gait cycles.

Conversely, the duration of each strap-down double integration of the gravity-compensated linear acceleration vector is related, for either Method A or B, to the duration of the corresponding movement epoch, see Fig. 7. Table 1 reports the RMS values of Δp achieved by Method A and B (about 0.6% of the total walked distance). If the EKF is run continuously, the positioning errors sum up to 129 m (horizontal) and 2 m (vertical). The DR trajectory, projected in the horizontal plane of the Earth's reference frame, is reported in Fig. 8, with the coordinates of the GPS way-points superimposed to it.

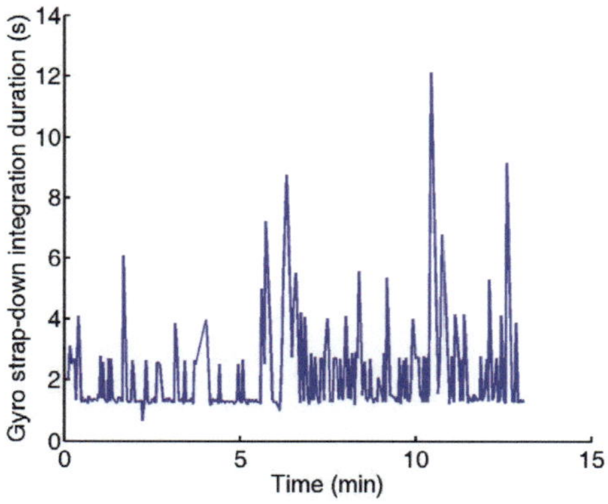

Fig. 6. Time duration of each EKF run, as a function of the time from start.

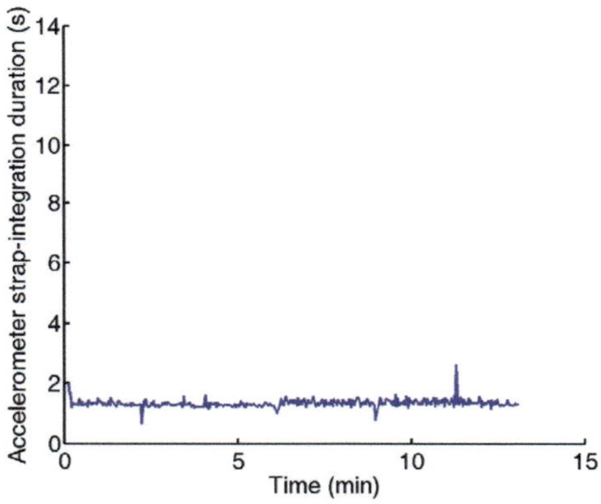

Fig. 7. Time duration of each gait cycle, as a function of the time from start.

	Δp_h [m]	Δp_v [m]	Δp [m]
A	2.1	3.6	4.1
B	2.4	3.7	4.4

Table 1. Values of horizontal, vertical, total positioning errors incurred by Method A and B.

The mean ± SD of the Euler angles of the foot (roll and pitch), measured at the time of alignment from the rotation quaternion delivered by the EKF (Method A), are reported in Table 2.

	uphill	downhill
roll angle [°]	21.6 ± 2.1	36.7 ± 1.5
pitch angle [°]	-16.2 ± 3.3	-5.9 ± 2.5

Table 2. Values of mean and standard deviation of the roll, pitch Euler angles measured at the time of alignment with Method A.

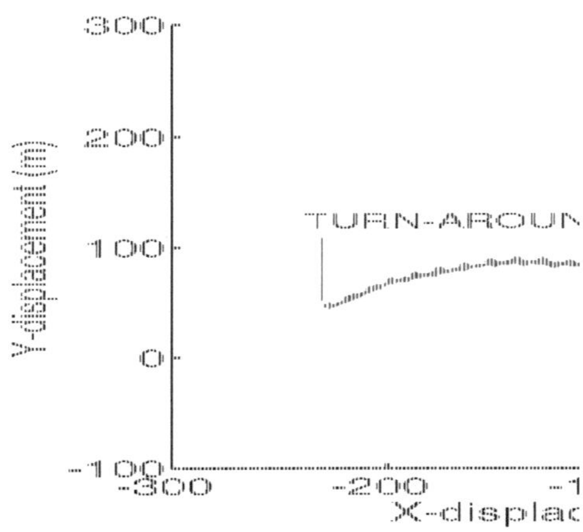

Fig. 8. Dead-reckoning trajectory reconstructed by the IMMU, and superimposed way-points collected from the GPS unit.

The statistics are averaged over the downhill and the uphill portions of the path, separately. Based on these data, the incline of the walking surface (in the direction of travel) turns out to be, on average, 7.5° (relative to the horizontal plane in the Earth's reference frame). The incline, estimated from the horizontal and vertical components of the DR trajectory, turns out to be 7.6° and 7.3° (downhill and uphill portions of the path, respectively).

5. Discussion and conclusions

Both methods A and B behave exactly in the same way when g-rejections do not occur: the procedure of alternation between TRIAD-based EKF initializations and EKF runs in both methods is, indeed, identical, since the movement detection module works for both methods on the same noisy angular velocity vector. However, in the interplay between initialization and run of the EKF, and in the face of the difficulty of performing double integration of gravity-compensated linear accelerations, the movement detector plays a very important role. It is the movement detector which identifies movement epochs based on signal thresholding. In our previous work, we have verified that movement detection is better handled by feeding gyro output signals, rather than acceleration output signals, to a movement detector. In (Sabatini et al., 2005) the signal from a gyro oriented in the user's medio-lateral direction is used for detecting a number of gait events, including heel-strike and toe-off. In order to detect movement epochs based on non-walking patterns, we propose to use here the norm of the angular velocity vector. Figs. 3-4 shows the difference between using the norm or a single component of the angular velocity vector, i.e., the X-axis component, which is approximately in the user's medio-lateral direction. While, for a representative gait cycle, the difference is minimal, the movement detector introduces a small delay when the turn-around maneuver is analyzed via the X-axis gyro output signal.

In the configuration of shoe-mounted IMMU studied in this paper, the threshold setting is not overly difficult, unless the walking speed increases too much, such that time intervals when the body part (the foot instep, here) is steady are critical to identify. In this regard, however, it should be pointed out that the accurate tracking of foot movements involved in fast walking, jogging or running is, above all, undermined by limitations in the gyro maximum sensing range. When the thresholds are too low, gyro measurement noise may erroneously lead to identify movement epochs when they do not exist; however, provided that the duration of these movement artifacts is not excessive, their effect on the overall positioning/orientation accuracy is generally quite limited. Due to an inadequately low threshold setting, the motion detector may be missing the end of a movement epoch, with the consequence of delaying the time of the zero velocity update; conversely, when the thresholds are too high, either the start of a movement epoch is delayed, or its end is anticipated, so that a moving body part is misleadingly considered motionless; the consequences are that the EKF initialization step and the zero velocity update are applied at the wrong time. The threshold setting used in this paper is hand-crafted to work properly on the outdoor walking trial data-set.

The DR algorithm we have designed allocates different roles to the IMMU sensors. The gyro is given the task to provide short-term accurate a priori estimates of the state vector, in particular the rotation quaternion. During each EKF run, the acceleration measurements taken from a swinging leg are in fact prevented from influencing the filter behavior by properly applying the measurement validation test (18); meanwhile, the measurement validation test (18) tends to increase the measurement noise variance of the magnetic sensor when it is exposed to external magnetic disturbances over the value prescribed in a magnetically clean environment, so that, when the a posteriori estimate of the vector state has to be formed, the EKF tends to put more confidence on the a priori estimate than on the actual sensor measurements. Since the tri-axis gyro in our shoe-mounted IMMU is thermally compensated, it is sufficient to capture the bias offset at the start of the experimental session to have a well-calibrated sensor for several minutes before the next bias capture, which can be performed anytime the tri-axis gyro is detected to be motionless. In our approach, the effects of random walk errors due to gyro wideband noise integration are counteracted by letting the EKF to run over single movement epochs, i.e., single strides in the case of normal gait. We remind that, in Method A, the g-rejections tend to increase the duration of the EKF run, and to delay the application of the TRIAD algorithm until quasi-static gravity read-outs are available. The magnetic measurements are bias-compensated for use by the iterated-TRIAD algorithm, depending on whether an h-rejection occurs at the time of alignment or not; conversely, the zero velocity updates are applied to gravity-compensated linear accelerations as frequently as possible.

The results of the outdoor walking trial indicate that positioning errors are less than 0.6% for both Method A and B, with a slight preference for Method A. Of course, this conclusion would be taken with care, because the truth-reference is, on its own, affected by errors (RMS of about 5 m are declared by the manufacturer). However, it is interesting that a relatively low-cost GPS unit shows similar levels of accuracy of a simple IMMU when a) the GPS works in nearly optimal conditions b) the IMMU works over a temporal horizon for which, it is quoted, would be very difficult to keep the error growth small (Foxlin, 2002).

It is interesting to note that the outdoor walking trial is traveled over an asphalt road, whose incline (in the direction of movement) is approximately constant. After few strides taken on a level surface, the path is traveled, first downhill, up to the time of turning around, and then uphill. That the first strides are taken on a level surface, it is important, because the first step of our computational procedure is to register the sensor frame to the reference frame. First, the unit is calibrated; second, the unit is placed on the level walking surface, and the expression of the referential magnetic field is estimated from the calibrated magnetic sensor measurements.

Because of the axis arrangement, the difference in the roll angle estimated uphill and downhill would give an indication of the slope of the walking surface. An estimation of the same quantity comes from taking the horizontal and vertical displacements. Since the agreement between these two estimates turns out to be quite good, we can speculate that the foot posture at the time of alignment is estimated reasonably well in terms of roll and pitch angles. By closer examination of the filtering results, it is the foot yaw angle estimate to be critical, which may lead to catastrophic results especially when the gyro integration is left free running.

In conclusion, an adaptive quaternion-based EKF algorithm is developed in this paper to process the sensory data from a fully integrated IMMU, deployed in a shoe-mounted PNS. The traveled path is then reconstructed by stride-wise strap-down double integration of foot accelerations resolved in the navigation frame. In order to make the filtering process robust against the disturbances which may affect the IMMU sensors , several tricks are considered:

- adaptation of the measurement noise covariance matrix during EKF runs;
- adaptive alternation between initialization and run of the EKF, so as to refine the estimation of either the rotation quaternion or the magnetic sensor bias vector - this is based on stance/swing phase gait detection driven by gyroscopic data, and accelerometric/magnetic measurement validation;
- bias-correction of the magnetic sensor measurements before using them for initializing each EKF run;
- stride-wise integration of gravity-compensated acceleration components with zero velocity updates performed once every movement epoch is detected.

Preliminary experimental results are offered in support of the use of inertial/magnetic sensing and EKF for implementing dead-reckoning algorithms in applications of personal navigation.

6. Acknowledgement

This work has been supported, in part, by funds from the Italian Ministry of University and Research. The author is indebted to Dr. Vincenzo Genovese, for his help in programming the PC sensor interface used for data collection.

7. References

Elwell J. (1999). Inertial navigation for the urban warrior. *Proceedings SPIE,* vol. 3709, pp. 196-204, Orlando, FL, USA, 7-8 April 1999.

Fang L.; Antsaklis, P.J., Montestruque, L.A., McMickell, B., Lemmon, M., Sun, Y., Fang H., Koutroulis, I., Haenggi, M., Xie, M. & Xie, X. (2005). Design of a wireless assisted pedestrian dead reckoning system - The NavMote experience. *IEEE Trans. Instrum. Meas.*, Vol. 54, No. 6, pp. 2342-2358.

Foxlin, E. (2002). Motion tracking requirements and technologies, In: *Handbook of virtual environment technologies,* K. Stanney, (Ed.), pp. 163-210, Lawrence Erlbaum Publishers, Hillsdale, NJ, USA.

Gebre-Egziabher D.; Elkaim G.H., Powell J.D. & Parkinson B.W. (2000). A gyro-free quaternion-based attitude determination system suitable for implementation using low cost sensors. *Proc. IEEE Position, Location and Navigation Symposium,* pp. 185-192, San Diego, CA, USA, 13-16 March, 2000.

Jirawimut, R.; Ptasinski, P., Garaj, V., Cecelja, F. & Balachandran, W. (2003). A method for dead reckoning parameter correction in pedestrian navigation system. *IEEE Trans. Instrum. Meas.*, Vol. 52, No. 1, pp. 209-215.

Ladetto, Q. & Merminod B. (2002). In step with INS - navigation for the blind, tracking emergency crews. *GPS World,* October 2002, pp. 30-38.

Lee, S.-W. & Mase K. (2002). Activity and location recognition using wearable sensors. *Pervasive Computing,* Vol. 1, No. 1, pp. 24-32.

Perrin O.; Terrier, P., Ladetto, Q., Merminod, B. & Schutz, Y. (2000). Improvement of walking speed prediction by accelerometry and altimetry, validated by satellite positioning. *Med. Biol. Eng. Comput.*, Vol. 38, No. 2, pp. 164—168.

Sabatini, A.M. (2005). Quaternion based strap-down integration method for applications of inertial sensing to gait analysis. *Med. Biol. Eng. Comp.,* Vol. 43, No. 1, pp. 94-101.

Sabatini, A.M.; Martelloni, C., Scapellato, S., & Cavallo, F. (2005). Assessment of walking features from foot inertial sensing. *IEEE Trans. Biomed. Eng.*, Vol. 52, No. 3, pp. 486-494.

Sabatini, A.M. (2006). Quaternion based Extended Kalman filter for determining orientation by inertial and magnetic sensing. *IEEE Trans. Biomed. Eng.*, Vol. 53, No. 7, pp. 1346-1356.

Shuster, M.D. & Oh S.D. (1981). Three-axis attitude determination from vector observations. *J. Guidance and Control,* Vol. 4, No. 1, pp. 70-77.

Stirling, R.; Fyfe, K. & Lachapelle, G. (2005). Evaluation of a new method of heading estimation for pedestrian dead reckoning using shoe mounted sensors. *Journal of Navigation,* Vol. 58, No. 1, pp. 31-45.

Veltink, P.H.; Slycke, P. , Hemssems, J., Buschman, R., Bulstra, G. & Hermens, H. (2003). Three dimensional inertial sensing of foot movements for automatic tuning of a two-channel implantable drop-foot stimulator. *Med. Eng. Phys.*, Vol. 25, No. 1, pp. 21—28.

Welch, G. & Foxlin E. (2002). Motion tracking: no silver bullet, but a respectable arsenal. *IEEE Computer Graphics and Applications,* Vol. 22, No. 6, pp. 24-38.

Yun, X. & Bachmann, E.R. (2006). Design, implementation, and experimental results of a quaternion-based Kalman filter for human body motion tracking. *IEEE Trans. Robotics*, Vol. 22, No. 6, pp. 1216–1227.

12

Ultrasonic-Based Distance Measurement Through Discrete Extended Kalman Filter

Leopoldo Angrisani, Aldo Baccigalupi and Rosario Schiano Lo Moriello
Università degli Studi di Napoli
Italy

1. Introduction

Ultrasonic-based measurements are extensively used both in research and production field, spanning in endless applications: environment sensing of autonomous mobile robots, high definition imaging of biomedical devices, precise location of micro-flaws in materials, accurate estimation of the level of flammable fluids or dangerous rivers, and so on. The reason of this success mainly relies upon the opportunity offered by ultrasonics of conceiving rather simple methods or building up relatively cheap meters, characterized by satisfactory accuracy, reduced measurement time, and, above all, high level of intrinsic safety.

The measuring principle of most methods is the estimation of the time-of-flight (TOF) of an ultrasonic burst (high-frequency sinusoidal pulse train) generated by a proper transducer; i.e. the time elapsing between the firing up of the transducer and the detection of the echo originated by any discontinuity or reflector in the propagation medium. The desired information, x, concerning distance (the object of unknown distance acts like a reflector), or level (the surface of the fluid of unknown level gives rise to a discontinuity), or integrity (any crack in the structure under test disturbs medium continuity) is then gained through a very common and straightforward expression:

$$x = \frac{c \cdot t}{2} \tag{1}$$

where c is the propagation velocity of the ultrasonic burst, and t is the TOF estimate.

Two sequential steps generally characterize TOF-based measurements. The first step provides for the digitization of the received ultrasonic signal through a data acquisition system (DAS), while in the second one a suitable digital signal-processing (DSP) algorithm is applied to the acquired samples for the desired TOF to be estimated. Major sources of inaccuracy can be found in additive noise affecting the acquired ultrasonic signal, shape distortion of the received echo, and dependence on temperature of the propagation velocity.

To face noise problems, DSP algorithms implementing the cross-correlation estimator (CCE), or matched filter, have been proposed. In the presence of additive, zero mean, white Gaussian noise, the CCE is, in fact, proven to be optimal according to maximum likelihood criterion, provided that no shape distortion of the received echo occurs. When the last assumption is violated, TOF estimates become significantly biased, and the amount of bias can be much greater than the experimental standard deviation.

To mitigate distortion effects, generalized versions of the conventional CCE have been defined and implemented. More specifically, parametric models of the echo envelope, which produce a sort of correlation function, are built concurrently with the process of TOF estimation. Benefits in bias reduction are, however, gained to the detriment of noise sensitivity and, above all, computational burden.

Concerning the influence of temperature in TOF-based measurements, the most popular method for avoiding accuracy loss is to duly check its value by an external sensor. Straightforward relations, in fact, apply for establishing the actual propagation velocity according to the current value of the temperature.

An original use of *discrete extended Kalman filter* (DEKF) is presented in the following to face the aforementioned problems. The novelty of the method mainly relies upon its capability of jointly estimating the whole set of parameters (A_0, α, T, and τ) that characterize the well-known model of echo envelope, $A(t)$:

$$A(t) = A_0\left(\frac{t-\tau}{T}\right)^{\alpha} \exp\left(\frac{t-\tau}{T}\right) \tag{2}$$

A_0 accounts for echo amplitude, α and T are peculiar to the specific ultrasonic transducer, and τ is the desired TOF [4]-[6]. The main advantage of the new approach is that TOF estimation inherently accounts for distortions the ultrasonic echo eventually undergoes, with a consequent positive effect on bias reduction. An original use of the DEKF allows the desired joint estimation of the aforementioned four parameters to be pursued. Specifically, after modeling the echo envelope as a stochastic process whose state is identified by the considered parameters, the DEKF provides a robust and reliable solution of the non-linear equation system involved.

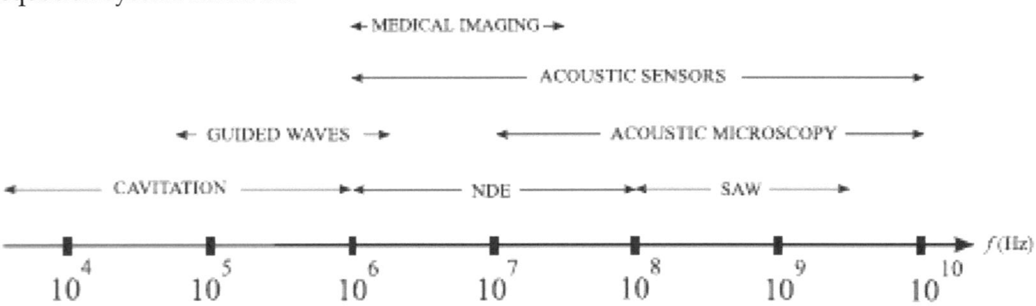

Fig. 1. Common frequency ranges for various ultrasonic processes.

2. Ultrasonic-based distance measurement: state of the art

The contactless and cheap measurement of distances in the range of a few millimiters to a few meters is a strategic task in several fields [1]-[3]. Although several solutions providing good accuracy can be conceived, for example optical solutions which are based on lasers or position sensitive devices, such solutions are usually rather expensive. In addition, in several cases the use of lasers or other high-power systems cannot be accepted in hazardous environments or when low energy devices are prescribed [4]. In these cases low-power ultrasonic sensors are a cost-effective solution, especially when low-frequency devices (30-50 kHz) are used [5]-[7]. What are ultrasounds? Like the visible spectrum, the audio spectrum corresponds to the standard human receptor response function and covers a frequency range from 20 Hz to 20 kHz, although, with age, the upper limit is reduced significantly. For both light and sound, the "human band" is only a tiny slice of the total available bandwidth. In each case the full bandwidth can be described by a complete and unique theory, that of electromagnetic waves for optics and the theory of stress waves in material media for acoustics. Ultrasonics is defined as that band above 20 kHz. It continues up into the MHz range and finally, at around 1 GHz, goes over into what is conventionally called the *hypersonic* regime. The full spectrum is shown in Fig.1, where typical ranges for the phenomena of interest are indicated. Most of the applications of interest take place in the range of 1 to 100 MHz, corresponding to wavelengths in a typical solid of approximately 1 mm to 10 μm, where an average sound velocity is about 5000 m/s. In water—the most widely used liquid—the sound velocity is about 1500 m/s, with wavelengths of the order of 3 mm to 30 μm for the above frequency range.

An advantage of measuring methods exploiting ultrasonic waves is that they enable the direct accomplishment of a digital measurement without the need for conversion of an analog signal to a digital one by an analog-to digital converter (ADC). In most applications, either the velocity of the ultrasonic wave or the time of flight of a wave over the measured distance is utilized. From a technological point of view, another advantage is that the propagation velocity of ultrasonic waves is many orders lower than that of electromagnetic waves. Because of this, less stringent demands are required on the transducers and associated electronic circuits. On the other hand, the use of ultrasonic waves has certain drawbacks too, in particular the large dependence of their propagation velocity on the parameters of the propagation medium, and their high attenuation and scattering, especially in air.

These circumstances determine the boundaries for the full exploitation of ultrasonic measuring methods. In the first instance, they are limited to relatively small distances, compared with methods employing electromagnetic radiation. In case where more accurate measurements are required, ultrasonic techniques become more complicated due to the need to compensate for the effects of fluctuations of the parameters of the propagation medium. In the following, some general methods are described which are most often used for in-air distance measurement.

2.1 Classification of measurement methods

Measuring methods can roughly be divided into two fundamental groups. One of them uses a continuous (harmonic, periodic) wave motion, the other one uses discontinuous (pulsed) waves. The case of harmonic ultrasonic waves is commonly used to evaluate the phase shift between the transmitted and the received signals. The phase change is dependent on the measured quantity, e.g. a distance, in an unchanged and stationary medium, on the composition the (fluid) medium at a stationary distance between the transducers, and on the medium flow rate, temperature, etc. Therefore, these methods can be included in the group of methods which use phase modulation.

In the case of measurements involving a pulsed ultrasonic wave, the duration of the pulse propagation, from the transmitter (pulse generator) to the receiver (pulse front detector), is usually evaluated. The duration of the pulse propagation depends on the transmitter-receiver distance, as well as on the properties (and the motion) of the intervening medium.

It is worth noting that it is possible for the same transducer to act as transmitter and receiver, thus allowing a reduction of complexity of the meter. Generally this method can be classified among those using time-pulse modulation. In the case of the detection of a reflected pulsed ultrasonic wave from an object, the method is analogous to the radiolocation method. Both methods have advantages and drawbacks of their own.
It is worth noting that, although accurate, the phase determination is insufficient for the evaluation of the pulse propagation because the result has a periodicity of one carrier wavelength. This way, in the following, measuring methods using pulsed ultrasonic waves will only be analyzed in details; in particular, the most interesting solutions, in order of increasing measurement reliability, are presented.

2.2 Measurement method based on threshold detection

As stated above, pulse methods evaluate the time of propagation (i.e. the time of flight, TOF) of an ultrasonic pulse wave from a transmitted to a receiver. For the case of distance measurement, a typical example of a digital evaluation of the TOF [8] is illustrated in Fig.2.
At the start of a measurement, a pulse generator excites a voltage pulse, V_i. This is converted in the transmitter to an ultrasonic pulse which propagates towards the receiver at a velocity *c*. After the front edge of the pulse wave falls on the active surface of the receiver, a voltage, V_a, appears at the amplifier output. When the amplitude of the received signal overcome a fixed threshold the echo is assumed to be detected, and the time measuring pulse, V_p is stopped. The conversion of the pulse propagation time into a number N_x is then carried out by a circuit depicted in the lower part of Fig.2.a; at its input there is a bistable circuit whose output is set to the active (logical one) state.

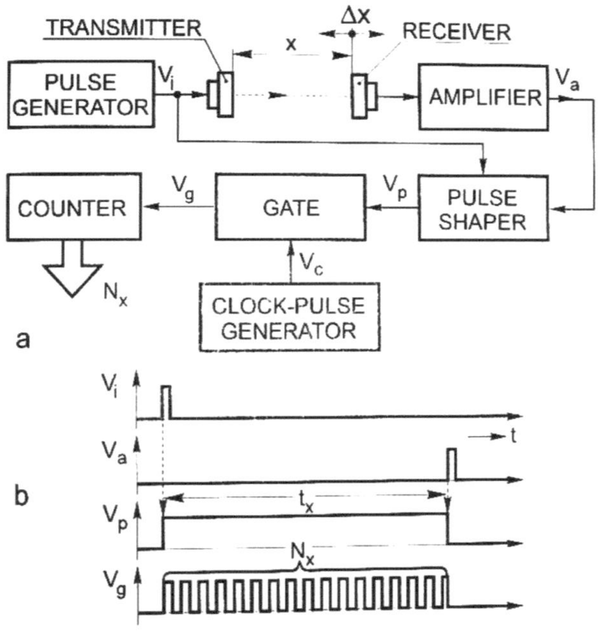

Fig. 2. Measurement of distance through threshold-based method.

This results in the opening of the gate through which pulses, V_c, begin to pass from the clock (time mark) generator to a reversible counter. After arrival of the pulse V_a, the bistable

returns to its initial (zero) state and the measurement is over. On the counter display, a number N_x appears which corresponds to the measured distance. The process described is illustrated in the time diagrams of Fig.2.b.
The measured distance, x, can be expressed through the propagation time, TOF, of the ultrasonic wave as

$$x = cTOF \quad or \quad x = \frac{c}{2}TOF \tag{3}$$

according to the type (direct or reflected) of performed measurement. At the same time, it is also true that N_x=fTOF, where f stands for the clock fundamental frequency. By considering the inherent error of the time-to-digital conversion (i.e. the quantization error), it can be written

$$x = \left(\frac{c}{f}\right)(N_x \pm 1) \tag{4}$$

In order to read the distance in a straightforward way in length units, its value should be expressed in decimal order of tens. In order to lower the discretization error, the working frequency of the clock is chosen sufficiently high (as a rule, tens of MHz are used). As an example, if 20 °C is the environmental temperature in the working space, the frequency can be 34.37 MHz. On measuring a distance of x=1 m, there is a reading N_x of 100000±1 on the counter display; the resolution is then 10 μm.
The threshold method proves itself very easy and simple to realize on actual sensor. Its main drawback is the uncertainty associated to the instant of detection of the received signal. As for all the similar threshold method, the echo receiver suffers from noise sensitivity: in fact, spike superimposed to the useful signal can give rise to spurious identification of the TOF. Finally, the threshold does not identify the right onset of the signal; this way, the obtained measurements are unavoidably biased. The problem is makes worse in the presence of signal shape distortion.

2.3 Measurement methods based on cross-correlation estimator

Measurement method based only on cross-correlation estimator

When higher accuracy are required, methods based on cross correlation estimator are suggested [9]. Measurement of the time of flight can be considered in the general framework of time delay estimation. The transducer generates a signal, $s(t)$, that propagates to the target and is reflected back, being detected after a delay D. The TOF measurement system has to determine this time interval.
The propagating medium introduces attenuation that increases with frequency, and can distort the reflected wave. However, if the pulse is narrow-band, attenuation by a constant coefficient α can be assumed for the delayed echo, so that one can express it in the form $\alpha s(t\text{-}D)$. In practice, these hypotheses are satisfied only approximately. Furthermore, external disturbances such as turbulence and vibrations may affect the signal waveform, and quantization noise is introduced by the conversion process. The measurement system acquires the two digital sequences $x_T(nT)$ and $x_E(nT)$ representing the transmitted and echo signals, respectively, that can be written in the form

$$x_T(nT) = s(nT) + v(nT)$$
$$x_E(nT) = \alpha s(nT) + n(nT) \tag{5}$$

where T is the sampling interval, while $v(nT)$ and $n(nT)$ take into account the discrepancies from the ideal model and can be considered as zero mean uncorrelated random processes. It is worth noting that the transmitted signal, $x_T(nT)$, is taken as reference, and the cross-correlation function is always evaluated through this signal. The cross-correlation of the two sequences is given by:

$$C(kT) = \sum_{n=-\infty}^{n=\infty} x_T(nT) x_E(nT + kT) \tag{6}$$

According to the hypotheses given above on $v(nT)$ and $n(nT)$, the statistical expectation of this sequence is:

$$E[C(kT)] = \alpha C_{ss}(\tau - D)\big|_{\tau = kT} \tag{7}$$

where $C_{SS}(\tau)$ is the auto-correlation function of the continuous signal $s(t)$. Therefore, if k_D is the index of the peak of $E[C(kT)]$, it can be stated that $D = k_D T$ when the delay is an integer multiple of the sampling interval, and $D = (k_D + \delta)T$, with $|\delta| < 0.5$, otherwise. In practice, the delay can be estimated by finding the maximum of the cross-correlation function (6). A typical expression of the ultrasonic signal is:

$$s(t) = a(t)\sin(2\pi f_0 t + \phi) \tag{8}$$

where f_0 is the transducer resonant frequency, and the pulse $a(t)$ represents the signal envelope and has finite duration. For this class of signals, the following expression holds:

$$C_{ss}(\tau) = C_{aa}(\tau)\frac{1}{2}\cos(2\pi f_0 \tau) \tag{9}$$

$C_{aa}(\tau)$ stands for the auto-correlation function of the signal envelope $a(t)$. This suggests the possibility of estimating the delay from the cross-correlation function, $C_{aa}(\tau)$, of signal envelopes, with the advantage that improved resolution can be expected, since the sinusoidal term is no longer present. Depending on the distance to be measured, the TOF can be quite large, resulting in very long data sequence if the echo signal is sampled continuously. However, since $s(t)$ in (6) has finite duration, an interval occurs between the transmitted and echo pulses, where the only relevant information is the count of samples falling within.

If the onset of the echo can be detected by some simple experiment, the sequence of echo samples, $x_E(nT)$, can be much shorter. In fact, it suffices that its length N is equal to that of the sampled transmission sequence $x_T(nT)$, the only requirements being that the time interval NT is longer than the duration of $s(t)$ and that the echo is entirely contained in the sequence. If this is the case, the TOF is determined by algebraically adding the delay estimate provided by the algorithm to the number of samples that were counted before the

acquisition of the echo sequence. The main advantage lies in the reduced computations involved in processing shorter sequences.
The first step of the algorithm is to recover from the sequences $x_T(nT)$ and $x_E(nT)$ their sampled envelopes, that will be indicated as $y_T(nT)$ and $y_E(nT)$, respectively. It is apparent from (4) that the transducer output can be interpreted as an amplitude modulated signal having carrier frequency f_0; this suggests the use of demodulation. After analyzing and trying different methods, an usual choice is to realize in digital form a square law envelope detector. This is a simple kind of demodulator that does not require accurately determining the carrier frequency f_0, thus avoiding the need for a specific setup of the system if different ultrasonic transducers must be used. After demodulated, the cross-correlation function of transmitted and received envelope is evaluated according to:

$$C(kKT) = \sum_{n=0}^{(N/K)-1} y_T(nKT) y_E(nKT + kKT)$$
$$k = -\frac{N}{K}+1,\ldots,\frac{N}{K}-1 \tag{10}$$

where K is a suitable decimation factor needed to reduce the number of acquired samples. If the delay D has a fractional component (i.e., $\delta \neq 0$), the peak of the corresponding continuous correlation function does not coincide with the position of the sample of index k_D.
The fractional index δ can be determined from the samples of $C(kKT)$ through an interpolation formula. Although its analytical expression can be given, in most practical cases the relationship is unlikely to be satisfied exactly. Therefore, it was decided to avoid this complication and rely instead on an approximate interpolation formula. Given the samples with index k_D, $k_D - 1$ and $k_D + 1$, a simple second-order polynomial approximation of $C(t)$ yields a parabola, and the fractional index δ is obtained as the abscyssa of its vertex. Dropping for simplicity the term KT from the argument of $C(kKT)$, it can be written:

$$\delta = \frac{C(k_D+1)-C(k_D-1)}{2[2C(k_D)-C(k_D-1)-C(k_D+1)]} \tag{11}$$

Results provided by the cross-correlation estimator have been reported for a set of experiments carried out in the presence of different transducer-to-target distances, with reference distance measurements being obtained by laser interferometry. Experimental data are reported in Tab.1. As suggested by the authors of the paper, all distances are measured with respect to a common reference point; that represents zero distance; the TOF related to this point is always subtracted from subsequent measurements. This enables compensation for a number of possible factors that introduce offsets, such as time delays between the digitizer trigger and the actual start of the transmit pulse, in the evaluation of the origin for measuring distance.

Measurement method based on combined use of cross-correlation estimator and phase shift evaluation

The phase shift method, in addition to the correlation method, has been suggested in order to enhance the accuracy [10]. It relies on the property that, for a sampled cosine signal, one can determine the phase shift from the origin by computing the coefficient of the discrete

Fourier transform (DFT) corresponding to the frequency of this cosine wave. This calculation is more or less complex, depending mainly on the relation between the cosine frequency and the sampling rate.

Reference (mm)	Measured Distances (points)	(mm)	Difference (mm)
0	0	0	—
100.0	146.0	100.7	+0.7
203.5	296.8	204.8	+1.3
306.0	443.7	306.1	+0.1
407.2	589.1	406.5	−0.7
503.8	729.5	503.4	−0.4
600.8	869.8	600.2	−0.6
698.8	1013.6	699.4	+0.6
799.4	1159.1	799.8	+0.4
898.9	1303.5	899.4	+0.5
998.7	1448.7	999.6	+0.9
1101.1	1598.1	1102.7	+1.6
1200.2	1736.9	1198.5	−1.7

Tab. 1. TOF-based distance measurement

If the sampling time is strictly synchronized with the transmission signal, the *phase shift* between transmission and reception *carriers* can be evaluated by computing the phase shift of the received signal from the sampling time reference. A good choice of the sampling rate can simplify the calculation of the corresponding DFT coefficient.
The final TOF resulting from using both methods simultaneously is

$$TOF = \frac{\left(k_D + \dfrac{\alpha}{2\pi}\right)}{f_0} \tag{12}$$

where k_D is the integer number of carrier wavelengths inferred from the correlation result, α the phase shift, and f_0 the carrier frequency. It is worth noting that, although accurate, the phase determination is insufficient for the evaluation of the TOF because the result has a periodicity of one carrier wavelength. Among the positions determined by phase computation, the one which is nearest to the maximum of the cross-correlation parabolic approximation previously determined, is the final value of the measured TOF.
From an operative point of view, the first step of the method consists of applying the aforementioned cross-correlation approach (upper evaluation path in Fig.3). The second path calculates the phase difference between the transmitted and received waves. This value can be computed by using the DFT coefficient of the acquired sample *r(n)* corresponding to the carrier frequency (the transmitted signal is replaced by the synchronous sampling clock). The proper choice of the sampling rate simplifies the calculation of the phase difference. The computed phase-shift has an accuracy mainly limited by the amplitude accuracy of the

samples and thus the resolution of the A/D converter used for digitization. Moreover, simulations has shown that the phase evaluation is significantly less affected by the additive white noise than the cross-correlation peak determination.

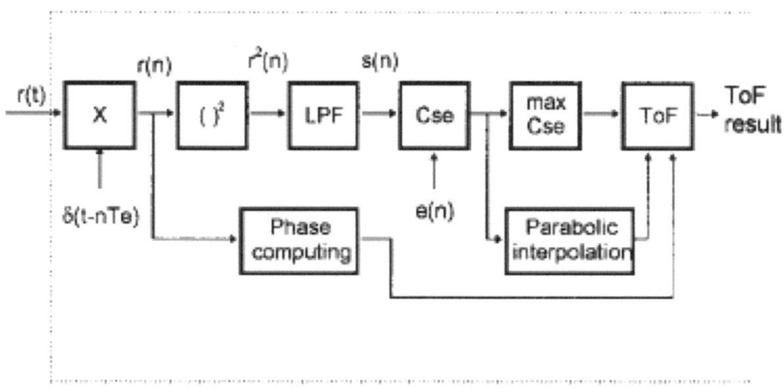

Fig. 3. Measurement algorithm combining cross-correlation estimator and phase shift methods

Results presented by the authors highlight the strong improvement due to the combination of the two methods (Fig.4). For each trial reported in abscissa, gives the distance (expressed in number of carrier wavelengths, λ) computed successively by the correlation-only method (Fig.4.a) and the combined (correlation plus phase; λ = 9 mm) method (Fig.4.b).

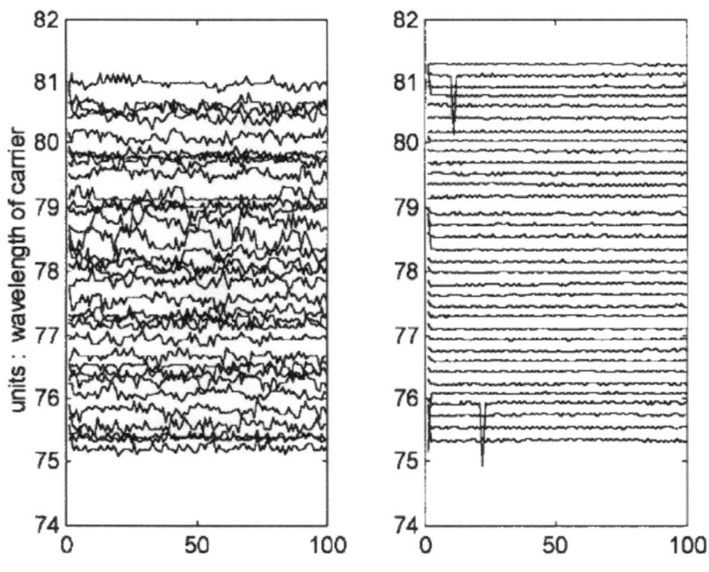

Fig. 4. Measurement results (a) from correlation method and (b) from correlation plus phase method.

Moreover, Fig.5 shows the difference in distance versus the position, of each result for both methods, with reference to the linear regression of the mean results (evaluated upon 100 independent measurements for each distance value) obtained by the combined method ("phase results"). The continuous curves (combined method is the upper curve) are the fluctuations of the mean, the vertical segments are the total excursion of the results at each position, and the dots represent the standard deviations. The pseudoperiodicity of about 4.8 mm, about half of a wavelength at the sampling frequency, of the results obtained by the correlation-only method is explained by a residual effect of the squaring in the computing algorithm due to an imperfect filtering. The computation of the mean standard deviation averaged over all the positions gives for the combined method a value of 0.07 mm.

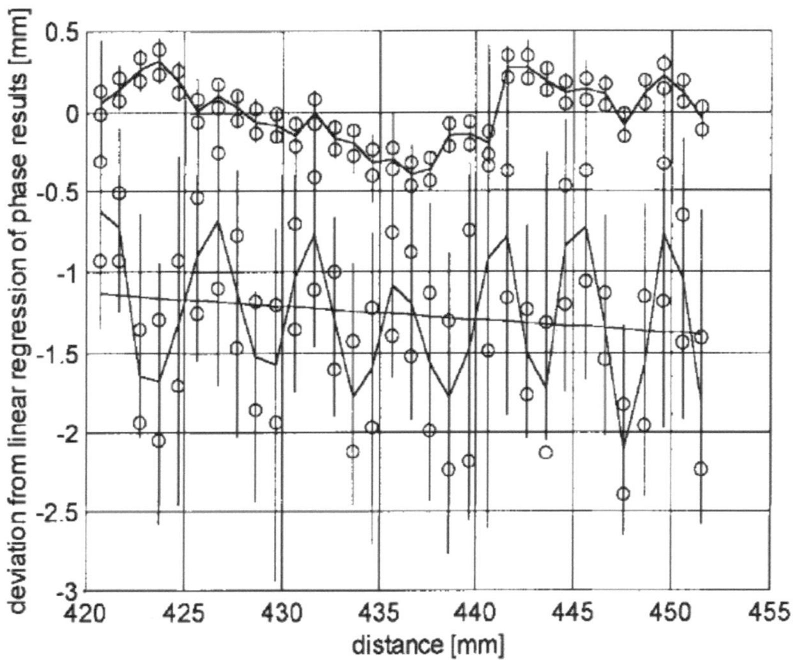

Fig. 5. Distance deviations from linear regression of the mean of results obtained by the combined ("phase") method.

Drawbacks

Despite of the its simplicity, cross-correlation estimation suffers from a dramatic drawback. As aforementioned, it aims at identifying the maximum value of the cross-correlation between the return signal and a properly chosen reference signal [11]. The cross-correlation estimator, or matched filter (MF) is proven to be optimal according to the maximum likelihood (ML) criterion for signals embedded in additive white Gaussian noise with zero mean, provided that time-delayed, amplitude-scaled, nonoverlapping replicas of the reference signal are actually contained in the return signal [12].

When the assumption that the shapes of the received echoes do not change is violated, the estimator is no longer optimal. Usually, the efficiency of non-matched filters is taken as the peak signal-to-noise ratio (SNR) from the non-matched filter divided by the peak SNR from the MF [13]. Actually, the consequence of shape distortions is that the cross-correlation estimator becomes biased, and the amount of bias can be much greater than the standard deviation of the TOF estimates [14]. Echo shape distortions occur in consequence of many factors. The geometrical properties of the insonified reflector play a major role in modifying the echo shape; the position and orientation of the object relative to the ultrasonic sensor, the propagation path, and some environmental factors such as temperature and humidity also have an influence. The ability of modeling the echo shape is thus a requisite that correlation-based ultrasonic sensor systems should possess in order to accomplish object ranging and identification. To overcome the problem of the polarization, some authors suggested the possibility of simultaneously estimating the envelope of a narrowband signal embedded in additive noise and its time delay in the case that the a priori information about the shape of the signal is minimal.

2.4 Measurement method based on generalized cross-correlation estimator

As stated above, most methods facing the problem of the polarization involve techniques for joint distance measurement and model-based estimation of the echo shape. One of the most successful solution is a method based on a truncated series expansion of the echo envelope by a set of Laguerre basis functions [20]. Laguerre functions are widely used in the field of system identification to approximate the impulse response of a causal linear time-invariant stable system [15]. They are exploited in the context of simultaneous system identification and TOF estimation. The outputs of the Laguerre filter bank that computes the running Laguerre transform are used to build a generalized correlation function. The envelope of the echo from an unknown object is represented by the set of expansion coefficients, e.g., the Laguerre spectrum, which we need to estimate together with the unknown TOF. Differently from other generalized cross-correlation techniques [14], a reference signal is not required (unconstrained signal modeling); the only a priori information available to the receiver that may be used to attenuate its noise sensitivity is given by some smoothness conditions regarding the value of the unknown reference signal and of its first time derivative at the signal onset (constrained signal modeling). These signal constraints are motivated by empirical observations of typical ultrasonic sensor signals in a variety of experimental conditions. Let us suppose that the signal observation model is of the form:

$$r(t) = s(t-\tau) + n(t) \tag{13}$$

Here, τ is the TOF to be estimated. $s(t)$ is assumed to be a narrowband signal, with center frequency f_0 (the ultrasonic carrier frequency) and bandwidth $B \ll f_0$. Accordingly, $s(t)$ can be represented in terms of its complex envelope $s(t)$ as follows:

$$s(t) = \Re\{\tilde{s}(t)\exp(j2\pi f_0 t)\} \tag{14}$$

$\Re\{\cdot\}$ indicates the real part of its argument. By definition, the complex envelope of a narrowband signal is a low-pass, complex-valued signal with bandwidth B. Its magnitude $\mu_s(t)$ is the envelope of $s(t)$. The task to be accomplished concerns the joint estimation of $\mu_s(t)$ and τ, in the case that the additive noise $n(t)$ is white Gaussian, having zero mean and power spectral density $N_o/2$.

A typical expression of the envelope $A(t)$ is given in terms of functions

$$A(t) = \left(\frac{t}{T}\right)^m \exp\left(-\frac{t}{T}\right) U(t) \tag{15}$$

with $1 < m < 3$ (damped exponential model with exponent m). T is a transducer-dependent time constant and $U(t)$ is the unit step function.
The Laguerre functions are obtained by orthonormalizing the functions $t^i \exp(-at)$, $i \in N$, $a>0$:

$$l_i(t,a) = \sqrt{2a}\,\exp(-at)\sum_{j=0}^{i} C_j^i \frac{(-2at)^j}{j!} \tag{16}$$

where C_j^i is the binomial coefficient [16], and the parameter a, also called the time scaling factor of the Laguerre series, is related to the pole position of the Laplace transforms of the Laguerre functions. Laguerre functions act the same role of the sinusoidal functions in the Fourier transform; in fact, the nature of typical signals produced by in-air ultrasonic sensors is strongly in support of using a set of Laguerre functions which decay exponentially to zero at a controllable rate for their representation:

$$A(t) \triangleq \sum_{i=0}^{Q} c_i(a) l_i(t,a) \tag{17}$$

Q stands for the model order, and $c_i(a)$ is the i-th coefficient of the Laguerre spectrum. Along with the time-of-flight, t, they are unknown and needed to be estimated from noisy observations of the signal $s(t)$. It should be noted that the time scaling factor a is critical for achieving accurate approximations of a given signal by a truncated series of Laguerre functions. In fact, for any value of the time scaling factor, the Laguerre coefficients are computed by minimizing the approximation error in the least-square sense. Optimal values of a are thus to be computed by searching for the global minimum of the squared error surface of these approximations; the numerical techniques that are available for this purpose are expensive in computational terms [17]. An optimal choice of the time scaling factor also should provide a minimum of significant coefficients of the Laguerre spectrum [18].
In spite that the theory presented concerns Laguerre functions and analog signals, it can take advantage of using sampled signals to implement an equivalent discrete-time version of the correlation receivers. The block diagram of a correlation receiver of order M is depicted in Fig.6. The magnitude $\mu_r(kt)$ of the complex envelope of the return signal is computed by means of the Hilbert transform method [19].
The output of the receiver are the M-th order discrete-time generalized correlation function (GCF) and constraining function (CF). TOF is identified by means of both the functions: in particular, GCF is employed to achieve a rough TOF estimate. One local minimum of the CF then occurs at the same time instant when the GCF takes its global peak, thus allowing TOF to be reliably located (Fig.7).
The performance of the GCF method has been assessed through computer simulations and experimental results using a simple US sensor system. At high SNRs the proposed constrained correlation receiver performs better than conventional matched filters if echo shape distortions not properly accounted for in the selection of the reference signal of the matched filters are present; in fact, such distortions are known to produce biased TOF estimates. The proposed receiver trades the bias removal for the increased noise sensitivity at low SNRs (Fig.8).

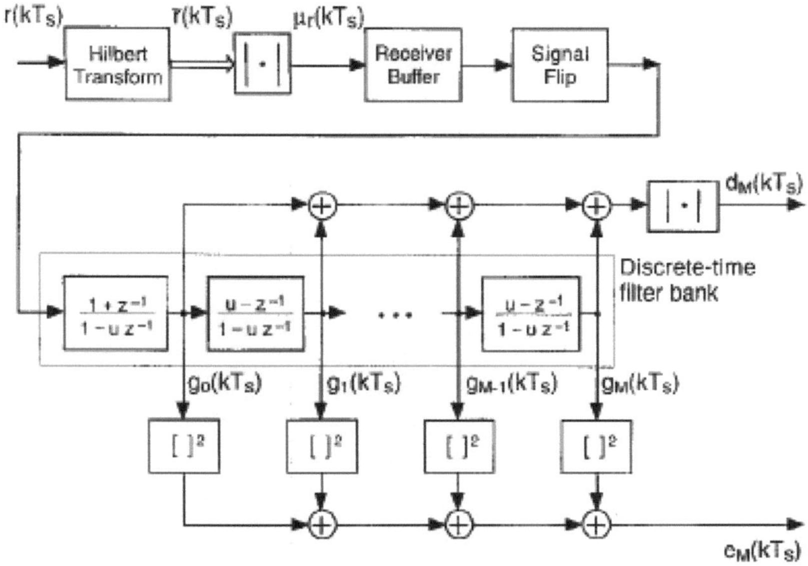

Fig. 6. Block diagram of the correlation receiver.

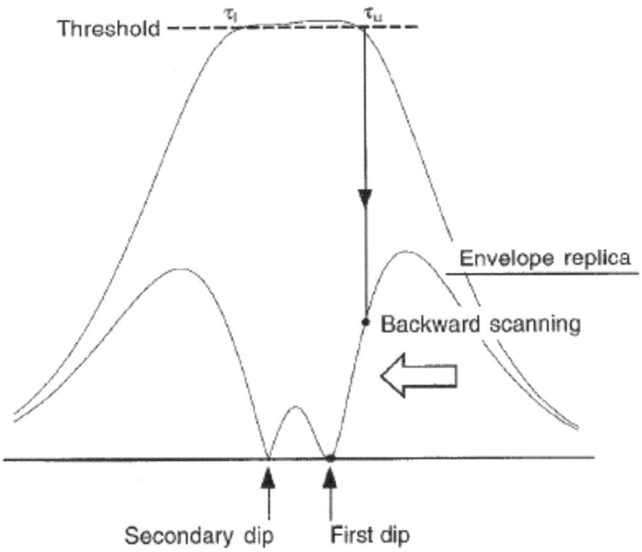

Fig. 7. Explanation of the proposed TOF algorithm (constrained correlation receiver).

3. Measurement method based on discrete extended Kalman filter

3.1 Discrete extended Kalman filter

The Discrete Kalman Filter (DKF) is generally adopted to estimate the state of a linear stochastic process. It uses a kind of feedback control based on measurement results of quantities that are linear functions of the state [9]. More specifically, the filter estimates the process state at a given time instant, and then obtains feedback by incorporating a new measurement result into the *a-priori* estimate in order to gain an improved *a-posteriori* estimate.

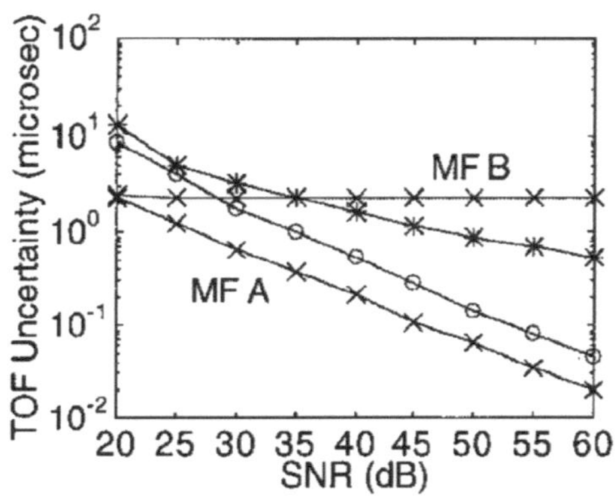

Fig. 8. - TOF estimation accuracy for M=4. MFA stands for unbiased cross correlation estimator, MFB is the biased version, symbol o indicate Constrained correlation receiver, and * identify unconstrained correlation receiver.

In the presence of a non-linear process, the DKF can still be adopted, provided that suitable linearization techniques are applied. Non-linear behaviors should affect the process through either dynamics or measurement equations. In the absence of control inputs, the evolution of a generic, discrete-time, non-linear process can be analyzed through the following non-linear equation system:

$$\begin{cases} x_k = f(x_{k-1}, k-1) + w_{k-1} \\ z_k = h(x_k, k) + v_k \end{cases} \tag{18}$$

where x_k is the current n-dimensional vector of the process state, z_k is the m-dimensional vector of current measurement results, f and h are known functions; $w_k \sim N(0,Q_k)$ and $v_k \sim N(0,R_k)$ are uncorrelated, noisy, Gaussian sequences [7].

Two linearization techniques are available in the literature: *discrete linearized Kalman filter* (DLKF) and *discrete extended Kalman filter* (DEKF). Both of them provides for linear approximation of the effect of small perturbation from a "nominal" value in the state of the non-linear system. DLKF is tailored to applications, such as guidance and control, in which the nominal values of the state variables are fairly well known beforehand. Thus, the estimation problem can effectively be linearized around the nominal trajectory (i.e. the sequence of nominal state vectors). When the process under analysis exhibits hard non-linear behavior, the deviation value of the actual trajectory from the nominal one usually tends to increase with time. In such cases, the higher-order approximation terms cannot be neglected, preventing DLKF to be extensively used.

DEKF gives a simple but effective remedy for this problem; the nominal trajectory is defined "on the fly" as the current best estimate of the actual trajectory. According to the DEKF theory, the actual state vector may be written as:

$$x_k = x_k^N + \delta x_k \tag{19}$$

$x_k^N = \hat{x}_{k-1}^+$ is the nominal trajectory assumed equal to the *a-posteriori* estimate of the state vector obtained at the previous step. If the perturbation, δx_k , has small value, f and h functions can be approximated through their first-order, Taylor's series expansions with respect to x. With this assumption, the evolution of the process may be analyzed through the following implementation equations:

$$\begin{aligned} \hat{x}_k^- &= f(\hat{x}_{k-1}^+, k-1) + \Phi_{k-1}\delta x_{k-1} \\ \hat{P}_k^- &= \Phi_{k-1}\hat{P}_{k-1}^+\Phi_{k-1}^T + Q_k \\ \hat{z}_k^- &= h(\hat{x}_k^-, k) + \mathrm{H}_k \delta x_k \end{aligned} \tag{20}$$

where $\Phi_k = \left.\frac{\partial f(x,k)}{\partial x}\right|_{x=\hat{x}_{k-1}^+}$ is the state transition matrix and $\mathrm{H}_k = \left.\frac{\partial h(x,k)}{\partial x}\right|_{x=\hat{x}_k^-}$ is the measurement sensitivity matrix; $\hat{x}_k^-$, P_k^- and $\hat{z}_k^-$ stands respectively for *a-priori* (predicted) estimate of state vector, error covariance matrix and measurement results.
The resulting discrete-time update equations are

$$\begin{aligned} \hat{x}_k^+ &= \hat{x}_k^- + \overline{K}_k\left(z_k - \hat{z}_k^-\right) \\ \hat{P}_k^+ &= \left(I - \overline{K}_k \mathrm{H}_k\right)\hat{P}_k^- \end{aligned} \tag{21}$$

where $\hat{x}_k^+$ and $\hat{P}_k^+$ are *a-posteriori* (corrected) estimates, and $\overline{K}_k = \hat{P}_k^- \mathrm{H}_k^T \left(\mathrm{H}_k \hat{P}_k^- \mathrm{H}_k^T + R_k\right)^{-1}$ is the Kalman gain. Once evaluated the expression (21) the filter is ready to execute another recursive loop.
In recent scientific works [10],[11], the DEKF has been used to improve the accuracy of ultrasonic-based location systems of robots. In particular, TOF data provided by several ultrasonic sensors and collected as temporal readings are properly fused thanks to the exploitation of some nice properties of the DEKF.
In the following [12],[13], the DEKF is, instead, proposed as an original tool to jointly determine the TOF and shape parameters (A_0, α, and T) characterizing an ultrasonic echo envelope modeled according to:

$$A(t) = A_0\left(\frac{t-\tau}{T}\right)^{\alpha} \exp\left(\frac{t-\tau}{T}\right) \tag{22}$$

Details concerning the suggested use of the DEKF and its action in the framework of the adopted measurement procedure are given below.

3.2 Application of DEKF to ultrasonic echoes

The key idea underlying the proposed use of the DEKF consists of defining the state vector $x=[A_0, \alpha, T, \tau]$ through the considered parameters of the ultrasonic echo envelope. This way, the generic equations system (18) is simplified, since these parameters can be considered constant once the ultrasonic echo has been acquired. Moreover, once $\hat{x}_k^+$ is determined, it is taken as the nominal trajectory for the subsequent recursive loop. With the last assumptions, the perturbation δx_k of the expression (19) is null for each k, while the state transition matrix, Φ_k, reduces itself to the unity matrix, I. Finally, since the state has no superimposed noise, Q_k matrix is always null. The time update equations (21) take so the form:

$$\hat{x}_k^- = \hat{x}_{k-1}^+$$
$$\hat{P}_k^- = \hat{P}_{k-1}^+ \tag{23}$$

With regard to the matrix R_k, it has 1x1 dimension, and its element is the variance of the superimposed measurement noise.
The basic loop of the recursive procedure to evaluate the discrete-time Kalman estimator of the state vector x_k is as follows (Fig.9).

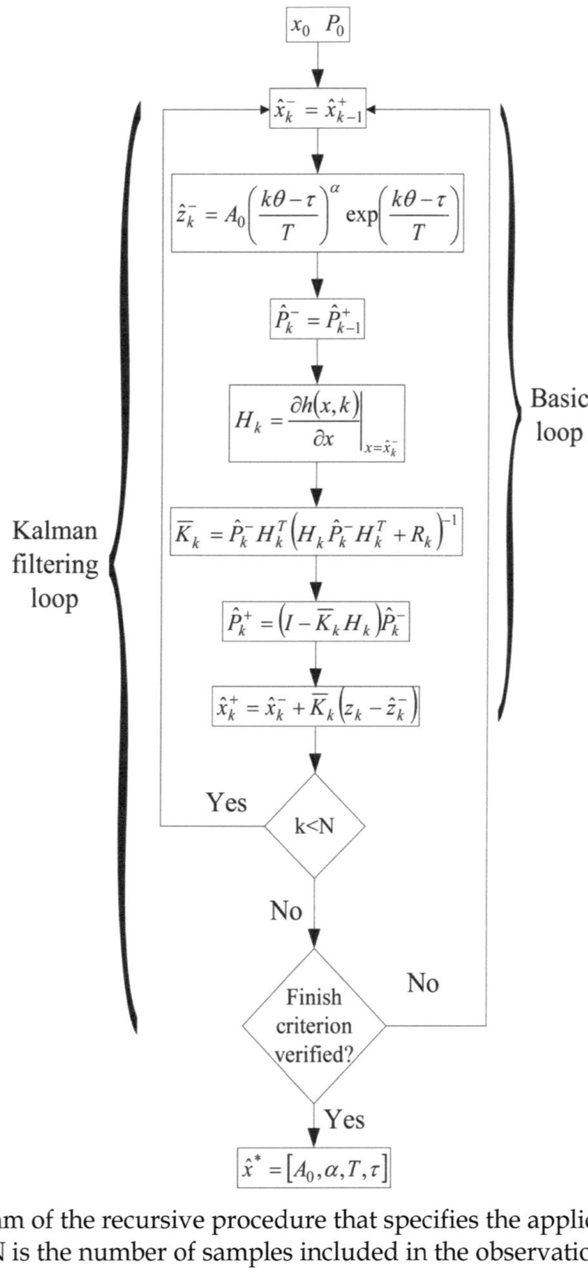

Fig. 9. - Flow diagram of the recursive procedure that specifies the application of DEKF to ultrasonic echoes; N is the number of samples included in the observation interval.

1. *A-priori* estimation of the state vector:

$$\hat{x}_k^- = \hat{x}_{k-1}^+$$

2. *A-priori* estimation of the measurement result through the equation (22):

$$\hat{z}_k^- = A_0 \left(\frac{k\theta - \tau}{T} \right)^{\alpha} \exp\left(\frac{k\theta - \tau}{T} \right)$$

   where θ is the sampling period, and A_0, α, T, and τ represent the values of the parameters obtained at the previous step.

3. *A-priori* estimation of the error covariance matrix:

$$\hat{P}_k^- = \hat{P}_{k-1}^+$$

   the matrix has 4x4 dimension.

4. Evaluation of the measurement sensitivity matrix:

$$\mathrm{H}_k = \left. \frac{\partial h(x,k)}{\partial x} \right|_{x=\hat{x}_k^-}$$

   the matrix has 4x1 dimension.

5. Calculation of the Kalman gain:

$$\overline{K}_k = \hat{P}_k^- \mathrm{H}_k^T \left(\mathrm{H}_k \hat{P}_k^- \mathrm{H}_k^T + R_k \right)^{-1}$$

6. *A-posteriori* estimation of the state vector conditioned on the current measurement result:

$$\hat{x}_k^+ = \hat{x}_k^- + \overline{K}_k \left(z_k - \hat{z}_k^- \right)$$

7. *A-posteriori* estimation of the error covariance matrix:

$$\hat{P}_k^+ = \left(I - \overline{K}_k H_k \right) \hat{P}_k^-$$

The basic loop is iterated all along the observation interval including the echo envelope of interest. Once the iteration is over (i.e. the whole observation interval has been examined), a single Kalman filtering loop of the recursive procedure is completed (Fig.9). The recursive procedure stops when a suitable finish condition is met; the elements of the state vector $\hat{x}^*$ corresponding to the last state estimate give the desired parameters of the ultrasonic echo envelope.

3.3 Initial conditions and recursion finish criterion

The described recursive procedure can be executed once *(i)* the starting estimates of the state vector and error covariance matrix, referred to respectively as x_0 and P_0, *(ii)* the experimental variance of measurement noise, R_0, and *(iii)* the recursion finish criterion are available.
With regard to *(i)*, some preliminary considerations are needed. Specifically, the generic element x_i is modeled as random variate, and it can take values in a specific interval $[x_{i1}, x_{i2}]$.

For each parameter, in fact, a suitable range of values has to be fixed according both to their typical interval of variation [14] and user's knowledge and experience. In particular:

1. with regard to A_0, typical values of the amplitude of received echoes should be considered;
2. concerning α, typical slopes that the rising edge of received echoes exhibits in proximity to the onset should be accounted for;
3. referring to T, typical durations of the ultrasonic transmission burst should be enlisted;
4. as for TOF, the related interval is automatically established after the signal preprocessing step of the measurement procedure, details of which are given below.

Assuming a rectangular probability density function for each element x_i, the starting estimates of the element and its variance are given by:

$$\hat{x}_{i0} = \frac{1}{2}(x_{i2} + x_{i1})$$
$$\sigma_{i0}^2 = \frac{1}{12}(x_{i2} - x_{i1})^2 \tag{24}$$

This way, P_0 is a diagonal matrix, the elements of which correspond to the variances of the starting estimates.

As for *(ii)*, the variance of the noise floor of the adopted data acquisition system should be measured.

Concerning *(iii)*, it is worth noting that, if the problem is well-conditioned, a better state vector estimate is achieved for each execution of the Kalman filtering loop. A suitable finish criterion is thus needed. At this aim, the value of the modulus of the difference between the state vector estimates provided by two consecutive Kalman filtering loops is compared to a proper threshold value (empirical tests suggest the value of $1 \cdot 10^{-4}$). If the difference is lower than the threshold, the recursive procedure stops, and the best estimate of the four parameters of the echo envelope is delivered; otherwise, a new Kalman filtering loop is executed.

3.4 Measurement procedure

The fundamental steps of the DEKF-based measurement procedure are described with reference to a clarifying example.

- *Digitization*

The ultrasonic signal is at first digitized by means of a data acquisition system, the characteristics of which, in terms of sample rate and memory depth, have to be chosen appropriately. Specifically, the adopted sample rate, f_c, has to satisfy the Nyquist lower bound, and, along with the memory depth, has to grant an appropriate observation interval according to the desired TOF measurement range.

Fig.10 shows an ultrasonic signal characterized by a center frequency of 43.8 kHz and digitized at sample rate of 250 kS/s; multiple echoes can be noted.

- *Signal pre-processing*

As already stated, the proposed recursive procedure is expected to work on the envelope of the ultrasonic echo of interest. After digitization, pre-processing operations are, thus, needed. In particular, the portion of the digitized signal, accounting for the ultrasonic transmission burst, is firstly cut; in the application example the removed portion covers 2 ms. The envelope of the remaining signal is, then, given by the modulus of its analytical version, attained through an ordinary Hilbert transform (Fig.11). If the transmitted ultrasonic burst undergoes multiple reflections, more than one echo is present in the obtained envelope. As a consequence, the echo of interest (generally, the main one) is, finally, isolated through the location of the maximum of the envelope and the selection of the portion, including this maximum, whose values are not buried in the noise floor (Fig.12).

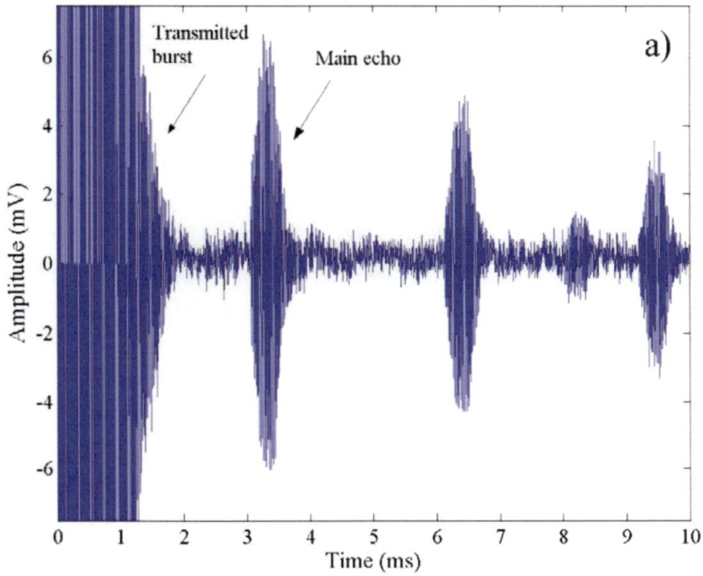

Fig. 10. Fundamental steps of the measurement procedure. a) Original ultrasonic signal digitized at a sample rate of 250 kS/s.

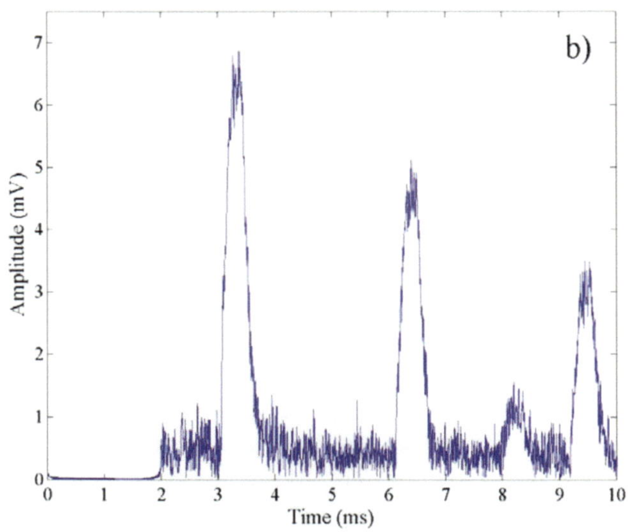

Fig. 11. Fundamental steps of the measurement procedure. b) envelope provided by the Hilbert transform: its null portion accounts for the cut that the original digitized signal has undergone;

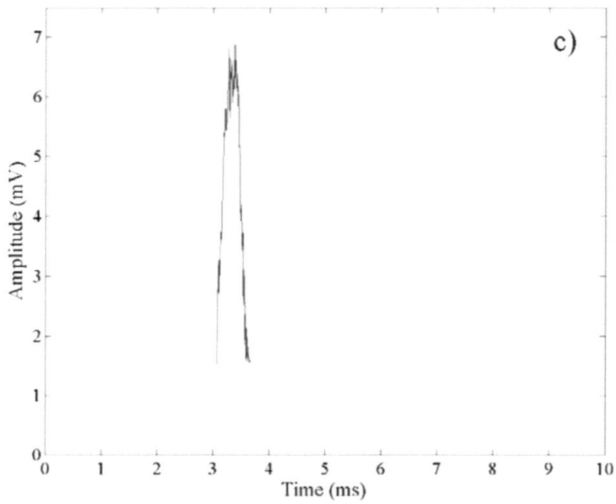

Fig. 12. Fundamental steps of the measurement procedure. c) location and isolation results of the echo of interest.

- *TOF and shape parameters estimation*

Before applying the proposed recursive procedure, the variation interval, $[x_{i1}, x_{i2}]$, of the TOF has to be assigned in order to fix the starting estimates of the TOF itself and its variance, according to what stated above. The upper bound, x_{i2}, is given by the time instant characterizing the first value of the echo of interest obtained at the end of the previous step; in the considered example it is equal to 3.068 ms. The lower bound, x_{i1}, is then gained by subtracting from x_{i1} a suitable number of sampling intervals; the experimental tests have shown that 50 sampling intervals are appropriate to the purpose.

After fixing the initial estimates of the state vector and error covariance matrix, the recursive procedure can run, thus giving, at the end, the wanted values of the TOF and shape parameters of the echo of interest.

Concerning the application example, Fig.13 shows the superposition of the envelope reconstructed by substituting in (22) the values of A_0, α, T, and τ provided by the proposed method to the original digitized signal; it can be appreciated how well the obtained envelope fits the experimental data.

3.5 Performance assessment

To assess the performance of the proposed method, a number of tests on simulated and actual ultrasonic signals have been carried out.

Tests conducted on simulated signals

Ultrasonic echo envelopes have been synthesized numerically in the hypothesis of a sample rate equal to 250 kS/s. The values of the shape parameters are very similar to those peculiar to the actual signals involved in the successive experimental tests. The obtained envelopes have then modulated a sinusoidal carrier, the frequency of which matches that of the ultrasonic transmitter (43.8 kHz) adopted in the experimental tests. The resulting signals have finally been corrupted by additive, white, Gaussian noise.

After fixing the interval of variation of the shape parameters, [3 mV, 30 mV] for A_0, [1, 3] for α, and [100 μs, 150 μs] for T, several tests have been conducted for different values both of

TOF, in order to account for various distances or levels (within 35-175 cm) to be measured, and signal-tonoise ratio, SNR (within 20-60 dB), in order to simulate diverse noise conditions of the measurement chain. For the sake of clarity, Fig.14 shows the superposition of an envelope reconstructed by the proposed method to the related, original signal, characterized by a TOF of 4.5 ms.

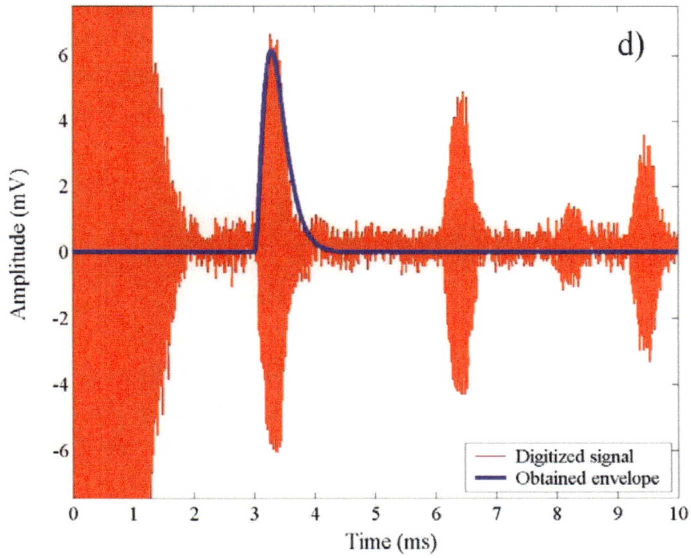

Fig. 13. Fundamental steps of the measurement procedure. d) superposition of the envelope reconstructed by the proposed method to the original digitized signal.

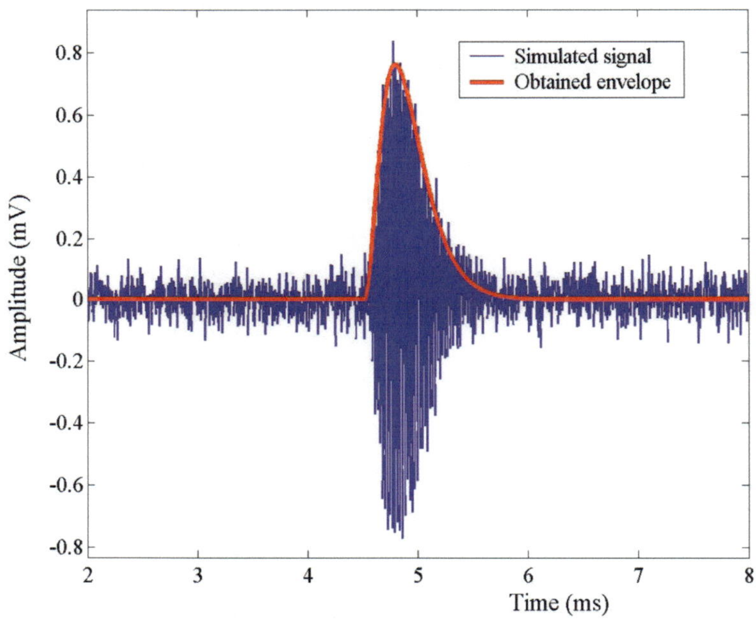

Fig. 14. Superposition of an envelope reconstructed by the proposed method to the related, original signal, characterized by a TOF of 4.5 ms.

For each couple of values of TOF and SNR, about 100 ultrasonic signals have been analyzed. From the obtained results, bias and experimental standard deviation, σ, on TOF estimates have been evaluated. In particular, the bias is given by the difference between the mean value of the TOF estimates and the imposed one. Values of bias and σ lower respectively than 2.8 μs and 5.3 μs have always been experienced. In the presence of a temperature equal to 24°C, these values correspond to a bias and experimental standard deviation on distance estimates equal respectively to 970 μm and 1834 μm. Moreover, a proper figure of merit, *MSE*, which quantifies the performance exhibited by the proposed method in reconstructing ultrasonic echo envelopes, has also been evaluated. *MSE* is given by

$$MSE = 10\log_{10}\frac{\sum_{k=1}^{N}(Ar_k - A_k)^2}{\sum_{k=1}^{N}{A_k}^2} \tag{25}$$

where N is the number of samples included the observation interval; A_k and Ar_k stands for the amplitude of respectively reference and reconstructed echo at the time instant $k\theta$. Values of *MSE* lower than -20 dB have been achieved also in critical measurement conditions (very low SNR values and high degree of echo distortion).

Tests conducted on actual signals

Some experiments have been conducted through a suitable measurement station capable of generating and acquiring ultrasonic signals. It has included (i) a processing and control unit (PCU), namely a personal computer, (ii) an ultrasonic transmitter/receiver (UT), *Polaroid 9000 Series,* (10°x40° beam angle, 43.8 kHz carrier frequency), (iii) a data acquisition system (DAQ), *Tektronix 210,* (8-bit resolution, 60-MHz bandwidth, 1-GS/s maximum sample rate) and (iv) a set of reference distances realized by a calibrated sliding plane. The PCU and the DAQ have been linked together by means of an IEEE-488 interface bus.

The PCU has driven the UT (acting as transmitter) with a rectangular burst, consisting of 16 cycles, through the line-0 of its parallel port. At the same time, it has generated a synchronization pulse on the line-1 of the same parallel port. The signal coming from the UT, accounting both for the transmitted ultrasonic pulse and received echo, has been digitized by the DAQ, and stored in a record covering a time-window of 10 ms (2500 samples). The DAQ has exhibited a vertical scale of 2 mV/div, and it has externally been triggered through the synchronization pulse generated by the PCU. To accurately estimate the propagation velocity, the temperature of the coupling medium, namely the air, has duly been checked throughout the measurement process; a standard RTD probe has been adopted.

In the following sub-sections, results are presented in terms of bias, δ, and experimental standard deviation, σ, obtained by statistically processing the values provided by about one hundred acquisitions for each value of distance or tilt angle.

- *Tests conducted in free-space propagation.*

A number of experimental tests in free-space propagation have preliminarily been conducted to assess the performance of the method in the best measurement conditions (i.e.

perfect orthogonality between the source and target, and measurement environment without acoustic interferences). The ultrasonic source has been mounted on a sliding plane, while the target has been realized by means of a fixed metallic surface. The distance between the source and target has been measured with a proper reference (Fig.15).

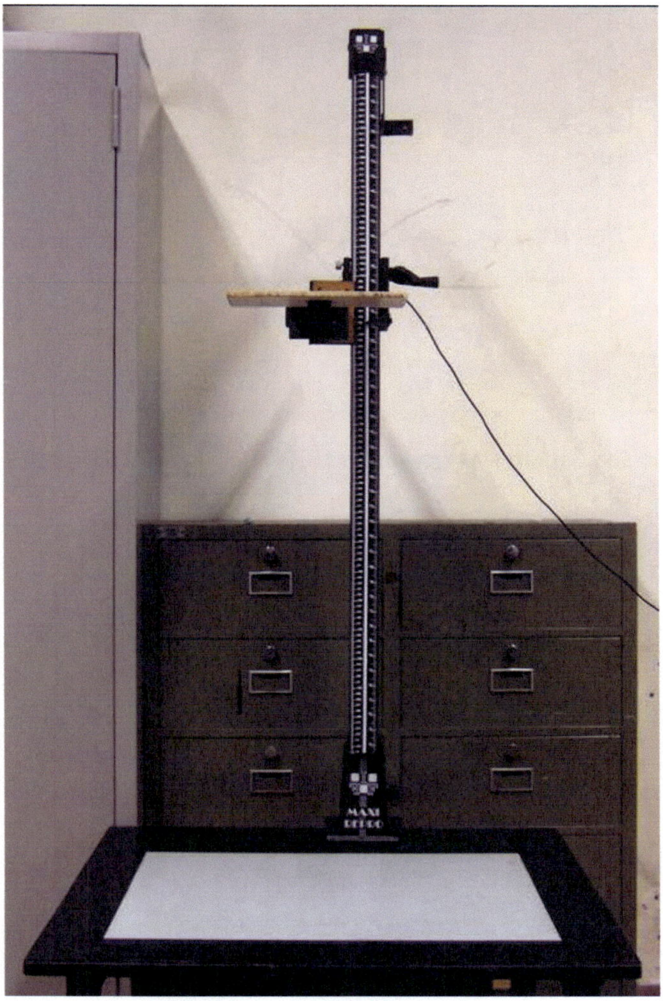

Fig. 15. Experimental apparatus adopted in tests in free-space propagation.

The performance of the method has been investigated upon the distance's varying in the interval equal to 400-1000 mm. The obtained results, both expressed in percentage relative terms, are given in Fig.16; values of δ and σ respectively lower than 0.2% and 0.4% have always been experienced.

- *Tests conducted in closed-tank configuration*

This kind of tests has been conducted to assess the robustness of the proposed method in the presence of multiple echoes or reverberation. At this aim, the worst measurement configuration has been adopted: the ultrasonic source has been positioned on the axis of a

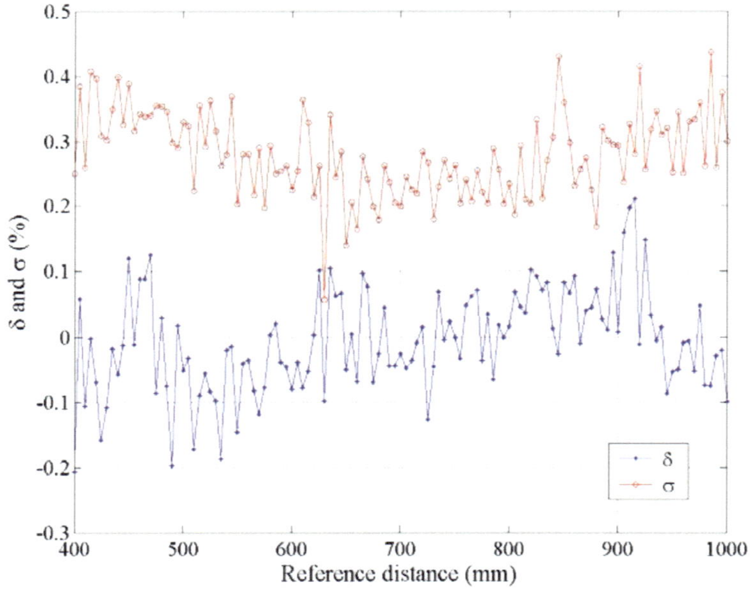

Fig. 16. Values of δ and σ, both expressed in relative percentage terms, obtained in tests in free-space propagation.

Fig. 17. Experimental apparutus adopted in tests in closed-tank configuration.

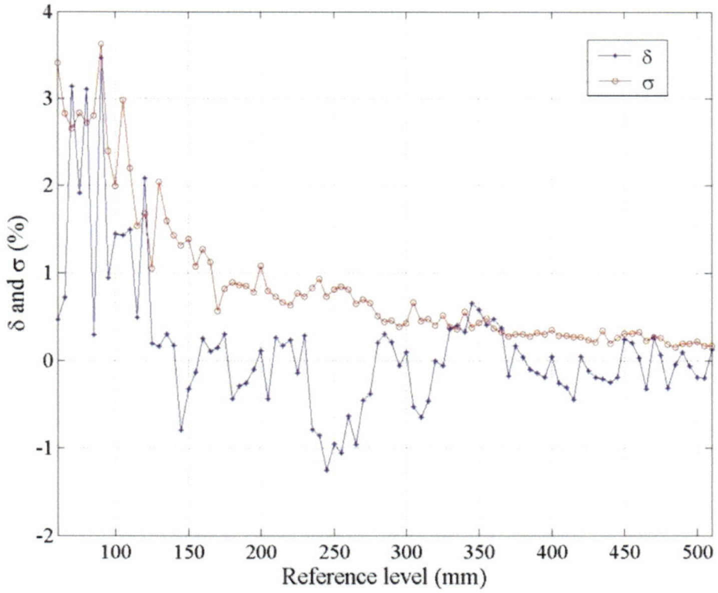

Fig. 18. Values of δ and σ, both expressed in relative percentage terms, obtained in tests in closed tank configuration.

Fig. 19. Experimental apparatus adopted in tests in misalignment conditions.

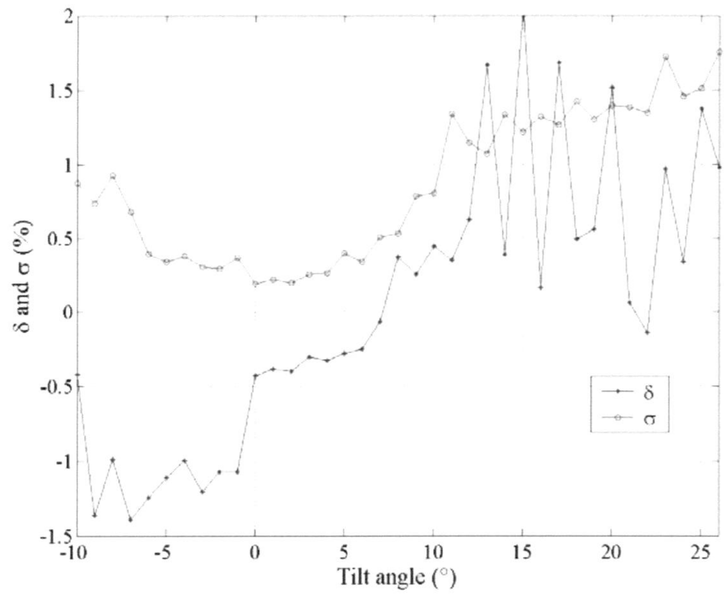

Fig. 20. Values of δ and σ, both expressed in relative percentage terms, obtained in tests in misalignment condition for a reference distance of 41 cm.

cylindrical tank (Fig.17). The level of the fluid is then calculated as difference between the measured distance of liquid-air interface and the known distance of tank bottom.
The performance of the method has been investigated upon the level's varying in the interval equal to 60-510 mm. The obtained results, both expressed in percentage relative terms, are given in Fig.18; values of δ and σ similar to those granted in free-space propagation tests have been experienced, except for the lowest levels.

- *Tests conducted in misalignment conditions*

The effect on measurement results of misalignment between the reflecting plane and ultrasonic source has then been investigated. The adopted apparatus is represented in Fig.19. It consists of the same sliding plane of the free-space propagation test and a target plane that rotates around its own axes; the angular position of the rotating plane has been measured through a reference goniometer.
It has been experienced, as expected, that the amplitude of the received echo was decreased upon the increasing of the tilt angle or distance. As an example, results, both expressed in percentage relative terms, obtained for a reference distance of 41 cm are given in Fig.20; similar results have been obtained for the other examined distances.
Values of δ and σ similar to those granted in free-space propagation tests have been experienced in a wide range of examined angular positions of the target plane.

4. References

[1] P. Kleinschmidt and V. Magori, Ultrasonic robotic-sensors for exact short range distance measurement and object identification, *Ultrasonics Symp. Proc*, IEEE, 1985, Vol.1, pp.457-462.

[2] D. Marioli, E. Sardini and A. Taroni, Ultrasonic distance measurement for linear and angular position control, IEEE Trans. lustrum. Meas. Vol.37, N.4, December 1988, pp.578-581.

[3] C. Lougblin, Ultrasonic measurement: keeping your distance, *Sensor Rev.*, April 1989, pp.85- 89.

[4] G. Hayward and Y. Gorfu, A digital hardware correlation system for fast ultrasonic data acquisition in peak power limited applications, *IEEE Trans. Ultrason. Ferroelec. Freq. Control*, Vol.35, N.6, November 1988, pp. 800-808.

[5] LM 1812 Ultrasonic Transceiver, National Semiconductor Special Purpose Linear Devices Databook, 1989, pp. 9/77-9/84.

[6] Murata ultrasonic sensors, Murata Products 1991, 1991, p. 77.

[7] Honeywell ultrasonic distance sensors Series 942, Honeywell Data Sheet El 01, 1989.

[8] S. Kocis, Z. Figura, Ultrasonic Measurements and Technologies, Chapman and Hall, London, 1996.

[9] D. Marioli, C. Narduzzi, C. Offelli, D. Petri, E. Sardini, A. Taroni, Digital time-of-flight measurement for ultrasonic sensors, IEEE Trans, lustrum. Meas., Vol.41, N.1, February 1992, pp.93-97.

[10] F.E. Gueuning, M. Varlan, C.E. Eugene, P. Dupuis, Accurate Distance Measurement by an Autonomous Ultrasonic System Combining Time-of-Flight and Phase-Shift Methods, IEEE Trans. on Instr. and Meas., Vol.46, N.6, December 1997, pp.1236-1241.

[11] P. Kleinschmidt and V. Magori, "Ultrasonic remote sensors for noncontact object detection," Siemens Forsch. Entwickl.ber., vol. 10, no. 2, pp. 110-118, 1981.

[12] H. Peremans, K. Audenaert, and J. Van Campenhout, "A high-resolution sensor based on triaural perception," IEEE Trans. Robot. Automat, vol. 9, no. 1, pp. 36-48, 1993.

[13] N. J. Nilsson, "On the optimum range resolution of radar signals in noise," IRE Trans. Inform. Theory, vol. 32, no. 7, pp. 245— 253, 1961.

[14] H. Eriksson, P. O. Borjesson, P. Odling and N.-G. Holmer, "A robust correlation receiver for distance estimation," IEEE Trans. Ultrason., Ferroelect., Freq. Contr., vol. 41, no. 5, pp. 596— 603, 1994.

[15] P. Eykhoff, System Identification. New York: Wiley, 1974.

[16] Y. W. Lee, Statistical Theory of Communication. New York: Wiley, 1960.

[17] T. Oliveira e Silva, "On the determination of the optimal pole position of Laguerre filters," IEEE Trans. Signal Processing, vol. 43, no. 9, pp. 2079-2087, 1995.

[18] A. C. Den Brinker, "Adaptive modified Laguerre filters," Signal Process., vol. 31, pp. 69-79, 1993.

[19] P. M. Gammell, "Improved ultrasonic detection using the analytic signal magnitude," Ultrasonics, vol. 19, no. 2, pp. 73-76, 1981.

[20] A. M. Sabatini, "Correlation receivers using Laguerre filter banks for modelling narrowband ultrasonic echoes and estimating their time-of-flights," IEEE Trans. on Ultr., Ferr. and Freq. Contr., vol.44, No.6, pp.1253–1263, Nov. 1997.

[21] M.S.Grewal, A.P.Andrews, Kalman filtering. Theory and practice, Englewood Cliffs, NJ, Prentice Hall, 1993.

[22] C.Tsai, "A Localization System of a Mobile Robot by Fusing Dead-Reckoning and Ultrasonic Measurements," IEEE Trans. on Instr. and Meas., vol.45, No.5, pp.1399-1404, October 1998.
[23] P.Ramuhalli, J.Kim, L.Udpa, S.S.Udpa, "Multichannel signal processing methods for ultrasonic nondestructive evaluation," Proc. of Sensor Array and Multichannel Signal Processing Workshop, pp.229 233, Aug. 2002.

13

Localization Using Extended Kalman Filters in Wireless Sensor Networks

Ali Shareef and Yifeng Zhu
Electrical and Computer Engineering
University of Maine
United States of America

1. Introduction

Localization arises repeatedly in many location-aware applications such as navigation, autonomous robotic movement, and asset tracking. Analytical localization methods include *triangulation* and *trilateration*. Triangulation uses angles, distances, and trigonometric relationships to locate an object. Trilateration, on the other hand, uses only distance measurements to identify the position of the target. Figure 1A, describes a simple example of trilateration. Using three reference points S_1, S_2, and S_3 with known locations and distances d_1, d_2, and d_3 to the target object, the object can be located at the intersecting point of the three circles.

However, in a dynamic system where distance measurements are noisy and fluctuate, the task of localizing becomes difficult. This can be seen in Figure 1B, where with fluctuating distances, regions within the circles become possible locations for the tracked object. In this case, rather than the object being located at a single point at the intersection of the circles as in Figure 1A, the object can be located anywhere in the dark overlapped region in Figure 1B.

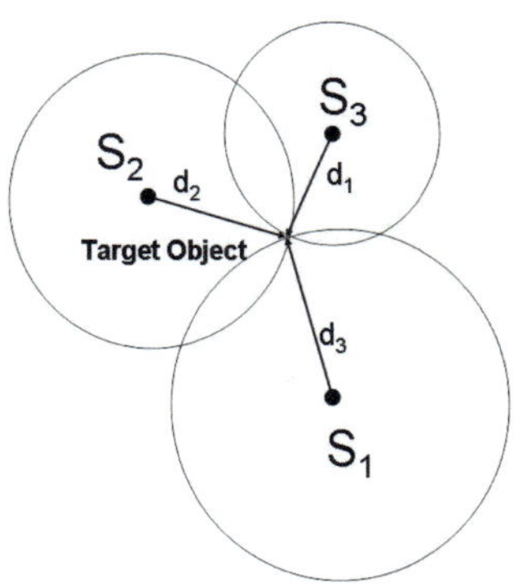

A.

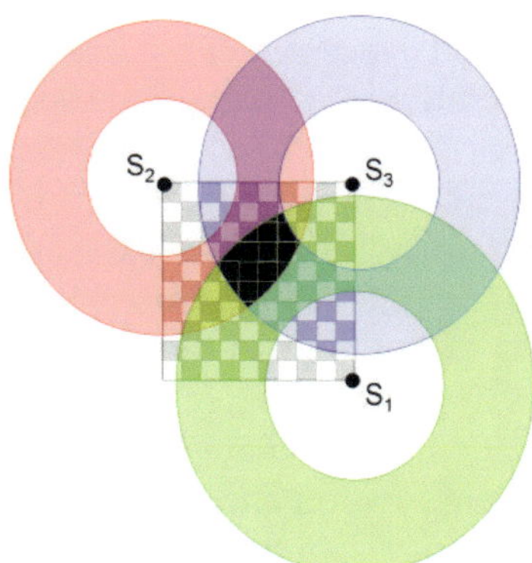

B.

Fig. 1A. Trilateration

Fig. 1B. Trilateration with noise

This uncertainty due to measurement noises renders analytical methods almost useless. Localization methods capable of accounting for and filtering out the measurement noises are

desired. The method by which the distance measurements are carried out determines the sources of noise in these measurements.
Typically devices known as "beacons" are placed at known locations and emit either radio or acoustic signals or both. It is possible for a "mobile node" to determine the distance to a beacon by using properties of these signals such as the signal strength of the RF signal, Received Signal Strength (RSS) (Patwari, et al., 2003). Other methods utilize both RF and acoustic signals by computing the time difference between the reception of an RF pulse and an acoustic pulse generated by a beacon. RF signals travel at the speed of light and the time it takes for a RF signal to get to a mobile node is almost instantaneous and can be considered zero while the propagation time of an acoustic signal in air is much longer (about 1.13 ft/ms at room temperature). This is exactly the way the Crickets (Priyantha, et al., 2000) operate where the RF and ultrasound signals are emitted simultaneously by the beacons. The mobile node computes the distance by using the time it takes for the first instance of the acoustic pulse to reach the sensor after the RF signal. However, wave reflection is common to both RF and acoustic signals and it is possible that the mobile node erroneously identifies a pulse due to the reflected wave of the original pulse as a new pulse (Ward, et al., 1997). This, of course, results in skewed distance measurements.

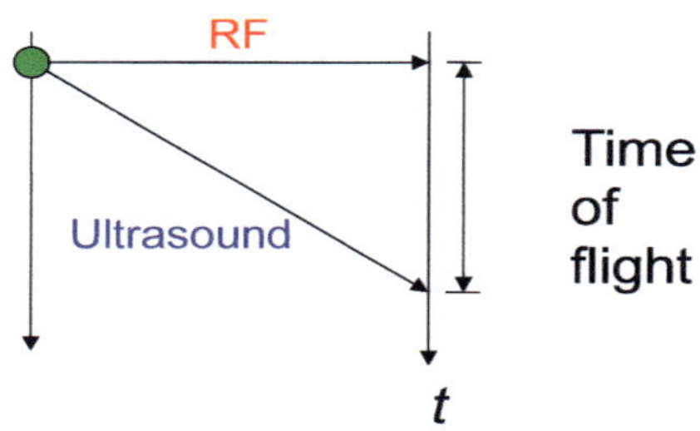

Fig. 2. Distance computation using time of flight between RF and Ultrasound signals

The Kalman filter is an iterative state estimator and it is widely used to locate an object with noisy measurements. However, the formalization of the filter states will dictate its computational and memory efficiency. The computation and memory efficiency of the Kalman filter is of concern because it is frequently implemented on embedded systems with limited computation and memory resources. A formalization of the Kalman filter with excessive states will potentially overburden a sensor system and result in a performance decrease. A trade-off must be made that balances the timely computation of the position and the desired accuracy necessary for the application. This chapter will examine the accuracy, robustness, computational and memory efficiencies of localization utilizing three different formalizations of the Kalman filters, including the position (*P*), position-velocity (*PV*), and position-velocity-acceleration (*PVA*) models. Our experiments conclude that all Kalman filter models are robust and are capable of handling large erroneous data. While the P model has the least computation and memory complexity, one of these models may have the best localization accuracy than the others depending upon the motion of the moving object.

2. Related work

The Active Badge Location System (Want, et al., 1992) is often credited as one of the earliest implementations of an indoor sensor network used to localize a mobile node. While this

system, utilizing infrared signals, was only capable of localizing the room that the mobile node was located in, many other systems based on this concept have been proposed.
The Bat system (Harter, et al., 1999), much like the Active-Badge System, also utilizes a network of sensors. A central controller broadcasts an RF query to a mobile node and resets a network of serially linked receivers at the same time. The mobile node responds by emitting an ultrasonic pulse which is picked up by the receivers. The time it takes for the ultrasound pulse to reach different receivers in the network indicates the distance the mobile node is from those receivers and the position of the mobile node can then be trilaterated.
Researchers at MIT have utilized similar concepts from the Bat System in their Cricket sensors, albeit using a more decentralized structure. However, one drawback to the Crickets is the risk of collisions during the RF and Ultrasound transmissions between different beacons. The Cricket Location System (Smith, et al., 2004) uses a hybrid approach involving the use of an Extended Kalman filter, Least Square Minimization to reset the Kalman filter during the Active state, and Outlier Rejection to eliminate bad distance readings.
Other researchers at MIT have proposed another method of localization utilizing the Cricket system exploiting properties of robust quadrilaterals to localize an ad-hoc collection of sensors without the use of beacons (Moore, et al., 2004).
It is also possible to localize optically as in the HiBall head tracking system (Welch, et al., 2001). Arrays of LEDs flash synchronously, and cameras capture the position of these LEDs. The system utilizes information about the geometry of the system and computes the position.
Localization using signal strength of RF signals has been studied extensively, (Alippi, et al., 2005) and (Patwari, et al., 2003) are all examples of methods that were devised using this approach.
Neural networks have also been used for localization (Shareef, et al., 2008). In fact, neural networks have been shown to perform better than the Kalman filter in a low-noise environment. However, neural networks suffer from weak self-adaptivity and have a high over-head due to training costs. A neural network, once trained for a particular set of parameters can only be used in the scenario corresponding to those parameters. If the number or the position of beacons or the size of the localization area was to change, then the neural network would have to be trained again.

3. Kalman filter applied to localization

The Kalman filter is an iterative approach that uses prior knowledge of noise characteristics to account for and filter out the noise. However, problems arise when attempting to model noise. Attempts at measuring noise are only approximations and do not indicate the real distribution of the noise. The Kalman filter can only be used for linear stochastic processes and for non-linear processes the *Extended Kalman Filter* (EKF) must be used. The assumption with these two methods is that the process and noise measurements are independent, white, and with normal probability.
There are different parameters that the EKF can use in modeling the trajectory of a moving object. It is possible to model the motion of an object using just the state of the X and Y position to obtain the position (*P*) model of the Kalman filter. The velocity can also be incorporated in the state in addition to the position to form the position-velocity (*PV*) model.

Of course, if acceleration is included also, this results in the position-velocity-acceleration (*PVA*) model.
In two-dimensional space, the distances to three known beacons returned by a sensor can be related to the position of this sensor (x, y) using the distance formula given in (1),

$$d_i = \sqrt{(x - x_i)^2 + (y - y_i)^2} \quad (1)$$

where (x_i, y_i) is the coordinations of beacon *i* (*i* = 1, 2, and 3).
A way of modeling motion is by setting up a linear system composed of the kinematics equations for each dimension of tracked motion. The following example of a linear system describes an object's two-dimensional motion using the position, velocity, and acceleration (PVA) at time step *k*.

$$\begin{bmatrix} x_k \\ y_k \\ \dot{x}_k \\ \dot{y}_k \\ \ddot{x}_k \\ \ddot{y}_k \end{bmatrix} = A \cdot \begin{bmatrix} x_{k-1} \\ y_{k-1} \\ \dot{x}_{k-1} \\ \dot{y}_{k-1} \\ \ddot{x}_{k-1} \\ \ddot{y}_{k-1} \end{bmatrix} + B \cdot \begin{bmatrix} u_{xk} \\ u_{yk} \end{bmatrix} + Q \quad (2)$$

Equation (2) can be written in a simpler way.

$$X_k = A \cdot X_{k-1} + B \cdot U_k + Q$$

The state transition matrix *A* arises from the respective kinematics equations. For a *PVA* model, the *A* matrix becomes:

$$A = \begin{bmatrix} 1 & 0 & T & 0 & \frac{1}{2}T^2 & 0 \\ 0 & 1 & 0 & T & 0 & \frac{1}{2}T^2 \\ 0 & 0 & 1 & 0 & T & 0 \\ 0 & 0 & 0 & 1 & 0 & T \\ 0 & 0 & 0 & 0 & 1 & 0 \\ 0 & 0 & 0 & 0 & 0 & 1 \end{bmatrix} \quad (3)$$

The u_{xk} and u_{yk} are the inputs to the system, and the *B* matrix is the input matrix. However, the input kinematics parameters of the moving object to be tracked are not known so the u_{xk}, u_{yk}, and *B* can be dropped from the linear system. If this information had been known, then there would be no need to, "track" the object. The inputs to this system are the distance measurements d_k, and these distance measurement will be used to update the state of the object as given in step 4 of the Kalman filter procedure in Table 1.
The process noise covariance matrix *Q* accounts for the unmodeled factors of the system that will be treated as random noise. For example, in the systems of equations above, while the change of velocity is accounted for by acceleration, the change in acceleration is not considered. The contribution of this effect to the state is accounted for as random noise. See (Welch, et al., 2007) for a more in depth discussion. In this example, q_x and q_y can be considered as the standard deviations of the acceleration noise in the *x* and *y* direction, respectively.

$$Q = \begin{bmatrix} q_x\frac{\partial t^5}{20} & 0 & q_x\frac{\partial t^4}{8} & 0 & q_x\frac{\partial t^3}{6} & 0 \\ 0 & q_y\frac{\partial t^5}{20} & 0 & q_y\frac{\partial t^4}{8} & 0 & q_y\frac{\partial t^3}{6} \\ q_x\frac{\partial t^4}{8} & 0 & q_x\frac{\partial t^3}{3} & 0 & q_x\frac{\partial t^2}{2} & 0 \\ 0 & q_y\frac{\partial t^4}{8} & 0 & q_y\frac{\partial t^3}{3} & 0 & q_y\frac{\partial t^2}{2} \\ q_x\frac{\partial t^3}{3} & 0 & q_x\frac{\partial t^2}{2} & 0 & q_x\partial t & 0 \\ 0 & q_y\frac{\partial t^3}{3} & 0 & q_y\frac{\partial t^2}{2} & 0 & q_y\partial t \end{bmatrix} \tag{4}$$

At time step k, the three measured distances d_{ik} (i=1, 2, 3) to the locations of the three beacons (x_i, y_i), can be used to relate the location of the target object (x_k, y_k) using the following equation:

$$\begin{aligned} d_{1k} &= \sqrt{(x_k - x_1)^2 + (y_k - y_1)^2} + \tilde{d}_{1k} \\ d_{2k} &= \sqrt{(x_k - x_2)^2 + (y_k - y_2)^2} + \tilde{d}_{2k} \\ d_{3k} &= \sqrt{(x_k - x_3)^2 + (y_k - y_3)^2} + \tilde{d}_{3k} \end{aligned} \tag{5}$$

where $\tilde{d}_{1k}, \tilde{d}_{2k}$ and $\tilde{d}_{3k}$ are distance measurement errors. The equation (5) can be expressed as (6).

$$\begin{bmatrix} d_{1k} \\ d_{2k} \\ d_{3k} \end{bmatrix} = H \cdot \begin{bmatrix} x_k \\ y_k \\ \dot{x}_k \\ \dot{y}_k \\ \ddot{x}_k \\ \ddot{y}_k \end{bmatrix} + \begin{bmatrix} \tilde{d}_{1k} \\ \tilde{d}_{2k} \\ \tilde{d}_{3k} \end{bmatrix} \tag{6}$$

Where H is the measurement matrix that relates the current state to the output. Since the output equations (5) are non-linear, the Jacobian needs to be used, where

$$H = \begin{bmatrix} \frac{\partial d_1}{\partial x} & \frac{\partial d_1}{\partial y} & 0 & 0 & 0 & 0 \\ \frac{\partial d_2}{\partial x} & \frac{\partial d_2}{\partial y} & 0 & 0 & 0 & 0 \\ \frac{\partial d_3}{\partial x} & \frac{\partial d_3}{\partial y} & 0 & 0 & 0 & 0 \end{bmatrix} \tag{7}$$

and the partial derivatives are given in (8) and (9) below.

$$\frac{\partial d_i}{\partial x} = \frac{x - x_i}{\sqrt{(x-x_i)^2 + (y-y_i)^2}} \tag{8}$$

$$\frac{\partial d_i}{\partial y} = \frac{y - y_i}{\sqrt{(x-x_i)^2 + (y-y_i)^2}} \tag{9}$$

The assumption that, the measurement noise associated with the distance measurements of a beacon is independent among the three beacons, will be made. This will result in measurement noise values for the appropriate beacon only along the diagonal of the measurment noise matrix R.

$$R = \begin{bmatrix} MN_1 & 0 & 0 \\ 0 & MN_2 & 0 \\ 0 & 0 & MN_3 \end{bmatrix} \tag{10}$$

Where MN_1, MN_2, and MN_3 are the measurement noises to beacon 1, 2 and 3, respectively. Using the formulation of the problem as described above, the following equations can be evaluated iteratively to track the target object. In each iteration, five steps are performed, as shown in Table 1. The current state X_{k-1} is used to estimate the location at the next time instant. The error covariance matrix P_k^- in the next time step is also projected using the state space model A and the process noise matrix Q in step 2. In step 3, the Kalman gain K_k is computed. The Kalman gain is used in step 4, when the distance measurements $D_k = [d_{k1}, d_{k2}, d_{k3}]^T$ from the beacons to the target object are obtained and are used to update the state X_k. The current position (x_k, y_k) is a subset of the state vector X_k.

Procedure of Extended Kalman Filter		
1. Project the state ahead	$X_k^- = A \cdot X_{k-1} + B \cdot U_k$	(11)
2. Project the error covariance ahead	$P_k^- = A \cdot P_{k-1} \cdot A^T + Q$	(12)
3. Compute the Kalman gain	$K_k = P_k^- \cdot H^T \cdot (H \cdot P_k^- \cdot H^T + R)^{-1}$	(13)
4. Update estimation with measurements	$X_k = X_k^- + K_k \cdot (D_k - H \cdot X_k^-)$	(14)
5. Update the error covariance	$P_k = (I - K_k \cdot H) \cdot P_k^-$	(15)

Table 1. Procedure of Extended Kalman Filter

Figure 3 depicts the iterative process described in Table 1. The current state and the error covariance matrix are projected for the next time step using equations (11) and (12). The next state is then computed by correcting the estimate that was made in step 1. This is done by using the measurement noise matrix R to compute the Kalman gain K. The Kalman gain K is used to scale the contribution of the distance measurement inputs to the next state estimate in step 4. The error covariance matrix that was projected for the next time step is corrected, and the process repeats all over again.

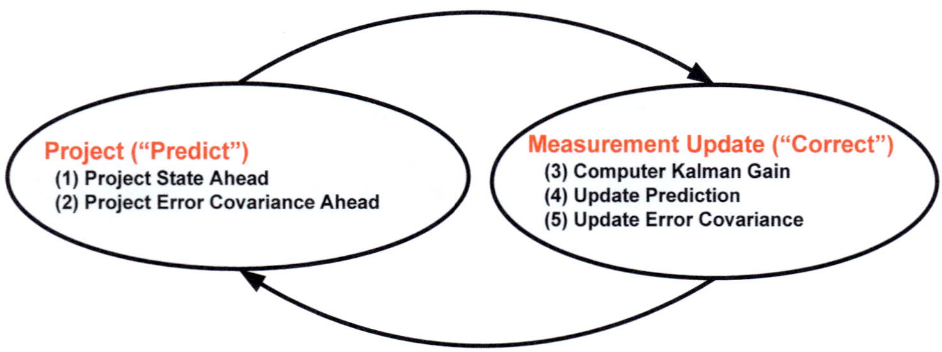

Fig. 3. Extended Kalman filter operation

In this chapter, the performance of the *P*, *PV*, and *PVA* extended Kalman filter models will be compared. The benefit of one over the other depends upon the characteristics of the motion of the object. A system modeled using just *P* will work when the position is mostly constant and the velocity can be treated as noise. In the case of a *PV* model, it will tend to work better when velocity is mostly constant, and the acceleration can be treated as noise. *PVA* on the other hand works better when the acceleration is mostly constant (Welch, et al., 2007).

4. Experiment design

We will explore the performance of the *P*, *PV*, and *PVA* models of the Kalman filters using MIT's Cricket sensors (Priyantha, et al., 2000). However, as was discussed, the use of ultrasound introduces noise. The distance measurements returned by the sensors fluctuate often and these measurements are the inputs to the Kalman filters. We simulate the two dimensional motion of an object by collecting distance measurements of the mobile node while physically moving it in a network composed of Cricket sensors (see Figure 4). A tile floor provided a very regular grid of 30 cm in size upon which the sensors could be accurately located. Four Cricket sensors are used, three as beacons and the other as the mobile node.

Fig. 4. Cricket sensor

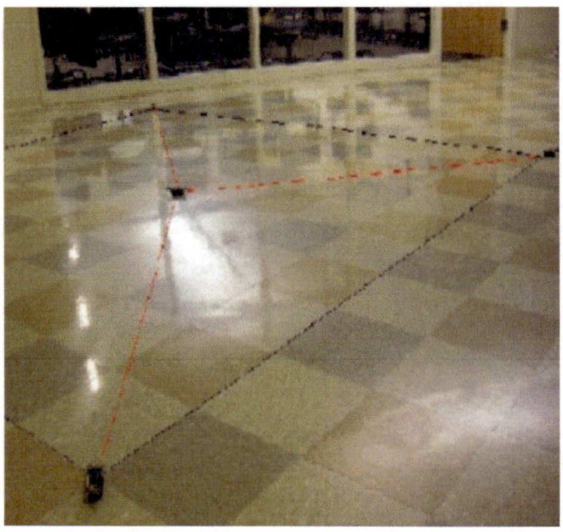

Fig. 5. Experiment Test Bed

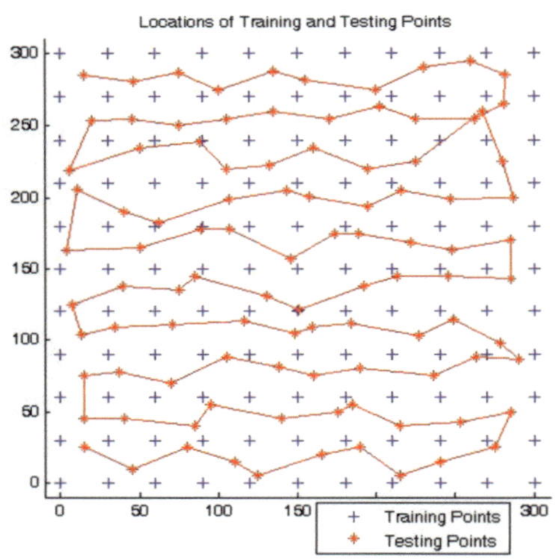

Fig. 6. Locations of Testing Data Collected

Using a grid of 300 cm × 300 cm, beacons were placed at the coordinates of (0, 300), (300, 300), and (300, 0) of the grid as shown in Figure 5. For each of the 121 tested position, distances measurements were collected from the three beacons. This is indicated using the "*" sign in Figure 6. The distances are input as D_k in step 4 of the Kalman filter procedure to update the state estimate, as shown in Table 1.
The measurement noise for each of the sensors was assumed to be independent of the others. The measurement noise was obtained by taking the average difference between the actual and estimated distances from the beacons to the nodes. However, it should be noted that for the path generated in Figure 6, the measurement noise was restricted to 30 cm. Any measurement with error greater than this was discarded. In the next section, the robustness of the Kalman filter will be analyzed using the raw distance measurements of another path traced out by a moving object.
The process noise matrix Q is more difficult to obtain. Approximate behavior such as the standard deviation of the position for the P model about the estimated movement of the object can be used. Of course, the standard deviation of velocity would be applied for the PV model, and the standard deviation of the acceleration for the PVA model.
Determination of the correct process noise parameters are key to accurate localization as will be seen in the next section. The process noise parameters for comparing the three models of the Kalman filter were obtained by computing the average error in localization for varying values of process noise, and the noise parameters that correspond to the least localization error were used.

5. Results

5.1 Performance comparison

Figures 7A, 7C, and 7E show the localization accuracy of the P, PV, and PVA methods, respectively. Two metrics were utilized in comparing the performances of the Kalman filters. The first is the average distance error in localization per estimate, as defined by equation (16).
Another metric that was used is the Root Mean Square Error (RMSE). This metric computes the error in localization for the X and Y coordinates and squares it. The sum of all errors are computed, divided by the number of estimates, and the square root is taken of the resulting value. The benefit of the RMSE given in equation (17) is that the error in localization of the X and Y coordinates is available. The X and Y RMSE values can be combined using equation (18) to result in the Net RMSE that describes the net error. An interesting characteristics of the RMSE is that it is biased towards large errors. A large error make a larger contribution in RMSE than in average distance error.

$$Distance\ Error = \frac{\sum\sqrt{(X_{Actual} - X_{Est})^2 + (Y_{Actual} - Y_{Est})^2}}{Number\ of\ Estimates} \tag{16}$$

$$RMSE = \sqrt{\frac{\sum(Actual - Estimated)^2}{Number\ of\ Estimates}} \tag{17}$$

$$Net\ RMSE = \sqrt{X_{RMSE}^{\ 2} + Y_{RMSE}^{\ 2}} \tag{18}$$

As Table 2 indicates, the P model has the least distance error per estimate and the least Net RMSE and hence the best localization performance. This is followed closely by the PV

model, and finally the *PVA* model. It should be noted, that Table 2 lists the minimum error that can possibly be attained by these methods. This was done, by evaluating the Kalman filter for a variety of process noise parameters and selecting the resulting minimum error. The discussion that follows will clarify this point.

Method	Avg. Distance Error Per Estimate (cm)	RMSE (cm)	Net RMSE (cm)
P	8.1626	(6.8520, 7.2268)	9.9587
PV	8.5811	(6.8160, 7.5349)	10.1603
PVA	9.4023	(7.7226, 7.9404)	11.0741

Table 2. Accuracy Comparison between *P*, *PV* and *PVA* models

There is an interesting anomaly between the RMSE values of the X coordinates for the *P* and *PV* models. Although the *P* model has the lower distance error per estimate and Net RMSE, its localization in the X direction is not as good as the *PV* model. This anomaly indicates that the *PV* model can potentially be a better candidate in some scenarios.

A good portion of the error for all of the methods seems to be along the edge of the testing boundary in the vicinity of the beacons. This may be due to the fact that the use of ultrasound on the Cricket sensors results in large interferences between signals close to the beacons.

The experiments also show that the Kalman filters display relatively large errors at the edges of the boundaries. This may be due to the fact that the Kalman filters iteratively close in on the localized position. At the boundaries, where the object's motion takes a sudden turn, the Kalman filter's estimates require a few iterations before it can "catch up" with the object. This may be due to the process noise of the simulated motion of the object not adhering to Gaussian characteristics, which is assumed in Kalman filter.

In the case of the *P* model, the assumption that velocity and acceleration are just random noise allow it to take these turns with less error. The *PV* and *PVA* models are forced to maintain rigidly to the Kinematic equations.

Figures 7B, 7D, and 7F depict the percentage of varying magnitudes of error for the *P*, *PV*, and *PVA* models respectively. It is observed that the *P* model has a greater percentage of errors of low magnitude, whereas the *PV* and *PVA* models have lower percentages, but of greater magnitude. The *P* model seems to make many small errors at each step, whereas the *PV* and *PVA* make large errors, typically at the edge of the boundary.

Table 3 summerizes the maximum error values and their locations in our experiments. Note that the *PV* and *PVA* models have their maximum error values close to the same locations.

Method	Max Error (cm)	Coordinate of Max Error
P	38.0901	(285, 50)
PV	31.7478	(20, 254)
PVA	32.6776	(45, 255)

Table 3. Maximum error and location of maximum error

The process noise is an independent variable of the system, and it attempts to predict the motion and future estimates of the position of the object. For this reason, it is impossible to exactly ascertain this paramter. Even when points on the path of the object are given, this is not sufficient since they are just samples of a coarse simulation of the movement of an object.

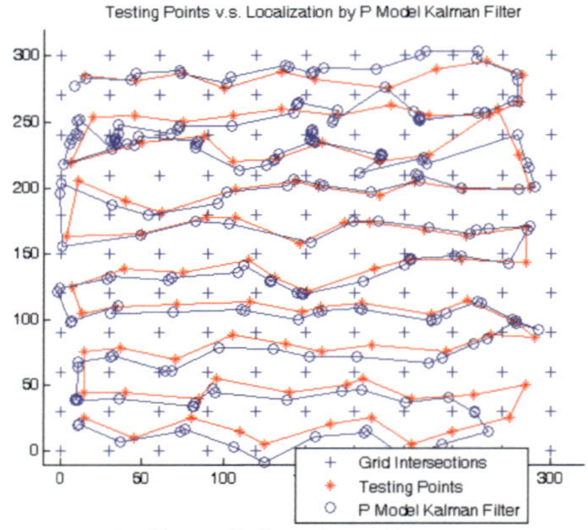

A. *P* model estimation

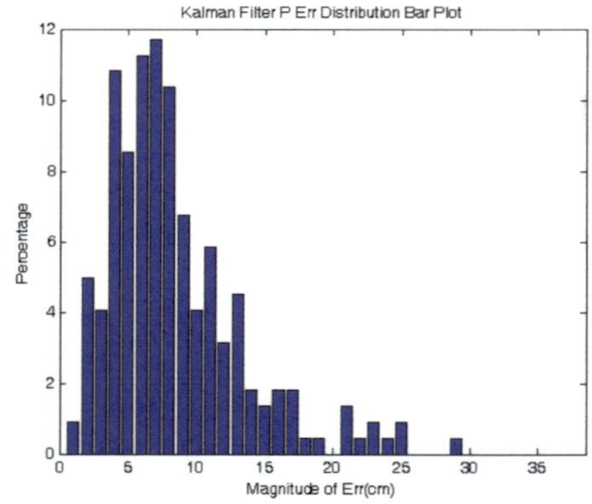

B. *P* model error distribution

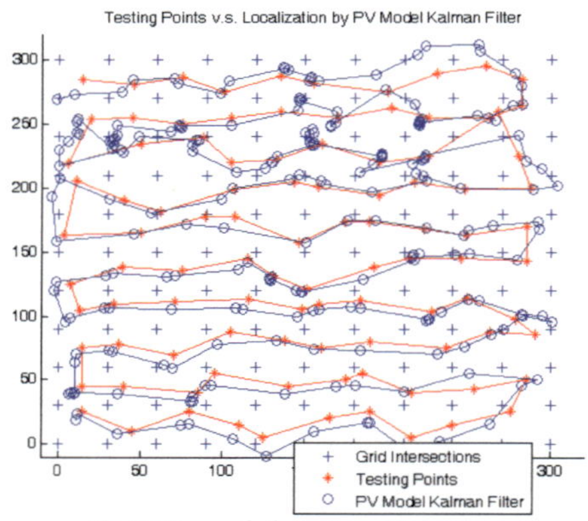

C. *PV* model estimation

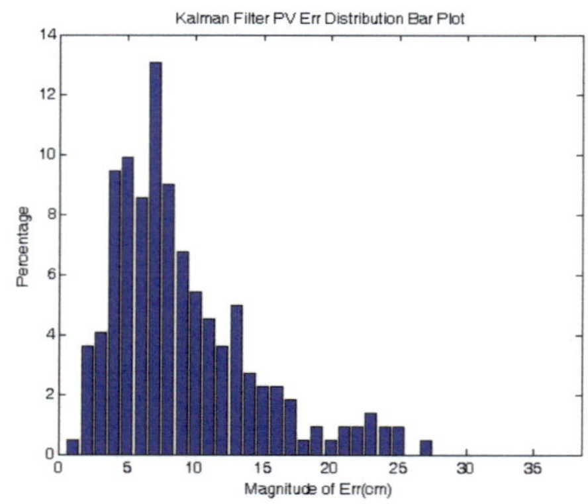

D. *PV* model error distribution

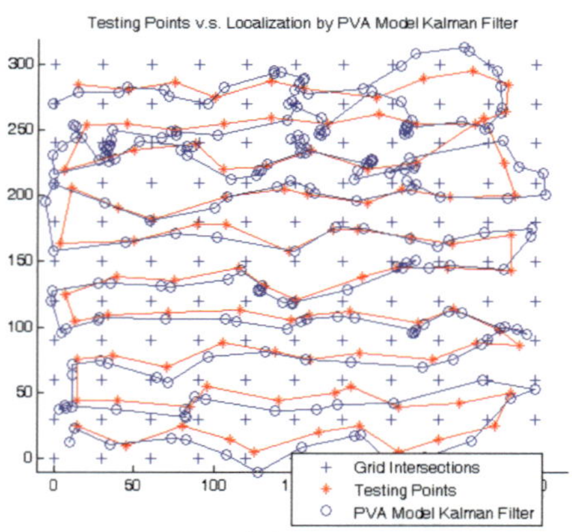

E. *PVA* model estimation

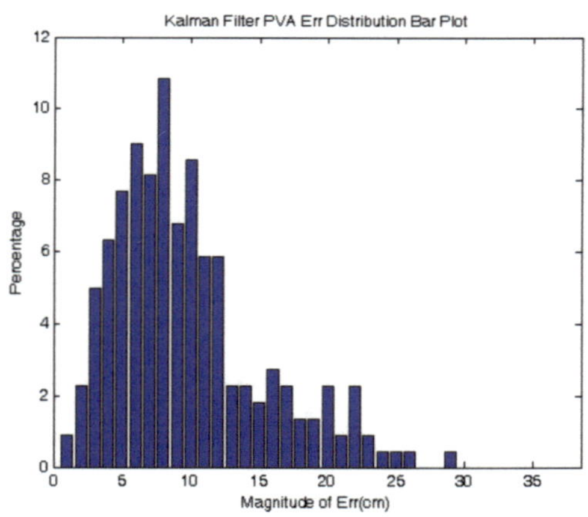

F. *PVA* model error distribution

Fig. 7A, 7C, 7E. Comparison between actual and estimated tracked paths as given by *P*, *PV*, and *PVA* models

Fig. 7B, 7D, 7F. Distribution of the magnitude of error for localized positions for P, PV, and PVA models.

The process noise parameter matrix Q was obtained by using varying values of the X and Y process noise parameters, and computing the average distance error for the entire path for that set. Figure 8 depicts a surface plot of X and Y process noise parameters versus the resulting average distance error. It is interesting how the use of inaccurate process noise parameters effects the perfomance; for low value of the X component of the process noise, the resulting error is very high. The minimum average distance error as given in Table 2, was found for process noise paramters, (300,100), which interestingly implies that the process noise parameters don't seem to matter a great deal for the P model. In this model, the velocity is considered as the process noise, and hence the units can be considered as cm. The minimum error that was listed in Table 2 was obtained for the process noise parameters listed in Table 4.

The same steps were taken to obtain the process noise parameters for the PV model. However, here the acceleration is considered as the process noise, and the unit are cm/sec.

Method	Avg Distance Error Per Estimate (cm)	Process Noise	Units
P	8.1626	(300,100)	cm
PV	8.5811	(300,62)	cm/sec
PVA	9.4023	(37,18)	cm/sec^2

Table 4. Process noise parameters corresponding to the minimum distance error

The PVA model presents an interesting relationship between the process noise and its performance unlike the P and PV models. The process noise parameters for the PVA model corroborate well with the movement of the object, since the object moves almost 30 cm along the X-axis and almost 20 cm along the Y-axis at each step as depicted in Figures 7A, 7C, and 7E.

The process noise values listed in Table 4 are input to the Kalman filter by setting q_x of the process noise matrix Q in equation 4 to the x component, and q_y to the y component.

In the analysis presented above, the average distance error in localization was used as a metric in determining the process noise paramters. However, it is also possible to use the RMSE value to do the same. Suprisingly, there is a strong correlation between the process noise obtained using the average distance error and RMSE metrics indicating the suitability of this procedure. Table 5 lists the appropriate process noise values corresponding to the minimum RMSE value. In the interest of space and brevity, the surface graphs that were used to obtain these values will not be displayed.

Method	RMSE (cm)	Process Noise	Units
P	9.9587	(300,100)	cm
PV	10.1572	(300,71)	cm/sec
PVA	11.0584	(34,13)	cm/sec^2

Table 5. Process noise parameters corresponding to the minimum RMSE

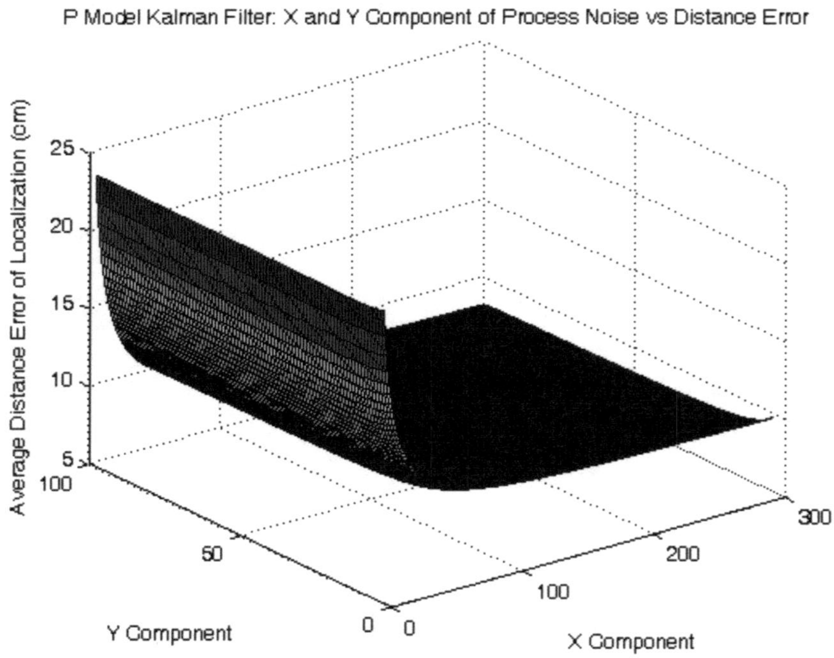

Fig. 8. Process noise versus average distance error of localization for P model.

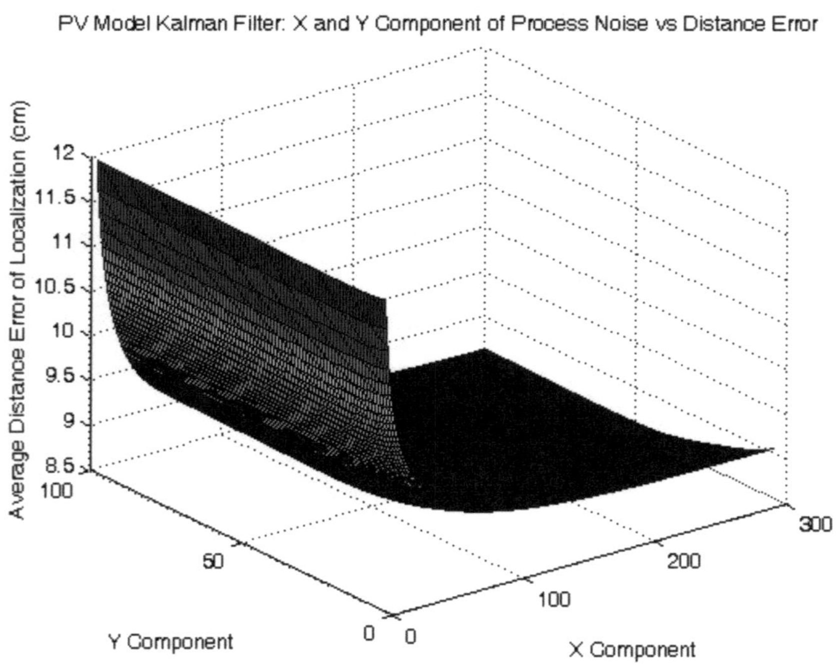

Fig. 9. Process noise versus average distance error of localization for PV model

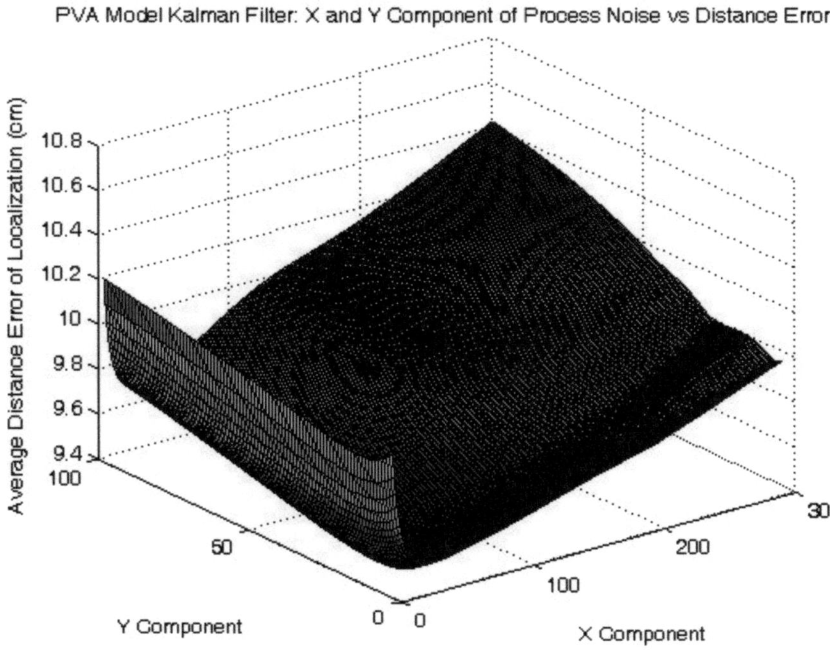

Fig. 10. Process noise versus average distance error of localization for *PVA* model

5.2 Robustness comparison

Armed with the analysis procedure given above , the robustness of these methods will now be evaluated. A new path traced out by a moving node was generated as shown in Figure 11 that contains nearly 271 points with an average step size of 10.48 cm whereas the path in Figure 6 contains 222 points with an average step size of 14.13 cm.

The robustness of each of these Kalman filter models was examined by comparing the performance of each of these models for various magnitudes of erroroneous distance measurements. This is unlike the first path generated, where the error in distance measurements exceeding 30 cm was discarded. The distance measurements to the path traced out by the moving object as shown in Figure 11 were collected and categorized into six data sets. In the first data set, no distance measurements were removed. All spurious distance measurements of any magnitude were kept. The maximum threshold for the error was set to 10,000 cm to include all distance measurements regardless of the size of the error. (No distance measure error exceeded 10,000 cm.) In the second set of data, distance measurements with errors of only 300 cm or less were kept. In the third, distance measurements with errors of only 200 cm or less were kept. In the fourth, distance measurements with errors of 100 cm or less were kept. In the fifth, distance measurements with errors of 50 cm or less were kept, and in the last data set, only measurements with errors that did not exceed 30 cm were kept. In this way, the method most capable of localizing under these demanding conditions can be identified.

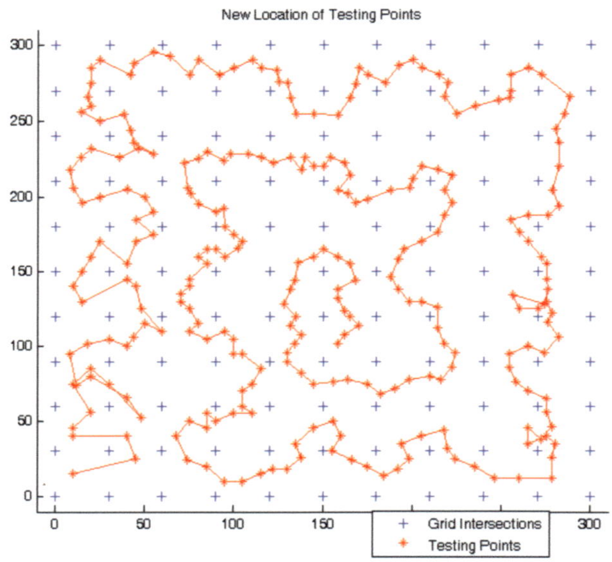

Fig. 11. New path generated for testing robustness

Error Method	Maximum Error Threshold (cm)	*P* Model		*PV* Model		*PVA* Model	
		Avg Error (cm)	Process Noise (cm)	Avg Error (cm)	Process Noise (cm/s)	Avg Error (cm)	Process Noise (cm/s²)
Dist. Error	10000	278.6226	(6,11)	328.0187	(8,7)	479.274	(5,5)
RMSE	10000	376.3137	(6,5)	480.9813	(7,6)	645.7573	(5,6)
Dist. Error	300	22.149	(16,26)	28.039	(72,50)	35.0343	(6,38)
RMSE	300	29.6411	(5,10)	46.7252	(34,5)	59.0939	(6,26)
Dist. Error	200	15.4266	(35,100)	17.5227	(10,5)	19.2767	(8,9)
RMSE	200	20.5447	(8,20)	24.5717	(5,5)	27.8166	(8,9)
Dist. Error	100	11.8554	(69,100)	12.6885	(150,67)	13.3489	(38,5)
RMSE	100	14.5468	(33,100)	15.7661	(10,71)	16.2669	(8,5)
Dist. Error	50	10.9748	(82,100)	11.4858	(300,100)	11.9595	(107,52)
RMSE	50	12.7345	(63,100)	13.6644	(300,100)	14.2215	(121,5)
Dist. Error	30	10.5008	(125,100)	10.9549	(300,100)	11.2604	(174,50)
RMSE	30	11.8822	(100,100)	12.6447	(300,100)	13.0828	(300,10)

Table 6. Six different data sets and the minimum averge distance error and the RMSE error and the corresponding process noise parameters for the *P*, *PV*, and *PVA* models.

Figure 12, 13, and 14 depict the surface plots of the process noise versus the average distance error measurement of localization for the *P*, *PV*, and *PVA* models. In Figure 12, the average distance error increases at a nearly smooth and steady rate. This is in contrast to Figure 8, where the error decreased for increasing process noise. In Figure 13 and 14, the average distance error flutuates wildly with changing process noise, while the general trend seems to indicate that the error increases with increasing process noise.

Surface plots examining the behaviour of the RMSE instead of the average distance error were also generated, however, for the sake of brevity they will not be presented here. The first rows in Table 6 lists the minimum average distance error, 278.6226 cm, for process noise at (6,11) cm for the set of data containing up to 10,000 cm error in distance measurements. The minimum average distance errors and the corresponding process noise values for the PV and PVA models are listed next. The next row in Table 6 lists the minimum RMSE values and corresponding process noise parameters for the P, PV, and PVA models respectively. The next two rows deal with the minimum average distance error and RMSE for a maximum of 300 cm error in the distance measurements for the P, PV, and PVA. The results for maximum thresholds of 200, 100, 50, and 30 cm follow.

It is clear from the graph that the P model consistently has lower error than the other models, and the PV model performs better than the PVA. It is also interesting to note that at a high error threshold, the process noise for the P, PV and PVA models is low. As the error threshold decreases, the process noise increases.

It is a testament to the Kalman filters that the error rates between error threshold 100 cm and 30 cm for the P, PV, and PVA does not change much. For example, the average distance error for P changes only 1.3546 cm (11.8554 - 10.5008) and the error rates for PV and PVA change by only 1.7336 and 2.0885 cm. That is at most a 16 percent drop in error for nearly a 70 percent decrease in the magnitude of erroneous distance measurements. In other words, even with errors of up to 100 cm in distance measurments, the Kalman filter models were still capable of localizing fairly accurately. Figures 15A, 15C, and 15E reveal the performance of the P, PV, and PVA models for error threshold of 100 cm. Figures 15B, 15D, and 15F reveal the performance of the P, PV, and PVA models for error threshold of 30 cm. It is apparent between Figures 15A and 15C that the P model is better adept at tracking the irratic motion of the object. The PV and PVA models overshoot sudden turns and require several iterations before they close in on the object's position again.

Table 6 show that pre-filtering of the distance measurements can result in a significant decrease of errors in localization, especially between error thresholds of 10,000 and 100 cm. The level of pre-filtering does not need to be very rigorous since the Kalman filter is very robust. Extremely large errors in distance measurements can be easily spotted and eliminated. One such method is utilizing the past distance measurements and the maximum rate at which the object is expected to move. This projection can be used as a threshold against which the current distance measurements can be compared and if necessary discarded. Assuming that the last distance measuments for three becons are stored in d_1, d_2, and d_3. Maximum velocity and acceleration attainable by the object are v_{max} and a_{max} . Using the distance from beacon 1, the mobile node can either be moving away from the beacon or approaching it. In case that the object is moving away from the beacon, the distance from the beacon will increase as given by equation (19) for d_{1max}^{+} where T is the time step. However, if the object is approaching the beacon, then the distance will decrease as given by equation (20) for d_{1max}^{-} .

$$d_{1max}^{+} = d_1 + T \cdot v_{max} + \frac{1}{2}T^2 \cdot a_{max} \tag{19}$$

$$d_{1max}^{-} = d_1 - T \cdot v_{max} + \frac{1}{2}T^2 \cdot a_{max} \tag{20}$$

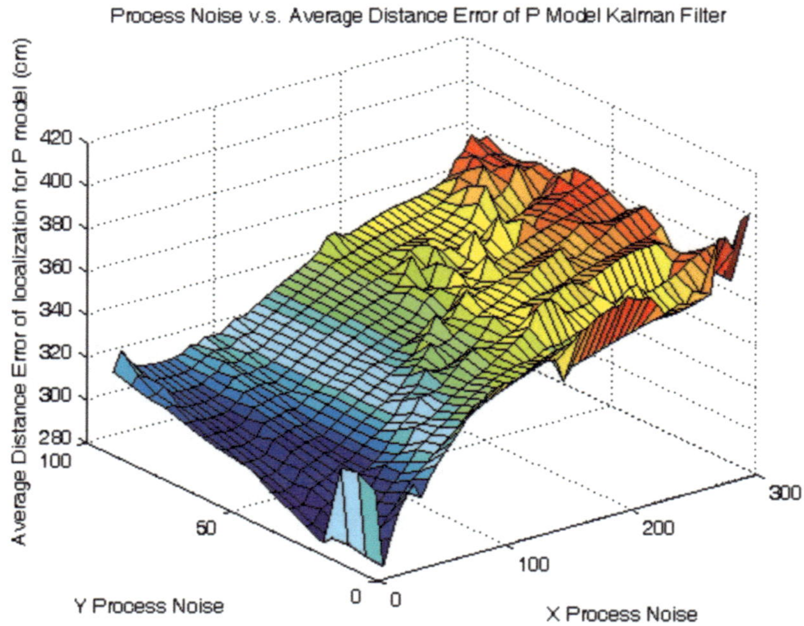

Fig. 12. Process noise versus localization error for *P* model using a maximum error threshold of 10,000 cm

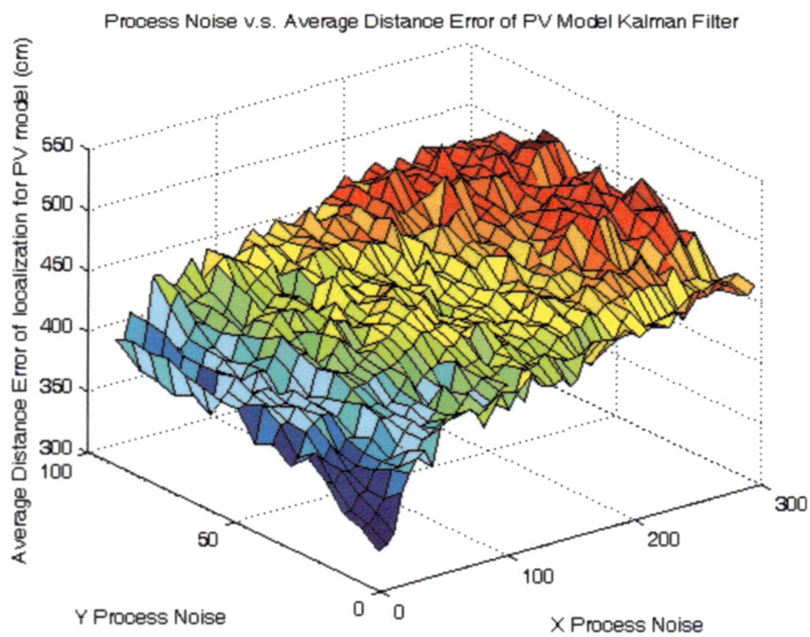

Fig. 13. Process noise versus localization error for *PV* model using a maximum error threshold of 10,000 cm

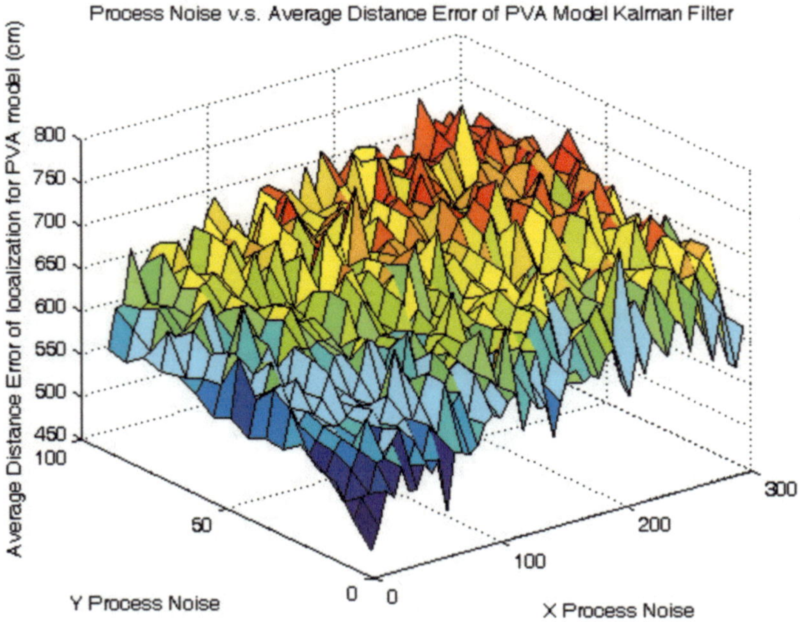

Fig. 14. Process noise versus localization error for *PVA* model using a maximum error threshold of 10,000 cm

Subtracting equation (20) from (19) results in:

$$\begin{aligned}\Delta d_1 &= d_{1max}^{+} - d_{1max}^{-} \\ &= \left(d_1 + T\cdot v_{max} + \tfrac{1}{2}T^2\cdot a_{max}\right) - \left(d_1 - T\cdot v_{max} + \tfrac{1}{2}T^2\cdot a_{max}\right) \\ &= 2\cdot T\cdot v_{max} + T^2\cdot a_{max}\end{aligned} \tag{21}$$

Equation (21) results in a threshold against which we can compare future distance measurements from beacon $B1$. Thresholds for the other beacons 2 and 3 can be obtained similarly. If the absolute value of the current distance measurement minus the previous measurement is greater than than the predefined threshold ΔD, then this current distance measurement can be discarded.

5.3 Computation requirement comparison

Thus far, only the accuracy of the localization methods has been examined without any discussion of the computation requirements associated with them. As mentioned before, these localization methods will be implemented on an embedded system with limited capabilities. Based on the application, an appropriate localization method must be used that balances accuracy with the capabilities of the system.

The following analysis utilizes the number of floating point operations as a metric to compare the different methods. For simplicity of presentation, this analysis assumes that the embedded system has native floating point capabilities and does not rely on integer computations to mimic floating point operations. Further, this analysis only accounts for

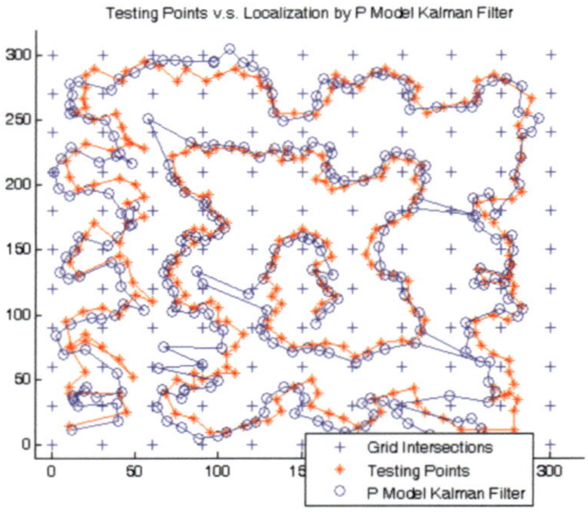

A. *P* model, Error threshold = 100 cm

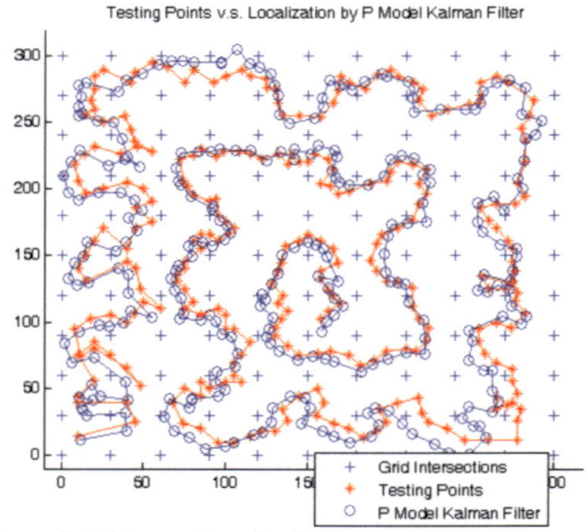

B. *P* model, Error threshold = 30 cm

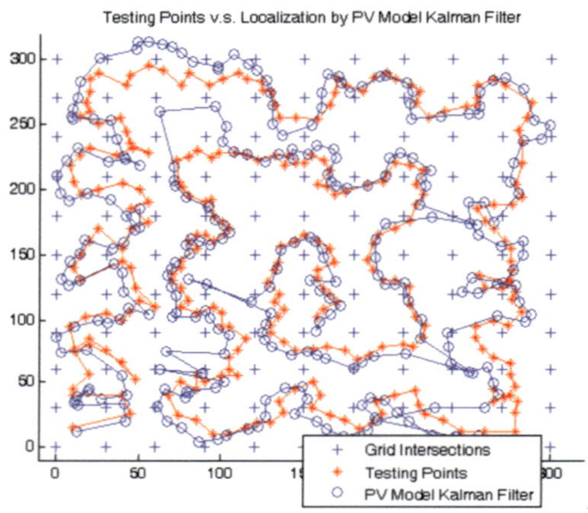

C. *PV* model, Error threshold = 100 cm

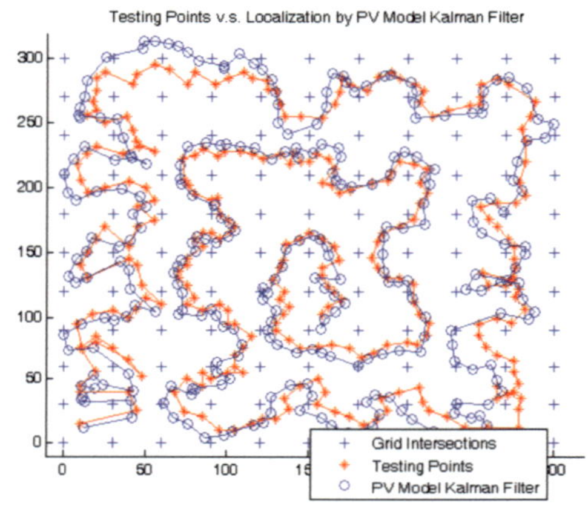

D. *PV* model, Error threshold = 30 cm

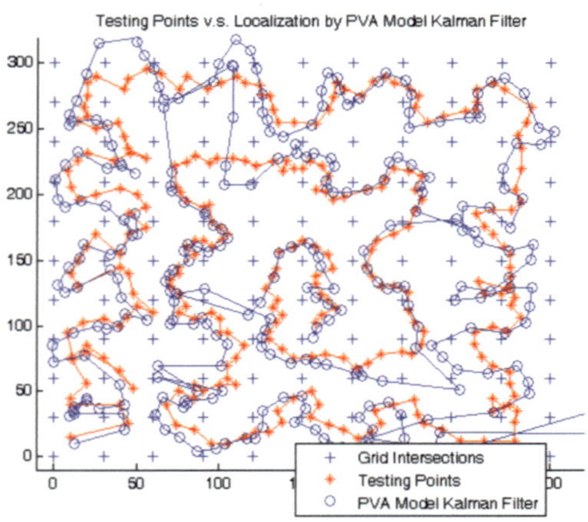

E. *PVA* model, Error threshold = 100 cm

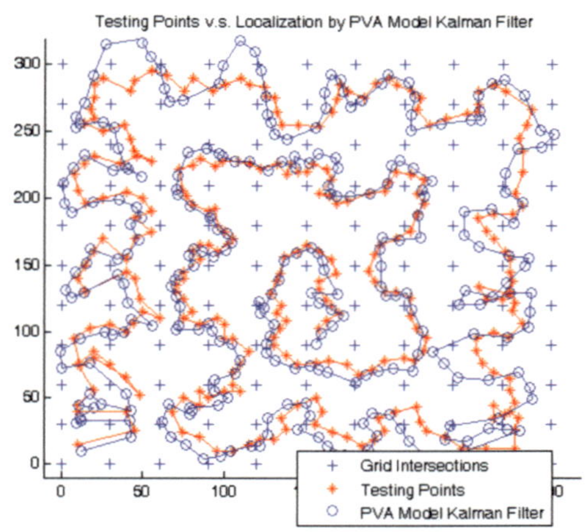

F. F. *PVA* model Error threshold = 30 cm

Fig. 15A, C, and E. Performance of *P*, *PV*, and *PVA* models with error threshold of 100 cm.

Fig. 15B, 15D, and 15F. Performance of *P*, *PV*, and *PVA* models with error threshold of 30 cm.

steady-state computation, meaning the initialization and setup computations are not considered. All the addition, subtraction, multiplication, and division steps that must be evaluated for each matrix operation for the equations given in Table 1 were considered.

Method	Number of Floating Point Operations per Iteration
P	268
PV	884
PVA	2220

Table 7. Comparison of Floating Point Operations between methods

As Table 7 reveals, the *P* model is the least computationally intensive. It is followed by the PV and PVA Kalman filters. This is intuitive since the *P* model has only two element in its state, and the dimensions of the state space model *A*, process noise Q, covariance P_k, and Kalman gain $K_k$matrices will be much smaller. Whereas the larger number of elements in the *PV* and *PVA* state result in greater dimensional matrices used during the evaulation of the Kalman filter equations, and hence a greater number of computations.
The Kalman filter equations involve many matrix multiplications and an inverse operation for computing the Kalman gain *K*. These two operations have complexity $O(n^3)$ and as a result the Kalman filter is also of complexity $O(n^3)$ where n is the number of parameters in the state.

Method	Order of Magnitude	Comment
P	$O(n^3)$	n is the number of elements in the state variable.
PV	$O(n^3)$	n is the number of elements in the state variable.
PVA	$O(n^3)$	n is the number of elements in the state variable.

Table 8. Computational complexity between methods

5.4 Memory requirement comparison

This section takes a cursory glance at the memory needs of the three Kalman filter models. It should be noted that the memory usage described here is the steady state memory, this does not take into account any initializations that may be required for different applications. It is also assumed that floats are four bytes long and that all variables in the Kalman filter equations require the float type.
In the expressions for the three Kalman filters, n is the number of elements in the state variable and m is the number of distance readings. The expressions for the memory requirements of the Kalman filters include an additional $(n^2 + n + 2nm + m + m^2)$ bytes of memory for temporary variables.
Since the measurement noises for each of the sensors in the experiment was assumed to be independent, R (measurement noise matrix) in Equation (12) of the Kalman filter contains values only along the diagonal. Instead of a matrix, a vector (mx1) can be used to represent each of the values along the diagonal and saving some space.

Name of Variable	Kalman Filter Variable	Matrix Dimension	Total Size
State model	A	$n\times n$	n^2
State estimate	X_k^-	$n\times 1$	n
Last state estimate	X_{k-1}	$n\times 1$	n
Estimated covariance	P_k^-	$n\times n$	n^2
Last estimated covariance	P_{k-1}	$n\times n$	n^2
Process noise	Q	$n\times n$	n^2
Output measurement matrix	H	$n\times m$	nm
Measurement noise	R	$m\times 1$	m
Kalman gain	K_k	$n\times m$	nm
Next state	X_k	$n\times 1$	n
Distance vector	D_k	$m\times 1$	m
Next covariance	P_k	$n\times n$	n^2
Position of sensors	Sensor location	$m\times 2$	$2m$
		Total	$5n^2 + 3n + 2nm + 4m$

Table 9. Computation of memory usage of Kalman filter variables.

The temporary variables listed in Table 10 are used during the Kalman filter operation to hold intermediate values during matrix multiplication and other operations. It should be noted that during the computation of the error covariance matrix P_k, it requires a temporary variable of size($n\times n$). However, while projecting the error covariance matrix P_k^-, a temporary variable of size ($n\times n$) is utilized. This same temporary variable can be used during the computation of P_k as well.

$$\begin{aligned}\text{Total Memory} &= [\text{Kalman Filter Variables} + \text{Temporary Variables}] \times 4 \text{ Bytes}\\ &= [(5n^2 + 3n + 2nm + 4m) + (n^2 + n + 2nm + m + m^2)] \times 4 \text{ Bytes}\\ &= [6n^2 + 4n + 4nm + 5m + m^2] \times 4 \text{ Bytes} \qquad (22)\end{aligned}$$

Equation (22), describes the total memory required for the computation of the Kalman filter equations. The number of distance measurements m is assumed to be 3, since this is the smallest number of distance measurements required to localize. The value for n for each of the P, PV, and PVA models depends upon the number of elements in each of their states which is outlined in Table 11.

Kalman Filter Equations		Terms Requiring Temporary Variables	Variable Size	Total Size
$X_k^- = A \cdot X_{k-1} + B \cdot U_k$	(10)			
$P_k^- = A \cdot P_{k-1} \cdot A^T + Q$	(11)	$\{A \cdot P_{k-1}\}$	$n \times n$	n^2
$K_k = P_k^- \cdot H^T \cdot (H \cdot P_k^- \cdot H^T + R)^{-1}$	(12)	$\{P_k^- \cdot H^T\}$ $\{H \cdot P_k^-\}$ $\{H \cdot P_k^- \cdot H^T\}$	$n \times m$ $m \times n$ $m \times m$	nm nm m^2
$X_k = X_k^- + K_k \cdot (D_k - H \cdot X_k^-)$	(13)	$\{H \cdot X_k^-\}$ $\{K_k \cdot (D_k - H \cdot X_k^-)\}$	$m \times 1$ $n \times 1$	m n
$P_k = (I - K_k \cdot H) \cdot P_k^-$	(14)	$\{K_k \cdot H\}$	$n \times n$	
		Total Size	$n^2 + n + 2nm + m + m^2$	

Table 10. Computation of memory usage of temporary variables for Kalman filter.

Method	Number of elements (n)
P	2
PV	4
PVA	6

Table 11. Number of elements in the state variable for each of the methods

Method	Total Memory Usage	Number of Bytes
P	$6n^2 + 4n + 4nm + 5m + m^2$	320
PV	$6n^2 + 4n + 4nm + 5m + m^2$	736
PVA	$6n^2 + 4n + 4nm + 5m + m^2$	1344

Table 12. Comparison between memory requirments between localization methods

6. Summary

The Kalman filter is very capable of localizing using noisy distance measurements in a wireless sensor network. The P model of the Kalman filter was found to have the best performance in these examples, however, depending on the motion of the tracked object the

PV or *PVA* model could be better. In the examples studied in this chapter, the *P* model is more adept at tracking the movement of an object with sporadic motion with sharp turns. Since the *P* model treats velocity and acceleration as random noise, it is less bound by these parameters. The *PV* and *PVA* models are bound by the Kinematics equations which do not allow for motion that is discontinuos in velocity and acceleration.

Two metrics were introduced that can be used to measure the accuracy of localiztion: the average distance error in localization and the Root Mean Square Error (RMSE). The average distance error in localization and the RMSE are very consistent metrics, although the RMSE method will return a higher error rate due to the squaring of the error.

The process noise parameters allow the Kalman filter to project the position of the object in the next time instant. If the proper process noise parameters are not used, the performance of the Kalman filters will be severly affected. In oder to obtain process noise parameters, the error rates can be computed for a variety of process noise paramters and the process noise parameters that result in minimum localization error can be used. This needs to be done each time a new path is expected to be taken by a mobile node because by comparing Table 4 and the section of Table 6 with error threshold of 30 cm, we can see that the process noise that results in the minimum localization error does indeed change between the two paths.

The Kalman filters are robust, and as the results indicated, there was very little difference in performance when the magnitude of errors in distance measurements was 100 cm and when the magnitude of error was 30 cm. However, despite the Kalman filters robustness, significant performance gains can be attained if the distance measurements used for localization are pre-filtered to ensure that they are not too erroneous. A method that was suggested was using the past distance measurements and the maximum velocity and acceleration attainable by the mobile node to project the next distance measurement. If the next distance measurement exceeds this threshold, it can be discarded.

Since localization methods well suited for wireless sensor networks using embedded systems with limited resources was desired, there is a need to analyze the computation and memory requirements. The *P* model Kalman filter was found to have the best computation and memory requirements due to the small number of elements in its state variable. This is followed by the *PV* model, and then the *PVA* model.

Although, in the experiments outlined in this chapter the process noise corresponding to reasonable low localization error was obtained, the task of obtaining process noise values in a real world scenario with a real moving object may be challenging. Especially if the path of the object is not known beforehand.

An assumtion that was made during these experiments was that the measurement noise R of each beacon is independent of the other which resulted in values only along the diagonal. However, in actuality, this is not the case especially when dealing with ultrasound pulses; the ultrasound pulses from each of the beacons may interfere with each other. This means that the measurement noise matrix, R, has values in all positions. Future work is needed to study the effects of interferances between beacons.

The experiments in this chapter focused only on the use of three beacons. Further study is needed to determine the effects of having more than three beacons and determine a policy for selecting the beacons to use the distance measurements from.

7. Acknowledgements

This research work is sponsored by National Science Foundation (NSF) IGERT-0504494, GK-12 0538457, CCF-0621493, and CNS-0723093.

8. References

Alippi, C.; Mottarella, A. & Vanini, G. (2005). A RF map-based localization algorithm for indoor environments, *Proceedings of IEEE International Symposium on Circuits and Systems*, 2005. ISCAS 2005, pp.652-655, ISBN: 0-7803-8834-8, Kobe, May 2005, IEEE CNF, Piscataway

Harter, A.; Steggles, P.; Ward, A. & Webster, P. (1999). The Anatomy of a Context-Aware Application , *Proceedings of the 5th Annual ACM/IEEE International Conference on Mobile Computing and Networking*, pp. 59-68, ISBN:1-58113-142-9 , Seattle, August 1999, ACM Press, New York.

Moore, D.; Leonard, J.; Rus, D. & Teller, S. (2004). Robust distributed network localization with noisy range measurements, *Proceedings of the 2nd international conference on Embedded networked sensor systems*, pp. 50-61, ISBN:1-58113-879-2, Baltimore, November 2004, ACM Press, New York

Patwari, N. & Hero, A. (2003). *Using proximity and quantized RSS for sensor localization in wireless networks*, Proceedings of the 2nd ACM international conference on Wireless sensor networks and applications, pp. 20-29, ISBN:1-58113-764-8, San Diego, September 2003, ACM Press, New York

Priyantha, B.; Chakraborty, A. & Balakrishnan, H. (2000). The Cricket location-support system, *Proceedings of the 6th annual international conference on Mobile computing and networking*, pp. 32-43, ISBN:1-58113-197-6, Boston, August 2000, ACM Press, New York

Shareef, A.; Zhu, Y.; & Musavi, M. (2008). Localization Using Neural Networks in Wireless Sensor Networks, *Proceedings of ACM First International Conference on Mobile Wireless Middleware, Operating Systems, and Applications*, pp. 1-7, ISBN:978-1-59593-984-5, Innsbruck, February 2008, ICST, Brussels

Smith, A.; Balakrishnan, H.; Goraczko, M. & Priyantha, N. (2004). Tracking moving devices with the cricket location system, *Proceedings of the 2nd international conference on Mobile systems, Applications, and Services*, pp. 190-202, ISBN:1-58113-793-1, Boston, June 2004, ACM Press, New York

Want, R.; Hopper, A.; Falcao, V. & Gibbons, J. (1992). The Active Badge Location System. *ACM Transactions on Information Systems*, Vol. 10, Issue 1., (January 1992), page numbers (91-102), ISSN:1046-8188

Ward, A.; Jones, A. & Hopper, A. (1997). A new location technique for the active office. *IEEE Personal Communications*, Vol. 4, Issue 5., (October 1997) page numbers (42-47), ISSN: 1070-9916

Welch, G.; Bishop, G.; Vicci, L.; Brumback, S.; Keller, K. & Colucci, D. (2001) High-Performance Wide-Area Optical Tracking: The HiBall Tracking System. *Presence: Teleoperators and Virtual Environments*, Vol. 10, Issue 1., (February 2001) page numbers (1-22), ISSN 1054-7460

Welch, G.; Allen, B.; Ilie, A. & Bishop, G. (2007). Measurement Sample Time Optimization for Human Motion Tracking/Capture Systems, *Proceedings of Trends and Issues in Tracking for Virtual Environments, Workshop at the IEEE Virtual Reality 2007 Conference,* ISBN: 978-3-8322-5967-9, Charlotte, March 2007, Shaker Verlag, Aachen

14

Adaptive and Nonlinear Kalman Filtering for GPS Navigation Processing

Dah-Jing Jwo[1], Mu-Yen Chen[1], Chien-Hao Tseng[1] and Ta-Shun Cho[2]
[1]*National Taiwan Ocean University*
[2]*National Chi Nan University*
Taiwan

1. Introduction

The Global Positioning System (GPS) is a satellite-based navigation system that provides a user with the proper equipment access to useful and accurate positioning information anywhere on the globe. The well-known Kalman filter (Gelb, 1974; Brown & Hwang, 1997; Axelrad & Brown, 1996) provides optimal (minimum mean square error) estimate of the system state vector, and has been widely applied to the fields of navigation such as GPS receiver position/velocity determination.

To obtain good estimation solutions using the EKF approach, the designers are required to have good knowledge on both dynamic process (plant dynamics, using an estimated internal model of the dynamics of the system) and measurement models, in addition to the assumption that both the process and measurement are corrupted by zero-mean white noises. A conventional Kalman filter fails ensure error convergence due to limited knowledge of the system's dynamic model and measurement noise. If the Kalman filter is provided with information that the process behaves a certain way, whereas, in fact, it behaves a different way, the filter will continually intend to fit an incorrect process signal.

In actual navigation filter designs, there exist model uncertainties which cannot be expressed by the linear state-space model. The linear model increases modelling errors since the actual vehicle motions are non-linear process. It is very often the case that little *a priori* knowledge is available concerning the manoeuvring. Hence, compensation of the uncertainties is an important task in the navigation filter design. In the modelling strategy, some phenomena are disregarded and a way to take them into account is to consider a nominal model affected by uncertainty.

The adaptive algorithm has been one of the approaches to prevent divergence problem of the EKF when precise knowledge on the system models are not available. To prevent divergence problem due to modelling errors using the EKF approach, the adaptive filter algorithm has been one of the strategies considered for estimating the state vector. Many efforts have been made to improve the estimation of the covariance matrices. Mehra (1970; 1971; 1972) classified the adaptive approaches into four categories: Bayesian, maximum likelihood, correlation and covariance matching. These methods can be applied to the Kalman filtering algorithm for realizing the adaptive Kalman filtering (Mehra, 1972; Mohamed & Schwarz, 1999). One of the adaptive fading methods (Ding, et al., 2007; Jwo & Weng, 2008) is called the strong tracking Kalman filter (STKF) (Zhou & Frank, 1996), which is essentially a nonlinear smoother algorithm that employs suboptimal multiple fading factors, in which the softening factors are involved. STKF has several merits, such as: (1) strong robustness against model uncertainties; (2) good real-time state tracking ability even when a state jump occurs, no matter whether the system has reached steady state or not.

Although it has been very common that additional fictitious process noise can be added to the system model, however, the more suitable cure for non convergence caused by un-modelled states is to correct the model. For the nonlinear estimation problem, alternatives for the model-based EKF can be employed, such as the unscented Kalman filter (UKF) approach. The UKF is a nonlinear, distribution approximation method, which uses a finite number of sigma points to propagate the probability of state distribution through the nonlinear dynamics of system. The UKF exhibits superior performance when compared with classical EKF since the series approximations in the EKF algorithm can lead to poor representations of the nonlinear functions and probability distributions of interest.

Another adaptive-like approach, referred to as the interacting multiple model (IMM) algorithm (Bar-Shalom, et al., 2001; Chen & Harigae, 2001; Deshpande & Challa, 2007; Johnston & Krishnamurthy, 2001; Kim & Hong, 2004; Lee, et al., 2005 ; Li & Bar-Shalom, 1993; Xu & Cui, 2007.), takes into account a set of models to represent the system behaviour patterns or system model. The overall estimates is obtained by a combination of the estimates from the filters running in parallel based on the individual models that match the system modes. The IMM-based method is realized to allow the possibility of using highly dynamic models just when required, diminishing unrealistic noise considerations in non-manoeuvring situations of the system.

The fuzzy logic adaptive system (FLAS) can be employed into the filter design, where the fuzzy logic reasoning system based on the Takagi-Sugeno (T-S) model is employed, for dynamically adjusting the softening factor according to the change in vehicle dynamics. The philosophy is based on combination of the merits by UKF and strong tracking feature. Navigation algorithm and performances evaluation based on the above various filters are to be discussed.

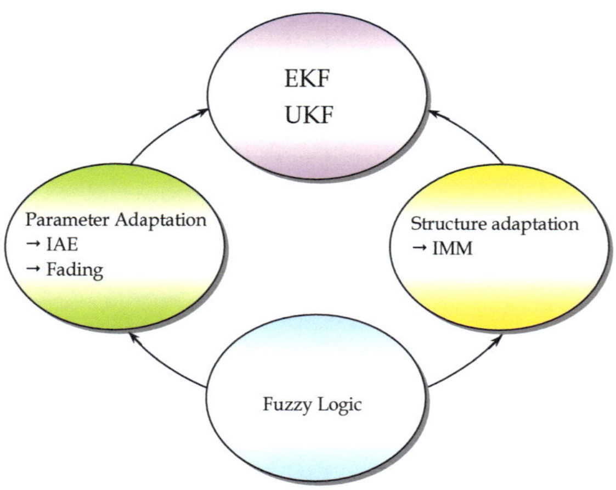

Fig. 1. Techniques involved for filter design in this chapter

In the GPS navigation processing, three feasible ways to avoid the divergence problem and improve the navigation accuracy are discussed: (1) adaptive approaches assisted by heuristic search techniques to fit the dynamic model process of interest as precisely as possible; (2) utilization of an appropriate nonlinear estimation approach after deriving a better nonlinear dynamic process model; and (3) interactive multiple model approach accounting for different manoeuvring conditions. Based on the consideration, this chapter is organized as follows. In Section 2, preliminary background on GPS navigation processing using the extended Kalman filter is reviewed. The adaptive Kalman filter is discussed in Section 3. In Section 4, the unscented Kalman filter (UKF) with nonlinear dynamic modelling approach is presented. Discussion on the IMM estimator is provided in Section 5. In Section 6, Incorporation of the fuzzy logic adaptive system (FLAS) to the GPS navigation processing is presented. Three illustrative examples on GPS navigation processing are provided in Section 7 for illustrating the performance for various approaches. Conclusion is given in Section 8.

2. GPS navigation processing using the extended Kalman filter

The discrete-time extended Kalman filter deals with the case governed by the nonlinear stochastic differential equations:

$$\mathbf{x}_{k+1} = \mathbf{f}_k(\mathbf{x}_k) + \mathbf{w}_k \tag{1a}$$

$$\mathbf{z}_k = \mathbf{h}_k(\mathbf{x}_k) + \mathbf{v}_k \tag{1b}$$

where the state vector $\mathbf{x}_k \in \Re^n$, process noise vector $\mathbf{w}_k \in \Re^n$, measurement vector $\mathbf{z}_k \in \Re^m$, and measurement noise vector $\mathbf{v}_k \in \Re^m$. In Equation (1), both the vectors $\mathbf{w}_k$ and $\mathbf{v}_k$ are zero mean Gaussian white sequences having zero crosscorrelation with each other:

$$\mathbf{E}[\mathbf{w}_k\mathbf{w}_i^{\mathrm{T}}] = \begin{cases} \mathbf{Q}_k, & i = k \\ 0, & i \neq k \end{cases}; \ \mathbf{E}[\mathbf{v}_k\mathbf{v}_i^{\mathrm{T}}] = \begin{cases} \mathbf{R}_k, & i = k \\ 0, & i \neq k \end{cases}; \ \mathbf{E}[\mathbf{w}_k\mathbf{v}_i^{\mathrm{T}}] = \mathbf{0} \quad \textit{for all i and k} \tag{2}$$

where $\mathbf{Q}_k$ is the process noise covariance matrix, $\mathbf{R}_k$ is the measurement noise covariance matrix, $E[\cdot]$ represents expectation, and superscript "T" denotes matrix transpose.
The discrete-time extended Kalman filter algorithm for the GPS navigation processing is summarized as follow:

1. Initialize state vector and state covariance matrix: $\hat{\mathbf{x}}_0^-$ and $\mathbf{P}_0^-$
2. Compute Kalman gain matrix from state covariance and estimated measurement covariance:

$$\mathbf{K}_k = \mathbf{P}_k^- \mathbf{H}_k^{\mathrm{T}} [\mathbf{H}_k \mathbf{P}_k^- \mathbf{H}_k^{\mathrm{T}} + \mathbf{R}_k]^{-1} \tag{3}$$

3. Multiply prediction error vector by Kalman gain matrix to get state correction vector and update state vector:

$$\hat{\mathbf{x}}_k = \hat{\mathbf{x}}_k^- + \mathbf{K}_k[\mathbf{z}_k - \hat{\mathbf{z}}_k^-], \text{ where } \hat{\mathbf{z}}_k^- = \mathbf{h}_k(\hat{\mathbf{x}}_k^-) \tag{4}$$

4. Update error covariance

$$\mathbf{P}_k = [\mathbf{I} - \mathbf{K}_k \mathbf{H}_k]\mathbf{P}_k^- \tag{5}$$

5. Predict new state vector and state covariance matrix

$$\hat{\mathbf{x}}_k^- = \mathbf{f}_{k-1}(\hat{\mathbf{x}}_{k-1}^-) \tag{6}$$

$$\mathbf{P}_{k+1}^- = \mathbf{\Phi}_k \mathbf{P}_k \mathbf{\Phi}_k^{\mathbf{T}} + \mathbf{Q}_k \tag{7}$$

where the linear approximation equations for system and measurement matrices are obtained through the relations

$$\mathbf{\Phi}_k \approx \left.\frac{\partial \mathbf{f}_k}{\partial \mathbf{x}}\right|_{\mathbf{x}=\hat{\mathbf{x}}_k^-} \ ; \ \mathbf{H}_k \approx \left.\frac{\partial \mathbf{h}_k}{\partial \mathbf{x}}\right|_{\mathbf{x}=\hat{\mathbf{x}}_k^-} \tag{8}$$

Equations (3-5) are the measurement update equations, and Equations (6-7) are the time update equations of the algorithm from k to step $k+1$. These equations incorporate a measurement value into *a priori* estimation to obtain an improved *a posteriori* estimation. In the above equations, $\mathbf{P}_k$ is the error covariance matrix defined by $E[(\mathbf{x}_k - \hat{\mathbf{x}}_k)(\mathbf{x}_k - \hat{\mathbf{x}}_k)^{\mathrm{T}}]$. The Kalman filter algorithm starts with an initial condition value, $\hat{\mathbf{x}}_0^-$ and $\mathbf{P}_0^-$. When new measurement $\mathbf{z}_k$ becomes available with the progression of time, the estimation of states and the corresponding error covariance would follow recursively ad infinity. Fig 2 shows GPS navigation using the filter approach and the flow chart for the GPS Kalman filter. Further detailed discussion can be referred to Brown and Hwang (1997), Gelb (1974), and Jwo & Cho (2007).

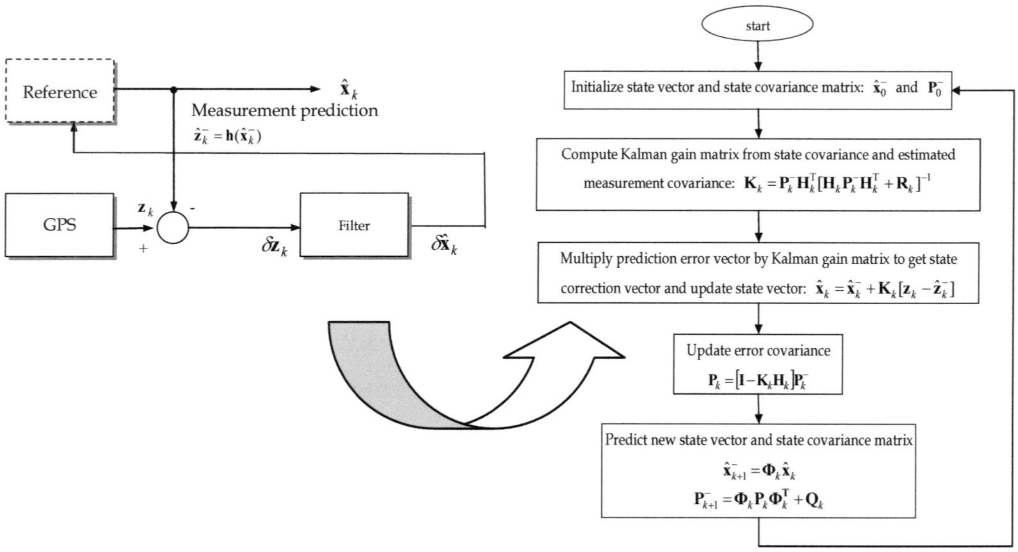

Fig. 2. GPS navigation using the filter approach and the flow chart for the GPS Kalman filter

3. The adaptive extended Kalman filter

The implementation of Kalman filter requires the *a priori* knowledge of both the process and measurement models. It is widely known that poorly designed mathematical model for the

EKF may lead to the divergence. Clearly, if the plant parameters are subject to perturbations and dynamics of the system are too complex to be characterized by an explicit mathematical model, an adaptive scheme is needed. An adaptive Kalman filter can be utilized as the noise-adaptive filter to adjust the parameters. It is well known that the process model is dependent on the dynamical characteristics of the vehicle onto which the navigation system is placed. In order to overcome the defect of the conventional Kalman filtering, several approaches of adaptive Kalman filter have been proposed.

Mehra classified the adaptive approaches into four categories: Bayesian, maximum likelihood, correlation and covariance matching. The innovation sequences have been utilized by the correlation and covariance-matching techniques to estimate the noise covariances. The basic idea behind the covariance-matching approach is to make the actual value of the covariance of the residual consistent with its theoretical value. From the incoming measurement $\mathbf{z}_k$ and the optimal prediction $\hat{\mathbf{x}}_k^-$ obtained in the previous step, the innovation sequence is defined as: $\boldsymbol{\upsilon}_k = \mathbf{z}_k - \hat{\mathbf{z}}_k^-$. The innovation represents the additional information available to the filter as a consequence of the new observation $\mathbf{z}_k$. An innovation of zero means that the two are in complete agreement. The mean of the corresponding error of an unbiased estimator is zero.

The innovation sequences have been utilized to estimate the noise covariance matrices (Mohamed & Schwarz, 1999; Hide et al., 2003) and system fault detection (Caliskan & Hajiyev, 2000; Jwo & Cho, 2007). The innovation-based adaptive estimation (IAE) approach is essentially a type of variance estimation (scaling to the $\mathbf{Q}_k$ or $\mathbf{R}_k$ matrices) method. The basic idea behind the covariance-matching approach is to make the actual value of the covariance of the residual consistent with its theoretical value. This leads to the estimate of process noise matrix $\mathbf{Q}_k$ and measurement noise matrix $\mathbf{R}_k$. For more detailed information derivation for these equations, see Mohamed & Schwarz (1999), and Hide et al. (2003).

One of the approaches for adaptive processing is on the incorporation of fading factors. Xia et al. (1994) proposed a concept of adaptive fading Kalman filter (AFKF) and solved the state estimation problem. The AFKF is essentially a covariance scaling-based Kalman filter (scaling to the P matrix). The approach tries to estimate a scale factor to increase the predicted variance components of the state vector. In the AFKF, suboptimal fading factors are introduced into the algorithm. The idea of fading Kalman filtering is to apply a factor matrix to the predicted covariance matrix to deliberately increase the variance of the predicted state vector:

$$\mathbf{P}_{k+1}^- = \boldsymbol{\lambda}_k \boldsymbol{\Phi}_k \mathbf{P}_k \boldsymbol{\Phi}_k^T + \mathbf{Q}_k \tag{9}$$

where $\boldsymbol{\lambda}_k = diag(\lambda_1, \lambda_2 \ldots, \lambda_m)$. The main difference between different adaptive fading algorithms is on the calculation of scale factor $\boldsymbol{\lambda}_k$ (Ding, et al., 2007; Jwo & Weng, 2008). One approach is to assign the scale factors as constants. When $\lambda_i \le 1$ ($i = 1,2,\ldots,m$), the filtering is in a steady state processing while $\lambda_i > 1$, the filtering may tend to be unstable. For the case $\lambda_i = 1$, it deteriorates to the standard Kalman filter. There are some drawbacks with constant factors, e.g., as the filtering proceeds, the precision of the filtering will decrease because the effects of old data tend to become less and less. The ideal way is to use time varying factors that are determined according to the dynamic and observation model accuracy.

To increase the tracking capability, the time-varying suboptimal scaling factor is incorporated, for on-line tuning the covariance of the predicted state, which adjusts the filter gain, and accordingly the improved version of AFKF is developed. Various formulations have been modified by multiplying the weighting factor, see Ding, et al. (2007), and Jwo & Weng (2008).

Zhou et al. proposed a concept of strong tracking Kalman filter (STKF) and solved the state estimation problem of a class of nonlinear systems with white noise. In the so called STKF algorithm, suboptimal fading factors are introduced into the nonlinear smoother algorithm. The STKF has several important merits, including (1) strong robustness against model uncertainties; (2) good real-time state tracking capability even when a state jump occurs, no matter whether the system has reached steady state or not. Zhou & Frank (1996) proved that a filter is called the STKF only if the filter satisfies the orthogonal principle stated as follows:

Orthogonal principle: The sufficient condition for a filter to be called the STKF only if the time-varying filter gain matrix be selected on-line such that the state estimation mean-square error is minimized and the innovations remain orthogonal:

$$E[\mathbf{x}_k - \hat{\mathbf{x}}_k][\mathbf{x}_k - \hat{\mathbf{x}}_k]^T = \min$$

$$E[\boldsymbol{\upsilon}_{k+j}\boldsymbol{\upsilon}_k^T] = 0\,,\; k = 0,1,2...,\; j = 1,2... \tag{10}$$

Equation (10) is required for ensuring that the innovation sequence will be remained orthogonal. The time-varying suboptimal scaling factor is incorporated, for on-line tuning the covariance of the predicted state, which adjusts the filter gain, and accordingly the STKF is developed. The suboptimal scaling factor in the time-varying filter gain matrix is given by:

$$\lambda_{i,k} = \begin{cases} \alpha_i c_k & ,\alpha_i c_k \ge 1 \\ 1 & ,\alpha_i c_k < 1 \end{cases} \tag{11}$$

where

$$c_k = \frac{tr[\mathbf{N}_k]}{tr[\boldsymbol{\alpha}\mathbf{M}_k]} \tag{12}$$

and

$$\mathbf{N}_k = \mathbf{V}_k - \beta\mathbf{R}_k - \mathbf{H}_k\mathbf{Q}_k\mathbf{H}_k^T \tag{13a}$$

$$\mathbf{M}_k = \mathbf{H}_k\mathbf{\Phi}_k\mathbf{P}_k\mathbf{\Phi}_k^T\mathbf{H}_k^T \tag{14}$$

$$\mathbf{V}_k = \begin{cases} \boldsymbol{\upsilon}_0\boldsymbol{\upsilon}_0^T, k = 0 \\ \dfrac{[\rho\mathbf{V}_{k-1} + \boldsymbol{\upsilon}_k\boldsymbol{\upsilon}_k^T]}{1+\rho}, k \ge 1 \end{cases} \tag{15}$$

Equation (13a) can be modified by multiplying an additional parameter $\boldsymbol{\gamma}$, which can be a scalar of a diagonal matrix:

$$\mathbf{N}_k = \boldsymbol{\gamma}\mathbf{V}_k - \beta\mathbf{R}_k - \mathbf{H}_k\mathbf{Q}_k\mathbf{H}_k^T \tag{13b}$$

This parameter is introduced for increasing the tracking capability through the increase of covariance matrix of the innovation.
The key parameter in the STKF is the fading factor matrix $\boldsymbol{\lambda}_k$, which is dependent on three parameters, including (1) α_i; (2) the forgetting factor (ρ); (3) and the softening factor (β). These parameters are usually selected empirically. $\alpha_i \geq 1, i = 1,2,\ldots,m$, which are *a priori* selected. If from *a priori* knowledge, we have the knowledge that $\mathbf{x}$ will have a large change, then a large α_i should be used so as to improve the tracking capability of the STKF. On the other hand, if no *a priori* knowledge about the plant dynamic, it is commonly select $\alpha_1 = \alpha_2 = \cdots = \alpha_m = 1$. In such case, the STKF based on multiple fading factors deteriorates to a STKF based on a single fading factor. The range of the forgetting factor is $0 < \rho \leq 1$, for which 0.95 is commonly used. The softening factor β is utilized to improve the smoothness of state estimation. A larger β (with value no less than 1) leads to better estimation accuracy; while a smaller β provides stronger tracking capability. The value is usually determined empirically through computer simulation and $\beta = 4.5$ is a commonly selected value.

4. The unscented Kalman filter

In the EKF, the state distribution is approximated by a Gaussian random variable (GRV), which is then propagated analytically through the first-order linearization of the nonlinear system. Wan and van der Merwe (2000) pointed out that this will introduce large errors in the true posterior mean and covariance of the transformed GRV and lead to sub-optimal performance and sometimes filter divergence. The UKF addresses this problem by using a deterministic sampling approach (Crassidis, 2006). The state distribution is also approximated by a GRV, but is represented using a minimal set of sample points. These sample points are carefully chosen so as to completely capture the true mean and covariance of the GRV. When the sample points are propagated through the true nonlinear system, the posterior mean and covariance can be captured accurately to the 3rd order of Taylor series expansion for any nonlinear system.

4.1 Unscented transformation

The first step in the UKF is to sample the prior state distribution, i.e., generate the sigma points through the unscented transformation (UT) (Julier et al. 2000; Julier & Uhlmann 2002; Julier 2002). The unscented transform is a method for calculating the statistics of a random variable which undergoes a nonlinear transformation. The basic premise is that to approximate a probability distribution is easier than to approximate an arbitrary nonlinear transformation. A set of weighted samples or sigma points are deterministically chosen so that they completely capture the true mean and covariance of the random variable. The samples are propagated through true nonlinear equations without linearization of the model. Suppose the mean $\bar{\mathbf{x}}$ and covariance $\mathbf{P}$ of vector $\mathbf{x}$ are known, a set of deterministic vector called sigma points can then be found. The ensemble mean and covariance of the sigma points are equal to $\bar{\mathbf{x}}$ and $\mathbf{P}$. The nonlinear function $\mathbf{y} = f(\mathbf{x})$ is applied to each deterministic vector to obtain transformed vectors. The ensemble mean and covariance of the transformed vectors will give a good estimate of the true mean and covariance of $\mathbf{y}$, which is the key to the unscented transformation. Illustration of properties of UKF and EKF is shown in Fig. 3. The UKF approach estimates are expected to be closer to the true values than the EKF approach.

Consider an n dimensional random variable $\mathbf{x}$, having the mean $\hat{\mathbf{x}}$ and covariance $\mathbf{P}$, and suppose that it propagates through an arbitrary nonlinear function $\mathbf{f}$. The unscented transform creates $2n+1$ sigma vectors $\mathbf{X}$ (a capital letter) and weighted points W, given by

$$\mathbf{X}_{(0)} = \hat{\mathbf{x}} \tag{16}$$

$$\mathbf{X}_{(i)} = \hat{\mathbf{x}} + (\sqrt{(n+\lambda)\mathbf{P}})_i^T \;, \; i = 1,...,n \tag{17}$$

$$\mathbf{X}_{(i+n)} = \hat{\mathbf{x}} - (\sqrt{(n+\lambda)\mathbf{P}})_i^T \;, \; i = 1,...,n \tag{18}$$

$$W_0^{(m)} = \frac{\lambda}{(n+\lambda)} \tag{19}$$

$$W_0^{(c)} = W_0^{(m)} + (1-\alpha^2+\beta) \tag{20}$$

$$W_i^{(m)} = W_i^{(c)} = \frac{1}{2(n+\lambda)} \;, \; i = 1,...,2n \tag{21}$$

where $(\sqrt{(n+\lambda)\mathbf{P}})_i$ is the ith row (or column) of the matrix square root. $\sqrt{(n+\lambda)\mathbf{P}}$ can be obtained from the lower-triangular matrix of the Cholesky factorization; $\lambda = \alpha^2(n+k)-n$ is a scaling parameter; α determines the spread of the sigma points around $\hat{\mathbf{x}}$ and is usually set to a small positive(e.g., $1e-4 \le \alpha \le 1$); k is a secondly scaling parameter (usually set as 0); β is used to incorporate prior knowledge of the distribution of $\bar{\mathbf{x}}$ (When $\mathbf{x}$ is normally distributed, $\beta = 2$ is an optimal value); $W_i^{(m)}$ is the weight for the mean associated with the i*th* point; and $W_i^{(c)}$ is the weigh for the covariance associated with the i*th* point.

The sigma vectors are propagated through the nonlinear function to yield a set of transformed sigma points,

$$\mathbf{y}_i = f(\mathbf{X}_i) \quad i = 0,...,2n \tag{22}$$

The mean and covariance of $\mathbf{y}_i$ are approximated by a weighted average mean and covariance of the transformed sigma points as follows:

$$\bar{\mathbf{y}}_u = \sum_{i=0}^{2n} W_i^{(m)} \mathbf{y}_i \tag{23}$$

$$\bar{\mathbf{P}}_u = \sum_{i=0}^{2n} W_i^{(c)} (\mathbf{y}_i - \bar{\mathbf{y}}_u)(\mathbf{y}_i - \bar{\mathbf{y}}_u)^T \tag{24}$$

As compared to the EKF's linear approximation, the unscented transformation is accurate to the second order for any nonlinear function.

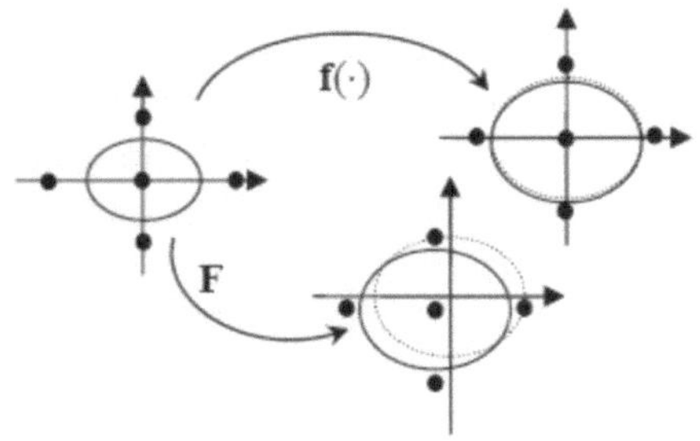

Fig. 3. The mapping of the UKF versus that of the EKF, through the transformation of: (1) the nonlinear function $\mathbf{f}(\cdot)$, shown on the top portion of the figure, and (2) its Jacobian $\mathbf{F}$, shown at the bottom portion of the figure. The dot-line ellipse represents the true covariance; the solid-line ellipse represents the calculated covariance (Li et al. 2006)

4.2 The unscented Kalman filter

The basic premise behind the unscented Kalman filter is it is easier to approximate a Gaussian distribution than it is to approximate an arbitrary nonlinear function. Instead of linearizing using Jacobian matrices as in the EKF and achieving first-order accuracy, the UKF uses a deterministic sampling approach to capture the mean and covariance estimates with a minimal set of sample points. To look at the detailed algorithm of the UKF, firstly, the set of sigma points are created by Equations (12) and (13). A high level of operation of the unscented Kalman filter and the flow chart for the UKF approach is shown in Fig. 4. After

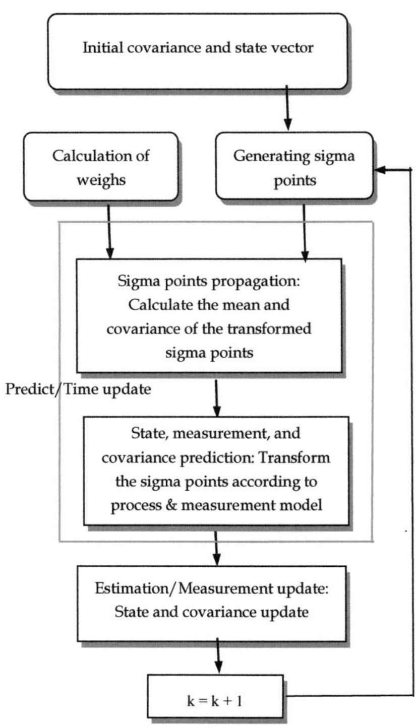

(1) The transformed set is given by instantiatin point through the process model

$$(\boldsymbol{\zeta}_k^-)_i = f((\mathbf{X}_k^-)_i)$$

(2) Predicted mean

$$\hat{\mathbf{x}}_k^- = \sum_{i=0}^{2n} W_i^{(m)} (\boldsymbol{\zeta}_k^-)_i$$

(3) Predicted covariance

$$\mathbf{P}_k^- = \sum_{i=0}^{2n} W_i^c [(\boldsymbol{\zeta}_k^-)_i - \hat{\mathbf{x}}_k^-][(\boldsymbol{\zeta}_k^-)_i - \hat{\mathbf{x}}_k^-]^T + \mathbf{Q}_k$$

(4) Instantiate each of the prediction points thr observation model

$$(\mathbf{Z}_k^-)_i = \mathbf{h}((\boldsymbol{\zeta}_k^-)_i)$$

(5) Predicted observation

$$\hat{\mathbf{z}}_k^- = \sum_{i=0}^{2n} W_i^{(m)} (\mathbf{Z}_k^-)_i$$

(6) Innovation covariance

$$\mathbf{P}_{yy} = \sum_{i=0}^{2n} W_i^{(c)} [(\mathbf{Z}_k^-)_i - \hat{\mathbf{z}}_k^-][(\mathbf{Z}_k^-)_i - \hat{\mathbf{z}}_k^-]^T + \mathbf{R}_k$$

(7) Cross covariance

$$\mathbf{P}_{xz} = \sum_{i=0}^{2n} W_i^{(c)} [(\boldsymbol{\zeta}_k^-)_i - \hat{\mathbf{x}}_k^-][(\mathbf{Z}_k^-)_i - \hat{\mathbf{z}}_k^-]^T$$

(8) Performing update using the nominal KF

$$\mathbf{K}_k = \mathbf{P}_{xz}\mathbf{P}_{yy}^{-1}$$
$$\hat{\mathbf{x}}_k = \hat{\mathbf{x}}_k^- + \mathbf{K}_k(\mathbf{z}_k - \hat{\mathbf{z}}_k^-)$$
$$\mathbf{P}_k = \mathbf{P}_k^- - \mathbf{K}_k \mathbf{P}_{yy} \mathbf{K}_k^T$$

Fig. 4. High level of operation of the unscented Kalman filter (left) and the flow chart (right) for the unscented Kalman Filter the sigma points are generated, the time update (prediction) step and the measurement update (correction) step are involved. The samples are propagated through true nonlinear equations; the linearization is unnecessary (i.e., calculation of Jacobian is not necessary). They can capture the states up to at least second order, where as the EKF is only a first order approximation. Further detailed discussion on the UKF can be referred to Wan & Van der Merwe (2001), Julier & Uhlmann (1997), and Julier, et al. (1995). Although recently the particle filter (Gordon, 1993; 2004) has been studied and shown promising potential, especially for nonlinear, non-Gaussian problems, the content will not be covered this chapter.

4.3 A nonlinear model

Derivation of a better, nonlinear, dynamic model not only alleviates the divergence problem by resorting to modelling the system dynamic process as precisely as possible but also improves the estimation accuracy. To construct the nonlinear dynamic model, consider a vehicle moving at the velocity represented as $\mathbf{V}_b = u_b\vec{i} + v_b\vec{j} + w_b\vec{k}$. The velocity in the fixed frame in terms of Euler angles and body velocity components has the relation

$$\mathbf{V} = \begin{bmatrix} \dot{x} \\ \dot{y} \\ \dot{z} \end{bmatrix} = \begin{bmatrix} C_\theta C_\psi & S_\Phi S_\theta C_\psi - C_\Phi S_\psi & C_\Phi S_\theta C_\psi + S_\Phi S_\psi \\ C_\theta S_\psi & S_\Phi S_\theta S_\psi + C_\Phi C_\psi & C_\Phi S_\theta S_\psi - S_\Phi C_\psi \\ -S_\theta & S_\Phi C_\theta & C_\Phi C_\theta \end{bmatrix} \begin{bmatrix} u_b \\ v_b \\ w_b \end{bmatrix}$$

where the following notations are used: $S_\Phi \equiv \sin(\Phi)$, $C_\Phi \equiv \cos(\Phi)$, $S_\theta \equiv \sin(\theta)$, $C_\theta \equiv \cos(\theta)$, $S_\psi \equiv \sin(\psi)$, and $C_\psi \equiv \cos(\psi)$. Based on the idea, the dynamic process model of the GPS receiver can be represented by the nonlinear model. Suppose that, as the non-holonomic constraint, only the longitudinal movement is considered and the lateral slippage is neglected. In case the velocity in the x-component of body frame is considered, $\| \mathbf{V}_b \| \approx \| u_b\vec{i} \| \approx V$, the model can be simplified

$$\begin{aligned} \dot{x} &= V\cos\theta\cos\psi \\ \dot{y} &= V\cos\theta\sin\psi \\ \dot{z} &= -V\sin\theta \end{aligned} \tag{25}$$

In this case, we consider the GPS navigation filter with three position states, three angles states, and two clock states, so that the state to be estimated is a 9×1 vector. The dynamic model governed by Equation (25) with additive noise can be represented by

$$\begin{bmatrix} \dot{x} \\ \dot{y} \\ \dot{z} \\ \dot{\Phi} \\ \dot{\theta} \\ \dot{\psi} \\ \dot{V} \\ \dot{b} \\ \dot{d} \end{bmatrix} = \begin{bmatrix} \dot{x}_1 \\ \dot{x}_2 \\ \dot{x}_3 \\ \dot{x}_4 \\ \dot{x}_5 \\ \dot{x}_6 \\ \dot{x}_7 \\ \dot{x}_8 \\ \dot{x}_9 \end{bmatrix} = \begin{bmatrix} V\cos\theta\cos\psi \\ V\cos\theta\sin\psi \\ -V\sin\theta \\ 0 \\ 0 \\ 0 \\ 0 \\ d \\ 0 \end{bmatrix} + \begin{bmatrix} u_1 \\ u_2 \\ u_3 \\ u_4 \\ u_5 \\ u_6 \\ u_7 \\ u_8 \\ u_9 \end{bmatrix} \tag{26}$$

and

$$\mathbf{F} = \frac{\partial \mathbf{f}}{\partial \mathbf{x}} = \begin{bmatrix} 0 & 0 & 0 & 0 & -VS_\theta C_\psi & -VC_\theta S_\psi & C_\theta C_\psi & 0 & 0 \\ 0 & 0 & 0 & 0 & -VS_\theta S_\psi & VC_\theta C_\psi & C_\theta S_\psi & 0 & 0 \\ 0 & 0 & 0 & 0 & -VC_\theta & 0 & -S_\theta & 0 & 0 \\ 0 & 0 & 0 & 0 & 0 & 0 & 0 & 0 & 0 \\ 0 & 0 & 0 & 0 & 0 & 0 & 0 & 0 & 0 \\ 0 & 0 & 0 & 0 & 0 & 0 & 0 & 0 & 0 \\ 0 & 0 & 0 & 0 & 0 & 0 & 0 & 0 & 0 \\ 0 & 0 & 0 & 0 & 0 & 0 & 0 & 0 & 1 \\ 0 & 0 & 0 & 0 & 0 & 0 & 0 & 0 & 0 \end{bmatrix} \tag{27}$$

In this nonlinear dynamic model, attitude angles are introduced. As part of the state variables, these angles can be estimated from the GPS filter in a single-antenna receiver with pseudorange observables. The process noise covariance matrix for this nonlinear model is given by the form

$$\mathbf{Q}_k = \begin{bmatrix} q_{11} & & & & & & & & \\ & q_{22} & & & & & & 0 & \\ & & q_{33} & & & & & & \\ & & & q_{44} & & & & & \\ & & & & q_{55} & & & & \\ & & & & & q_{66} & & & \\ & & & & & & q_{77} & & \\ & 0 & & & & & & q_{88} & q_{98} \\ & & & & & & & q_{89} & q_{99} \end{bmatrix} \tag{28}$$

in which the q_{ii} are set to be constants, $i = 1 \ldots 7$; $q_{88} = S_f \Delta t + S_g \frac{\Delta t^3}{2}$; $q_{98} = S_g \frac{\Delta t^2}{2}$; $q_{89} = S_g \frac{\Delta t^2}{2}$; $q_{99} = S_g \Delta t$. The linearized measurement equation based on n observables for this nonlinear model is given by:

$$\begin{bmatrix} \rho_1 \\ \rho_2 \\ \vdots \\ \rho_n \end{bmatrix} = \begin{bmatrix} \hat{\rho}_1 \\ \hat{\rho}_2 \\ \vdots \\ \hat{\rho}_n \end{bmatrix} + \begin{bmatrix} h_x^{(1)} & h_y^{(1)} & h_z^{(1)} & 0 & 0 & 0 & 0 & 1 & 0 \\ h_x^{(2)} & h_y^{(2)} & h_z^{(2)} & 0 & 0 & 0 & 0 & 1 & 0 \\ \vdots & \vdots & \vdots & \vdots & \vdots & \vdots & \vdots & \vdots & 0 \\ h_x^{(3)} & h_y^{(3)} & h_z^{(3)} & 0 & 0 & 0 & 0 & 1 & 0 \end{bmatrix} \begin{bmatrix} x_1 \\ x_2 \\ x_3 \\ x_4 \\ x_5 \\ x_6 \\ x_7 \\ x_8 \\ x_9 \end{bmatrix} + \begin{bmatrix} v_{\rho 1} \\ v_{\rho 2} \\ \vdots \\ v_{\rho n} \end{bmatrix} \tag{29}$$

where, as defined previously, the elements of the measurement model $\mathbf{H}_k$ are the partial derivatives of the predicted measurements with respect to each state, which is an $(n \times 9)$ matrix.

$$\mathbf{H}_k = \begin{bmatrix} h_x^{(1)} & h_y^{(1)} & h_z^{(1)} & 0 & 0 & 0 & 0 & 1 & 0 \\ h_x^{(2)} & h_y^{(2)} & h_z^{(2)} & 0 & 0 & 0 & 0 & 1 & 0 \\ \vdots & \vdots & \vdots & \vdots & \vdots & \vdots & \vdots & \vdots & 0 \\ h_x^{(3)} & h_y^{(3)} & h_z^{(3)} & 0 & 0 & 0 & 0 & 1 & 0 \end{bmatrix} \tag{30}$$

The expected pseudorange $\mathbf{h}_k(\hat{\mathbf{x}}_k^-)$ based on the GPS satellite position and the *a priori* state estimate $\hat{\mathbf{x}}_k^-$ is given by

$$\mathbf{h}_k(\hat{\mathbf{x}}_k^-) = [x_k^- \quad y_k^- \quad z_k^-]^T$$

with norm

$$\hat{r}_i = \| \mathbf{h}_k(\hat{\mathbf{x}}_k^-) \| = \sqrt{(\hat{x}_k^- - x_i)^2 + (\hat{y}_k^- - y_i)^2 + (\hat{z}_k^- - z_i)^2}$$

The vector $(h_x^{(i)}, h_y^{(i)}, h_z^{(i)})$, $i = 1, \ldots, n$, denotes the line-of-sight vector from the user to the satellites:

$$h_x^{(i)} = \frac{\hat{x}_k^- - x_i}{\hat{r}_i}\,;\; h_y^{(i)} = \frac{\hat{y}_k^- - y_i}{\hat{r}_i}\,;\; h_z^{(i)} = \frac{\hat{z}_k^- - z_i}{\hat{r}_i} \tag{31}$$

Discussion on the linear position-velocity (PV) model can be referred to Axelrad & Brown (1996) and Brown & Hwang (1997). More detailed treatment to the nonlinear model are referred to Jwo & Lai (2008).

5. The IMM algorithm

As a structure adaptation algorithm (for tuning the $\mathbf{\Phi}_k$ and/or $\mathbf{Q}_k$), the IMM estimators can substantially improve navigation accuracy during vehicle manoeuvring (such as circular motion and acceleration) as well as during constant velocity straight-line motion over the conventional EKF. The IMM algorithm takes into account a set of models to represent the system behaviour patterns or system model. The approach uses model (Markov chain state) probabilities to weight the input and output of a bank of parallel Kalman filters at each time instant. The overall estimates is obtained by a combination of the estimates from the filters running in parallel based on the individual models that match the system modes. In each cycle it consists of four major steps: interaction (mixing), filtering, mode probability calculation, and combination.

According to the summary given by Lin et al. (2001) , the IMM has the following properties: (1) it consists of a low bandwidth filter for the nearly uniform motion and a high bandwidth filter for the manoeuvring situations; (2) these filters interact (exchange information) with time-varying weights; (3) the final estimate is a combination of each filter's estimate, with the weights being the mode probabilities; (4) the weights for interaction and combination are based on which model fits better the data and other factors, such as the expected transition from one mode to another.

The IMM algorithm is summarized as follows.

1. Calculation of mixing probabilities. The probability that mode $\mathbf{M}^i$ was in effect at $k-1$ given that $\mathbf{M}^j$ is in effect at k conditioned on $\mathbf{z}_{k-1}$ is given by

$$\boldsymbol{\mu}_{k-1}^{i|j} = \frac{1}{\bar{\mathbf{c}}_j} P\{\mathbf{M}_k^j \mid \mathbf{M}_{k-1}^i, \mathbf{z}_{k-1}\} P\{\mathbf{M}_{k-1}^i \mid \mathbf{z}_{k-1}\} \tag{32}$$

which are the mixing probabilities and can be written as

$$\boldsymbol{\mu}_{k-1}^{i|j} = \frac{1}{\bar{\mathbf{c}}_j} \mathbf{P}_{ij} \boldsymbol{\mu}_{k-1}^{i}, \; i, j = 1, \ldots, r \tag{33}$$

where

$$\mathbf{P}_{ij} = P\{\mathbf{M}_k^j \mid \mathbf{M}_{k-1}^i, \mathbf{z}_{k-1}\}, \; \boldsymbol{\mu}_{k-1}^{i} = P\{\mathbf{M}_{k-1}^i \mid \mathbf{z}_{k-1}\}$$

and the normalizing constants

$$\bar{\mathbf{c}}_j = \sum_{i=1}^{r} \mathbf{P}_{ij} \boldsymbol{\mu}_{k-1}^{i} \tag{34}$$

2. Mixing. Starting with $\hat{\mathbf{x}}_{k-1}^i$, the mixed initial condition for the filter matched to $\mathbf{M}_k^j$ is computed

$$\hat{\mathbf{x}}_{k-1}^{0j} = \sum_{i=1}^{r} \hat{\mathbf{x}}_{k-1}^{i} \boldsymbol{\mu}_{k-1}^{i|j} \tag{35}$$

The corresponding covariance is

$$\mathbf{P}_{k-1}^{0j} = \sum_{i=1}^{r} \boldsymbol{\mu}_{k-1}^{i|j} \left\{ \mathbf{P}_{k-1}^{i} + [\hat{\mathbf{x}}_{k-1}^{i} - \hat{\mathbf{x}}_{k-1}^{0j}] \cdot [\hat{\mathbf{x}}_{k-1}^{i} - \hat{\mathbf{x}}_{k-1}^{0j}]^T \right\} \tag{36}$$

3. Mode-matched filtering. The estimate Equation (35) and covariance Equation (36) are used as input to the filter matched to $\mathbf{M}_k^j$, which uses $\mathbf{z}_k$ to yield $\hat{\mathbf{x}}_k^j$ and $\mathbf{P}_k^j$. The likelihood function corresponding to the r filters

$$\boldsymbol{\Lambda}_k^j = p[\mathbf{z}_k \mid \mathbf{M}_k^j, \mathbf{z}_{k-1}] \tag{37}$$

are computed using the mixed initial condition Equation (35) and the associated covariance Equation (36) as

$$\boldsymbol{\Lambda}_k^j = p[\mathbf{z}_k \mid \mathbf{M}_k^j, \hat{\mathbf{x}}_{k-1}^{0j}, \mathbf{P}_{k-1}^{0j}]$$

that is

$$\boldsymbol{\Lambda}_k^j = N\{\mathbf{z}_k ; \hat{\mathbf{z}}^j[k \mid k-1; \hat{\mathbf{x}}_{k-1}^{0j}], s^j[k, \mathbf{P}_{k-1}^{0j}]\}$$

4. Mode probability update

$$\boldsymbol{\mu}_k^j = \frac{1}{\mathbf{C}} \boldsymbol{\Lambda}_k^j \bar{\mathbf{c}}_j \tag{38}$$

where

$$\mathbf{C} = \sum_{j=1}^{r} \boldsymbol{\Lambda}_k^j \bar{\mathbf{c}}_j \tag{39}$$

is the normalization constant.

5. State estimate and covariance calculation through combination. Combination of the model-conditioned estimates and covariance is done according to the mixture equations given by

$$\hat{\mathbf{x}}_k = \sum_{j=1}^{r} \hat{\mathbf{x}}_k^j \boldsymbol{\mu}_k^j \tag{40}$$

$$\mathbf{P}_k = \sum_{j=1}^{r} \boldsymbol{\mu}_k^j \left\{ \mathbf{P}_k^j + [\hat{\mathbf{x}}_k^j - \hat{\mathbf{x}}_k] \cdot [\hat{\mathbf{x}}_k^j - \hat{\mathbf{x}}_k]^T \right\} \tag{41}$$

The filters in the bank of parallel filters could be EKFs or UKFs to describe their individual nonlinear behaviour in each manoeuvring stage, resulting in the IMM-based extended Kalman filter (IMM-EKF) or IMM-based unscented Kalman filter (IMM-UKF) to emphasize its nonlinear consideration on system modelling. To deal with the vehicle manoeuvring in tracking and navigation applications, the two-stage estimator has been an alternative. The content will not be discussed here and the related information can be found in Alouani & Xia (1991), Blair (1993), and Keller & Darouach (1997).

6. Incorporation of the fuzzy logic adaptive system

Fuzzy logic was first developed by Zadeh in the mid-1960s for representing uncertain and imprecise knowledge. It provides an approximate but effective means of describing the behaviour of systems that are too complex, ill-defined, or not easily analyzed mathematically. A typical fuzzy system consists of three components, that is, fuzzification, fuzzy reasoning (fuzzy inference), and fuzzy defuzzification. The fuzzification process converts a crisp input value to a fuzzy value, the fuzzy inference is responsible for drawing calculations from the knowledge base, and the fuzzy defuzzification process converts the fuzzy actions into a crisp action.

The fuzzification modules: (1) transforms the error signal into a normalized fuzzy subset consisting of a subset for the range of the input values and a normalized membership function describing the degree of confidence of the input belonging to this range; (2) selects reasonable and good, ideally optimal, membership functions under certain convenient criteria meaningful to the application. The characteristics of the fuzzy adaptive system depend on the fuzzy rules and the effectiveness of the rules directly influences its performance. To obtain the best deterministic output from a fuzzy output subset, a procedure for its interpretation, known as defuzzification should be considered. The defuzzification is used to provide the deterministic values of a membership function for the output. Using fuzzy logic to infer the consequent of a set of fuzzy production rules invariably leads to fuzzy output subsets.

Fuzzy modelling is the method of describing the characteristics of a system using fuzzy inference rules. A Takagi-Sugeno (T-S) fuzzy system can be used to detect the divergence of EKF and adapt the filter. Takagi and Sugeno proposed a fuzzy modelling approach to model nonlinear systems. The T-S fuzzy system represents the conclusion by functions. The typical T-S system is shown as in Fig. 5. The output is the weighted average of the y_k :

$$y = \sum_{k=1}^{M} w_k \cdot y_k \tag{30}$$

where the weights w_k are computed as

$$w_k = \frac{\prod_{i=1}^{n} \mu_{F_i^k}(x_i)}{\sum_{j=1}^{M} [\prod_{i=1}^{n} \mu_{F_i^j}(x_i)]} \tag{31}$$

with $\sum_{i=1}^{M} w_i = 1$, and the μ 's represent the membership functions.

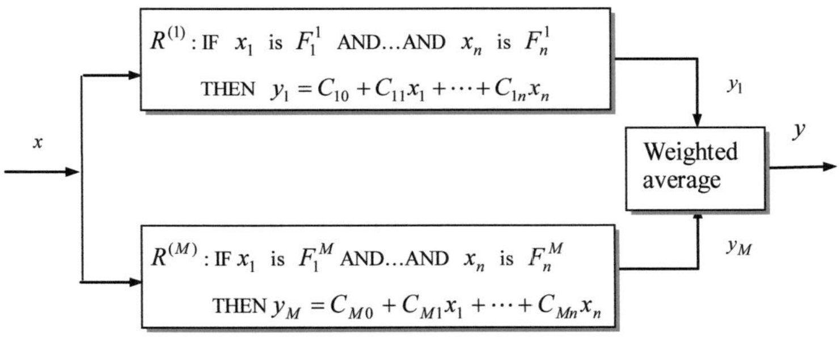

Fig. 5. Takagi-Sugeno (T-S) fuzzy system

The application of fuzzy logic to adaptive Kalman filtering has been becoming popular, e.g., (Sasiadek et al., 2000; Abdelnour et al, 1993; Kobayashi et al, 1995; Mostov & Soloviev, 1996). Sasiadek, Wang, and Zeremba introduced the Fuzzy Logic Adaptive System (FLAS) for adapting the process and measurement noise covariance matrices in navigation data fusion design (Sasiadek et al., 2000). Abdelnour, et al. (1993) used the exponential-weighting algorithm for detecting and correcting the divergence of the Kalman filter. Kobayashi, et al. (1995) proposed a method for generating an accurate estimate of the absolute speed of a vehicle from noisy acceleration and erroneous wheel speed information. The method employed the fuzzy logic rule-based Kalman filter to handle abrupt wheel skid and slip, and poor signal-to-noise sensor data. Mostov and Soloviev (1996) proposed the method to increase the Kalman filter order, which in turn enhances the accuracy of smoothing and thus location finding for kinematic GPS.

The process model of the KF is dependent on the dynamical characteristics of the vehicle. It is widely known that poorly designed mathematical model for the EKF may lead to the divergence. The fuzzy logic adaptive system (FLAS) can be used to adapt the gain and therefore prevent the Kalman filter from divergence. The FLAS is employed to make the necessary trade-off between accuracy and computational burden due to the increased dimension of the state vector and associated matrices. When the FLAS is employed, the lower order state model can be used without significantly compromising accuracy. In other words, for a given accuracy, the fuzzy adaptive Kalman filter is allowed to use a lower order state model. When a designer lacks sufficient information to develop complete model or the parameters will slowly change with time, the fuzzy system can be used to adjust the performance of EKF on-line, and it will remain sensitive to parameter variations by 'remembering' most recent data samples.

Examples for possible approaches are given as follows. The covariance matrix of the innovation can be written as $\mathbf{C}_{\upsilon_k} = E[\boldsymbol{\upsilon}_k \boldsymbol{\upsilon}_k^{\mathrm{T}}] = \mathbf{H}_k \mathbf{P}_k^- \mathbf{H}_k^{\mathrm{T}} + \mathbf{R}_k$. The trace of innovation covariance matrix can be obtained through the relation: $\boldsymbol{\upsilon}_k^{\mathrm{T}} \boldsymbol{\upsilon}_k = tr(\boldsymbol{\upsilon}_k \boldsymbol{\upsilon}_k^{\mathrm{T}})$. The degree of divergence (DOD) parameters for identifying the degree of change in vehicle dynamics can be determined. The innovation information at the present epoch is employed for timely reflect the change in vehicle dynamics. The DOD parameter ξ can be defined as the trace of innovation covariance matrix at present epoch (i.e., the window size is one) divided by the number of satellites employed for navigation processing:

$$\xi = \frac{\boldsymbol{\upsilon}_k^{\mathrm{T}} \boldsymbol{\upsilon}_k}{m} \tag{34}$$

where $\boldsymbol{\upsilon}_k = [\upsilon_1 \quad \upsilon_2 \quad \cdots \quad \upsilon_m]^T$, m is the number of measurements (number of satellites). Alternatively, the averaged magnitude (absolute value) of innovation at the present epoch can also be used:

$$\zeta = \frac{1}{m} \sum_{i=1}^{m} |\upsilon_i| \tag{35}$$

In the FLAS, the DOD parameters are employed as the inputs for the fuzzy inference engines. By monitoring the DOD parameters, the FLAS is able to on-line tune the filter parameters according to the fuzzy rules. Fig. 6 illustrates the system architecture for GPS navigation using the FLAS-assisted filter. The block diagram of the FLAS-assisted IMM algorithm (an example on one cycle with two models) is shown in Fig. 7.

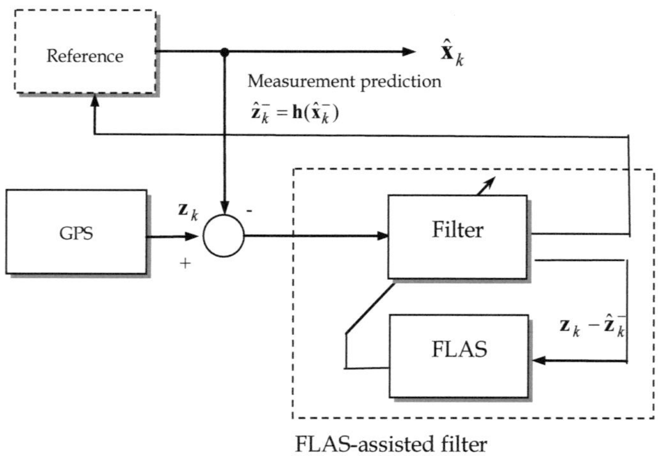

Fig. 6. System architecture for GPS navigation using the FLAS-assisted filter

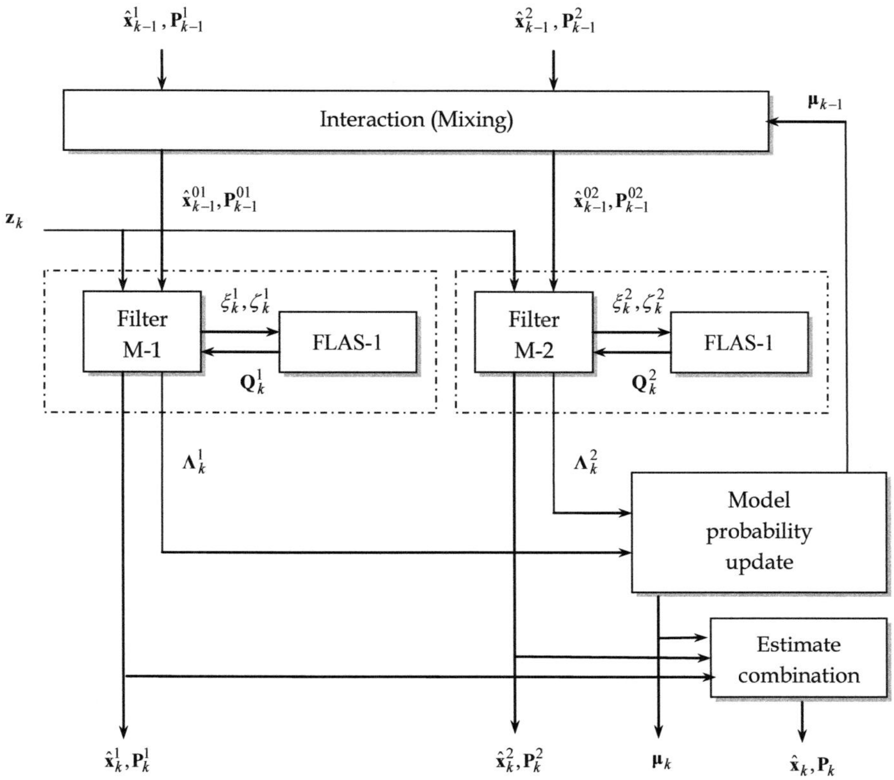

Fig. 7. The block diagram of the FLAS-assisted IMM algorithm (an example on one cycle with two models)

7. Examples

In this section, three examples are provided to illustrate the performance for various types of filter algorithms.

(A) Example 1: Incorporation of FLAS to the adaptive Kalman filter

Example 1 is taken from Jwo & Wang (2007). The simulation scenario is as follows. The simulated vehicle trajectory originates from the position of North 25.1492 degrees and East 121.7775 degrees at an altitude of 100m. This is equivalent to $[-3042329.2 \quad 4911080.2 \quad 2694074.3]^{\mathrm{T}}$ m in the WGS-84 ECEF coordinate system. The location of the origin is defined as the (0,0,0) m location in the local tangent East-North-Up (ENU) frame. The three dimensional plot of trajectory and vehicle velocity are shown in Fig. 8. The description of the vehicle motion is listed in Table 1. Assuming that the differential GPS (DGPS) mode is used most of the errors can be corrected, but the multipath and receiver measurement thermal noise cannot be eliminated. The measurement noise variances r_{ρ_i} value are assumed *a priori* known, which is set to be $(3m)^2$. Let each of the white-noise spectral amplitudes that drive the random walk position states be $S_p = 0.1(m/\sec^2)/(rad/\sec)$. Also, let the clock model spectral amplitudes be

$S_f = 0.4 \cdot 10^{-18}$ sec and $S_g = 1.58 \cdot 10^{-18}$ sec^{-1}. These spectral amplitudes can be used to find the $\mathbf{Q}_k$. The measurement noise covariance matrix is set as

$$\mathbf{R}_k = \begin{bmatrix} 15 & & & \mathbf{0} \\ & 15 & & \\ & & \ddots & \\ \mathbf{0} & & & 15 \end{bmatrix}$$

The parameter β in STKF is a constant and does not change subject to the change in dynamics. When the vehicle is in high dynamic environments, a smaller softening factor (β) will be required for better tracking capability; when the vehicle is in lower dynamic environments, a larger β will be needed for better estimation precision. Therefore, the improved versioned of STKF, which incorporates the FLAS, can be introduced for automatically adjust the value of β. For the vehicle in a very low dynamic environment, β should be increased to a very large value, which leads $\lambda_{i,k}$ to 1 and results in the standard Kalman filter. The philosophy for defining the rules is straightforward: (1) for the case that the DOD parameter is small, our objective is to obtain results with better estimation accuracy, and a larger softening factor (β) should be applied; (2) for the case that the DOD parameter is increased, our objective is to increase the tracking capability, and a smaller softening factor should be applied. The membership functions (MFs) of input fuzzy variable DOD parameters are triangle MFs, obtained by the function:

$$\mu(x) = \begin{cases} 0 & x \le a \\ \dfrac{x-a}{b-a} & a \le x \le b \\ \dfrac{c-x}{c-b} & b \le x \le c \\ 0 & c \le x \end{cases}$$

Time interval (sec)	Motion
[0-50]	Constant velocity
[51-100]	Constant acceleration
[101-150]	Constant velocity
[151-200]	Variable acceleration
[201-250]	Constant velocity
[251-350]	Circular motion, clockwise turn
[351-450]	Constant velocity

Table 1. Description of vehicle motion for Examples 1 and 2

The first-order T-S model is given. The zero-order model needs more complicated MFs and rule base and is therefore more difficult to determine. The presented FLAS is the *If-Then* form and consists of 3 rules. Two methods corresponding to four DOD parameters are presented.

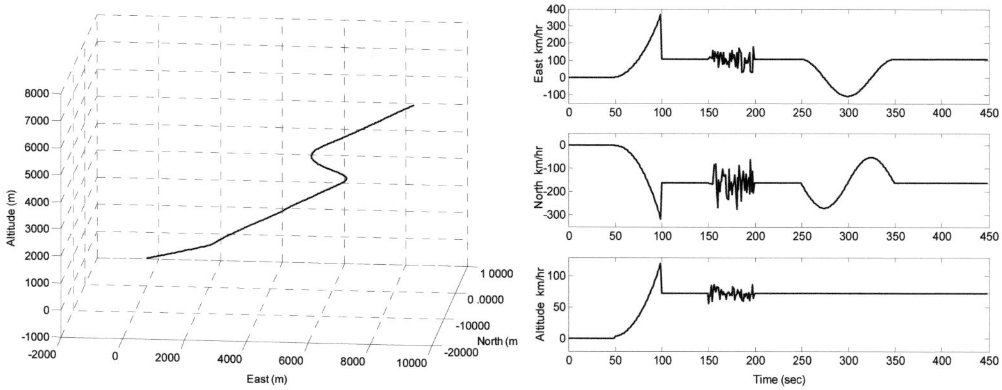

Fig. 8. Three dimensional vehicle trajectory (left) and velocity (right) in the east, north, and vertical components

(1) Method 1 - use ξ in Equation (34) as the DOD parameter

1. IF ξ is zero THEN β is $\xi+10$
2. IF ξ is small THEN β is $\xi+4$
3. IF ξ is large THEN β is 1

(2) Method 2 - use ζ in Equation (35) as the DOD parameter

1. IF ζ is zero THEN β is $3\zeta+8$
2. IF ζ is small THEN β is $2\zeta+4$
3. IF ζ is large THEN β is 1

The membership functions of input fuzzy variable ξ and ζ are provided in Fig. 9.

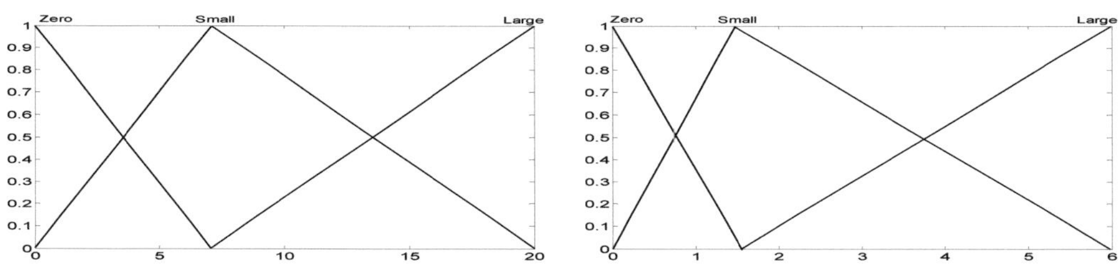

Fig. 9. Membership functions of input fuzzy variable ξ (left) and ζ (right)

Figs. 10 and 11 provide the GPS navigation results for the EKF, STKF and AFSTKF approaches. It can be seen that substantial estimation accuracy improvement is obtained by using the proposed technique. In the three time intervals, 51~100, 151~200, 251~350 sec, the vehicle is manoeuvring. The mismatch of the model leads the conventional EKF to large navigation error while the FLAS timely detects the increase of DOD parameter, and then reduces softening factor so as to maintain good tracking capability. The AFSTKF has good capability to detect the change in vehicle dynamics and adjust the softening factor for preventing the divergence and remaining better navigation accuracy. The softening factors determined by the FLAS, and the corresponding fading factors are given in Fig. 12. It can be seen that when the vehicle is in high dynamic environment, β will be tuned to a smaller value; in a low dynamic case, β will be tuned to a very larger value. The case that β is very large will lead the fading factor $\lambda_{i,k}$ to 1, and the AFSTKF becomes the standard extended Kalman filter. The fact, as was predicted, can be seen in the time intervals 0-50 sec, 101-150 sec, 201-250 sec and 351-405 sec.

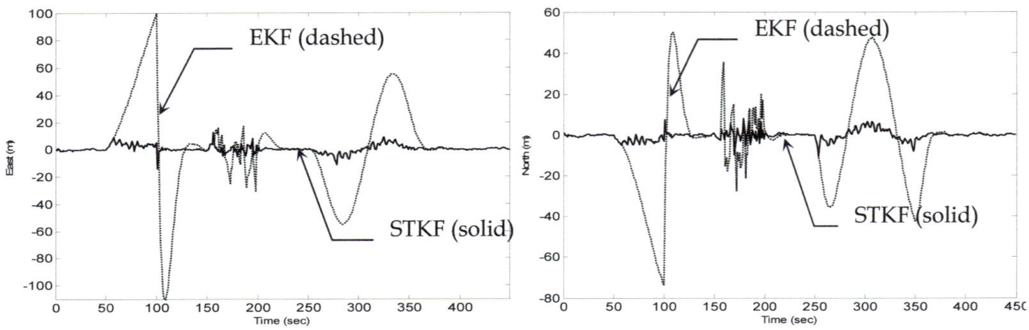

Fig. 10. Navigation errors for the STKF method (left) and the EKF method (right)

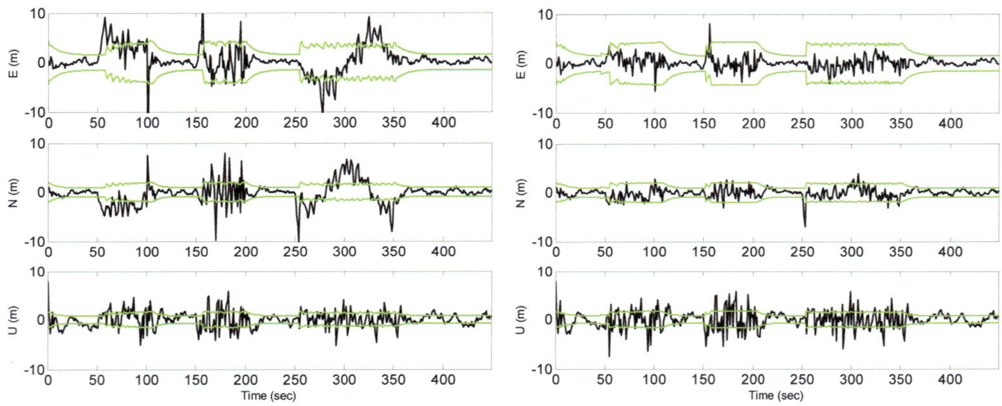

Fig. 11. East, north and up components of the navigation errors and the corresponding $1-\sigma$ bound based on the STKF method (left) and AFSTKF method (right)

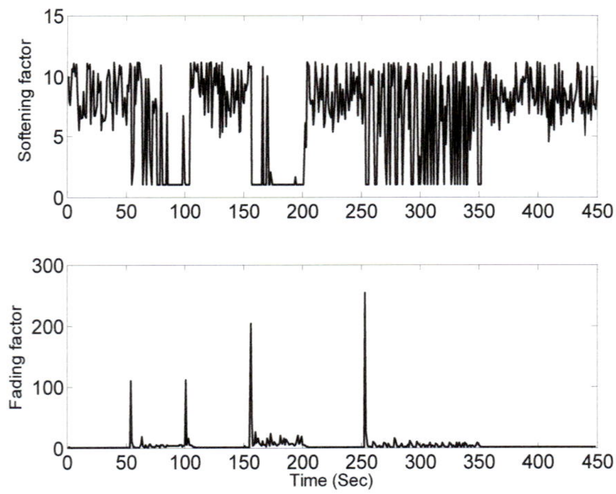

Fig. 12. The softening factors (top) and fading factors (bottom)

(B) Example 2: utilization of the UKF - the higher order filter

Example 2 is taken from Jwo & Lai (2008), which has the same simulation scenario as used in Example 1. In order to improve the navigation estimation accuracy, utilization of a nonlinear model for better description on the vehicle dynamic will be more plausible to achieve better estimation accuracy. For comparison purpose, the same values of process noise covariance parameters are utilized for both the EKF and UKF: $q_{ii} = 3$, $i = 1 \ldots 7$, for which

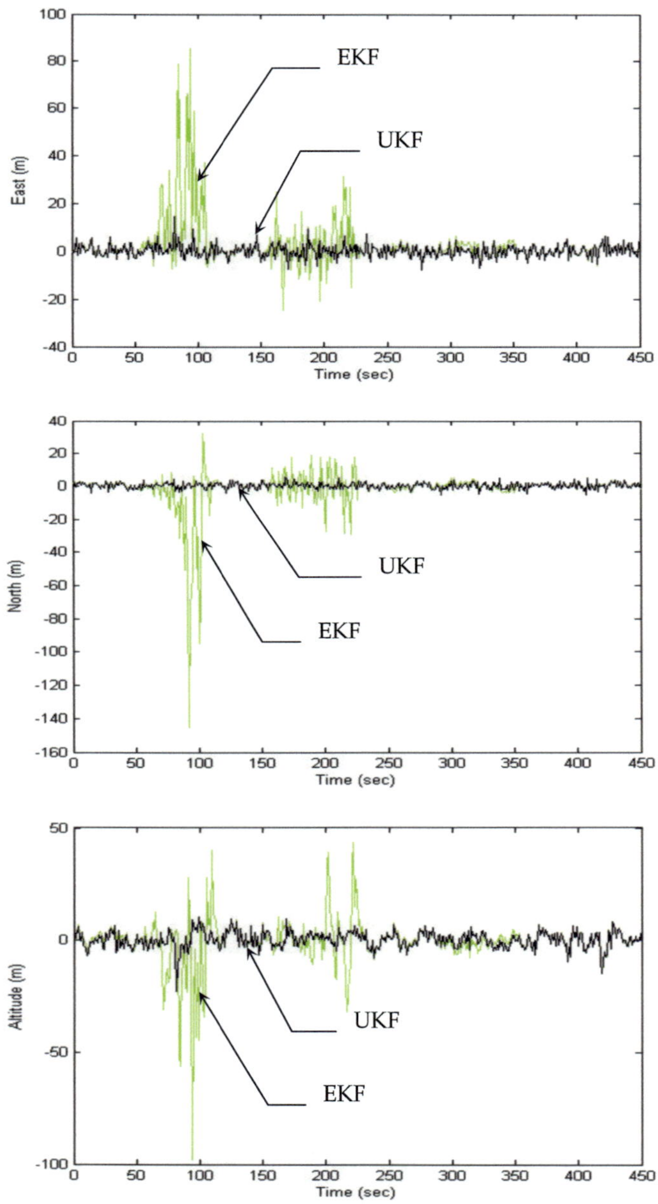

Fig. 13. Comparison of GPS positioning errors for EKF and UKF when the proposed nonlinear dynamic model is used

case $\alpha = 0.007$, $\beta = 2$, $\gamma = 0$. In the three time intervals, 51~100, 151~200, 251~350 s, the vehicle is conducting manoeuvring. The significant mismatch of the model leads the large errors in the conventional EKF solution, while the UKF with nonlinear model that better describes the vehicle dynamics is more able to achieve better navigation accuracy. Comparison of the positioning errors is shown in Fig. 13.

(C) Example 3: utilization of the IMM algorithm

Example 3 is taken from Jwo & Tseng (2008). Two models of the vehicle are defined: the non-manoeuvring model (constant velocity) reproduces properly straight trajectories of the vehicle; the manoeuvring model (constant acceleration) considers sharp turns and brusque accelerations. In the lower dynamic environment, the dynamic process of the GPS receiver is represented by the CV or PV (Position-Velocity) model, in which the state to be estimated is a 8×1 vector, including three position states, three velocity states, and two clock states. While considering the vehicle manoeuvring (or turning), the CA or PVA (Position-Velocity-Acceleration) model will be more suitable than the PV one. The PVA model adds three acceleration variables to the original PV model, leading to the 11×1 state vector. The following transition probability matrices of the Markov chain were used

$$\mathbf{P}_{ij} = \begin{bmatrix} 0.99 & 0.01 \\ 0.01 & 0.99 \end{bmatrix} \tag{85}$$

The simulation scenario in this example is made as follows. The location of the origin is defined as the (0,0,0) m location in the local tangent East-North-Up (ENU) coordinate frame. The two dimensional simulated vehicle trajectory and vehicle velocity are shown in Fig. 14. Furthermore, the description of the vehicle motion is listed in Table 2.

The mode probability of the IMM filter is depicted in Fig. 15. Fig. 16 provides the GPS navigation results for the standard EKF and IMM-EKF approaches. In the three time intervals, 1001-3000, 4001-5000, 5501-6500s, the vehicle is manoeuvring. The mismatch of the model leads the conventional EKF to large navigation error. Using the IMM-EKF, a reduction of approximately 8.14 m RMSE has been achieved.

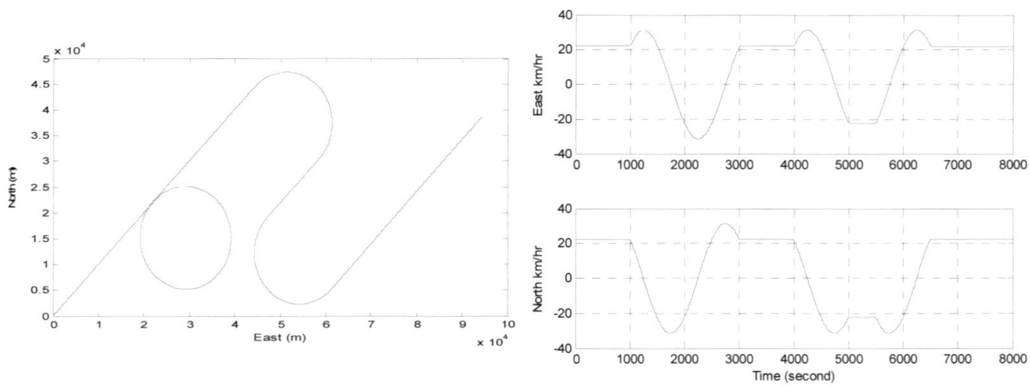

Fig. 14. Simulated vehicle trajectory (left) and the corresponding vehicle velocity (right) in the east and north components

Time interval (sec)	Motion
[0-1000]	Constant velocity
[1001-3000]	Circular motion
[3001-4000]	Constant velocity
[4001-5000]	Clockwise turn
[5001-5500]	Constant velocity
[5501-6500]	Counter-clockwise turn
[6501-8000]	Constant velocity

Table 2. Description of vehicle motion for example 3

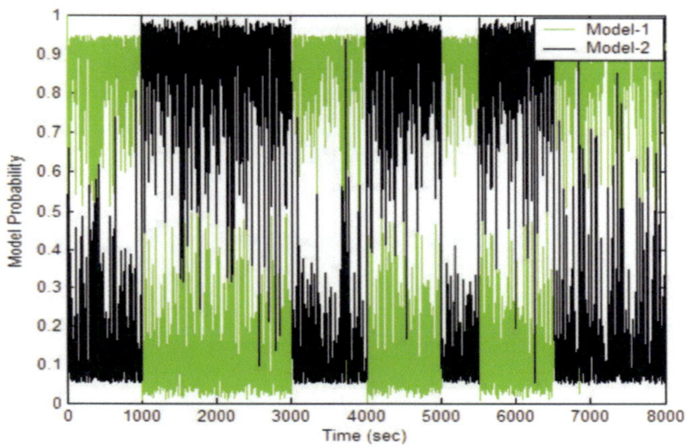

Fig. 15. Model probability of the IMM-EKF

8. Conclusion

The divergence problem due to modelling errors is critical in Kalman filter applications. The conventional extended Kalman filter does not present the capability to monitor the change of parameters due to changes in vehicle dynamics. In this chapter, three feasible ways to avoid the divergence problem and to further improve the GPS navigation accuracy are discussed: (1) adaptive approaches assisted by heuristic search techniques to fit the dynamic model process of interest as precisely as possible; (2) utilization of an appropriate nonlinear estimation approach after deriving a better nonlinear dynamic process model; and (3) interactive multiple model approach accounting for different manoeuvring conditions.

In Example 1, the FLAS is incorporated into the traditional strong tracking Kalman filter (STKF) approach for determining the softening factors, resulting in the adaptive fuzzy strong tracking Kalman filter (AFSTKF). Through the use of fuzzy logic, the FLAS has been employed as a mechanism for timely detecting the dynamical changes and implementing the on-line tuning of filter parameters by monitoring the innovation information so as to maintain good tracking capability. By use of the FLAS, lower order of filter model can be utilized and, therefore, less computational effort will be sufficient without compromising estimation accuracy significantly.

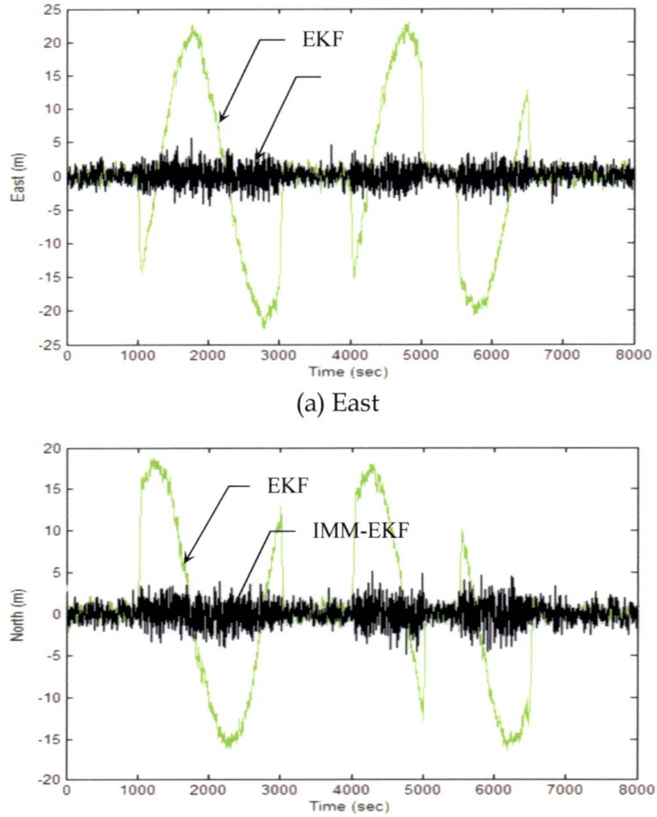

(a) East

(b) North

Fig. 16. Navigation accuracy comparison for EKF and IMM-EKF

An unscented Kalman filtering approach with nonlinear modelling has been presented to be superior to the EKF, due to the fact that the UKF is able to deal with the nonlinear formulation, while the linear model does not reflect the actual dynamic behaviour when the vehicle is manoeuvring. The UKF with nonlinear model ensures better description on the vehicle dynamics and will be able to achieve better navigation accuracy.

The other alternative approach for designing an adaptive Kalman filter is the interacting multiple model (IMM) algorithm. The use of an IMM method also allows exploiting the benefits of high dynamic models in the problem of vehicle navigation. An IMM-based method has been presented to be able to improve the estimation accuracy. Two models that represent different manoeuvring conditions have been conducted. Simulation experiments for GPS navigation have been carried out to discuss the accessibility and performance improvement using various approaches.

9. Acknowledgements

The authors gratefully acknowledge the support of the National Science Council of the Republic of China.

10. References

Abdelnour, G.; Chand, S. & Chiu, S. (1993). Applying fuzzy logic to the Kalman filter divergence problem. *IEEE Int. Conf. On Syst., Man and Cybernetics, Le Touquet, France,* pp. 630-634

Alouani, A. T. & Xia, P. (1991). A two-stage Kalman estimator for state estimation in the presence of random bias and for tracking maneuvering targets, *Proc. IEEE 30th Conf. Decision and Control,* pp. 2059-2062

Axelrad, P. & Brown, R. G. (1996). GPS navigation algorithms, in *Global Positioning System: Theory and Applications*: B. W. Parkinson, J. J. Spilker, P. Axelrad, , and P. Enga, (Ed.), Volume I, Chap. 9, AIAA, Washington DC, 1996.

Bar-Shalom, Y.; Li, X. R. & Kirubarajan, T. (2001). *Estimation with Applications to Tracking and Navigation,* John Wiley & Sons, Inc

Blair, W. D. (1993). Fixed gain two-stage estimators for tracking manoeuvring targets. *IEEE Transactions on Aerospace and Electronic System, 29(3),* pp. 1004-1014

Brown, R. G. & Hwang, P. Y. C. (1997). *Introduction to Random Signals and Applied Kalman Filtering,* John Wiley & Sons, New York, 3rd edn

Caliskan, F. & Hajiyev, C. M. (2000). Innovation sequence application to aircraft sensor fault detection: comparison of checking covariance matrix algorithms, *ISA Transactions,* 39, pp. 47-56

Chen, G. & Harigae, M. (2001). Using IMM adaptive estimator in GPS positioning, *SICE,* pp. 25-27

Crassidis, JL. (2006). Sigma-point Kalman filtering for integrated GPS and inertial navigation. *IEEE Transactions on Aerospace and Electronic System 42 (2),* pp. 750-756

Deshpande, S. K. & Challa, S. (2007). Robust background estimator using IMM, *Proc. IEEE Conf. Decision and Control,* pp. 130-135

Ding, W.; Wang, J. & Rizos, C. (2007). Improving adaptive Kalman estimation in GPS/INS Integration. *The Journal of Navigation,* 60, pp. 517-529

Gelb, A. (1974). *Applied optimal estimation,* M. I. T. Press, MA

Gordon, N.; Ristic, B. & Arulampalam, S. (2004). *Beyond the Kalman Filter: Particle Filter for Tracking Applications,* Artech House, Boston. London

Gordon, N.; Salmond, D. J. & Smith, A. F. M. (1993). Novel approach to nonlinear/non-Gaussian Bayesian state estimation. *IEE Proc.-F, 140 (2),* pp. 107-113

Hide, C.; Moore, T. & Smith, M. (2003). Adaptive Kalman filtering for low cost INS/GPS. *The Journal of Navigation,* 56, pp. 143-152

Johnston, L. A. & Krishnamurthy, V. (2001). An improvement to the interacting multiple model (IMM) algorithm. *IEEE Transactions on Signal Processing,* 49(12), pp. 2909-2923

Julier, S. J. (2002). The scaled unscented transformation, *Proceedings of the American Control Conference,* pp. 4555-4559, Anchorage, USA

Julier, S. J. & Uhlmann, J. K. (1997). A new extension of the Kalman filter to nonlinear systems. *Proceedings of the 11th International Symposium on Aerospace/Defence Sensing, Simulation and Control,* pp. 54-65

Julier, S. J.; Uhlmann, J. K. & Durrant-whyte, H. F. (1995). A new approach for filtering nonlinear system. *Proceedings of the American Control Conference,* pp. 1628-1632

Julier, S. J.; Uhlmann, J. K. & Durrant-whyte, H. F. (2000). A new mehhod for the nonlinear transformation of means and covariances in filers and estimators. *IEEE Transactions on Automatic Control 5(3),* pp. 477-482

Julier, S. J. & Uhlmann, J. K. (2002). Reduced sigma point filters for the propagation of means and covariances through nonlinear transformations, *Proceedings of the American Control Conference,* pp. 887-892

Jwo, D. J. & Cho, T. S. (2007). A practical note on evaluating Kalman filter performance Optimality and Degradation. *Applied Mathematics and Computation, 193,* pp. 482-505

Jwo, D. J. & Lai, C. N. (2008). Unscented Kalman filter with nonlinear dynamic process modeling for GPS navigation, *GPS Solutions*, 12, pp. 249-260

Jwo, D. J. & Tseng, C. H. (2008). GPS Navigation processing using the IMM-based EKF, *The 3rd International Conference on Sensing Technology*, (to appear)

Jwo, D. J. & Wang, S. H. (2007). Adaptive fuzzy strong tracking extended Kalman filtering for GPS navigation, *IEEE Sensors Journal*, 7(5), pp. 778-789.

Jwo, D. J. & Weng, T. P. (2008). An adaptive sensor fusion method with applications in integrated navigation. *The Journal of Navigation*, 61, pp. 705-721

Keller, J. Y. & Darouach, M. (1997). Optimal two-stage Kalman filter in the presence of random bias, *Automatica*, 33(9), pp. 1745-1748

Kim, Y. S. & Hong, K. S. (2004). An IMM Algorithm for tracking manoeuvring vehicles in an adaptive cruise control environment. *International Journal of control Automation and System*, Vol. 2, No. 3, pp. 310-318

Kobayashi, K.; Cheok, K. & Watanabe, K. (1995). Estimation of the absolute vehicle speed using fuzzy logic rule-based Kalman filter, *Proceedings of the American Control Conf.*, pp. 3086-3090, Seattle

Lee, B. J.; Park, J. B.; Lee, H. J. & Joo, Y. H. (2005). Fuzzy-logic-based IMM algorithm for tracking a manoeuvring target, *IEE Radar Sonar Navig*, Vol. 152, No. 1, pp. 16-22

Li, X. R. & Bar-Shalom, Y. (1993). Performance prediction of the interacting multiple model algorithm. *IEEE Transactions on Aerospace and Electronic System*, 29(3), pp. 755-771

Li, Y.; Wang, J.; Rizos, C.; Mumford, P. J. & Ding, W. (2006). Low-cost tightly couple GPS/INS integration based on a nonlinear Kalman filter design, *Proceedings of the U.S. Institute of Navigation National Tech. Meeting*, pp. 958-966

Lin, X.; Kirubarajan, T.; Bar-Shalom, Y. & Li, X. (2001). Enhanced accuracy GPS navigation using the interacting multiple model estimator, *IEEE Proceedings on Aerospace Conference*, 4, pp. 1911-1923

Mehra, R. K. (1970). On the identification of variance and adaptive Kalman filtering. *IEEE Trans. Automat. Contr., AC-15*, pp. 175-184

Mehra, R. K. (1971). On-line identification of linear dynamic systems with applications to Kalman filtering. *IEEE Trans. Automat. Contr.*, AC-16, pp. 12-21

Mehra, R. K. (1972). Approaches to adaptive filtering. *IEEE Trans. Automat. Contr.*, Vol. AC-17, pp. 693-698

Mostov, K. & Soloviev, A. (1996). Fuzzy adaptive stabilization of higher order Kalman filters in application to precision kinematic GPS, *ION GPS-96*, Vol. 2, pp. 1451-1456, Kansas

Mohamed, A. H. & Schwarz, K. P. (1999). Adaptive Kalman filtering for INS/GPS. *Journal of Geodesy, 73 (4)*, pp. 193-203

Sasiadek, J. Z.; Wang, Q. & Zeremba, M. B. (2000). Fuzzy adaptive Kalman filtering for INS/GPS data fusion. *15th IEEE int. Symp. on intelligent control, Rio Patras, Greece*, pp. 181-186

Wan, E. A. & Van der Merwe, R. (2000). The unscented Kalman filter for nonlinear estimation, *Proceedings of Adaptive Systems for Signal Processing, Communication and Control (AS-SPCC) Symposium*, pp. 153-156, Alberta, Canada

Wan, E. A. & Van der Merwe, R. (2001). *The Unscented Kalman Filter*, Simon Haykin (Ed.), Kalman Filtering and Neural Networks, Wiley, (Chapter 7)

Xia, Q.; Rao, M.; Ying, Y. & Shen, X. (1994). Adaptive fading Kalman filter with an application, *Automatica*, 30, pp. 1333-1338

Xu, T. & Cui, P. (2007). Fuzzy adaptive interacting multiple model algorithm for INS/GPS, *IEEE International Conference on Mechatronics and Automation* pp. 2963-2967

Zhou, D.H. & Frank, P. H. (1996). Strong tracking Kalman filtering of nonlinear time-varying stochastic systems with coloured noise: application to parameter estimation and empirical robustness analysis. *Int. J control*, Vol. 65, No. 2, pp. 295-307

15

Innovation Approach Based Sensor FDI in LEO Satellite Attitude Determination and Control System

Chingiz Hajiyev
Istanbul Technical University
Turkey

1. Introduction

In this study Fault Detection and Isolation (FDI) in the attitude determination and control system of Low Earth Orbit (LEO) satellite is investigated. Attitude determination system uses algebraic method. This method is based on computing any two analytical vectors in the reference frame and measuring these vectors in the body coordinate system (Barishev & Krilov, 1968; Wertz, 1988). As measuring devices, magnetometers and sun sensors are used. The satellite attitude is estimated via Extended Kalman Filter (EKF).

The Kalman filter approach to attitude determination and control is quite sensitive to the any measurement malfunctions (abnormal measurements, sudden shifts in the measurement channel, and other difficulties such as decrease of instrument accuracy, an increase of background noise, etc.). If the condition of operation of the measurement system does not correspond to the models, used in the synthesis of filter, then these changes resulting from some possible failures at the measurement channels significantly decrease the effectiveness of the attitude determination and control system. It is important to achieve fault-tolerance in the design of satellite attitude determination and control systems. For this purpose it is required to perform the sensor FDI in these systems.

Many fault detection methods have been developed to detect and identify faults in dynamic systems by using analytical redundancy (Zhang & Li, 1997; Rago et al., 1998; Larson et al., 2002; Lee & Lyou, 2002). In (Zhang & Li, 1997; Rago et al., 1998) the algorithms for detection and diagnosis of multiple failures in the dynamic systems are described. They are based on the Interacting Multiple-Model (IMM) estimation algorithm, which is one of the most cost-effective adaptive estimation techniques for systems involving structural as well as parametric changes. The proposed algorithms provide an integrated framework for fault detection, diagnosis, and state estimation. In methods, described in these works, the faults are assumed to be known, and the Kalman filters are designed for the known types of faults. As the approach requires several parallel Kalman filters, and the faults should be known, it can be used in limited applications.

In (Larson et al., 2002) an analytical redundancy-based approach for detecting and isolating sensor, actuator, and component (i.e., plant) faults in complex dynamical systems, such as aircraft and spacecraft is developed. The method is based on the use of constrained Kalman filters, which are able to detect and isolate such faults by exploiting functional relationships that exist among various subsets of available actuator input and sensor output data. A statistical change detection technique based on a modification of the standard generalized likelihood ratio (GLR) statistic is used to detect faults in real time. The GLR test requires the statistical characteristics of the system to be known before and after the fault occurs. As this information is usually not available after the fault, the method has limited applications in practice.

An integrated robust FDI and fault tolerant control (FTC) scheme for a fault in actuators or sensors of linear stochastic systems subjected to unknown inputs (disturbances) is presented in (Lee & Lyou, 2002). The FDI modules is constructed using banks of robust two-stage Kalman filters, which simultaneously estimate the state and the fault bias, and generate residual sets decoupled from unknown disturbances. All elements of residual sets are evaluated by using a hypothesis statistical test, and the fault is declared according to the prepared decision logic. In this work it is assumed that single fault occurs at a time and the treated fault is of random bias type. The diagnostic method presented in the article is valid only for the control surface FDI.

Fault tolerant attitude control system architecture presented in (Bak, et al., 1996) is based on the sensor reconfiguration. Part of the fault handling is dedicated to the duplicate components. Faults in non-dublicated sensors are detected using analytic redundancy methods based on different sensors. This approach deals with the hardware redundancy and it is very expensive.

In the references (Borairi & Wang, 1998; Alessandri, 2003) the neural network based methods to detect sensor, control surface/actuator failures are developed and discussed. In (Borairi & Wang, 1998) an approach for the fault detection and diagnosis of the actuators and sensors in non-linear systems is presented. First, a known non-linear system is considered, where an adaptive diagnostic model incorporating the estimate of the fault is constructed. Further, unknown nonlinear systems are studied and a feed forward neural network trained to estimate the system under healthy conditions. Genetic algorithms is proposed as a means of optimising the weighting connections of neural network and to assist the diagnosis of the fault.

In (Alessandri, 2003) a neural network based method to detect faults in nonlinear systems is proposed. Fault diagnosis is accomplished by means of a bank of estimators, which provide estimates of parameters that describe actuator, plant, and sensor faults. The problem of designing such estimators for general nonlinear systems is solved by searching for optimal estimation functions. These functions are approximated by feed forward neural networks and the problem is reduced to find the optimal neural weights. The methods based on artificial neural networks and genetic algorithms do not have physical bases. Therefore according to the different data corresponding to the same event, the model gives different solutions. Thus, the model should continuously be trained by using the new data.

To recover the possible malfunctions in the estimation system, the Adaptive Kalman Filters can be used (Sasiadek & Wang, 1999; Zhang & Wei, 2003) The Adaptive KF presented in (Sasiadek & Wang, 1999) has been applied to fuse position signals from the GPS and INS for the autonomous mobile vehicles. The EKF and the noise characteristic have been modified using the Fuzzy Logic Adaptive System. In the paper (Zhang & Wei, 2003), a method of multi-sensor data fusion based on the Adaptive Fuzzy Kalman Filter is presented. This method is applied in fusing position and orientation signals from Dead Reckoning (DR) system and the GPS for landing vehicle navigation. The EKF and the characteristics of the measurement noise are modified by using the Fuzzy Adaptive system, and Fuzzy Adaptive system is based on a covariance matching technique. It has been demonstrated that the Fuzzy Adaptive Kalman Filter gives better results (more accurate) than the EKF (Sasiadek & Wang, 1999; Zhang & Wei, 2003). However, the fuzzy logic is a knowledge-based system operating on linguistic variables. These methods are based on the human experiences and are not widely applicable to the vital systems such as flight control systems.

Faults in multidimensional dynamic systems can be detected with the aid of an innovation sequence of Kalman filter (Mehra & Peschon, 1971; Willsky, 1976; Gadzhiev, 1992; Gadzhiev, 1994). This approach does not require a priori statistical characteristics of the faults, and the computational burden is not very heavy. Generally, fault detection algorithms developed to check the statistical characteristics of the innovation sequence in real-time are based on the following fact. If a system of estimation operates normally, the normalized innovation sequence in the Kalman filter coordinated with a dynamics model, represents the white Gauss noise with zero average value and unitary covariance matrix. Change of indicated statistical characteristics of the normalized innovation sequence are caused by a variety of problems: faults of measuring sensors, anomalous measurements, sudden shifts arising in the measurement channel, changing the statistical characteristics of the object or measurements noises, computer malfunctions, troubles with the deterioration precision of instruments, increasing noise background of instruments, as well as divergence of real process trajectories and divergence of estimations generated by the Kalman filter. The task of efficiently detecting such changes has to be undertaken in real operating conditions in order to correct the estimations. It is also essential to take decisions in a timely manner to change test and operating conditions.

The ways of checking a correspondence of the innovation sequence to the white noise and revealing a change in its mathematical expectation are considered in (Mehra & Peschon, 1971; Willsky, 1976; Hajiyev & Caliskan, 2003). The approaches that verify the covariance matrix of the innovation process are addressed in (Mehra & Peschon, 1971; Gadzhiev, 1992; Gadzhiev, 1994; Hajiyev & Caliskan, 2003).

In this study, fault detection algorithm for LEO satellite attitude determination and control system based on statistic for the mathematical expectation of the spectral norm of the normalized innovation matrix of the Kalman filter is presented. A real-time detection of sensor failures effecting the mean and variance of the innovation sequence, applied to satellite attitude dynamics, is examined and an effective approach to isolate the sensor failures is proposed.

2. Algebraic method based attitude determination and error analysis

2.1 Two-vector algorithms using Sun, Earth's magnetic field and Nadir vectors

The goal of the attitude determination is to find the orientation of the satellite relative to an inertial reference or to some specific object of interest (for example the Earth). In order to do this, there must be one or more available reference vectors, i.e. unit vectors in the known directions with respect to the satellite. Commonly used reference vectors are the Earth's magnetic field and unit vectors in the direction of the Sun, a known star or the centre of the Earth. Given reference vectors, and these vectors' orientations in the frame of the reference of the satellite can be obtained by using the measurements of the attitude sensor. Thus, the orientation of the satellite with respect to these vectors can be computed with some ambiguity (Wertz, 1988; Hajiyev & Bahar, 1998).

As an attitude specification of the satellite in space, Euler angles were selected. An attitude determination procedure that frequently used on three-axis stabilised satellite, is to determine the attitude by measuring the orientation in satellite coordinate system of two reference vectors fixed in inertial space. This is known as two-vector algorithm or algebraic method.

To determine the attitude matrix by using the method, mentioned above, at least components of two vectors have to be known in orbital frame and body frame (Barishev & Krilov, 1968; Wertz, 1988). The direction cosine matrix has to be found also from the orbital frame to the body frame. This gives an opportunity to express the attitude of a satellite in the reference coordinate system. The algorithms' output become "bad" when the reference vectors used in the algorithms are close to parallel or the value of pitch angle (θ) approaches (90°+nπ) degrees.

The aim of this study is to improve these "bad" results as much as possible. As a result, the two-vector algorithm may be used more along the satellite's orbit with better accuracy. To do this, three different algorithms, based on the selected reference vectors (Earth's magnetic field, unit vectors in the direction of the Sun and the center of the Earth), were designed and redundant data processing method was used.

In order to find the expressions of the reference vectors in the reference frame, the satellite's orbital parameters are required. Orbital parameters of a satellite can be determined using $x, y, z, \dot{x}, \dot{y}, \dot{z}$ quantities, which can be obtained by radio-technique measurements (Brandin et al., 1984). The two-vector algorithm includes the following steps (Hajiyev and Bahar, 2002):

1. determination of the orbital parameters,
2. estimation of the orbital parameters,
3. determination of the expressions of the reference vectors in the orbital frame,
4. measurement of the components of these vectors in the body coordinate system,
5. determination of the satellite's attitude.

As it was stated above, the two-vector algorithm requires two reference vectors. Let these vectors be the unit vector in the direction of the Sun (Sun vector) and the Earth's magnetic field. In orbital frame, these vectors are indicated by $\mathbf{S}_0$ and $\mathbf{H}_0$ respectively. In the body frame, these vectors are measured by sun sensors and magnetometers. The resultant measurement vectors are denoted with $\mathbf{S}_k$ and $\mathbf{H}_k$. A transformation matrix between the mentioned coordinate systems has to be formed. If the transformation matrix between these frames is A, and if $\mathbf{n}_0 = \mathbf{S}_0 \times \mathbf{H}_0, \mathbf{n}_k = \mathbf{S}_k \times \mathbf{H}_k$, then the following equalities can be written (Wertz, 1988):

$$\mathbf{S}_k = A\mathbf{S}_0, \mathbf{H}_k = A\mathbf{H}_0, \mathbf{n}_k = A\mathbf{n}_0 \tag{1}$$

Let's form the matrices C and C', which columns are made up of the above vectors:

$$C = [\mathbf{S}_0, \mathbf{H}_0, \mathbf{n}_0] \, \text{ve} \, C' = [\mathbf{S}_k, \mathbf{H}_k, \mathbf{n}_k] \tag{2}$$

Then

$$C' = AC, A = C'C^{-1} \tag{3}$$

equalities can be written ($|\mathbf{n}_0| \neq 0$ and $|\mathbf{n}_k| \neq 0$). So, forming the transformation matrix A, it was found that (Wertz, 1988):

$$[A]=\begin{bmatrix} \cos\theta\cos\varphi & \cos\theta\sin\varphi & -\sin\theta \\ -\sin\varphi\cos\psi+\sin\psi\sin\theta\cos\varphi & \cos\varphi\cos\psi+\sin\varphi\sin\theta\sin\psi & \sin\psi\cos\theta \\ \sin\psi\sin\varphi+\sin\theta\cos\psi\cos\varphi & -\cos\varphi\sin\psi+\cos\psi\sin\theta\sin\varphi & \cos\theta\cos\psi \end{bmatrix} \quad (4)$$

Using Eq.(1)-(4) attitude angles pitch (θ), yaw (ψ) and roll (φ) are found as functions of $\mathbf{H}_0$, $\mathbf{S}_0$, $\mathbf{H}_k$, $\mathbf{S}_k$ vectors

$$\theta=f_\theta(\mathbf{H}_0,\mathbf{S}_0,\mathbf{H}_k,\mathbf{S}_k),\ \psi=f_\psi(\mathbf{H}_0,\mathbf{S}_0,\mathbf{H}_k,\mathbf{S}_k),\ \varphi=f_\varphi(\mathbf{H}_0,\mathbf{S}_0,\mathbf{H}_k,\mathbf{S}_k) \quad (5)$$

The detailed expression of the Eq.(5) is given in Appendix-1. These expressions will be used in computing the accuracy of the satellite's attitude angles.
In this study three reference vectors were selected. Thus, three different two-vector algorithms can be designed. The studied algorithms are:

1. algorithm - Earth's magnetic field and Sun vector
2. algorithm - Earth's magnetic field and Nadir vector
3. algorithm - Nadir vector and Sun vector

The first of these algorithms was studied, and the attitude angles were expressed as functions of the reference vectors, included in this algorithm, and their measurements in the body frame. That was done in order to study the accuracy.
To examine the accuracy of the outputs of the other two-vector algorithms, it is necessary to express them like the first algorithm. The results will be similar to these of the first algorithm. Appropriately, adaptation of Eq.(A1) to the new state is sufficient. The result for the second algorithm can be obtained by replacing $S_{x_k}, S_{y_k}, S_{z_k}, S_{x_0}, S_{y_0}$ and S_{z_0} components in Eq.(A1) with $N_{x_k}, N_{y_k}, N_{z_k}, N_{x_0}, N_{y_0}$ and N_{z_k} components respectively. In a similar manner for the third algorithm the components $H_{x_k}, H_{y_k}, H_{z_k}, H_{x_0}, H_{y_0}$ and H_{z_k} taking place in Eq.(A1) have to be changed by $N_{x_k}, N_{y_k}, N_{z_k}, N_{x_0}, N_{y_0}$ and N_{z_k} components respectively.

2.2 Analysis of the LEO satellite attitude determination accuracy

There are a lot of factors affecting the LEO satellite's attitude determination. The most important of these factors are,

- errors due to the determination of the satellite's orbit,
- errors due to the determination and estimation of the satellite's orbital parameters,
- errors due to the models of the reference vectors in the orbital frame,
- errors due to the measurements of the reference vectors in the in body frame,
- errors due to the algorithm itself.

The scheme of the Earth's magnetic field and Sun vector based two-vector algorithm, used for determination of satellite's attitude, is shown in Fig.1.
Determination of attitude angles with two-vector algorithm includes the following procedures:

- determination of the orbit

$$q_{\ddot{o}}=\Phi_1 \mathrm{d},$$

here Φ_1 is the algorithm for determination of the orbital parameters

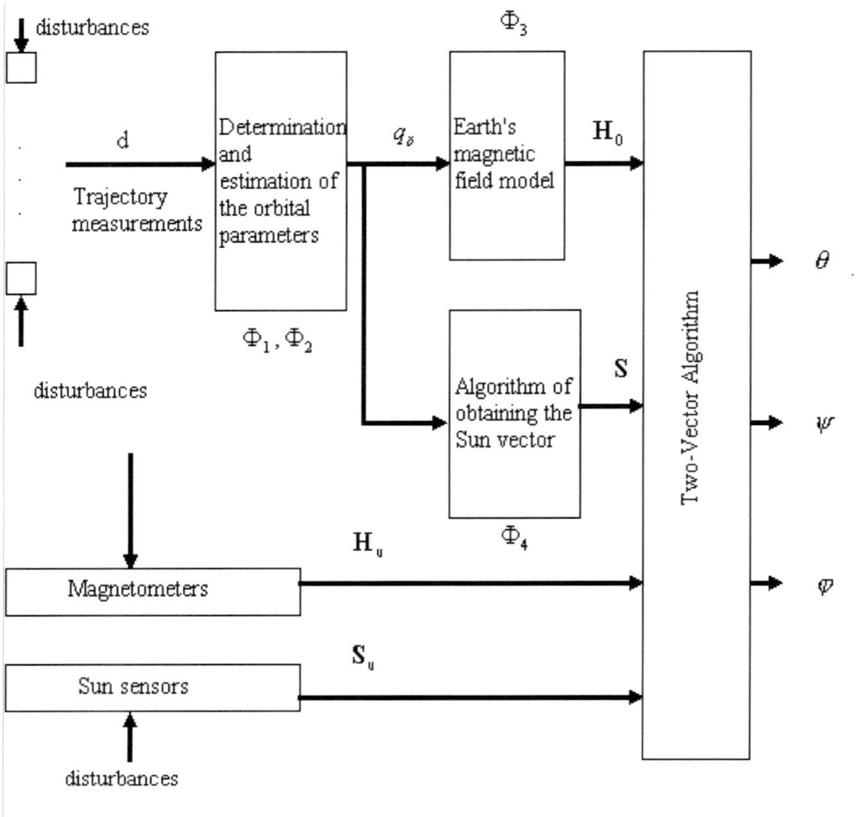

Fig. 1. Earth's magnetic field and Sun vector based two-vector algorithm scheme

- estimation of the orbit

$$q_{\ddot{o}} = \Phi_2 \mathrm{d}$$

here Φ_2 is the algorithm for estimation of the orbital parameters

- determination of the Earth's magnetic field components in orbital frame

$$\mathbf{H}_0 = \Phi_3 q_{\ddot{o}},$$

here Φ_3 is the algorithm for Earth's magnetic field determination

- determination of the Sun vector components in orbital frame

$$\mathbf{S}_0 = \Phi_4 q_{\ddot{o}},$$

here Φ_4 is the algorithm for Sun vector determination

- determination of the satellite's attitude

$$\theta = f_\theta(\mathbf{H}_0, \mathbf{S}_0, \mathbf{H}_k, \mathbf{S}_k),\ \psi = f_\psi(\mathbf{H}_0, \mathbf{S}_0, \mathbf{H}_k, \mathbf{S}_k),\ \varphi = f_\varphi(\mathbf{H}_0, \mathbf{S}_0, \mathbf{H}_k, \mathbf{S}_k)$$

In general, the attitude determination algorithm is a nonlinear function of random variables. Thus, in order to find the error of the algorithm given, it was linearised by expanding to

Taylor series. Correlation between different parameters were ignored. So, after linearization, accuracy (variance) of the algorithm is found as:

$$D_{i\varphi} = \left(\frac{\partial f_\varphi}{\partial \mathbf{H}_0}\right)_m^2 D_{i\mathbf{H}_0} + \left(\frac{\partial f_\varphi}{\partial \mathbf{S}_0}\right)_m^2 D_{i\mathbf{S}_0} + \left(\frac{\partial f_\varphi}{\partial \mathbf{H}_k}\right)_m^2 D_{i\mathbf{H}_k} + \left(\frac{\partial f_\varphi}{\partial \mathbf{S}_k}\right)_m^2 D_{i\mathbf{S}_k} \tag{6}$$

here $D_{i\varphi}$ -is φ's computing error variance at step *i*.; $\left(\frac{\partial f}{\partial(\,)}\right)_m$ is the partial differentiation.

The subscript of the Eq.(6) means that, mean values of the parameters have to be used in the equation. In a similar way

$$D_{i\theta} = \left(\frac{\partial f_\theta}{\partial \mathbf{H}_0}\right)_m^2 D_{i\mathbf{H}_0} + \left(\frac{\partial f_\theta}{\partial \mathbf{S}_0}\right)_m^2 D_{i\mathbf{S}_0} + \left(\frac{\partial f_\theta}{\partial \mathbf{H}_k}\right)_m^2 D_{i\mathbf{H}_k} + \left(\frac{\partial f_\theta}{\partial \mathbf{S}_k}\right)_m^2 D_{i\mathbf{S}_k} \tag{7}$$

$$D_{i\psi} = \left(\frac{\partial f_\psi}{\partial \mathbf{H}_0}\right)_m^2 D_{i\mathbf{H}_0} + \left(\frac{\partial f_\psi}{\partial \mathbf{S}_0}\right)_m^2 D_{i\mathbf{S}_0} + \left(\frac{\partial f_\psi}{\partial \mathbf{H}_k}\right)_m^2 D_{i\mathbf{H}_k} + \left(\frac{\partial f_\psi}{\partial \mathbf{S}_k}\right)_m^2 D_{i\mathbf{S}_k} \tag{8}$$

The equations (6)-(8) can easily be adapted for second and third algorithm.

In the simulation, the satellite's orbital parameters are taken as: inclination i=97°; right ascension of the ascending node λ=15°. The orbit height is h=550 km; the Earth radius is R=6378.140 km; the Earth angular velocity is ω_D=7.28e-5 rad/s; the Earth magnetic field moment is M_{yer}=7.86e+15 Wb.m; the angle between geographical north and magnetic north is δ=11.4°. The accuracy of the orbital parameters i, λ and u are 5e-6 rad, 1e-5 rad and 1.5e-4 rad respectively. The attitude sensors' accuracy are ~1° for magnetometer, 0.1° for sun sensor and 0.36° for horizon sensor (horizon sensor determines the roll and pitch angles). It is assumed that eccentric anomaly is equal to the mean anomaly. Only one orbital period was simulated. In Fig.2 the change of the satellite attitude accuracy throughout the orbit is shown when the first algorithm is used (required accuracy is 1°). As accuracy characteristics pitch (θ), yaw (ψ) and roll (φ) angles' variances are taken.

When the results were examined it was seen that, when the reference vectors became near parallel or the value of the pitch angle θ approaches to (90°+nπ) degrees, the accuracy of the outputs are bellow the requirement. Furthermore, depending on the orbit, the Sun may be out of sight for some periods of orbit (as it is for the most low Earth orbits). It makes the first and third algorithm unusable. Similar results are obtained for the other two-vector algorithms.

It is obvious from the simulation results that the main effect on the accuracy is the magnetometer error, when the first algorithm is used. When the other two algorithms are used, horizon sensor error is more influent on the accuracy of the results.

According to the simulation results, the following conclusions are drawn: a) the accuracy of the spacecraft's attitude is changing in a wide range along the orbit; the accuracy is worst when the reference vectors are close to parallel or the value of the pitch angle θ approaches to 90°+nπ degrees; b) the attitude determination accuracy is affected by different factors in a different manner; the most influent factors on the accuracy are used initial values and the sensor errors; c) to increase the accuracy of attitude determination, redundant data processing methods (statistical methods) can be used (Hajiyev & Bahar, 1998; 2000).

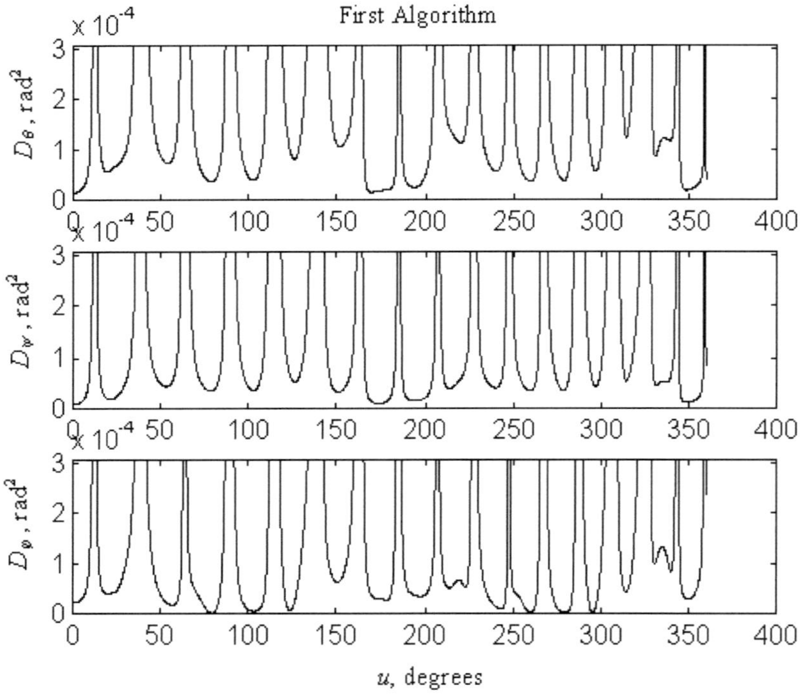

Fig. 2. Change of the variance of the attitude angles, obtained by the first algorithm, along one whole orbit

2.3 Increasing accuracy of the LEO satellite attitude determination using redundancy techniques

In order to increase the attitude determination accuracy, the redundant data processing algorithm, based on the Maximum Likelihood Method (MLM), was used to make the statistical operation on the measurements of the three algorithms mentioned above and appropriate formulas were derived.

Let's assume that the output x of a system is measured simultaneously with n different measurement devices with different measuring principles. Then the measurement equation of the ith device will be

$$z_{x_i} = x + \delta_i, \quad i = 1..n$$

here z_{x_i} -is the measurement of the ith device; δ_i -is the measurement error of the ith device. It is assumed that there is no correlation between the measurement errors of the measurement channels. Another assumption is that the measurement errors are subject to normal distribution with zero mean and finite σ_i^2 variance,

$$p(\delta_i) = \frac{1}{\sqrt{2\pi}\sigma_i}\exp\left\{-\frac{\delta_i^2}{2\sigma_i^2}\right\}, i = 1\ ..n$$

Thus, the distribution density of measurement is known as a function of evaluated parameter,

$$p(z_{x_i}/x) = \frac{1}{\sqrt{2\pi}\sigma_i}\exp\left\{-\frac{(z_{x_i}-x)^2}{2\sigma_i^2}\right\}.$$

It is desired to find the optimal value of x which maximizes the Likelihood function. With the assumption that the measurements z_{x_i} (i =1..n) are independent, the Likelihood function $p(z_{x_1}, z_{x_2}, ..., z_{x_n} / x)$ can be expressed as (Hajiyev, 1999),

$$p(z_{x_i}, z_{x_2}, ..., z_{x_n}/x) = \frac{1}{\sqrt{(2\pi)^n \prod_{i=1}^{n}\sigma_i}}\exp\left\{-\sum_{i=1}^{n}\frac{(z_{x_i}-x)^2}{2\sigma_i^2}\right\}. \tag{9}$$

After mathematical operations the expression for the estimated value that is searched is found as,

$$\hat{x} = \left(\sum_{i=1}^{n}\frac{z_{x_i}}{\sigma_i^2}\right) \Bigg/ \left(\sum_{i=1}^{n}\frac{1}{\sigma_i^2}\right) \tag{10}$$

which covariance can be shown like,

$$D = \left\{-E\left[\frac{\partial^2 \ln p(z_{x_1}, z_{x_2}, ... z_{x_n}/x)}{\partial x^2}\right]\right\}^{-1} = \left(\sum_{i=1}^{n}\frac{1}{\sigma_i^2}\right)^{-1}, \tag{11}$$

here E -denotes the operator for mathematical expectation.

Theorem 1. The inequality $D < \sigma_i^2, \forall i \in [1, n]$, is true for the variance of the estimated value (11).

Proof of the theorem is given in (Hajiyev, 1999).

In this study the pitch, roll and yaw angles that characterizes the angular position of the satellite was found with three different algorithms. Which means that, there is more information than required. Thus, adapting the redundant data processing method based on MLM to the case examined, the following results are obtained (Hajiyev & Bahar, 2002):

$$\hat{\varphi} = \frac{D_{\varphi_1}D_{\varphi_2}z_{\varphi_3} + D_{\varphi_3}D_{\varphi_2}z_{\varphi_1} + D_{\varphi_1}D_{\varphi_3}z_{\varphi_2}}{D_{\varphi_1}D_{\varphi_2} + D_{\varphi_1}D_{\varphi_3} + D_{\varphi_2}D_{\varphi_3}}, \tag{12}$$

$$\psi = \frac{D_{\psi_1}z_{\psi_N} + D_{\psi_N}z_{\psi_1}}{D_{\psi_1} + D_{\psi_N}}, \quad D_{\hat{\psi}} = \frac{D_{\psi_1}D_{\psi_N}}{D_{\psi_1} + D_{\psi_N}}, \quad \hat{\theta} = \frac{D_{\theta_1}z_{\theta_N} + D_{\theta_N}z_{\theta_1}}{D_{\theta_1} + D_{\theta_N}}, \quad D_{\hat{\theta}} = \frac{D_{\theta_1}D_{\theta_N}}{D_{\theta_1} + D_{\theta_N}}$$

where, $D_{(\bullet)_i}$ - is the variance of the appropriate angle found via i^{th} algorithm.

In Fig.3 the change of the satellite attitude accuracy is shown, when the redundant data processing method based on MLM is used. It can be seen that the accuracy of the values found with redundant data processing are better than the values found with each other three algorithms. In order to get good results from the redundant data method, at least one of the three algorithms should produce available output (values with equal or better accuracy than required). The "bad" intervals (intervals where the accuracy is worse than required), formed due to the co-linearity of the reference vectors, can be removed by using redundant data processing method. But the "bad" intervals formed due to the pitch angle's value can not be removed with this method. Because, in that case the three algorithms give unavailable results. So, it can be said that, it is possible to increase the satellite's attitude determination accuracy by using redundant data processing method.

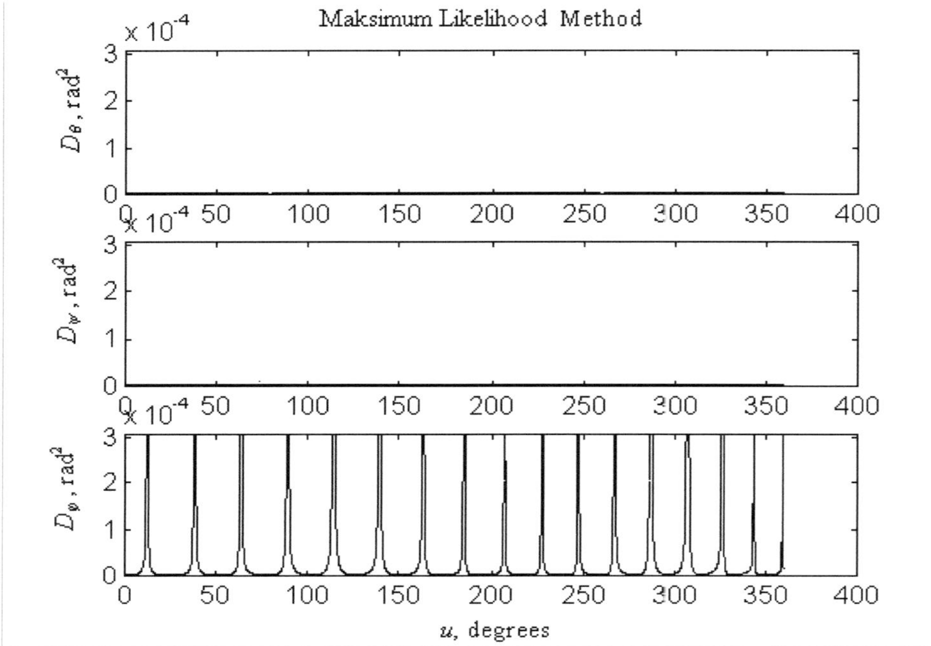

Fig. 3. Change of the variance of the attitude angles obtained by redundant data processing algorithm through the whole orbit

When the results, given in Fig. 2 are compared with results, given in Fig. 3, it is obvious that the result obtained by redundant data processing algorithm are better than all other results given. In order to get good results from the redundant data processing method, at least one of the other algorithms have to produce available data (equal or better than the required accuracy). The "*bad areas*" (areas where the attitude accuracy is worse than the required one), formed due to the parallelism of the reference vectors, can be removed by using the redundant data processing algorithm. But it is impossible to remove the "*bad areas*", formed due to the pitch angle's value.

3. Satellite attitude estimation via extended Kalman filter

3.1 Extended Kalman filter design

The mathematical model of the satellite's rotational motion about its center of mass, is given bellow

$$\dot{\bar{\omega}}_c = J^{-1}\left\{-\bar{\omega}_c \times \left[J\bar{\omega}_c + \bar{H}_m\right] + \bar{m} + \bar{\xi}\right\} \tag{13}$$

where ω_c is the satellite's angular velocity in body coordinate system; $\bar{H}_m{}^T = \begin{bmatrix}0 & H_m & 0\end{bmatrix}$, H_m is the kinetic momentum of the momentum wheel; J is the inertia matrix of the LEO satellite and is equal to $J = \begin{bmatrix}J_{xc} & 0 & 0; 0 & J_{yc} & 0; 0 & 0 & J_{zc}\end{bmatrix}$; $\bar{m}$ is the vector of constant unknown disturbances acting on the satellite; $\bar{\xi}$ is the vector containing the random components of the forces acting on the satellite whose mathematical expectation and correlation matrix are as bellow,

$$E[\xi] = 0, \quad E\left[\xi_t \xi_{t-\tau}^T\right] = D_\xi \delta(t-\tau)$$

it is assumed that D_ξ is known.
The relations among the LEO satellite's rotation angles and angular velocities, are given below

$$\begin{bmatrix}\dot{\varphi} \\ \dot{\theta} \\ \dot{\psi}\end{bmatrix} = T_c\bar{\omega}_c + \bar{\omega}_{orb} \tag{14}$$

where,

$$T_c = \begin{bmatrix}\cos\psi & -\sin\psi & 0 \\ \dfrac{\sin\psi}{\cos\varphi} & \dfrac{\cos\psi}{\cos\varphi} & 0 \\ \sin\psi\ \mathrm{tg}\varphi & \cos\psi\ \mathrm{tg}\varphi & 1\end{bmatrix}, \quad \bar{\omega}_{orb}^T = \begin{bmatrix}0 & \omega_{orb} & 0\end{bmatrix}$$

ω_{orb} is the LEO satellite's angular orbit velocity.
The determination model of the angles that are characterizing LEO satellite's attitude, is given bellow,

$$z_{\varphi_i} = \varphi_i + \mathrm{v}_{\varphi_i}, \; z_{\theta_i} = \theta_i + \mathrm{v}_{\theta_i}, \; z_{\psi_i} = \psi_i + \mathrm{v}_{\psi_i} \tag{15}$$

here $\mathrm{v}(\bullet)_i$ is the error of the attitude angles, determined by the MLM based redundant data processing algorithm which is given above. The mathematical expectations and variances of these errors are $E[\mathrm{v}] = 0$, $E\left[\mathrm{v}_{\varphi_i}, \mathrm{v}_{\varphi_j}\right] = D_{\varphi_i}\delta_{ij}$, $E\left[\mathrm{v}_{\theta_i}, \mathrm{v}_{\theta_j}\right] = D_{\theta_i}\delta_{ij}$ and $E\left[\mathrm{v}_{\psi_i}, \mathrm{v}_{\psi_j}\right] = D_{\psi_i}\delta_{ij}$; δ_{ij} is Kronecker's delta symbol.
The angular velocities $\omega_x, \omega_y, \omega_z$ of satellite are measured through the rate gyroscopes.
If the general vector

$$\bar{U}^T = \begin{bmatrix}\varphi & \theta & \psi & \omega_x & \omega_y & \omega_z & m_x & m_y & m_z\end{bmatrix}$$

is arranged and the mathematical model of the LEO satellite's rotational motion about its center of mass, is linearized using quasi-linearization method,

$$U_i = f\left(\hat{U}_{i-1}, \bar{\omega}_{orb_{i-1}}\right) + F_{U_{i-1}}\left(U_{i-1} - \hat{U}_{i-1}\right) + F_{orb}\left(\bar{\omega}_{orb_{i-1}} - \omega_{orb_{i-1}}^{comp}\right) + h_{i-1} \tag{16}$$

where θ_i, ψ_i, φ_i - are pitch, yaw and roll angles respectively; ω_{x_i}, ω_{y_i}, ω_{z_i} - are angular rates; m_x, m_y, m_z - are the unknown constant components of the external moments acting on the satellite; $f\left(\hat{U}_{i-1}, \bar{\omega}_{orb_{i-1}}\right)$ - is the right hand side of the LEO satellite's rotational motion mathematical model based on estimated values; ω_{orb} - is the satellite's angular orbit velocity; F_{orb}-is the coefficient matrix of the entrance effects;

$$F_U = \left[\frac{\partial f}{\partial U}\right]_{\hat{U}_{i-1}, \bar{\omega}_{orb_{i-1}}}, F_{orb} = \left[\frac{\partial f}{\partial \omega_{orb}}\right]_{\hat{U}_{i-1}, \bar{\omega}_{orb_{i-1}}}, h_{i-1} = \left[\frac{\partial f}{\partial \delta}\right]_{\hat{U}_{i-1}, \bar{\omega}_{orb_{i-1}}}.$$

Minimum of the error's standard deviation was selected as an optimum criterion. It is suggested to derive LEO satellite attitude estimation algorithm using Bayes' method.
The problem of finding the values of the system's parameters and output coordinates, takes us to evaluation of $p\left(U_i / \bar{z}_i, \bar{\omega}_{orb_i}\right)$ conditional probability density. To the Bayes' formula, this probability density can be written as (Hajiyev & Bahar, 2003),

$$p\left(U_i / Z^i, \bar{\omega}_{orb_i}\right) = p\left(U_i / Z^{i-1}, z_i, \bar{\omega}_{orb_i}\right) = \frac{p\left(U_i / Z^{i-1}, \bar{\omega}_{orb_i}\right) p\left(z_i / U_i, Z^{i-1}, \bar{\omega}_{orb_i}\right)}{p\left(z_i / Z^{i-1}\right)}, \tag{17}$$

where $z_i^T = \left[z_{\varphi_i}, z_{\theta_i}, z_{\psi_i}, z_{w_{xi}}, z_{w_{yi}}, z_{w_{zi}}\right]$ is the measurement vector; $Z^i = \{z_1 \quad z_2 \quad \dots \quad z_i\}$, $Z^{i-1} = \{z_1 \quad z_2 \quad \dots \quad z_{i-1}\}$.

Finding and substituting terms respectively into Eq.(17) and via taking into consideration that the minimum of the standard deviation, which was chosen as an optimum criterion (in this case the conditional mathematical expectation of the value's a posteriori distribution will be the best value and as for the value's accuracy, the covariance matrix of this distribution will be used) and $p\left(U_i / Z^i, \bar{\omega}_{orb_i}\right)$, is a Gauss distribution, the recursive algorithm for the satellite's attitude estimation is obtained as bellow,

$$\hat{U}_i = f\left(\hat{U}_{i-1}, \bar{\omega}_{orb_{i-1}}\right) + K_i\left[z_i - Hf\left(\hat{U}_{i-1}, \bar{\omega}_{orb_{i-1}}\right)\right], \tag{18}$$

$$P_i = M_i - M_i H^T \left[D_{v_i} + H M_i H^T\right]^{-1} H M_i, \tag{19}$$

$$M_i = F_U P_{i-1} F_U^T + F_{orb} D_{orb_{i-1}} F_{orb}^T + D_{h_{i-1}}. \tag{20}$$

where M_i is the covariance matrix of the extrapolation error, P_i is the covariance matrix of the estimation error, $K_i = P_i H^T D_{v_i}^{-1}$ is the gain matrix of Kalman filter.
The Eqs.(18)-(20) are representing the Extended Kalman Filter (EKF) which fulfils recursive estimation of the satellite's rotational motion parameters about its mass center.

3.2 LEO satellite attitude estimation results

Portion of simulation results are given in Fig. 4 (a,b,c).

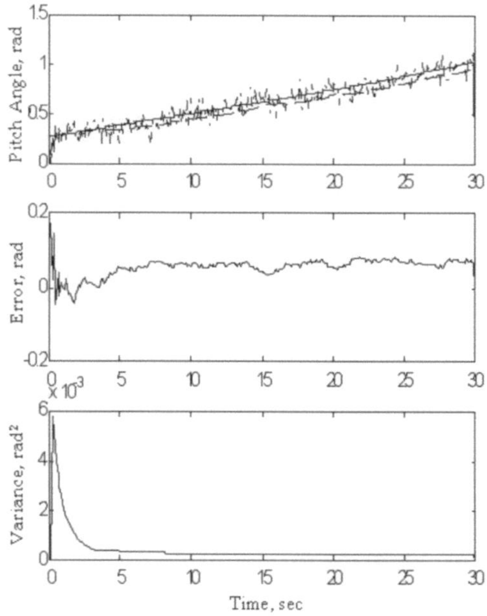

(a)

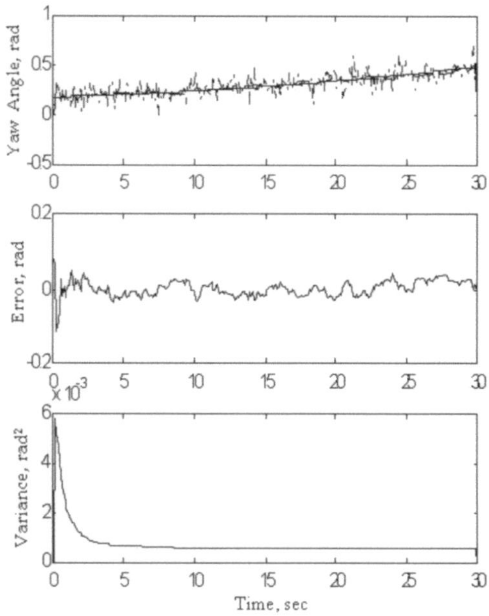

(b)

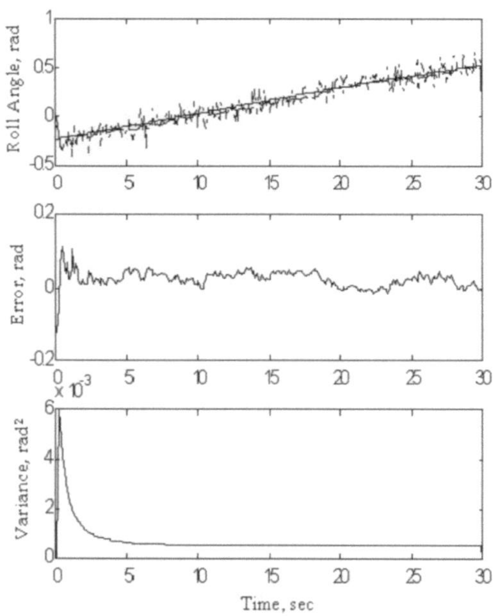

(c)

Fig. 4. Results by using EKF for a) pitch angle; b) yaw angle; c) roll angle (solid line - actual value; dash and dotted line - measurement value; dashed line - EKF output)

Graphics of the roll, pitch and yaw angles' estimated values, their error variances and the error between the actual values of the attitude angles and their estimated values are shown.

As it is seen from the graphics, for the taken orbit interval, the proposed EKF estimates the satellite rotational motion parameters with high accuracy.

3.3 Structure of attitude estimation and control system

The scheme of the proposed attitude estimation and control system is given in Fig. 5. As it seen, the system includes magnetometers, sun sensors, and horizon sensors to measure the above mentioned vectors. The system also includes three different two-vector algorithms based on the Earth magnetic field vector, nadir vector, and the Sun vector; redundant data processing algorithm based on Maximum likelihood method; EKF, and controller. The controlling action is done with the help of the momentum wheels. The system mentioned gives a possibility to stabilize the satellite through out the orbit.

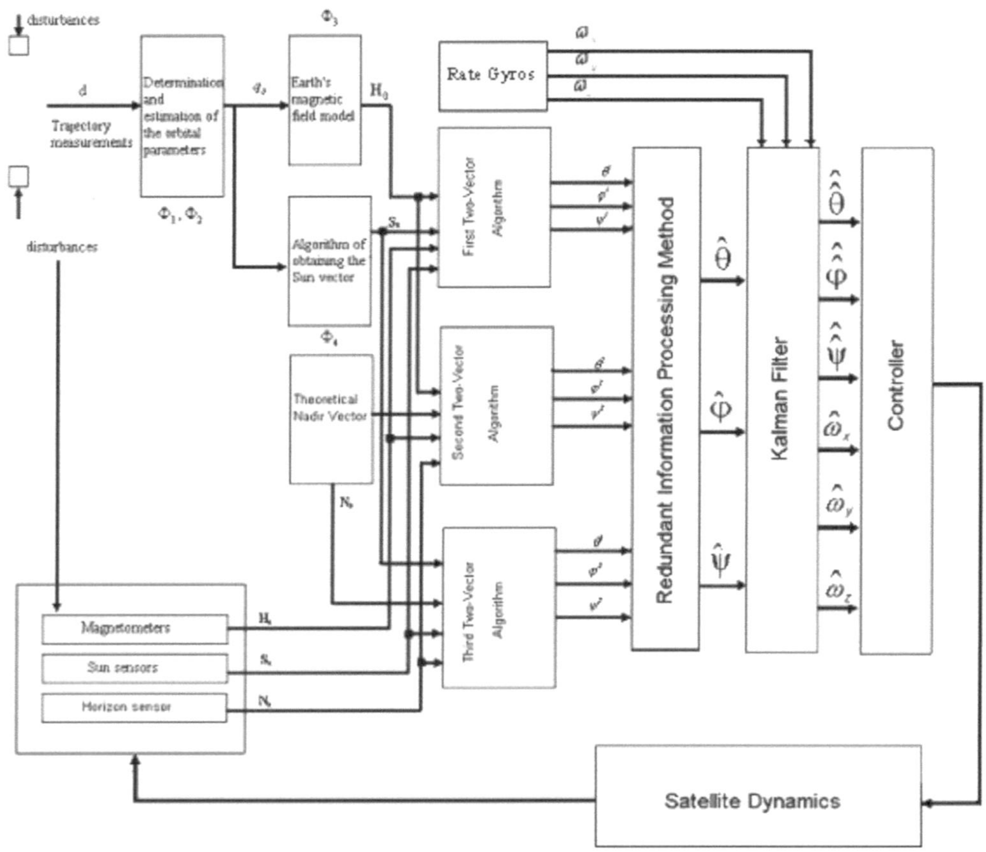

Fig. 5. Attitude estimation and control system scheme of LEO satellite

4. Innovation approach based sensor FDI

4.1 Fault detection via mathematical expectation statistic of spectral norm of normalized innovation matrix

In the Eq.(18)

$$\Delta_i = \left[z_i - Hf\left(\hat{U}_{i-1}, \bar{\omega}_{orb_{i-1}} \right) \right] \tag{21}$$

is the innovation sequence of EKF. If there is no trouble in the estimation system, the normalized innovation sequence

$$\tilde{\Delta}_i = \left[HM_i H^T + D_{v_i} \right]^{-1/2} \Delta_i, \tag{22}$$

of the EKF (18)-(20) accords with the dynamic model representing the white Gauss noise with zero average value and unitary covariance matrix (Mehra & Peschon, 1971):

$$E\left[\tilde{\Delta}_i\right] = 0; E\left[\tilde{\Delta}_k \tilde{\Delta}_j^T\right] = P_{\tilde{\Delta}_i} = I\delta_{kj}.$$

Faults causing abrupt changes in the characteristics of the measurement channel, malfunctions in the computer, as well as divergence of real process trajectories and estimations generated by the Kalman filter (which we shall hereafter name as faults of the estimation system) can cause changes in the demonstrated characteristics of the sequence $\tilde{\Delta}_i$ and can make it different from white noise, displace the zero average value and change the unitary covariance matrix.

It is important to develop an efficient method for simultaneous checking of the mathematical expectation and the variance of the normalized innovation sequence (22), which does not require a priori information on variation values in the fault case and makes it possible to find the faults of the estimation system in real-time.

Let us introduce two hypotheses: γ_0 - the estimation system operates properly; γ_1 - there is a trouble in the estimation system. To find a fault, we build a matrix with the columns of innovation vectors of EKF (18)-(20) and introduce the following definitions (Gadzhiev, 1996).

Definition 1. The innovation matrix of EKF (18)-(20) is rectangular $n \times m$ - matrix (n - dimension of innovation vector; $n \geq 2$; $m \geq 2$), with columns which are innovation vectors Δ_i corresponding to m different moments of time.

Definition 2. The innovation matrix, made up from normalized innovation vectors $\tilde{\Delta}_i$, is named as the normalized innovation matrix of EKF (18)-(20).

Hereafter for simplicity, we shall use the normalized innovation matrices A consisting of a finite number of innovation vectors. If the check is realized in real time, it is reasonable to form the matrix A_i at the i-th instant ($i \geq m$) of time from finite number m ($m \geq 2$) of sequential innovation vectors $\underbrace{\cdots \tilde{\Delta}_{i-2}, \tilde{\Delta}_{i-1}, \tilde{\Delta}_i}_{m}$. In order to check the hypotheses γ_0 and γ_1, we use a spectral norm of matrix A_i built in this way. As it is known (Horn and Johnson, 1986), the spectral norm $\|.\|_2$ of the real matrix A_i is defined by the formula $\|A_i\|_2 \equiv \max\left\{ (\lambda_l \left[A^T{}_i A_i \right])^{1/2} \right\}$, where $\lambda_l\left[A^T{}_i A_i \right]$ are eigenvalues of the matrix $A^T{}_i A_i$. Square roots from eigenvalues of the matrix $A^T{}_i A_i$ i.e. values $(\lambda_l\left[A^T{}_i A_i \right])^{1/2}$ are named as singular values of the matrix A_i. Hence the spectral norm of the matrix A_i is equal to its maximum singular value. The singular values are real and non-negative (Horn and Johnson, 1986). By that reasoning, a determination of singular values and, consequently, spectral norm represents a simpler problem in computing than determination of eigenvalues for arbitrary matrix. It explains the choice of the controlled scalar measure for the spectral norm of normalized innovation matrix of Kalman filter. In order to check the hypotheses γ_0 and γ_1, one-dimensional statistic for mathematical expectation of spectral norm of the matrix A_i for large values of k is introduced:

$$E\{\|A_i\|_2\} \approx \overline{\|A_i\|_2} = \frac{1}{k}\sum_{j=1}^{k}\|A_j\|_2 . \tag{23}$$

As it is clear from (23), the mathematical expectation of spectral norm of the matrix A_i is substituted by its average arithmetical estimate. For determining upper and lower limit $E\{\|A_i\|_2\}$ use results obtained in (Hansen, 1988), where a number of bounds have been found for the mathematical expectation of spectral norm of random matrix $A_i \in R^{n \times m}$, constituted of random Gaussian values, having zero mathematical expectation and σ standard deviation. Let us consider some of them. Assume, r_k^T and a_j are rows and columns of the matrix A. Introduce maximum row-column norm

$$\mu \equiv \max\left[\|r_k\|_2, \|a_j\|_2\right], \tag{24}$$

where $\|r_k\|_2$ and $\|a_j\|_2$ are corresponding Euclid vector norms. The following bounds for $E\{\|A_i\|_2\}$ have been obtained in (Hansen, 1988) by means of norm μ introduced:

$$E\{\mu\} \le E\{\|A_i\|_2\} \le \left[\max(n,m)\right]^{1/2} E\{\mu\}. \tag{25}$$

Using the formula (25) in practical calculations represents a complex problem, because of the difficulty of estimation of $E\{\mu\}$. So, the value $E\{\mu\}$ is replaced by its lower bound

$$\sigma\sqrt{\max(n,m)} = \max\left[E\{\|r_i\|_2\}, E\{\|a_j\|_2\}\right] \le E\{\mu\}. \tag{26}$$

Then the equation (25) can be written as follows:

$$\sigma\sqrt{\max(n,m)} \le E\{\|A_i\|_2\} \le f(\max(n,m))\sigma\sqrt{\max(n,m)}, \tag{27}$$

where f is an unknown function to be determined. It is shown in (Hansen, 1988) by means of computer simulation, the value $\sigma\sqrt{\max(n,m)}$ is good lower bound for $E\{\|A_i\|_2\}$. It is also shown by numeric calculations that function f asymptotically approaches value 2 as $n=m\to\infty$, and f is always between values 1 and 2. So the value 2 is suggested to be used for estimating function f . Taking the above mentioned fact into consideration the following simple bounds are obtainable for $E\{\|A_i\|_2\}$:

$$\sigma\sqrt{\max(n,m)} \le E\{\|A\|_2\} \le 2\sigma\sqrt{\max(n,m)} . \tag{28}$$

The expression (28) characterizes the connection between the standard deviation σ of elements of the random matrix A and its spectral norm.

The normalized innovation matrix A_i, used for finding the troubles in the estimation system consists of the Gaussian random elements with zero mathematical expectation and finite variance $a_{kj} \in N(0,1)$. The inequality (28) can be applied for solving the diagnostic problem formulated in this study. Thus it is possible to say, if elements a_{kj} of the controlled normalized innovation matrix of EKF are subordinated to distribution $N(0,1)$, the inequality (28) is fulfilled. Nonfulfilment of the inequality (28) indicates a shifting zero average value of elements a_{kj}, changing the unitary variance or that $\{a_{kj}\}$ is other than white noise.
The algorithm offered for real system operation conditions is reduced to the following sequence of calculations to be executed at every step of measurements.

1. The EKF evaluating system state vector and vector value of the normalized innovation sequence on given step i are calculated by means of expressions (18)-(22).
2. The normalized innovation matrix of the EKF is formed for given $n \geq 2$ and $m \geq 2$. The eigenvalues of the matrix $A^T{}_i A_i$ as roots of equation

$$\det[A_i^T A_i - \lambda I] = 0 \tag{29}$$

   and the spectral norm

$$\left\| A_i \right\|_2 \equiv \max\left\{ (\lambda_1\left[A_i^T A_i \right])^{1/2} \right\} \tag{30}$$

   are determined.
3. The statistic of mathematical expectation of spectral norm of the matrix A_i is calculated by means of (23).
4. The fulfilment of inequality (28) is checked and the solution is made according to the faulty operation of system.
5. The sequence of calculations is repeated as from the operation 1 for the following moment of time $i+1$.

It is necessary to note that the offered algorithm does not permit the realization of checking the nondiagonal elements of the covariance matrix of the normalized innovation sequence, but permits checks only on its mathematical expectation and variance. In spite of this fact, the given approach (due to its simplicity and ease of application) can bring good results when deciding the problems of check and diagnostics under conditions of relatively limited computer memory.

4.2 Sensor failure isolation based on innovation sequence

If the sensor fault is detected, then it is necessary to determine what sensor is faulty. For this purpose, the s-dimensional sequence $\tilde{\Delta}$ is transformed into n one-dimensional sequences to isolate the faulty sensor, and for each one-dimensional sequence $\tilde{\Delta}_i\,(i = 1,2,\ldots,n)$ corresponding monitoring algorithm is run. The statistic of the faulty sensor is assumed to be affected much more than those of the other sensors. Let the statistics is denoted as $\xi_i(k)$. When $\max\{\xi_i(k)/i = 1,2,\ldots,n\} = \xi_p(k)$ for $i \neq j$, and $\xi_i(k) \neq \xi_j(k)$, it is judged that p-th control channel has failed.

Let the statistics, which is a rate of sample and theoretical variances; $\hat{\sigma}_i^2 / \sigma_i^2$ be used to verify the variances of one-dimensional innovation sequences $\tilde{\Delta}_i(k), i = 1,2,\ldots,n$. When $\tilde{\Delta}_i \sim N(0,\sigma_i)$ it is known that,

$$\frac{\nu_i}{\sigma_i^2} \sim \chi^2_{M-1}, \forall i, i = 1,2,...,n \tag{31}$$

where

$$\nu_i = (M-1)\hat{\sigma}_i^2 . \tag{32}$$

As $\sigma_i^2 = 1$ for normalized innovation sequence, it follows that,

$$\nu_i \sim \chi^2_{M-1}, \forall i, i = 1,2,...,n . \tag{33}$$

By selecting α level of significance as,

$$P\{\chi^2 > \chi^2_{\alpha,M-1}\} = \alpha \; ; 0 < \alpha < 1$$

So from the equation above, the threshold value $\chi^2_{\alpha,M-1}$ will be determined.
When a fault affecting the variance of the innovation sequence, occurs in the system, the statistics V_i exceeds the threshold value $\chi^2_{\alpha,M-1}$ depending on the confidence probability (1-α), and degree of freedom $(M-1)$. Using (33) it can be proved that any change in the mean of the normalized innovation sequence can be detected. Let a change in the mean of the innovation sequence occur at the time τ, and let $\tilde{\Delta}^*(k)$ denote the unchanged normalized innovation sequence, then the changed normalized innovation sequence is given by,

$$\tilde{\Delta}(k) = \tilde{\Delta}^*(k) \qquad k = 1,2,...,\tau - 1 \tag{34}$$

$$\tilde{\Delta}(k) = \tilde{\Delta}^*(k) + \mu(k-\tau) \qquad k = \tau, \tau + 1, ... \tag{35}$$

where $\mu(.)$ is an unknown change and may vary with respect to time, but there exists a quantity $L > 0$ such that $|\mu(j)| < L$, for $\forall j$. (34) and (35) yield,

$$\tilde{\Delta}(k) \sim N(0,1) \;\; k = 1,2,...,\tau - 1 \tag{36}$$

$$\tilde{\Delta}(k) \sim N(\mu(k-\tau),1) \;\; k = \tau, \tau + 1, ... \tag{37}$$

Let the number of shifted values from $j = k - M + 1$ to k in a window be denoted by N. When $k<\tau$ it can be easily shown that the mathematical expectation of investigated statistic (32) is $E[\nu_i] = M - 1$. When a fault occurs, the mathematical expectation of (32) can be determined by the following theorem.
Theorem 2. When $k \geq \tau$, i.e. the hypothesis H_1 is true, the following equation is also true,

$$E[\upsilon(k)] = (M-1)\sigma^2 + E\left\{ \sum_{j=k-M+1}^{k} \left[\mu(j-\tau) - \frac{\sum_{j=k-M+1}^{k} \mu(j-\tau)}{M} \right]^2 \right\} \tag{38}$$

where

$$\mu(j-\tau)=\begin{cases} 0 & j<\tau \\ \mu^{*}=\text{constant} & j\geq\tau \end{cases}$$

The proof is given in (Hajiyev, 2006).
Let the number of shifted innovation values from $j=k-M+1$ to k in a window be denoted by N. Two distinct cases may be considered;

a. N=M, in this case,

$$E\left\{\sum_{j=k-M+1}^{k}\left[\mu(j-\tau)-\frac{\sum_{j=k-M+1}^{k}\mu(j-\tau)}{M}\right]^{2}\right\}=0 \tag{39}$$

and so, $E[\nu(k)]=(M-1)\sigma^2$. When the values $\tilde{\Delta}(j)$ have shifted by the same amount $\mu(j-\tau)$ in a window, it is impossible to detect the change by using (32).

b. $N<M$, in this case

$$\left[\mu(j-\tau)-\frac{\sum_{j=k-M+1}^{k}\mu(j-\tau)}{M}\right]^{2}=\left[\mu(j-\tau)-\frac{N\mu^{*}}{M}\right]^{2}\geq 0 \tag{40}$$

and a shift in the innovation sequence will cause an asymptotic increase in the expected value of the statistic $\nu(k)$, and $\nu(k)$ will exceed the threshold $\chi^{2}_{\alpha,M-1}$. The larger μ^* the faster detection is.

The sample variances $\hat{\sigma}_i$ are the diagonal components of the sample covariance matrix $S(k)$. Therefore there is no need to make heavy additional computation in the existent algorithm, but only the diagonal components of the matrix $S(k)$ are multiplied by $(M-1)$, and compared with $\chi^{2}_{\alpha,M-1}$ and with one another at each iteration. The decision making for isolation is done as follows; if the hypothesis H_1 is true and $S_{ii}(k)\neq S_{jj}(k), i\neq j$ and $\max\{S_{ii}(k)/i=1,2,...,n\}=S_{pp}(k)$ where $S_{ii}(k)$ is the ii th component of $S(k)$, then it is judged that there is a fault in the pth channel.

4.3 Simulation results of FDI algorithms

To test the proposed algorithm, it is applied to the mathematical model of the LEO satellite's rotational motion about its center of mass. It is demonstrated that the faults in a measurement channel can be detected by checking the mathematical expectation and the variance of the EKF innovation sequence. Under computer simulation of the above specified problem, as the estimation of system state vector is calculated, the values of normalized innovation sequence were determined by means of the expression (22). The spectral norm of matrix A_i for the case $n=6$, $m=6$ was determined by means of expression (30); the mathematical expectation of spectral norm $\|A_i\|_2$ was determined by means of (23). Decisions on finding a system fault were made on the basis of inequality (28), written for the case $n=6$, $m=6$. If the case is $\sigma=1$, $n=6$ and $m=6$,the inequality (28) can be written in a simpler form

$$\sqrt{6} \le E\{\|A\|_2\} \le 2\sqrt{6} \tag{41}$$

The results of calculations are shown in Figures 5-7.

One can see in Fig.5 that the values of statistic $E\{\|A_i\|_2\}$ fall within the permissible domain (between lower and upper thresholds) when no sensor fault occurs. The graphs of the values of statistic $E\{\|A\|_2\}$ are shown in Fig.6 when a shift occurs in the pitch rate gyroscope at the step 30.The behavior of the appropriate normalized innovation sequences $\tilde{\Delta}_{\omega_y}(k)$ is presented in the Fig. 7.

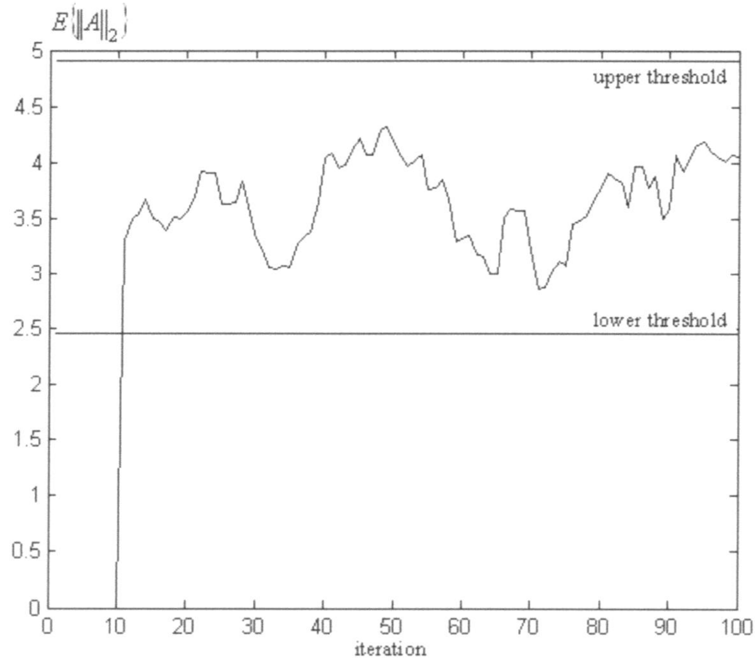

Fig. 5. The behavior of the statistic $E\{\|A\|_2\}$ for a normal operating system

This fault causes a change in the mean of the innovation sequence. As seen in Fig.6, when there is no sensor fault the values of statistic $E\{\|A\|_2\}$ fall within the permissible domain, and when a fault occurs in the pitch rate gyroscope $E\{\|A\|_2\}$ grows rapidly and after 1 steps it exceeds the upper threshold. Hence γ_1 hypotheses is judged to be true.

The Fig.8 shows detection of faults changing the noise variance of the pitch rate gyroscope.

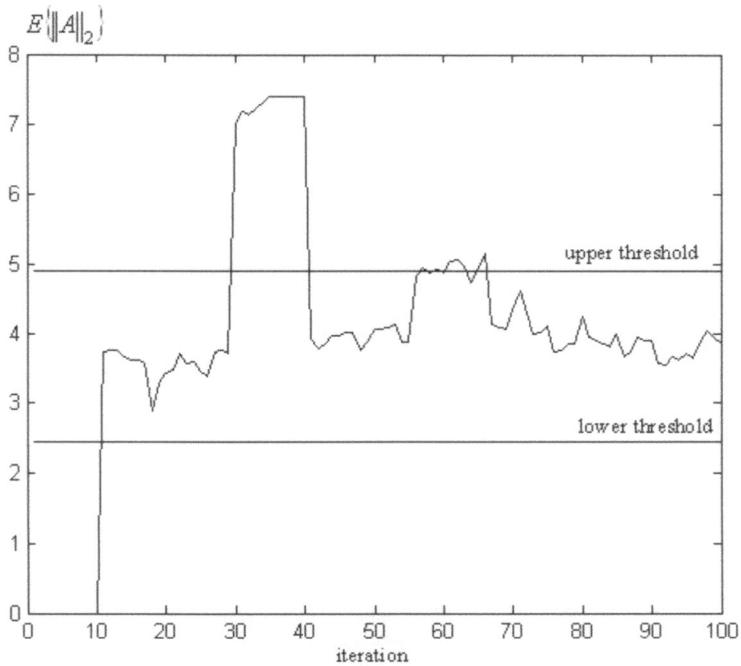

Fig. 6. The behavior of the statistic $E\{\|A\|_2\}$ in case of shift in the pitch rate gyroscope (the moment of the shift appears at k=30, the moment reveals the shift at k=31)

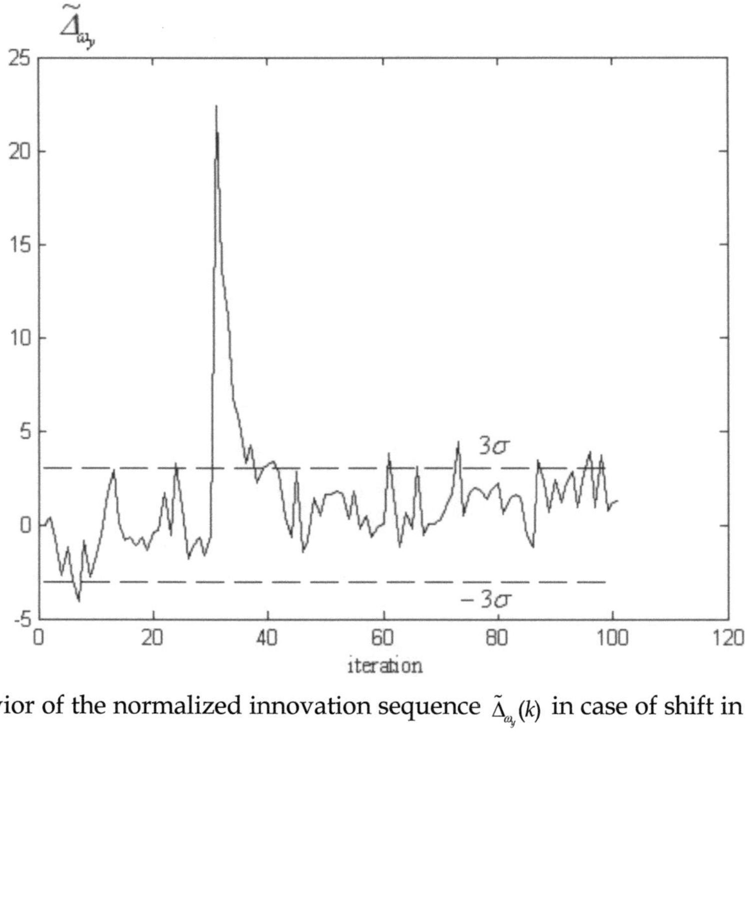

Fig. 7. Behavior of the normalized innovation sequence $\tilde{\Delta}_{\omega_y}(k)$ in case of shift in the pitch rate gyroscope

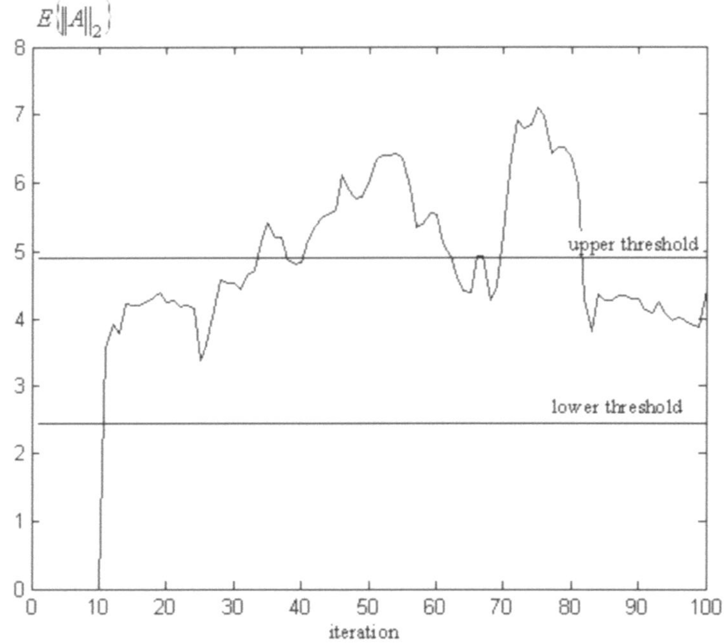

Fig. 8. The behavior of the statistic $E\{\|A\|_2\}$ in case of changes in noise variance of the pitch rate gyroscope (the moment of variance changes at k=30, the moment of revealing variance changes at k=34)

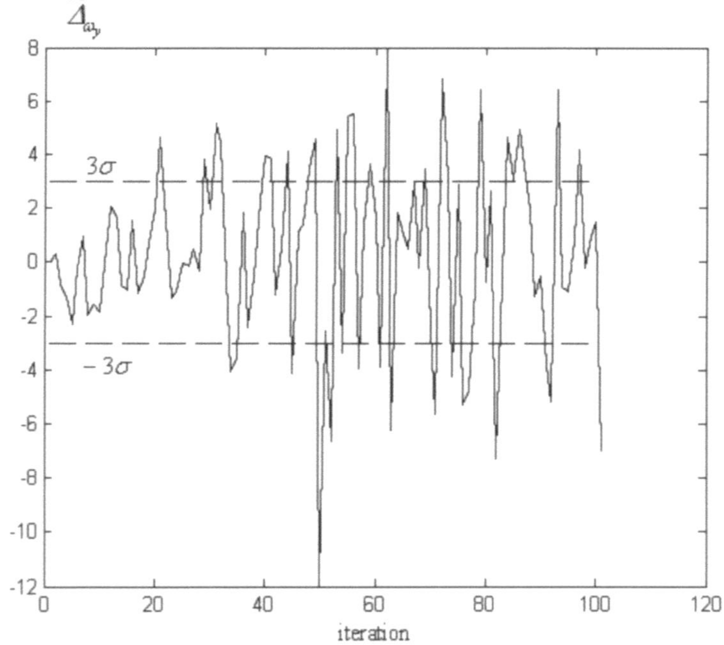

Fig. 9. Behavior of the normalized innovation sequence $\tilde{\Delta}_{\omega_y}(k)$ in case of changes in noise variance of the pitch rate gyroscope

In this case, the mean value of the innovation sequence does not change, but the variance changes. The graphs of the values of statistic $E\{\|A\|_2\}$ are shown in Fig.8 when a fault occurs in the pitch rate gyroscope at the step 30. This fault causes a change in the variance of the innovation sequence. As seen in Fig.8, when there is no sensor fault $E\{\|A\|_2\}$ fall between lower threshold and upper threshold lines, and when a fault occurs in the pitch rate gyroscope $E\{\|A\|_2\}$ grows rapidly and after 4 steeps it exceeds the threshold. Hence γ_1 hypotheses is judged to be true. The behavior of the appropriate normalized innovation sequences $\tilde{\Delta}_{\omega_y}(k)$ is presented in the Fig. 9.
The results of computer simulation have confirmed the practical possibility of simultaneous real-time check of mathematical expectation and variance of normalized innovation sequence with the aid of the statistic introduced (32).
Sensor failure isolation results in case of shift in the pitch rate gyroscope are given in Fig. 10(a,b) and in case of changes in noise variance of the pitch rate gyroscope in Fig. 11(a,b). As it is shown from presented figures, only the *(5,5)* element of the covariance matrix *S* ($S(5,5)$) exceeds the threshold $\chi^2_{\alpha,M-1}$ (for M=15 and $\alpha = 0.1$ the threshold value $\chi^2_{\alpha,M-1} = 21.1$) which indicates a failure in the pitch rate gyro. *S(j,j)*, $j \neq 5$ elements do not exceed the thresholds.

5. Conclusion

Fault detection and isolation algorithms for LEO satellite attitude determination and control system using an approach for checking the statistical characteristics of EKF innovation sequence are proposed. The fault detection algorithm is based on statistic for the mathematical expectation of the spectral norm of the normalized innovation matrix of the EKF. This approach permits simultaneous real-time checking of the mathematical expectation and the variance of the innovation sequence and does not require a priori information about the faults and statistical characteristics of the system in fault cases.
In this study an attitude estimation and control system for LEO satellite is proposed. To determine the attitude of the satellite, this system use algebraic method (two-vector algorithm). As a reference direction, the unit vectors toward the Sun, the Earth's center, and the Earth magnetic field are used. Thus, it includes three different two-vector algorithms based on using the Earth's magnetic field - the Sun vector, the Earth's magnetic field - nadir vector, and nadir vector - the Sun vector couples. In order to increase the attitude determination accuracy, the redundant data processing algorithm, based on the Maximum Likelihood Method, is used.
An extended Kalman filter has been developed for nonlinear rotational dynamics estimation of LEO satellite. Failures in the sensors affect the characteristics of the innovation sequence of the EKF. The failures that affect the mean and variance of the innovation sequence have been considered. The application of the proposed fault detection algorithm to the LEO satellite attitude determination and control system has shown that, sensor fault detection by the presented algorithm is possible in real time.
Assuming that the effect of the faulty sensor on its channel is more significant than on the other channels, a sensor isolation method is presented by transforming *n*-dimensional innovation process to n one-dimensional processes. The simulations, carried out on a nonlinear dynamic model of the rotational motion of LEO satellite, confirm the theoretical results.
The future work is to investigate the faults affecting the attitude dynamics e.g., actuator faults and to perform the integrated sensor/actuator FDI via innovation approach.

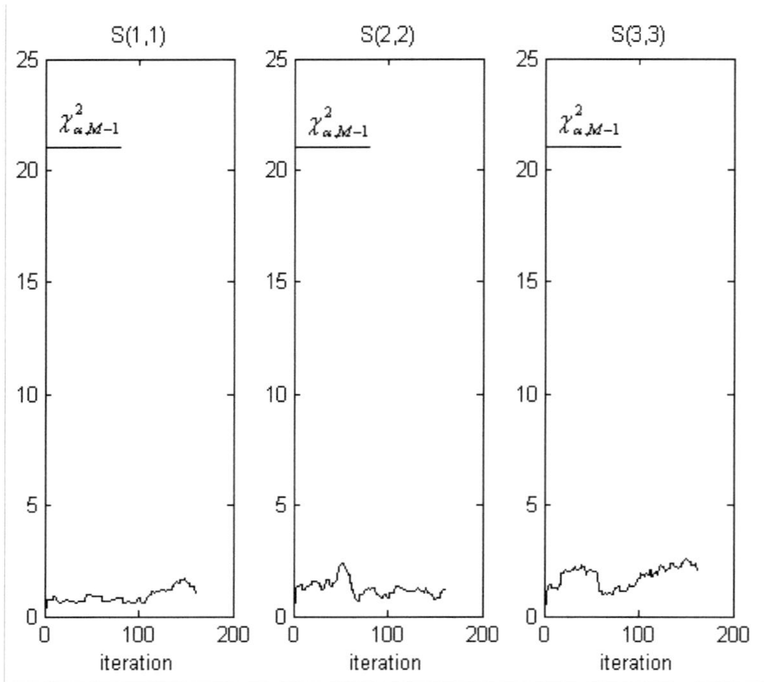

(a)

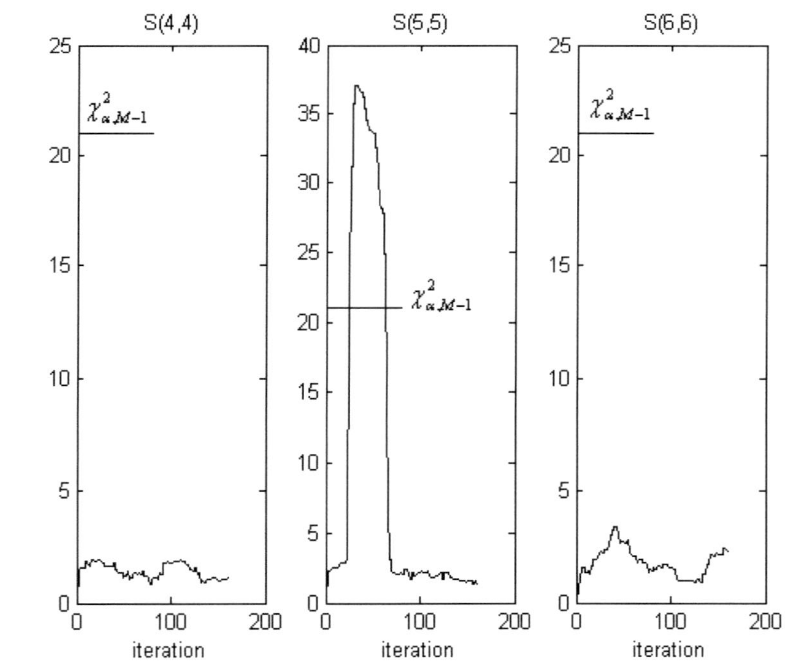

(b)

Fig. 10. Sensor failure isolation in case of shift in the pitch rate gyroscope

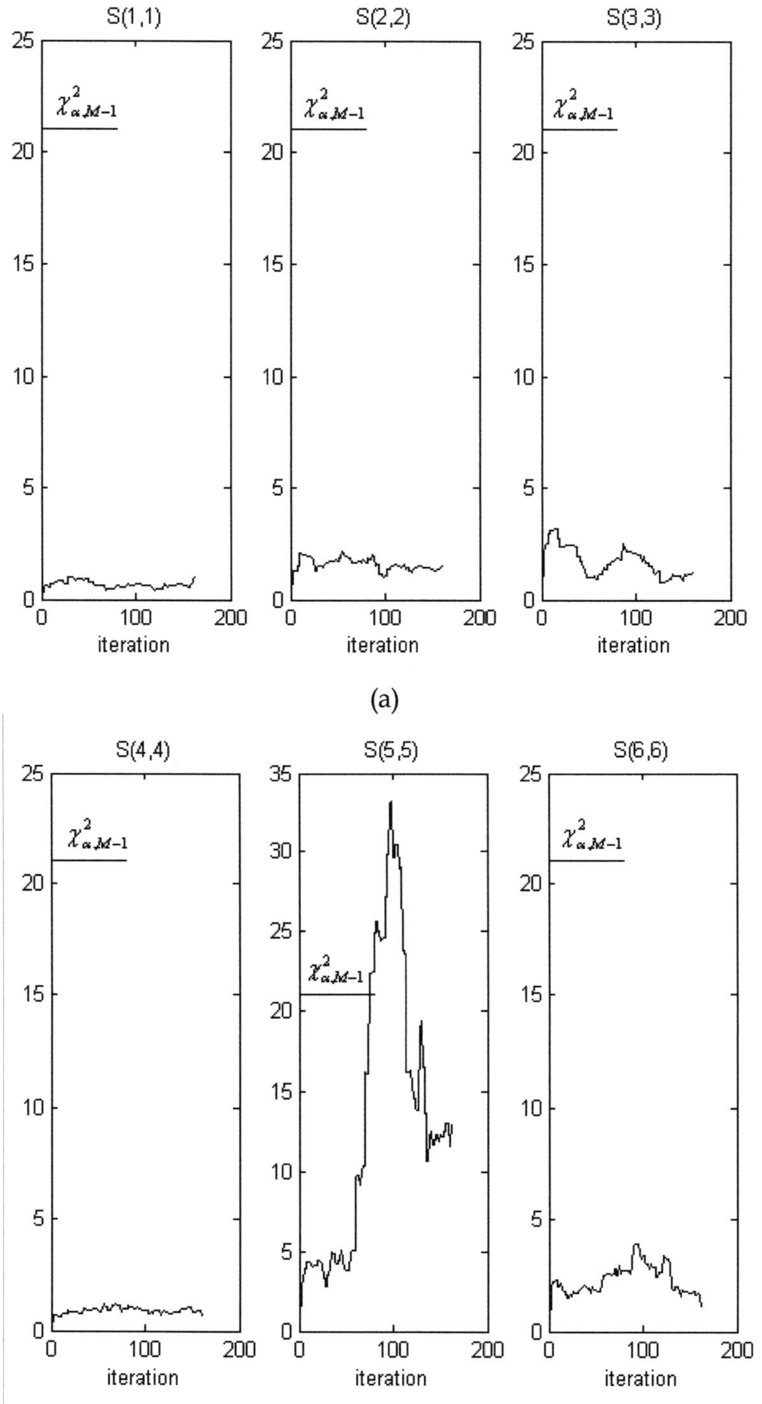

(b)

Fig. 11. Sensor failure isolation in case of changes in noise variance in the pitch rate gyroscope

7. References

Alessandri, A. (2003). Fault Diagnosis for Nonlinear Systems Using a Bank of Neural Estimators. *Computers in Industry*, Vol 52(3), pp. 271-289

Bak, T, Wisniewski, R. and Blanke, M. (1996). Autonomous Attitude Determination and Control System for the Orsted Satellite. *Proceedings of the 1996 IEEE Aerospace Applications Conference*, V. 2, pp. 173-185, Snowmass, CO, USA, Feb 9-10 1996

Barishev, V.A. and Krilov, G.N. (1968). *Tracking of Meteorological Satellites*, (in Russian), Gidrometeoizdat, Moscow

Borairi, M., Wang, H. (1998). Actuator and Sensor Fault Diagnosis of Non-Linear Dynamic Systems via Genetic Neural Networks and Adaptive Parameter Estimation Technique. *Proceedings of the IEEE Conference on Control Applications*, V 1, pp. 278-282

Brandin, V. N., Vasilyev, A. A. and Kunetskiy, A. A., (1984). *Experimental Ballistic of Space Vehicles.*, (in Russian), Maschinostroyeniye, Moscow

Hajiyev, Ch.M. and Bahar, M. (1998). Approach to the Increase of Accuracy of the Satellite Attitude Determination. *Proceedings of 5Th Saint Petersburg International Conference on Integrated Navigation Systems,* pp. 111-118, Russia, 25-27 May 1998

Hajiyev, Ch., M. (1999). Radio Navigation, (in Turkish), Istanbul Technical University Press, Istanbul, Turkey

Hajiyev, Ch. and Bahar, M. (2000). Multichannel Kalman Filter Based on Preliminary Data Compression for the Satellite Rotational Motion Parameters Identification. *Proceedings of the 3rd International Conference on Nonlinear Problems in Aviation and Aerospace*, European Conference Publications, V.1, pp.277-284, Daytona Beach, Florida, USA, May,2000

Hajiyev, Ch.M. and Bahar, M. (2002). Increase of Accuracy of the Small Satellite Attitude Determination Using Redundancy Techniques. *Acta Astronautica,* vol. 50, No. 11, 2002, pp. 673-679

Hajiyev, Ch. And Bahar, M. (2003). Attitude Determination and Control System Design of the ITU-UUBF LEO1 Satellite. *Acta Astronautica*, Vol. 52, Issues 2-6, 2003, pp. 493-499

Hajiyev, Ch. and Caliskan, F. (2003). Fault Diagnosis and Reconfiguration in Flight Control Systems, Kluwer Academic Publishers, Boston.

Hajiyev, Ch. (2006). Innovation Approach Based Measurement Error Self-Correction in Dynamic Systems. Measurement, 39, pp. 585-593

Hansen, P.C. (1988). The 2-Norm of Random Matrices. *J.Comput. & Appl. Math,* vol. 23, pp.117-120

Horn, R. and Johnson, C. (1986). *Matrix Analysis,* England, Cambridge University Press

Gadzhiev, Ch.M. (1992). Dynamic Systems Diagnosis Based on Kalman Filter Updating Sequences. *Automation and Remote Control*, No 1, pp.147-150

Gadzhiev, Ch.M. (1994). Check of the Generalized Variance of the Kalman Filter Updating Sequence in Dynamic Diagnosis. Automation and Remote Control,Vol.55, No. 8, pp.1165-1169

Gadzhiev, Ch.M. (1996). A New Method of Kalman Filter Innovation Sequence Statistical Characteristics Checking. *Engineering Simulation*, No.1, pp. 83-91

Larson, E.C., et al. (2002). Model-Based Sensor and Actuator Fault Detection and Isolation. Proceedings of the American Control Conference, vol 5, pp. 4215-4219

Lee, J. H, Lyou, J. (2002). Fault Diagnosis and Fault Tolerant Control of Linear Stochastic Systems with Unknown Inputs. *Systems Science*, Vol 27(3), pp.59-76

Mehra, R.K. and Peschon, J. (1971). An Innovations Approach to Fault Detection and Diagnosis in Dynamic Systems. *Automatica*, vol.7, pp.637-640

Rago, C., et al. (1998). Failure Detection and Identification and Fault Tolerant Control Using the IMM-KF with Applications to the Eagle-Eye UAV. Proceedings of the IEEE Conference on Decision and Control, vol 4,pp. 4208-4213

Sasiadek, J.Z. and Wang, Q. (1999). Sensor Fusion Based on Fuzzy Kalman Filtering for Autonomous Robot Vehicle Proceedings of the 1999 IEEE International Conference on Robotics & Automation, pp. 2970-2975, Detroit, Michigan, May 1999

Wertz, J.R., ed. (1988). *Spacecraft Attitude Determination and Control,* Kluwer Academic, Dordrecht, The Netherlands

Willsky, A.S.. (1976). A Survey of Design Methods for Failure Detection in Dynamic Systems. *Automatic*a, vol.12, No.6, pp. 601-611

Zhang, S-T. and Wei, X-Y. (2003). Fuzzy Adaptive Kalman Filtering for DR/GPS. Proceedings of the Second International Conference on Machine Learning and Cybernetics, pp.2634-2637, Xi'an, 2-5 November 2003

Zhang Y. and Li, X.R. (1997). Detection and Diagnosis of Sensor and Actuator Failures using Interacting Multiple-Model Estimator. *Proceedings of the IEEE Conference on Decision and Control,* vol. 5, pp. 4475-4480

Appendix-1

It is possible to express the attitude angles with the components of the vectors used in the algorithm. For that purpose, first it have to be found the inverse of matrix C. Then using the Eq.(3) the transformation matrix *A* could be formed. Once the transformation matrix is formed, the following relations can be written,

$$\theta = \sin^{-1}\left(R'/P'\right)$$
$$\varphi = \tan^{-1}\left(R''/P''\right)$$
$$\psi = \tan^{-1}\left(R'''/P'''\right)$$

here,

$$\begin{aligned} R' = {} & H_{z_0} S_{x_0}^2 H_{x_k} - H_{x_0} S_{x_0} S_{z_0} H_{x_k} - H_{y_0} S_{y_0} S_{z_0} H_{x_k} + H_{z_0} S_{y_0}^2 H_{x_k} + H_{y_0}^2 S_{z_0} S_{x_k} - \\ & - H_{y_0} H_{z_0} S_{y_0} S_{x_k} - H_{x_0} H_{z_0} S_{x_0} S_{x_k} + H_{x_0}^2 S_{x_0} S_{x_k} + H_{x_0} S_{y_0} H_{y_k} S_{z_k} - H_{y_0} S_{x_0} H_{y_k} S_{z_k} - \\ & - H_{x_0} S_{y_0} H_{z_k} S_{y_k} + H_{y_0} S_{x_0} H_{z_k} S_{y_k} \end{aligned}$$

$$\begin{aligned} P' = {} & H_{x_0}^2 S_{y_0}^2 + H_{x_0}^2 S_{z_0}^2 + H_{y_0}^2 S_{x_0}^2 + H_{y_0}^2 S_{z_0}^2 + H_{z_0}^2 S_{x_0}^2 + H_{z_0}^2 S_{y_0}^2 - 2H_{x_0} H_{y_0} S_{x_0} S_{y_0} - \\ & - 2H_{x_0} H_{z_0} S_{x_0} S_{z_0} - 2H_{y_0} H_{z_0} S_{y_0} S_{z_0} \end{aligned}$$

$$
\begin{aligned}
R'' = {} & H_{y_0} H_{x_k} S_{z_0}^2 - H_{z_0} H_{x_k} S_{y_0} S_{z_0} - H_{x_0} H_{x_k} S_{x_0} S_{y_0} + H_{y_0} H_{x_k} S_{x_0}^2 + H_{x_0}^2 S_{y_0} S_{x_k} - \\
& - H_{x_0} H_{y_0} S_{x_0} S_{x_k} - H_{y_0} H_{z_0} S_{z_0} S_{x_k} + H_{z_0}^2 S_{y_0} S_{x_k} + H_{z_0} H_{y_k} S_{x_0} S_{z_k} - H_{x_0} H_{y_k} S_{z_0} S_{z_k} - \\
& - H_{z_0} H_{z_k} S_{x_0} S_{y_k} + H_{x_0} H_{z_k} S_{z_0} S_{y_k}
\end{aligned} \tag{A1}
$$

$$
\begin{aligned}
P'' = {} & H_{x_0} H_{x_k} S_{y_0}^2 - H_{y_0} H_{x_k} S_{x_0} S_{y_0} - H_{z_0} H_{x_k} S_{x_0} S_{z_0} + H_{x_0} H_{x_k} S_{z_0}^2 + H_{z_0}^2 S_{z_0} S_{x_k} - \\
& - H_{x_0} H_{z_0} S_{z_0} S_{x_k} - H_{x_0} H_{y_0} S_{y_0} S_{x_k} + H_{y_0}^2 S_{x_0} S_{x_k} + H_{y_0} H_{y_k} S_{z_0} S_{z_k} - H_{z_0} H_{y_k} S_{y_0} S_{z_k} - \\
& - H_{y_0} H_{z_k} S_{z_0} S_{y_k} + H_{z_0} H_{z_k} S_{y_0} S_{y_k}
\end{aligned}
$$

$$
\begin{aligned}
R''' = {} & H_{z_0} H_{y_k} S_{x_0}^2 - H_{x_0} H_{y_k} S_{x_0} S_{z_0} - H_{y_0} H_{y_k} S_{y_0} S_{z_0} + H_{z_0} H_{y_k} S_{y_0}^2 + H_{y_0}^2 S_{z_0} S_{y_k} - \\
& - H_{y_0} H_{z_0} S_{y_0} S_{y_k} - H_{x_0} H_{z_0} S_{x_0} S_{y_k} + H_{x_0}^2 S_{z_0} S_{y_k} + H_{x_0} H_{z_k} S_{y_0} S_{x_k} - H_{y_0} H_{z_k} S_{x_0} S_{x_k} - \\
& - H_{x_0} H_{x_k} S_{y_0} S_{z_k} + H_{y_0} H_{x_k} S_{x_0} S_{z_k}
\end{aligned}
$$

$$
\begin{aligned}
P''' = {} & H_{z_0} H_{z_k} S_{x_0}^2 - H_{x_0} H_{z_k} S_{x_0} S_{z_0} - H_{y_0} H_{z_k} S_{y_0} S_{z_0} + H_{z_0} H_{z_k} S_{y_0}^2 + H_{y_0}^2 S_{z_0} S_{z_k} - \\
& - H_{y_0} H_{z_0} S_{y_0} S_{z_k} - H_{x_0} H_{z_0} S_{x_0} S_{z_k} + H_{x_0}^2 S_{z_0} S_{z_k} + H_{x_0} H_{x_k} S_{y_0} S_{y_k} - H_{y_0} H_{x_k} S_{x_0} S_{y_k} - \\
& - H_{x_0} H_{y_k} S_{y_0} S_{x_k} + H_{y_0} H_{y_k} S_{x_0} S_{x_k}
\end{aligned}
$$

Electrical Engineering

16

Estimation of Electrical Power Quantities by Means of Kalman Filtering

Alberto Pigazo and Víctor M. Moreno
University of Cantabria
Spain

1. Introduction

The presence of non-linear loads and the increasing number of distributed generation power systems (DGPS) in electrical grids contribute to change the characteristics of voltage and current waveforms in power systems, which differ from pure sinusoidal constant amplitude signals. Under these conditions advanced signal processing techniques are required for accurate measurement of electrical power quantities. The impact of non-linear loads in electrical power systems has been increasing during the last decades. Such electrical loads, which introduce non-sinusoidal current consumption patterns (current harmonics), can be found in rectification front-ends in motor drives, electronic ballasts for discharge lamps, personal computers or electrical appliances. Current harmonics reduce the efficiency of low and medium voltage electrical grids (Dugan et al., 2003). It must be also considered that renewable energy sources in electrical grids can also deteriorate the electrical power quality. For instance, wind turbines can introduce flickering (Larson, 2000) and PV systems, due to solar radiance variations, generate variable output power. Moreover, such resources, especially in low-voltage systems, change their status (grid connection or disconnection) continuously, contributing to the electrical system instability.
Diverse approaches can be applied to characterize electrical signal waveforms in real-time: windowed or recursive Fourier transforms, wavelets, artificial neural networks (ANN) (Bollen & Gu, 2006). Kalman filtering can be applied to estimate electrical quantities in power systems, such as voltage and/or current magnitude, grid balance and/or frequency. The obtained signal measurements can be employed for revenue purposes, electrical grid characterization and/or active compensation of power system disturbances. This chapter is focused on Kalman filtering based approaches for estimation of electrical power quantities, such as voltage amplitude, current harmonics amplitude or grid frequency, under sinusoidal, non-sinusoidal, balanced or unbalanced conditions. Moreover, steady-state signals and transients in power systems are also analysed.
The second section in this chapter describes the characteristics of power quality disturbances in electrical grids, considering time and frequency domains. The following section reviews the applications of Kalman filters in electrical power systems. The fundamentals of Kalman and extended Kalman filtering techniques for estimation of power system signal waveforms are given in the fourth section. The implementations of Kalman filtering loops in MatLab/Simulink, as well as a new signal model for frequency estimation, are also given in this section. Section five will give the obtained simulation results under diverse conditions of the electrical grid. Finally, the conclusions of this chapter are shown.

2. Power quality disturbances in electrical power systems

Electrical power networks integrate generation and distribution systems and electrical loads. Due to the environmental issues related to conventional generation systems, such as coal or nuclear plants, and the rising price of fossil fuels renewable energy sources, such as wind or photovoltaic generation systems, are becoming more and more interesting. In case of the European Union, the target is 20% of generation from renewable energy sources by 2020. Electrical loads are also being changed due to the impact of power electronics, which allow the efficiency, reliability and controllability to be increased at low cost. This is the case of electrical machines which are connected to the electrical grid through electronic power converters or switched power supplies in computers.

Due to this scenario, the waveforms of voltage and current signals in electrical grids present multiple disturbances which can reduce the efficiency and reliability of electrical systems. In order to manage the electrical grids such disturbances must be properly measured and their impact evaluated. Generally speaking, the electrical disturbances can arrive to a certain customer, maybe due to a fault (Fig. 1.a), or can be produced by a customer (Fig. 1.b). In the most general case, measurement equipments must consider both possibilities and their interaction (Fig. 1.c). Fig. 1.a shows a passive load connected to the electrical grid and a sudden variation of the voltage magnitude which, due to the passive load impedance, is translated to the current waveform. The effect of a distorting load is shown in Fig 1.b. As it can be seen, the electrical load contains a full-bridge diode rectifier with a capacitive dc side wich produce current peaks at the grid side. Due to the impedance of distribution lines, such current pattern will distort the pure sinusoidal grid voltage. Finally, Fig. 1.c shows a more general case where a fault appears changing the current pattern of the non-linear load.

According to (Bollen & Gu, 2006), power quality disturbances can be classified as variations and events. Variations are defined as *steady-state or quasi-steady-state disturbances that require continuous measurement* while events correspond to *sudden disturbances with a beginning and an ending* (time bounded disturbances). Frequency and voltage magnitude variations, unbalances, voltage fluctuations as well as waveform distortion (harmonics and interharmonics) are included in the first group while interruptions, voltage dips/swells and transients can be grouped as events.

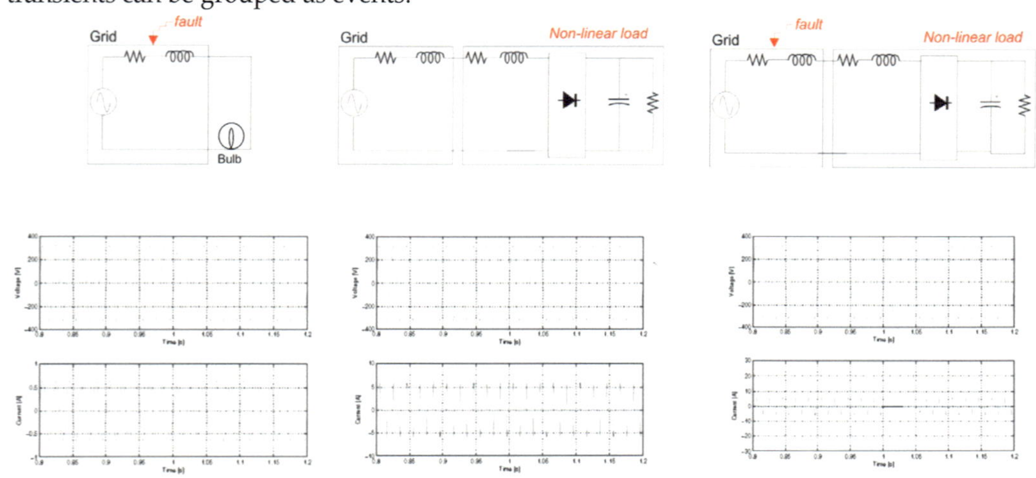

Fig. 1. Disturbances. a) From the electrical grid, b) from the load and c) both.

Frequency variations are due to active power mismatches between generators and electrical loads. A power-frequency control strategy is needed in order to maintain the fundamental frequency of the electrical grid. The frequency variations measured at the School of Nautical Studies, University of Cantabria, Santander, by means of Dranetz PowerPlatform1 are shown in Fig. 2.a. As it can be seen, the average value of the measured frequency is 50 Hz and the measured values variate between 49.93 Hz and 50.07 Hz continuously. According to IEC-61000-2-2 standard, the allowable frequency variations must be in range ± 1 Hz. Voltage magnitude variations cause problems to sensitive electrical loads, such as electronic devices. Fig 2.b shows magnitude variations in a three-phase power system. The average measured value of voltage in phase A is 232.40 Vrms. Maximum and minimum values are 243.15 Vrms and 222.39 Vrms respectively. Such magnitude variations are limited by IEC-61000-2-2 to a 3% of the nominal voltage. Voltage unbalances are also classified as variations and they are due to unbalanced loads, such as single-phase electrical loads connected to three-phase systems, or unbalanced system impedances. They can reduce the efficiency of rotating machines and produce erroneous firing angles in controlled rectifiers. Standard IEC-61000-2-2 allows 2% inverse sequences during unbalanced conditions.

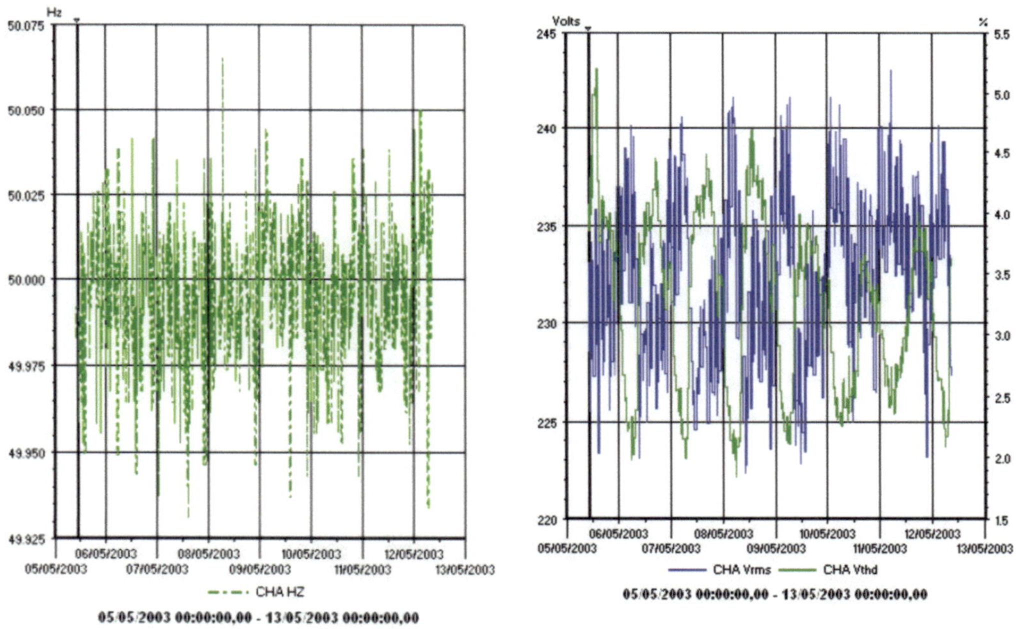

(a) (b)

Fig. 2. a) Frequency and b) voltage magnitude variations measured at the School of Nautical Studies, Santander, Spain.

Voltage fluctuations, shown in fig. 3.a, denote fast changes in the voltage magnitude which can be produced by repetitive current changes, such as continuous starts and stops in air conditioning or heating systems, or fast current variations. They can generate braking or accelerating moments for electrical motors or light flickering. The short and long term allowable flickers are 1 and 0.8 respectively according to standard IEC-61000-2-2. Waveform distortions are due to non-linear elements in electrical power systems. This is the case of grid-connected power converters or fluorescent lighting. Fig. 3.b shows the evolution of per-phase and neutral currents during the afternoon and night at the Economics Faculty, University of Cantabria, Santander, Spain. As it can be seen, depending on the daily power consumption, the current magnitude and its spectral distribution change. Fig. 3.c shows the spectral distribution of the phase-current, which presents a 47.32% Total Harmonic Distortion (THD). The voltage THD and the magnitude of individual voltage harmonics are limited in standard IEC-61000-2-2. Current harmonics can cause extra losses in transformers, neutral cable overheating in three-phase four-wire electrical systems and resonances in capacitor banks.

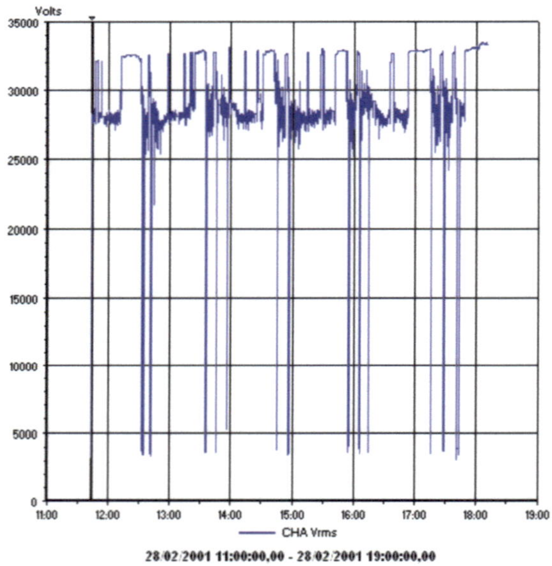

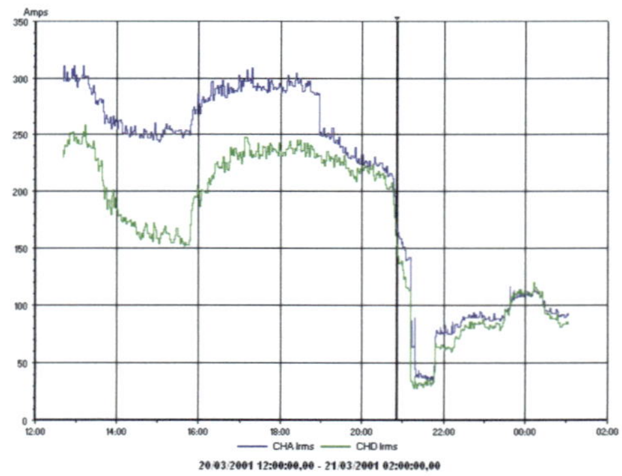

(b)

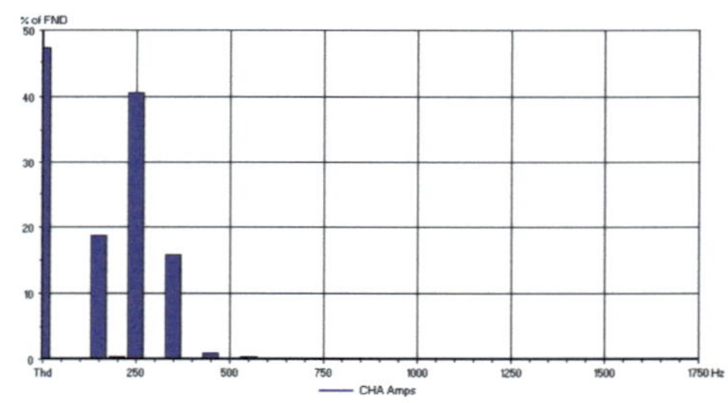

(a) (c)

Fig. 3. a) Measured voltage fluctuations at the point of connection of an arc furnace. b) Per-phase and neutral current magnitudes (rms) and c) harmonic distribution of the phase current.

Short and long interruptions (fig. 4.a) occur when one or more customers are disconnected from the electrical grid and the voltage magnitude falls to zero or close to zero. They are produced by short circuits, earth faults, inadvertent operation of circuit breakers or intentional disconnection due to maintenance tasks. The consequences depend on the edge. Falling transients can cause electrical equipment malfunction while rising transients can cause transformers saturation or protections tripping in case of high start-up currents. Voltage transients (fig. 4.b) can be due to lightning or switching transients and can cause voltage dips or interruptions as well as voltage magnification, in case of switch on transients in capacitors, or restrikes during capacitors or inductances de-energizing.

Voltage magnitude reductions with short duration, typically less than one second, can be considered as voltage dips (fig. 5). They are produced by short circuits, earth faults, starting of induction motors or energizing of transformers and can cause undervoltages at the dc-bus of uncontrolled rectifiers.

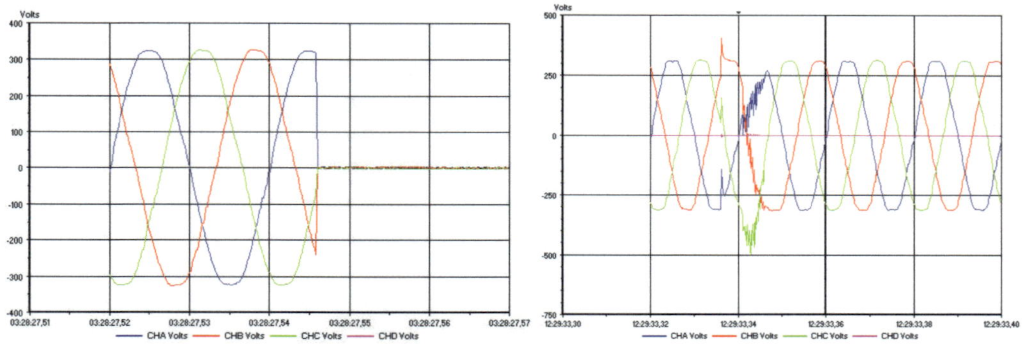

(a) (b)

Fig. 4. a) Interruption, with a 1.018 s length, and b) voltage transient measured at the School of Nautical Studies, Santander, Spain.

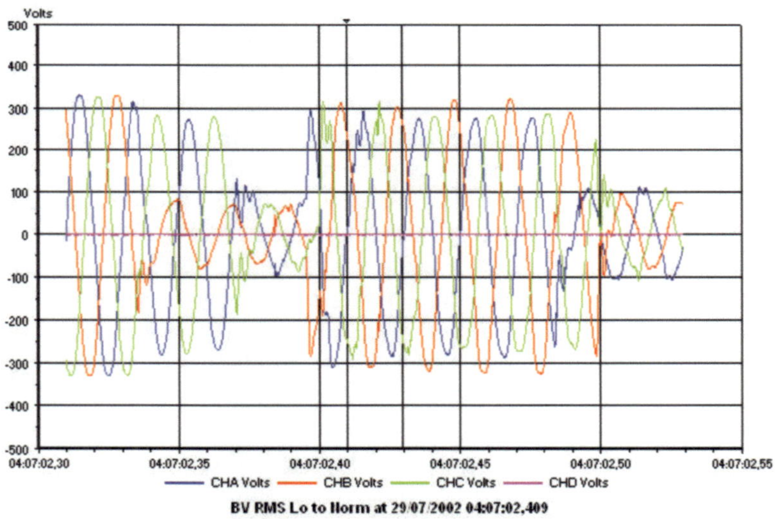

Fig. 5. Voltage dip measured at the School of Nautical Studies, Santander, Spain.

3. Application of Kalman filters to electrical power systems

An overview of the main power system disturbances has been given in the previous section. Once the importance of accurate measurements of the electrical power quantities has been established, this section is devoted to review previous works on Kalman filtering for estimation of frequency, amplitude and/or spectra of voltage and current signals in electrical power systems.

The fundamental frequency of the electrical power system can be accurately estimated for grid management purposes by means of Kalman filters. Firstly proposed in (Girgis & Hwang, 1984), an extended Kalman filter (EKF) is applied to a signal model composed by three state variables which only considers the fundamental component (grid frequency, in-phase and in-quadrature components). (Dash et al., 1999) considers a three-phase configuration by means of a complex signal model; again, voltage harmonics are not modelled. In order to reduce the response time of the Kalman filter, (Dash et al., 2000) proposed to include a hysteresis method for resetting the covariance matrix after a signal transient. A new signal model, which considers three consecutive points of a pure sinusoidal signal, is applied to an EKF in (Routray et al., 2002). The effect of grid voltage harmonics is considered in (Aghazadeh et al., 2005) by including two state variables per modelled signal harmonic. In this case, a fixed axes signal model is proposed. The computational burden associated to EKFs can be reduced, as proposed in (Zhang et al., 2007), by means of an unscented Kalman filter (UKF) which avoids the computation of Jacobian matrices. A predictive frequency estimation algorithm, which models the frequency considering the slop and the previous estimation, is shown in (Adanir, 2007). In order to evaluate the frequency components of a certain power signal, an accurate measurement of the fundamental grid frequency is required. (Shaw & Laughman, 2007) proposed a signal model which considers zero crossings of the voltage signal and the number of samples between two zero crossings.

Harmonics in voltage and current signals can be tracked by means of linear Kalman filters. The harmonics are modelled, considering stationary and rotating reference frames, in (Girgis et al., 1991). Two state variables are required per modelled harmonic (Beides & Heydt, 1991). A rotating reference frame model is employed in (Ma & Girgis, 1996), discussing the optimal location of the harmonic meters. The computational burden of the KF can be reduced by storing the pre-calculated filter gains (Moreno & Barros, 1997). (Al-Hamadi & Soliman, 2002) proposed a fuzzy signal model for linear Kalman filters in order to detect harmonic components. A complex linear model for harmonics estimation, which reduces the number of required state variables, is introduced in (Pradhan et al., 2004). Continuous and discrete approaches for harmonic identification are compared in (Alcaraz et al., 2006). Extended Kalman filters, as proposed in (Kumar et al., 2006), can be applied to a certain power system bus in order to measure active and reactive powers. (Yu et al., 2005) analyses the dynamical response of Kalman filters during power system transients and proposes an Adaptive Kalman filter in order to improve the performance of the estimation process. In case of (Macías & Exposito, 2006), such problem is solved by applying a self-tuning algorithm to the covariance matrix. As it is shown in (Moreno et al., 2007), the frequency resolution of Kalman filters for tracking of power system harmonics can be adjusted by a proper selection of the signal model frequencies.

Power system unbalances can be also detected by applying Kalman filters. (Rosolowski & Michalik, 1994) proposed a stationary reference frame signal model in order to track Clarke transformation components. (Soliman & El-Hawary, 1996) extended this analysis by considering the effects of the frequency drift and the sampling frequency. (Pigazo & Moreno, 2008) proposed a rotating reference frame signal model for unbalances identification which allowed Park transformation components to be estimated directly.

Previously paragraphs in this section were centred on variations. Voltage dips caused by power system faults can be classified as events. (Girgis & Brown, 1981) proposed a three-state signal model which allowed transient voltage variations to be tracked for computer relaying. First two states correspond to the fundamental grid frequency in a rotating reference frame while the third one, an exponentially decaying signal, is employed for fault detection purposes. This signal model was extended in (Girgis et al., 1990) by including two state variables per harmonic component to be tracked. An analysis of Kalman filters applied to voltage phasors estimation is also given in (Woxd et al., 1985). A ground fault relaying schema based on Kalman filters is also proposed in (Murty & Smolinski, 1990). In this case only harmonic components are employed. An expert system for classification and analysis of power system events is proposed in (Styvaktakis et al., 2002). Three Kalman filters, one per phase, are applied in order to obtain frequency and harmonic measurements as well as a detection index. (Dash & Chilukuri, 2004) proposed to integrate wavelet transforms and Kalman filters in order to characterize short duration power quality disturbances. The phase-corrected wavelet transform, S-transform, allows the disturbances to be detected and time localized while the Kalman filter characterizes the disturbance. The impact of arc furnaces in electrical power systems can be also analysed by means of Kalman filters (Wang et al., 2005). In this case, the states-variables model considers the arc furnace characteristics and the electrical grid topology. Three Kalman filters are also considered in (Barros & Pérez, 2006) in order to detect voltage dips and swells. The voltage signals, which consist of fundamental component and harmonics, are modelled in a rotating reference frame. (González et al., 2006) proposed an equivalent approach without harmonic components in the signal model. (Ukil & Živanović, 2007) proposed several Kalman filters to be executed in parallel, each one using a different model, in order to reveal the power system disturbance. An extended Kalman filter, where the instantaneous phase at the fundamental grid frequency is also tracked, is proposed in (Pérez & Barros, 2008) for detection and analysis of voltage dips.

Due to the characteristics of discrete Kalman filters (accurate estimation of power signals and fast response time), they have been included in control algorithms in power converters. This is the case of (Liserre et al., 2006), where Kalman filters are employed in grid-connected photovoltaic inverters in order to detect the islanding operation mode. Such inverters in distributed generation systems are also analysed in (Prodanovic et al., 2007), where Kalman filters are proposed in order to support the operation of the electrical grid. (Ahmed et al., 2008) discusses the compensation of the controller delays by applying Kalman filters. The synchronization, a key issue in distributed generation systems based on inverters, is discussed in (Cardoso et al., 2008). Special attention must be paid to applications where precision is a main issue, such as power converters for compensation of electrical grid disturbances. (Moreno et al., 2002) proposed a Kalman filter, using previously calculated Kalman gains and a stationary reference frame for current harmonic compensation in electrical grids by means of a shunt active power filter (SAPF). (Barros & Pérez, 2003) employed a synchronously rotating reference frame model in SAPF which requires an external phase locked loop (PLL) for synchronization. (Moreno et al., 2004) extended the stationary reference frame model in order to compensate the load reactive power. The employed model allowed the external synchronisation mechanism to be avoided. (Kwan et al., 2007), (Elnady & Salama, 2007) and (Griffo et al., 2007) proposed Kalman filters in order to control a Unified Power Quality Conditioner which allows both grid and load disturbances to be compensated.

Kalman filters have been also successfully applied to electrical grid management issues and electrical loads forecasting. First application of Kalman filters for electrical grid management is probably given in (Girgis, 1982), where faults are located by estimation of the apparent impedance to the fault. Kalman filters, modelling the fundamental grid frequency, are applied to voltage and current signals in order to estimate the impedance. (Heydt, 1989) proposed to analyse the optimal location of harmonic meters by means of Kalman filters.

Walsh transformations and Kalman filters cooperates in (Bhattacharya & Basu, 1993) in order to obtain medium range forecasts of power system load. Walsh transformations are substituted in (Zheng et al., 2000) by Wavelet transforms. Previously presented signal models are modified in (Soliman et al., 1995) by including time decaying amplitudes at each harmonic frequency in order to evaluate transient stability swings in large interconnected power systems. According to (Kim et al., 2001), Kalman filters can be also applied in order to determine the switching status of capacitive banks in electrical utilities. Load forecasting is analyzed again in (Trudnowski et al., 2001). In this case, Kalman filters allow very short load forecasting, typically less than two hours, to be carried out. The weather conditions are also considered in the signal model proposed in (Al-Hamadi & Soliman, 2004) in order to improve the load forecasting.
The characteristics of the electrical loads can be also estimated by applying Kalman filters. This is the case of (Soliman & Alammari, 2004), where a general passive electrical load (capacitive, inductive and resistive) is modelled in order to obtain its parameters under sinusoidal and non-sinusoidal conditions. The characterization of electrical loads becomes especially difficult in case of electrical machines, where mechanical forces must be also considered. This is the case of (Abu-Al-Feilat et al., 1999), where a two-state Kalman filter was proposed in order to estimate the synchronizing and damping torque coefficients of a synchronous electrical machine, or (Caruana et al., 2003), that estimates the flux position in cage induction machines by applying Kalman filters and high-frequency injection.

4. Linear and extended discrete Kalman filtering loops

This section reviews the principles of discrete Kalman filtering loops (Chui & Chen, 1999), both linear and extended, and gives their implementation in MatLab/Simulink. Commonly employed signal models in literature, and their implementation, are also given. Finally, a new three phase signal model for frequency estimation and harmonics tracking in three-phase three-wire power systems is proposed. Simulation results which have been obtained by applying this model are given in the following section.

4.1 Linear Kalman filtering loop

Considering a discrete-time state-space representation of a linear system:

$$\begin{cases} \mathbf{x}_{k+1} = \mathbf{A}_k \mathbf{x}_k + \mathbf{B}_k \mathbf{u}_k + \Gamma \xi_k \\ \mathbf{s}_k = \mathbf{C}_k \mathbf{x}_k + \mathbf{D}_k \mathbf{u}_k + \boldsymbol{\eta}_k \end{cases} \tag{1}$$

where ξ and η are uncorrelated noise sequences with normal probability distributions, u is a deterministic input sequence, x contains the system state variables, s is a vector with the available measurements, A is the state transition matrix, C the measurement matrix and B and D matrices allow the deterministic input sequence to be considered. The recursive Kalman filtering loop for time instants k=1,2,... can be written as:

$$\mathbf{P}_{k|k+1} = \mathbf{A}_{k-1}\mathbf{P}_{k-1|k-1}\mathbf{A}_{k-1}^T + \mathbf{\Gamma}_{k-1}\mathbf{Q}_{k-1}\mathbf{\Gamma}_{k-1}^T \tag{2.1}$$

$$\mathbf{G}_k = \mathbf{P}_{k|k-1}\mathbf{C}_k^T\left(\mathbf{C}_k\mathbf{P}_{k|k-1}\mathbf{C}_k^T + \mathbf{R}_k\right)^{-1} \tag{2.2}$$

$$\mathbf{P}_{k|k} = \left(\mathbf{I} - \mathbf{G}_k\mathbf{C}_k\right)\mathbf{P}_{k|k-1} \tag{2.3}$$

$$\hat{\mathbf{x}}_{k|k-1} = \mathbf{A}_{k-1}\hat{\mathbf{x}}_{k-1|k-1} + \mathbf{B}_{k-1}\mathbf{u}_{k-1} \tag{2.4}$$

$$\hat{\mathbf{x}}_{k|k} = \hat{\mathbf{x}}_{k|k-1} + \mathbf{G}_k\left(\mathbf{s}_k - \mathbf{C}_k\hat{\mathbf{x}}_{k|k-1} - \mathbf{D}_k\mathbf{u}_k\right) \tag{2.5}$$

where **P** is the covariance matrix and **G** is a matrix containing the Kalman gains, which allows a least-squares sense optimal estimation of the state variables by adjusting the information which arrives from the process model and the measurements, $\hat{\mathbf{x}}_{k|k-1}$ is the estimation of the state variables at instant *k* from values at instant *k-1*. The filtering loop generates a prediction of the covariance matrix in (2.1), which is employed in (2.2) in order to obtain the Kalman gains, then, in (2.3) the covariance matrix is updated. Finally, the state variables are estimated in (2.4) according to the model and then, in (2.5), such estimation is updated by means of the obtained measurements. It must be considered that in most linear Kalman filters applied to the estimation of electrical power quantities the terms corresponding to ***u*** can be avoided. Moreover, as initial values:

$$\mathbf{P}_{0|0} = Var(\mathbf{x}_0), \quad \hat{\mathbf{x}}_{0|0} = E(\mathbf{x}_0) \tag{3}$$

In case of correlated noise sequences, a complete description of the filtering loop can be found in (Chui & Chen, 1999). In certain cases where time independent ***A*** and ***C*** matrices are employed, as well as ***u*** is neglected, the limiting Kalman filtering loop can be employed, where the time dependent $\mathbf{G}_k$ can be substituted using its value at $\mathbf{G} = \lim_{k\to\infty} \mathbf{G}_k$ and, hence, the overall computational burden can be reduced.
Fig. 6 shows the implementation of the discrete Kalman filtering loop in MatLab/Simulink. As it can be seen, a triggered subsystem has been selected in order to apply an external synchronization signal. Moreover, the depicted structure can be repeated, independently of the employed model, and only ***A*** and ***C*** matrices must be changed in each case. Each Simulink block implements equations (2.1)-(2.5). In case the limiting approach is employed, and considering that the values of ***G*** can be stored in the memory, the filtering loop can be simplified obtaining the block depicted in fig. 7. As it can be seen, in this case, **G** must be supplied for each specific model.

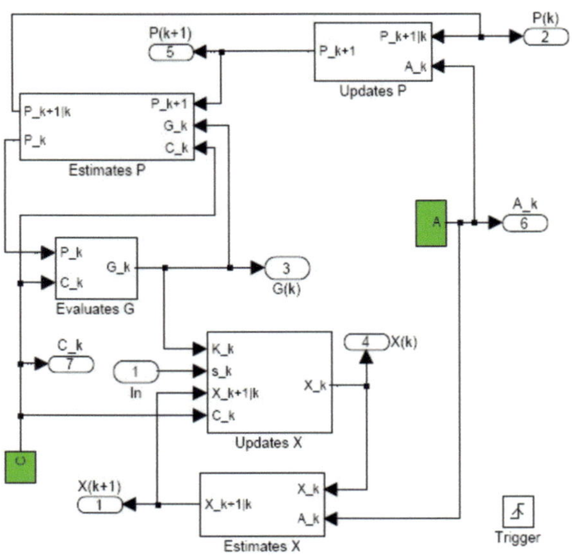

Fig. 6. Discrete Kalman filtering loop implementation in MatLab/Simulink.

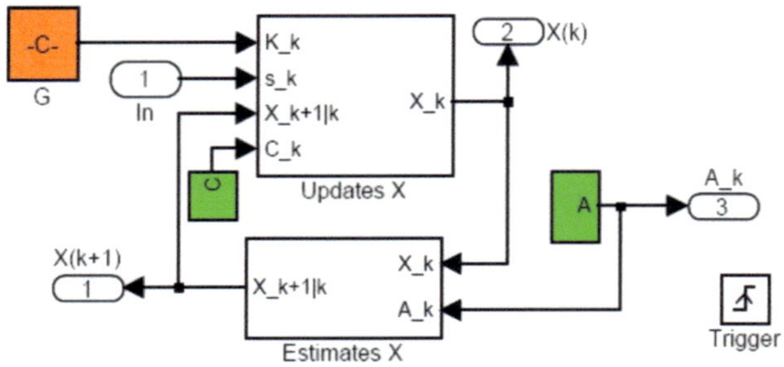

Fig. 7. Limiting approach of the discrete Kalman filtering loop implemented in MatLab/Simulink.

4.2 Extended Kalman filtering loop

In case the model is non-linear, the filtering loop in (2.1)-(2.5) can not be applied but the model can be linearized in order to estimate the state variables (Chui & Chen, 1999). Considering the system:

$$\begin{cases} \mathbf{x}_{k+1} = \mathbf{f}_k(\mathbf{x}_k) + \mathbf{H}_k(\mathbf{x}_k)\boldsymbol{\xi}_k \\ \mathbf{s}_k = \mathbf{g}_k(\mathbf{x}_k) + \boldsymbol{\eta}_k \end{cases} \tag{4}$$

$\mathbf{f}_k(\mathbf{x}_k)$ and $\mathbf{g}_k(\mathbf{x}_k)$ can be linearized around $\hat{\mathbf{x}}_k$ and $\hat{\mathbf{x}}_{k|k-1}$ respectively by means of a Taylor approximation and, hence, the filering loop results on:

$$\mathbf{P}_{k|k-1} = \left[\frac{\partial \mathbf{f}_{k-1}}{\partial \mathbf{x}_{k-1}}(\hat{\mathbf{x}}_{k-1})\right]\mathbf{P}_{k-1|k-1}\left[\frac{\partial \mathbf{f}_{k-1}}{\partial \mathbf{x}_{k-1}}(\hat{\mathbf{x}}_{k-1})\right]^T + \mathbf{H}_{k-1}(\hat{\mathbf{x}}_{k-1})\mathbf{Q}_{k-1}\mathbf{H}_{k-1}^T(\hat{\mathbf{x}}_{k-1}) \tag{5.1}$$

$$\hat{\mathbf{x}}_{k|k-1} = \mathbf{f}_{k-1}(\hat{\mathbf{x}}_{k-1}) \tag{5.2}$$

$$\mathbf{G}_k = \mathbf{P}_{k|k-1}\left[\frac{\partial \mathbf{g}_k}{\partial \mathbf{x}_k}(\hat{\mathbf{x}}_{k|k-1})\right]^T\left(\left[\frac{\partial \mathbf{g}_k}{\partial \mathbf{x}_k}(\hat{\mathbf{x}}_{k|k-1})\right]\mathbf{P}_{k|k-1}\left[\frac{\partial \mathbf{g}_k}{\partial \mathbf{x}_k}(\hat{\mathbf{x}}_{k|k-1})\right]^T + \mathbf{R}_k\right)^{-1} \tag{5.3}$$

$$\mathbf{P}_{k|k} = \left(\mathbf{I} - \mathbf{G}_k\left[\frac{\partial \mathbf{g}_k}{\partial \mathbf{x}_k}(\hat{\mathbf{x}}_{k|k-1})\right]\right)\mathbf{P}_{k|k-1} \tag{5.4}$$

$$\hat{\mathbf{x}}_{k|k} = \hat{\mathbf{x}}_{k|k-1} + \mathbf{G}_k\left(\mathbf{s}_k - \mathbf{g}_k(\hat{\mathbf{x}}_{k|k-1})\right) \tag{5.5}$$

Despite of the algorithm complexity, where partial derivatives must be computed, depending on the employed model the computational burden of this filtering loop can be quite low. The evaluation of the inverse matrix in (5.3) requires the most of the execution time.
The implementation of the extended Kalman filtering loop in MatLab/Simulink is shown in fig. 8. In this case, the simulink blocks require also partial derivatives evaluated from the state variables, as it is shown in the block labelled as *nonlinear H_O*, which is employed to evaluate ***A***, ***C*** and their derivatives each time instant from the state variables values. It must be noted that one sample delay must be included before this block in order to avoid execution inconsistencies. Moreover, this is the block whose inner structure must be changed depending on the employed model.

4.3 Conventional signal models

Three signal model shown in literature are described in this section in order to show the principles of the method that will be proposed in the following subsection. Signals models for harmonics tracking, considering both fixed and rotating axes approaches, and frequency estimation are explained and MatLab/Simulink implementations, which can be employed with the filtering loops described in 4.2 and 4.3, are given.

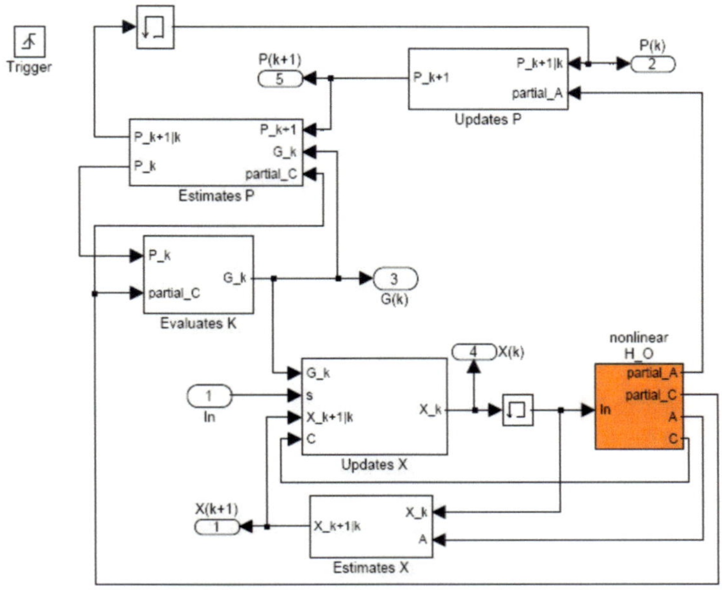

Fig. 8. Extended Kalman filtering loop implemented in MatLab/Simulink.

Firstly of all, it must be considered that in case of harmonics tracking, both in fixed and rotating axes approaches, two state variables are required per each considered frequency (fundamental, harmonics, interharmonics or subharmonics). Moreover, the dc component can be also included in both models by means of one state variable. The fixed axes approach considers that there is a stationary complex reference frame where all the considered harmonic components rotate. Due to this fact, and considering two consecutive samples of the mth harmonic, its phasor can be tracked by means of two in-quadrature state variables

$$\begin{cases} x_{m,k}^{\alpha} = X_k \cos\left(m\dfrac{2\pi}{N}k\right) \\ x_{m,k}^{\beta} = X_k \sin\left(m\dfrac{2\pi}{N}k\right) \end{cases} \tag{6}$$

where $x_{m,k}^{\alpha}$ and $x_{m,k}^{\beta}$ are the orthogonal projections of its phasor at instant k, X_m is its amplitude and N is the number of considered samples at the fundamental grid frequency. At instant k+1, the phasor associated to this harmonic will rotate on these stationary axes at its frequency:

$$\begin{cases} x_{m,k+1}^{\alpha} = X_k \cos\left(m\dfrac{2\pi}{N}(k+1)\right) = x_{m,k}^{\alpha}\cos\left(m\dfrac{2\pi}{N}\right) - x_{m,k}^{\beta}\sin\left(m\dfrac{2\pi}{N}\right) \\ x_{m,k+1}^{\beta} = X_k \sin\left(m\dfrac{2\pi}{N}(k+1)\right) = x_{m,k}^{\alpha}\sin\left(m\dfrac{2\pi}{N}\right) + x_{m,k}^{\beta}\cos\left(m\dfrac{2\pi}{N}\right) \end{cases} \tag{7}$$

Selecting α and β components as state-variables, and considering *k* and *k+1* instants, the harmonic m[th] can be represented through a rotation matrix $\boldsymbol{A}_n$ which is time independent:

$$A_m = \begin{pmatrix} \cos\left(m\dfrac{2\pi}{N}\right) & -\sin\left(m\dfrac{2\pi}{N}\right) \\ \sin\left(m\dfrac{2\pi}{N}\right) & \cos\left(m\dfrac{2\pi}{N}\right) \end{pmatrix} \tag{8}$$

The complete signal, including all harmonics can be reconstructed by adding the real component, α , of each harmonic phasor. As a consequence, harmonics up to order n can be considered by employing *2n* state variables:

$$A = \begin{pmatrix} A_1 & 0 & 0 \\ 0 & \ddots & 0 \\ 0 & 0 & A_n \end{pmatrix}, \quad C = \begin{pmatrix} 1 & 0 & \cdots & 1 & 0 \end{pmatrix} \tag{9}$$

Being time independent and constant matrices, they can be directly implemented in the schema depicted in fig. 6.
In case of the rotating axes approach, it is considered that each phasor is modelled in a certain complex frame which rotates at the frequency of the considered harmonic. Fig. 9 shows the principle for the fundamental component (in red) and the 5th harmonic (in blue). As it can be seen, each harmonic frequency is decomposed in its rotating reference frame resulting on two orthogonal components. As a consequence, $\boldsymbol{A}$ corresponds to the identity matrix while the measurement matrix becomes time dependent:

$$C = \begin{pmatrix} \cos\left(\dfrac{2\pi}{N}k\right) & -\sin\left(\dfrac{2\pi}{N}k\right) & \cdots & \cos\left(n\dfrac{2\pi}{N}k\right) & -\sin\left(n\dfrac{2\pi}{N}k\right) \end{pmatrix} \tag{10}$$

Due to the nature of $\boldsymbol{C}$, the computational burden of the Kalman filter is increased in this case. In order to reduce the complexity, it is proposed in the literature to employ an external phase locked loop (PLL) which moves a pointer over the values stored in memory corresponding to the elements in (10).

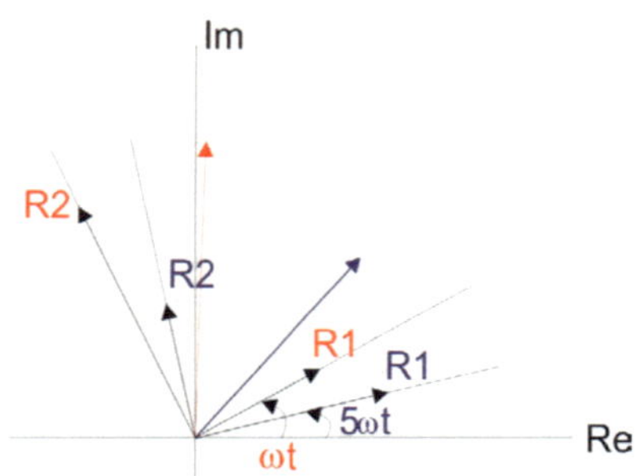

Fig. 9. Phasors for the fundamental component and the 5th harmonic in rotating reference frames.

In previous signal models, the fundamental grid frequency is considered constant, or in case of the rotating axes approach with PLL, the sampling frequency is dynamically changed in order to maintain constant the number of samples per cycle at the fundamental grid frequency. If frequency measurements are required, the extended Kalman filtering loop depicted in fig. 8 must be employed. A first approach which can be applied to single phase power systems is:

$$A = \begin{pmatrix} A_1 & 0 & 0 & 0 \\ 0 & \ddots & 0 & \vdots \\ 0 & 0 & A_n & 0 \\ 0 & \cdots & 0 & 1 \end{pmatrix}, \quad C = \begin{pmatrix} 1 & 0 & 1 & 0 & \cdots & 0 \end{pmatrix} \tag{11}$$

where:

$$A_n = \begin{pmatrix} \cos(n2\pi T_s f) & -\sin(n2\pi T_s f) \\ \sin(n2\pi T_s f) & \cos(n2\pi T_s f) \end{pmatrix} \tag{12}$$

and T_s is the employed sampling frequency and f is the fundamental grid frequency to be estimated. As a consequence, the computational burden associated to the linearization process through the derivatives can be very high. In order to reduce it, (Routray et al., 2002) proposed a signal model considering three-consecutive points of a sinusoidal signal, as it is shown in fig. 10. From this figure, the relationship between these points is:

$$y_{k+1} = (2\cos(2\pi f T_s))y_k - y_{k-1} \tag{13}$$

Considering y_k, y_{k-1} and $2\cos(2\pi f T_s)$ as state variables, the nonlinear signal model can be written as:

$$\begin{cases} x_{1,k+1} = x_{3,k}x_{1,k} - x_{2,k} \\ x_{2,k+1} = x_{1,k} \\ x_{3,k+1} = x_{3,k} \end{cases} \tag{14}$$

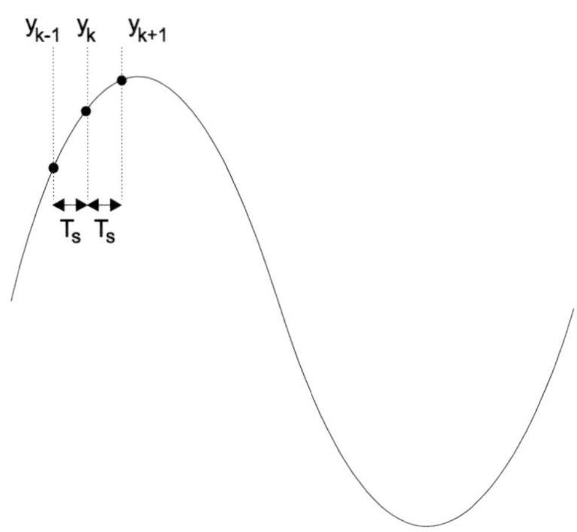

Fig. 10. Three consecutive sampling points of a sinusoidal signal in order to obtain a frequency measurement

As a consequence, the Simulink blocks to be employed in fig. 8 must implement the matrices:

$$\mathbf{x}_k = \begin{pmatrix} x_{1,k} & x_{2,k} & x_{3,k} \end{pmatrix} \tag{15.1}$$

$$\mathbf{A}_k = \begin{pmatrix} x_{3,k} & -1 & 0 \\ 1 & 0 & 0 \\ 0 & 0 & 1 \end{pmatrix} \tag{15.2}$$

$$\mathbf{C}_k = \begin{pmatrix} x_{3,k} & -1 & 0 \end{pmatrix} \tag{15.3}$$

$$\frac{\partial \mathbf{f}_k}{\partial \mathbf{x}_k} = \begin{pmatrix} x_{3,k} & -1 & x_{1,k} \\ 1 & 0 & 0 \\ 0 & 0 & 1 \end{pmatrix} \tag{15.4}$$

$$\frac{\partial \mathbf{g}_k}{\partial \mathbf{x}_k} = \begin{pmatrix} x_{3,k} & -1 & x_{1,k} \end{pmatrix} \tag{15.5}$$

Their implementation in MatLab/Simulink is shown in fig. 11.

4.4 Proposed signal model for frequency measurement

This section proposes a signal model for three-phase three-wire power systems which allows the fundamental grid frequency to be estimated accurately under unbalanced phase voltages. The signal model considers positive and negative sequences of the three voltage signals, as well as voltage harmonics, in order to estimate the fundamental grid frequency:

$$\mathrm{s}_k = \begin{pmatrix} v_{A,k} & v_{B,k} & v_{C,k} \end{pmatrix} \tag{16.1}$$

$$\mathrm{x}_k = \begin{pmatrix} x_{1_p^+} & x_{1_q^+} & \cdots & x_{n_p^{sign}} & x_{n_q^{sign}} & f \end{pmatrix}^T \tag{16.2}$$

where n is the harmonic order, sign denotes the sequence of the modelled harmonic and subindexes p and q correspond to in-phase and in-quadrature components of the considered harmonic. As a consequence, the measurement equation can be designed by applying the Clarke's transformation to the phase voltages:

$$\mathrm{C} = \begin{pmatrix} 1 & 0 \\ -\frac{1}{2} & -\frac{\sqrt{3}}{2} \\ -\frac{1}{2} & \frac{\sqrt{3}}{2} \end{pmatrix} \begin{pmatrix} \mathrm{I} & \mathrm{I} & \cdots & \mathrm{I} & 0 \\ & & & & 0 \end{pmatrix} \tag{17}$$

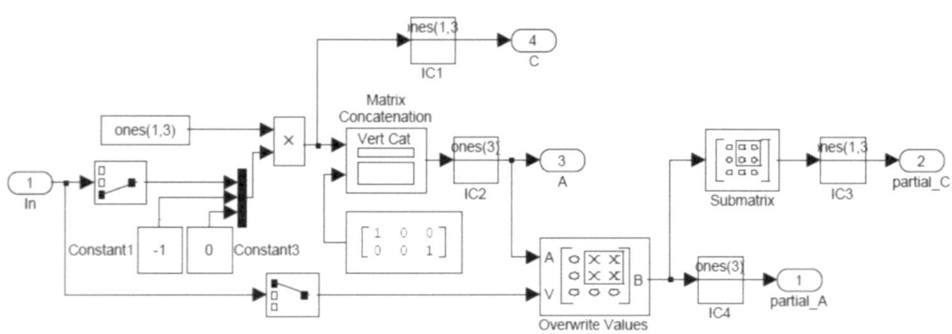

Fig. 11. Implementation of equations (15.1)-(15.5) in MatLab/Simulink

The second matrix in (17), where $\boldsymbol{I}$ is a 2x2 identity matrix, allows $\alpha\beta$ components of the grid voltage to be decomposed on the considered harmonics and sequences. The non-linearity appears inside the transition matrix:

$$\mathbf{A}_k = \begin{pmatrix} \mathbf{A}_1^+ & 0 & \cdots & \cdots & 0 \\ 0 & \mathbf{A}_1^- & \ddots & & \vdots \\ \vdots & \ddots & \ddots & \ddots & \vdots \\ \vdots & & \ddots & \mathbf{A}_n^{sign} & 0 \\ 0 & \cdots & \cdots & 0 & 1 \end{pmatrix} \tag{18}$$

where, considering T_s as the sampling time:

$$\mathbf{A}_n^{sign} = \begin{pmatrix} sign \cdot \sin(n2\pi T_s f) & \cos(n2\pi T_s f) \\ \cos(n2\pi T_s f) & -sign \cdot \sin(n2\pi T_s f) \end{pmatrix} \tag{19}$$

The MatLab/Simulink implementation of (18) and its derivative is shown in fig. 12. As it can be seen, the implementation allows the positive and negative sequences of the fundamental component, as well as 5th and 7th harmonics with negative and positive sequences respectively, are modelled.

5. Simulation results

The results shown in this section have been obtained by means of MatLab/Simulink and considering a three-phase three-wire balanced non-linear load, a full bridge diode rectifier with highly inductive dc side, which has been fed by diverse test source voltages. Both the proposed signal model and the model in (Routray et al., 2002) has been applied in order to evaluate the performance of the proposed method. The Simulink model considers the A/D subsystem (T_s=156.25 μs and time delays due to the signal acquisition) and includes anti-aliasing filters (Butterworth, 4th order and 3.2 kHz cut-off frequency).

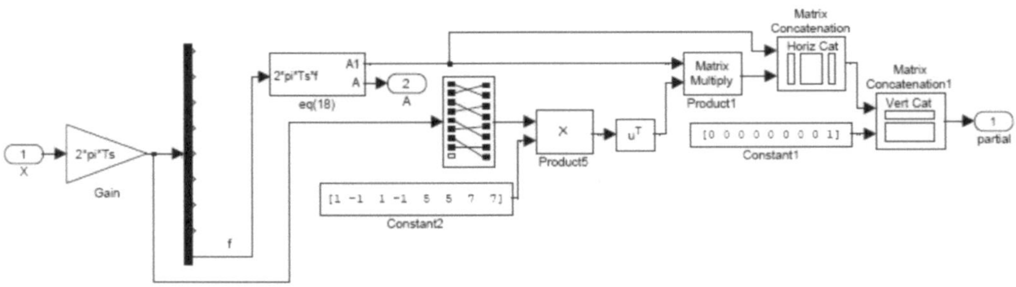

Fig. 12. Simulink implementation of (18) and its partial derivative.

5.1 Balanced grid voltages

The grid voltages are balanced and pure sinusoidal at 50 Hz. In order to test the tracking capability of each method, a frequency variation is applied from 0.4 s to 0.5 s by means of a frequency ramp where the final frequency reaches 48Hz. The obtained results are shown in fig. 13. As it can be seen in fig. 13.a, the proposed method tracks the frequency variation with a 2.97 ms delay, which corresponds to 19 samples, while the signal model described in

(Routray et al., 2002) oscillates around the applied grid frequency and generates spikes during the frequency variation (fig. 13.b). The proposed method generates a smoother and slower response due to the selected state variables.

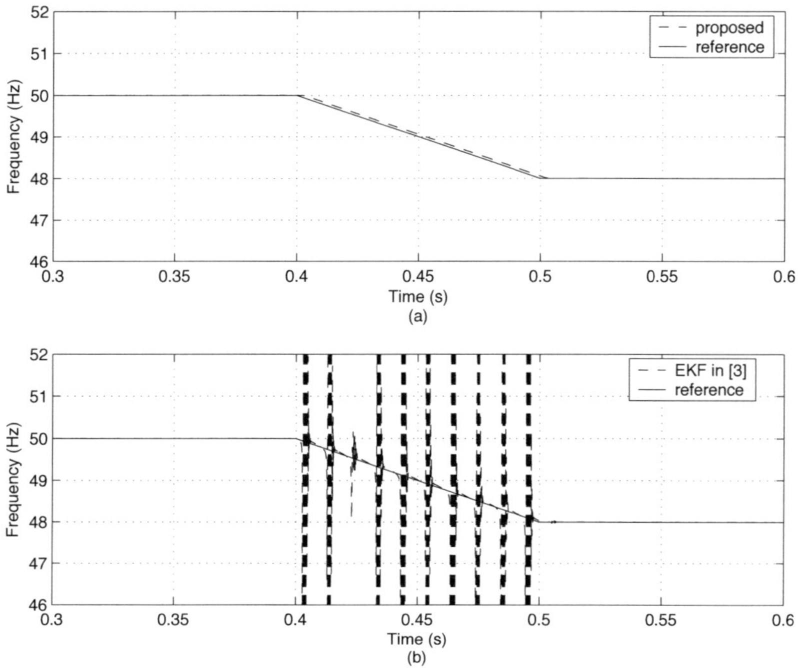

Fig. 13. Simulation results under a ramp frequency variation. Measured frequency applying a) the proposed signal model and b) the EKF in (Routray et al., 2002).

5.2 Unbalanced grid voltages

The initially balanced and pure sinusoidal grid voltages at 50 Hz become unbalanced at 0.4 s while both EKF are being applied to the measured voltages. The applied voltage unbalance is shown in fig. 14.a. From fig. 14.b and 14.c, both methods results on frequency transients during the unbalance transients. The maximum deviation of the proposed signal model is 2.43 Hz while the signal model described in (Routray et al., 2002) reaches 464.22 Hz. The measured response times are 12.8 ms and 15.3 ms, with the proposed method being the faster one due to simultaneous measurement of the three phase voltages.

5.3 Harmonically distorted grid voltages with a voltage dip

This last simulation test applies balanced grid voltages with harmonic distortion between IEEE Std. 519-1992 limits (1st is 100%, 5th is 2% and 7th is 4% with VTHD<5%). A 40% voltage dip occurs at 0.4 s and finishes at 0.6 s. Fig. 15.a shows the applied test conditions. The proposed signal model, due to the modelled harmonic components, track the fundamental grid frequency properly (fig. 15.b) while the signal model described in (Routray et al., 2002) generates spikes in the frequency estimation (fig. 15.c). Moreover, the proposed signal model allows the voltage dip to be detected due to the measured frequency transients.

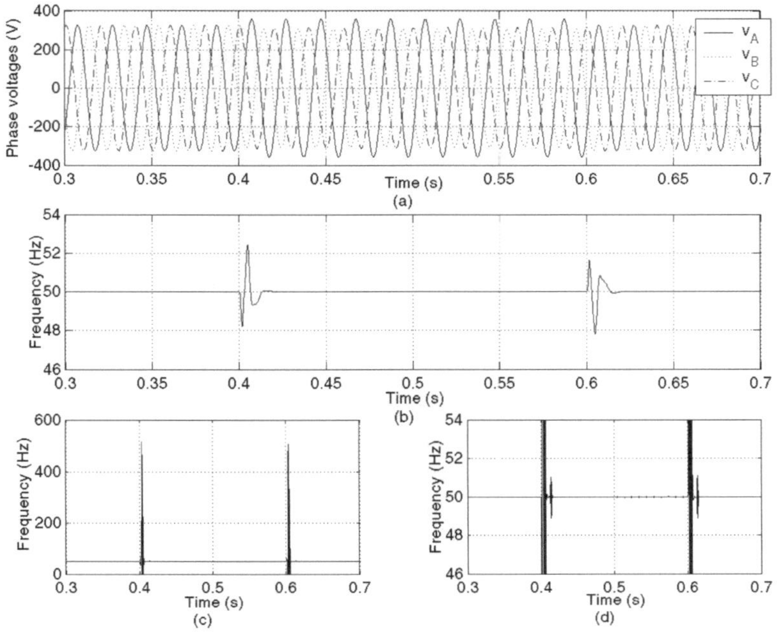

Fig. 14. a) Applied test grid voltages and the obtained frequency measurements by applying the b) proposed signal model and c) the EKF in (Routray et al., 2002), which is detailed in d).

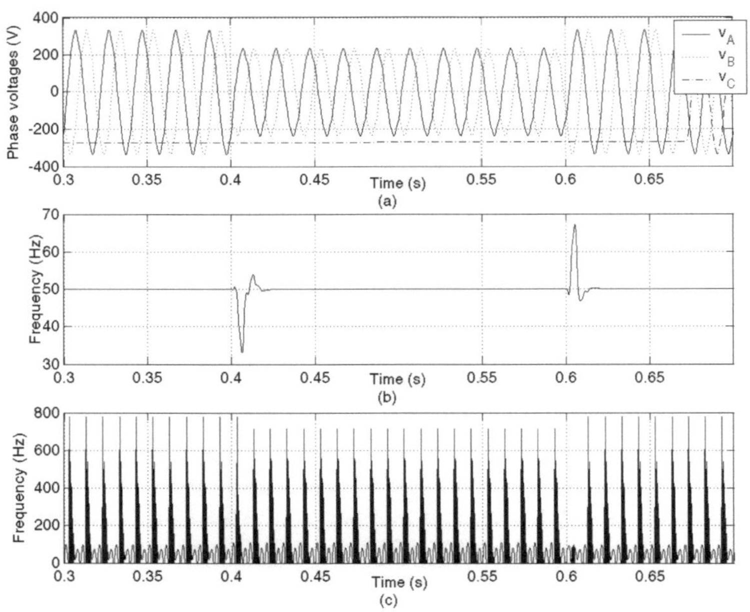

Fig. 15. a) Test grid voltages and the obtained frequency measurements applying b) the proposed signal model and c) the EKF in (Routray et al., 2002).

6. Conclusion

This chapter gives an introduction to the applications of Kalman filtering in electrical power systems. Power quality disturbances are introduced, considering their sources and impact, and monitoring examples are given. The literature on this researching area is reviewed, given a detailed analysis of the most applied signal models as well as their implementation in MatLab/Simulink. Moreover, a new signal model which considers a three-phase three-wires power system with voltage unbalances and harmonically distorted grid voltages is given. The proposed signal model is compared to a previously proposed signal model in single phase power systems by means of simulation tests carried out using MatLab/Simulink.

7. References

Abu-Al-Feilat, E. A.; Younan, N. & Grzybowski, S. (1999). Estimating the synchronizing and damping torque coefficients using Kalman filtering. *Electric Power Systems Research*, Vol. 52, No. 2, (November 1999) 145-149, ISSN: 0378-7796.

Aghazadeh, R.; Lesani, H.; Sanaye-Pasand, M. & Ganji, B. (2005). New technique for frequency and amplitude estimation of power system signals. *IEE Proceedings – Generation, Transmission and Distribution*, Vol. 152, No. 3, (May 2005) 435-440, ISSN: 1350-2360.

Ahmed, K. H.; Massoud, A. M.; Finney, S. J. & Williams, B. W. (2008). Autonomous control of a PWM inverter in islanded distributed generation with different feedback signals, *Proceedings of 4th IET Conference on Power Electronics, Machines and Drives 2008 (PEMD 2008)*, pp. 573-577, ISBN: 978-0-86341-900-3, York, UK, April 2008, Institution of Engineering and Technology (IET), London.

Alcaraz, R; Bueno, E. J.; Cóbreces, S.; Rodríguez, F. J., Espinosa, F. & Muyulema, S. (2006). Power System Voltage Harmonic Identification Using Kalman Filter, *Proceedings of 12th International Power Electronics and Motion Control Conference (EPE-PEMC 2006)*, pp. 1283-1288, ISBN: 1-4244-0120-8, Portoroz, August 2006.

Adanir, T. (2007). Extremely short term frequency estimation (ESTFE) algorithm for underfrequency protection. *International Journal of Electrical Power & Energy Systems*, Vol. 29, No. 4, (May 2007), 329-337, ISSN: 0142-0615.

Al-Hamadi, H. M. & Soliman, S. A. (2002). Kalman filter for identification of power system fuzzy harmonic components. *Electric Power Systems Research*, Vol. 62, No. 3, (July 2002) 241-248, ISSN: 0378-7796.

Al-Hamadi, H. M. & Soliman, S. A. (2004). Short-term electric load forecasting based on Kalman filtering algorithm with moving window weather and load model. *Electric Power Systems Research*, Vol. 68, No. 1, (January 2004) 47-59, ISSN: 0378-7796.

Barros, J. & Pérez, E. (2003). An adaptive method for determining the reference compensating current in single-phase shunt active power filters. *IEEE Transactions on Power Delivery*, Vol. 18, No. 4, (October 2003) 1578-1580, ISSN: 0885-8977.

Barros, J. & Pérez, E. (2006). Automatic Detection and Analysis of Voltage Events in Power Systems. *IEEE Transactions on Instrumentation and Measurement*, Vol. 55, No. 5, (October 2006) 1487-1493, ISSN: 0018-9456.

Beides, H. M. & Heydt, G. T. (1991). Dynamic state estimation of power system harmonics using Kalman filter methodology. *IEEE Transactions on Power Delivery*, Vol. 6, No. 4, (October 1991) 1663-1670, ISSN: 0885-8977.

Bhattacharya, T. K. & Basu, T. K. (1993). Medium range forecasting of power system load using modified Kalman filter and Walsh transform. *International Journal of Electrical Power & Energy Systems*, Vol. 15, No. 2, (April 1993) 109-115, ISSN: 0142-0615.

Bollen, M. H. J. & Gu, I. (2006). *Signal Processing of Power Quality Disturbances*, Wiley-IEEE Press, 978-0-471-73168-9, USA.

Brown, R. G. (1983). *Introduction to Random Signal Analysis and Kalman Filtering,* Wiley, 0-471-08732-7, USA.

Cardoso, R.; de Camargo, R. F.; Pinheiro, H. & Gründling, H. A. (2008). Kalman filter based synchronisation methods. *IET Generation, Transmission & Distribution*, Vol. 2, No. 4, (July 2008) 542-555, ISSN: 1751-8687.

Caruana, C.; Asher, G. M.; Bradley, K. J. & Woolfson, M. (2003). Flux position estimation in cage induction machines using synchronous HF injection and Kalman filtering. *IEEE Transactions on Industry Applications*, Vol. 39, No. 5, (September 2003) 1372-1378, ISSN: 0093-9994.

Chui, C. K. & Chen, G. (1999). *Kalman filtering with real-time applications*. 3rd Edition, Springer-Verlag, 3-540-64611-6, Germany.

Dash, P. K.; Pradhan, A. K. & Panda, G. (1999). Frequency estimation of distorted power system signals using extended complex Kalman filter. *IEEE Transactions on Power Delivery*, Vol. 14, No. 3, (July 1999) 761-766, ISSN: 0885-8977.

Dash, P. K.; Jena, R. K.; Panda, G. & Routray, A. (2000). An extended complex Kalman filter for frequency measurement of distorted signals. *IEEE Transactions on Instrumentation and Measurement*, Vol. 49, No. 4, (August 2000) 746-753, ISSN: 0018-9456.

Dash, P. K. & Chilukuri, M. V. (2004). Hybrid S-transform and Kalman filtering approach for detection and measurement of short duration disturbances in power networks. *IEEE Transactions on Instrumentation and Measurement*, Vol. 53, No. 2, (April 2004) 588-596, ISSN: 0018-9456.

Dugan, R. C.; McGranaghan, M. F.; Santoso, S. & Beaty, H. W. (2003). *Electrical Power Systems Quality, 2nd Edition*, McGraw-Hill, 0-07-138622-X, USA.

Elnady, A. & Salama, M. M. A. (2007). Mitigation of the voltage fluctuations using an efficient disturbance extraction technique. *Electric Power Systems Research*, Vol. 77, No. 3-4, (March 2007) 266-275. ISSN: 0378-7796.

Girgis, A. A. & Brown, R. G. (1981). Application of Kalman Filtering in Computer Relaying. *IEEE Transactions on Power Apparatus and Systems*, Vol. PAS-100, No. 7, (July 1981) 3387-3397, ISSN: 0018-9510.

Girgis, A. A. (1982). A New Kalman Filtering Based Digital Distance Relay. *IEEE Transactions on Power Apparatus and Systems*, Vol. PAS-101, No. 9, (September 1982) 3471 - 3480, ISSN: 0018-9510.

Girgis, A. A. & Hwang, T. L. D. (1984). Optimal Estimation Of Voltage Phasors And Frequency Deviation Using Linear And Non-Linear Kalman Filtering: Theory And Limitations. *IEEE Transactions on Power Apparatus and Systems*, Vol. PAS-103, No. 10, (October 1984) 2943-2951, ISSN: 0018-9510.

Girgis, A. A., Chang, W. & Makram, E. B. (1990). Analysis of high-impedance fault generated signals using a Kalman filtering approach. *IEEE Transactions on Power Delivery*, Vol. 5, No. 4, (October 1990) 1714-1724, ISSN: 0885-8977.

Girgis, A. A.; Chang, W. B. & Makram, E. B. (1991). A digital recursive measurement scheme for online tracking of power system harmonics. *IEEE Transactions on Power Delivery*, Vol. 6, No. 3, (July 1991) 1153-1160, ISSN: 0885-8977.

González, M.; Cárdenas, V. & Álvarez, V. (2006). Detection of sags, swells, and interruptions using the digital RMS method and Kalman filter with fast response. *Proceedings of IEEE 32nd Annual Conference on Industrial Electronics (IECON 2006)*, pp. 2249-2254, ISSN: 1553-572X, Paris, France, November 2006, Institute of Electrical and Electronics Engineers.

Griffo, A.; Carpinelli, G.; Lauria, D. & Russo, A. (2007). An optimal control strategy for power quality enhancement in a competitive environment. *International Journal of Electrical Power & Energy Systems*, Vol. 29, No. 7, (September 2007) 514-525, ISSN: 0142-0615.

Heydt, G. T. (1989). Identification of harmonic sources by a state estimation technique. *IEEE Transactions on Power Delivery*, Vol. 4, No. 1, (Jan. 1989) 569 - 576, ISSN: 0885-8977.

Kim, J.; Grady, W. M.; Arapostathis, A.; Soward, J. & Bhatt, S. C. (2001). A time-domain procedure for locating switched capacitors in power distribution systems. *IEEE Transactions on Power Delivery*, Vol. 17, No. 4, (October 2002) 1044-1049, ISSN: 0885-8977.

Kumar, A.; Das, B. & Sharma, J. (2006). Robust dynamic state estimation of power system harmonics. *International Journal of Electrical Power & Energy Systems*, Vol. 28, No. 1, (January 2006) 65-74, ISSN: 0142-0615.

Kwan, K. H., So, P. L. & Chu, Y. C. (2007). A harmonic selective unified power quality conditioner using MVR with Kalman filters. *Proceedings of the International Power Engineering Conference 2007 (IPEC 2007)*, pp. 332-337, ISBN: 978-981-05-9423-7, Singapore, December 2007.

Larson, A. (2000). *The power quality of wind turbines.* Ph.D. thesis, Chalmers University of Technology, 0346-718X, Göteborg, Sweden.

Liserre, M.; Pigazo, A.; Dell'Aquila, A. & Moreno, V. M. (2006). An Anti-Islanding Method for Single-Phase Inverters Based on a Grid Voltage Sensorless Control. *IEEE Transactions on Industrial Electronics*, Vol. 53, No. 5, (October 2006) 1418-1426, ISSN: 0278-0046.

Ma, H. & Girgis, A. A. (1996). Identification and tracking of harmonic sources in a power system using a Kalman filter. *IEEE Transactions on Power Delivery*, Vol. 11, No. 3, (July 1996) 1659-1665, ISSN: 0885-8977.

Macías, J. A. R. & Exposito, A. G. (2006). Self-tuning of Kalman filters for harmonic computation. *IEEE Transactions on Power Delivery*, Vol. 21, No. 1, (January 2006) 501-503, ISSN: 0885-8977.

Moreno, V. M. & Barros, J. (1997). Application of Kalman filtering for continuous real-time tracking of power system harmonics. *IEE Proceedings - Generation, Transmission and Distribution*, Vol. 144, No. 1, (January 1997) 13-20, ISSN: 1350-2360.

Moreno, V. M.; Pigazo, A. & Diego, R. I. (2002). Reference estimation technique for active power filters using a digital Kalman algorithm, *Proceedings of 10th International*

Conference on Harmonics and Quality of Power (ICHQP'02), pp. 490-494, ISBN: 0-7803-7671-4, Brazil, 2002.

Moreno, V. M.; Pigazo, A. & Diego, R. I. (2004). Reference current estimation under distorted line voltage for control of shunt active power filters, *IEEE Transactions on Power Electronics*, Vol. 19, No. 4, (July 2004) 988-994, ISSN: 0885-8993.

Moreno, V. M.; Liserre, M.; Pigazo, A. & Dell'Aquila, A. (2007). A comparative analysis of real-time algorithms for power signal decomposition in multiple synchronous reference frames. *IEEE Transactions on Power Electronics*, Vol. 22, No. 4, (July 2007) 1280-1289, ISSN: 0885-8993.

Murty, Y. V. V. S. & Smolinski, W. J. (1990). A Kalman filter based digital percentage differential and ground fault relay for a 3-phase power transformer. *IEEE Transactions on Power Delivery*, Vol. 5, No. 3, (July 1990) 1299-1308, ISSN: 0885-8977.

Pecen, R.; Ula, S. & Timmerman, M. (2004). Modeling and simulation of a Kalman filter based control scheme for an AC/DC power system. *International Journal of Electrical Power & Energy Systems*, Vol. 26, No. 3, (March 2004) 173-189, ISSN: 0142-0615.

Pérez, E. & Barros, J (2008). An extended Kalman filtering approach for detection and analysis of voltage dips in power systems. *Electric Power Systems Research*, Vol. 78, No. 4, (April 2008) 618-625, ISSN: 0378-7796.

Pigazo, A. & Moreno, V. M. (2008). 3Φ -3w Signal Model for Power System Harmonics and Unbalance Identification Using Kalman Filtering. *IEEE Transactions on Power Delivery*, Vol. 23, No. 2, (April 2008) 1260-1261, ISSN: 0885-8977.

Pradhan, A. K.; Routray, A. & Sethi, D. (2004). Voltage phasor estimation using complex linear Kalman filter, *Proceedings of 8th IEE International Conference on Developments in Power System Protection*, pp. 24-27, ISBN: 0-86341-385-4, Amsterdam, Netherlands, April 2004.

Prodanovic, M.; De Brabandere, K.; Van den Keybus, J.; Green, T. & Driesen, J. (2007). Harmonic and reactive power compensation as ancillary services in inverter-based distributed generation. *IET Generation, Transmission & Distribution*, Vol. 1, No. 3, (May 2007) 432-438, ISSN: 1751-8687.

Rosolowski, E. & Michalik, M. (1994). Fast identification of symmetrical components by use of a state observer. *IEE Proceedings - Generation, Transmission and Distribution*, Vol. 141, No. 6, (November 1994) 617-622, ISSN: 1350-2360.

Routray, A.; Pradhan, A. K. & Rao, K. P. (2002). A novel Kalman filter for frequency estimation of distorted signals in power systems. *IEEE Transactions on Instrumentation and Measurement*, Vol. 51, No. 3, (June 2002) 469-479, ISSN: 0018-9456.

Shaw, S. R. & Laughman, C. R. (2007). A Kalman-filter spectral envelope preprocessor. *IEEE Transactions on Instrumentation and Measurement*, Vol. 56, No. 5, (October 2007) 2010-2017, ISSN: 0018-9456.

Soliman, S. A.; Al-Kandari, A. M. & El-Hawary, M. E. (1995). Linear Kalman filter algorithm for analysis of transient stability swings in large interconnected power systems. *Electric Power Systems Research*, Vol. 34, No. 3, (Sept. 1995) 173-178, ISSN: 0378-7796.

Soliman, S. A. & El-Hawary, M. E. (1996). Application of Kalman filtering for online estimation of symmetrical components for power system protection. *Electric Power Systems Research*, Vol. 38, No. 2, (August 1996) Pages 113-123, ISSN: 0378-7796.

Soliman, S. A. & Alammari, R. A. (2004). Harmonic modeling of linear and nonlinear loads based on Kalman filtering algorithm. *Electric Power Systems Research*, Vol. 72, No. 2, (December 2004) 147-155, ISSN: 0378-7796.

Styvaktakis, E.; Bollen, M. H. J. & Gu, I. Y. H. (2002). Expert system for classification and analysis of power system events. *IEEE Transactions on Power Delivery*, Vol. 17, No. 2, (April 2002) 423-428, ISSN: 0885-8977.

Trudnowski, D. J.; McReynolds, W. L. & Johnson, J. M. (2001). Real-time very short-term load prediction for power-system automatic generation control. *IEEE Transactions on Control Systems Technology*, Vol. 9, No. 2, (March 2001) 254-260, ISSN: 1558-0865.

Ukil, A. & Živanović, R. (2007). The detection of abrupt changes using recursive identification for power system fault analysis. *Electric Power Systems Research*, Vol. 77, No. 3-4, (March 2007) 259-265, ISSN: 0378-7796.

Wang, F.; Jin, Z.; Zhu, Z. & Wang, X. (2005). Application of Extended Kalman Filter to the Modeling of Electric Arc Furnace for Power Quality Issues, *Proceedings of International Conference on neural Networks and Brain (ICNN&B'05)*, pp. 991-996, ISBN: 0-7803-9422-4, Beijing, China, October 2005.

Woxd, H. C.; Johnson, N. G. & Sachdev, M.S. (1985). Kalman Filtering Applied to Power System Measurements Relaying. IEEE Transactions on Power Apparatus and Systems, Vol. PAS-104, No. 12, (December 1985) 3565 – 3573. ISSN: 0018-9510.

Yu, K. K. C.; Watson, N. R. & Arrillaga, J. (2005). An adaptive Kalman filter for dynamic harmonic state estimation and harmonic injection tracking. *IEEE Transactions on Power Delivery*, Vol. 20, No. 2, Part 2, (April 2005) 1577-1584, ISSN: 0885-8977.

Zhang, J.; Swain, A.; Nair, N.-K. C. & Liu, J. J. (2007). Estimation of power quality using an unscented Kalman filter. *Proceedings of 2007 IEEE Region 10 Conference (TENCON 2007)*, pp. 1-4, ISBN: 978-1-4244-1272-3, Taipei, October 2007.

Zheng, T.; Girgis, A. A. & Makram, E. B. (2000). A hybrid wavelet-Kalman filter method for load forecasting. *Electric Power Systems Research*, Vol. 54, No. 1, (April 2000) 11-17, ISSN: 0378-7796.

17

Kalman Filter on Power Electronics and Power Systems Applications

Fernando P. Marafão[1], Diego Colón[1], Marcelo S. de Padua[2] and Sigmar M. Deckmann[2]
São Paulo State University[1],
University of Campinas[2]
Brazil

1. Introduction

For decades, developments have been taking place, separately, in the areas of power systems, digital signal processing and automatic control. Despite of some isolated cases, where the "trajectories" touched, there never was a time when these areas more benefited from each other than in the last few years. Traditionally, power systems problems and applications have been solved by means of purely analog circuits, while an enormous number of digital signal processing and control algorithms have been developed by people working in the communications and control areas. The ever increasing improvement of the semiconductor industry on one hand, and the rising of power electronics applications on the other, have changed this scenario forever, paving the way to the very fruitful area of digital control and signal processing applied on power systems and power electronics. This new area has been applying successfully all the knowledge gathered to improve processes, like power quality monitoring, power system's protection, power conditioning and synchronization of distributed generators (among others), and the most used digital techniques have been digital filtering, discrete Fourier transform, phased-locked loop tracking methods and more recently, the Kalman filtering (Kalman, 1960).
The Kalman filter (KF) was originally proposed to solve a control theoretic problem: considering a linear time-invariant (LTI) system, including state disturbances and measurement errors, how to obtain the best process' LTI state-estimator (in a stochastic sense, that is, minimizing the covariance of the estimation error), in order to be used in a state feedback control law? In conjunction with optimal linear quadratic regulator, the KF found its first application in the well known LQG control (Linear Quadratic Gaussian). After, it became very popular in other areas, according to (Papoulis, 1991), when people became aware of its desirable properties as an estimator. Then several different applications progressively emerged in economics, image processing and biomedical instrumentation, to name a few. More recently, the KF found applications as part of more complex systems, as in an adaptive control system - see for example (Sastry & Bodson, 1989), where it is shown that the RLS (recursive least mean square) algorithm is a particular case of the KF - and attempts to find a nonlinear KF have been taking place, as in (Wong & Yau, 1999) and (Colón & Pait, 2004).

This chapter presents a concise survey of applications of KF to power systems and power electronics, giving emphasis on the topic of signal's fundamental component identification, which has a key role in most of them. The text is divided as follows: In section two, a review of the fundamental aspects of the KF, as well as a qualitatively explanation of its properties, are given. In section three, a brief description of different applications of the KF is presented. In section four, it is demonstrated how to achieve the fundamental component of measured voltages and/or current signals (their magnitude, frequency and phase angle), independently of input signal distortions or frequency and amplitude deviations. Simulation and experimental results concerning the fundamental component identification are presented in section five. Finally, section six summarizes the main discussions and results presented in this chapter.

2. Theoretical foundations

In order to design systems that use the KF, it is important to distinguish between three different concepts: 1) the real process; 2) the state-space mathematical model and 3) the KF itself. The real process can be interpreted as a "black box", producing signals by mean of sensors, which could be disposed in m-dimensional vectors and it could be a power plant or an airplane to be controlled or a signal to be decomposed in harmonics. The state-space mathematical model, on the other hand, is a way to predict the future behaviour of the real process, and consists of a set o first-order (differential or difference) equations, one for each state variable describing its dynamics. This model does not exist physically. Finally, the KF is a system whose objective is to produce *on-line* estimates for the state-variables, based on *on-line* measurements of the real process (the outputs). The KF is a system to be implemented digitally.

It is important to note that: 1) the state variables do not necessarily represent a physical quantity and as far as signal processing is concerned, not even one of them does; 2) The KF and the state-space model must be linear time-variant systems, but the KF is a deterministic system, in the sense that all of their inputs are deterministic signals. The state-space model, on the other hand, must have some stochastic inputs to account for the randomness of the real process. In the following, a detailed description of both systems is given. It is supposed also that the process is of discrete-time nature, so only the theory for discrete-time system is considered.

2.1 Stochastic state-space mathematical models

The state-space mathematical model must be, as said above, a linear (possibly time-variant) system of the form:

$$\begin{cases} \boldsymbol{x}(k+1) = \boldsymbol{A}(k)\boldsymbol{x}(k) + \boldsymbol{B}(k)\boldsymbol{u}(k) + \boldsymbol{H}(k)\boldsymbol{w}(k) \\ \boldsymbol{y}(k) = \boldsymbol{C}(k)\boldsymbol{x}(k) + \boldsymbol{G}(k)\boldsymbol{z}(k) \end{cases} \tag{1}$$

where $\boldsymbol{x}(k)$ is the n-vector state (containing the n-state variables), $\boldsymbol{y}(k)$ is the output m-vector, $\boldsymbol{u}(k)$ is a deterministic input p-vector signal (control sequence) and $\boldsymbol{w}(k)$ and $\boldsymbol{z}(k)$ are stochastic processes (process noise and measurement noise, respectively), representing, respectively, the uncertainty in the model and in the measurements. The matrices $\boldsymbol{A}(k), \boldsymbol{B}(k), \boldsymbol{C}(k), \boldsymbol{H}(k)$ and $\boldsymbol{G}(k)$ are generally time-invariant and represent the dynamic of

the process modelled and the noise. The initial state $\boldsymbol{x}(0) = \boldsymbol{x_0}$ is a random n-vector uncorrelated to the others $\boldsymbol{w}(k)$ and $\boldsymbol{z}(k)$.
Additional restrictions must be done in the stochastic processes $\boldsymbol{w}(k)$ and $\boldsymbol{z}(k)$ in order to derive a KF, that is, they must be Wide Sense Stationary (WSS) white noise. The mathematical formalism behind stochastic systems, putting altogether, can be a little clumsy. On the other hand, if one works with WSS processes as inputs, and models with matrices varying in a known way, it is easier to cope with. As could be expected, one can only determine statistical parameters of the states/outputs given the statistics of the inputs. In the WSS case, on the other hand, if one knows the input's expected value and auto-covariance functions, one can determine the same functions for the states and outputs.
It is a basic result that a sufficiently rich class of spectral power density function can be obtained as the output of a LTI model excited by white noise process. The class of linear time-varying models excited by WSS stochastic process is sufficiently vast to the purposes of this work, as it exhibits sufficient complex correlations between different instants.

2.2 Kalman filter

The KF to a state-space model must be a deterministic linear (possibly time-variant) system, as it must be implemented in, for example, a computer, and its inputs must be deterministic signals. The equations for the KF are:

$$\begin{cases} \widehat{\boldsymbol{x}}(k+1|k) & = & \boldsymbol{A}(k)\widehat{\boldsymbol{x}}(k|k-1) + \boldsymbol{B}(k)\boldsymbol{u}(k) + \boldsymbol{K}(k)[\boldsymbol{y}(k) - \boldsymbol{C}(k)\widehat{\boldsymbol{x}}(k|k-1)] \\ \widehat{\boldsymbol{y}}(k) & = & \boldsymbol{C}(k)\widehat{\boldsymbol{x}}(k|k-1) \end{cases} \tag{2}$$

where $\widehat{\boldsymbol{x}}(k|k-1)$ represents the current state-estimate based in the information collected up to instant $k-1, \widehat{\boldsymbol{y}}(k)$ is the current estimate of the real process output, $\boldsymbol{y}(k)$ is the current real process output and $\boldsymbol{K}(k)$, known as the Kalman open-loop gain, is given by the formula (Davis & Vinter, 1985):

$$\boldsymbol{K}(k) = [\boldsymbol{A}(k)\boldsymbol{P}(k)\boldsymbol{C}^T(k) + \boldsymbol{H}(k)\boldsymbol{G}^T(k)][\boldsymbol{C}(k)\boldsymbol{P}(k)\boldsymbol{C}^T(k) + \boldsymbol{G}(k)\boldsymbol{G}^T(k)]^{-1} \tag{3}$$

The matrix $\boldsymbol{P}(k)$ is the estimates' error covariance, given by $\boldsymbol{P}(k) = E[(\boldsymbol{x}(k) - \widehat{\boldsymbol{x}}(k+1|k))(\boldsymbol{x}(k) - \widehat{\boldsymbol{x}}(k+1|k))^T]$, which can be calculated by the Riccati difference equation:

$$\begin{aligned} \boldsymbol{P}(k+1) = \boldsymbol{A}(k)\boldsymbol{P}(k)\boldsymbol{A}^T(k) + \boldsymbol{H}(k)\boldsymbol{H}^T(k) \\ - [\boldsymbol{A}(k)\boldsymbol{P}(k)\boldsymbol{C}^T(k) + \boldsymbol{H}(k)\boldsymbol{G}^T(k)][\boldsymbol{C}(k)\boldsymbol{P}(k)\boldsymbol{C}^T(k) \\ + \boldsymbol{G}(k)\boldsymbol{G}^T(k)]^{-1}[\boldsymbol{A}(k)\boldsymbol{P}(k)\boldsymbol{C}^T(k) \\ + \boldsymbol{H}(k)\boldsymbol{G}^T(k)]^T \end{aligned} \tag{4}$$

where $\boldsymbol{P}(0) = \boldsymbol{P}_0$ is the initial covariance (given by the user).
It can be shown (Davis & Vinter, 1985) and (Yeh, 1990) that a KF is the best estimator for the states of (1) in the sense of minimum covariance of the estimations and least square estimation.
Some observations are now in order:

I. $\boldsymbol{H}(k)\boldsymbol{H}^T(k)$ is the covariance matrix of the process noise and $\boldsymbol{G}(k)\boldsymbol{G}^T(k)$ is the covariance matrix of the measurement noise inside the system (not white anymore). Those parameters strongly influence the KF performance in the following way: 1) If the model is known to have more process than measurement noise (that is, $\boldsymbol{G}(k)\boldsymbol{G}^T(k)$ is smaller than $\boldsymbol{H}(k)\boldsymbol{H}^T(k)$, what makes sense given that both are positive-definite), the

KF should put more confidence in $\boldsymbol{y}(k)$, what means to have greater $\boldsymbol{K}(k)$. As a consequence, the dynamic response become faster (the bandwidth becomes larger and the filter closed-loop gain tends to one); 2) In the opposite situation, on the other hand, the model output (KF input) is heavily influenced by the measurement noise, and a better result would be achieved giving less weight to $\boldsymbol{y}(k)$, that is, smaller values in the entries of $\boldsymbol{K}(k)$. In consequence, the bandwidth would be narrower and the closed-loop gain less than one. In fact, according to (Yeh, 1990), the Kalman gain can be interpreted as being proportional to the ratio of the norms of $\boldsymbol{G}(k)\boldsymbol{G}^T(k)$ over $\boldsymbol{H}(k)\boldsymbol{H}^T(k)$. Therefore, the KF design depends on a compromise between desired accuracy and dynamic response, what can be achieved by a proper choice of matrices $\boldsymbol{H}(k)$ and $\boldsymbol{G}(k)$, taking into account input waveform distortions and desired characteristics of final applications.

II. The system in (2) and (3) is to be implemented in a digital processor, and calculates the state-estimates recursively and *on-line*, as it depends on the current output of the process. The equation (4), however, could be solved *off-line*, that is, before the KF starts to "filter", if the values of the model's matrices are known in advance. This implementation significantly reduces the memory and CPU time needed in digital systems, what is essential in practical applications.

III. Independently of its final use, which can be either on open or closed-loop applications, the KF is itself a closed-loop system, in the sense that the estimation $\hat{\boldsymbol{y}}(k)$ generated is constantly compared to the real signal $\boldsymbol{y}(k)$ and the discrepancy is used in calculating the future estimates. Also, the optimality guarantees robustness and stability.

IV. Substituting (3) in (4), it is easy to see that the equation (4) could be restated in the form

$$\boldsymbol{P}(k+1) = \boldsymbol{A}(k)\boldsymbol{P}(k)\boldsymbol{A}^T(k) + \boldsymbol{C}(k)\boldsymbol{C}^T(k)$$
$$-\boldsymbol{K}(k)[\boldsymbol{A}(k)\boldsymbol{P}(k)\boldsymbol{C}^T(k) + \boldsymbol{H}(k)\boldsymbol{G}^T(k)]^T \quad (5)$$

V. The optimality of the KF is guaranteed under the hypothesis of (uncorrelated) Gaussian white noise $\boldsymbol{w}(k)$ and $\boldsymbol{z}(k)$. Of course, some modifications in the covariance matrices can change the spectral power density in order to produce the kind of correlation necessary to turn the KF optimal in these cases.

VI. In case of all the matrices being time-invariant (that is, LTI model), it is expected that, after the transient, the estimation process would result in more accurate results than in the beginning, as the process reaches a stationary condition. In fact, equation (4) is deterministic and tends to stabilize in a final value.

3. KF on power electronics and power systems – state of the art

A concise description of different applications of the KF in power electronics and power systems areas is summarized in next sections. Even if some of them have been proposed more than 20 years ago, especially those based on *off-line* processing, the applications are quite limited if compared with other digital techniques applied in such areas. Probably, it happened because of the computational complexity of the KF for *on-line* applications that could not have the equation (4) solved *off-line* (for example, when the model's matrices change in not *a priori* known pattern).

Nevertheless, considering the ever increasing capacity of digital processor's technology, this line has been broken down and new KF applications have emerged, including *on-line* approaches. Most of them are based on the identification of the fundamental 60Hz components (x_1) of phase voltages and/or currents (amplitude, phase and frequency) or even based on the fundamental positive sequence components (x_1^+).

3.1 Load forecasting and modal estimation

One of the first applications of the KF in the power system area had been to forecast the total load demanded by a multi-node system (Abu-El-Magd et al., 1981; Park et al., 1991). Temporal load data, collected by the various agents in the power system administration, are used in order to predict load conditions, and the KF is frequently a fundamental part of the algorithm. Normally, the collected data are hourly based, and the prediction algorithm must yield short-term results, that would be useful in scheduling the actual system in order to supply the daily demand, and medium and long-term results, what would be useful in, for example, expansion planning and annual maintenance scheduling. Load forecasting has been gaining more importance as long as the electricity market becomes deregulated and the power sources become more and more distributed in the interconnected grid (Song et al., 2006).

In this kind of application, there is not much difference from the forecasting of economic data, as presented in (Clements & Hendry, 1998). There is a temporal series of power consumption and several periodicities and trends can be detected. The most evident is the daily periodicity on weekdays, which assumes the peak value around the beginning of the night. On Sundays and holydays, however, the pattern consumption tends to be less correlated. This pattern also reveals a weekly and monthly periodicity, and a yearly periodicity can obviously be assumed. Trends are always present in this kind of data, and the most important is the rising consumption that can be observed in the series. It is also important to mention the parameter dependence variations coming from the climate (mostly temperature). In tropical countries, the load is expected to be higher in summer, by the use of air conditioning systems, for example.

On the technical side, it is always possible to associate to a temporal series a model like (1), where $\boldsymbol{y}(k)$ is the series itself. The states, on the other hand, could be the periodic components (in a Fourier series sense) or even non-periodic, and the matrices could be determined in order to generate those components (obviously time-invariant in this case). Disturbances and noise covariance should be adequately selected. The KF would act in order to estimate those components, which would be the states and could represent trends and seasonal behaviour. The matrices could even be time-varying, if the process is known to be more complex.

In a similar way, other interesting application is the modal estimation of the power system. Based on power system's measurements under normal conditions and defining a stochastic model relating different disturbance inputs (e.g., load changes), the KF is adjusted to estimate the outputs produced by the disturbances. Then, by monitoring the difference between the measured output and the estimated output, one can recognize if there is any change in the model parameters (Wiltshire et al., 2007).

3.2 Protection and digital relaying

Other key application of KF in power systems is to detect fault conditions and to control protection devices, a task normally done by digital relays. Based on information coming from voltages and currents, decisions must be taken in order to detect and protect the power system from more severe faults and maintain its stable operation (Girgis & Brown, 1981).

The discrete signals coming from several sensors do contain valuable information, but it is necessary to extract it from input disturbances, what means that it is necessary to identify the signals fundamental component (v_1), given that during transient conditions the fundamental voltages or currents are corrupted (Girgis, 1982; Mir & McCleer, 1984; Sachdev et al., 1985).
Of course, this information is in the transient condition and depending on the kind, frequency of occurrence and location of the fault, the effects produced in the 60 Hz components (and other frequencies), are of very particular type, allowing gathering valuable information in order to control a protective device or to plan a repair as soon as possible.

3.3 Analysis and control of electrical machinery

Considering the digital control or analysis of induction motors, the KF has been applied in some different ways, e.g., to estimate the rotor time constant in PWM motor drives (Zai et al., 1992); to estimate the airgap flux in order to implement a direct flux control strategy (Pietrzak-David et al., 1992) or also to identify the rotor resistance in order to propose adaptive vector control schemes (Wade et al., 1997). In addition, KF has been also applied in order to reduce or avoid the use of additional sensors in the motor controlling or monitoring, considering the so called sensorless applications (Bolognani et al., 2001).
It is interesting to mention that these applications use the KF as part of an automatic closed-loop control system, that is, in the same way as its first applications (see section 1). Conversely, in the others mentioned in sections 3.1 and 3.2, the information from the estimates was used by people in decision making processes or open-loop applications.

3.4 Power conditioners control and synchronization

The requirement of synchronization of several electronic devices (such as active rectifiers, active power filters, uninterruptible power suppliers, dynamic voltage restorers, distributed generators, etc.) has been motivating the development of different algorithms to detect the amplitude, frequency and phase angle of the power grid fundamental voltage (Padua et al., 2007; Moreno et al., 2007). Such required information can be provided by the KF output (Padua et al., 2007a; Cardoso, et al., 2007; Huang et al., 2008), as it will be demonstrated in the following.
In the matter of power conditioning, several closed-loop control schemes have been applied in order to control the voltages and currents waveforms, frequency, and amplitudes of an electrical load or point of common coupling (PCC) (Peng, 2001). Many control laws can be used in order to guarantee the voltage/current to track the references, and to compensate for disturbances, running from classically inspired techniques (Marafão et al., 2008) to those including a KF in the control loop (Moreno et al., 2004; Kwan et al., 2005; Rosendo et al, 2007).
An active rectifier, e.g., should drain a sinusoidal current from the supply system, which should be in-phase with the fundamental component of the grid voltage, even if this one is distorted. This will ensure a high power factor for the resulting active rectifier. In case of three-phase devices, it is also desired to ensure equal phase currents, it means that the three-phase rectifier will act as resistive balanced load.
An active power filter, either in series or parallel to the loads, should ensure, e.g., that voltages and/or currents (depending of the configuration) are sinusoidal, balanced, symmetrical and with constant magnitude. It is possibly based on the identification of the

disturbing signals, which will become the references for the control scheme in order to be injected in or filtered out of the power system. In this case, the KF should be responsible for the detection of the ideal signals (fundamental positive sequence components x_1^+) and by the difference with the original voltages or currents, the deteriorated signals (harmonic distortions, voltage sags and swells, low power factor, unbalances, etc.) could be identified ($x_d = x - x_1^+$).

In the matter of distributed generation, the control of different power sources (AC or DC) have been carried out by means of electronic power converters and usually, it depends on some synchronized signal, in order to ensure that the generated voltages have the same frequency and phase angle of the main power grid (Padua et al., 2007). Again in this case, the required information could be achieved by means of the KF.

3.5 Revenue metering and power quality monitoring

The continuously increasing demand for electronic equipments and power converter applications has been the most important cause of power quality deterioration phenomena, including voltage and current distortions and imbalances. The impacts of such disturbing effects can be directly related to power losses, insulation stress, over voltages, power oscillations or even malfunction and damage on sensitive loads (Bollen, 2000).

Among a number of different areas related to this question, during the last decades intensive research has been directed to the definition of power quality indices and revenue metering techniques, suitable for monitoring nonlinear and unbalanced systems (Ferrero et al, 1998; Marafão et al., 2002; Farghal et al, 2002).

Considering the power quality monitoring, important indices have been defined to estimate the amount of harmonic distortion or unbalances on the measured voltage (v) and currents (i) or also how these distortions affect other indicators, such as, e.g., the power factor (PF). Once more, the KF can be applied in order to identify the fundamental components (v_1, i_1) and the positive sequence components (v_1^+, i_1^+), which could be used to the calculation of the mentioned indices. Thus, indices such as: the voltage Total Harmonic Distortion $THD_V = \frac{\sqrt{\sum_{h=2}^{N} V_h^2}}{V_1}$ or Negative Unbalance Factor $K^- = \frac{V_1^-}{V_1^+}$ are defined.

In the matter of revenue metering, considering for example the IEEE STD 1459-2000, which brings the definition of several power quantities related to fundamental components, positive sequence components, harmonic components, among others, the KF application could be responsible for the calculation of, e.g., the Fundamental Active Power (P_1), the Fundamental Equivalent Apparent Power (S_{e1}), the Fundamental Power Factor (FP_1), the Fundamental Positive Sequence Power Factor (FP_1^+).

The KF has also been applied to the development of expert systems focused on the analysis, classification and possible cause's identification of short term power quality disturbances, such as: voltage sags, swells and interruptions (Styvaktakis et al., 2002; Dash & Chilukuri, 2004; González et al., 2006).

4. Fundamental component identification

As stated in the above section, in many power system and power electronics' applications, it is necessary to identify the fundamental component of voltages and/or currents signals, independently of frequency fluctuations, amplitude variations and waveform distortions.

phase-locked loop (PLL) has been one of the most applied algorithms to get the required information (Kaura & Blasko, 1997; Zhan et al, 2001; Padua et al, 2005). Recent researches, however, have shown that recursive discrete Fourier transform (RDFT) could also be applied (Andria & Salvatore, 1990; McGrath et al., 2005). Other possibility is the KF. All of the mentioned techniques can be used in single-phase systems. Moreover, the PLL and KF can also be applied in three-phase systems with a suitable model (Padua et al., 2007; Moreno et al., 2007).

In the following sections, two distinct ways of using the KF in fundamental component identification are presented. One method uses a second order KF, treating all the signal components as disturbances (except for the fundamental). The other uses a 2n-order KF, and includes the harmonics in the deterministic part of the model (Cardoso et al., 2006; Mustafa, 2007). It can be shown that the last KF represents a great computational burden, and the performance of both, as long as fundamental component identification is concerned, is very similar. The first section presents both KF for the single-phase case, and the following section presents the three-phase case.

4.1 Single-phase case

The filter design begins with determining a state-space model to the real signal to be measured, including the fundamental component, harmonics, inter-harmonics, and other disturbances. In stationary regime, the harmonic of order i of a (voltage) signal (with N samples per period) is given by

$$v_i(k) = V_i \sin\left[\frac{2\pi k i}{N} + \theta_i\right]$$

where V_i is the fundamental amplitude, θ_i is the phase angle and $N = f_s/f_1$, that is, the number of samples in the fundamental component. By using the values of this sequence in successive steps, one can show, by basic trigonometric properties, that

$$v_i(k) = v_i(k-1)\cos\frac{2\pi i}{N} - v_i^q\,(\mathrm{k}-1)\sin\frac{2\pi i}{N}$$

The signal $v_i^q(k)$ is known as the *in quadrature* component and is orthogonal to $v_i(k)$. Searching for a similar identity for $v_i^q(k)$, it is possible to write down a recursive formula for both components in a vector form. By defining the vector $\boldsymbol{V_i}(k) = \begin{bmatrix} v_i(k) & v_i^q(k) \end{bmatrix}^T$, the formula becomes:

$$\boldsymbol{V_i}(k) = \boldsymbol{A_i}.\boldsymbol{V_i}(k-1), \text{ where the matrix } \boldsymbol{A_i} \text{ is given by}$$

$$\boldsymbol{A_i} = \begin{bmatrix} \cos\frac{2\pi i}{N} & -\sin\frac{2\pi i}{N} \\ \sin\frac{2\pi i}{N} & \cos\frac{2\pi i}{N} \end{bmatrix}$$

The formula above represents a dynamical state-variable model of a harmonic of order i and could be used, in combination with other similar systems, to represent a periodic signal, (with harmonics till order n), which would have a matrix of the form:

$$\mathbf{A}=\begin{bmatrix} \boldsymbol{A}_1 & \cdots & 0 \\ \vdots & \ddots & \vdots \\ 0 & \cdots & \boldsymbol{A}_n \end{bmatrix}$$

The state-vector would have the form $\boldsymbol{V}(k) = [\boldsymbol{V_1} \quad \dots \quad \boldsymbol{V}_n]^{\mathrm{T}}$, and the fundamental component of periodic signal would be given by

$$v(k) = [1 \quad 0 \quad 0 \quad \dots \quad 0 \quad 0].\boldsymbol{V}(k) = \boldsymbol{C}.\boldsymbol{V}(k)$$

In order to represent the disturbances (all the components other than the harmonics till order n) and the measurement noise and errors (for example, the quantization noise), process and measurement noise should be added, which put the model in the form presented in (1), but with null exogenous control input $\boldsymbol{B}(k) = 0$. Thus, the complete signal model is:

$$\begin{cases} \boldsymbol{V}(k+1) &= \boldsymbol{A}(k).\boldsymbol{V}(k) + \boldsymbol{H}.\boldsymbol{w}(k) \\ v(k) &= \boldsymbol{C}.\boldsymbol{V}(k) + \boldsymbol{G}.\boldsymbol{z}(k) \end{cases} \tag{6}$$

All the matrices in the model, except $\boldsymbol{A}(k)$, do not vary with time, and $\boldsymbol{H}$ and $\boldsymbol{G}$ are related to the covariance matrices of the process and measurement noises, that could be conveniently chosen if *a priori* information about the nature of the disturbances is available. The model to be used in case of complete lack of prior information is Gaussian white noise, and both matrices would be proportional to the identity matrix.

Having the estimates coming from the KF, it is possible to calculate the fundamental component's magnitude and phase, by the formulas:

$$M = \sqrt{\hat{v}_1^2(k) + (\hat{v}_1^q(k))^2}$$

and

$$\theta(k) = \tan^{-1}\left[\frac{\hat{v}_1\,(k)}{\hat{v}_1^q(k)}\right] \tag{7}$$

and the fundamental frequency f_1 can be estimated from zero-crossing detection of the signal $\theta(k)$ and improved with an average of the last four estimates.

In these applications, if the sample frequency f_s is kept constant, the $\boldsymbol{A}(k)$ matrix must be varied according to the most recent estimation of f_1. It means that the difference Riccati equation have to be solved *on-line*. Of course, the greater the number of harmonics represented in the $\boldsymbol{A}$ matrix, the greater the computational burden.

A more attractive alternative, as presented in (Padua et al, 2007), is to consider only the fundamental component in the $\boldsymbol{A}(k)$ matrix, and by choosing $\boldsymbol{H}$ and $\boldsymbol{G}$ adequately, the other harmonics would be represented in the noise models. The performance of this simplified model is as good as in the first case, and the computational burden is significantly reduced. In section 5, simulation and experimental results for this case are presented.

Another possible alternative can be applied if the sampling frequency were a free parameter, it means, if it were possible to change its value *on-line*, in order to ensure a fixed number of samples regarding to the fundamental component (N).

4.2 Three-phase case

In the same spirit of the single-phase model, a set of three-phase fundamental voltages can also be represented by means of a state space model of the form (1), but where the matrix $\boldsymbol{A}$ is given by:

$$\boldsymbol{A} = \begin{bmatrix} \cos\left(\frac{2\pi}{N}\right) & \frac{1}{\sqrt{3}}\sin\left(\frac{2\pi}{N}\right) & -\frac{1}{\sqrt{3}}\sin\left(\frac{2\pi}{N}\right) & 0 \\ -\frac{1}{\sqrt{3}}\sin\left(\frac{2\pi}{N}\right) & \cos\left(\frac{2\pi}{N}\right) & \frac{1}{\sqrt{3}}\sin\left(\frac{2\pi}{N}\right) & 0 \\ \frac{1}{\sqrt{3}}\sin\left(\frac{2\pi}{N}\right) & -\frac{1}{\sqrt{3}}\sin\left(\frac{2\pi}{N}\right) & \cos\left(\frac{2\pi}{N}\right) & 0 \\ \sin\left(\frac{2\pi}{N}\right) & 0 & 0 & \cos\left(\frac{2\pi}{N}\right) \end{bmatrix}$$

And the state vector is given by $\boldsymbol{V}(k) = \left[\boldsymbol{v_{a1}}(k) \quad \boldsymbol{v_{b1}}(k) \quad \boldsymbol{v_{c1}}(k) \quad \boldsymbol{v^{q}_{a1}}(k)\right]^{\boldsymbol{T}}$, where the first three components are three-phase signals and the last component is orthogonal to the first. The matrix $\boldsymbol{C}$, that represents the output of the model, that is, the three-phase components, is given by:

$$\boldsymbol{C} = \begin{bmatrix} 1 & 0 & 0 & 0 \\ 0 & 1 & 0 & 0 \\ 0 & 0 & 1 & 0 \end{bmatrix}$$

The signals $\boldsymbol{w}(k)$ and $\boldsymbol{z}(k)$ are Gaussian white noise vectors, as expected, and represents the distortions. The instantaneous phase angle can thus be obtained by:

$$\theta(k) = \tan^{-1}\left[\frac{\hat{v}_{a1}(k)}{\hat{v}^{q}_{a1}(k)}\right]$$

and the fundamental frequency f_1 can be calculated in the same way as in the simplified single-phase model. In case of unbalanced (amplitudes), but symmetrical (phase angle) input voltages, such KF model has the advantage to be able to identify the positive sequence component, in such a way that its magnitude can be calculated by:

$$V^{+}(k) = \sqrt{\frac{2}{3}\left[\hat{v}^{2}_{a1}(k) + \hat{v}^{2}_{b1}(k) + \hat{v}^{2}_{c1}(k)\right]} \tag{8}$$

In addition, it has been verified that if $\boldsymbol{H}$ and $\boldsymbol{G}$ were set to attenuating harmonic distortions, the dynamic convergence of the three-phase model is better than the single-phase one, since, statistically, its model has more information than the previous. However, it should be considered that its implementation complexity is also superior (4 x 4 systems instead of 2 x 2).

5. Simulation and experimental results

5.1 Simulation results

In order to compare different KF´s for the same application, some simulations were realized and the results are presented in the sequel. The sampling frequency fs was chosen to be 12 kHz, what means that the number of samples per period N varies with f_1 (N = 200 for f_1 = 60 Hz). In order to find the ideal balance between velocity of response and filtering quality, different matrices $GG^T(k)$ and $HH^T(k)$ were tested. Considering adequate results for both, the filtering and dynamic response, appropriate values were defined as, for the single-phase system:

$$GG^T = \begin{bmatrix} 0.01 & 0 \\ 0 & 0.01 \end{bmatrix} \quad \text{e} \quad HH^T = [25],$$

and for the three-phase system:

$$GG^T = \begin{bmatrix} 0.0025 & 0 & 0 & 0 \\ 0 & 0.0025 & 0 & 0 \\ 0 & 0 & 0.0025 & 0 \\ 0 & 0 & 0 & 0.0025 \end{bmatrix} \text{ e } HH^T = \begin{bmatrix} 16 & 0 & 0 \\ 0 & 16 & 0 \\ 0 & 0 & 16 \end{bmatrix},$$

These values were found following the suggestion of (Simon, 2001) and references therein. Note that the entries of $HH^T(k)$ are much greater than the ones in $GG^T(k)$, what is the way to attenuate the harmonic distortion.
It is worth mentioning that in order to guarantee the same performance, different values of these matrices must be used for different voltage levels.

5.1.1 Single-phase case

In order to evaluate the performance of the simplified single-phase KF on the fundamental component identification, four different input voltage conditions were simulated:

Case 1 - Sinusoidal 60 Hz voltage with amplitude equal to 127 Vrms and 90° phase angle;
Case 2 - The same conditions of *Case 1*, but with the addition of 5% of harmonic distortion in each 3rd, 5th and 7th harmonics;
Case 3 - The same conditions of *Case 2*, but with a voltage sag of 50%;
Case 4 - The same conditions of *Case 2*, but with the addition of an abrupt frequency transition from 60 Hz to 59 Hz.

Fig. 1 shows the influence of the initial state of the filter, which must be set by the user. In this case, values were chosen such that the initial phase of the signal should be 0°. In the uppermost graphic, the sinusoidal voltage v (output of the KF) along with their in-phase ($v1$) and orthogonal (vq) components are presented. Note that the convergence is achieved in about six cycles. In the bottom graphic, the fundamental frequency f_1 calculated as indicated earlier, converges to 60 Hz. The observed transient comes from the difference between the real state of the system ($\theta = 90°$) and the one fixed in the algorithm ($\theta = 0°$). Just for comparison, in Fig. 2 the initial phase angle was set to ($\theta = 0°$), as the KF initial state definition. It is obvious that the closer the initial value to the real phase, the faster the convergence. Observe that the convergence in this case is achieved in less than 3 cicles.
The good filtering performance of KF-1ϕ can be observed in Fig. 3 (*Case* 2). The Total Harmonic Distortion (THD), which would be 8.66% in the modelled signal (v), was reduced to about 1% in the fundamental output ($v1$).
Figs. 4 e 5 show the performance of KF-1ϕ when there are abrupt transitions in amplitude and frequency. In the first case, estimated voltages converge in less than 2 cycles, while fundamental frequency estimate practically does not change. In the second case, $v1$ and vq follow v while f_1 stabilizes in 9 cycles. Little ripple in frequency (58.90 Hz -59.04 Hz) can be observed as the ratio fs/f_1 is no longer an integer number. If necessary, such frequency ripple could be minimized updating the matrix A or the sampling frequency in order to maintain a fixed number of samples per fundamental period (N).

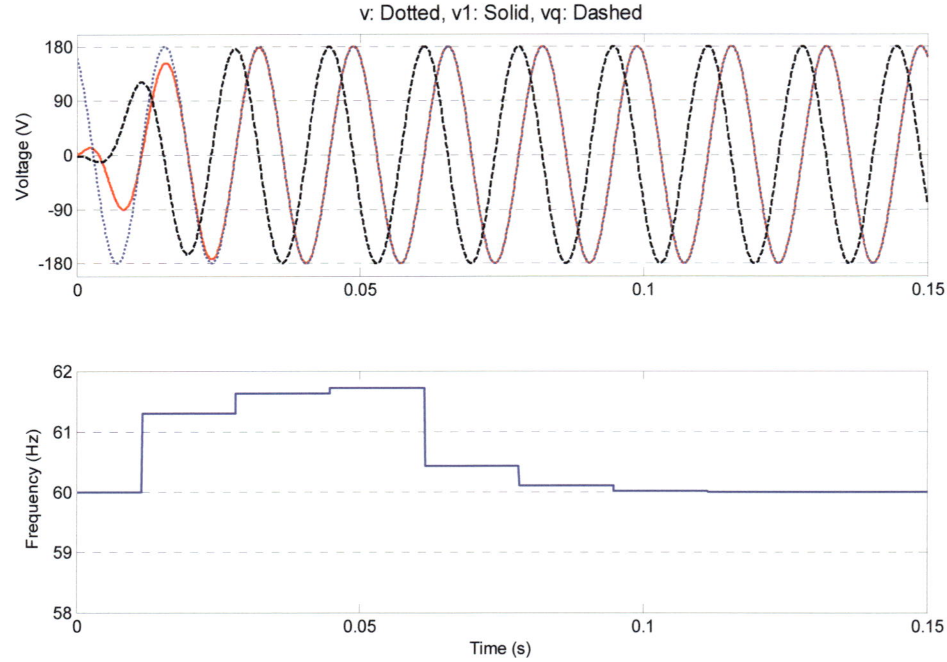

Fig. 1. KF-1ϕ (Case 1): Input voltages (127 Vrms, 60 Hz, **90°**) and filter outputs: v1, vq e f_1.

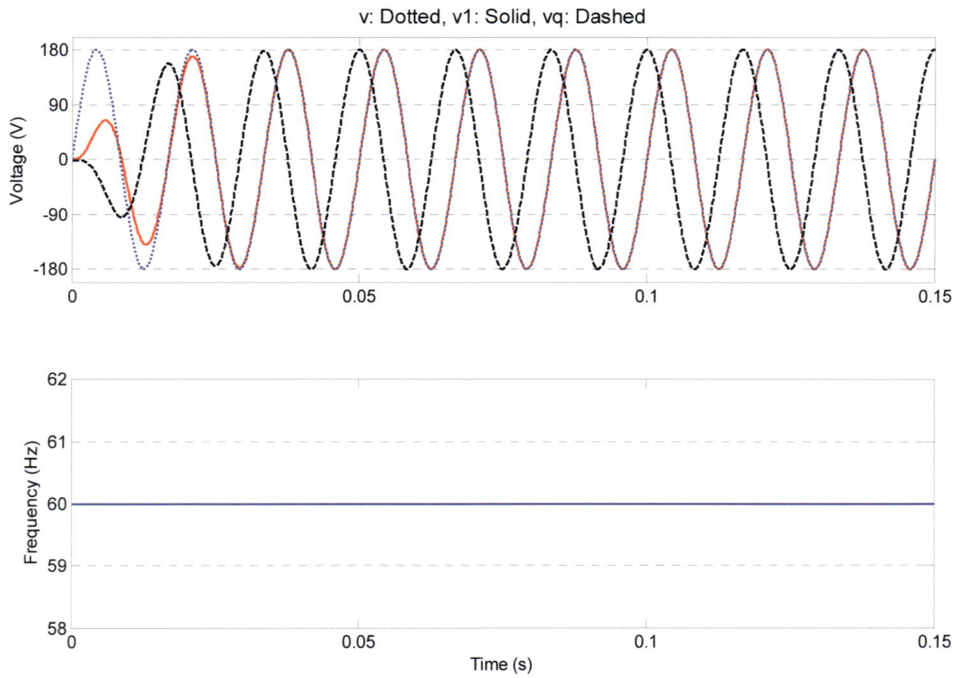

Fig. 2. KF-1ϕ (Case 1): Input voltages (127 Vrms, 60 Hz, **0°**) and filter outputs: v1, vq e f_1.

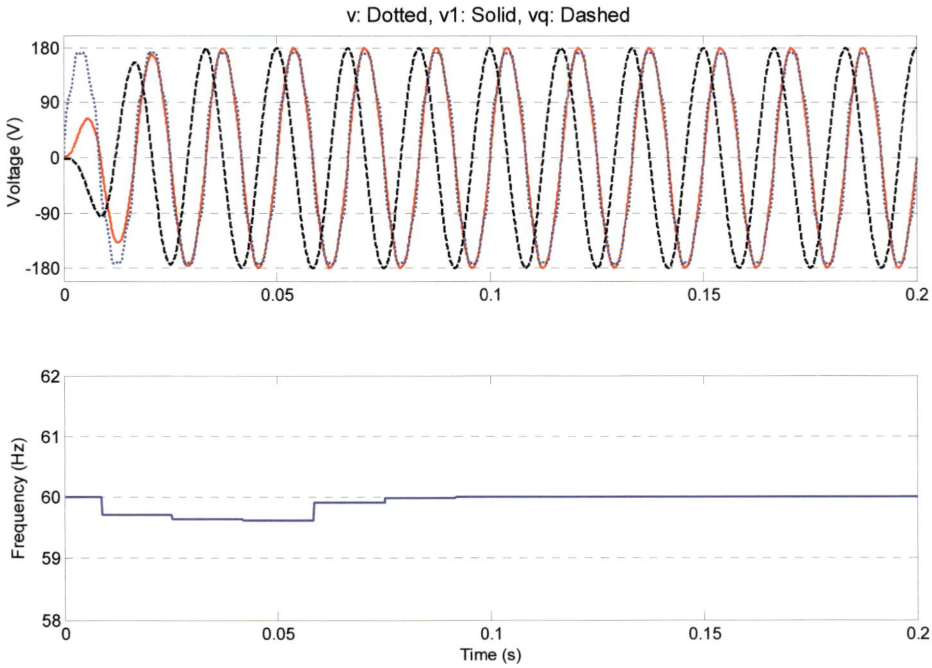

Fig. 3. KF-1ϕ (Case 2): Input voltage (127 Vrms, 60 Hz, 0°), with 5% of distortion in 3rd, 5th and 7th harmonics and filter outputs: v1, vq e f_1.

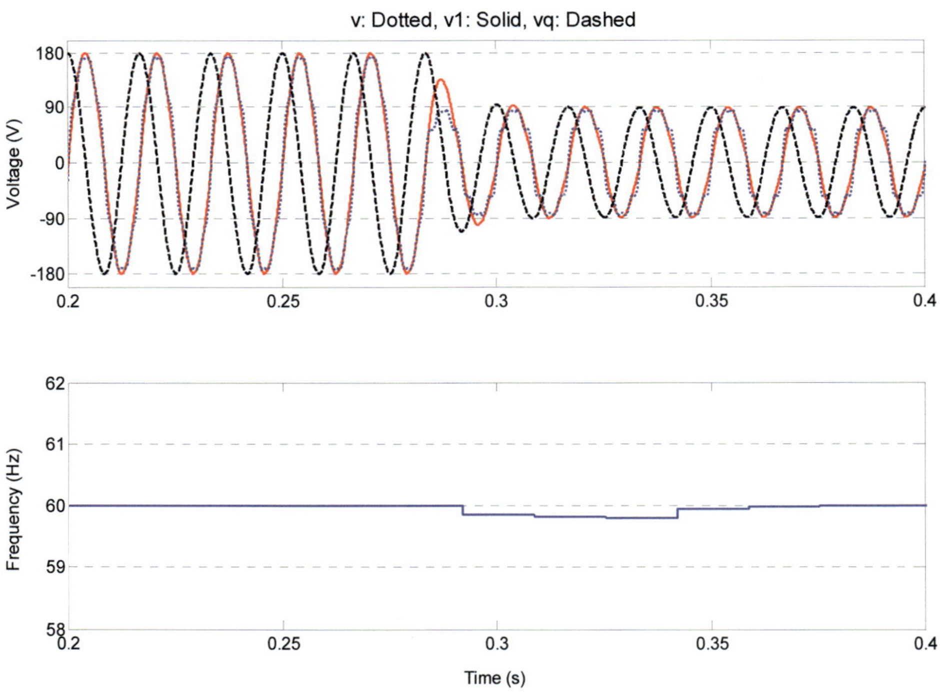

Fig. 4. KF-1ϕ (Case 3): Input voltage and filter outputs: v1, vq e f_1, after a voltage sag.

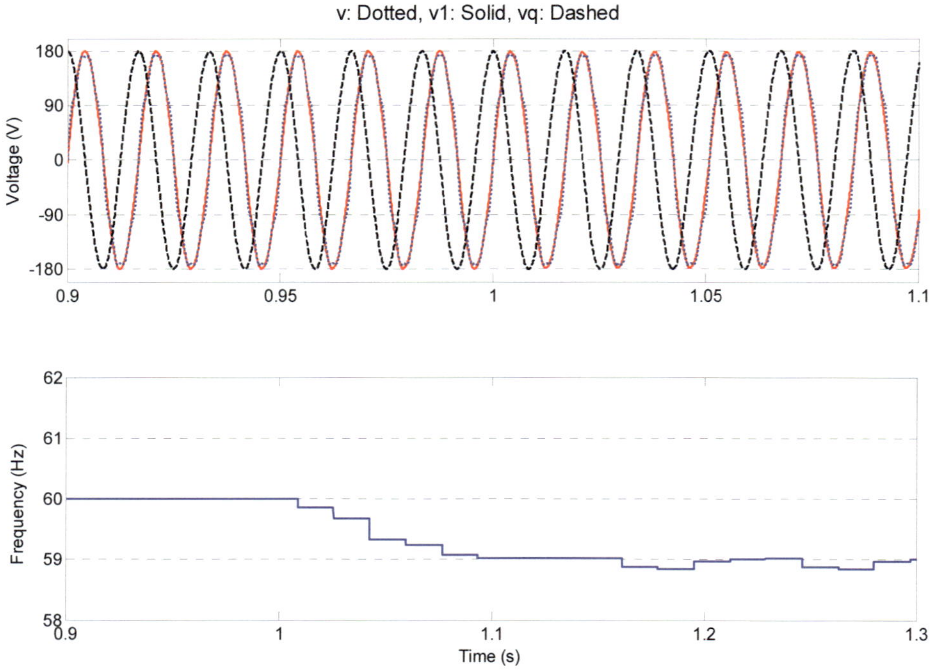

Fig. 5. KF-1ϕ (Case 4): Input voltage and filter outputs: v1, vq e f_1, after a frequency transient.

5.1.2 Three-phase case

In the same way of the previous section, four different conditions were imposed to the three-phase KF in order to evaluate its performance. The results are discussed in the following.

Case 1 - Sinusoidal and balanced (60Hz, 127 Vrms) three-phase voltages, with $\theta a = 0\,°$ (initial phase-a angle);
Case 2 - Unbalanced voltages (70% in phase b and 85% in phase c), with 5% of 3rd, 5th and 7th harmonic distortion;
Case 3 - The same conditions of *Case 2*, but with a voltage sag of 50%;
Case 4 - The same conditions of *Case 2*, but with the addition of an abrupt frequency transition from 60 Hz to 59 Hz.

Fig. 6 shows the fast dynamic response of the KF-3ϕ outputs considering *Case 1*. In the central graphic, the sinusoidal phase voltage (va) and its fundamental component (va1), that comes from the KF are put together. One can see the convergence in less than 2 cycles. In the bottom, the left graphic indicates the evolution of the positive sequence magnitude (Seq+) and the right-side graphic shows the fundamental frequency convergence.
In Fig. 7, a case with unbalanced and distorted (THD=8.66%) three-phase voltages is analyzed. Once more, one can see the convergence in about 2 cycles (with the same initial state in the KF) and the good filtering behaviour of the KF (fundamental output with a distortion reduction to THD=0.8%). Besides, the amplitudes of va1 and of the others resulting fundamental components are equal to 179,6x(1+0,7+0,85)/3 ≅ 152,66 V, what is the mean value of the measured amplitudes, which in this case, coincides with the positive sequence magnitude (Seq+).

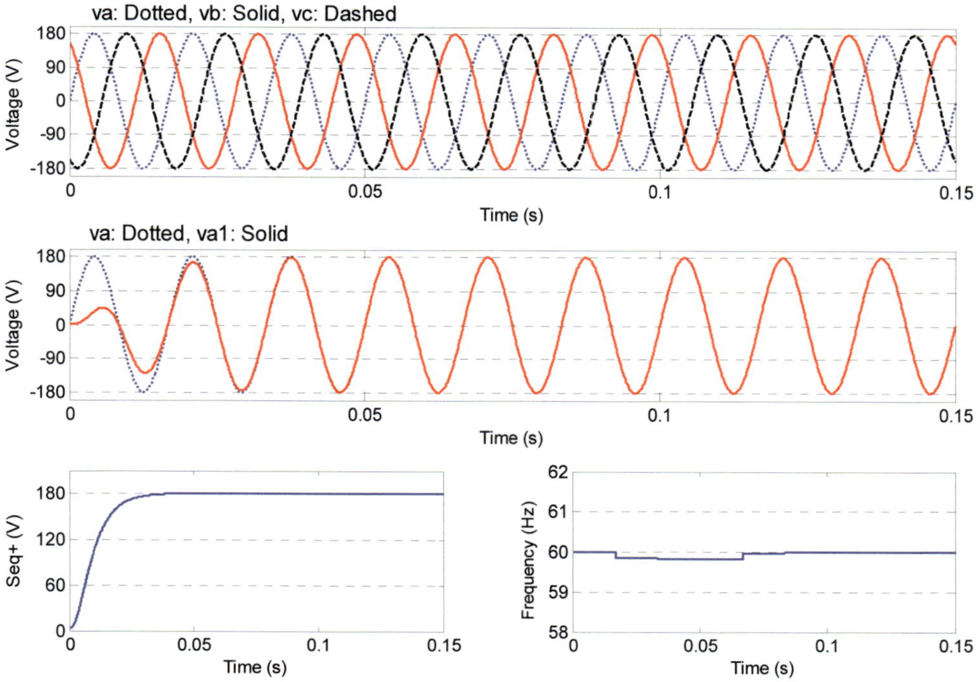

Fig. 6. KF-3ϕ (Case 1): Sinusoidal and balanced input voltages (127 Vrms, 60 Hz, 0° - phase a), and KF outputs - va1, Seq+ and f_1.

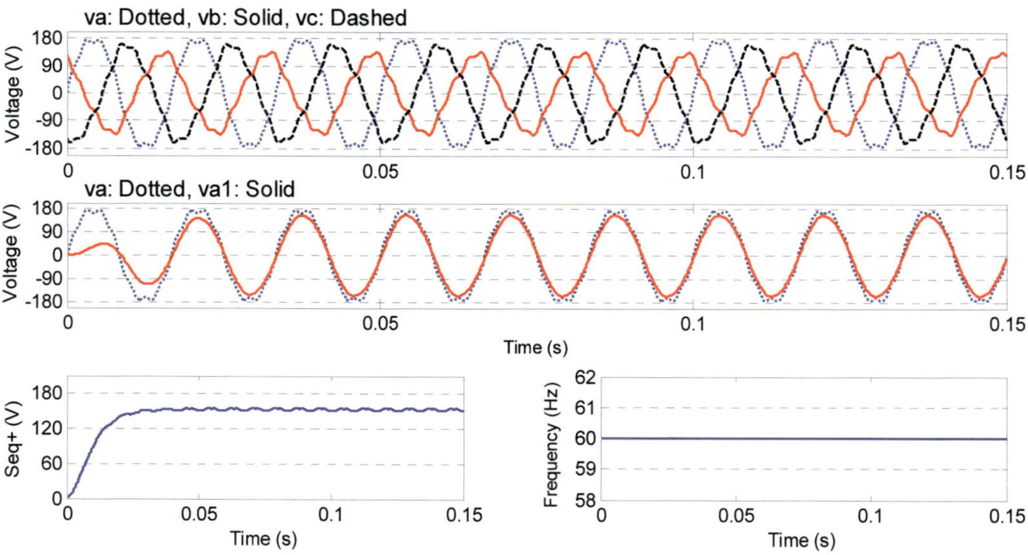

Fig. 7. KF-3ϕ (Case 2): filter response with unbalanced and distorted three-phase input voltages.

Fig. 8 and 9 show the performance of the KF-3ϕ when the power system voltages present an abrupt amplitude and frequency variations. In the case of amplitude variation (Fig. 8), the filtered voltages converge in 1 cycle while the frequency practically does not alter. In case of frequency variation, f_1 stabilizes in about 9 cycles.

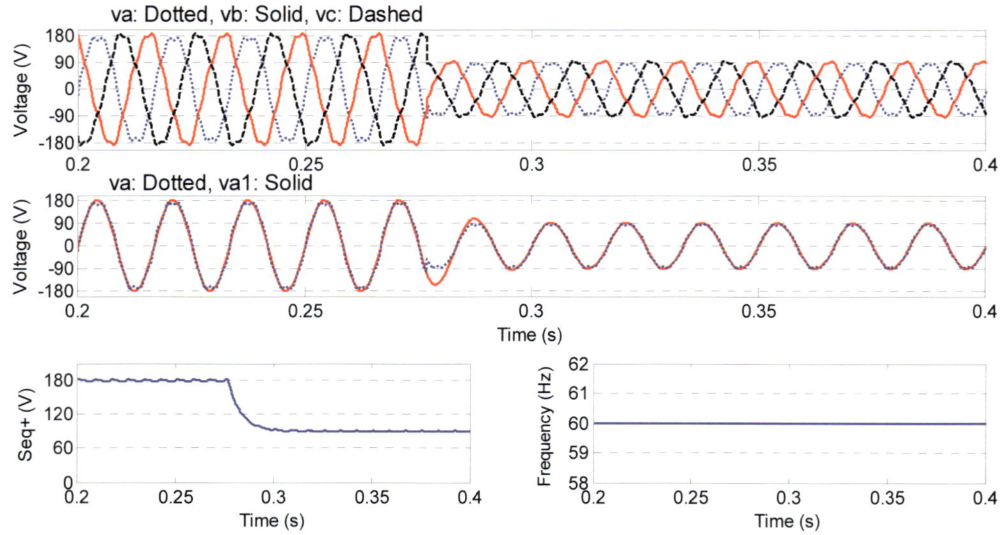

Fig. 8. KF-3ϕ (Case 3): outputs with distorted voltages and a three-phase voltage sag.

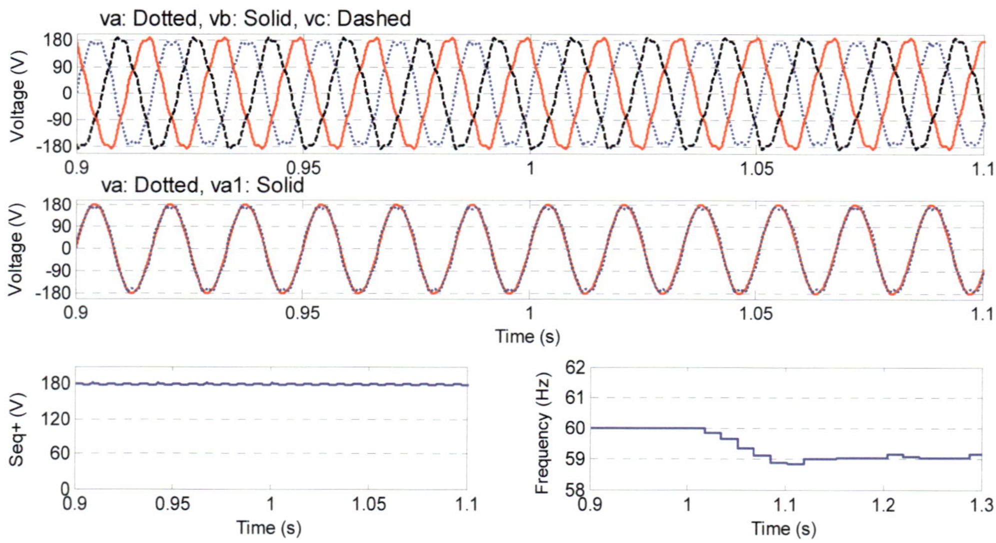

Fig. 9. KF-3ϕ outputs with distorted voltages and abrupt frequency deviation.

In order to demonstrate the influence of the matrices GG^T and HH^T, the conditions of Case 1 were simulated considering the following parameters:

$$GG^T = \begin{bmatrix} 0.1 & 0 & 0 & 0 \\ 0 & 0.1 & 0 & 0 \\ 0 & 0 & 0.1 & 0 \\ 0 & 0 & 0 & 0.1 \end{bmatrix} \text{ e } HH^T = \begin{bmatrix} 250 & 0 & 0 \\ 0 & 250 & 0 \\ 0 & 0 & 250 \end{bmatrix}$$

Fig. 10 shows the performance of the KF in such condition. Comparing to Fig. 6, note that in this case the KF convergence is faster than in the previous configuration.

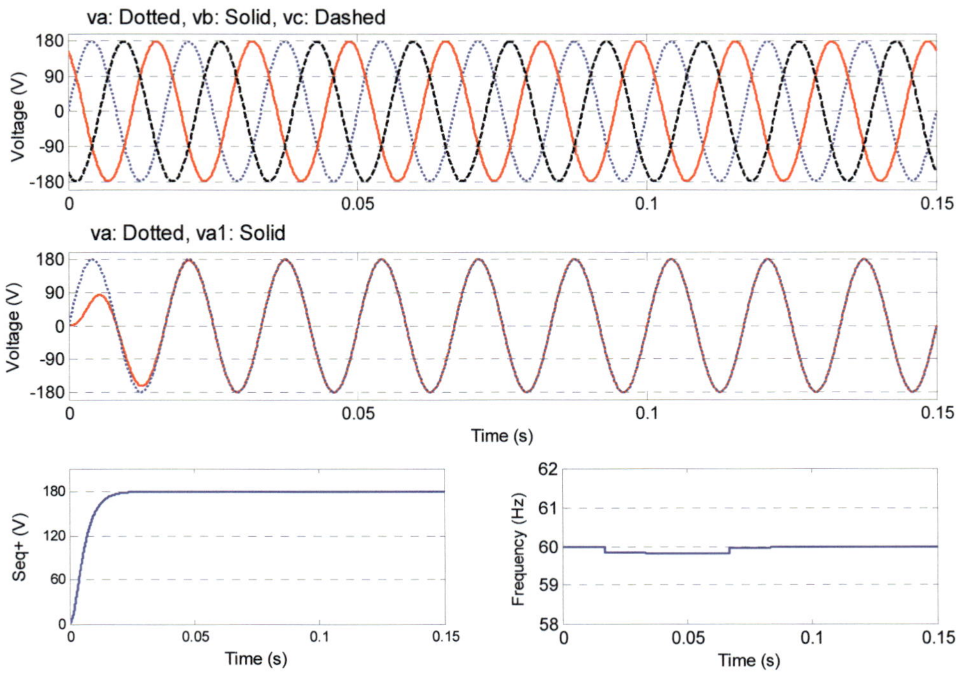

Fig. 10. KF-3ϕ (Case 1): Sinusoidal and balanced input voltages and KF outputs considering a different configuration in matrices $\boldsymbol{H}$ and $\boldsymbol{G}$.

5.2 Experimental results

For the purpose of evaluating the KF in practical real-time applications, the single-phase model was implemented in a high performance acquisition system and the three-phase model was implemented in a fixed point digital signal processor (DSP). The obtained results are presented in next sections.

5.2.1 High performace acquisition system

The single-phase algorithm was tested in a data acquisition and processing system based on the concept of virtual instrumentation (Moreira et al., 2005). The experimental apparatus was composed by an eight-channel simultaneous acquisition board with 16-bit AD converter (PCI-6143 from National Instruments - NI) with maximum frequency of 200 kHz. The analog signals were measured by current and voltage Hall-effect sensors (LV-25P and LA-55P from LEM) and the computational part was implemented in a Pentium 4 desktop with LabView 7.1 software (National Instruments). The voltages were generated by a programmable three-phase generator from California Instruments, model 4500iL.

Initially, the KF-1ϕ algorithm was tested for different voltage conditions. In the uppermost graphic of Fig. 11, one has a sinusoidal 127 Vrms, 60 Hz input voltage with 10% of 3rd, 5th and 7th harmonic distortion. In the middle graphic, one has the estimated and filtered voltage v1. In the bottom, the estimated fundamental frequency f_1 can be seen.

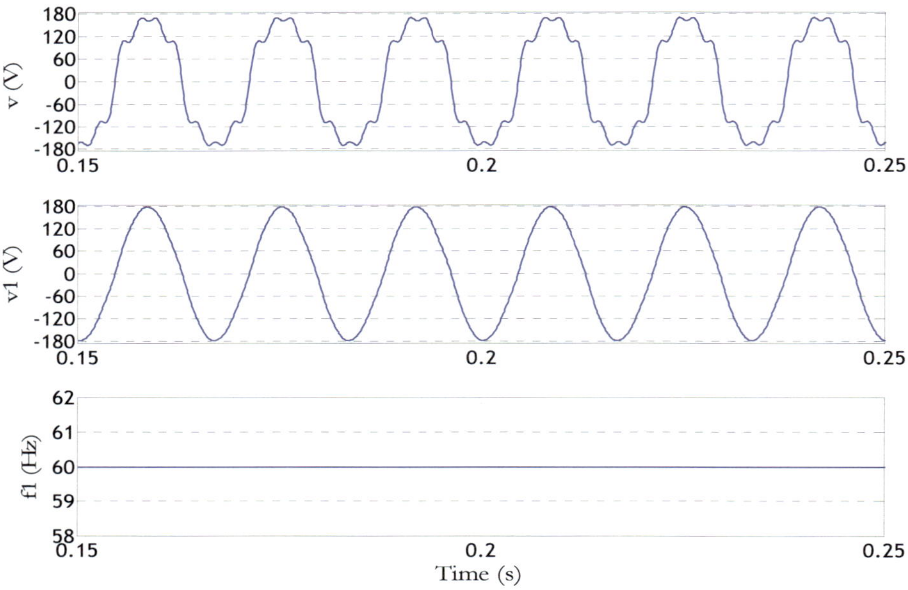

Fig. 11. KF-1ϕ: Top - input voltage (127 Vrms, 60 Hz), with 10% of 3rd, 5th and 7th harmonic distortion; middle - fundamental component and bottom - fundamental frequency estimated by the KF.

In Fig. 12, the input voltage suffers a voltage sag of 50%, but despite that, the algorithm manages to converge in about one cycle. In Fig. 13, the amplitude remains constant but there is an abrupt change in the fundamental frequency from 60 to 59 Hz. There is no change in the filtered voltage, but the frequency stabilizes in about 10 cycles.

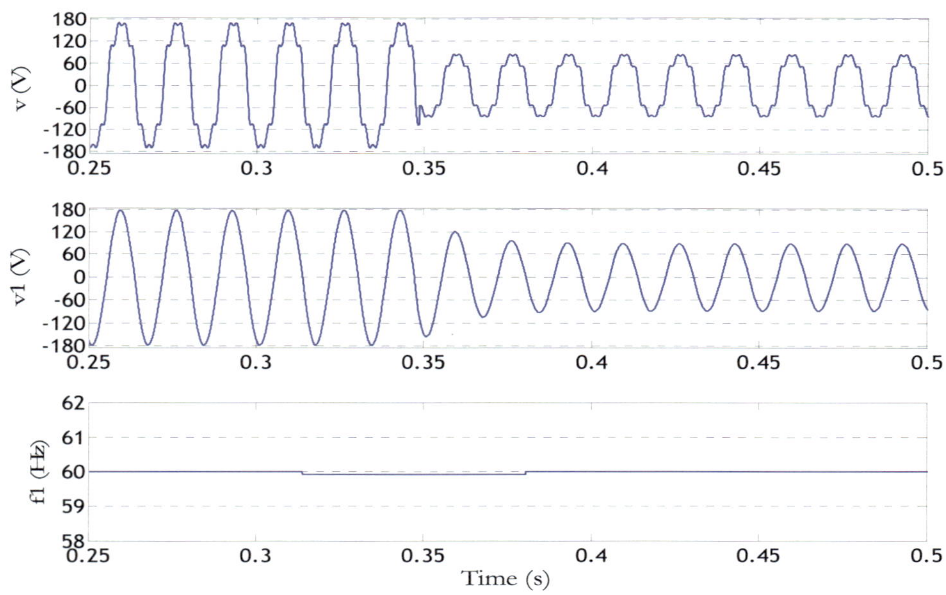

Fig. 12. KF-1ϕ: Performance of the KF output under 50% voltage sag.

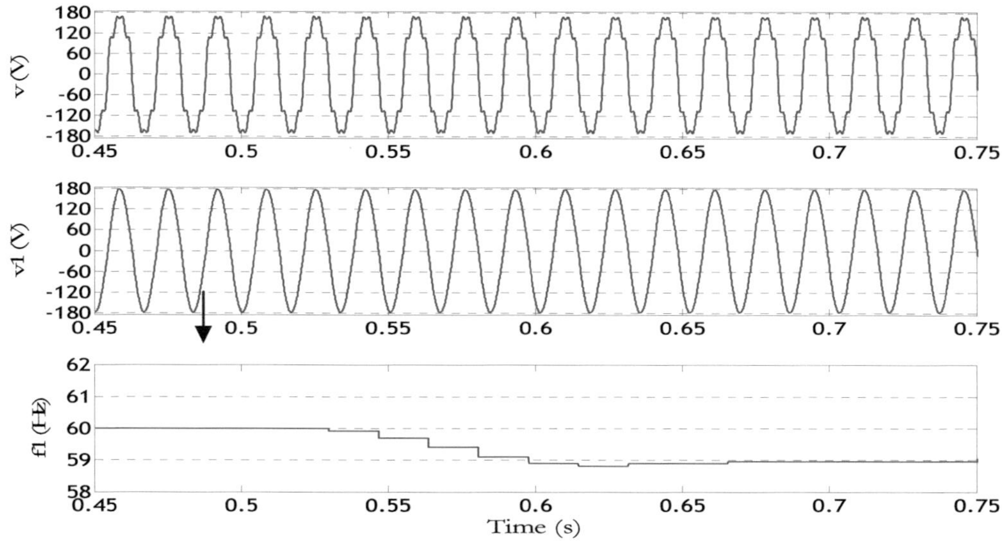

Fig. 13. KF-1ϕ: Performance of the KF output under an abrupt frequency deviation (from 60 to 59 Hz).

5.2.1 32-bits fixed point DSP

In order to demonstrate that the KF can be implemented even in fixed-point discrete systems, the three-phase model was implemented in a fixed-point 32-bit DSP, from Texas Instruments (TMS320F2812). The sampling frequency was set to 12kHz.

Fig. 14 shows the three-phase input voltages, which became distorted (20% of 3rd and 10% of 5th harmonics and each phase) after a 50% voltage sag. Considering just one of the phase voltages, Fig. 15 shows the convergence of the KF estimated fundamental component. Note that it converges in less than 2 fundamental cycles. Observe that the magnitudes in both figures are normalized by the digital to analog (DA) converter applied to reconstruct the KF output and the digitalized input voltages.

6. Conclusion

This chapter has discussed the main characteristics of the Kalman Filter and possible applications in the areas of power electronics and power systems. Since a great number of this applications are based on the identification of the fundamental voltage and/or current signals, it was demonstrated how the KF can be applied to estimate the fundamental component from a distorted signal (and/or an unbalanced set of signals in case of three-phase systems) like those present in real power system. The filter was designed by adopting a stochastic state-space model for the power system voltage, what is a very reasonable hypothesis. The performance of the zero-crossing detection method, based on the estimated voltage, was shown to be very effective as a way to calculate the fundamental frequency f_1, even in the presence of harmonic distortion.

Complex matrix calculations are not a concern here because their dimensions never exceed two, in the single-phase case (and four, in the three-phase case). It makes possible to do calculations elementwise. In the three-phase case, the algorithm also estimates the mean-

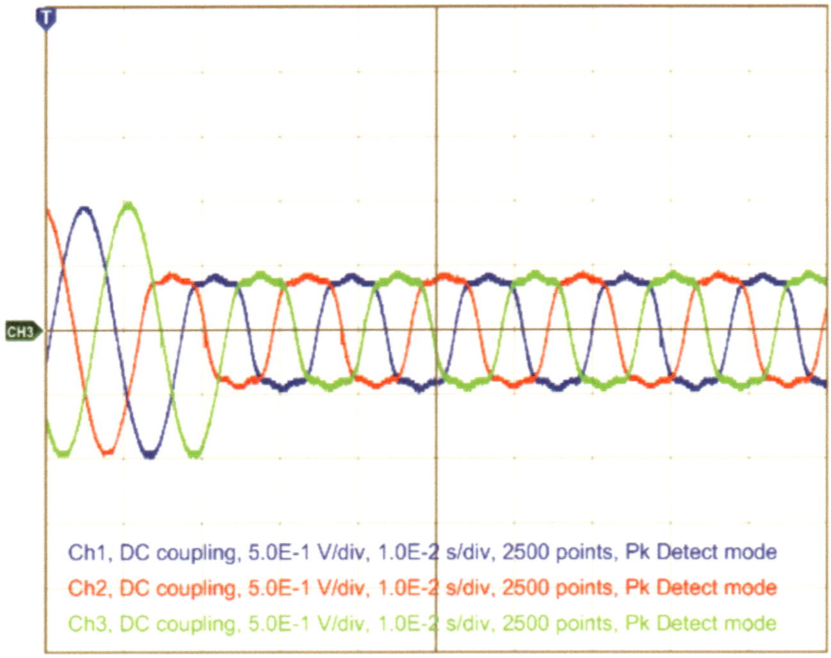

Fig. 14. KF-3ϕ: DSP input voltages considering a 50% voltage sag and 20% of 3rd and 10% of 5th harmonics and each phase.

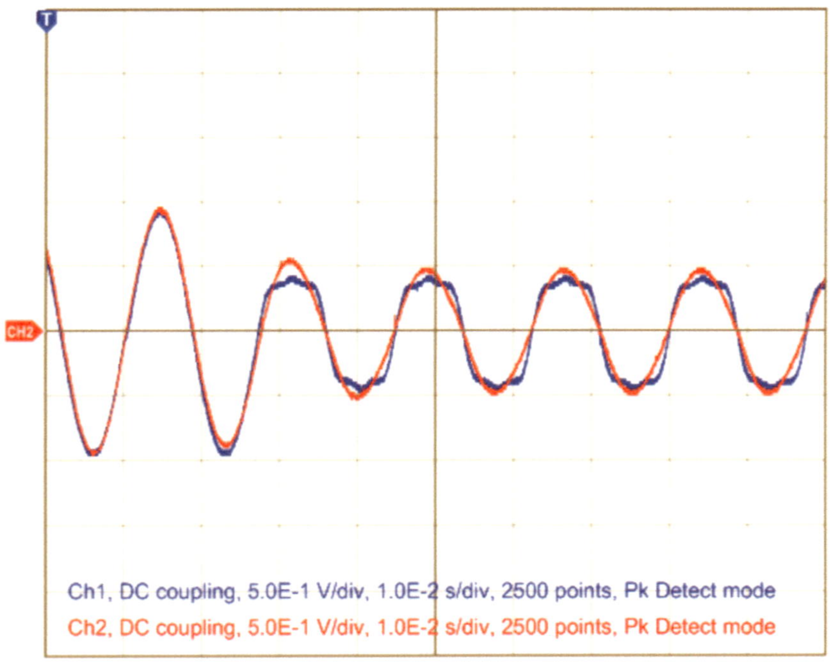

Fig. 15. KF-3ϕ: Fundamental component estimation after the 50% voltage sag, with corresponding voltage distortion (for one of the phases).

amplitude in the presence of unbalanced voltages, what could be used, in some cases, in place of a positive-sequence detector (Padua et al., 2005). It was also shown that, setting adequate values to ***H*** and ***G***, the performance of the three-phase could be better than the single-phase case.
Simulated and experimental results illustrate the suitable performance of the KF (single and three-phase models) in different conditions and tuning. So the proposed models are interesting alternatives for power systems and power electronics applications, even if real-time and fixed-point implementations are required.
Comparing with other synchronization algorithms, like those in (Kaura & Blasko, 1997; Zhan et al., 2001 ; McGrath et al., 2005 ; Cardoso et al, 2006; Mostata, 2007), as to say the PLL-based and the DFT-based, one can say that the proposed Kalman filter based algorithm is 1) so precise in steady-state as the others two; 2) as fast and sensible to voltage distortions as the PLL-based and 3) computationally simpler than other Kalman-based algorithms presented in literature.
It is important to point out that no matter how complex the detection algorithm is, there is always a compromise between precision (or in a wide sense, robustness) and rapidity of the response. The designer should thus know how to adjust ***H*** and ***G*** matrices in the most convenient way for the application in hand. Besides, the computational complexity can be a major concern, as in real-time analysis and control.
Considering future works, the author's intend to modify the three-phase KF in order to obtain the fundamental positive sequence components in the presence of phase-angle asymmetries, since in this case, equation (8) does not represent correctly such information.

7. References

Andria, G. & Salvatore, L. (1990). Inverter Drive Signal Processing Via DFT and EKF, *IEE Proceedings Electric Power Applications*, Vol. 137, No. 2, (March 1990), pages (111 119), ISSN 0143-7038.

Bollen, M. H. J. (2000). Understanding power quality problems: Voltage Sags And Interruptions. IEEE Press Series on Power Engineering, P. M. Anderson Series Editor , New York USA.

Bolognani, S.; Zigliotto, M. & Zordan, M. (2001). Extended-Range PMSM Sensorless Speed Drive Based on Stochastic Filtering, *IEEE Transactions on Power Electronics*, Vol. 16, No. 1, (January 2001), pages (110-117), ISSN 0885-8993.

Cardoso, R.; de Camargo, R. F.; Pinheiro, H. & Gründling, H. A. (2006). Kalman Filter Based Synchronisation Methods, *The 37th IEEE Power Electronics Specialists Conference PESC,* pp. 1-7, ISBN 0-7803-9716-9, June 2006, Jeju Korea.

Chien-Hung Huang; Chien-Hsing Lee; Kuang-Jung Shih; Yaw-Juen Wang (2008). Frequency Estimation of Distorted Power System Signals Using a Robust Algorithm, *IEEE Transactions on Power Delivery*, Vol. 23, No. 1, (January 2008), pages (41-51), ISSN 0885-8977.

Clements, M. P. & Hendry, D. F. (1998). Forecasting Economic Time Series, Cambridge University Press, ISBN 0521632420, United Kingdom.

Colón, D. & Pait, F. M. (2004). Geometry of Adaptive Control: Optimization and Geodesics, *International Journal of Adaptive Control and Signal Processing*, Vol. 18, No. 4, (May 2004), pages (381 - 392), ISSN 0890-6327.

Dash, P. K. & Chilukuri, M. V. (2004). Hybrid S-transform and Kalman Filtering Approach for Detection and Measurement of Short Duration Disturbances in Power Networks, *IEEE Transaction on Instrumentation and Measurement*, Vol. 53, No. 2, (April 2004), pages (588-596), ISSN 0018-9456.

Davis, M. H. A. & Vinter, R. B. (1985). *Stochastic Modelling and Control, Monographs on Statistics and Applied Probability 24*, Chapman and Hall, ISBN MR86f:93118, London/New York USA.

Farghal, S. A.; Kandil, M. S. & Elmitwally, A. (2002). Quantifying Electric Power Quality Via Fuzzy Modelling and Analytic Hierarchy Processing, *IEE Proceeding Generation, Transmission and Distribution*, Vol. 149, No. 1, (January 2002), pages (44-49), ISSN 1350-2360.

Ferrero, A. ; Peretto, L. & Sasdelli, R. (1998). Revenue metering in the presence of distortion and unbalance: myths and reality, Proceedings of the IEEE International Conference on Harmonics and Quality of Power, pp. 42-47, ISBN 0-7803-7671-4, Greece.

Girgis, A. A. & Brown, R. G. (1981). Application of Kalman Filtering in Computer Relaying, *IEEE Transactions on Power Apparatus and Systems*, Vol. PAS-100, No. 7, (July 1981), pages (3387-3397), ISSN 0018-9510.

Girgis, A. A. (1982). A New Kalman Filtering Based Digital Distance Relay, *IEEE Transactions on Power Apparatus and Systems*, Vol. PAS-101, No. 9, (September 1982), pages (3471-3480), ISSN 0018-9510.

Gonzalez, M.; Cardenas, V. & Alvarez, R. (2006). Detection of Sags, Swells, and Interruptions Using the Digital RMS Method and Kalman Filter with Fast Response, *The 32nd Conference of the IEEE Industrial Electronics Society IECON*, pp. 2249-2254, ISBN: 1-4244-0391-X, November 2006, Paris, France.

IEEE Trial-Use Standard Definitions for the Measurement of Electric Power Quantities Under Sinusoidal, Nonsinusoidal, Balanced or Unbalanced Conditions, *IEEE Standard 1459-2000*, (June, 2000), ISBN 0-7381-1963-6.

Kalman, R. E. (1960). A New Approach to Linear Filtering and Prediction Problems, Transaction of the ASME - Journal of Basic Engineering, 82 Seires D, (March 1960), pagues (35-45), ISSN 0021-9223.

Kaura, V. & Blasko, V. (1997). Operation of a Phase Locked Loop System under Distorted Utility Conditions, *IEEE Transaction on Industry Applications*, Vol. 33, No. 1, (January/February 1997), pages (58-63), ISSN 0093-9994.

Kwan, K. H.; So, P. L. & Chu, Y. C. (2005). Unified Power Quality Conditioner for Improving Power Quality using MVR with Kalman Filters, *The 7th International Power Engineering Conference IPEC*, vol. 2, pp. 980-985, ISBN 981-05-5702-7, December 2005, Singapore.

Li-Cheng Zai; DeMarco, C.L. & Lipo, T.A. (1992). An Extended Kalman Filter Approach to Rotor Time Constant Measurement in PWM Induction Motor Drives, *IEEE Transactions on Industry Applications*, Vol. 28 , No. 1, (January/February 1992), pages (96-104), ISSN: 0093-9994.

Marafão, F. P.; Deckmann, S. M. & Marafão, J. A. G. (2002). Power Factor Analysis under Nonsinusoidal and Unbalanced Systems, *The 10th International Conference on Harmonics and Quality of Power ICHQP*, pp. 266-271, ISBN 0-7803-7671-4, October 2002, Rio de Janeiro, Brazil.

Marafão, F. P. et al, (2008). Multiloop Controller and Reference generator for a Dynamic Voltage Restorer Implementarion, *Proceedings of the 13th IEEE International Conference on Harmonics and Quality of Power ICHQP*, October 2008, Australia.

McGrath, B. P.; Holmes, D. G.; & Galloway, J. (2005). Power Converter Line Synchronization Using a Discrete Fourier Transform (DFT) Based on a Variable Sample Rate, *IEEE Transactions on Power Electronics*, Vol. 20, No. 4, (July 2005), pages (877-844), ISSN 0885-8993.

Mir, M. & Mccleer, P. J. (1984). Simulation Methods for Optimum Performance Estimation of Analog and Computer Impedance Relays, *IEEE Transactions on Power Apparatus and Systems*, Vol. PAS-103, No 6, (June 1984), pages (1147-1154), ISSN 0018-9510.

Mohamed A.; Abu-El-Magd & Naresh K. S. (1981). Two New Algotihms for On-Line Modelling and Forecasting of the Load Demand of a Multinode Power System, *IEEE Transactions on Power Apparatus and Systems*, Vol. PAS-100, No. 7 (July 1981), pages (3246-3253), ISSN 0018-9510.

Moreira, A. C.; Deckmann, S. M.; Marafão, F. P.; Lima, E. G.; & Bini, M. A. (2005). Virtual Instrumentation Applied to the Implementation of IEEE STD 1459-2000 Power Definitions, *The IEEE 36th Power Electronics Specialists Conference PESC*, pp. 1712-1718, ISBN 0-7803-9033-4, June 2005, Recife Brazil.

Moreno, V. M.; Lopez, A. P. & Garcias, R. I. D. (2004). Reference Current Estimation under Distorted Line Voltage for Control of Shunt Active Power Filters, *IEEE Transactions on Power Electronics*, Vol. 19, No. 4, (July 2004), pages (988-994), ISSN: 0885-8993.

Moreno, V. M.; Liserre, M.; Pigazo, A. & Dell'Aquila, A. (2007). A Comparative Analysis of Real-Time Algorithms for Power Signal Decomposition in Multiple Synchronous Reference Frames, *IEEE Transactions on Power Electronics*, Vol. 22, No. 4, (July 2007), pages (1280-1289), ISSN 0885-8993.

Mostafa, M. A. (2003). Kalman Filtering Algorithm for Electric Power Quality Analysis: Harmonics and Voltage Sags Problems. *The IEEE Large Engineering Systems Conference on power Engineering LESCOPE*, pp. 110-119, ISBN 0-7803-7863-6, May 2003, Montreal, Canada.

Oppenheim, A. V. & Schafer, R. W. (1999). *Discrete-Time Signal Processing*. (2nd Edition), Prentice Hall, ISBN 013216292X, New Jersey, USA.

Pádua, M. S.; Deckmann, S. M. & Marafão, F. P. (2005). Frequency-Adjustable Positive Sequence Detector for Power Conditioning Applications, *IEEE 36th Power Electronics Specialists Conference*, pp. 1928-1934, ISBN 0-7803-9033-4, Recife, Brazil.

Pádua, M. S.; Deckmann, S. M.; Sperandio, G. S. ; Marafão, F. P. & Colón, D. (2007). Comparative Analysis of Synchronization Algorithmos based on PLL, RDFT and Kalman Filter, *Proceedings of the IEEE International Symposium on Industrial Electronics ISIE*, June 2007, Vigo, Spain.

Pádua, M. S.; Deckmann, S. M.; Marafão, F. P. & Colón, D. (2007a). Simplified Models of Kalman Filter for Fundamental Frequency, Amplitude and Phase Angle Detection, *Proceedings of the Brazilian Power Electronics Conference (COBEP)*, Blumenau Brazil.

Papoulis, A. (1991). Probability, Random Variables, and Stochastic Processes, MacGraw-Hill Series in Electrical Engineering, Comunnication and signal processing, Third Edition, MacGraw-Hill Companies, ISBN 0070484771, USA.

Park, J. H. ; Park, Y. M. & Lee, K. Y. (1991). Composite Modeling for Adaptive Short-Term Load Forecasting, *IEEE Transactions on Power Systems*, Vol. 6. No. 2, (May 1991), pages (450-457), ISSN 1558-0679.

Peng. F. Z. (2001). Harmonic Sources and Filtering Approaches. *IEEE Industry application Magazine*. Vol. 7, No. 4, (July/August 2001), pages (18-25), ISSN 1077-2618.

Pietrzak-David, M.; de Fornel, B.; Lima, A. M. N. & Jelassi, K. (1992). Digital Control of an Induction Motor Drive by a Stochastic Estimator and Airgap Magnetic Flux Feedback Loop, *IEEE Transactions on Power Electronics*, Vol. 7 No. 2, (April 1992), pages (393 - 403), ISSN 0885-8993.

Rosendo, J. A.; Bachiller, A. & Gomez, A. (2007). Application of Self-Tuned Kalman Filters to Control of Active Power Filters, *The IEEE Power Tech*, pp. 1262-1265, ISBN: 978-1-4244-2189-3, July 2007, Lausanne Switzerland.

Sachdev, M. S.; Wood, H. C. & Johnson, N. G. (1985). Kalman Filtering Applied to Power System Measurements for Relaying, *IEEE Transactions on Power Apparatus and Systems*, Vol. PAS-104, No. 12, pages (3565-3573), ISSN 0018-9510.

Satry, S. & Bodson, M. (1989). *Adaptive Control: Stability, Convergence, and Robustness*, Prentice-Hall, ISBN 0-13-004326-5, USA.

Song, K. B.; Ha, S. K.; Park, J. W.; Kweon, D. J. & Kim, K. H. (2006). Hybrid Load Forecasting Method With Analysis of Temperature Sensitivities, *IEEE Transactions on Power Systems*, Vol. 21, No. 2, (May 2006), pegas (869-876), ISSN 1558-0679.

Styvaktakis, E.; Bollen, M. H. J. & Gu, I. Y. H. (2002). Expert System for Classification and Analysis of Power System Events, *IEEE Transactions on Power Delivery*, Vol. 17, No. 2, (April 2002), pages (423 - 428), ISSN 0885-8977.

Zhan, C.; Fitzer, C.; Ramachandaramurthy, V. K.; Arulampalam, A.; Barnes, M. & Jenkins, N. (2001). Software Phase-Locked Loop Applied to Dynamic Voltage Restorer (DVR), *IEEE Power Engineering Society Winter Meeting*, pp. 1033-1038, ISBN: 0-7803-6672-7, January/February 2001, Columbus USA.

Yeh, H. G. (1990). Real-Time Implementation of a Narrow-Band Kalman Filter With a Floating-Point Processor DSP32, *IEEE Transactions on Industrial Electronics*, Vol. 37, No. 1, (February 1990), pages (13-18), ISSN 0278-0046.

Wade, S.; Dunnigan, M. W. & Williams, B. W. (1997). Modeling and simulation of induction machine vector control with rotor resistance identification, *IEEE Transactions on Power Electronics*, Vol. 12, No. 3, (May 1997), pages (495-506), ISSN 0885-8993.

Wiltshire, R. A.; Ledwich, G. & O'Shea, P. (2007). A Kalman Filtering Approach to Rapidly Detecting Modal Changes in Power Systems, *IEEE Transactions on Power Systems*, Vol. 22, No. 4, (November 2007), pages (1698- 1706), ISSN 1558-0679.

Wong, W. S. & Yau, S. S. T. (1998), The Estimation Algebra of Nonlinear Filtering Systems, *In : Mathematical Control Theory*, pages 33-65, Springer, ISBN 0387983171, USA.

Woxd, H. C.; Johnson, N. G. & Sachdev, M. S. (1985). Kalman Filtering Applied to Power System Measurements Relaying, *IEEE Transactions on Power Apparatus and Systems*, Vol. PAS-104, No. 12, (December 1985), pages (3565-3573), ISSN 0018-9510.

18

Application of the Kalman Filters in the Self-Commissioning High-Performance Drive System with an Elastic Joint

Krzysztof Szabat and Teresa Orlowska-Kowalska
Wroclaw University of Technology
Poland

1. Introduction

Torsional vibrations limit the performance of many industrial drives. They decrease the system reliability, product quality in some specific cases they can even lead to instability of the whole control structure. The problem of damping of torsional vibrations originates from the rolling-mill drive, where large inertias of the motor and load parts with a long shaft create an elastic system (Hori et al., 1999), (Szabat & Orlowska-Kowalska 2007), (Pittner & Simaan, 2008). Similar problems exist in paper and textile industry, where the electromagnetic torque goes through complex mechanical parts of the drive (Valenzuela et al., 2005). The damping ability of the system is also a critical issue in conveyer and cage-host drives (Hace et al., 2006). Originally the elastic system has been recognized in high-power applications. However, due to the progress in power electronic and microprocessor systems, which allow controlling the electromagnetic torque almost without delay, the torsional vibrations appear in many medium and small power applications. Today they are acknowledged in servo-drives, throttle drives, robot arm drives including space applications, and others (Hamamoto et al., 2003), (O'Sullivan et al., 2007), (Shen & Tsai, 2006), (Katsura & Ohnishi,, 2005) and (Vasak et al., 2007).

Since the classical PI controller is not effective in the two-mass drive system different control concepts have been developed. As has been shown in (Zhang & Furusho, 2000), the application of the PID controller ensures effective suppression of the torsional vibrations. This approach is easy to implement and designated for the system with an accurate speed sensor. Torsional vibrations can be damped effectively by inserting additional feedback from selected state variable(s) of the two-mass system. The survey of those structures is presented in (Szabat & Orlowska-Kowalska 2007) and (Nordin & Gutman, 2002). The structure with one additional feedback can damp the torsional vibration effectively, yet the settling time of the system cannot be set freely. The more advanced control concept relies on the inserting of all states of the control structure, which allows the free location of the system closed-loop poles. The cascade control structure with two additional feedbacks or the structure with the state controller are illustrated in (O'Sullivan et al., 2007) and (Szabat & Orlowska-Kowalska, 2008).

Also the nonlinear and adaptive control have been proposed to control the two-mass system in order to eliminate the effect of the parameter uncertainties and disturbances e.g. in papers

(Erbatur et al., 1999) and (Erenturk, 2008) the sliding mode control have been applied. In all cases the authors claim that the robustness to the parameter variation is one of the major advantages of this type of control. Different way to eliminate the effect of the disturbances is to apply the adaptive control. The application of the Kalman filter in the two-mass drive structure is presented in (Szabat & Orlowska-Kowalska, 2008) and (Hirovonen et al., 2006). The damping of the torsional vibration using adaptive neuro-fuzzy controller has been presented in (Wang & Frayman, 2002), (Szabat & Orlowska-Kowalska, 2008b). In all cases the authors report an improved performance of the controlled drives.

Despite the advantages of the nonlinear and adaptive control, about 95% of all controllers used in the industry rely on the PI concept (Äström & Hägglund, 2001). It results from the following reasons. To begin with, the classical PI concept is well-known by industrial engineers. The tuning methodologies and stability analysis methods are well established. Therefore, the PI-control structure with two additional feedbacks from the shaft torque and difference between the motor and the load speed is selected in this paper to work in the real system (Szabat & Orlowska-Kowalska, 2008). It should be noted that this structure ensures the free location of the system closed-loop poles, which means that the responses of the system can be shaped in the linear range of the system work.

During the design process of the above-mentioned structure the acknowledgment of the value of the system parameters is necessary. However, in industrial application only the mechanical parameters of the motor calculated according to the nominal data are known. The parameters of the shaft and load machine are uncertain or even unknown in many cases. Therefore, the special identification methods have been developed in order to identify the plant parameters (Schutte et al., 1997), (Wertz et al., 1999), (Eker & Vular, 2003), (Schröder et al., 2001) and (Angerer et al., 2004). They can be divided into two different groups. The basic assumption of all methods dedicated to industry is that only the signals of the electromagnetic torque and motor speed are accessible for identification procedure.

The first group encompasses the off-line identification methods. In this methodology the plant is stimulated by specific types of signals and the response of object is saved. Then on the basis of those signals the plant parameters are calculated. This first framework is presented in (Schutte et al., 1997) and (Wertz et al., 1999). In the paper (Schutte et al., 1997), the plant has been stimulated by step signal of the electromagnetic torque. Then from the response (driving motor speed) the oscillation part of the speed has been extracted. Later this part has been transformed into a frequency domain and the resonant frequency of the system has been identified. From the physical relationship of the plant the stiffness coefficient of the plant and the inertia of the load machine have been calculated. In the following work (Wertz et al., 1999) the excitation signal has been changed to the PRBS so as to extracting the additional information from frequency domain, namely the anti-resonant frequency of the plant. On the basis on the values of the antiresonant and resonant frequency all the main parameters of the plant can be calculated (inertia of the motor and load machines, stiffness coefficient). Additionally, by adjusting the frequency characteristics of the model to the plant the internal damping coefficient of the shaft can be determined. The next framework is based on the parametric identification method (Wertz et al., 1999) and (Eker & Vular, 2003). On the basis of the responses of the object, the parameters of the linear model of the plant are selected in order to minimise the difference between the real system and the model outputs. As the advantage of this method, the authors report (Wertz et al., 1999) the possibility of the identification of the friction in the system. However, they claim the problems with the determination of the order of the model which is the main disadvantage of this method. The application of this method to identification of the multi-mass system is presented in (Eker & Vular, 2003). The authors report good accuracy of the estimated parameters.

The second group includes so-called the on-line identification methods, in which special observers are applied to calculate the plants parameters in the real time. In (Szabat & Orlowska-Kowalska, 2008) the mechanical parameters are estimated on-line with the help of the Kalman filter. The obtained results show the advantages of the proposed estimation technique. A different approach is presented in (Schröder et al., 2001). The so-called intelligent observers have been used to identify the nonlinear parts of the system. Nevertheless, the parameters of the linear parts have to be known exactly. The extension of the mentioned works has been presented in (Angerer et al., 2004). The assumed parameter of the linear parts can be incorrect (up to 20% of errors is acceptable). Additionally the existence of the some delay elements in the nonlinear part is acceptable.

The main goal of the paper is to present the application of the Kalman filters in the self-commissioning high-performance drive system with an elastic joint. Two main topic are discussed in the paper. Firstly the issues related to estimation of the mechanical parameters of the drives are discussed. The nonlinear extended Kalman filter is applied for this purpose. Then on the basis of the obtained parameters the advanced control structures with two additional feedbacks is designed. In order to provide the information of the non-measurable state variables (shaft torque, load speed) the linear Kalman filter is applied. The drive system is tested under different conditions. The theoretical considerations and simulation works are supported by the experimental results.

2. The mathematical model of the two-mass system and the control structure

In the paper the commonly-used model of the drive system with the resilient coupling is considered. The system is described by the following state equation (in per unit system) (Szabat & Orlowska-Kowalska, 2007):

$$\frac{d}{dt}\begin{bmatrix}\omega_1(t)\\ \omega_2(t)\\ m_s(t)\end{bmatrix}=\begin{bmatrix}0 & 0 & \frac{-1}{T_1}\\ 0 & 0 & \frac{1}{T_2}\\ \frac{1}{T_c} & \frac{-1}{T_c} & 0\end{bmatrix}\begin{bmatrix}\omega_1(t)\\ \omega_2(t)\\ m_s(t)\end{bmatrix}+\begin{bmatrix}\frac{1}{T_1}\\ 0\\ 0\end{bmatrix}\left[m_e\right]+\begin{bmatrix}0\\ \frac{-1}{T_2}\\ 0\end{bmatrix}\left[m_L\right] \tag{1}$$

where: ω_1 - motor speed, ω_2 - load speed, m_e - motor torque, m_s - shaft (torsional) torque, m_L - disturbance torque, T_1- mechanical time constant of the motor, T_2 - mechanical time constant of the load machine, T_c - stiffness time constant. The nominal values are T_1=T_2=203ms and T_c=2.6ms.

A typical electrical drive system is composed of a power converter-fed motor coupled to a mechanical system, a microprocessor-based controllers, current, rotor speed and/or position sensors used as feedback signals. Typically, a cascade speed control structure containing two major control loops is used, as presented in Fig 1.

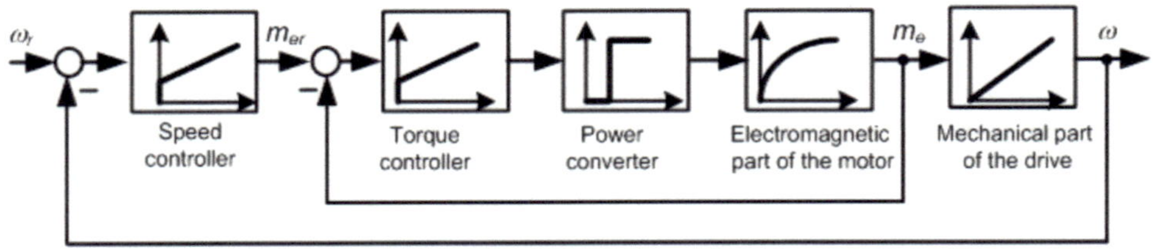

Fig. 1. The classical cascade control structure

The inner control loop performs the motor torque regulation and consists of the power converter, electromagnetic part of the motor, current sensor and respective current or torque controller. As this control loop is designed to provide sufficiently fast torque control, it can be approximated by an equivalent first order term. If the suitable torque control is ensured, the driven machine could be an AC or DC motor, with no difference in the outer speed control loop. The outer loop consists of the mechanical part of the motor, speed sensor, speed controller, and is cascaded to the inner loop. It provides speed control according to the reference value. The classical structure (without additional feedbacks) works well only for specific inertia ratio (T_2/T_1) of the two-mass system. When the mechanical time constant of the load machine is low, transients of the system are not proper. To improve the dynamical characteristics of the drive, a modification of the cascade structure is necessary. It is obtained by inserting to the control structure the additional feedbacks from selected state variables (Szabat & Orlowska-Kowalska, 2007) and (Szabat & Orlowska-Kowalska, 2008). The pattern of the speed control structure for the two-mass system with a simplified inner control loop and additional feedbacks from the shaft torque and the difference between the motor and load speed is presented in Fig 2.

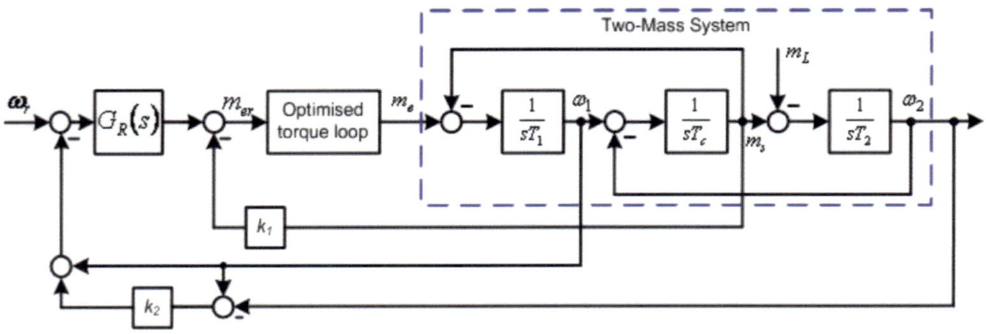

Fig. 2. Schematic diagram of the control structure with additional feedbacks

The closed-loop transfer functions from reference input to the motor and load speed are given by the following equations (with the assumption that the optimized transfer function of the electromagnetic torque control loop equals 1):

$$G_{p\omega_1}(s)=\frac{\Delta\omega_1(s)}{\Delta\omega_r(s)}=\frac{G_r\left(s^2T_2T_c+1\right)}{s^3T_1T_2T_c+s^2T_2T_cG_r\left(1+k_2\right)+s\left(T_1+T_2\left(1+k_1\right)\right)+G_r} \tag{2}$$

$$G_{p\omega_2}(s)=\frac{\Delta\omega_2(s)}{\Delta\omega_r(s)}=\frac{G_r}{s^3T_1T_2T_c+s^2T_2T_cG_r(1+k_2)+s(T_1+T_2(1+k_1))+G_r} \tag{3}$$

where:

$$G_r = K_p + {K_I}/{s} \tag{4}$$

is the transfer function of the controller.
The parameters of the control structures are set using the pole-placement method, according to the following equations (Szabat & Orlowska-Kowalska, 2008):

$$K_I = \omega_0^4 T_1 T_2 T_c \tag{5}$$

$$K_P = 4\xi_r \omega_0^3 T_1 T_2 T_c \tag{6}$$

$$k_2 = \left(\omega_0^2 T_2 T_c\right)^{-1} - 1 \tag{7}$$

$$k_1 = T_1 T_2^{-1}\left(4\xi_r^2 - k_2\right)\left(1 + k_2\right)^{-1} - 1 \tag{8}$$

where: ξ_r - required damping coefficient, ω_0- required resonant frequency of the system.
The cascade control structure with additional feedbacks requires information of the values of the two-mass system parameters and signals from the hard measurable state variables, i.e. shaft torque and load speed. Therefore, the application of state estimators like the state observers or Kalman Filters is advisable.

3. Mathematical model of the Kalman filters

3.1 Linear Kalman Filter (LKF)

In the case of the drive system with elastic joint, the state vector of the drive system (1) is extended by the load torque, to obtain the estimation of all mechanical state variables of the system:

$$\mathbf{x_R} = [\omega_1 \quad \omega_2 \quad m_S \quad m_L]^T \tag{9}$$

The motor electromagnetic torque and speed are used as input and output variables of the LKF, respectively:

$$\mathbf{u} = m_e \quad \mathbf{y_R} = \omega_1 \tag{10}$$

The mechanical part of the drive system (1) can be described in the following form, where according to the KF theory, the system is disturbed by Gaussian white noises, which represent process and measurement errors (**w**(t), **v**(t)):

$$\frac{d}{dt}\mathbf{x_R}(t) = \mathbf{A_R}\mathbf{x_R}(t) + \mathbf{B_R}\,\mathbf{u}(t) + \mathbf{w}(t) = \mathbf{f_R}(\mathbf{x_R}(t), \mathbf{u}(t)) + \mathbf{w}(t) \tag{11a}$$

$$\mathbf{y_R}(t) = \mathbf{C_R}\mathbf{x_R}(t) + \mathbf{v}(t) \tag{11b}$$

Thus the state, control and output matrices of this extended LKF are following:

$$\mathbf{A_R} = \begin{bmatrix} 0 & 0 & -\frac{1}{T_1} & 0 \\ 0 & 0 & \frac{1}{T_2} & -\frac{1}{T_2} \\ \frac{1}{T_c} & -\frac{1}{T_c} & 0 & 0 \\ 0 & 0 & 0 & 0 \end{bmatrix} \mathbf{B_R} = \begin{bmatrix} \frac{1}{T_1} \\ 0 \\ 0 \\ 0 \end{bmatrix} \mathbf{C_R} = \begin{bmatrix} 1 \\ 0 \\ 0 \\ 0 \end{bmatrix}^T \tag{12}$$

After discretisation of Eq. (11) with the sampling step T_p, the state estimation using LKF algorithm is calculated by Eq. (13):

$$\hat{\mathbf{x}}_\mathbf{R}(k+1/k+1) = \hat{\mathbf{x}}_\mathbf{R}(k+1/k) + \mathbf{K}(k+1)[\mathbf{y}_\mathbf{R}(k+1) - \mathbf{C}_\mathbf{R}(k+1)\hat{\mathbf{x}}_\mathbf{R}(k+1/k)] \tag{13}$$

where the gain matrix **K** is obtained by the following numerical procedure:

$$\mathbf{P}(k+1/k) = A_\mathbf{R}(k)\mathbf{P}(k)A_\mathbf{R}^\mathbf{T}(k) + \mathbf{Q}(k) \tag{14}$$

$$\mathbf{K}(k+1) = \mathbf{P}(k+1/k)\mathbf{C}_\mathbf{R}^\mathbf{T}(k+1)[\mathbf{C}_\mathbf{R}(k+1)\mathbf{P}(k+1/k)\mathbf{C}_\mathbf{R}^\mathbf{T}(k+1) + \mathbf{R}(k)]^{-1} \tag{15}$$

$$\mathbf{P}(k+1/k+1) = [\mathbf{I} - \mathbf{K}(k+1)\mathbf{C}_\mathbf{R}(k+1)]\mathbf{P}(k+1/k) \tag{16}$$

with state and measurement covariance matrices **Q** and **R**.The estimation accuracy of the Kalman Filter strictly depends on proper setting of the covariance matrix **Q** and **R** elements. Usually to solve this problem the trial and error tuning procedure is applied. However, this approach can not guarantee the best selection of the covariance matrices. In this work the covariance matrices **Q** and **R** were determined using the genetic algorithm (GA) with the following cost function:

$$F = \min\left\{\sum_1^n(|m_s - m_{se}|)\sum_1^n(|\omega_2 - \omega_{2e}|)\sum_1^n(|m_L - m_{Le}|)\right\} \tag{17}$$

where m_{se}, ω_{2e}, m_{Le} – denote the estimated state variables

3.2 Non-linear Kalman Filter (NKF)

In the presence of the unknown parameters (T_2 and T_c), there is a need to extend the two-mass system state vector (1) with the additional elements $1/T_2$ and $1/T_c$:

$$\mathbf{x_R}(t) = \begin{bmatrix} \omega_1(t) & \omega_2(t) & m_s(t) & \frac{1}{T_2}(t) & \frac{1}{T_c}(t) \end{bmatrix}^T \tag{18}$$

where T_2 and T_c denotes the time constant of the load side inertia and the stiffness, respectively. The extended, nonlinear state and output equations can be written in the following form:

$$\mathbf{A}_R\left(\frac{1}{T_2}(t),\frac{1}{T_c}(t)\right)=\begin{bmatrix} 0 & 0 & \frac{-1}{T_1} & 0 & 0 \\ 0 & 0 & \frac{1}{T_2(t)} & 0 & 0 \\ \frac{1}{T_c(t)} & \frac{-1}{T_c(t)} & 0 & 0 & 0 \\ 0 & 0 & 0 & 0 & 0 \\ 0 & 0 & 0 & 0 & 0 \end{bmatrix} \quad \mathbf{B}_R=\begin{bmatrix} \frac{1}{T_1} \\ 0 \\ 0 \\ 0 \\ 0 \end{bmatrix} \quad \mathbf{C}_R=\begin{bmatrix} 1 \\ 0 \\ 0 \\ 0 \\ 0 \end{bmatrix}^T \tag{19}$$

The matrix $\mathbf{A}_R$ depends on the changeable parameters T_2 and T_c . It means that in every calculation step this matrix must be updated due to the estimated value of those parameters, which means that the linearized state equation (3) must be updated in each calculation step. The input and the output vectors of the Kalman filter are electromagnetic torque and motor speed, respectively. After the discretization of (11) the state estimate is calculated using (13). The gain matrix **K** is obtained by the following numerical procedure. First, the state vector predictor is calculated:

$$\mathbf{P}(k+1/k)=\mathbf{F}_\mathbf{R}(k)\mathbf{P}(k)\mathbf{F}_\mathbf{R}^\mathbf{T}(k)+\mathbf{Q}(k) \tag{20}$$

where:

$$\mathbf{F}_\mathbf{R}(k)=\left.\frac{\partial \mathbf{f}_\mathbf{R}\left(\mathbf{x}_\mathbf{R}(k/k),\mathbf{u}(k),k\right)}{\partial x_\mathbf{P}(k/k)}\right|_{\mathbf{x}_\mathbf{R}=\hat{\mathbf{x}}_\mathbf{R}(k/k)} \tag{20}$$

$\mathbf{F}_R$ is the state matrix of the system (3) after its linearization in the actual operating point. It must be updated in every calculation step:

$$\mathbf{F}_\mathbf{R}=\begin{bmatrix} 1 & 0 & \frac{-T_p}{T_1} & 0 & 0 \\ 0 & 1 & \frac{T_p}{T_2(k)} & T_p m_s(k) & 0 \\ \frac{T_p}{T_c(k)} & \frac{-T_p}{T_c(k)} & 1 & 0 & T_p[\omega_1(k)-\omega_2(k)] \\ 0 & 0 & 0 & 1 & 0 \\ 0 & 0 & 0 & 0 & 1 \end{bmatrix} \tag{22}$$

The NKF gain matrix and the covariance matrix of the state estimation error are calculated using (15) and (16).
In this paper covariance matrix elements are set by means of the genetic algorithm with the following cost function:

$$F=\min\left\{\left(\sum_1^n |T_s-T_{se}|\right)*\left(\sum_1^n |T_c-T_{ce}|\right)\right\} \tag{23}$$

where T_{se} and T_{2e} denote the estimated value of the system parameters. The cost function defined in this way ensures the optimal setting of covariance matrices **Q** and **R** for unknown drive parameters.

4. Simulation results

4.1 Identification case (NKF)

In the following section the properties of the proposed identification procedure is investigated. The drive system is working under reverse condition. The electromagnetic torque and the motor speed, used as the input and output vectors of NEKF, are disturbed with white noises. The parameters of the covariance matrices are set with the GA in order to ensure the shortest identification time. The resulting value of the covariance matrices are as follows **R**=10, diag(**Q**)=[12 2 5 300 10e5] The transients of the electromagnetic torque and motor speed during the system operation drive are presented in Fig.3.

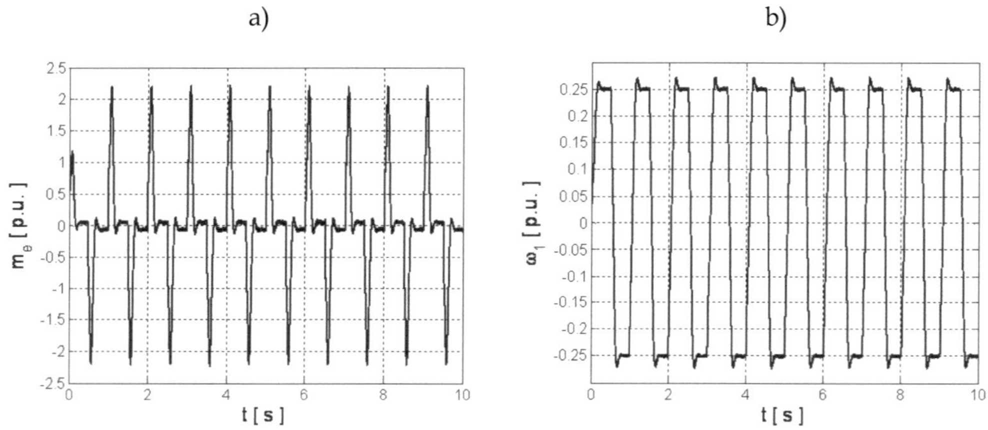

Fig. 3. Transients of the input signal of the Kalman Filter: the electromagnetic torque (a) and the motor speed (b)

The drive system starts with misidentified time constant of the load machine T_2=406ms and the stiffness time constant T_c=5.2ms (Fig. 4a,b). During the start-up the estimated value of the T_2 reaches its real value. The value of T_c equals 3.2ms after the first reversal and reaches its real value after 3s. Some small disturbances are visible during every reversal in transients of both estimated parameters.

Then the smaller initial values of the system parameters are tested (T_2=101.5ms, T_c=1.3ms). The input signals of the Kalman filter are presented in Fig. 4. The transients of the estimated parameters are presented in Fig. 4c,d. The values of the covariance matrices **Q** and **R** are the same as in the previous case (i.e. they are not optimal). During the start-up the time constant of the load machine reaches the value of about 140ms, then after the first reversal it is about 215ms and then slowly converges to its real value. After 3s the estimate of T_2 approaches its real value. The estimated value of the T_c reaches its real value also after 3 s. However, it should be emphasized that the convergence is slower in this case; it can be accelerated by increasing the values of the covariance matrix **Q** parameters, which will be demonstrated under experimental study.

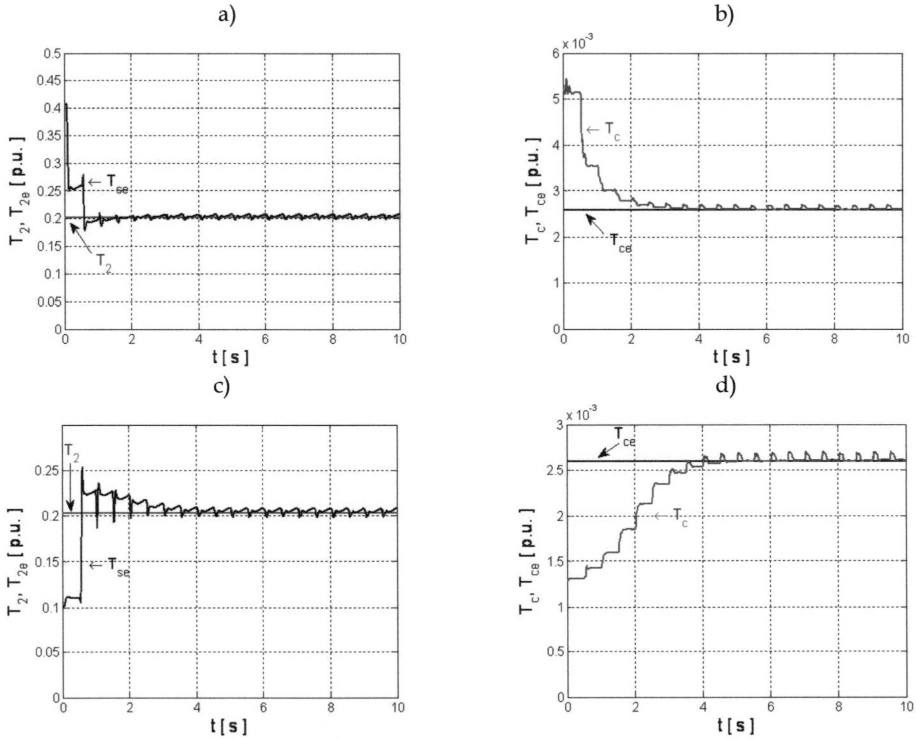

Fig. 4. Transients of the estimated time constant: of the load machine (a,c) and the shaft (b,d) in the case of the bigger (a,b) and smaller (c,d) initial values of those parameters

3.2 Open and closed-loop control structure (LKF)

In the following section the issues related to the application of the LKF are presented. First, the quality of the estimated states is investigated. The electromagnetic torque and the motor speed are taken from the closed-loop control structure. Then in order to emulate the real conditions these signals are disturbed with noises which imitates the measurement sensor quality (5% for the electromagnetic torque and 0.5% for the motor speed). Additionally the values of the parameters used in the Kalman filter are decreased by 3% in order to account for the identification errors. The transients of the input signal of the LKF are presented in Fig. 5.

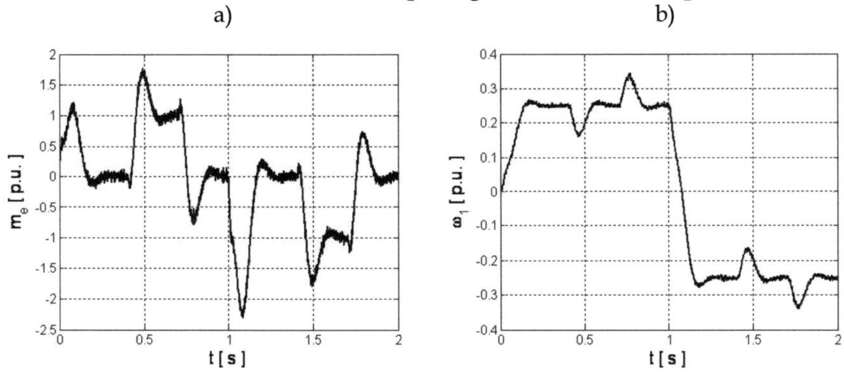

Fig. 5. Transients of the input signal of the Kalman Filter: the electromagnetic torque (a) and the motor speed (b)

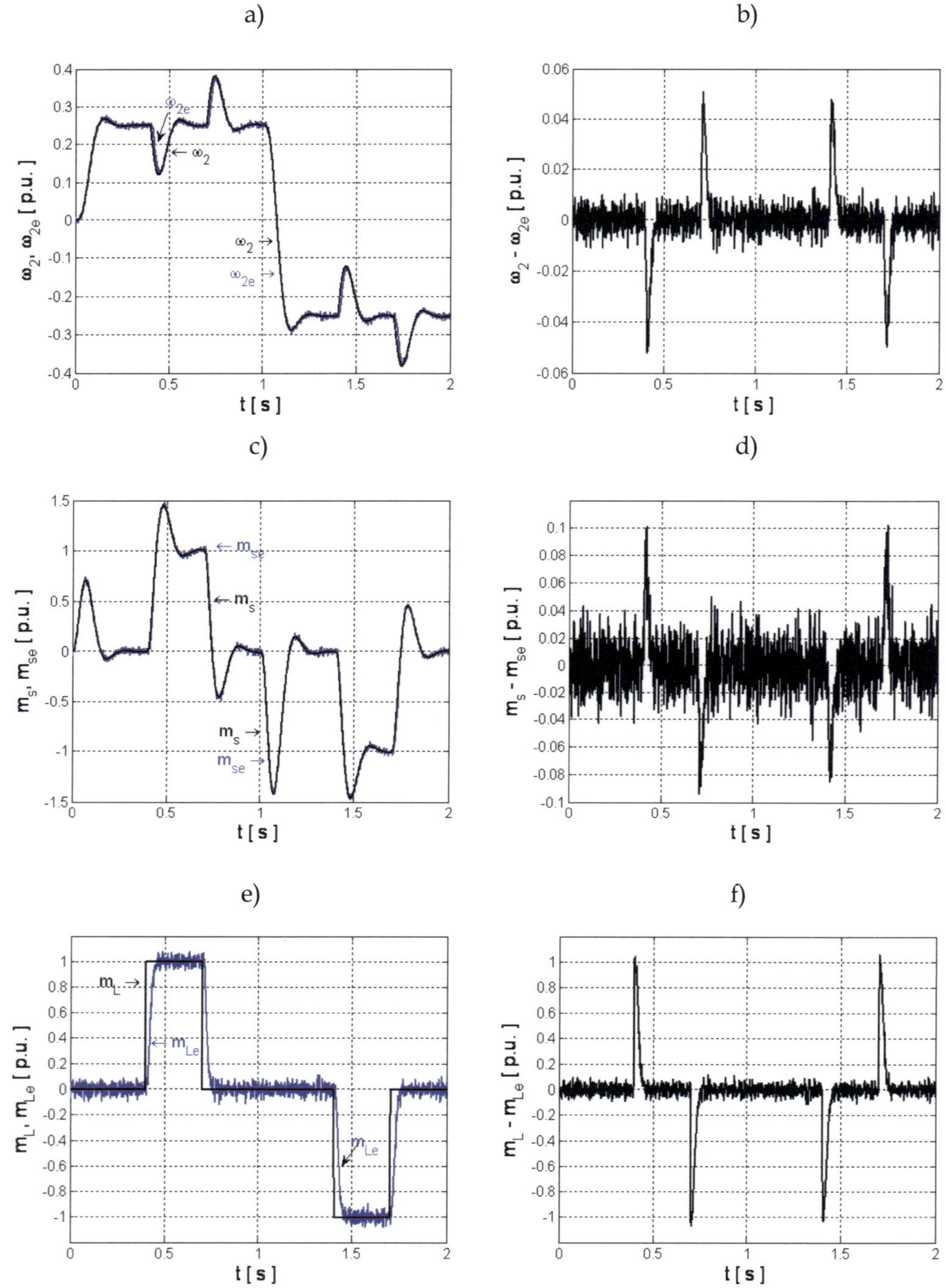

Fig. 6. Transients of the real and estimated variables and their estimation errors: load speed (a,b), shaft torque (c,d) and load torque (e,f) for the closed-lop system with measured and estimated variables

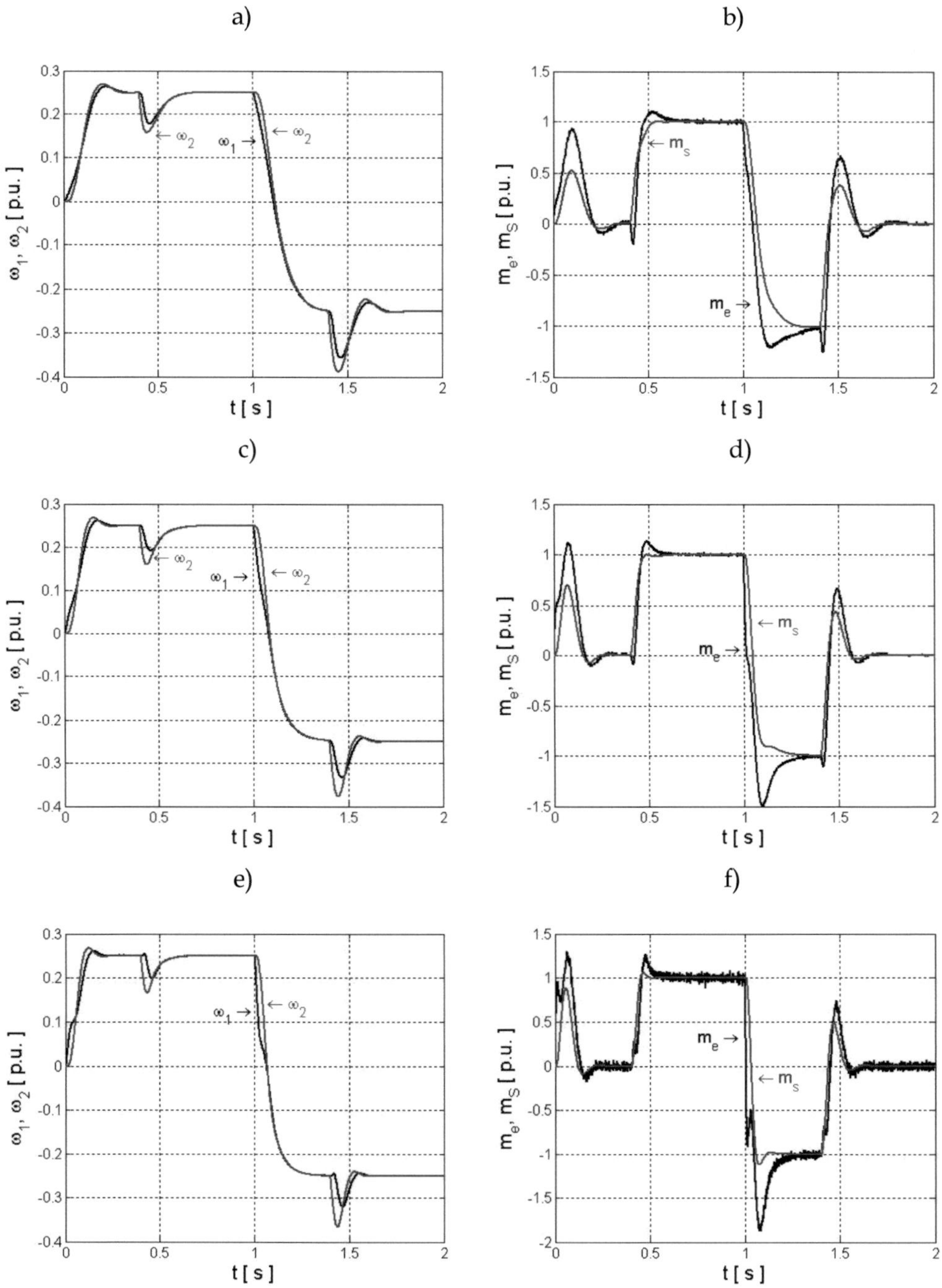

Fig. 7. Transients of the motor and the load speeds (a,c,e) and the electromagnetic and the shaft torques (b,d,f) in the control structure working with the Kalman filter for ξ_r=0.7 and ω_0=30s^{-1} (a,b), ω_0=40s^{-1} (c,d) i ω_0=50 s^{-1} (e,f)

The LKF is working in the open-loop structures. The real and estimated system states as well as the estimation errors are presented in Fig. 6.

The LKF works properly. The reconstructed values of the states cover the real ones with small errors. The biggest estimation errors exist in all system state variables in the case of the rapid changing of the load torque. The faster covariance between the real and estimated parameters can be obtained by increasing the values of the covariance matrices. However, at the same time the noise level during the steady-stay condition will increase.

Next the closed-loop control structure (Fig. 8) working with the Kalman filter has been tested. The additional signals from the shaft torque and the load speed are taken from the estimator. The transients of the system for assumed values of the control structure parameters ξ_r=0.7 and ω_0=30s^{-1}(a,b), ω_0=40s^{-1}(a,b), ω_0=50s^{-1}(a,b) are presented in Fig. 7.

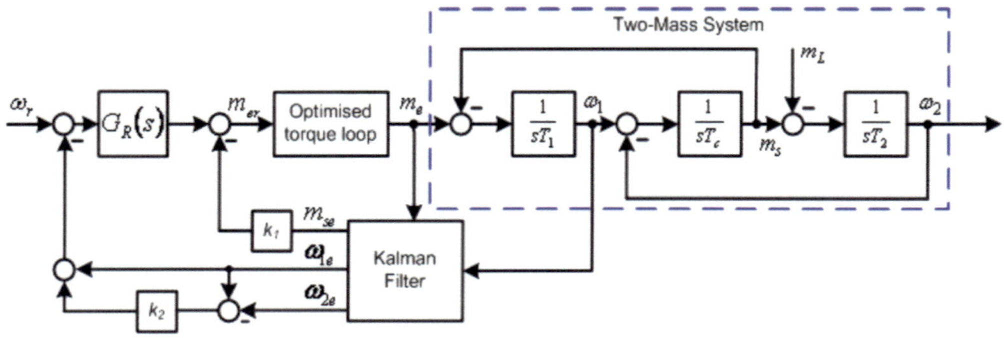

Fig. 8. Schematic diagram of the control structure with LKF

The drive system working under the reverse condition with the reference speed set to the ω_r=0.25 is tested. After the start-up, at the time t_1=0.4s the nominal load torque is applied to the system. Next at the time t_2=1s the reference signal is changing to ω_r=-0.25. Under the reversal the passive load torque is applied to the system. Later at the time t_3=1.4s the load torque is switched off. The drive system works properly. The bigger assumed value of the resonant frequency, the shorter setting time obtained. In the transients of the electromagnetic torque some noises are visible. Their amplitude increases for the bigger values of the resonant frequency. It comes from the fact that the bigger value of the resonant frequency requires the bigger value of the coefficients (k_1, k_2), which gain the noises from the estimated variables.

5. Experimental results

5.1 Experimental set-up

In this section the experimental validation of the analysed algorithms are presented. The laboratory set-up is composed of the two DC-motors (500W each) connected by long shaft.

The driving motor is supplied by the power converter. The speeds of the two motors are measured by two incremental encoders (36000 per rotation). The signal from the second encoder is not used in the control structure but only to display the real velocity of the load machine. The current of the motor is measured by LED sensor. The identification and the control algorithms are implemented by digital signal processor using DSpace 1102 control card. The schematic diagram of the control structure is presented in Fig 9.

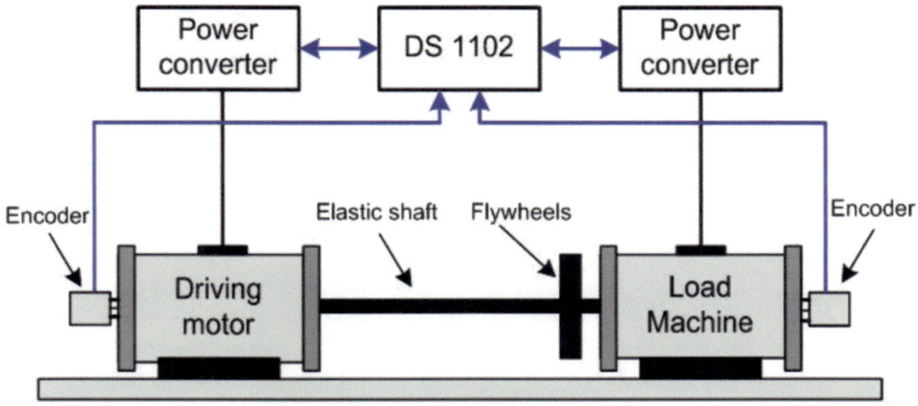

Fig. 9. The schematic diagram of laboratory set-up

5.2 Identification case (NKF)

First the identification procedure has been tested. Similarly as in the simulation study the drive system is stimulated by the square-type of the reference speed signal. The signals of the electromagnetic torque and the motor speed (Fig. 10a,b) are passed to the Kalman Filter. On the basis on these signals the estimated procedure is carried out. The value of the parameters standing for the real one (in the Fig. 10) have been obtained using different identification methodology as presented in (Wertz et al., 1999).

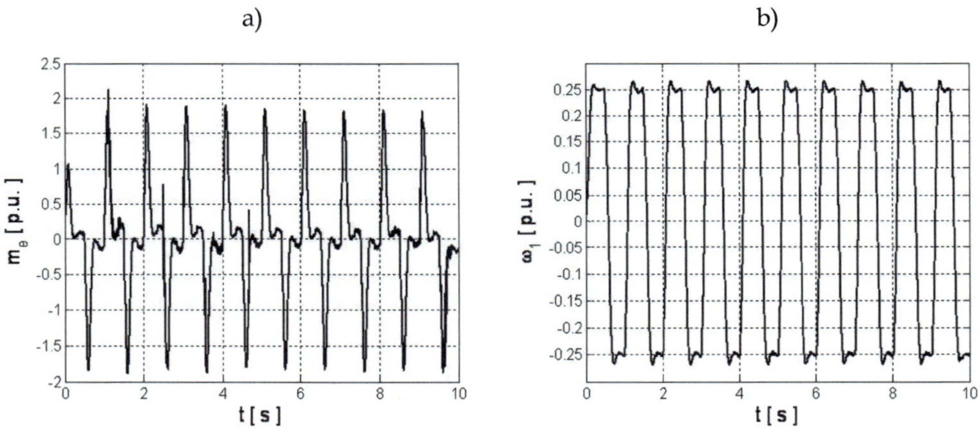

Fig. 10. Transients of the input signal of the Kalman Filter: the electromagnetic torque (a) and the motor speed (b)

Transients of the identified parameters T_2 and T_c are presented in Fig 11. The transients marked as q_{55}=10e5 represent the case of the optimal (found by GA) values of the covariance matrices. First the case of the bigger initial values of the identified parameters is considered (Fig. 11a,b). As in the simulation study the estimate of the T_2 tends to its real value very fast. The convergence of T_c is slower. It can be accelerated by increasing the value of the covariance matrix **Q**. This case is marked in Fig. 11 as q_{55}=10e6. However, the increasing the value of q_{55} can bring about the stability problem of the KF algorithm as well as it gain the disturbances visible in the transients in every reversal. Then the case of the smaller initial value of the mechanical parameters is considered (Fig. 11c,d). Similarly as in the simulation study the identification process is slower. Especially the estimate of the T_c needs more time to reach its real value.

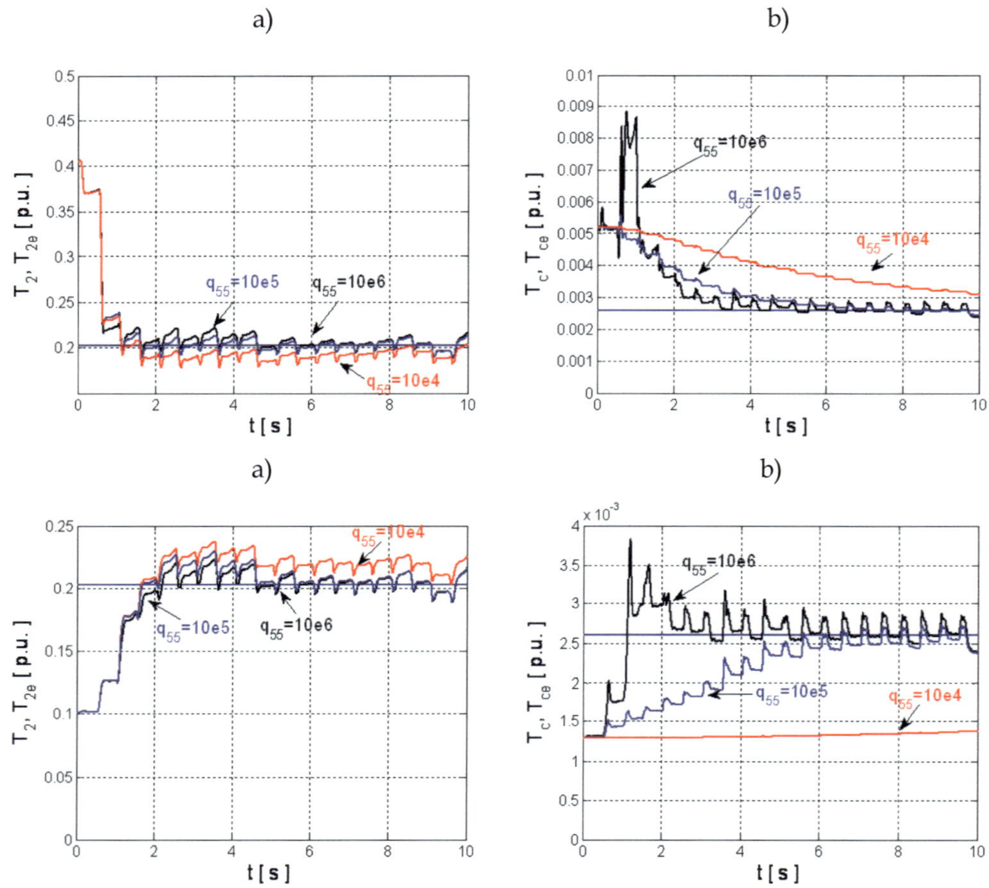

Fig. 11. Transients of the estimated time constant: of load machine (a) and shaft (b) in the case of bigger initial values of those parameters

5.3 Closed-loop control structure (LKF)

The estimated parameters of the two-mass system from the previous section have been used to tune the control structure coefficients according to eq. 5-8. The KF presented in section 3.2 is applied to obtain the information of the shaft torque and the load speed. First the control structure under the reverse condition for the reference speed ω_r=0.25 is tested. The transients of the motor and the load speed for the assumed value oft eh damping coefficient ξ_r=0.7 and different value of the resonant frequency are presented in Fig. 12.

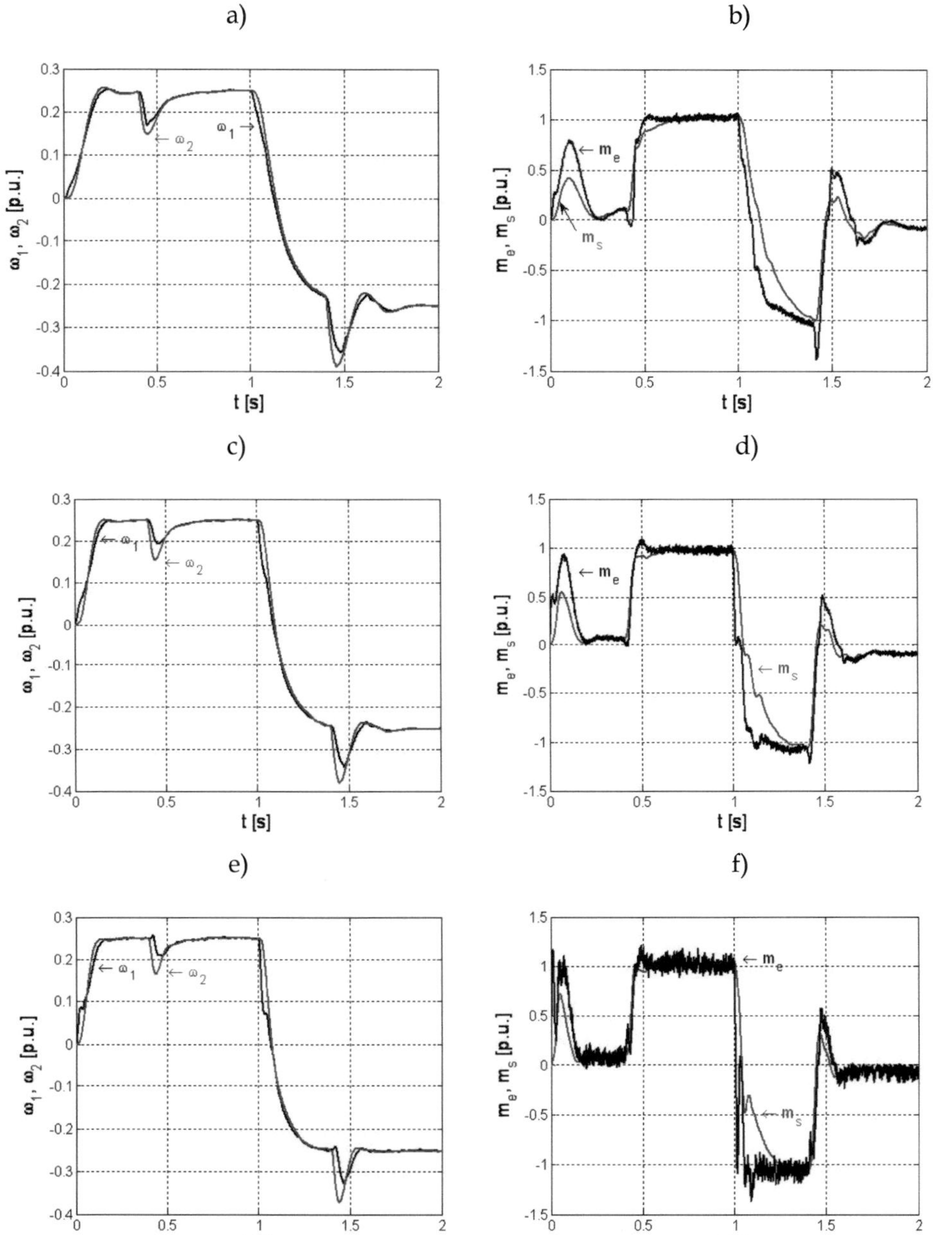

Fig. 12. Experimental transients of the motor and the load speeds (a,c,e) and the electromagnetic and the shaft torques (b,d,f) in the control structure working with the Kalman filter for ξ_r=0.7 and ω_r=30s^{-1} (a,b), ω_r=40s^{-1} (c,d) i ω_r=50 s^{-1} (e,f)

The drive system works under the some conditions as described in section 4.2. Similarly as in the simulation study, the faster response of the system is obtained when the value of the resonant frequency is bigger. The level of the noises visible into the electromagnetic torque transients depends also on the assumed dynamic of the control structure. The faster system , the bigger amplitude of the noises characterize the system. Next the drive system working for the nominal value of the reference speed ω_r=1 is examined. The transients of the system are shown in Fig. 13.

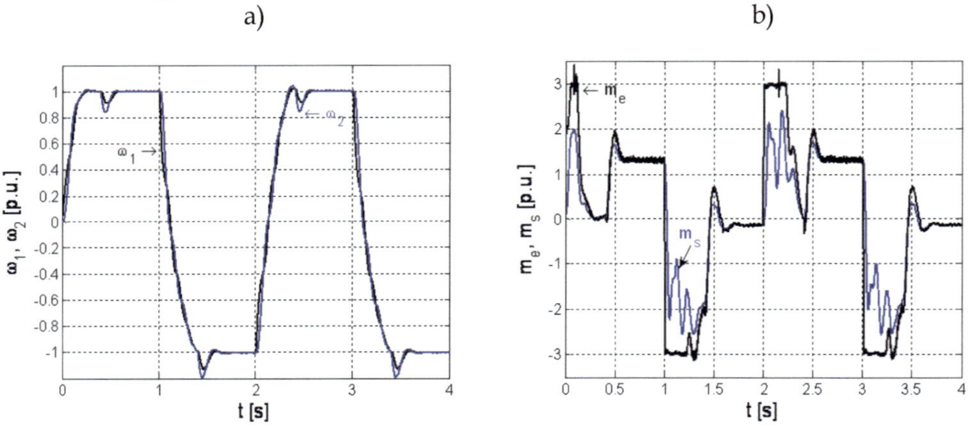

Fig. 13. Experimental transients of the system states for the reference speed ω_r=1

During start-up as well as during the reversal the electromagnetic torque reaches the limitation value (set to 3). The load torque is switched on at the time t_1=0.4 and t_2=2.4s and switched off at the time t_3=1.4s and t_4=2.4s. Despite the system is being overloaded the control structure works properly.

6. Conclusion

In the paper the issues related to identification and control of the drive system with an elastic joint has been presented. The NKF is proposed to provide on-line identification of the mechanical parameters of the two-mass system. The time constants of the shaft and the load machine are estimated simultaneously with high accuracy on the basis of the electromagnetic torque and motor speed. These parameters are used to calculate the gain coefficients of the advanced control structure for the two-mass system. Then the control structure with additional feedbacks, which allows to damp the torsional vibrations of the two-mass system effectively, is introduced. In this case the LKF is applied as an estimator of the non-measurable state variables such as the shaft torque, load speed as well as the load torque.

Parameters of the covariance matrices **Q** and **R** of both considered estimators are selected using the genetic algorithm with special cost functions. The application of the global optimization technique allows to reach the global solution according to the defined cost function. However, the application of the genetic algorithm is possible only as an off-line process due to a long calculation time.

The presented methods are complex and useful of the industrial drive with mechanical elasticity. They allow to ensure the optimal dynamics of the used estimators as well as the whole control structure. The proposed identification and control methods have been examined under simulation and experimental tests. The slight difference between the simulation and experimental results comes from the fact that the additional elements neglected under simulation study such as friction, nonlinear characteristics of the drive exit in the experimental set-up.

7. References

Angerer B. T., Hintz C. & Schröder D. (2004) Online identification of a nonlinear mechatronic system, *Control Engineering Practice,* Vol. 12, No. , pp. 1465 - 1478.

Äström K. J. & Hägglund T. (2001) The future of PID control, *Control Engineering Practice,* Vol. 9, No. , pp. 1163-1175.

Eker I. & Vular M. (2003) Experimantal On-Line Identification of a Three-Mass Mechanical System, *Proc. of IEEE Conference on Control Applications CCA 2003,* Istanbul, Turkey, pp. 60-65.

Erbatur, K., Kaynak, O. & Sabanovic A. (1999). A Study on Robustness Property of Sliding Mode Controllers: A Novel Design and Experimental Investigations, *IEEE Transaction on Industrial Electronics,* Vol. 46, No. 5 , pp. 1012-1018.

Erenturk, K. (2008). Nonlinear two-mass system control with sliding-mode and optimised proportional and integral derivative controller combined with a grey estimator, *Control Theory & Applications, IET,* Vol. 2, No. 7, pp. 635 - 642.

Hace, A., Jezernik, K., & Sabanovic, A. (2006). SMC With Disturbance Observer for a Linear Belt Drive, *IEEE Transaction on Industrial Electronics,* Vol. 53, No. 6, pp. 3402-3412.

Hamamoto, K., Fukuda, T. & Sugie, T. (2003). Iterative feedback tuning of controllers for a two-mass-spring system with friction, *Control Engineering Practice,* Vol. 11, No. 9, pp. 1061–1068.

Hirovonen, M., Pyrhonen, O. & Handroos H. (2006). Adaptive nonlinear velocity controller for a flexible mechanism of a linear motor, Mechatronic, *Elsevier,* Vol. 16, No. 5, pp. 279-290.

Hori, Y., Sawada, H., & Chun, Y. (1999). Slow resonance ratio control for vibration suppression and disturbance rejection in torsional system, *IEEE Transaction on Industrial Electronics,* Vol. 46, No. 1, pp. 162-168.

Katsura, S. & Ohnishi, K. (2005). Force Servoing by Flexible Manipulator Based on Resonance Ratio Control, *Proc. of the IEEE International Symposium on Industrial Electronics ISIE 2005,* Croatia, pp. 1343-1348.

Nordin, M. & Gutman, P. O. (2002), Controlling Mechanical Systems with Backlash - a Survey, *Automatica,* Vol. 38, No. 10, pp. 1633-1649.

Orlowska-Kowalska, T. & Szabat, K. (2008). Damping of Torsional Vibrations in Two-Mass System Using Adaptive Sliding Neuro-Fuzzy Approach, *IEEE Transactions on Industrial Informatics,* Vol. 4, No. 1, pp. 47-57.

O'Sullivan, T., Bingham, C. C. & Schofield, N. (2007). Enhanced Servo-Control Performance of Dual-Mass System, *IEEE Transaction on Industrial Electronics,* Vol. 54, No. 3, pp. 1387-1398.

Pittner, J., & Simaan, M. A. (2008). Control of a continuous tandem cold metal rolling process, *Control Engineering Practice,* Vol. 16, No. 11, pp. 1379– 1390.

Schröder D., Hintz C. & Rau M. (2001) Intelligent Modeling, Observation, and Control for Nonlinear Systems, *IEEE/ASME Trans. on Mechatronics,* Vol. 6, No. 2, pp. 122-131.

Schutte F., Beineke S., Grotstollen H., Witkowski U., Ruckert U. & Ruping S. (1997) Structure- and Parameter Identification for a Two-Mass System with Backlash and Fraction using Self-Organizing Map, *Proc. of the International Conference of European Power Electronics EPE'97,* Trondheim, Norway, pp. 3.358-3.363.

Shen, B. H. & Tsai, M. C. (2006). Robust dynamic stiffness design of linear servomotor drives, *Control Engineering Practice,* Vol. 14, No. 11, pp. 1325-1336.

Szabat, K., & Orlowska-Kowalska, T., (2007). Vibration suppression in two-mass drive system using PI speed controller and additional feedbacks - comparative study, *IEEE Transaction on Industrial Electronics,* Vol. 54, No. 2, pp. 1193-1206.

Szabat, K. & Orlowska-Kowalska, T. (2008). Performance Improvement of Industrial Drives With Mechanical Elasticity Using Nonlinear Adaptive Kalman Filter, *IEEE Transactions on Industrial Electronics,* Vol. 55, No. 3, pp. 1075-1084.

Valenzuela, M. A., Bentley, J. M., Villablanca, A., & Lorenz, R. D. (2005). Dynamic compensation of torsional oscillation in paper machine sections, *IEEE Transaction on Industry Applications,* Vol. 41, No. 6, pp. 1458- 1466.

Vasak, M., Baotic, M., Petrovic, I. & Peric, N. (2007). Hybrid Theory-Based Time-Optimal Control of an Electronic Throttle, *IEEE Transaction on Industrial Electronic,* Vol. 436, No. 3, pp. 1483-1494.

Wang, L. & Frayman Y. (2002). A dynamically generated fuzzy neural network and its application to torsional vibration control of tandem cold rolling mill spindles, *Engineering Applications of Artificial Intelligence,* Vol. 15, No. 6, pp. 541-550.

Wertz H., Beineke S., Frőhleke N., Bolognani S., Unterkofler K., Zigliotto M. & Zordan M. (1999) Computer Aided Commissioning of Speed and Position Control for Electrical Drives with Identification of Mechanical Load, *Proc. of the Thirty-Fourth IAS Annual Meeting Industry Applications Conference,* Phoenix, USA, pp. 4.1372-4.2379.

Zhang, G. & Furusho, J. (2000). Speed Control of Two-Inertia System by PI/PID Control, *IEEE Trans. on Industrial Electronic,* Vol. 47, No. 3, pp. 603-609.

19

Grid Synchronization and Voltage Analysis Based on the Kalman Filter

Rafael Cardoso[1] and Hilton Abílio Gründling[2]
[1]*Federal University of Technology – Paraná*
Energy Processing and Analysis Research Group
[2]*Federal University of Santa Maria*
Power Electronics and Control Research Group
Brazil

1. Introduction

This chapter deals with the problem of grid synchronization in the presence of several perturbations such as harmonics, voltage unbalance, measurement noise, transients and frequency deviation. The development of two synchronization structures is presented, one for single-phase systems and the other for three-phase systems. These schemes are based on the Kalman filter and all the aforementioned perturbations are incorporated, explicitly, in the problem formulation. A voltage analyser is also developed based on the three-phase synchronization structure.

Determining the phase angle of grid voltages is important for many power conditioning devices such as active power filters, reactive power compensators, uninterruptible power supplies, distributed power generation systems, among others, that must be appropriately synchronized with grid voltages. Due to the dynamic nature of the power system, the synchronization method chosen must be capable of rejecting many perturbations inherent to the system, such as harmonics, voltage sags and swells, imbalance, frequency deviations, measurement noise and phase angle jump (Svensson, 2001; Karimi-Ghartemani & Iravani, 2004; Blaabjerg et al., 2006).

A traditional approach to the extraction of the phase angle is the use of closed-loop techniques, such as Phase-Locked Loops (PLLs) (Hsieh & Hung, 1996). For three-phase applications, the phase angle is usually obtained by means of the well-known synchronous reference frame PLL. Implementation of these methods is straightforward but they suffer from the presence of harmonics and voltage imbalance as described in (Chung, 2000). Further analysis of the behaviour of the synchronous reference frame PLL under distorted and unbalanced utility conditions can be found in (Kaura & Blasko, 1997), where some tuning recommendations are also made to minimize the impact of the harmonics and voltage unbalance in phase angle tracking. In (Timbus et al., 2006), an improved PLL, based on a repetitive controller, is proposed. This PLL has a simple structure and is capable of rejecting the negative sequence.

Another closed-loop approach is the Enhanced Phase-Locked Loop (EPLL) (Karimi-Ghartemani & Iravani, 2004). This structure is based on use of the gradient method and three gains are used to tune the algorithm. Like the PLL, the choice of its gains will influence its tracking capability. Since there is no rule to guide the choice of gains, tuning them by trial and error can be tedious. The concept of the EPLL is further elaborated in (Rodríguez et al., 2006) and a new Dual EPLL (DEPLL) is discussed. According to the authors, the DEPLL can lead to detection errors under certain grid conditions. The Dual Second Order Generalized Integrator-Frequency Locked Loop (DSOGI-FLL) was later proposed to overcome the drawbacks of the DEPLL.

Open-loop techniques have also been described in the literature. In (Song & Nam, 2000) an approach based on weighted least-squares that is capable of rejecting the effects of the negative-sequence and of accommodating frequency variations is proposed. However, it is sensitive to the presence of noise and harmonics in the voltages and presents long transients in detecting frequency variations. Another simple method is the PLL based on low-pass filters (LPF-PLL) (Svensson, 2001). This method is simple but has shortcomings. The filtering process introduces a phase shift that must be compensated by a rotation matrix. The phase shift is a function of the frequency and, since this method does not consider frequency variations, full compensation of the phase shift is not possible. Voltage imbalance is also not considered and there must be a trade-off between harmonic rejection and convergence speed, defined by the cut-off frequency of the low-pass filters. Because of oscillatory behaviour, its use is not recommended for systems subjected to phase jumps (Svensson, 2001).

The Normalized Positive Synchronous Frame (NPSF) is another synchronization method that is also based on low-pass filters and considers voltage imbalance and frequency deviations (De Camargo & Pinheiro, 2006). In this method, the cut-off frequency of the low-pass filters tracks the grid frequency based on an adaptation algorithm. The main drawback is that the only tuning parameter is the convergence rate of the frequency identifier. Neither the convergence speed nor harmonic rejection can be modified since the cut-off frequencies of low-pass filters must be the same as the grid frequency.

A possible alternative to extract the phase angle of a signal is the use of the Kalman filter (Kalman, 1960). This filter is well known due to its ability to deal with linear systems corrupted by uncertainties in the states of the plant as well as measurement noise. The spectrum of this type of noise is usually distributed over a wide range of frequencies which can be modelled as white noise (Gelb et al., 1996). The elimination of this perturbation by traditional filtering methods is not straightforward because of the significant phase changes that the signal can suffer. Since the Kalman filter is an optimal algorithm that considers this type of perturbation in its formulation, it is a promising alternative for extracting the phase information from a noisy signal of interest.

Some authors have studied the relation between the Kalman filter and PLL (Gupta, 1975; Christiansen, 1994; Driessen 1994; Patapounian, 1999; Izadi & Leung, 2002). Synchronization methods based on the Kalman filter are mostly used in telecommunication systems and do not consider the presence of disturbances in the signal of interest, such as harmonics and voltage sags and swells that occur in the power system; nor are they appropriate for three-phase systems. Another approach is the use of the extended Kalman filter (Svensson, 2001). However, the extended Kalman filter uses linearizations around the estimates provided by the filter. Since the linearizations are applied using the last available estimate, the propagation equations are only valid if the estimate is not very distant from the actual state (Boutayeb et al., 1997). Moreover, an arbitrary choice of filter covariance matrices together with initial filter states not sufficiently close to the actual states may lead to a filter that fails to converge (Boutayeb et al., 1999).

This chapter describes single and three-phase synchronization methods based on the Kalman filter. They are termed the Kalman Filter-Phase Locked Loop (KF-PLL) and were first introduced in (Cardoso et al., 2006) with further developments presented in (Cardoso et al., 2008). As will be shown, the Kalman gain can be evaluated off-line, so that the filter can be implemented using fixed gains, simplifying its digital implementation. The proposed method is capable of generating synchronization signals even with input signals that contain harmonics and measurement noise. To achieve this, a mathematical model that considers the existence of harmonics in the signal, and also allows for the possible occurrence of transient voltages is used. As this model involves the grid frequency, the performance of the filter may be reduced if the grid frequency deviates from the value considered in the filter. Therefore, the fundamental grid frequency is also identified and is used to update the mathematical model used in the filter. The identification procedure is based on the internal model principle (Francis & Wonham, 1976) in a way similar to that presented in (Brown & Zhang, 2004). However, the present identification method uses a modified input signal and, in contrast to (Brown & Zhang, 2004), the algorithm is entirely derived in discrete form. The first discrete implementation of such an algorithm appeared in (Zhao & Brown, 2004) but their derivation is not clear. In this chapter, the discrete derivation is presented entirely for a better understanding of its discrete implementation. For the three-phase case, the possibility of voltage imbalance is also considered, and since the Kalman filter is an optimum algorithm, the results represent a good compromise between transient response and disturbance rejection. If the stochastic model of the process to be filtered is completely known, the obtained results are optimum according to several optimization criteria (Maybeck, 1979). Performance comparisons of the proposed synchronization structures with other methods presented in literature are available in (Cardoso et al., 2008).
The use of the KF-PLL is also presented for purposes of voltage analysis, where several data about the grid voltages are extracted. For instance, harmonic content with their respective amplitudes, total harmonic distortion, positive, negative and zero sequence components, and further comments on synchronization with negative and zero sequences are also addressed.
This chapter is organized as follows: Section 2 presents the Kalman filter equations. Section 3 introduces the mathematical modeling of a signal with harmonics. The grid frequency identification is described in Section 4. The proposed synchronization methods are developed in Section 5. The use of the KF-PLL for voltage analysis is presented in Section 6. Digital implementation in a fixed point DSP TMS320F2812 is described in Section 7. Finally, the results of real time experiments are given in Section 8 and conclusions are presented in Section 9.

2. The Kalman filter

Consider a discrete linear dynamic stochastic system modeled by

$$\mathbf{x}_{k+1} = \mathbf{\Phi}_k \mathbf{x}_k + \mathbf{\Gamma}_k \boldsymbol{\gamma}_k , \tag{1}$$

$$\mathbf{y}_k = \mathbf{F}_k \mathbf{x}_k + \boldsymbol{\upsilon}_k , \tag{2}$$

$$\dim \mathbf{x}_k = n \times 1, \dim \mathbf{y}_k = r \times 1, \dim \boldsymbol{\gamma}_k = p \times 1 , \tag{3}$$

where $\boldsymbol{\gamma}_k$ and $\boldsymbol{\upsilon}_k$ are independent Gaussian white noise sequences with means and covariances given by

$$E\{\boldsymbol{\gamma}_i\} = 0,\ E\{\boldsymbol{\gamma}_i \boldsymbol{\gamma}_j^T\} = \mathbf{Q}_i \delta_{ij}, \quad (4)$$

$$E\{\boldsymbol{\upsilon}_i\} = 0,\ E\{\boldsymbol{\upsilon}_i \boldsymbol{\upsilon}_j^T\} = \mathbf{R}_i \delta_{ij}, \quad (5)$$

$$E\{\boldsymbol{\gamma}_i \boldsymbol{\upsilon}_j^T\} = 0,\ E\{\boldsymbol{\gamma}_i \mathbf{x}_j^T\} = 0,\ E\{\boldsymbol{\upsilon}_i \mathbf{x}_j^T\} = 0,\ \forall i, j, \quad (6)$$

where $E\{\cdot\}$ denotes the expectation mathematical operator and δ_{ij} denotes the Kronecker Delta function. The matrices $\mathbf{\Phi}_k$, $\mathbf{\Gamma}_k$ and $\mathbf{F}_k$ have appropriate dimensions.
Denoting by $\hat{\mathbf{x}}_{k+1|k}$ the estimate of $\mathbf{x}_{k+1}$ based on all the measurements up to k, the filtering equation as given in (Brown, 1992) is

$$\hat{\mathbf{x}}_{k+1|k} = \mathbf{\Phi}_k \hat{\mathbf{x}}_{k|k-1} + \mathbf{K}_k \left(\mathbf{y}_k - \mathbf{F}_k \hat{\mathbf{x}}_{k|k-1}\right) \quad (7)$$

where

$$\mathbf{K}_k = \mathbf{\Phi}_k \mathbf{P}_{k|k-1} \mathbf{F}_k^T \left(\mathbf{F}_k \mathbf{P}_{k|k-1} \mathbf{F}_k^T + \mathbf{R}_k\right)^{-1} \quad (8)$$

is the Kalman gain and

$$\mathbf{P}_{k+1|k} = \mathbf{\Phi}_k \mathbf{P}_{k|k-1} \mathbf{\Phi}_k^T - \mathbf{K}_k \mathbf{F}_k \mathbf{P}_{k|k-1} \mathbf{\Phi}_k^T + \mathbf{\Gamma}_k \mathbf{Q}_k \mathbf{\Gamma}_k^T \quad (9)$$

is the covariance matrix of the estimation error of the vector $\mathbf{x}_{k+1}$ evaluated at time $\boldsymbol{t}_k$:

$$\mathbf{P}_{k+1|k} \overset{\Delta}{=} E\left\{\left(\mathbf{x}_{k+1} - \hat{\mathbf{x}}_{k+1|k}\right)\left(\mathbf{x}_{k+1} - \hat{\mathbf{x}}_{k+1|k}\right)^T\right\}. \quad (10)$$

The initial conditions are given by $\hat{\mathbf{x}}_{0|-1}$ and $\mathbf{P}_{0|-1}$. Further details can be found in (Brown, 1992).

3. Describing a signal with harmonics

To use the Kalman filter presented in section 2 a mathematical model that describes the process to be filtered is needed. Thus, to obtain a mathematical model that adequately represents grid voltage dynamics, a signal that contains only the fundamental component is initially considered; harmonic components are introduced subsequently. Hence, consider a signal with amplitude A_k, angular frequency ω_k and phase θ_k

$$S_k = A_k \sin\left(\omega_k t_k + \theta_k\right). \quad (11)$$

Let

$$x_{1_k} = A_k \sin\left(\omega_k t_k + \theta_k\right) \quad (12)$$

and

$$x_{2_k} = A_k \cos\left(\omega_k t_k + \theta_k\right). \quad (13)$$

Initially, consider $A_{k+1} \approx A_k$, $\omega_{k+1} \approx \omega_k$ and $\theta_{k+1} \approx \theta_k$. At the time $t_{k+1} = t_k + T_s$ the signal S_{k+1} can be expressed as

$$\begin{aligned} S_{k+1} &= A_{k+1} \sin(\omega_k t_k + \omega_k T_s + \theta_{k+1}) = x_{1_{k+1}} \\ &= x_{1_k} \cos(\omega_k T_s) + x_{2_k} \sin(\omega_k T_s) \end{aligned} \tag{14}$$

where T_s is the sampling period.
Additionally,

$$\begin{aligned} x_{2_{k+1}} &= A_{k+1} \cos(\omega_k t_k + \omega_k T_s + \theta_{k+1}) \\ &= -x_{1_k} \sin(\omega_k T_s) + x_{2_k} \cos(\omega_k T_s). \end{aligned} \tag{15}$$

To model amplitude or phase variations in the signal, a perturbation vector $[\gamma_1 \quad \gamma_2]_k^T$ in the system states is considered. The state-space representation of the signal then becomes

$$\begin{bmatrix} x_1 \\ x_2 \end{bmatrix}_{k+1} = \begin{bmatrix} \cos(\omega_k T_s) & \sin(\omega_k T_s) \\ -\sin(\omega_k T_s) & \cos(\omega_k T_s) \end{bmatrix} \begin{bmatrix} x_1 \\ x_2 \end{bmatrix}_k + \begin{bmatrix} \gamma_1 \\ \gamma_2 \end{bmatrix}_k, \tag{16}$$

$$y_k = \begin{bmatrix} 1 & 0 \end{bmatrix} \begin{bmatrix} x_1 \\ x_2 \end{bmatrix}_k + \upsilon_k \tag{17}$$

where υ_k represents the measurement noise.
If there are n frequencies in the signal S_k, i. e.,

$$S_k = \sum_{i=1}^{n} A_{i_k} \sin(i\omega_k t_k + \theta_{i_k}), \tag{18}$$

the state-space representation of the signal becomes

$$\begin{bmatrix} x_1 \\ x_2 \\ \vdots \\ x_{2n-1} \\ x_{2n} \end{bmatrix}_{k+1} = \begin{bmatrix} \mathbf{M_1} & \cdots & 0 \\ \vdots & \ddots & \vdots \\ 0 & \cdots & \mathbf{M_n} \end{bmatrix}_k \begin{bmatrix} x_1 \\ x_2 \\ \vdots \\ x_{2n-1} \\ x_{2n} \end{bmatrix}_k + \begin{bmatrix} \gamma_1 \\ \gamma_2 \\ \vdots \\ \gamma_{2n-1} \\ \gamma_{2n} \end{bmatrix}_k, \tag{19}$$

$$y_k = \begin{bmatrix} 1 & 0 & \cdots & 1 & 0 \end{bmatrix} \begin{bmatrix} x_1 \\ x_2 \\ \vdots \\ x_{2n-1} \\ x_{2n} \end{bmatrix}_k + \upsilon_k \tag{20}$$

where

$$\mathbf{M_i} = \begin{bmatrix} \cos(i\omega_k T_s) & \sin(i\omega_k T_s) \\ -\sin(i\omega_k T_s) & \cos(i\omega_k T_s) \end{bmatrix}. \quad (21)$$

The perturbation vector $[\gamma_1 \quad \gamma_2 \quad \cdots \quad \gamma_{2n-1} \quad \gamma_{2n}]_k^T$ models amplitude or phase variations of each harmonic component of the signal and its covariance is given by matrix **Q**, defined by (4). The covariance of the measurement noise υ_k is given by $\mathbf{R}$ as defined in (5).
The mathematical model (19)-(21) has the same form as the mathematical model (1)-(2) used in the Kalman filter. Note that this model needs the value of the angular grid frequency that may be subject to deviations from its nominal value. If the frequency considered in the mathematical model differs from the real value, the estimates provided by the filter will not be accurate. It is therefore necessary to identify the grid frequency in real time to update the model used in the Kalman filter. This is accomplished by the method given in next section.

4. Real time frequency identification

The grid frequency identification method proposed here is based on the internal model principle (Francis & Wonham, 1976), in which a stable closed-loop dynamic system is considered, as shown in Fig. 1, with

$$G(z) = \frac{N(z)}{D(z)} \quad (22)$$

proper and coprime and a sinusoidal input signal $R_\omega(z)$, i. e.,

$$R_\omega(z) = \frac{N_R(z)}{D_R(z)} = \frac{z^2 \sin(\omega_\omega T_s)}{z^2 - 2\cos(\omega_\omega T_s) z + 1}, \quad (23)$$

if the unstable poles of $R_\omega(z)$ are reproduced by $G(z)$, i. e., $D(z)=D_R(z)$, then

$$\lim_{k\to\infty} e(kT_s) = \lim_{k\to\infty} [r_\omega(kT_s) - y_\omega(kT_s)] = 0. \quad (24)$$

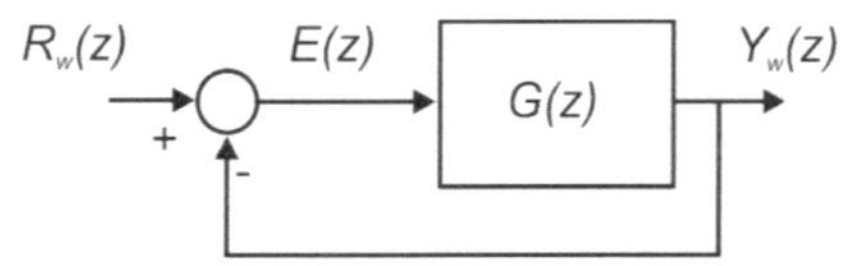

Fig. 1. Dynamic system based on the internal model principle

With these considerations, a possible transfer function $G(z)$, for the dynamic system shown in Fig. 1, from which the frequency identifier is derived, is

$$G(z) = K_\omega \frac{z^2 - \cos(\omega T_s)}{z^2 - 2\cos(\omega T_s) z + 1}. \quad (25)$$

The transfer function (25) can be realized in state-space as

$$\begin{bmatrix} x_{\omega 1} \\ x_{\omega 2} \end{bmatrix}_{k+1} = \begin{bmatrix} 0 & 1 \\ -1 & 2\cos(\omega_k T_s) \end{bmatrix} \begin{bmatrix} x_{\omega 1} \\ x_{\omega 2} \end{bmatrix}_k + \begin{bmatrix} 0 \\ K_\omega \end{bmatrix} e_k, \quad (26)$$

$$y_{\omega_k} = \begin{bmatrix} -1 & \cos(\omega_k T_s) \end{bmatrix} \begin{bmatrix} x_{\omega 1} \\ x_{\omega 2} \end{bmatrix}_k + K_\omega e_k \quad (27)$$

where ω_k, at $k=0$, is initialized with the nominal value of the grid angular frequency. Subsequently, this value will be updated by the identification algorithm that will be developed to satisfy (24). The value of ω_k will be the identified grid frequency.

Let

$$r_{\omega_k} = A_{\omega_k} \sin\left(\omega_{\omega_k} t_k + \theta_{\omega_k}\right) \quad (28)$$

be a sinusoidal reference with amplitude A_{ω_k}, angular frequency ω_{ω_k} and phase θ_{ω_k} at time t_k. Now, consider a reference as described by (28) with constant values for A_{ω_k}, ω_{ω_k} and θ_{ω_k}, i. e.,

$$A_{\omega_{k+1}} = A_{\omega_k} = A_\omega, \quad (29)$$

$$\omega_{\omega_{k+1}} = \omega_{\omega_k} = \omega_\omega, \quad (30)$$

$$\theta_{\omega_{k+1}} = \theta_{\omega_k} = \theta_\omega \quad (31)$$

and the model described by (26) and (27) with ω_k constant, i. e.,

$$\omega_{k+1} = \omega_k = \omega. \quad (32)$$

Then, if we define

$$a = \cos(\omega_\omega T_s) - \cos(\omega T_s) \quad (33)$$

and

$$b = \sin(\omega_\omega T_s), \quad (34)$$

the state $x_{\omega 2_k}$, the output y_{ω_k} and the error e_k will converge to

$$y_{\omega_k} = A_{y_\omega} \sin\left(\omega_\omega t_k + \theta_\omega + \varphi_{y_\omega}\right), \quad (35)$$

$$x_{\omega 2_k} = \frac{A_{y_\omega}}{\sqrt{a^2 + b^2}} \sin\left(\omega_\omega t_k + \theta_\omega + \varphi_{x_{\omega 2}}\right), \quad (36)$$

and

$$e_k = A_e \sin\left(\omega_\omega t_k + \theta_\omega + \varphi_{x_{e\omega}}\right), \quad (37)$$

respectively, where

$$A_{y_\omega} = A_\omega K_\omega \sqrt{\frac{a^2 + b^2}{(2 + K_\omega)^2 a^2 + K_\omega^2 b^2}}, \quad (38)$$

$$A_e = 2A_\omega \sqrt{\frac{a^2}{(2+K_\omega)^2 a^2 + K_\omega^2 b^2}}, \tag{39}$$

$$\varphi_{y_\omega} = \arctan\left(\frac{2ab}{(2+K_\omega)a^2 + K_\omega b^2}\right), \tag{40}$$

$$\varphi_{x_{\omega 2}} = -\arctan\left(\frac{K_\omega b}{(2+K_\omega)a}\right) \tag{41}$$

and

$$\varphi_{x_{e\omega}} = -\arctan\left(\frac{K_\omega ab}{(2+K_\omega)a^2}\right). \tag{42}$$

When the angular frequency of the driving signal is the same as the frequency considered in the state space representation of $G(z)$, i. e., when $\omega_\omega = \omega$, y_{ω_k} will track the input signal r_{ω_k} by virtue of (35). Hence, from (37), in steady-state, $e_k = 0$. Therefore, the error e_k provides useful information for the identification of the angular frequency ω_ω of the driving signal.

For the proposed discrete model (26)-(27), considering $\omega_\omega \approx \omega$, in steady-state, two orthogonal signals are obtained,

$$y_{\omega_k} \approx A_\omega \sin(\omega_\omega t_k + \theta_\omega) \tag{43}$$

and

$$x_{\omega 2_k} \approx -\frac{A_\omega}{\sin(\omega_\omega)} \cos(\omega_\omega t_k + \theta_\omega). \tag{44}$$

Defining ϕ_k as

$$\phi_k = \omega_\omega t_k + \theta_\omega \tag{45}$$

then, the frequency ω_ω can be obtained by

$$\omega_\omega = \frac{\phi_{k+1} - \phi_k}{T_s} \tag{46}$$

Using (43) and (44) leads to

$$\tan(\phi_k) = \frac{\sin(\omega_\omega t_k + \theta_\omega)}{\cos(\omega_\omega t_k + \theta_\omega)} = \frac{y_{\omega_k}}{-\sin(\omega_\omega T_s) x_{\omega 2_k}}, \tag{47}$$

which gives

$$\phi_k = \arctan(\tan(\phi_k)) \tag{48}$$

To obtain $\tan(\phi_k)$ in (47), we need to know the angular frequency ω_ω of the driving signal, which is unknown. By putting $\omega_\omega \approx \omega$, ω_ω is replaced by ω. Hence,

$$\tan(\phi_k) \approx \frac{y_{\omega_k}}{-\sin(\omega T_s)x_{\omega 2_k}} \tag{49}$$

and

$$\phi_k \approx \arctan\left(\frac{y_{\omega_k}}{-\sin(\omega T_s)x_{\omega 2_k}}\right). \tag{50}$$

Instead of using (46) to obtain the derivative of ϕ_k, (48) is used together with the definition of the continuous derivative of arctan. Then, the continuous values are replaced by the discrete ones available at time t_k, with continuous derivatives approximated by

$$\frac{d}{dt}(\cdot) \approx \frac{(\cdot)_{k+1} - (\cdot)_k}{T_s}. \tag{51}$$

The derivative of arctan is given by

$$\frac{d}{dt}\arctan[\tan(\phi(t))] = \frac{1}{1+\tan(\phi(t))^2}\frac{d}{dt}\tan(\phi(t)). \tag{52}$$

which, by replacing $\tan(\phi(t))$ by its value at time t_k as given by (49), using (26)-(27) and re-introducing the subscript of time k, gives an estimate of the frequency ω_ω of the driving signal denoted by $\hat{\omega}_{\omega_k}$,

$$\hat{\omega}_{\omega_k} \approx \omega_k - \frac{1}{T_s}\frac{K_\omega \sin(\omega_k T_s)x_{\omega 2_k} e_k}{\left[\sin(\omega_k T_s)x_{\omega 2_k}\right]^2 + \left[y_{\omega_k}\right]^2} \tag{53}$$

giving the error $\hat{\omega}_{\omega_k} - \omega_k$,

$$\hat{\omega}_{\omega_k} - \omega_k \approx -\frac{1}{T_s}\frac{K_\omega \sin(\omega_k T_s)x_{\omega 2_k} e_k}{\left[\sin(\omega_k T_s)x_{\omega 2_k}\right]^2 + \left[y_{\omega_k}\right]^2} = -\frac{1}{T_s}\varepsilon_k \tag{54}$$

where

$$\varepsilon_k = \frac{K_\omega \sin(\omega_k T_s)x_{\omega 2_k} e_k}{\left[\sin(\omega_k T_s)x_{\omega 2_k}\right]^2 + \left[y_{\omega_k}\right]^2}. \tag{55}$$

Therefore, ω_k can be updated by

$$\frac{\omega_{k+1} - \omega_k}{T_s} = -K_u \frac{1}{T_s}\varepsilon_k \tag{56}$$

giving

$$\omega_{k+1} = \omega_k - K_u \varepsilon_k \tag{57}$$

where K_u is again a scalar value.

Based on (57) the model (26)-(27) is updated. The structure of the identifier is shown in Fig. 2, where the internal model is given by (26)-(27), the error ε_k is given by (55) and the integrator is given by (57).

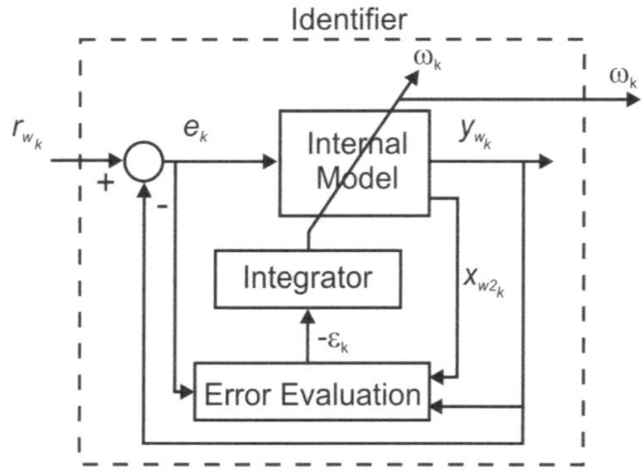

Fig. 2. Complete structure of the frequency identifier with signals involved.

Since the voltage measurements may be corrupted by measurement noise and harmonics and suffer from voltage sags and swells, the use of these measurements directly as r_{ω_k} may result in undesirable behavior of the frequency identifier. To avoid this, the synchronization signal is used, which is generated by the structures proposed in the next section. As will be shown, these signals are already filtered and normalized.

5. Synchronization methods

5.1 Single-phase synchronization

For single-phase synchronization, it is necessary to generate a signal in phase with the fundamental component of the grid voltage. From (19), it is clear that

$$x_{1_k} = A_k \sin\left(\omega_k t_k + \theta_{1_k}\right) \tag{58}$$

and

$$x_{2_k} = A_k \cos\left(\omega_k t_k + \theta_{1_k}\right), \tag{59}$$

are the orthogonal components of the fundamental voltage phasor of the grid voltage. Its instantaneous phase is

$$\phi_{V1_k} = \omega_k t_k + \theta_{1_k} \,. \tag{60}$$

From the Kalman filter described in section 2, with a mathematical model of the signal S_k given by (19)-(21), the estimates of the components of the fundamental voltage phasor $\hat{x}_{1_{k|k-1}}$ and $\hat{x}_{2_{k|k-1}}$ are obtained. Based on these estimates, and assuming $A_k \neq 0$, the sine and cosine functions are given by

$$\sin\left(\phi_{V1_k}\right) = \frac{\hat{x}_{1_{k|k-1}}}{A_k} = r_{\omega_k} \tag{61}$$

and

$$\cos\left(\phi_{V1_k}\right) = \frac{\hat{x}_{2_{k|k-1}}}{A_k} \tag{62}$$

where

$$A_k = \sqrt{\hat{x}_{1_{k|k-1}}^2 + \hat{x}_{2_{k|k-1}}^2}\ . \tag{63}$$

The angular frequency ω_k needed in the mathematical model used by the Kalman filter is updated by the algorithm described in section 4. The reference signal r_{ω_k} is obtained from (61). This signal contains only the fundamental component of the measured signal and is normalized. The influence of harmonics or amplitude variations of the measured signal is therefore minimized. Fig. 3 shows the proposed single-phase synchronization structure. In this figure, the block termed the Kalman Filter is implemented by (7)-(9). The input of the filter, that is, $\mathbf{y}_k$ in (7), is the voltage measurement of the phase of interest. In Fig. 3, the input of the filter is represented by v_k. The Kalman filter will provide the estimates of the harmonics included in the mathematical model (19)-(21) used to describe the signal. Since the interest is on the fundamental component, only the first two estimated states $\hat{x}_{1_{k|k-1}}$ and $\hat{x}_{2_{k|k-1}}$ are used. These estimates are the two orthogonal signals used to obtain the synchronization signals as depicted in Fig. 3.

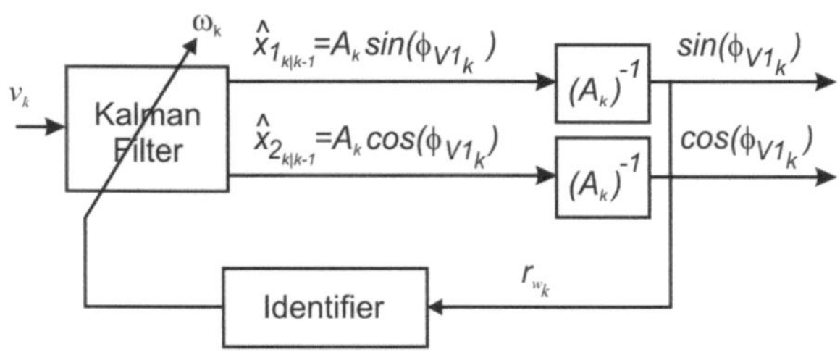

Fig. 3. Single-phase synchronization structure.

From (61) and (62) the instantaneous phase of the fundamental grid voltage component is found to be

$$\phi_{V1_k} = \arctan\left(\frac{\hat{x}_{1_{k|k-1}}}{\hat{x}_{2_{k|k-1}}}\right). \tag{64}$$

5.2 Three-phase synchronization

In some applications, such as power conditioning equipment (Campos et al., 1994; Song & Nam, 2000), distributed generation (Karimi-Ghartemani & Iravani, 2004; Blaabjerg et al., 2006), PWM rectifiers (De Camargo & Pinheiro, 2006) among others, it is desirable that the synchronization method be able to provide synchronism signals in phase with the positive sequence of the fundamental component of the grid voltages.

Given the fundamental phase voltages $v_{a_k}^f$, $v_{b_k}^f$ and $v_{c_k}^f$, the positive sequence components can be obtained through (Fortescue, 1918)

$$\begin{bmatrix} v_a^+ \\ v_b^+ \\ v_c^+ \end{bmatrix}_k = \frac{1}{3}\begin{bmatrix} 1 & \alpha & \alpha^2 \\ \alpha^2 & 1 & \alpha \\ \alpha & \alpha_2 & 1 \end{bmatrix}\begin{bmatrix} v_a^f \\ v_b^f \\ v_c^f \end{bmatrix}_k \tag{65}$$

where $\alpha = e^{j120^\circ}$. Considering $e^{\pm j120^\circ} = -\left(1/2\right) \pm \left(\sqrt{3}/2\right) e^{j90^\circ}$ and defining S_{90} as the 90° phase shift operator, i. e., $S_{90} = e^{j90^\circ}$, (65) can be rewritten as

$$\begin{aligned} v_{a_k}^+ &= \frac{1}{3} v_{a_k}^f - \frac{1}{6}\left(v_{b_k}^f + v_{c_k}^f\right) + \frac{\sqrt{3}}{6} S_{90}\left(v_{b_k}^f - v_{c_k}^f\right), \\ v_{b_k}^+ &= -v_{a_k}^+ - v_{c_k}^+, \\ v_{c_k}^+ &= \frac{1}{3} v_{c_k}^f - \frac{1}{6}\left(v_{a_k}^f + v_{b_k}^f\right) + \frac{\sqrt{3}}{6} S_{90}\left(v_{a_k}^f - v_{b_k}^f\right) \end{aligned} \tag{66}$$

The values of $v_{a_k}^f$, $v_{b_k}^f$, $v_{c_k}^f$ and their orthogonal components $S_{90}\left(v_{a_k}^f\right)$, $S_{90}\left(v_{b_k}^f\right)$ and $S_{90}\left(v_{c_k}^f\right)$ are obtained directly from the Kalman filter due to (58) and (59). That is, $v_{a_k}^f = \hat{x}_{1_{k|k-1}}^a$, $v_{b_k}^f = \hat{x}_{1_{k|k-1}}^b$, $v_{c_k}^f = \hat{x}_{1_{k|k-1}}^c$ and $S_{90}\left(v_{a_k}^f\right) = \hat{x}_{2_{k|k-1}}^a$, $S_{90}\left(v_{b_k}^f\right) = \hat{x}_{2_{k|k-1}}^b$, $S_{90}\left(v_{c_k}^f\right) = \hat{x}_{2_{k|k-1}}^c$, where the superscripts *a*, *b* and *c* indicate the filter associated to each phase. This avoids the need for additional filters to provide the phase shift required in the fundamental component to obtain the orthogonal components of the voltages.

To obtain the synchronism signals, the positive sequence components are represented in the stationary reference frame $\alpha\beta$:

$$\begin{bmatrix} v_\alpha^+ \\ v_\beta^+ \end{bmatrix}_k = \frac{2}{3}\begin{bmatrix} 1 & -1/2 & -1/2 \\ 0 & -\sqrt{3}/2 & \sqrt{3}/2 \end{bmatrix}\begin{bmatrix} v_a^+ \\ v_b^+ \\ v_c^+ \end{bmatrix}_k . \tag{67}$$

To simplify the transforms (66) and(67), they can be combined as

$$\mathbf{v}_{\boldsymbol{\alpha\beta}}^+ = \mathbf{T_1} \mathbf{v}_{\mathbf{abc}_k}^{\mathbf{f}} + \mathbf{T_2} S_{90} \mathbf{v}_{\mathbf{abc}_k}^{\mathbf{f}} \tag{68}$$

where

$$\mathbf{v}_{\boldsymbol{\alpha\beta}_k}^+ = \begin{bmatrix} v_\alpha^+ \\ v_\beta^+ \end{bmatrix}_k, \quad \mathbf{v}_{\mathbf{abc}_k}^{\mathbf{f}} = \begin{bmatrix} v_a^f \\ v_b^f \\ v_c^f \end{bmatrix}_k, \tag{69}$$

$$\mathbf{T}_1 = \frac{2}{3}\begin{bmatrix} 1/2 & -1/4 & -1/4 \\ 0 & -\sqrt{3}/4 & \sqrt{3}/4 \end{bmatrix}, \tag{70}$$

and

$$\mathbf{T}_2 = \frac{2}{3}\begin{bmatrix} 0 & \sqrt{3}/4 & -\sqrt{3}/4 \\ 1/2 & -1/4 & -1/4 \end{bmatrix}. \tag{71}$$

Therefore, considering $\left\|\mathbf{v}^{+}_{\boldsymbol{\alpha\beta}_k}\right\| \neq 0$ the synchronism signals are given by

$$\sin\left(\phi^{+}_{Va_k}\right) = \frac{v^{+}_{\alpha_k}}{\left\|\mathbf{v}^{+}_{\boldsymbol{\alpha\beta}_k}\right\|} = r_{\omega_k} \tag{72}$$

and

$$\cos\left(\phi^{+}_{Va_k}\right) = \frac{v^{+}_{\beta_k}}{\left\|\mathbf{v}^{+}_{\boldsymbol{\alpha\beta}_k}\right\|} \tag{73}$$

where

$$\left\|\mathbf{v}^{+}_{\boldsymbol{\alpha\beta}_k}\right\| = \sqrt{\left(v^{+}_{\alpha_k}\right)^2 + \left(v^{+}_{\beta_k}\right)^2}\,. \tag{74}$$

The angular frequency in the mathematical model used by the Kalman filter is updated again by the algorithm set out in section 4. The reference signal r_{ω_k} is obtained from (72). Fig. 4 shows the proposed three-phase synchronization method. Similar to the single-phase case, the signals v_{a_k}, v_{b_k} and v_{c_k}, in Fig. 4, are the inputs of three Kalman filters used to decompose the grid voltages of each phase in the harmonic components considered in the signal model. From each filter, the first two orthogonal estimated states are used by the positive sequence extractor block, i. e., $v^{f}_{a_k}$, $v^{f}_{b_k}$, $v^{f}_{c_k}$ and its orthogonal components $S_{90}\left(v^{f}_{a_k}\right)$, $S_{90}\left(v^{f}_{b_k}\right)$ and $S_{90}\left(v^{f}_{c_k}\right)$. Note that to reduce the processing time, the positive sequence extractor and abc to $\alpha\beta$ blocks are combined as shown by (68).

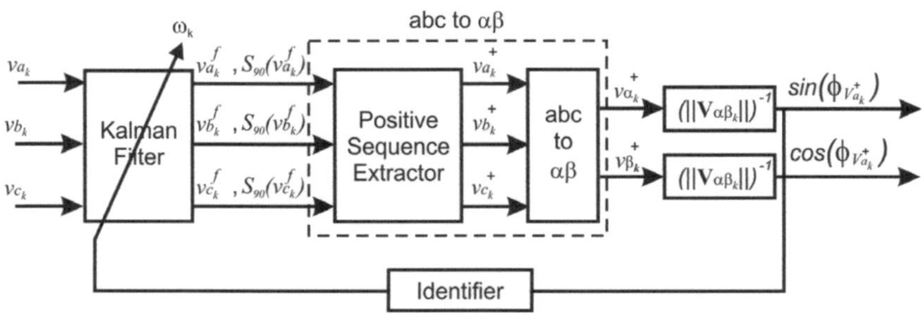

Fig. 4. Three-phase synchronization structure.

The instantaneous phase can be obtained from (72) and (73),

$$\phi_{V\alpha_k}^{+} = \arctan\left(\frac{v_{\alpha_k}^{+}}{v_{\beta_k}^{+}}\right) \tag{75}$$

while the amplitude of the positive sequence component is

$$A_k^{+} = \left\|\mathbf{v}_{\boldsymbol{\alpha\beta}_k}^{+}\right\|. \tag{76}$$

6. Voltage analysis

In Fig. 4, which shows the structure of the three-phase KF-PLL, it can be observed that some information about the grid voltages can be directly obtained, for instance, fundamental components, harmonics, symmetrical components and frequency. This indicates that the KF-PLL can also be used for purposes of voltage analysis. This section describes how the information provided by the different blocks of the KF-PLL can be used for this purpose.
The three-phase KF-PLL uses three Kalman filters in its first block. Each filter is associated to one of the phase voltages. Based on these filters, it is possible to optimally extract the harmonics of each phase voltage and their orthogonal components. Hence, the amplitude of the considered harmonic component can be obtained straightforwardly as shown by (58), (59) and (63). In this case, the fundamental component was considered. Obviously, it can be extended to any harmonic component considered in the model (19)-(21).
Based on the harmonic components extracted by the Kalman filters, the total harmonic distortion (THD) can also be evaluated in real time, that is,

$$THD_k = \frac{\sqrt{\sum_{i=2}^{n} A_{i_k}^2}}{A_k} \tag{77}$$

where A_k is the amplitude of the fundamental component and A_{i_k} is the amplitude of the i-th harmonic component.
The detection of the symmetrical components is important for purposes of monitoring unbalance. In the KF-PLL, the positive sequence is promptly available. To measure the degree of unbalance, the negative and possibly the zero sequence components must be also detected. The zero sequence component can be obtained from

$$v_k^0 = \frac{1}{3}(v_{a_k}^f + v_{b_k}^f + v_{c_k}^f), \tag{78}$$

while its magnitude can be evaluated from

$$A_k^0 = \sqrt{\left(v_k^0\right)^2 + \left(S_{90} v_k^0\right)^2} \tag{79}$$

where

$$S_{90}v_k^0 = \frac{1}{3}(S_{90}v_{a_k}^f + S_{90}v_{b_k}^f + S_{90}v_{c_k}^f). \tag{80}$$

The negative sequence components are obtained straightforwardly from

$$v_{i_k}^- = v_{i_k}^f - v_{i_k}^+ - v_k^0, \quad i = a,b,c\,, \tag{81}$$

while its magnitude is given by

$$A_k^- = \sqrt{\frac{2}{3}\left(\left(v_{a_k}^-\right)^2 + \left(v_{b_k}^-\right)^2 + \left(v_{c_k}^-\right)^2\right)}. \tag{82}$$

Note that representing the negative sequence components in the $\alpha\beta$ reference frame, that is,

$$\begin{bmatrix} v_\alpha^- \\ v_\beta^- \end{bmatrix}_k = \frac{2}{3}\begin{bmatrix} 1 & -\frac{1}{2} & -\frac{1}{2} \\ 0 & -\frac{\sqrt{3}}{2} & \frac{\sqrt{3}}{2} \end{bmatrix}\begin{bmatrix} v_a^- \\ v_b^- \\ v_c^- \end{bmatrix}_k, \tag{83}$$

the synchronization signals with these components can be obtained by

$$\sin\left(\phi_{Va_k}^-\right) = \frac{v_{\alpha_k}^-}{\left\|\mathbf{v}_{\alpha\beta_k}^-\right\|}, \qquad \cos\left(\phi_{Va_k}^-\right) = \frac{v_{\beta_k}^-}{\left\|\mathbf{v}_{\alpha\beta_k}^-\right\|} \tag{84}$$

where

$$\left\|\mathbf{v}_{\alpha\beta_k}^-\right\| = A_k^- = \sqrt{\left(v_{\alpha_k}^-\right)^2 + \left(v_{\beta_k}^-\right)^2}. \tag{85}$$

Hence, the instantaneous phase of the negative sequence component is

$$\phi_{Va_k}^- = \arctan\left(\frac{v_{\alpha_k}^-}{v_{\beta_k}^-}\right). \tag{86}$$

Similarly,

$$\sin\left(\phi_{V_k}^0\right) = \frac{v_k^0}{A_k^0}, \qquad \cos\left(\phi_{Va_k}^-\right) = \frac{S_{90}v_k^0}{A_k^0} \tag{87}$$

And the instantaneous phase of the zero sequence component is given by

$$\phi_{V_k}^0 = \arctan\left(\frac{v_k^0}{S_{90}v_k^0}\right). \tag{88}$$

Further details on voltage analysis based on Kalman filter can be found in (Cardoso et. al., 2007).

7. Digital implementation

This section describes the digital implementation of the synchronization methods in a 32 bits fixed-point DSP (TI-TMS320F2812). Because of the finite word length and precision of the device, the IQmath library (Texas Instruments, 2002) was used to improve the performance of the algorithms. To determine the sampling frequency, two factors must be considered: calculation time and the sampling frequency usually used in the power electronic apparatus. If neither the calculation time nor the equipment sampling frequency impose restrictions, higher sampling frequencies will provide better results. The sampling frequency used here is 10.5 kHz.

The mathematical model used in the Kalman filter incorporates the fundamental, 3rd, 5th, 7th and 11th harmonics. The covariance of the measurement noise is set to $\mathbf{R} = 200V^2$ while the covariance of the process noise is set to $\mathbf{Q} = 0.05I_{10\times 10}V^2$. In fact, in practice, both matrices $\mathbf{Q}$ and $\mathbf{R}$ can be identified by using whitening techniques as presented in (Mehra, 1970; Cardoso et al., 2005).

To design the transfer function gain K_ω, see (25), the natural frequency is set equal to the nominal angular frequency of the grid, i. e., $\omega_n = \omega = 377\, rad/s$ and a damping coefficient $\xi = 0.707$ is used. Therefore, from the well known relationships (Ogata, 1994)

$$|z| = e^{-T_s \xi \omega_n} \tag{89}$$

and

$$\angle z = T_s \omega_n \sqrt{1-\xi^2}\ (rad) \tag{90}$$

replacing the values of ω_n and ξ by those defined for them gives the roots of the closed loop characteristic equation, i. e.,

$$z = 0.975 \pm j0.025\,. \tag{91}$$

From (91) and the closed loop characteristic equation, solving for K_ω we have $K_\omega = 0.052$.

The gain K_u is responsible for the speed of convergence of the frequency identifier. For fast convergence, K_u must have a large value. However, a high value for K_u may lead to an undesirable behavior of the identifier. In the following experiments $K_u = 20$. This gain provides a satisfactory performance for the integrator.

When implementing the Kalman filter, it is necessary to evaluate the Kalman gain K_k, given by (8), for which the covariance matrix (9) must be computed at every sampling time k. Since the standards (IEC 60034, 1996; IEC 61000-2-2, 2001; IEEE Std C37.106, 2003) limit the range of frequency deviation in the grid, a fixed Kalman gain can be evaluated at the nominal grid frequency. This simplification imposes a negligible reduction in the performance of the Kalman filter when compared with the use of the Kalman gain evaluated for the actual grid frequency, as will be shown below.

Considering $f = 60\, Hz$ and based on the values $\mathbf{Q} = 0.05I_{10\times 10}V^2$ and $\mathbf{R} = 200V^2$, previously defined, the following steady-state Kalman filter gain is obtained

$$\begin{aligned}\mathbf{K}_{\infty_{60}} = [&21.1726 \quad -0.0848 \quad 21.1721 \quad -0.1728 \quad 21.1727 \quad \cdots \\ &\cdots \quad 0.0693 \quad 21.1161 \quad 1.5481 \quad 21.0486 \quad -2.2893]^T \times 10^{-3}\end{aligned}. \tag{92}$$

Based on this gain, Fig. 5 shows the frequency response of the Kalman filter states $\hat{x}_1$ and $\hat{x}_2$. The proposed synchronization schemes strongly reject the harmonics at the frequencies used in the mathematical model. At the fundamental frequency, the gains equal unity and the difference in phase is 0° and -90° for the states $\hat{x}_1$ and $\hat{x}_2$, respectively. Figs. 6a and 6b present the errors in magnitude, in dB, and in phase, in degrees, that arise when fixed gains are used. When fixed gains are evaluated for the nominal grid frequency, i. e., $f = 60\,Hz$, both errors, in magnitude and phase, are negligible if the actual grid frequency is updated in the mathematical model of the filter.

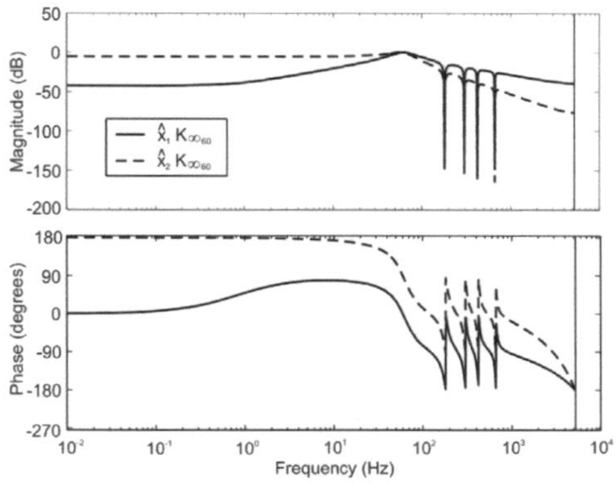

Fig. 5. Frequency response of the Kalman filter considering $f = 60\,Hz$.

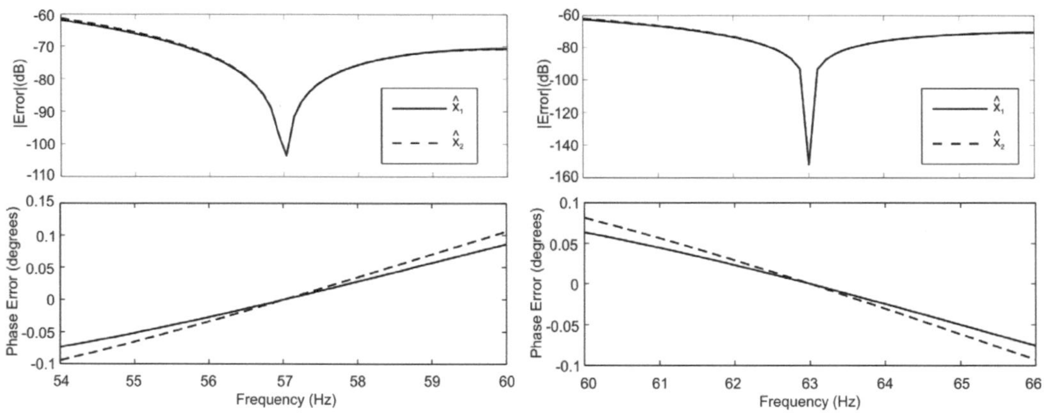

a) Error introduced by using fixed Kalman gains but considering $f = 57\,Hz$ in the mathematical model of the Kalman filter.

b) Error introduced by using fixed Kalman gains but considering $f = 63\,Hz$ in the mathematical model of the Kalman filter.

Fig. 6. Frequency response errors for different conditions of operation of the Kalman filter.

8. Experimental results

The single and three-phase synchronization methods were implemented in a fixed point DSP (TI-TMS320F2812) to evaluate their performance in real time. The Kalman gain used and sampling frequency are the same as described in section 7. Fig. 7a and Fig. 7b depict the synchronization signals obtained with the proposed single and the three-phase KF-PLLs superimposed with the distorted grid voltage ($THD = 5.8\%$).Fig. 7c and Fig. 7d show the synchronization signals for a sinusoidal grid voltage. The good behavior of both proposed structures can be noted, even when voltage waveforms are distorted.

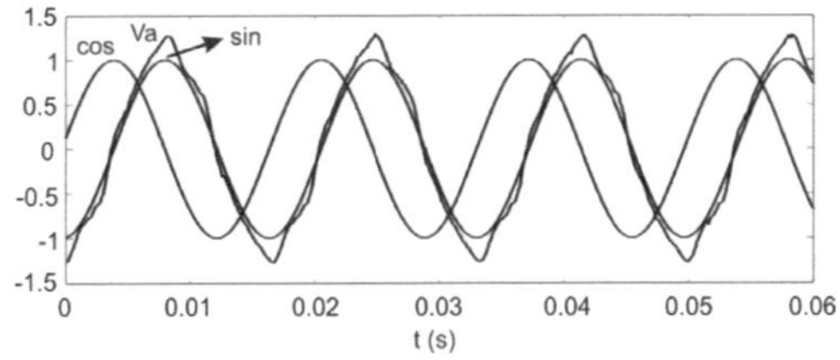

a) Single-phase under distorted grid voltages (THD=5.8%)

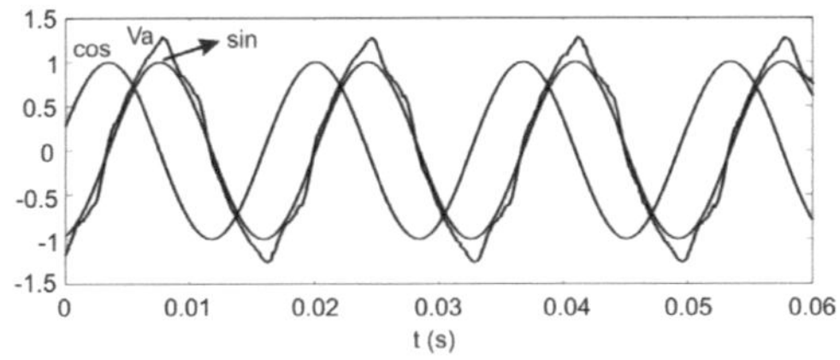

b) Three-phase under distorted grid voltages (THD=5.8%)

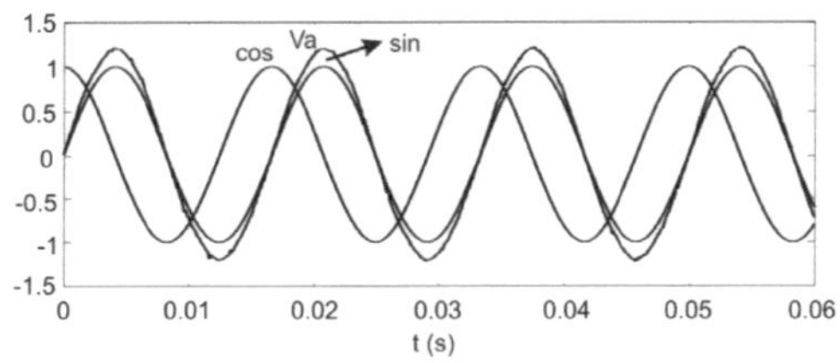

c) Single-phase under sinusoidal grid voltages

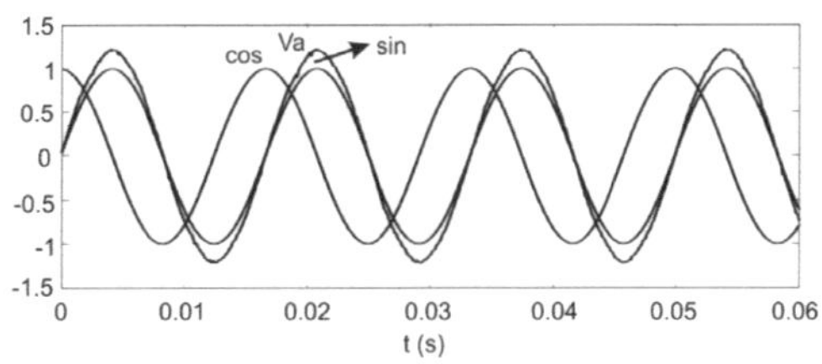

d) Three-phase under sinusoidal grid voltages

Fig. 7. Synchronization signals obtained.

The use of the KF-PLL for purposes of voltage analysis is exemplified in the following set of experimental results. Again, the results are based on a fixed point DSP (TI-TMS320F2812) implementation. The voltages are composed of a 220 V fundamental component and the following harmonics are present: 5th, 7th, and 11th, with amplitudes given by 0.3 p.u., 0.15 p.u. and 0.09 p.u., respectively, referring to the fundamental peak value. Therefore, the total harmonic distortion of the voltages is $THD = 34.7\%$. At $t = 0.0832\,s$ a voltage drop of 30% occurs in all phases. Additionally, an unbalance of 50% is considered in phase *c*. The KF-PLL was tuned considering: $\mathbf{Q} = 0.01 I_{10\times10} V^2$, $\mathbf{R} = 20V^2$, $Ku = 20$ and $Kw = 0.052$.

Fig. 8a shows the measured grid voltages while Fig 8b depicts the extracted fundamental components of each phase with their amplitudes. Note that the fundamental components are adequately detected. The same occurs with the peak values. The convergence of the signals is fast and occurs in less than one cycle.

Fig. 9 presents the extraction of the harmonics in the measured signal with their amplitudes evaluated in real time. Note that the non-existent 3rd harmonic is also correctly detected.

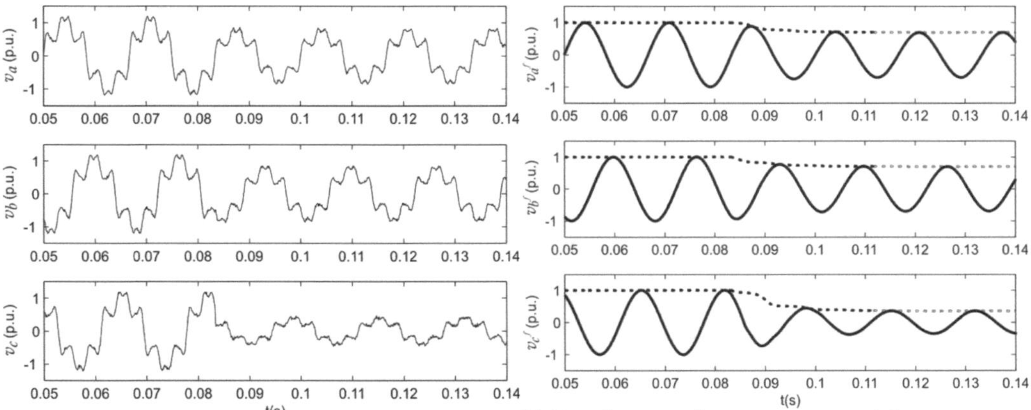

a) Measured voltages.

b) Fundamental components with amplitudes.

Fig. 8. Measured grid voltages and fundamental extraction.

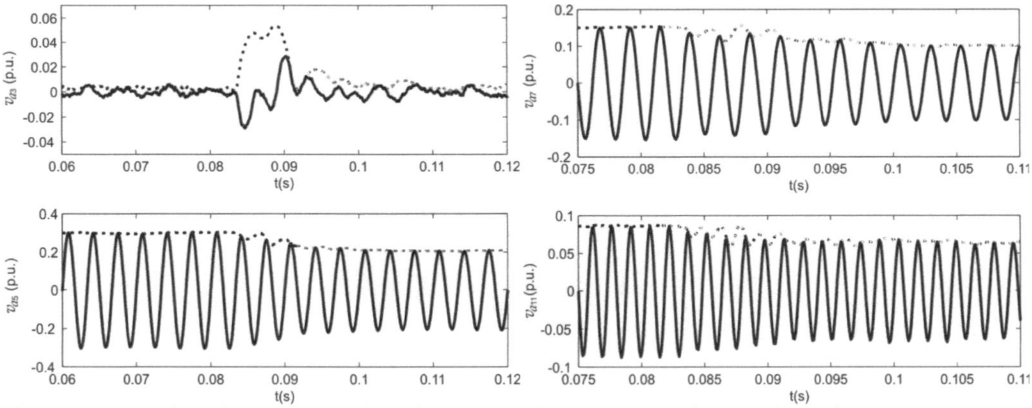

a) Extraction of 3rd (non-existent) and 5th harmonics.

b).Extraction of 7th and 11th harmonics.

Fig. 9. Harmonic decomposition and amplitude detection.

The detection of the symmetrical components is depicted in Fig. 10a. Until t=0.0832s the grid voltages are balanced and the negative and zero sequence are zero. After t=0.0832s, the voltages are unbalanced and the proposed method detects the presence of negative and zero sequences adequately. The amplitude of the positive, negative and zero sequences are also correctly identified.

Fig. 10b shows the generation of the synchronization signals with the negative sequence components of the fundamental voltages. It also presents the associated instantaneous phase. Similar results can also be obtained with the zero sequence component or any harmonic signal of interest.

Finally, Fig. 11 depicts the THD of the phase a voltage, evaluated in real time. It also shows the identified grid frequency, which due to the normalized signal used to drive the identifier, is practically immune to transients in grid voltages.

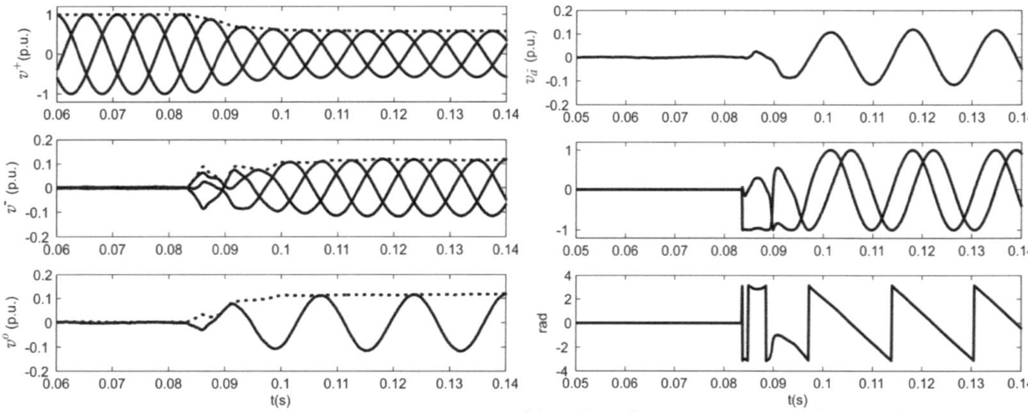

a) Positive, negative and zero sequences.

b) Synchronism signals with negative sequence and instantaneous phase.

Fig. 10. Symmetrical components and synchronism signals.

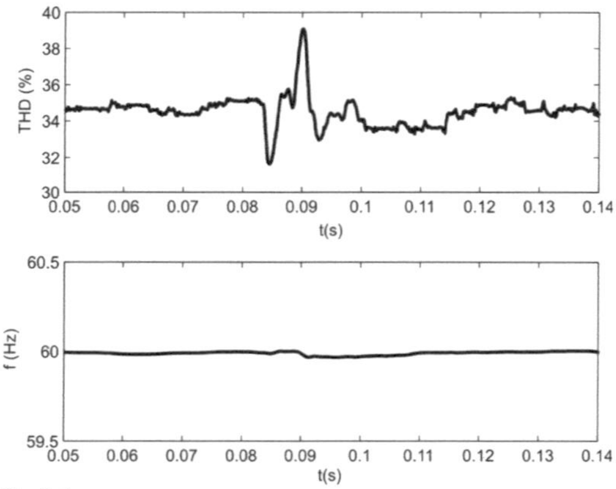

Fig. 11. THD and identified frequency.

9. Conclusions

This chapter presented a description of how the Kalman filter can be used to obtain the synchronization signals with the grid voltages as well as how it can also be helpful for voltage analysis. As for synchronization, the described methods are capable of dealing with signals corrupted by harmonics and measurement noise. For three-phase systems the method also considers voltage imbalance.

To deal with voltage frequency variations, the fundamental grid frequency is identified in real time to update the Kalman filter model. It was shown that for frequency deviations within the limits allowed by several standards, fixed Kalman gains can be used, which simplifies digital implementation. The formulation of the proposed synchronization schemes deals explicitly with the following phenomena that can occur in a real system: presence of harmonics, voltage transients, measurement noise, voltage imbalance and frequency deviation.

As mentioned, the synchronization methods can also provide information about the grid voltages such as harmonic analysis, amplitude detection, instantaneous phase, extraction of symmetrical components and frequency, useful for the analysis of power quality.
The experimental results show that the proposed synchronization methods can be implemented without great difficulty in a fixed-point DSP. The implementation based on fixed Kalman gains simplifies the DSP implementation, and it was shown that the effect on performance of the fixed gains is small.

10. References

BLAABJERG, F.; TEODORESCU, R.; LISERRE, M.; TIMBUS, A. V. (2006). Overview of control and grid synchronization for distributed power generation systems. *IEEE Transactions on Industrial Electronics*, Vol. 53, No. 5, October 2006, pp. 1398-1409

BOUTAYEB, M., RAFARALAHY, H., DAROUACH, M. (1997). Convergence analysis of the extended Kalman filter used as an observer for nonlinear deterministic discrete-time systems, *IEEE Transactions on Automatic Control*, Vol. 42, No. 4, April 1997, pp. 581-586

BOUTAYEB, M., AUBRY, D. (1999). A strong tracking extended Kalman observer for nonlinear discrete-time systems, *IEEE Transactions on Automatic Control*, Vol. 44, No. 8, August 1999, pp. 1550-1556

BROWN, R. G. (1992) *Introduction to Random Signals and Applied Kalman Filtering*, John Wiley & Sons, New York

BROWN, L. J., ZHANG, Q. (2004). Periodic disturbance cancellation with uncertain frequency, *Automatica*, Vol. 40, No. 4, April 2004, pp. 631-637

CAMPOS, A., JOOS, G., ZIOGAS, P. D., LINDSAY, J. F. (1994). Analysis and design of a series voltage unbalance compensator based on a three-phase VSI operating with unbalance switching functions, *IEEE Transactions on Power Electronics*, Vol. 9, No. 3, May 1994, pp. 269-274

CARDOSO, R., CÂMARA, H. T., GRÜNDLING, H. A. (2005). Sensorless induction motor control using low cost electrical sensors, *Proceedings of 36th IEEE Power Electronics Specialists Conference*, pp. 1600-1606, June 2005, IEEE, Recife

CARDOSO, R., DE CAMARGO, R. F., PINHEIRO, H., GRÜNDLING, H. A. (2006). Kalman filter based synchronization methods, *Proceedings of 37th IEEE Power Electronics Specialists Conference*, pp. 1935-1941, June 2006, IEEE, Jeju

CARDOSO, R.; KANIESKI, J. M.; PINHEIRO, H. & GRÜNDLING, H. A. (2007). Power quality evaluation based on optimum filtering theory for time-varying frequencies, *Proceedings of 9th Brazilian Power Electronics Conference*, pp. 462-467, September-October 2007, Sobraep, Blumenau

CARDOSO, R.; DE CAMARGO, R. F.; PINHEIRO, H. & GRÜNDLING, H. A. (2008). Kalman filter based synchronization methods. *IET Generation, Transmition & Distribution*, Vol. 2, No. 4, July 2008, pp. 542-555

CHUNG, S.-K. (2000). A phase tracking system for three phase utility interface inverters. *IEEE Transactions on Power Electronics*, Vol. 15, No. 3, May 2000, pp. 431-438

CHRISTIANSEN, G. S. (1994). Modelling of a PRML timing loop as a Kalman filter, *Proceedings of IEEE Global Telecommunications Conference*, pp. 1157-1161, November-December 1994, IEEE, San Francisco

DE CAMARGO, R. F., PINHEIRO, H. (2006). Synchronization method for three-phase PWM converters under unbalance and distorted grid. *IEE Proceedings Electric Power Applications*, Vol. 153, No. 5, September 2006, pp. 763-772

DRIESSEN, P. F. (1994). DPLL bit synchronizer with rapid acquisition using adaptive Kalman filtering techniques. *IEEE Transactions on Communications*, Vol. 42, No. 9, September 1994, pp. 2673-2675

FORTESCUE, C. L. (1918). Method of symmetrical coordinates applied to the solution of polyphase networks. *Trans. AIEE*, Vol. 37, 1918, pp. 1027-1140

FRANCIS, B. A., WONHAM, W. M. (1976). The internal model principle of control theory, *Automatica*, Vol. 12, No. 5, 1976, pp. 457-465

GELB, A., KASPER JR., J. F., NASH JR., R. A., PRICE, C. F., SUTHERLAND JR. A. A. (1996). *Applied Optimal Estimation*, M.I.T. Press, Cambridge

GUPTA, S. C. (1975). Phase-locked loops. *Proceedings of the IEEE*, Vol. 63, 1975, pp. 291-306

HSIEH, G.-C., HUNG, J. C. (1996). Phase-locked loop techniques-a survey. *IEEE Transactions on Industrial Electronics*, Vol. 43, No. 6, December 1996, pp. 609-615

IZADI, M. H., LEUNG, B. (2002). PLL-based frequency discriminator using the loop filter as an estimator. *IEEE Transactions on Circuit and Systems-II: Analog and Digital Signal Processing*, Vol. 49, No. 11, November 2002, pp. 721-727

IEC 60034 (1996). *Rotating electrical machines part 3: Specific requirements for turbine-type synchronous machines*, IEC

IEC 61000-2-2 (2001). *Electromagnetic compatibility (EMC) part 2-2: Environment-Compatibility levels for low frequency conducted disturbances and signaling in public low-voltage power supply systems*, IEC

IEEE Std C37.106 (2003). *IEEE guide for abnormal frequency protection for power generating plants*, IEEE

KALMAN, R. E. (1960). A new approach to linear filtering and prediction problems. *Journal of Basic Engineering*, Series 82D, March 1960 , pp. 35-45

KARIMI-GHARTEMANI, M., IRAVANI, M. R. (2004). A method for synchronization of power electronic converters in polluted and variable-frequency environments. *IEEE Transactions on Power Systems*, Vol. 19, No. 3, August 2004, pp. 1263-1270

KAURA, V., BLASKO, V. (1997). Operation of a phase locked loop system under distorted utility conditions. *IEEE Transactions on Industry Applications*, Vol. 33, No. 1, January/February 1997, pp. 58-63

MAYBECK, P. S. (1979). *Stochastic Models, Estimation and Control-Vol. 1*, Academic Press, New York

MEHRA, R. K. (1970). On the identification of variances and adaptive Kalman filtering. *IEEE Transactions on Automatic Control*, Vol. AC-15, No. 3, April 1970, pp. 175-184

OGATA, K. (1994). *Discrete-Time Control Systems*, Prentice-Hall, Upper Saddle River

PATAPOUNIAN, A. (1999). On phase-locked loops and Kalman filters. *IEEE Transactions on Communications*, Vol. 47, No. 5, May 1999, pp. 670-672

RODRÍGUEZ, P., LUNA, A., CIOBOTARU, M., TEODORESCU, R., BLAABJERG, F. (2006). Advanced grid synchronization system for power converters under unbalanced and distorted operating conditions, *Proceedings of Annual Conference of the IEEE Industrial Electronics Society*, pp. 5173-5178, November 2006, IEEE, Paris

SONG, H.-S., NAM, K. (2000). Instantaneous phase-angle estimation algorithm under unbalanced voltage-sag conditions. *IEE Proc. Gener. Transm. Distrib.*, Vol. 147, No. 6, November 2000, pp. 409-415

SVENSSON, J. (2001). Synchronization methods for grid-connected voltage source converters, *IEE Proc. Gener. Transm. Distrib.*, Vol. 148, No. 3, May 2001, pp. 229-235

TEXAS INSTRUMENTS (2002). *IQ Math Library-Module User's Guide-C28x Foundation Software*, TI, Dallas

TIMBUS, A. V., BLAABJERG, F., TEODORESCU, R., LISERRE, M., RODRIGUEZ, P. (2006). PLL algorithm for power generation systems robust to grid voltage faults, *Proceedings of 37th IEEE Power Electronics Specialists Conference*, pp. 1360-1366, June 2006, IEEE, Jeju

ZHAO, Z., BROWN L. (2004). Fast estimation of power system frequency using adaptive internal-model control technique, *Proceedings of 43rd IEEE Conference on Decision and Control*, pp. 845-850, December 2004, Bahamas

Industrial Applications and Communications

20

Application of the Unscented Kalman Filter (UKF) Estimation Techniques for Fault Detection Diagnosis and Isolation (FDDI) in Attitude Control (AC) and Heating Ventilation Air Conditioning (HVAC) Systems

Nicolae Tudoroiu[1], Kash Khorasani[1], Mohammed Zaheeruddin[1], Eshan Sobhani-Tehrani[1], Dumitru Burdescu[2] and Elena-Roxana Tudoroiu[3]
[1]*Concordia University, Montreal,*
[2]*University of Craiova,*
[3]*West University Politehnica Timisoara,*
[1]*Canada*
[2,3]*Romania*

1. Introduction

In this work we investigate two main applications of the detection and isolation of partial (soft) and total (hard) failures in the reaction wheel (RW) actuators of the satellite attitude control systems (ACS) and in the Heating Ventilation and Air Conditioning (HVAC) valve actuators respectively. The fault detection diagnosis and isolation (FDDI) is accomplished using a probabilistic approach based on the interactive multiple models (IMM) schemes embedded with Extended Kalman Filter (EKF) or Unscented Kalman Filter (UKF) estimation techniques. Towards this objective, the healthy modes of the ACS and HVAC systems under different operating conditions as well as a number of different fault scenarios including changes and anomalies in the temperature, power supply bus voltage, and unexpected current variations in the actuators of each axis of the satellite, or leakage, stuck-open and stuck-close fault modes in the HVAC actuator valves are considered. We describe and develop a bank of interacting multiple model Extended Kalman Filters (IMM_EKF) or Unscented Kalman Filters (IMM_UKF) to detect and isolate the above mentioned reaction wheel and valve failures in the ACS and HVAC systems. Also, it should be emphasized that the proposed IMM_EKF and IMM_UKF techniques are implemented based on high-fidelity highly nonlinear models of a commercial ITHACO RWA and discharge air temperature (DAT) cooling or heating coils. Compared to other fault detection diagnosis and isolation (FDDI) strategies developed in the control systems literature, the proposed FDDI schemes is shown, through extensive numerical simulations by using MATLAB and SIMULINK software packages, to be more accurate, less computationally demanding, and more robust with the potential of extending to a number of other engineering applications. Also, the proposed algorithms deal directly with the nonlinear dynamics of the system, the unanticipated valve actuator failures and statistic properties of the process noise and measurements such as the mean and covariance matrices in the most general formulation based on the Extended Kalman Filter (EKF) or Unscented Kalman Filter (UKF) estimation theory [Tudoroiu & Khorasani, 2007; Tudoroiu et al., 2006; Plett, 2004; Haykin 2003; Joseph, 2003; Wan & Merwe, 2000; Julier & Uhlman, 1997]. The satellite's attitude control system (ACS) faults caused by malfunctions in its components, actuators, and sensors result from unexpected interferences or gradual aging of system components. These faults could result in higher energy consumption, loss of the vehicle control, and in case of total failures catastrophic loss of the satellite. With increasing emphasis recently placed on energy efficiency and equipment safety and reliability, there is a need to develop robust intelligent and autonomous tools capable of detecting, isolating and diagnosing any sensor, actuator or system component fault so that remedial reconfiguration and recovery actions could be taken as soon as possible with minimal support from ground station and operators. The increasing complexity of space vehicles and the prevailing cost reduction measures have necessitated calls for fewer satellite operators and an increasingly larger drive toward more autonomy in the satellite diagnostics and control systems. Current methods for detecting and correcting anomalies onboard the satellite and specifically on the ground are primarily ad hoc and manual and, therefore, slow and error-prone. Traditionally, health monitoring and trend analysis of satellite telemetry data have been a time consuming, repetitive, and labour-intensive activity. Operators normally inspect telemetry plots downloaded to the ground stations to determine the current satellite state and health. Given this fact, relieving operators of portions of the telemetry monitoring and anomaly diagnosis task is highly desirable and necessary. It should be recognized that satellite monitoring and fault diagnosis could be automated using advanced decision support systems such as rule-based, expert systems, and intelligent-based methodologies .Conventionally various forms of statistical evaluation techniques are employed and comparisons with prediction and estimation models are performed. However, the evaluations still require extensive human expertise that is subject to error, and could result in catastrophic failures if operators fail to detect and identify critical faults in safety critical components and subsystems such as the ACS. In this work, an advanced decision support system is proposed to accurately and expeditiously monitor the telemetry data in the reaction wheels of a satellite. Our goal is to improve the efficiency, accuracy, and reliability of trend analysis and diagnosis techniques through utilization of estimation and model-based methodologies. Health monitoring of the attitude control system is the process that involves:

i. examining satellite telemetry data,
ii. developing mathematical or functional representations of the data,
iii. analyzing the derived information to formulate an evaluation of the state and condition of the satellite components, and
iv. determining if safety critical trends exist that could lead to catastrophes and loss of the vehicle.

If serious and critical trends are detected, corrective or preventive measures are then identified and reconfiguration and recovery mechanisms are invoked. Specifically, based on the set of fault characteristics and scenarios considered, models that represent the most likely possible system behaviour patterns and structures will be first constructed. Bank of filters based on these models are then designed to operate in parallel at all times [Haykin, 2001; Zang & Xiao, 1998; Zang & Xiao, 1997]. Each filter is designed and tuned to a particular model (normal or faulty mode) for obtaining a model-based state estimator. The overall state estimate is a "certain" combination of these model-based estimates and the jump or switching in the system mode is modeled as a transition between the estimated models, assuming that this transition is described by a first order Markov chain. By considering various scenarios corresponding to the evolution of the ACS, and based on our preliminary results in [Tudoroiu & Khorasani, 2007; Tudoroiu et al., 2006; Tudoroiu & Zaheeruddin, 2006], we will develop a fault detection, diagnosis, and isolation (FDDI) strategy for the reaction wheel actuators. Subsequently, appropriate remedial actions could be undertaken in the shortest time and as expeditiously as possible to maintain the desired specifications and requirements of the mission. Conventionally, for regulating variables such as temperature, currents, and torques in the ACS various SISO (single input single output) or MIMO (multi input multi output) PI/PID (proportional, integral and derivative), self-tuning, or adaptive feedback control strategies are utilized. The design of a closed-loop control system for achieving the stringent performance specifications of the ACS is a very challenging task since the system:

i. exhibits inherently a highly nonlinear behaviour,
ii. has a multivariable structure, and
iii. is subjected to multiple sources of uncertainties and disturbances.

In this work, we treat the satellite as a MIMO system that is managed by PID controllers yielding good tracking and dynamic performance for the healthy ACS. We then investigate the development of our proposed FDDI strategy for the reaction wheels failures by utilizing bank of interacting Kalman Filter estimators. The FDDI scheme is applied to a highly nonlinear model of the reaction wheel considered as well as a nonlinear attitude dynamics of the satellite [Bialke, 1998]. Regarding the HVAC systems for most of them several failures caused by malfunctions in components, actuators, and sensors can be as result of unexpected interference, or gradual aging of system components. Consequently these failures have a great impact on the energy consumption, thermal comfort and generate severe equipment operating problems. To increase the energy efficiency and equipment reliability, there is a need to develop robust fault detection and diagnosis tools capable of detecting and isolating any sensor, actuator or system component faults so that remedial actions could be taken as soon as possible. The FDDI based on the IMM algorithm is implemented in a simulation environment, and the fault diagnosis results are presented for a several fault scenarios in terms of mode probabilities and mode probability indices.

2. The satellite's ACS model and the discharge air temperature (DAT) system

2.1 The satellite's ACS model

A hypothetical satellite is considered here having a scientific mission to study the Earth. This is a three-axis stabilized satellite which consumes a maximum of approximately 200 Watts of power that is generated by solar arrays and stored power from batteries, of approximately 24 V each, designated by V_{bus}. The attitude control system (ACS) consists of three-axis stabilized system making use of 4-reaction wheels assembly (3 Active + 1 Redundant) type ITHACO. The ACS could be conceptualized as either a MIMO system or as a SISO system if each axis is considered independent and having no interactions with other axes. In this paper, a high fidelity nonlinear representation of a reaction wheel, as shown in Figure 1, is considered. A detailed mathematical model of this reaction wheel is described and derived below. The satellite's attitude control is achieved by using three reaction wheels to generate control torques in each of the three axes independently. The reaction wheel actuators utilized are essentially torque motors with high inertial rotors. They can spin in either direction and provide one axis of control for each wheel. Each reaction wheel (Roll, Pitch or Yaw) is aligned with one of the body axes of the satellite. The Roll, Pitch or Yaw reaction wheels act as actuators for the Roll, Pitch or Yaw control loops, respectively. Each reaction wheel consists of several internal and external loops that have to be integrated to yield an accurate overall mathematical model. The following loops play an important role in the dynamics of each reaction wheel (refer to Figure 1 and [Bialke, 1998] for further details):

i. The negative feedback EMF torque limiting loop τ_{EMF} due to low bus voltage, V_{bus}, condition that may limit the motor torque at high speeds because of increasing back-EMF voltage gain, K_e, of the motor,

ii. The negative feedback viscous and coulomb friction loop. Viscous friction is generated due to the bearing lubricant, and it has a strong sensitivity to temperature, T. The relationship between temperature and drag torque model is given by:

$$\tau_V = (0.049 - 0.0002(T + 30)) \tag{1}$$

Coulomb friction is caused by friction within bearings, and is independent of the wheel speed and temperature, and therefore is primarily of interest as a disturbance source. This loop is included only for modeling purpose; we don't measure these frictions to be used in the control loop, only we take into consideration their effect in the reaction wheel system.

iii. The negative feedback speed limiter loop is to prevent the flywheel from reaching unsafe speeds,

iv. The motor torque control is included since the motor driver is essentially a voltage controlled current source with a gain G_d. In our research, we consider the motor current I_m to be directly proportional to the torque command voltage. The motor has a torque constant gain K_i, which delivers a torque proportional to the current driver. By changing the torque constant gain K_i, we have the possibility of generating another source of a fault, due to unexpected changes in motor current value, and

v. The torque noise disturbance τ_{noise} is a very low frequency torque variation from bearings due to lubricant dynamics. This torque can be specified as a deviation from the ideal location of rotor at any constant speed, and is connected directly to satellite jitter by the ratio of flywheel inertia to the satellite inertia, according to

$$\theta_{sat} = \theta_{noise} \frac{J}{I_{sat}} \tag{2}$$

The torque noise is assumed as a sine wave having a high pass filter frequency ω_n

$$\tau_{noise} = J\theta_{noise}\omega_n^2 \sin(\omega_n t) \tag{3}$$

where θ_{sat} represents the satellite angular jitter and θ_{noise} represents the torque noise angle. The speed limiter and EMF torque limiting loops use three conditional Heveaside functions to enable the high-gain negative feedback K_s, when the reaction wheel exceeds an established speed threshold ω_s, and to eliminate the voltage drop when the power is not being drawn from the bus during a deceleration (since the energy is being removed from the wheel). The EMF torque limiting loop could be controlled by the voltage feedback gain, K_f.. The above models and existing governing relationships as shown in Figure 1 could be combined to yield a state-space representation for the reaction wheel, such in [Tudoroiu et al., 2006; Tudoroiu & Khorasani, 2007].

2.2 Discharge Air Temperature (DAT) system

Figure 2 shows a schematic diagram of a DAT loop of a HVAC system. A central air supply provides air at a controlled temperature and water flow rate for use in heating coil, T_{a0} and $\dot{m}_w$ respectively. A heating coil interposed in the central air supply space heats the discharged air using hot water. The temperature of the air leaving the heating coil T_a is controlled by regulating the rate at which the hot water flows through the heating coil as shown by the feedback control loop. The discharged air flow rate is regulated to maintain a predetermined static air pressure within the temperature controlled space. In Figure 2, u represents the hot water flow rate, i.e., the DAT loop subsystem input, and T_a, is the DAT output. The entering air temperature T_{a0} is considered as a disturbance on the system.
The DAT system is modeled as a SISO system as shown by the block diagram in Figure 3. The model is nonlinear and described by the following equations [Zaheeruddin & Patel, 1995]:

$$\frac{dT_a}{dt} = c_1 h_a \eta_{ov} (\overline{T}_a - \overline{T}_t) + c_2 \dot{m}_a (T_a - T_{a,in}) \tag{4}$$

$$\frac{dT_w}{dt} = c_3 h_w (\overline{T}_t - \overline{T}_w) + c_4 \dot{m}_w (T_w - T_{w,in}) \tag{5}$$

$$\begin{aligned}\frac{d\overline{T}_t}{dt} = \frac{1-\eta_s}{\eta_s + c_5}[c_6 \dot{m}_a (T_a - T_{a,in}) + \frac{c_7}{1-\eta_s} h_w (\overline{T}_t - \overline{T}_w) + \\ + (c_8 + \frac{c_9}{1-\eta_s}) h_a \eta_{ov} (\overline{T}_a - \overline{T}_t)]\end{aligned} \tag{6}$$

For the simulations we use the following values for the coefficients:

$$c_1 = -1.2046, c_2 = -38.9034, c_3 = 4.5714 \times 10^{-5}, c_4 = -0.2023,$$

$$c_5 = 1.1192, c_6 = 38.9034, c_7 = -1.4926 \times 10^{-5}, c_8 = 1.2046,$$

$c_9 = 4.8995 \times 10^{-4}$, and the air and water heat transfer coefficients h_a, h_w, the sensitive efficiency quadratic functions η_s, η_{ov} are given by:

$$h_a = -17.58 \dot{m}_a^{\ 2} + 70.562 \dot{m}_a + 8.1796\,, \tag{7}$$

$$h_w = 1403.2 (\dot{m}_w)^{0.8}\,, \tag{8}$$

$$\eta_s = 0.16375 \dot{m}_a^2 - 0.39483 \dot{m}_a + 0.92805\,, \tag{9}$$

$$\eta_{ov} = 1 - 0.9(1 - \eta_s). \tag{10}$$

The variation ranges for the disturbance inputs $\dot{m}_a, T_{a,in}, T_{w,in}$, and the control input $\dot{m}_w$, are given by:

$$\dot{m}_a \in [0.1,\ 0.8]\left[\frac{kg}{s}\right], T_{a,in} \in [16, 22][^0C],\ T_{w,in} \in [35, 50][^0C]$$

The variables that appear in this DAT model have the following significance:

T_a $[^0C]$ -the air temperature leaving the heating coil,

T_w $[^0C]$ - the hot water supply temperature, with their average values given by

$$\overline{T}_a = \frac{T_a + T_{a,in}}{2}, \overline{T}_w = \frac{T_w + T_{w,in}}{2},$$

$\overline{T}_t$ $[^0C]$ - the average tube temperature, $T_{a,in}$ $[^0C]$ -the inlet air temperature leaving the heating coil, $T_{w,in}$ $[^0C]$ -the inlet water supply temperature, $\dot{m}_a$ $\left[\frac{kg}{s}\right]$ -the input air flow rate, and $\dot{m}_w$ $\left[\frac{kg}{s}\right]$ -the water flow rate.

The input of the simplified *SISO* model is hot water flow rate, $\dot{m}_w$, $u(k)$, and the output is the temperature of air leaving the heating coil, T_a [°C], $y(k)$. Hot water supply temperature T_w[°C] and the average tube temperature $\overline{T}_t$ [°C] act as disturbances on the DAT loop of HVAC system. Also such as input disturbances could be considered $\dot{m}_a, T_{a,in}$, and $T_{w,in}$. In practice the hot water flow rate is regulated such that the temperature of air leaving the heating coil is maintained closed to a chosen set-point. In this representation the heating coil output temperature set point is more directly related to the overall DAT subsystem performance, and the model uncertainties are due to variable heat and mass transfer rates. The equivalent discrete time space system representation of the DAT system (4)-(6) has the following form:

$$\begin{aligned} x_1(k+1) = x_1(k) + c_1 h_a(k)\eta_{ov}(k)T_s(\overline{x}_1(k) - x_3(k)) + \\ c_2 T_s(x_1(k) - p_1(k))p_2(k) \end{aligned} \tag{11}$$

$$\begin{aligned} x_2(k+1) = x_2(k) + c_3 h_w(k)T_s(x_3(k) - \overline{x}_2(k)) + \\ c_4 T_s(x_2(k) - p_3(k))u(k) \end{aligned} \tag{12}$$

$$\begin{aligned} x_3(k+1) = x_3(k) + \frac{1-\eta_s}{\eta_s + c_5} T_s[c_6 u(x_1(k) - p_2(k))p_1(k) + \\ \frac{c_7}{1-\eta_s} h_w(k)(x_3(k) - \overline{x}_2(k))p_2(k) + \\ (c_8 + \frac{c_9}{1-\eta_s})h_a(k)\eta_{ov}(k)(\overline{x}_1(k) - x_3(k))] \end{aligned} \tag{13}$$

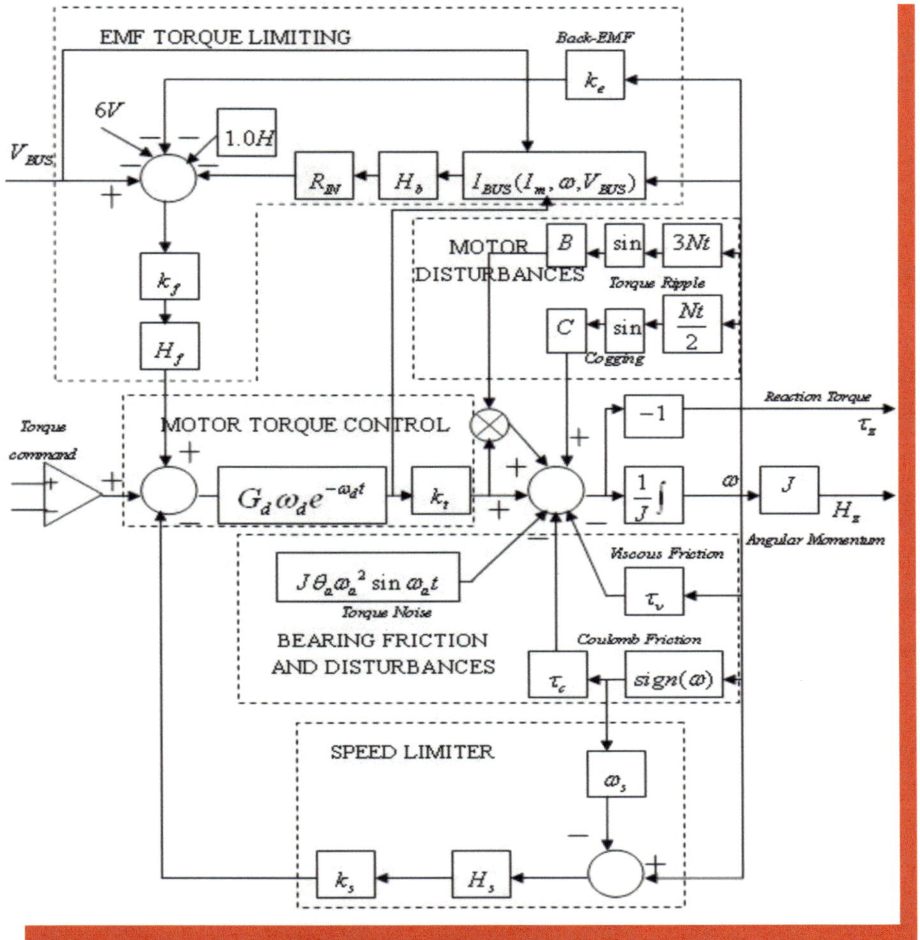

Fig. 1. A detailed block diagram of a high fidelity reaction wheel model.

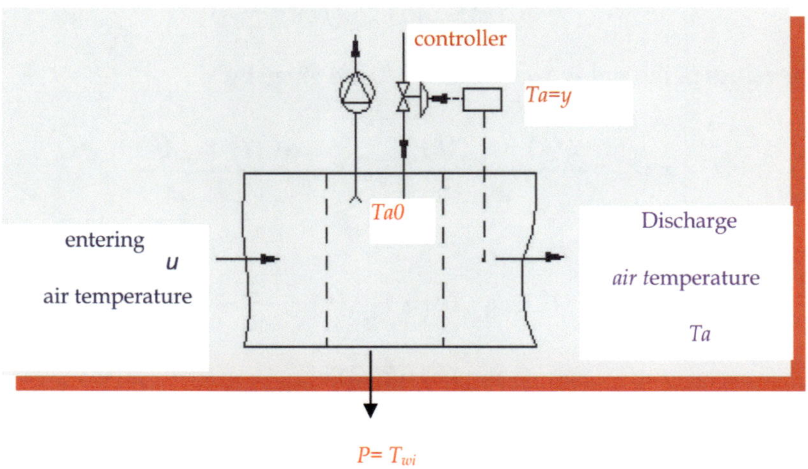

Fig. 2. Schematic diagram of DAT system

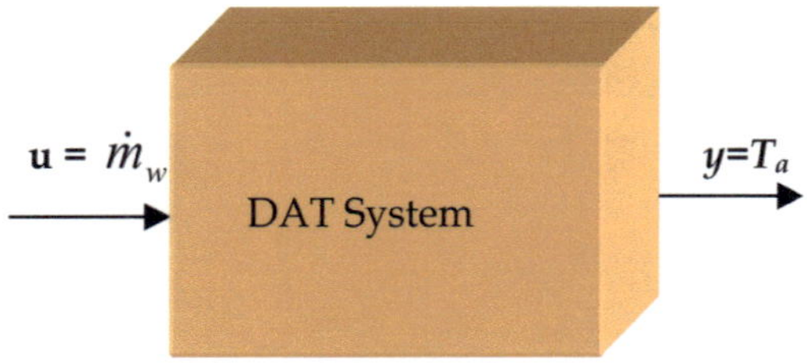

Fig. 3. SISO DAT oriented system

$$y(k) = x_1(k) \tag{14}$$

where
$x(k) = [x_1(k)\ \ x_2(k)\ \ x_3(k)]^T = [T_a(k)\ \ T_w(k)\ \ \overline{T}_t(k)]^T$ represents the state space vector,
$u(k) = \dot{m}_w(k)$ is the DAT subsystem input,
$y(k) = [T_a(k)]$ is the DAT subsystem output, and
$p(k) = [p_1(k)\ \ p_2(k)\ \ p_3(k)]^T = [T_{a,in}(k)\ \ \dot{m}_a(k)\ \ T_{w,in}(k)\ ]^T$ represents the disturbance input vector. In simulation environment we consider the sampling time T_s = 4 seconds.
The sensitive efficiency quadratic functions η_s, η_{ov} and the time variable water heat transfer coefficients h_a, h_w, become:

$$\eta_s(k) = 0.16375 p_2^{\ 2}(k) - 0.39483 p_2(k) + 0.92805 \tag{15}$$

$$\eta_{ov}(k) = 1 - 0.9(1 - \eta_s(k)) \tag{16}$$

$$h_a(k) = -17.58 p_2^{\ 2}(k) + 70.562 p_2(k) + 8.1796 \tag{17}$$

$$h_w(k) = 1403.2(u(k))^{0.8} \tag{18}$$

The average values of the states $x_1(k)$ and $x_2(k)$ are given by

$$\overline{x}_1(k) = \frac{x_1(k) + x_{1,in}(k)}{2},\ \overline{x}_2(k) = \frac{x_2(k) + x_{2,in}(k)}{2} \tag{19}$$

where

$$x_{1,in}(k) = T_{a,in}(k),$$

$$x_{2,in}(k) = T_{w,in}(k)\,.$$

The dynamics of the valve actuator is integrated in the plant dynamics, and will be represented by a nonlinear block with backlash characteristic of dead zone width =2r, such in Figure 4.

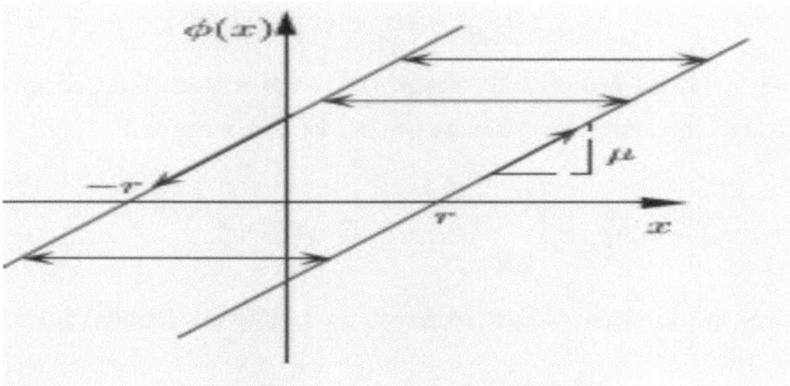

Fig. 4. The backslash nonlinearity

The input-output behaviour of the backlash nonlinearity can be described by two modes of operation, as either tracking or in the dead zone:

Tracking described by the following differential equation:

$$\dot{w} = \mu \dot{y} \tag{20}$$

with the solution given by:

$$w = \mu(y - r) \text{ for } \frac{dy}{dx} > 0 \text{, and} \tag{21}$$

$$w = \mu(y + r) \text{ for } \frac{dy}{dx} < 0 \tag{22}$$

Dead zone described by the following differential equation:

$$\dot{w} = 0 \quad |w - \mu y| \le \mu r \tag{23}$$

where r is the dead zone width and μ is the slope of tracking region such as depicted in the Figure 4, with

$$y = \phi(x) \text{, and} \tag{24}$$

$$w(t) = \phi(\phi_0, x([0,t)) = \Phi[x, \phi_0](t) \text{, } t \in [0,T] \tag{25}$$

Unlike memory less nonlinearities, hysteresis output at any given time is function of the entire history of the input, and the initial condition of the output, ϕ_0.

3. Kalman filter estimation techniques

3.1 Extended Kalman Filter (EKF)

Consider the dynamics of a *linear* stochastic system expressed in the state-space difference representation

$$x_{k+1} = Fx_k + Gu_k + w_k \tag{26}$$

$$y_k = Hx_k + v_k \tag{27}$$

where w_k and v_k are the process and measurement noise, respectively, that are assumed to be independent white Gaussian random processes with zero mean and

$$E[w_n w_k^T] = \begin{cases} Q_w, n = k \\ 0, n \neq k \end{cases}, \quad E[v_n v_k^T] = \begin{cases} R_v, n = k \\ 0, n \neq k \end{cases} \tag{28}$$

The process and measurement noise have normal probability distributions governed by

$$\mathrm{p}(w) \sim N(0, Q_w), \ \mathrm{p}(v) \sim N(0, R_v) \tag{29}$$

The covariance matrices Q_w (process noise covariance) and R_v (measurement noise covariance) might change with each time step or measurement, but in our approach we assume that they are constant. Due to the process noise injected in the state space equation (26)-(27), the state vector $x_k \in R^n$ becomes random variable with its distribution approximated by a Gaussian distribution function $\mathrm{p}(x) \sim G(\hat{x}, P_x)$. The general formulation of EKF algorithm used for the state estimation of the dynamical system (26)-(27) is well presented in the literature and we recommend for documentation some of the several fundamental papers such as [Plett, 2004; Haykin 2003;Joseph, 2003; Wan & Merwe, 2000; Julier & Uhlman, 1997]. The covariance matrices Q_w (process noise covariance) and R_v (measurement noise covariance), together with the initial error covariance $P_{0|0}$ are the three tuning parameters in the EKF algorithm. The matrices Q_w and R_v are determined empirically and account for uncertainty in the tracking data. Setting these matrices "properly" significantly contributes in making the EKF filter robust. The error covariance matrix P indicates uncertainty in the state estimate and provides criterion for the error bound.

3.2 Unscented Transform Techniques (UTT)

Compared to EKF the UKF addresses the approximation issues presented in [Haykin, 2003; Joseph, 2003; Wan & Merwe, 2000; Julier & Uhlman, 1997]. The state distribution is represented by a Gaussian Random Variable, specified using a minimal set of carefully chosen sigma points. These sigma points completely capture the true mean and covariance of the Gaussian random variable, and when propagated through the true non-linear system, capture the posterior mean and covariance accurately until the 3rd order (Taylor series expansion) for any nonlinearity. The Unscented Transformation (UT), is a method for calculating the statistics of a random variable, which undergoes a nonlinear transformation. Consider propagating a random variable x (dimension L) through a nonlinear function, $y = g(x)$. We assume that x has the mean $\overline{x}$ and the covariance P_x. To calculate the statistics of y we will build a matrix X of $2L+1$ sigma vectors X_i (with corresponding weights W_i), as follows:

$$
\begin{aligned}
X_0 &= \bar{x} \\
X_i &= \bar{x} + (\sqrt{(L+\lambda)\times P_x})_i, i = 1,2...,L \\
X_i &= \bar{x} - (\sqrt{(L+\lambda)\times P_x})_{i-L}, i = L+1,...,2L \\
W_0^m &= \frac{\lambda}{L+\lambda} \\
W_0^c &= \frac{\lambda}{L+\lambda} + (1-\alpha^2+\beta) \\
W_i^m &= W_i^c = \frac{1}{2\times(L+\lambda)}, i = 1,2...,2L
\end{aligned} \tag{30}
$$

where the parameter λ is selected in deterministic manner

$$
\lambda = \alpha^2 \times (L+\kappa) - L \tag{31}
$$

and α represents a scaling parameter, which determines the spread of the sigma points around mean state value $\bar{x}$ and is usually set to a small positive value. k is a secondary scaling parameter which is usually set to 0, β is used to incorporate prior knowledge of the distribution of x (for Gaussian distribution, β =2 is optimal), and $\sqrt{(L+\lambda)P_x)}_i$ is the *i-th* row of the matrix square root. The Unscented Transform determine the mean and covariance of system output y by approximation, using a weighted sample mean and covariance of the posterior sigma points. A simple example is shown in Figure 5 for a two-dimensional system. The left plot shows the true mean and covariance propagation using Monte-Carlo sampling [Haykin, 2003; Joseph, 2003; Julier & Uhlman, 1997], the center plots show the results using a linearization approach as would be done in the Unscented Transform (UT), and the right plots show the performance of the UT.

$$
\begin{aligned}
Y_i &= g(X_i) \\
\bar{y} &\approx \sum_{i=0}^{2L} W_i^m Y_i \\
P_y &\approx \sum_{i=0}^{2L} W_i^c [Y_i - \bar{y}][Y_i - \bar{y}]^T
\end{aligned} \tag{32}
$$

3.3 Unscented Kalman Filter (UKF) technique

The Unscented Kalman Filter (UKF) technique is based on the unscented transformation (UT) [Haykin, 2003; Joseph, 2003; Wan & Merwe, 2000; Julier & Uhlman, 1997] and addresses the general problem of state estimation $\mathbf{x}_k \in R^n$ of a discrete-time controlled process that is governed by the nonlinear stochastic difference state-space equation with a measurement $\mathbf{y}_k \in \mathbf{R}^m$ that is given by the output equation

$$
\mathbf{x}_{k+1} = f(\mathbf{x}_k, \mathbf{u}_k) + \mathbf{w}_k \tag{33}
$$

$$
\mathbf{y}_k = g(\mathbf{x}_k, \mathbf{u}_k) + \mathbf{v}_k \tag{34}
$$

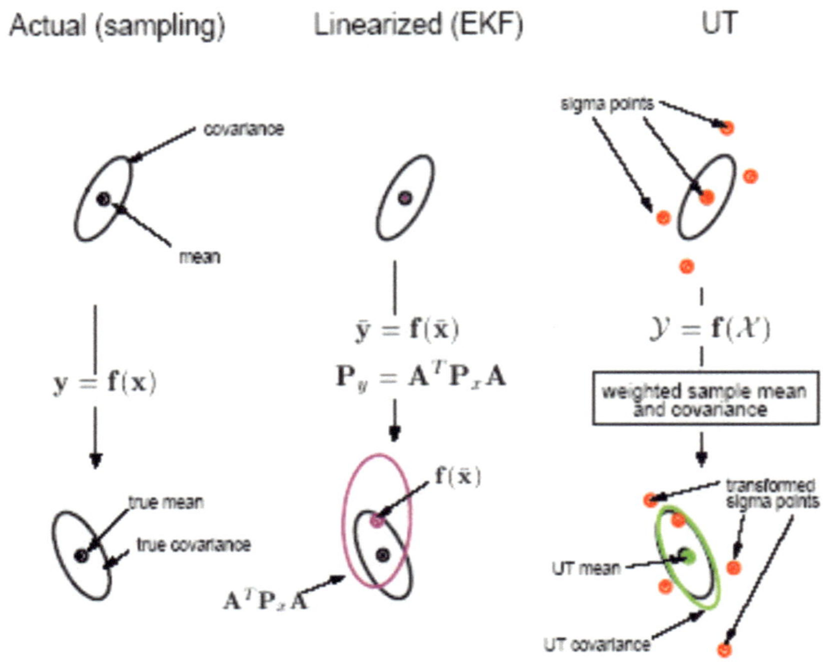

Fig. 5. Two-dimensional example of the Unscented Transform [1]-[4]

The random variables $\mathbf{w}_k$ and $\mathbf{v}_k$ representing the process and measurement noise injected to drive the system dynamics are generated by the additive noise sources. They are assumed to be independent, zero mean, white, and with normal probability distributions:

$$p(\mathbf{w}) \sim N(0, \mathbf{Q}_\mathbf{w})$$

$$p(\mathbf{v}) \sim N(0, \mathbf{R}_\mathbf{v}) \tag{35}$$

The covariance matrices $\mathbf{Q}_w$ (process noise covariance) and $\mathbf{R}_v$ (measurement noise covariance) might change with each time step or measurement, but in our approach we assume they are constant. Due to the process noise injected in the state space equation the state vector $\mathbf{x}_k \in \mathbf{R}^n$ becomes random variable with its distribution approximated by a Gaussian distribution function:

$$p(\mathbf{x}) \sim G(\hat{\mathbf{x}}, \mathbf{P}_\mathbf{x}) \tag{36}$$

The vital operation performed in the Kalman Filter is the propagation of a Gaussian random state variable $\mathbf{x}_k \in \mathbf{R}^n$ through the system dynamics. In the Extended Kalman Filter (EKF) estimator the Gaussian random state variable $\mathbf{x}_k \in \mathbf{R}^n$ is propagated analytically through the first-order linearization of the nonlinear system.

This can introduce large errors in the true posterior mean and covariance of the transformed Gaussian random state variable, which may lead to sub-optimal performance and sometimes divergence of the filter. The UKF estimator approach is developed such as an

alternative to the EKF estimator and addresses this problem by using a deterministic sampling approach.
Using the principle that a minimal set of carefully chosen sample points can be used to parameterize mean and covariance, the UKF estimator yields superior performance compare to EKF estimator, specially for nonlinear systems. These sample points completely capture the true mean and covariance of the Gaussian random state variable $\mathbf{x}_k \in \mathbf{R}^n$, and are propagated through the true nonlinear system dynamics. The main advantage of the UKF estimator is that does not require the calculation of the Jacobean matrices that could lead to implementation difficulties In this work we developed an augmented UKF architecture [Haykin, 2003; Joseph, 2003; Wan & Merwe, 2000; Julier & Uhlman, 1997].
The algorithm is developed to compute a collection of sigma points corresponding to the state vector $\mathbf{x}_k$ or noise signals $\mathbf{w}_k$ and $\mathbf{v}_k$ stored in the column of the $L \times (2L+1)$ sigma point matrix $\mathbf{X}_{k-1}$, where $L = \dim(X) + \dim(W) + \dim(V)$.

4. Design of the IMM Fault Detection and Diagnosis (FDDI) strategy

4.1 Jump Markov linear hybrid dynamic model

The multiple model approach for fault detection and diagnosis (FDD) assumes that the actual system at any time can be modeled sufficiently accurately by the following jump Markov hybrid nonlinear system:

$$x(k+1) = F(k, m(k+1), x(k), u(k)) + T(k, m(k+1))w(k, m(k+1)),\ x(0) \sim N(\hat{x}_0, P_0) \quad (37)$$

$$z(k) = G(k, m(k), x(k), u(k)) + v(k, m(k)) \quad (38)$$

The mode of the system (normal or faulty) at time k is selected by a discrete process m_j and modeled as a s-state, first-order Markov chain with transition probabilities $\pi_{ij}(k)$ given by:

$$\pi_{ij}(k) = P\{m_j(k+1) \mid m_i(k)\},\ \forall m_i, m_j \in S \quad (39)$$

and

$$0 \le \pi_{ij}(k) \le 1,\ i = \overline{1,N}, j = \overline{1,N}, \qquad \sum_j \pi_{ij}(k) = 1,\ i = \overline{1,N} \quad (40)$$

The initial state distribution of the Markov chain is $\pi(0) = [\pi_1\ \pi_2\ \pi_3 \ldots\ldots \pi_N]$, where

$$0 \le \pi_j \le 1,\ \forall j = \overline{1,N},\ \sum_{j=1}^{N} \pi_j = 1 \quad (41)$$

and where $x(k)$ is the state vector, $z(k)$ is the mode-dependent measurement vector, and $u(k)$ is the control input vector. The process and measurement noise vectors $w(k)$ and $v(k)$, respectively, are mutually independent, additive, white Gaussian of zero mean and covariance matrices $Q_w(k)$ and $R_v(k)$, and are independent of the initial state $x(0)$. In expression (39), P{.} denotes the probability operator. The event that m_j is in effect at time

k is denoted as $m_j(k) = \{m(k) = m_j\}$, and $S = \{m_1, m_2, ..., m_N\}$ represents the set of all possible system modes. The system (37)-(38) may jump from one such system to another at a random time. It can be observed from (37) that the state vector observations are in general noisy and dependent. Therefore, the mode information is embedded in the measurement sequence. The system mode sequence is an indirectly observed Markov chain, from which the transition probability matrix $\pi = \{\pi_{ij}\}$ represents a design parameter. The FDD problem for the above hybrid system (37)-(38) can be stated as that of determining the current model state. In other words, it involves determining whether the normal or a faulty mode is currently in effect from a sequence of noisy observations. How to design set of modes to represent the possible system modes is a key issue in multiple model approach, which is problem-dependent. This design should be achieved by attempting to have models (approximately) that represent or cover all possible system modes at any given time. This represents the model set design that is critical for multiple model based FDD. To design a good set of models requires *a priori* knowledge of possible faults in the system. These issues are formally described in the next subsection.

4.2 IMM Fault Detection and Diagnosis and Isolation (FDDI) strategy

In application of multiple model estimation techniques for fault detection and diagnosis, the following tasks should be implemented:

i. model set design,
ii. filter selection,
iii. estimate fusion, and
iv. filter re-initialization.

Filter selection deals with the problem of selecting a model-based recursive filter such as an unscented Kalman Filter (UKF) for each model of the nonlinear system. The estimate fusion task combines model-conditional estimates to obtain an overall estimate. Towards this end, three approaches could be investigated, namely soft, hard and random decisions. The procedure for reinitializing each single-model based filter from time to time is of significant importance for multi-model estimation. The simplest approach for reinitializing each filter is to use its previous state estimate and filter covariance at the current cycle. In this case filters are operating in parallel and no interactions exist among them. However, this may lead to unsatisfactory performance when the system structure or its mode changes. For this reason, it would be more appropriate to reinitialize each filter using the previous overall state estimate and covariance matrix which does lead to an interacting multiple model estimation technique. For each faulty mode corresponding to a set of possible ACS reaction wheel or HVAC faults and a normal operating mode, one can apply an EKF or UKF based on measurements collected from the reaction wheel or valve actuators. The input considered can be taken as the torque command voltage vector ***u***, or water flow rate. The dynamics of a Kalman Filter estimation technique associated with each mode is described by the following nonlinear state space representation:

$$
\begin{aligned}
x_j(k+1) &= F_j(k, x_j(k), u_j(k)) + T_j(k) w_j(k) \\
z_j(k) &= G_j(k, x_j(k), u_j(k)) + v_j(k)
\end{aligned}
\tag{42}
$$

where the subscript j denotes the quantities pertaining to mode m_j. The nonlinear functions F_j, G_j and the weighting matrix T_j may have different structures for different values of j. The process noise and measurement noise vectors w_j and v_j are white Gaussian of zero mean with covariance matrices Q_{wj} and R_{vj}, respectively. In principle the probability of a given model matches the system mode provides the required information for the fault detection and diagnosis. Taking into account historical behaviour of modes at time $\boldsymbol{k}$ ensures that the interacting multiple model (IMM) algorithm yields a good estimate. Consequently, exponential increase in complexity of a detection algorithm is avoided by mixing previous estimates at beginning of each cycle. The model probabilities provide an indication of the mode in effect at any given time, and therefore can provide an indication of the reaction wheel actuator fault. By using model probabilities information, both fault detection and diagnosis can be achieved. This decision making process is formally stated according to:

$$\begin{aligned} &\mu_j(k+1) = \max_j \mu_j(k+1) = \mu \\ &\textit{If} \quad \mu > \mu_T \quad \textit{then} \quad \text{mode} \ j \ \textit{is faulty} \\ &\textit{Otherwise} \quad \textit{no} \quad \textit{fault} \quad \textit{occurs} \end{aligned} \tag{43}$$

where $\mu_{Threshold}$ represents the fault detection threshold value. The interacting estimation algorithm runs each parallel filter banks only once in each cycle. Each of these filters at time $t_{k+1} = k+1$ has its own input, the state estimate at time t_k, $\hat{x}^0(k\,|\,k)$, and its own covariance matrix, $P^0(k\,|\,k)$, which form a valid quasi-sufficient statistics of all the past information, under the assumption that model of each filter matches the system mode. The above decision rule yields not only fault detection capability but also information about the type (sensor or actuator), the location (which sensor or actuator), the size (total failure or partial failure with fault severity), and the fault occurrence time.

4.3 Interacting Multiple Model (IMM) algorithm

A detailed procedure for an IMM algorithm that utilizes the standard Kalman Filter estimation technique is included in references [Zhang & Xiao, 1997; Narendra & Balakrishnan, 1997; Zhang & Xiao, 1998]. Similarly, the steps for an IMM algorithm that utilizes an UKF estimation technique are also developed in [Tudoroiu & al., 2006, Tudoroiu & Zaheeruddin, 2006, Tudoroiu & Khorasani, 2005]. Based on the standard IMM algorithm described in details in [Zhang & Xiao, 1997; Zhang & Xiao, 1998] we could embed without difficulties the dynamics of the EKF or UKF estimation techniques to obtain an IMM_EKF or IMM_UKF structures. A simplified flowchart representing the FDDI scheme with the process dynamics of the IMM_ EKF and IMM_UKF estimators is shown in Figure 6. The results of applying EKF and UKF algorithms for fault detection and diagnosis (FDDI) of the faults in reaction wheel actuators (ACS) of the satellite and in valve actuators (HVAC systems). These results will be presented in the next section.

Parameter Settings

The set of parameters chosen for the EKF and UKF algorithms is given by

$$\alpha = 0.0001,\ k = 0,\ \beta = 2,\ \mathbf{P}_0 = 1*10^{-6}*\mathbf{I}_3,\ \mathbf{Q}_w = 2*10^{-6}*\mathbf{I}_3,\ R_v = 10^{-6}.$$

5. Simulation results

5.1 ACS systems

EKF and UKF-based interacting multiple model (IMM) algorithms are now applied for fault detection and diagnosis of a reaction wheel under different kinds of uncertainty (unknown model structure and parameters). In this work, we consider only transitions between the normal mode and faulty modes as well as between faulty modes and the normal mode. The root-causes of faults injected to the reaction wheels are due to the following sources:

i. unexpected viscous friction changes generating anomalies in the temperature *T*,

ii. unexpected changes in the bus voltage V_{bus}, and

iii. loss of effectiveness in the motor torque as represented by unexpected changes in the coefficient k_t.

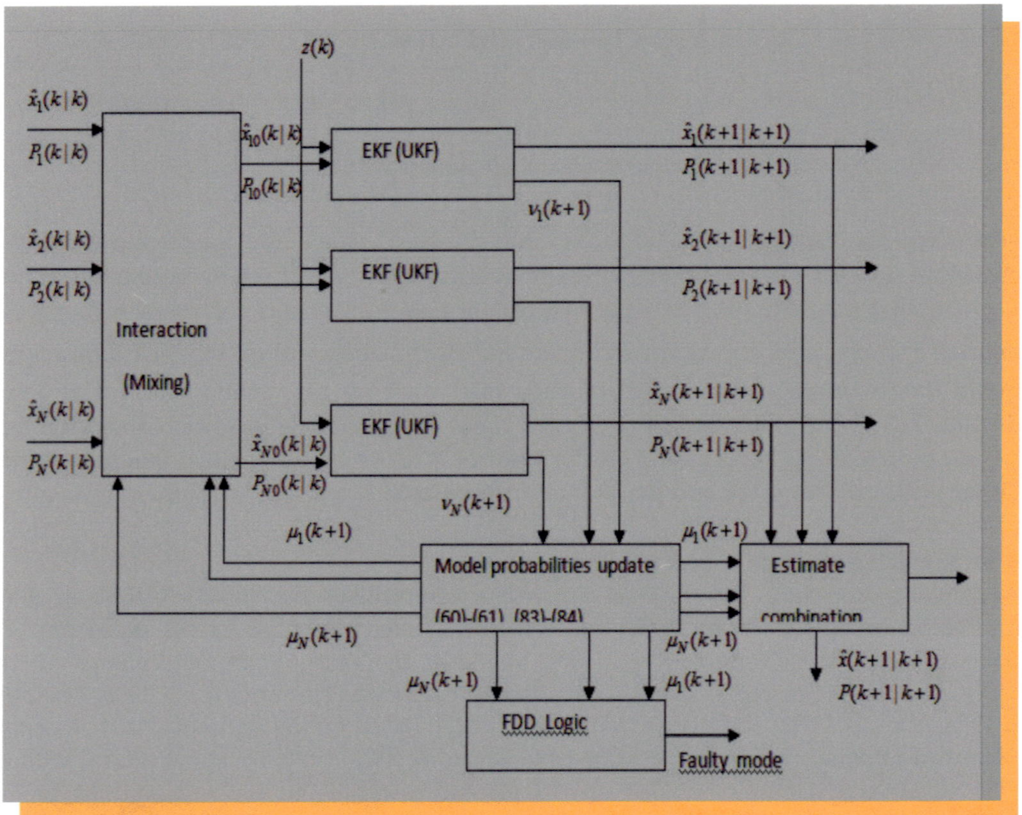

Fig. 6. FDD Block Scheme

Let us now to designate by $(z_1,u_1),(z_2,u_2),(z_3,u_3),(z_4,u_4)$ measurement observations and inputs of the filter banks for the normal mode, first, second, and third faulty modes, respectively. We also designate by $(z_{23},u_{23}),(z_{24},u_{24}),(z_{34},u_{34})$ measurement observations and inputs of the filter banks for simultaneous two faulty modes $(z_2z_3,u_{23}),(z_2z_4,u_{24}),(z_3z_4,u_{34})$, respectively. These modes are labelled from *j*=1 to *j*=7 as an alternative to a mode probability graphical representation. In this way it is easier to identify the occurrence and dynamic evolution of fault modes within each window horizon. These modes have the following specifications:

i. The normal mode (z_1,u_1), labelled *j*=1, is generated according to the nonlinear state equations corresponding to the nominal parameters, $T_1 = 30\ [{}^0C]$, $k_{t_1} = 0.029$, and $V_{bus_1} = 24[V]$.

ii. The faulty mode (z_2, u_2), labelled *j*=2, is generated by an abnormal increase of temperature from $T_1 = 30[{}^0C]$ to $T_2 = 200[{}^0C]$, $k_{t_2} = 0.029$, and $V_{bus_2} = 24[V]$.

iii. The faulty mode (z_3, u_3), labelled *j*=3, is generated by a sudden change of V_{bus} from $V_{bus_1} = 24[V]$ to $V_{bus_3} = 12[V]$, $T_3 = 30\ [{}^0C]$, and $k_{t_3} = 0.029$.

iv. The faulty mode (z_4, u_4), labelled *j*=4, is generated by a sudden change in the motor current corresponding to a loss of effectiveness of k_t from $k_{t_1} = 0.029$ to $k_{t_4} = 0.002$, $T_4 = 30\ [{}^0C]$, and $V_{bus_4} = 24[V]$.

v. The faulty mode (z_{23}, u_{23}), labelled *j*=5, is generated by an abnormal increase of temperature from $T_1 = 30[{}^0C]$ to $T_5 = 100[{}^0C]$ and a sudden change of V_{bus} from $V_{bus_1} = 24[V]$ to $V_{bus_5} = 12[V]$, and $k_{t_5} = 0.029$.

vi. The faulty mode (z_{24}, u_{24}), labelled *j*=6, is generated by an abnormal increase of temperature T from $T_1 = 30\,{}^0[C]$ to $T_6 = 100[{}^0C]$ and a sudden change in the motor current corresponding to a loss of effectiveness k_t from $k_{t_1} = 0.029$ to $k_{t_6} = 0.002$, and $V_{bus_6} = 24[V]$.

vii. The faulty mode (z_{34}, u_{34}), labelled *j*=7, is generated by a sudden change of V_{bus} from $V_{bus_1} = 24[V]$ to $V_{bus_7} = 12[V]$ and a change in the motor current corresponding to a loss of effectiveness of k_t from $k_{t_1} = 0.029$ to $k_{t_7} = 0.002$, and $T_7 = 30\,{}^0[C]$.

The specific level of process and measurement noise, and the selected parameters and initialization settings are given below:

$$\hat{x}_1 = \hat{x}_2 = \hat{x}_3 = \hat{x}_4 = \begin{bmatrix} 0 \\ 0 \end{bmatrix},\ P_1 = P_2 = P_3 = P_4 = 10^{-4}\begin{bmatrix} 1 & 0 \\ 0 & 1 \end{bmatrix},$$

$T_1 = T_2 = T_3, = T_4 = \begin{bmatrix} 1 & 0 \\ 0 & 1 \end{bmatrix}$, the process and measurement noise covariance matrices are

$$Q_1 = Q_2 = Q_3 = Q_4 = 2\times 10^{-2}\begin{bmatrix} 1 & 0 \\ 0 & 1 \end{bmatrix},\ R_1 = R_2 = R_3 = R_4 = 5\times 10^{2}\begin{bmatrix} 1 & 0 \\ 0 & 1 \end{bmatrix},$$

$\mu_1(1,1) = \mu_2(1,1) = \mu_3(1,1) = \mu_4(1,1) = \dfrac{1}{N}$, $N = 4$ represents the number of modes, the threshold mode probability is $\mu_{Threshold} = 0.3$, and the IMM transition mode probability is selected as

$$\pi = \begin{bmatrix} \frac{117}{120} & \frac{1}{120} & \frac{1}{120} & \frac{1}{120} \\ \frac{3}{120} & \frac{117}{120} & 0 & 0 \\ \frac{3}{120} & 0 & \frac{117}{120} & 0 \\ \frac{3}{120} & 0 & 0 & \frac{117}{120} \end{bmatrix}.$$

The simulation results are presented in Figure 7.

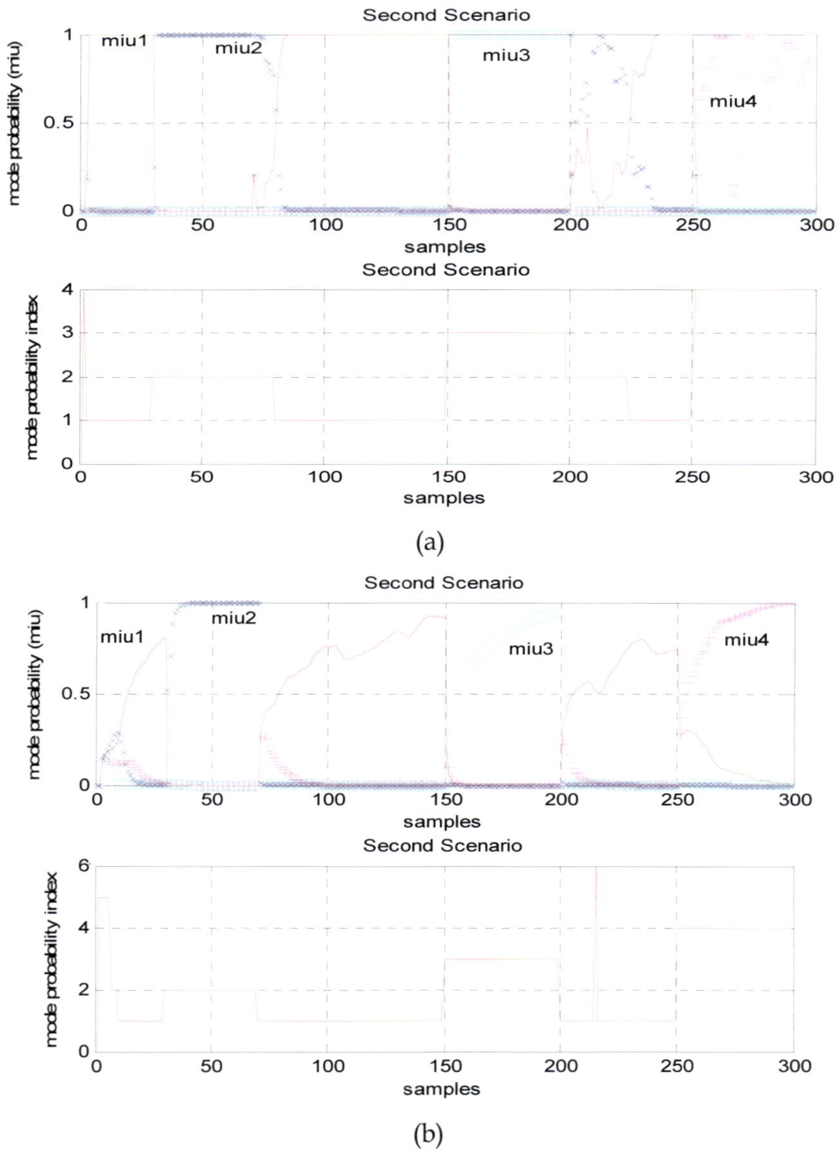

Fig. 7. The evolution of the mode probability and of the index of the mode probability for the second scenario.

It should be noted that there are short transient responses in the first window horizon [0, 30] and in the sixth window horizon [200, 250] for the IMM UKF algorithm (Figure 7(b)), but a long transient response time of at least 25 samples inside the window horizon [200, 250], for the IMM EKF algorithm (Figure 7(a)). Results reveal that a very good faulty mode detection and classification are obtained with a very fast transient response for the EKF algorithm and a small transient response for the UKF algorithm. For the simulation purpose we consider in our research the sequence of multiple fault modes (second scenario) $z=[z_1\ z_2\ z_1\ z_3\ z_1\ z_4]$, $u=[u_1\ u_2\ u_1\ u_3\ u_1\ u_4]$, where the first, second, and the third wheel's fault occur at the beginning of window horizons [30,70], [150,200], and [250,300], respectively. These faults persist for the duration of 40, 50, and 50 samples, respectively within each window. The evolution of mode probabilities and their index for this scenario are presented in Figures 7(a) and 7(b).

5.2 HVAC systems

The simulation results for the UKF estimator and IMM_UKF analysis approach in the simple estimation and fault detection (valve leakage) cases of the HVAC systems are presented in Figures 8-11. The step responses of the healthy DAT system ($\propto$ = r = 0) and of the faulty modes ($\propto$ = r =2, 4, and 6, representing different severity levels of the valve leakage) are represented and described in detail in [Tudoroiu & Zaheeruddin, 2006, Tudoroiu & Zaheeruddin 2005]. These responses reveal a progressive degradation of the system performance with the increasing of the backlash width $\propto$. In practice, it is very important to detect all these intermediate phases of progressive increase in backlash width to avoid complete failure of the valve actuator and consequently the total degradation of the system performance.

For state estimation purpose we consider the following two cases:

a. State estimation with the same state initial conditions with the process model, as in Figure 8:
   (15[°C], 35[°C] ,34[°C]), p_1=10[°C], p_3=40[°C])
b. State estimation with different state initial conditions than the process model, as in Figure 9:
   (20[°C], 38[°C] ,37[°C]), p_1=10[°C], p_3=40[°C]) for process model and (25[°C], 32[°C], 30[°C]), p_1=10[°C], p_3=40[°C]) the initial conditions for the state estimates.

The simulations results presented in Figures 8-9 reveal the robustness of the UKF algorithm to the changes in the initial conditions of the state estimates. The IMM_UKF algorithm could be applied for a wide engineering applications field for estimation and fault detection, diagnosis and isolation (FDDI) of stochastic systems under different kinds of uncertainties (unknown model structure or parameters) or system failures (valve leakage, stuck-open valve, stuck close valve). In our paper we have applied IMM_UKF algorithm to detect the following faulty modes:

1. **First scenario (healthy system)**, labeled by j=1 is obtained for the following parameters values: p_1=10, p_2=0.8, p_3=40.
2. **Second scenario (first fault)**, labeled by j=2 is obtained for p_1=16, p_2=0.8, p_3=40.
3. **Third scenario (second fault)**, labeled by j=3 is obtained for p_1=10, p_2=0.8, p_3=40.
4. **Fourth scenario (third fault)**, labeled by j=4 is obtained for p_1=10, p_2=0.6, p_3=50.

For the simulation purposes we consider the following scenarios:

i. $z = z_j, u = u_j\ ,\ j = 1,2,3,4.$

ii. $z = [z_1\ z_2\ z_1], u = [u_1\ u_2\ u_1]$, when the first actuator's failure occurs inside the horizon window [50,150].

iii. $z = [z_1\ z_3\ z_1], u = [u_1\ u_3\ u_1]$, when the second actuator's failure occurs inside the horizon window [150, 200].

iv. $z = [z_1\ z_4\ z_1], u = [u_1\ u_4\ u_1]$, when the third actuator's failure occurs inside the horizon window [150, 250].

v. $z = [z_1\ z_2\ z_1\ z_3\ z_1\ z_4\ z_1], u = [u_1\ u_2\ u_1\ u_3\ u_1 u_4\ u_1]$, when the first actuator's failure occurs inside the horizon window [50,100], the second actuator's failure inside the horizon window [150, 200], and the third actuator's failure inside the horizon window [250, 300]. In this paper we consider only the transitions between the normal mode and the fault modes, and also between the fault modes and the normal mode. The output measurements z_1, z_2, z_3, z_4 could be obtained from the deterministic part of the model equations. The process will be initialized by the following values:

$$\hat{x}_1 = \hat{x}_2 = \hat{x}_3 = \hat{x}_4 = \begin{bmatrix} 0 \\ 0 \\ 0 \end{bmatrix}, P_1 = P_2 = P_3 = P_4 = diag(0.0001,\ 0.0001,\ 0.0001)\ ,$$

$$T_1 = T_2 = T_3 = T_4 = \begin{bmatrix} 1 & 0 & 0 \\ 0 & 1 & 0 \\ 0 & 0 & 1 \end{bmatrix},$$

The initial values of the mode probabilities are assumed to be equal: $\mu_1 = \mu_2 = \mu_3 = \mu_4 = \frac{1}{n} = 0.25$, where $n = 4$, represents the number of modes, the threshold mode probability $\mu_{Threshold} = 0.02$, and the transition mode probability used for simulations is

$$\pi = \begin{bmatrix} \frac{117}{120} & \frac{1}{120} & \frac{1}{120} & \frac{1}{120} \\ \frac{3}{120} & \frac{117}{120} & 0 & 0 \\ \frac{3}{120} & 0 & \frac{117}{120} & 0 \\ \frac{3}{120} & 0 & 0 & \frac{117}{120} \end{bmatrix}$$

It seems that the last scenario is more complex and we will present the simulation results only for this sequence of multiple faults such in Figures 10-11. In Figure 10 is presented the evolution of the mode probabilities and in Figures 11 is presented the probability index of the active fault. These simulation results reveal robustness and an accurate identification of the sequence of the multiple faults. We remark also some false alarms during the transient period of the fault injection within the windows [50,100], [150,200]. These false alarms occur due to the fact that the IMM_UKF algorithm is based on the steady-state residual measurements.

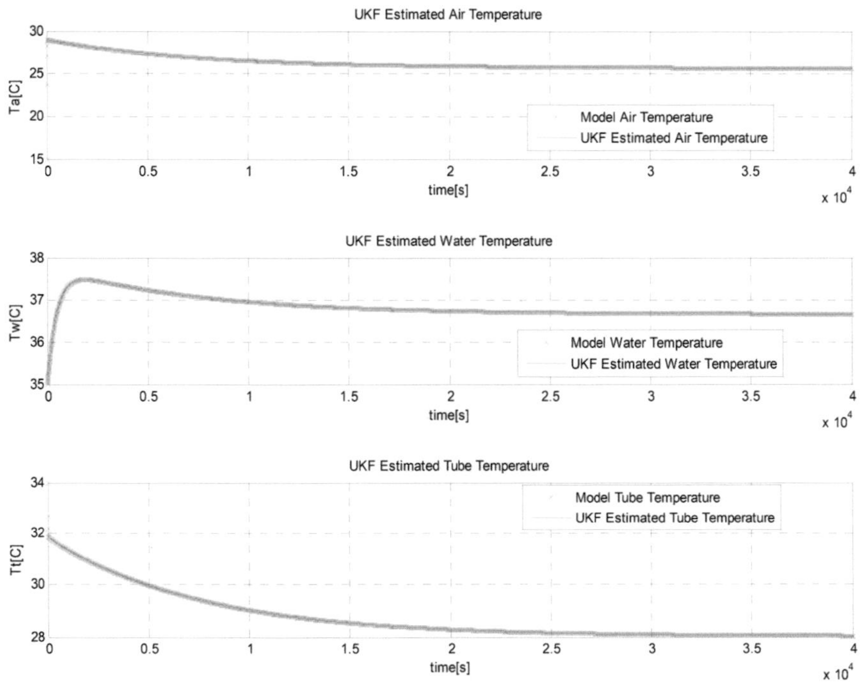

Fig. 8. The UKF state estimation with the same initial conditions with the process model

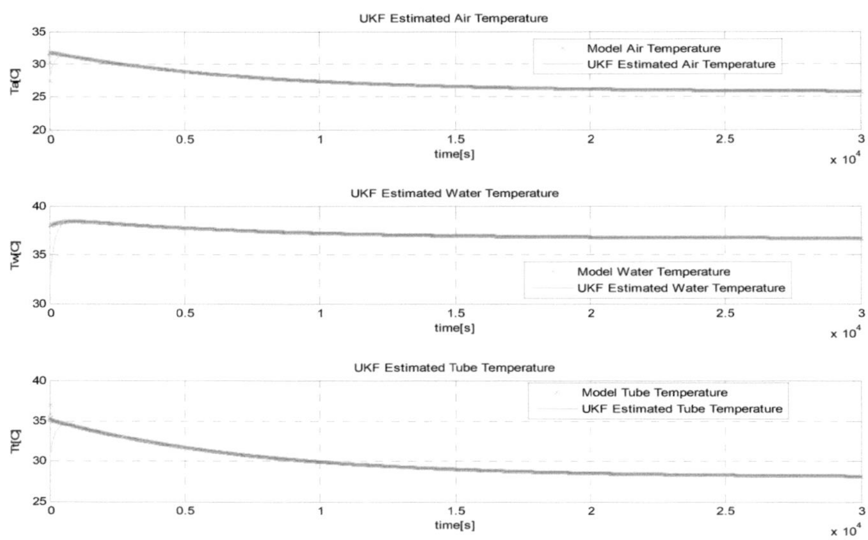

Fig. 9. The UKF state estimation with different initial conditions than the process model

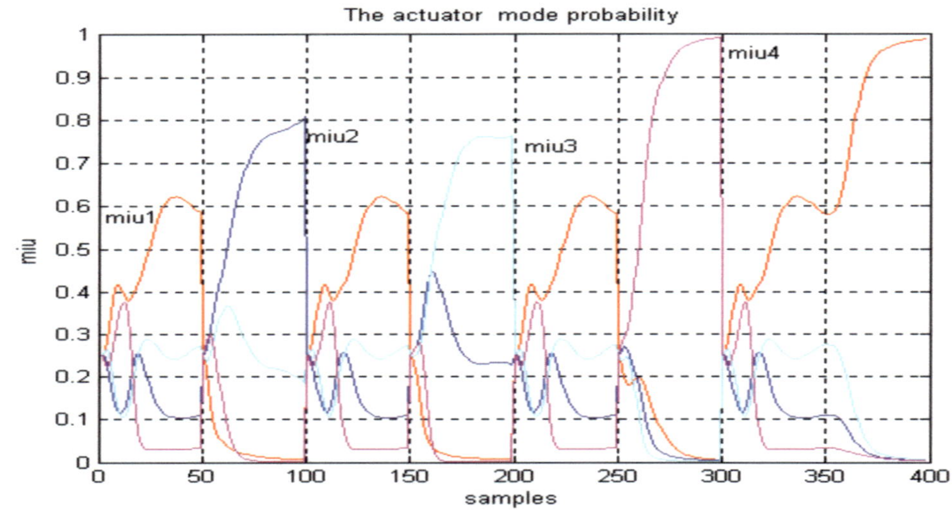

Fig. 10. The evolution of the mode probability for the sequence
$z = [z_1\ z_2\ z_1\ z_3\ z_1\ z_4\ z_1],\ u = [u_1\ u_2\ u_1\ u_3\ u_1\ u_4\ u_1]$

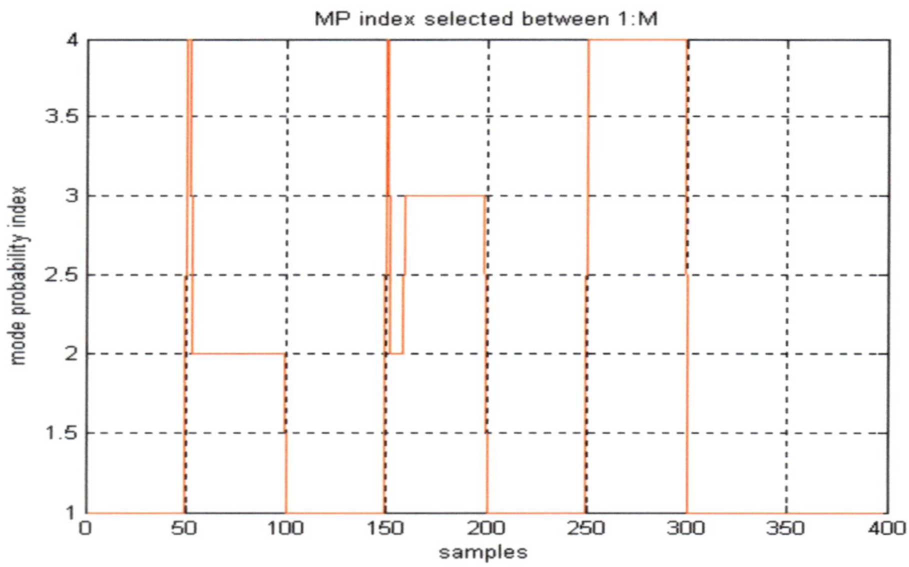

Fig. 11. The index of the mode probability for the sequence
$z = [z_1\ z_2\ z_1\ z_3\ z_1\ z_4\ z_1],\ u = [u_1\ u_2\ u_1\ u_3\ u_1\ u_4\ u_1]$

6. Conclusion

In this paper, we present two fault detection model-based approaches, namely frequency analysis and an Interactive Multiple Model based on Unscented Kalman Filter (IMM_UKF) state estimation. The frequency analysis method is simple and practical, but not accurate and robust. The results of IMM_UKF algorithm obtained in simulation environment reveal the superiority of this algorithm compare to frequency analysis approach. The IMM_UKF algorithm is more accurate and capable to estimate the dynamic evolution of the state variables for monitoring purposes in HVAC systems. The IMMM_UKF algorithm is faster and eliminates completely the linearization of the process dynamics. Also the robustness to the measurement and process noises as well as parameter changes is a further benefit of this algorithm. Also the superiority of the UKF algorithm is well documented in the literature [Haykin, 2003; Joseph, 2003; Tudoroiu et al., 2006]. However the gain of the UKF algorithm is for nonlinear cases, but sometimes it is very difficult to obtain the analytical model of the nonlinear system. Based on these results we will be capable to identify the degradation level of the faulty valve. The approach is probabilistic and gives results more accurate than the spectral analysis. The results obtained are encouraging and the performance of the IMM_UKF algorithm will be tested. The recovery mode development to complete the IMM_UKF algorithm in order to avoid the degrading in performance of the closed-loop HVAC systems during the failures periods will be explored in the future work. In our research, we have studied the possibility of using two interacting multiple models based on extended (IMM_EKF) and unscented (IMM_UKF) Kalman Filter estimation techniques for detection and diagnosis of faults in reaction wheels of the attitude control system (ACS) in a satellite and the valve actuators of HVAC systems. The main contributions are summarized briefly as follows:

a. Detection and identification of reaction wheel faults of the ACS and HVAC systems due to a number of possible sources that generate soft and hard anomalies during a scientific mission of a satellite or valve operation.
b. Implementation of a bank of parallel Kalman filters for faulty modes covering a rather broad set of the most likely and commonly possible scenarios of reaction wheel and valve actuators failures,
c. Detection and diagnosis of both partial and significant reaction wheel and valve actuators failures for different scenarios using the IMM_EKF and IMM_UKF estimation algorithms,
d. Comparison of performance capabilities and advantages of IMM_ UKF estimation algorithm with respect to the IMM_EKF estimation algorithm, and
e. Robustness analysis of both the IMM_EKF and IMM_UKF estimation algorithms to the selection of model transition probabilities, modeling errors, and noise statistics under different scenarios.

The approach proposed in this paper is probabilistic in nature and yields results that are more accurate and having good fault classification capabilities than the spectral analysis that are well studied in the literature [Tornhill et al., 2001; Tudoroiu & Zaheeruddin, 2005]. Based on fault identification analysis that is carried out it can be observed that the IMM_UKF estimation algorithm is robust to modeling uncertainties, and to statistics of noise measurements and process noise. Our proposed algorithms work similar to a neural network estimator and classifier that is described in e.g. [Li, 2005; Sobhani, 2006] where dynamic neural network architectures are employed to perform satisfactory FDDI. Compared to a neural network estimator and classifier, IMM_UKF estimation algorithm doesn't need an on-line training that takes an extensive amount of computational resources. Another similar approach uses observer banks of autoregressive time series models for fault diagnosis, based on Box-Jenkins linear autoregressive models, back-propagation neural networks, and radial function networks. Compared to the above approaches and IMM_EKF estimation algorithm, the IMM_UKF estimation algorithm performs better and has a much less computational burden and complexity, and it furthermore operates much faster. Perhaps the biggest drawback of predictive model-based approaches is the need for a suitable quantity of data for training and testing the system during the development phase. Moreover, stability of the IMM_UKF estimation algorithm still remains an open question, which needs further investigation. Also, the behavior of the IMM_UKF estimation algorithm for diagnosis in a fast or rapidly changing process dynamics needs to be explored further.

7. References

Bialke B. (1998). High Fidelity Mathematical Modeling of Reaction Wheel Performance, *Advances in the Astronautical Sciences*, pp. 483-496, 1998.

Haykin S. (2003). *Adaptive filter theory - Fourth edition*, Prentice Hall, 2003.

Joseph, LaViola Jr. (2003). A Comparison of Unscented and Extended Kalman Filtering forEstimating Quaternion Motion, *Proceedings of the American Control Conference* Denver, Colorado June 4-6, 2003.

Julier S. J., Uhlman J.K. (1997). A New Extension of the Kalman Filter to Nonlinear Systems, *Proceedings of Aero Sense, the 11th International Symposium on Aerospace/Defense Sensing, Simulation and Controls*, 1997, pp.182-193.

Li Z., Ma L. & Khorasani K. (2005). Fault Detection in Reaction Wheel of a Satellite using Observer-based Dynamic Neural Networks, *Proceedings of International Symposium on Neural Networks*, May 2005.

Plett G. (2004). Extended Kalman filtering for battery management systems of LiPB-based HEV battery packs - Part 3. State and parameter estimation, *J. Power Source.*, 134, no. 2,pp. 277-292, 2004.

Mihaylova L. & E. Semerdjiev E. (1999). An Interacting Multiple Model Algorithm for Stochastic Systems Control, *Information and Security*, Vol. 2, 1999.

Mihaylova L. & E. Semerdjiev E. (1999). Interacting Multiple Model Algorithm for Maneuvering Ship Tracking Based on New Ship Models, *Information and Security*, Vol. 2, 1999.

Semerdjiev E. & Mihaylova L. (1998). Variable and Fixed Structure Augmented InteractingMultiple Model Algorithms for Maneuvering Ship Tracking Based on New Ship Models, *Bulgarian Academy of Sciences, Central laboratory for Parallel processing*, Report, 1998.

Sobhani E., K. Khorasani K. & Tafazoli S. (2005). Dynamic Neural Network-based Estimatorfor Fault Diagnosis in Reaction Wheel Actuator of Satellite Attitude Control System, *Proceedings of the 2005 International Joint Conference on Neural Networks*, August 2005.

Thornhill N.F., Shah S.L. & Huang B. (2001). Detection of Distribution Oscillations andRoot-Cause Diagnosis, *Proceedings of the IFAC Workshop on on-line Fault*

Detection and Supervision in the chemical process industries, Korea, pp. 167-172, June 2001.

Tudoroiu N., Zaheeruddin M. (2004). Fault Detection and Diagnosis of the ValveActuators In HVAC Systems Using Interactive Parallel Kalman Filters Bank, *Proceedings of the 29th Annual Congress of the American Romanian Academy of Arts and Sciences (ARA)*, Bochum, Germany, September 7-12, 2004, pp 395-398.

Tudoroiu N., Zaheeruddin M. (2005). Frequency Analysis Approach to Detect and Diagnosis Faults in Discharge Air Temperature (DAT) Systems, *Proceedings of the 30th Annual ARA Congress*, July 5-10, 2005, Chisinau, Republic of Moldova, pp.597-600.

Tudoroiu N., Zaheeruddin M. (2005). Fault Detection and Diagnosis of Valve Actuators in HVAC Systems, *Proceeding of the 2005 IEEE International Conference on Control Applications*, August 29-31, 2005, Toronto, Canada, ISBN:0- 7803-9354-6.

Tudoroiu N., Khorasani K. (2005). State estimation of the Vinyl Acetate Reactor using Unscented Kalman Filters (UKF), *2005 International Conference on Industrial electronics and Control Applications, ICIECA 2005*, Quito, IEEE, ISBN :0-7803-9420-8.

Tudoroiu N., Zaheeruddin M. (2006). Fault Detection and Diagnosis of Valve Actuators in Discharge Air Temperature (DAT) Systems, using Interactive Unscented Kalman Filter Estimation, *International Symposium on Industrial Electronics, ISIE2006*, 9-13 July 2006, Montreal.

Tudoroiu N., Sobhani-Tehrani E. & Khorasani K. (2006). Interactive Bank of Unscented Kalman Filters for Fault Detection and Isolation in Reaction Wheel Actuators of Satellite Attitude Control System, *IECON'2006, Paris, 32nd Annual Conference of the IEEE Industrial Electronics Society*, November 2006.

Tudoroiu N. & Khorasani K. (2007). Satellite Fault Diagnosis using a Bank of Interacting Kalman Filters, *IEEE Transactions on Aerospace and Electronic Systems*, Vol. 43, No.4, October 2007, ISSN 0018-9251, pp.1334-1350.

Narendra K. & Balakrishnan J. (1997). Adaptive Control Using Multiple Models, *IEEE Transaction on Automatic Control*, Vol. 42, N0.2, pp.171-187, 1997.

R. J. Patton R.J., Frank P.M. & Clark R. N. (1989), *Fault Diagnosis in Dynamic Systems, Theory and Applications,* Englewood Cliffs, NJ: Prentice Hall, 1989.

Zaheeruddin M., Patel R. V. (1995), Optimal Tracking Control of Multi Zone Indoor Environnemental Space, *ASME Journal Dynamic Systems, Measurement and Control*, Vol. 117, pp. 292-303, 1995.

Zhang Y., & Xiao Rong-Li. (1997). Detection and Diagnosis of Sensor and Actuator Failures using interacting multiple-model estimator, *Proceedings of the 36th IEEE Conference on Decision and Control*, pp. 4475-4480, San Diego, CA, Dec. 1997.

Zhang Y., & Xiao Rong-Li. (1998). Detection and Diagnosis of Sensor and Actuator Failures using IMM Estimator, *IEEE Transaction On Aerospace and Electronic Systems*, Vol.34, No.4, pp. 1293-1311, October 1998.

Wan E. A, Merwe R. (2000). The Unscented Kalman Filter for Nonlinear Estimation, *Proceedings IEEE Symposium 2000 (AS-SPCC)*, Lake Louise, Alberta, Canada, Oct. 2000.

21

Kalman Filtering for Manufacturing Processes

Thomas Oakes, Lie Tang, Robert G. Landers and S. N. Balakrishnan
Missouri University of Science and Technology
United States of America

1. Introduction

Unwanted signal variation commonly occurs in manufacturing process measurements. This variation, due to both random electrical noise and noise in the manufacturing process itself, can be quantified by calculating the steady-state process data variance

$$\sigma^2 = \frac{1}{N-1}\sum_{k=1}^{N}\left(x_k - \bar{x}\right)^2 \tag{1}$$

where x_k is the measurement at iteration k, $\bar{x}$ is the measurement average, and N is the number of samples. Noise due to the manufacturing process itself is often greater in magnitude than the electrical noise. Examples of process noise include: (1) high frequency cyclic variations due to tool eccentricity in a turning process, (2) low frequency variations due to discrete solidification of deposited material in Laser Metal Deposition (LMD) processes, and (3) chaotic mixing of materials in Friction Stir Welding (FSW) processes.

Manufacturing process measurements must be filtered before the data can be used for dynamic modeling or control. First principle modeling is generally unable to capture inherent nonlinear dynamics such as non-uniform friction and system wear. Therefore, dynamic manufacturing process models are often developed empirically. Estimation techniques such as Recursive Least Squares and Particle Swarm Optimization are commonly used for system identification to create a "best fit" model based on collected measurements. However, the fidelity of an empirical model greatly depends upon the measurements used to create it and processes with high-magnitude variations in the measurement signals are often difficult to model due to the low signal-to-noise ratio. Manufacturing process models are often used to design process controllers. Process control is the on-line adjustment of process parameters to enhance operation productivity and improve part quality. Variations in the measurement signal are generally higher in frequency than the available actuator bandwidth, which can lead to increased actuator wear and possible instability. A filter must be developed for (1) post processing of data to compensate for large signal variations prior to use by a model identification method and (2) on-line filtering capable of preserving signal phase and magnitude with minimal computational burden.

The fourth-order Butterworth filter is used in a number of manufacturing processes. Bhattacharyya and Sengupta (2007) used a fourth-order Butterworth filter on a face milling process to remove high frequency variation due to spindle rotation harmonics. Liang et al. (2002) employed a Butterworth filter on the spindle power signal of an end milling process for use in a fuzzy logic controller. Ghosh et al. (2007) used a Butterworth filter for neural-

based sensor fusion to estimate tool wear. Another common filter is a point-averaging filter. Freitag (2004) used a 50 ms Finite Impulse Response moving average filter to smooth command signals sent to the process controller of a miniature ball end mill. Zhao et al. (2007) employed a five-point moving average filter to reduce the standard deviation of the axial force signal of a FSW process for the purposes of modeling and process control.
The objective of this chapter is to present a methodology for filtering manufacturing process measurement signals. The rest of the chapter is organized as follows. A general filtering methodology is established that uses a stochastic model and a two-step Kalman filter. The filtering methodology is compared to other common filters via simulation studies. Post process filtering is performed on FSW and LMD processes to develop dynamic process models. Then, on-line filtering is performed for FSW and LMD processes for use in process controllers.

2. Filtering methodology

Unlike standard frequency-based filters, the Kalman filter is a time domain filter that recursively estimates process states using data from both a dynamic system model and collected measurements. Selection of a reliable dynamic process model is vital in maximizing the filter performance. A Markov process is a model that expresses the stochastic evolution of a system. This implies that knowledge of the present system states completely describes all relevant information necessary for the process evolution. Past and future states of a Markov Process are statistically independent. The excessive signal variation observed in many manufacturing processes leads to the realization that these processes can be modeled as Markov processes. A general stochastic model of a manufacturing process is

$$\dot{x}(t) = \lambda x(t) + w(t) \tag{2}$$

where $x(t)$ is the system state, λ is the system pole, and $w(t)$ is the process noise, which accounts for the system's stochastic nature, as well as changes in the input. It is assumed the process noise is Gaussian with a zero mean normal distribution and variance, Q. Transforming equation (2) into the discrete-time domain using a zero order hold

$$x(k) = e^{\lambda T_s} x(k-1) + w(k-1) \tag{3}$$

where k is the time step and T_s is the sample period (s). The two-step discrete-time Kalman filter uses the model

$$x(k) = Fx(k-1) + Gu(k-1) + w(k-1) \tag{4}$$

where $F = e^{\lambda T_s}$ and $u(k\text{-}1) = 0$ to fit the form of equation (3). The input term in equation (4) is set to zero to allow the process noise term to account for all deviations in the state due to model uncertainty and input changes. Equation (4) has process noise characteristics

$$w \sim N(0,Q) \qquad E\left(w(k)w(k)^T\right) = Q \tag{5}$$

The measurement is

$$y(k) = Hx(k) + v(k) \tag{6}$$

Equation (6) has measurement noise characteristics

$$v \sim N(0, R) \qquad E\left(v(k)v(k)^T\right) = R \tag{7}$$

where R is the measurement variance. Initial values of the state estimate and covariance, respectively, are

$$\hat{x}^+(0) = x(0) \tag{8}$$

$$P^+(0) = E\left|\left(x(0) - \hat{x}^+(0)\right)\left(x(0) - \hat{x}^+(0)\right)^T\right| \tag{9}$$

where $\hat{x}^+$ is the state estimate after the filter's measurement update (aposteriori) and P^+ is the covariance after the filter's measurement update. A large initial covariance matrix is required to ensure the estimates convergence. Equation (4) is rewritten in terms of its estimates

$$\hat{x}^-(k) = e^{\lambda T}\hat{x}^+(k-1) \tag{10}$$

where $\hat{x}^-$ is the state estimate before the filter's measurement update (apriori). Equation (10) is used to propagate the state estimate to the next time step. The covariance is propagated to the next time step using

$$P^-(k) = FP^+(k-1)F^T + Q \tag{11}$$

where P^- is the covariance prior to the filter's measurement update. The Kalman gain matrix is

$$K(k) = P^-(k)H^T\left[HP^-(k)H^T + R\right] \tag{12}$$

Then the measurement is used to update, respectively, the state estimate and covariance

$$\hat{x}^+(k) = \hat{x}^-(k) + K(k)\left[y(k) - H\hat{x}^-(k)\right] \tag{13}$$

$$P^+(k) = \left[I - K(k)H\right]P^-(k)\left[I - K(k)H\right]^T + K(k)RK^T(k) \tag{14}$$

The computations in equations (10)-(14) are repeated at each time step.

2.1 Filter tuning

A generic first order system is used to illustrate the tuning required for the filtering methodology. The system's transfer function is

$$G(s) = \frac{K}{\tau s + 1} = \frac{6}{0.6s + 1} \tag{15}$$

where K is the gain and τ is the time constant. The system is converted into the discrete-time domain using a zero order hold and $T_s = 0.01$ s

$$G(z) = \frac{9.917 \cdot 10^{-2}}{z - 0.9835} \tag{16}$$

The unit step response is shown in Fig. 1. Random noise with variance 0.25 is added to the output to simulate a noisy measurement. The measurement variance, R, is calculated directly from the measurement data while values of λ and Q are tuned to optimize the filter's performance. This can be accomplished by first setting $Q = R$, implying equal faith in the measurements and model, and tuning λ while leaving Q and R constant until the disparity between the filtered and measured data is minimized.

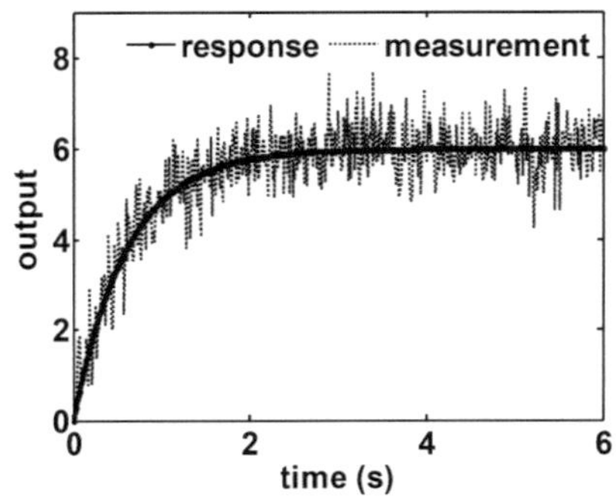

Fig. 1. Unit step response of system described by equation (16)

Figure 2 illustrates the effect of tuning λ. As λ approaches zero, the observable offset between the measurement data and the estimated state is eliminated. For this particular portion of the tuning process, it can be assumed that the optimal value of λ is zero.

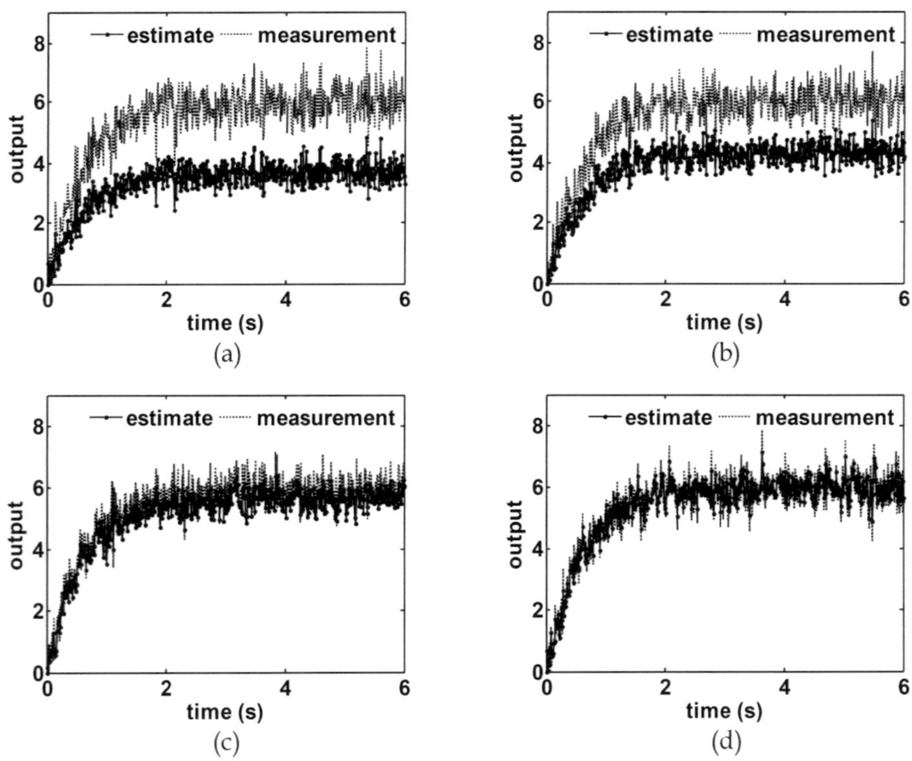

Fig. 2. Outputs and estimates for system described by equation (16) with a unit step input and (a) $\lambda = -1000$, (b) $\lambda = -100$, (c) $\lambda = -10$, and (d) $\lambda = 0$, with $Q = R = 0.25$ and $T_s = 0.01$ s

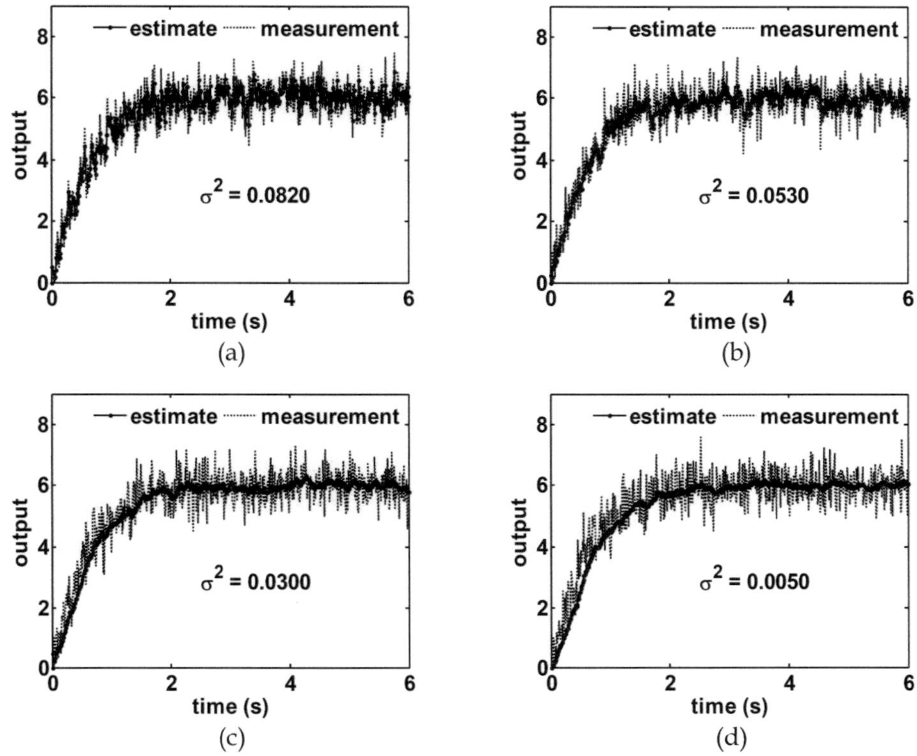

Fig. 3. Outputs and estimates for system described by equation (16) with a unit step input and (a) $Q = 0.5R$, (b) $Q = 0.1R$, (c) $Q = 0.01R$, and (d) $Q = 0.005R$, with $\lambda = 0$ and $T_s = 0.01$ s

The sampling period also has a tremendous affect on the filter performance. Applying a zero order hold to equation (15) with $T_s = 0.1$ s

$$G(z) = \frac{0.9288}{z - 0.8465} \tag{17}$$

With $\lambda = 0$, the same tuning process of Q is performed to illustrate the affect the sample rate has on the filter performance. The results are shown in Fig. 4. The larger sample period impacts the degree to which adjusting the value of Q will affect the phase. Lowering the value of Q significantly reduces the variance when compared to Fig. 3; however, it also significantly increases the phase due to less data being available to the filter during the transient portion of the process.

2.2 Filter comparison

The performances of two common filters are compared to that of the proposed filtering methodology. A first order low-pass filter is

$$\frac{X_f(s)}{X(s)} = \frac{1}{\tau s + 1} \tag{18}$$

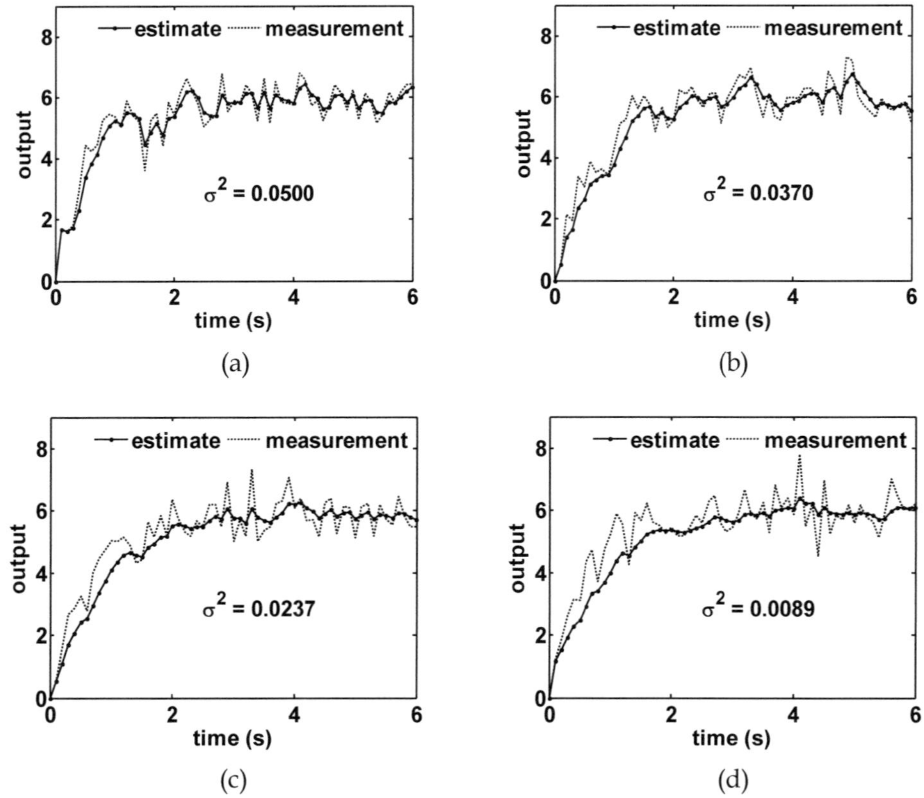

Fig. 4. Outputs and estimates for system described by equation (17) with a unit step input and (a) $Q = 0.5R$, (b) $Q = 0.25R$, (c) $Q = 0.1R$, and (d) $Q = 0.05R$, with $\lambda = 0$ and $T_s = 0.1$ s

where $X_f(s)$ is the filtered signal, $X(s)$ is the unfiltered signal, τ is the time constant and τ–1 is the filter break frequency (rad/s). The break frequency is selected to be 2π to provide a cut off frequency of 1 Hz; therefore, $\tau = 0.1592$ s. Transforming equation (18) into the discrete-time domain with a zero order hold and $T_s = 0.01$ s

$$\frac{X_f(z)}{X(z)} = \frac{6.882 \cdot 10^{-2}}{z - 0.9391} \tag{19}$$

Transforming equation (18) into the discrete–time domain with a zero order hold and T_s = 0.01 s

$$\frac{X_f(z)}{X(z)} = \frac{0.4664}{z - 0.5336} \tag{20}$$

A fourth–order Butterworth filter with a 1 Hz cutoff frequency and $T_s = 0.01$ s is

$$\frac{X_f(z)}{X(z)} = \frac{8.982 \cdot 10^{-7} z^4 + 3.594 \cdot 10^{-6} z^3 + 5.391 \cdot 10^{-6} z^2 + 3.594 \cdot 10^{-6} z + 8.982 \cdot 10^{-7}}{z^4 - 3.836 z^3 + 5.521 z^2 - 3.534 z + 0.8486} \tag{21}$$

A fourth order Butterworth filter with a 1 Hz cutoff frequency and $T_s = 0.1$ s is

$$\frac{X_f(z)}{X(z)}=\frac{4.824\cdot10^{-3}z^4+1.937\cdot10^{-2}z^3+2.891\cdot10^{-2}z^2+1.937\cdot10^{-2}z+4.824\cdot10^{-3}}{z^4-2.366z^3+2.314z^2-1.055z+0.1874} \quad (22)$$

Plots of filters' performances are shown for the transient portion of the response in Fig. 5 for T_s = 0.01 s and in Fig 6 for T_s = 0.1 s. Values of Q = 0.01 and Q = 0.25 are selected for the Kalman filter with T_s = 0.01 and 0.1 s, respectively. Figures 5 and 6 show that the filtering methodology outperforms the low-pass and Butterworth filters. All three filters underpredict the measurement for both sample periods. The maximum error of the Butterworth filter is approximately 44% for both sample periods while the low-pass and Kalman filters contain comparable maximum errors at approximately 13%. Less error is present in the Kalman filter estimates in both plots through the majority of the transient portion of the response.

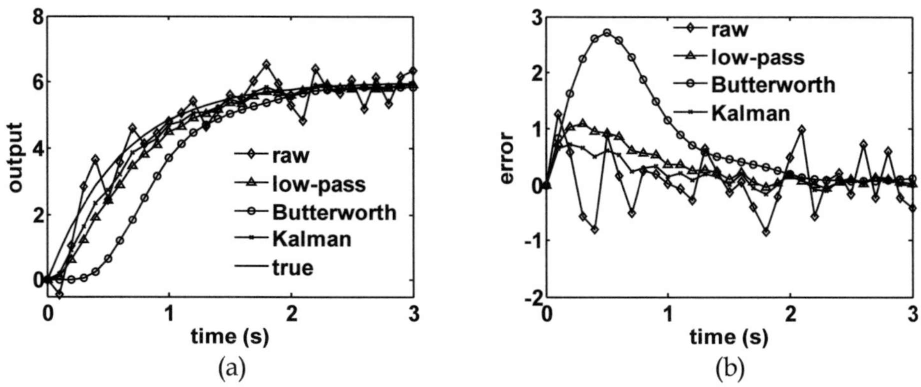

Fig. 5. (a) Output and (b) error for low-pass, Butterworth, and Kalman filters, T_s = 0.01 s

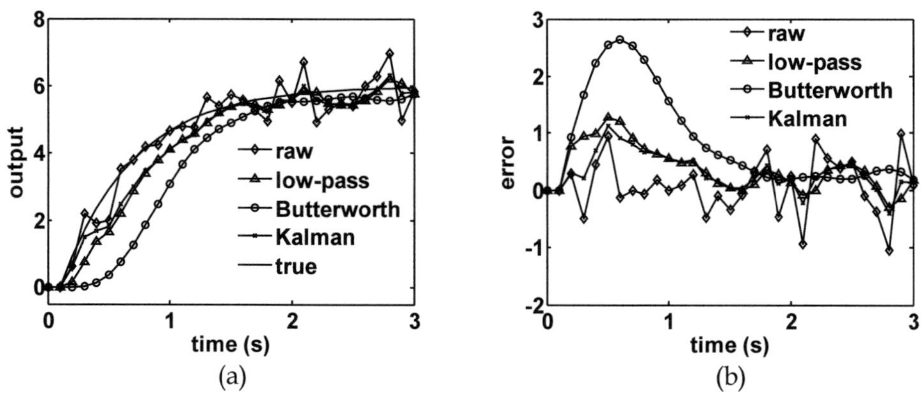

Fig. 6. (a) Output and (b) error for low-pass, Butterworth, and Kalman filters, T_s = 0.1 s

2.3 Modeling

The Recursive Least Squares technique (Åström & Wittenmark, 1995) is used to develop system models from the filtered and raw signals. The model responses for a step input are shown in Figs. 7 and 8 for T_s = 0.01 and 0.1 s, respectively. The model coefficients and percent error are shown in Tables 1 and 2 for T_s = 0.01 and 0.1 s, respectively. The model constructed from the data processed with the Kalman filter is the most accurate in terms of coefficient estimates, transient response, and steady-state error. The model constructed from the data processed with the Butterworth filter has significant errors due to the phase shift created by the Butterworth filter. The model constructed from the raw data contains the most error since the noise distorts the system dynamics.

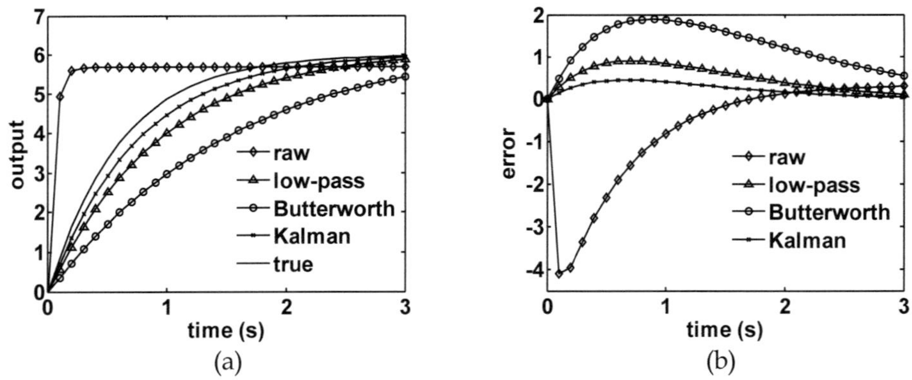

Fig. 7. Model (a) output and (b) error using raw data, low-pass, Butterworth, and Kalman filters, $T_s = 0.01$ s

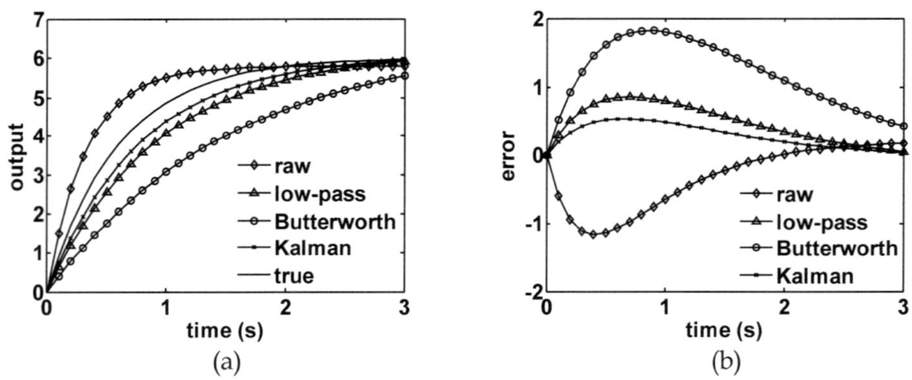

Fig. 8. Model (a) output and (b) error using raw data, low-pass, Butterworth, and Kalman filters, $T_s = 0.1$ s

	a		b	
	estimate	error (%)	estimate	error (%)
raw data	-0.797	19.0	1.15	1060
low-pass	-0.989	0.596	$6.57 \cdot 10^{-2}$	34.1
Butterworth	-0.994	1.04	$4.05 \cdot 10^{-2}$	59.3
Kalman	-0.986	0.315	$8.15 \cdot 10^{-2}$	18.2

Table 1. Coefficient estimates for models with $T_s = 0.01$ s, a = -0.983, and b = 9.917·10–2

	a		b	
	estimate	error (%)	estimate	error (%)
raw data	-0.737	12.9	1.52	64.8
low-pass	-0.897	6.04	0.631	31.5
Butterworth	-0.938	10.8	0.404	56.2
Kalman	-0.879	3.88	0.732	20.6

Table 2. Coefficient estimates for models with $T_s = 0.01$ s, a = -0.846, and b = 0.922

The filtering methodology can be used to filter data prior to empirical modeling to acquire a more reliable model. Since this filter relies on model-based estimation, it has always been necessary to have a precise model of the system dynamics to ensure proper filter performance. However, the stochastic process model provides a way to use a Kalman filter for state estimation with limited knowledge of the system behavior.

3. Friction Stir Welding example

Friction Stir Welding is a new welding technique capable of joining traditionally hard to join materials such as 2000 and 7000 series aluminum alloys (Mishra & Ma, 2005). The process utilizes a rotating, non-consumable tool containing a shoulder and profiled pin to induce gross plastic deformation along a weld path. In a FSW process, the tool is plunged into the material at a specified spindle speed, ω, until the shoulder contacts the material and is then left to dwell for a specified period of time to soften the surrounding area. The tool then advances along its weld path at a traverse speed, v, joining the material as it leaves the processing zone. Schematics of the FSW process are shown in Fig. 9.

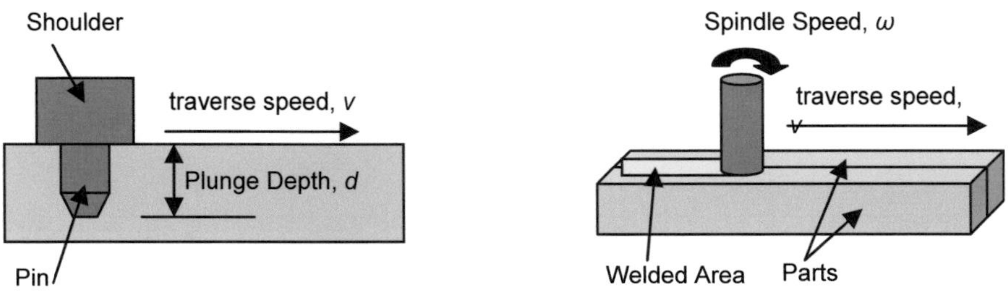

Fig. 9. FSW Process Schematics

Constant process parameter runs in FSW processes can lead to internal defects known as wormholes and surface voids due to improper fixturing of the parts and machine geometric errors. Therefore, the process is typically run in a force control mode in which the traverse speed and spindle speed are held constant while the plunge depth is adjusted on-line to maintain a desired axial force profile. Before a controller can be designed, the system is modeled empirically through a series of step tests. An example of a step test is shown in Fig. 10. It can be seen that small changes in plunge depth create large changes in axial force. If no

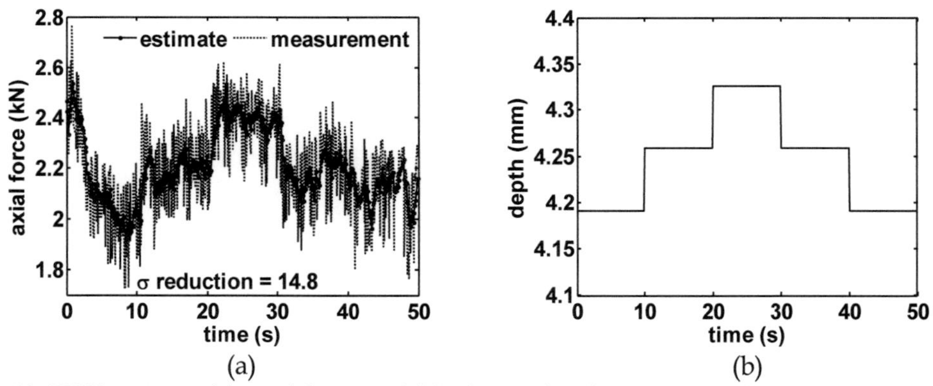

Fig. 10. FSW step test (a) axial force and (b) plunge depth, v = 2.6 mm/s and ω = 1600 rpm

post signal processing is used, the combined process and sensor noise is so large in magnitude that it is difficult to detect changes in the axial force due to changes in the plunge depth. This is particularly apparent between the fourth and fifth step changes. From the experimental data, $R = 1.63 \cdot 10^{-2}$ kN^2. The filtering methodology is applied using $\lambda = 0$ and $Q = 0.05R$ to the measurement data in Fig. 10. It is seen that the variance is greatly reduced (i.e., nearly a factor of fifteen) without compromising the phase and magnitude fidelity.

3.a FSW process modeling

Twelve experiments are conducted based on a central composite Design of Experiments (DOE) over the operating range of all three process parameters. The filtering methodology is applied with $\lambda = 0$ and $Q = 0.05R$ to all twelve runs. Table 3 shows the process parameters, heat index, and variance reduction ratio for each run. The variance reduction ratio is the unfiltered signal variance divided by the filtered signal variance. The results demonstrate the filtering methodology can reduce signal variance by a factor of 3 to nearly a factor of seventeen for FSW processes.

The results from runs 11 and 12 were deemed to be unacceptable and, therefore, were not used to create the dynamic model. This can be explained by the heat index, which is

$$HI = \frac{\omega^2}{10^4 v} \tag{23}$$

Note the traverse speed is given in inches per minute when calculating the heat index. Runs 11 and 12 had particularly low heat indices, although they were not the lowest. A low heat index can lead to a "cold run" that sometimes produces poor welds.

Run	v (mm/s)	ω (rpm)	HI (rpm^2/ipm)	Variance Reduction Ratio
1	2.60	1600	41.7	11.3
2	2.60	1900	58.8	3.11
3	2.18	1810	63.6	4.91
4	3.02	1390	27.1	12.9
5	2.60	1600	41.7	7.08
6	3.02	1810	45.9	8.25
7	2.18	1390	37.5	16.9
8	3.02	1390	27.1	5.22
9	2.18	1810	63.6	3.07
10	2.00	1600	54.2	7.23
11	3.20	1600	33.9	12.1
12	2.60	1300	27.5	6.01

Table 3. Process parameters and variance reduction ratio for FSW runs used for process modeling

An empirical second order model of the process and equipment dynamics is

$$\frac{F(z)}{U(z)} = v^{\alpha} \omega^{\beta} \frac{b_1 z + b_2}{z^2 + a_1 z + a_2} z^{-n_d} \tag{24}$$

where $F(z)$ is the axial force, $U(z)$ is the control signal, n_d is the number of delay periods, and b_1, b_2, a_1, a_2, α, and β are model coefficients. The model structure is based upon visual inspection of the runs in Table 3. The control signal and plunge depth are related by

$$u(k) = d^{\gamma}(k) \tag{25}$$

where γ is a model coefficient. The model coefficients α, β, and γ are found by using the steady-state model

$$F_{ss} = C v^{\alpha} \omega^{\beta} d^{\gamma} \tag{26}$$

where F_{ss} is the average steady-state axial force and C is the steady-state gain. Taking the natural log of both sides of equation (19)

$$\ln(F_{ss}) = \ln(C) + \alpha \ln(v) + \beta \ln(\omega) + \gamma \ln(d) \tag{27}$$

and applying Least Squares to the data in runs 1–10, $C = 6.18 \cdot 10^{-2}$, $\alpha = 0.185$, $\beta = -0.374$, and $\gamma = 2.65$. Transforming equation (24) into the discrete-time domain

$$F(k) = -a_1 F(k-1) - a_2 F(k-2) + v^{\alpha} \omega^{\beta} \left[b_1 u(k-1-n_d) + b_2 u(k-2-n_d) \right] \tag{28}$$

where n_d is determined to be 5 iterations by visually inspecting the step tests. Recursive Least Squares is used to determine the model coefficients $b1$, $b2$, $a1$, and $a2$. A complete covariance reset is employed if any of the diagonals of the covariance matrix become less than ten percent of their initial value. After the algorithm is executed for runs 1–10, the model coefficient sets are averaged and the transfer function is

$$\frac{F(z)}{U(z)} = v^{0.185} \omega^{-0.374} \frac{1.22 \cdot 10^{-2} z}{z^2 - 0.848z + 4.77 \cdot 10^{-2}} z^{-5} \tag{29}$$

The empirical model is now constructed in the same manner as above using the unfiltered data. In this case the transfer function is

$$\frac{F(z)}{U(z)} = v^{0.189} \omega^{-0.372} \frac{6.04 \cdot 10^{-2} z - 6.2 \cdot 10^{-3}}{z^2 - 7.34 \cdot 10^{-2} z - 3.48 \cdot 10^{-2}} z^{-5} \tag{30}$$

The response of each model is now compared to the measured data. An example is shown in Fig. 11. Both dynamic models predict steady-state values within five percent of each other.

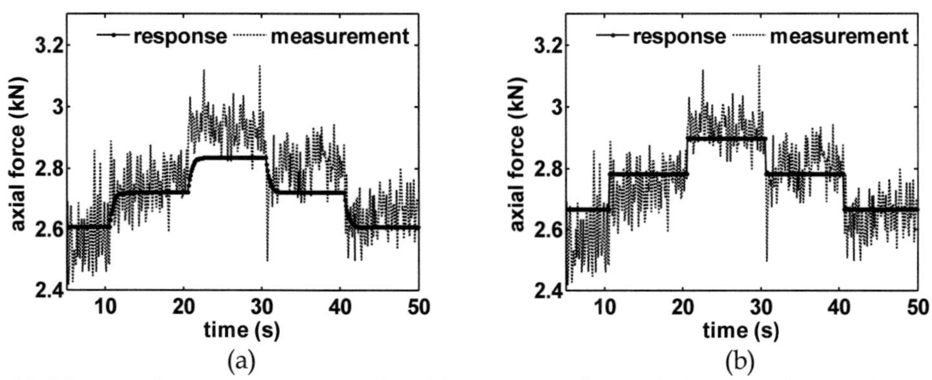

Fig. 11. Measured response compared to (a) response of model developed using filtered data and (b) response of model developed using unfiltered data, with v = 3.02 mm/s, ω = 1810 rpm, and plunge depth profile in Fig. 10b.

The model in equation (29) contains two overdamped poles with time constants of $3.57 \cdot 10^{-2}$ and 0.418 s. The model in equation (30) contains two overdamped poles with time constants of $6.74 \cdot 10^{-2}$ and $5.33 \cdot 10^{-2}$ s. Based on the work of Zhao et al. (2007), the system is dominated by a time constant of 0.519 s. This implies the model acquired through the use of the unfiltered data is not reliable and should not be used for controller design.

3.b FSW process control

A general tracking controller with constant disturbance rejection is designed to control the axial force. The block diagram is shown in Fig. 12. The transfer function is

$$G(z) = \frac{b(z)}{a(z)} \tag{31}$$

The disturbance generating polynomial is

$$v(z) = z - 1 \tag{32}$$

The controller polynomial is

$$g(z) = g_1 z^2 + g_2 z + g_3 \tag{33}$$

where $g1$, $g2$, and $g3$ are chosen to shape the closed-loop system error dynamics. The closed-loop error dynamics are third order with one overdamped pole and two underdamped poles. The time constant of the overdamped pole is $\tau 1$ = 0.03 s and the two underdamped poles are characterized by a natural frequency of 10 rad/s and a damping ratio of 0.5. Equating the actual and desired closed-loop characteristic polynomials

$$v(z)a(z) - g(z) = z^3 - 0.8216z^2 + 0.3959z - 1.311 \cdot 10^{-2} \tag{34}$$

Equating like coefficients in z in equation (34), g_1 = -1.026, g_2 = 0.4994, and g_3 = -0.3460. The control signal is

$$\begin{aligned} u(k) = & \frac{1}{b_1}\left[F_r(k+1) + (a_1 - 1)F_r(k) + (a_2 - a_1)F_r(k-1) - a_2 F_r(k-2)\right] \\ & - \frac{1}{b_1}\left[g_1 E_1(k) - g_2 E_1(k-1) - g_3 E_1(k-2)\right] \\ & + \frac{1}{b_1}\left[(b_2 - b_1)u(k-1) + b_2 u(k-2)\right] \end{aligned} \tag{35}$$

The controller is implemented on the FSW platform with saturation limits on the plunge depth set between 4.17 mm and 4.8 mm to ensure the shoulder does not lose contact with the material surface. The imposed rate limitation on change in plunge depth is 0.5 mm/s to prevent tool breakage.

Four control experiments are now presented. In the first experiment the axial force controller uses the unfiltered measurement to track $F_r(t)$ = 2.7 kN. The traverse speed and spindle speed are 2.18 mm/s and 1810 rpm, respectively. The results are plotted in Fig. 13. The controller maintains a constant force with an average 2.74 kN and standard deviation of

0.372 kN; however, the average absolute error during the steady-state response is 0.341 kN and large axial force oscillations occur due to the large amounts of variation present in the raw measurement signal. The plunge depth signal has large oscillations and often saturates at its lower limit.

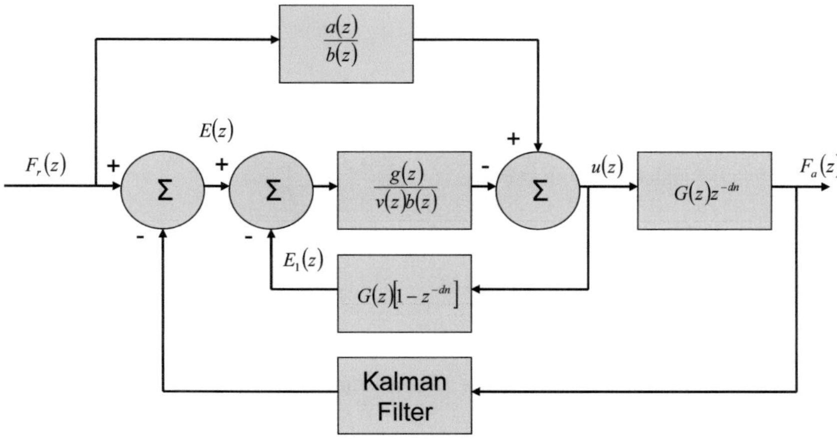

Fig. 12. Axial force closed-loop system block diagram

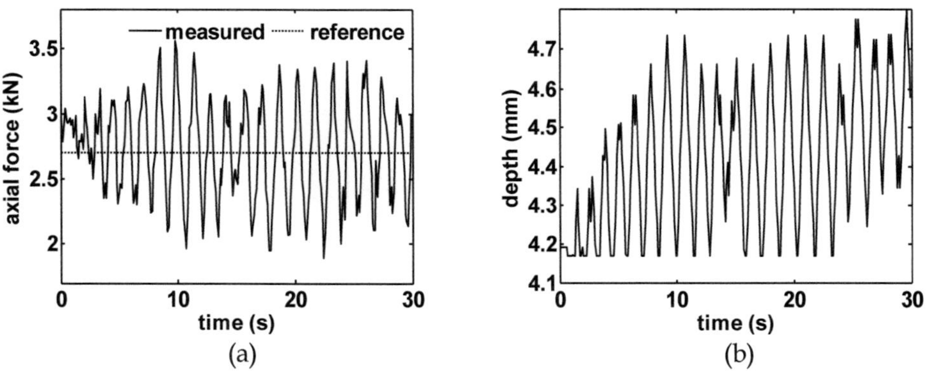

Fig. 13. Axial force controller results using unfiltered measurement and $F_r(t)$ = 2.7 kN, (a) axial force and (b) plunge depth

In the second experiment the axial force controller uses the filtered measurement to track $F_r(t)$ = 2.7 kN. The traverse speed and spindle speed are 2.18 mm/s and 1810 rpm, respectively. The results are shown in Fig. 14. In this case the average axial force is 2.705 kN, the standard deviation is 0.141 kN, and the absolute average error is 0.106 kN during the steady-state response. The filter effectively reduces the magnitude of the oscillations in both the axial force and plunge depth signals. Implementation of the filtering methodology allows for a wider range of reference tracking as the controller no longer saturates.

Next, the axial force controller is used to track the time varying reference

$$F_r(t) = 2.7 + 0.1\sin(0.8\pi t) \tag{36}$$

In the third experiment the axial force controller uses the unfiltered measurement to track the reference signal in equation (36). The traverse speed and spindle speed are 2.18 mm/s and 1810 rpm, respectively. The results are shown in Fig. 15. As in Fig. 13, the controller is able to adequately track the desired reference, but with considerable oscillations and plunge depth saturation at both its upper and lower limits. For this experiment the average absolute error is 0.413 kN during the steady-state response.

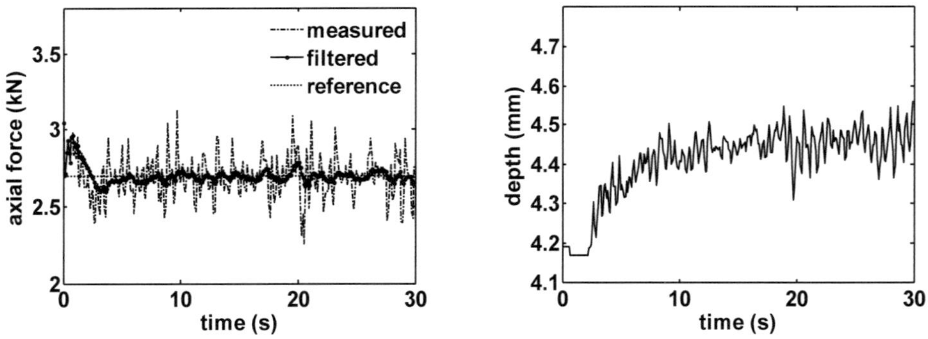

(a) (b)

Fig. 14. Axial force controller results using filtered measurement and $F_r(t)$ = 2.7 kN, (a) axial force and (b) plunge depth

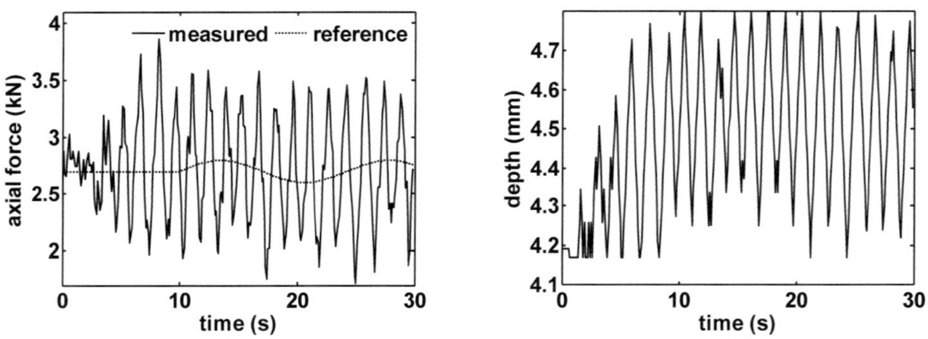

(a) (b)

Fig. 15. Axial force controller results using unfiltered measurement and reference force in equation (36), (a) axial force and (b) plunge depth

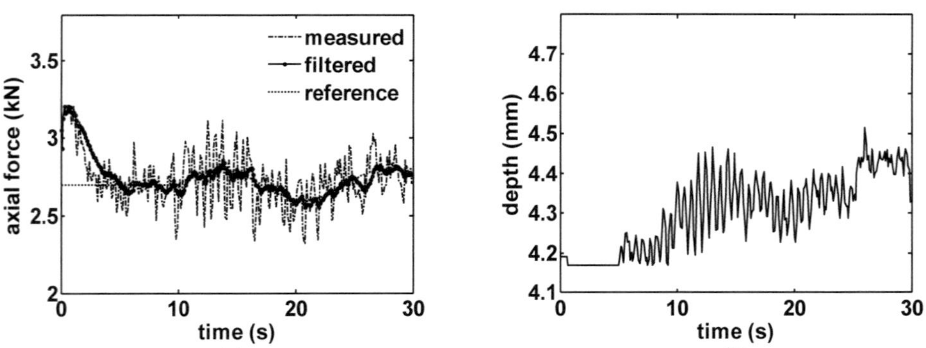

(a) (b)

Fig. 16. Axial force controller results using filtered measurement and reference force in equation (36), (a) axial force and (b) plunge depth

In the fourth experiment the axial force controller uses the filtered measurement to track the reference signal in equation (36). The traverse speed and spindle speed are 2.18 mm/s and 1810 rpm, respectively. The results are shown in Fig. 16. Similar to Fig. 14, the filter effectively reduces the magnitude of the axial force oscillations and allows for a wider range of reference signals to be utilized since the plunge depth is not saturating during the steady-state response. For this experiment the average absolute error is 0.124 kN during the steady-state response.

4. Laser metal deposition example

Laser Metal Deposition is an important Solid Freeform Fabrication technique that allows direct fabrication of functional metal parts directly from CAD solid models (Liou et al., 2007). The process can also be used for part repair, thereby extending product service life. Generally an LMD system consists of a multiple-axis motion system, a laser, and a powder feeder (see Fig. 17). During the process, a powder stream is injected into a laser generated melt pool on the substrate. With the axis moving, the melt pool quickly solidifies and forms a clad; thus, the injected powder is metallurgically bonded with the substrate. Depending on the trajectory of the motion system, parts with complex geometries can be fabricated in a layer-by-layer manner. Melt pool temperature control is an important control problem in LMD because it affects the part microstructure, which is highly related to the material properties. The measurement signal has tremendous variations that may deteriorate the controller performance. The application of the filtering methodology to the temperature measurement signal will significantly reduce measurement signal variation, resulting in improved controller performance.

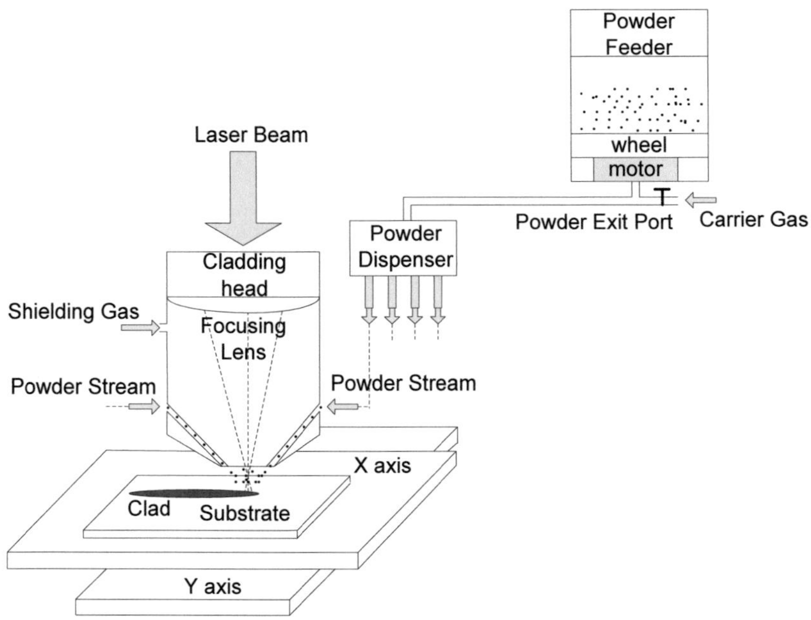

Fig. 17. LMD system schematic

To illustrate the affect the filtering methodology has on the measured temperature signal, an open-loop test is conducted. In this experiment the powder flow rate is 4 g/min and the traverse speed is 4 ipm. The powder material is H13 tool steel with particles having a mean diameter of 100 μm. The filtered and measured temperature signals are shown in Fig. 18. The filtering methodology reduces the standard deviation from 39.2 °C in the raw signal to 30.2 °C in the filtered signal.

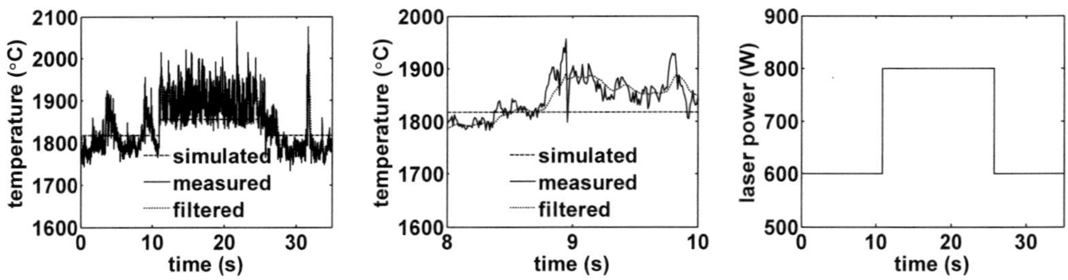

(a) (b) (c)

Fig. 18. Open-loop LMD test with T_s = 0.01 s, λ = 0, R = 2500, and Q = 25, (a) temperature versus time, (b) zoomed-in view of temperature versus time, and (c) laser power versus time

4.a LMD process modeling

The melt pool temperature is modeled using the following transfer function

$$T(s) = \frac{K}{\tau s + 1} V^{\alpha}(s) Q^{\beta}(s) M^{\gamma}(s) \tag{37}$$

where T is the melt pool temperature (°C), V is the traverse speed (ipm), Q is the laser power (W), M is the powder flow rate (g/min), K is the system gain, and τ is the time constant (s). Transforming equation (37) into the discrete-time domain using a zero order hold

$$T(z) = \frac{b_0}{z + a_0} V^{\alpha}(z) Q^{\beta}(z) M^{\gamma}(z) \tag{38}$$

where $a_0 = -e^{-T_s/\tau}$ and $b_0 = K\left(1 - e^{-T_s/\tau}\right)$. To determine the model coefficients K, α, β, and γ, the steady-state portion of equation (38) is considered

$$T_{ss} = K v^{\alpha} q^{\beta} m^{\gamma} \tag{39}$$

where T_{ss} is the average steady-state temperature. A series of experiments, covering the process operating range, are designed using DOE. The results are listed in Table 4. The parameters are estimated using the Least Squares method based on the data listed in Table 4 and are found to be K = 1170, α = $-8.18 \cdot 10^{-3}$, β = $7.16 \cdot 10^{-2}$, and γ = $3.42 \cdot 10^{-3}$. The filtering methodology is applied to the data in Table 4 and it is seen the signal variance has been reduced by 16 to nearly 60%.

To determine the time constant, an experiment is conducted where the laser power is increased and decreased in a step-wise manner. For this experiment, m = 4 g/min and v = 4 ipm. The measured temperature data is processed using the filtering methodology with λ = 0, R = 2500, and Q = 25. Recursive Least Squares is then applied to estimate the time constant. The value of the time constant is determined to be τ = 7.27·10^{-2} s. The model response is compared to the filtered measurement data in Fig. 18.

Run	*Q* (W)	*m* (g/min)	*v* (ipm)	ave(*T*) (°C)	Variance Reduction (%)
1	600	4	8	1851	16.1
2	700	4	4	1861	27.4
3	800	6	4	1911	59.6
4	600	6	6	1835	22.6
5	700	8	6	1854	26.6
6	800	4	6	1854	42.6
7	600	8	4	1842	35.1
8	700	6	8	1857	33.5
9	800	8	8	1881	25.6

Table 4. Experimental results for model coefficient identification of LMD process

4.b LMD process control

Letting $U(z) = V^{\alpha}(z)Q^{\beta}(z)M^{\gamma}(z)$, equation (38) becomes

$$T(z) = \frac{b_0}{z + a_0} U(z) \tag{40}$$

A general tracking controller using the Internal Model Principle is designed to regulate the melt pool temperature. The block diagram is shown in Fig. 19.

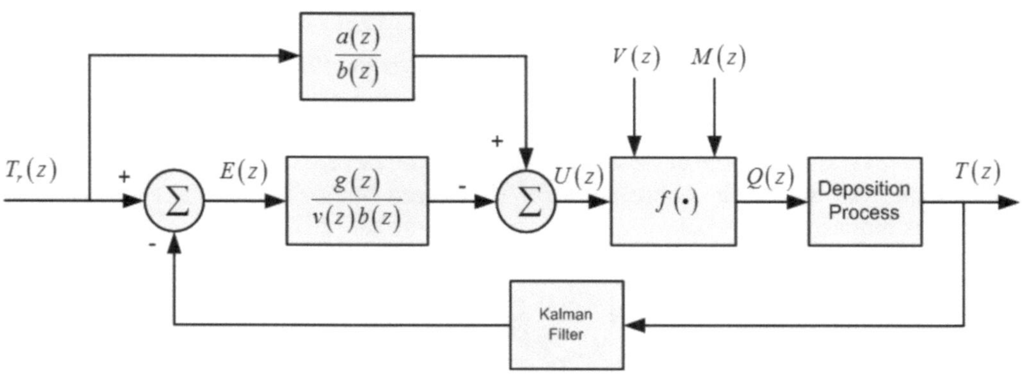

Fig. 19. Melt pool temperature closed-loop control system block diagram

With the disturbance generating polynomial given in equation (32) and a closed-loop characteristic polynomial $v(z)a(z)$–$g(z)$ with two poles located at $-e^{-T_s/\tau_1}$ and $-e^{-T_s/\tau_2}$, where τ_1 = 0.1 s and τ_2 = 0.11 s, the controller polynomial is

$$g(z) = g_1 z + g_0 = \left(e^{-T_s/\tau_1} + e^{-T_s/\tau_2} - 1 - e^{-T_s/\tau}\right) z + \left(e^{-T_s/\tau} - e^{-T_s/\tau_1 - T_s/\tau_2}\right) \tag{41}$$

The control signal is

$$u(k) = u(k-1) + \frac{T_r(k+1) - \left(1 + e^{-T_s/\tau}\right) T_r(k) + e^{-T_s/\tau} T_r(k-1) - g_1 e(k) - g_0 e(k-1)}{K\left(1 - e^{-T_s/\tau}\right)} \tag{42}$$

and the commanded laser power is

$$q(k)=\left(\frac{u(k)}{v(k)^{\alpha}\,m(k)^{r}}\right)^{1/\beta} \tag{43}$$

Four control experiments are now presented. In the first experiment the temperature controller uses the unfiltered measurement to track $T_r(t)$ = 1900 °C. The mass flow rate and traverse speed are 6 g/min and 6 ipm, respectively. The results are shown in Fig. 20. For this experiment, the average melt pool temperature is 1904 °C, the average absolute error is 61.8 °C, and error standard deviation is 76.8 °C. The results show that significant variation exists in both the temperature and the laser power signals.

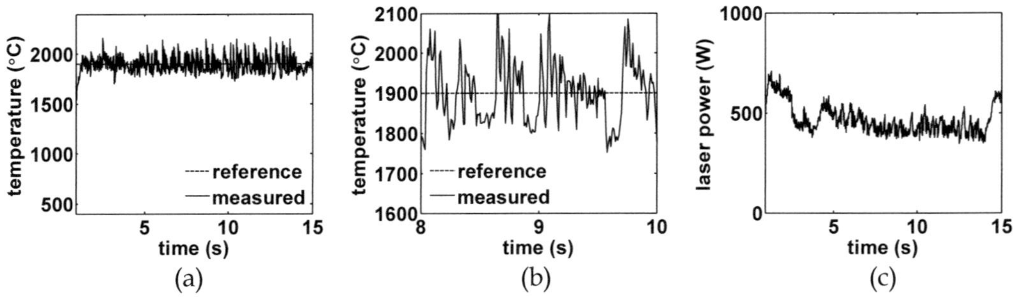

Fig. 20. Temperature controller results using unfiltered measurement and $T_r(t)$ = 1900 °C, (a) temperature, (b) zoomed-in view of temperature, and (c) laser power

In the second experiment the temperature controller uses the filtered measurement to track $T_r(t)$ = 1900 °C. The mass flow rate and traverse speed are 6 g/min and 6 ipm, respectively. The results are shown in Fig. 21. For this experiment, the average melt pool temperature is 1901 °C, the average absolute error is 42.3 °C, and error standard deviation is 57.9 °C. The results show that the average absolute error is reduced by 31.6% and the error standard deviation is reduced by 24.6%.

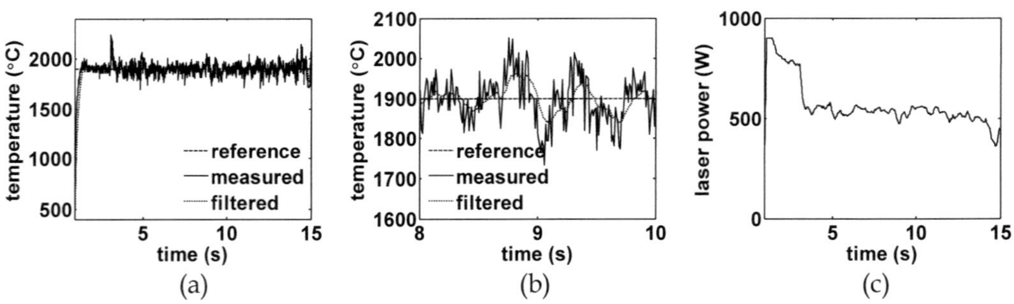

Fig. 21. Temperature controller results using filtered measurement and $T_r(t)$ = 1900 °C, (a) temperature, (b) zoomed-in view of temperature, and (c) laser power

The performances of the controllers are now compared when tracking a time varying reference. The temperature reference for these experiments is

$$T_r(t)=1850+50\sin(t) \tag{44}$$

In the third experiment the temperature controller uses the unfiltered measurement to track the temperature reference given in equation (44). The mass flow rate and traverse speed are 6 g/min and 6 ipm, respectively. The results are shown in Fig. 22. The average absolute error is 52.9 °C and error standard deviation is 71.0 °C. The results show that significant variation exists in both the temperature and the laser power signals due to the fact that the controller operates on the unfiltered signal.

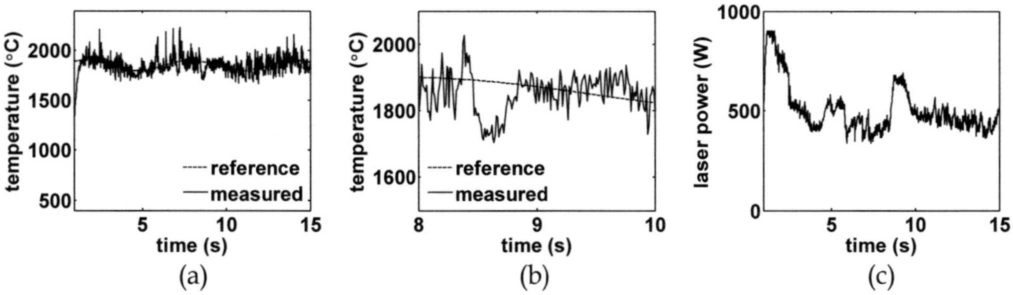

Fig. 22. Temperature controller results using unfiltered measurement and reference temperature given in equation (44), (a) temperature, (b) zoomed-in view of temperature, and (c) laser power

In the fourth experiment the temperature controller uses the filtered measurement to track the temperature reference given in equation (44). The mass flow rate and traverse speed are 6 g/min and 6 ipm, respectively. The results are shown in Fig. 23. The average absolute error is 40.8 °C and error standard deviation is 55.7 °C. Compared with the results in Fig. 22, the average absolute error is reduced by 22.9% and error standard deviation is reduced by 21.6%. Also, the oscillations in the temperature and laser power signals have been greatly reduced.

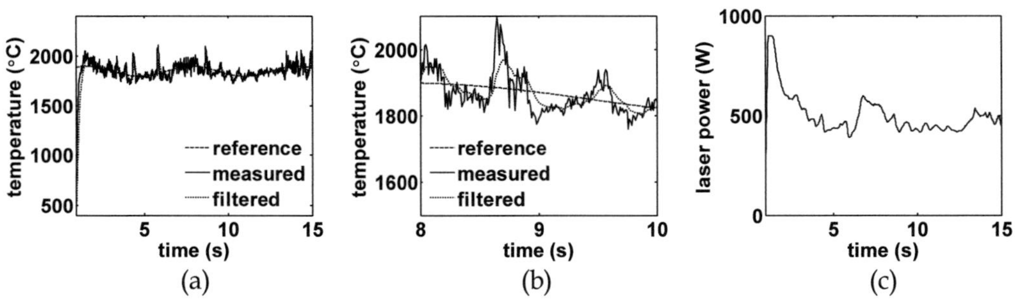

Fig. 23. Temperature controller results using filtered measurement and reference temperature given in equation (44), (a) temperature, (b) zoomed-in view of temperature, and (c) laser power

5. Summary and conclusions

This chapter presented a methodology, based on stochastic process modeling and Kalman filtering, to filter manufacturing process measurements, which are known to be inherently noisy. Via simulation studies, the methodology was compared to low pass and Butterworth filters. The methodology was applied in a Friction Stir Welding (FSW) process to filter data

used to construct a dynamic axial force process model and by an on-line axial force controller. Also, the methodology was applied to a Laser Metal Deposition (LMD) process to filter data used to construct a dynamic melt pool temperature process model and by an on-line melt pool temperature controller.
The simulation studies demonstrated that the filter methodology was able to reduce signal variation and maintain signal phase and magnitude fidelity better than the low-pass and Butterworth filters. Also, the dynamic response generated from the model constructed from data processed with the filtering methodology was closer to the true response than those generated from models constructed from data processed with the low-pass and Butterworth filters. The experimental results demonstrated that models for the FSW and LMD process constructed from data processed by the filtering methodology provided more accurate responses than models constructed from the raw data. Also, when the filtering methodology was used to process the measurements in the FSW and LMD controllers, better closed-loop response was realized as compared to the closed-loop response when implementing the controllers using unprocessed measurements.

6. References

Åström, K.J. and Wittenmark, B., 1995, Adaptive Control, Addison-Wesley, New York.

Bhattacharyya, P. and Sengupta, D., 2007, "Estimation of Tool Wear Based on Adaptive Sensor Fusion of Force and Power in Face Milling," *International Journal of Production Research*, Vol. 43, pp. 1-17.

Freitag, K.P., 2004, "Two-Axis Force Feedback Deflection Compensation of Miniature Ball End Mills," Mechanical Engineering Department, North Carolina State University.

Ghosh, N., Ravi, Y.B., Patra, A., Mukhopadhyay, S., Paul, S., Mohanty, A.R., and Chattopadhyay, A.B., 2007, "Estimation of Tool Wear during CNC Milling Using Neural Network Based Sensor Fusion," *Mechanical Systems and Signal Processing*, Vol. 21, pp. 466-479.

Liang, M., Yeap, T., Rahmati, S., and Han, Z., 2002, "Fuzzy Control of Spindle Power in End Milling Processes," *International Journal of Machine Tools and Manufacture*, Vol. 42, pp. 1487-1496.

Liou, F.W., Slattery, K., Kinsella, M., Newkirk, J., Chou, J-N., and Landers, R.G., 2007, "Applications of a Hybrid Manufacturing Process for Fabrication of Metallic Structures," *Journal of Rapid Prototyping*, Vol. 13, No. 4, pp. 236-244.

Mishra, R.S. and Ma, Z.Y., 2005, "Friction Stir Welding and Processing," *Materials Science and Engineering: R*, Vol. 50, No. 1-2, pp. 1-78.

22

Applications of Robust Descriptor Kalman Filter in Robotics

João Y. Ishihara[1], Marco H. Terra[2], Geovany A. Borges[1],
Glauco G. Scandaroli[1], Roberto S. Inoue[2] and Valdir Grassi Jr[2]
[1]*University of Brasilia, CP 4386, Brasilia,*
[2]*University of São Paulo at São Carlos, CP 359, São Carlos,*
Brazil

1. Introduction

In this chapter we are interested in designing estimators for the internal variables of two kind of robots, wheeled mobile and robotic leg prosthesis, based on a recently developed robust descriptor Kalman filter. The proposed approach is reasonable since descriptor formulation can cope with algebraic restrictions on system's signals. Further, the recursiveness of this class of filter is useful for on-line applications.

Different procedures have been used to deal with mobile robots localization problem. Measurement systems based on odometric, inertial sensors and ultrasounds are self-contained, simple to use, and able to guarantee a high data rate. However, the problem of these systems is that they integrate the relative increments, and the localization errors considerably grow over time if an appropriate sensor fusion algorithm is not used, see for instance [17], [18] and references therein. The examples developed in these references do not take into account robust approaches, in the line we are proposing here.

In the context of robotic leg prosthesis, we deal with the development of devices for above knee amputees. Robotic prosthesis are devices intended to replace parts of the human body. They should be able to sense the environment and complain with the movement of the body in such a way to aid the user to perform the most common tasks. This is a very interesting and current research topic [7]. Environment sensing is one of the most difficult tasks, mainly in the case of leg prosthesis because of the great diversity of walking conditions and terrains. The use of Electromyographic (EMG) signal processing for detecting the main properties of the walking terrain is the focus of [15]. However, in the case of above knee prosthesis, there is no EMG signal available to allow automatic reorientation of the robotic foot. When the foot of a robotic leg is not in contact with ground, its configuration should be estimated to allow its control with respect to ground. This can be useful for controlling its orientation, mainly in the end of phase where the foot is not in contact with ground. In this chapter, it is shown a solution for this problem using multisensor data fusion by a robust descriptor Kalman filter.

This chapter is divided in three main parts. In the first part we present basic definitions and concepts of descriptor systems and some examples to clarify the use of this kind of approach. In the second part we present three algorithms for the computation of the descriptor robust Kalman filter for its filtered, predicted, and time and measurement update forms. Finally we present two practical examples of application in robotics.

2. Descriptor systems and the robust estimation problem

In dynamical systems modeling, it is usually obtained a set of differential equations (by first principles like Newton's law, Ohm's law,...)

$$\begin{aligned} \dot{x}_1(t) &= f_1(x_1(t), ..., x_n(t), u_1(t), ..., u_m(t), t) \\ &\vdots \\ \dot{x}_n(t) &= f_n(x_1(t), ..., x_n(t), u_1(t), ..., u_m(t), t) \end{aligned}$$

and a set of algebraic restrictions (conservative laws, Kirchoff rules,...)

$$\begin{aligned} g_1(x_1(t), ..., x_n(t), u_1(t), ..., u_m(t), t) &= 0 \\ &\vdots \\ g_p(x_1(t), ..., x_n(t), u_1(t), ..., u_m(t), t) &= 0 \end{aligned}$$

or in matricial notation

$$\begin{aligned} \dot{x}(t) &= f(x(t), u(t), t) \\ g(x(t), u(t), t) &= 0. \end{aligned} \tag{1}$$

A dynamic system in this formulation is called descriptor system or differential-algebraic system. These nonlinear sets of dynamic and constraint equations are usually obtained by modeling softwares. Therefore, systems in descriptor formulation frequently arises naturally in the process of modeling of economical systems [21], image modeling [9], robotics [22], and so on.

Note that the descriptor formulation of a dynamical system states that the input $u(t) = [u_1(t) ... u_m(t)]^T$, the descriptor variable $x(t) = [x_1(t) ... x_n(t)]^T$ and its dynamics $\dot{x}(t)$ are related implicitly as

$$F(\dot{x}(t), x(t), u(t), t) = 0 \tag{2}$$

where the function $F(*)$ is usually considered differentiable. Due to this alternative general formulation, a descriptor system is also known as implicit system and the descriptor variable is also called internal latent variable, generalized state, semi-state or simply, state variable. In many cases (those called regular), it is possible to obtain some descriptor variables in terms of others and thus obtain a minimum set of equations in state-space form

$$\dot{x}(t) = f(x(t), u(t), t).$$

However, there are cases (those called singular) where it is not possible to reduce to a state-space formulation. Therefore, the descriptor formulation is more general than the state-space formulation in the sense that it can describe some dynamical systems for which state-space description does not exist [31]. Descriptor formulation arises naturally in several situations:

1. **Proportional derivative (PD) controller**. The state derivative feedback leads to a closed loop system

$$(I + BK)\,\dot{x}(t) = Ax(t)$$

where the matrix $(I + BK)$ is in general nonsingular. [20]

2. **Systems interconnection**. The feedback closed system

$$\begin{aligned} \dot{x}(t) &= Ax(t) + Bu(t) \\ y(t) &= Cx(t) + Du(t) \\ u(t) &= Ky(t) + v(t) \end{aligned}$$

can be written in descriptor form as

$$\begin{bmatrix} I & 0 & 0 \\ 0 & 0 & 0 \\ 0 & 0 & 0 \end{bmatrix} \begin{bmatrix} \dot{x}(t) \\ \dot{u}(t) \\ \dot{y}(t) \end{bmatrix} = \begin{bmatrix} A & B & 0 \\ C & D & -I \\ 0 & -I & K \end{bmatrix} \begin{bmatrix} x(t) \\ u(t) \\ y(t) \end{bmatrix} + \begin{bmatrix} 0 \\ 0 \\ I \end{bmatrix} v(t)$$

The closed loop system is singular if the matrix $\begin{bmatrix} D & -I \\ -I & K \end{bmatrix}$ is singular.

3. **System with unknown imputs.** The system

$$\dot{x}(t) = Ax(t) + d(t)$$

where the input $d(t)$ is considered unknown can be written as

$$\begin{bmatrix} I & 0 \\ 0 & 0 \end{bmatrix} \begin{bmatrix} \dot{x}(t) \\ \dot{d}(t) \end{bmatrix} = \begin{bmatrix} A & I \\ 0 & I \end{bmatrix} \begin{bmatrix} x(t) \\ d(t) \end{bmatrix}.$$

For more details on descriptor systems see for instance [2], [19], [5], [30] and references therein, in which an extensive list of applications can be found.

After the first step of obtaining the general descriptor equation (1) or (2), in order to deal with computer implementations, usually it is performed a linearization and time discretization on (2) and it is chosen an output signal z leading to a linear discrete-time descriptor system

$$E_{i+1}x_{i+1} = F_i x_i + G_{u,i}u_i$$

$$z_i = H_i x_i + K_{u,i}u_i.$$

This linear model is suitable in many cases, but its main hypothesis is that the system parameters are exactly known. In most situations the effects of some uncertainties cannot be neglected. For these situations, a more appropriate model can be considered as

$$\begin{aligned}(E_{i+1} + \Delta E_{i+1})\, x_{i+1} &= (F_i + \Delta F_i)\, x_i + (G_i + \Delta G_i)\, u_i + w_i \\ z_i &= (H_i + \Delta H_i)\, x_i + (K_i + \Delta K_i)\, u_i + v_i\end{aligned} \tag{3}$$

where ΔE_{i+1}, ΔF_i, ΔG_i, ΔH_i, and ΔK_i deal with the disturbances in the model parameters (to cope with approximations or nonlinearities) and w_i and v_i are random vectors (to cope with noisy signals).

In the last years, the robust estimation problem of descriptor systems has been considered in the literature by several authors. This chapter deals with a class of robust descriptor filters based on recursive algorithms. They are extensions of the robust filters developed in [25] for standard state space systems.

A. The problem of generalized state estimation

In this subsection, we consider the problem of the general internal variable estimation and its solution. The theoretical presentation is reduced and most proofs are omitted to easy reading. The detailed proofs can be found in the references.

Consider that we have a set of measured or observed signals $z = \{z_0, z_1, ..., z_k\}$ from a certain real dynamical system in discrete-time. We are interested in obtaining a suitable dynamical model which 'explains' the observed measurements and even obtain some knowledge about the values of next measurements, as z_{k+1}, for example. As a first attempt, we can consider that z is the output of a linear system. An ideal linear dynamical system in its more general form is an implicit or descriptor system

$$\begin{aligned}E_{i+1}x_{i+1} &= F_i x_i, \; i = 0, 1, 2, ... \\ z_i &= H_i x_i\end{aligned} \tag{4}$$

where x_i is the descriptor variable which describes the internal behavior of the system; E_{i+1}, F_i, and H_i are real rectangular matrices of appropriated dimensions. Then, we can state a deterministic data fitting problem over the entire trajectory as follows. Suppose that are given a sequence of measurements $\{z_i\}_{i=0}^{k}$, the matrices E_i, F_i, H_i of appropriate dimensions, and an initial value $\bar{x}_0$. For each state sequence $\{x_{0|k}, x_{1|k}, ..., x_{k|k}, x_{k+1|k}\}$ we can define the following fitting errors

$$\begin{aligned}w_{i|k} &:= E_{i+1}x_{i+1|k} - F_i x_{i|k} \\ v_{i|k} &:= z_i - H_i x_{i|k}, \; i = 0, 1, ..., k \\ p_{0|k} &:= E_0 x_{0|k} - F_{-1}\bar{x}_0\end{aligned} \tag{5}$$

where the matrices E_0 and F_{-1} are supposed of appropriate dimensions. These matrices can deal with the *a priori* information on the initial state x_0, and usually it is supposed $E_0 = F_{-1} = I$. Now, the deterministic optimal fitting problem is to find a state sequence which minimizes some predefined error functional (the actual expression of the functional is not considered in this chapter. The interested reader can see [12]). Once obtained the minimizing sequence $\{\hat{x}_{i|k}\}$, we can define from (5) the corresponding minimum fitting errors $\hat{w}_{i|k},\ \hat{v}_{i|k},\ \hat{p}_{0|k}$ so that the complete model which 'explains' the set of measured signals $z = \{z_i\}_{i=0}^{k}$ can be written as

$$E_0\hat{x}_{0|k} = F_{-1}\bar{x}_0 + \hat{p}_{0|k} \tag{6}$$

$$E_{i+1}\hat{x}_{i+1|k} = F_i\hat{x}_{i|k} + \hat{w}_{i|k} \tag{7}$$

$$z_i = H_i\hat{x}_{i|k} + \hat{v}_{i|k},\ i = 0, 1, ..., k. \tag{8}$$

As the model (6)-(8) also gives the next internal value $\hat{x}_{k+1|k}$, we could try to obtain a prevision for the value of the next measurement z_{k+1}. From the process followed until now (with fixed $k + 1$ observations), we do not have $\hat{v}_{k+1|k+1}$ nor $\hat{v}_{k+1|k}$, and so, the best knowledge we have about a possible value for the next measurement is the estimate

$$\hat{z}_{k+1|k} := H_{k+1}\hat{x}_{k+1|k}. \tag{9}$$

This is a reasonable guess since for the last available measurement we have, z_k, we see from (8) that the estimate

$$\hat{z}_{k|k} := H_k\hat{x}_{k|k} \tag{10}$$

differs from the actually measured value by the fitting error $\hat{v}_{k|k}$, which was minimized.

Note that the estimates (10) and (9) are completely determined by the estimates for the present and next descriptor variables. Therefore, our original problem is solved if we consider the following two problems:

1. The filtering problem: obtain the best $x_{k|k},\ \hat{x}_{k|k}$, from the measurements $\{z_0,\ z_1, ..., z_k\}$;
2. The prediction problem: obtain the best $x_{k+1|k},\ \hat{x}_{k+1|k}$, from the measurements $\{z_0,\ z_1, ..., z_k\}$.

The nomenclature 'filtering' is justified by the observation that if $H_k = I$ in the model (6)-(8), then we have from (8)

$$z_k = \hat{x}_{k|k} + \hat{v}_{k|k} \tag{11}$$

and so, if the signal $\hat{x}_{k|k}$ was obtained from the actually measured signal z_k, the error signal $\hat{v}_{k|k}$ has been suppressed.

So far, we have considered a fixed set of measurements $\{z_0, ..., z_k\}$. However, for many practical dynamical systems, it is usual that the set of measurements is constantly updated forming the sets $\{z_0, ..., z_k,\ z_{k+1}\}$, $\{z_0, ..., z_k,\ z_{k+1},\ z_{k+2}\}$ and so on. Therefore, it is natural to ask if we could obtain $\hat{x}_{k+1|k},\ \hat{x}_{k+1|k+1}$ based on $\hat{x}_{k|k-1},\ \hat{x}_{k|k}$. The answer is given by the elegant recursive algorithm of the Kalman filter which can be obtained considering recursively the one-step deterministic optimum data fitting problem

$$\min_{x_i,\, x_{i+1}} \left[\left\| x_i - \hat{x}_{i|i} \right\|^2_{P^{-1}_{i|i}} + \| E_{i+1}x_{i+1} - F_i x_i \|^2_{Q_i^{-1}} + \| z_{i+1} - H_{i+1}x_{i+1} \|^2_{R^{-1}_{i+1}} \right]. \quad (12)$$

The resulting descriptor Kalman filter in filtered form is given by the following theorem (cf. [6], [24], [23], [12]).

Theorem 1: Suppose that $\begin{bmatrix} E_i \\ H_i \end{bmatrix}$ has full column rank for all $i \geq 0$. The Kalman filter to estimate $\hat{x}_{i|i}$ can be obtained from the following recursive algorithm
Step 0: (Initial Conditions): $P_{0|0} := \left(P_0^{-1} + H_0^T R_0^{-1} H_0\right)^{-1}; \quad \hat{x}_{0|0} := P_{0|0} H_0^T R_0^{-1} z_0.$
Step *i*: Update $\{\hat{x}_{i|i}, P_{i|i}\}$ to $\{\hat{x}_{i+1|i+1}, P_{i+1|i+1}\}$

$$P_{i+1|i+1} := \left(E^T_{i+1}\left(Q_i + F_i P_{i|i} F_i^T\right)^{-1} E_{i+1} + H^T_{i+1} R^{-1}_{i+1} H_{i+1}\right)^{-1}; \quad (13)$$

$$\hat{x}_{i+1|i+1} := P_{i+1|i+1} E^T_{i+1} (Q_i + F_i P_{i|i} F_i^T)^{-1} F_i \hat{x}_{i|i} + P_{i+1|i+1} H^T_{i+1} R^{-1}_{i+1} z_{i+1}. \quad \square \quad (14)$$

Analogously, the predicted estimates recursion can be obtained by solving recursively the following optimization problem

$$\begin{aligned} &\min_{x_i, x_{i+1}} [(x_i - \hat{x}_{i|i-1})^T P^{-1}_{i|i-1}(x_i - \hat{x}_{i|i-1}) + (z_i - H_i x_i)^T R_i^{-1}(z_i - H_i x_i) \\ &+ (E_{i+1}x_{i+1} - F_i x_i)^T Q_i^{-1}(E_{i+1}x_{i+1} - F_i x_i)] \end{aligned} \quad (15)$$

and is given by the following theorem.

Theorem 2: Suppose that E_i has full column rank for all $i \geq 0$. The optimum predicted estimates $\widehat{x}_{i+1|i}$ can be obtained from the following recursive algorithm
Step 0: (Initial Conditions): $P_{0|-1} := P_0; \quad \hat{x}_{0|-1} := \bar{x}_0 = 0.$
Step *i*: Update $\{\hat{x}_{i|i-1}, P_{i|i-1}\}$ to $\{\hat{x}_{i+1|i}, P_{i+1|i}\}$

$$P_{i+1|i} := \left(\begin{bmatrix} E_{i+1} \\ 0 \end{bmatrix}^T \begin{bmatrix} Q_i + F_i P_{i|i-1} F_i^T & -F_i P_{i|i-1} H_i^T \\ -H_i P_{i|i-1} F_i^T & R_i + H_i P_{i|i-1} H_i^T \end{bmatrix}^{-1} \begin{bmatrix} E_{i+1} \\ 0 \end{bmatrix} \right)^{-1}; \quad (16)$$

$$\hat{x}_{i+1|i} := P_{i+1|i} \begin{bmatrix} E_{i+1} \\ 0 \end{bmatrix}^T \begin{bmatrix} Q_i + F_i P_{i|i-1} F_i^T & -F_i P_{i|i-1} H_i^T \\ -H_i P_{i|i-1} F_i^T & R_i + H_i P_{i|i-1} H_i^T \end{bmatrix}^{-1} \begin{bmatrix} F_i \hat{x}_{i|i-1} \\ z_i - H_i \widehat{x}_{i|i-1} \end{bmatrix}. \quad \square \quad (17)$$

Remark II.1: The underling descriptor model in the above theorems is

$$\begin{aligned} E_{i+1}x_{i+1} &= F_i x_i + w_i, \\ z_i &= H_i x_i + v_i. \end{aligned} \quad (18)$$

Remark II.2: The data fitting approach is suitable for general descriptor systems and therefore is valid for state-space systems. However, it is important to remember that what is natural for state-space systems is not directly valid for descriptor systems. For example, in (18), the matrix E_{i+1} restrict the allowed directions of the vectors x_i and w_i. In particular, for some values of x_i and w_i, the value of x_{i+1} may be non-determinable. Therefore, in the descriptor setting, a naive approach of considering w_i a normal random vector can lead to very difficult technical problems as admissible initial conditions and admissible inputs.
Remark II.3: In the fitting functionals, the intuitive notion of (relative) degree of uncertainty or, how big we allow each error to be, is dealt with the introduction of positive definite weighting matrices W_j, V_i, and P_0 to the errors $w_{j|k}$, $v_{i|k}$, and $p_{0|k}$, respectively, for all i and j. This is the deterministic counterpart of covariance matrices.
Remark II.4: Note that it was used one quadratic functional to obtain the best filtered estimate recursion and other quadratic functional to obtain the best predicted estimate recursion. The two functionals have to be considered since for general descriptor systems, the predictor and filtered recursions do not correspond to a same filter transfer matrix as occur in the state-space setting.

B. Robust filtered estimates

The optimum robust fitting problem for the filtered estimates is defined as follows. It is assumed that at step i an estimate for the state x_i, denoted by $\hat{x}_{i|i}$, and there exists a positive-definite weighting matrix $P_{i|i}$ for the state estimation error $x_i - \hat{x}_{i|i}$, along with the new observation at time $i + 1$, i.e., z_{i+1}. To update the estimate of x_i from $\hat{x}_{i|i}$ to $\hat{x}_{i+1|i+1}$, it is proposed the following sequence of robust data fitting problems: Solve

$$\min_{x_0} \max_{\delta H_0} \left[\|x_0\|^2_{P_0^{-1}} + \|z_0 - (H_0 + \delta H_0)x_0\|^2_{R_0^{-1}} \right] \qquad \text{for } i = 0; \tag{19}$$

$$\begin{aligned} \min_{\{x_i,\, x_{i+1}\}} \max_{\{\delta E_{i+1}, \delta F_i, \delta H_{i+1}\}} & \left[\|x_i - \hat{x}_{i|i}\|^2_{P_{i|i}^{-1}} + \|(E_{i+1} + \delta E_{i+1})x_{i+1} - (F_i + \delta F_i)x_i\|^2_{Q_i^{-1}} \right. \\ & \left. + \|z_{i+1} - (H_{i+1} + \delta H_{i+1})x_{i+1}\|^2_{R_{i+1}^{-1}} \right] \qquad \text{for } i > 0 \end{aligned} \tag{20}$$

where the uncertainties are assumed modeled with the following structures

$$\delta F_i = M_{f,i}\Delta_i N_{f,i}; \quad \delta E_{i+1} = M_{f,i}\Delta_i N_{e,i+1}; \quad \delta H_i = M_{h,i}\Delta_i N_{h,i}; \quad \|\Delta_i\| \leq 1 \tag{21}$$

where $M_{f,i}$, $M_{h,i}$, $N_{e,i+1}$, $N_{f,i}$, $N_{h,i}$ are known matrices and Δ_i is a bounded matrix (with norm less or equal to 1) but otherwise arbitrary. The robust filtering algorithms we present in this section are based on the following auxiliary functions

$$G(\lambda) := \|x(\lambda)\|^2_Q + \lambda \|N_a x(\lambda) - N_b\|^2 + \|Ax(\lambda) - b\|^2_{W(\lambda)}; \tag{22}$$

$$x(\lambda) := [Q(\lambda) + A^T W(\lambda) A]^{-1}[A^T W(\lambda) b + \hat{\lambda} N_a^T N_b]; \tag{23}$$

$$Q(\lambda) := Q + \lambda N_a^T N_a; \quad W(\lambda) := W + WH(\lambda I - H^T W H)^{\dagger} H^T W. \tag{24}$$

The optimum robust filtered estimates $\hat{x}_{i|i}$ resulting from (20) can be obtained recursively from Algorithm 1.

Algorithm 1: Robust Filtered Estimates

Step 0: (Initial Conditions): If $M_{h,0} = 0$ then $P_{0|0} := \left(P_0^{-1} + H_0^T R_0^{-1} H_0\right)^{-1}$; $\hat{x}_{0|0} := P_{0|0} H_0^T R_0^{-1} z_0$. Otherwise determine the optimum scalar parameter $\hat{\lambda}_{-1}$ by minimizing over the interval $\lambda > \left\|M_{h,0}^T R_0^{-1} M_{h,0}\right\|$ the function $G(\lambda)$ of (22) corresponding to

$$A \leftarrow H_0;\ b \leftarrow z_0;\ Q \leftarrow P_0^{-1};\ W \leftarrow R_0^{-1};\ H \leftarrow M_{h,0};\ N_a \leftarrow N_{h,0};\ N_b \leftarrow 0. \tag{25}$$

Then set

$$\hat{R}_0 := R_0 - \hat{\lambda}_{-1}^{-1} M_{h,0} M_{h,0}^T;\quad P_{0|0} := \left(P_0^{-1} + H_0^T \hat{R}_0^{-1} H_0 + \hat{\lambda}_{-1} N_{h,0}^T N_{h,0}\right)^{-1};\quad \hat{x}_{0|0} := P_{0|0} H_0^T \hat{R}_0^{-1} z_0. \tag{26}$$

Step 1: If $M_{f,i} = 0$ and $M_{h,i+1} = 0$ then $\hat{\lambda}_i := 0$. Otherwise determine the optimum scalar parameter $\hat{\lambda}_i$ by minimizing over the interval

$$\hat{\lambda}_i > \lambda_{l,i} := \|diag\{M_{f,i}^T Q_i^{-1} M_{f,i}, M_{h,i+1}^T R_{i+1}^{-1} M_{h,i+1}\}\| \tag{27}$$

the function $G(\lambda)$ of (22) corresponding to

$$A \leftarrow \begin{bmatrix} -F_i & E_{i+1} \\ 0 & H_{i+1} \end{bmatrix};\ b \leftarrow \begin{bmatrix} F_i \hat{x}_{i|i} \\ z_{i+1} \end{bmatrix};\ Q \leftarrow \begin{bmatrix} P_{i|i}^{-1} & 0 \\ 0 & 0 \end{bmatrix}$$

$$W \leftarrow \begin{bmatrix} Q_i^{-1} & 0 \\ 0 & R_{i+1}^{-1} \end{bmatrix};\ N_a \leftarrow \begin{bmatrix} -N_{f,i} & N_{e,i+1} \\ 0 & N_{h,i+1} \end{bmatrix};\ N_b \leftarrow \begin{bmatrix} N_{f,i} \hat{x}_{i|i} \\ 0 \end{bmatrix};\ H \leftarrow \begin{bmatrix} M_{f,i} & 0 \\ 0 & M_{h,i} \end{bmatrix}. \tag{28}$$

Step 2: If $\hat{\lambda}_i \neq 0$, the given parameters $\{Q_i, R_{i+1}, E_{i+1}, F_i, H_{i+1}\}$ are replaced by the corrected parameters

$$\hat{\mathcal{Q}}_i := \begin{bmatrix} \hat{Q}_i & 0 \\ 0 & I \end{bmatrix},\ \hat{Q}_i := Q_i - \hat{\lambda}_i^{-1} M_{f,i} M_{f,i}^T;\quad \hat{E}_{i+1} := \begin{bmatrix} E_{i+1} \\ \sqrt{\hat{\lambda}_i} N_{e,i+1} \end{bmatrix};\quad \hat{F}_i := \begin{bmatrix} F_i \\ \sqrt{\hat{\lambda}_i} N_{f,i} \end{bmatrix}$$

$$\hat{\mathcal{R}}_{i+1} := \begin{bmatrix} \hat{R}_{i+1} & 0 \\ 0 & I \end{bmatrix},\ \hat{R}_{i+1} := R_{i+1} - \hat{\lambda}_i^{-1} M_{h,i+1} M_{h,i+1}^T;\quad \hat{H}_{i+1} := \begin{bmatrix} H_{i+1} \\ \sqrt{\hat{\lambda}_i} N_{h,i+1} \end{bmatrix}.$$

Step 3: If $rank \begin{bmatrix} \hat{E}_{i+1} \\ \hat{H}_{i+1} \end{bmatrix} = n$, update $\{P_{i|i}, \hat{x}_{i|i}\}$ to $\{P_{i+1|i+1}, \hat{x}_{i+1|i+1}\}$ as follows

$$P_{i+1|i+1} := \left(\hat{E}_{i+1}^T \left(\hat{\mathcal{Q}}_i + \hat{F}_i P_{i|i} \hat{F}_i^T\right)^{-1} \hat{E}_{i+1} + \hat{H}_{i+1}^T \hat{\mathcal{R}}_{i+1}^{-1} \hat{H}_{i+1}\right)^{-1}, \tag{29}$$

$$\hat{x}_{i+1|i+1} = P_{i+1|i+1}\left(\hat{E}_{i+1}^T\left(\hat{\mathcal{Q}}_i+\hat{F}_iP_{i|i}\hat{F}_i^T\right)^{-1}\hat{F}_i\hat{x}_{i|i}+\hat{H}_{i+1}^T\hat{\mathcal{R}}_{i+1}\begin{bmatrix} z_{i+1} \\ 0 \end{bmatrix}\right). \quad (30)$$

Remark II.5: $\begin{bmatrix} -F_i & E_{i+1} \\ 0 & H_{i+1} \end{bmatrix}$ full column rank is a sufficient condition for the existence of the robust filter.

Remark II.6: From (29) and (30), it is easy to verify that for descriptor systems without uncertainties ($M_{f,i}=0$, $M_{h,i+1}=0$, $N_{e,i+1}=0$, $N_{f,i}=0$, $N_{h,i+1}=0$), this algorithm collapses to the standard descriptor Kalman filter of Theorem 1.

The next theorem gives necessary and sufficient conditions for the convergence of the Riccati equation (29) and the stability of the filter (30) in steady-state. In the following, for the constant parameters over time, we drop the index *i*.

Theorem 3: Consider that all system parameters $\{Q, R, E, F, H, M_f, M_h, N_e, N_f, N_h\}$ are constant and that the parameter $\hat{\lambda}$ is a constant value which satisfies (27). If $rank\begin{bmatrix} \hat{E} \\ \hat{H} \end{bmatrix} = n$ and $P_{0|0} > 0$, then $rank\begin{bmatrix} z\hat{E}-\hat{F} \\ \hat{H} \end{bmatrix} = n(\forall z \in C, |z| \geq 1)$, is a necessary and sufficient condition for $\lim_{i\to\infty} P_{i|i} = P$ where $P_{i|i}$ is the solution of (29) and P is the unique solution of

$$P := \left(\hat{E}^T\left(\hat{\mathcal{Q}}+\hat{F}P\hat{F}^T\right)^{-1}\hat{E}+\hat{H}^T\hat{\mathcal{R}}^{-1}\hat{H}\right)^{-1}, \quad (31)$$

for which all roots of the state transition matrix $F_p = P\hat{E}^T\left(\hat{\mathcal{Q}}+\hat{F}P\hat{F}^T\right)^{-1}\hat{F}$ of the filter (30) are inside the unit circle.

□

The above theorem indicates that for practical implementations, one can use a fixed value for $\hat{\lambda}$. Therefore, if the system's parameters are almost constant, it is expected that even with a constant $\hat{\lambda}$, the filter follows well the input sequence. This is interesting since the computation of $\hat{\lambda}_i$ as indicated in Step 1 of Algorithm 1 can be very time consuming.

C. Robust predictor estimates

The successive robust predicted estimates $\hat{x}_{i+1|i}$ can be obtained recursively from Algorithm 2.

Algorithm 2: Robust Predictor Estimates

Step 0: (Existence and Initial Conditions): Check if E_{i+1} is full column rank, $N_{e,i+1}^T N_{f,i} = 0$ and $N_{e,i+1}^T N_{e,i+1}$ is invertible. Set $P_{0|-1} := P_0$ and $\hat{x}_{0|-1} := \bar{x}_0 = 0$.

Step 1: If $M_{f,i} = 0$ and $M_{h,i} = 0$, then set $\hat{\lambda}_i = 0$. Otherwise determine the optimum scalar parameter $\hat{\lambda}_i$ by minimizing over the interval

$$\hat{\lambda}_i > \lambda_{l,i} := \|diag\{M_{f,i}^T Q_i^{-1} M_{f,i}, M_{h,i}^T R_i^{-1} M_{h,i}\}\|; \quad (32)$$

the function $G(\lambda)$ of (22) corresponding to

$$A \leftarrow \begin{bmatrix} F_i & E_{i+1} \\ H_i & 0 \end{bmatrix}; b \leftarrow \begin{bmatrix} F_i\hat{x}_{i|i-1} \\ H_i\hat{x}_{i|i-1} - z_i \end{bmatrix}; \quad Q \leftarrow \begin{bmatrix} P_{i|i-1}^{-1} & 0 \\ 0 & 0 \end{bmatrix}; \tag{33}$$

$$W \leftarrow \begin{bmatrix} Q_i^{-1} & 0 \\ 0 & R_i^{-1} \end{bmatrix}; \quad H \leftarrow \begin{bmatrix} M_{f,i} & 0 \\ 0 & M_{h,i+1} \end{bmatrix}; N_b \leftarrow \begin{bmatrix} N_{f,i} \\ N_{h,i} \end{bmatrix} \hat{x}_{i|i-1}; N_a \leftarrow \begin{bmatrix} N_{f,i} & N_{e,i+1} \\ N_{h,i} & 0 \end{bmatrix}. \tag{34}$$

Step 2: If $\hat{\lambda}_i \neq 0$, replace the given parameters $\{Q_i, R_i, P_{i|i-1}, F_i\}$ by the corrected parameters

$$\hat{Q}_i := Q_i - \hat{\lambda}_i^{-1} M_{f,i} M_{f,i}^T; \quad \hat{R}_i := R_i - \hat{\lambda}_i^{-1} M_{h,i} M_{h,i}^T; \tag{35}$$

$$\hat{P}_{i|i-1} := (P_{i|i-1}^{-1} + \hat{\lambda}_i N_{f,i}^T N_{f,i})^{-1}; \quad \hat{F}_i := F_i(I - \hat{\lambda}_i(\hat{P}_{i|i-1}^{-1} + L_i^T J_i^{-1} L_i)^{-1} N_{f,i}^T N_{f,i}). \tag{36}$$

If $\hat{\lambda}_i = 0$, there is no correction: $\{\hat{Q}_i, \hat{R}_i, \hat{P}_{i|i-1}, \hat{F}_i\} := \{Q_i, R_i, P_{i|i-1}, F_i\}$
Step 3: Update $\{P_{i|i-1}, \hat{x}_{i|i-1}\}$ to $\{P_{i+1|i}, \hat{x}_{i+1|i}\}$ as follows

$$P_{i+1|i} := \left(\begin{bmatrix} E_{i+1}^T & 0 \end{bmatrix} \begin{bmatrix} \hat{Q}_i + F_i\hat{P}_{i|i-1}F_i^T & -F_i\hat{P}_{i|i-1}L_i^T \\ -L_i\hat{P}_{i|i-1}F_i^T & J_i + L_i\hat{P}_{i|i-1}L_i^T \end{bmatrix}^{-1} \begin{bmatrix} E_{i+1} \\ 0 \end{bmatrix} + \lambda_i N_{e,i+1}^T N_{e,i+1} \right)^{-1} \tag{37}$$

$$\hat{x}_{i+1|i} := P_{i+1|i} \begin{bmatrix} E_{i+1}^T & 0 \end{bmatrix} \begin{bmatrix} \hat{Q}_i + F_i\hat{P}_{i|i-1}F_i^T & -F_i\hat{P}_{i|i-1}L_i^T \\ -L_i\hat{P}_{i|i-1}F_i^T & J_i + L_i\hat{P}_{i|i-1}L_i^T \end{bmatrix}^{-1} \begin{bmatrix} \hat{F}_i\hat{x}_{i|i-1} \\ \begin{bmatrix} z_i \\ 0 \end{bmatrix} - L_i\hat{x}_{i|i-1} \end{bmatrix} \tag{38}$$

$$J_i := \begin{bmatrix} \hat{R}_i & 0 \\ 0 & I \end{bmatrix}; L_i := \begin{bmatrix} H_i \\ \lambda_i N_{h,i} \end{bmatrix}. \tag{39}$$

C.1 Robust descriptor estimator in time and measurement update form

For the examples of applications we are proposing in this chapter, it is important to compute the estimates in two steps, leading to the so-called time and measurement update form. In this section we rewrite the Algorithm 2 in this form. Furthermore, we incorporate the control input and a practical rule to adjust $\hat{\lambda}_i$ in the recursions presented in the Algorithm 3. The underling uncertain model considered in the Algorithm 3 is given by

$$(E_{i+1} + \delta E_{i+1})x_{i+1} = (F_i + \delta F_i)x_i + G_i u_i + w_i, \tag{40}$$

$$z_i = (H_i + \delta H_i)x_i + v_i, \tag{41}$$

where the perturbations δE_{i+1}, δF_i e δH_i are modeled as in (21).

Algorithm 3: Time and measurement update robust descriptor filter

Initial conditions: $\hat{x}_{0|-1} = 0$ and $P_{0|-1} = P_0$.

Step 1: If $M_{f,i} = 0$ and $M_{h,i} = 0$, then set $\hat{\lambda}_i = 0$. Otherwise, select $\alpha_f > 0$ and set

$$\hat{\lambda}_i = (1+\alpha_f)\|diag\{M_{f,i}^T Q_i^{-1} M_{f,i}, M_{h,i}^T R_i^{-1} M_{h,i}\}\|. \tag{42}$$

Step 2: Replace $\{Q_i, R_i, P_{i|i}, E_{i+1}, F_i, H_i\}$ by the corrected parameters:

$$\hat{\mathcal{Q}}_i = \begin{bmatrix} \hat{Q}_i & 0 \\ 0 & I \end{bmatrix}, \text{ where } \hat{Q}_i = Q_i - \hat{\lambda}_i^{-1} M_{f,i} M_{f,i}^T,$$

$$\hat{\mathcal{R}}_i = \begin{bmatrix} \hat{R}_i & 0 \\ 0 & I \end{bmatrix}, \text{ where } \hat{R}_i = R_i - \hat{\lambda}_i^{-1} M_{h,i} M_{h,i}^T,$$

$$\hat{\mathcal{E}}_{i+1} = \begin{bmatrix} E_{i+1} \\ \sqrt{\hat{\lambda}_i} N_{e,i+1} \end{bmatrix}, \quad \hat{\mathcal{F}}_i = \begin{bmatrix} F_i \\ \sqrt{\hat{\lambda}_i} N_{f,i} \end{bmatrix}, \quad \hat{\mathcal{H}}_i = \begin{bmatrix} H_i \\ \sqrt{\hat{\lambda}_i} N_{h,i} \end{bmatrix}.$$

Step 3: Update $\{\hat{x}_{i|i-1}, \ P_{i|i-1}\}$ to $\{\hat{x}_{i|i}, \hat{x}_{i+1|i}, P_{i+1|i}\}$ as follows:

$$\hat{x}_{i+1|i} = (\hat{\mathcal{E}}_{i+1}^T \hat{\mathcal{Q}}_i^{-1} \hat{\mathcal{E}}_{i+1})^{-1} \hat{\mathcal{E}}_{i+1}^T \hat{\mathcal{Q}}_i^{-1} \hat{\mathcal{F}}_i \hat{x}_{i|i} + G_i u_i \tag{43}$$

$$\begin{aligned} \hat{x}_{i|i} = \hat{x}_{i|i-1} + \begin{bmatrix} I & 0 \end{bmatrix} & \begin{bmatrix} P_{i|i-1}^{-1} + \hat{\mathcal{F}}_i^T \hat{\mathcal{Q}}_i^{-1} \hat{\mathcal{F}}_i + \hat{\mathcal{H}}_i^T \hat{\mathcal{R}}_i^{-1} \hat{\mathcal{H}}_i & -\hat{\mathcal{F}}_i^T \hat{\mathcal{Q}}_i^{-1} \hat{\mathcal{E}}_{i+1} \\ -\hat{\mathcal{E}}_{i+1}^T \hat{\mathcal{Q}}_i^{-1} \hat{\mathcal{F}}_i & \hat{\mathcal{E}}_{i+1}^T \hat{\mathcal{Q}}_i^{-1} \hat{\mathcal{E}}_{i+1} \end{bmatrix}^{-1} \\ \times & \begin{bmatrix} -\hat{\mathcal{F}}_i^T \hat{\mathcal{Q}}_i^{-1} \hat{\mathcal{F}}_i \hat{x}_{i|i-1} + \hat{\mathcal{H}}_i^T \hat{\mathcal{R}}_i^{-1} (\mathcal{Z}_i - \hat{\mathcal{H}}_i \hat{x}_{i|i-1}) \\ -\hat{\mathcal{E}}_{i+1}^T \hat{\mathcal{Q}}_i^{-1} \hat{\mathcal{F}}_i \hat{x}_{i|i-1} \end{bmatrix} \end{aligned} \tag{44}$$

$$P_{i+1|i} = \left(\begin{bmatrix} \hat{\mathcal{E}}_{i+1} \\ 0 \end{bmatrix}^T \begin{bmatrix} \hat{\mathcal{Q}}_i + \hat{\mathcal{F}}_i P_{i|i-1} \hat{\mathcal{F}}_i^T & -\hat{\mathcal{F}}_i P_{i|i-1} \hat{\mathcal{H}}_i^T \\ -\hat{\mathcal{H}}_i P_{i|i-1} \hat{\mathcal{F}}_i^T & \hat{\mathcal{R}}_i + \hat{\mathcal{H}}_i P_{i|i-1} \hat{\mathcal{H}}_i^T \end{bmatrix}^{-1} \begin{bmatrix} \hat{\mathcal{E}}_{i+1} \\ 0 \end{bmatrix} \right)^{-1} \tag{45}$$

where $\mathcal{Z}_i = \begin{bmatrix} z_i \\ 0 \end{bmatrix}$.

Remark II.7: The presented robust descriptor Kalman filters can estimate the state of a rectangular descriptor system (that is, when the matrix E in (3) is rectangular). The proposed filters collapse to the nominal descriptor Kalman filters when the system is not subject to uncertainties. When they are reduced to the standard state space systems, they provide robust Kalman-type recursions.

In the next section, we apply these robust filters in two practical robotic systems. It is possible to use many other estimation algorithms but this chapter is not meant to be exhaustive.

3. Application examples

A. Robust estimation of mobile robot localization

This section provides an example of application for the robust filters aforementioned to estimate mobile robots localization. Measurement systems based on odometric, inertial sensors and ultrasounds are self-contained, simple to use, and able to guarantee a high data rate. However, the problem of these systems is that they integrate the relative increments, and the localization errors considerably grow over time if an appropriate sensor fusion algorithm is not used. Extended Kalman filters (EKF) have been used to solve this kind of problem [3], [4], [8], [16], [26], [29]. They have been widely used mainly for position tracking [28], where the initial robot pose is known, and the problem is to compensate small incremental errors in the robot odometry. The localization approaches developed in [10], [11], [14], [13] are based on the kinematic model of the mobile robot, where the positions are performed through numerical integration of the encoders increments. Due to the several variables involved, the mobile robot localization is subject to several sources of uncertainties. They include deterministic and stochastic factors coming from robots actuators, inaccuracies of the sensors and odometry errors. This set of problems motivates the use of robust estimation methods in order to limit the performance degradation of optimal estimates. In [17] and [18], a robust localization method for mobile robot based on the combination of a Kalman filter with a perturbation estimator was presented with simulated and experimental results. We have observed that all approaches aforementioned were not based on robust filters where the parameters uncertainties are taken into account. The design procedure we present in this section aims to solve this problem.

A.1 Mobile robot and sensors model

The kinematic model of an unicyle mobile robot shown in Fig. 1 is described by:

$$\dot{x}(t) = \nu(t)cos\theta(t), \tag{46}$$

$$\dot{y}(t) = \nu(t)sin\theta(t), \tag{47}$$

$$\dot{\theta}(t) = \omega(t), \tag{48}$$

and the nonholonomic kinematic constraint is given by:

$$-sin\theta(t)\dot{x}(t) + cos\theta(t)\dot{y}(t) = 0, \tag{49}$$

where x and y are the coordinates between the two driving wheels, θ is the angle between the main axis of the robot and the x-direction, $\nu(t)$ and $\omega(t)$ are, respectively, the displacement and angular velocities of the robot. The discrete displacement and angular velocities $\overline{\nu}_i$ and $\overline{\omega}_i$ are given by odometric measures at time instant $t_i = iT$, where T is the sampling period.

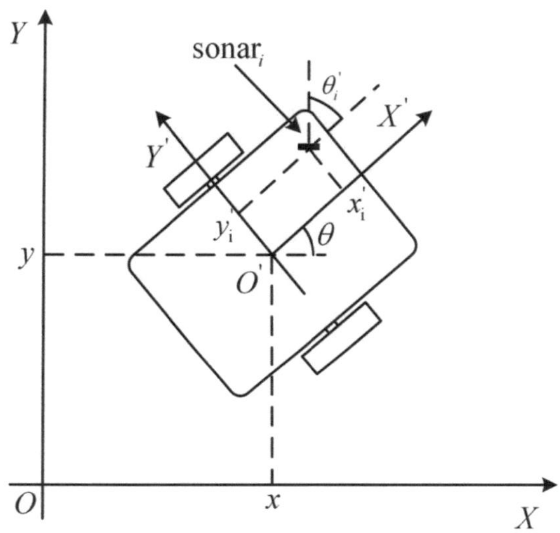

Fig. 1. Geometry of the wheeled mobile robot.

The distances of the sonars readings can be related to the model of the indoor environment and the configuration of the mobile robot as shown in [14] and [13]. Consider a planar distribution of n_s sonar sensors on the robot. Denote x'_m, y'_m, θ'_m the planar position and orientation of the m-th sonar, $m = 1, 2, \ldots, n_s$, referring to the coordinate system (O', X', Y'), as reported in Fig. 1. The position x_m, y_m and orientation θ_m of the m-th sonar referred to the inertial coordinate system (O, X, Y) at the time instant t_i, are given by:

$$x_{m,i} = x_i + x'_m cos\theta_i - y'_m sin\theta_i, \tag{50}$$

$$y_{m,i} = y_i + x'_m sin\theta_i + y'_m cos\theta_i, \tag{51}$$

$$\theta_{m,i} = \theta_i + \theta_m. \tag{52}$$

The walls and the obstacles in indoor environment are represented by a proper set of orthogonal planes to the plane XY of the inertial coordinate system. As shown in Fig. 2, δ is the beam-width of the sonar sensor and each plane P^j, $j = 1, 2, \ldots, n_p$ (n_p is the number of planes which describe the indoor environment). These planes are grouped in a vector Π, which is composed of geometric parameters P^j_r, the normal distance of the plane from the origin O; P^j_n, the angle between the normal line to the plane and the x-direction; and P^j_ν, a binary variable. $P^j_\nu \in \{-1, 1\}$ defines the face of the plane reflecting the sonar beam. Then, if

$P_n^j \in [\theta_m(t_i) - \delta/2, \theta_m(t_i) + \delta/2]$, the distance d_m^j from the m-th sonar to the plane P^j is given by the following equation:

$$d_{m,i}^j = P_\nu^j(P_r^j - x_{m,i}cosP_n^j - y_{m,i}sinP_n^j), \tag{53}$$

otherwise, the sonar measure is rejected.

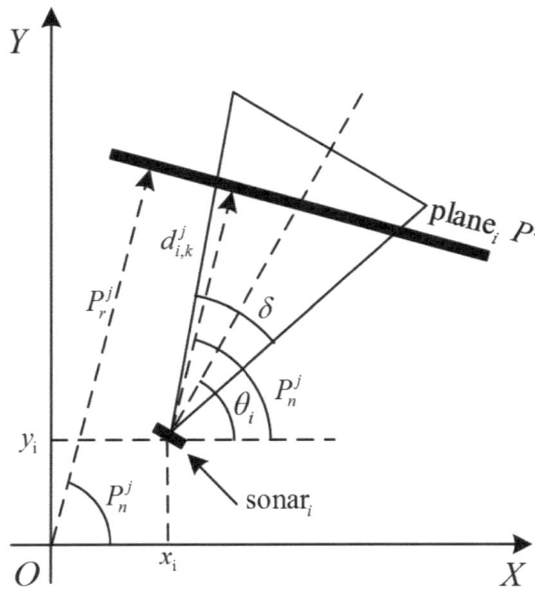

Fig. 2. Sonar measurement.

A.2 Descriptor system

The mobile robot in descriptor form is obtained by the discretization of the equations (46), (47), (48), and (49):

$$E_i\mathbf{x}_{i+1} = F_i\mathbf{x}_i + G_i\mathbf{u}_i + \mathbf{w}_i, \tag{54}$$

where $\mathbf{x}_i := [x_i \quad y_i \quad \theta_i]^T$ is the robot state, $\mathbf{u}(t) := [\nu_i \quad \omega_i]^T$, $\mathbf{w}_i \sim N(0, Q_i)$ is a zero mean white Gaussian noise,

$$E_i = \begin{bmatrix} \frac{1}{T} & 0 & 0 \\ 0 & \frac{1}{T} & 0 \\ 0 & 0 & \frac{1}{T} \\ -\frac{1}{T}sin\theta_i & \frac{1}{T}cos\theta_i & 0 \end{bmatrix}, \; F_i = \begin{bmatrix} \frac{1}{T} & 0 & 0 \\ 0 & \frac{1}{T} & 0 \\ 0 & 0 & \frac{1}{T} \\ -\frac{1}{T}sin\theta_i & \frac{1}{T}cos\theta_i & 0 \end{bmatrix}, \text{ and } G_i = \begin{bmatrix} cos\theta_i & 0 \\ sin\theta_i & 0 \\ 0 & 1 \\ 0 & 0 \end{bmatrix}. \tag{55}$$

The sampled nonlinear measurement equation, with sampling period T, is given by:

$$\mathbf{z}_i = \mathbf{s}(\mathbf{x}_i, \Pi) + \mathbf{v}_i \tag{56}$$

where $\mathbf{z}_i$ is the vector containing sonar and odometer measures and $\mathbf{v}_i \sim N(0,R_i)$ is a white sequence. The dimension p_i of $\mathbf{z}_i$ varies, it depends on the number of sonar sensors that are actually used at each time instant. The measurement vector $\mathbf{z}_i$ is composed of two subvectors

$$\mathbf{z}_{1,i} = \begin{bmatrix} z_{1,i} & z_{2,i} & z_{3,i} \end{bmatrix}^T \text{ and}$$

$$\mathbf{z}_{2,i} = \begin{bmatrix} z_{4,i} & z_{5,i} & \dots & z_{p_i,i} \end{bmatrix}^T,$$

where

$$z_{1,i} = x_i + v_{1,i}, \qquad z_{2,i} = y_i + v_{2,i}, \qquad z_{3,i} = \theta_i + v_{3,i} \tag{57}$$

are the measurements provided by the odometric device, and

$$z_{(3+m),i} = d^j_{m,i} + v_{(3+m),i} \tag{58}$$

is the distance measure provided by the m-th sonar sensor from the P_j plane with $j \in [1, n_p]$, and $d^j_{m,i}$, given by (53). The environment map provides the information needed to know which plane P_j is in front of the m-th sonar. By definition the measurement vector has the following form:

$$\mathbf{s}(\mathbf{x}_i, \Pi) = \begin{bmatrix} d^{j_1}_{1,i} \\ d^{j_2}_{2,i} \\ \vdots \\ d^{\overline{p}_i}_{\overline{p}_i,i} \end{bmatrix}, \; j_1, j_2, \dots, j_{\overline{p_i}} \in [1, n_p] \tag{59}$$

where $\overline{p}_i := p_i - 3$. The number of measures p_i may vary from 3 to n_s+3. In order to present Equation (56) in a form useful to implement the robust filter, it is rewritten as:

$$\mathbf{z}_i = H_i \mathbf{x}_i + \mathbf{v}_i \tag{60}$$

where

$$H_i := \begin{bmatrix} H_{1i} \\ H_{2i} \\ \vdots \\ H_{p_i i} \end{bmatrix}, \; [H^T_{1i} \;\; H^T_{2i} \;\; H^T_{3i}]^T = I_3,$$

$$\begin{aligned} H_{(m+3)i} &= P^j_\nu[-cosP^j_n \quad - sinP^j_n \quad x'_i cos(\theta_i - P^j_n) - y'_i sin(\theta_i - P^j_n)] \\ m &= 1, 2, \dots, \overline{p_i}, \; \leq n_s, \;\; j \in [1, n_p]. \end{aligned} \tag{61}$$

Here a sonar readings selection algorithm is used to reduce the probability of an inadequate interpretation of erroneous sensor data (see [11] for more details): at each step, for each sonar measure z_{3+m}, the residual $\gamma_{m,i} = z_{(3+m),i} - \hat{d}^j_m$ represents the difference between the actual sonar measure $z_{(3+m),i}$ and its expected value $\hat{d}^j_m$, $m = 1, 2, \cdots, p_i - 3$, $j = 1, 2, \cdots, n_p$, which is computed by (53) on the basis of the current estimate of $\mathbf{x}_i$ and on a *priori* knowledge of the environment. As $\gamma_{m,i} \sim N(0, s_{m,i})$, the current read of $z_{(3+m),i}$ is only accepted if $|\gamma_{m,i}| \leq 2\sqrt{s_{m,i}}$. For this chapter $s_{m,i} = 0.15$.

A.3 Simulation

The simulation was performed in MATLAB ® with nominal parameters of a Pioneer 2 DX mobile robot. The Pioneer has sixteen sonars range finders: 8 on the front and 8 on the back. The locations and directions of the sonar range finders on the Pioneer are listed in Table I and shown in Figure 3.

m	x'_m (m)	y'_m (m)	θ'_m (degrees)
1	0.115	0.130	90
2	0.155	0.115	50
3	0.190	0.080	30
4	0.210	0.025	10
5	0.210	-0.025	- 10
6	0.190	-0.080	- 30
7	0.155	-0.115	- 50
8	0.115	-0.130	- 90
9	-0.115	-0.130	- 90
10	-0.155	-0.115	-130
11	-0.190	-0.080	-150
12	-0.210	-0.025	-170
13	-0.210	0.025	170
14	-0.190	0.080	150
15	-0.155	0.115	130
16	-0.115	0.130	90

Table 1. Mounting positions and directions of the sonar range finders on the Pioneer 2DX.

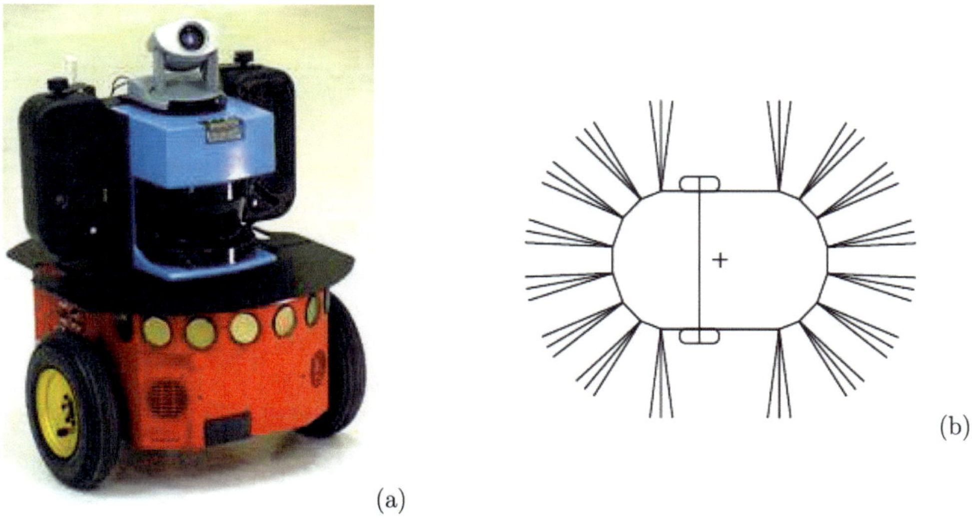

Fig. 3. Pioneer 2 DX: (a) Picture and (b) Locations and directions of the sonars.

A.4 Noise models

There are several kinds of noise typically observed when robots operate in real-world environments. On one hand there is a typical Gaussian noise in the odometry and proximity sensors coming from the inherent inaccuracy of the sensors. On the other hand there are non-Gaussian errors arising from collision with obstacles, or from interference with the sensors. In this chapter, the odometry errors coming from wheel slippage, uneven floors, or different payloads are characterized according to three parameters of the odometry model [27] displayed in Fig. 4.

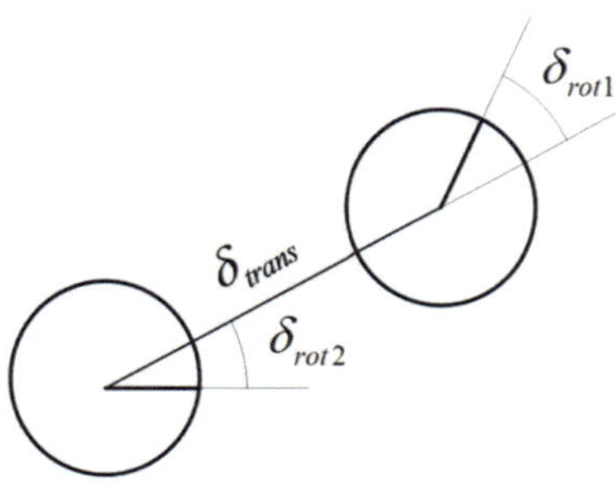

Fig. 4. Odometry Model

The robot motion in the time interval $(t - 1, t]$ is approximated by a rotation δ_{rot1}, followed by a translation δ_{trans} and a second rotation δ_{rot2}. Each element is corrupted by independent noise:

$$\begin{pmatrix} \hat{\delta}_{rot1} \\ \hat{\delta}_{trans} \\ \hat{\delta}_{rot2} \end{pmatrix} = \begin{pmatrix} \delta_{rot1} \\ \delta_{trans} \\ \delta_{rot2} \end{pmatrix} + \begin{pmatrix} \epsilon_{rot1} \\ \epsilon_{trans} \\ \epsilon_{rot2} \end{pmatrix} \tag{62}$$

where

$$\epsilon_{rot1} = (\alpha_1 \delta_{rot1} + \alpha_2 \delta_{trans}), \tag{63}$$

$$\epsilon_{trans} = (\alpha_3 \delta_{trans} + \alpha_4 (\delta_{rot1} + \delta_{rot2})), \tag{64}$$

$$\epsilon_{rot2} = (\alpha_1 \delta_{rot2} + \alpha_2 \delta_{trans}). \tag{65}$$

The α_t, $t = 1 \ldots 4$, parameters are the influences of translation and rotation on themselves and on each other. The parameters α_t used in simulation were $\alpha_1 = 0.6$, $\alpha_2 = 0.2$, $\alpha_3 = 0.7$ and $\alpha_4 = 0.0$. Finally, the inaccuracies of the sonars were simulated as:

$$z_{(3+m),i} = d^j_m + \beta p_{random}, \tag{66}$$

where $z_{(3+m),i}$ is the actual sonar measure, d^j_m is computed by (53), β is the inaccuracy of the sonar and p_{random} is pseudo-random value drawn from a normal distribution with mean zero and standard deviation one. The beam width and the imprecision of the sonar considered in this simulation were$\delta = 30°$ and $\beta = 0.03$ m, respectively.

A.5 Descriptor filter

The descriptor robust filter presented in the Algorithm 3 was set with

$$Q_i = \sigma^2 I_4, \text{ com } \sigma = 1000,$$

$$R_i = \begin{bmatrix} 0.0035 & 0 & 0 & 0 & \cdots & 0 \\ 0 & 0.0035 & 0 & 0 & \cdots & 0 \\ 0 & 0 & 0.0126 & 0 & \cdots & 0 \\ 0 & 0 & 0 & 0.03 & \cdots & 0 \\ \vdots & \vdots & \vdots & \vdots & \ddots & 0 \\ 0 & 0 & 0 & 0 & 0 & 0.03 \end{bmatrix},$$

$$M_{f,i} = I_4, \quad M_{h,i} = I_{p_i}, \tag{67}$$

$$N_{e,i} = N_{f,i} = \begin{bmatrix} 0 & 0 & 0 \\ 0 & 0 & 0 \\ 0 & 0 & 0 \\ 0.3077 & 0.3869 & 0 \end{bmatrix} \text{ and } N_{h,i} = \begin{bmatrix} 0 & 0 & 0 \\ 0 & 0 & 0 \\ 0 & 0 & 0 \\ 0_{(\overline{p_i},1)} & 0_{(\overline{p_i},1)} & H(4:p_i,3)_i \end{bmatrix} \tag{68}$$

and $\alpha_f = 10$. The results obtained are shown in figures 5, 6 and 7.

A.6 Comparative study

The simulation of the Pioneer 2 DX localization (equipped with sonar sensors and odometry) was performed using three different methods: only odometry measures integration; sonar and odometry measures fusion through nominal descriptor filter; and sonar and odometry measures fusion using descriptor robust filter. The following $\mathcal{L}_2$ norm of the state vector is used to compare the performance of these procedures:

$$\mathcal{L}_2[\tilde{\mathbf{x}}] = \left(\frac{1}{(t_r - t_0)} \int_{t_0}^{t_r} \|\tilde{\mathbf{x}}(t)\|_2^2 \, dt \right)^2, \tag{69}$$

where $\|\cdot\|_2$ is the Euclidean norm, $\tilde{\mathbf{x}}(t)$ is the state vector error and $t_0 = 0$, $t_r = 30(s)$ is the experimental time interval. As expected, both filters presented better results on tracking the robot's pose than using only odometry integration. However, the Robust filter obtained an average improvement of 16.7% over the EKF in the position error. These results can be seen in Table II. In future works, we intend to perform experiments with an actual Pioneer 2 DX mobile robot.

Algorithms	$\mathcal{L}_2[\tilde{\mathbf{x}}]$
Odometry	0.4618
Nominal Descriptor Filter	0.1315
Robust Descriptor Filter	0.1095

Table 2. Performance Index

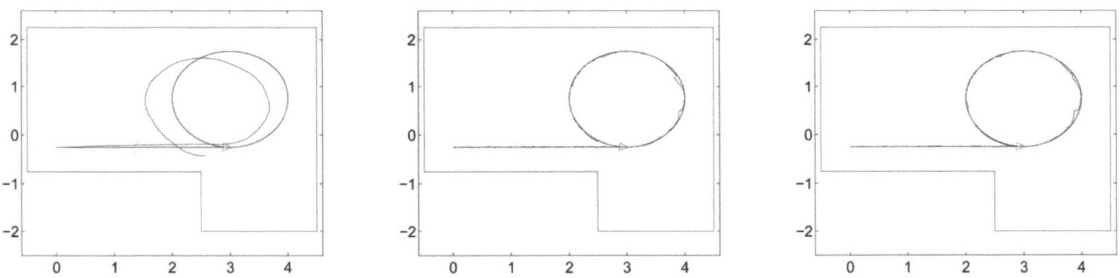

(a) (b) (c)

Fig. 5. Robot poses estimation: (a) Only using odometry measures, (b) Nominal filter and (c)Descriptor filter.

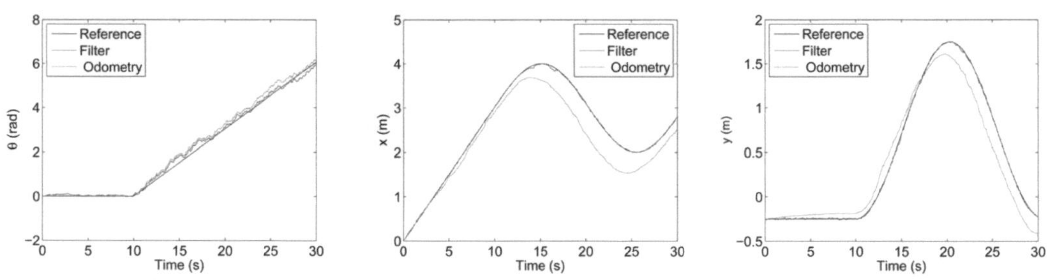

(a) (b) (c)

Fig. 6. Robot poses estimation using nominal filter: (a) θ, (b) x and (c) y.

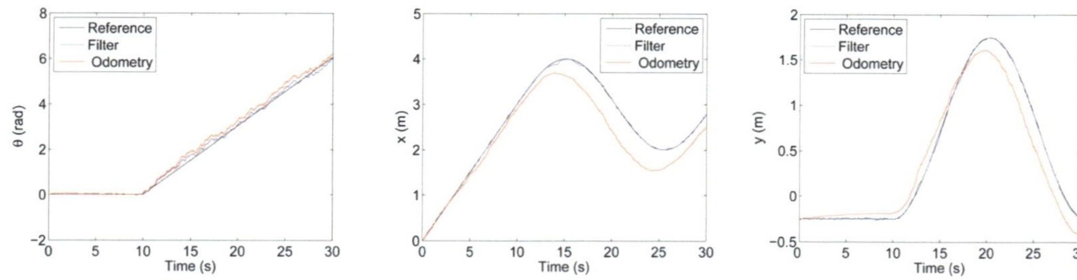

(a) (b) (c)

Fig. 7. Robot poses estimation using the descriptor filter: (a) θ, (b) x and (c) y.

B. Estimation of robotic prosthesis configuration with respect to ground

In this section it is presented a new application of stochastic filtering in the field of rehabilitation robotics. It is part of a research project which consists in the development of a robotic prosthesis for above knee amputees. Fig. 8(a) shows a picture of this device, which has three degrees of actuation: one for the knee and two for the ankle. Each joint is controlled by a direct current motor and a switched current source actuator. Concerning the foot, it is equipped with two Analog Devices ADXRS300 gyroscopes, and four Sharp GP2D120 distance measuring infrared sensors mounted underneath the foot (*c.f.*, Fig. 8(b)) [1].

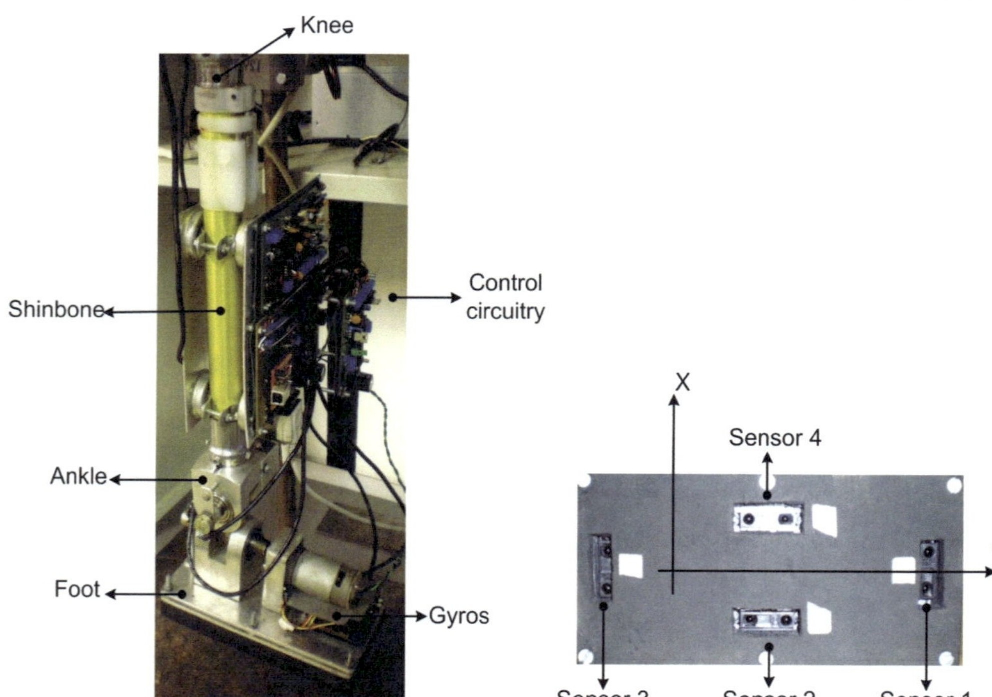

Fig. 8. (a) picture of the prosthesis and (b) infrared sensors placement underneath the foot

The aim of this application is to provide real-time estimates of the prosthesis foot configuration with respect to ground. A solution to this problem would allow the use of the prosthesis for natural terrain walking, where foot positioning with respect to ground should be controlled. Robust descriptor filter allows to deal with uncertainties in model structure as well as to cope with constraints in estimated variables. Experimental results show the main properties of the system as well as the need of formulating this problem in a descriptor model framework.

B.1 Prosthesis configuration variables and sensing

In order to describe the configuration of the foot with respect to ground, denote $X \times Y \times Z$ the reference cartesian system as depicted in Fig. 9. $X \times Y$ is the foot plan, and Ξ represents the ground plan. Prosthesis foot configuration with respect to ground is described by $n = \begin{bmatrix} n_x & n_y & n_z \end{bmatrix}^T$, the unit length vector coordinates of the normal to Ξ described in the $X \times Y \times Z$ the reference system, and d is the distance in Z axis of the ground plan to the origin of $X \times Y \times Z$.

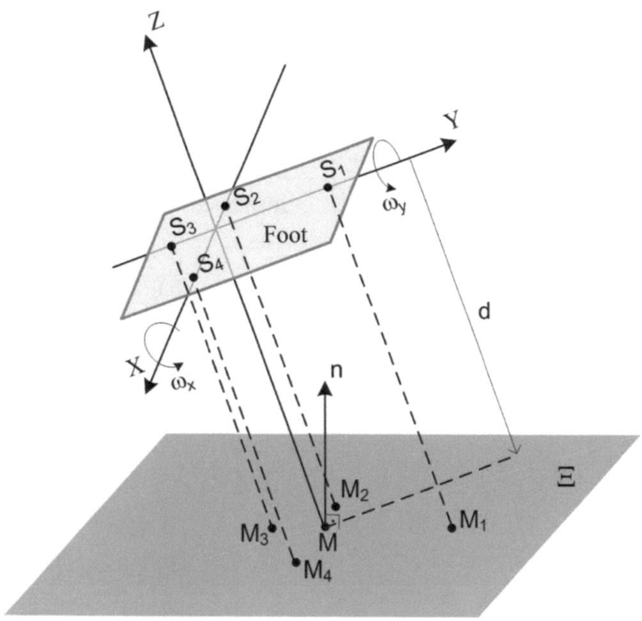

Fig. 9. Foot configuration with respect to ground and sensor measurements

S_1, S_2, S_3 and S_4 are the positioning in foot plan of the infrared sensors. It is considered such sensors make measurements perpendicular to $X \times Y$ plan in the direction of Ξ. Such measurements are taken in points M_1, M_2, M_3 and M_4, and denoted d_j, $j = 1, \ldots, 4$, all of them with the same variance σ_d^2, meaning that infrared sensors have the same uncertainty. The coordinates m_j of $M_j \in \Xi$ are given by

$$m_j = s_j + \begin{bmatrix} 0 \\ 0 \\ -d_j \end{bmatrix} = \begin{bmatrix} s_{j,x} \\ s_{j,y} \\ -d_j \end{bmatrix}. \tag{70}$$

where $s_j = \begin{bmatrix} s_{j,x} & s_{j,y} & 0 \end{bmatrix}^T$ are the coordinates of S_j corresponding to the placement of the *j*-th infrared sensor. Since $M \in \Xi$, with coordinates $m = \begin{bmatrix} 0 & 0 & -d \end{bmatrix}^T$, one has

$$n^T(m_j - m) = 0$$

for each infrared sensor measurement, resulting in

$$d_j = \frac{dn_z + s_{j,y}n_y + s_{j,x}n_x}{n_z} \tag{71}$$

as equation relating the *j*th sensor distance measurement d_j to foot configuration variables n and d.

The two gyroscopes provide angular motion measurements of the foot in X and Y axis. Such measurements are angular velocities ω_x and ω_y as shown in Fig. 9, and take effect in n according to

$$\dot{n} = \frac{\partial n}{\partial \phi_x}\omega_x + \frac{\partial n}{\partial \phi_y}\omega_y$$

where $\omega_x = \frac{d\phi_x}{dt}$ and $\omega_y = \frac{d\phi_y}{dt}$ with ϕ_x and ϕ_y being small rotation angles in axis X and Y, respectively. The partial derivatives are computed as

$$\begin{aligned} \frac{\partial n}{\partial \phi_x} &= \lim_{\Delta\phi_x \longrightarrow 0} \frac{\Delta n}{\Delta \phi_x} = \lim_{\Delta\phi_x \longrightarrow 0} \frac{R_X(\Delta\phi_x)n - n}{\Delta\phi_x} \\ \frac{\partial n}{\partial \phi_y} &= \lim_{\Delta\phi_y \longrightarrow 0} \frac{\Delta n}{\Delta \phi_y} = \lim_{\Delta\phi_y \longrightarrow 0} \frac{R_Y(\Delta\phi_y)n - n}{\Delta\phi_y} \end{aligned}$$

with

$$R_X(\theta) = \begin{bmatrix} 1 & 0 & 0 \\ 0 & \cos(\theta) & \sin(\theta) \\ 0 & -\sin(\theta) & \cos(\theta) \end{bmatrix}, \quad R_Y(\theta) = \begin{bmatrix} \cos(\theta) & 0 & -\sin(\theta) \\ 0 & 1 & 0 \\ \sin(\theta) & 0 & \cos(\theta) \end{bmatrix}$$

being the basic rotations of angle θ about X and Y axis, respectively. Further development results in

$$\dot{n} = \begin{bmatrix} -n_z\omega_y \\ n_z\omega_x \\ -n_y\omega_x + n_x\omega_y \end{bmatrix}. \tag{72}$$

It should be pointed out that the angular velocity about Z axis is considered small when compared to ω_x and ω_y. This is usually the case for general movement of foot.

B.2 System modeling as descriptor model

Let $x_i = \begin{bmatrix} n_i^T & d_i \end{bmatrix}^T = \begin{bmatrix} n_{x,i} & n_{y,i} & n_{z,i} & d_i \end{bmatrix}^T$ the system state variable corresponding to foot configuration at discrete time i. The following model describes the evolution of state variables between measurements:

$$x_{i+1} = \begin{pmatrix} n_{x,i} - Tn_{z,i}\omega_{y,i} \\ n_{y,i} + Tn_{z,i}\omega_{x,i} \\ n_{z,i} - Tn_{y,i}\omega_{x,i} + Tn_{x,i}\omega_{y,i} \\ d_i \end{pmatrix} + w_i \tag{73}$$

In above, concerning evolution of the normal vector n_i, it has been used (72) in a first order Euler approximation with sampling period T. w_i is a Gaussian random noise encompassing gyroscope uncertainty as well as neglecting rotation about Z axis. Further, it has been considered a random evolution for d_i with Gaussian distribution, represented by the last entry of w_i. Rewriting (73) as

$$x_{i+1} = \begin{bmatrix} 1 & 0 & -T\omega_{y,i} & 0 \\ 0 & 1 & T\omega_{x,i} & 0 \\ T\omega_{y,i} & -T\omega_{x,i} & 1 & 0 \\ 0 & 0 & 0 & 1 \end{bmatrix} x_i + w_i \tag{74}$$

$$x_{i+1} = F\left(\omega_{x,i}; \omega_{y,i}\right) x_i + w_i \tag{75}$$

the evolution of the state variables becomes linear given the pair $(\omega_{x,i}; \omega_{y,i})$. It should be pointed out that (75) does not guarantee n_{i+1} with unit length. Thus, the following constraint should be considered:

$$n_{x,i+1}^2 + n_{y,i+1}^2 + n_{z,i+1}^2 = 1. \tag{76}$$

According to (71), a set $z_i = \begin{bmatrix} d_{1,i} & d_{2,i} & d_{3,i} & d_{4,i} \end{bmatrix}^T$ of measurements from infrared sensors are related to system state as

$$z_i = \begin{pmatrix} \frac{d_i n_{z,i} + s_{1,y} n_{y,i} + s_{1,x} n_{x,i}}{n_{z,i}} \\ \frac{d_i n_{z,i} + s_{2,y} n_{y,i} + s_{2,x} n_{x,i}}{n_{z,i}} \\ \frac{d_i n_{z,i} + s_{3,y} n_{y,i} + s_{3,x} n_{x,i}}{n_{z,i}} \\ \frac{d_i n_{z,i} + s_{4,y} n_{y,i} + s_{4,x} n_{x,i}}{n_{z,i}} \end{pmatrix} + v_i \tag{77}$$

$$z_i = h\left(x_i\right) + v_i \tag{78}$$

with $v_i \sim N(0, \sigma_d^2 I_4)$ being the measurement noise. The above equation corresponds to a non-linear measurement model which, when linearized at some given $\bar{x}_{i-1}$ results in

$$z_i' = z_i - h\left(\bar{x}_{i-1}\right) + H\left(\bar{x}_{i-1}\right)\bar{x}_{i-1} \tag{79}$$

$$= H\left(\bar{x}_{i-1}\right)x_i + v_i \tag{80}$$

with

$$H\left(x_i\right) = \begin{bmatrix} \frac{s_{1,x}}{n_{z,i}} & \frac{s_{1,y}}{n_{z,i}} & \frac{s_{1,x}n_{x,i}+s_{1,y}n_{y,i}}{n_{z,i}^2} & 1 \\ \frac{s_{2,x}}{n_{z,i}} & \frac{s_{2,y}}{n_{z,i}} & \frac{s_{2,x}n_{x,i}+s_{2,y}n_{y,i}}{n_{z,i}^2} & 1 \\ \frac{s_{3,x}}{n_{z,i}} & \frac{s_{3,y}}{n_{z,i}} & \frac{s_{3,x}n_{x,i}+s_{3,y}n_{y,i}}{n_{z,i}^2} & 1 \\ \frac{s_{4,x}}{n_{z,i}} & \frac{s_{4,y}}{n_{z,i}} & \frac{s_{4,x}n_{x,i}+s_{4,y}n_{y,i}}{n_{z,i}^2} & 1 \end{bmatrix}. \tag{81}$$

Equations (75), (76), and (80) correspond to a descriptor model when defining a new state variable:

$$x_i' = \begin{bmatrix} x_i^T & u_i \end{bmatrix}^T \tag{82}$$

with $u_i = u_{i-1}$, and $u_0 = 1$ the norm of vector n at all instants i, thus:

$$E_{i+1}x_{i+1}' = F_i x_i' + w_i' \tag{83}$$

$$z_{i+1}' = H_i x_i' + v_i \tag{84}$$

$$E_{i+1} = \begin{bmatrix} I_4 & 0_{4\times 1} \\ D_{i+1} & 0 \\ 0_{1\times 4} & 1 \end{bmatrix}, \qquad D_{i+1} = \begin{bmatrix} \bar{n}_{x,i-1} & \bar{n}_{y,i-1} & \bar{n}_{z,i-1} & 0 \end{bmatrix} \tag{85}$$

$$F_i = \begin{bmatrix} F\left(\omega_{x,i}, \omega_{y,i}\right) & 0_{4\times 1} \\ 0 & 1 \\ 0 & 1 \end{bmatrix}, \qquad w_i' = \begin{bmatrix} w_i \\ 0 \end{bmatrix} \tag{86}$$

$$H_i = \begin{bmatrix} H\left(\bar{x}_{i-1}\right) & 0_{4\times 1} \end{bmatrix} \tag{87}$$

Remark III.1: In this example, we have chosen $\bar{x}_{i-1} = \hat{x}_{i-1|i-1}$, that is, we linearized at the last estimate. Since we have the expression (81), there is no need to perform differentiations in the filter algorithm iterations. We further incorporate the effects of the neglected nonlinearities in the uncertainties δE_{i+1}, δF_i and δH_i.

B.3 Experimental results

In this section, it is presented an experimental evaluation of the proposed foot configuration estimator. The prosthesis shinbone was set in a perpendicular position with respect to floor and several movement signals were sent to the motors responsible for rotation in X and Y axis. Gyroscope and infrared measurements were gathered in real-time during 35 s at 10 ms sampling period. Further, a potentiometer installed at foot provided direct angular measurements in X axis, which can be used to evaluate the performance in estimating the n_x normal vector component. This sensor can be used to partially validate the results of the proposed filter by giving a ground truth reference for n_x. However, it cannot be used in replacement of the proposed system because its measurement is taken with respect to the prosthesis shinbone, which only in this experiment is has approximately known configuration with respect to ground. This is not the case with the prostheses installed in a human patient.

The robust descriptor filter of Algorithm 1 presented in Subsection II-B is used to estimate x_i. Equations (83) and (84) are rewritten as an uncertain system based on the following:

- $\hat{n}_{i-1}$ does not represent exactly n_{i+1}, thus the descriptor matrix E_{i+1} is replaced by $\left(\bar{E}_{i+1} + \delta E_{i+1}\right)$, in order to consider a range of possible n_{i+1} that must satisfy the unit norm constraint (76);
- Gyroscope measurements may have scale factor errors, bias, and also suffer from analog-to-digital conversion noise. Thus, the process matrix F_i is replaced by $\left(\bar{F}_i + \delta F_i\right)$ in order to consider the range of possible $F\left(\omega_{x,i}, \omega_{y,i}\right)$;
- Measurement matrix H_i is the linearized form of Eq. (77) at $\bar{x}_{i-1} = \hat{x}_{i-1|i-1}$, and thus H_i is replaced by $\left(\bar{H}_i + \delta H_i\right)$ in order to incorporate linearization errors.

By using

$$M_{d,i} = \begin{bmatrix} 10^{-6} & 10^{-6} & 10^{-8} & 0 \end{bmatrix}, \quad M_{a,i} = 10^{-2} \begin{bmatrix} 0 & 0 & -T\omega_{y,i} & 0 \\ 0 & 0 & T\omega_{x,i} & 0 \\ T\omega_{y,i} & -T\omega_{x,i} & 0 & 0 \\ 0 & 0 & 0 & 0 \end{bmatrix} \tag{88}$$

$$M_{f,i} = \begin{bmatrix} M_{a,i} & 0_{4\times1} & 0_4 & 0_4 \\ 0_{1\times4} & 0 & M_{d,i} & 0_{1\times4} \\ 0_{1\times4} & 0 & 0_{1\times4} & 0_{1\times4} \end{bmatrix}, \quad M_{h,i} = 10^{-2} \begin{bmatrix} 1_{4\times3} & 0_{4\times2} \end{bmatrix} \tag{89}$$

$$N_{e,i} = \begin{bmatrix} 0_4 & 0_{4\times1} \\ 0_{1\times4} & 1 \\ I_4 & 0_{4\times1} \\ 0_4 & 0 \end{bmatrix}, \quad N_{f,i} = \begin{bmatrix} I_4 & 0 \\ 0_{1\times4} & 0 \\ 0_4 & 0_{4\times1} \\ 0_4 & 0 \end{bmatrix}, \quad N_{h,i} = I_5 \tag{90}$$

$$\lambda = 25 \tag{91}$$

in (29) and (30), the estimated configuration variables are presented in Fig. 10. In the first plot of Fig. 10(a), it is shown the estimated n_x and the corresponding measured projection based on potentiometer readings. It can be seen in Fig. 10(a) that the estimated n_x component is very close to that measured by the potentiometer throughout the whole experiment. A small difference at 25 s and at 30 s is possibly caused by an instantaneous error in gyroscope that could not be completely corrected by the estimator. However, as a robust estimator, that error presented limited influence in the estimate. The obtained robust filter has limited bandwidth according to the parameters used in its design. Otherwise, the estimate could be very sensitive to fast changes in infrared sensor measurements. Thus,

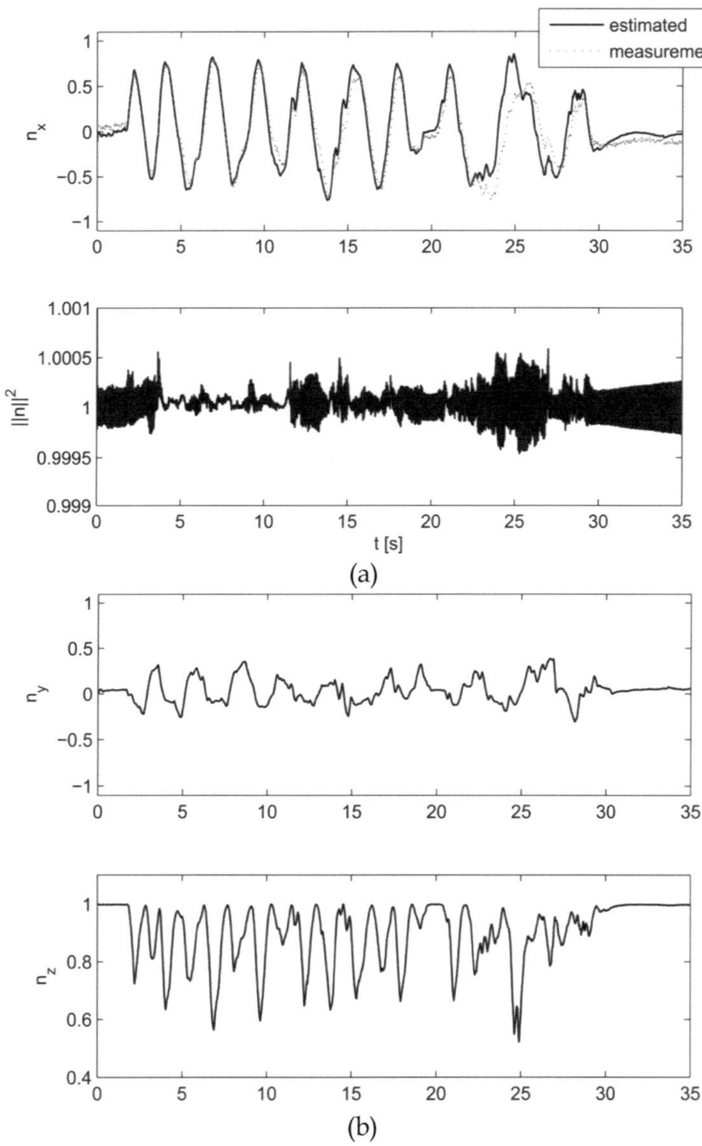

Fig. 10. (a) Vector n component n_x estimated (solid black), measured (dotted red), and unitary norm $||n||^2 = n_x^2 + n_y^2 + n_z^2$. (b) Vector n components n_y, n_z estimated

there is a trade off between satisfactory bandwidth and sensitivity to fast changes in infrared sensor measurements due to moving in irregular terrain.

The second plot in Fig. 10(a) presents the norm of vector n. It can be seen that the estimated n has norm very close to unity through the experiment.

Fig. 10(b) presents results on components n_y, and n_z. For these estimates there is no ground truth measurements for comparison. The proposed system is currently used to provide foot configuration estimates to a controller responsible for keeping the foot parallel to ground.

4. Conclusion

Many classes of systems, such as systems with fast and low dynamics and systems with equality constraints on the state or inputs can be treated at once in the framework of descriptor systems. In this chapter we presented an extension of the well known Kalman filter to general rectangular descriptor systems subject to uncertainties. We presented the robust *a priori, a posteriori* estimates recursions and one version of predictor-corrector recursions. Applications of the filters are illustrated in the robotics field by two practical problems: the robust estimation of the localization of a mobile robot and the robust estimation of the configuration with respect to ground of a robotic prosthesis. The position estimation of a mobile robot is naturally formulated as an estimation problem of a system with algebraic constraints and subject to parametric uncertainties. In the proposed sensing system for the robotic prosthesis, the physical meaning of the signals imposes constraints in the estimates. For both examples, the constraints as well as the model structure uncertainties were fully addressed by the presented robust descriptor Kalman filter.

5. References

[1] D. A. Brasil. Controle de orientação do pé de uma prótese robótica para amputados acima do joelho. B. Sc. Thesis Report, Electrical Engineering Department, University of Brasilia, 2008.

[2] S. L. Campbell. Singular Systems of Differential Equations II. Pitman, 1982.

[3] L. Charbonnier and A. Fournier. Heading guidance and obstacles localization for indoor mobile robot. In *International Conference on Advanced Robotics*, Barcelons, Spain, 1995.

[4] A. Curran and K. J. Kyriakopoulos. Sensor-based self-localization for wheeled mobile robots. In *IEEE Mediterranean Symposium New Directions in Control and Automation*, Chania, Creta, 1993.

[5] L. Dai. Singular Control Systems. Lectures Notes in Control and Information Sciences Series, volume 118. Springer-Verlag, 1989.

[6] M. Darouach, M. Zasadzinski, and D. Mehdi. State estimation of stochastic singular linear systems. *Int. J. Syst. Sci.*, 24(2):345–354, 1993.

[7] B. Dellon and Y. Matsuoka. Prosthetics, exoskeletons, and rehabilitation. *IEEE Robotics & Automation Magazine*, 14(1):30–34, 2007.

[8] G. Garcia, P. Bonnifait, and F.-F. le Corre. A multisensor fusion localization algorithm with self-calibration of error-corrupted mobile robot parameters. In *International Conference on Advanced Robotics*, Barcelons, Spain, 1995.

[9] M. A. Hasan and M. R. Azim-Sadjani. Noncausal image modeling using descriptor approach. *IEEE Trans. Circuits Syst. II*, 42(8):536–540, 1995.

[10] G. Ippoliti, L. Jetto, and S. Longhi. Localization of mobile robots: development and comparative evaluation of algorithms based on odometric and inertial sensors. *Journal of Robotic Systems*, pages 725–735, 2005.

[11] G. Ippoliti, L. Jetto, A. La Manna, and S. Longhi. Improving the robustness properties of robot localization procedures with respect do enviroment features uncertainties. In *IEEE International Conference on Robotics and Automation*, Barcelona, Spain, 2005.

[12] J. Y. Ishihara, M. H. Terra, and J. C. T. Campos. Optimal recursive estimation for discrete-time descriptor systems. *International Journal of Systems Science*, 36(10):605–615, 2005.

[13] L. Jetto, S. Longhi, and G. Venturini. Development and experimental validation of an adaptive extend kalman filter. *IEEE Transaction on Robotics and Automation*, 15(2):219–229, April 1999.

[14] L. Jetto, S. Longhi, and D. Vitali. Localization of a wheeled mobile robot by sensor data fusion based on a fuzzy logic adapted kalman filter. *Control Engineering Practice*, 7:763–771, 1999.

[15] D. Jin, R. Zhang, J. Zhang, R. Wang, and W.A. Gruver. An intelligent above-knee prosthesis with emg-based terrain identification. In *IEEE International Conference on Systems, Man, and Cybernetics*, pages 1859–1864, 2000.

[16] D. J. Kriegman, E. Triendl, and T. O. Binford. Stereo vision and navigation in buildings for mobile robots. *IEEE Transactions on Robotics and Automation*, 5(6):792–803, December 1989.

[17] S. J. Kwon, K. W. Yang, and S. Park. An effective kalman filter localization method for mobile robots. In *Proceedings of the2006 IEEE/RSJ International Conference on Intelligent Robots and Systems*, Beijing, China, 2006.

[18] S. J. Kwon, K. W. Yang, S. Park, and Y. Ryuh. Robust mobile robot localization with combined kalman filter-perturbation estimator. In *IEEE/RSJ International Conference on Intelligent Robots and Systems*, Alberta,Canada, 2005.

[19] F. L. Lewis. A survey of singular linear systems. *Circuits, Systems and Signal Processing*, (5):3–36, 1986.

[20] F. L. Lewis. A tutorial on the geometric analysis of linear time-invariant implicit systems. *Automatica*, 28(1):119–137, 1992.

[21] D. V. Luenberger. Dynamic equations in descriptor form. *IEEE Trans. Automat. Contr.*, 22(3):312–321, 1977.

[22] J. K. Mills and A. A. Goldenberg. Force and position control of manipulators during constrained motion tasks. *IEEE Trans.* Robot. Automat., 68:30–46, 1989.

[23] R. Nikoukhah, S. L. Campbell, and F. Delebecque. Kalman filtering for general discrete-time linear systems. *IEEE Trans. Automat. Contr.*, 44(10):1829–1839, 1999.

[24] R. Nikoukhah, A. L. Willsky, and B. C. Levy. Kalman filtering and Riccati equations for decriptor systems. *IEEE Trans. Automat. Contr.*, 37(9):1325–1342, 1992.

[25] A. H. Sayed. A framework for state-space estimation with uncertain models. *IEEE Trans. Automat. Contr.*, 46(7):998–1013, 2001.

[26] R. Smith, M. Self, and P. Cheeseman. Estimating uncertain spatial relationships in robotics. In I. J. Cox and G. T. Wilfong, editors, *Autonomous Robot Vehicles*, pages 167– 193. Springer-Verlag, 1990.

[27] S. Thrun, W. Burgard, and D. Fox. *Probabilistic Robotics*. The MIT Press, 2005.

[28] S. Thrun, D. Fox, W. Burgard, and F. Dellaert. Robust monte carlo localization dor mobile robots. *Artificial Intelligence*, 2001.

[29] J. Vaganay, M. J. Aldon, and A. Fournier. Mobile robot attitude estimation by fusion of inertial data. In *IEEE International Conference on Robotics and Automation*, Atlanta, GA, 1993.

[30] S. Xu and J. Lam. Robust Control and Filtering of Singular Systems. Springer, 2006.

[31] M. E. Zaghloul and W. N. Newcomb. Semistate implementation: Differentiator example. *Circ. Syst. Sig. Proces.*, 5(1):171–183, 1986.

23

Joint MIMO Channel Tracking and Symbol Decoding

B. Balakumar and T. Kirubarajan
McMaster University
Canada

1. Introduction

The objective of fourth generation (4G) wireless communication systems is to achieve broadband connectivity anytime, anywhere and between anything. It is anticipated that in the next two decades, this is likely to be achieved by employing multiple antennas at the base station (service provider) as well as at the end user devices. In this regard, the past decade has seen an explosion of interest in multi antenna systems, especially, multi-input multi-output (MIMO) communication systems. MIMO communication systems provide a promising approach to deliver higher data throughput without the need for increased power and bandwidth. Space-time coding adds time as another dimension to the diversity, in addition to the spatial diversity achieved by multiple antennas in MIMO system.

Among different space-time coding schemes presented in the literature, orthogonal space-time block codes (OSTBCs, Alamouti, 1998) are of particular interest since they achieve full diversity at a lower receiver complexity. Indeed, many practical systems and standards such as WiFi and WiMAX have already adopted OSTBC for MIMO communications.

The primary interest of this Chapter is to delve into the receiver aspect of the MIMO system where continuous interest has been shown in developing blind-adaptive decoding algorithms. Blind decoding algorithms improve data throughput by enabling the system designer to replace training symbols with data. On the other hand, considering the fact that the wireless end user environment is becoming increasingly mobile, adaptive algorithms have the ability to improve the performance of a system regardless of whether it is a blind system or training based one. The difficulty faced by blind and adaptive algorithms is that they are generally computationally intense. Further, the possible use of higher frequency carriers and the appeal of broadband communication for a wide variety of applications as well as the emergence of newer technologies such as cooperative communications have been contributing to the growing interest in a general $M \times N$ MIMO system over the 2×1 Alamouti's scheme which was the subject of intense research in the past decade. Hence, any blind-adaptive algorithm should be computationally efficient before they can be implemented in practical systems. This Chapter presents blind decoding algorithms that are adaptive in nature as well as computationally efficient for any $M \times N$ MIMO system.

In (Liu et al., 2002), Kalman filtering has been studied in application to channel tracking for MIMO communication systems. The method proposed in (Liu et al., 2002) is based on two assumptions. First, the underlying space-time coding scheme is based on Alamouti code

(Alamouti, 1998), and therefore its application is limited to the case of two transmit antennas. Second, the channel is assumed to be time-varying during the transmission of each block. The latter assumption implies that the linear ML receiver is optimal in a mean sense (Liu et al., 2002). Kalman filtering has been applied to the problem of MIMO channel tracking in several other research reports (Schafhuber et al., 2003). Also, in (Coon et al., 2005), a frequency domain equalization method has been proposed for single carrier MIMO systems. Particle filtering has also been used in other studies (Haykin et al., 2004) for MIMO channel tracking. In (AlNauffouri et al., 2004), a Kalman filtering approach has been used in the maximization step of an expectation-maximization (EM) method to track the frequency selective MIMO channel when the underlying code is an OSTBC and when an orthogonal frequency division multiplexing (OFDM) is used.

This chapter also focuses on the MIMO channel tracking and data decoding algorithms (Balakumar et al., 2007) that are a) suitable for any $M \times N$ MIMO system and b) computationally efficient to be able to implement in practical systems. By considering a class of MIMO systems where OSTBCs are used as the underlying space-time coding schemes and assuming a fixed channel during the transmission of each block of data a two-step channel tracking algorithm is developed. In the first step, Kalman filtering is used at the beginning of each block to obtain an initial channel estimate for that block based on the channel estimate obtained for previous block. In the second step, to improve the quality of the channel estimate obtained by Kalman filtering, a simple iterative channel estimation technique is proposed. This iterative method is in fact a decision-directed algorithm and it consists of sequential use of a linear receiver and a linear channel estimator. In addition, it is shown that, due to specific properties of orthogonal space-time block codes, both the Kalman filter and the decision-directed algorithm can be significantly simplified.

2. Background

Consider a MIMO system with N transmit and M receive antennas. We consider a block transmission scheme and assume that within the block period T the channel is fixed, i.e., the channel is assumed to be quasi-static. However, between different blocks the channel can change. As such, the n th received block can be written as

$$\mathbf{Y}(n) = \mathbf{X}(n)\mathbf{H}(n) + \mathbf{V}(n) \tag{1}$$

where $\mathbf{Y}(n)$ is the $T \times M$ matrix of the received signals, $\mathbf{X}(n)$ is the $T \times N$ matrix of transmitted signals, $\mathbf{V}(n)$ is the $T \times M$ matrix of noise, and $\mathbf{H}(n)$ is the $N \times M$ channel matrix during the n th block period. The noise $\mathbf{V}(n)$ is assumed to be zero-mean complex Gaussian and both spatially and temporally white with variance $\sigma_v^2 / 2$ per real dimension.

In space-time block coding, the matrix $\mathbf{X}(n)$ is a mapping that transforms a block of complex symbols to a $T \times N$ complex matrix. Hence, we hereafter replace $\mathbf{X}(n)$ with $\mathbf{X}(\mathbf{s}(n))$ where $s(n)$ is the n th symbol vector of length K . Let us define $\mathbf{s}(n)$ as

$$\mathbf{s}(n) = [s_1(n)\, s_2(n) \cdots s_K(n)]^T \tag{2}$$

where $(\cdot)^T$ denotes the transpose operator. The $T \times N$ matrix $\mathbf{X}(s(n))$ is called an OSTBC (Alamouti, 1998; Tarokh et al., 1999) if i) all elements of $\mathbf{X}(\mathbf{s}(n))$ are linear functions of the

K complex variables $s_1(n), s_2(n), \ldots, s_K(n)$ and their complex conjugates, ii) and if, for any arbitrary $\mathbf{s}(n)$, $\mathbf{X}(\mathbf{s}(n))$ satisfies

$$\mathbf{X}^H(\mathbf{s}(n))\mathbf{X}(\mathbf{s}(n)) = \| \mathbf{s}(n) \|^2 \, \mathbf{I}_N \tag{3}$$

where $\mathbf{I}_N$ is the $N \times N$ identity matrix, $\| \cdot \|$ is the Euclidean norm, and $(\cdot)^H$ denotes Hermitian transpose.
It follows from the definition of OSTBC that matrix $\mathbf{X}(\mathbf{s}(n))$ can be written as

$$\mathbf{X}(\mathbf{s}(n)) = \sum_{k=1}^{K} (\mathbf{C}_k \, Re\{s_k(n)\} + \mathbf{D}_k \, Im\{s_k(n)\}) \tag{4}$$

where $Re\{\cdot\}$ and $Im\{\cdot\}$ denote the real and imaginary parts, respectively, and C_k and D_k matrices are defined as[1]

$$\mathbf{C}_k = X(\mathbf{u}_k) \tag{5}$$

$$\mathbf{D}_k = X(j\mathbf{u}_k) \tag{6}$$

where $\mathbf{u}_k$ is the kth column of identity matrix $\mathbf{I}_K$ and $j = \sqrt{-1}$. Let us define the "underline" operator for a matrix $\mathbf{P}$ as

$$\underline{\mathbf{P}} \triangleq \begin{bmatrix} vec\{Re(\mathbf{P})\} \\ vec\{Im(\mathbf{P})\} \end{bmatrix} \tag{7}$$

where $vec\{\cdot\}$ refers to the vectorization operator stacking all the columns of a matrix on top of each other. Using (4) and (7), one can re-write (1) as (Gharavi-Alkhansari & Gershman, 2005)

$$\mathbf{y}(n) \triangleq \underline{\mathbf{Y}(n)} = \mathbf{A}(\mathbf{H}(n))\mathbf{s}_n + \mathbf{v}_n \tag{8}$$

where $\mathbf{s}_n \triangleq \underline{\mathbf{s}(n)}$, $\mathbf{v}_n \triangleq \underline{\mathbf{V}(n)}$ and the $2MT \times 2K$ real matrix $\mathbf{A}(\mathbf{H}(n))$ is given by

$$\mathbf{A}(\mathbf{H}(n)) = [\underline{\mathbf{C}_1\mathbf{H}(n)} \ldots \underline{\mathbf{C}_K\mathbf{H}(n)}\underline{\mathbf{D}_1\mathbf{H}(n)} \ldots \underline{\mathbf{D}_K\mathbf{H}(n)}]. \tag{9}$$

It has been shown that for any channel matrix $\mathbf{H}(n)$, the matrix $A(\mathbf{H}(n))$ satisfies the so-called *decoupling* property, i.e., its columns are orthogonal to each other and have identical norms (Larsson & Stoica, 2003). More specifically, it satisfies

$$\mathbf{A}^T(\mathbf{H}(n))\mathbf{A}(\mathbf{H}(n)) = \| \mathbf{H}(n) \|_F^2 \, \mathbf{I}_{2K} \tag{10}$$

where $\|.\|_F$ denotes the Frobenius norm. Let us define the $2MN \times 1$ time-varying channel vector $\mathbf{h}(n)$ as $\mathbf{h}(n) \triangleq \underline{\mathbf{H}(n)}$. With a small abuse of notation, we hereafter replace $A(\mathbf{H}(n))$ with $A(\mathbf{h}(n))$. Therefore, we rewrite (10) as

---

[1]In fact, any OSTBC is completely defined by the set of matrices $\{\mathbf{C}_k, \mathbf{D}_k\}_{k=1}^K$.

$$\mathbf{A}^T(\mathbf{h}(n))\mathbf{A}(\mathbf{h}(n)) = \|\mathbf{h}(n)\|^2 \mathbf{I}_{2K} \tag{11}$$

Since $\mathbf{A}(\mathbf{h}(n))$ is linear in $\mathbf{h}(n)$, there exists a unique $4KMT \times 2MN$ matrix $\mathbf{\Phi}$ such that $vec\{\mathbf{A}(\mathbf{h}(n))\} = \mathbf{\Phi h}(n)$ where $\mathbf{\Phi}$ is a $4KMT \times 2MN$ matrix whose k th column is given by

$$[\mathbf{\Phi}]_k = vec\{\mathbf{A}(\mathbf{e}_k)\}. \tag{12}$$

Here, $[\cdot]_k$ denotes the k th column of a matrix and $\mathbf{e}_k$ is the k th column of identity matrix $\mathbf{I}_{2MN}$. Note that matrix $\mathbf{\Phi}$ can be written as $\mathbf{\Phi} = [\mathbf{\Phi}_1^T \, \mathbf{\Phi}_2^T \cdots \mathbf{\Phi}_{2K}^T]^T$ where each sub-matrix $\mathbf{\Phi}_k$, ($k = 1,\ldots 2K$) describes the linear relationship between the k th column of $\mathbf{A}(\mathbf{h}(n))$ and $\mathbf{h}(n)$, $[\mathbf{A}(\mathbf{h})]_k = \mathbf{\Phi}_k \mathbf{h}(n)$.

Given the channel vector $\mathbf{h}(n)$, the optimal ML decoder for OSTBCs consists of a linear receiver followed by a symbol-by-symbol decoder (Ganesan & Stoica, 2001). Indeed, the linear receiver computes $\hat{\mathbf{s}}_n$, the estimate of $\mathbf{s}_n$ as

$$\hat{\mathbf{s}}_n = \frac{1}{\|\mathbf{h}(n)\|^2}\mathbf{A}^T(\mathbf{h}(n))\mathbf{y}_n. \tag{13}$$

Then, the symbol-by-symbol decoder builds the estimate $\mathbf{s}(n)$, of vector $\mathbf{s}(n)$ as

$$\hat{\mathbf{s}}(n) = [\mathbf{I}_K \, j\mathbf{I}_K]\hat{\mathbf{s}}_n \tag{14}$$

The k th element of $\mathbf{s}(n)$ is compared with all points in the constellation corresponding to $\mathbf{s}_k(n)$ and the closest point in this constellation to the k th element of $\mathbf{s}(n)$ is accepted as the k th decoded symbol.

Note however that implementation of the ML decoder requires the knowledge of the time-varying channel. If the channel is fixed, one can use training to estimate the channel in a non-blind fashion. However, in practice, the channel is time-varying, and hence tracking of the MIMO channel is required. Recently, blind channel estimation has been studied in the literature (see for example (Shahbazpanahi et al., 2005)). The blind channel estimation of (Shahbazpanahi et al., 2005) is based on the assumption that the channel is fixed, and hence, it is not applicable to time-varying channels.

Without assuming any model for the MIMO channel, the problem of joint channel tracking and symbol detection is ill-posed. Fortunately, in many practical scenarios, the wireless channels can be modeled with a few parameters. It has been shown in (Wang & Chang, 1996) that the first-order AR model can be used as a sufficiently precise method to describe the time-varying behavior of wireless channels. Based on this model, we assume that the channel variation between adjacent blocks is modeled as a first order autoregressive (AR) model, i.e.,

$$\mathbf{H}(n) = \alpha\mathbf{H}(n-1) + \mathbf{W}(n) \tag{15}$$

where $\mathbf{W}(n)$ is an $N \times M$ noise matrix that is assumed to be zero-mean complex Gaussian with independent entries and variance of $\sigma_w^2 / 2$ per real dimension. This implies that $\mathbf{W}(n)$, and consequently $\mathbf{H}(n)$, are zero-mean wide-sense stationary processes. The parameter α is a complex scalar that can be estimated using the method of (Tsatsanis et al., 1999), and hence, it is herein assumed to be known. The noise variance σ_w^2 and α are related as $\sigma_w^2 = \sigma_h^2(1-|\alpha|^2)$ where σ_h^2 is the variance of each element of $\mathbf{H}(n)$ and $|\cdot|$ denotes the amplitude of a complex number.

3. Kalman filter based channel tracking

In this Section, the problem of channel tracking via Kalman filtering is addressed. Subsequently, a two-step channel tracking algorithm is proposed. In the first step of this algorithm, Kalman filtering is used to obtain an initial channel estimate for each block based on the channel estimates obtained for the previous blocks. In the second step, the so-obtained initial channel estimate is refined using an iterative decision-directed technique, which involves a linear ML channel estimator based on the decoded symbols. In fact, the linearity of such an ML channel estimator follows from the interesting properties of OSTBCs. It is also demonstrated that due to the specific structure of OSTBCs, Kalman filtering based channel tracking can be significantly simplified.
To derive the two-step channel tracking algorithm, we rewrite (8) as

$$\mathbf{y}_n = \mathbf{B}(\mathbf{s}_n)\mathbf{h}(n) + \mathbf{v}_n \tag{16}$$

where the $2MT \times 2MN$ real matrix $\mathbf{B}(\mathbf{s}_n)$ is defined as

$$\mathbf{B}(\mathbf{s}_n) \triangleq [A(\mathbf{e}_1)\mathbf{s}_n \quad A(\mathbf{e}_2)\mathbf{s}_n \ldots A(\mathbf{e}_{2MN})\mathbf{s}_n] \tag{17}$$

and $\mathbf{e}_k$, as defined earlier, is the k th column of the identity matrix $\mathbf{I}_{2MN}$. The following Lemma plays an important role in simplifying the forthcoming Kalman filtering algorithm.
Lemma 1: The matrix $\mathbf{B}(s_n)$ *satisfies*

$$\mathbf{B}^T(\mathbf{s}_n)\mathbf{B}(\mathbf{s}_n) = \|\mathbf{s}(n)\|^2 \mathbf{I}_{2MN} \tag{18}$$

Proof: We first show that the sub-matrices $\{\mathbf{\Phi}_k\}_{k=1}^{2K}$ satisfy the following equations:

$$\mathbf{\Phi}_l^T\mathbf{\Phi}_m = \begin{cases} \mathbf{I}_{2MN} & \text{if } l = m, \\ -\mathbf{\Phi}_m^T\mathbf{\Phi}_l & \text{if } l \neq m. \end{cases} \tag{19}$$

To prove (19), we use the decoupling property in (11). Indeed, for any channel vector $\mathbf{h}$, the decoupling property in (11) implies that

$$[A(\mathbf{h})]_l^T[A(\mathbf{h})]_l = \|\mathbf{h}\|^2 \tag{20}$$

or

$$\mathbf{h}^T\mathbf{\Phi}_l^T\mathbf{\Phi}_l\mathbf{h} = \mathbf{h}^T\mathbf{h} \tag{21}$$

Since (21) holds true for any $\mathbf{h}$ and because $\mathbf{\Phi}_l^T\mathbf{\Phi}_l$ is a symmetric matrix, we conclude that $\mathbf{\Phi}_l^T\mathbf{\Phi}_l = \mathbf{I}_{2MN}$. To prove the second part of (19), based on the fact that different columns of $A(\mathbf{h})$ are orthogonal to each other, we can write

$$\left.\begin{array}{lll}[A(\mathbf{h})]_l^T[A(\mathbf{h})]_m & = \mathbf{h}^T\mathbf{\Phi}_l^T\mathbf{\Phi}_m\mathbf{h} & = 0 \\ {[A(\mathbf{h})]_m^T[A(\mathbf{h})]_l} & = \mathbf{h}^T\mathbf{\Phi}_m^T\mathbf{\Phi}_l\mathbf{h} & = 0\end{array}\right\} \Rightarrow \mathbf{h}^T(\mathbf{\Phi}_l^T\mathbf{\Phi}_m + \mathbf{\Phi}_m^T\mathbf{\Phi}_l)\mathbf{h} = 0 \tag{22}$$

Since (22) holds true for any vector $\mathbf{h}$ and since $\mathbf{\Phi}_l^T\mathbf{\Phi}_m + \mathbf{\Phi}_m^T\mathbf{\Phi}_l$ is a symmetric matrix, we conclude that $\mathbf{\Phi}_l^T\mathbf{\Phi}_m + \mathbf{\Phi}_m^T\mathbf{\Phi}_l = 0$. This completes the proof of (19).
We now use (19) to prove (18). To do so, we note that

$$\mathbf{B}^T(\mathbf{s}_n)\mathbf{B}(\mathbf{s}_n) = \begin{bmatrix} \mathbf{s}_n^T A^T(\mathbf{e}_1)A(\mathbf{e}_1)\mathbf{s}_n & \cdots & \mathbf{s}_n^T A^T(\mathbf{e}_1)A(\mathbf{e}_{2MN})\mathbf{s}_n \\ \mathbf{s}_n^T A^T(\mathbf{e}_2)A(\mathbf{e}_1)\mathbf{s}_n & \cdots & \mathbf{s}_n^T A^T(\mathbf{e}_2)A(\mathbf{e}_{2MN})\mathbf{s}_n \\ \vdots & \ddots & \vdots \\ \mathbf{s}_n^T A^T(\mathbf{e}_{2MN})A(\mathbf{e}_1)\mathbf{s}_n & \cdots & \mathbf{s}_n A^T(\mathbf{e}_{2MN})A(\mathbf{e}_{2MN})\mathbf{s}_n \end{bmatrix} \tag{23}$$

where we have used (17). Note also that

$$\mathbf{s}_n^T \underbrace{A^T(\mathbf{e}_l)A(\mathbf{e}_l)}_{\|\mathbf{e}_l\|^2\mathbf{I}_{2K}}\mathbf{s}_n = \|\mathbf{s}_n^T\|^2 \tag{24}$$

which follows from the decoupling property. For $l \neq m$, the following set of equalities holds true:

$$\begin{aligned}
\mathbf{s}_n^T A^T(\mathbf{e}_l)A(\mathbf{e}_m)\mathbf{s}_n &= \sum_{r=1}^{2K}\sum_{s=1}^{2K}\tilde{\mathbf{s}}_{n,r}[A(\mathbf{e}_l)]_r^T[A(\mathbf{e}_m)]_s\mathbf{s}_{n,s} \\
&= \sum_{r=1}^{2K}\sum_{s=1,s\neq r}^{2K}\mathbf{s}_{n,r}\left(\mathbf{e}_l^T\mathbf{\Phi}_r^T\mathbf{\Phi}_s\mathbf{e}_m\right)\mathbf{s}_{n,s} \\
&+\sum_{r=1}^{2K}\mathbf{s}_{n,r}(\mathbf{e}_l^T\overbrace{\mathbf{\Phi}_r^T\mathbf{\Phi}_r}^{\mathbf{I}_{2MN}}\mathbf{e}_m)\mathbf{s}_{n,r} \\
&= \sum_{r=1}^{2K}\sum_{s=1,s\neq r}^{2K}\mathbf{s}_{n,r}(\mathbf{e}_l^T\mathbf{\Phi}_r^T\mathbf{\Phi}_s\mathbf{e}_m)\mathbf{s}_{n,s} + \sum_{r=1}^{2K}\mathbf{s}_{n,r}\overbrace{\mathbf{e}_l^T\mathbf{e}_m}^{\mathbf{0}}\mathbf{s}_{n,r} \\
&= -\sum_{r=1}^{2K}\sum_{s=1,s\neq r}^{2K}\mathbf{s}_{n,s}(\mathbf{e}_l^T\mathbf{\Phi}_s^T\mathbf{\Phi}_r\mathbf{e}_m)\mathbf{s}_{n,r} + 0 \\
&= -\sum_{s=1}^{2K}\sum_{r=1,r\neq s}^{2K}\mathbf{s}_{n,s}(\mathbf{e}_l^T\mathbf{\Phi}_s^T\mathbf{\Phi}_r\mathbf{e}_m)\mathbf{s}_{n,r} \\
&= -\mathbf{s}_n^T A^T(\mathbf{e}_l)A(\mathbf{e}_m)\mathbf{s}_n
\end{aligned}$$

where $\mathbf{s}_{n,r}$ is the r th element of $\mathbf{s}_n$. Therefore, we obtain that, for $l \neq m$

$$\mathbf{s}_n^T A^T(\mathbf{e}_l)A(\mathbf{e}_m)\mathbf{s}_n = 0 \tag{25}$$

It follows from (24) and (25) that $\mathbf{B}^T(\mathbf{s}_n)\mathbf{B}(\mathbf{s}_n) = \|\mathbf{s}(n)\|^2\,\mathbf{I}_{2MN}$ and the proof is complete.

It follows from (16) and (18) that given $\mathbf{s}_n$, the ML estimate of the channel vector $\mathbf{h}(n)$ can be obtained as

$$\mathbf{h}_{ML}(n) = \frac{1}{\| \mathbf{s}(n) \|^2} \mathbf{B}^T(\mathbf{s}_n)\mathbf{y}_n. \tag{26}$$

Therefore, if the information symbols were available, the optimal ML channel estimation would involve a linear estimator as in (26). However, in practice, the information symbols are not available and they have to be estimated. To overcome this problem, one can use an iterative decision-directed channel estimation scheme. That is, given an initial channel estimate for the n th block, say $\mathbf{h}^{(0)}(n)$, one can replace $\mathbf{h}(n)$ in (13) with $\mathbf{h}^{(0)}(n)$ and obtain an estimate for $\mathbf{s}_n$, say $\hat{\mathbf{s}}_n^{(0)}$. This estimate of $\mathbf{s}_n$ will, in turn, be used in (26) instead of $\mathbf{s}(n)$ to obtain a new estimate for $\mathbf{h}(n)$, say $\mathbf{h}^{(1)}(n)$. This new channel estimate will again be used in (13) instead of $\mathbf{h}(n)$ to obtain a new estimate of $\mathbf{s}(n)$. This procedure is repeated until the normalized difference between two consecutive channel estimates is negligible. The accuracy of this iterative decision-directed channel estimation scheme depends on the availability of a precise enough initial channel vector estimate $\mathbf{h}^{(0)}(n)$. The proposal here is to use Kalman filtering to obtain the initial channel estimate, $\mathbf{h}^{(0)}(n)$, based on the channel estimates obtained for the previous blocks as well as the n th block received data. In what follows, the details of the Kalman filtering technique when applied to our MIMO channel tracking problem are discussed. It is shown that using Lemma 1, the Kalman filter can be simplified significantly. To show this, (16) is used as the observation model of the Kalman filter (Bar-Shalom et al., 2002). Note that the data model in (16) is real-valued. To obtain a real-valued state transition equation, (15) can be rewritten as

$$\mathbf{h}(n) = \mathbf{F}\mathbf{h}(n-1) + \mathbf{w}(n) \tag{27}$$

where

$$\mathbf{F} \triangleq \begin{bmatrix} Re(\alpha)\mathbf{I}_{MN} & -Im(\alpha)\mathbf{I}_{MN} \\ Im(\alpha)\mathbf{I}_{MN} & Re(\alpha)\mathbf{I}_{MN} \end{bmatrix} \tag{28}$$

and $\mathbf{w}(n) = \underline{\mathbf{W}(n)}$ is the real-valued process noise with covariance matrix $\mathbf{Q} = (\sigma_w^2 / 2)\mathbf{I}_{2MN}$. We can use (27) as the real-valued state transition equation required for Kalman filtering.

The Kalman filtering problem for channel tracking in OSTBC-based MIMO communication system can now be formally stated as follows: Given the measurement-to-state matrix $\mathbf{B}(\mathbf{s}_n)$, use the observed data $\mathbf{y}_n$ to find the minimum mean squared error (MMSE) estimate of the components of the state vector $\mathbf{h}(n)$ for each $n \geq 1$.

Given the estimate of the state at time $n-1$, i.e., $\mathbf{h}(n-1|n-1)$, and the associated error covariance matrix $\mathbf{P}(n-1|n-1)$, the Kalman filter (Bar-Shalom et al., 2002) is used to obtain the estimate of the state at time n, i.e., $\mathbf{h}(n|n)$ and the associated error covariance matrix $\mathbf{P}(n|n)$. The Kalman filtering algorithm can be summarized as follows:

$$\mathbf{h}(n|n-1) = \mathbf{F}\mathbf{h}(n-1|n-1) \tag{29}$$

$$\mathbf{P}(n|n-1) = \mathbf{F}\mathbf{P}(n-1|n-1)\mathbf{F}^T + \mathbf{Q} \tag{30}$$

$$\mathbf{y}_n = \mathbf{B}(\mathbf{s}_n)\mathbf{h}(n \mid n-1) \tag{31}$$

$$\mathbf{v}(n) = \mathbf{y}_n - \mathbf{y}_n \tag{32}$$

$$\mathbf{P}_v(n) = \mathbf{R} + \mathbf{B}(\mathbf{s}_n)\mathbf{P}(n \mid n-1)\mathbf{B}^T(\mathbf{s}_n) \tag{33}$$

$$\mathbf{G}(n) = \mathbf{P}(n \mid n-1)\mathbf{B}^T(\mathbf{s}_n)\mathbf{P}_v^{-1}(n) \tag{34}$$

$$\mathbf{h}(n \mid n) = \mathbf{h}(n \mid n-1) + \mathbf{G}(n)\ \mathbf{v}(n) \tag{35}$$

$$\mathbf{P}(n \mid n) = \mathbf{P}(n \mid n-1) - \mathbf{G}(n)\mathbf{P}_v(n)\mathbf{G}^T(n) \tag{36}$$

where $\mathbf{h}(n \mid n-1)$ is the predicted state, $\mathbf{P}(n \mid n-1)$ is the covariance matrix of the predicted state, $\mathbf{y}_n$ is the predicted observation, $\mathbf{v}(n)$ is the innovation process, $\mathbf{P}_v(n)$ is the innovation covariance matrix, $\mathbf{G}(n)$ is the Kalman gain (Bar-Shalom et al., 2002), and $\mathbf{R} = E\{\mathbf{v}_n\mathbf{v}_n^T\}$ is the covariance matrix of the measurement noise $\mathbf{v}_n$. As we assumed that the measurement noise is spatio-temporally white with a variance of $\sigma_v^2/2$ per real dimension, $\mathbf{R} = (\sigma_v^2/2)\mathbf{I}_{2MT}$ holds true.
The following Lemma uses the result of Lemma 1 to reduce the computational complexity of finding $\mathbf{P}_v^{-1}(n)$ in (34).

Lemma 2: If $\mathbf{P}(n-1 \mid n-1)$ *is a diagonal matrix, then,* $\mathbf{P}(n \mid n-1)$ *in (30) and* $\mathbf{P}(n \mid n)$ *in (36) are also diagonal, i.e., if*

$$\mathbf{P}(n-1 \mid n-1) = \delta_{n-1}\mathbf{I}_{2MN} \tag{37}$$

then

$$\mathbf{P}(n \mid n-1) = \beta_n\mathbf{I}_{2MN} \tag{38}$$

$$\mathbf{P}(n \mid n) = \delta_n\mathbf{I}_{2MN} \tag{39}$$

where

$$\beta_n = \delta_{n-1} \mid \alpha \mid^2 + \frac{\sigma_w^2}{2} \qquad \text{and} \qquad \delta_n = \frac{\sigma_v^2\beta_n}{2\,\| s(n) \|^2\, \beta_n + \sigma_v^2}. \tag{40}$$

Proof: Substituting (37) into the predicted state in (30), we can rewrite it as

$$\mathbf{P}(n \mid n-1) = \delta_{n-1}\mathbf{F}\mathbf{F}^T + \mathbf{Q} = \mid \alpha \mid^2 \delta_{n-1}\mathbf{I}_{2MN} + \mathbf{Q} = \underbrace{\left(\mid \alpha \mid \delta_{n-1}^2 + \frac{\sigma_w^2}{2} \right)}_{\beta_n}\mathbf{I}_{2MN}. \tag{41}$$

Inserting (41) into (33) and using matrix inversion lemma, $\mathbf{P}_v^{-1}(n)$ in (33) can be written as

$$\mathbf{P}_v^{-1}(n) = \mathbf{R}^{-1} - \mathbf{R}^{-1}\mathbf{B}(\mathbf{s}_n)(\mathbf{B}^T(\mathbf{s}_n)\mathbf{R}^{-1}\mathbf{B}(\mathbf{s}_n) + \mathbf{P}^{-1}(n \mid n-1))^{-1}\mathbf{B}^T(\mathbf{s}_n)\mathbf{R}^{-1}$$
$$= \frac{2}{\sigma_v^2}\mathbf{I}_{2MT} - \frac{4}{\sigma_v^4}\mathbf{B}(\mathbf{s}_n)\left(\frac{2}{\sigma_v^2}\mathbf{B}^T(\mathbf{s}_n)\mathbf{B}(\mathbf{s}_n) + \frac{1}{\beta_n}\mathbf{I}_{2MN} \right)^{-1}\mathbf{B}^T(\mathbf{s}_n)$$

$$=\frac{2}{\sigma_v^2}\mathbf{I}_{2MT}-\left(\frac{4\beta_n}{2\|\mathbf{s}(n)\|^2\beta_n\sigma_v^2+\sigma_v^4}\right)\mathbf{B}(\mathbf{s}_n)\mathbf{B}^T(\mathbf{s}_n) \quad (42)$$

where the fact that $\mathbf{B}^T(\mathbf{s}_n)\mathbf{B}(\mathbf{s}_n)=\|\mathbf{s}(n)\|^2\mathbf{I}_{2MN}$ has been used.
Using (34) and (42), we rewrite (36) as

$$\mathbf{P}(n|n)=\mathbf{P}(n|n-1)-\mathbf{P}(n|n-1)\mathbf{B}^T(\mathbf{s}_n)$$

$$\left(\frac{2}{\sigma_v^2}\mathbf{I}_{2MT}-\left(\frac{4\beta_n}{2\|\mathbf{s}(n)\|^2\beta_n\sigma_v^2+\sigma_v^4}\right)\mathbf{B}(\mathbf{s}_n)\mathbf{B}^T(\mathbf{s}_n)\right)\mathbf{B}(\mathbf{s}_n)\mathbf{P}(n|n-1)$$

$$=\left(\frac{\sigma_v^2\beta_n}{2\|\mathbf{s}(n)\|^2\beta_n+\sigma_v^2}\right)\mathbf{I}_{2MN}. \quad (43)$$

The proof is complete.
Based on Lemma 2, if $\mathbf{P}(0|0)$ is initialized as a diagonal matrix, $\mathbf{P}(n|n-1)$ and $\mathbf{P}(n|n)$ always take the form of (38) and (39), respectively. Hence, $\mathbf{P}_v^{-1}$ in (34) is simplified as in (42). It is also noteworthy that using (41) and (42) the Kalman filter gain $\mathbf{G}(n)$ in (34) can be written as

$$\mathbf{G}(n)=\underbrace{\beta_n\left(\frac{2}{\sigma_v^2}-\frac{4\beta_n\|\mathbf{s}(n)\|^2}{2\|\mathbf{s}(n)\|^2\beta_n\sigma_v^2+\sigma_v^4}\right)}_{\overset{\Delta}{=}\mu_n}\mathbf{B}^T(\mathbf{s}_n). \quad (44)$$

Using (31), (32) and (44), we can simplify (35) as

$$\mathbf{h}(n|n)=\mathbf{h}(n|n-1)+\mu_n\mathbf{B}^T(\mathbf{s}_n)(\mathbf{y}(n)-\mathbf{B}(\mathbf{s}_n)\mathbf{h}(n|n-1))$$

$$=(1-\mu_n\|\mathbf{s}(n)\|^2)\mathbf{h}(n|n-1)+\mu_n\mathbf{B}^T(\mathbf{s}_n)\mathbf{y}(n). \quad (45)$$

Therefore, the Kalman filtering algorithm presented in (29)--(36) can be simplified as it follows:

$$\mathbf{h}(n|n-1)=\mathbf{F}\mathbf{h}(n-1|n-1) \quad (46)$$

$$\beta_n=\delta_{n-1}|\alpha|^2+\frac{\sigma_w^2}{2},\qquad \mu_n=\beta_n\left(\frac{2}{\sigma_v^2}-\frac{4\beta_n\|\mathbf{s}(n)\|^2}{2\|\mathbf{s}(n)\|^2\beta_n\sigma_v^2+\sigma_v^4}\right) \quad (47)$$

$$\mathbf{h}^{(0)}(n)=\mathbf{h}(n|n)=(1-\mu_n\|\mathbf{s}(n)\|^2)\mathbf{h}(n|n-1)+\mu_n\mathbf{B}^T(\mathbf{s}_n)\mathbf{y}(n) \quad (48)$$

$$\delta_n=\frac{\sigma_v^2\beta_n}{2\|\mathbf{s}(n)\|^2\beta_n+\sigma_v^2}. \quad (49)$$

We then use the so-obtained $\mathbf{h}^{(0)}(n)$ in the aforementioned iterative procedure to improve its accuracy.

Remark 1: Note that the simplified Kalman filter requires the knowledge of the symbol vector $\mathbf{s}_n$ (or $\mathbf{B}(\mathbf{s}(n))$). However, the primary objective is to decode $\mathbf{s}(n)$. To overcome this obstacle, we propose to replace $\mathbf{s}_n$ in the Kalman filter equations (46)--(49), by its estimate, which is obtained by replacing the true channel vector in (13) by the predicted channel vector $\mathbf{h}(n|n-1)$ as

$$\mathbf{s}_n = \frac{1}{\|\mathbf{h}(n|n-1)\|^2} A^T(\mathbf{h}(n|n-1))\mathbf{y}_n . \tag{50}$$

Note that given the predicted channel vector $\mathbf{h}(n|n-1)$, the symbol estimate in (50) is optimal in the ML sense.

Remark 2: To initiate the whole process, we also need to obtain an accurate channel estimate $\mathbf{h}(0)$ as well as its initial covariance $\delta_0 \mathbf{I}_{2MN}$. To obtain such an initial channel estimate, one can use a training block $\mathbf{s}(0)$, which is known at the receiver. At the beginning of the tracking process, the receiver can then use (26) to obtain the ML estimate of $\mathbf{h}(0)$ as

$$\mathbf{h}(0) = \frac{1}{\|\mathbf{s}(0)\|^2}\mathbf{B}^T(\mathbf{s}_0)\mathbf{y}_0 \tag{51}$$

where $\mathbf{s}_0 = \underline{\mathbf{s}(0)}$ is defined.

To find δ_0, we note that

$$\delta_0 \mathbf{I}_{2MN} = E\left\{\left(\mathbf{h}(0)-\hat{\mathbf{h}}(0)\right)\left(\mathbf{h}(0)-\hat{\mathbf{h}}(0)\right)^T\right\}$$

$$= E\left\{\mathbf{h}(0)\mathbf{h}^T(0)\right\} + E\left\{\mathbf{h}(0)\mathbf{h}^T(0)\right\} - 2E\left\{\mathbf{h}(0)\mathbf{h}^T(0)\right\} \tag{52}$$

where channel is assumed zero-mean and

$$E\left\{\mathbf{h}(0)\mathbf{h}^T(0)\right\} = \frac{1}{\|\mathbf{s}(0)\|^4}\mathbf{B}^T(\mathbf{s}_0)E\left\{\mathbf{y}_0\mathbf{y}_0^T\right\}\mathbf{B}(\mathbf{s}_0)$$

$$= \frac{1}{\|s(0)\|^4}\mathbf{B}^T(\mathbf{s}_0)\left(\mathbf{B}(\mathbf{s}_0)\underbrace{E\{\mathbf{h}(0)\mathbf{h}^T(0)\}}_{(\sigma_h^2/2)\mathbf{I}_{2MN}}\mathbf{B}^T(\mathbf{s}_0) + (\sigma_v^2/2)\mathbf{I}_{2MT}\right)\mathbf{B}(\mathbf{s}_0)$$

$$= \left(\frac{\sigma_h^2}{2} + \frac{\sigma_v^2}{2\|\mathbf{s}(0)\|^2}\right)\mathbf{I}_{2MN}$$

$$= \frac{1}{\|\mathbf{s}(0)\|^2}\mathbf{B}^T(\mathbf{s}_0)E\left\{\left(\mathbf{B}(\mathbf{s}_0)\mathbf{h}(0)+\mathbf{v}_0\right)\mathbf{h}^T(0)\right\} = \frac{\sigma_h^2}{2}\mathbf{I}_{2MN} \tag{53}$$

Therefore, one can obtain δ_0 as

$$\delta_0 = \frac{1}{2}\frac{\sigma_v^2}{\|\mathbf{s}(0)\|^2}. \tag{54}$$

Remark 3: To avoid error propagation, training should be repeated at regular intervals. The training repetition period (TRP) determines the bandwidth efficiency of the system and it is defined as the distance, in terms of number of blocks, between two consecutive training blocks.

Remark 4: In terms of computational complexity, the proposed channel tracking method enjoys the low computational complexity of linear processing. More specifically, the first step requires the computation of $\mathbf{B}^T(\mathbf{s}_n)\mathbf{y}(n)$, and therefore, $2MT$ real multiplications are required for computation of each entry of $\mathbf{h}(n|n)$. Taking into account that $\mathbf{h}(n|n)$ is of length $2MN$, the total computational complexity of the first step is of order $O(M^2NT)$. The second step is indeed an iterative algorithm. In each iteration, we need to compute four quantities: $\|\mathbf{h}^{(k-1)}(n)\|^2$, $\mathbf{A}^T(\mathbf{h}^{(k-1)}(n))\mathbf{y}_n$, $\|\mathbf{s}_n^k\|^2$, and $\mathbf{B}^T(\mathbf{s}_n^{(k)})\mathbf{y}_n$. Computing these four quantities requires $2MN$, $4KMT$, $2K$, and $4M^2NT$ real multiplications, respectively. Therefore, the computational complexity of the second step is of the order $O(M^2NT)$ per iteration of the first step. The traditional Kalman filtering method involves the computation of $\mathbf{P}_v^{-1}(n)$. This amounts to a computational complexity of the order $O(M^3T^3)$ per iteration. Therefore, the proposed method significantly reduces the computational complexity of the traditional Kalman filtering.

4. Simulation results

In our numerical example, we consider the 3/4 rate code of (Larsson & Stoica, 2003) with $N = M = T = 4$, and $K = 3$. The SNR is defined as σ_h^2 / σ_v^2. In each simulation run, the elements of $H(n)$ are generated according to Jakes model (Jakes Jr, 1974) corresponding to $F_m T_s = 0.0045$ where F_m is the doppler frequency and T_s is the sampling time. This results in $\alpha = J_0(0.2\pi F_m T_s)e^{j2\pi F_o T_s} = 0.9998e^{j0.0283}$ where $J_0(\cdot)$ is the zeroth order Bessel function of first kind. In terms of channel estimation accuracy, we compare our Kalman filtering based channel tracking technique with the online implementation of the technique developed in (Shahbazpanahi et al., 2005). In order to implement the method of (Shahbazpanahi et al., 2005) in an online manner, we have used the subspace tracking approach proposed in section III.G of (Shahbazpanahi et al., 2005). In our comparison, we use normalized mean squared error (NMSE) of the channel estimates defined as

$$\textbf{NMSE} = E\left\{\frac{\|\mathbf{H}(n) - \widehat{\mathbf{H}}(n)\|^2}{\|\mathbf{H}(n)\|^2}\right\}. \tag{55}$$

In terms of symbol error rate (SER), we compare our method not only with the method of (Shahbazpanahi et al., 2005) but also with the differential space-time coding scheme (Larsson & Stoica, 2003).

Figure 1 illustrates the SERs of different methods, versus SNR, for TRP = 10. In this figure, we have also plotted the SER for the (clairvoyant) coherent ML receiver that is aware of the time-varying channel. It is noteworthy that the latter receiver does not correspond to any practical application and it is herein considered only for the sake of comparison. We have also plotted the performance of a differential coding scheme which uses the same OTSTBC which we have used in our method. As can be seen from this figure, for TRP = 10, our Kalman filtering based technique outperforms the differential space-time coding scheme by 1 dB.

It is worthwhile to observe that our technique outperforms the technique of (Shahbazpanahi et al., 2005) by more than 2 dB. In fact, when applied to track a time-varying MIMO channel, the algorithm of (Shahbazpanahi et al., 2005) performs even worse than the differential scheme. This is not surprising as (Shahbazpanahi et al., 2005) assumes that the MIMO channel is fixed within the observation interval. Therefore, the method of (Shahbazpanahi et al., 2005) is not applicable whenever the MIMO channel variations are fairly fast.

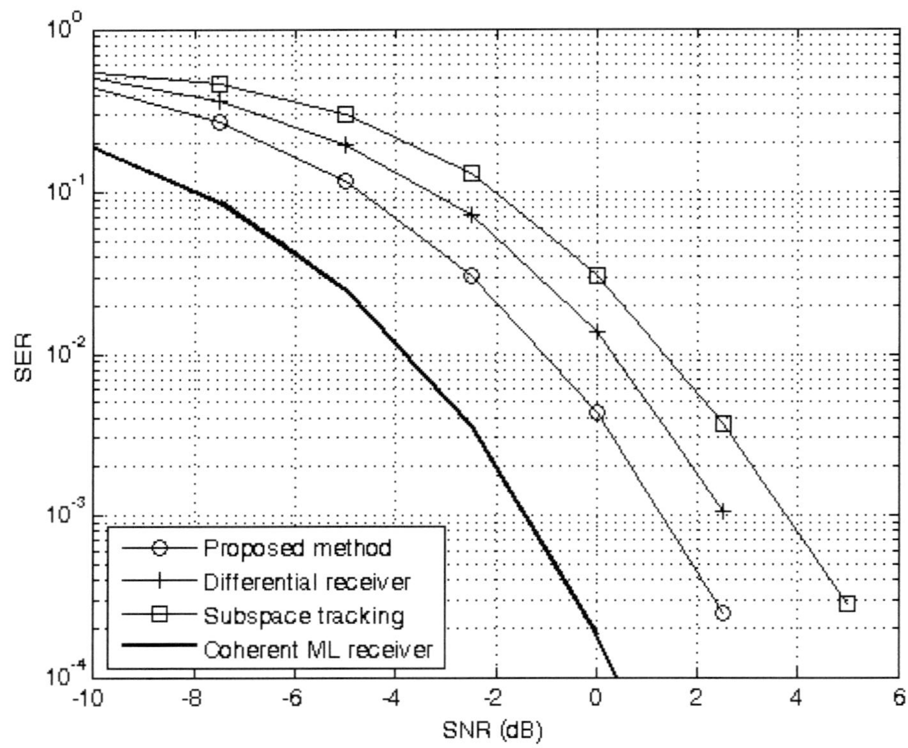

Fig. 1. The SERs versus SNR for different methods and for TRP = 10.

5. Conclusions

In this Chapter, an efficient Kalman filtering solution for the problem of channel tracking in MIMO communication systems where the MIMO channel is time-varying is presented. Considering the type of MIMO systems where orthogonal space-time block codes are used to encode the information symbols a two-step MIMO channel tracking algorithm is presented. As the first step, Kalman filtering is used to obtain an initial channel estimate for the current block based on the channel estimates obtained for previous blocks. In the second step, the so-obtained initial channel estimate is refined using a decision-directed iterative method. In is shown that due to the interesting properties of orthogonal space-time block codes, both the Kalman filter and the decision-directed algorithm can be significantly simplified.

6. References

Al-Naffouri, T., Awoniyi, O., Oteri, O., and Paulraj, A. (2004). Receiver design for MIMO-OFDM transmission over time variant channels, *IEEE Global Telecommunications Conference*, volume 4, pages 2487–2492.

Alamouti, S. (1998). A simple transmit diversity technique for wireless communications. *IEEE Journal on Selected Areas in Communications*, Vol. 16, No. 8, pp. 1451–1458.

Balakumar, B., Shahbazpanahi, S., and Kirubarajan, T. (2007), Joint MIMO channel tracking and symbol decoding using Kalman filtering, *IEEE Transactions on Signal Processing*, Vol. 55, No. 12, pp. 5873–5879.

Bar-Shalom, Y., Kirubarajan, T., and Li, X.-R. (2002), *Estimation with Applications to Tracking and Navigation*, John Wiley & Sons, Inc., New York.

Coon, J., Armour, S., Beach, M., and McGeehan, J. (2005), Adaptive frequency-domain equalization for single-carrier multiple-input multiple-output wireless transmissions, *IEEE Transactions on Signal Processing*, Vol. 53, No. 8, pp. 3247–3256.

Ganesan, G. and Stoica, P. (2001), Space-time block codes: a maximum SNR approach, *IEEE Transactions on Information Theory*, Vol. 47, No. 4, pp. 1650–1656.

Gharavi-Alkhansari, M. and Gershman, A. B. (2005), Constellation space invariance of space-time block codes, *IEEE Transactions on Information Theory*, Vol. 51, No. 1, pp. 331–334.

Haykin, S., Huber, K., and Chen, Z. (2004), Bayesian sequential state estimation for MIMOwireless communications, *Proceedings of the IEEE*, Vol. 92, No. 3, pp. 439–454.

Jakes Jr, W. (1974). *Microwave Moble Communication*. John Wiley & Sons, Inc., New York.

Larsson, E. G. and Stoica, P. (2003), *Space-time block coding for wireless communications*, Cambridge UniversityPress.

Liu, Z., Ma, X., and Giannakis, G. (2002), Space-time coding and Kalman filtering for time-selective fading channels, *IEEE Transactions on Communications*, Vol. 50, No. 2, pp. 183–186.

Schafhuber,D.,Matz, G., and Hlawatsch, F. (2003), Kalman tracking of time-varying channels in wireless MIMO-OFDM systems, *In Thirty-Seventh Asilomar Conference on Signals, Systems and Computers*, Vol. 2, pp. 1261–1265.

Shahbazpanahi, S., Gershman, A., and Manton, J. (2005), Closed-form blind MIMO channel estimation for orthogonal space-time block codes, *IEEE Transactions on Signal Processing*, Vol. 53, No. 12, pp. 4506–4517.

Tarokh, V., Jafarkhani, H., and Calderbank, A. (1999), Space-time block codes from orthogonal designs, *IEEE Transactions on Information Theory*, Vol. 45, No. 5, pp. 1456–1467.

Tsatsanis, M., Giannakis, G., and Zhou, G. (1996), Estimation and equalization of fading channels with random coefficients, *IEEE International Conference on Acoustics, Speech, and Signal Processing*, Vol. 2, pp. 1093–1096.

Wang, H. S. and Chang, P.-C. (1996), On verifying the first-order Markovian assumption for a Rayleigh fading channel model, *IEEE Transactions on Vehicular Technology,* Vol. 45, No. 2, pp. 353–357.

24

Kalman Filtering Based Motion Estimation for Video Coding

Assist. Prof. Nai-Chung Yang[1], Prof. Chaur Heh Hsieh[2]
and Prof. Chung Ming Kuo[1]
[1]Dept. of information Engineering, I-Shou University, Dahsu Kaohsiung, 840,
[2]Dept. of Computer and Communication Engineering, Ming Chuan University,
Gui-Shan, Taoyuan, 333,
Taiwan, R.O.C.

1. Introduction

Video compression is a very efficient method for storage and transmission of digital video signal. The applications include multimedia transmission, teleconferencing, videophone, high-definition television (HDTV), CD-ROM storages, etc. The hybrid coding techniques based on predictive and transform coding are the most popular and adopted by many video coding standards such as MPEG-1/2/4 [1] and H.261/H.263/H.264 [2, 3], owing to its high compression efficiency. In the hybrid coding system, the motion compensation, first proposed by Netravali and Robbins in 1997, plays a key role from the view point of coding efficiency and implementation cost [4-11]. A generic hybrid video coder is depicted in Figure 1.

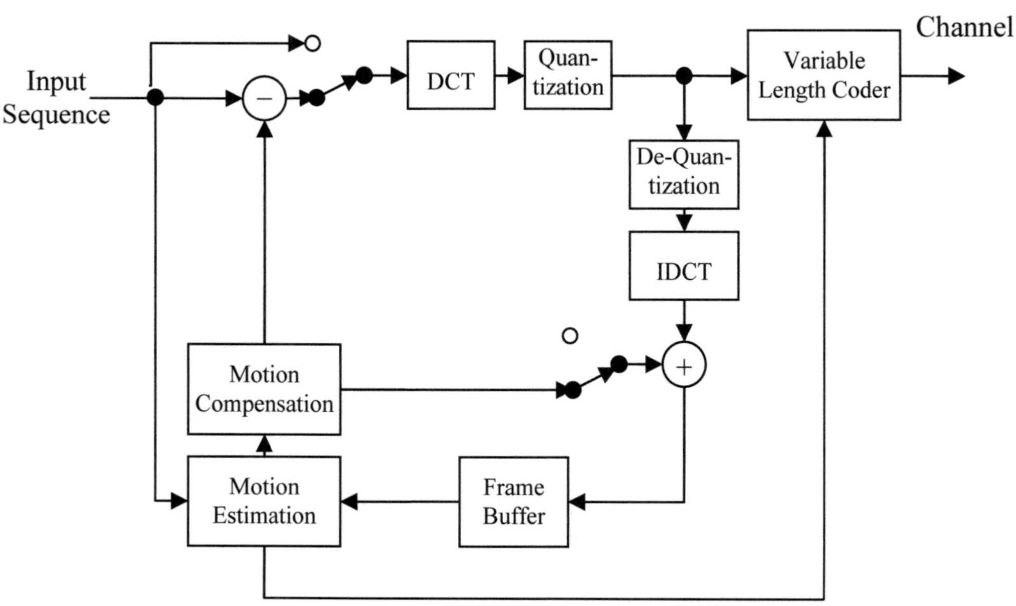

Fig. 1. A generic hybrid motion compensated DCT video coder.

The main idea of video compression to achieve compression is to remove spatial and temporal redundancies existing in video sequences. The temporal redundancy is usually removed by a motion compensated prediction scheme, whereas the spatial redundancy left in the prediction error is commonly reduced by a discrete cosine transform (DCT) coder. Motion compensated is a predictive technique in temporal direction, which compensates for the displacements of moving objects from the reference frame to the current frame. The displacement is obtained with the so-called motion vector estimation. Motion estimation obtains the motion compensated prediction by finding the motion vector (MV) between the reference frame and the current frame.

The most popular technique used for motion compensation (MC) is the block-matching algorithm (BMA) due to its simplicity and reasonable performance. In a typical BMA, the current frame of a video sequence is divided into non-overlapping square blocks of $N \times N$ pixels. For each reference block in the current frame, BMA searches for the best matched block within a search window of size $(2P+1)\times(2P+1)$ in the previous frame, where P stands for the maximum allowed displacement. Figure 2 depicts the basic principle of block matching.

In general, BMAs are affected by following factors: (i) search area, (ii) matching criterion, and (iii) searching scheme. The matching criterion is to measure the similarity between the block of the current frame and candidate block of the reference frame. Two typical matching criteria are mean square error (MSE) and mean absolute error (MAE), which are defined respectively as below:

$$MSE(u,v) = \frac{1}{N^2}\sum_{x=0}^{N-1}\sum_{y=0}^{N-1}\left[f(x,y,k) - f(x+u,y+v,k-1)\right]^2 \text{, for } u,v \in [-P,P]$$

$$MAE(u,v) = \frac{1}{N^2}\sum_{x=0}^{N-1}\sum_{y=0}^{N-1}\left|f(x,y,k) - f(x+u,y+v,k-1)\right| \text{, for } u,v \in [-P,P]$$

where $f(x,y,k)$ denotes the coordinate of the top left corner of the searching block of the current frame k, and (u,v) is the displacement of the matching block of frame $k-1$. The MAE is the most popular matching criterion due to its simplicity of hardware implementation.

The searching scheme is very important because it is significantly related to with the computational complexity and accuracy of motion estimation for general video applications. A straightforward way to obtain the motion vector is the full search algorithm (FSA), which searches all locations in the search window and selects the position with minimal matching error. However, its high computational complexity makes it often not suitable for real-time implementation. Therefore, many fast search algorithms have been developed to reduce the computational cost. In general, fast search algorithms reduce the computational burden by limiting the number of search locations or by sub-sampling the pixels of a block. However, they often converge to a local minimum, which leads to worse performance.

Most search algorithms estimate the motion vector (MV) for each block independently. In general moving scenes, it is very likely that a large homogeneous area in the picture frame will move in the same direction with similar velocities. Therefore, the displacements between neighboring blocks are highly correlated. Some schemes take advantage of this correlation to reduce the computational complexity [14-16].

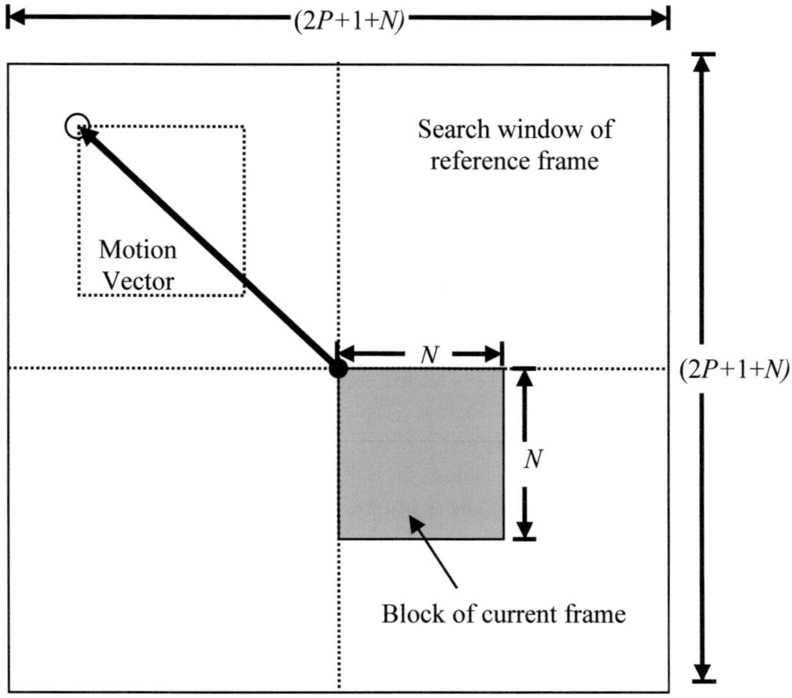

Fig. 2. Block matching algorithm.

There are two major problems for the existing fast search algorithms. One is that the estimation accuracy in terms of the energy or the entropy of the motion-compensated prediction error (MCPE) signal is worse than that of FSA. The other is that the true motion may not be obtained even with FSA, which is very important in some applications such as motion compensated interpolation and frame (field) rate conversion. Bierling [17] proposed a hierarchical search scheme to achieve a truer (smoother) motion vector field over FSA, but it results in a worse performance in terms of the energy of the MCPE signal.

The above two problems may arise from the following reasons [18]: (i) the basic assumptions, including pure translation, unchanged illumination in consecutive frames and noiseless environment, are not exactly correct; furthermore, another assumption that the occlusion of one object by another and uncovered background are neglected is also not exactly correct, (ii) the size of a moving object may not be equal to the prescribed block size, (iii) the fast search schemes often converge to a local optimum. In Section 2, we will introduce how to overcome these problems with a relatively low computational cost. We neither relax the above assumptions nor develop a globally optimal search scheme. Instead, we use the Kalman filter to compensate the incorrect and/or inaccurate estimates of motion. We first obtain a measurement of motion vector of a block by using a conventional fast search scheme. We then generate the predicted motion vector utilizing the motion correlation between spatial neighboring blocks. Based on the predicted and measured motion information, a Kalman filter is employed to obtain the optimal estimate of motion vector. In the new method, a local Kalman filter is developed, which is based on a novel motion model that exploits both spatial and temporal motion correlations. The proposed local Kalman filter successfully addresses the difficulty of multi-dimensional state space representation, and thus it is simpler and more computationally efficient than the conventional 2-D Kalman filter such as reduced update Kalman filter (RUKF) [19]. In addition, we will also introduce an adaptive scheme to further improve estimate accuracy while without sending extra side information to the decoder.

In low- or very low- bit rate applications such as videoconference and videophone, the percentage of MV bit rate increases when overall rate budget decreases. Thus, the coding of MVs takes up a significant portion of the bandwidth [20]. Then in very low bit rate compression, the motion compensation must consider the assigned MV rate simultaneously. A joint rate and distortion (R-D) optimal motion estimation has been developed to achieve the trade-off between MV coding and residue coding [20-28]. In [25], a global optimum R-D motion estimation scheme is developed. The scheme achieves significant improvement of performance, but it employs Viterbi algorithm for optimization, which is very complicated and results in a significant time delay. In [26], a local optimum R-D motion estimation criterion was presented. It effectively reduces the complexity at the cost of performance degradation.

In Section 3, we will introduce two Kalman filter-based methods to improve the conventional R-D motion estimation, which are referred to as enhanced algorithm and embedded algorithm, respectively. In the enhanced algorithm, the Kalman filter is employed as a post processing of MV, which extends the integer-pixel accuracy of MV to fractional-pixel accuracy, thus enhancing the performance of motion compensation. Because the Kalman filter exists in both encoder and decoder, the method achieves higher compensation quality without increasing the bit rate for MV.

In the embedded algorithm, the Kalman filter is applied directly during the process of optimization of motion estimation. Since the R-D motion estimation consider compensation error (distortion) and bit rate simultaneously, when Kalman filter is applied the distortion will be reduced, and thus lowering the cost function. Therefore, the embedded algorithm can improve distortion and bit rate simultaneously. Specifically, this approach can be combined with existing advanced motion estimation algorithms such as overlapped block motion compensation (OBMC) [29,30], and those recommended in H.264 or MPEG-4 AVC [31, 32].

2. Motion estimation with Kalman filter

2.1 Review of Kalman filter

The Kalman filtering algorithm estimates the states of a system from noisy measurement [33-36]. There are two major features in Kalman filter. One is its mathematical formulation is described in terms of state-space representation, and the other is that its solution is computed recursively. It consists of two consecutive stages: prediction and updating. We summarize the Kaman filter algorithm as follows:

$$\text{Predicted equation: } \mathbf{v}(k) = \mathbf{\Phi}(k-1)\mathbf{v}(k-1) + \mathbf{\Gamma}(k)\mathbf{w}(k), \tag{1}$$

$$\text{Measurement equation: } \mathbf{z}(k) = \mathbf{H}(k)\mathbf{v}(k) + \mathbf{n}(k), \tag{2}$$

where **v**(k) and **z**(k) are state and measurement vector at time k, and □H and □ are state transition, measurement and driving matrix, respectively. The model error **w**(k), with covariance matrix **Q**(k), and measurement error **n**(k), with covariance matrix **R**(k), are often assumed to be Gaussian white noises; we assume that **w**(k)~N(0,**Q**(k)), **n**(k)~N(0,**R**(k)) and E[**w**(k)**n**^{T}(l)]=0 for all k and l. Let $E[\mathbf{v}(0)] = \hat{\mathbf{v}}(0)$, and $E[(\mathbf{v}(0) - \hat{\mathbf{v}}(0))(\mathbf{v}(0) - \hat{\mathbf{v}}(0))^T] = \mathbf{P}(0)$ be initial values. The prediction and updating are given as follows.

Prediction:

$$\text{State prediction: } \hat{\mathbf{v}}^-(k) = \mathbf{\Phi}(k-1)\hat{\mathbf{v}}^+(k-1) \tag{3}$$

Prediction-error covariance:

$$\mathbf{P}^-(k) = \mathbf{\Phi}(k-1)\mathbf{P}^+(k-1)\mathbf{\Phi}^T(k-1) + \mathbf{\Gamma}(k)\mathbf{Q}(k-1)\mathbf{\Gamma}^T(k) \tag{4}$$

Updating:

$$\text{State updating: } \hat{\mathbf{v}}^+(k) = \hat{\mathbf{v}}^-(k) + \mathbf{K}(k)[\mathbf{z}(k) - \mathbf{H}(k)\hat{\mathbf{v}}^-(k)] \tag{5}$$

$$\text{Updating-error covariance: } \mathbf{P}^+(k) = [\mathbf{I} - \mathbf{K}(k)\mathbf{H}(k)]\mathbf{P}^-(k) \tag{6}$$

$$\text{Kalman gain matrix: } \mathbf{K}(k) = \mathbf{P}^-(k)\mathbf{H}(k)[\mathbf{H}(k)\mathbf{P}^-(k)\mathbf{H}^T(k) + \mathbf{R}(k)]^{-1} \tag{7}$$

The **P**(k) is the error covariance matrix that is associated with the state estimate **v**(k), and is defined as

$$\mathbf{P}(k) = E[(\mathbf{v}(k) - \hat{\mathbf{v}}(k))(\mathbf{v}(k) - \hat{\mathbf{v}}(k))^T]. \tag{8}$$

The superscripts "-" and "+" denote "before" and "after" measurement, respectively. The error covariance matrix **P**(k) provides a statistical measure of the uncertainty in **v**(k).

2.2 The overview of motion estimation with Kalman filter

In general, for moving scenes, the motion vectors among neighboring blocks are highly correlated. Therefore, the MV of the current block can be predicted from its neighboring blocks if an appropriate motion model is employed. Furthermore, any existing searching algorithms can be used to measure the MV. Using the predicted MV and the measured MV, a motion estimation method was developed, as depicted in Figure 3. The MV obtained with any conventional searching algorithm is defined as measurement, **z**(k). The measurement is then inputted to the Kalman filter and the updating estimate of MV could be obtained [37]. Because an identical Kalman filter will be used in the decoder, we can only send z(k), which is an integer, instead of $\hat{\mathbf{v}}(k)$, which is a real in general, to the receiver. By the same procedure, we can estimate $\hat{\mathbf{v}}(k)$ in the receiver, therefore we can achieve fractional-pixel accuracy with the bit rate of integer motion vector. In summary, there are two advantages for the new method: (i) it improves the performance of any conventional motion estimation due to the fractional-pixel accuracy; (ii) the transmitted bit rate for the motion vector is the same as that of the input integer motion vector, therefore, the new method is compatible with the current video coding standards.

In the following, we will first introduce a motion model that exploits both spatial and temporal motion correlations, and then a local Kalman filter is developed accordingly. The local Kalman filter is simpler and more computationally efficient than the conventional 2-D Kalman filter such as RUKF. Therefore, it is more suitable for the real-time applications [48-49]. In addition, to further improve the motion estimate accuracy, we also introduce an adaptive scheme. The scheme can automatically adjust the uncertainty of prediction and measurement; however, it needs not to send side information to the decoder.

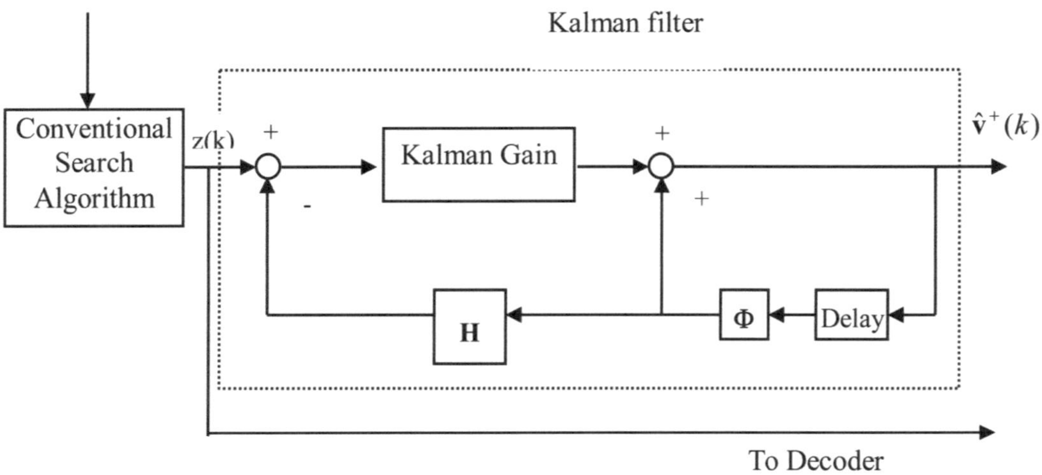

Fig. 3. Block diagram of motion estimation with Kalman filter

2.3 Motion estimation using Local Kalman Filter (LKF)

Let B(m,n,i) be the block at the location (m,n) in the ith frame, and $\mathbf{V}(m,n,i)=[v_x(m,n,i),v_y(m,n,i)]^T$ be the MV of B(m,n,i), where $v_x(m,n,i)$ and $v_y(m,n,i)$ denote the horizontal and vertical components, respectively. Assume that the MV is a random process, and the two components are independent. Then we can model these two components separately. In this work, we present a three-dimensional (3-D) AR model that exploits the relationship of motion vectors for only 3-D neighboring blocks that arrive at before the current block. We only choose the nearest neighboring blocks, in which the motion vectors are strongly correlated. We refer to this model as 3-D local model, which is expressed as

$$v_x(m,n,i)=\sum\sum\sum_{(k,l,p)\in S^{\oplus}} a_{klp}v_x(m-k,n-l,i-p)+w_x(m,n,i), \tag{9}$$

$$v_y(m,n,i)=\sum\sum\sum_{(k,l,p)\in S^{\oplus}} a_{klp}v_y(m-k,n-l,i-p)+w_y(m,n,i), \tag{10}$$

where $S^{\oplus}=\{l=0,k=1,p=0\}\cup\{l=1,|k|\le 1,p=0\}\cup\{|l|\le 1,|k|\le 1,p=1\}$. The support of the model mentioned above is depicted in Figure 4.

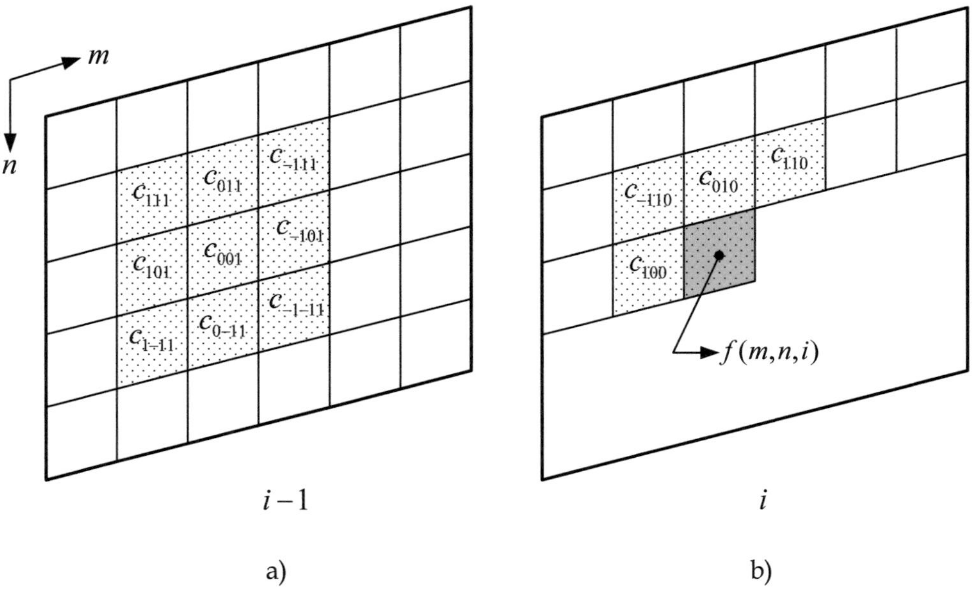

Fig. 4. Causal AR models for motion vector associated with spatial and temporal neighborhood system.

2.3.1 State space representation of MV model

For the fully state propagation, we must represent the proposed models of Eqs. (9) and (10) in a state space. This will yield a 13-dimensional state vector. The high-dimension state vector will result in a huge computation for estimating the motion vector. To attack the computation problem, we decompose the AR model into two parts: filtering and prediction. The prediction part will not affect the state propagation; thus it is considered as a deterministic input. Consequently, the state space representation can be formulated as

$$\mathbf{v}(m,n,i) = \Phi\mathbf{v}(m-1,n,i) + \Lambda\mathbf{u}(m,n,i) + \Gamma\mathbf{w}(m,n,i)\,, \tag{11}$$

$$\mathbf{z}(m,n,i) = \mathrm{H}\mathbf{v}(m,n,i) + \mathbf{e}(m,n,i)\,. \tag{12}$$

In the above equations, $\mathbf{v}(m,n,i)$ represents the state vector at the location (m,n,i); $\mathrm{u}(m,n,i)$ denotes a deterministic input; and $\mathbf{\Phi}$, $\mathbf{\Lambda}$, $\mathbf{\Gamma}$ and $\mathbf{H}$ are the corresponding matrices. In our work, the deterministic input is defined as the prediction part of the model, which will be used to implement the local Kalman filter (LKF). Since the motion estimation processes the block one by one according to the order of raster scan, the state propagation should be performed in one-dimensional manner, as depicted in Eq. (11).

The main idea in LKF is the approximation of the MV $\mathbf{v}(m,n,i)$, which can not be represented in terms of $\mathbf{v}(m\text{-}1,n,i)$. We will demonstrate the state space representation in Eqs. (13) and (14) as follows.

$$\mathbf{v}(m,n,i) = \Phi\mathbf{v}(m-1,n,i) + \Lambda\mathbf{u}(m,n,i) + \Gamma\mathbf{w}(m,n,i) \tag{13}$$

where

$$\mathbf{v}(m,n,i)=\begin{bmatrix} v(m,n,i) \\ v(m-1,n,i) \\ v(m+2,n-1,i) \\ v(m+1,n-1,i) \\ v(m,n-1,i) \\ v(m+1,n,i-1) \end{bmatrix},\ \mathbf{v}(m-1,n,i)=\begin{bmatrix} v(m-1,n,i) \\ v(m-2,n,i) \\ v(m-1,n-1,i) \\ v(m,n-1,i) \\ v(m-1,n,i) \\ v(m,n,i-1) \end{bmatrix},\ \mathbf{u}(m,n,i)=\begin{bmatrix} v(m+1,n-1,i-1) \\ v(m,n-1,i-1) \\ v(m-1,n-1,i-1) \\ v(m+1,n,i-1) \\ v(m-1,n,i-1) \\ v(m+1,n+1,i-1) \\ v(m,n+1,i-1) \\ v(m-1,n+1,i-1) \end{bmatrix},$$

$$\mathbf{w}(m,n,i)=\begin{bmatrix} w(m,n,i) \\ w(m+1,n,i-1) \end{bmatrix},$$

$$\mathbf{\Phi}=\begin{bmatrix} c_{100} & 0 & c_{-110} & c_{010} & c_{110} & c_{001} \\ 1 & 0 & 0 & 0 & 0 & 0 \\ 0 & 0 & 0 & 0 & 0 & 0 \\ 0 & 0 & 1 & 0 & 0 & 0 \\ 0 & 0 & 0 & 1 & 0 & 0 \\ 0 & 0 & 0 & 0 & 0 & 0 \end{bmatrix},\ \mathbf{\Lambda}=\begin{bmatrix} c_{-111} & c_{011} & c_{111} & c_{-101} & c_{101} & c_{-1-11} & c_{0-11} & c_{1-11} \\ 0 & 0 & 0 & 0 & 0 & 0 & 0 & 0 \\ 0 & 0 & 0 & 0 & 0 & 0 & 0 & 0 \\ 0 & 0 & 0 & 0 & 0 & 0 & 0 & 0 \\ 0 & 0 & 0 & 0 & 0 & 0 & 0 & 0 \\ 0 & 0 & 1 & 0 & 0 & 0 & 0 & 0 \end{bmatrix}$$

and $\mathbf{\Gamma}=\begin{bmatrix} 1 & 0 \\ 0 & 0 \\ 0 & 0 \\ 0 & 0 \\ 0 & 0 \\ 0 & 1 \end{bmatrix}$.

$$\mathbf{z}(m,n,i)=\mathbf{H}\mathbf{v}(m,n,i)+\mathbf{e}(m,n,i) \tag{14}$$

where $\mathbf{z}(m,n,i)=\begin{bmatrix} z(m,n,i) \\ z(m+2,n-1,i) \end{bmatrix}$, $\mathbf{H}=\begin{bmatrix} 1 & 0 & 0 & 0 & 0 & 0 \\ 0 & 0 & 1 & 0 & 0 & 0 \end{bmatrix}$ and $\mathbf{e}(m,n,i)=\begin{bmatrix} e(m,n,i) \\ e(m+2,n-1,i) \end{bmatrix}$.

The motion vector $\mathbf{v}(m,n,i)$, which can not be represented in terms of $\mathbf{v}(m\text{-}1,n,i)$, consists of two components: $v(m+2,n\text{-}1,i)$ and $v(m+1,n,i\text{-}1)$. We use the most recent estimate with uncertainty to approximate them, i.e.,

$$v(m+2,n-1,i)=\hat{v}(m+2,n-1,i)+e(m+2,n-1,i), \tag{15}$$

$$v(m+1,n,i-1)=\hat{v}(m+1,n,i-1)+w(m+1,n,i-1), \tag{16}$$

The above equations indicate that the best available estimate is the most recent update of the MV, which is available at time (m,n,i). The current frame MV, $v(m+2,n\text{-}1,i)$, is incorporated into measurement, and the previous frame MV, $v(m+1,n,i\ \text{-}1)$, is incorporated into deterministic input. In our work, the covariance of these two uncertainties is given a small

value for simplicity. Through the above process, the motion estimation with 3-D AR model can be realized by 1-D recursive manner.
Given these models, the Kalman filter is described in the following:
<1> Prediction

$$\text{State prediction: } \hat{\mathbf{v}}^{-}(m,n,i) = \Phi\hat{\mathbf{v}}^{+}(m-1,n,i) + \Lambda\mathbf{u}(m,n,i) \tag{17}$$

$$\text{Prediction-error covariance: } \mathbf{P}^{-}(m,n,i) = \Phi\mathbf{P}^{+}(m-1,n,i)\Phi^{T} + \Gamma\,\mathbf{Q}(m,n,i)\Gamma^{T} \tag{18}$$

<2> Updating:

$$\text{State updating: } \hat{\mathbf{v}}^{+}(m,n,i) = \hat{\mathbf{v}}^{-}(m,n,i) + \mathbf{K}(m,n,i)[\mathbf{z}(m,n,i) - \mathbf{H}\hat{\mathbf{v}}^{-}(m,n,i)] \tag{19}$$

$$\text{Updating-error covariance: } \mathbf{P}^{+}(m,n,i) = [\mathbf{I} - \mathbf{K}(m,n,i)\mathbf{H}]\mathbf{P}^{-}(m,n,i) \tag{20}$$

$$\text{Kalman gain matrix: } \mathbf{K}(m,n,i) = \mathbf{P}^{-}(m,n,i)\mathbf{H}^{T}[\mathbf{H}\mathbf{P}^{-}(m,n,i)\mathbf{H}^{T} + \mathbf{R}(m,n,i)]^{-1} \tag{21}$$

The $\mathbf{P}(m,n,i)$ is the error covariance matrix that is associated with the state estimate $\mathbf{v}(m,n,i)$, $\mathbf{R}(m,n,i)$ and $\mathbf{Q}(m,n,i)$ are the covariance of $\mathbf{e}(m,n,i)$ and $\mathbf{w}(m,n,i)$, respectively.
However, the local model can be simplified to consider only spatial or temporal support, and then the motion model and the corresponding state space representation are modified accordingly.

2.3.2 Spatial causal AR models for MV

Let $B(m,n,i)$ be the block at the location (m,n) in the ith frame, and $\mathbf{V}(m,n,i)=[v_x(m,n,i),v_y(m,n,i)]^T$ be the MV of $B(m,n,i)$, where $v_x(m,n,i)$ and $v_y(m,n,i)$ denote the horizontal and vertical components, respectively. Assume that the MV is a random process, and the two components are independent. A 2-D AR model exploits the motion information of only 2-D neighboring blocks that arrived before the current block. In the block matching, the calculation of matching criterion is performed block-by-block in a raster scan manner, i.e., from left to right and top to bottom. Thus we can define the 2-D AR model for a motion vector as

$$v_{i,x} = \sum\sum_{(k,l)\in S^{+}} a_{kl0} v_{i,x}(m-k,n-l,i) + w_{i,x}(m,n,i), \tag{22}$$

$$v_{i,y} = \sum\sum_{(k,l)\in S^{+}} a_{kl0} v_{i,y}(m-k,n-l,i) + w_{i,y}(m,n,i), \tag{23}$$

where $S^{+} = \{k \geq l,\ \forall l\} \cup \{k = 0,\ l \geq 1\}$ is the model support, and a_{kl0} are the model coefficients, which can be space varying or space invariant. For simplicity, we assume that the model is space invariant. Eq. (22) and (23) are also called the nonsymmetric half-plane (NSHP) model [19].
We only chose the nearest neighboring blocks in both horizontal and vertical direction because their motions are strongly correlated. We call this model as 2-D local motion model. In such case, Eq. (22) and (23) can be simplified as

$$v_{i,x}(m,n,i) = a_{100}v_{i,x}(m-1,n,i) + a_{-110}v_{i,x}(m+1,n-1,i) + a_{010}v_{i,x}(m,n-1,i) + a_{110}v_{i,x}(m-1,n-1,i) + w_{i,x}(m,n,i), \tag{24}$$

$$v_{i,y}(m,n,i) = a_{100}v_{i,y}(m-1,n,i) + a_{-110}v_{i,y}(m+1,n-1,i) + a_{010}v_{i,y}(m,n-1,i) + a_{110}v_{i,y}(m-1,n-1,i) + w_{i,y}(m,n,i). \tag{25}$$

The support of the model mentioned above is depicted in Figure 5.

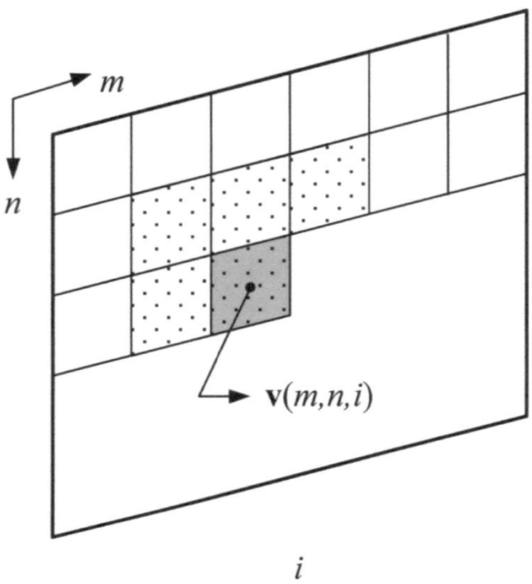

Fig. 5. Causal AR models for motion vector associated with spatial neighboring blocks.

2.3.3 State space representation of spatial local AR model

For the full state propagation, we must represent the proposed models, Eq. (11) and (12), in a state space. Since the Kalman filter is implemented by one-dimensional recursion, it is very difficult to transfer the two-dimensional AR model into one-dimensional state space representation [39,40]. To attack this problem, we introduce an extra deterministic input into the conventional state-space equations, and then we have the state-space representation as follows.

Predicted equation:

$$\mathbf{v}(m,n,i) = \Phi\mathbf{v}(m-1,n,i) + \Lambda\mathbf{u}(m,n,i) + \Gamma\mathbf{w}(m,n,i)\,, \tag{26}$$

where $\mathbf{v}(m,n,i)$ represents the state vector at the location (m,n,i); $\mathbf{u}(m,n,i)$ is the introduced deterministic input; and $\mathbf{\Phi}$, $\mathbf{\Lambda}$, $\mathbf{\Gamma}$ and $\mathbf{H}$ are the corresponding matrices. They are respectively defined as

$$\mathbf{v}(m,n,i)=\begin{bmatrix} v(m,n,i) \\ v(m-1,n,i) \\ v(m+2,n-1,i) \\ v(m+1,n-1,i) \\ v(m,n-1,i) \end{bmatrix},\ \mathbf{v}(m-1,n,i)=\begin{bmatrix} v(m-1,n,i) \\ v(m-2,n,i) \\ v(m+1,n-1,i) \\ v(m,n-1,i) \\ v(m-1,n-1,i) \end{bmatrix},$$

$$\mathbf{u}(m,n,i)=\hat{v}(m+2,n-1,i),\qquad \mathbf{w}(m,n)=\begin{bmatrix} w(m,n,i) \\ w(m+2,n-1,i) \end{bmatrix},$$

$$\mathbf{\Phi}=\begin{bmatrix} a_{100} & 0 & a_{-110} & a_{010} & a_{110} \\ 1 & 0 & 0 & 0 & 0 \\ 0 & 0 & 0 & 0 & 0 \\ 0 & 0 & 1 & 0 & 0 \\ 0 & 0 & 0 & 1 & 0 \end{bmatrix},\ \mathbf{\Lambda}=\begin{bmatrix} 0 \\ 0 \\ 1 \\ 0 \\ 0 \end{bmatrix},\text{ and } \mathbf{\Gamma}=\begin{bmatrix} 1 & 0 \\ 0 & 0 \\ 0 & 1 \\ 0 & 0 \\ 0 & 0 \end{bmatrix}.$$

Measurement equation:

$$z(m,n,i)=\mathbf{H}\ \mathbf{v}(m,n,i)+e(m,n,i), \tag{27}$$

where $\mathbf{H}=\begin{bmatrix}1 & 0 & 0 & 0 & 0\end{bmatrix}$.

Because the element $v(m+2,n\text{-}1,i)$ of the motion vector $\mathbf{v}(m,n,i)$ can not be written in terms of its previous state, here we use the most recent estimate to approximate it, i.e.,

$$v(m+2,n-1,i)=\hat{v}(m+2,n-1,i)+w(m+2,n-1,i). \tag{28}$$

The above equations indicate that the best available estimate is the most recent update of the MV, which is available at time (m,n,i). Through the above process, the motion estimation based on 2-D AR model can be realized by 1-D recursive manner.

2.3.4 Temporal causal AR models for MV

Using the similar definition of the above spatial model, the AR models in the temporal direction are defined as

$$v_x(m,n,i)=\sum\sum\sum_{(k,l,p)\in S^{\oplus}} a_{klp} v_x(m-k,n-l,i-p)+w_x(m,n,i), \tag{29}$$

$$v_y(m,n,i)=\sum\sum\sum_{(k,l,p)\in S^{\oplus}} a_{klp} v_y(m-k,n-l,i-p)+w_y(m,n,i), \tag{30}$$

where $S^{\oplus}=\{|l|\le 1,\ |k|\le 1,\ p=1\}$. Like the spatial local model, only the adjacent neighboring blocks are considered as model support, as shown in Figure 6. In such case, the state-space representation of Eq. (29) and (30) are

Predicted equation:

$$v(m,n,i) = a_{001}v(m,n,i-1) + \Lambda \begin{bmatrix} v(m+1,n-1,i-1) \\ v(m,n-1,i-1) \\ v(m-1,n-1,i-1) \\ v(m+1,n,i-1) \\ v(m-1,n,i-1) \\ v(m+1,n+1,i-1) \\ v(m,n+1,i-1) \\ v(m-1,n+1,i-1) \end{bmatrix} + w(m,n,i), \tag{31}$$

where $\Lambda = [a_{-111} \quad a_{011} \quad a_{111} \quad a_{-101} \quad a_{101} \quad a_{-1-11} \quad a_{0-11} \quad a_{1-11}]$.

Measurement equation:

$$z(m,n,i) = v(m,n,i) + e(m,n,i). \tag{32}$$

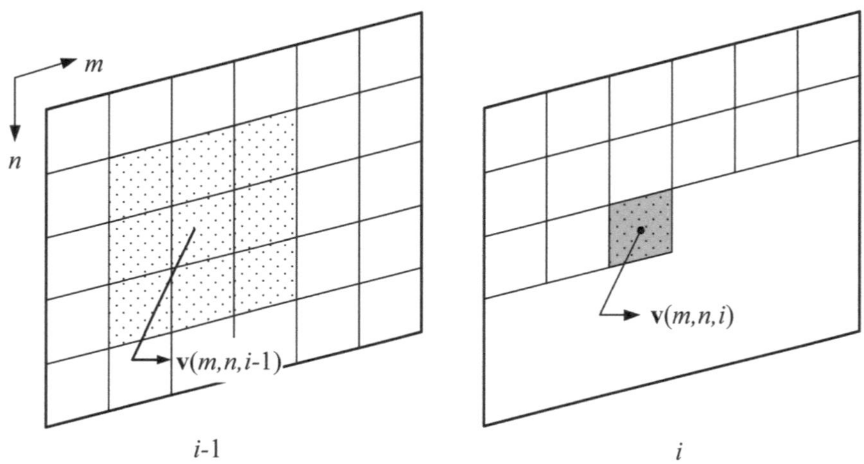

Fig. 6. Causal AR models for motion vector associated with temporal neighboring blocks.

Once the motion models and their state space representation are available, same procedure can then be obtained as in Section 2.3.1.

2.4 Adaptive Kalman filtering

In general, the motion correlation between the adjacent blocks cannot be modeled exactly. Similarly, the measurement of motion vector may have error due to incorrect, inaccurate and low precision estimation algorithms. Therefore, there exist uncertainties in both prediction and measurement processes. The uncertainties of prediction and measurement are represented by zero mean white Gaussian noise $\mathbf{w}(m,n,i)$ and $\mathbf{e}(m,n,i)$ with variance $\mathbf{q}(m,n,i)$ and $\mathbf{r}(m,n,i)$, respectively. In Kalman filtering algorithm, the Kalman gain depends on $\mathbf{q}(m,n,i)$ and $\mathbf{r}(m,n,i)$; therefore, the variances will determine the relative amount of updating using prediction or measurement information [41]. Due to the nonstationary nature of motion vector fields, the values of the variances $\mathbf{q}(m,n,i)$ and $\mathbf{r}(m,n,i)$ should be adjusted block by block to achieve better performance.

In [37], we introduced a distortion function, D_1 and D_2, to measure the uncertainty for both prediction and measurement, and use the distortion function as a reliability criterion. Based on such concept, we calculate the covariance $\mathbf{q}(m,n,i)$ and $\mathbf{r}(m,n,i)$ that are closely related to D_1 and D_2, and then obtain a time-varying Kalman gain. This results in more reliable estimate of MV. The idea behind the procedure is that we use the actual distortion of prediction and measurement to adjust the covariance instead of the conventional complex statistical on-line approaches [37]. Because the distortion measured is more trustworthy than any assumption, the developed scheme achieves very good performance as demonstrated in [37]. The major disadvantages of the scheme are: (i) it needs to send extra side-information, (ii) it increases the overall bit rate, and (iii) the bit stream may be not compatible with the current video coding standard. To overcome this problem, we will introduce an adaptive scheme, which is simpler and more effective than the previous schemes and it does not need to send extra side-information.

We first calculate the errors compensated by predicted MV and measured MV. And then investigate the relation between the difference of the two errors, Δd, and the difference of two motion vectors, ΔMV. Let D_1 and D_2 be the block distortion of motion compensation due to the measurement error and prediction error, respectively, which are defined as

$$\begin{aligned} D_1 &= \frac{1}{M \times N} \sum_{j=0}^{N-1} \sum_{l=0}^{N-1} \left| B(m+j, n+l, i) - \tilde{B}(m+j+z(m,n,i), n+l+z(m,n,i), i-1) \right|, \\ &= MAD(z_x, z_y) \end{aligned} \tag{33}$$

and

$$\begin{aligned} D_2 &= \frac{1}{M \times N} \sum_{j=0}^{N-1} \sum_{l=0}^{N-1} \left| B(m+j, n+l, i) - \tilde{B}(m+j+\hat{v}_x^-(m,n,i), n+l+\hat{v}_y^-(m,n,i), i-1) \right|, \\ &= MAD(\hat{v}_x^-, \hat{v}_y^-) \end{aligned} \tag{34}$$

where B_i and B_{i-1} are the current block and motion compensated block, respectively. The Δd is defined as

$$\Delta d = |\, D_1 - D_2 \,|. \tag{35}$$

When ΔMV increases, Δd first increased approximately exponentially, and then decreased exponentially; the increasing rate is larger than the decreasing rate. In general, the measurement is obtained by a real matching; thus a large ΔMV means that the prediction is far away from optimal location. This results in a large value of Δd. However, when ΔMV exceeds a certain value, the measurement may find incorrect position due to the restrictions of block matching, such as cover/uncover-background, complex motion types, etc. Hence Δd will decrease gradually according to the increase of ΔMV. Therefore, we can use two exponential functions to model the variance of prediction as:

$$q(m,n,i) = \begin{cases} 1 - a_1 \exp(-b_1 \|\mathbf{z}(m,n,i) - \hat{\mathbf{v}}^-(m,n,i)\|), & \|\mathbf{z} - \hat{\mathbf{v}}^-\| \le th \\ a_2 \exp(-b_2 (\|\mathbf{z}(m,n,i) - \hat{\mathbf{v}}^-(m,n,i)\| - th)), & \|\mathbf{z} - \hat{\mathbf{v}}^-\| > th \end{cases} \tag{36}$$

$$r(m,n,i) = 1 - q(m,n,i), \tag{37}$$

where *th* is the turning point, which is a reliable index of measurement. If ΔMV is less than *th,* the measurement is reliable compared with prediction. However, when ΔMV is far away from *th,* the measurement is less reliable and the prediction should give more contribution. The parameters a and b affect the shape of the exponential function and are related with searching methods. The parameter values for full search are larger than those for fast search. Because the prediction can be calculated in the receiver, no extra-information needs to be sent. Therefore, this method is also suitable for real-time application.

2.5 Simulation results

Several image sequences including "Miss America", "Salesman", "Flower Garden" and "Susie" are evaluated to compare the performances of different motion estimation algorithms. The first two sequences are typical videoconference situations. In order to create larger motion displacement, each of the two sequences is reduced to 15 Hz with frame skipping. The last two sequences contain more complex motion such as rotation, and covered/uncovered background. They are converted from CCIR 601 format using the decimation filters recommended by the ISO/MPEG standard committee. The 30 successive frames of each sequence are used in simulation.

Four different algorithms are compared: (i) full search algorithm (FSA), (ii) new three-step algorithm (NTSS), (iii) NTSS combined with 3-D Kalman filter (3DLKF), and (iv) NTSS combined with adaptive Kalman filter (3DALKF). The size of the image block is 16×16. The search window is 15×15 pixels (i.e., S = 7) for “Miss America”, “Salesman” and “Susie”, 31×31(S = 15) for “Flower Garden”. The threshold for the motion detection is 2 for each algorithm. The model parameters are obtained by off-line least-squared estimate. In our work, the parameters are given by $c_{100}=7/C$, $c_{-110}=2/C$, $c_{010}=7/C$, $c_{110}=2/C$, $c_{001}=5/C$, $c_{-111}=0.25/C$, $c_{011}=0.5/C$, $c_{111}=0.25/C$, $c_{-101}=0.5/C$, $c_{101}=0.5/C$, $c_{-1-11}=0.25/C$, $c_{0-11}=0.5/C$, and $c_{1-11}=0.25/C$. Where C is a normalization factor, and C=26 in our simulation. For non-adaptive algorithm, the covariance of $\mathbf{w}(m,n,i)$ and $\mathbf{e}(m,n,i)$ should be given *a priori*. In this work, the $q(m+2,n\text{-}1,i)$ and $r(m+1,n,i\text{-}1)$ are 0.095, $q(m,n,i)$ and $r(m,n,i)$ are 0.85 and 0.15, respectively. In the adaptive algorithm, $q(m,n,i)$ and $r(m,n,i)$ are adjusted automatically, the parameters a, b and th are set as a_1=0.55, a_2=1.10, b_1=0.985, b_2=0.009 and th=5.8 for "Flower Garden", a_1=1.10, a_2=0.98, b_1=0.735, b_2=0.008 and th=4.2 for others sequences. The value is obtained experimentally. The $q(m+2,n\text{-}1,i)$ and $r(m+1,n,i\text{-}1)$ are the same as the non-adaptive algorithm.

The motion-compensated prediction frame is obtained by displacing the previous reconstructed blocks using the estimated motion vectors. Since the estimated motion vector is a real value instead of an integer, the displaced pixels may not be on the sampling grid. Therefore, the well-known bilinear interpolation [17] is adopted to generate a motion compensated prediction frame.

Table 1 summarizes the comparison of the average PSNRs for various algorithms. It indicates that all our algorithms perform better than NTSS. The 3DLKF also obtains better performance than FSA on the average. It is noted that the 3DLKF needs few additional computations over NTSS. The 3DALKF give much better PSNR performance than FSA.

Figures 7-10 displays the comparison of PSNR of the test sequences obtained by various algorithms. It indicates that the proposed method improves the performance. The most important point to note is that the adaptive algorithm can compensate poor measurement and thereby raise the PSNR significantly. In addition, the visual quality of the reconstructed image is also improved considerably. This can be seen from Figure 11, which shows the reconstructed images of frame 74 obtained by NTSS and 3DALKF, respectively. The NTSS algorithm yields the obvious distortion on some regions such as the left ear and the mouth, as shown in Figure 11 (a). The 3DLKF algorithm, as shown in Figure 11 (c), improves this significantly.

Image Sequence	Algorithm			
	NTSS	FSA	3DLKF	3DALKF
Miss America	38.2581	38.3956	38.6473	38.9077
Salesmen	34.6905	34.7827	34.9477	35.1080
Susie	37.8381	37.8742	38.2893	38.5298
Flower Garden	28.2516	28.4485	28.3836	28.5340
Average	34.7596	34.8753	35.067	35.2699

Table 1. Average PSNR for various algorithms

Figure 12 shows the motion vector fields of "Miss America" obtained by FSA, NTSS and 3DALKF, respectively. The motion vector fields obtained by 3DLKF algorithm are obviously smoother than those by the other algorithms. Although the hierarchical search algorithm presented in [17] can also achieve smooth motion vector fields, it obtains lower PSNR than FSA.

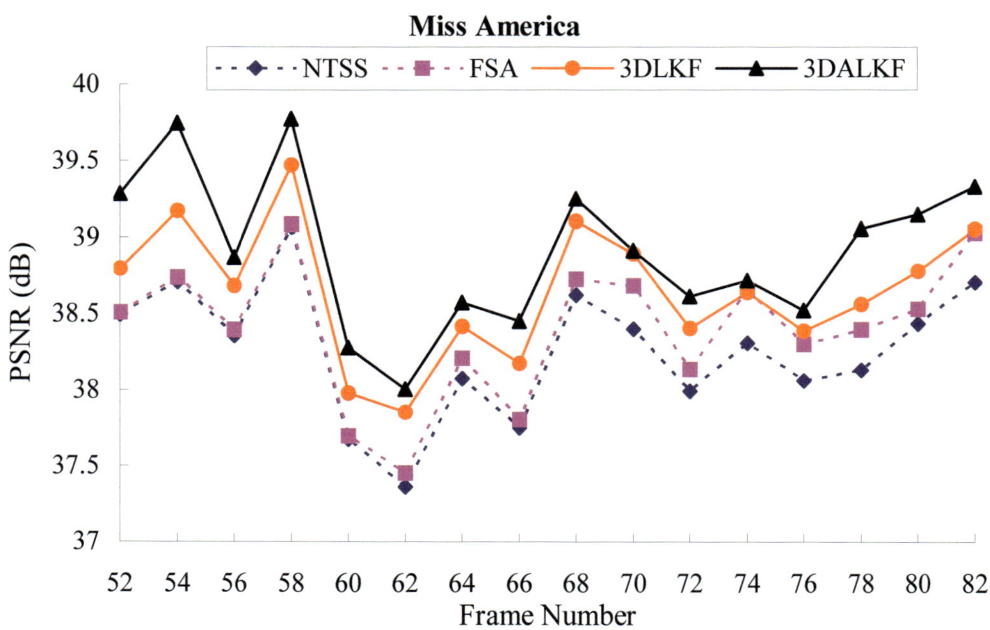

Fig. 7. The PSNR comparison for Miss America sequence at 15Hz

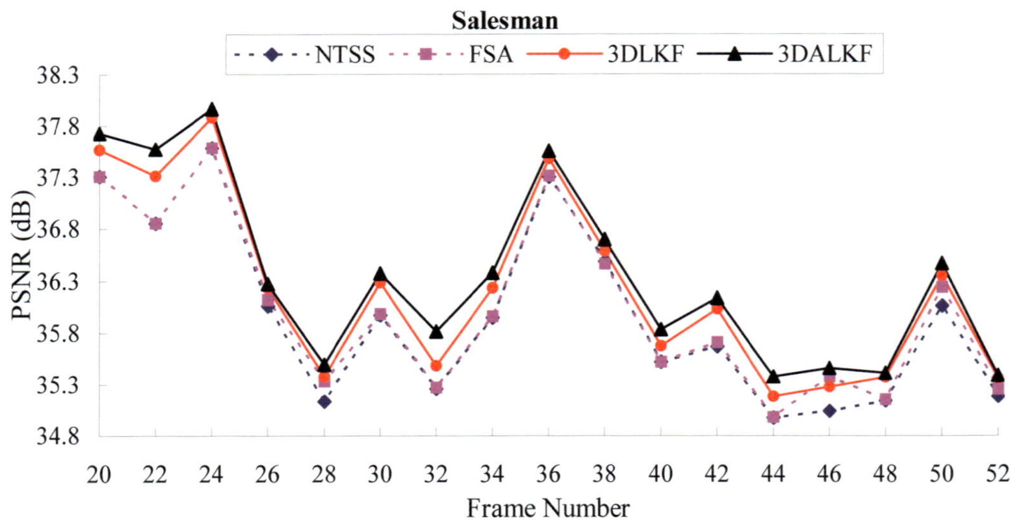

Fig. 8. The PSNR comparison for Salesman sequence at 15Hz

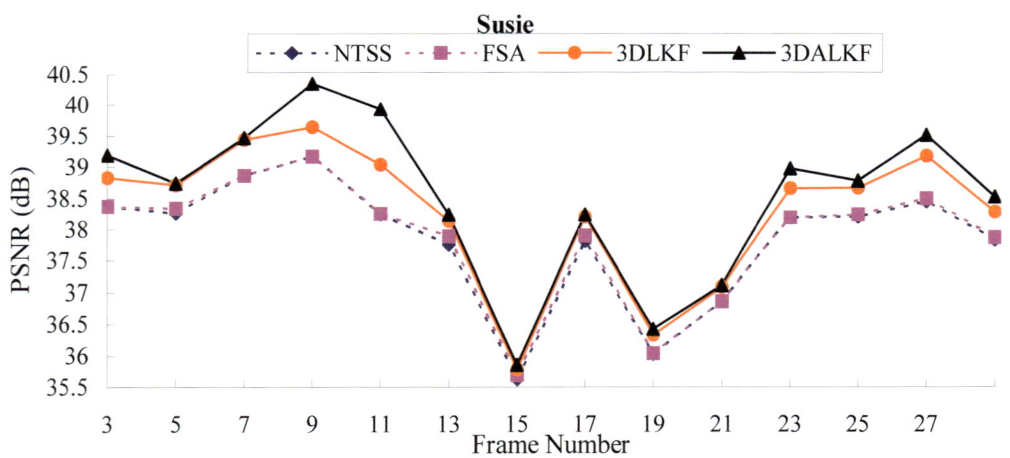

Fig. 9. The PSNR comparison for Susie sequence at 15Hz

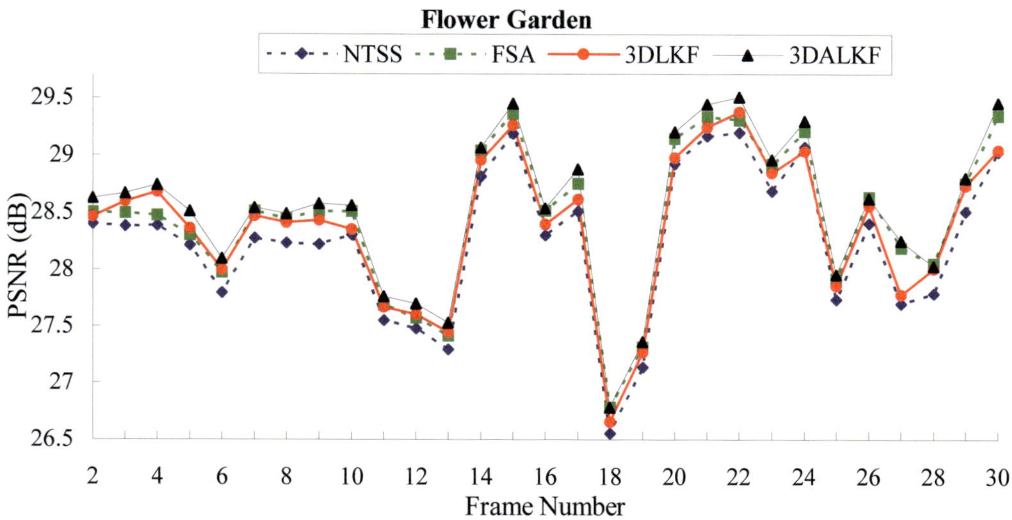

Fig. 10. The PSNR comparison for Flower Garden sequence at 30Hz

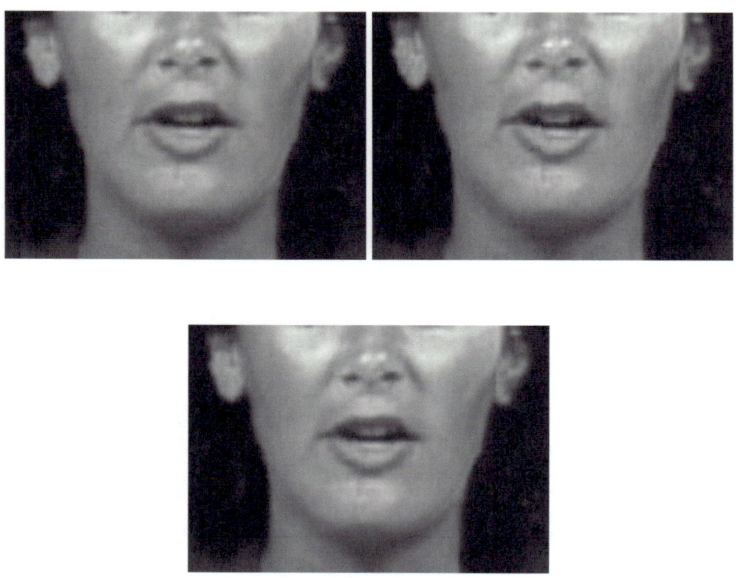

Fig. 11. The comparison of reconstructed image (a) Original image (b) NTSS and (c) 3DALKF.

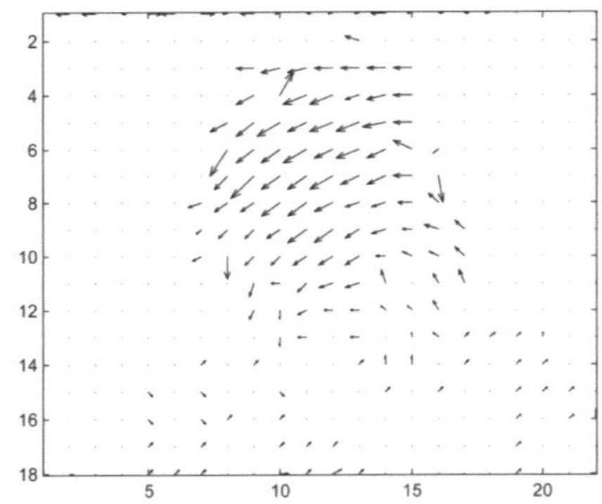

(a) FAS

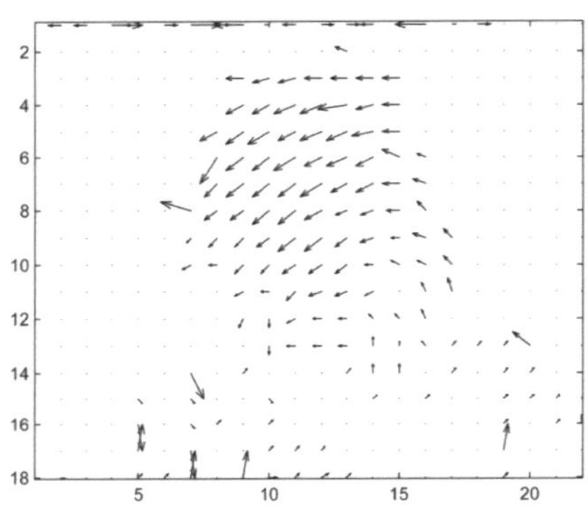

(b) NTSS

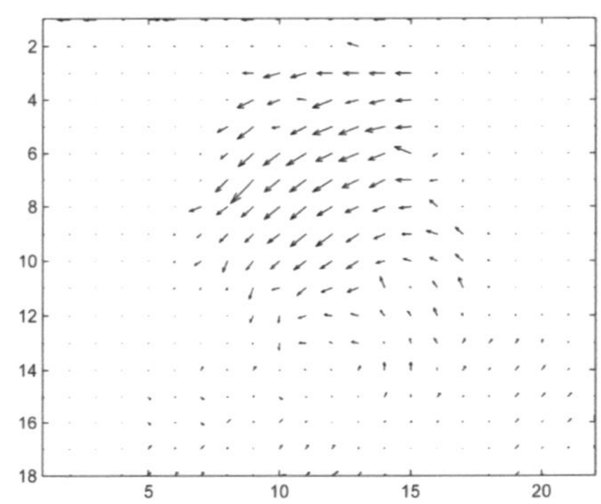

(c) 3DALKF

Fig. 12. The motion vector fields obtained by (a) FSA, (b) NTSS (c) 3DALKF

In the proposed methods, the 3DALKF is the most computationally expensive scheme. The computation time for FSA, NTSS, and 3DALKF are listed in Table 2. It is obvious that the computation time of the KF methods are only about 2/5 of the FSA, and is slightly more than that of NTSS. Thus it is suitable for real-time application.

Image Sequence	Computation time (second/frame)			
	NTSS	FSA	3DLKF	3DALKF
Miss America	1.0881	6.4162	2.4000	2.6950
Salesmen	0.5559	3.1694	1.5559	1.8147
Susie	0.9846	7.0262	2.0477	2.2954
Flower Garden	1.5017	44.3021	2.5297	2.8367
Average	1.0326	15.2285	2.1333	2.4105

Table 2. The computation time for various algorithms

3. Rate-constrained motion estimation with Kalman filter

In BMA, the motion compensated prediction difference blocks (called residue blocks) and the motion vectors are encoded and sent to the decoder. In high-quality applications, the bit rate for motion vectors, R_{mv}, is much less than that for residues, R_{res}; thus R_{mv} can be neglected in motion vector estimation. However, in low- or very low- bit rate applications such as videoconference and videophone, the percentage of motion vector bit rate is increased when overall rate budget decreases. Thus, the coding of motion vectors takes up a significant portion of the bandwidth [20]. Then in very low bit rate compression, the motion compensation must consider the assigned motion vector rate and residue rate simultaneously, which yields the so-called rate-constrained motion estimation. In this section, we will present two Kalman filtering based rate-constrained motion estimation algorithms.

3.1 Rate-distortion motion estimation

In conventional motion estimation, a major consideration is to reduce the motion compensated prediction error such that the coding rate for the prediction error can be reduced. This is true for high-rate applications because the bit rate for motion vector (R_{mv}) is only a very small part of the overall transmission rates. However, in low bit-rate or very low bit-rate situation, R_{mv} is a significant part of the available rate budget. For this reason, R_{mv} should be considered into the process of motion estimation. Therefore, the criterion of motion estimation must be modified accordingly.
In 1994, Bernd Girod addressed this problem first. He proposed a theoretical framework for rate-constrained motion estimation, and a new region based motion estimation scheme [22]. In motion compensated hybrid coding, the bit-rate can be divided into the displacement vector field, the prediction error, and additional side information. Very accurate motion compensation is not the key to achieve a better picture quality at low or very low bit-rates.
In 1998, Chen and Willson confirmed this point again [25], and analyzed this issue thoroughly. They explained a new estimation criterion in detail, and proposed a rate-constrained motion estimation for general video coding system. The performance of video compression depends on not only the motion compensation but also the rate budget, which include bit-rate for motion vector and bit-rate for prediction error. Therefore, the optimal solution can then be searched throughout the convex hull of all possible R-D pairs by minimizing the total Lagrangian cost function:

$$J_{\min}(\vec{v},q,\lambda) = \min_{D\in S^k, q\in Q^k} \sum_{k=1}^{K} D_k(\vec{v}_{k,}q_k) + \lambda\left[R_k^{mv}(\vec{v}) + R_k^{res}(\vec{v},q)\right], \tag{38}$$

where Q^K is the quantization parameter for K blocks, respectively. This approach, however, is computationally intensive, involving a joint optimization between motion estimation/ compensation and prediction residual coding schemes. From Eq. (38), we see that the DCT and quantization operations must be performed on an MV candidate basis in order to obtain $R_k^{res}(\vec{v},q)$ and $D_k(\vec{v}_k,q_k)$. The significant computations make the scheme unacceptable for most practical applications, no matter what software or hardware implementation is adopted. Thus, they simplify Eq. (38) by only considering motion estimation error and bit-rate for MV.

Assume a frame is partitioned into K block sets. Let $\hat{v}_k \in U^K$ be the motion vector estimated for block k. Then the motion field of a frame is described by the K_1-tuple vector, $V = \left(\hat{v}_1, \hat{v}_2, \ldots \hat{v}_{K_1}\right) \in U^K$. The joint rate and distortion optimization can be interpreted as finding a motion vector field that minimizes the distortion under a given rate constraint, which can be formulated by the Lagrange multiplier method as

$$J_{\min}(v, \lambda) = \sum_{U^k} \min_{V \in U^k} \{ \sum_{k=1}^{K} D_k(\hat{v}_k) + \lambda R_k(\hat{v}_k) \} , \tag{39}$$

where λ is the Lagrange multiplier; D_k and R_k are the motion-compensated distortion and the number of bits associated with motion vector of the block k, respectively. In most video coding standards, the motion vectors of blocks are differentially coded using Huffman code. Thus, the blocks are coded dependently. However, this simplification has two evident defects: (i) it is still too complex, and (ii) the performance is degraded.

In the same year, Coban and Merserau proposed different scheme on the RD-optimal problem [26]. They think that Eq. (39) is a principle for global optimal of R-D problem, but it is difficult in implementation. They supposed, if each block is coded independently, the solution Eq. (39) can be reduced to minimizing the Lagrangian cost function of each block, i.e.,

$$J_{\min}(v, \lambda) = \min_{V \in U^k} \{ D_k(\hat{v}_k) + \lambda R_k(\hat{v}_k) \} . \tag{40}$$

In order to simplify the problem, although the MV's are coded differentially, the blocks will be treated as if they are being coded independently. This will lead to a locally optimal, globally sub-optimal solution. By this way, the framework of R-D optimal motion estimation is close to conventional motion estimation. Although it saves computation by ignoring the relation of blocks, it reduces the overall performance.

3.2 Enhanced R-D motion estimation using Kalman filter

The R-D motion estimation often yields smooth motion vector fields, as compared with conventional BMAs [25,26]. In other words, the resulting motion vectors are highly correlated. In this work, we try to fully exploit the correlation of motion vectors by using the Kalman filter. This is motivated by our previous works [37,40] that the Kalman filter is combined with the conventional BMA's to improve the estimate accuracy of motion vectors. The system consists of two cascaded stages: measurement of motion vector and Kalman filtering. We can employ a R-D fast search scheme [20,23-26] to obtain the measured motion vector. Then we model the motion vectors and generate the predicted motion vector utilizing the inter-block correlation. Based on the measured and predicted motion vectors, a Kalman filter is applied to obtain an optimal estimate of motion vector.

For the sake of simplicity in implementation, we employ the first-order AR (autoregressive) model to characterize the motion vector correlation. The motion vector of the block at location (m,n) of the i-th frame is denoted by $\mathrm{v}_i(m,n) = [v_{i,x}(m,n), v_{i,y}(m,n)]$, and its two components in horizontal and vertical directions are modeled as

$$v_{i,x}(m,n) = a_1 v_{i,x}(m,n-1) + w_{i,x}(m,n) \tag{41}$$

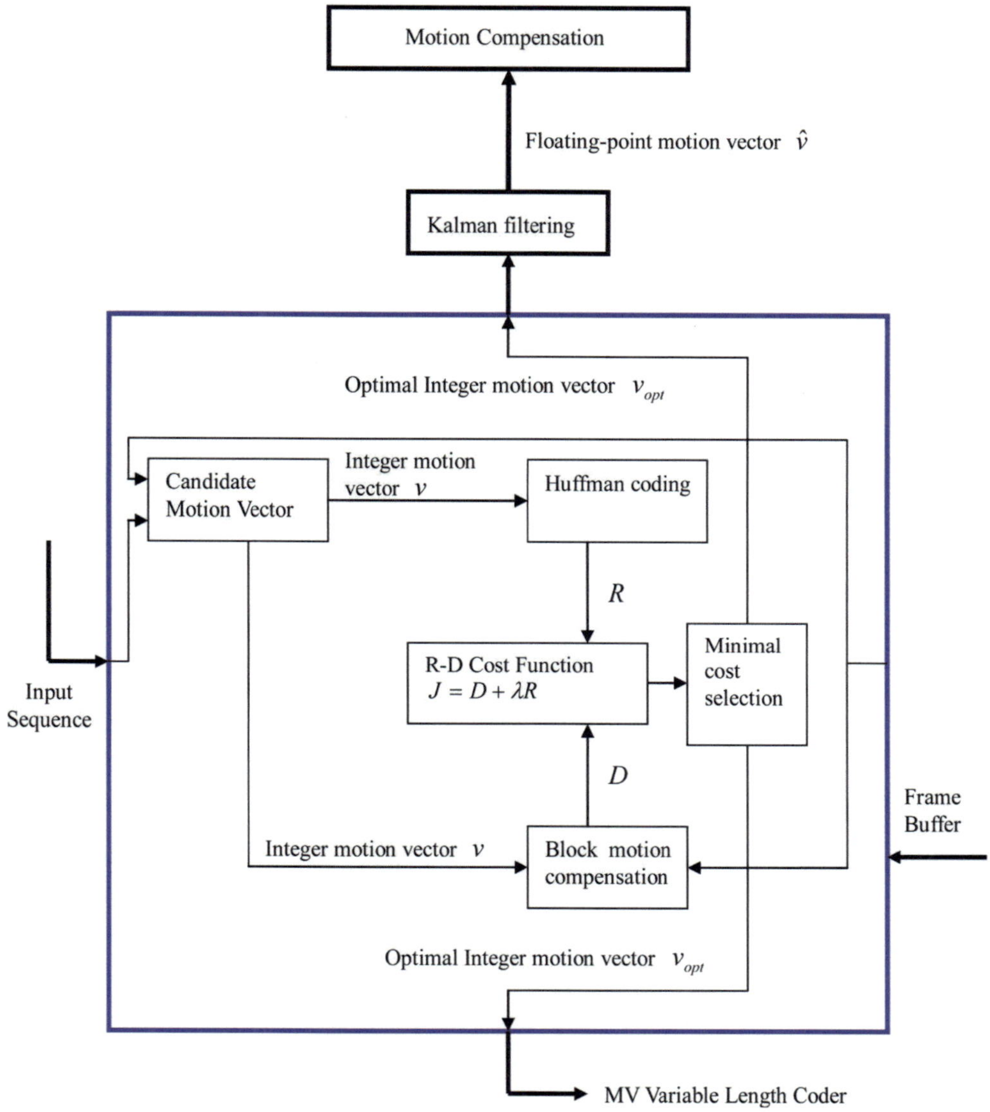

Fig. 13. The block diagram of the proposed enhanced R-D motion estimation algorithm

$$v_{i,y}(m,n) = b_1 v_{i,y}(m,n-1) + w_{i,y}(m,n). \tag{42}$$

where $w_{i,x}(m,n)$ and $w_{i,y}(m,n)$ represent the model error components. In order to derive the state-space representation, the time indexes k and $k-1$ are used to represent the current block location (m,n), and the left-neighbor block location $(m-1,n)$, respectively. Consequently, the state-space representation of (41) and (42) are

$$\begin{bmatrix} x_1(k) \\ x_2(k) \end{bmatrix} = \begin{bmatrix} a_1 & 0 \\ 0 & b_1 \end{bmatrix} \begin{bmatrix} x_1(k-1) \\ x_2(k-1) \end{bmatrix} + \begin{bmatrix} w_{i,x}(k) \\ w_{i,y}(k) \end{bmatrix}, \tag{43}$$

or

$$\mathbf{V}_x(k) = \mathbf{\Phi}_x(k-1)\mathbf{V}_x(k-1) + \mathbf{\Gamma}(k)\mathbf{w}_x(k), \tag{44}$$

where we let $x_1(k) = v_{i,x}(k)$, $x_1(k-1) = v_{i,x}(k-1)$, $x_2(k) = v_{i,y}(k)$ and $x_2(k-1) = v_{i,y}(k-1)$. The error components, $w_{i,x}(k)$ and $w_{i,y}(k)$, are assumed to be Gaussian distribution with zero mean and the same variance $q(k)$.
The measurement equations for the horizontal and vertical directions are expressed by

$$\mathbf{z}(k) = \begin{bmatrix} 1 & 0 \\ 0 & 1 \end{bmatrix} \begin{bmatrix} x_1(k) \\ x_2(k) \end{bmatrix} + \begin{bmatrix} n_x(k) \\ n_y(k) \end{bmatrix}$$

$$= \mathbf{H}(k)\mathbf{V}_\mathbf{x}(k) + \mathbf{n}_x(k), \tag{45}$$

where $n_x(k)$, $n_y(k)$ denote two measurement error components with the same variance $r(k)$.
In general, the model error $\mathbf{W}(k)$ and measurement error $\mathbf{n}(k)$ may have colored noises. We can model each colored noise by a low-order difference equation that is excited by white Gaussian noise, and augment the states associated colored noise models to the original state space representation. Finally, we apply the recursive filter to the augmented system. However, the procedure requires considerable computational complexity and is not suitable for our application. Moreover, the blocks are processed independently when the measurements are obtained by the R-D fast search algorithm [26]. Thus, we can assume that the measurement error is independent. For simplicity but without loss of generality, the prediction error and measurement error are assumed to be zero-mean Gaussian distribution with the same variances $q(k)$ and $r(k)$, respectively.

In the above equations, the measurement matrix $\mathbf{H}(k)$ is constant, and state transition matrix $\mathbf{\Phi}(k)$ can be estimated by the least square method. Since the motion field for low bit-rate applications is rather smooth, we assume that $q(k)$ and $r(k)$ are fixed values.

The algorithm is summarized as follows.
<Step 1> Measure motion vector
Measure the motion vector of a moving block, $\mathbf{z}(k) = [z_x(k) \quad z_y(k)]^T$, by any R-D search algorithms [20][23]-[26]. Encode the motion vector by H.263 Huffman table [7][9].
<Step 2> Kalman filtering

a. The predicted motion vector is obtained by

$$\hat{\mathbf{V}}^-(k) = \mathbf{\Phi}(k-1)\hat{\mathbf{V}}^+(k-1).$$

b. Calculate prediction-error covariance by

$$\mathbf{P}^-(k) = \mathbf{\Phi}(k-1)\mathbf{P}^+(k-1)\mathbf{\Phi}^T(k-1) + \mathbf{\Gamma}(k)\mathbf{Q}(k)\mathbf{\Gamma}^T(k).$$

c. Obtain Kalman gain by

$$\mathbf{K}(k) = \mathbf{P}^-(k)\mathbf{H}^T(k)[\mathbf{H}(k)\mathbf{P}^-(k)\mathbf{H}^T(k) + \mathbf{R}(k)]^{-1}.$$

d. The motion vector estimate is updated by

$$\hat{\mathbf{V}}^{+}(k) = \hat{\mathbf{V}}^{-}(k) + \mathbf{K}(k)[\mathbf{z}(k) - \mathbf{H}(k)\hat{\mathbf{V}}^{-}(k)] .$$

This is the final estimate output.

e. Calculate the filtering-error covariance by

$$\mathbf{P}^{+}(k) = [\mathrm{I} - \mathbf{K}(k)\mathbf{H}(k)]\mathbf{P}^{-}(k) .$$

<Step 3> Go to <step 1> for next block.

In the above algorithm, the optimal estimate $\hat{\mathrm{V}}(k)$ is usually real, which yields fractional-pixel accuracy estimate. The conventional BMA can also obtain the fractional-pixel motion vector by increasing resolution with interpolation and matching higher-resolution data on the new sampling grid. However, this not only increases computational complexity significantly, but also raises overhead bit rate for motion vector. On the contrast, the required computational overhead is much lower than that of the conventional BMA with fractional-pixel matching. In addition, using the same Kalman filter as in the encoder, the decoder can estimate the fractional part of motion vector by receiving integer motion vector. In summary, this method achieves fractional pixel performance with the same bit-rate for motion vector as an integer-search BMA, at the cost of a small increase of computational load at the decoder. Furthermore, because the Kalman filter is independent with motion estimation, it can be combined with any existing R-D motion estimation scheme with performance improvement.

3.3 Kalman filter embedded R-D motion estimation

The main feature of the above enhanced scheme is to obtain fractional pixel accuracy of motion vector with estimation instead of actual searching. Hence, no extra bit rate is needed for the fractional part of motion vector. However, because the enhanced algorithm does not involve the estimation process of motion vector, the obtained motion vector is not optimum from viewpoint of distortion. To address the problem, here we introduce a method for R-D motion estimation in which the Kalman filter is embedded. We refer to it as Kalman filter embedded R-D motion estimation and describe the details as follows.

The cost function of Kalman filter embedded R-D motion estimation can be formulated as

$$J_{\min}(v,\lambda) = \min_{V \in U^k}\{Kalman\ [D_k(\hat{v}_k)] + \lambda R_k(\hat{v}_k)\} , \tag{46}$$

where the $Kalman[D_k(\hat{v}_k)]$ is a distortion of Kalman filter-based motion compensation. It is obtained by Kalman filtering the integer-point motion vector and the resulting floating-point motion vector is used to generate motion compensation prediction. In such case, the motion vector is represented in integer-point, but it can generate motion compensation with fractional pixel accuracy. Therefore, the assigned bit rate for motion vector is not affected by $Kalman[D_k(\hat{v}_k)]$, but the total cost function is reduced due to the accuracy increase in compensation. Figure 14 is the block diagram of the embedded algorithm. For simplicity, we select Eq. (46) as the criterion for motion estimation.

The Kalman filter embedded R-D motion estimation algorithm is summarized as follows.

<Step 1> Kalman filter-based motion estimation

a. Select a location in the search range and denote it as a candidate measurement of motion vector $[z_x, z_y]$.

b. Apply the Kalman filter to $[z_x, z_y]$ using the procedure of Step 2 in the previous section. Then we obtain an optimal estimate of motion vector $[\hat{v}_x, \hat{v}_y]$, which is with fractional accuracy. Calculate the distortion $Kalman[D_k(\hat{v}_k)]$ according to the $[\hat{v}_x, \hat{v}_y]$.

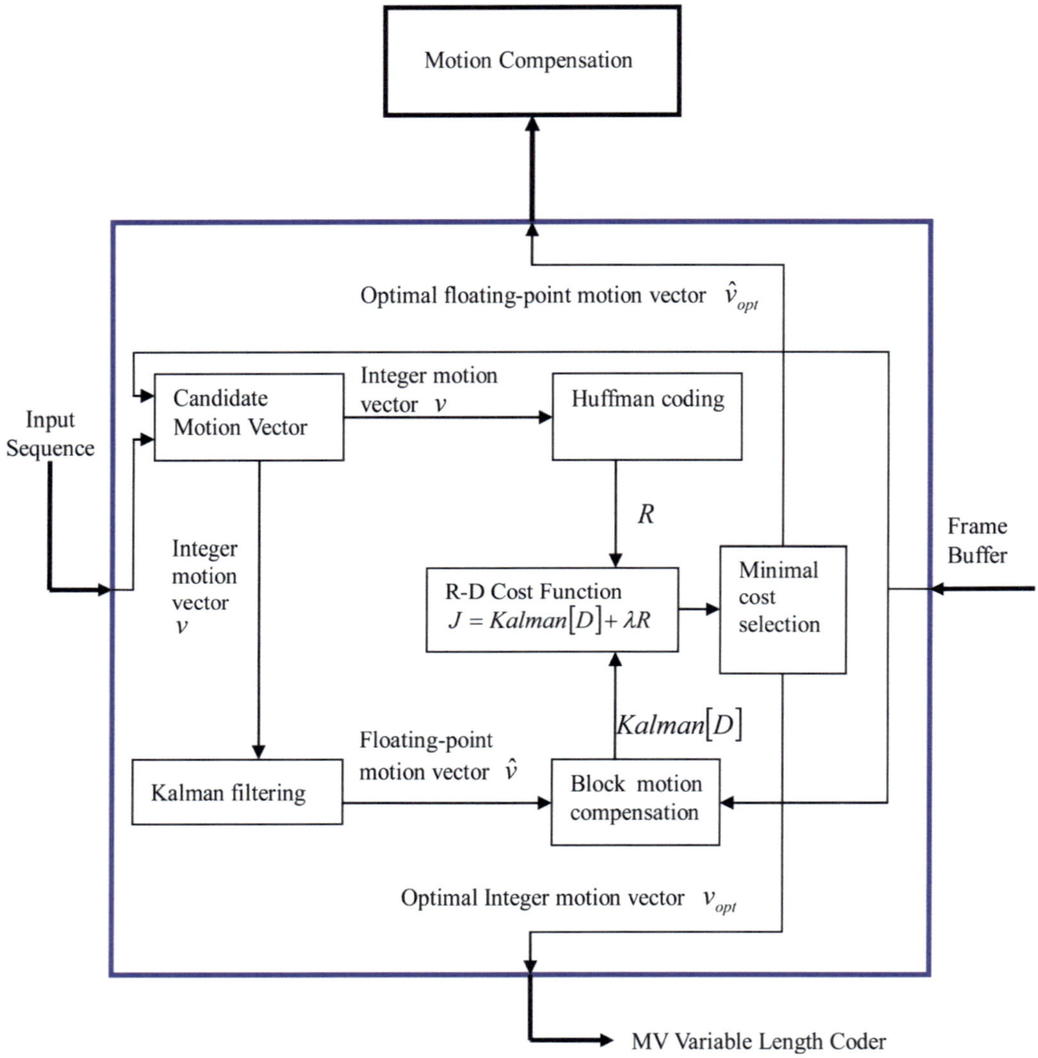

Fig. 14. The block diagram of the proposed embedded R-D motion estimation algorithm

<Step 2> Calculate the bit rate of the motion vector $[z_x, z_y]$ according to the H.263 Huffman table [7][9]. Notice that transmission motion vector is $[z_x, z_y]$, which is an integer; thus the required bit rate of motion vector is not affected by Kalman filter.

<Step 3> Using (46), we calculate the cost function. If the best match is found, go to <step 4>; otherwise, go back <Step 1> to select the next location for estimation.

<Step 4> Go to <step 1> for next block.

In the enhanced algorithm, the Kalman filter is not applied during the block searching. It is only used to enhance the performance when motion vector is obtained by R-D motion estimation. Therefore, the Kalman filter can be viewed as a post processing of motion estimation. However, in the embedded algorithm, the Kalman filter is applied for every block searching by employing the joint rate-distortion. Thus, it can be considered as a new R-D motion estimation approach. Since it includes the Kalman filter into the optimization process, the embedded method performs better than the enhanced version at the cost of computational complexity.

3.4 Simulation results

The performance of the RD-motion estimation with Kalman filter (RD-Kalman) was evaluated using a set of standard image sequences including Forman, Mother and Daughter, Carphone, Salesman and Claire. All sequences are with CIF (352×288) or QCIF (176×144) resolution and frame rate of 10 Hz. Since the RD-Kalman motion estimation has fractional pel accuracy, the results are compared with the conventional RD algorithm and MSE-optimal scheme with both integer and half-pixel accuracy. The block size 16×16 and search range 64×64 for CIF format and block size 16×16 (or 8×8) and search range 31×31 for QCIF format were chosen, respectively. The conventional RD and RD-Kalman adopted the same motion estimation strategy as that in [25]. Specifically, for the current block, the motion vectors of the left-neighbor block and up-neighbor block, and the motion vector obtained with MSE criterion, were selected as the predicted search center, and then a small search of 3×3 is performed.

For the KF-based motion estimation, the parameters are chosen experimentally as follows: the model coefficients $a_1 = b_1 = 1$, model error variance $q(k)$=0.8, measurement error variance $r(k)$=0.2, initial error covariance **P(0)=I**, and initial state $\hat{\mathbf{V}}(0) = 0$. It is evident that from [31], the estimated motion vectors are real values rather than integer. The displaced pixels may not be on the sampling grid. Therefore, the well-known bilinear interpolation is adopted to generate a motion compensated prediction frame. A Huffman codebook adopted from H.263 standard was used in the coding of 2-D differentially coded motion vectors. The various algorithms were compared in terms of rate and distortion performance. The common PSNR measure defined in the following was selected to evaluate distortion performance.

$$PSNR = 10 \cdot \log_{10} \frac{255^2}{MSE} \tag{47}$$

Moreover, rate performance was evaluated by the number of bits required to encode an image frame or a motion field.

The Lagrange multiplier λ, which controls the overall performance in the rate distortion sense, is a very important parameter. Generally, an iterative method is needed to determine the value of λ. However, it is very computational expensive. As pointed out in [26], for typical video coding applications λ is insensitive to different frames of a video sequence; thus a constant λ of 20 is adopted in the simulations.

The simulations were carried out by incorporating various motion estimation algorithms into an H.263 based MC-DCT video coding system. To be fair in the comparisons, we fixed the overall coding bit-rate at 4000 bits per frame for CIF-Claire and CIF-Salesman. For QCIF format, two block sizes are conducted for each sequence, which are assigned two different bit-rates per frame, respectively. The bit rates preset are 2000 bits (8×8) and 1600 bits (16×16) for Forman, 1400 bits and 1000 bits for Mother & Daughter, and 2000 bits and 1300 bits for Carphone, respectively.

	CIF-Claire Sequence, fixed coding bit-rate at 4000 bits				
	Block size, 16 x 16				
	MC psnr	MC+Res psnr	MV rate	Res rate	Overall rate
Full Search	38.86	39.67	1620	2424	4048
Half Pixel	40.32	40.92	2089	1989	4078
Half Pixel(RD)	39.23	41.53	1349	2637	3986
Half Pixel(RD) + KF(en)	39.46	41.79	1349	2637	3986
Half Pixel(RD) + KF(em)	39.57	42.43	1133	2686	3849
RD Optimal	38.82	41.76	1326	2628	3954
RD + KF(en)	38.93	41.82	1326	2628	3954
RD + KF(em)	39.20	42.33	947	2784	3731

Table 3. Comparisons of compression performance, in terns of PSNR, Overall Bit Rate, and MV Bit Rate for various motion estimation algorithms using the CIF-Clair 100 frames under 15 frames/s

	CIF-Salesman Sequence, fixed coding bit-rate at 4000 bits				
	Block size, 16 x 16				
	MC psnr	MC+Res psnr	MV rate	Res rate	Overall rate
Full Search	37.42	40.56	1042	2802	3844
Half Pixel	38.94	41.28	1268	2770	4038
Half Pixel(RD)	37.88	40.82	1043	2773	3816
Half Pixel(RD) + KF(en)	38.23	41.13	1043	2773	3816
Half Pixel(RD) + KF(em)	38.78	41.67	977	2786	3763
RD Optimal	37.33	40.93	1028	2805	3833
RD + KF(en)	37.45	41.16	1028	2805	3833
RD + KF(em)	38.54	41.51	950	2878	3828

Table 4. Comparisons of compression performance, in terns of PSNR, Overall Bit Rate, and MV Bit Rate for various motion estimation algorithms using the CIF-Salesman 100 frames under 15 frames/s

The averaged results for 100 frames of CIF format sequences are summarized in Tables 3 and 4. The Kalman-based R-D motion estimation approach outperforms the MSE-optimal and conventional RD algorithms in terms of PSNR. Since the Kalman filter has fractional pel accuracy with the rates of integer motion vector, it achieves significant PSNR improvement, as expected. When the integer-based Kalman filter is compared to the motion estimation methods in half pixel accuracy, it still achieves better PSNR, but not so significantly. It can be seen that the Kalman filter with half pixel accuracy performs better slightly than that with integer pixel accuracy. This may be due to the limitation of bilinear interpolation; i.e., the accuracy improvement is saturated when too many interpolations are performed. The performance may be further enhanced with the advanced interpolation filters [45,46].

	QCIF-Foreman Sequence, fixed coding bit-rate at 2000 bits				
	Block size, 8 x 8				
	MC psnr	MC+Res psnr	MV rate	Res rate	Overall rate
Full Search	32.37	33.49	1274	776	2050
Half Pixel	33.75	34.38	1438	626	2064
Half Pixel(RD)	33.44	34.57	1162	844	2006
Half Pixel(RD) + KF(en)	33.59	34.61	1162	844	2006
Half Pixel(RD) + KF(em)	33.71	34.93	1047	956	2003
RD Optimal	31.83	34.27	1096	903	1999
RD + KF(en)	31.92	34.33	1096	903	1999
RD + KF(em)	32.11	34.62	1022	971	1993

*MV: Motion Vector *MC : Motion Compensation. *Res : Prediction Residuals. (DFD)

Table 5. Comparisons of compression performance, in terns of PSNR, Overall Bit Rate, and MV Bit Rate for various motion estimation algorithms using the QCIF-Foreman 100 frames under 10 frames/s

	QCIF-Foreman Sequence, fixed coding bit-rate at 1600 bits				
	Block size, 16 x 16				
	MC psnr	MC+Res psnr	MV rate	Res rate	Overall rate
Full Search	30.75	32.79	635	970	1605
Half Pixel	31.83	33.55	728	893	1621
Half Pixel(RD)	31.69	33.72	655	948	1603
Half Pixel(RD) + KF(en)	31.76	33.79	655	948	1603
Half Pixel(RD) + KF(em)	31.89	33.97	604	993	1597
RD Optimal	30.62	33.13	583	1028	1611
RD + KF(en)	30.72	33.39	583	1028	1611
RD + KF(em)	31.04	33.67	553	1051	1604

Table 6. Comparisons of compression performance, in terns of PSNR, Overall Bit Rate, and MV Bit Rate for various motion estimation algorithms using the QCIF-Foreman 100 frames under 10 frames/s

At the same bite rate level and integer pixel accuracy, the enhanced algorithm achieved an average of 1.23 dB gain over MSE-optimal and 0.34 dB gain over the conventional RD. The embedded version achieved an average of 1.77 dB gain over MSE-optimal, and 0.88 dB gain over the conventional RD. Note that the new methods have lower bit rate. Tables 5-7 summarized the average results for QCIF format sequences. For both block sizes of 16×16 and 8×8, the Kalman filter-based R-D motion estimation approaches achieve significant PSNR improvement. Particularly, the embedded Kalman R-D algorithm achieves the best performance due to its ability in reduction of motion vector rate as well as the compensation distortion.

	QCIF-Mother & Daughter Sequence, fixed coding bit-rate at 1400 bits				
	Block size, 8 x 8				
	MC psnr	**MC+Res psnr**	**MV rate**	**Res rate**	**Overall rate**
Full Search	37.21	38.79	762	654	1216
Half Pixel	38.57	39.88	816	603	1419
Half Pixel(RD)	37.72	40.14	638	670	1308
Half Pixel(RD) + KF(en)	37.98	40.66	638	670	1308
Half Pixel(RD) + KF(em)	38.32	41.98	463	694	1157
RD Optimal	37.15	40.28	431	705	1136
RD + KF(en)	37.23	41.31	431	705	1136
RD + KF(em)	37.55	42.06	216	806	1022

Table 7. Comparisons of compression performance, in terns of PSNR, Overall Bit Rate, and MV Bit Rate for various motion estimation algorithms using the QCIF-Mother & Daughter 120 frames under 10 frames/s

Figures 15 and 16 compare the MSE-Optimal, conventional R-D, enhanced Kalman R-D and embedded Kalman R-D schemes with both integer and half pixel accuracy in terms of PSNR with approximately fixed bit rate for each sequence, respectively. Figures 17 to 19 compare these algorithms in terms of bit rate with approximately fixed PSNR for each sequence, respectively. The results indicate that the proposed schemes achieve better rate-distortion performance.

The motion vector fields generated by various algorithms are shown in Figures 20-21, respectively. The test sequences contain mainly small rotation and camera panning. This algorithm produces smoother motion fields because of the filtering effect of Kalman filter.

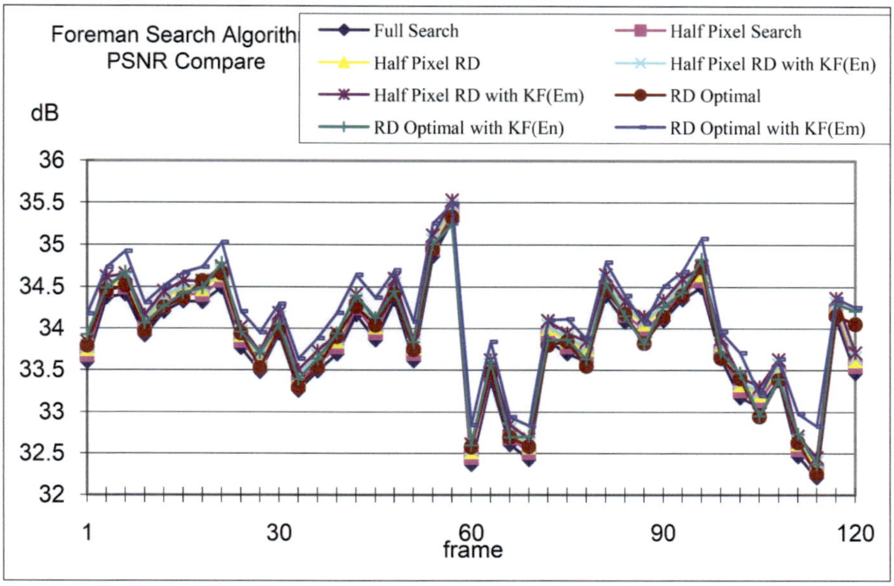

Fig. 15. Comparisons of PSNR performance using the QCIF-Froeman sequence, 120 frames at 10 frames/s, fixed coding bit-rate at 2000 bits. Block size = 8 x 8, search range = [-15, 16].

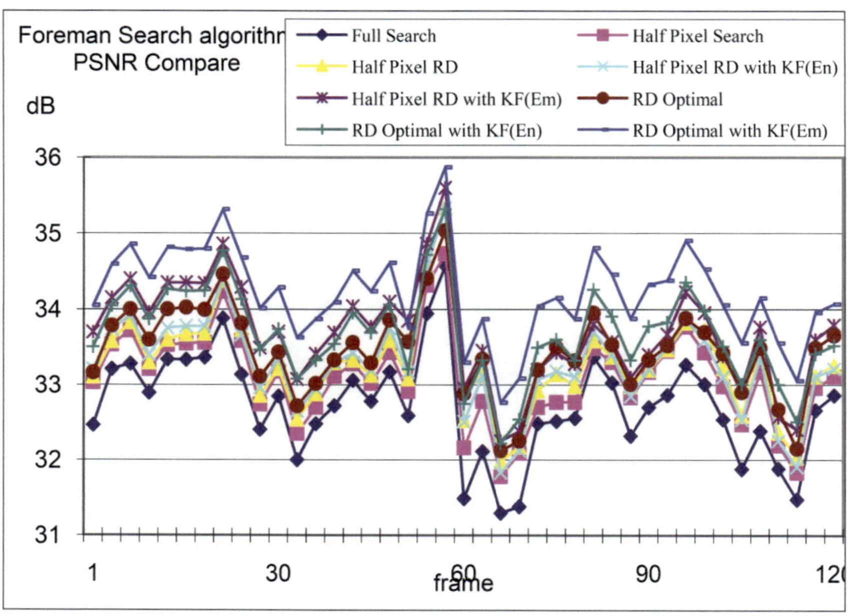

Fig. 16. Comparisons of PSNR performance using the QCIF-Froeman sequence, 120 frames at 10 frames/s, fixed coding bit-rate at 2000 bits. Block size = 16 x 16, search range = [-31, 32].

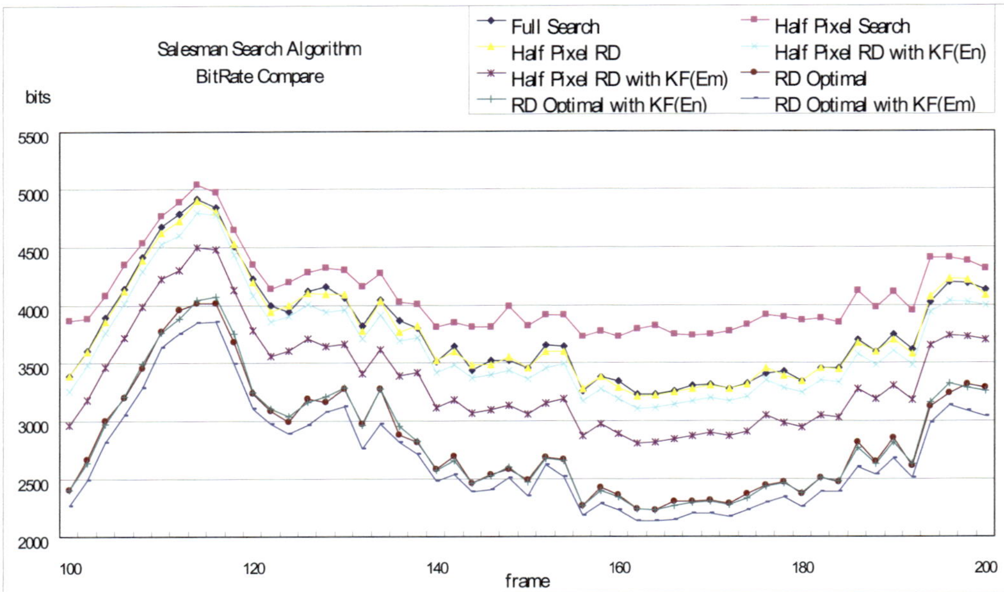

Fig. 17. Comparisons of bit-rate performance using the CIF-Salesman sequence, 120 frames at 10 frames/s, fixed average PSNR Full Search at 39.93 dB, Half Pixel Search at 40.01 dB, Half Pixel RD at 39.92 dB, Half Pixel RD with KF(En) at 39.95 dB, Half Pixel RD with KF(Em) at 40.05 dB, RD-Optimal at 39.88 dB, RD with KF(En) at 39.95 dB, and RD with KF(Em) at 39.98 dB.

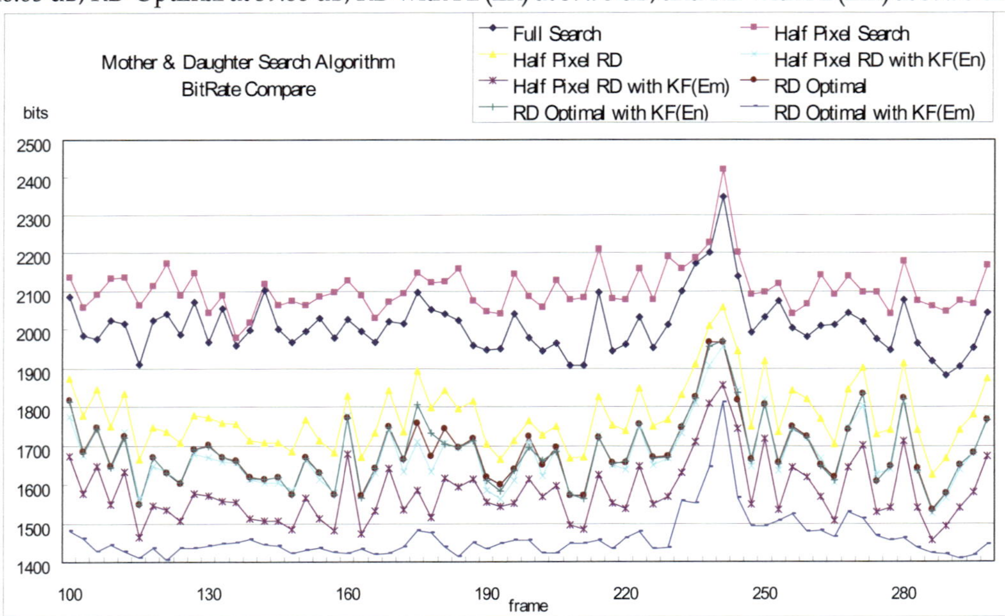

Fig. 18. Comparisons of bit-rate performance using the QCIF-Mother & Daughter sequence, 200 frames at 10 frames/s, fixed average PSNR Full Search at 38.80 dB, Half Pixel Search at 38.82 dB, Half Pixel RD at 38.75 dB, Half Pixel RD with KF(En) at 38.81 dB, Half Pixel RD with KF(Em) at 38.89 dB, RD-Optimal at 38.77 dB, RD with KF(En) at 38.83 dB, and RD with KF(Em) at 38.87 dB.

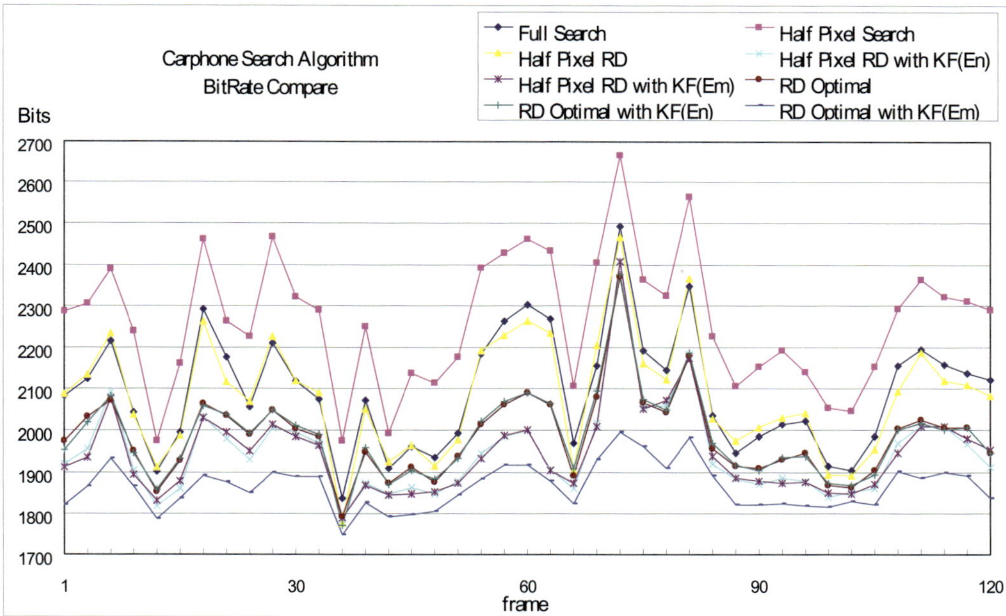

Fig. 19. Comparisons of bit-rate performance using the QCIF-Carphone sequence, 120 frames at 10 frames/s, fixed average PSNR Full Search at 37.23 dB, Half Pixel Search at 37.32 dB, Half Pixel RD at 37.20 dB, Half Pixel RD with KF(En) at 37.29 dB, Half Pixel RD with KF(Em) at 37.37 dB, RD-Optimal at 37.14 dB, RD with KF(En) at 37.28 dB, and RD with KF(Em) at 37.30 dB.

Fig. 20 (a). Motion field estimated by the conventional Half Pixel scheme on the QCIF-Foreman sequence frame 204. The PSNR quality is 34.56 dB and it requires 1230 bits to encode using the H.263 Huffman codebook.

Fig. 20 (b). Motion field estimated by the Half Pixel with RD-Optimal on the QCIF-Foreman sequence frame 204. The PSNR quality is 34.15 dB and it requires 1158 bits to encode using the H.263 Huffman codebook.

Fig. 20 (c). Motion field estimated by the Half Pixel RD with Enhanced Algorithm scheme on the QCIF-Foreman sequence frame 204. The PSNR quality is 34.27 dB and it requires 1158 bits to encode using the H.263 Huffman codebook.

Fig. 20 (d). Motion field estimated by the Half Pixel RD with Embedded Algorithm scheme on the QCIF-Foreman sequence frame 204. The PSNR quality is 34.66 dB and it requires 889 bits to encode using the H.263 Huffman codebook.

Fig. 21 (a). Motion field estimated by the conventional Half Pixel scheme on the QCIF-Mother & Daughter sequence frame 28. The PSNR quality is 34.83 dB and it requires 1476 bits to encode using the H.263 Huffman codebook.

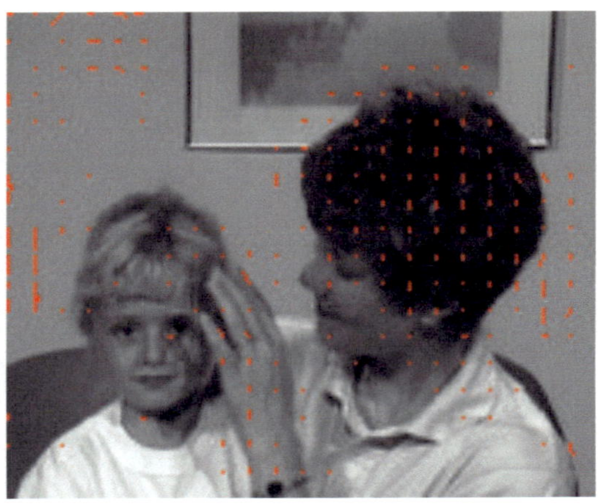

Fig. 21 (b). Motion field estimated by the Half Pixel with RD-Optimal scheme on the QCIF- Mother & Daughter sequence frame 28. The PSNR quality is 34.52 dB and it requires 1112 bits to encode using the H.263 Huffman codebook.

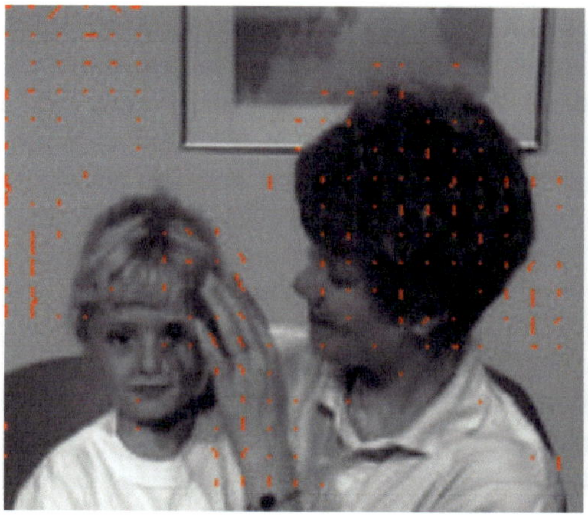

Fig. 21(c). Motion field estimated by the Half Pixel RD with Enhanced Algorithm scheme on the QCIF- Mother & Daughter sequence frame 28. The PSNR quality is 34.67 dB and it requires 1120 bits to encode using the H.263 Huffman codebook.

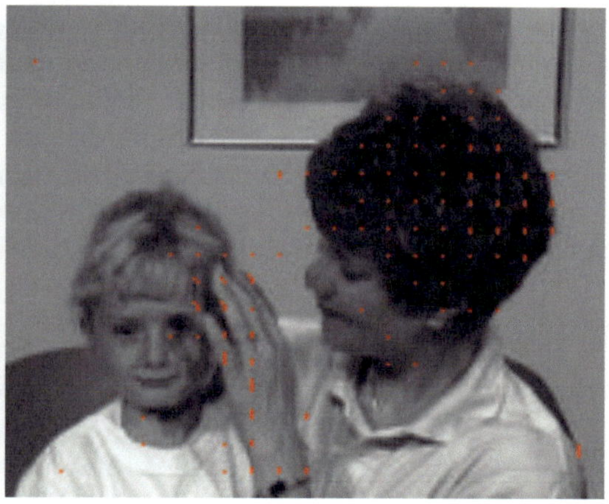

Fig. 21(d). Motion field estimated by the Half Pixel RD with Embedded Algorithm scheme on the QCIF- Mother & Daughter frame 28. The PSNR quality is 34.95 dB and it requires 868 bits to encode using the H.263 Huffman codebook.

In general, the Kalman filtering is computationally expensive. However, both the computational complexities of the enhanced and embedded algorithms are relatively small because the calculation of Kalman filtering can be significantly simplified. The extra computational load required for the algorithms is summarized in Table 8 [47]. It indicates the extra computation introduced by the proposed method is small.

Motion Estimation Algorithms	Computational Complexity		
	Additions	Multiplications	Bilinear interpolation
Enhanced algorithm (per block)	5	3	1 ($8N^2(\times)+6N^2(+)$)
Embedded algorithm (per search)	5	3	1 ($8N^2(\times)+6N^2(+)$)

Table 8. Extra computation required by Kalman filtering for each algorithm

4. Conclusions

In this chapter, we have introduced two types of motion estimation based on Kalman filter, without and with rate-constraint. The first type employs the predicted motion information and the measured motion information to obtain an optimal estimate of motion vector. The predicted motion is achieved through the use of AR models which characterize the motion correlation of neighboring blocks. The measurement motion is obtained by using any conventional block-matching fast search scheme. The results indicate that the method provides smoother motion vector fields than that of the full search scheme, and saves computational cost significantly.

For the rate-constraint case, we have introduced two efficient Kalman filter-based R-D motion estimation algorithms in which a simple 1-D Kalman filter is applied to improve the performance of conventional RD motion estimation. Since equivalent Kalman filters are used in both encoder and decoder, no extra information bit for motion vector is needed to send to the decoder. The algorithm achieves significantly PSNR gain with only a slight increase of complexity. The enhanced algorithm is a post processing, and can be easily combined with any conventional R-D motion estimation schemes. The embedded algorithm can more effectively exploit the correlation of block motion.

5. References

J. R. Jain and A. K. Jain. Displacement measurement and its application in interframe image coding. *IEEE Transactions on Communications*, 29: pages 1799-1808, 1981. [1]

S. Kappagantula and K. R. Rao. Motion compensated interframe image prediction. *IEEE Transactions on Communications*, 33(9): pages 1011-1015, 1985. [2]

M. Ghanbari. The cross-search algorithm for motion estimation. *IEEE Transcations on Communications*, 38(7): pages 950-953, 1990. [3]

L. W. Lee, J. F. Wang, J. Y. Lee, and J. D. Shie. Dynamic search-window adjustment and interlaced search for block-matching algorithm. *IEEE Trans. Circuits and Systems for Video Technology*. 3(1): pages 85-85, 1993. [4]

R. Li, B. Zeng, and M. L. Liou. A new three step search algorithm for block motion estimation. *IEEE Trans Circuits and Systems for Video Technology*. 4(4): pages 438-442, 1994. [5]

L. M. Po and W. C. Ma. A novel four-step search algorithm for fast block motion estimation. *IEEE Transactions Circuits and Systems for Video Technology*. 6(3): pages 313-317, 1996. [6]

Video Coding for Low Bitrate Communication. ITU Telecom. Standardization sector of ITU, ITU-T Recommendation H.263, 1996. [7]

B. Zeng, R. Li and M.L. Liou. Optimization of fast block motion estimation algorithms. *IEEE Transactions Circuits and Systems for Video Technology*. 7(6): pages 833-844, 1997. [8]

Video Coding for Low Bitrate Communication. ITU Telecom. Standardization sector of ITU, Draft ITU-T Rec. H.263 Version 2, 1997. [9]

MPEG-4 Visual Fixed Draft International Standard. ISO/IEC 14 496-2, 1998. [10]

S. Zhu, K.K. Ma. A new diamond search algorithm for fast block-matching motion estimation. *IEEE Transactions Image Process*. 9(2): pages 287-290, 2000. [11]

MPEG-4VideoVerification ModelVersion 18.0. MPEGVideo Group, ISO/IEC JTC1/SC29/WG11 N3908, 2001. [12]

C. Zhu, X. Lin, L.P. Chau. An enhanced hexagonal search algorithm for block motion estimation. *In Proceedings of ISCAS* (2), pages 392-395, 2003. [13]

C. Hsieh, P.C. Lu, J.S. Shyu aud E. H. Lu. A motion estimation algorithm using inter-block correlation. *Electronic Letters,* 26(5): pages 276-277, Mar. 1990. [14]

S. Zafar, Y.Zhang and J. Baras. Predictive block-matching motion estimation for TV coding-part I: inter-block prediction. *IEEE Transactions Broadcasting*. 37(3): pages 97-101, 1991. [15]

Y. Zhang and S. Zafar. Predictive block-matching motion estimation for TV coding-part I: inter-frame prediction. *IEEE Transactions Broadcasting,* 37(3): pages 102- 105, 1991. [16]

M. Bierling. Displacement estimation by hierarchical block-matching. *SPIE, Visual Communications and Image Processing*, 1011: pages 942-951, 1988. [17]

A. N. Netravali and B. G. Haskell. *Digital Pictures: Representation and Compression.* New York: Plenum, 1988. [18]

J. W. Woods and C. H. Radewan. Kalman filtering in two dimensions. *IEEE Transactions Inform. Theory*, 23: pages 473-482, 1977. [19]

T. Wiegand, M. Lightstone, D. Mukherjee, T. G. Cambell, and S. K. Mitra. Rate- distortion optimized mode selection for very low bit rate video coding and the emerging H.263 standard. *IEEE Transactions on Circuits and Systems for Video Technology.* 6(2): pages 482–190, 1996. [20]

H. li, A. Lundmark, and R. Forchheimer. Image sequence coding at very low-bit bitrates: A review. *IEEE Transactions Image Process.*3(9): pages 589–609, 1994. [21]

B. Girod. Rate-constrained motion estimation. *Proc. SPIE Visual Commun. Image Process.* 2308: pages 1026–1034, 1994. [22]

F. Kossentini, Y.-W. Lee, M. J. T. Smith, and R. K.Ward. Predictive RD optimized motion estimation for very low bit rate video coding. *IEEE Journal on Selected Areas in Communitions.* 15(6): pages 1752–1763, 1997. [23]

D. T. Hoang, P. M. Long, and J. S. Vitter. Efficient cost measure for motion estimation at low bit rate. *IEEE Transactions on Circuits and Systems for Video Technology.* 8(5): pages 488–500, 1998. [24]

M. C. Chen and A. N.Willson. Rate-distortion optimal motion estimation algorithm for motion-compensated transform video coding. *IEEE Transactions on Circuits and Systems for Video Technology.* 8(3): pages 147–158, 1998. [25]

M. Z. Coban and R. M. Mersereau. A fast exhaustive search algorithm for rate-constrained motion estimation. *IEEE Transactions Image Process.*, 7(5): pages 769–773, 1998. [26]

J. C. H. Ju, Y. K. Chen, and S. Y. Kung. A fast rate-optimized motion estimation algorithm for low-bit rate video coding. *IEEE Transactions on Circuits and Systems for Video Technology.* 9(7): pages 994–1002, 1999. [27]

Y. Y. Sheila and S. Hemami. Generalized rate-distortion optimization for motion-compensated video coders. *IEEE Transactions on Circuits and Systems for Video Technology.* 10(6): pages 942–955, 2000. [28]

M. T. Orchard and G. J. Sullivan. Overlapped block motion compensation: An estimation-theoretic approach. *IEEE Transactions Image Process.* 3(5): pages 693–699, 1994. [29]

J. K. Su and R. M. Mersereau. Motion estimation methods for overlapped block motion compensation. *IEEE Transactions Image Process.* 9(6): pages 1509–1521, 2000. [30]

Draft ITU-T Recommendation and Final Draft International Standard of Joint Video Specification (ITU-T Rec. H.264 ISO/IEC 14496-10AVC) Joint Video Team (JVT). Doc. JVT-G050, 2003. [31]

T. Wiegand, G. Sullivan, G. Bjøntegaard, and A. Luthra. Overview of the H.264/AVC video coding standard. *IEEE Transactions on Circuits and Systems for Video Technology.*13(7): pages 560–576, Jul. 2003. [32]

C. K. Chui, and G. Chen. Kalman Filtering with Real-Time Applications. Springer Series in Information Sciences, 17: New York: Springer, 1987. [33]

S. Haykin. Adaptive Filter Theory, Prentice-Hall Inc., Englewood Cliffs, 1991. [34]

J. M. Mendel. Lessons in Digital Estimation Theory for signal processing, communications, and control. Prentice-Hall Inc., Englewood Cliffs, 1995. [35]

M. S. Grewal, and A. P. Andrews. Kalman Filtering Theory and Practice, Prentice-Hall Inc., Englewood Cliffs, 1993. [36]

C. M. Kuo, C. H. Hsieh, H. C. Lin and P. C. Lu. A new motion estimation method for video coding. *IEEE Transactions Broadcasting*. 42(2): pages 110-116, 1996. [37]

J. Kim and J. W. Woods. 3D Kalman Filter for Image Motion Estimation. *IEEE Transactions Image Processing*, 7: pages 42-52, 1998. [38]

D. Angwin and H. Kaufman. Image restoration using a reduced order model. *IEEE Transactions on Signal Processing*, 16: pages 21-28, 1989. [39]

C. M. Kuo, C. H. Hsieh, H. C. Lin and P. C. Lu. Motion Estimation Algorithm with Kalman Filetring. *IEE Electronic Letters*, 30(15): pages 1204-1206, 1994. [40]

R. K. Mehra. On the identification of variance and adaptive Kalman filtering. *IEEE Transactions Automat. Contr.* 15: 1970. [41]

R. A. HOWARD, .Systems Analysis of Semi-Markov Processes. *IEEE Transactions on Military Electronics*, 8(2): pages 114-124, 1964. [42]

M. T. Orchard and G. J. Sullivan. Overlapped block motion compensation: an estimation-theoretic approach. *IEEE Transactions Image Processing*, 3(5): pages 693-699, 1994. [43]

J. K. Su, R. M. Mersereau. Motion estimation methods for overlapped block motion compensation. *IEEE Transactions Image Processing*, 9(9): pages 1509-1521, 2000. [44]

T. Wedi, H.G. Musmann. Motion- and aliasing-compensated prediction for hybrid video coding. *IEEE Transactions of Circuits and Systems for Video Technology*, 13(7): pages 577 – 586, 2003.[45]

T. Wedi. Adaptive interpolation filter for motion compensated prediction. *In proceedings of the 2002 IEEE International Conference on Image Processing*. 2: pages 22-25, 2002.[46]

C. M. Kuo, S. C. Chung, P. Y. Shih. Kalman Filtering Based Rate-Constrained Motion Estimation for Very Low Bit Rate Video Coding. *IEEE Transactions Circuit and Systems for Video Technology*, 16(1): pages 3-18, 2006.[47]

C. M. Kuo, C. P. Chao and C. H. Hsieh. An Efficient Motion Estimation Algorithm for Video Coding Using Kalman Filter. *Real-Time Imaging*, 8, pp.253-264, 2002.[48]

C. M. Kuo, C. P. Chao and C. H. Hsieh. A New Motion estimation algorithm for Video Coding Using Adaptive Kalman Filter. *Real-Time Imaging*, 8, pp.387-398, 2002.[49]